D1197668

mini

Spanish
dictionary

Spanish > English   English > Spanish

First published in this edition 2001

© HarperCollins Publishers 2001
Glasgow G64 2QT

ISBN 0-00-712814-2

A catalogue record for this book
is available from the British Library.

Typeset by Morton Word Processing Ltd,
Scarborough, England

Printed and bound in Great Britain by
Omnia Books Ltd, Glasgow, G64

ÍNDICE

CONTENTS

INTRODUCCIÓN

Estamos muy satisfechos de que hayas decidido comprar este diccionario y esperamos que lo disfrutes y que te sirva de gran ayuda ya sea en el colegio, en el trabajo, en tus vacaciones o en casa.

Esta introducción pretende darte algunas indicaciones para ayudarte a sacar el mayor provecho de este diccionario; no sólo de su extenso vocabulario, sino de toda la información que te proporciona cada entrada. Esta te ayudará a leer y comprender — y también a comunicarte y a expresarte — en inglés moderno.

El diccionario comienza con una lista de abreviaturas utilizadas en el texto y con una ilustración de los sonidos representados por los símbolos fonéticos. Al final del diccionario encontrarás una tabla de los verbos irregulares del inglés, y para terminar, una sección sobre el uso de los números y de las expresiones de tiempo.

EL MANEJO DE TU DICCIONARIO

La amplia información que te ofrece este diccionario aparece presentada en distintas tipografías, con caracteres de diversos tamaños y con distintos símbolos, abreviaturas y paréntesis. Los apartados siguientes explican las reglas y símbolos utilizados.

Entradas

Las palabras que consultas en el diccionario — las "entradas" — aparecen ordenadas alfabéticamente y en **caracteres gruesos** para una identificación más rápida. Las dos palabras que ocupan el margen superior de cada página indican la primera y la última entrada de la página en cuestión.

La información sobre el uso o la forma de determinadas entradas aparece entre paréntesis, detrás de la transcripción fonética, y generalmente en forma abreviada y en cursiva (p.ej.: *(fam)*, *(COM)*.

En algunos casos se ha considerado oportuno agrupar palabras de una misma familia (**nación, nacionalismo; accept, acceptance**) bajo una misma entrada, en caracteres gruesos de tamaño algo más pequeño que los de la entrada principal.

Las expresiones de uso corriente en las que aparece una entrada se dan en negrita (p.ej.: **to be in a hurry**).

Símbolos fonéticos

La transcripción fonética de cada entrada (que indica su pronunciación) aparece entre corchetes, inmediatamente después de la entrada (p.ej.: **knead** [ni:d]). En la página x encontrarás una lista de los símbolos fonéticos utilizados en este diccionario.

Traducciones

Las traducciones de las entradas aparecen en caracteres normales, y en los casos en los que existen significados o usos diferentes, éstos aparecen separados mediante un punto y coma. A menudo encontrarás también otras palabras en cursiva y entre paréntesis antes de las traducciones. Estas sugieren contextos en los que la entrada podría aparecer (p.ej.: **rough** (*voice*) o (*weather*)) o proporcionan sinónimos (p.ej.: **rough** (*violent*)).

Palabras clave

Particular relevancia reciben ciertas palabras inglesas y españolas que han sido consideradas palabras "clave" en cada lengua. Estas pueden, por ejemplo, ser de utilización muy corriente o tener distintos usos (**de, haber; get, that**). La combinación de rombos ♦ y números te permitirá distinguir las diferentes categorías gramaticales y los diferentes significados. Las indicaciones en cursiva y entre paréntesis proporcionan además importante información adicional.

Información gramatical

Las categorías gramaticales aparecen en forma abreviada y en cursiva después de la transcripción fonética de cada entrada (*vt, adv, conj*).

También se indican la forma femenina y los plurales irregulares de los sustantivos del ingeIs (**child, ~ren**).

INTRODUCTION

We are delighted you have decided to buy this dictionary and hope you will enjoy and benefit from using it at school, at home, on holiday or at work.

This introduction gives you a few tips on how to get the most out of your dictionary — not simply from its comprehensive wordlist but also from the information provided in each entry. This will help you to read and understand modern Spanish, as well as communicate and express yourself in the language.

The dictionary begins by listing the abbreviations used in the text and illustrating the sounds shown by the phonetic symbols. You will find Spanish verb tables at the back, followed by a final section on numbers and time expressions.

USING YOUR DICTIONARY

A wealth of information is presented in the dictionary, using various typefaces, sizes of type, symbols, abbreviations and brackets. The conventions and symbols used are explained in the following sections.

Headwords
The words you look up in a dictionary — "headwords" — are listed alphabetically. They are printed in **bold type** for rapid identification. The two headwords appearing at the top of each page indicate the first and last word dealt with on the page in question.

Information about the usage or form of certain headwords is given in brackets after the phonetic spelling. This usually appears in abbreviated form and in italics (e.g. (*fam*), (*COMM*)).

Where appropriate, words related to headwords are grouped in the same entry (**nación, nacionalismo; accept, acceptance**) in a slightly smaller bold type than the headword.

Common expressions in which the headword appears are shown in a different bold roman type (e.g. **hacer calor**).

Phonetic spellings
The phonetic spelling of each headword (indicating its pronunciation) is given in square brackets immediately after the headword (e.g. **dónde** ['donde]). A list of these symbols is given on page x.

Translations

Headword translations are given in ordinary type and, where more than one meaning or usage exists, these are separated by a semi-colon. You will often find other words in italics in brackets before the translations. These offer suggested contexts in which the headword might appear (e.g. **grande** (*de tamaño*)) or provide synonyms (e.g. **grande** (*alto*) *o* (*distinguido*)).

The gender of the translation also appears in *italics* immediately following the key element of the translation, except where this is a regular masculine singular noun ending in "o", or a regular singular feminine noun ending in "a".

"Key" words

Special status is given to certain Spanish and English words which are considered as "key" words in each language. They may, for example, occur very frequently or have several types of usage (e.g. **de, haber**). A combination of lozenges ♦ and numbers helps you to distinguish different parts of speech and different meanings. Further helpful information is provided in brackets and in italics.

Grammatical information

Parts of speech are given in abbreviated form in *italics* after the phonetic spellings of headwords (e.g. *vt, adv, conj*).

Genders of Spanish nouns are indicated as follows: *nm* for a masculine and *nf* for a feminine noun. Feminine and irregular plural forms of nouns are also shown (**irlandés, esa; luz,** (*pl* **luces**)).

ABREVIATURAS

ABBREVIATIONS

abreviatura	ab(b)r	abbreviation
adjetivo, locución adjetiva	adj	adjective, adjectival phrase
administración	ADMIN	administration
adverbio, locución adverbial	adv	adverb, adverbial phrase
agricultura	AGR	agriculture
América Latina	AM	Latin America
anatomía	ANAT	anatomy
arquitectura	ARQ, ARCH	architecture
el automóvil	AUT(O)	the motor car and motoring
aviación, viajes aéreos	AVIAT	flying, air travel
biología	BIO(L)	biology
botánica, flores	BOT	botany
inglés británico	BRIT	British English
química	CHEM	chemistry
comercio, finanzas, banca	COM(M)	commerce, finance, banking
informática	COMPUT	computers
conjunción	conj	conjunction
construcción	CONSTR	building
compuesto	cpd	compound element
cocina	CULIN	cookery
economía	ECON	economics
electricidad, electrónica	ELEC	electricity, electronics
enseñanza, sistema escolar y universitario	ESCOL	schooling, schools and universities
España	Esp	Spain
especialmente	esp	especially
exclamación, interjección	excl	exclamation, interjection
femenino	f	feminine
lengua familiar (! vulgar)	fam (!)	colloquial usage (! particularly offensive)
ferrocarril	FERRO	railways
uso figurado	fig	figurative use
fotografía	FOTO	photography
(verbo inglés) del cual la partícula es inseparable	fus	(phrasal verb) where the particle is inseparable
generalmente	gen	generally
geografía, geología	GEO	geography, geology
geometría	GEOM	geometry
uso familiar (! vulgar)	inf (!)	colloquial usage (! particularly offensive)
infinitivo	infin	infinitive
informática	INFORM	computers
invariable	inv	invariable
irregular	irreg	irregular
lo jurídico	JUR	law
América Latina	LAM	Latin America
gramática, lingüística	LING	grammar, linguistics

ABREVIATURAS		ABBREVIATIONS
masculino	m	masculine
matemáticas	MATH	mathematics
masculino/femenino	m/f	masculine/feminine
medicina	MED	medicine
lo militar, ejército	MIL	military matters
música	MUS	music
sustantivo, nombre	n	noun
navegación, náutica	NAUT	sailing, navigation
sustantivo numérico	num	numeral noun
complemento	obj	(grammatical) object
	o.s.	oneself
peyorativo	pey, pej	derogatory, pejorative
fotografía	PHOT	photography
fisiología	PHYSIOL	physiology
plural	pl	plural
política	POL	politics
participio de pasado	pp	past participle
preposición	prep	preposition
pronombre	pron	pronoun
psicología, psiquiatría	PSICO, PSYCH	psychology, psychiatry
tiempo pasado	pt	past tense
química	QUÍM	chemistry
ferrocarril	RAIL	railways
religión	REL	religion
	sb	somebody
enseñanza, sistema escolar y universitario	SCH	schooling, schools and universities
singular	sg	singular
España	SP	Spain
	sth	something
sujeto	su(b)j	(grammatical) subject
subjuntivo	subjun	subjunctive
tauromaquia	TAUR	bullfighting
también	tb	also
técnica, tecnología	TEC(H)	technical term, technology
telecomunicaciones	TELEC, TEL	telecommunications
imprenta, tipografía	TIP, TYP	typography, printing
televisión	TV	television
universidad	UNIV	university
inglés norteamericano	US	American English
verbo	vb	verb
verbo intransitivo	vi	intransitive verb
verbo pronominal	vr	reflexive verb
verbo transitivo	vt	transitive verb
zoología	ZOOL	zoology
marca registrada	®	registered trademark
indica un equivalente cultural	≈	introduces a cultural equivalent

SPANISH PRONUNCIATION

Consonants

c	[k]	caja	c before a, o or u is pronounced as in cat
ce, ci	[θe, θi]	cero cielo	c before e or i is pronounced as in thin
ch	[tʃ]	chiste	ch is pronounced as ch in chair
d	[d, ð]	danés ciudad	at the beginning of a phrase or after l or n, d is pronounced as in English. In any other position it is pronounced like th in the
g	[g, ɤ]	gafas paga	g before a, o or u is pronounced as in gap, if at the beginning of a phrase or after n. In other positions the sound is softened
ge, gi	[xe, xi]	gente girar	g before e or i is pronounced similar to ch in Scottish loch
h		haber	h is always silent in Spanish
j	[x]	jugar	j is pronounced similar to ch in Scottish loch
ll	[ʎ]	talle	ll is pronounced like the lli in million
ñ	[ɲ]	niño	ñ is pronounced like the ni in onion
q	[k]	que	q is pronounced as k in king
r, rr	[r, rr]	quitar garra	r is always pronounced in Spanish, unlike the silent r in dancer. rr is trilled, like a Scottish r
s	[s]	quizás isla	s is usually pronounced as in pass, but before b, d, g, l, m or n it is pronounced as in rose
v	[b, ß]	vía dividir	v is pronounced something like b. At the beginning of a phrase or after m or n it is pronounced as b in boy. In any other position the sound is softened
z	[θ]	tenaz	z is pronounced as th in thin

b, f, k, l, m, n, p, t and x are pronounced as in English.

Vowels

a	[a]	p**a**ta	not as long as *a* in f**a**r. When followed by a consonant in the same syllable (i.e. in a closed syllable), as in am**a**nte, the *a* is short, as in b**a**t
e	[e]	m**e**	like *e* in th**e**y. In a closed syllable, as in g**e**nte, the *e* is short as in p**e**t
i	[i]	p**i**no	as in m**ea**n or mach**i**ne
o	[o]	l**o**	as in l**o**cal. In a closed syllable, as in c**o**ntrol, the *o* is short as in c**o**t
u	[u]	l**u**nes	as in r**u**le. It is silent after *q*, and in *gue, gui*, unless marked *güe, güi* e.g. antig**ü**edad

Diphthongs

ai, ay	[ai]	b**ai**le	as *i* in r**i**de
au	[au]	**au**to	as *ou* in sh**ou**t
ei, ey	[ei]	b**ue**y	as *ey* in gr**ey**
eu	[eu]	d**eu**da	both elements pronounced independently [e]+[u]
oi, oy	[oi]	h**oy**	as *oy* in t**oy**

Stress

The rules of stress in Spanish are as follows:
(a) when a word ends in a vowel or in *n* or *s*, the second last syllable is stressed: pat**a**ta, pat**a**tas, c**o**me, c**o**men
(b) when a word ends in a consonant other than *n* or *s*, the stress falls on the last syllable: par**e**d, habl**a**r
(c) when the rules set out in a and b are not applied, an acute accent appears over the stressed vowel: com**ú**n, geograf**í**a, ingl**é**s

In the phonetic transcription, the symbol ['] precedes the syllable on which the stress falls.

PRONUNCIACIÓN INGLESA

Vocales y diptongos

	Ejemplo inglés	*Ejemplo español/explicación*
ɑ	f**a**ther	Entre *a* de p**a**dre y *o* de n**o**che
ʌ	b**u**t, c**o**me	*a* muy breve
æ	m**a**n, c**a**t	Se mantienen los labios en la posición de *e* en p**e**na y luego se pronuncia el sonido *a*
ə	f**a**ther, **a**go	Sonido indistinto parecido a una *e* u *o* casi mudas
əː	b**i**rd, h**ea**rd	Entre *e* abierta, y *o* cerrada, sonido alargado
ɛ	g**e**t, b**e**d	como en p**e**rro
ɪ	**i**t, b**i**g	Más breve que en s**i**
iː	t**ea**, s**ee**	Como en f**i**no
ɔ	h**o**t, w**a**sh	Como en t**o**rre
ɔː	s**a**w, **a**ll	Como en p**o**r
u	p**u**t, b**oo**k	Sonido breve, más cerrado que b**u**rro
uː	t**oo**, y**o**u	Sonido largo, como en **u**no
aɪ	fl**y**, h**igh**	Como en fr**ai**le
au	h**ow**, h**ou**se	Como en p**au**sa
ɛə	th**ere**, b**ear**	Casi como en v**ea**, pero el sonido *a* se mezcla con el indistinto [ə]
eɪ	d**ay**, ob**ey**	*e* cerrada seguida por una *i* débil
ɪə	h**ere**, h**ear**	Como en man**ía**, mezclándose el sonido *a* con el indistinto [ə]
əu	g**o**, n**o**te	[ə] seguido por una breve *u*
ɔɪ	b**oy**, **oi**l	Como en v**oy**
uə	p**oor**, s**ure**	*u* bastante larga más el sonido indistinto [ə]

Consonantes

	Ejemplo inglés	*Ejemplo español/explicación*
d	men*d*ed	Como en con*d*e, an*d*ar
g	*g*o, *g*et, bi*g*	Como en *g*rande, *g*ol
dʒ	*g*in, *j*u*dg*e	Como en la *ll* andaluza y en *G*eneralitat (catalán)
ŋ	si*ng*	Como en ví*n*culo
h	*h*ouse, *h*e	Como en la *j*ota hispanoamericana
j	*y*oung, *y*es	Como en *y*a
k	*c*ome, mo*ck*	Como en *c*aña, Es*c*ocia
r	*r*ed, t*r*ead	Se pronuncia con la punta de la lengua hacia atrás y sin hacerla vibrar
s	*s*and, ye*s*	Como en *c*asa, *s*esión
z	ro*s*e, *z*ebra	Como en de*s*de, mi*s*mo
ʃ	*sh*e, ma*ch*ine	Como en *ch*ambre (francés), ro*x*o (portugués)
tʃ	*ch*in, ri*ch*	Como en *ch*ocolate
v	*v*alley	Como en f, pero se retiran los dientes superiores vibrándolos contra el labio inferior
w	*w*ater, *wh*ich	Como en la *u* de h*u*evo, p*u*ede
ʒ	vi*s*ion	Como en *j*ournal (francés)
θ	*th*ink, my*th*	Como en re*c*eta, *z*apato
ð	*th*is, *th*e	Como en la *d* de habla*d*o, verda*d*

b, p, f, m, n, l, t iguales que en español

El signo * indica que la r final escrita apenas se pronuncia en inglés británico cuando la palabra siguiente empieza con vocal.
El signo ['] indica la sílaba acentuada.

ESPAÑOL · INGLÉS
SPANISH · ENGLISH

ESPAÑOL - INGLÉS
SPANISH - ENGLISH

A, a

PALABRA CLAVE

a [a] (a+ el = al) prep **1** (dirección) to; **fueron ~ Madrid/Grecia** they went to Madrid/Greece; **me voy ~ casa** I'm going home

2 (distancia): **está ~ 15 km de aquí** it's 15 kms from here

3 (posición): **estar ~ la mesa** to be at table; **al lado de** next to, beside; ver tb **puerta**

4 (tiempo): **~ las 10/~ medianoche** at 10/midnight; **~ la mañana siguiente** the following morning; **~ los pocos días** after a few days; **estamos ~ 9 de julio** it's the ninth of July; **~ los 24 años** at the age of 24; **al año/~ la semana** (AM) a year/week later

5 (manera): **~ la francesa** the French way; **~ caballo** on horseback; **~ oscuras** in the dark

6 (medio, instrumento): **~ lápiz** in pencil; **~ mano** by hand; **cocina ~ gas** gas stove

7 (razón): **~ 30 ptas el kilo** at 30 pesetas a kilo; **~ más de 50 km/h** at more than 50 kms per hour

8 (dativo): **se lo di ~ él** I gave it to him; **vi al policía** I saw the policeman; **se lo compré ~ él** I bought it from him

9 (tras ciertos verbos): **voy ~ verle** I'm going to see him; **empezó ~ trabajar** he started working o to work

10 (+ infin): **al verle, le reconocí inmediatamente** when I saw him I recognized him at once; **el camino ~ recorrer** the distance we (etc) have to travel; **¡~ callar!** keep quiet!; **¡~ comer!** let's eat!

abad, esa [a'βað, 'ðesa] nm/f abbot/abbess; **~ía** nf abbey

abajo [a'βaxo] adv (situación) (down) below, underneath; (en edificio) downstairs; (dirección) down, downwards; **el piso ~** the downstairs flat; **la parte de ~** the lower part; **¡~ el gobierno!** down with the government!; **cuesta/río ~** downhill/downstream; **de arriba ~** from top to bottom; **más ~** lower o further down

abalanzarse [aβalan'θarse] vr: **~ sobre** o **contra** to throw o.s. at

abandonado, a [aβando'naðo, a] adj derelict; (desatendido) abandoned; (desierto) deserted; (descuidado) neglected

abandonar [aβando'nar] vt to leave; (persona) to abandon, desert; (cosa) to abandon, leave behind; (descuidar) to neglect; (renunciar a) to give up; (INFORM) to quit; **~se** vr: **~se a** to abandon o.s. to; **abandono** nm (acto) desertion, abandonment; (estado) abandon, neglect; (renuncia) withdrawal, retirement; **ganar por abandono** to win by default

abanicar [aβani'kar] vt to fan; **abanico** nm fan; (NAUT) derrick

abaratar [aβara'tar] vt to lower the price of; **~se** vr to go o come down in price

abarcar [aβar'kar] vt to include, embrace; (AM) to monopolize

abarrotado, a [aβarro'taðo, a] adj packed

abarrotar [aβarro'tar] vt (local, estadio, teatro) to fill, pack

abarrotero, a [aβarro'tero, a] (AM) nm/f grocer; **abarrotes** nmpl (AM) groceries, provisions

abastecer [aβaste'θer] vt: ~ (de) to supply (with); **abastecimiento** nm supply

abasto [a'βasto] nm supply; **no dar ~ a** to be unable to cope with

abatido, a [aβa'tiðo, a] adj dejected, downcast

abatimiento [aβati'mjento] nm (depresión) dejection, depression

abatir [aβa'tir] vt (muro) to demolish; (pájaro) to shoot o bring down; (fig) to depress; **~se** vr to get depressed; **~se sobre** to swoop o pounce on

abdicación [aβðika'θjon] nf abdication

abdicar [aβði'kar] vi to abdicate

abdomen [aβ'ðomen] nm abdomen; **abdominales** nmpl (tb: ejercicios abdominales) sit-ups

abecedario [aβeθe'ðarjo] nm alphabet

abedul [aβe'ðul] nm birch

abeja [a'βexa] nf bee

abejorro [aβe'xorro] nm bumblebee

abertura [aβer'tura] nf = apertura

abeto [a'βeto] nm fir

abierto, a [a'βjerto, a] pp de **abrir** ♦ adj open; (AM) generous

abigarrado, a [aβiɣa'rraðo, a] adj multi-coloured

abismal [aβis'mal] adj (fig) vast, enormous

abismar [aβis'mar] vt to humble, cast down; **~se** vr to sink; **~se en** (fig) to be plunged into

abismo [a'βismo] nm abyss

abjurar [aβxu'rar] vi: ~ **de** to abjure, forswear

ablandar [aβlan'dar] vt to soften; **~se**
vr to get softer

abnegación [aβneɣa'θjon] nf self-denial

abnegado, a [aβne'ɣaðo, a] adj self-sacrificing

abocado, a [aβo'kaðo, a] adj: **verse ~ al desastre** to be heading for disaster

abochornar [aβotʃor'nar] vt to embarrass

abofetear [aβofete'ar] vt to slap (in the face)

abogado, a [aβo'ɣaðo, a] nm/f lawyer; (notario) solicitor; (en tribunal) barrister (BRIT), attorney (US); **~ defensor** defence lawyer o attorney (US)

abogar [aβo'ɣar] vi: ~ **por** to plead for; (fig) to advocate

abolengo [aβo'lengo] nm ancestry, lineage

abolición [aβoli'θjon] nf abolition

abolir [aβo'lir] vt to abolish; (cancelar) to cancel

abolladura [aβoʎa'ðura] nf dent

abollar [aβo'ʎar] vt to dent

abominable [aβomi'naβle] adj abominable

abonado, a [aβo'naðo, a] adj (deuda) paid(-up) ♦ nm/f subscriber

abonar [aβo'nar] vt (deuda) to settle; (terreno) to fertilize; (idea) to endorse; **~se** vr to subscribe; **abono** nm payment; fertilizer; subscription

abordar [aβor'ðar] vt (barco) to board; (asunto) to broach

aborigen [aβo'rixen] nm/f aborigine

aborrecer [aβorre'θer] vt to hate, loathe

abortar [aβor'tar] vi (malparir) to have a miscarriage; (deliberadamente) to have an abortion; **aborto** nm miscarriage; abortion

abotonar [aβoto'nar] vt to button (up), do up

abovedado, a [aβoβe'ðaðo, a] adj vaulted, domed

abrasar [aβra'sar] vt to burn (up);

(AGR) to dry up, parch

abrazar [aβra'θar] vt to embrace, hug

abrazo [a'βraθo] nm embrace, hug; **un ~ en** (en carta) with best wishes

abrebotellas [aβreβo'teʎas] nm inv bottle opener

abrecartas [aβre'kartas] nm inv letter opener

abrelatas [aβre'latas] nm inv tin (BRIT) o can opener

abreviar [aβre'βjar] vt to abbreviate; (texto) to abridge; (plazo) to reduce;

abreviatura nf abbreviation

abridor [aβri'ðor] nm bottle opener; (de latas) tin (BRIT) o can opener

abrigar [aβri'var] vt (proteger) to shelter; (suj: ropa) to keep warm; (fig) to cherish

abrigo [a'βrivo] nm (prenda) coat, overcoat; (lugar protegido) shelter

abril [a'βril] nm April

abrillantar [aβriʎan'tar] vt to polish

abrir [a'βrir] vt to open (up) ♦ vi to open; **~se** vr to open (up); (extenderse) to open out; (cielo) to clear; **~se paso** to find o force a way through

abrochar [aβro'tʃar] vt (con botones) to button (up); (zapato, con broche) to do up

abrumar [aβru'mar] vt to overwhelm; (sobrecargar) to weigh down

abrupto, a [a'βrupto, a] adj abrupt; (empinado) steep

absceso [aβs'θeso] nm abscess

absentismo [aβsen'tismo] nm absenteeism

absolución [aβsolu'θjon] nf (REL) absolution; (JUR) acquittal

absoluto, a [aβso'luto, a] adj absolute; **en ~** adv not at all

absolver [aβsol'βer] vt to absolve; (JUR) to pardon; (: acusado) to acquit

absorbente [aβsor'βente] adj absorbent; (interesante) absorbing

absorber [aβsor'βer] vt to absorb; (embeber) to soak up

absorción [aβsor'θjon] nf absorption;

(COM) takeover

absorto, a [aβ'sorto, a] pp de **absorber** ♦ adj absorbed, engrossed

abstemio, a [aβs'temjo, a] adj teetotal

abstención [aβsten'θjon] nf abstention

abstenerse [aβste'nerse] vr: **~ (de)** to abstain o refrain (from)

abstinencia [aβsti'nenθja] nf abstinence; (ayuno) fasting

abstracción [aβstrak'θjon] nf abstraction

abstracto, a [aβ'strakto, a] adj abstract

abstraer [aβstra'er] vt to abstract; **~se** vr to be o become absorbed

abstraído, a [aβstra'iðo, a] adj absent-minded

absuelto [aβ'swelto] pp de **absolver**

absurdo, a [aβ'surðo, a] adj absurd

abuchear [aβutʃe'ar] vt to boo

abuelo, a [a'βwelo, a] nm/f grandfather/mother; **~s** nmpl grandparents

abulia [a'βulja] nf apathy

abultado, a [aβul'taðo, a] adj bulky

abultar [aβul'tar] vi to be bulky

abundancia [aβun'danθja] nf: **una ~ de** plenty of; **abundante** adj abundant, plentiful

abundar [aβun'dar] vi to abound, be plentiful

aburguesarse [aβurve'sarse] vr to become middle-class

aburrido, a [aβu'rriðo, a] adj (hastiado) bored; (que aburre) boring; **aburrimiento** nm boredom, tedium

aburrir [aβu'rrir] vt to bore; **~se** vr to be bored, get bored

abusar [aβu'sar] vi to go too far; **~ de** to abuse

abusivo, a [aβu'siβo, a] adj (precio) exorbitant

abuso [a'βuso] nm abuse

abyecto, a [aβ'jekto, a] adj wretched, abject

acá [a'ka] adv (lugar) here; ¿de cuándo ~? since when?

acabado, a [aka'βaðo, a] adj finished, complete; (perfecto) perfect; (agotado) worn out; (fig) masterly ♦ nm finish

acabar [aka'βar] vt (llevar a su fin) to finish, complete; (consumir) to use up; (rematar) to finish off ♦ vi to finish, end; ~se vr to finish, stop; (terminarse) to be over; (agotarse) to run out; ~ con to put an end to; ~ de llegar to have just arrived; ~ por hacer to end (up) by doing; ¡se acabó! it's all over!; ¡basta! that's enough!

acabóse [aka'βose] nm: esto es el ~ this is the last straw

academia [aka'ðemja] nf academy; **académico, a** adj academic

acaecer [akae'θer] vi to happen, occur

acallar [aka'ʎar] vt (persona) to silence; (protestas, rumores) to suppress

acalorado, a [akalo'raðo, a] adj (discusión) heated

acalorarse [akalo'rarse] vr (fig) to get heated

acampar [akam'par] vi to camp

acantilado [akanti'laðo] nm cliff

acaparar [akapa'rar] vt to monopolize; (acumular) to hoard

acariciar [akari'θjar] vt to caress; (esperanza) to cherish

acarrear [akarre'ar] vt to transport; (fig) to cause, result in

acaso [a'kaso] adv perhaps, maybe; (por) si ~ (just) in case

acatamiento [akata'mjento] nm respect; (ley) observance

acatar [aka'tar] vt to respect; (ley) obey

acatarrarse [akata'rrarse] vr to catch a cold

acaudalado, a [akauða'laðo, a] adj well-off

acaudillar [akauði'ʎar] vt to lead, command

acceder [akθe'ðer] vi: ~ a (petición etc) to agree to; (tener acceso a) to have access to; (INFORM) to access

accesible [akθe'siβle] adj accessible

acceso [ak'θeso] nm access, entry; (camino) access, approach; (MED) attack, fit

accesorio, a [akθe'sorjo, a] adj, nm accessory

accidentado, a [akθiðen'taðo, a] adj uneven; (montañoso) hilly; (azaroso) eventful ♦ nm/f accident victim

accidental [akθiðen'tal] adj accidental; **accidentarse** vr to have an accident

accidente [akθi'ðente] nm accident; ~s nmpl (de terreno) unevenness sg

acción [ak'θjon] nf action; (acto) action, act; (COM) share; (JUR) action, lawsuit; **accionar** vt to work, operate; (INFORM) to drive

accionista [akθjo'nista] nm/f shareholder, stockholder

acebo [a'θeβo] nm holly; (árbol) holly tree

acechar [aθe'tʃar] vt to spy on; (aguardar) to lie in wait for; **acecho** nm: estar al acecho (de) to lie in wait (for)

aceitar [aθei'tar] vt to oil, lubricate

aceite [a'θeite] nm oil; (de oliva) olive oil; ~ra nf oilcan; **aceitoso, a** adj oily

aceituna [aθei'tuna] nf olive

acelerador [aθelera'ðor] nm accelerator

acelerar [aθele'rar] vt to accelerate

acelga [a'θelγa] nf chard, beet

acento [a'θento] nm accent; (acentuación) stress

acentuar [aθen'twar] vt to accent; to stress; (fig) to accentuate

acepción [aθep'θjon] nf meaning

aceptable [aθep'taβle] adj acceptable

aceptación [aθepta'θjon] nf acceptance; (aprobación) approval

aceptar [aθep'tar] vt to accept; (aprobar) to approve

acequia [a'θekja] nf irrigation ditch

acera [a'θera] nf pavement (BRIT), sidewalk (US)

acerca [a'θerka]: ~ **de** prep about, concerning

acercar [aθer'kar] vt to bring o move nearer; ~**se** vr to approach, come near

acerico [aθe'riko] nm pincushion

acero [a'θero] nm steel

acérrimo, a [a'θerrimo, a] adj (partidario) staunch; (enemigo) bitter

acertado, a [aθer'taðo, a] adj correct; (apropiado) apt; (sensato) sensible

acertar [aθer'tar] vt (blanco) to hit; (solución) to get right; (adivinar) to guess ♦ vi to get it right, be right; ~ a to manage to; ~ **con** to happen o hit on

acertijo [aθer'tixo] nm riddle, puzzle

achacar [atʃa'kar] vt to attribute

achacoso, a [atʃa'koso, a] adj sickly

achantar [atʃan'tar] (fam) vt to scare, frighten; ~**se** vr to back down

achaque etc [a'tʃake] vb ver **achacar** ♦ nm ailment

achicar [atʃi'kar] vt to reduce; (NAUT) to bale out

achicharrar [atʃitʃa'rrar] vt to scorch, burn

achicoria [atʃi'korja] nf chicory

aciago, a [a'θjavo, a] adj ill-fated, fateful

acicalar [aθika'lar] vt to polish; (persona) to dress up; ~**se** vr to get dressed up

acicate [aθi'kate] nm spur

acidez [aθi'ðeθ] nf acidity

ácido, a ['aθiðo, a] adj sour, acid ♦ nm acid

acierto etc [a'θjerto] vb ver **acertar** ♦ nm success; (buen paso) wise move; (solución) solution; (habilidad) skill, ability

aclamación [aklama'θjon] nf acclamation; (aplausos) applause

aclamar [akla'mar] vt to acclaim; (aplaudir) to applaud

aclaración [aklara'θjon] nf clarification, explanation

aclarar [akla'rar] vt to clarify, explain; (ropa) to rinse ♦ vi to clear up; ~**se** vr (explicarse) to understand; ~**se la garganta** to clear one's throat

aclaratorio, a [aklara'torjo, a] adj explanatory

aclimatación [aklimata'θjon] nf acclimatization

aclimatar [aklima'tar] vt to acclimatize; ~**se** vr to become acclimatized

acné [ak'ne] nm acne

acobardar [akoβar'ðar] vt to intimidate

acodarse [ako'ðarse] vr: ~ **en** to lean on

acogedor, a [akoxe'ðor, a] adj welcoming; (hospitalario) hospitable

acoger [ako'xer] vt to welcome; (abrigar) to shelter; ~**se** vr to take refuge

acogida [ako'xiða] nf reception; refuge

acometer [akome'ter] vt to attack; (emprender) to undertake; **acometida** nf attack, assault

acomodado, a [akomo'ðaðo, a] adj (persona) well-to-do

acomodador, a [akomoða'ðor, a] nm/f usher(ette)

acomodar [akomo'ðar] vt to adjust; (alojar) to accommodate; ~**se** vr to conform; (instalarse) to install o.s.; (adaptarse) ~**se a** to adapt (to)

acompañar [akompa'ɲar] vt to accompany; (documentos) to enclose

acondicionar [akondiθjo'nar] vt to arrange, prepare; (pelo) to condition

acongojar [akoŋgo'xar] vt to distress, grieve

aconsejar [akonse'xar] vt to advise, counsel; ~**se** vr: ~**se con** to consult

acontecer [akonte'θer] vi to happen, occur; **acontecimiento** nm event

acopio [a'kopjo] nm store, stock

acoplamiento [akopla'mjento] nm coupling, joint; **acoplar** vt to fit; (ELEC) to connect; (vagones) to couple

acorazado, a [akora'θaðo, a] adj

armour-plated, armoured ♦ *nm* battleship

acordar [akor'ðar] *vt* (*resolver*) to agree, resolve; (*recordar*) to remind; **~se** *vr* to agree; **~se (de algo)** to remember (sth); agree

acorde *adj* (*MUS*) harmonious; **acorde con** (*medidas etc*) in keeping with ♦ *nm* chord

acordeón [akorðe'on] *nm* accordion

acordonado, a [akorðo'naðo, a] *adj* (*calle*) cordoned-off

acorralar [akorra'lar] *vt* to round up, corral

acortar [akor'tar] *vt* to shorten; (*duración*) to cut short; (*cantidad*) to reduce; **~se** *vr* to become shorter

acosar [ako'sar] *vt* to pursue relentlessly; (*fig*) to hound, pester; **acoso** *nm* harassment; **acoso sexual** sexual harassment

acostar [akos'tar] *vt* (*en cama*) to put to bed; (*en suelo*) to lay down; **~se** *vr* to go to bed; to lie down; **~se con uno** to sleep with sb

acostumbrado, a [akostum'braðo, a] *adj* usual; **~ a** used to

acostumbrar [akostum'brar] *vt*: **~ a uno a algo** to get sb used to sth ♦ *vi*: **~ (a) hacer** to be in the habit of doing; **~se** *vr*: **~se a** to get used to

acotación [akota'θjon] *nf* marginal note; (*GEO*) elevation mark; (*de límite*) boundary mark; (*TEATRO*) stage direction

ácrata ['akrata] *adj, nm/f* anarchist

acre ['akre] *adj* (*olor*) acrid; (*fig*) biting ♦ *nm* acre

acrecentar [akreθen'tar] *vt* to increase, augment

acreditar [akreði'tar] *vt* (*garantizar*) to vouch for, guarantee; (*autorizar*) to authorize; (*dar prueba de*) to prove; (*COM: abonar*) to credit; (*embajador*) to accredit; **~se** *vr* to become famous

acreedor, a [akree'ðor, a] *adj*: **~ de** worthy of ♦ *nm/f* creditor

acribillar [akriβi'ʎar] *vt*: **~ a balazos**

to riddle with bullets

acróbata [a'kroβata] *nm/f* acrobat

acta ['akta] *nf* certificate; (*de comisión*) minutes *pl*, record; **~ de nacimiento/de matrimonio** birth/ marriage certificate; **~ notarial** affidavit

actitud [akti'tuð] *nf* attitude; (*postura*) posture

activar [akti'βar] *vt* to activate; (*acelerar*) to speed up

actividad [aktiβi'ðað] *nf* activity

activo, a [ak'tiβo, a] *adj* active; (*vivo*) lively ♦ *nm* (*COM*) assets *pl*

acto ['akto] *nm* act, action; (*ceremonia*) ceremony; (*TEATRO*) act; **en el ~** immediately

actor [ak'tor] *nm* actor; (*JUR*) plaintiff ♦ *adj*: **parte ~a** prosecution

actriz [ak'triθ] *nf* actress

actuación [aktwa'θjon] *nf* action; (*comportamiento*) conduct, behaviour; (*JUR*) proceedings *pl*; (*desempeño*) performance

actual [ak'twal] *adj* present(-day), current; **~idad** *nf* present; **~idades** *nfpl* (*noticias*) news *sg*; **en la ~idad** at present; (*hoy día*) nowadays

actualizar [aktwali'θar] *vt* to update, modernize

actualmente [aktwal'mente] *adv* at present; (*hoy día*) nowadays

actuar [ak'twar] *vi* (*obrar*) to work, operate; (*actor*) to act, perform ♦ *vt* to work, operate; **~ de** to act as

acuarela [akwa'rela] *nf* watercolour

acuario [a'kwarjo] *nm* aquarium; (*ASTROLOGÍA*): **A~** Aquarius

acuartelar [akwarte'lar] *vt* (*MIL*) to confine to barracks

acuático, a [a'kwatiko, a] *adj* aquatic

acuchillar [akutʃi'ʎar] *vt* (*TEC*) to plane (down), smooth

acuciante [aku'θjante] *adj* urgent

acuciar [aku'θjar] *vt* to urge on

acudir [aku'ðir] *vi* (*asistir*) to attend; (*ir*) to go; **~ a** (*fig*) to turn to; **~ en**

ayuda de to go to the aid of

acuerdo *etc vb ver* **acordar**
♦ *nm* agreement; **¡de ~!** agreed!; **de ~ con** (*persona*) in agreement with; (*acción, documento*) in accordance with; **estar de ~** to be agreed, agree

acumular |akumu'lar| *vt* to accumulate, collect

acuñar |aku'ɲar| *vt* (*moneda*) to mint; (*frase*) to coin

acupuntura |akupun'tura| *nf* acupuncture

acurrucarse |akurru'karse| *vr* to crouch; (*ovillarse*) to curl up

acusación |akusa'θjon| *nf* accusation

acusar |aku'sar| *vt* to accuse; (*revelar*) to reveal; (*denunciar*) to denounce

acuse |a'kuse| *nm:* **~ de recibo** acknowledgement of receipt

acústica |a'kustika| *nf* acoustics *pl*

acústico, a |a'kustiko, a| *adj* acoustic

adaptación |aðapta'θjon| *nf* adaptation

adaptador |aðapta'ðor| *nm* (*ELEC*) adapter

adaptar |aðap'tar| *vt* to adapt; (*acomodar*) to fit

adecuado, a |aðe'kwaðo, a| *adj* (*apto*) suitable; (*oportuno*) appropriate

adecuar |aðe'kwar| *vt* to adapt; to make suitable

a. de J.C. *abr* (= *antes de Jesucristo*) B.C.

adelantado, a |aðelan'taðo, a| *adj* advanced; (*reloj*) fast; **pagar por ~** to pay in advance

adelantamiento |aðelanta'mjento| *nm* (*AUTO*) overtaking

adelantar |aðelan'tar| *vt* to move forward; (*avanzar*) to advance; (*acelerar*) to speed up; (*AUTO*) to overtake ♦ *vi* to go forward, advance; **~se** *vr* to go forward, advance

adelante |aðe'lante| *adv* forward(s), ahead ♦ *excl* come in!; **de hoy en ~** from now on; **más ~** later on; (*más allá*) further on

adelanto |aðe'lanto| *nm* advance; (*mejora*) improvement; (*progreso*) progress

adelgazar |aðelɣa'θar| *vt* to thin (down) ♦ *vi* to get thin; (*con régimen*) to slim down, lose weight

ademán |aðe'man| *nm* gesture; **ademanes** *nmpl* manners; **en ~ de** as if to

además |aðe'mas| *adv* besides; (*por otra parte*) moreover; (*también*) also; **~ de** besides, in addition to

adentrarse |aðen'trarse| *vr:* **~ en** to go into, get inside; (*penetrar*) to penetrate (into)

adentro |a'ðentro| *adv* inside, in; **mar ~** out at sea; **tierra ~** inland

adepto, a |a'ðepto, a| *nm/f* supporter

aderezar |aðere'θar| *vt* (*ensalada*) to dress; (*comida*) to season; **aderezo** *nm* dressing; seasoning

adeudar |aðeu'ðar| *vt* to owe; **~se** *vr* to run into debt

adherirse |aðe'rirse| *vr:* **~ a** to adhere to; (*partido*) to join

adhesión |aðe'sjon| *nf* adhesion; (*fig*) adherence

adicción |aðik'θjon| *nf* addiction

adición |aði'θjon| *nf* addition

adicto, a |a'ðikto, a| *adj:* **~ a** addicted to; (*dedicado*) devoted to ♦ *nm/f* supporter, follower; (*toxicómano etc*) addict

adiestrar |aðjes'trar| *vt* to train, teach; (*conducir*) to guide, lead; **~se** *vr* to practise; (*enseñarse*) to train o.s.

adinerado, a |aðine'raðo, a| *adj* wealthy

adiós |a'ðjos| *excl* (*para despedirse*) goodbye!, cheerio!; (*al pasar*) hello!

aditivo |aði'tiβo| *nm* additive

adivinanza |aðiβi'nanθa| *nf* riddle

adivinar |aðiβi'nar| *vt* to prophesy; (*conjeturar*) to guess; **adivino, a** *nm/f* fortune-teller

adj *abr* (= *adjunto*) encl.

adjetivo |aðxe'tiβo| *nm* adjective

adjudicación [aðxuðika'θjon] nf
award; adjudication

adjudicar [aðxuði'kar] vt to award;
~se vr: **~se algo** to appropriate sth

adjuntar [aðxun'tar] vt to attach,
enclose; **adjunto, a** adj attached,
enclosed ♦ nm/f assistant

administración [aðministra'θjon] nf
administration; (dirección)
management; **administrador, a** nm/f
administrator; manager(ess)

administrar [aðminis'trar] vt to
administer; **administrativo, a** adj
administrative

admirable [aðmi'raβle] adj admirable

admiración [aðmira'θjon] nf
admiration; (asombro) wonder; (LING)
exclamation mark

admirar [aðmi'rar] vt to admire;
(extrañar) to surprise; **~se** vr to be
surprised

admisible [aðmi'siβle] adj admissible

admisión [aðmi'sjon] nf admission;
(reconocimiento) acceptance

admitir [aðmi'tir] vt to admit;
(aceptar) to accept

admonición [aðmoni'θjon] nf
warning

adobar [aðo'βar] vt (CULIN) to season

adobe [a'ðoβe] nm adobe, sun-dried
brick

adoctrinar [aðoktri'nar] vt: **~ en** to
indoctrinate with

adolecer [aðole'θer] vi: **~ de** to suffer
from

adolescente [aðoles'θente] nm/f
adolescent, teenager

adonde [a'ðonde] conj (to) where

adónde [a'ðonde] adv = **dónde**

adopción [aðop'θjon] nf adoption

adoptar [aðop'tar] vt to adopt

adoptivo, a [aðop'tiβo, a] adj (padres)
adoptive; (hijo) adopted

adoquín [aðo'kin] nm paving stone

adorar [aðo'rar] vt to adore

adormecer [aðorme'θer] vt to put to
sleep; **~se** vr to become sleepy;

(dormirse) to fall asleep

adornar [aðor'nar] vt to adorn

adorno [a'ðorno] nm ornament;
(decoración) decoration

adosado, a [aðo'saðo, a] adj: **casa
adosada** semi-detached house

adquiero etc vb ver **adquirir**

adquirir [aðki'rir] vt to acquire, obtain

adquisición [aðkisi'θjon] nf
acquisition

adrede [a'ðreðe] adv on purpose

adscribir [aðskri'βir] vt to appoint

adscrito pp de **adscribir**

aduana [a'ðwana] nf customs pl

aduanero, a [aðwa'nero, a] adj
customs cpd ♦ nm/f customs officer

aducir [aðu'θir] vt to adduce; (dar
como prueba) to offer as proof

adueñarse [aðwe'narse] vr: **~ de** to
take possession of

adulación [aðula'θjon] nf flattery

adular [aðu'lar] vt to flatter

adulterar [aðulte'rar] vt to adulterate

adulterio [aðul'terjo] nm adultery

adúltero, a [a'ðultero, a] adj
adulterous ♦ nm/f adulterer/adulteress

adulto, a [a'ðulto, a] adj, nm/f adult

adusto, a [a'ðusto, a] adj stern;
(austero) austere

advenedizo, a [aðβene'ðiθo, a] nm/f
upstart

advenimiento [aðβeni'mjento] nm
arrival; (al trono) accession

adverbio [að'βerβjo] nm adverb

adversario, a [aðβer'sarjo, a] nm/f
adversary

adversidad [aðβersi'ðað] nf adversity;
(contratiempo) setback

adverso, a [að'βerso, a] adj adverse

advertencia [aðβer'tenθja] nf
warning; (prefacio) preface, foreword

advertir [aðβer'tir] vt to notice;
(avisar): **~ a uno de** to warn sb about
o of

Adviento [að'βjento] nm Advent

advierto etc vb ver **advertir**

adyacente [aðja'θente] adj adjacent

aéreo, a [a'ereo, a] *adj* aerial

aerobic [ae'roßik] *nm* aerobics *sg*

aerodeslizador [aeroðesliða'ðor] *nm* hovercraft

aeromozo, a [aero'moθo, a] (*AM*) *nm/f* air steward(ess)

aeronáutica [aero'nautika] *nf* aeronautics *sg*

aeronave [aero'naße] *nm* spaceship

aeroplano [aero'plano] *nm* aeroplane

aeropuerto [aero'pwerto] *nm* airport

aerosol [aero'sol] *nm* aerosol

afabilidad [afaßili'ðað] *nf* friendliness; **afable** *adj* affable

afamado, a [afa'maðo, a] *adj* famous

afán [a'fan] *nm* hard work; (*deseo*) desire

afanar [afa'nar] *vt* to harass; (*fam*) to pinch; ~**se** *vr*: ~**se por hacer** to strive to do

afear [afe'ar] *vt* to disfigure

afección [afek'θjon] *nf* (*MED*) disease

afectación [afekta'θjon] *nf* affectation; **afectado, a** *adj* affected

afectar [afek'tar] *vt* to affect

afectísimo, a [afek'tisimo, a] *adj* affectionate; **suyo** ~ yours truly

afectivo, a [afek'tißo, a] *adj* (*problema etc*) emotional

afecto [a'fekto] *nm* affection; **tenerle** ~ **a uno** to be fond of sb

afectuoso, a [afek'twoso, a] *adj* affectionate

afeitar [afei'tar] *vt* to shave; ~**se** *vr* to shave

afeminado, a [afemi'naðo, a] *adj* effeminate

Afganistán [afyanis'tan] *nm* Afghanistan

afianzamiento [afjanθa'mjento] *nm* strengthening; security

afianzar [afjan'θar] *vt* to strengthen; to secure; ~**se** *vr* to become established

afiche [a'fitʃe] (*AM*) *nm* poster

afición [afi'θjon] *nf* fondness, liking; **la** ~ **the fans** *pl*; **pinto por** ~ I paint as a

hobby; **aficionado, a** *adj* keen, enthusiastic; (*no profesional*) amateur ♦ *nm/f* enthusiast; fan; amateur; **ser aficionado a algo** to be very keen on o fond of sth

aficionar [afiθjo'nar] *vt*: ~ **a uno a algo** to make sb like sth; ~**se** *vr*: ~**se a algo** to grow fond of sth

afilado, a [afi'laðo, a] *adj* sharp

afilar [afi'lar] *vt* to sharpen

afiliarse [afi'ljarse] *vr* to affiliate

afín [a'fin] *adj* (*parecido*) similar; (*conexo*) related

afinar [afi'nar] *vt* (*TEC*) to refine; (*MUS*) to tune ♦ *vi* (*tocar*) to play in tune; (*cantar*) to sing in tune

afincarse [afin'karse] *vr* to settle

afinidad [afini'ðað] *nf* affinity; (*parentesco*) relationship; **por** ~ by marriage

afirmación [afirma'θjon] *nf* affirmation

afirmar [afir'mar] *vt* to affirm, state; **afirmativo, a** *adj* affirmative

aflicción [aflik'θjon] *nf* affliction; (*dolor*) grief

afligir [afli'xir] *vt* to afflict; (*apenar*) to distress; ~**se** *vr* to grieve

aflojar [aflo'xar] *vt* to slacken; (*desatar*) to loosen, undo; (*relajar*) to relax ♦ *vi* to drop; (*bajar*) to go down; ~**se** *vr* to relax

aflorar [aflo'rar] *vi* to come to the surface, emerge

afluente [aflu'ente] *adj* flowing ♦ *nm* tributary

afluir [aflu'ir] *vi* to flow

afmo, a *abr* (= *afectísimo(a) suyo(a)*) Yours

afónico, a [a'foniko, a] *adj*: **estar** ~ to have a sore throat; to have lost one's voice

aforo [a'foro] *nm* (*de teatro etc*) capacity

afortunado, a [afortu'naðo, a] *adj* fortunate, lucky

afrancesado, a [afranθe'saðo, a] *adj*

francophile; (*pey*) Frenchified

afrenta [a'frenta] *nf* affront, insult; (*deshonra*) dishonour, shame

África ['afrika] *nf* Africa; **africano, a** *adj, nm/f* African

afrontar [afron'tar] *vt* to confront; (*poner cara a cara*) to bring face to face

afuera [a'fwera] *adv* out, outside; ~**s** *nfpl* outskirts

agachar [aɣa'tʃar] *vt* to bend, bow; ~**se** *vr* to stoop, bend

agalla [a'ɣaʎa] *nf* (*ZOOL*) gill; **tener ~s** (*fam*) to have guts

agarradera [aɣarra'ðera] (*esp AM*) *nf* handle

agarrado, a [aɣa'rraðo, a] *adj* mean, stingy

agarrar [aɣa'rrar] *vt* to grasp, grab; (*AM*) to take, catch; (*recoger*) to pick up ♦ *vi* (*planta*) to take root; ~**se** *vr* to hold on (tightly)

agarrotar [aɣarro'tar] *vt* (*persona*) to squeeze tightly; (*reo*) to garrotte; ~**se** *vr* (*motor*) to seize up; (*MED*) to stiffen

agasajar [aɣasa'xar] *vt* to treat well, fête

agazaparse [aɣaθa'parse] *vr* to crouch down

agencia [a'xenθja] *nf* agency; **~ inmobiliaria** estate (*BRIT*) o real estate (*US*) agent's (office); **~ de viajes** travel agency

agenciarse [axen'θjarse] *vr* to obtain, procure

agenda [a'xenda] *nf* diary

agente [a'xente] *nm/f* agent; (*de policía*) policeman/policewoman; **~ inmobiliario** estate agent (*BRIT*), realtor (*US*); **~ de seguros** insurance agent

ágil ['axil] *adj* agile, nimble; **agilidad** *nf* agility, nimbleness

agilizar [axili'θar] *vt* (*trámites*) to speed up

agitación [axita'θjon] *nf* (*de mano etc*) shaking, waving; (*de líquido etc*)

stirring; (*fig*) agitation

agitado, a [axi'taðo, a] *adj* hectic; (*viaje*) bumpy

agitar [axi'tar] *vt* to wave, shake; (*líquido*) to stir; (*fig*) to stir up, excite; ~**se** *vr* to get excited; (*inquietarse*) to get worried o upset

aglomeración [aɣlomera'θjon] *nf*: **~ de tráfico/gente** traffic jam/mass of people

aglomerar [aɣlome'rar] *vt* to crowd together; ~**se** *vr* to crowd together

agnóstico, a [aɣ'nostiko, a] *adj, nm/f* agnostic

agobiar [aɣo'βjar] *vt* to weigh down; (*oprimir*) to oppress; (*cargar*) to burden

agolparse [aɣol'parse] *vr* to crowd together

agonía [aɣo'nia] *nf* death throes *pl*; (*fig*) agony, anguish

agonizante [aɣoni'θante] *adj* dying

agonizar [aɣoni'θar] *vi* to be dying

agosto [a'ɣosto] *nm* August

agotado, a [aɣo'taðo, a] *adj* (*persona*) exhausted; (*libros*) out of print; (*acabado*) finished; (*COM*) sold out

agotador, a [aɣota'ðor, a] *adj* exhausting

agotamiento [aɣota'mjento] *nm* exhaustion

agotar [aɣo'tar] *vt* to exhaust; (*consumir*) to drain; (*recursos*) to use up, deplete; ~**se** *vr* to be exhausted; (*acabarse*) to run out; (*libro*) to go out of print

agraciado, a [aɣra'θjaðo, a] *adj* (*atractivo*) attractive; (*en sorteo etc*) lucky

agradable [aɣra'ðaßle] *adj* pleasant, nice

agradar [aɣra'ðar] *vt*: **él me agrada** I like him

agradecer [aɣraðe'θer] *vt* to thank; (*favor etc*) to be grateful for; **agradecido, a** *adj* grateful; **¡muy agradecido!** thanks a lot!; **agradecimiento** *nm* thanks *pl*;

gratitude

agradezco etc vb ver **agradecer**

agrado |a'vraðo| nm: **ser de tu** etc ~ to be to your etc liking

agrandar |avran'dar| vt to enlarge; (fig) to exaggerate; ~**se** vr to get bigger

agrario, a |a'vrarjo, a| adj agrarian, land cpd; (política) agricultural, farming

agravante |avra'ßante| adj aggravating ♦ nm: **con el** ~ **de que** ... with the further difficulty that ....

agravar |avra'ßar| vt (pesar sobre) to make heavier; (irritar) to aggravate; ~**se** vr to worsen, get worse

agraviar |avra'ßjar| vt to offend; (ser injusto con) to wrong; ~**se** vr to take offence; **agravio** nm offence; wrong; (JUR) grievance

agredir |avre'ðir| vt to attack

agregado, a |avre'xaðo, a| nm/f: A~ = teacher (who is not head of department) ♦ nm aggregate; (persona) attaché

agregar |avre'xar| vt to gather; (añadir) to add; (persona) to appoint

agresión |avre'sjon| nf aggression

agresivo, a |avre'sißo, a| adj aggressive

agriar |a'vrjar| vt (to turn) sour; ~**se** vr to turn sour

agrícola |a'vrikola| adj farming cpd, agricultural

agricultor, a |avrikul'tor, a| nm/f farmer

agricultura |avrikul'tura| nf agriculture, farming

agridulce |avri'ðulθe| adj bittersweet; (CULIN) sweet and sour

agrietarse |avrje'tarse| vr to crack; (piel) to chap

agrimensor, a |avrimen'sor, a| nm/f surveyor

agrio, a |'avrjo, a| adj bitter

agrupación |avrupa'θjon| nf group; (acto) grouping

agrupar |avru'par| vt to group

agua |'avwa| nf water; (NAUT) wake; (ARQ) slope of a roof; ~**s** nfpl (de piedra) water sg, sparkle sg; (MED) water sg, urine sg; (NAUT) waters; ~**s abajo/arriba** downstream/upstream; ~ **bendita/destilada/potable** holy/ distilled/drinking water; ~ **caliente** hot water; ~ **corriente** running water; ~ **de colonia** eau de cologne; ~ **mineral (con/sin gas)** (carbonated/uncarbonated) mineral water; ~ **oxigenada** hydrogen peroxide; ~**s jurisdiccionales** territorial waters

aguacate |avwa'kate| nm avocado (pear)

aguacero |avwa'θero| nm (heavy) shower, downpour

aguado, a |a'vwaðo, a| adj watery, watered down

aguafiestas |avwa'fjestas| nm/f inv spoilsport, killjoy

aguanieve |avwa'njeße| nf sleet

aguantar |avwan'tar| vt to bear, put up with; (sostener) to hold up ♦ vi to last; ~**se** vr to restrain o.s.; **aguante** nm (paciencia) patience; (resistencia) endurance

aguar |a'vwar| vt to water down

aguardar |avwar'ðar| vt to wait for

aguardiente |avwar'ðjente| nm brandy, liquor

aguarrás |avwa'rras| nm turpentine

agudeza |avu'ðeθa| nf sharpness; (ingenio) wit

agudizar |avuði'θar| vt (crisis) to make worse; ~**se** vr to get worse

agudo, a |a'vuðo, a| adj sharp; (voz) high-pitched, piercing; (dolor, enfermedad) acute

agüero |a'vwero| nm: **buen/mal** ~ good/bad omen

aguijón |avi'xon| nm sting; (fig) spur

águila |'avila| nf eagle; (fig) genius

aguileño, a |avi'leno, a| adj (nariz) aquiline; (rostro) sharp-featured

aguinaldo |avi'naldo| nm Christmas

box

aguja [a'γuxa] nf needle; (de reloj) hand; (ARQ) spire; (TEC) firing-pin; **~s** nfpl (ZOOL) ribs; (FERRO) points

agujerear [aγuxere'ar] vt to make holes in

agujero [aγu'xero] nm hole

agujetas [aγu'xetas] nfpl stitch sg; (rigidez) stiffness sg

aguzar [aγu'θar] vt to sharpen; (fig) to incite

ahi [a'i] adv there; **de ~ que** so that, with the result that; **~ llega** here he comes; **por ~ that** way; (allá) over there; **200 o por ~** 200 or so

ahijado, a [ai'xaðo, a] nm/f godson/ daughter

ahínco [a'inko] nm earnestness

ahogar [ao'γar] vt to drown; (asfixiar) to suffocate, smother; (fuego) to put out; **~se** vr (en el agua) to drown; (por asfixia) to suffocate

ahogo [a'oγo] nm breathlessness; (fig) financial difficulty

ahondar [aon'dar] vt to deepen, make deeper; (fig) to study thoroughly ♦ vi: **~ en** to study thoroughly

ahora [a'ora] adv now; (hace poco) a moment ago, just now; (dentro de poco) in a moment; **~ voy I'm** coming; **~ mismo** right now; **~ bien** now then; **por ~** for the present

ahorcar [aor'kar] vt to hang

ahorita [ao'rita] adv (fam: esp AM) right now

ahorrar [ao'rrar] vt (dinero) to save; (esfuerzos) to save, avoid; **ahorro** nm (acto) saving; **ahorros** nmpl (dinero) savings

ahuecar [awe'kar] vt to hollow (out); (voz) to deepen; **~se** vr to give o.s. airs

ahumar [au'mar] vt to smoke, cure; (llenar de humo) to fill with smoke ♦ vi to smoke; **~se** vr to fill with smoke

ahuyentar [aujen'tar] vt to drive off, frighten off; (fig) to dispel

airado, a [ai'raðo, a] adj angry

airar [ai'rar] vt to anger; **~se** vr to get angry

aire ['aire] nm air; (viento) wind; (corriente) draught; (MUS) tune; **~** nmpl: **darse ~s** to give o.s. airs; **al ~ libre** in the open air; **~ acondicionado** air conditioning; **airearse** vr (persona) to go out for a breath of fresh air; **airoso, a** adj windy; draughty; (fig) graceful

aislado, a [ais'laðo, a] adj isolated; (incomunicado) cut-off; (ELEC) insulated

aislar [ais'lar] vt to isolate; (ELEC) to insulate

ajardinado, a [axarði'naðo, a] adj landscaped

ajedrez [axe'ðreθ] nm chess

ajeno, a [a'xeno, a] adj (que pertenece a otro) somebody else's; **~ a** foreign to

ajetreado, a [axetre'aðo, a] adj busy

ajetreo [axe'treo] nm bustle

ají [a'xi] (AM) nm chil(l)i, red pepper; (salsa) chil(l)i sauce

ajillo [a'xiλo] nm: **gambas al ~** garlic prawns

ajo ['axo] nm garlic

ajuar [a'xwar] nm household furnishings pl; (de novia) trousseau; (de niño) layette

ajustado, a [axus'taðo, a] adj (tornillo) tight; (cálculo) right; (ropa) tight(-fitting); (resultado) close

ajustar [axus'tar] vt (adaptar) to adjust; (encajar) to fit; (TEC) to engage; (IMPRENTA) to make up; (apretar) to tighten; (concertar) to agree (on); (reconciliar) to reconcile; (cuentas, deudas) to settle ♦ vi to fit; **~se** vr: **~se** (a precio etc) to be in keeping with, fit in with; **~ las cuentas a uno** to get even with sb

ajuste [a'xuste] nm adjustment; (COSTURA) fitting; (acuerdo) compromise; (de cuenta) settlement

al [al] (= a + el) ver **a**

ala ['ala] nf wing; (de sombrero) brim; (futbolista) winger; **~ delta** nf hang-glider

alabanza [ala'βanθa] nf praise

alabar [ala'βar] vt to praise

alacena [ala'θena] nf kitchen cupboard (*BRIT*), kitchen closet (*US*)

alacrán [ala'kran] nm scorpion

alambique [alam'bike] nm still

alambrada [alam'braða] nf wire fence; (*red*) wire netting

alambrado [alam'braðo] nm = alambrada

alambre [a'lambre] nm wire; ~ de púas barbed wire

alameda [ala'meða] nf (*plantío*) poplar grove; (*lugar de paseo*) avenue, boulevard

álamo ['alamo] nm poplar; ~ temblón aspen

alarde [a'larðe] nm show, display; hacer ~ de to boast of

alargador [alarva'ðor] nm (*ELEC*) extension lead

alargar [alar'var] vt to lengthen, extend; (*paso*) to hasten; (*brazo*) to stretch out; (*cuerda*) to pay out; (*conversación*) to spin out; ~se vr to get longer

alarido [ala'riðo] nm shriek

alarma [a'larma] nf alarm

alarmar vt to alarm; ~se to get alarmed; **alarmante** [alar'mante] adj alarming

alba ['alβa] nf dawn

albacea [alβa'θea] nm/f executor/executrix

albahaca [al'βaka] nf basil

Albania [al'βanja] nf Albania

albañil [alβa'ɲil] nm bricklayer; (*cantero*) mason

albarán [alβa'ran] nm (*COM*) delivery note, invoice

albaricoque [alβari'koke] nm apricot

albedrío [alβe'ðrio] nm: libre ~ free will

alberca [al'βerka] nf reservoir; (*AM*) swimming pool

albergar [alβer'var] vt to shelter

albergue etc [al'βerɣe] vb ver albergar ♦ nm shelter, refuge; ~ juvenil youth hostel

albóndiga [al'βondiɣa] nf meatball

albornoz [alβor'noθ] nm (*de los árabes*) burnous; (*para el baño*) bathrobe

alborotar [alβoro'tar] vi to make a row ♦ vt to agitate, stir up; ~se vr to get excited; (*mar*) to get rough; **alboroto** nm row, uproar

alborozar [alβoro'θar] vt to gladden; ~se vr to rejoice

alborozo [alβo'roθo] nm joy

álbum ['alβum] (*pl* ~s, ~es) nm album; ~ de recortes scrapbook

alcachofa [alka'tʃofa] nf artichoke

alcalde, esa [al'kalde, esa] nm/f mayor(ess)

alcaldía [alkal'dia] nf mayoralty; (*lugar*) mayor's office

alcance etc [al'kanθe] vb ver alcanzar ♦ nm reach; (*COM*) adverse balance

alcantarilla [alkanta'riʎa] nf (*de aguas cloacales*) sewer; (*en la calle*) gutter

alcanzar [alkan'θar] vt (*algo: con la mano, el pie*) to reach; (*alguien: en el camino etc*) to catch up with; (*autobús*) to catch; (*suj: bala*) to hit, strike ♦ vi (*ser suficiente*) to be enough; ~ a hacer to manage to do

alcaparra [alka'parra] nf caper

alcayata [alka'jata] nf hook

alcázar [al'kaθar] nm fortress; (*NAUT*) quarter-deck

alcoba [al'koβa] nf bedroom

alcohol [al'kol] nm alcohol; ~ metílico methylated spirits pl (*BRIT*), wood alcohol (*US*); **alcohólico, a** adj, nm/f alcoholic

alcoholímetro [alko'limetro] nm Breathalyser ® (*BRIT*), drunkometer (*US*)

alcoholismo [alko'lismo] nm alcoholism

alcornoque [alkor'noke] nm cork tree; (*fam*) idiot

alcurnia [al'kurnja] *nf* lineage
aldaba [al'daβa] *nf* (door) knocker
aldea [al'dea] *nf* village; **~no, a** *adj* village *cpd* ♦ *nm/f* villager
aleación [alea'θjon] *nf* alloy
aleatorio, a [alea'torjo, a] *adj* random
aleccionar [alekθjo'nar] *vt* to instruct; (*adiestrar*) to train
alegación [aleɣa'θjon] *nf* allegation
alegar [ale'ɣar] *vt* to claim; (*JUR*) to plead ♦ *vi* (*AM*) to argue
alegato [ale'ɣato] *nm* (*JUR*) allegation; (*AM*) argument
alegoría [aleɣo'ria] *nf* allegory
alegrar [ale'ɣrar] *vt* (*causar alegría*) to cheer (up); (*fuego*) to poke; (*fiesta*) to liven up; **~se** *vr* (*fam*) to get merry o tight; **~se de** to be glad about
alegre [ale'ɣre] *adj* happy, cheerful; (*fam*) merry, tight; (*chiste*) risqué, blue; **alegría** *nf* happiness; merriment
alejamiento [alexa'mjento] *nm* removal; (*distancia*) remoteness
alejar [ale'xar] *vt* to remove; (*fig*) to estrange; **~se** *vr* to move away
alemán, ana [ale'man, ana] *adj*, *nm/f* German ♦ *nm* (*LING*) German
Alemania [ale'manja] *nf*: **~ Occidental** West Germany
alentador, a [alenta'ðor, a] *adj* encouraging
alentar [alen'tar] *vt* to encourage
alergia [a'lerxja] *nf* allergy
alero [a'lero] *nm* (*de tejado*) eaves *pl*; (*de carruaje*) mudguard
alerta [a'lerta] *adj, nm* alert
aleta [a'leta] *nf* (*de pez*) fin; (*de ave*) wing; (*de foca, DEPORTE*) flipper; (*AUTO*) mudguard
aletargar [aletar'ɣar] *vt* to make drowsy; (*entumecer*) to make numb; **~se** *vr* to grow drowsy; to become numb
aletear [alete'ar] *vi* to flutter
alevín [ale'βin] *nm* fry, young fish
alevosía [aleβo'sia] *nf* treachery
alfabeto [alfa'βeto] *nm* alphabet

alfalfa [al'falfa] *nf* alfalfa, lucerne
alfarería [alfare'ria] *nf* pottery; (*tienda*) pottery shop; **alfarero, a** *nm/f* potter
alféizar [al'feiθar] *nm* window-sill
alférez [al'fereθ] *nm* (*MIL*) second lieutenant; (*NAUT*) ensign
alfil [al'fil] *nm* (*AJEDREZ*) bishop
alfiler [alfi'ler] *nm* pin; (*broche*) clip
alfiletero [alfile'tero] *nm* needlecase
alfombra [al'fombra] *nf* carpet; (*más pequeña*) rug; **alfombrar** *vt* to carpet; **alfombrilla** *nf* rug, mat; (*INFORM*) mouse mat o pad
alforja [al'forxa] *nf* saddlebag
algarabía [alɣara'βia] *nf* (*fam*) gibberish; (*griterío*) hullabaloo
algas ['alɣas] *nfpl* seaweed
álgebra ['alxeβra] *nf* algebra
álgido, a [al'xiðo, a] *adj* (*momento etc*) crucial, decisive
algo ['alɣo] *pron* something; anything ♦ *adv* somewhat, rather; **¿~ más?** anything else?; (*en tienda*) is that all?; **por ~ será** there must be some reason for it
algodón [alɣo'ðon] *nm* cotton; (*planta*) cotton plant; **~ de azúcar** candy floss (*BRIT*), cotton candy (*US*); **~ hidrófilo** cotton wool (*BRIT*), absorbent cotton (*US*)
algodonero, a [alɣoðo'nero, a] *adj* cotton *cpd* ♦ *nm/f* cotton grower ♦ *nm* cotton plant
alguacil [alɣwa'θil] *nm* bailiff; (*TAUR*) mounted official
alguien ['alɣjen] *pron* someone, somebody; (*en frases interrogativas*) anyone, anybody
alguno, a [al'ɣuno, a] *adj* (*delante de nm*: **algún**) some; (*después de n*): **no tiene talento** ~ he has no talent, he doesn't have any talent ♦ *pron* (*alguien*) someone, somebody; **algún que otro libro** some book or other; **algún día iré** I'll go one o some day; **sin interés** ~ without the slightest interest; **~ que otro** an occasional

one; **~s piensan** some (people) think

alhaja [a'laxa] *nf* jewel; (*tesoro*) precious object, treasure

alhelí [ale'li] *nm* wallflower, stock

aliado, a [a'ljaðo, a] *adj* allied

alianza [a'ljanθa] *nf* alliance; (*anillo*) wedding ring

aliar [a'ljar] *vt* to ally; **~se** *vr* to form an alliance

alias ['aljas] *adv* alias

alicates [ali'kates] *nmpl* pliers; **~ de uñas** nail clippers

aliciente [ali'θjente] *nm* incentive; (*atracción*) attraction

alienación [aljena'θjon] *nf* alienation

aliento [a'ljento] *nm* breath; (*respiración*) breathing; **sin ~** breathless

aligerar [alixe'rar] *vt* to lighten; (*reducir*) to shorten; (*aliviar*) to alleviate; (*mitigar*) to ease; (*paso*) to quicken

alijo [a'lixo] *nm* consignment

alimaña [ali'maɲa] *nf* pest

alimentación [alimenta'θjon] *nf* (*comida*) food; (*acción*) feeding; (*tienda*) grocer's (shop); **alimentador** *nm*: **alimentador de papel** sheet-feeder

alimentar [alimen'tar] *vt* to feed; (*nutrir*) to nourish; **~se** *vr* to feed

alimenticio, a [alimen'tiθjo, a] *adj* food *cpd*; (*nutritivo*) nourishing, nutritious

alimento [ali'mento] *nm* (*nutrición*) nourishment

alineación [alinea'θjon] *nf* alignment; (*DEPORTE*) line-up

alinear [aline'ar] *vt* to align; **~se** *vr* (*DEPORTE*) to line up; **~se en** to fall in with

aliñar [ali'ɲar] *vt* (*CULIN*) to season; **aliño** *nm* (*CULIN*) dressing

alioli [ali'oli] *nm* garlic mayonnaise

alisar [ali'sar] *vt* to smooth

aliso [a'liso] *nm* alder

alistarse [alis'tarse] *vr* to enlist; (*inscribirse*) to enrol

aliviar [ali'βjar] *vt* (*carga*) to lighten; (*persona*) to relieve; (*dolor*) to relieve, alleviate

alivio [a'liβjo] *nm* alleviation, relief

aljibe [al'xiβe] *nm* cistern

allá [a'ʎa] *adv* (*lugar*) there; (*por ahí*) over there; (*tiempo*) then; **~ abajo** down there; **más ~** further on; **más ~ de** beyond; **¡~ tú!** that's your problem!

allanamiento [aʎana'mjento] *nm*: **~ de morada** burglary

allanar [aʎa'nar] *vt* to flatten, level (out); (*igualar*) to smooth (out); (*fig*) to subdue; (*JUR*) to burgle, break into

allegado, a [aʎe'ɣaðo, a] *adj* near, close ♦ *nm/f* relation

allí [a'ʎi] *adv* there; **~ mismo** right there; **por ~** over there; (*por ese camino*) that way

alma ['alma] *nf* soul; (*persona*) person

almacén [alma'θen] *nm* (*depósito*) warehouse, store; (*MIL*) magazine; (*AM*) shop; **(grandes) almacenes** *nmpl* department store *sg*; **almacenaje** *nm* storage

almacenar [almaθe'nar] *vt* to store, put in storage; (*proveerse*) to stock up with; **almacenero** *nm* (*AM*) shopkeeper

almanaque [alma'nake] *nm* almanac

almeja [al'mexa] *nf* clam

almendra [al'mendra] *nf* almond; **almendro** *nm* almond tree

almíbar [al'miβar] *nm* syrup

almidón [almi'ðon] *nm* starch; **almidonar** *vt* to starch

almirante [almi'rante] *nm* admiral

almirez [almi'reθ] *nm* mortar

almizcle [al'miθkle] *nm* musk

almohada [almo'aða] *nf* pillow; (*funda*) pillowcase; **almohadilla** *nf* cushion; (*TEC*) pad; (*AM*) pincushion

almohadón [almoa'ðon] *nm* large pillow; bolster

almorranas [almo'rranas] *nfpl* piles, haemorrhoids

almorzar [almor'θar] vt: ~ **una tortilla** to have an omelette for lunch ♦ vi to (have) lunch

almuerzo etc [al'mwerθo] vb ver **almorzar** ♦ nm lunch

alocado, a [alo'kaðo] adj crazy

alojamiento [aloxa'mjento] nm lodging(s) (pl); (viviendas) housing

alojar [alo'xar] vt to lodge; ~**se** vr to lodge, stay

alondra [a'londra] nf lark, skylark

alpargata [alpar'ɣata] nf rope-soled sandal, espadrille

Alpes ['alpes] nmpl: **los ~** the Alps

alpinismo [alpi'nismo] nm mountaineering, climbing; **alpinista** nm/f mountaineer, climber

alpiste [al'piste] nm birdseed

alquilar [alki'lar] vt (suj: propietario: inmuebles) to let, rent (out); (: coche) to hire out; (: TV) to rent (out); (suj: alquilador: inmuebles, TV) to rent; (: coche) to hire; "**se alquila casa**" "house to let (BRIT) o for rent (US)"

alquiler [alki'ler] nm renting; letting; hiring; (arriendo) rent, hire charge; ~ **de automóviles** car hire; **de ~** for hire

alquimia [al'kimja] nf alchemy

alquitrán [alki'tran] nm tar

alrededor [alreðe'ðor] adv around, about; ~ **de** around, about; mirar a su ~ to look (round) about one; ~**es** nmpl surroundings

alta ['alta] nf (certificate of) discharge; **dar de ~** to discharge

altanería [altane'ria] nf haughtiness, arrogance; **altanero, a** adj arrogant, haughty

altar [al'tar] nm altar

altavoz [alta'βoθ] nm loudspeaker; (amplificador) amplifier

alteración [altera'θjon] nf alteration; (alboroto) disturbance

alterar [alte'rar] vt to alter; to disturb; ~**se** vr (persona) to get upset

altercado [alter'kaðo] nm argument

alternar [alter'nar] vt to alternate ♦ vi to alternate; (turnar) to take turns; ~**se** vr to alternate; to take turns; ~ **con** to mix with; **alternativa** nf alternative; (elección) choice; **alternativo, a** adj alternative; (alterno) alternating; **alterno, a** adj alternate; (ELEC) alternating

Alteza [al'teθa] nf (tratamiento) Highness

altibajos [alti'βaxos] nmpl ups and downs

altiplanicie [altipla'niθje] nf high plateau

altiplano [alti'plano] nm = **altiplanicie**

altisonante [altiso'nante] adj high-flown, high-sounding

altitud [alti'tuð] nf height; (AVIAT, GEO) altitude

altivez [alti'βeθ] nf haughtiness, arrogance; **altivo, a** adj haughty, arrogant

alto, a ['alto, a] adj high; (persona) tall; (sonido) high, sharp; (noble) high, lofty ♦ nm halt; (MUS) alto; (GEO) hill; (: de coche) to hire; **alto, a** pile ♦ adv (de sitio) high; (de sonido) loud, loudly ♦ excl halt!; **la pared tiene 2 metros de ~** the wall is 2 metres high; **en alta mar** on the high seas; **en voz alta** in a loud voice; **las altas horas de la noche** the small o wee hours; **en lo ~** at the top of; **pasar por ~** to overlook

altoparlante [altopar'lante] (AM) nm loudspeaker

altruismo [altru'ismo] nm altruism

altura [al'tura] nf height; (NAUT) depth; (GEO) latitude; **la pared tiene 1.80 de ~** the wall is 1 metre 80cm high; **a estas ~s** at this stage; **a estas ~s del año** at this time of the year

alubia [a'luβja] nf bean

alucinación [aluθina'θjon] nf hallucination

alucinar [aluθi'nar] vi to hallucinate ♦ vt to deceive; (fascinar) to fascinate

alud [a'luð] nm avalanche; (fig) flood

aludir [alu'ðir] vi: ~ **a** to allude to;
darse por aludido to take the hint

alumbrado [alum'braðo] nm lighting;
alumbramiento nm lighting; (MED)
childbirth, delivery

alumbrar [alum'brar] vt to light (up)
♦ vi (MED) to give birth

aluminio [alu'minjo] nm aluminium
(BRIT), aluminum (US)

alumno, a [a'lumno, a] nm/f pupil,
student

alunizar [aluni'θar] vi to land on the
moon

alusión [alu'sjon] nf allusion

alusivo, a [alu'siβo, a] adj allusive

aluvión [alu'βjon] nm alluvium; (fig)
flood

alverja [al'βerxa] (AM) nf pea

alza ['alθa] nf rise; (MIL) sight

alzada [al'θaða] nf (de caballos) height;
(JUR) appeal

alzamiento [alθa'mjento] nm
(rebelión) rising

alzar [al'θar] vt to lift (up); (precio,
muro) to raise; (cuello de abrigo) to turn
up; (AGR) to gather in; (IMPRENTA) to
gather; ~**se** vr to get up, rise;
(rebelarse) to revolt; (COM) to go
fraudulently bankrupt; (JUR) to appeal

ama ['ama] nf lady of the house;
(dueña) owner; (institutriz) governess;
(madre adoptiva) foster mother; ~ **de
casa** housewife; ~ **de llaves**
housekeeper

amabilidad [amaβili'ðað] nf kindness;
(simpatía) niceness; **amable** adj kind;
nice; **es usted muy amable** that's
very kind of you

amaestrado, a [amaes'traðo, a] adj
(animal: en circo etc) performing

amaestrar [amaes'trar] vt to train

amago [a'maɣo] nm threat; (gesto)
threatening gesture; (MED) symptom

amainar [amai'nar] vi (viento) to die
down

amalgama [amal'ɣama] nf amalgam;

amalgamar vt to amalgamate;
(combinar) to combine, mix

amamantar [amaman'tar] vt to
suckle, nurse

amanecer [amane'θer] vi to dawn
♦ nm dawn; ~ **afiebrado** to wake up
with a fever

amanerado, a [amane'raðo, a] adj
affected

amansar [aman'sar] vt to tame;
(persona) to subdue; ~**se** vr (persona)
to calm down

amante [a'mante] adj: ~ **de** fond of
♦ nm/f lover

amapola [ama'pola] nf poppy

amar [a'mar] vt to love

amargado, a [amar'ɣaðo, a] adj
embittered

amargar [amar'ɣar] vt to make bitter;
(fig) to embitter; ~**se** vr to become
embittered

amargo, a [a'marɣo, a] adj bitter;
amargura nf bitterness

amarillento, a [amari'ʎento, a] adj
yellowish; (tez) sallow; **amarillo, a**
adj, nm yellow

amarrar [ama'rrar] vt to moor;
(sujetar) to tie up

amarras [a'marras] nfpl: **soltar** ~ to
set sail

amasar [ama'sar] vt (masa) to knead;
(mezclar) to mix, prepare;
(confeccionar) to concoct; **amasijo** nm
kneading; mixing; (fig) hotchpotch

amateur ['amatur] nm/f amateur

amazona [ama'θona] nf horsewoman;
A~s nm: **el A~s** the Amazon

ambages [am'baxes] nmpl: **sin** ~ in
plain language

ámbar ['ambar] nm amber

ambición [ambi'θjon] nf ambition;
ambicionar vt to aspire to;
ambicioso, a adj ambitious

ambidextro, a [ambi'ðekstro, a] adj
ambidextrous

ambientación [ambjenta'θjon] nf
(CINE, TEATRO etc) setting; (RADIO)
sound effects

ambiente [am'bjente] nm (tb fig) atmosphere; (medio) environment

ambigüedad [ambiɣwe'ðað] nf ambiguity; **ambiguo, a** adj ambiguous

ámbito ['ambito] nm (campo) field; (fig) scope

ambos, as ['ambos, as] adj pl, pron pl both

ambulancia [ambu'lanθja] nf ambulance

ambulante [ambu'lante] adj travelling cpd, itinerant

ambulatorio [ambula'torio] nm state health-service clinic

amedrentar [ameðren'tar] vt to scare

amén [a'men] excl amen; **~ de** besides

amenaza [ame'naθa] nf threat

amenazar [amena'θar] vt to threaten
♦ vi: **~ con hacer** to threaten to do

amenidad [ameni'ðað] nf pleasantness

ameno, a [a'meno, a] adj pleasant

América [a'merika] nf America; **~ del Norte/del Sur** North/South America; **~ Central/Latina** Central/Latin America; **americana** nf coat, jacket; ver tb **americano; americano, a** adj, nm/f American

amerizar [ameri'θar] vi (avión) to land (on the sea)

ametralladora [ametraʎa'ðora] nf machine gun

amianto [a'mjanto] nm asbestos

amigable [ami'ɣaßle] adj friendly

amígdala [a'miɣðala] nf tonsil; **amigdalitis** nf tonsillitis

amigo, a [a'miɣo, a] adj friendly
♦ nm/f friend; (amante) lover; **ser ~ de algo** to be fond of sth; **ser muy ~s** to be close friends

amilanar [amila'nar] vt to scare; **~se** vr to get scared

aminorar [amino'rar] vt to diminish; (reducir) to reduce; **~ la marcha** to slow down

amistad [amis'tað] nf friendship; **~es** nfpl (amigos) friends; **amistoso, a** adj friendly

amnesia [am'nesja] nf amnesia

amnistía [amnis'tia] nf amnesty

amo ['amo] nm owner; (jefe) boss

amodorrarse [amoðo'rrarse] vr to get sleepy

amoldar [amol'dar] vt to mould; (adaptar) to adapt

amonestación [amonesta'θjon] nf warning; **amonestaciones** nfpl (REL) marriage banns

amonestar [amones'tar] vt to warn; (REL) to publish the banns of

amontonar [amonto'nar] vt to collect, pile up; **~se** vr to crowd together; (acumularse) to pile up

amor [a'mor] nm love; (amante) lover; **hacer el ~** to make love; **~ propio** self-respect

amoratado, a [amora'taðo, a] adj purple

amordazar [amorða'θar] vt to muzzle; (fig) to gag

amorfo, a [a'morfo, a] adj amorphous, shapeless

amoroso, a [amo'roso, a] adj affectionate, loving

amortajar [amorta'xar] vt to shroud

amortiguador [amortiɣwa'ðor] nm shock absorber; (parachoques) bumper; **~es** nmpl (AUTO) suspension sg

amortiguar [amorti'ɣwar] vt to deaden; (ruido) to muffle; (color) to soften

amortización [amortiθa'θjon] nf (de deuda) repayment; (de bono) redemption

amotinar [amoti'nar] vt to stir up, incite (to riot); **~se** vr to mutiny

amparar [ampa'rar] vt to protect; **~se** vr to seek protection; (de la lluvia etc) to shelter; **amparo** nm help, protection; **al amparo de** under the protection of

amperio [am'perjo] nm ampère, amp

ampliación [amplja'θjon] nf enlargement; (extensión) extension

ampliar [am'pljar] vt to enlarge; to extend

amplificación [amplifika'θjon] nf enlargement; **amplificador** nm amplifier

amplificar [amplifi'kar] vt to amplify

amplio, a ['ampljo, a] adj spacious; (de falda etc) full; (extenso) extensive; (ancho) wide; **amplitud** nf spaciousness; extent; (fig) amplitude

ampolla [am'poʎa] nf blister; (MED) ampoule

ampuloso, a [ampu'loso, a] adj bombastic, pompous

amputar [ampu'tar] vt to cut off, amputate

amueblar [amwe'ßlar] vt to furnish

amurallar [amura'ʎar] vt to wall up o in

anacronismo [anakro'nismo] nm anachronism

anales [a'nales] nmpl annals

analfabetismo [analfaße'tismo] nm illiteracy; **analfabeto, a** adj, nm/f illiterate

analgésico [anal'xesiko] nm painkiller, analgesic

análisis [a'nalisis] nm inv analysis

analista [ana'lista] nm/f (gen) analyst

analizar [anali'θar] vt to analyse

analogía [analo'xia] nf analogy

analógico, a [ana'loxiko, a] adj (INFORM) analog; (reloj) analogue (BRIT), analog (US)

análogo, a [a'naloxo, a] adj analogous, similar

ananá(s) [ana'na(s)] (AM) nm pineapple

anaquel [ana'kel] nm shelf

anarquía [anar'kia] nf anarchy; **anarquismo** nm anarchism; **anarquista** nm/f anarchist

anatomía [anato'mia] nf anatomy

anca ['anka] nf rump, haunch; **~s** nfpl (fam) behind sg

ancho, a ['antʃo, a] adj wide; (falda) full; (fig) liberal ♦ nm width; (FERRO)

gauge; **ponerse ~** to get conceited; **estar a sus anchas** to be at one's ease

ancho [an'tʃoa] nf anchovy

anchura [an'tʃura] nf width; (extensión) wideness

anciano, a [an'θjano, a] adj old, aged ♦ nm/f old man/woman; elder

ancla ['ankla] nf anchor; **~dero** nm anchorage; **anclar** vi to (drop) anchor

andadura [anda'ðura] nf gait; (de caballo) pace

Andalucía [andalu'θia] nf Andalusia; **andaluz, a** adj, nm/f Andalusian

andamiaje [anda'mjaxe] nm = **andamio**

andamio [an'damjo] nm scaffold(ing)

andar [an'dar] vt to go, cover, travel ♦ vi to go, walk, travel; (funcionar) to go, work; (estar) to be ♦ nm walk, gait, pace; **~se** vr to go away; **~ a pie/a caballo/en bicicleta** to go on foot/on horseback/by bicycle; **~ haciendo algo** to be doing sth; **¡anda!** (sorpresa) go on!; **anda por** o **en los 40** he's about 40

andén [an'den] nm (FERRO) platform; (NAUT) quayside; (AM: de la calle) pavement (BRIT), sidewalk (US)

Andes ['andes] nmpl: **los ~** the Andes

Andorra [an'dorra] nf Andorra

andrajo [an'draxo] nm rag; **~so, a** adj ragged

anduve etc [an'duße] vb ver **andar**

anécdota [a'nekðota] nf anecdote, story

anegar [ane'xar] vt to flood; (ahogar) to drown; **~se** vr to drown; (hundirse) to sink

anejo, a [a'nexo, a] adj, nm = **anexo**

anemia [a'nemja] nf anaemia

anestesia [anes'tesja] nf (sustancia) anaesthetic; (proceso) anaesthesia

anexar [anek'sar] vt to annex; (documento) to attach; **anexión** nf annexation; **anexionamiento** nm annexation; **anexo, a** adj attached

♦ *nm* annexe

anfibio, a [an'fiβjo, a] *adj* amphibious ♦ *nm* amphibian

anfiteatro [anfite'atro] *nm* amphitheatre; (*TEATRO*) dress circle

anfitrión, ona [anfi'trjon, ona] *nm/f* host(ess)

ángel ['anxel] *nm* angel; ~ **de la guarda** guardian angel; **tener** ~ to be charming; **angelical; angélico, a** *adj* angelic(al)

angina [an'xina] *nf* (*MED*) inflammation of the throat; ~ **de pecho** angina; **tener** ~**s** to have tonsillitis

anglicano, a [angli'kano, a] *adj*, *nm/f* Anglican

anglosajón, ona [anglosa'xon, ona] *adj* Anglo-Saxon

angosto, a [an'gosto, a] *adj* narrow

anguila [an'gila] *nf* eel

angula [an'gula] *nf* elver, baby eel

ángulo ['angulo] *nm* angle; (*esquina*) corner; (*curva*) bend

angustia [an'gustja] *nf* anguish; **angustiar** *vt* to distress, grieve

anhelar [ane'lar] *vt* to be eager for; (*desear*) to long for, desire ♦ *vi* to pant, gasp; **anhelo** *nm* eagerness; desire

anidar [ani'ðar] *vi* to nest

anillo [a'niʎo] *nm* ring; ~ **de boda** wedding ring

animación [anima'θjon] *nf* liveliness; (*vitalidad*) life; (*actividad*) activity; bustle

animado, a [ani'maðo, a] *adj* lively; (*vivaz*) animated; **animador, a** *nm/f* (*TV*) host(ess), compère; (*DEPORTE*) cheerleader

animadversión [animaðβer'sjon] *nf* ill-will, antagonism

animal [ani'mal] *adj* animal; (*fig*) stupid ♦ *nm* animal; (*fig*) fool; (*bestia*) brute

animar [ani'mar] *vt* (*BIO*) to animate, give life to; (*fig*) to liven up, brighten up, cheer up; (*estimular*) to stimulate;

~**se** *vr* to cheer up; to feel encouraged; (*decidirse*) to make up one's mind

ánimo ['animo] *nm* (*alma*) soul; (*mente*) mind; (*valentía*) courage ♦ *excl* cheer up!

animoso, a [ani'moso, a] *adj* brave; (*vivo*) lively

aniquilar [aniki'lar] *vt* to annihilate, destroy

anís [a'nis] *nm* aniseed; (*licor*) anisette

aniversario [aniβer'sarjo] *nm* anniversary

anoche [a'notʃe] *adv* last night; **antes de** ~ the night before last

anochecer [anotʃe'θer] *vi* to get dark ♦ *nm* nightfall, dark; **al** ~ at nightfall

anodino, a [ano'ðino, a] *adj* dull, anodyne

anomalía [anoma'lia] *nf* anomaly

anonadado, a [anona'ðaðo, a] *adj*: **estar/quedar/sentirse** ~ to be overwhelmed o amazed

anonimato [anoni'mato] *nm* anonymity

anónimo, a [a'nonimo, a] *adj* anonymous; (*COM*) limited ♦ *nm* (*carta*) anonymous letter; (: *maliciosa*) poison-pen letter

anormal [anor'mal] *adj* abnormal

anotación [anota'θjon] *nf* note; annotation

anotar [ano'tar] *vt* to note down; (*comentar*) to annotate

anquilosamiento [ankilosa'mjento] *nm* (*fig*) paralysis; stagnation

anquilosarse [ankilo'sarse] *vr* (*fig*: *persona*) to get out of touch; (*método*, *costumbres*) to go out of date

ansia ['ansja] *nf* anxiety; (*añoranza*) yearning; **ansiar** *vt* to long for

ansiedad [ansje'ðað] *nf* anxiety

ansioso, a [an'sjoso, a] *adj* anxious; (*anhelante*) eager; ~ **de** *o* **por algo** greedy for sth

antagónico, a [anta'γoniko, a] *adj* antagonistic; (*opuesto*) contrasting; **antagonista** *nm/f* antagonist

antaño [an'taɲo] *adv* long ago, formerly

Antártico [an'tartiko] *nm*: **el ~** the Antarctic

ante ['ante] *prep* before, in the presence of; (*problema etc*) faced with ♦ *nm* (*piel*) suede; **~ todo** above all

anteanoche [antea'notʃe] *adv* the night before last

anteayer [antea'jer] *adv* the day before yesterday

antebrazo [ante'βraθo] *nm* forearm

antecedente [anteθe'ðente] *adj* previous ♦ *nm* antecedent; **~s** *nmpl* (*JUR*): **~s penales** criminal record; (*procedencia*) background

anteceder [anteθe'ðer] *vt* to precede, go before

antecesor, a [anteθe'sor, a] *nm/f* predecessor

antedicho, a [ante'ðitʃo, a] *adj* aforementioned

antelación [antela'θjon] *nf*: **con ~** in advance

antemano [ante'mano]: **de ~** *adv* beforehand, in advance

antena [an'tena] *nf* antenna; (*de televisión etc*) aerial; **~ parabólica** satellite dish

anteojo [ante'oxo] *nm* eyeglass; **~s** *nmpl* (*AM*) glasses, spectacles

antepasados [antepa'saðos] *nmpl* ancestors

anteponer [antepo'ner] *vt* to place in front; (*fig*) to prefer

anteproyecto [antepro'jekto] *nm* preliminary sketch; (*fig*) blueprint

anterior [ante'rjor] *adj* preceding, previous; **~idad** *nf*: **con ~idad a** prior to, before

antes ['antes] *adv* (*con prioridad*) before ♦ *prep*: **~ de** before ♦ *conj*: **~ de ir/de que te vayas** before going/before you go; **~ bien** (but) rather; **dos días ~** two days before ♦ previously; **no quise venir ~** she didn't want to come any earlier; **tomo**

el avión ~ que el barco I take the plane rather than the boat; **~ que yo** before me; **lo ~ posible** as soon as possible; **cuanto ~ mejor** the sooner the better

antiaéreo, a [antia'ereo, a] *adj* anti-aircraft

antibalas [anti'βalas] *adj inv*: **chaleco ~** bullet-proof jacket

antibiótico [anti'βjotiko] *nm* antibiotic

anticipación [antiθipa'θjon] *nf* anticipation; **con 10 minutos de ~** 10 minutes early

anticipado, a [antiθi'paðo, a] *adj* (*pago*) advance; **por ~** in advance

anticipar [antiθi'par] *vt* to anticipate; (*adelantar*) to bring forward; (*COM*) to advance; **~se** *vr*: **~se a su época** to be ahead of one's time

anticipo [anti'θipo] *nm* (*COM*) advance

anticonceptivo, a [antikonθep'tiβo, a] *adj, nm* contraceptive

anticongelante [antikonxe'lante] *nm* antifreeze

anticuado, a [anti'kwaðo, a] *adj* out-of-date, old-fashioned; (*desusado*) obsolete

anticuario [anti'kwarjo] *nm* antique dealer

anticuerpo [anti'kwerpo] *nm* (*MED*) antibody

antidepresivo [antiðepre'siβo] *nm* antidepressant

antídoto [an'tiðoto] *nm* antidote

antiestético, a [anties'tetiko, a] *adj* unsightly

antifaz [anti'faθ] *nm* mask; (*velo*) veil

antigualla [anti'ɣwaʎa] *nf* antique; (*reliquia*) relic

antiguamente [antiɣwa'mente] *adv* formerly; (*hace mucho tiempo*) long ago

antigüedad [antiɣwe'ðað] *nf* antiquity; (*artículo*) antique; (*rango*) seniority

antiguo, a [an'tiɣwo, a] *adj* old,

ancient; *(que fue)* former

Antillas [an'tiʎas] *nfpl:* **las ~** the West Indies

antílope [an'tilope] *nm* antelope

antinatural [antinatu'ral] *adj* unnatural

antipatía [antipa'tia] *nf* antipathy, dislike; **antipático, a** *adj* disagreeable, unpleasant

antirrobo [anti'rroβo] *adj inv (alarma etc)* anti-theft

antisemita [antise'mita] *adj* anti-Semitic ♦ *nm* anti-Semite

antiséptico, a [anti'septiko, a] *adj* antiseptic ♦ *nm* antiseptic

antítesis [an'titesis] *nf inv* antithesis

antojadizo, a [antoxa'ðiθo, a] *adj* capricious

antojarse [anto'xarse] *vr (desear):* **se me antoja comprarlo** I have a mind to buy it; *(pensar):* **se me antoja que** I have a feeling that

antojo [an'toxo] *nm* caprice, whim; *(rosa)* birthmark; *(lunar)* mole

antología [antolo'xia] *nf* anthology

antorcha [an'tortʃa] *nf* torch

antro ['antro] *nm* cavern

antropófago, a [antro'pofaxo, a] *adj, nm/f* cannibal

antropología [antropolo'xia] *nf* anthropology

anual [a'nwal] *adj* annual

anuario [a'nwarjo] *nm* yearbook

anudar [anu'ðar] *vt (unir)* to knot, tie; *(unir)* to join; **~se** *vr* to get tied up

anulación [anula'θjon] *nf* annulment; *(cancelación)* cancellation

anular [anu'lar] *vt (contrato)* to annul, cancel; *(ley)* to revoke, repeal; *(suscripción)* to cancel ♦ *nm* ring finger

Anunciación [anunθja'θjon] *nf (REL)* Annunciation

anunciante [anun'θjante] *nm/f (COM)* advertiser

anunciar [anun'θjar] *vt* to announce; *(proclamar)* to proclaim; *(COM)* to advertise

anuncio [a'nunθjo] *nm* announcement; *(señal)* sign; *(COM)* advertisement; *(cartel)* poster

anzuelo [an'θwelo] *nm* hook; *(para pescar)* fish hook

añadidura [aɲaði'ðura] *nf* addition, extra; **por ~** besides, in addition

añadir [aɲa'ðir] *vt* to add

añejo, a [a'ɲexo, a] *adj* old; *(vino)* mellow

añicos [a'ɲikos] *nmpl:* **hacer ~** to smash, shatter

añil [a'ɲil] *nm (BOT, color)* indigo

año ['aɲo] *nm* year; **¡Feliz A~ Nuevo!** Happy New Year!; **tener 15 ~s** to be 15 (years old); **los ~s 90** the nineties; **~ bisiesto/escolar** leap/school year; **el ~ que viene** next year

añoranza [aɲo'ranθa] *nf* nostalgia; *(anhelo)* longing

apabullar [apaβu'ʎar] *vt (tb fig)* to crush, squash

apacentar [apaθen'tar] *vt* to pasture, graze

apacible [apa'θiβle] *adj* gentle, mild

apaciguar [apaθi'ɣwar] *vt* to pacify, calm (down)

apadrinar [apaðri'nar] *vt* to sponsor, support; *(REL)* to be godfather to

apagado, a [apa'ɣaðo, a] *adj (volcán)* extinct; *(color)* dull; *(voz)* quiet; *(sonido)* muted, muffled; *(persona: apático)* listless; **estar ~** *(fuego, luz)* to be out; *(RADIO, TV etc)* to be off

apagar [apa'ɣar] *vt* to put out; *(ELEC, RADIO, TV)* to turn off; *(sonido)* to silence, muffle; *(sed)* to quench

apagón [apa'ɣon] *nm* blackout; power cut

apalabrar [apala'βrar] *vt* to agree to; *(contratar)* to engage

apalear [apale'ar] *vt* to beat, thrash

apañar [apa'ɲar] *vt (reparar)* to mend, patch up; *(asir)* to take hold of, grasp; *(reparar)* to mend, patch up; **~se** *vr* to manage, get along

aparador [apara'ðor] *nm* sideboard; *(AM: escaparate)* shop window

aparato [apa'rato] nm apparatus; (máquina) machine; (doméstico) appliance; (boato) ostentation; ~ de facsímil facsimile (machine), fax; ~ digestivo (ANAT) digestive system; ~so, a adj showy, ostentatious

aparcamiento [aparka'mjento] nm car park (BRIT), parking lot (US)

aparcar [apar'kar] vt, vi to park

aparear [apare'ar] vt (objetos) to pair, match; (animales) to mate; ~se vr to make a pair; to mate

aparecer [apare'θer] vi to appear; ~se vr to appear

aparejado, a [apare'xaðo, a] adj fit, suitable; llevar o traer ~ to involve; **aparejador, a** nm/f (ARQ) master builder

aparejo [apa'rexo] nm harness; rigging; (de poleas) block and tackle

aparentar [aparen'tar] vt (edad) to look; (fingir): ~ tristeza to pretend to be sad

aparente [apa'rente] adj apparent; (adecuado) suitable

aparezco etc vb ver aparecer

aparición [apari'θjon] nf appearance; (de libro) publication; (espectro) apparition

apariencia [apa'rjenθja] nf (outward) appearance; en ~ outwardly, seemingly

apartado, a [apar'taðo, a] adj separate; (lejano) remote ♦ nm (tipográfico) paragraph; ~ (de correos) post office box

apartamento [aparta'mento] nm apartment, flat (BRIT)

apartamiento [aparta'mjento] nm separation; (aislamiento) remoteness, isolation; (AM) apartment, flat (BRIT)

apartar [apar'tar] vt to separate; (quitar) to remove; ~se vr to separate, part; (irse) to move away; to keep away

aparte [a'parte] adv (separadamente) separately; (además) besides ♦ nm

aside; (tipográfico) new paragraph

aparthotel [aparto'tel] nm serviced apartments

apasionado, a [apasjo'naðo, a] adj passionate

apasionar [apasjo'nar] vt to excite; le **apasiona el fútbol** she's crazy about football; ~se vr to get excited

apatía [apa'tia] nf apathy

apático, a [a'patiko, a] adj apathetic

Apdo abr (= Apartado (de Correos)) PO Box

apeadero [apea'ðero] nm halt, stop, stopping place

apearse [ape'arse] vr (jinete) to dismount; (bajarse) to get down o out; (AUTO, FERRO) to get off o out

apechugar [apetʃu'xar] vr: ~ con algo to face up to sth

apedrear [apeðre'ar] vt to stone

apegarse [ape'xarse] vr: ~ a to become attached to; **apego** nm attachment, devotion

apelación [apela'θjon] nf appeal

apelar [ape'lar] vi to appeal; ~ a (fig) to resort to

apellidar [apeʎi'ðar] vt to call, name; ~se vr: **se apellida Pérez** her (sur)name's Pérez

apellido [ape'ʎiðo] nm surname

apelmazarse [apelma'θarse] vr (masa, arroz) to go hard; (prenda de lana) to shrink

apenar [ape'nar] vt to grieve, trouble; (AM: avergonzar) to embarrass; ~se vr to grieve; (AM) to be embarrassed

apenas [a'penas] adv scarcely, hardly ♦ conj as soon as, no sooner

apéndice [a'pendiθe] nm appendix; **apendicitis** nf appendicitis

aperitivo [ape'ritiβo] nm (bebida) aperitif; (comida) appetizer

apero [a'pero] nm (AGR) implement; ~s nmpl farm equipment sg

apertura [aper'tura] nf opening; (POL) liberalization

apesadumbrar [apesaðum'brar] vt to

grieve, sadden; **~se** vr to distress o.s.

apestar |apes'tar| vt to infect ♦ vi: **~ (a)** to stink (of)

apetecer |apete'θer| vt: **¿te apetece un café?** do you fancy a (cup of) coffee?; **apetecible** adj desirable; (comida) appetizing

apetito |ape'tito| nm appetite; **~so, a** adj appetizing; (fig) tempting

apiadarse |apja'ðarse| vr: **~ de** to take pity on

ápice |'apiθe| nm whit, iota

apilar |api'lar| vt to pile o heap up; **~se** vr to pile up

apiñarse |api'narse| vr to crowd o press together

apio |'apjo| nm celery

apisonadora |apisona'ðora| nf steamroller

aplacar |apla'kar| vt to placate; **~se** vr to calm down

aplanar |apla'nar| vt to smooth, level; (allanar) to roll flat, flatten

aplastante |aplas'tante| adj overwhelming; (lógica) compelling

aplastar |aplas'tar| vt to squash (flat); (fig) to crush

aplatanarse |aplata'narse| vr to get lethargic

aplaudir |aplau'ðir| vt to applaud

aplauso |a'plauso| nm applause; (fig) approval, acclaim

aplazamiento |aplaθa'mjento| nm postponement

aplazar |apla'θar| vt to postpone, defer

aplicación |aplika'θjon| nf application; (esfuerzo) effort

aplicado, a |apli'kaðo, a| adj diligent, hard-working

aplicar |apli'kar| vt (ejecutar) to apply; **~se** vr to apply o.s.

aplique |a'plike| vb ver **aplicar** ♦ nm wall light

aplomo |a'plomo| nm aplomb, self-assurance

apocado, a |apo'kaðo, a| adj timid

apodar |apo'ðar| vt to nickname

apoderado |apoðe'raðo| nm agent, representative

apoderarse |apoðe'rarse| vr: **~ de** to take possession of

apodo |a'poðo| nm nickname

apogeo |apo'xeo| nm peak, summit

apolillarse |apoli'ʎarse| vr to get moth-eaten

apología |apolo'xia| nf eulogy; (defensa) defence

apoltronarse |apoltro'narse| vr to get lazy

apoplejía |aople'xia| nf apoplexy, stroke

apoquinar |apoki'nar| (fam) vt to fork out, cough up

aporrear |aporre'ar| vt to beat (up)

aportar |apor'tar| vt to contribute ♦ vi to reach port; **~se** vr (AM: llegar) to arrive, come

aposento |apo'sento| nm lodging; (habitación) room

aposta |a'posta| adv deliberately, on purpose

apostar |apos'tar| vt to bet, stake; (tropas etc) to station, post ♦ vi to bet

apóstol |a'postol| nm apostle

apóstrofo |a'postrofo| nm apostrophe

apoyar |apo'jar| vt to lean, rest; (fig) to support, back; **~se** vr: **~se en** to lean on; **apoyo** nm (gen) support; backing, help

apreciable |apre'θjaβle| adj considerable; (fig) esteemed

apreciar |apre'θjar| vt to evaluate, assess; (COM) to appreciate, value; (persona) to respect; (tamaño) to gauge, assess; (detalles) to notice

aprecio |a'preθjo| nm valuation, estimate; (fig) appreciation

aprehender |apreen'der| vt to apprehend, detain

apremiante |apre'mjante| adj urgent, pressing

apremiar |apre'mjar| vt to compel, force ♦ vi to be urgent, press;

apremio nm urgency

aprender [apren'der] vt, vi to learn

aprendiz, a [apren'diθ, a] nm/f apprentice; (principiante) learner; ~ **de conductor** learner driver; ~**aje** nm apprenticeship

aprensión [apren'sjon] nm apprehension, fear; **aprensivo, a** adj apprehensive

apresar [apre'sar] vt to seize; (capturar) to capture

aprestar [apres'tar] vt to prepare, get ready; (TEC) to prime, size; ~**se** vr to get ready

apresurado, a [apresu'raðo, a] adj hurried, hasty; **apresuramiento** nm hurry, haste

apresurar [apresu'rar] vt to hurry, accelerate; ~**se** vr to hurry, make haste

apretado, a [apre'taðo, a] adj tight; (escritura) cramped

apretar [apre'tar] vt to squeeze; (TEC) to tighten; (presionar) to press together, pack ♦ vi to be too tight

apretón [apre'ton] nm squeeze; ~ **de manos** handshake

aprieto [a'prjeto] nm squeeze; (dificultad) difficulty; **estar en un** ~ to be in a fix

aprisa [a'prisa] adv quickly, hurriedly

aprisionar [aprisjo'nar] vt to imprison

aprobación [aproβa'θjon] nf approval

aprobar [apro'βar] vt to approve (of); (examen, materia) to pass ♦ vi to pass

apropiación [apropja'θjon] nf appropriation

apropiado, a [apro'pjaðo, a] adj suitable

apropiarse [apro'pjarse] vr: ~ **de** to appropriate

aprovechado, a [aproβe'tʃaðo, a] adj industrious, hard-working; (económico) thrifty; (pey) unscrupulous; **aprovechamiento** nm use; exploitation

aprovechar [aproβe'tʃar] vt to use; (explotar) to exploit; (experiencia) to

profit from; (oferta, oportunidad) to take advantage of ♦ vi to progress, improve; ~**se** vr: ~**se de** to make use of; to take advantage of; **¡que aproveche!** enjoy your meal!

aproximación [aproksima'θjon] nf approximation; (de lotería) consolation prize; **aproximado, a** adj approximate

aproximar [aproksi'mar] vt to bring nearer; ~**se** vr to come near, approach

apruebo etc vb ver **aprobar**

aptitud [apti'tuð] nf aptitude

apto, a [a'pto, a] adj suitable

apuesta [a'pwesta] nf bet, wager

apuesto, a [a'pwesto, a] adj neat, elegant

apuntador [apunta'ðor] nm prompter

apuntalar [apunta'lar] vt to prop up

apuntar [apun'tar] vt (con arma) to aim at; (con dedo) to point at o to; (anotar) to note (down); (TEATRO) to prompt; ~**se** vr (DEPORTE: tanto, victoria) to score; (ESCOL) to enrol

apunte [a'punte] nm note

apuñalar [apuɲa'lar] vt to stab

apurado, a [apu'raðo, a] adj needy; (difícil) difficult; (peligroso) dangerous; (AM) hurried, rushed

apurar [apu'rar] vt (agotar) to drain; (recursos) to use up; (molestar) to annoy, tease ♦ vr (preocuparse) to worry; (darse prisa) to hurry

apuro [a'puro] nm (aprieto) fix, jam; (escasez) want, hardship; (vergüenza) embarrassment; (AM) haste, urgency

aquejado, a [ake'xaðo, a] adj: ~ **de** (MED) afflicted by

aquél, aquélla [a'kel, a'keʎa] (pl aquéllos, as) pron that (one); (pl) those (ones)

aquel, aquella [a'kel, a'keʎa] (pl aquellos, as) adj that; (pl) those

aquello [a'keʎo] pron that, that business

aquí [a'ki] adv (lugar) here; (tiempo) now; ~ **arriba** up here; ~ **mismo**

right here; **~ yace** here lies; **de ~ a siete días** a week from now

aquietar [akje'tar] *vt* to quieten (down), calm (down)

ara ['ara] *nf*: **en ~s de** for the sake of

árabe [a'raße] *adj, nm/f* Arab ♦ *nm* (*LING*) Arabic

Arabia [a'raßja] *nf*: **~ Saudí** o **Saudita** Saudi Arabia

arado [a'raðo] *nm* plough

Aragón [ara'ɣon] *nm* Aragon; **aragonés, esa** *adj, nm/f* Aragonese

arancel [aran'θel] *nm* tariff, duty; **~ de aduanas** customs (duty)

arandela [aran'dela] *nf* (*TEC*) washer

araña [a'raɲa] *nf* (*ZOOL*) spider; (*lámpara*) chandelier

arañar [ara'ɲar] *vt* to scratch

arañazo [ara'ɲaθo] *nm* scratch

arar [a'rar] *vt* to plough, till

arbitraje [arßi'traxe] *nm* arbitration

arbitrar [arßi'trar] *vt* to arbitrate in; (*DEPORTE*) to referee ♦ *vi* to arbitrate

arbitrariedad [arßitrarje'ðað] *nf* arbitrariness; (*acto*) arbitrary act; **arbitrario, a** *adj* arbitrary

arbitrio [ar'ßitrjo] *nm* free will; (*JUR*) adjudication, decision

árbitro ['arßitro] *nm* arbitrator; (*DEPORTE*) referee; (*TENIS*) umpire

árbol ['arßol] *nm* (*BOT*) tree; (*NAUT*) mast; (*TEC*) axle, shaft; **arbolado, a** *adj* wooded; (*camino etc*) tree-lined ♦ *nm* woodland

arboleda [arßo'leða] *nf* grove, plantation

arbusto [ar'ßusto] *nm* bush, shrub

arca ['arka] *nf* chest, box

arcada [ar'kaða] *nf* arcade; (*de puente*) arch, span; **~s** *nfpl* (*náuseas*) retching *sg*

arcaico, a [ar'kaiko, a] *adj* archaic

arce ['arθe] *nm* maple tree

arcén [ar'θen] *nm* (*de autopista*) hard shoulder; (*de carretera*) verge

archipiélago [artʃi'pjelaɣo] *nm* archipelago

archivador [artʃißa'ðor] *nm* filing cabinet

archivar [artʃi'ßar] *vt* to file (away); **archivo** *nm* file, archive(s) (*pl*)

arcilla [ar'θiʎa] *nf* clay

arco ['arko] *nm* arch; (*MAT*) arc; (*MIL, MUS*) bow; **~ iris** rainbow

arder [ar'ðer] *vi* to burn; **estar que arde** (*persona*) to fume

ardid [ar'ðið] *nm* ploy, trick

ardiente [ar'ðjente] *adj* burning, ardent

ardilla [ar'ðiʎa] *nf* squirrel

ardor [ar'ðor] *nm* (*calor*) heat; (*fig*) ardour; **~ de estómago** heartburn

arduo, a ['arðwo, a] *adj* arduous

área ['area] *nf* area; (*DEPORTE*) penalty area

arena [a'rena] *nf* sand; (*de una lucha*) arena; **~ movedizas** quicksand *sg*

arenal [are'nal] *nm* (*arena movediza*) quicksand

arengar [aren'gar] *vt* to harangue

arenisca [are'niska] *nf* sandstone; (*cascajo*) grit

arenoso, a [are'noso, a] *adj* sandy

arenque [a'renke] *nm* herring

argamasa [arva'masa] *nf* mortar, plaster

Argel [ar'xel] *n* Algiers; **Argelia** *nf* Algeria; **argelino, a** *adj, nm/f* Algerian

Argentina [arxen'tina] *nf*: **(la) ~** Argentina

argentino, a [arxen'tino, a] *adj* Argentinian; (*de plata*) silvery ♦ *nm/f* Argentinian

argolla [ar'voʎa] *nf* (*large*) ring

argot [ar'vo] (*pl* **~s**) *nm* slang

argucia [ar'vuθja] *nf* subtlety, sophistry

argüir [ar'vwir] *vt* to deduce; (*discutir*) to argue; (*indicar*) to indicate, imply; (*censurar*) to reproach ♦ *vi* to argue

argumentación [arvumenta'θjon] *nf* (line of) argument

argumentar [arvumen'tar] *vt, vi* to argue

argumento [arvu'mento] *nm*

aria

arrastrar

argument; (*razonamiento*) reasoning; (*de novela etc*) plot; (*CINE, TV*) storyline

aria ['arja] *nf* aria

aridez [ari'ðeθ] *nf* aridity, dryness

árido, a ['ariðo, a] *adj* arid, dry; **~s** *nmpl* (*COM*) dry goods

Aries ['arjes] *nm* Aries

ario, a ['arjo, a] *adj* Aryan

arisco, a [a'risko, a] *adj* surly; (*insociable*) unsociable

aristócrata [aris'tokrata] *nm/f* aristocrat

aritmética [arit'metika] *nf* arithmetic

arma ['arma] *nf* arm; **~s** *nfpl* arms; **~ blanca** blade, knife; (*espada*) sword; **~ de fuego** firearm; **~s cortas** small arms

armada [ar'maða] *nf* armada; (*flota*) fleet

armadillo [arma'ðiʎo] *nm* armadillo

armado, a [ar'maðo, a] *adj* armed; (*TEC*) reinforced

armador [arma'ðor] *nm* (*NAUT*) shipowner

armadura [arma'ðura] *nf* (*MIL*) armour; (*TEC*) framework; (*ZOOL*) skeleton; (*FÍSICA*) armature

armamento [arma'mento] *nm* armament; (*NAUT*) fitting-out

armar [ar'mar] *vt* (*soldado*) to arm; (*máquina*) to assemble; (*navío*) to fit out; **~la, ~ un lío** to start a row, kick up a fuss

armario [ar'marjo] *nm* wardrobe; (*de cocina, baño*) cupboard

armatoste [arma'toste] *nm* (*mueble*) monstrosity; (*máquina*) contraption

armazón [arma'θon] *nf o m* body, chassis; (*de mueble etc*) frame; (*ARQ*) skeleton

armería [arme'ria] *nf* gunsmith's

armiño [ar'miɲo] *nm* stoat; (*piel*) ermine

armisticio [armis'tiθjo] *nm* armistice

armonía [armo'nia] *nf* harmony

armónica [ar'monika] *nf* harmonica

armonioso, a [armo'njoso, a] *adj* harmonious

armonizar [armoni'θar] *vt* to harmonize; (*diferencias*) to reconcile ♦ *vi*: **~ con** (*fig*) to be in keeping with; (*colores*) to tone in with, blend

arnés [ar'nes] *nm* armour; **arneses** *nmpl* (*de caballo etc*) harness *sg*

aro ['aro] *nm* ring; (*tejo*) quoit; (*AM: pendiente*) earring

aroma [a'roma] *nm* aroma, scent

aromático, a [aro'matiko, a] *adj* aromatic

arpa ['arpa] *nf* harp

arpía [ar'pia] *nf* shrew

arpillera [arpi'ʎera] *nf* sacking, sackcloth

arpón [ar'pon] *nm* harpoon

arquear [arke'ar] *vt* to arch, bend; **~se** *vr* to arch, bend

arqueología [arkeolo'xia] *nf* archaeology; **arqueólogo, a** *nm/f* archaeologist

arquero [ar'kero] *nm* archer, bowman

arquetipo [arke'tipo] *nm* archetype

arquitecto [arki'tekto] *nm* architect; **arquitectura** *nf* architecture

arrabal [arra'ßal] *nm* suburb; (*AM*) slum; **~es** *nmpl* (*afueras*) outskirts

arraigado, a [arrai'xaðo, a] *adj* deep-rooted; (*fig*) established

arraigar [arrai'xar] *vt* to establish ♦ *vi* to take root; **~se** *vr* to take root; (*persona*) to settle

arrancar [arran'kar] *vt* (*sacar*) to extract, pull out; (*arrebatar*) to snatch (away); (*INFORM*) to boot; (*fig*) to extract ♦ *vi* (*AUTO, máquina*) to start; (*ponerse en marcha*) to get going; **~ de** to stem from

arranque *etc* [a'rranke] *vb ver* **arrancar** ♦ *nm* sudden start; (*AUTO*) start; (*fig*) fit, outburst

arrasar [arra'sar] *vt* (*aplanar*) to level, flatten; (*destruir*) to demolish

arrastrado, a [arras'traðo, a] *adj* poor, wretched; (*AM*) servile

arrastrar [arras'trar] *vt* to drag

(along); (fig) to drag down, degrade; (suj: agua, viento) to carry away ♦ vi to drag, trail on the ground; ~se vr to crawl; (fig) to grovel; **llevar algo arrastrado** to drag sth along

arrastre [a'rrastre] nm drag, dragging

arre ['arre] excl gee up!

arrear [arre'ar] vt to drive on, urge on ♦ vi to hurry along

arrebatado, a [arreβa'taðo, a] adj rash, impetuous; (repentino) sudden, hasty

arrebatar [arreβa'tar] vt to snatch (away), seize; (fig) to captivate; ~se vr to get carried away, get excited

arrebato [arre'βato] nm fit of rage, fury; (éxtasis) rapture

arrecife [arre'θife] nm (tb: ~ de coral) reef

arredrarse [arre'ðrarse] vr: ~ (ante algo) to be intimidated (by sth)

arreglado, a [arre'vlaðo, a] adj (ordenado) neat, orderly; (moderado) moderate, reasonable

arreglar [arre'vlar] vt (poner orden) to tidy up; (algo roto) to fix, repair; (problema) to solve; ~se vr to reach an understanding; **arreglárselas** (fam) to get by, manage

arreglo [a'rreɣlo] nm settlement; (orden) order; (acuerdo) agreement; (MUS) arrangement, setting

arrellanarse [arreʎa'narse] vr: ~ en to sit back in/on

arremangar [arreman'gar] vt to roll up, turn up; ~se vr to roll up one's sleeves

arremeter [arreme'ter] vi: ~ contra to attack, rush at

arrendamiento [arrenda'mjento] nm letting; (alquilar) hiring; (contrato) lease; (alquiler) rent; **arrendar** vt to let, lease; to rent; **arrendatario, a** nm/f tenant

arreos [a'rreos] nmpl (de caballo) harness sg, trappings

arrepentimiento [arrepenti'mjento] nm regret, repentance

arrepentirse [arrepen'tirse] vr to repent; ~ **de** to regret

arrestar [arres'tar] vt to arrest; (encarcelar) to imprison; **arresto** nm arrest; (MIL) detention; (audacia) boldness, daring; **arresto domiciliario** house arrest

arriar [a'rrjar] vt (velas) to haul down; (bandera) to lower, strike; (cable) to pay out

---

PALABRA CLAVE

---

arriba [a'rriβa] adv **1** (posición) above; **desde** ~ from above; ~ **de todo** at the very top, right on top; **Juan está** ~ Juan is upstairs; **lo** ~ **mencionado** the aforementioned

2 (dirección): **calle** ~ up the street

3: **de** ~ **abajo** from top to bottom; **mirar a uno de** ~ **abajo** to look sb up and down

4: para ~: **de 5000 pesetas para** ~ from 5000 pesetas up(wards)

♦ adj: **de** ~: **el piso de** ~ the upstairs flat (BRIT) o apartment; **la parte de** ~ the top o upper part

♦ prep: ~ **de** (AM) more than; ~ **de 200 dólares** more than 200 dollars

♦ excl: ¡~! up!; ¡manos ~! hands up!; ¡~ **España**! long live Spain!

---

arribar [arri'βar] vi to put into port; (llegar) to arrive

arribista [arri'βista] nm/f parvenu(e), upstart

arriendo etc [a'rrjendo] vb ver **arrendar** ♦ nm = **arrendamiento**

arriero [a'rrjero] nm muleteer

arriesgado, a [arrjes'xaðo, a] adj (peligroso) risky; (audaz) bold, daring

arriesgar [arrjes'xar] vt to risk; (poner en peligro) to endanger; ~se vr to take a risk

arrimar [arri'mar] vt (acercar) to bring close; (poner de lado) to set aside; ~se vr to come close o closer; ~se a to lean on

arrinconar |arrinko'nar| vt (colocar) to put in a corner; (enemigo) to corner; (fig) to put on one side; (abandonar) to push aside

arrodillarse |arroði'ʎarse| vr to kneel (down)

arrogancia |arro'ɣanθja| nf arrogance; **arrogante** adj arrogant

arrojar |arro'xar| vt to throw, hurl; (humo) to emit, give out; (COM) to yield, produce; **~se** vr to throw o hurl o.s.

arrojo |a'rroxo| nm daring

arrollador, a |arroʎa'ðor, a| adj overwhelming

arrollar |arro'ʎar| vt (AUTO etc) to run over, knock down; (DEPORTE) to crush

arropar |arro'par| vt to cover, wrap up; **~se** vr to wrap o.s. up

arroyo |a'rrojo| nm stream; (de la calle) gutter

arroz |a'rroθ| nm rice; **~ con leche** rice pudding

arruga |a'rruɣa| nf (de cara) wrinkle; (de vestido) crease

arrugar |arru'ɣar| vt to wrinkle; to crease; **~se** vr to get creased

arruinar |arrwi'nar| vt to ruin, wreck; **~se** vr to be ruined, go bankrupt

arrullar |arru'ʎar| vt to coo ♦ vt to lull to sleep

arsenal |arse'nal| nm naval dockyard; (MIL) arsenal

arsénico |ar'seniko| nm arsenic

arte |'arte| nm (gen m en sg y siempre f en pl) nm art; (maña) skill, guile; **~s** nfpl (bellas ~s) arts

artefacto |arte'fakto| nm appliance

arteria |ar'terja| nf artery

artesanía |artesa'nia| nf craftsmanship; (artículos) handicrafts pl; **artesano, a** nm/f artisan, craftsman/woman

ártico, a |'artiko, a| adj Arctic ♦ nm: **el Á~** the Arctic

articulación |artikula'θjon| nf

articulation; (MED, TEC) joint;

articulado, a |artiku'laðo, a| adj articulated; jointed

articular |artiku'lar| vt to articulate; to join together

artículo |ar'tikulo| nm article; (cosa) thing, article; **~s** nmpl (COM) goods

artífice |ar'tifiθe| nm/f architect

artificial |artifi'θjal| adj artificial

artificio |arti'fiθjo| nm art, skill; (astucia) cunning

artillería |artiʎe'ria| nf artillery

artillero |arti'ʎero| nm artilleryman, gunner

artilugio |arti'luxjo| nm gadget

artimaña |arti'maɲa| nf trap, snare; (astucia) cunning

artista |ar'tista| nm/f (pintor) artist, painter; (TEATRO) artist, artiste; **~ de cine** film actor/actress; **artístico, a** adj artistic

artritis |ar'tritis| nf arthritis

arveja |ar'ßexa| (AM) nf pea

arzobispo |arθo'ßispo| nm archbishop

as |as| nm ace

asa |'asa| nf handle; (fig) lever

asado |a'saðo| nm roast (meat); (AM: barbacoa) barbecue

asador |asa'ðor| nm spit

asadura |asa'ðura| nf entrails pl, offal

asalariado, a |asala'rjaðo, a| adj paid, salaried ♦ nm/f wage earner

asaltante |asal'tante| nm/f attacker

asaltar |asal'tar| vt to attack, assault; (fig) to assail; **asalto** nm attack, assault; (DEPORTE) round

asamblea |asam'blea| nf assembly; (reunión) meeting

asar |a'sar| vt to roast

asbesto |as'ßesto| nm asbestos

ascendencia |asθen'denθja| nf ancestry; (AM) ascendancy; **de ~ francesa** of French origin

ascender |asθen'der| vi (subir) to ascend, rise; (ser promovido) to gain promotion ♦ vt to promote; **~ a** to amount to; **ascendiente** nm influence ♦ nm/f ancestor

ascensión [asθen'sjon] nf ascent; (REL): la A~ the Ascension

ascenso [as'θenso] nm ascent; (promoción) promotion

ascensor [asθen'sor] nm lift (BRIT), elevator (US)

ascético, a [as'θetiko, a] adj ascetic

asco ['asko] nm: ¡qué ~! how revolting o disgusting; **el ajo me da ~** I hate o loathe garlic; **estar hecho un ~** to be filthy

ascua ['askwa] nf ember; **estar en ~s** to be on tenterhooks

aseado, a [ase'aðo, a] adj clean; (arreglado) tidy; (pulcro) smart

asear [ase'ar] vt to clean, wash; to tidy (up)

asediar [ase'ðjar] vt (MIL) to besiege, lay siege to; (fig) to chase, pester; **asedio** nm siege; (COM) run

asegurado, a [aseɣu'raðo, a] adj insured

asegurador, a nm/f insurer

asegurar [aseɣu'rar] vt (consolidar) to secure, fasten; (dar garantía de) to guarantee; (preservar) to safeguard; (afirmar, dar por cierto) to assure, affirm; (tranquilizar) to reassure; (tomar un seguro) to insure; **~se** vr to assure o.s., make sure

asemejarse [aseme'xarse] vr to be alike; **~ a** to be like, resemble

asentado, a [asen'taðo, a] adj established, settled

asentar [asen'tar] vt (sentar) to seat, sit down; (poner) to place, establish; (alisar) to level, smooth down o out; (anotar) to note down ♦ vi to be suitable, suit

asentir [asen'tir] vi to assent, agree; **~ con la cabeza** to nod (one's head)

aseo [a'seo] nm cleanliness; **~s** nmpl (servicios) toilet sg (BRIT), cloakroom sg (BRIT), restroom sg (US)

aséptico, a [a'septiko, a] adj germ-free, free from infection

asequible [ase'kiβle] adj (precio) reasonable; (meta) attainable; (persona) approachable

aserradero [aserra'ðero] nm sawmill; **aserrar** vt to saw

asesinar [asesi'nar] vt to murder; (POL) to assassinate; **asesinato** nm murder; assassination

asesino, a [ase'sino, a] nm/f murderer, killer; (POL) assassin

asesor, a [ase'sor, a] nm/f adviser, consultant

asesorar [aseso'rar] vt (JUR) to advise, give legal advice to; (COM) to act as consultant to; **~se** vr: **~se con o de** to take advice from, consult; **asesoría** nf (cargo) consultancy; (oficina) consultant's office

asestar [ases'tar] vt (golpe) to deal, strike

asfalto [as'falto] nm asphalt

asfixia [as'fiksja] nf asphyxia, suffocation

asfixiar [asfik'sjar] vt to asphyxiate, suffocate; **~se** vr to be asphyxiated, suffocate

asgo etc vb ver **asir**

así [a'si] adv (de esta manera) in this way, like this, thus; (aunque) although; (tan pronto como) as soon as; **~ que** so; **~ como** as well as; **~ y todo** even so; **¿no es ~?** isn't it?, didn't you? etc; **~ de grande** this big

Asia ['asja] nf Asia; **asiático, a** adj, nm/f Asian, Asiatic

asidero [asi'ðero] nm handle

asiduidad [asiðwi'ðað] nf assiduousness; **asiduo, a** adj assiduous; (frecuente) frequent ♦ nm/f regular (customer)

asiento [a'sjento] nm (mueble) seat, chair; (de coche, en tribunal etc) seat; (localidad) seat, place; (fundamento) site; **~ delantero/trasero** front/back seat

asignación [asiɣna'θjon] nf (atribución) assignment; (reparto) allocation; (sueldo) salary; **~ (semanal)**

pocket money

asignar |asiɣ'nar| vt to assign, allocate

asignatura |asiɣna'tura| nf subject; course

asilado, a |asi'laðo, a| nm/f inmate; (POL) refugee

asilo |a'silo| nm (refugio) asylum, refuge; (establecimiento) home, institution; **~ político** political asylum

asimilación |asimila'θjon| nf assimilation

asimilar |asimi'lar| vt to assimilate

asimismo |asi'mismo| adv in the same way, likewise

asir |a'sir| vt to seize, grasp

asistencia |asis'tenθja| nf audience; (MED) attendance; (ayuda) assistance; **asistente** nm/f assistant; **los asistentes** those present; **asistente social** social worker

asistido, a |asis'tiðo, a| adj: **~ por ordenador** computer-assisted

asistir |asis'tir| vt to assist, help ♦ vi: **~ a** to attend, be present at

asma |'asma| nf asthma

asno |'asno| nm donkey; (fig) ass

asociación |asoθja'θjon| nf association; (COM) partnership; **asociado, a** adj associate ♦ nm/f associate; (COM) partner

asociar |aso'θjar| vt to associate

asolar |aso'lar| vt to destroy

asomar |aso'mar| vt to show, stick out ♦ vi to appear; **~se** vr to appear, show up; **~ la cabeza por la ventana** to put one's head out of the window

asombrar |asom'brar| vt to amaze, astonish; **~se** vr (sorprenderse) to be amazed; (asustarse) to get a fright; **asombro** nm amazement, astonishment; (susto) fright; **asombroso, a** adj astonishing, amazing

asomo |a'somo| nm hint, sign

aspa |'aspa| nf (cruz) cross; (de molino) sail; **en ~** X-shaped

aspaviento |aspa'βjento| nm

exaggerated display of feeling; (fam) fuss

aspecto |as'pekto| nm (apariencia) look, appearance; (fig) aspect

aspereza |aspe'reθa| nf roughness; (agrura) sourness; (de carácter) surliness; **áspero, a** adj rough; bitter, sour; harsh

aspersión |asper'sjon| nf sprinkling

aspiración |aspira'θjon| nf breath, inhalation; (MUS) short pause; **aspiraciones** nfpl (ambiciones) aspirations

aspirador |aspira'ðor| nm = **aspiradora**

aspiradora |aspira'ðora| nf vacuum cleaner, Hoover ®

aspirante |aspi'rante| nm/f (candidato) candidate; (DEPORTE) contender

aspirar |aspi'rar| vt to breathe in ♦ vi: **~ a** to aspire to

aspirina |aspi'rina| nf aspirin

asquear |aske'ar| vt to sicken ♦ vi to be sickening; **~se** vr to feel disgusted; **asqueroso, a** adj disgusting, sickening

asta |'asta| nf lance; (arpón) spear; (mango) shaft, handle; (ZOOL) horn; **a media ~** at half mast

asterisco |aste'risko| nm asterisk

astilla |as'tiʎa| nf splinter; (pedacito) chip; **~s** nfpl (leña) firewood sg

astillero |asti'ʎero| nm shipyard

astringente |astrin'xente| adj, nm astringent

astro |'astro| nm star

astrología |astrolo'xia| nf astrology; **astrólogo, a** nm/f astrologer

astronauta |astro'nauta| nm/f astronaut

astronave |astro'naβe| nm spaceship

astronomía |astrono'mia| nf astronomy; **astrónomo, a** nm/f astronomer

astucia |as'tuθja| nf astuteness; (ardid) clever trick

asturiano, a |astu'rjano, a| adj, nm/f

Asturian

astuto, a [as'tuto, a] adj astute; (taimado) cunning

asumir [asu'mir] vt to assume

asunción [asun'θjon] nf assumption; (REL): **A~** Assumption

asunto [a'sunto] nm (tema) matter, subject; (negocio) business

asustar [asus'tar] vt to frighten; **~se** vr to be (o become) frightened

atacar [ata'kar] vt to attack

atadura [ata'ðura] nf bond, tie

atajar [ata'xar] vt (enfermedad, mal) to stop ♦ vi (persona) to take a short cut

atajo [a'taxo] nm short cut

atañer [ata'ɲer] vi: **~ a** to concern

ataque etc [a'take] vb ver **atacar** ♦ nm attack; **~ cardíaco** heart attack

atar [a'tar] vt to tie, tie up

atardecer [atarðe'θer] vi to get dark ♦ nm evening; (crepúsculo) dusk

atareado, a [atare'aðo, a] adj busy

atascar [atas'kar] vt to clog up; (obstruir) to jam; (fig) to hinder; **~se** vr to stall; (cañería) to get blocked up; **atasco** nm obstruction; (AUTO) traffic jam

ataúd [ata'uð] nm coffin

ataviar [ata'βjar] vt to deck, array; **~se** vr to dress up

atavío [ata'βio] nm attire, dress; **~s** nmpl finery sg

atemorizar [atemori'θar] vt to frighten, scare; **~se** vr to get scared

Atenas [a'tenas] n Athens

atención [aten'θjon] nf attention; (bondad) kindness ♦ excl (be) careful!, look out!

atender [aten'der] vt to attend to, look after ♦ vi to pay attention

atenerse [ate'nerse] vr: **~ a** to abide by, adhere to

atentado [aten'taðo] nm crime, illegal act; (asalto) assault; **~ contra la vida de uno** attempt on sb's life

atentamente [atenta'mente] adv: Le saluda **~** Yours faithfully

atentar [aten'tar] vi: **~ a o contra** to commit an outrage against

atento, a [a'tento, a] adj attentive, observant; (cortés) polite, thoughtful

atenuante [ate'nwante] adj extenuating

atenuar [ate'nwar] vt (disminuir) to lessen, minimize

ateo, a [a'teo, a] adj atheistic ♦ nm/f atheist

aterciopelado, a [aterθjope'laðo, a] adj velvety

aterido, a [ate'riðo, a] adj: **~ de frío** frozen stiff

aterrador, a [aterra'ðor, a] adj frightening

aterrar [ate'rrar] vt to frighten; to terrify

aterrizaje [aterri'θaxe] nm landing

aterrizar [aterri'θar] vi to land

aterrorizar [aterrori'θar] vt to terrify

atesorar [ateso'rar] vt to hoard

atestado, a [ates'taðo, a] adj packed ♦ nm (JUR) affidavit

atestar [ates'tar] vt to pack, stuff; (JUR) to attest, testify to

atestiguar [atesti'ɣwar] vt to testify, bear witness to

atiborrar [atiβo'rrar] vt to fill, stuff; **~se** vr to stuff o.s.

ático ['atiko] nm attic; **~ de lujo** penthouse (flat (BRIT) o apartment)

atinado, a [ati'naðo, a] adj (sensato) wise; (correcto) right, correct

atinar [ati'nar] vi (al disparar): **~ al blanco** to hit the target; (fig) to be right

atisbar [atis'βar] vt to spy on; (echar una ojeada) to peep at

atizar [ati'θar] vt to poke; (horno etc) to stoke; (fig) to stir up, rouse

atlántico, a [at'lantiko, a] adj Atlantic ♦ nm: el (océano) **A~** the Atlantic (Ocean)

atlas ['atlas] nm atlas

atleta [at'leta] nm athlete; **atlético, a** adj athletic; **atletismo** nm athletics sg

atmósfera [at'mosfera] nf atmosphere

atolladero [atoʎa'ðero] nm (fig) jam, fix

atolondramiento [atolondra'mjento] nm bewilderment; (insensatez) silliness

atómico, a [a'tomiko, a] adj atomic

atomizador [atomiθa'ðor] nm atomizer; (de perfume) spray

átomo [f'atomo] nm atom

atónito, a [a'tonito, a] adj astonished, amazed

atontado, a [aton'taðo, a] adj stunned; (bobo) silly, daft

atontar [aton'tar] vt to stun; **~se** vr to become confused

atormentar [atormen'tar] vt to torture; (molestar) to torment; (acosar) to plague, harass

atornillar [atorni'ʎar] vt to screw on o down

atosigar [atosi'var] vt to harass, pester

atracador, a [atraka'ðor, a] nm/f robber

atracar [atra'kar] vt (NAUT) to moor; (robar) to hold up, rob ♦ vi to moor; **~se** vr: **~se (de)** to stuff o.s. (with)

atracción [atrak'θjon] nf attraction

atraco [a'trako] nm holdup, robbery

atracón [atra'kon] nm: **darse** o **pegarse un ~ (de)** (fam) to stuff o.s. (with)

atractivo, a [atrak'tiβo, a] adj attractive ♦ nm appeal

atraer [atra'er] vt to attract

atragantarse [atravan'tarse] vr: **~ (con)** to choke (on); **se me ha atragantado el chico** I can't stand the boy

atrancar [atran'kar] vt (puerta) to bar, bolt

atrapar [atra'par] vt to trap; (resfriado etc) to catch

atrás [a'tras] adv (movimiento) back (-wards); (lugar) behind; (tiempo) previously; **ir hacia ~** to go back(wards); **ir a ~** to go to the rear; **estar ~** to be behind o at the back

atrasado, a [atra'saðo, a] adj slow; (pago) overdue, late; (país) backward

atrasar [atra'sar] vi to be slow; **~se** vr to remain behind; (tren) to be o run late; **atraso** nm slowness; lateness, delay; (de país) backwardness; **atrasos** nmpl (COM) arrears

atravesar [atraβe'sar] vt (cruzar) to cross (over); (traspasar) to pierce; to go through; (poner al través) to lay o put across; **~se** vr to come in between; (intervenir) to interfere

atravieso etc vb ver **atravesar**

atrayente [atra'jente] adj attractive

atreverse [atre'βerse] vr to dare; (insolentarse) to be insolent; **atrevido, a** adj daring; insolent; **atrevimiento** nm daring; insolence

atribución [atriβu'θjon] nf: **atribuciones** (POL) powers; (ADMIN) responsibilities

atribuir [atriβu'ir] vt to attribute; (funciones) to confer

atribular [atriβu'lar] vt to afflict, distress

atributo [atri'βuto] nm attribute

atril [a'tril] nm (para libro) lectern; (MUS) music stand

atrocidad [atroθi'ðað] nf atrocity, outrage

atropellar [atrope'ʎar] vt (derribar) to knock over o down; (empujar) to push (aside); (AUTO) to run over, run down; (agraviar) to insult; **~se** vr to act hastily; **atropello** nm (AUTO) accident; (empujón) push; (agravio) wrong; (atrocidad) outrage

atroz [a'troθ] adj atrocious, awful

ATS nmf abr (= Ayudante Técnico Sanitario) nurse

atto, a adj abr = **atento**

atuendo [a'twendo] nm attire

atún [a'tun] nm tuna

aturdir [atur'ðir] vt to stun; (de ruido) to deafen; (fig) to dumbfound, bewilder

atusar [atu'sar] vt to smooth (down)

audacia [au'ðaθja] nf boldness, audacity; **audaz** adj bold, audacious
audible [au'ðiβle] adj audible
audición [auði'θjon] nf hearing; (TEATRO) audition
audiencia [au'ðjenθja] nf audience; **A~** (JUR) High Court
audífono [au'ðifono] nm (para sordos) hearing aid
auditor [auði'tor] nm (JUR) judge advocate; (COM) auditor
auditorio [auði'torjo] nm audience; (sala) auditorium
auge ['auxe] nm boom; (clímax) climax
augurar [auɣu'rar] vt to predict; (presagiar) to portend
augurio [au'ɣurjo] nm omen
aula ['aula] nf classroom; (en universidad etc) lecture room
aullar [au'ʎar] vi to howl, yell
aullido [au'ʎiðo] nm howl, yell
aumentar [aumen'tar] vt to increase; (precios) to put up; (producción) to step up; (con microscopio, anteojos) to magnify ♦ vi to increase, be on the increase; **~se** vr to increase, be on the increase; **aumento** nm increase; rise
aun [a'un] adv even; **~ así** even so; **~ más** even o yet more
aún [a'un] adv: **~ está aquí** he's still here; **~ no lo sabemos** we don't know yet; **¿no ha venido ~?** hasn't she come yet?
aunque [a'unke] conj though, although, even though
aúpa [a'upa] excl come on!
aureola [aure'ola] nf halo
auricular [auriku'lar] nm (TEL) receiver; **~es** mpl (cascos) headphones
aurora [au'rora] nf dawn
auscultar [auskul'tar] vt (MED: pecho) to listen to, sound
ausencia [au'senθja] nf absence
ausentarse [ausen'tarse] vr to go away; (por poco tiempo) to go out
ausente [au'sente] adj absent
auspicios [aus'piθjos] nmpl auspices

austero, a [aus'tero, a] adj austere
austral [aus'tral] adj southern ♦ nm monetary unit of Argentina
Australia [aus'tralja] nf Australia; **australiano, a** adj, nm/f Australian
Austria ['austrja] nf Austria; **austríaco, a** adj, nm/f Austrian
auténtico, a [au'tentiko, a] adj authentic
auto ['auto] nm (JUR) edict, decree; (: orden) writ; (AUTO) car; **~s** nmpl (JUR) proceedings; (: acta) court record sg
autoadhesivo [autoaðe'siβo] adj self-adhesive; (sobre) self-sealing
autobiografía [autoβjoɣra'fia] nf autobiography
autobronceador [autoβronθea'ðor] adj self-tanning
autobús [auto'βus] nm bus
autocar [auto'kar] nm coach (BRIT), (passenger) bus (US)
autóctono, a [au'toktono, a] adj native, indigenous
autodefensa [autoðe'fensa] nf self-defence
autodeterminación [autoðetermina'θjon] nf self-determination
autodidacta [autoði'ðakta] adj self-taught
autoescuela [autoes'kwela] nf driving school
autógrafo [au'toɣrafo] nm autograph
autómata [au'tomata] nm automaton
automático, a [auto'matiko, a] adj automatic ♦ nm press stud
automotor, triz [automo'tor, 'triθ] adj self-propelled ♦ nm diesel train
automóvil [auto'moβil] nm (motor) car (BRIT), automobile (US)
automovilismo nm (actividad) motoring; (DEPORTE) motor racing; **automovilista** nm/f motorist, driver; **automovilístico, a** adj (industria) motor cpd
autonomía [autono'mia] nf autonomy; **autónomo, a** adj (ESP),

autonómico, a [autoˈnomiko, a] (ESP) adj (POL) autonomous

autopista [autoˈpista] nf motorway (BRIT), freeway (US); **~ de peaje** toll road (BRIT), turnpike road (US)

autopsia [auˈtopsja] nf autopsy, postmortem

autor, a [auˈtor, a] nm/f author

autoridad [autoriˈðað] nf authority; **autoritario, a** adj authoritarian

autorización [autoriθaˈθjon] nf authorization; **autorizado, a** adj authorized; (aprobado) approved

autorizar [autoriˈθar] vt to authorize; (aprobar) to approve

autorretrato [autorreˈtrato] nm self-portrait

autoservicio [autoserˈβiθjo] nm (tienda) self-service shop (BRIT) o store (US); (restaurante) self-service restaurant

autostop [autoˈstop] nm hitch-hiking; **hacer ~** to hitch-hike; **~ista** nm/f hitch-hiker

autosuficiencia [autosufiˈθjenθja] nf self-sufficiency

autovía [autoˈβia] nf ≈ A-road (BRIT), dual carriageway (BRIT), ≈ state highway (US)

auxiliar [auksiˈljar] vt to help ♦ nm/f assistant; **auxilio** nm assistance, help; **primeros auxilios** first aid sg

Av abr (= Avenida) Av(e).

aval [aˈβal] nm guarantee; (persona) guarantor

avalancha [aβaˈlantʃa] nf avalanche

avance [aˈβanθe] nm advance; (pago) advance payment; (CINE) trailer

avanzar [aβanˈθar] vt, vi to advance

avaricia [aβaˈriθja] nf avarice, greed; **avaricioso, a** adj avaricious, greedy

avaro, a [aˈβaro, a] adj miserly, mean ♦ nm/f miser

avasallar [aβasaˈʎar] vt to subdue, subjugate

Avda abr (= Avenida) Av(e).

AVE [ˈaβe] nm abr (= Alta Velocidad Española) ≈ bullet train

ave [ˈaβe] nf bird; **~ de rapiña** bird of prey

avecinarse [aβeθiˈnarse] vr (tormenta, fig) to be on the way

avellana [aβeˈʎana] nf hazelnut; **avellano** nm hazel tree

avemaría [aβemaˈria] nm Hail Mary, Ave Maria

avena [aˈβena] nf oats pl

avenida [aβeˈniða] nf (calle) avenue

avenir [aβeˈnir] vt to reconcile; **~se** vr to come to an agreement, reach a compromise

aventajado, a [aβentaˈxaðo, a] adj outstanding

aventajar [aβentaˈxar] vt (sobrepasar) to surpass, outstrip

aventura [aβenˈtura] nf adventure; **aventurado, a** adj risky; **aventurero, a** adj adventurous

avergonzar [aβerɣonˈθar] vt to shame; (desconcertar) to embarrass; **~se** vr to be ashamed; to be embarrassed

avería [aβeˈria] nf (TEC) breakdown, fault

averiado, a [aβeˈrjaðo, a] adj broken down; **"~~"** "out of order"

averiguación [aβeriɣwaˈθjon] nf investigation; (descubrimiento) ascertainment

averiguar [aβeriˈɣwar] vt to investigate; (descubrir) to find out, ascertain

aversión [aβerˈsjon] nf aversion, dislike

avestruz [aβesˈtruθ] nm ostrich

aviación [aβjaˈθjon] nf aviation; (fuerzas aéreas) air force

aviador, a [aβjaˈðor, a] nm/f aviator, airman/woman

avicultura [aβikulˈtura] nf poultry farming

avidez [aβiˈðeθ] nf avidity, eagerness; **ávido, a** adj avid, eager

avinagrado, a [aβinaˈɣraðo, a] adj sour, acid

avión [aˈβjon] nm aeroplane; (ave)

martin; ~ **de reacción** jet (plane)

avioneta [aβjo'neta] nf light aircraft

avisar [aβi'sar] vt (advertir) to warn, notify; (informar) to tell; (aconsejar) to advise, counsel; **aviso** nm warning; (noticia) notice

avispa [a'βispa] nf wasp

avispado, a [aβis'paðo, a] adj sharp, clever

avispero [aβis'pero] nm wasp's nest

avispón [aβis'pon] nm hornet

avistar [aβis'tar] vt to sight, spot

avituallar [aβitwa'ʎar] vt to supply with food

avivar [aβi'βar] vt to strengthen, intensify; ~**se** vr to revive, acquire new life

axila [ak'sila] nf armpit

axioma [ak'sjoma] nm axiom

ay [ai] excl (dolor) ow!, ouch!; (aflicción) oh!, oh dear!; **¡~ de mi!** poor me!

aya ['aja] nf governess; (niñera) nanny

ayer [a'jer] adv, nm yesterday; **antes de ~** the day before yesterday

ayote [a'jote] (AM) nm pumpkin

ayuda [a'juða] nf help, assistance ♦ nm page; **ayudante, a** nm/f assistant, helper; (ESCOL) assistant; (MIL) adjutant

ayudar [aju'ðar] vt to help, assist

ayunar [aju'nar] vi to fast; **ayunas** nfpl: **estar en ayunas** to be fasting; **ayuno** nm fast; fasting

ayuntamiento [ajunta'mjento] nm (consejo) town (o city) council; (edificio) town (o city) hall

azabache [aθa'βatʃe] nm jet

azada [a'θaða] nf hoe

azafata [aθa'fata] nf air stewardess

azafrán [aθa'fran] nm saffron

azahar [aθa'ar] nm orange/lemon blossom

azar [a'θar] nm (casualidad) chance, fate; (desgracia) misfortune, accident; **por ~** by chance; **al ~** at random

azoramiento [aθora'mjento] nm alarm; (confusión) confusion

azorar [aθo'rar] vt to alarm; ~**se** vr to

get alarmed

Azores [a'θores] nfpl: **las ~** the Azores

azotar [aθo'tar] vt to whip, beat; (pegar) to spank; **azote** nm (látigo) whip; (latigazo) lash, stroke; (en las nalgas) spank; (calamidad) calamity

azotea [aθo'tea] nf (flat) roof

azteca [aθ'teka] adj, nm/f Aztec

azúcar [a'θukar] nm sugar;
azucarado, a adj sugary, sweet

azucarero, a [aθuka'rero, a] adj sugar cpd ♦ nm sugar bowl

azucena [aθu'θena] nf white lily

azufre [a'θufre] nm sulphur

azul [a'θul] adj, nm blue; ~ **marino** navy blue

azulejo [aθu'lexo] nm tile

azuzar [aθu'θar] vt to incite, egg on

B, b

B.A. abr (= Buenos Aires) B.A.

baba ['baβa] nf spittle, saliva; **babear** vi to drool, slaver

babero [ba'βero] nm bib

babor [ba'βor] nm port (side)

baboso, a [ba'βoso, a] (AM: fam) adj silly

baca ['baka] nf (AUTO) luggage o roof rack

bacalao [baka'lao] nm cod(fish)

bache ['batʃe] nm pothole, rut; (fig) bad patch

bachillerato [batʃiʎe'rato] nm higher secondary school course

bacteria [bak'terja] nf bacterium, germ

báculo ['bakulo] nm stick, staff

bagaje [ba'vaxe] nm baggage, luggage

Bahama [ba'ama]: **las (Islas) ~** nfpl the Bahamas

bahía [ba'ia] nf bay

bailar [bai'lar] vt, vi to dance; ~**ín, ina** nm/f (ballet) dancer; **baile** nm dance; (formal) ball

baja ['baxa] nf drop, fall; (MIL) casualty; **dar de ~** (soldado) to discharge;

(*empleado*) to dismiss

bajada [ba'xaða] *nf* descent; (*camino*) slope; (*de aguas*) ebb

bajar [ba'xar] *vi* to go down, come down; (*temperatura, precios*) to drop, fall ♦ *vt* (*cabeza*) to bow; (*escalera*) to go down, come down; (*precio, voz*) to lower; (*llevar abajo*) to take down; ~se *vr* (*de coche*) to get out; (*de autobús, tren*) to get off; ~ **de** (*coche*) to get out of; (*autobús, tren*) to get off

bajeza [ba'xeθa] *nf* baseness *no pl*; (*una ~*) vile deed

bajío [ba'xio] *nm* (*AM*) lowlands *pl*

bajo, a [ˈbaxo, a] *adj* (*mueble, edificio, precio*) low; (*piso*) ground; (*de estatura*) small, short; (*color*) pale; (*sonido*) faint, soft, low; (*voz: en tono*) deep; (*metal*) base; (*humilde*) low, humble ♦ *adv* (*hablar*) softly, quietly; (*volar*) low ♦ *prep* under, below, underneath ♦ *nm* (*MUS*) bass; ~ **la lluvia** in the rain

bajón [ba'xon] *nm* fall, drop

bakalao [baka'lao] (*fam*) *nm* rave (music)

bala [ˈbala] *nf* bullet

balance [ba'lanθe] *nm* (*COM*) balance; (: *libro*) balance sheet; (: *cuenta general*) stocktaking

balancear [balanθe'ar] *vt* to balance ♦ *vi* to swing (to and fro); (*vacilar*) to hesitate; ~se *vr* to swing (to and fro); to hesitate; **balanceo** *nm* swinging

balanza [ba'lanθa] *nf* scales *pl*, balance; (*ASTROLOGÍA*): **B~ Libra**; ~ **comercial** balance of trade; ~ **de pagos** balance of payments

balar [ba'lar] *vi* to bleat

balaustrada [balaus'traða] *nf* balustrade; (*pasamanos*) banisters *pl*

balazo [ba'laθo] *nm* (*golpe*) shot; (*herida*) bullet wound

balbucear [balβuθe'ar] *vi, vt* to stammer, stutter; **balbuceo** *nm* stammering, stuttering

balbucir [balβu'θir] *vi, vt* to stammer, stutter

balcón [bal'kon] *nm* balcony

balde [ˈbalde] *nm* bucket, pail; **de ~** (for) free, for nothing; **en ~** in vain

baldío, a [bal'dio, a] *adj* uncultivated; (*terreno*) waste ♦ *nm* waste land

baldosa [bal'dosa] *nf* (*azulejo*) floor tile; (*grande*) flagstone; **baldosín** *nm* (small) tile

Baleares [bale'ares] *nfpl*: **las (Islas) ~** the Balearic Islands

balido [ba'liðo] *nm* bleat, bleating

baliza [ba'liθa] *nf* (*AVIAT*) beacon; (*NAUT*) buoy

ballena [ba'ʎena] *nf* whale

ballesta [ba'ʎesta] *nf* crossbow; (*AUTO*) spring

ballet [ba'le] (*pl* **~s**) *nm* ballet

balneario [balne'arjo, a] *adj*: **estación balnearia** (*AM*) (bathing) resort ♦ *nm* spa, health resort

balón [ba'lon] *nm* ball

baloncesto [balon'θesto] *nm* basketball

balonmano [balon'mano] *nm* handball

balonvolea [balombo'lea] *nm* volleyball

balsa [ˈbalsa] *nf* raft; (*BOT*) balsa wood

bálsamo [ˈbalsamo] *nm* balsam, balm

baluarte [ba'lwarte] *nm* bastion, bulwark

bambolear [bambole'ar] *vi* to swing, sway; (*silla*) to wobble; ~se *vr* to swing, sway; to wobble; **bamboleo** *nm* swinging, swaying; wobbling

bambú [bam'bu] *nm* bamboo

banana [ba'nana] (*AM*) *nf* banana; **banano** (*AM*) *nm* banana tree

banca [ˈbanka] *nf* (*COM*) banking

bancario, a [ban'karjo, a] *adj* banking *cpd*, bank *cpd*

bancarrota [banka'rrota] *nf* bankruptcy; **hacer ~** to go bankrupt

banco [ˈbanko] *nm* bench; (*ESCOL*) desk; (*COM*) bank; (*GEO*) stratum; ~ **de crédito/de ahorros** credit/savings bank; ~ **de arena** sandbank; ~ **de**

datos databank

banda ['banda] nf band; (pandilla) gang; (NAUT) side, edge; **la B~ Oriental** Uruguay; **~ sonora** soundtrack

bandada [ban'daða] nf (de pájaros) flock; (de peces) shoal

bandazo [ban'daθo] nm: **dar ~s** to sway from side to side

bandeja [ban'dexa] nf tray

bandera [ban'dera] nf flag

banderilla [bande'riʎa] nf banderilla

banderín [bande'rin] nm pennant, small flag

bandido [ban'diðo] nm bandit

bando ['bando] nm (edicto) edict, proclamation; (facción) faction; **los ~s** (REL) the banns

bandolera [bando'lera] nf: **llevar en ~** to wear across one's chest

bandolero [bando'lero] nm bandit, brigand

banquero [ban'kero] nm banker

banqueta [ban'keta] nf stool; (AM: en la calle) pavement (BRIT), sidewalk (US)

banquete [ban'kete] nm banquet; (para convidados) formal dinner

banquillo [ban'kiʎo] nm (JUR) dock, prisoner's bench; (banco) bench; (para los pies) footstool

bañador [baɲa'ðor] nm swimming costume (BRIT), bathing suit (US)

bañar [ba'ɲar] vt to bath, bathe; (objeto) to dip; (de barniz) to coat; **~se** vr (en el mar) to bathe, swim; (en la bañera) to have a bath

bañera [ba'ɲera] nf bath(tub)

bañero, a [ba'ɲero, a] (AM) nm/f lifeguard

bañista [ba'ɲista] nm/f bather

baño ['baɲo] nm (en bañera) bath; (en río) dip, swim; (cuarto) bathroom; (bañera) bath(tub); (capa) coating

baqueta [ba'keta] nf (MUS) drumstick

bar [bar] nm bar

barahúnda [bara'unda] nf uproar, hubbub

baraja [ba'raxa] nf pack (of cards); **barajar** vt (naipes) to shuffle; (fig) to jumble up

baranda [ba'randa] nf = **barandilla**

barandilla [baran'diʎa] nf rail, railing

baratija [bara'tixa] nf trinket

baratillo [bara'tiʎo] nm (tienda) junkshop; (subasta) bargain sale; (conjunto de cosas) secondhand goods pl

barato, a [ba'rato, a] adj cheap ♦ adv cheap, cheaply

baraúnda [bara'unda] nf = **barahúnda**

barba ['barßa] nf (mentón) chin; (pelo) beard

barbacoa [barßa'koa] nf (parrilla) barbecue; (carne) barbecued meat

barbaridad [barßari'ðað] nf barbarity; (acto) barbarism; (atrocidad) outrage; **una ~** (fam) loads; **¡qué ~!** (fam) how awful!

barbarie [bar'ßarje] nf barbarism, savagery; (crueldad) barbarity

barbarismo [barßa'rismo] nm = **barbarie**

bárbaro, a ['barßaro, a] adj barbarous, cruel; (grosero) rough, uncouth ♦ nm/f barbarian ♦ adv: **lo pasamos ~** (fam) we had a great time; **¡qué ~!** (fam) how marvellous!; **un éxito ~** (fam) a terrific success; **es un tipo ~** (fam) he's a great bloke

barbecho [bar'ßetʃo] nm fallow land

barbero [bar'ßero] nm barber, hairdresser

barbilla [bar'ßiʎa] nf chin, tip of the chin

barbo ['barßo] nm barbel; **~ de mar** red mullet

barbotear [barßote'ar] vt, vi to mutter, mumble

barbudo, a [bar'ßuðo, a] adj bearded

barca ['barka] nf (small) boat; **~ pesquera** fishing boat; **~ de pasaje** ferry; **~za** nf barge; **~za de desembarco** landing craft

Barcelona [barθe'lona] *n* Barcelona

barcelonés, esa [barθelo'nes, esa] *adj* o from Barcelona

barco ['barko] *nm* boat; *(grande)* ship; **~ de carga** cargo boat; **~ de vela** sailing ship

baremo [ba'remo] *nm* (MAT, fig) scale

barítono [ba'ritono] *nm* baritone

barman ['barman] *nm* barman

Barna *n* = **Barcelona**

barniz [bar'niθ] *nm* varnish; *(en la loza)* glaze; *(fig)* veneer; **~ar** *vt* to varnish; *(loza)* to glaze

barómetro [ba'rometro] *nm* barometer

barquero [bar'kero] *nm* boatman

barquillo [bar'kiʎo] *nm* cone, cornet

barra ['barra] *nf* bar, rod; *(de un bar, café)* bar; *(de pan)* French stick; *(palanca)* lever; **~ de carmín** o **de labios** lipstick; **~ libre** free bar

barraca [ba'rraka] *nf* hut, cabin

barranco [ba'rranko] *nm* ravine; *(fig)* difficulty

barrena [ba'rrena] *nf* drill; **barrenar** *vt* to drill (through), bore; **barreno** *nm* large drill

barrer [ba'rrer] *vt* to sweep; *(quitar)* to sweep away

barrera [ba'rrera] *nf* barrier

barriada [ba'rrjaða] *nf* quarter, district

barricada [barri'kaða] *nf* barricade

barrido [ba'rriðo] *nm* sweep, sweeping

barrido [ba'rriðo] *nm* = **barrida**

barriga [ba'rriɣa] *nf* belly; *(panza)* paunch; **barrigón, ona** *adj* potbellied; **barrigudo, a** *adj* potbellied

barril [ba'rril] *nm* barrel, cask

barrio ['barrjo] *nm* (*vecindad*) area, neighborhood (US); *(las afueras)* suburb; **~ chino** red-light district

barro ['barro] *nm* (*lodo*) mud; *(objetos)* earthenware; *(MED)* pimple

barroco, a [ba'rroko, a] *adj, nm* baroque

barrote [ba'rrote] *nm* (*de ventana*) bar

barruntar [barrun'tar] *vt* (*conjeturar*)

to guess; *(presentir)* to suspect; **barrunto** *nm* guess; suspicion

bartola [bar'tola]: **a la ~** *adv*: **tirarse a la ~** to take it easy, be lazy

bártulos ['bartulos] *nmpl* things, belongings

barullo [ba'ruʎo] *nm* row, uproar

basar [ba'sar] *vt* to base; **~se** *vr*: **~se en** to be based on

báscula ['baskula] *nf* (platform) scales

base ['base] *nf* base; **a ~ de** on the basis of; *(mediante)* by means of; **~ de datos** (INFORM) database

básico, a ['basiko, a] *adj* basic

basílica [ba'silika] *nf* basilica

┌─────────────────────────┐
│ PALABRA CLAVE │
└─────────────────────────┘

bastante [bas'tante] *adj* **1** *(suficiente)* enough; **~ dinero** enough o sufficient money; **~s libros** enough books
2 *(valor intensivo)*: **~ gente** quite a lot of people; **tener ~ calor** to be rather hot

♦ *adv*: **~ bueno/malo** quite good/ rather bad; **~ rico** pretty rich; **(lo) ~ inteligente (como) para hacer algo** clever enough o sufficiently clever to do sth

bastar [bas'tar] *vi* to be enough o sufficient; **~se** *vr* to be self-sufficient; **~ para** to be enough to; **¡basta!** (that's) enough!

bastardilla [bastar'ðiʎa] *nf* italics

bastardo, a [bas'tarðo, a] *adj, nm/f* bastard

bastidor [basti'ðor] *nm* frame; *(de coche)* chassis; *(TEATRO)* wing; **entre ~es** *(fig)* behind the scenes

basto, a ['basto, a] *adj* coarse, rough; **~s** *nmpl* (NAIPES) ≈ clubs

bastón [bas'ton] *nm* stick, staff; *(para pasear)* walking stick

bastoncillo [baston'θiʎo] *nm* cotton bud

basura [ba'sura] *nf* rubbish (BRIT), garbage (US)

basurero [basu'rero] nm (hombre) dustman (BRIT), garbage man (US); (lugar) dump; (cubo) (rubbish) bin (BRIT), trash can (US)

bata ['bata] nf (gen) dressing gown; (cubretodo) smock, overall; (MED, TEC etc) lab(oratory) coat

batalla [ba'taʎa] nf battle; **de ~** (fig) for everyday use

batallar [bata'ʎar] vi to fight

batallón [bata'ʎon] nm battalion

batata [ba'tata] nf sweet potato

batería [bate'ria] nf battery; (MUS) drums; **~ de cocina** kitchen utensils

batido, a [ba'tiðo, a] adj (camino) beaten, well-trodden ♦ nm (CULIN): **~ (de leche)** milk shake

batidora [bati'ðora] nf beater, mixer; **~ eléctrica** food mixer, blender

batir [ba'tir] vt to beat, strike; (vencer) to beat, defeat; (revolver) to beat, mix; **~se** vr to fight; **~ palmas** to applaud

batuta [ba'tuta] nf baton; **llevar la ~** (fig) to be the boss, be in charge

baúl [ba'ul] nm trunk; (AUTO) boot (BRIT), trunk (US)

bautismo [bau'tismo] nm baptism, christening

bautizar [bauti'θar] vt to baptize, christen; (fam: diluir) to water down; **bautizo** nm baptism, christening

baya ['baja] nf berry

bayeta [ba'jeta] nf floorcloth

baza ['baθa] nf trick; **meter ~** to butt in

bazar [ba'θar] nm bazaar

bazofia [ba'θofja] nf trash

BCE nm abr (= Banco Central Europeo) ECB

beato, a [be'ato, a] adj blessed; (piadoso) pious

bebé [be'ße] (pl **~s**) nm baby

bebedor, a [beße'ðor, a] adj hard-drinking

beber [be'ßer] vt, vi to drink

bebida [be'ßiða] nf drink; **bebido, a** adj drunk

beca ['beka] nf grant, scholarship

becario, a [be'karjo, a] nm/f scholarship holder, grant holder

bedel [be'ðel] nm (ESCOL) janitor; (UNIV) porter

béisbol ['beisßol] nm (DEPORTE) baseball

belén [be'len] nm (de navidad) nativity scene, crib; **B~** Bethlehem

belga ['belɣa] adj, nm/f Belgian

Bélgica ['belxika] nf Belgium

bélico, a ['beliko, a] adj (actitud) warlike; **belicoso, a** adj (guerrero) warlike; (agresivo) aggressive, bellicose

beligerante [belixe'rante] adj belligerent

belleza [be'ʎeθa] nf beauty

bello, a ['beʎo, a] adj beautiful, lovely; **Bellas Artes** Fine Art

bellota [be'ʎota] nf acorn

bemol [be'mol] nm (MUS) flat; **esto tiene ~es** (fam) this is a tough one

bencina [ben'θina] (AM) nf (gasolina) petrol (BRIT), gasoline (US)

bendecir [bende'θir] vt to bless

bendición [bendi'θjon] nf blessing

bendito, a [ben'dito, a] pp de **bendecir** ♦ adj holy; (afortunado) lucky; (feliz) happy; (sencillo) simple ♦ nm/f simple soul

beneficencia [benefi'θenθja] nf charity

beneficiar [benefi'θjar] vt to benefit, be of benefit to; **~se** vr to benefit, profit; **~io, a** nm/f beneficiary

beneficio [bene'fiθjo] nm (bien) benefit, advantage; (ganancia) profit, gain; **~so, a** adj beneficial

benéfico, a [be'nefiko, a] adj charitable

beneplácito [bene'plaθito] nm approval, consent

benevolencia [beneßo'lenθja] nf benevolence, kindness; **benévolo, a** adj benevolent, kind

benigno, a [be'niɣno, a] adj kind; (suave) mild; (MED: tumor) benign, non-malignant

berberecho [berβe'retʃo] nm (ZOOL, CULIN) cockle

berenjena [beren'xena] nf aubergine (BRIT), eggplant (US)

Berlin [ber'lin] n Berlin; **berlinés, esa** adj of o from Berlin ♦ nm/f Berliner

bermudas [ber'muðas] nfpl Bermuda shorts

berrear [berre'ar] vi to bellow, low

berrido [be'rriðo] nm bellow(ing)

berrinche [be'rrintʃe] (fam) nm temper, tantrum

berro ['berro] nm watercress

berza ['berθa] nf cabbage

besamel [besa'mel] nf (CULIN) white sauce, bechamel sauce

besar [be'sar] vt to kiss; (fig: tocar) to graze; **~se** vr to kiss (one another); **beso** nm kiss

bestia ['bestja] nf beast, animal; (fig) idiot; **~ de carga** beast of burden

bestial [bes'tjal] adj bestial; (fam) terrific; **~idad** nf bestiality; (fam) stupidity

besugo [be'suɣo] nm sea bream; (fam) idiot

besuquear [besuke'ar] vt to cover with kisses; **~se** vr to kiss and cuddle

betún [be'tun] nm shoe polish; (QUÍM) bitumen

biberón [biβe'ron] nm feeding bottle

Biblia ['biβlja] nf Bible

bibliografía [biβljoɣra'fia] nf bibliography

biblioteca [biβljo'teka] nf library; (mueble) bookshelves; **~ de consulta** reference library; **~rio, a** nm/f librarian

bicarbonato [bikarβo'nato] nm bicarbonate

bicho ['bitʃo] nm (animal) small animal; (sabandija) bug, insect; (TAUR) bull

bici ['biθi] (fam) nf bike

bicicleta [biθi'kleta] nf bicycle, cycle; **ir en ~** to cycle

bidé [bi'ðe] (pl **~s**) nm bidet

bidón [bi'ðon] nm (de aceite) drum; (de gasolina) can

PALABRA CLAVE

bien [bjen] nm 1 (bienestar) good; **te lo digo por tu ~** I'm telling you for your own good; **el ~ y el mal** good and evil

2 (posesión): **~es** goods; **~es de consumo** consumer goods; **~es inmuebles** o **raíces/~es muebles** real estate sg/personal property sg

♦ adv 1 (de manera satisfactoria, correcta etc) well; **trabaja/come ~** she works/eats well; **contestó ~** he answered correctly; **me siento ~** I feel fine; **no me siento ~** I don't feel very well; **se está ~ aquí** it's nice here

2 (frases): **hiciste ~ en llamarme** you were right to call me

3 (valor intensivo) very; **un cuarto ~ caliente** a nice warm room; **~ se ve que ...** it's quite clear that ...

4: **estar ~: estoy muy ~ aquí** I feel very happy here; **está ~ que vengan** it's all right for them to come; **¡está ~! lo haré** oh all right, I'll do it

5 (de buena gana): **yo ~ que iría pero ...** I'd gladly go but ...

♦ excl: **¡~!** (aprobación) O.K.!; **¡muy ~!** well done!

♦ adj inv (matiz despectivo): **niño ~** rich kid; **gente ~** posh people

♦ conj 1: **~ ... ~ ...: ~ en coche ~ en tren** either by car or by train

2: **no ~** (esp AM): **no ~ llegue te llamaré** as soon as I arrive I'll call you

3: **si ~** even though; ver tb **más**

bienal [bje'nal] adj biennial

bienaventurado, a [bjenaβentu'raðo, a] adj (feliz) happy, fortunate

bienestar [bjenes'tar] nm well-being, welfare

bienhechor, a [bjene'tʃor, a] adj beneficent ♦ nm/f benefactor/ benefactress

bienvenida [bjembe'niða] nf welcome; **dar la ~ a uno** to welcome sb

bienvenido, a [bjembe'niðo] excl welcome!

bife ['bife] (AM) nm steak

bifurcación [bifurka'θjon] nf fork

bifurcarse [bifur'karse] vr (camino, carretera, río) to fork

bigamia [bi'vamja] nf bigamy; **bígamo, a** adj bigamous ♦ nm/f bigamist

bigote [bi'vote] nm moustache; **bigotudo, a** adj with a big moustache

bikini [bi'kini] nm bikini; (CULIN) toasted ham and cheese sandwich

bilbaíno, a [bilßa'ino, a] adj from o of Bilbao

bilingüe [bi'lingwe] adj bilingual

billar [bi'ʎar] nm billiards sg; (lugar) billiard hall; (mini-casino) amusement arcade; **~ americano** pool

billete [bi'ʎete] nm ticket; (de banco) (bank)note (BRIT), bill (US); (carta) note; **~ sencillo, ~ de ida solamente** single (BRIT) o one-way (US) ticket; **~ de ida y vuelta** return (BRIT) o round-trip (US) ticket; **~ de 20 libras** £20 note

billetera [biʎe'tera] nf wallet

billetero [biʎe'tero] nm = **billetera**

billón [bi'ʎon] nm billion

bimensual [bimen'swal] adj twice monthly

bimotor [bimo'tor] adj twin-engined ♦ nm twin-engined plane

bingo ['bingo] nm bingo

biodegradable [bioðevraða'ßle] adj biodegradable

biografía [bjovra'fia] nf biography; **biógrafo, a** nm/f biographer

biología [bjolo'xia] nf biology; **biológico, a** adj biological; (cultivo, producto) organic; **biólogo, a** nm/f biologist

biombo ['bjombo] nm (folding) screen

biquini [bi'kini] nm bikini

birlar [bir'lar] (fam) vt to pinch

Birmania [bir'manja] nf Burma

birria ['birrja] nf: **ser una ~** (película, libro) to be rubbish

bis [bis] excl encore! ♦ adv: **viven en el 27 ~** they live at 27a

bisabuelo, a [bisa'ßwelo, a] nm/f great-grandfather/mother

bisagra [bi'savra] nf hinge

bisiesto [bi'sjesto] adj: **año ~** leap year

bisnieto, a [bis'njeto, a] nm/f great-grandson/daughter

bisonte [bi'sonte] nm bison

bisté [bis'te] nm = **bistec**

bistec [bis'tek] nm steak

bisturí [bistu'ri] nm scalpel

bisutería [bisute'ria] nf imitation o costume jewellery

bit [bit] nm (INFORM) bit

bizco, a ['biθko, a] adj cross-eyed

bizcocho [biθ'kotʃo] nm (CULIN) sponge cake

blanca ['blanka] nf (MUS) minim; **estar sin ~** to be broke; ver tb **blanco**

blanco, a ['blanko, a] adj white ♦ nm/f white man/woman, white ♦ nm (color) white; (en texto) blank; (MIL, fig) target; **en ~** blank; **noche en ~** sleepless night

blancura [blan'kura] nf whiteness

blandir [blan'dir] vt to brandish

blando, a ['blando, a] adj soft; (tierno) tender, gentle; (carácter) mild; (fam) cowardly; **blandura** nf softness; tenderness; mildness

blanquear [blanke'ar] vt to whiten; (fachada) to whitewash; (paño) to bleach ♦ vi to turn white; **blanquecino, a** adj whitish

blasfemar [blasfe'mar] vi to blaspheme, curse; **blasfemia** nf blasphemy

blasón [bla'son] nm coat of arms

bledo ['bleðo] nm: **me importa un ~** I couldn't care less

blindado, a [blin'daðo, a] adj (MIL) armour-plated; (antibala) bullet-proof; **coche** (ESP) o **carro** (AM) ~ armoured car

blindaje [blin'daxe] nm armour, armour-plating

bloc [blok] (pl ~s) nm writing pad

bloque ['bloke] nm block; (POL) bloc; ~ **de cilindros** cylinder block

bloquear [bloke'ar] vt to blockade; **bloqueo** nm blockade; (COM) freezing, blocking

blusa ['blusa] nf blouse

boato [bo'ato] nm show, ostentation

bobada [bo'βaða] nf foolish action; foolish statement; **decir ~s** to talk nonsense

bobería [boβe'ria] nf = **bobada**

bobina [bo'βina] nf (TEC) bobbin; (FOTU) spool; (ELEC) coil

bobo, a ['boβo, a] adj (tonto) daft, silly; (cándido) naïve ♦ nm/f fool, idiot ♦ nm (TEATRO) clown, funny man

boca ['boka] nf mouth; (de crustáceo) pincer; (de cañón) muzzle; (de entrada) mouth, entrance; ~s (de río) mouth sg; ~ **abajo/arriba** face down/up; **se me hace agua la ~** my mouth is watering

bocacalle [boka'kaʎe] nf (entrance to a) street; **la primera ~** the first turning o street

bocadillo [boka'ðiʎo] nm sandwich

bocado [bo'kaðo] nm mouthful, bite; (de caballo) bridle; ~ **de Adán** Adam's apple

bocajarro [boka'xarro]: **a ~** adv (disparar, preguntar) point-blank

bocanada [boka'naða] nf (de vino) mouthful, swallow; (de aire) gust, puff

bocata [bo'kata] (fam) nm sandwich

bocazas [bo'kaθas] (fam) nm inv bigmouth

boceto [bo'θeto] nm sketch, outline

bochorno [bo'tʃorno] nm (vergüenza) embarrassment; (calor): **hace ~** it's very muggy; **~so, a** adj muggy;

embarrassing

bocina [bo'θina] nf (MUS) trumpet; (AUTO) horn; (para hablar) megaphone

boda ['boða] nf (tb: ~s) wedding, marriage; (fiesta) wedding reception; **~s de plata/de oro** silver/golden wedding

bodega [bo'ðexa] nf (de vino) (wine) cellar; (depósito) storeroom; (de barco) hold

bodegón [boðe'xon] nm (ARTE) still life

bofe ['bofe] nm (tb: ~s: de res) lights

bofetada [bofe'taða] nf slap (in the face)

bofetón [bofe'ton] nm = **bofetada**

boga ['boxa] nf: **en ~** (fig) in vogue

bogar [bo'xar] vi (remar) to row; (navegar) to sail

bogavante [boxa'βante] nm lobster

Bogotá [boxo'ta] n Bogotá

bohemio, a [bo'emjo, a] adj, nm/f Bohemian

boicot [boi'kot] (pl ~s) nm boycott; **~ear** vt to boycott; **~eo** nm boycott

boina ['boina] nf beret

bola ['bola] nf ball; (canica) marble; (NAIPES) (grand) slam; (betún) shoe polish; (mentira) tale, story; ~s (AM) nfpl bolas sg; ~ **de billar** billiard ball; ~ **de nieve** snowball

bolchevique [boltʃe'βike] adj, nm/f Bolshevik

boleadoras [bolea'ðoras] (AM) nfpl bolas sg

bolera [bo'lera] nf skittle o bowling alley

boleta [bo'leta] (AM) nf (billete) ticket; (permiso) pass, permit

boletería [bolete'ria] (AM) nf ticket office

boletín [bole'tin] nm bulletin; (periódico) journal, review; ~ **de noticias** news bulletin

boleto [bo'leto] nm ticket

boli ['boli] (fam) nm Biro ®, pen

bolígrafo [bo'lixrafo] nm ball-point

pen, Biro ®

bolívar [bo'liβar] nm monetary unit of Venezuela

Bolivia [bo'liβja] nf Bolivia; **boliviano, a** adj, nm/f Bolivian

bollería [boλe'ria] nf cakes pl and pastries pl

bollo ['boλo] nm (pan) roll; (bulto) bump, lump; (abolladura) dent

bolo ['bolo] nm skittle; (píldora) (large) pill; **(juego de) ~s** nmpl skittles pl

bolsa ['bolsa] nf bag; (AM) pocket; (ANAT) cavity, sac; (COM) stock exchange; (MINERÍA) pocket; **de ~** pocket cpd; **~ de agua caliente** hot water bottle; **~ de aire** air pocket; **~ de papel** paper bag; **~ de plástico** plastic bag

bolsillo [bol'siλo] nm pocket; (cartera) purse; **de ~** pocket(-size)

bolsista [bol'sista] nm/f stockbroker

bolso ['bolso] nm (bolsa) bag; (de mujer) handbag

bomba ['bomba] nf (MIL) bomb; (TEC) pump ♦ (fam) adj: **noticia ~** bombshell ♦ (fam) adv: **pasarlo ~** to have a great time; **~ atómica/de humo/de efecto retardado** atomic/smoke/time bomb

bombardear [bombarðe'ar] vt to bombard; (MIL) to bomb; **bombardeo** nm bombardment; bombing

bombardero [bombar'ðero] nm bomber

bombear [bombe'ar] vt (agua) to pump (out o up); **~se** vr to warp

bombero [bom'bero] nm fireman

bombilla [bom'biλa] (ESP) nf (light) bulb

bombín [bom'bin] nm bowler hat

bombo ['bombo] nm (MUS) bass drum; (TEC) drum

bombón [bom'bon] nm chocolate

bombona [bom'bona] nf (de butano, oxígeno) cylinder

bonachón, ona [bona'tʃon, ona] adj good-natured, easy-going

bonanza [bo'nanθa] nf (NAUT) fair weather; (fig) bonanza; (MINERÍA) rich pocket o vein

bondad [bon'daδ] nf goodness, kindness; **tenga la ~ de** (please) be good enough to; **~oso, a** adj good, kind

bonificación [bonifika'θjon] nf bonus

bonito, a [bo'nito, a] adj pretty; (agradable) nice ♦ nm (atún) tuna (fish)

bono ['bono] nm voucher; (FIN) bond

bonobús [bono'βus] (ESP) nm bus pass

bonoloto [bono'loto] nf state-run weekly lottery

boquerón [boke'ron] nm (pez) (kind of) anchovy; (agujero) large hole

boquete [bo'kete] nm gap, hole

boquiabierto, a [bokja'βjerto, a] adj: **quedar ~** to be amazed o flabbergasted

boquilla [bo'kiλa] nf (para riego) nozzle; (para cigarro) cigarette holder; (MUS) mouthpiece

borbotón [borβo'ton] nm: **salir a borbotones** to gush out

borda ['borða] nf (NAUT) (ship's) rail; **tirar algo/caerse por la ~** to throw sth/fall overboard

bordado [bor'ðaðo] nm embroidery

bordar [bor'ðar] vt to embroider

borde ['borðe] nm edge, border; (de camino etc) side; (de la costura) hem; **al ~ de** (fig) on the verge o brink of; **ser ~** (ESP: fam) to be rude; **~ar** vt to border

bordillo [bor'ðiλo] nm kerb (BRIT), curb (US)

bordo ['borðo] nm (NAUT) side; **a ~** on board

borinqueño, a [borin'kenjo, a] adj, nm/f Puerto Rican

borla ['borla] nf (adorno) tassel

borrachera [borra'tʃera] nf (ebriedad) drunkenness; (orgía) spree, binge

borracho, a [bo'rratʃo, a] adj drunk ♦ nm/f (habitual) drunkard, drunk; (temporal) drunk, drunk man/woman

borrador [borra'ðor] nm (escritura) first draft, rough sketch; (goma) rubber (BRIT), eraser

borrar [bo'rrar] vt to erase, rub out

borrasca [bo'rraska] nf storm

borrico, a [bo'rriko, a] nm/f donkey/she-donkey; (fig) stupid man/woman

borrón [bo'rron] nm (mancha) stain

borroso, a [bo'rroso, a] adj vague, unclear; (escritura) illegible

bosque [boske] nm wood; (grande) forest

bosquejar [boske'xar] vt to sketch; **bosquejo** nm sketch

bostezar [boste'θar] vi to yawn; **bostezo** nm yawn

bota ['bota] nf (calzado) boot; (para vino) leather wine bottle; ~s de agua, ~s de goma Wellingtons

botánica [bo'tanika] nf (ciencia) botany; ver tb **botánico**

botánico, a [bo'taniko, a] adj botanical ♦ nm/f botanist

botar [bo'tar] vt to throw, hurl; (NAUT) to launch; (AM) to throw out ♦ vi to bounce

bote ['bote] nm (salto) bounce; (golpe) thrust; (vasija) tin, can; (embarcación) boat; de ~ en ~ packed, jammed full; ~ de la basura (AM) dustbin (BRIT), trashcan (US); ~ salvavidas lifeboat

botella [bo'teʎa] nf bottle; **botellín** nm small bottle

botica [bo'tika] nf chemist's (shop) (BRIT), pharmacy; ~rio, a nm/f chemist (BRIT), pharmacist

botijo [bo'tixo] nm (earthenware) jug

botín [bo'tin] nm (calzado) half boot; (polaina) spat; (MIL) booty

botiquín [boti'kin] nm (armario) medicine cabinet; (portátil) first-aid kit

botón [bo'ton] nm button; (BOT) bud; ~ de oro buttercup

botones [bo'tones] nm inv bellboy; bellhop (US)

bóveda ['boßeða] nf (ARQ) vault

boxeador [boksea'ðor] nm boxer

boxear [bokse'ar] vi to box

boxeo [bok'seo] nm boxing

boya ['boja] nf (NAUT) buoy; (de caña) float

boyante [bo'jante] adj prosperous

bozal [bo'θal] nm (de caballo) halter; (de perro) muzzle

bracear [braθe'ar] vi (agitar los brazos) to wave one's arms

bracero [bra'θero] nm labourer; (en el campo) farmhand

bragas ['braɣas] nfpl (de mujer) panties, knickers (BRIT)

bragueta [bra'ɣeta] nf fly, flies pl

braille [breil] nm braille

bramar [bra'mar] vi to bellow, roar; **bramido** nm bellow, roar

brasa ['brasa] nf live o hot coal

brasero [bra'sero] nm brazier

Brasil [bra'sil] nm: (el) ~ Brazil; **brasileño, a** adj, nm/f Brazilian

bravata [bra'ßata] nf boast

braveza [bra'ßeθa] nf (valor) bravery; (ferocidad) ferocity

bravío, a [bra'ßio, a] adj wild; (feroz) fierce

bravo, a ['braßo, a] adj (valiente) brave; (feroz) ferocious; (salvaje) wild; (mar etc) rough, stormy ♦ excl bravo!; **bravura** nf bravery; ferocity

braza ['braθa] nf fathom; **nadar a la** ~ to swim (the) breast-stroke

brazada [bra'θaða] nf stroke

brazado [bra'θaðo] nm armful

brazalete [braθa'lete] nm (pulsera) bracelet; (banda) armband

brazo ['braθo] nm arm; (ZOOL) foreleg; (BOT) limb, branch; **luchar a** ~ **partido** to fight hand-to-hand; **ir cogidos del** ~ to walk arm in arm

brea ['brea] nf pitch, tar

brebaje [bre'ßaxe] nm potion

brecha ['bretʃa] nf (hoyo, vacío) gap, opening; (MIL, fig) breach

brega ['breɣa] nf (lucha) struggle; (trabajo) hard work

breva ['breßa] nf early fig

breve ['breθe] *adj* short, brief ♦ *nf* (*MUS*) breve; **~dad** *nf* brevity, shortness

brezo ['breθo] *nm* heather

bribón, ona [bri'βon, ona] *adj* idle, lazy ♦ *nm/f* (*pícaro*) rascal, rogue

bricolaje [briko'laxe] *nm* do-it-yourself, DIY

brida ['briða] *nf* bridle, rein; (*TEC*) clamp; **a toda ~** at top speed

bridge [britʃ] *nm* bridge

brigada [bri'βaða] *nf* (*unidad*) brigade; (*trabajadores*) squad, gang ♦ *nm* ≈ staff-sergeant, sergeant-major

brillante [bri'ʎante] *adj* brilliant ♦ *nm* diamond

brillar [bri'ʎar] *vi* (*tb fig*) to shine; (*joyas*) to sparkle

brillo ['briʎo] *nm* shine; (*brillantez*) brilliance; (*fig*) splendour; **sacar ~ a** to polish

brincar [brin'kar] *vi* to skip about, hop about, jump about; **está que brinca** he's hopping mad

brinco ['brinko] *nm* jump, leap

brindar [brin'dar] *vi*: **~ a o por** to drink (a toast) to ♦ *vt* to offer, present

brindis ['brindis] *nm inv* toast

brío ['brio] *nm* spirit, dash; **brioso, a** *adj* spirited, dashing

brisa ['brisa] *nf* breeze

británico, a [bri'taniko, a] *adj* British ♦ *nm/f* Briton, British person

brizna ['briθna] *nf* (*de hierba, paja*) blade; (*de tabaco*) leaf

broca ['broka] *nf* (*TEC*) drill, bit

brocal [bro'kal] *nm* rim

brocha ['brotʃa] *nf* (*large*) paintbrush; **~ de afeitar** shaving brush

broche ['brotʃe] *nm* brooch

broma ['broma] *nf* joke; **en ~** in fun, as a joke; **~ pesada** practical joke; **bromear** *vi* to joke

bromista [bro'mista] *adj* fond of joking ♦ *nm/f* joker, wag

bronca ['bronka] *nf* row; **echar una ~ a uno** to tick sb off

bronce ['bronθe] *nm* bronze; **~ado, a**

adj bronze; (*por el sol*) tanned ♦ *nm* (*sun*)tan; (*TEC*) bronzing

bronceador [bronθea'ðor] *nm* suntan lotion

broncearse [bronθe'arse] *vr* to get a suntan

bronco, a ['bronko, a] *adj* (*manera*) rude, surly; (*voz*) harsh

bronquio ['bronkjo] *nm* (*ANAT*) bronchial tube

bronquitis [bron'kitis] *nf inv* bronchitis

brotar [bro'tar] *vi* (*BOT*) to sprout; (*aguas*) to gush (forth); (*MED*) to break out

brote ['brote] *nm* (*BOT*) shoot; (*MED, fig*) outbreak

bruces ['bruθes]: **de ~** *adv*: **caer o dar de ~** to fall headlong, fall flat

bruja ['bruxa] *nf* witch; **brujería** *nf* witchcraft

brujo ['bruxo] *nm* wizard, magician

brújula ['bruxula] *nf* compass

bruma ['bruma] *nf* mist; **brumoso, a** *adj* misty

bruñir [bru'ɲir] *vt* to polish

brusco, a ['brusko, a] *adj* (*súbito*) sudden; (*áspero*) brusque

Bruselas [bru'selas] *n* Brussels

brutal [bru'tal] *adj* brutal

brutalidad [brutali'ðað] *nf* brutality

bruto, a ['bruto, a] *adj* (*idiota*) stupid; (*bestial*) brutish; (*peso*) gross; **en ~** raw, unworked

Bs.As. *abr* (= *Buenos Aires*) B.A.

bucal [bu'kal] *adj* oral; **por vía ~** orally

bucear [buθe'ar] *vi* to dive ♦ *vt* to explore; **buceo** *nm* diving

bucle ['bukle] *nm* curl

budismo [bu'ðismo] *nm* Buddhism

buen [bwen] *adj m ver* **bueno**

buenamente [bwena'mente] *adv* (*fácilmente*) easily; (*voluntariamente*) willingly

buenaventura [bwenaβen'tura] *nf* (*suerte*) good luck; (*adivinación*) fortune

bueno, a [ˈbweno, a] *adj* (*antes de nmsg:* **buen**) **1** (*excelente etc*) good; **es un libro ~,** es un buen libro it's a good book; **hace ~,** hace buen tiempo the weather is fine, it is nice; **el ~ de Paco** good old Paco; **fue muy ~ conmigo** he was very nice o kind to me

2 (*apropiado*): **ser ~ para** to be good for; **creo que vamos por buen camino** I think we're on the right track

3 (*irónico*): **le di un buen rapapolvo** I gave him a good o real ticking off; **¡buen conductor estás hecho!** some o a fine driver you are!; **¡estaría ~ que ...!** a fine thing it would be if ...!

4 (*atractivo, sabroso*): **está ~ este bizcocho** this sponge is delicious; **Carmen está muy buena** Carmen is gorgeous

5 (*saludos*): **¡buen día!, ¡~s días!** (good) morning!; **¡buenas (tardes)!** (good) afternoon!; (*más tarde*) (good) evening!; **¡buenas noches!** good night!

6 (*otras locuciones*): **estar de buenas** to be in a good mood; **por las buenas o por las malas** by hook or by crook; **de buenas a primeras** all of a sudden

♦ *excl* **¡~!** all right!; **~, ¿y qué?** well, so what?

Buenos Aires *nm* Buenos Aires
buey [bwei] *nm* ox
búfalo [ˈbufalo] *nm* buffalo
bufanda [buˈfanda] *nf* scarf
bufar [buˈfar] *vi* to snort
bufete [buˈfete] *nm* (*despacho de abogado*) lawyer's office
buffer [ˈbufer] *nm* (INFORM) buffer
bufón [buˈfon] *nm* clown
buhardilla [buarˈðiʎa] *nf* attic

búho [ˈbuo] *nm* owl; (*fig*) hermit, recluse
buhonero [buoˈnero] *nm* pedlar
buitre [ˈbwitre] *nm* vulture
bujía [buˈxia] *nf* (*vela*) candle; (ELEC) candle (power); (AUTO) spark plug
bula [ˈbula] *nf* (*papal*) bull
bulbo [ˈbulβo] *nm* bulb
bulevar [buleˈβar] *nm* boulevard
Bulgaria [bulˈγarja] *nf* Bulgaria;
búlgaro, a *adj, nm/f* Bulgarian
bulla [ˈbuʎa] *nf* (*ruido*) uproar; (*de gente*) crowd
bullicio [buˈʎiθjo] *nm* (*ruido*) uproar; (*movimiento*) bustle
bullir [buˈʎir] *vi* (*hervir*) to boil; (*burbujear*) to bubble
bulto [ˈbulto] *nm* (*paquete*) package; (*fardo*) bundle; (*tamaño*) size, bulkiness; (MED) swelling, lump; (*silueta*) vague shape
buñuelo [buˈɲwelo] *nm* ≈ doughnut (BRIT), ≈ donut (US); (*fruta de sartén*) fritter
BUP [bup] *nm abr* (ESP: = *Bachillerato Unificado Polivalente*) *secondary education and leaving certificate for 14–17 age group*
buque [ˈbuke] *nm* ship, vessel
burbuja [burˈβuxa] *nf* bubble;
burbujear *vi* to bubble
burdel [burˈðel] *nm* brothel
burdo, a [ˈburðo, a] *adj* coarse, rough
burgués, esa [burˈγes, esa] *adj* middle-class, bourgeois; **burguesía** *nf* middle class, bourgeoisie
burla [ˈburla] *nf* (*mofa*) gibe; (*broma*) joke; (*engaño*) trick
burladero [burlaˈðero] *nm* (*bullfighter's*) refuge
burlar [burˈlar] *vt* (*engañar*) to deceive ♦ *vi* to joke; **~se** *vr* to joke; **~se de** to make fun of
burlesco, a [burˈlesko, a] *adj* burlesque
burlón, ona [burˈlon, ona] *adj* mocking

burocracia [buro'kraθja] nf civil service

burócrata [bu'rokrata] nm/f civil servant

burrada [bu'rraða] nf: **decir/soltar ~s** to talk nonsense; **hacer ~s** to act stupid; **una ~** (mucho) a (hell of a) lot

burro, a ['burro, a] nm/f donkey/she-donkey; (fig) ass, idiot

bursátil [bur'satil] adj stock-exchange cpd

bus [bus] nm bus

busca ['buska] nf search, hunt ♦ nm (TEL) bleeper; **en ~ de** in search of

buscar [bus'kar] vt to look for, search for, seek ♦ vi to look, search, seek; **se busca secretaria** secretary wanted

busque etc vb ver **buscar**

búsqueda ['buskeða] nf = **busca**

busto ['busto] nm (ANAT, ARTE) bust

butaca [bu'taka] nf armchair; (de cine, teatro) stall, seat

butano [bu'tano] nm butane (gas)

buzo ['buθo] nm diver

buzón [bu'θon] nm (en puerta) letter box; (en la calle) pillar box

C, c

C. abr (= centígrado) C; (= compañía) Co.

c. abr (= capítulo) ch.

C/ abr (= calle) St

c.a. abr (= corriente alterna) AC

cabal [ka'βal] adj (exacto) exact; (correcto) right, proper; (acabado) finished, complete; **~es** nmpl: **estar en sus ~es** to be in one's right mind

cábalas ['kaβalas] nfpl: **hacer ~** to guess

cabalgar [kaβal'ɣar] vt, vi to ride

cabalgata [kaβal'ɣata] nf procession

caballa [ka'βaʎa] nf mackerel

caballeresco, a [kaβaʎe'resko, a] adj noble, chivalrous

caballería [kaβaʎe'ria] nf mount; (MIL)

cavalry

caballeriza [kaβaʎe'riθa] nf stable;

caballerizo nm groom, stableman

caballero [kaβa'ʎero] nm gentleman; (de la orden de caballería) knight; (trato directo) sir

caballerosidad [kaβaʎerosi'ðað] nf chivalry

caballete [kaβa'ʎete] nm (ARTE) easel; (TEC) trestle

caballito [kaβa'ʎito] nm (caballo pequeño) small horse, pony; **~s** nmpl (en verbena) roundabout, merry-go-round

caballo [ka'βaʎo] nm horse; (AJEDREZ) knight; (NAIPES) queen; **ir en ~** to ride; **~ de vapor** o **de fuerza** horsepower; **~ de carreras** racehorse

cabaña [ka'βaɲa] nf (casita) hut, cabin

cabaré [kaβa're] (pl **~s**) nm cabaret

cabaret [kaβa're] (pl **~s**) nm cabaret

cabecear [kaβeθe'ar] vt, vi to nod

cabecera [kaβe'θera] nf head; (IMPRENTA) headline

cabecilla [kaβe'θiʎa] nm ringleader

cabellera [kaβe'ʎera] nf (head of) hair; (de cometa) tail

cabello [ka'βeʎo] nm (tb: **~s**) hair

caber [ka'βer] vi (entrar) to fit, go; **caben 3 más** there's room for 3 more

cabestrillo [kaβes'triʎo] nm sling

cabestro [ka'βestro] nm halter

cabeza [ka'βeθa] nf head; (POL) chief, leader; **~ rapada** skinhead; **~da** nf (golpe) butt; **dar ~da** to nod off; **cabezón, ona** adj (vino) heady; (fam: persona) pig-headed

cabida [ka'βiða] nf space

cabildo [ka'βildo] nm (de iglesia) chapter; (POL) town council

cabina [ka'βina] nf cabin; (de camión) cab; **~ telefónica** telephone box (BRIT) o booth

cabizbajo, a [kaβiθ'βaxo, a] adj crestfallen, dejected

cable ['kaβle] nm cable

cabo ['kaβo] nm (de objeto) end,

extremity; (MIL) corporal; (NAUT) rope, cable; (GEO) cape; **al ~ de 3 días** after 3 days

cabra [ˈkaßra] nf goat

cabré etc vb ver **caber**

cabrear [kaßreˈar] (fam) vt to bug; **~se** vr (enfadarse) to fly off the handle

cabrio, a [kaˈßrio, a] adj goatish; **macho ~** (he-)goat, billy goat

cabriola [kaˈßrjola] nf caper

cabritilla [kaßriˈtiλa] nf kid, kidskin

cabrito [kaˈßrito] nm kid

cabrón [kaˈßron] nm cuckold; (fam!) bastard (!)

caca [ˈkaka] (fam) nf pooh

cacahuete [kakaˈwete] (ESP) nm peanut

cacao [kaˈkao] nm cocoa; (BOT) cacao

cacarear [kakareˈar] vi (persona) to boast; (gallina) to crow

cacería [kaθeˈria] nf hunt

cacerola [kaθeˈrola] nf pan, saucepan

cachalote [katʃaˈlote] nm (ZOOL) sperm whale

cacharro [kaˈtʃarro] nm earthenware pot; **~s** nmpl pots and pans

cachear [katʃeˈar] vt to search, frisk

cachemir [katʃeˈmir] nm cashmere

cacheo [kaˈtʃeo] nm searching, frisking

cachete [kaˈtʃete] nm (ANAT) cheek; (bofetada) slap (in the face)

cachiporra [katʃiˈporra] nf truncheon

cachivache [katʃiˈßatʃe] nm (trasto) piece of junk; **~s** nmpl junk sg

cacho [ˈkatʃo] nm (small) bit; (AM: cuerno) horn

cachondeo [katʃonˈdeo] (fam) nm farce, joke

cachondo, a [kaˈtʃondo, a] adj (ZOOL) on heat; (fam: sexualmente) randy; (: gracioso) funny

cachorro, a [kaˈtʃorro, a] nm/f (perro) pup, puppy; (león) cub

cacique [kaˈθike] nm chief, local ruler; (POL) local party boss; **caciquismo** nm system of control by the local boss

caco [ˈkako] nm pickpocket

cacto [ˈkakto] nm cactus

cactus [ˈkaktus] nm inv cactus

cada [ˈkaða] adj inv each; (antes de número) every; **~ día** each day, every day; **~ dos días** every other day; **~ uno/a** each one, every one; **~ vez más/menos** more and more/less and less; **uno de ~ diez** one out of every ten

cadalso [kaˈðalso] nm scaffold

cadáver [kaˈðaßer] nm (dead) body, corpse

cadena [kaˈðena] nf chain; (TV) channel; **trabajo en ~** assembly line work; **~ perpetua** (JUR) life imprisonment

cadencia [kaˈðenθja] nf rhythm

cadera [kaˈðera] nf hip

cadete [kaˈðete] nm cadet

caducar [kaðuˈkar] vi to expire; **caduco, a** adj expired; (persona) very old

caer [kaˈer] vi to fall (down); **~se** vr to fall (down); **me cae bien/mal** I get on well with him/I can't stand him; **~ en la cuenta** to realize; **su cumpleaños cae en viernes** her birthday falls on a Friday

café [kaˈfe] (pl **~s**) nm (bebida, planta) coffee; (lugar) café ♦ adj (color) brown; **~ con leche** white coffee; **~ solo** black coffee

cafetera [kafeˈtera] nf coffee pot

cafetería [kafeteˈria] nf (gen) café

cafetero, a [kafeˈtero, a] adj coffee cpd; **ser muy ~** to be a coffee addict

cagar [kaˈvar] (fam!) vt to bungle, mess up ♦ vi to have a shit (!)

caída [kaˈiða] nf fall; (declive) slope; (disminución) fall, drop

caído, a [kaˈiðo, a] adj drooping

caiga etc vb ver **caer**

caimán [kaiˈman] nm alligator

caja [ˈkaxa] nf box; (para reloj) case; (de ascensor) shaft; (COM) cashbox; (donde se hacen los pagos) cashdesk; (: en supermercado) checkout, till; **~ de**

ahorros savings bank; **~ de cambios** gearbox; **~ fuerte**, **~ de caudales** safe, strongbox

cajero, a [ka'xero, a] *nm/f* cashier; **~ automático** cash dispenser

cajetilla [kaxe'tiʎa] *nf* (*de cigarrillos*) packet

cajón [ka'xon] *nm* big box; (*de mueble*) drawer

cal [kal] *nf* lime

cala ['kala] *nf* (*GEO*) cove, inlet; (*de barco*) hold

calabacín [kalaβa'θin] *nm* (*BOT*) baby marrow; (: *más pequeño*) courgette (*BRIT*), zucchini (*US*)

calabaza [kala'βaθa] *nf* (*BOT*) pumpkin

calabozo [kala'βoθo] *nm* (*cárcel*) prison; (*celda*) cell

calada [ka'laða] *nf* (*de cigarrillo*) puff

calado, a [ka'laðo, a] *adj* (*prenda*) lace *cpd* ♦ *nm* (*NAUT*) draught

calamar [kala'mar] *nm* squid *nv ~s*

calambre [ka'lambre] *nm* (*tb: ~s*) cramp

calamidad [kalami'ðað] *nf* calamity, disaster

calar [ka'lar] *vt* to soak, drench; (*penetrar*) to pierce, penetrate; (*comprender*) to see through; (*vela*) to lower; **~se** *vr* (*AUTO*) to stall; **~se las gafas** to stick one's glasses on

calavera [kala'βera] *nf* skull

calcar [kal'kar] *vt* (*reproducir*) to trace; (*imitar*) to copy

calcetín [kalθe'tin] *nm* sock

calcinar [kalθi'nar] *vt* to burn, blacken

calcio ['kalθjo] *nm* calcium

calcomanía [kalkoma'nia] *nf* transfer

calculador, a [kalkula'ðor, a] *adj* (*persona*) calculating

calculadora [kalkula'ðora] *nf* calculator

calcular [kalku'lar] *vt* (*MAT*) to calculate, compute; **~ que ...** to reckon that ...; **cálculo** *nm* calculation

caldear [kalde'ar] *vt* to warm (up), heat (up)

caldera [kal'dera] *nf* boiler

calderilla [kalde'riʎa] *nf* (*moneda*) small change

caldero [kal'dero] *nm* small boiler

caldo ['kaldo] *nm* stock; (*consomé*) consommé

calefacción [kalefak'θjon] *nf* heating; **~ central** central heating

calendario [kalen'darjo] *nm* calendar

calentador [kalenta'ðor] *nm* heater

calentamiento [kalenta'mjento] *nm* (*DEPORTE*) warm-up

calentar [kalen'tar] *vt* to heat (up); **~se** *vr* to heat up, warm up; (*fig: discusión etc*) to get heated

calentura [kalen'tura] *nf* (*MED*) fever, (high) temperature

calibrar [kali'βrar] *vt* to gauge, measure; **calibre** *nm* (*de cañón*) calibre, bore; (*diámetro*) diameter; (*fig*) calibre

calidad [kali'ðað] *nf* quality; **de ~** quality *cpd*; **en ~ de** in the capacity of, as

cálido, a ['kaliðo, a] *adj* hot; (*fig*) warm

caliente *etc* [ka'ljente] *vb ver* **calentar** ♦ *adj* hot; (*fig*) fiery; (*disputa*) heated; (*fam: cachondo*) randy

calificación [kalifika'θjon] *nf* qualification; (*de alumno*) grade, mark

calificar [kalifi'kar] *vt* to qualify; (*alumno*) to grade, mark; **~ de** to describe as

calima [ka'lima] *nf* (*cerca del mar*) mist

cáliz ['kaliθ] *nm* chalice

caliza [ka'liθa] *nf* limestone

calizo, a [ka'liθo, a] *adj* lime *cpd*

callado, a [ka'ʎaðo, a] *adj* quiet

callar [ka'ʎar] *vt* (*asunto delicado*) to keep quiet about, say nothing about; (*persona, opinión*) to silence ♦ *vi* to keep quiet, be silent; **~se** *vr* to keep quiet, be silent; **¡cállate!** be quiet!, shut up!

calle ['kaʎe] *nf* street; (*DEPORTE*) lane; **~ arriba/abajo** up/down the street;

~ de un solo sentido one-way street
calleja [ka'ʎexa] *nf* alley, narrow street;
callejear *vi* to wander (about) the streets; **callejero, a** *adj* street *cpd*
♦ *nm* street map; **callejón** *nm* alley, passage; **callejón sin salida** cul-de-sac; **callejuela** *nf* side-street, alley
callista [ka'ʎista] *nm/f* chiropodist
callo ['kaʎo] *nm* callus; (*en el pie*) corn; **~s** *nmpl* (CULIN) tripe *sg*
calma ['kalma] *nf* calm
calmante [kal'mante] *nm* sedative, tranquillizer
calmar [kal'mar] *vt* to calm, calm down ♦ *vi* (*tempestad*) to abate; (*mente etc*) to become calm
calmoso, a [kal'moso, a] *adj* calm, quiet
calor [ka'lor] *nm* heat; (*agradable*) warmth; **hace ~** it's hot; **tener ~** to be hot
caloría [kalo'ria] *nf* calorie
calumnia [ka'lumnja] *nf* calumny, slander; **calumnioso, a** *adj* slanderous
caluroso, a [kalu'roso, a] *adj* hot; (*sin exceso*) warm; (*fig*) enthusiastic
calva ['kalβa] *nf* bald patch; (*en bosque*) clearing
calvario [kal'βarjo] *nm* stations *pl* of the cross
calvicie [kal'βiθje] *nf* baldness
calvo, a ['kalβo, a] *adj* bald; (*terreno*) bare, barren; (*tejido*) threadbare
calza ['kalθa] *nf* wedge, chock
calzada [kal'θaða] *nf* roadway, highway
calzado, a [kal'θaðo, a] *adj* shod ♦ *nm* footwear
calzador [kalθa'ðor] *nm* shoehorn
calzar [kal'θar] *vt* (*zapatos etc*) to wear; (*un mueble*) to put a wedge under; **~se** *vr*: **~se los zapatos** to put on one's shoes; **¿qué (número) calza?** what size do you take?
calzón [kal'θon] *nm* (tb: **calzones** *nmpl*) shorts; (AM: *de hombre*) (under)pants; (: *de mujer*) panties

calzoncillos [kalθon'θiʎos] *nmpl* underpants
cama ['kama] *nf* bed; **~ individual/de matrimonio** single/double bed
camafeo [kama'feo] *nm* cameo
camaleón [kamale'on] *nm* chameleon
cámara ['kamara] *nf* chamber; (*habitación*) room; (*sala*) hall; (CINE) cine camera; (*fotográfica*) camera; **~ de aire** inner tube; **~ de comercio** chamber of commerce; **~ frigorífica** cold-storage room
camarada [kama'raða] *nm* comrade, companion
camarera [kama'rera] *nf* (*en restaurante*) waitress; (*en casa, hotel*) maid
camarero [kama'rero] *nm* waiter
camarilla [kama'riʎa] *nf* clique
camarón [kama'ron] *nm* shrimp
camarote [kama'rote] *nm* cabin
cambiable [kam'bjaβle] *adj* (*variable*) changeable, variable; (*intercambiable*) interchangeable
cambiante [kam'bjante] *adj* variable
cambiar [kam'bjar] *vt* to change; (*dinero*) to exchange ♦ *vi* to change; **~se** *vr* (*mudarse*) to move; (*de ropa*) to change; **~ de idea** to change one's mind; **~ de ropa** to change (one's clothes)
cambio ['kambjo] *nm* change; (*trueque*) exchange; (COM) rate of exchange; (*oficina*) bureau de change; (*dinero menudo*) small change; **en ~** on the other hand; (*en lugar de*) instead; **~ de divisas** foreign exchange; **~ de velocidades** gear lever
camelar [kame'lar] *vt* to sweet-talk
camello [ka'meʎo] *nm* camel; (*fam: traficante*) pusher
camerino [kame'rino] *nm* dressing room
camilla [ka'miʎa] *nf* (MED) stretcher
caminante [kami'nante] *nm/f* traveller
caminar [kami'nar] *vi* (*marchar*) to walk, go ♦ *vt* (*recorrer*) to cover, travel

caminata [kami'nata] nf long walk; (por el campo) hike

camino [ka'mino] nm way, road; (sendero) track; **a medio** ~ halfway (there); **en el** ~ on the way, en route; ~ **de** on the way to; ~ **particular** private road

---

Camino de Santiago

The Camino de Santiago is a medieval pilgrim route stretching from the Pyrenees to Santiago de Compostela in north-west Spain, where tradition has it the body of the Apostle James is buried. Nowadays it is a popular tourist route as well as a religious one.

---

camión [ka'mjon] nm lorry (BRIT), truck (US); ~ **cisterna** tanker; **camionero, a** nm/f lorry o truck driver

camioneta [kamjo'neta] nf van, light truck

camisa [ka'misa] nf shirt; (BOT) skin; ~ **de fuerza** straitjacket; **camisería** nf outfitter's (shop)

camiseta [kami'seta] nf (prenda) tee-shirt; (: ropa interior) vest; (de deportista) top

camisón [kami'son] nm nightdress, nightgown

camorra [ka'morra] nf: **buscar** ~ to look for trouble

campamento [kampa'mento] nm camp

campana [kam'pana] nf bell; ~ **de cristal** bell jar; ~**da** nf peal; ~**rio** nm belfry

campanilla [kampa'niʎa] nf small bell

campaña [kam'paɲa] nf (MIL, POL) campaign

campechano, a [kampe'tʃano, a] adj (franco) open

campeón, ona [kampe'on, ona] nm/f champion; **campeonato** nm championship

campesino, a [kampe'sino, a] adj country cpd, rural; (gente) peasant cpd ♦ nm/f countryman/woman; (agricultor) farmer

campestre [kam'pestre] adj country cpd, rural

camping ['kampin] (pl ~s) nm camping; (lugar) campsite; **ir de** o **hacer** ~ to go camping

campo ['kampo] nm (fuera de la ciudad) country, countryside; (AGR, ELEC) field; (de fútbol) pitch; (de golf) course; (MIL) camp; ~ **de batalla** battlefield; ~ **de deportes** sports ground, playing field

camposanto [kampo'santo] nm cemetery

camuflaje [kamu'flaxe] nm camouflage

cana ['kana] nf white o grey hair; **tener** ~**s** to be going grey

Canadá [kana'ða] nm Canada; **canadiense** adj, nm/f Canadian ♦ nf fur-lined jacket

canal [ka'nal] nm canal; (GEO) channel, strait; (de televisión) channel; (de tejado) gutter; ~ **de Panamá** Panama Canal; ~**izar** vt to channel

canalla [ka'naʎa] nf rabble, mob ♦ nm swine

canalón [kana'lon] nm (conducto vertical) drainpipe; (del tejado) gutter

canapé [kana'pe] (pl ~s) nm sofa, settee; (CULIN) canapé

Canarias [ka'narjas] nfpl: **(las Islas)** ~ the Canary Islands, the Canaries

canario, a [ka'narjo, a] adj, nm/f (native) of the Canary Isles ♦ nm (ZOOL) canary

canasta [ka'nasta] nf (round) basket; **canastilla** nf small basket; (de niño) layette

canasto [ka'nasto] nm large basket

cancela [kan'θela] nf gate

cancelación [kanθela'θjon] nf cancellation

cancelar [kanθe'lar] vt to cancel; (una

deuda) to write off

cáncer ['kanθer] nm (MED) cancer; (ASTROLOGÍA): **C~** Cancer

cancha ['kantʃa] nf (de baloncesto, tenis etc) court; (AM: de fútbol) pitch

canciller [kanθi'ʎer] nm chancellor

canción [kan'θjon] nf song; **~ de cuna** lullaby; **cancionero** nm song book

candado [kan'daðo] nm padlock

candente [kan'dente] adj red-hot; (fig: tema) burning

candidato, a [kandi'ðato, a] nm/f candidate

candidez [kandi'ðeθ] nf (sencillez) simplicity; (simpleza) naiveté; **cándido, a** adj simple; naive

candil [kan'dil] nm oil lamp; **~ejas** nfpl (TEATRO) footlights

candor [kan'dor] nm (sinceridad) frankness; (inocencia) innocence

canela [ka'nela] nf cinnamon

canelones [kane'lones] nmpl cannelloni

cangrejo [kan'grexo] nm crab

canguro [kan'guro] nm kangaroo; **hacer de ~** to babysit

caníbal [ka'nißal] adj, nm/f cannibal

canica [ka'nika] nf marble

canijo, a [ka'nixo, a] adj frail, sickly

canino, a [ka'nino, a] adj canine ♦ nm canine (tooth)

canjear [kanxe'ar] vt to exchange

cano, a [ˈkano, a] adj grey-haired, white-haired

canoa [ka'noa] nf canoe

canon [ˈkanon] nm canon; (pensión) rent; (COM) tax

canónigo [ka'noniγo] nm canon

canonizar [kanoni'θar] vt to canonize

canoso, a [ka'noso, a] adj grey-haired

cansado, a [kan'saðo, a] adj tired, weary; (tedioso) tedious, boring

cansancio [kan'sanθjo] nm tiredness, fatigue

cansar [kan'sar] vt (fatigar) to tire, tire out; (aburrir) to bore; (fastidiar) to

bother; **~se** vr to tire, get tired; (aburrirse) to get bored

cantábrico, a [kan'taßriko, a] adj Cantabrian; **mar C~** Bay of Biscay

cantante [kan'tante] adj singing ♦ nm/f singer

cantar [kan'tar] vt to sing ♦ vi to sing; (insecto) to chirp ♦ nm (acción) singing; (canción) song; (poema) poem

cántara [ˈkantara] nf large pitcher

cántaro [ˈkantaro] nm pitcher, jug; **llover a ~s** to rain cats and dogs

cante [ˈkante] nm: **~ jondo** flamenco singing

cantera [kan'tera] nf quarry

cantidad [kanti'ðað] nf quantity, amount

cantimplora [kantim'plora] nf (frasco) water bottle, canteen

cantina [kan'tina] nf canteen; (de estación) buffet

canto [ˈkanto] nm singing; (canción) song; (borde) edge, rim; (de un cuchillo) back; **~ rodado** boulder

cantor, a [kan'tor, a] nm/f singer

canturrear [kanturre'ar] vi to sing softly

canuto [ka'nuto] nm (tubo) small tube; (fam: droga) joint

caña [ˈkaɲa] nf (BOT: tallo) stem, stalk; (carrizo) reed; (vaso) tumbler; (de cerveza) glass of beer; (ANAT) shinbone; **~ de azúcar** sugar cane; **~ de pescar** fishing rod

cañada [ka'ɲaða] nf (entre dos montañas) gully, ravine; (camino) cattle track

cáñamo [ˈkaɲamo] nm hemp

cañería [kaɲe'ria] nf (tubo) pipe

caño [ˈkaɲo] nm (tubo) tube, pipe; (de albañal) sewer; (MUS) pipe; (de fuente) jet

cañón [ka'ɲon] nm (MIL) cannon; (de fusil) barrel; (GEO) canyon, gorge

caoba [ka'oßa] nf mahogany

caos [ˈkaos] nm chaos

cap. abr (= capítulo) ch.

capa ['kapa] nf cloak, cape; (GEO) layer, stratum; **so ~ de** under the pretext of; **~ de ozono** ozone layer

capacidad [kapaθi'ðað] nf (medida) capacity; (aptitud) capacity, ability

capacitar [kapaθi'tar] vt: **~ a algn para (hacer)** to enable sb to (do)

capar [ka'par] vt to castrate, geld

caparazón [kapara'θon] nm shell

capataz [kapa'taθ] nm foreman

capaz [ka'paθ] adj able, capable; (amplio) capacious, roomy

capcioso, a [kap'θjoso, a] adj wily, deceitful

capellán [kape'ʎan] nm chaplain; (sacerdote) priest

caperuza [kape'ruθa] nf hood

capicúa [kapi'kua] adj inv (número, fecha) reversible

capilla [ka'piʎa] nf chapel

capital [kapi'tal] adj capital ♦ nm (COM) capital ♦ nf (ciudad) capital; **~ social** o authorized capital

capitalismo [kapita'lismo] nm capitalism; **capitalista** adj, nm/f capitalist

capitán [kapi'tan] nm captain

capitanear [kapitane'ar] vt to captain

capitulación [kapitula'θjon] nf (rendición) capitulation, surrender; (acuerdo) agreement, pact; **capitulaciones (matrimoniales)** nfpl marriage contract sg

capitular [kapitu'lar] vi to make an agreement

capítulo [ka'pitulo] nm chapter

capó [ka'po] nm (AUTO) bonnet

capón [ka'pon] nm (gallo) capon

capota [ka'pota] nf (de mujer) bonnet; (AUTO) hood (BRIT), top (US)

capote [ka'pote] nm (abrigo: de militar) greatcoat; (: de torero) cloak

capricho [ka'pritʃo] nm whim, caprice; **~so, a** adj capricious

Capricornio [kapri'kornjo] nm Capricorn

cápsula ['kapsula] nf capsule

captar [kap'tar] vt (comprender) to understand; (RADIO) to pick up; (atención, apoyo) to attract

captura [kap'tura] nf capture; (JUR) arrest; **capturar** vt to capture; to arrest

capucha [ka'putʃa] nf hood, cowl

capullo [ka'puʎo] nm (BOT) bud; (ZOOL) cocoon; (fam) idiot

caqui ['kaki] nm khaki

cara ['kara] nf (ANAT, de moneda) face; (de disco) side; (descaro) boldness; **~ a** facing; **de ~** opposite, facing; **dar la ~** to face the consequences; **¿~ o cruz?** heads or tails?; **¡qué ~ (más dura)!** what a nerve!

carabina [kara'ßina] nf carbine, rifle; (persona) chaperone

Caracas [ka'rakas] n Caracas

caracol [kara'kol] nm (ZOOL) snail; (concha) (sea) shell

carácter [ka'rakter] (pl **caracteres**) nm character; **tener buen/mal ~** to be good natured/bad tempered

característica [karakte'ristika] nf characteristic

característico, a [karakte'ristiko,a] adj characteristic

caracterizar [karakteri'θar] vt to characterize, typify

caradura [kara'ðura] nm/f: **es un ~** he's got a nerve

carajillo [kara'xiʎo] nm coffee with a dash of brandy

carajo [ka'raxo] (fam!) nm: **¡~!** shit! (!)

caramba [ka'ramba] excl good gracious!

carámbano [ka'rambano] nm icicle

caramelo [kara'melo] nm (dulce) sweet; (azúcar fundida) caramel

caravana [kara'ßana] nf caravan; (fig) group; (AUTO) tailback

carbón [kar'ßon] nm coal; **papel ~** carbon paper; **carboncillo** [-'θiʎo] (ARTE) charcoal; **carbonero, a** nm/f coal merchant; **carbonilla** [-'niʎa] nf coal dust

carbonizar [karßoni'θar] vt to carbonize; (*quemar*) to char

carbono [kar'ßono] nm carbon

carburador [karßura'ðor] nm carburettor

carburante [karßu'rante] nm (*para motor*) fuel

carcajada [karka'xaða] nf (loud) laugh, guffaw

cárcel ['karθel] nf prison, jail; (*TEC*) clamp; **carcelero, a** adj prison cpd ♦ nm/f warder

carcoma [kar'koma] nf woodworm

carcomer [karko'mer] vt to bore into, eat into; (*fig*) to undermine; **~se** vr to become worm-eaten; (*fig*) to decay

cardar [kar'ðar] vt (*pelo*) to backcomb

cardenal [karðe'nal] nm (*REL*) cardinal; (*MED*) bruise

cardíaco, a [kar'ðiako, a] adj cardiac, heart cpd

cardinal [karði'nal] adj cardinal

cardo ['karðo] nm thistle

carearse [kare'arse] vr to come face to face

carecer [kare'θer] vi: **~ de** to lack, to be in need of

carencia [ka'renθja] nf lack; (*escasez*) shortage; (*MED*) deficiency

carente [ka'rente] adj: **~ de** lacking in, devoid of

carestía [kares'tia] nf (*escasez*) scarcity, shortage; (*COM*) high cost

careta [ka'reta] nf mask

carga ['karva] nf (*peso, ELEC*) load; (*de barco*) cargo, freight; (*MIL*) charge; (*responsabilidad*) duty, obligation

cargado, a [kar'vaðo, a] adj loaded; (*ELEC*) live; (*café, té*) strong; (*cielo*) overcast

cargamento [karva'mento] nm (*acción*) loading; (*mercancías*) load, cargo

cargar [kar'var] vt (*barco, arma*) to load; (*ELEC*) to charge; (*COM: algo en cuenta*) to charge; (*INFORM*) to load ♦ vi (*MIL*) to charge; (*AUTO*) to load (up);

~ con to pick up, carry away; (*peso, fig*) to shoulder, bear; **~se** (fam) vr (*estropear*) to break; (*matar*) to bump off

cargo ['karvo] nm (*puesto*) post, office; (*responsabilidad*) duty, obligation; (*JUR*) charge; **hacerse ~ de** to take charge of o responsibility for

carguero [kar'vero] nm freighter, cargo boat; (*avión*) freight plane

Caribe [ka'riße] nm: **el ~** the Caribbean; **del ~** Caribbean

caribeño, a [kari'ßeno, a] adj Caribbean

caricatura [karika'tura] nf caricature

caricia [ka'riθja] nf caress

caridad [kari'ðað] nf charity

caries ['karjes] nf inv tooth decay

cariño [ka'riɲo] nm affection, love; (*caricia*) caress; (*en carta*) love ...; **tener ~ a** to be fond of; **~so, a** adj affectionate

carisma [ka'risma] nm charisma

caritativo, a [karita'tißo, a] adj charitable

cariz [ka'riθ] nm: **tener o tomar buen/mal ~** to look good/bad

carmesí [karme'si] adj, nm crimson

carmín [kar'min] nm lipstick

carnal [kar'nal] adj carnal; **primo ~** first cousin

carnaval [karna'ßal] nm carnival

---

carnaval

Carnaval is the traditional period of fun, feasting and partying which takes place in the three days before the start of Lent ("Cuaresma"). Although in decline during the Franco years the carnival has grown in popularity recently in Spain. Cádiz and Tenerife are particularly well-known for their flamboyant celebrations with fancy-dress parties, parades and firework displays being the order of the day.

carne ['karne] nf flesh; (CULIN) meat; **~ de cerdo/cordero/ternera/vaca** pork/lamb/veal/beef; **~ de gallina** (fig): **se me pone la ~ de gallina sólo verlo** I get the creeps just seeing it

carné [kar'ne] (pl **~s**) nm: **~ de conducir** driving licence (BRIT), driver's license (US); **~ de identidad** identity card

carnero [kar'nero] nm sheep, ram; (carne) mutton

carnet [kar'ne] (pl **~s**) nm = **carné**

carnicería [karniθe'ria] nf butcher's (shop); (fig: matanza) carnage, slaughter

carnicero, a [karni'θero, a] adj carnivorous ♦ nm/f (tb fig) butcher; (carnívoro) carnivore

carnívoro, a [kar'niβoro, a] adj carnivorous

carnoso, a [kar'noso, a] adj beefy, fat

caro, a ['karo, a] adj dear; (COM) dear, expensive ♦ adv dear, dearly

carpa ['karpa] nf (pez) carp; (de circo) big top; (AM: de camping) tent

carpeta [kar'peta] nf folder, file

carpintería [karpinte'ria] nf carpentry, joinery; **carpintero** nm carpenter

carraspear [karraspe'ar] vi to clear one's throat

carraspera [karras'pera] nf hoarseness

carrera [ka'rrera] nf (acción) run(ning); (espacio recorrido) run; (competición) race; (trayecto) course; (profesión) career; (ESCOL) course

carreta [ka'rreta] nf wagon, cart

carrete [ka'rrete] nm reel, spool; (TEC) coil

carretera [karre'tera] nf (main) road, highway; **~ de circunvalación** ring road; **~ nacional** A road (BRIT), ≈ state highway (US)

carretilla [karre'tiΛa] nf trolley; (AGR) (wheel)barrow

carril [ka'rril] nm furrow; (de autopista) lane; (FERRO) rail

carrillo [ka'rriΛo] nm (ANAT) cheek; (TEC) pulley

carrito [ka'rrito] nm trolley

carro ['karro] nm cart, wagon; (MIL) tank; (AM: coche) car

carrocería [karroθe'ria] nf bodywork, coachwork

carroña [ka'rroɲa] nf carrion no pl

carroza [ka'rroθa] nf (carruaje) coach

carrusel [karru'sel] nm merry-go-round, roundabout

carta ['karta] nf letter; (CULIN) menu; (naipe) card; (mapa) map; (JUR) document; **~ de crédito** credit card; **~ certificada** registered letter; **~ marítima** chart; **~ verde** (AUTO) green card

cartabón [karta'ßon] nm set square

cartel [kar'tel] nm (anuncio) poster, placard; (ESCOL) wall chart; (COM) cartel; **~era** nf hoarding, billboard; (en periódico etc) entertainments guide; **"en ~era"** "showing"

cartera [kar'tera] nf (de bolsillo) wallet; (de colegial, cobrador) satchel; (de señora) handbag; (para documentos) briefcase; (COM) portfolio; **ocupa la ~ de Agricultura** she is Minister of Agriculture

carterista [karte'rista] nm pickpocket

cartero [kar'tero] nm postman

cartilla [kar'tiΛa] nf primer, first reading book; **~ de ahorros** savings book

cartón [kar'ton] nm cardboard; **~ piedra** papier-mâché

cartucho [kar'tutʃo] nm (MIL) cartridge

cartulina [kartu'lina] nf card

casa ['kasa] nf house; (hogar) home; (COM) firm, company; **en ~** at home; **~ consistorial** town hall; **~ de huéspedes** boarding house; **~ de socorro** first aid post

casado, a [ka'saðo, a] adj married ♦ nm/f married man/woman

casamiento [kasa'mjento] *nm* marriage, wedding

casar [ka'sar] *vt* to marry; (*JUR*) to quash, annul; **~se** *vr* to marry, get married

cascabel [kaska'ßel] *nm* (small) bell

cascada [kas'kaða] *nf* waterfall

cascanueces [kaska'nweθes] *nm inv* nutcrackers *pl*

cascar [kas'kar] *vt* to crack, split, break (open); **~se** *vr* to crack, split, break (open)

cáscara ['kaskara] *nf* (*de huevo, fruta seca*) shell; (*de fruta*) skin; (*de limón*) peel

casco ['kasko] *nm* (*de bombero, soldado*) helmet; (*NAUT: de barco*) hull; (*ZOOL: de caballo*) hoof; (*botella*) empty bottle; **el ~ antiguo** the old part; **el ~ urbano** the town centre; **los ~s azules** the UN peace-keeping force, the blue berets

cascote [kas'kote] *nm* rubble

caserío [kase'rio] *nm* hamlet; (*casa*) country house

casero, a [ka'sero, a] *adj* (*pan etc*) home-made ♦ *nm/f* (*propietario*) landlord/lady; **ser muy ~** to be home-loving; **"comida casera"** "home cooking"

caseta [ka'seta] *nf* hut; (*para bañista*) cubicle; (*de feria*) stall

casete [ka'sete] *nm o f* cassette

casi ['kasi] *adv* almost, nearly; **~ nada** hardly anything; **~ nunca** hardly ever, almost never; **~ te caes** you almost fell

casilla [ka'siʎa] *nf* (*casita*) hut, cabin; (*AJEDREZ*) square; (*para cartas*) pigeonhole; **casillero** *nm* (*para cartas*) pigeonholes *pl*

casino [ka'sino] *nm* club; (*de juego*) casino

caso ['kaso] *nm* case; **en ~ de ...** in case of ...; **en ~ de que ...** in case ...; **el ~ es que** the fact is that; **en ese ~** in that case; **hacer ~ a** to pay

attention to; **hacer o venir al ~** to be relevant

caspa ['kaspa] *nf* dandruff

cassette [ka'sete] *nm o f* = **casete**

casta ['kasta] *nf* caste; (*raza*) breed; (*linaje*) lineage

castaña [kas'taɲa] *nf* chestnut

castañetear [kastaɲete'ar] *vi* (*dientes*) to chatter

castaño, a [kas'taɲo, a] *adj* chestnut (-coloured), brown ♦ *nm* chestnut tree

castañuelas [kasta'ɲwelas] *nfpl* castanets

castellano, a [kaste'ʎano, a] *adj, nm/f* Castilian ♦ *nm* (*LING*) Castilian, Spanish

castidad [kasti'ðað] *nf* chastity, purity

castigar [kasti'ɣar] *vt* to punish; (*DEPORTE*) to penalize; **castigo** *nm* punishment; (*DEPORTE*) penalty

Castilla [kas'tiʎa] *nf* Castille

castillo [kas'tiʎo] *nm* castle

castizo, a [kas'tiθo, a] *adj* (*LING*) pure

casto, a ['kasto, a] *adj* chaste, pure

castor [kas'tor] *nm* beaver

castrar [kas'trar] *vt* to castrate

castrense [kas'trense] *adj* (*disciplina, vida*) military

casual [ka'swal] *adj* chance, accidental; **~idad** *nf* chance, accident; (*combinación de circunstancias*) coincidence; **¡qué ~idad!** what a coincidence!

cataclismo [kata'klismo] *nm* cataclysm

catador, a [kata'ðor, a] *nm/f* wine taster

catalán, ana [kata'lan, ana] *adj, nm/f* Catalan ♦ *nm* (*LING*) Catalan

catalizador [kataliθa'ðor] *nm* catalyst; (*AUT*) catalytic convertor

catalogar [katalo'ɣar] *vt* to catalogue; **~ a algn (de)** (*fig*) to categorize sb (as)

catálogo [ka'taloɣo] *nm* catalogue

Cataluña [kata'luɲa] *nf* Catalonia

catar [ka'tar] *vt* to taste, sample

catarata [kata'rata] *nf* (*GEO*) waterfall;

(MED) cataract

catarro [ka'tarro] nm catarrh; (constipado) cold

catástrofe [ka'tastrofe] nf catastrophe

catear [kate'ar] (fam) vt (examen, alumno) to fail

cátedra ['kateðra] nf (UNIV) chair, professorship

catedral [kate'ðral] nf cathedral

catedrático, a [kate'ðratiko, a] nm/f professor

categoría [kateɣo'ria] nf category; (rango) rank, standing; (calidad) quality; **de ~** (hotel) top-class

categórico, a [kate'ɣoriko, a] adj categorical

cateto, a ['kateto, a] (pey) nm/f peasant

catolicismo [katoli'θismo] nm Catholicism

católico, a [ka'toliko, a] adj, nm/f Catholic

catorce [ka'torθe] num fourteen

cauce ['kauθe] nm (de río) riverbed; (fig) channel

caucho ['kautʃo] nm rubber; (AM: llanta) tyre

caución [kau'θjon] nf bail; **caucionar** vt (JUR) to bail, go bail for

caudal [kau'ðal] nm (de río) volume, flow; (fortuna) wealth; (abundancia) abundance; **~oso, a** adj (río) large

caudillo [kau'ðiʎo] nm leader, chief

causa ['kausa] nf cause; (razón) reason; (JUR) lawsuit, case; **a ~ de** because of

causar [kau'sar] vt to cause

cautela [kau'tela] nf caution, cautiousness; **cauteloso, a** adj cautious, wary

cautivar [kauti'ßar] vt to capture; (atraer) to captivate

cautiverio [kauti'ßerjo] nm captivity

cautividad [kautißi'ðað] nf = **cautiverio**

cautivo, a [kau'tißo, a] adj, nm/f captive

cauto, a ['kauto, a] adj cautious, careful

cava ['kaßa] nm champagne-type wine

cavar [ka'ßar] vt to dig

caverna [ka'ßerna] nf cave, cavern

cavidad [kaßi'ðað] nf cavity

cavilar [kaßi'lar] vt to ponder

cayado [ka'jaðo] nm (de pastor) crook; (de obispo) crozier

cayendo etc vb ver **caer**

caza ['kaθa] nf (acción: gen) hunting; (: con fusil) shooting; (una ~) hunt, chase; (animales) game ♦ nm (AVIAT) fighter

cazador, a [kaθa'ðor, a] nm/f hunter; **cazadora** nf jacket

cazar [ka'θar] vt to hunt; (perseguir) to chase; (prender) to catch

cazo ['kaθo] nm saucepan

cazuela [ka'θwela] nf (vasija) pan; (guisado) casserole

CD abbr (= compact disc) CD

CD-ROM abbr m CD-ROM

CE nf abr (= Comunidad Europea) EC

cebada [θe'ßaða] nf barley

cebar [θe'ßar] vt (animal) to fatten (up); (anzuelo) to bait; (MIL, TEC) to prime

cebo ['θeßo] nm (para animales) feed, food; (para peces, fig) bait; (de arma) charge

cebolla [θe'ßoʎa] nf onion; **cebolleta** nf spring onion; **cebollín** nm spring onion

cebra ['θeßra] nf zebra

cecear [θeθe'ar] vi to lisp; **ceceo** nm lisp

ceder [θe'ðer] vt to hand over, give up, part with ♦ vi (renunciar) to give in, yield; (disminuir) to diminish, decline; (romperse) to give way

cedro ['θeðro] nm cedar

cédula ['θeðula] nf certificate, document

cegar [θe'ɣar] vt to blind; (tubería etc) to block up, stop up ♦ vi to go blind; **~se** vr: **~se (de)** to be blinded (by)

ceguera [θe'ɣera] nf blindness

CEI abbr (= *Confederación de Estados Independientes*) CIS

ceja ['θexa] nf eyebrow

cejar [θe'xar] vi (fig) to back down

celador, a [θela'ðor, a] nm/f (de edificio) watchman; (de museo etc) attendant

celda ['θelda] nf cell

celebración [θeleβra'θjon] nf celebration

celebrar [θele'βrar] vt to celebrate; (alabar) to praise ♦ vi to be glad; ~se vr to occur, take place

célebre ['θelebre] adj famous

celebridad [θeleβri'ðað] nf fame; (persona) celebrity

celeste [θe'leste] adj (azul) sky-blue

celestial [θeles'tjal] adj celestial, heavenly

celibato [θeli'βato] nm celibacy

célibe ['θeliβe] adj, nm/f celibate

celo¹ ['θelo] nm zeal; (REL) fervour; (ZOOL): **en ~** on heat; **~** nmpl jealousy sg; **tener ~s** to be jealous

celo² ® ['θelo] nm Sellotape ®

celofán [θelo'fan] nm cellophane

celoso, a [θe'loso, a] adj jealous; (trabajador) zealous

celta ['θelta] adj Celtic ♦ nm/f Celt

célula ['θelula] nf cell; **~ solar** solar cell

celulitis [θelu'litis] nf cellulite

cementerio [θemen'terjo] nm cemetery, graveyard

cemento [θe'mento] nm cement; (hormigón) concrete; (AM: cola) glue

cena ['θena] nf evening meal, dinner

cenagal [θena'xal] nm bog, quagmire

cenar [θe'nar] vt to have for dinner ♦ vi to have dinner

cenicero [θeni'θero] nm ashtray

cenit [θe'nit] nm zenith

ceniza [θe'niθa] nf ash, ashes pl

censo ['θenso] nm census; **~ electoral** electoral roll

censura [θen'sura] nf (POL) censorship

censurar [θensu'rar] vt (idea) to

censure; (cortar: película) to censor

centella [θen'teʎa] nf spark

centellear [θenteʎe'ar] vi (metal) to gleam; (estrella) to twinkle; (fig) to sparkle

centenar [θente'nar] nm hundred

centenario, a [θente'narjo, a] adj centenary; hundred-year-old ♦ nm centenary

centeno [θen'teno] nm (BOT) rye

centésimo, a [θen'tesimo, a] adj hundredth

centígrado [θen'tixraðo] adj centigrade

centímetro [θen'timetro] nm centimetre (BRIT), centimeter (US)

céntimo [θen'timo] nm cent

centinela [θenti'nela] nm sentry, guard

centollo [θen'toʎo] nm spider crab

central [θen'tral] adj central ♦ nf head office; (TEC) plant; (TEL) exchange; **~ eléctrica** power station; **~ nuclear** nuclear power station; **~ telefónica** telephone exchange

centralita [θentra'lita] nf switchboard

centralizar [θentrali'θar] vt to centralize

centrar [θen'trar] vt to centre

céntrico, a ['θentriko, a] adj central

centrifugar [θentrifu'xar] vt to spin-dry

centrista [θen'trista] adj centre cpd

centro ['θentro] nm centre; **~ comercial** shopping centre; **~ juvenil** youth club; **~ de atención al cliente** call centre

centroamericano, a [θentroameri'kano, a] adj, nm/f Central American

ceñido, a [θe'niðo, a] adj (chaqueta, pantalón) tight(-fitting)

ceñir [θe'nir] vt (rodear) to encircle, surround; (ajustar) to fit (tightly)

ceño [θe'no] nm frown, scowl; **fruncir el ~** to frown, knit one's brow

CEOE nf abr (ESP: = Confederación

Española de Organizaciones Empresariales) ≈ CBI (BRIT), employers' organization

cepillar [θepiˈʎar] *vt* to brush; *(madera)* to plane (down)

cepillo [θeˈpiʎo] *nm* brush; *(para madera)* plane; **~ de dientes** toothbrush

cera [ˈθera] *nf* wax

cerámica [θeˈramika] *nf* pottery; *(arte)* ceramics

cerca [ˈθerka] *nf* fence ♦ *adv* near, nearby, close; **~ de** near, close to

cercanías [θerkaˈnias] *nfpl (afueras)* outskirts, suburbs

cercano, a [θerˈkano, a] *adj* close, near

cercar [θerˈkar] *vt* to fence in; *(rodear)* to surround

cerciorar [θerθjoˈrar] *vt (asegurar)* to assure; **~se** *vr (asegurarse)* to make sure

cerco [ˈθerko] *nm (AGR)* enclosure; *(AM)* fence; *(MIL)* siege

cerdo, a [ˈθerðo, a] *nm/f* pig/sow

cereal [θereˈal] *nm* cereal; **~es** *nmpl* cereals, grain *sg*

cerebro [θeˈreβro] *nm* brain; *(fig)* brains *pl*

ceremonia [θereˈmonja] *nf* ceremony; **ceremonial** *adj, nm* ceremonial; **ceremonioso, a** *adj* ceremonious

cereza [θeˈreθa] *nf* cherry

cerilla [θeˈriʎa] *nf (fósforo)* match

cernerse [θerˈnerse] *vr* to hover

cero [ˈθero] *nm* nothing, zero

cerrado, a [θeˈrraðo, a] *adj* closed, shut; *(con llave)* locked; *(tiempo)* cloudy, overcast; *(curva)* sharp; *(acento)* thick, broad

cerradura [θerraˈðura] *nf (acción)* closing; *(mecanismo)* lock

cerrajero [θerraˈxero] *nm* locksmith

cerrar [θeˈrrar] *vt* to close, shut; *(paso, carretera)* to close; *(grifo)* to turn off; *(cuenta, negocio)* to close ♦ *vi* to close, shut; *(la noche)* to come down; **~se** *vr*

to close, shut; **~ con llave** to lock; **~ un trato** to strike a bargain

cerro [ˈθerro] *nm* hill

cerrojo [θeˈrroxo] *nm (herramienta)* bolt; *(de puerta)* latch

certamen [θerˈtamen] *nm* competition, contest

certero, a [θerˈtero, a] *adj (gen)* accurate

certeza [θerˈteθa] *nf* certainty

certidumbre [θertiˈðumbre] *nf* = **certeza**

certificado [θertifiˈkaðo] *nm* certificate

certificar [θertifiˈkar] *vt (asegurar, atestar)* to certify

cervatillo [θerβaˈtiʎo] *nm* fawn

cervecería [θerβeθeˈria] *nf (fábrica)* brewery; *(bar)* public house, pub

cerveza [θerˈβeθa] *nf* beer

cesante [θeˈsante] *adj* redundant

cesar [θeˈsar] *vi* to cease, stop ♦ *vt (funcionario)* to remove from office

cesárea [θeˈsarea] *nf (MED)* Caesarean operation o section

cese [ˈθese] *nm (de trabajo)* dismissal; *(de pago)* suspension

césped [ˈθespeð] *nm* grass, lawn

cesta [ˈθesta] *nf* basket

cesto [ˈθesto] *nm (large)* basket, hamper

cetro [ˈθetro] *nm* sceptre

cfr *abr (= confróntese)* cf.

chabacano, a [tʃaβaˈkano, a] *adj* vulgar, coarse

chabola [tʃaˈβola] *nf* shack; **barrio de ~s** shanty town sg

chacal [tʃaˈkal] *nm* jackal

chacha [ˈtʃatʃa] *nf (fam)* maid

cháchara [ˈtʃatʃara] *nf* chatter; **estar de ~** to chatter away

chacra [ˈtʃakra] *nf (AM)* smallholding

chafar [tʃaˈfar] *vt (aplastar)* to crush; *(plan etc)* to ruin

chal [tʃal] *nm* shawl

chalado, a [tʃaˈlaðo, a] *adj (fam)* crazy

chalé [tʃaˈle] *(pl ~s) nm* villa; ≈

detached house

chaleco [tʃa'leko] nm waistcoat, vest (US); ~ **salvavidas** life jacket

chalet [tʃa'le] (pl ~**s**) nm = **chalé**

champán [tʃam'pan] nm champagne

champaña [tʃam'paɲa] nm = **champán**

champiñón [tʃampi'ɲon] nm mushroom

champú [tʃam'pu] (pl **champúes**, **champús**) nm shampoo

chamuscar [tʃamus'kar] vt to scorch, sear, singe

chance ['tʃanθe] (AM) nm chance

chancho, a ['tʃantʃo, a] (AM) nm/f pig

chanchullo [tʃan'tʃuʎo] (fam) nm fiddle

chandal [tʃan'dal] nm tracksuit

chantaje [tʃan'taxe] nm blackmail

chapa ['tʃapa] nf (de metal) plate, sheet; (de madera) board, panel; (AM: AUTO) number (BRIT) o license (US) plate; **~do, a** adj: **~do en oro** gold-plated

chaparrón [tʃapa'rron] nm downpour, cloudburst

chapotear [tʃapote'ar] vi to splash about

chapurrear [tʃapurre'ar] vt (idioma) to speak badly

chapuza [tʃa'puθa] nf botched job

chapuzón [tʃapu'θon] nm: **darse un ~** to go for a dip

chaqueta [tʃa'keta] nf jacket

chaquetón [tʃake'ton] nm long jacket

charca ['tʃarka] nf pond, pool

charco ['tʃarko] nm pool, puddle

charcutería [tʃarkute'ria] nf (tienda) shop selling chiefly pork meat products; (productos) cooked pork meats pl

charla ['tʃarla] nf talk, chat; (conferencia) lecture

charlar [tʃar'lar] vi to talk, chat

charlatán, ana [tʃarla'tan, ana] nm/f (hablador) chatterbox; (estafador) trickster

charol [tʃa'rol] nm varnish; (cuero)

patent leather

chascarrillo [tʃaska'rriʎo] (fam) nm funny story

chasco ['tʃasko] nm (desengaño) disappointment

chasis ['tʃasis] nm inv chassis

chasquear [tʃaske'ar] vt (látigo) to crack; (lengua) to click; **chasquido** [tʃas'kiðo] nm crack; click

chatarra [tʃa'tarra] nf scrap (metal)

chato, a ['tʃato, a] adj flat; (nariz) snub

chaval, a [tʃa'ßal, a] nm/f kid, lad/lass

checo, a ['tʃeko, a] adj, nm/f Czech ♦ nm (LING) Czech

checo(e)slovaco, a [tʃeko(e)slo'ßako, a] adj, nm/f Czech, Czechoslovak

Checo(e)slovaquia [tʃeko(e)slo'ßakja] nf Czechoslovakia

cheque ['tʃeke] nm cheque (BRIT), check (US); ~ **de viajero** traveller's cheque (BRIT), traveler's check (US)

chequeo [tʃe'keo] nm (MED) check-up; (AUTO) service

chequera [tʃe'kera] (AM) nf chequebook (BRIT), checkbook (US)

chicano, a [tʃi'kano, a] adj, nm/f chicano

chícharo ['tʃitʃaro] (AM) nm pea

chichón [tʃi'tʃon] nm bump, lump

chicle ['tʃikle] nm chewing gum

chico, a ['tʃiko, a] adj small, little ♦ nm/f (niño) child; (muchacho) boy/girl

chiflado, a [tʃi'flaðo, a] adj crazy

chiflar [tʃi'flar] vt to hiss, boo

Chile ['tʃile] nm Chile; **chileno, a** adj, nm/f Chilean

chile ['tʃile] nm chilli pepper

chillar [tʃi'ʎar] vi (persona) to yell, scream; (animal salvaje) to howl; (cerdo) to squeal

chillido [tʃi'ʎiðo] nm (de persona) yell, scream; (de animal) howl

chillón, ona [tʃi'ʎon, ona] adj (niño) noisy; (color) loud, gaudy

chimenea [tʃime'nea] nf chimney; (hogar) fireplace

China ['tʃina] *nf*: **(la) ~** China

chinche ['tʃintʃe] *nf (insecto)* (bed)bug; *(TEC)* drawing pin *(BRIT)*, thumbtack *(US)* ♦ *nm/f* nuisance, pest

chincheta [tʃin'tʃeta] *nf* drawing pin *(BRIT)*, thumbtack *(US)*

chino, a ['tʃino, a] *adj, nm/f* Chinese ♦ *nm (LING)* Chinese

chipirón [tʃipi'ron] *nm (ZOOL, CULIN)* squid

Chipre ['tʃipre] *nf* Cyprus; **chipriota** *adj, nm/f* Cypriot

chiquillo, a [tʃi'kiʎo, a] *nm/f (fam)* kid

chirimoya [tʃiri'moja] *nf* custard apple

chiringuito [tʃirin'vito] *nm* small open-air bar

chiripa [tʃi'ripa] *nf* fluke

chirriar [tʃi'rrjar] *vi* to creak, squeak

chirrido [tʃi'rriðo] *nm* creak(ing), squeak(ing)

chis [tʃis] *excl* sh!

chisme ['tʃisme] *nm (habladurías)* piece of gossip; *(fam: objeto)* thingummyjig

chismoso, a [tʃis'moso, a] *adj* gossiping ♦ *nm/f* gossip

chispa ['tʃispa] *nf* spark; *(fig)* sparkle; *(ingenio)* wit; *(fam)* drunkenness

chispear [tʃispe'ar] *vi (lloviznar)* to drizzle

chisporrotear [tʃisporrote'ar] *vi (fuego)* to throw out sparks; *(leña)* to crackle; *(aceite)* to hiss, splutter

chiste ['tʃiste] *nm* joke, funny story

chistoso, a [tʃis'toso, a] *adj* funny, amusing

chivo, a ['tʃiβo, a] *nm/f* (billy-/nanny-) goat; **~ expiatorio** scapegoat

chocante [tʃo'kante] *adj* startling; *(extraño)* odd; *(ofensivo)* shocking

chocar [tʃo'kar] *vi (coches etc)* to collide, crash ♦ *vt* to shock; *(sorprender)* to startle; **~ con** to collide with; *(fig)* to run into, run up against; **¡chócala!** *(fam)* put it there!

chochear [tʃotʃe'ar] *vi* to be senile

chocho, a ['tʃotʃo, a] *adj* doddering, senile; *(fig)* soft, doting

chocolate [tʃoko'late] *adj, nm* chocolate; **chocolatina** *nf* chocolate

chofer [tʃo'fer] *nm* = **chófer**

chófer ['tʃofer] *nm* driver

chollo ['tʃoʎo] *(fam)* *nm* bargain, snip

choque *etc* [tʃoke] *vb ver* **chocar** ♦ *nm (impacto)* impact; *(golpe)* jolt; *(AUTO)* crash; *(fig)* conflict; **~ frontal** head-on collision

chorizo [tʃo'riθo] *nm* hard pork sausage, (type of) salami

chorrada [tʃo'rraða] *(fam) nf*: **¡es una ~!** that's crap! *(!)*; **decir ~s** to talk crap *(!)*

chorrear [tʃorre'ar] *vi* to gush (out), spout (out); *(gotear)* to drip, trickle

chorro ['tʃorro] *nm* jet; *(fig)* stream

choza ['tʃoθa] *nf* hut, shack

chubasco [tʃu'βasko] *nm* squall

chubasquero [tʃuβas'kero] *nm* lightweight raincoat

chuchería [tʃutʃe'ria] *nf* trinket

chuleta [tʃu'leta] *nf* chop, cutlet

chulo ['tʃulo] *nm (de prostituta)* pimp

chupar [tʃu'par] *vt* to suck; *(absorber)* to absorb; **~se** *vr* to grow thin

chupete [tʃu'pete] *nm* dummy *(BRIT)*, pacifier *(US)*

chupito [tʃu'pito] *(fam) nm* shot

churro ['tʃurro] *nm (type of)* fritter

chusma ['tʃusma] *nf* rabble, mob

chutar [tʃu'tar] *vi* to shoot (at goal)

Cía *abr (= compañía)* Co.

cianuro [θja'nuro] *nm* cyanide

cibercafé [θiβerka'fe] *nm* cybercafé

cicatriz [θika'triθ] *nf* scar; **~arse** *vr* to heal (up), form a scar

ciclismo [θi'klismo] *nm* cycling

ciclista [θi'klista] *adj* cycle *cpd* ♦ *nm/f* cyclist

ciclo ['θiklo] *nm* cycle; **~turismo** *nm*: **hacer ~turismo** to go on a cycling holiday

ciclón [θi'klon] nm cyclone

ciego, a ['θjeɣo, a] adj blind ♦ nm/f blind man/woman

cielo ['θjelo] nm sky; (REL) heaven; **¡~s!** good heavens!

ciempiés [θjem'pjes] nm inv centipede

cien [θjen] num ver **ciento**

ciénaga ['θjenaɣa] nf marsh, swamp

ciencia ['θjenθja] nf science; **~s** nfpl (ESCOL) science sg; **~-ficción** nf science fiction

cieno ['θjeno] nm mud, mire

científico, a [θjen'tifiko, a] adj scientific ♦ nm/f scientist

ciento ['θjento] num; **pagar al 10 por ~** to pay at 10 per cent

cierre etc ['θjerre] vb ver **cerrar** ♦ nm closing, shutting; (con llave) locking; **~ de cremallera** zip (fastener)

cierro etc vb ver **cerrar**

cierto, a ['θjerto, a] adj sure, certain; (un tal) a certain; (correcto) right, correct; **~ hombre** a certain man; **ciertas personas** certain o some people; **sí, es ~** yes, that's correct

ciervo ['θjerßo] nm deer; (macho) stag

cierzo ['θjerθo] nm north wind

cifra ['θifra] nf number; (secreta) code

cifrar [θi'frar] vt to code, write in code

cigala [θi'ɣala] nf Norway lobster

cigarra [θi'ɣarra] nf cicada

cigarrillo [θiɣa'rriʎo] nm cigarette

cigarro [θi'ɣarro] nm cigarette; (puro) cigar

cigüeña [θi'ɣweɲa] nf stork

cilíndrico, a [θi'lindriko, a] adj cylindrical

cilindro [θi'lindro] nm cylinder

cima ['θima] nf (de montaña) top, peak; (de árbol) top; (fig) height

cimbrearse [θimbre'arse] vr to sway

cimentar [θimen'tar] vt to lay the foundations of; (fig: fundar) to found

cimiento [θi'mjento] nm foundation

cinc [θink] nm zinc

cincel [θin'θel] nm chisel; **~ar** vt to chisel

cinco ['θinko] num five

cincuenta [θin'kwenta] num fifty

cine ['θine] nm cinema

cineasta [θine'asta] nm/f film director

cinematográfico, a [θinemato'-ɣrafiko, a] adj cine-, film cpd

cínico, a ['θiniko, a] adj cynical ♦ nm/f cynic

cinismo [θi'nismo] nm cynicism

cinta ['θinta] nf band, strip; (de tela) ribbon; (película) reel; (de máquina de escribir) ribbon; **~ adhesiva** sticky tape; **~ de vídeo** videotape; **~ magnetofónica** tape; **~ métrica** tape measure

cintura [θin'tura] nf waist

cinturón [θintu'ron] nm belt; **~ de seguridad** safety belt

ciprés [θi'pres] nm cypress (tree)

circo ['θirko] nm circus

circuito [θir'kwito] nm circuit

circulación [θirkula'θjon] nf circulation; (AUTO) traffic

circular [θirku'lar] adj, nf circular ♦ vi, vt to circulate ♦ vi (AUTO) to drive; **"circule por la derecha"** "keep (to the) right"

círculo ['θirkulo] nm circle; **~ vicioso** vicious circle

circuncidar [θirkunθi'dar] vt to circumcise

circundar [θirkun'dar] vt to surround

circunferencia [θirkunfe'renθja] nf circumference

circunscribir [θirkunskri'ßir] vt to circumscribe; **~se** vt to be limited

circunscripción [θirkunskrip'θjon] nf (POL) constituency

circunspecto, a [θirkuns'pekto, a] adj circumspect, cautious

circunstancia [θirkuns'tanθja] nf circumstance

cirio ['θirjo] nm (wax) candle

ciruela [θi'rwela] nf plum; **~ pasa** prune

cirugía [θiruˈxia] nf surgery;
~ **estética** o **plástica** plastic surgery
cirujano [θiruˈxano] nm surgeon
cisne [ˈθisne] nm swan
cisterna [θisˈterna] nf cistern, tank
cita [ˈθita] nf appointment, meeting;
(*de novios*) date; (*referencia*) quotation
citación [θitaˈθjon] nf (*JUR*) summons
sg
citar [θiˈtar] vt (*gen*) to make an
appointment with; (*JUR*) to summons;
(*un autor, texto*) to quote; ~**se** vr: **se
citaron en el cine** they arranged to
meet at the cinema
cítricos [ˈθitrikos] nmpl citrus fruit/s
ciudad [θjuˈðað] nf town; (*más grande*)
city; ~**anía** nf citizenship; ~**ano, a**
nm/f citizen
cívico, a [ˈθiβiko, a] adj civic
civil [θiˈβil] adj civil ♦ nm (*guardia*)
policeman
civilización [θiβiliθaˈθjon] nf
civilization
civilizar [θiβiliˈθar] vt to civilize
civismo [θiˈβismo] nm public spirit
cizaña [θiˈθaɲa] nf (*fig*) discord
cl. abr (= *centilitro*) cl.
clamar [klaˈmar] vt to clamour for, cry
out for ♦ vi to cry out, clamour
clamor [klaˈmor] nm clamour, protest
clandestino, a [klandesˈtino, a] adj
clandestine; (*POL*) underground
clara [ˈklara] nf (*de huevo*) egg white
claraboya [klaraˈβoja] nf skylight
clarear [klareˈar] vi (*el día*) to dawn; (*el
cielo*) to clear up, brighten up; ~**se** vr
to be transparent
clarete [klaˈrete] nm rosé (wine)
claridad [klariˈðað] nf (*del día*)
brightness; (*de estilo*) clarity
clarificar [klarifiˈkar] vt to clarify
clarinete [klariˈnete] nm clarinet
clarividencia [klariβiˈðenθja] nf
clairvoyance; (*fig*) far-sightedness
claro, a [ˈklaro, a] adj clear; (*luminoso*)
bright; (*color*) light; (*evidente*) clear,
evident; (*poco espeso*) thin ♦ nm (*en

bosque*) clearing ♦ adv clearly ♦ excl
(*tb*: ~ *que sí*) of course!
clase [ˈklase] nf class; ~ **alta/media/
obrera** upper/middle/working class;
~**s particulares** private lessons,
private tuition sg
clásico, a [ˈklasiko, a] adj classical
clasificación [klasifikaˈθjon] nf
classification; (*DEPORTE*) league (table)
clasificar [klasifiˈkar] vt to classify
claudicar [klauðiˈkar] vi to give in
claustro [ˈklaustro] nm cloister
cláusula [ˈklausula] nf clause
clausura [klauˈsura] nf closing, closure;
clausurar vt (*congreso etc*) to bring to
a close
clavar [klaˈβar] vt (*clavo*) to hammer
in; (*cuchillo*) to stick, thrust
clave [ˈklaβe] nf key; (*MUS*) clef
clavel [klaˈβel] nm carnation
clavícula [klaˈβikula] nf collar bone
clavija [klaˈβixa] nf peg, dowel, pin;
(*ELEC*) plug
clavo [ˈklaβo] nm (*de metal*) nail; (*BOT*)
clove
claxon [ˈklakson] (pl ~**s**) nm horn
clemencia [kleˈmenθja] nf mercy,
clemency
cleptómano, a [klepˈtomano, a] nm/f
kleptomaniac
clérigo [ˈkleriβo] nm priest
clero [ˈklero] nm clergy
cliché [kliˈtʃe] nm cliché; (*FOTO*)
negative
cliente, a [ˈkljente, a] nm/f client,
customer
clientela [kljenˈtela] nf clientele,
customers pl
clima [ˈklima] nm climate
climatizado, a [klimatiˈθaðo, a] adj
air-conditioned
clímax [ˈklimaks] nm inv climax
clínica [ˈklinika] nf clinic; (*particular*)
private hospital
clip [klip] (pl ~**s**) nm paper clip
clítoris [ˈklitoris] nm inv (*ANAT*) clitoris
cloaca [kloˈaka] nf sewer

cloro |'kloro| nm chlorine

club |klub| (pl **~s** o **~es**) nm club; **~ de jóvenes** youth club

cm abr (= centímetro, centímetros) cm

C.N.T. (ESP) abr = Confederación Nacional de Trabajo

coacción |koak'θjon| nf coercion, compulsion; **coaccionar** vt to coerce

coagular |koaxu'lar| vt (leche, sangre) to clot; **~se** vr to clot; **coágulo** nm clot

coalición |koali'θjon| nf coalition

coartada |koar'taða| nf alibi

coartar |koar'tar| vt to limit, restrict

coba |'koßa| nf: **dar ~ a uno** to soft-soap sb

cobarde |ko'ßarðe| adj cowardly ♦ nm coward; **cobardía** nf cowardice

cobaya |ko'ßaja| nf guinea pig

cobertizo |koßer'tiθo| nm shelter

cobertura |koßer'tura| nf cover

cobija |ko'ßixa| nf (AM) blanket

cobijar |koßi'xar| vt (cubrir) to cover; (proteger) to shelter; **cobijo** nm shelter

cobra |'koßra| nf cobra

cobrador, a |koßra'ðor, a| nm/f (de autobús) conductor/conductress; (de impuestos, gas) collector

cobrar |ko'ßrar| vt (cheque) to cash; (sueldo) to collect, draw; (objeto) to recover; (precio) to charge; (deuda) to collect ♦ vi to be paid; **cóbrese al entregar** cash on delivery

cobre |'koßre| nm copper; **~s** nmpl (MUS) brass instruments

cobro |'koßro| nm (de cheque) cashing; **presentar al ~** to cash

cocaína |koka'ina| nf cocaine

cocción |kok'θjon| nf (CULIN) cooking; (en agua) boiling

cocear |koθe'ar| vi to kick

cocer |ko'θer| vt, vi to cook; (en agua) to boil; (en horno) to bake

coche |'kotʃe| nm (AUTO) car (BRIT), automobile (US); (de tren, de caballos) coach, carriage; (para niños) pram (BRIT), baby carriage (US); **ir en ~ to**

drive; **~ celular** Black Maria, prison van; **~ de bomberos** fire engine; **~ fúnebre** hearse; **coche-cama** (pl **coches-cama**) nm (FERRO) sleeping car, sleeper

cochera |ko'tʃera| nf garage; (de autobuses, trenes) depot

coche restaurante (pl **coches restaurante**) nm (FERRO) dining car, diner

cochinillo |kotʃi'niʎo| nm (CULIN) suckling pig, sucking pig

cochino, a |ko'tʃino, a| adj filthy, dirty ♦ nm/f pig

cocido |ko'θiðo| nm stew

cocina |ko'θina| nf kitchen; (aparato) cooker, stove; (acto) cookery; **~ eléctrica/de gas** electric/gas cooker; **~ francesa** French cuisine; **cocinar** vt, vi to cook

cocinero, a |koθi'nero, a| nm/f cook

coco |'koko| nm coconut

cocodrilo |koko'ðrilo| nm crocodile

cocotero |koko'tero| nm coconut palm

cóctel |'koktel| nm cocktail

codazo |ko'ðaθo| nm: **dar un ~ a uno** to nudge sb

codicia |ko'ðiθja| nf greed; **codiciar** vt to covet; **codicioso, a** adj covetous

código |'koðixo| nm code; **~ de barras** bar code; **~ civil** common law; **~ de (la) circulación** highway code; **~ postal** postcode

codillo |ko'ðiʎo| nm (ZOOL) knee; (TEC) elbow (joint)

codo |'koðo| nm (ANAT, de tubo) elbow; (ZOOL) knee

codorniz |koðor'niθ| nf quail

coerción |koer'θjon| nf coercion

coetáneo, a |koe'taneo, a| adj, nm/f contemporary

coexistir |koe(k)sis'tir| vi to coexist

cofradía |kofra'ðia| nf brotherhood, fraternity

cofre |'kofre| nm (de joyas) case; (de dinero) chest

coger [ko'xer] (*ESP*) *vt* to take (hold of); (*objeto caído*) to pick up; (*frutas*) to pick, harvest; (*resfriado, ladrón, pelota*) to catch ♦ *vi*: **~ por el buen camino** to take the right road; **~se** *vr* (*el dedo*) to catch; **~se a algo** to get hold of sth

cogollo [ko'yoʎo] *nm* (*de lechuga*) heart

cogote [ko'yote] *nm* back o nape of the neck

cohabitar [koaβi'tar] *vi* to live together, cohabit

cohecho [ko'etʃo] *nm* (*acción*) bribery; (*soborno*) bribe

coherente [koe'rente] *adj* coherent

cohesión [koe'sjon] *nm* cohesion

cohete [ko'ete] *nm* rocket

cohibido, a [koi'βiðo, a] *adj* (*PSICO*) inhibited; (*tímido*) shy

cohibir [koi'βir] *vt* to restrain, restrict

coincidencia [koinθi'ðenθja] *nf* coincidence

coincidir [koinθi'ðir] *vi* (*en idea*) to coincide, agree; (*en lugar*) to coincide

coito ['koito] *nm* intercourse, coitus

coja *etc vb ver* **coger**

cojear [koxe'ar] *vi* (*persona*) to limp, hobble; (*mueble*) to wobble, rock

cojera [ko'xera] *nf* limp

cojín [ko'xin] *nm* cushion; **cojinete** *nm* (*TEC*) ball bearing

cojo, a [a ['koxo, a] *vb ver* **coger** ♦ *adj* (*que no puede andar*) lame, crippled; (*mueble*) wobbly ♦ *nm/f* lame person, cripple

cojón [ko'xon] (*fam*) *nm*: **¡cojones!** shit! (*!*); **cojonudo, a** (*fam*) *adj* great, fantastic

col [kol] *nf* cabbage; **~es de Bruselas** Brussels sprouts

cola ['kola] *nf* tail; (*de gente*) queue; (*lugar*) end, last place; (*para pegar*) glue, gum; **hacer ~** to queue (up)

colaborador, a [kolaβora'ðor, a] *nm/f* collaborator

colaborar [kolaβo'rar] *vi* to collaborate

colada [ko'laða] *nf*: **hacer la ~** to do the washing

colador [kola'ðor] *nm* (*de líquidos*) strainer; (*para verduras etc*) colander

colapso [ko'lapso] *nm* collapse; **~ nervioso** nervous breakdown

colar [ko'lar] *vt* (*líquido*) to strain off; (*metal*) to cast ♦ *vi* to ooze, seep (through); **~se** *vr* to jump the queue; **~se en** to get into without paying; (*fiesta*) to gatecrash

colcha ['koltʃa] *nf* bedspread

colchón [kol'tʃon] *nm* mattress; **~ inflable** o **neumático** air bed, air mattress

colchoneta [koltʃo'neta] *nf* (*en gimnasio*) mat; (*de playa*) air bed

colección [kolek'θjon] *nf* collection; **coleccionar** *vt* to collect; **coleccionista** *nm/f* collector

colecta [ko'lekta] *nf* collection

colectivo, a [kolek'tiβo, a] *adj* collective, joint ♦ *nm* (*AM*) (small) bus

colega [ko'leya] *nm/f* colleague

colegial, a [kole'xjal, a] *nm/f* schoolboy/girl

colegio [ko'lexjo] *nm* college; (*escuela*) school; (*de abogados etc*) association; **~ electoral** polling station; **~ mayor** hall of residence

---

colegio

A **colegio** is normally a private primary or secondary school. In the state system it means a primary school although these are also called **escuelas**. State secondary schools are called **institutos**.

---

colegir [kole'xir] *vt* to infer, conclude

cólera ['kolera] *nf* (*ira*) anger; (*MED*) cholera; **colérico, a** [ko'leriko, a] *adj* irascible, bad-tempered

colesterol [koleste'rol] *nm* cholesterol

coleta [ko'leta] *nf* pigtail

colgante [kol'xante] *adj* hanging ♦ *nm* (*joya*) pendant

colgar [kol'ɣar] *vt* to hang (up); (*ropa*) to hang out ♦ *vi* to hang; (*TELEC*) to hang up

cólico ['koliko] *nm* colic

coliflor [koli'flor] *nf* cauliflower

colilla [ko'liʎa] *nf* cigarette end, butt

colina [ko'lina] *nf* hill

colisión [koli'sjon] *nf* collision; **~ de frente** head-on crash

collar [ko'ʎar] *nm* necklace; (*de perro*) collar

colmar [kol'mar] *vt* to fill to the brim; (*fig*) to fulfil, realize

colmena [kol'mena] *nf* beehive

colmillo [kol'miʎo] *nm* (*diente*) eye tooth; (*de elefante*) tusk; (*de perro*) fang

colmo ['kolmo] *nm*: **¡es el ~!** it's the limit!

colocación [koloka'θjon] *nf* (*acto*) placing; (*empleo*) job, position

colocar [kolo'kar] *vt* to place, put, position; (*dinero*) to invest; (*poner en empleo*) to find a job for; **~se** *vr* to get a job

Colombia [ko'lombja] *nf* Colombia; **colombiano, a** *adj*, *nm/f* Colombian

colonia [ko'lonja] *nf* colony; (*de casas*) housing estate; (*agua de ~*) cologne

colonización [koloniθa'θjon] *nf* colonization; **colonizador, a** [koloniθa'ðor, a] *adj* colonizing ♦ *nm/f* colonist, settler

colonizar [koloni'θar] *vt* to colonize

coloquio [ko'lokjo] *nm* conversation; (*congreso*) conference

color [ko'lor] *nm* colour

colorado, a [kolo'raðo, a] *adj* (*rojo*) red; (*LAM: chiste*) rude

colorante [kolo'rante] *nm* colouring

colorear [kolore'ar] *vt* to colour

colorete [kolo'rete] *nm* blusher

colorido [kolo'riðo] *nm* colouring

columna [ko'lumna] *nf* column; (*pilar*) pillar; (*apoyo*) support

columpiar [kolum'pjar] *vt* to swing; **~se** *vr* to swing; **columpio** *nm* swing

coma ['koma] *nf* comma ♦ *nm* (*MED*)

coma

comadre [ko'maðre] *nf* (*madrina*) godmother; (*chismosa*) gossip; **comadrona** *nf* midwife

comandancia [koman'danθja] *nf* command

comandante [koman'dante] *nm* commandant

comarca [ko'marka] *nf* region

comba ['komba] *nf* (*curva*) curve; (*cuerda*) skipping rope; **saltar a la ~** to skip

combar [kom'bar] *vt* to bend, curve

combate [kom'bate] *nm* fight; **combatiente** *nm* combatant

combatir [komba'tir] *vt* to fight, combat

combinación [kombina'θjon] *nf* combination; (*QUÍM*) compound; (*prenda*) slip

combinar [kombi'nar] *vt* to combine

combustible [kombus'tiβle] *nm* fuel

combustión [kombus'tjon] *nf* combustion

comedia [ko'meðja] *nf* comedy; (*TEATRO*) play, drama

comediante [kome'ðjante] *nm/f* (comic) actor/actress

comedido, a [kome'ðiðo, a] *adj* moderate

comedor, a [kome'ðor, a] *nm* (*habitación*) dining room; (*cantina*) canteen

comensal [komen'sal] *nm/f* fellow guest (o diner)

comentar [komen'tar] *vt* to comment on

comentario [komen'tarjo] *nm* comment, remark; (*literario*) commentary; **~s** *nmpl* (*chismes*) gossip *sg*

comentarista [komenta'rista] *nm/f* commentator

comenzar [komen'θar] *vt*, *vi* to begin, start; **~ a hacer algo** to begin o start doing sth

comer [ko'mer] *vt* to eat; (*DAMAS,*

AJEDREZ) to take, capture ♦ vi to eat; (*almorzar*) to have lunch; **~se** vr to eat up

comercial [komer'θjal] adj commercial; (*relativo al negocio*) business cpd; **comercializar** vt (*producto*) to market; (*pey*) to commercialize

comerciante [komer'θjante] nm/f trader, merchant

comerciar [komer'θjar] vi to trade, do business

comercio [ko'merθjo] nm commerce, trade; (*negocio*) business; (*fig*) dealings pl; **~ electrónico** e-commerce

comestible [komes'tiβle] adj eatable, edible; **~s** nmpl food sg, foodstuffs

cometa [ko'meta] nm comet ♦ nf kite

cometer [kome'ter] vt to commit

cometido [kome'tiðo] nm task, assignment

comezón [kome'θon] nf itch, itching

cómic ['komik] nm comic

comicios [ko'miθjos] nmpl elections

cómico, a ['komiko, a] adj comic(al) ♦ nm/f comedian

comida [ko'miða] nf (*alimento*) food; (*almuerzo, cena*) meal; (*de mediodía*) lunch

comidilla [komi'ðiʎa] nf: **ser la ~ de la ciudad** to be the talk of the town

comienzo etc [ko'mjenθo] vb ver **comenzar** ♦ nm beginning, start

comillas [ko'miʎas] nfpl quotation marks

comilona [komi'lona] (*fam*) nf blow-out

comino [ko'mino] nm: **(no) me importa un ~** I don't give a damn

comisaría [komisa'ria] nf (*de policía*) police station; (*MIL*) commissariat

comisario [komi'sarjo] nm (*MIL etc*) commissary; (*POL*) commissar

comisión [komi'sjon] nf commission

comité [komi'te] (*pl* **~s**) nm committee

comitiva [komi'tiβa] nf retinue

como ['komo] adv as; (*tal ~*) like; (*aproximadamente*) about, approximately ♦ conj (*ya que, puesto que*) as, since; **¡~ no!** of course!; **no lo haga hoy** unless he does it today; **~ si** as if; **es tan alto ~ ancho** it is as high as it is wide

cómo ['komo] adv how?, why? ♦ excl what?, I beg your pardon? ♦ nm: **el ~ y el porqué** the whys and wherefores

cómoda ['komoða] nf chest of drawers

comodidad [komoði'ðað] nf comfort; **venga a su ~** come at your convenience

comodín [komo'ðin] nm joker

cómodo, a ['komoðo, a] adj comfortable; (*práctico, de fácil uso*) convenient

compact disc nm compact disk player

compacto, a [kom'pakto, a] adj compact

compadecer [kompaðe'θer] vt to pity, be sorry for; **~se** vr: **~se de** to pity, be sorry for

compadre [kom'paðre] nm (*padrino*) godfather; (*amigo*) friend, pal

compañero, a [kompa'ɲero, a] nm/f companion; (*novio*) boy/girlfriend; **~ de clase** classmate

compañía [kompa'ɲia] nf company

comparación [kompara'θjon] nf comparison; **en ~ con** in comparison with

comparar [kompa'rar] vt to compare

comparecer [kompare'θer] vi to appear (in court)

comparsa [kom'parsa] nm/f (*TEATRO*) extra

compartimiento [komparti'mjento] nm (*FERRO*) compartment

compartir [kompar'tir] vt to share; (*dinero, comida etc*) to divide (up), share (out)

compás [kom'pas] nm (*MUS*) beat, rhythm; (*MAT*) compasses pl; (*NAUT etc*) compass

compasión [kompa'sjon] *nf* compassion, pity

compasivo, a [kompa'siβo, a] *adj* compassionate

compatibilidad [kompatiβili'ðað] *nf* compatibility

compatible [kompa'tiβle] *adj* compatible

compatriota [kompa'trjota] *nm/f* compatriot, fellow countryman/woman

compendiar [kompen'djar] *vt* to summarize; **compendio** *nm* summary

compenetrarse [kompene'trarse] *vr* to be in tune

compensación [kompensa'θjon] *nf* compensation

compensar [kompen'sar] *vt* to compensate

competencia [kompe'tenθja] *nf* (*incumbencia*) domain, field; (*JUR, habilidad*) competence; (*rivalidad*) competition

competente [kompe'tente] *adj* competent

competición [kompeti'θjon] *nf* competition

competir [kompe'tir] *vi* to compete

compilar [kompi'lar] *vt* to compile

complacencia [kompla'θenθja] *nf* (*placer*) pleasure; (*tolerancia excesiva*) complacency

complacer [kompla'θer] *vt* to please; **~se** *vr* to be pleased

complaciente [kompla'θjente] *adj* kind, obliging, helpful

complejo, a [kom'plexo, a] *adj, nm* complex

complementario, a [komplemen'tarjo, a] *adj* complementary

completar [komple'tar] *vt* to complete

completo, a [kom'pleto, a] *adj* complete; (*perfecto*) perfect; (*lleno*) full ♦ *nm* full complement

complicado, a [kompli'kaðo, a] *adj* complicated; **estar ~ en** to be mixed up in

cómplice ['kompliθe] *nm/f* accomplice

complot [kom'plo(t)] (*pl* **~s**) *nm* plot

componer [kompo'ner] *vt* (*MUS, LITERATURA, IMPRENTA*) to compose; (*algo roto*) to mend, repair; (*arreglar*) to arrange; **~se** *vr* to consist of; **componérselas para hacer algo** to manage to do sth

comportamiento [komporta'mjento] *nm* behaviour, conduct

comportarse [kompor'tarse] *vr* to behave

composición [komposi'θjon] *nf* composition

compositor, a [komposi'tor, a] *nm/f* composer

compostura [kompos'tura] *nf* (*actitud*) composure

compra ['kompra] *nf* purchase; **ir de ~s** to go shopping; **comprador, a** *nm/f* buyer, purchaser

comprar [kom'prar] *vt* to buy, purchase

comprender [kompren'der] *vt* to understand; (*incluir*) to comprise, include

comprensión [kompren'sjon] *nf* understanding; **comprensivo, a** *adj* (*actitud*) understanding

compresa [kom'presa] *nf*: **~ higiénica** sanitary towel (*BRIT*) o napkin (*US*)

comprimido, a [kompri'miðo, a] *adj* compressed ♦ *nm* (*MED*) pill, tablet

comprimir [kompri'mir] *vt* to compress

comprobante [kompro'βante] *nm* proof; (*COM*) voucher; **~ de recibo** receipt

comprobar [kompro'βar] *vt* to check; (*probar*) to prove; (*TEC*) to check, test

comprometer [komprome'ter] *vt* to compromise; (*poner en peligro*) to endanger; **~se** *vr* (*involucrarse*) to get involved

compromiso [kompro'miso] *nm*
(*obligación*) obligation; (*cometido*)
commitment; (*convenio*) agreement;
(*apuro*) awkward situation

compuesto, a [kom'pwesto, a] *adj*:
~ **de** composed of, made up of ♦ *nm*
compound

computador [komputa'ðor] *nm*
computer; ~ **central** mainframe
computer; ~ **personal** personal
computer

computadora [komputa'ðora] *nf* =
computador

cómputo ['komputo] *nm* calculation

comulgar [komul'xar] *vi* to receive
communion

común [ko'mun] *adj* common ♦ *nm*:
el ~ the community

comunicación [komunika'θjon] *nf*
communication; (*informe*) report

comunicado [komuni'kaðo] *nm*
announcement; ~ **de prensa** press
release

comunicar [komuni'kar] *vt, vi* to
communicate; ~**se** *vr* to communicate;
está comunicando (*TEL*) the line's
engaged (*BRIT*) o busy (*US*)

comunicativo, a *adj* communicative

comunidad [komuni'ðað] *nf*
community; ~ **autónoma** (*POL*)
autonomous region; C~ **Económica
Europea** European Economic
Community

comunión [komu'njon] *nf*
communion

comunismo [komu'nismo] *nm*
communism; **comunista** *adj, nm/f*
communist

─────────────────
PALABRA CLAVE
─────────────────

con [kon] *prep* **1** (*medio, compañía*)
with; **comer** ~ **cuchara** to eat with a
spoon; **pasear** ~ **uno** to go for a walk
with sb

2 (*a pesar de*): ~ **todo, merece
nuestros respetos** all the same, he
deserves our respect

3 (*para* ~): **es muy bueno para
~ los niños** he's very good with (the)
children

4 (+ *infin*): ~ **llegar tan tarde se
quedó sin comer** by arriving so late
he missed out on eating

♦ *conj*: ~ **que**: **será suficiente ~ que
le escribas** it will be sufficient if you
write to her

conato [ko'nato] *nm* attempt; ~ **de
robo** attempted robbery

concebir [konθe'βir] *vt, vi* to conceive

conceder [konθe'ðer] *vt* to concede

concejal, a [konθe'xal, a] *nm/f* town
councillor

concentración [konθentra'θjon] *nf*
concentration

concentrar [konθen'trar] *vt* to
concentrate; ~**se** *vr* to concentrate

concepción [konθep'θjon] *nf*
conception

concepto [kon'θepto] *nm* concept

concernir [konθer'nir] *vi* to concern;
en lo que concierne a ... as far as ...
is concerned; **en lo que a mí
concierne** as far as I'm concerned

concertar [konθer'tar] *vt* (*MUS*) to
harmonize; (*acordar: precio*) to agree;
(: *tratado*) to agree; (*trato*) to
arrange, fix up; (*combinar: esfuerzos*) to
coordinate ♦ *vi* to harmonize, be in
tune

concesión [konθe'sjon] *nf* concession

concesionario [konθesjo'narjo] *nm*
(licensed) dealer, agent

concha ['kontʃa] *nf* shell

conciencia [kon'θjenθja] *nf*
conscience; **tener/tomar ~ de** to be/
become aware of; **tener la ~ limpia/
tranquila** to have a clear conscience

concienciar [konθjen'θjar] *vt* to make
aware; ~**se** *vr* to become aware

concienzudo, a [konθjen'θuðo, a]
adj conscientious

concierto *etc* [kon'θjerto] *vb ver*
concertar ♦ *nm* concert; (*obra*)

concerto

conciliar [konθi'ljar] vt to reconcile

concilio [kon'θiljo] nm council

conciso, a [kon'θiso, a] adj concise

concluir [konklu'ir] vt, vi to conclude; **~se** vr to conclude

conclusión [konklu'sjon] nf conclusion

concluyente [konklu'jente] adj (prueba, información) conclusive

concordar [konkor'ðar] vt to reconcile ♦ vi to agree, tally

concordia [kon'korðja] nf harmony

concretar [konkre'tar] vt to make concrete, make more specific; **~se** vr to become more definite

concreto, a [kon'kreto, a] adj, nm (AM) concrete; **en ~** (en resumen) to sum up; (especificamente) specifically; **no hay nada en ~** there's nothing definite

concurrencia [konku'rrenθja] nf turnout

concurrido, a [konku'rriðo, a] adj (calle) busy; (local, reunión) crowded

concurrir [konku'rrir] vi (juntarse: ríos) to meet, come together; (: personas) to gather, meet

concursante [konkur'sante] nm/f competitor

concurso [kon'kurso] nm (de público) crowd; (ESCOL, DEPORTE, competencia) competition; (ayuda) help, cooperation

condal [kon'dal] adj: **la Ciudad C~** Barcelona

conde ['konde] nm count

condecoración [kondekora'θjon] nf (MIL) medal

condecorar [kondeko'rar] vt (MIL) to decorate

condena [kon'dena] nf sentence

condenación [kondena'θjon] nf condemnation; (REL) damnation

condenar [konde'nar] vt to condemn; (JUR) to convict; **~se** vr (REL) to be damned

condensar [konden'sar] vt to condense

condesa [kon'desa] nf countess

condición [kondi'θjon] nf condition; **condicional** adj conditional

condicionar [kondiθjo'nar] vt (acondicionar) to condition; **~ algo a** to make sth conditional on

condimento [kondi'mento] nm seasoning

condolerse [kondo'lerse] vr to sympathize

condón [kon'don] nm condom

conducir [kondu'θir] vt to take, convey; (AUTO) to drive ♦ vi to drive; (fig) to lead; **~se** vr to behave

conducta [kon'dukta] nf conduct, behaviour

conducto [kon'dukto] nm pipe, tube; (fig) channel

conductor, a [konduk'tor, a] adj leading, guiding ♦ nm (FÍSICA) conductor; (de vehículo) driver

conduje etc vb ver **conducir**

conduzco etc vb ver **conducir**

conectado, a [konek'taðo, a] adj (INFORM) on-line

conectar [konek'tar] vt to connect (up); (enchufar) plug in

conejillo [kone'xiʎo] nm: **~ de Indias** (ZOOL) guinea pig

conejo [ko'nexo] nm rabbit

conexión [konek'sjon] nf connection

confección [konfe(k)'θjon] nf preparation; (industria) clothing industry

confeccionar [konfekθjo'nar] vt to make (up)

confederación [konfeðera'θjon] nf confederation

conferencia [konfe'renθja] nf conference; (lección) lecture; (TEL) call

conferir [konfe'rir] vt to award

confesar [konfe'sar] vt to confess, admit

confesión [konfe'sjon] nf confession

confesionario [konfesjo'narjo] nm confessional

confeti [kon'feti] nm confetti

confiado, a [kon'fjaðo, a] adj (crédulo) trusting; (seguro) confident

confianza [kon'fjanθa] nf trust; (seguridad) confidence; (familiaridad) intimacy, familiarity

confiar [kon'fjar] vt to entrust ♦ vi to trust

confidencia [konfi'ðenθja] nf confidence

confidencial [konfiðen'θjal] adj confidential

confidente [konfi'ðente] nm/f confidant/e; (policial) informer

configurar [konfiɣu'rar] vt to shape, form

confín [kon'fin] nm limit; **confines** nmpl confines, limits

confinar [konfi'nar] vi to confine; (desterrar) to banish

confirmar [konfir'mar] vt to confirm

confiscar [konfis'kar] vt to confiscate

confite [kon'fite] nm sweet (BRIT), candy (US)

confitería [konfite'ria] nf (tienda) confectioner's (shop)

confitura [konfi'tura] nf jam

conflictivo, a [konflik'tiβo, a] adj (asunto, propuesta) controversial; (país, situación) troubled

conflicto [kon'flikto] nm conflict; (fig) clash

confluir [kon'flwir] vi (ríos) to meet; (gente) to gather

conformar [konfor'mar] vt to shape, fashion ♦ vi to agree; **~se** vr to conform; (resignarse) to resign o.s.

conforme [kon'forme] adj (correspondiente): **~ con** in line with; (de acuerdo): **estar ~s (con algo)** to be in agreement (with sth) ♦ adv as ♦ excl agreed! ♦ prep: **~ a** in accordance with; **quedarse ~ (con algo)** to be satisfied (with sth)

conformidad [konformi'ðað] nf (semejanza) similarity; (acuerdo) agreement; **conformista** adj, nm/f

conformist

confortable [konfor'taβle] adj comfortable

confortar [konfor'tar] vt to comfort

confrontar [konfron'tar] vt to confront; (dos personas) to bring face to face; (cotejar) to compare

confundir [konfun'dir] vt (equivocar) to mistake, confuse; (turbar) to confuse; **~se** vr (turbarse) to get confused; (equivocarse) to make a mistake; (mezclarse) to mix

confusión [konfu'sjon] nf confusion

confuso, a [kon'fuso, a] adj confused

congelado, a [konxe'laðo, a] adj frozen; **~s** nmpl frozen food(s); **congelador** nm (aparato) freezer, deep freeze

congelar [konxe'lar] vt to freeze; **~se** vr (sangre, grasa) to congeal

congeniar [konxe'njar] vi to get on (BRIT) o along (US) well

congestión [konxes'tjon] nf congestion

congestionar [konxestjo'nar] vt to congest

congoja [kon'goxa] nf distress, grief

congraciarse [kongra'θjarse] vr to ingratiate o.s.

congratular [kongratu'lar] vt to congratulate

congregación [kongreɣa'θjon] nf congregation

congregar [kongre'ɣar] vt to gather together; **~se** vr to gather together

congresista [kongre'sista] nm/f delegate, congressman/woman

congreso [kon'greso] nm congress

congrio ['kongrjo] nm conger eel

conjetura [konxe'tura] nf guess; **conjeturar** vt to guess

conjugar [konxu'ɣar] vt to combine, fit together; (LING) to conjugate

conjunción [konxun'θjon] nf conjunction

conjunto, a [kon'xunto, a] adj joint, united ♦ nm whole; (MUS) band; **en ~**

as a whole

conjurar [konxu'rar] vt (REL) to
exorcise; (fig) to ward off ♦ vi to plot

conmemoración [konmemora'θjon]
nf commemoration

conmemorar [konmemo'rar] vt to
commemorate

conmigo [kon'miγo] pron with me

conmoción [konmo'θjon] nf shock;
(fig) upheaval; **~ cerebral** (MED)
concussion

conmovedor, a [konmoβe'ðor, a] adj
touching, moving; (emocionante)
exciting

conmover [konmo'βer] vt to shake,
disturb; (fig) to move

conmutador [konmuta'ðor] nm
switch; (AM: TEL: centralita)
switchboard; (: central) telephone
exchange

cono ['kono] nm cone

conocedor, a [konoθe'ðor, a] adj
expert, knowledgeable ♦ nm/f expert

conocer [kono'θer] vt to know; (por
primera vez) to meet, get to know;
(entender) to know about; (reconocer)
to recognize; **~se** vr (una persona) to
know o.s.; (dos personas) to (get to)
know each other

conocido, a [kono'θiðo, a] adj (well-)
known ♦ nm/f acquaintance

conocimiento [konoθi'mjento] nm
knowledge; (MED) consciousness; **~s**
nmpl (saber) knowledge sg

conozco etc vb ver **conocer**

conque ['konke] conj and so, so then

conquista [kon'kista] nf conquest;
conquistador, a adj conquering
♦ nm conqueror

conquistar [konkis'tar] vt to conquer

consagrar [konsa'γrar] vt (REL) to
consecrate; (fig) to devote

consciente [kons'θjente] adj
conscious

consecución [konseku'θjon] nf
acquisition; (de fin) attainment

consecuencia [konse'kwenθja] nf

consequence, outcome; (coherencia)
consistency

consecuente [konse'kwente] adj
consistent

consecutivo, a [konseku'tiβo, a] adj
consecutive

conseguir [konse'γir] vt to get,
obtain; (objetivo) to attain

consejero, a [konse'xero, a] nm/f
adviser, consultant; (POL) councillor

consejo [kon'sexo] nm advice; (POL)
council; **~ de administración** (COM)
board of directors; **~ de guerra** court
martial; **~ de ministros** cabinet
meeting

consenso [kon'senso] nm consensus

consentimiento [konsenti'mjento]
nm consent

consentir [konsen'tir] vt (permitir,
tolerar) to consent to; (mimar) to
pamper, spoil; (aguantar) to put up
with ♦ vi to agree, consent; **~ que
uno haga algo** to allow sb to do sth

conserje [kon'serxe] nm caretaker;
(portero) porter

conservación [konserβa'θjon] nf
conservation; (de alimentos, vida)
preservation

conservador, a [konserβa'ðor, a] adj
(POL) conservative ♦ nm/f conservative

conservante [konser'βante] nm
preservative

conservar [konser'βar] vt to conserve,
keep; (alimentos, vida) to preserve; **~se**
vr to survive

conservas [kon'serβas] nfpl canned
food(s) (pl)

conservatorio [konserβa'torjo] nm
(MUS) conservatoire, conservatory

considerable [konsiðe'raβle] adj
considerable

consideración [konsiðera'θjon] nf
consideration; (estimación) respect

considerado, a [konsiðe'raðo, a] adj
(atento) considerate; (respetado)
respected

considerar [konsiðe'rar] vt to consider

consigna [kon'siɣna] nf (orden) order, instruction; (para equipajes) left-luggage office

consigo etc vb ver **conseguir** ♦ pron (m) with him; (f) with her; (Vd) with you; (reflexivo) with o.s.

consiguiendo etc vb ver **conseguir**

consiguiente [konsi'ɣjente] adj consequent; **por ~** and so, therefore, consequently

consistente [konsis'tente] adj consistent; (sólido) solid, firm; (válido) sound

consistir [konsis'tir] vi: **~ en** (componerse de) to consist of

consola [kon'sola] nf (mueble) console table; (de videojuegos) console

consolación [konsola'θjon] nf consolation

consolar [konso'lar] vt to console

consolidar [konsoli'ðar] vt to consolidate

consomé [konso'me] (pl **~s**) nm consommé, clear soup

consonante [konso'nante] adj consonant, harmonious ♦ nf consonant

consorcio [kon'sorθjo] nm consortium

conspiración [konspira'θjon] nf conspiracy

conspirador, a [konspira'ðor, a] nm/f conspirator

conspirar [konspi'rar] vi to conspire

constancia [kon'stanθja] nf constancy; **dejar ~ de** to put on record

constante [kons'tante] adj, nf constant

constar [kons'tar] vi (evidenciarse) to be clear o evident; **~ de** to consist of

constatar [konsta'tar] vt to verify

consternación [konsterna'θjon] nf consternation

constipado, a [konsti'paðo, a] adj: **estar ~** to have a cold ♦ nm cold

constitución [konstitu'θjon] nf constitution; **constitucional** adj constitutional

constituir [konstitu'ir] vt (formar, componer) to constitute, make up; (fundar, erigir, ordenar) to constitute, establish

constituyente [konstitu'jente] adj constituent

constreñir [konstre'nir] vt (restringir) to restrict

construcción [konstruk'θjon] nf construction, building

constructor, a [konstruk'tor, a] nm/f builder

construir [konstru'ir] vt to build, construct

construyendo etc vb ver **construir**

consuelo [kon'swelo] nm consolation, solace

cónsul ['konsul] nm consul; **consulado** nm consulate

consulta [kon'sulta] nf consultation; (MED): **horas de ~** surgery hours

consultar [konsul'tar] vt to consult

consultorio [konsul'torjo] nm (MED) surgery

consumar [konsu'mar] vt to complete, carry out; (crimen) to commit; (sentencia) to carry out

consumición [konsumi'θjon] nf consumption; (bebida) drink; (comida) food; **~ mínima** cover charge

consumidor, a [konsumi'ðor, a] nm/f consumer

consumir [konsu'mir] vt to consume; **~se** vr to be consumed; (persona) to waste away

consumismo [konsu'mismo] nm consumerism

consumo [kon'sumo] nm consumption

contabilidad [kontaβili'ðað] nf accounting, book-keeping; (profesión) accountancy; **contable** nm/f accountant

contacto [kon'takto] nm contact; (AUTO) ignition

contado, a [kon'taðo, a] adj: **~s**

(*escasos*) numbered, scarce, few ♦ *nm*:
pagar al ~ to pay (in) cash

contador [konta'ðor] *nm* (*aparato*)
meter; (*AM*: *contante*) accountant

contagiar [konta'xjar] *vt* (*enfermedad*)
to pass on, transmit; (*persona*) to
infect; **~se** *vr* to become infected

contagio [kon'taxjo] *nm* infection;
contagioso, a *adj* infectious; (*fig*)
catching

contaminación [kontamina'θjon] *nf*
contamination; (*polución*) pollution

contaminar [kontami'nar] *vt* to
contaminate; (*aire, agua*) to pollute

contante [kon'tante] *adj*: **dinero ~ (y
sonante)** cash

contar [kon'tar] *vt* (*páginas, dinero*) to
count; (*anécdota, chiste etc*) to tell ♦ *vi*
to count; **~ con** to rely on, count on

contemplación [kontempla'θjon] *nf*
contemplation

contemplar [kontem'plar] *vt* to
contemplate; (*mirar*) to look at

contemporáneo, a
[kontempo'raneo, a] *adj, nm/f*
contemporary

contendiente [konten'djente] *nm/f*
contestant

contenedor [kontene'ðor] *nm*
container

contener [konte'ner] *vt* to contain,
hold; (*retener*) to hold back, contain;
~se *vr* to control o restrain o.s.

contenido, a *adj* (*actitud*) restrained; (*risa etc*)
suppressed ♦ *nm* contents *pl*, content

contentar [konten'tar] *vt* (*satisfacer*)
to satisfy; (*complacer*) to please; **~se** *vr*
to be satisfied

contento, a [kon'tento, a] *adj* (*alegre*)
pleased; (*feliz*) happy

contestación [kontesta'θjon] *nf*
answer, reply

contestador [kontesta'ðor] *nm*:
~ automático answering machine

contestar [kontes'tar] *vt* to answer,
reply; (*JUR*) to corroborate, confirm

contexto [kon'te(k)sto] *nm* context

contienda [kon'tjenda] *nf* contest

contigo [kon'tiyo] *pron* with you

contiguo, a [kon'tiywo, a] *adj*
adjacent, adjoining

continente [konti'nente] *adj, nm*
continent

contingencia [kontin'xenθja] *nf*
contingency; (*riesgo*) risk;
contingente *adj, nm* contingent

continuación [kontinwa'θjon] *nf*
continuation; **a ~** then, next

continuar [konti'nwar] *vt* to continue,
go on with ♦ *vi* to continue, go on;
~ hablando to continue talking o to
talk

continuidad [kontinwi'ðað] *nf*
continuity

continuo, a [kon'tinwo, a] *adj* (*sin
interrupción*) continuous; (*acción
perseverante*) continual

contorno [kon'torno] *nm* outline;
(*GEO*) contour; **~s** *nmpl* neighbourhood
sg, surrounding area *sg*

contorsión [kontor'sjon] *nf*
contortion

contra ['kontra] *prep, ad* against ♦ *nm*
inv con ♦ *nf*: **la C~** (*de Nicaragua*) the
Contras *pl*

contraataque [kontraa'take] *nm*
counter-attack

contrabajo [kontra'βaxo] *nm* double
bass

contrabandista [kontraβan'dista]
nm/f smuggler

contrabando [kontra'βando] *nm*
(*acción*) smuggling; (*mercancías*)
contraband

contracción [kontrak'θjon] *nf*
contraction

contracorriente [kontrako'rrjente]:
(a) ~ *adv* against the current

contradecir [kontraðe'θir] *vt* to
contradict

contradicción [kontraðik'θjon] *nf*
contradiction

contradictorio, a [kontraðik'torjo, a]

adj contradictory

contraer [kontra'er] *vt* to contract; (*limitar*) to restrict; **~se** *vr* to contract; (*limitarse*) to limit o.s.

contraluz [kontra'luθ] *nf*: **a ~** against the light

contrapartida [kontrapar'tiða] *nf*: **como ~ (de)** in return (for)

contrapelo [kontra'pelo]: **a ~** *adv* the wrong way

contrapesar [kontrape'sar] *vt* to counterbalance; (*fig*) to offset; **contrapeso** *nm* counterweight

contraportada [kontrapor'taða] *nf* (*de revista*) back cover

contraproducente [kontraproðu'θente] *adj* counterproductive

contrariar [kontra'rjar] *vt* (*oponerse*) to oppose; (*poner obstáculo*) to impede; (*enfadar*) to vex

contrariedad [kontrarje'ðað] *nf* (*obstáculo*) obstacle, setback; (*disgusto*) vexation, annoyance

contrario, a [kon'trarjo, a] *adj* contrary; (*persona*) opposed; (*sentido, lado*) opposite ♦ *nm/f* enemy, adversary; (*DEPORTE*) opponent; **al/por el ~** on the contrary; **de lo ~** otherwise

contrarreloj [kontrarre'lo] *nf* (*tb*: **prueba ~**) time trial

contrarrestar [kontrarres'tar] *vt* to counteract

contrasentido [kontrasen'tiðo] *nm*: **es un ~ que él ...** it doesn't make sense for him to ...

contraseña [kontra'seɲa] *nf* (*INFORM*) password

contrastar [kontras'tar] *vt, vi* to contrast

contraste [kon'traste] *nm* contrast

contratar [kontra'tar] *vt* (*firmar un acuerdo para*) to contract for; (*empleados, obreros*) to hire, engage; **~se** *vr* to sign on

contratiempo [kontra'tjempo] *nm*

setback

contratista [kontra'tista] *nm/f* contractor

contrato [kon'trato] *nm* contract

contravenir [kontraβe'nir] *vi*: **~ a** to contravene, violate

contraventana [kontraβen'tana] *nf* shutter

contribución [kontriβu'θjon] *nf* (*municipal etc*) tax; (*ayuda*) contribution

contribuir [kontriβu'ir] *vt, vi* to contribute; (*COM*) to pay (in taxes)

contribuyente [kontriβu'jente] *nm/f* (*COM*) taxpayer; (*que ayuda*) contributor

contrincante [kontrin'kante] *nm* opponent

control [kon'trol] *nm* control; (*inspección*) inspection, check; **~ador, a** *nm/f* controller; **~ador aéreo** air-traffic controller

controlar [kontro'lar] *vt* to control; (*inspeccionar*) to inspect, check

controversia [kontro'βersja] *nf* controversy

contundente [kontun'dente] *adj* (*instrumento*) blunt; (*argumento, derrota*) overwhelming

contusión [kontu'sjon] *nf* bruise

convalecencia [kombale'θenθja] *nf* convalescence

convalecer [kombale'θer] *vi* to convalesce, get better

convaleciente [kombale'θjente] *adj, nm/f* convalescent

convalidar [kombali'ðar] *vt* (*título*) to recognize

convencer [komben'θer] *vt* to convince

convencimiento [kombenθi'mjento] *nm* (*certidumbre*) conviction

convención [komben'θjon] *nf* convention

conveniencia [kombe'njenθja] *nf* suitability; (*conformidad*) agreement; (*utilidad, provecho*) usefulness; **~s** *nfpl* (*convenciones*) conventions; (*COM*) property sg

conveniente [kombe'njente] *adj* suitable; (*útil*) useful

convenio [kom'benjo] *nm* agreement, treaty

convenir [kombe'nir] *vi* (*estar de acuerdo*) to agree; (*venir bien*) to suit, be suitable

convento [kom'bento] *nm* convent

convenza *etc vb ver* **convencer**

converger [komber'xer] *vi* to converge

convergir [komber'xir] *vi* = **converger**

conversación [kombersa'θjon] *nf* conversation

conversar [komber'sar] *vi* to talk, converse

conversión [komber'sjon] *nf* conversion

convertir [komber'tir] *vt* to convert

convicción [kombik'θjon] *nf* conviction

convicto, a [kom'bikto, a] *adj* convicted

convidado, a [kombi'ðaðo, a] *nm/f* guest

convidar [kombi'ðar] *vt* to invite

convincente [kombin'θente] *adj* convincing

convite [kom'bite] *nm* invitation; (*banquete*) banquet

convivencia [kombi'ßenθja] *nf* coexistence, living together

convivir [kombi'ßir] *vi* to live together

convocar [kombo'kar] *vt* to summon, call (together)

convocatoria [komboka'torja] *nf* (*de oposiciones, elecciones*) notice; (*de huelga*) call

convulsión [kombul'sjon] *nf* convulsion

conyugal [konju'ßal] *adj* conjugal; **cónyuge** [kon'juxe] *nm/f* spouse

coñac [ko'na(k)] (*pl* ~s) *nm* cognac, brandy

coño ['kono] (*faml*) *excl* (*enfado*) shit! (!); (*sorpresa*) bloody hell! (!)

cooperación [koopera'θjon] *nf* cooperation

cooperar [koope'rar] *vi* to cooperate

cooperativa [koopera'tißa] *nf* cooperative

coordinadora [koorðina'ðora] *nf* (*comité*) coordinating committee

coordinar [koorði'nar] *vt* to coordinate

copa ['kopa] *nf* cup; (*vaso*) glass; (*bebida*): (**tomar una**) ~ (to have a) drink; (*de árbol*) top; (*de sombrero*) crown; **~s** *nfpl* (*NAIPES*) ≈ hearts

copia ['kopja] *nf* copy; **~ de respaldo** *o* **seguridad** (*INFORM*) back-up copy; **copiar** *vt* to copy

copioso, a [ko'pjoso, a] *adj* copious, plentiful

copla ['kopla] *nf* verse; (*canción*) (popular) song

copo ['kopo] *nm*: **~ de nieve** snowflake; **~s de maíz** cornflakes

coqueta [ko'keta] *adj* flirtatious, coquettish; **coquetear** (*ni*) *vi* to flirt

coraje [ko'raxe] *nm* courage; (*ánimo*) spirit; (*ira*) anger

coral [ko'ral] *adj* choral ♦ *nf* (*MUS*) choir ♦ *nm* (*ZOOL*) coral

coraza [ko'raθa] *nf* (*armadura*) armour; (*blindaje*) armour-plating

corazón [kora'θon] *nm* heart

corazonada [koraθo'naða] *nf* impulse; (*presentimiento*) hunch

corbata [kor'ßata] *nf* tie

corchete [kor'tʃete] *nm* catch, clasp

corcho [kor'tʃo] *nm* cork; (*PESCA*) float

cordel [kor'ðel] *nm* cord, line

cordero [kor'ðero] *nm* lamb

cordial [kor'ðjal] *adj* cordial; **~idad** *nf* warmth, cordiality

cordillera [korði'ʎera] *nf* range (of mountains)

Córdoba ['korðoßa] *n* Cordova

cordón [kor'ðon] *nm* (*cuerda*) cord, string; (*de zapatos*) lace; (*MIL etc*) cordon

cordura [kor'ðura] *nf*: **con ~** *(obrar, hablar)* sensibly

corneta [kor'neta] *nf* bugle

cornisa [kor'nisa] *nf* *(ARQ)* cornice

coro ['koro] *nm* chorus; *(conjunto de cantores)* choir

corona [ko'rona] *nf* crown; *(de flores)* garland; **coronación** *nf* coronation; **coronar** *vt* to crown

coronel [koro'nel] *nm* colonel

coronilla [koro'niʎa] *nf* *(ANAT)* crown (of the head)

corporación [korpora'θjon] *nf* corporation

corporal [korpo'ral] *adj* corporal, bodily

corpulento, a [korpu'lento a] *adj* *(persona)* heavily-built

corral [ko'rral] *nm* farmyard

correa [ko'rrea] *nf* strap; *(cinturón)* belt; *(de perro)* lead, leash

corrección [korrek'θjon] *nf* correction; *(reprensión)* rebuke; **correccional** *nm* reformatory

correcto, a [ko'rrekto, a] *adj* correct; *(persona)* well-mannered

corredizo, a [korre'ðiθo, a] *adj* *(puerta etc)* sliding

corredor, a [korre'ðor, a] *nm* *(pasillo)* corridor; *(balcón corrido)* gallery; *(COM)* agent, broker ♦ *nm/f* *(DEPORTE)* runner

corregir [korre'xir] *vt* *(error)* to correct; **~se** *vr* to reform

correo [ko'rreo] *nm* post, mail; *(persona)* courier; **C~s** *nmpl* Post Office *sg*; **~ aéreo** airmail; **~ electrónico** electronic mail, e-mail

correr [ko'rrer] *vt* to run; *(cortinas)* to draw; *(cerrojo)* to shoot ♦ *vi* to run; *(líquido)* to run, flow; *(colores)* to run; **~se** *vr* to slide, move

correspondencia [korrespon'denθja] *nf* correspondence; *(FERRO)* connection

corresponder [korrespon'der] *vi* to correspond; *(convenir)* to be suitable; *(pertenecer)* to belong; *(concernir)* to

concern; **~se** *vr* *(por escrito)* to correspond; *(amarse)* to love one another

correspondiente [korrespon'djente] *adj* corresponding

corresponsal [korrespon'sal] *nm/f* correspondent

corrida [ko'rriða] *nf* *(de toros)* bullfight

corrido, a [ko'rriðo, a] *adj* *(avergonzado)* abashed; **3 noches corridas** 3 nights running; **un kilo ~** a good kilo

corriente [ko'rrjente] *adj* *(agua)* running; *(dinero etc)* current; *(común)* ordinary, normal ♦ *nf* current ♦ *nm* current month; **~ eléctrica** electric current

corrija *etc vb ver* **corregir**

corrillo [ko'rriʎo] *nm* ring, circle (of people); *(fig)* clique

corro ['korro] *nm* ring, circle (of people)

corroborar [korroβo'rar] *vt* to corroborate

corroer [korro'er] *vt* to corrode; *(GEO)* to erode

corromper [korrom'per] *vt* *(madera)* to rot; *(fig)* to corrupt

corrosivo, a [korro'siβo, a] *adj* corrosive

corrupción [korrup'θjon] *nf* rot, decay; *(fig)* corruption

corsé [kor'se] *nm* corset

cortacésped [korta'θespeð] *nm* lawn mower

cortado, a [kor'taðo, a] *adj* *(gen)* cut; *(leche)* sour; *(tímido)* shy; *(avergonzado)* embarrassed ♦ *nm* coffee (with a little milk)

cortar [kor'tar] *vt* to cut; *(suministro)* to cut off; *(un pasaje)* to cut out ♦ *vi* to cut; **~se** *vr* *(avergonzarse)* to become embarrassed; *(leche)* to turn, curdle; **~se el pelo** to have one's hair cut

cortauñas [korta'uɲas] *nm inv* nail clippers *pl*

corte ['korte] *nm* cut, cutting; *(de tela)*

piece, length ♦ nf: **las C~s** the Spanish Parliament; **~ y confección** dressmaking; **~ de luz** power cut

cortejar [korte'xar] vt to court

cortejo [kor'texo] nm entourage; **~ fúnebre** funeral procession

cortés [kor'tes] adj courteous, polite

cortesía [korte'sia] nf courtesy

corteza [kor'teθa] nf (de árbol) bark; (de pan) crust

cortijo [kor'tixo] nm farm, farmhouse

cortina [kor'tina] nf curtain

corto, a ['korto, a] adj (breve) short; (tímido) bashful; **~ de luces** not very bright; **~ de vista** short-sighted; **estar ~ de fondos** to be short of funds; **~circuito** nm short circuit; **~metraje** nm (CINE) short

cosa ['kosa] nf thing; **~ de** about; **eso es ~ mía** that's my business

coscorrón [kosko'rron] nm bump on the head

cosecha [ko'setʃa] nf (AGR) harvest; (de vino) vintage

cosechar [kose'tʃar] vt to harvest, gather (in)

coser [ko'ser] vt to sew

cosmético, a [kos'metiko, a] adj, nm cosmetic

cosquillas [kos'kiʎas] nfpl: **hacer ~** to tickle; **tener ~** to be ticklish

costa ['kosta] nf (GEO) coast; **C~ Brava** Costa Brava; **C~ Cantábrica** Cantabrian Coast; **C~ del Sol** Costa del Sol; **a toda ~** at all costs

costado [kos'taðo] nm side

costar [kos'tar] vt (valer) to cost; **me cuesta hablarle** I find it hard to talk to him

Costa Rica nf Costa Rica;
costarricense adj, nm/f Costa Rican;
costarriqueño, a adj, nm/f Costa Rican

coste ['koste] nm = **costo**

costear [koste'ar] vt to pay for

costero, a [kos'tero, a] adj (pueblecito, camino) coastal

costilla [kos'tiʎa] nf rib; (CULIN) cutlet

costo ['kosto] nm cost, price; **~ de la vida** cost of living; **~so, a** adj costly, expensive

costra ['kostra] nf (corteza) crust; (MED) scab

costumbre [kos'tumbre] nf custom, habit

costura [kos'tura] nf sewing, needlework; (zurcido) seam

costurera [kostu'rera] nf dressmaker

costurero [kostu'rero] nm sewing box o case

cotejar [kote'xar] vt to compare

cotidiano, a [koti'ðjano, a] adj daily, day to day

cotilla [ko'tiʎa] nm/f (fam) gossip;
cotillear vi to gossip; **cotilleo** nm gossip(ing)

cotización [kotiθa'θjon] nf (COM) quotation, price; (de club) dues pl

cotizar [koti'θar] vt (COM) to quote, price; **~se** vr: **~se a** to sell at, fetch; (BOLSA) to stand at, be quoted at

coto ['koto] nm (terreno cercado) enclosure; (de caza) reserve

cotorra [ko'torra] nf parrot

COU [kou] (ESP) nm abr (= Curso de Orientación Universitaria) 1 year course leading to final school-leaving certificate and university entrance examinations

coyote [ko'jote] nm coyote, prairie wolf

coyuntura [kojun'tura] nf juncture, occasion

coz [koθ] nf kick

crack nm (droga) crack

cráneo ['kraneo] nm skull, cranium

cráter ['krater] nm crater

creación [krea'θjon] nf creation

creador, a [krea'ðor, a] adj creative ♦ nm/f creator

crear [kre'ar] vt to create, make

crecer [kre'θer] vi to grow; (precio) to rise

creces ['kreθes] : **con ~** adv amply, fully

crecido, a [kre'θiðo, a] *adj* (*persona, planta*) full-grown; (*cantidad*) large

creciente [kre'θjente] *adj* growing; (*cantidad*) increasing; (*luna*) crescent ♦ *nm* crescent

crecimiento [kreθi'mjento] *nm* growth; (*aumento*) increase

credenciales [kreðen'θjales] *nfpl* credentials

crédito ['kreðito] *nm* credit

credo ['kreðo] *nm* creed

crédulo, a ['kreðulo, a] *adj* credulous

creencia [kre'enθja] *nf* belief

creer [kre'er] *vt, vi* to think, believe; **~se** *vr* to believe o.s. (to be); **~ en** to believe in; **¡ya lo creo!** I should think so!

creíble [kre'iβle] *adj* credible, believable

creído, a [kre'iðo, a] *adj* (*engreído*) conceited

crema ['krema] *nf* cream; **~ pastelera** (*confectioner's*) custard

cremallera [krema'ʎera] *nf* zip (fastener)

crematorio [krema'torjo] *nm* (tb: **horno ~**) crematorium

crepitar [krepi'tar] *vi* to crackle

crepúsculo [kre'puskulo] *nm* twilight, dusk

cresta ['kresta] *nf* (GEO, ZOOL) crest

creyendo *vb ver* **creer**

creyente [kre'jente] *nm/f* believer

creyó *etc vb ver* **creer**

crezco *etc vb ver* **crecer**

cría *etc* ['kria] *vb ver* **criar** ♦ *nf* (*de animales*) rearing, breeding; (*animal*) young; *ver tb* **crío**

criadero [kria'ðero] *nm* (ZOOL) breeding place

criado, a [kri'aðo, a] *nm* servant ♦ *nf* servant, maid

criador [kria'ðor] *nm* breeder

crianza [kri'anθa] *nf* rearing, breeding; (*fig*) breeding

criar [kri'ar] *vt* (*educar*) to bring up; (*producir*) to grow, produce; (*animales*)

to breed

criatura [kria'tura] *nf* creature; (*niño*) baby, (*small*) child

criba ['kriβa] *nf* sieve; **cribar** *vt* to sieve

crimen ['krimen] *nm* crime

criminal [krimi'nal] *adj, nm/f* criminal

crin [krin] *nf* (tb: **~es** *nfpl*) mane

crío, a ['krio, a] (*fam*) *nm/f* (*niño*) kid

crisis ['krisis] *nf inv* crisis; **~ nerviosa** nervous breakdown

crispar [kris'par] *vt* (*nervios*) to set on edge

cristal [kris'tal] *nm* crystal; (*de ventana*) glass, pane; (*lente*) lens; **~ino, a** *adj* crystalline; (*fig*) clear ♦ *nm* lens (of the eye); **~izar** *vt, vi* to crystallize

cristiandad [kristjan'dað] *nf* Christendom

cristianismo [kristja'nismo] *nm* Christianity

cristiano, a [kris'tjano, a] *adj, nm/f* Christian

Cristo ['kristo] *nm* Christ; (*crucifijo*) crucifix

criterio [kri'terjo] *nm* criterion; (*juicio*) judgement

crítica [kri'tika] *nf* criticism; *ver tb* **crítico**

criticar [kriti'kar] *vt* to criticize

crítico, a ['kritiko, a] *adj* critical ♦ *nm/f* critic

Croacia *nf* Croatia

croar [kro'ar] *vi* to croak

cromo ['kromo] *nm* chrome

crónica ['kronika] *nf* chronicle, account

crónico, a ['kroniko, a] *adj* chronic

cronómetro [kro'nometro] *nm* stopwatch

croqueta [kro'keta] *nf* croquette

cruce *etc* ['kruθe] *vb ver* **cruzar** ♦ *nm* crossing; (*de carreteras*) crossroads

crucificar [kruθifi'kar] *vt* to crucify

crucifijo [kruθi'fixo] *nm* crucifix

crucigrama [kruθi'xrama] *nm* crossword (puzzle)

crudo, a ['kruðo, a] *adj* raw; (*no maduro*) unripe; (*petróleo*) crude; (*rudo, cruel*) cruel ♦ *nm* crude (oil)

cruel [krwel] *adj* cruel; **~dad** *nf* cruelty

crujido [kru'xiðo] *nm* (*de madera etc*) creak

crujiente [kru'xjente] *adj* (*galleta etc*) crunchy

crujir [kru'xir] *vi* (*madera etc*) to creak; (*dedos*) to crack; (*dientes*) to grind; (*nieve, arena*) to crunch

cruz [kruθ] *nf* cross; (*de moneda*) tails *sg*; **~ gamada** swastika

cruzada [kru'θaða] *nf* crusade

cruzado, a [kru'θaðo, a] *adj* crossed ♦ *nm* crusader

cruzar [kru'θar] *vt* to cross; **~se** *vr* (*líneas etc*) to cross; (*personas*) to pass each other

Cruz Roja *nf* Red Cross

cuaderno [kwa'ðerno] *nm* notebook; (*de escuela*) exercise book; (*NAUT*) logbook

cuadra ['kwaðra] *nf* (*caballeriza*) stable; (*AM*) block

cuadrado, a [kwa'ðraðo, a] *adj* square ♦ *nm* (*MAT*) square

cuadrar [kwa'ðrar] *vt* to square ♦ *vi:* **~ con** to square with, tally with; **~se** *vr* (*soldado*) to stand to attention

cuadrilátero [kwaðri'latero] *nm* (*DEPORTE*) boxing ring; (*GEOM*) quadrilateral

cuadrilla [kwa'ðriʎa] *nf* party, group

cuadro ['kwaðro] *nm* square; (*ARTE*) painting; (*TEATRO*) scene; (*diagrama*) chart; (*DEPORTE, MED*) team; **tela a ~s** checked (*BRIT*) o chequered (*US*) material

cuádruple ['kwaðruple] *adj* quadruple

cuajar [kwa'xar] *vt* (*leche*) to curdle; (*sangre*) to congeal; (*CULIN*) to set; **~se** *vr* to curdle; to congeal; to set; (*llenarse*) to fill up

cuajo ['kwaxo] *nm*: **de ~** (*arrancar*) by the roots; (*cortar*) completely

cual [kwal] *adv* like, as ♦ *pron:* **el ~** *etc* which; (*persona: sujeto*) who; (*: objeto*) whom ♦ *adj such as;* **cada ~** each one; **déjalo tal ~** leave it just as it is

cuál [kwal] *pron interr* which one

cualesquier(a) [kwales'kjer(a)] *pl de* **cualquier(a)**

cualidad [kwali'ðað] *nf* quality

cualquier [kwal'kjer] *adj ver* **cualquiera**

cualquiera [kwal'kjera] (*pl* **cualesquiera**) *adj* (*delante de nm y f:* **cualquier**) any ♦ *pron* anybody; **un coche ~ servirá** any car will do; **no es un hombre ~** he isn't just anybody; **cualquier día/libro** any day/book; **eso ~ lo sabe hacer** anybody can do that; **es un ~** he's a nobody

cuando ['kwando] *adv* when; (*aún si*) if, even if ♦ *conj* (*puesto que*) since ♦ *prep:* **yo, ~ niño ...** when I was a child ...; **~ no sea así** even if it is not so; **~ más** at (the most); **~ menos** at least; **~ no** if not, otherwise; **de ~ en ~** from time to time

cuándo ['kwando] *adv* when; **¿desde ~?, ¿de ~ acá?** since when?

cuantía [kwan'tia] *nf* (*importe: de pérdidas, deuda, daños*) extent

cuantioso, a [kwan'tjoso, a] *adj* substantial

PALABRA CLAVE

---

cuanto, a ['kwanto, a] *adj* **1** (*todo*): **tiene todo ~ desea** he's got everything he wants; **le daremos ~s ejemplares necesite** we'll give him as many copies as o all the copies he needs; **~s hombres la ven** all the men who see her

2: **unos ~s:** **había unos ~s periodistas** there were a few journalists

3 (+ *más*): **~ más vino bebes peor te sentirás** the more wine you drink the worse you'll feel

♦ *pron:* **tiene ~ desea** he has

everything he wants; **tome ~/~s quiera** take as much/many as you want

♦ *adv*: **en ~**: **en ~ profesor** as a teacher; **en ~ a mí** as for me; *ver tb* **antes**

♦ *conj* **1**: **~ más gana menos gasta** the more he earns the less he spends; **~ más joven más confiado** the younger you are the more trusting you are

2: **en ~**: **en ~ llegue/llegué** as soon as I arrive/arrived

cuánto, a ['kwanto, a] *adj* (*exclamación*) what a lot of; (*interr*: *sg*) how much?; (: *pl*) how many? ♦ *pron, adv* how; (*interr*: *sg*) how much?; (: *pl*) how many?; **¡cuánta gente!** what a lot of people!; **¿~ cuesta?** how much does it cost?; **¿a ~s estamos?** what's the date?; **Señor no sé ~s** Mr. So-and-So

cuarenta [kwa'rɛnta] *num* forty

cuarentena [kwarɛn'tena] *nf* quarantine

cuaresma [kwa'rɛsma] *nf* Lent

cuarta ['kwarta] *nf* (MAT) quarter, fourth; (*palmo*) span

cuartel [kwar'tel] *nm* (MIL) barracks *pl*; **~ general** headquarters *pl*

cuarteto [kwar'teto] *nm* quartet

cuarto, a ['kwarto, a] *adj* fourth ♦ *nm* (MAT) quarter, fourth; (*habitación*) room; **~ de baño** bathroom; **~ de estar** living room; **~ de hora** quarter (of an) hour; **~ de kilo** quarter kilo

cuatro ['kwatro] *num* four

Cuba ['kußa] *nf* Cuba; **cubano, a** *adj, nm/f* Cuban

cuba ['kußa] *nf* cask, barrel

cubata [ku'ßata] *nm* (*fam*) large drink (*of rum and coke etc*)

cúbico, a ['kußiko, a] *adj* cubic

cubierta [ku'ßjɛrta] *nf* cover, covering; (*neumático*) tyre; (NAUT) deck

cubierto, a [ku'ßjɛrto, a] *pp de* **cubrir**

♦ *adj* covered ♦ *nm* cover; (*lugar en la mesa*) place; **~s** *nmpl* cutlery *sg*; **a ~** under cover

cubil [ku'ßil] *nm* den; **~ete** *nm* (*en juegos*) cup

cubito [ku'ßito] *nm*: **~ de hielo** ice-cube

cubo ['kußo] *nm* (MATH) cube; (*balde*) bucket, tub; (TEC) drum

cubrecama [kußre'kama] *nm* bedspread

cubrir [ku'ßrir] *vt* to cover; **~se** *vr* (*cielo*) to become overcast

cucaracha [kuka'ratʃa] *nf* cockroach

cuchara [ku'tʃara] *nf* spoon; (TEC) scoop; **~da** *nf* spoonful; **~dita** *nf* teaspoonful

cucharilla [kutʃa'riʎa] *nf* teaspoon

cucharón [kutʃa'ron] *nm* ladle

cuchichear [kutʃitʃe'ar] *vi* to whisper

cuchilla [ku'tʃiʎa] *nf* (*large*) knife; (*de arma blanca*) blade; **~ de afeitar** razor blade

cuchillo [ku'tʃiʎo] *nm* knife

cuchitril [kutʃi'tril] *nm* hovel

cuclillas [ku'kliʎas] *nfpl*: **en ~** squatting

cuco, a ['kuko, a] *adj* pretty; (*astuto*) sharp ♦ *nm* cuckoo

cucurucho [kuku'rutʃo] *nm* cornet

cuello ['kweʎo] *nm* (ANAT) neck; (*de vestido, camisa*) collar

cuenca ['kwenka] *nf* (ANAT) eye socket; (GEO) bowl, deep valley

cuenco ['kwenko] *nm* bowl

cuenta *etc* ['kwenta] *vb ver* **contar**

♦ *nf* (*cálculo*) count, counting; (*en café, restaurante*) bill (BRIT), check (US); (COM) account; (*de collar*) bead; **a fin de ~s** in the end; **caer en la ~** to catch on; **darse ~ de** to realize; **tener en ~** to bear in mind; **echar ~s** to take stock; **~ corriente/de ahorros** current/savings account; **~ atrás** countdown; **~kilómetros** *nm inv* = milometer; (*de velocidad*) speedometer

cuento *etc* ['kwento] *vb ver* **contar**

♦ *nm* story

cuerda ['kwerða] *nf* rope; (*fina*) string; (*de reloj*) spring; **dar ~ a un reloj** to wind up a clock; **~ floja** tightrope

cuerdo, a ['kwerðo, a] *adj* sane; (*prudente*) wise, sensible

cuerno ['kwerno] *nm* horn

cuero ['kwero] *nm* leather; **en ~s** stark naked; **~ cabelludo** scalp

cuerpo ['kwerpo] *nm* body

cuervo ['kwerßo] *nm* crow

cuesta *etc* ['kwesta] *vb ver* **costar ♦** *nf* slope; (*en camino etc*) hill; **~ arriba/abajo** uphill/downhill; **a ~s** on one's back

cueste *etc vb ver* **costar**

cuestión [kwes'tjon] *nf* matter, question, issue

cueva ['kweßa] *nf* cave

cuidado [kwi'ðaðo] *nm* care, carefulness; (*preocupación*) care, worry **♦** *excl* careful!, look out!

cuidadoso, a [kwiða'ðoso, a] *adj* careful; (*preocupado*) anxious

cuidar [kwi'ðar] *vt* (*MED*) to care for; (*ocuparse de*) to take care of, look after **♦** *vi*: **~ de** to take care of, look after; **~se** *vr* to look after o.s.; **~se de hacer algo** to take care to do sth

culata [ku'lata] *nf* (*de fusil*) butt

culebra [ku'leßra] *nf* snake

culebrón [kule'ßron] (*fam*) *nm* (*TV*) soap(-opera)

culinario, a [kuli'narjo, a] *adj* culinary, cooking *cpd*

culminación [kulmina'θjon] *nf* culmination

culo ['kulo] *nm* bottom, backside; (*de vaso, botella*) bottom

culpa ['kulpa] *nf* fault; (*JUR*) guilt; **por ~ de** because of; **tener la ~ (de)** to be to blame (for); **~bilidad** *nf* guilt; **~ble** *adj* guilty **♦** *nm/f* culprit

culpar [kul'par] *vt* to blame; (*acusar*) to accuse

cultivar [kulti'ßar] *vt* to cultivate

cultivo [kul'tißo] *nm* (*acto*) cultivation; (*plantas*) crop

culto, a ['kulto, a] *adj* (*que tiene cultura*) cultured, educated **♦** *nm* (*homenaje*) worship; (*religión*) cult

cultura [kul'tura] *nf* culture

culturismo [kultu'rismo] *nm* body-building

cumbre ['kumbre] *nf* summit, top

cumpleaños [kumple'aɲos] *nm inv* birthday

cumplido, a [kum'pliðo, a] *adj* (*abundante*) plentiful; (*cortés*) courteous **♦** *nm* compliment; **visita de ~** courtesy call

cumplidor, a [kumpli'ðor, a] *adj* reliable

cumplimentar [kumplimen'tar] *vt* to congratulate

cumplimiento [kumpli'mjento] *nm* (*de un deber*) fulfilment; (*acabamiento*) completion

cumplir [kum'plir] *vt* (*orden*) to carry out, obey; (*promesa*) to carry out, fulfil; (*condena*) to serve **♦** *vi*: **~ con** (*deberes*) to carry out, fulfil; **~se** *vr* (*plazo*) to expire; **hoy cumple dieciocho años** he is eighteen today

cúmulo ['kumulo] *nm* heap

cuna ['kuna] *nf* cradle, cot

cundir [kun'dir] *vi* (*noticia, rumor, pánico*) to spread; (*rendir*) to go a long way

cuneta [ku'neta] *nf* ditch

cuña ['kuɲa] *nf* wedge

cuñado, a [ku'ɲaðo, a] *nm/f* brother-/sister-in-law

cuota ['kwota] *nf* (*parte proporcional*) share; (*cotización*) fee, dues *pl*

cupiera *etc vb ver* **caber**

cupo *vb ver* **caber ♦** *nm* quota

cupón [ku'pon] *nm* coupon

cúpula ['kupula] *nf* dome

cura ['kura] *nf* (*curación*) cure; (*método curativo*) treatment **♦** *nm* priest

curación [kura'θjon] *nf* (*acción*) curing

curandero, a [kuran'dero, a] *nm/f* quack

curar [ku'rar] *vt* (MED: *herida*) to treat, dress; (: *enfermo*) to cure; (CULIN): to cure, salt; (*cuero*) to tan; **~se** *vr* to get well, recover

curiosear [kurjose'ar] *vt* to glance at, look over ♦ *vi* to look round, wander round; (*explorar*) to poke about

curiosidad [kurjosi'ðað] *nf* curiosity

curioso, a [ku'rjoso, a] *adj* curious ♦ *nm/f* bystander, onlooker

currante [ku'rrante] (*fam*) *nm/f* worker

currar [ku'rrar] (*fam*) *vi* to work

currículo [ku'rrikulo] = **curriculum**

curriculum [ku'rrikulum] *nm* curriculum vitae

cursi ['kursi] *adj* affected

cursillo [kur'siʎo] *nm* short course

cursiva [kur'siβa] *nf* italics *pl*

curso ['kurso] *nm* course; **en ~** (*año*) current; (*proceso*) going on, under way

cursor [kur'sor] *nm* (INFORM) cursor

curtido, a [kur'tiðo, a] *adj* (*cara etc*) weather-beaten; (*fig: persona*) experienced

curtir [kur'tir] *vt* (*cuero etc*) to tan

curva ['kurβa] *nf* curve, bend

cúspide ['kuspiðe] *nf* (GEO) peak; (*fig*) top

custodia [kus'toðja] *nf* safekeeping; custody; **custodiar** *vt* (*conservar*) to take care of; (*vigilar*) to guard

cutis ['kutis] *nm inv* skin, complexion

cutre ['kutre] (*fam*) *adj* (*lugar*) grotty

cuyo, a ['kujo, a] *pron* (*de quien*) whose; (*de que*) whose, of which; **en ~ caso** in which case

C.V. *abr* (= *caballos de vapor*) H.P.

D, d

D. *abr* (= *Don*) Esq.

Da. *abr* = **Doña**

dádiva ['daðiβa] *nf* (*donación*) donation; (*regalo*) gift; **dadivoso, a**

adj generous

dado, a ['daðo, a] *pp de* **dar** ♦ *nm* die; **~s** *nmpl* dice; **~ que** given that

daltónico, a [dal'toniko, a] *adj* colour-blind

dama ['dama] *nf* (*gen*) lady; (AJEDREZ) queen; **~s** *nfpl* (*juego*) draughts *sg*

damnificar [damnifi'kar] *vt* to harm; (*persona*) to injure

danés, esa [da'nes, esa] *adj* Danish ♦ *nm/f* Dane

danzar [dan'θar] *vt, vi* to dance

dañar [da'ɲar] *vt* (*objeto*) to damage; (*persona*) to hurt; **~se** *vr* (*objeto*) to get damaged

dañino, a [da'ɲino, a] *adj* harmful

daño ['daɲo] *nm* (*a un objeto*) damage; (*a una persona*) harm, injury; **~s y perjuicios** (JUR) damages; **hacer ~ a** to damage; (*persona*) to hurt, injure; **hacerse ~** to hurt o.s.

PALABRA CLAVE

---

dar [dar] *vt* **1** (*gen*) to give; (*obra de teatro*) to put on; (*film*) to show; (*fiesta*) to hold; **~ algo a uno** to give sb sth o sth to sb; **~ de beber a uno** to give sb a drink

2 (*producir: intereses*) to yield; (*fruta*) to produce

3 (*locuciones + n*): **da gusto escucharle** it's a pleasure to listen to him; *ver tb* **paseo** *y otros sustantivos*

4 (+ *n*: = *perífrasis de verbo*): **me da asco** it sickens me

5 (*considerar*): **~ algo por descontado/entendido** to take sth for granted/as read; **~ algo por concluido** to consider sth finished

6 (*hora*): **el reloj dio las 6** the clock struck 6 (o'clock)

7: **me da lo mismo** it's all the same to me; *ver tb* **igual, más**

♦ *vi* **1**: **~ con**: **dimos con él dos horas más tarde** we came across him two hours later; **al final di con la solución** I eventually came up with the answer

2: ~ **en** (blanco, suelo) to hit; **el sol me da en la cara** the sun is shining (right) on my face

3: ~ **de sí** (zapatos etc) to stretch, give ♦ ~**se** vr **1**: ~**se por vencido** to give up

2 (ocurrir): **se han dado muchos casos** there have been a lot of cases

3: ~**se a: se ha dado a la bebida** he's taken to drinking

4: **se me dan bien/mal las ciencias** I'm good/bad at science

5: **dárselas de: se las da de experto** he fancies himself o poses as an expert

dardo ['darðo] nm dart

datar [da'tar] vi: ~ **de** to date from

dátil ['datil] nm date

dato ['dato] nm fact, piece of information; ~**s personales** personal details

DC abbr m (= disco compacto) CD

dcha. abr (= derecha) r.h.

d. de J.C. abr (= después de Jesucristo) A.D.

PALABRA CLAVE

de [de] prep (de+ el = del) **1** (posesión) of; **la casa** ~ **Isabel/mis padres** Isabel's/my parents' house; **es** ~ **ellos** it's theirs

2 (origen, distancia, con números): **soy** ~ **Gijón** I'm from Gijón; ~ **8 a 20** from 8 to 20; **salir del cine** to go out of o leave the cinema; ~ **2 en 2 2** by 2, 2 at a time

3 (valor descriptivo): **una copa** ~ **vino** a glass of wine; **la mesa** ~ **la cocina** the kitchen table; **un billete** ~ **1000 pesetas** a 1000 peseta note; **un niño** ~ **tres años** a three-year-old (child); **una máquina** ~ **coser** a sewing machine; **ir vestido** ~ **gris** to be dressed in grey; **la niña del vestido azul** the girl in the blue dress; **trabaja**

~ **profesora** she works as a teacher; ~ **lado** sideways; ~ **atrás/delante** rear/front

4 (hora, tiempo): **a las 8** ~ **la mañana** at 8 o'clock in the morning; ~ **día/ noche** by day/night; ~ **hoy en ocho días** a week from now; ~ **niño era gordo** as a child he was fat

5 (comparaciones): **más/menos** ~ **cien personas** more/less than a hundred people; **el más caro** ~ **la tienda** the most expensive in the shop; **menos/más** ~ **lo pensado** less/more than expected

6 (causa): **del calor** from the heat; ~ **puro tonto** out of sheer stupidity

7 (tema): about; **clases** ~ **inglés** English classes; ¿**sabes algo** ~ **él?** do you know anything about him?; **un libro** ~ **física** a physics book

8 (adj + de + infin): **fácil** ~ **entender** easy to understand

9 (oraciones pasivas): **fue respetado** ~ **todos** he was loved by all

10 (condicional + infin): **si** ~ **ser posible** if possible; ~ **no terminarlo hoy** if I etc don't finish it today

dé vb ver **dar**

deambular [deambu'lar] vi to wander

debajo [de'βaxo] adv underneath; ~ **de** below, under; **por** ~ **de** beneath

debate [de'βate] nm debate; **debatir** vt to debate

deber [de'βer] nm duty ♦ vt to owe ♦ vi: **debe** (de) it must, it should; ~**es** nmpl (ESCOL) homework; **debo hacerlo** I must do it; **debe de ir** he should go; ~**se** vr: ~**se a** to be owing o due to

debido, a [de'βiðo, a] adj proper, just; ~ **a** due to, because of

débil ['deβil] adj (persona, carácter) weak; (luz) dim; **debilidad** nf weakness; dimness

debilitar [deβili'tar] vt to weaken; ~**se** vr to grow weak

debutar [deβu'tar] vi to make one's debut

década ['dekaða] nf decade

decadencia [deka'ðenθja] nf (estado) decadence; (proceso) decline, decay

decaer [deka'er] vi (declinar) to decline; (debilitarse) to weaken

decaído, a [deka'iðo, a] adj: **estar ~** (abatido) to be down

decaimiento [dekai'mjento] nm (declinación) decline; (desaliento) discouragement; (MED: estado débil) weakness

decano, a [de'kano, a] nm/f (de universidad etc) dean

decapitar [dekapi'tar] vt to behead

decena [de'θena] nf: **una ~** ten (or so)

decencia [de'θenθja] nf decency

decente [de'θente] adj decent

decepción [deθep'θjon] nf disappointment

decepcionar [deθepθjo'nar] vt to disappoint

decidir [deθi'ðir] vt, vi to decide; **~se** vr: **~se a** to make up one's mind to

décimo, a [de'θimo, a] adj tenth ♦ nm tenth

decir [de'θir] vt to say; (contar) to tell; (hablar) to speak ♦ nm saying; **~se** vr: **se dice que** it is said that; **~ para o entre sí** to say to o.s.; **querer ~** to mean; **¡dígame!** (TEL) hello!; (en tienda) can I help you?

decisión [deθi'sjon] nf (resolución) decision; (firmeza) decisiveness

decisivo, a [deθi'siβo, a] adj decisive

declaración [deklara'θjon] nf (manifestación) statement; (de amor) declaration; **~ de ingresos o de la renta o fiscal** income-tax return

declarar [dekla'rar] vt to declare ♦ vi (JUR) to testify; **~se** vr to propose

declinar [dekli'nar] vt (gen) to decline; (JUR) to reject ♦ vi (el día) to draw to a close

declive [de'kliβe] nm (cuesta) slope;

(fig) decline

decodificador [dekoðifika'ðor] nm decoder

decolorarse [dekolo'rarse] vr to become discoloured

decoración [dekora'θjon] nf decoration

decorado [deko'raðo] nm (CINE, TEATRO) scenery, set

decorar [deko'rar] vt to decorate; **decorativo, a** adj ornamental, decorative

decoro [de'koro] nm (respeto) respect; (dignidad) decency; (recato) propriety; **~so, a** adj (decente) decent; (modesto) modest; (digno) proper

decrecer [dekre'θer] vi to decrease, diminish

decrépito, a [de'krepito, a] adj decrepit

decretar [dekre'tar] vt to decree; **decreto** nm decree

dedal [de'ðal] nm thimble

dedicación [deðika'θjon] nf dedication

dedicar [deði'kar] vt (libro) to dedicate; (tiempo, dinero) to devote; (palabras: decir, consagrar) to dedicate, devote; **dedicatoria** nf (de libro) dedication

dedo ['deðo] nm finger; **~ (del pie)** toe; **~ pulgar** thumb; **~ índice** index finger; **~ corazón** middle finger; **~ anular** ring finger; **~ meñique** little finger; **hacer ~** (fam) to hitch (a lift)

deducción [deðuk'θjon] nf deduction

deducir [deðu'θir] vt (concluir) to deduce, infer; (COM) to deduct

defecto [de'fekto] nm defect, flaw; **defectuoso, a** adj defective, faulty

defender [defen'der] vt to defend

defensa [de'fensa] nf defence ♦ nm (DEPORTE) defender, back; **defensivo, a** adj defensive; **a la defensiva** on the defensive

defensor, a [defen'sor, a] adj defending ♦ nm/f (abogado ~)

defending counsel; (*protector*) protector

deficiencia [defi'θjenθja] *nf* deficiency

deficiente [defi'θjente] *adj* (*defectuoso*) defective; **~ en** lacking o deficient in; **ser un ~ mental** to be mentally handicapped

déficit ['defiθit] (*pl* **~s**) *nm* deficit

definición [defini'θjon] *nf* definition

definir [defi'nir] *vt* (*determinar*) to determine, establish; (*decidir*) to define; (*aclarar*) to clarify; **definitivo, a** *adj* definitive; **en definitiva** definitively; (*en resumen*) in short

deformación [deforma'θjon] *nf* (*alteración*) deformation; (*RADIO etc*) distortion

deformar [defor'mar] *vt* (*gen*) to deform; **~se** *vr* to become deformed; **deforme** *adj* (*informe*) deformed; (*feo*) ugly; (*malhecho*) misshapen

defraudar [defrau'ðar] *vt* (*decepcionar*) to disappoint; (*estafar*) to defraud

defunción [defun'θjon] *nf* death, demise

degeneración [dexenera'θjon] *nf* (*de las células*) degeneration; (*moral*) degeneracy

degenerar [dexene'rar] *vi* to degenerate

degollar [dexo'ʎar] *vt* to behead; (*fig*) to slaughter

degradar [dexra'ðar] *vt* to debase, degrade; **~se** *vr* to demean o.s.

degustación [dexusta'θjon] *nf* sampling, tasting

deificar [deifi'kar] *vt* to deify

dejadez [dexa'ðeθ] *nf* (*negligencia*) neglect; (*descuido*) untidiness, carelessness

dejar [de'xar] *vt* to leave; (*permitir*) to allow, let; (*abandonar*) to abandon, forsake; (*beneficios*) to produce, yield ♦ *vi*: **~ de** (*parar*) to stop; (*no hacer*) to fail to; **no dejes de comprar un billete** make sure you buy a ticket; **~ a un lado** to leave o set aside

dejo ['dexo] *nm* (*LING*) accent

del [del] (= **de** + **el**) *ver* **de**

delantal [delan'tal] *nm* apron

delante [de'lante] *adv* in front, (*enfrente*) opposite; (*adelante*) ahead; **~ de** in front of, before

delantera [delan'tera] *nf* (*de vestido, casa etc*) front part; (*DEPORTE*) forward line; **llevar la ~ (a uno)** to be ahead (of sb)

delantero, a [delan'tero, a] *adj* front ♦ *nm* (*DEPORTE*) forward, striker.

delatar [dela'tar] *vt* to inform on o against, betray; **delator, a** *nm/f* informer

delegación [deleɣa'θjon] *nf* (*acción, delegados*) delegation; (*COM: oficina*) office, branch; **~ de policía** police station

delegado, a [dele'ɣaðo, a] *nm/f* delegate; (*COM*) agent

delegar [dele'ɣar] *vt* to delegate

deletrear [deletre'ar] *vt* to spell (out)

deleznable [deleθ'naβle] *adj* brittle; (*excusa, idea*) feeble

delfín [del'fin] *nm* dolphin

delgadez [delɣa'ðeθ] *nf* thinness, slimness

delgado, a [del'ɣaðo, a] *adj* thin; (*persona*) slim, thin; (*tela etc*) light, delicate

deliberación [deliβera'θjon] *nf* deliberation

deliberar [deliβe'rar] *vt* to debate, discuss

delicadeza [delika'ðeθa] *nf* (*gen*) delicacy; (*refinamiento, sutileza*) refinement

delicado, a [deli'kaðo, a] *adj* (*gen*) delicate; (*sensible*) sensitive; (*quisquilloso*) touchy

delicia [de'liθja] *nf* delight

delicioso, a [deli'θjoso, a] *adj* (*gracioso*) delightful; (*exquisito*) delicious

delimitar [delimi'tar] *vt* (*funciones, responsabilidades*) to define

delincuencia [delin'kwenθja] nf
delinquency; **delincuente** nm/f
delinquent; (*criminal*) criminal

delineante [deline'ante] nm/f
draughtsman/woman

delinear [deline'ar] vt (*dibujo*) to draw;
(*fig, contornos*) to outline

delinquir [delin'kir] vi to commit an
offence

delirante [deli'rante] adj delirious

delirar [deli'rar] vi to be delirious, rave

delirio [de'lirjo] nm (MED) delirium;
(*palabras insensatas*) ravings pl

delito [de'lito] nm (*gen*) crime;
(*infracción*) offence

delta ['delta] nm delta

demacrado, a [dema'krado, a] adj:
estar ~ to look pale and drawn, be
wasted away

demagogo, a [dema'ɣoɣo, a] nm/f
demagogue

demanda [de'manda] nf (*pedido*, COM)
demand; (*petición*) request; (JUR)
action, lawsuit

demandante [deman'dante] nm/f
claimant

demandar [deman'dar] vt (*gen*) to
demand; (JUR) to sue, file a lawsuit
against

demarcación [demarka'θjon] nf (*de
terreno*) demarcation

demás [de'mas] adj: **los ~ niños** the
other children, the remaining children
♦ pron: **los/las ~** the others, the rest
(of them); **lo ~** the rest (of it)

demasía [dema'sia] nf (*exceso*) excess,
surplus; **comer en ~** to eat to excess

demasiado, a [dema'sjaðo, a] adj:
~ vino too much wine ♦ adv (*antes de
adj, adv*) too; (*verbo*) too much; **~ libros** too many
books; **¡esto es ~!** that's the limit!;
hace ~ calor it's too hot; **~ despacio**
too slowly; **~s too many**

demencia [de'menθja] nf (*locura*)
madness; **demente** nm/f lunatic ♦ adj
mad, insane

democracia [demo'kraθja] nf
democracy

demócrata [de'mokrata] nm/f
democrat; **democrático, a** adj
democratic

demoler [demo'ler] vt to demolish;
demolición nf demolition

demonio [de'monjo] nm devil,
demon; **¡~s!** hell!, damn!; **¿cómo ~s**
how the hell?

demora [de'mora] nf delay; **demorar**
vt (*retardar*) to delay, hold back;
(*detener*) to hold up ♦ vi to linger, stay
on; **~se** vr to be delayed

demos vb ver **dar**

demostración [demostra'θjon] nf
(MAT) proof; (*de afecto*) show, display

demostrar [demos'trar] vt (*probar*) to
prove; (*mostrar*) to show; (*manifestar*)
to demonstrate

demudado, a [demu'ðaðo, a] adj
(*rostro*) pale

den vb ver **dar**

denegar [dene'ɣar] vt (*rechazar*) to
refuse; (JUR) to reject

denigrar [deni'ɣrar] vt (*desacreditar,
infamar*) to denigrate; (*injuriar*) to insult

Denominación de Origen

The **Denominación de Origen**,
abbreviated to **D.O.**, *is a prestigious
classification awarded to food
products such as wines, cheeses,
sausages and hams which meet the
stringent quality and production
standards of the designated region.
D.O. labels serve as a guarantee of
quality.*

---

denotar [deno'tar] vt to denote

densidad [densi'ðað] nf density; (*fig*)
thickness

denso, a ['denso, a] adj dense;
(*espeso, pastoso*) thick; (*fig*) heavy

dentadura [denta'ðura] nf (*set of*)
teeth pl; **~ postiza** false teeth pl

dentera [den'tera] nf (*sensación
desagradable*) the shivers pl

dentífrico, a [den'tifriko, a] *adj* dental
♦ *nm* toothpaste

dentista [den'tista] *nm/f* dentist

dentro ['dentro] *adv* inside ♦ *prep*:
~ **de** in, inside, within; **por** ~ (on the)
inside; **mirar por** ~ to look inside;
~ **de tres meses** within three months

denuncia [de'nunθja] *nf* (*delación*)
denunciation; (*acusación*) accusation;
(*de accidente*) report; **denunciar** *vt* to
report; (*delatar*) to inform on o against

departamento [departa'mento] *nm*
(*sección administrativa*) department,
section; (*AM: apartamento*) flat (*BRIT*),
apartment

dependencia [depen'denθja] *nf*
dependence; (*POL*) dependency; (*COM*)
office, section

depender [depen'der] *vi*: ~ **de** to
depend on

dependienta [depen'djenta] *nf*
saleswoman, shop assistant

dependiente [depen'djente] *adj*
dependent ♦ *nm* salesman, shop
assistant

depilar [depi'lar] *vt* (*con cera*) to wax;
(*cejas*) to pluck; **depilatorio** *nm* hair
remover

deplorable [deplo'raβle] *adj*
deplorable

deplorar [deplo'rar] *vt* to deplore

deponer [depo'ner] *vt* to lay down
♦ *vi* (*JUR*) to give evidence; (*declarar*) to
make a statement

deportar [depor'tar] *vt* to deport

deporte [de'porte] *nm* sport; **hacer** ~
to play sports; **deportista** *adj* sports
cpd ♦ *nm/f* sportsman/woman;
deportivo, a *adj* (*club, periódico*)
sports *cpd* ♦ *nm* sports car

depositar [deposi'tar] *vt* (*dinero*) to
deposit; (*mercancías*) to put away,
store; ~**se** *vr* to settle; ~**io, a** *nm/f*
trustee

depósito [de'posito] *nm* (*gen*) deposit;
(*almacén*) warehouse, store; (*de agua,
gasolina etc*) tank; ~ **de cadáveres**
mortuary

depreciar [depre'θjar] *vt* to
depreciate, reduce the value of; ~**se** *vr*
to depreciate, lose value

depredador, a [depreða'ðor, a] *adj*
predatory ♦ *nm* predator

depresión [depre'sjon] *nf* depression

deprimido, a [depri'miðo, a] *adj*
depressed

deprimir [depri'mir] *vt* to depress;
~**se** *vr* (*persona*) to become depressed

deprisa [de'prisa] *adv* quickly,
hurriedly

depuración [depura'θjon] *nf*
purification; (*POL*) purge

depurar [depu'rar] *vt* to purify;
(*purgar*) to purge

derecha [de'retʃa] *nf* right(-hand) side;
(*POL*) right; **a la** ~ (*estar*) on the right;
(*torcer etc*) (to the) right

derecho, a [de'retʃo, a] *adj* right,
right-hand ♦ *nm* (*privilegio*) right;
(*lado*) right(-hand) side; (*leyes*) law
♦ *adv* straight, directly; ~**s** *nmpl* (*de
aduana*) duty *sg*; (*de autor*) royalties;
tener ~ **a** to have a right to

deriva [de'riβa] *nf*: **ir o estar a la** ~ to
drift, be adrift

derivado [deri'βaðo] *nm* (*COM*) by-
product

derivar [deri'βar] *vt* to derive; (*desviar*)
to direct ♦ *vi* to be derived; (*NAUT*) to
drift; ~**se** *vr* to derive, be
derived; to drift

derramamiento [derrama'mjento]
nm (*dispersión*) spilling; ~ **de sangre**
bloodshed

derramar [derra'mar] *vt* to spill;
(*verter*) to pour out; (*esparcir*) to
scatter; ~**se** *vr* to pour out;
~ **lágrimas** to weep

derrame [de'rrame] *nm* (*de líquido*)
spilling; (*de sangre*) shedding; (*de tubo
etc*) overflow; (*pérdida*) leakage; (*MED*)
discharge

derredor [derre'ðor] *adv*: **al** o **en** ~ **de**
around, about

derretido, a [derre'tiðo, a] *adj* melted; (*metal*) molten

derretir [derre'tir] *vt* (*gen*) to melt; (*nieve*) to thaw; **~se** *vr* to melt

derribar [derri'ßar] *vt* to knock down; (*construcción*) to demolish; (*persona, gobierno, político*) to bring down

derrocar [derro'kar] *vt* (*gobierno*) to bring down, overthrow

derrochar [derro'tʃar] *vt* to squander; **derroche** *nm* (*despilfarro*) waste, squandering

derrota [de'rrota] *nf* (*NAUT*) course; (*MIL, DEPORTE etc*) defeat, rout; **derrotar** *vt* (*gen*) to defeat; **derrotero** *nm* (*rumbo*) course

derruir [derru'ir] *vt* (*edificio*) to demolish

derrumbar [derrum'bar] *vt* (*edificio*) to knock down; **~se** *vr* to collapse

derruyendo *etc vb ver* **derruir**

des *vb ver* **dar**

desabotonar [desaßoto'nar] *vt* to unbutton, undo; **~se** *vr* to come undone

desabrido, a [desa'ßriðo, a] *adj* (*comida*) insipid, tasteless; (*persona*) rude, surly; (*respuesta*) sharp; (*tiempo*) unpleasant

desabrochar [desaßro'tʃar] *vt* (*botones, broches*) to undo, unfasten; **~se** *vr* (*ropa etc*) to come undone

desacato [desa'kato] *nm* (*falta de respeto*) disrespect; (*JUR*) contempt

desacertado, a [desaθer'taðo, a] *adj* (*equivocado*) mistaken; (*inoportuno*) unwise

desacierto [desa'θjerto] *nm* mistake, error

desaconsejado, a [desakonse'xaðo, a] *adj* ill-advised

desaconsejar [desakonse'xar] *vt* to advise against

desacreditar [desakreði'tar] *vt* (*desprestigiar*) to discredit, bring into disrepute; (*denigrar*) to run down

desacuerdo [desa'kwerðo] *nm* disagreement, discord

desafiar [desa'fjar] *vt* (*retar*) to challenge; (*enfrentarse a*) to defy

desafilado, a [desafi'laðo, a] *adj* blunt

desafinado, a [desafi'naðo, a] *adj*: **estar ~** to be out of tune

desafinar [desafi'nar] *vi* (*al cantar*) to be o go out of tune

desafío *etc* [desa'fio] *vb ver* **desafiar**
♦ *nm* (*reto*) challenge; (*combate*) duel; (*resistencia*) defiance

desaforado, a [desafo'raðo, a] *adj* (*grito*) ear-splitting; (*comportamiento*) outrageous

desafortunadamente [desafortunaða'mente] *adv* unfortunately

desafortunado, a [desafortu'naðo, a] *adj* (*desgraciado*) unfortunate, unlucky

desagradable [desaɣra'ðaßle] *adj* (*fastidioso, enojoso*) unpleasant; (*irritante*) disagreeable

desagradar [desaɣra'ðar] *vi* (*disgustar*) to displease; (*molestar*) to bother

desagradecido, a [desaɣraðe'θiðo, a] *adj* ungrateful

desagrado [desa'ɣraðo] *nm* (*disgusto*) displeasure; (*contrariedad*) dissatisfaction

desagraviar [desaɣra'ßjar] *vt* to make amends to

desagüe [des'aɣwe] *nm* (*de un líquido*) drainage; (*cañería*) drainpipe; (*salida*) outlet, drain

desaguisado [desaɣi'saðo] *nm* outrage

desahogado, a [desao'ɣaðo, a] *adj* (*holgado*) comfortable; (*espacioso*) roomy, large

desahogar [desao'ɣar] *vt* (*aliviar*) to ease, relieve; (*ira*) to vent; **~se** *vr* (*relajarse*) to relax; (*desfogarse*) to let off steam

desahogo [desa'oxo] *nm* (*alivio*) relief; (*comodidad*) comfort, ease

desahuciar [desau'θjar] *vt* (*enfermo*) to give up hope for; (*inquilino*) to evict;

desahucio nm eviction

desairar [desai'rar] vt (menospreciar) to slight, snub

desaire [des'aire] nm (menosprecio) slight; (falta de garbo) unattractiveness

desajustar [desaxus'tar] vt (desarreglar) to disarrange; (desconcertar) to throw off balance; **~se** vr to get out of order; (aflojarse) to loosen

desajuste [desa'xuste] nm (de máquina) disorder; (situación) imbalance

desalentador, a [desalenta'ðor, a] adj discouraging

desalentar [desalen'tar] vt (desanimar) to discourage

desaliento etc [desa'ljento] vb ver **desalentar ♦** nm discouragement

desaliño [desa'liɲo] nm slovenliness

desalmado, a [desal'maðo, a] adj (cruel) cruel, heartless

desalojar [desalo'xar] vt (expulsar, echar) to eject; (abandonar) to move out of **♦** vi to move out

desamor [desa'mor] nm (frialdad) indifference; (odio) dislike

desamparado, a [desampa'raðo, a] adj (persona) helpless; (lugar: expuesto) exposed; (desierto) deserted

desamparar [desampa'rar] vt (abandonar) to desert, abandon; (JUR) to leave defenceless; (barco) to abandon

desandar [desan'dar] vt: **lo andado** o **el camino** to retrace one's steps

desangrar [desan'grar] vt to bleed; (fig: persona) to bleed dry; **~se** vr to lose a lot of blood

desanimado, a [desani'maðo, a] adj (persona) downhearted; (espectáculo, fiesta) dull

desanimar [desani'mar] vt (desalentar) to discourage; (deprimir) to depress; **~se** vr to lose heart

desapacible [desapa'θiβle] adj (gen) unpleasant

desaparecer [desapare'θer] vi (gen) to disappear; (el sol, la luz) to vanish; **desaparecido, a** adj missing; **desaparición** nf disappearance

desapasionado, a [desapasjo'naðo, a] adj dispassionate, impartial

desapego [desa'pexo] nm (frialdad) coolness; (distancia) detachment

desapercibido, a [desaperθi'βiðo, a] adj (desprevenido) unprepared; **pasar ~** to go unnoticed

desaprensivo, a [desapren'siβo, a] adj unscrupulous

desaprobar [desapro'βar] vt (reprobar) to disapprove of; (condenar) to condemn; (no consentir) to reject

desaprovechado, a [desaproβe'tʃaðo, a] adj (oportunidad, tiempo) wasted; (estudiante) slack

desaprovechar [desaproβe'tʃar] vt to waste

desarmar [desar'mar] vt (MIL, fig) to disarm; (TEC) to take apart, dismantle; **desarme** nm disarmament

desarraigar [desarrai'xar] vt to uproot; **desarraigo** nm uprooting

desarreglar [desarre'xlar] vt (desordenar) to disarrange; (trastocar) to upset, disturb

desarreglo [desa'rrexlo] nm (de casa, persona) untidiness; (desorden) disorder

desarrollar [desarro'ʎar] vt (gen) to develop; **~se** vr to develop; (ocurrir) to take place; (FOTO) to develop; **desarrollo** nm development

desarticular [desartiku'lar] vt (hueso) to dislocate; (objeto) to take apart; (fig) to break up

desasir [desa'sir] vt to loosen

desasosegar [desasose'xar] vt (inquietar) to disturb, make uneasy; **~se** vr to become uneasy

desasosiego etc [desaso'sjexo] vb ver **desasosegar ♦** nm (intranquilidad) uneasiness, restlessness; (ansiedad) anxiety

desastrado, a [desas'traðo, a] adj

(*desaliñado*) shabby; (*sucio*) dirty

desastre [de'sastre] *nm* disaster;
desastroso, a *adj* disastrous

desatado, a [desa'taðo, a] *adj*
(*desligado*) untied; (*violento*) violent,
wild

desatar [desa'tar] *vt* (*nudo*) to untie;
(*paquete*) to undo; (*separar*) to detach;
~se *vr* (*zapatos*) to come untied;
(*tormenta*) to break

desatascar [desatas'kar] *vt* (*cañería*) to
unblock, clear

desatender [desaten'der] *vt* (*no
prestar atención a*) to disregard;
(*abandonar*) to neglect

desatento, a [desa'tento, a] *adj*
(*distraído*) inattentive; (*descortés*)
discourteous

desatinado, a [desati'naðo, a] *adj*
foolish, silly; **desatino** *nm* (*idiotez*)
foolishness, folly; (*error*) blunder

desatornillar [desatorni'ʎar] *vt* to
unscrew

desatrancar [desatran'kar] *vt* (*puerta*)
to unbolt; (*cañería*) to clear, unblock

desautorizado, a [desautori'θaðo, a]
adj unauthorized

desautorizar [desautori'θar] *vt*
(*oficial*) to deprive of authority;
(*informe*) to deny

desavenencia [desaβe'nenθja] *nf*
(*desacuerdo*) disagreement;
(*discrepancia*) quarrel

desayunar [desaju'nar] *vi* to have
breakfast ♦ *vt* to have for breakfast;
desayuno *nm* breakfast

desazón [desa'θon] *nf* anxiety

desazonarse [desaθo'narse] *vr* to
worry, be anxious

desbandarse [desβan'darse] *vr* (*MIL*)
to disband; (*fig*) to flee in disorder

desbarajuste [desβara'xuste] *nm*
confusion, disorder

desbaratar [desβara'tar] *vt* (*deshacer*,
destruir) to ruin

desbloquear [desβloke'ar] *vt*
(*negociaciones*, *tráfico*) to get going

again; (*COM*: *cuenta*) to unfreeze

desbocado, a [desβo'kaðo, a] *adj*
(*caballo*) runaway

desbordar [desβor'ðar] *vt* (*sobrepasar*)
to go beyond; (*exceder*) to exceed; **~se**
vr (*río*) to overflow; (*entusiasmo*) to
erupt

descabalgar [deskaβal'var] *vi* to
dismount

descabellado, a [deskaβe'ʎaðo, a]
adj (*disparatado*) wild, crazy

descafeinado, a [deskafei'naðo, a]
adj decaffeinated ♦ *nm* decaffeinated
coffee

descalabro [deska'laβro] *nm* blow;
(*desgracia*) misfortune

descalificar [deskalifi'kar] *vt* to
disqualify; (*desacreditar*) to discredit

descalzar [deskal'θar] *vt* (*zapato*) to
take off; **descalzo, a** *adj* barefoot(ed)

descambiar [deskam'bjar] *vt* to
exchange

descaminado, a [deskami'naðo, a]
adj (*equivocado*) on the wrong road;
(*fig*) misguided

descampado [deskam'paðo] *nm* open
space

descansado, a [deskan'saðo, a] *adj*
(*gen*) rested; (*que tranquiliza*) restful

descansar [deskan'sar] *vt* (*gen*) to rest
♦ *vi* to rest, have a rest; (*echarse*) to lie
down

descansillo [deskan'siʎo] *nm* (*de
escalera*) landing

descanso [des'kanso] *nm* (*reposo*) rest;
(*alivio*) relief; (*pausa*) break; (*DEPORTE*)
interval, half time

descapotable [deskapo'taßle] *nm* (*tb*:
coche ~) convertible

descarado, a [deska'raðo, a] *adj*
shameless; (*insolente*) cheeky

descarga [des'karva] *nf* (*ARQ*, *ELEC*,
MIL) discharge; (*NAUT*) unloading

descargar [deskar'var] *vt* to unload;
(*golpe*) to let fly; **~se** *vr* to unburden
o.s.; **descargo** *nm* (*COM*) receipt; (*JUR*)
evidence

descaro [des'karo] *nm* nerve

descarriar [deska'rrjar] *vt* (*descaminar*)
to misdirect; (*fig*) to lead astray; **~se** *vr*
(*perderse*) to lose one's way; (*separarse*)
to stray; (*pervertirse*) to err, go astray

descarrilamiento [deskarrila'mjento]
nm (*de tren*) derailment

descarrilar [deskarri'lar] *vi* to be
derailed

descartar [deskar'tar] *vt* (*rechazar*) to
reject; (*eliminar*) to rule out; **~se** *vr*
(*NAIPES*) to discard; **~se de** to shirk

descascarillado, a [deskaskari'ʎaðo,
a] *adj* (*paredes*) peeling

descendencia [desθen'denθja] *nf*
(*origen*) origin, descent; (*hijos*)
offspring

descender [desθen'der] *vt* (*bajar*:
escalera) to go down ♦ *vi* to descend;
(*temperatura, nivel*) to fall, drop; **~ de**
to be descended from

descendiente [desθen'djente] *nm/f*
descendant

descenso [des'θenso] *nm* descent; (*de
temperatura*) drop

descifrar [desθi'frar] *vt* to decipher;
(*mensaje*) to decode

descolgar [deskol'xar] *vt* (*bajar*) to
take down; (*teléfono*) to pick up; **~se**
vr to let o.s. down

descolorido, a [deskolo'riðo, a] *adj*
faded; (*pálido*) pale

descompasado, a [deskompa'saðo,
a] *adj* (*sin proporción*) out of all
proportion; (*excesivo*) excessive

descomponer [deskompo'ner] *vt*
(*desordenar*) to disarrange, disturb;
(*TEC*) to put out of order; (*dividir*) to
break down (into parts); (*fig*) to
provoke; **~se** *vr* (*corromperse*) to rot,
decompose; (*TEC*) to break down

descomposición [deskomposi'θjon]
nf (*de un objeto*) breakdown; (*de fruta
etc*) decomposition; **~ de vientre**
stomach upset, diarrhoea

descompuesto, a [deskom'pwesto,
a] *adj* (*corrompido*) decomposed; (*roto*)
broken

descomunal [deskomu'nal] *adj*
(*enorme*) huge

desconcertado, a [deskonθer'taðo,
a] *adj* disconcerted, bewildered

desconcertar [deskonθer'tar] *vt*
(*confundir*) to baffle; (*incomodar*) to
upset, put out; **~se** *vr* (*turbarse*) to be
upset

desconchado, a [deskon'tʃaðo, a] *adj*
(*pintura*) peeling

desconcierto *etc* [deskon'θjerto] *vb*
ver **desconcertar** ♦ *nm* (*gen*) disorder;
(*desorientación*) uncertainty; (*inquietud*)
uneasiness

desconectar [deskonek'tar] *vt* to
disconnect

desconfianza [deskon'fjanθa] *nf*
distrust

desconfiar [deskon'fjar] *vi* to be
distrustful; **~ de** to distrust, suspect

descongelar [deskonxe'lar] *vt* to
defrost; (*COM, POL*) to unfreeze

descongestionar [deskonxestjo'nar]
vt (*cabeza, tráfico*) to clear

desconocer [deskono'θer] *vt* (*ignorar*)
not to know, to be ignorant of

desconocido, a [deskono'θiðo, a] *adj*
unknown ♦ *nm/f* stranger

desconocimiento [deskonoθi'
mjento] *nm* (*falta de conocimientos*)
ignorance

desconsiderado, a [deskonsiðe'raðo,
a] *adj* inconsiderate; (*insensible*)
thoughtless

desconsolar [deskonso'lar] *vt* to
distress; **~se** *vr* to despair

desconsuelo *etc* [deskon'swelo] *vb*
ver **desconsolar** ♦ *nm* (*tristeza*)
distress; (*desesperación*) despair

descontado, a [deskon'taðo, a] *adj*:
dar por ~ (que) to take (it) for
granted (that)

descontar [deskon'tar] *vt* (*deducir*) to
take away, deduct; (*rebajar*) to
discount

descontento, a [deskon'tento, a] *adj*

dissatisfied ♦ *nm* dissatisfaction, discontent

descorazonar [deskoraθo'nar] *vt* to discourage, dishearten

descorchar [deskor'tʃar] *vt* to uncork

descorrer [desko'rrer] *vt* (*cortinas, cerrojo*) to draw back

descortés [deskor'tes] *adj* (*mal educado*) discourteous; (*grosero*) rude

descoser [desko'ser] *vt* to unstitch; **~se** *vr* to come apart (at the seams)

descosido, a [desko'siðo, a] *adj* (*COSTURA*) unstitched

descrédito [des'kreðito] *nm* discredit

descreído, a [deskre'iðo, a] *adj* (*incrédulo*) incredulous; (*falto de fe*) unbelieving

descremado, a [deskre'maðo, a] *adj* skimmed

describir [deskri'βir] *vt* to describe; **descripción** [deskrip'θjon] *nf* description

descrito [des'krito] *pp de* **describir**

descuartizar [deskwarti'θar] *vt* (*animal*) to cut up

descubierto, a [desku'βjerto, a] *pp de* **descubrir** ♦ *adj* uncovered, bare; (*persona*) bareheaded ♦ *nm* (*bancario*) overdraft; **al ~** in the open

descubrimiento [deskuβri'mjento] *nm* (*hallazgo*) discovery; (*revelación*) revelation

descubrir [desku'βrir] *vt* to discover, find; (*inaugurar*) to unveil; (*vislumbrar*) to detect; (*revelar*) to reveal, show; (*destapar*) to uncover; **~se** *vr* to reveal o.s.; (*quitarse sombrero*) to take off one's hat; (*confesar*) to confess

descuento *etc* [des'kwento] *vb ver* **descontar** ♦ *nm* discount

descuidado, a [deskwi'ðaðo, a] *adj* (*sin cuidado*) careless; (*desordenado*) untidy; (*olvidadizo*) forgetful; (*desprevenido*) unprepared

descuidar [deskwi'ðar] *vt* (*dejar*) to neglect; (*olvidar*) to overlook; **~se** *vr* (*distraerse*) to be careless;

(*abandonarse*) to let o.s. go; (*desprevenirse*) to drop one's guard; **¡descuida!** don't worry!; **descuido** *nm* (*dejadez*) carelessness; (*olvido*) negligence

---

PALABRA CLAVE

---

desde ['desðe] *prep* **1** (*lugar*) from; **~ Burgos hasta mi casa hay 30 km** it's 30 kms from Burgos to my house
2 (*posición*): **hablaba ~ el balcón** she was speaking from the balcony
3 (*tiempo: + ad, n*): **~ ahora** from now on; **~ la boda** since the wedding; **~ niño** since I *etc* was a child; **~ 3 años atrás** since 3 years ago
4 (*tiempo: + vb, fecha*) since; for; **nos conocemos ~ 1992/ ~ hace 20 años** we've known each other since 1992/for 20 years; **no le veo ~ 1997/~ hace 5 años** I haven't seen him since 1997/for 5 years
5 (*gama*): **~ los más lujosos hasta los más económicos** from the most luxurious to the most reasonably priced
6: **~ luego (que no)** of course (not)
♦ *conj*: **~ que**: **~ que recuerdo** for as long as I can remember; **~ que llegó no ha salido** he hasn't been out since he arrived

---

desdecirse [desðe'θirse] *vr* to retract; **~ de** to go back on

desdén [des'ðen] *nm* scorn

desdeñar [desðe'nar] *vt* (*despreciar*) to scorn

desdicha [des'ðitʃa] *nf* (*desgracia*) misfortune; (*infelicidad*) unhappiness; **desdichado, a** *adj* (*sin suerte*) unlucky; (*infeliz*) unhappy

desdoblar [desðo'βlar] *vt* (*extender*) to spread out; (*desplegar*) to unfold

desear [dese'ar] *vt* to want, desire, wish for

desecar [dese'kar] *vt* to dry up; **~se** *vr* to dry up

desechar [dese'tʃar] vt (basura) to throw out o away; (ideas) to reject, discard; **desechos** nmpl rubbish sg, waste sg

desembalar [desemba'lar] vt to unpack

desembarazar [desembara'θar] vt (desocupar) to clear; (desenredar) to free; **~se** vr: **~se de** to free o.s. of, get rid of

desembarcar [desembar'kar] vt (mercancías etc) to unload ♦ vi to disembark; **~se** vr to disembark

desembocadura [desemboka'ðura] nf (de río) mouth; (de calle) opening

desembocar [desembo'kar] vi (río) to flow into; (fig) to result in

desembolso [desem'bolso] nm payment

desembragar [desembra'ɣar] vi to declutch

desembrollar [desembro'ʎar] vt (madeja) to unravel; (asunto, malentendido) to sort out

desemejanza [deseme'xanθa] nf dissimilarity

desempaquetar [desempake'tar] vt (regalo) to unwrap; (mercancía) to unpack

desempatar [desempa'tar] vi to replay, hold a play-off; **desempate** nm (FÚTBOL) replay, play-off; (TENIS) tie-break(er)

desempeñar [desempe'ɲar] vt (cargo) to hold; (papel) to perform; (lo empeñado) to redeem; **~ un papel** (fig) to play a role)

desempeño [desem'peɲo] nm redeeming; (de cargo) occupation

desempleado, a [desemple'aðo, a] nm/f unemployed person; **desempleo** nm unemployment

desempolvar [desempol'βar] vt (muebles etc) to dust; (lo olvidado) to revive

desencadenar [desenkaðe'nar] vt to unchain; (ira) to unleash; **~se** vr to

break loose; (tormenta) to burst; (guerra) to break out

desencajar [desenka'xar] vt (hueso) to dislocate; (mecanismo, pieza) to disconnect, disengage

desencanto [desen'kanto] nm disillusionment

desenchufar [desentʃu'far] vt to unplug

desenfadado, a [desenfa'ðaðo, a] adj (desenvuelto) uninhibited; (descarado) forward; **desenfado** nm (libertad) freedom; (comportamiento) free and easy manner; (descaro) forwardness

desenfocado, a [desenfo'kaðo, a] adj (FOTO) out of focus

desenfrenado, a [desenfre'naðo, a] adj (descontrolado) uncontrolled; (inmoderado) unbridled; **desenfreno** nm wildness; (de las pasiones) lack of self-control

desenganchar [desengan'tʃar] vt (gen) to unhook; (FERRO) to uncouple

desengañar [desenga'ɲar] vt to disillusion; **~se** vr to become disillusioned; **desengaño** nm disillusionment; (decepción) disappointment

desenlace [desen'laθe] nm outcome

desenmarañar [desenmara'ɲar] vt (fig) to unravel

desenmascarar [desenmaska'rar] vt to unmask

desenredar [desenre'ðar] vt (pelo) to untangle; (problema) to sort out

desenroscar [desenros'kar] vt to unscrew

desentenderse [desenten'derse] vr: **~ de** to pretend not to know about; (apartarse) to have nothing to do with

desenterrar [desente'rrar] vt (tesoro, fig) to unearth, dig up

desentonar [desento'nar] vi (MÚS) to sing (o play) out of tune; (color) to clash

desentrañar [desentra'ɲar] vt (misterio) to unravel

desentumecer [desentume'θer] vt
(pierna etc) to stretch

desenvoltura [desenβol'tura] nf ease

desenvolver [desenβol'βer] vt
(paquete) to unwrap; (fig) to develop;
~**se** vr (desarrollarse) to unfold,
develop; (arreglárselas) to cope

deseo [de'seo] nm desire, wish; ~**so, a**
adj: **estar** ~**so de** to be anxious to

desequilibrado, a [desekili'βraðo, a]
adj unbalanced

desertar [deser'tar] vi to desert

desértico, a [de'sertiko, a] adj desert
cpd

desesperación [desespera'θjon] nf
(impaciencia) desperation, despair;
(irritación) fury

desesperar [desespe'rar] vt to drive to
despair; (exasperar) to drive to
distraction ♦ vi: ~ **de** to despair of;
~**se** vr to despair, lose hope

desestabilizar [desestaβili'θar] vt to
destabilize

desestimar [desesti'mar] vt
(menospreciar) to have a low opinion
of; (rechazar) to reject

desfachatez [desfatʃa'teθ] nf
(insolencia) impudence; (descaro)
rudeness

desfalco [des'falko] nm embezzlement

desfallecer [desfaʎe'θer] vi (perder las
fuerzas) to become weak;
(desvanecerse) to faint

desfasado, a [desfa'saðo, a] adj
(anticuado) old-fashioned; **desfase** nm
(diferencia) gap

desfavorable [desfaβo'raβle] adj
unfavourable

desfigurar [desfixu'rar] vt (cara) to
disfigure; (cuerpo) to deform

desfiladero [desfila'ðero] nm gorge

desfilar [desfi'lar] vi to parade; **desfile**
nm procession

desfogarse [desfo'xarse] vr (fig) to let
off steam

desgajar [desxa'xar] vt (arrancar) to
tear off; (romper) to break off; ~**se** vr

to come off

desgana [des'xana] nf (falta de apetito)
loss of appetite; (apatía) unwillingness;
~**do, a** adj: **estar** ~**do** (sin apetito) to
have no appetite; (sin entusiasmo) to
have lost interest

desgarrador, a [desxarra'ðor, a] adj
(fig) heartrending

desgarrar [desxa'rrar] vt to tear (up);
(fig) to shatter; **desgarro** nm (en tela)
tear; (aflicción) grief

desgastar [desxas'tar] vt (deteriorar) to
wear away o down; (estropear) to spoil;
~**se** vr to get worn out; **desgaste** nm
wear (and tear)

desglosar [desxlo'sar] vt (factura) to
break down

desgracia [des'xraθja] nf misfortune;
(accidente) accident; (vergüenza)
disgrace; (contratiempo) setback; **por** ~
unfortunately

desgraciado, a [desxra'θjaðo, a] adj
(sin suerte) unlucky, unfortunate;
(miserable) wretched; (infeliz) miserable

desgravación [desxraβa'θjon] nf
(COM): ~ **fiscal** tax relief

desgravar [desxra'βar] vt (impuestos)
to reduce the tax o duty on

deshabitado, a [desaβi'taðo, a] adj
uninhabited

deshacer [desa'θer] vt (casa) to break
up; (TEC) to take apart; (enemigo) to
defeat; (diluir) to melt; (contrato) to
break; (intriga) to solve; ~**se** vr
(disolverse) to melt; (despedazarse) to
come apart o undone; ~**se de** to get
rid of; ~**se en lágrimas** to burst into
tears

desharrapado, a [desarra'paðo, a]
adj (persona) shabby

deshecho, a [des'etʃo, a] adj undone;
(roto) smashed; (persona): **estar** ~ to
be shattered

desheredar [desere'ðar] vt to
disinherit

deshidratar [desiðra'tar] vt to
dehydrate

deshielo [des'jelo] *nm* thaw

deshonesto, a [deso'nesto, a] *adj* indecent

deshonra [des'onra] *nf* (*deshonor*) dishonour; (*vergüenza*) shame

deshora [des'ora]: **a ~** *adv* at the wrong time

deshuesar [deswe'sar] *vt* (*carne*) to bone; (*fruta*) to stone

desierto, a [de'sjerto, a] *adj* (*casa, calle, negocio*) deserted ♦ *nm* desert

designar [desiv'nar] *vt* (*nombrar*) to designate; (*indicar*) to fix

designio [de'sivnjo] *nm* plan

desigual [desi'wwal] *adj* (*terreno*) uneven; (*lucha etc*) unequal

desilusión [desilu'sjon] *nf* disillusionment; (*decepción*) disappointment; **desilusionar** *vt* to disillusion; to disappoint; **desilusionarse** *vr* to become disillusioned

desinfectar [desinfek'tar] *vt* to disinfect

desinflar [desin'flar] *vt* to deflate

desintegración [desintevra'θjon] *nf* disintegration

desinterés [desinte'res] *nm* (*desgana*) lack of interest; (*altruismo*) unselfishness

desintoxicarse [desintoksi'karse] *vr* (*drogadicto*) to undergo detoxification

desistir [desis'tir] *vi* (*renunciar*) to stop, desist

desleal [desle'al] *adj* (*infiel*) disloyal; (*COM: competencia*) unfair; **~tad** *nf* disloyalty

desleír [desle'ir] *vt* (*líquido*) to dilute; (*sólido*) to dissolve

deslenguado, a [deslen'gwaðo, a] *adj* (*grosero*) foul-mouthed

desligar [desli'var] *vt* (*desatar*) to untie, undo; (*separar*) to separate; **~se** *vr* (*de un compromiso*) to extricate o.s.

desliz [des'liθ] *nm* (*fig*) lapse; **~ar** *vt* to slip, slide

deslucido, a [deslu'θiðo, a] *adj* dull;

(*torpe*) awkward, graceless; (*deslustrado*) tarnished

deslumbrar [deslum'brar] *vt* to dazzle

desmadrarse [desma'ðrarse] (*fam*) *vr* (*descontrolarse*) to run wild; (*divertirse*) to let one's hair down; **desmadre** (*fam*) *nm* (*desorganización*) chaos; (*jaleo*) commotion

desmán [des'man] *nm* (*exceso*) outrage; (*abuso de poder*) abuse

desmandarse [desman'darse] *vr* (*portarse mal*) to behave badly; (*excederse*) to get out of hand; (*caballo*) to bolt

desmantelar [desmante'lar] *vt* (*deshacer*) to dismantle; (*casa*) to strip

desmaquillador [desmakiʎa'ðor] *nm* make-up remover

desmayar [desma'jar] *vi* to lose heart; **~se** *vr* (MED) to faint; **desmayo** *nm* (MED: *acto*) faint; (: *estado*) unconsciousness

desmedido, a [desme'ðiðo, a] *adj* excessive

desmejorar [desmexo'rar] *vt* (*dañar*) to impair, spoil; (MED) to weaken

desmembrar [desmem'brar] *vt* (MED) to dismember; (*fig*) to separate

desmemoriado, a [desmemo'rjaðo, a] *adj* forgetful

desmentir [desmen'tir] *vt* (*contradecir*) to contradict; (*refutar*) to deny

desmenuzar [desmenu'θar] *vt* (*deshacer*) to crumble; (*carne*) to chop; (*examinar*) to examine closely

desmerecer [desmere'θer] *vt* to be unworthy of ♦ *vi* (*deteriorarse*) to deteriorate

desmesurado, a [desmesu'raðo, a] *adj* disproportionate

desmontable [desmon'taßle] *adj* (*que se quita: pieza*) detachable; (*que se puede plegar etc*) collapsible, folding

desmontar [desmon'tar] *vt* (*deshacer*) to dismantle; (*tierra*) to level ♦ *vi* to dismount

desmoralizar [desmorali'θar] *vt* to

demoralize

desmoronar [desmoro'nar] vt to wear away, erode; **~se** vr (edificio, dique) to collapse; (economía) to decline

desnatado, a [desna'taðo, a] adj skimmed

desnivel [desni'ßel] nm (de terreno) unevenness

desnudar [desnu'ðar] vt (desvestir) to undress; (despojar) to strip; **~se** vr (desvestirse) to get undressed; **desnudo, a** adj naked ♦ nm/f nude; **desnudo de** devoid or bereft of

desnutrición [desnutri'θjon] nf malnutrition; **desnutrido, a** adj undernourished

desobedecer [desoßeðe'θer] vt, vi to disobey; **desobediencia** nf disobedience

desocupado, a [desoku'paðo, a] adj at leisure; (desempleado) unemployed; (deshabitado) empty, vacant

desocupar [desoku'par] vt to vacate

desodorante [desoðo'rante] nm deodorant

desolación [desola'θjon] nf (de lugar) desolation; (fig) grief

desolar [deso'lar] vt to ruin, lay waste

desorbitado, a [desorßi'taðo, a] adj (excesivo: ambición) boundless; (deseos) excessive; (: precio) exorbitant

desorden [des'orðen] nm confusion; (político) disorder, unrest

desorganizar [desorγani'θar] vt (desordenar) to disorganize; **desorganización** nf (de persona) disorganization; (en empresa, oficina) disorder, chaos

desorientar [desorjen'tar] vt (extraviar) to mislead; (confundir, desconcertar) to confuse; **~se** vr (perderse) to lose one's way

despabilado, a [despaßi'laðo, a] adj (despierto) wide-awake; (fig) alert, sharp

despabilar [despaßi'lar] vt (el ingenio) to sharpen ♦ vi to wake up; (fig) to get

a move on; **~se** vr to wake up; to get a move on

despachar [despa'tʃar] vt (negocio) to do, complete; (enviar) to send, dispatch; (vender) to sell, deal in; (billete) to issue; (mandar ir) to send away

despacho [des'patʃo] nm (oficina) office; (de paquetes) dispatch; (venta) sale; (comunicación) message

despacio [des'paθjo] adv slowly

desparpajo [despar'paxo] nm self-confidence; (pey) nerve

desparramar [desparra'mar] vt (esparcir) to scatter; (líquido) to spill

despavorido, a [despaßo'riðo, a] adj terrified

despecho [des'petʃo] nm spite; **a ~ de** in spite of

despectivo, a [despek'tißo, a] adj (despreciativo) derogatory; (LING) pejorative

despedazar [despeða'θar] vt to tear to pieces

despedida [despe'ðiða] nf (adiós) farewell; (de obrero) sacking

despedir [despe'ðir] vt (visita) to see off, show out; (empleado) to dismiss; (inquilino) to evict; (objeto) to hurl; (olor etc) to give out o off; **~se** vr: **~se de** to say goodbye to

despegar [despe'γar] vt to unstick ♦ vi (avión) to take off; **~se** vr to come loose, come unstuck; **despego** nm detachment

despegue etc [des'peγe] vb ver **despegar** ♦ nm takeoff

despeinado, a [despei'naðo, a] adj dishevelled, unkempt

despejado, a [despe'xaðo, a] adj (lugar) clear, free; (cielo) clear; (persona) wide-awake, bright

despejar [despe'xar] vt (gen) to clear; (misterio) to clear up ♦ vi (el tiempo) to clear; **~se** vr (tiempo, cielo) to become clearer; (cabeza) to clear

despellejar [despeʎe'xar] *vt* (*animal*) to skin

despensa [des'pensa] *nf* larder

despeñadero [despeɲa'ðero] *nm* (*GEO*) cliff, precipice

despeñarse [despe'ɲarse] *vr* to hurl o.s. down; (*coche*) to tumble over

desperdicio [desper'ðiθjo] *nm* (*despilfarro*) squandering; **~s** *nmpl* (*basura*) rubbish *sg* (*BRIT*), garbage *sg* (*US*); (*residuos*) waste *sg*

desperdigarse [desperði'varse] *vr* (*rebaño, familia*) to scatter, spread out; (*granos de arroz, semillas*) to scatter

desperezarse [despere'θarse] *vr* to stretch

desperfecto [desper'fekto] *nm* (*deterioro*) slight damage; (*defecto*) flaw, imperfection

despertador [desperta'ðor] *nm* alarm clock

despertar [desper'tar] *nm* awakening ♦ *vt* (*persona*) to wake up; (*recuerdos*) to revive; (*sentimiento*) to arouse ♦ *vi* to awaken, wake up; **~se** *vr* to awaken, wake up

despiadado, a [despja'ðaðo, a] *adj* (*ataque*) merciless; (*persona*) heartless

despido *etc* [des'piðo] *vb ver* **despedir** ♦ *nm* dismissal, sacking

despierto, a *etc* [des'pjerto, a] *vb ver* **despertar** ♦ *adj* awake; (*fig*) sharp, alert

despilfarro [despil'farro] *nm* (*derroche*) squandering; (*lujo desmedido*) extravagance

despistar [despis'tar] *vt* to throw off the track o scent; (*confundir*) to mislead, confuse; **~se** *vr* to take the wrong road; (*confundirse*) to become confused

despiste [des'piste] *nm* absent-mindedness; **un ~** a mistake, slip

desplazamiento [desplaθa'mjento] *nm* displacement

desplazar [despla'θar] *vt* to move; (*NAUT*) to displace; (*INFORM*) to scroll; (*fig*) to oust; **~se** *vr* (*persona*) to travel

desplegar [desple'var] *vt* (*tela, papel*) to unfold, open out; (*bandera*) to unfurl; **despliegue** *etc* [des'plexe] *vb ver* **desplegar** ♦ *nm* display

desplomarse [desplo'marse] *vr* (*edificio, gobierno, persona*) to collapse

desplumar [desplu'mar] *vt* (*ave*) to pluck; (*fam: estafar*) to fleece

despoblado, a [despo'βlaðo, a] *adj* (*sin habitantes*) uninhabited

despojar [despo'xar] *vt* (*alguien: de sus bienes*) to divest of, deprive of; (*casa*) to strip, leave bare; (*alguien: de su cargo*) to strip of

despojo [des'poxo] *nm* (*acto*) plundering; (*objetos*) plunder, loot; **~s** *nmpl* (*de ave, res*) offal *sg*

desposado, a [despo'saðo, a] *adj, nm/f* newly-wed

desposar [despo'sar] *vt* to marry; **~se** *vr* to get married

desposeer [despose'er] *vt*: **~ a uno de** (*puesto, autoridad*) to strip sb of

déspota ['despota] *nm/f* despot

despreciar [despre'θjar] *vt* (*desdeñar*) to despise, scorn; (*afrentar*) to slight; **desprecio** *nm* scorn, contempt; slight

desprender [despren'der] *vt* (*broche*) to unfasten; (*olor*) to give off; **~se** *vr* (*botón: caerse*) to fall off; (*broche*) to come unfastened; (*olor, perfume*) to be given off; **~se de algo que ...** to draw from sth that ...

desprendimiento [desprendi'mjento] *nm* (*gen*) loosening; (*generosidad*) disinterestedness; (*de tierra, rocas*) landslide

despreocupado, a [despreoku'paðo, a] *adj* (*sin preocupación*) unworried, nonchalant; (*negligente*) careless

despreocuparse [despreoku'parse] *vr* not to worry; **~ de** to have no interest in

desprestigiar [despresti'xjar] *vt* (*criticar*) to run down; (*desacreditar*) to discredit

desprevenido, a [despreße'niðo, a] *adj* (*no preparado*) unprepared, unready

desproporcionado, a [despropor'θjo'naðo, a] *adj* disproportionate, out of proportion

desprovisto, a [despro'ßisto, a] *adj*: ~ **de** devoid of

después [des'pwes] *adv* afterwards, later; (*próximo paso*) next; ~ **de comer** after lunch; **un año** ~ a year later; ~ **se debatió el tema** next the matter was discussed; ~ **de corregido el texto** after the text had been corrected; ~ **de todo** after all

desquiciado, a [deski'θjaðo, a] *adj* deranged

desquite [des'kite] *nm* (*satisfacción*) satisfaction; (*venganza*) revenge

destacar [desta'kar] *vt* (*enfatizar*) to emphasize, point up; (MIL) to detach ♦ *vi* (*resaltarse*) to stand out; (*persona*) to be outstanding o exceptional; **~se** *vr* to stand out; to be outstanding o exceptional

destajo [des'taxo] *nm*: **trabajar a ~** to do piecework

destapar [desta'par] *vt* (*botella*) to open; (*cacerola*) to take the lid off; (*descubrir*) to uncover; **~se** *vr* (*revelarse*) to reveal one's true character

destartalado, a [destarta'laðo, a] *adj* (*desordenado*) untidy; (*ruinoso*) tumbledown

destello [des'teʎo] *nm* (*de estrella*) twinkle, flash; (*de faro*) signal light

destemplado, a [destem'plaðo, a] *adj* (MUS) out of tune; (*voz*) harsh; (MED) out of sorts; (*tiempo*) unpleasant, nasty

desteñir [deste'nir] *vt* to fade ♦ *vi* to fade; **~se** *vr* to fade; **esta tela no destiñe** this fabric will not run

desternillarse [desterni'ʎarse] *vr*: ~ **de risa** to split one's sides laughing

desterrar [deste'rrar] *vt* (*exilar*) to

exile; (*fig*) to banish, dismiss

destiempo [des'tjempo]: **a ~** *adv* out of turn

destierro *etc* [des'tjerro] *vb ver* **desterrar** ♦ *nm* exile

destilar [desti'lar] *vt* to distil; **destilería** *nf* distillery

destinar [desti'nar] *vt* (*funcionario*) to appoint, assign; (*fondos*): ~ **(a)** to set aside (for)

destinatario, a [destina'tarjo, a] *nm/f* addressee

destino [des'tino] *nm* (*suerte*) destiny; (*de avión, viajero*) destination

destituir [destitu'ir] *vt* to dismiss

destornillador [destorniʎa'ðor] *nm* screwdriver

destornillar [destorni'ʎar] *vt* (*tornillo*) to unscrew; **~se** *vr* to unscrew

destreza [des'treθa] *nf* (*habilidad*) skill; (*maña*) dexterity

destrozar [destro'θar] *vt* (*romper*) to smash, break (up); (*estropear*) to ruin; (*nervios*) to shatter

destrozo [des'troθo] *nm* (*acción*) destruction; (*desastre*) smashing; **~s** *nmpl* (*pedazos*) pieces; (*daños*) havoc *sg*

destrucción [destruk'θjon] *nf* destruction

destruir [destru'ir] *vt* to destroy

desuso [des'uso] *nm* disuse; **caer en ~** to become obsolete

desvalido, a [desßa'liðo, a] *adj* (*desprotegido*) destitute; (*sin fuerzas*) helpless

desvalijar [desvali'xar] *vt* (*persona*) to rob; (*casa, tienda*) to burgle; (*coche*) to break into

desván [des'ßan] *nm* attic

desvanecer [desßane'θer] *vt* (*disipar*) to dispel; (*borrar*) to blur; **~se** *vr* (*humo etc*) to vanish, disappear; (*color*) to fade; (*recuerdo, sonido*) to fade away; (MED) to pass out; (*duda*) to be dispelled

desvanecimiento [desßaneθi'mjento| *nm* (*desaparición*) disappearance; (*de colores*) fading; (*evaporación*) evaporation; (MED) fainting fit

desvariar |desβa'rjar| *vi* (*enfermo*) to be delirious; **desvario** *nm* delirium

desvelar |desβe'lar| *vt* to keep awake; **~se** *vr* (*no poder dormir*) to stay awake; (*preocuparse*) to be vigilant *o* watchful

desvelos |des'βelos| *nmpl* worrying *pl*

desvencijado, a |desβenθi'xaðo, a| *adj* (*silla*) rickety; (*máquina*) broken-down

desventaja |desβen'taxa| *nf* disadvantage

desventura |desβen'tura| *nf* misfortune

desvergonzado, a |desβerγon'θaðo, a| *adj* shameless

desvergüenza |desβer'γwenθa| *nf* (*descaro*) shamelessness; (*insolencia*) impudence; (*mala conducta*) effrontery

desvestir |desβes'tir| *vt* to undress; **~se** *vr* to undress

desviación |desβja'θjon| *nf* deviation; (AUTO) diversion, detour

desviar |des'βjar| *vt* to turn aside; (*río*) to alter the course of; (*navío*) to divert, re-route; (*conversación*) to sidetrack; **~se** *vr* (*apartarse del camino*) to turn aside; (: *barco*) to go off course

desvío *etc* |des'βío| *vb ver* **desviar** ♦ *nm* (*desviación*) detour, diversion; (*fig*) indifference

desvirtuar |desβir'twar| *vt* to distort

desvivirse |desβi'βirse| *vr*: **~ por** (*anhelar*) to long for, crave for; (*hacer lo posible por*) to do one's utmost for

detallar |deta'ʎar| *vt* to detail

detalle |de'taʎe| *nm* detail; (*gesto*) gesture, token; **al ~** in detail; (COM) retail

detallista |deta'ʎista| *nm/f* (COM) retailer

detective |detek'tiβe| *nm/f* detective

detener |dete'ner| *vt* (*gen*) to stop; (JUR) to arrest; (*objeto*) to keep; **~se** *vr*

to stop; (*demorarse*): **~se en** to delay over, linger over

detenidamente |deteniða'mente| *adv* (*minuciosamente*) carefully; (*extensamente*) at great length

detenido, a |dete'niðo, a| *adj* (*arrestado*) under arrest ♦ *nm/f* person under arrest, prisoner

detenimiento |deteni'mjento| *nm*: **con ~** thoroughly; (*observar, considerar*) carefully

detergente |deter'xente| *nm* detergent

deteriorar |deterjo'rar| *vt* to spoil, damage; **~se** *vr* to deteriorate; **deterioro** *nm* deterioration

determinación |determina'θjon| *nf* (*empeño*) determination; (*decisión*) decision; **determinado, a** *adj* specific

determinar |determi'nar| *vt* (*plazo*) to fix; (*precio*) to settle; **~se** *vr* to decide

detestar |detes'tar| *vt* to detest

detractor, a |detrak'tor, a| *nm/f* slanderer, libeller

detrás |de'tras| *adv* behind; (*atrás*) at the back; **~ de** behind

detrimento |detri'mento| *nm*: **en ~ de** to the detriment of

deuda |'deuða| *nf* debt

devaluación |deβalwa'θjon| *nf* devaluation

devanar |deβa'nar| *vt* (*destruir*) to devastate

devoción |deβo'θjon| *nf* devotion

devolución |deβolu'θjon| *nf* (*reenvío*) return, sending back; (*reembolso*) repayment; (JUR) devolution

devolver |deβol'βer| *vt* to return; (*lo extraviado, lo prestado*) to give back; (*carta al correo*) to send back; (COM) to repay, refund ♦ *vi* (*vomitar*) to be sick

devorar |deβo'rar| *vt* to devour

devoto, a |de'βoto, a| *adj* devout ♦ *nm/f* admirer

devuelto *pp de* **devolver**

devuelva *etc vb ver* **devolver**

di *vb ver* **dar**; **decir**

día ['dia] nm day; ¿qué ~ es? what's the date?; **estar/poner al** ~ to be/ keep up to date; **el** ~ **de hoy/de mañana** today/tomorrow; **al** ~ **siguiente** (on) the following day; **vivir al** ~ to live from hand to mouth; **de** ~ by day, in daylight; **en pleno** ~ in full daylight; **D~ de Reyes** Epiphany; ~ **festivo** (ESP) o **feriado** (AM) holiday; ~ **libre** day off

diabetes [dja'βetes] nf diabetes

diablo ['djaβlo] nm devil; **diablura** nf prank

diadema [dja'ðema] nf tiara

diafragma [dja'fraɣma] nm diaphragm

diagnosis [djaɣ'nosis] nf inv diagnosis

diagnóstico [djaɣ'nostiko] nm = diagnosis

diagonal [djaɣo'nal] adj diagonal

diagrama [dja'ɣrama] nm diagram; ~ **de flujo** flowchart

dial [djal] nm dial

dialecto [dja'lekto] nm dialect

dialogar [djalo'ɣar] vi: ~ **con** (POL) to hold talks with

diálogo ['djaloɣo] nm dialogue

diamante [dja'mante] nm diamond

diana ['djana] nf (MIL) reveille; (de blanco) centre, bull's-eye

diapositiva [djaposi'tiβa] nf (FOTO) slide, transparency

diario, a ['djarjo, a] adj daily ♦ nm newspaper; **a** ~ daily; **de** ~ everyday

diarrea [dja'rrea] nf diarrhoea

dibujar [diβu'xar] vt to draw, sketch; **dibujo** nm drawing; **dibujos animados** cartoons

diccionario [dikθjo'narjo] nm dictionary

dice etc vb ver **decir**

dicho, a ['ditʃo, a] pp de **decir** ♦ adj: **en ~s países** in the aforementioned countries ♦ nm saying

dichoso, a [di'tʃoso, a] adj happy

diciembre [di'θjembre] nm December

dictado [dik'taðo] nm dictation

dictador [dikta'ðor] nm dictator;

dictadura nf dictatorship

dictamen [dik'tamen] nm (opinión) opinion; (juicio) judgment; (informe) report

dictar [dik'tar] vt (carta) to dictate; (JUR: sentencia) to pronounce; (decreto) to issue; (AM: clase) to give

didáctico, a [di'ðaktiko, a] adj educational

diecinueve [djeθi'nweβe] num nineteen

dieciocho [djeθi'otʃo] num eighteen

dieciséis [djeθi'seis] num sixteen

diecisiete [djeθi'sjete] num seventeen

diente ['djente] nm (ANAT, TEC) tooth; (ZOOL) fang; (: de elefante) tusk; (de ajo) clove; **hablar entre ~s** to mutter, mumble

diera etc vb ver **dar**

diesel ['disel] adj: **motor** ~ diesel engine

diestro, a ['djestro, a] adj (derecho) right; (hábil) skilful

dieta ['djeta] nf diet; **dietética** nf: **tienda de dietética** health food shop; **dietético, a** adj diet (atr), dietary

diez [djeθ] num ten

diezmar [djeθ'mar] vt (población) to decimate

difamar [difa'mar] vt (JUR: hablando) to slander; (: por escrito) to libel

diferencia [dife'renθja] nf difference; **diferenciar** vt to differentiate between ♦ vi to differ; **diferenciarse** vr to differ, be different; (distinguirse) to distinguish o.s.

diferente [dife'rente] adj different

diferido [dife'riðo] nm: **en** ~ (TV etc) recorded

difícil [di'fiθil] adj difficult

dificultad [difikul'taθ] nf difficulty; (problema) trouble

dificultar [difikul'tar] vt (complicar) to complicate, make difficult; (estorbar) to obstruct

difteria [dif'terja] nf diphtheria

difundir [difun'dir] vt (calor, luz) to diffuse; (RADIO, TV) to broadcast; **~ una noticia** to spread a piece of news; **~se** vr to spread (out)

difunto, a [di'funto, a] adj dead, deceased ♦ nm/f deceased (person)

difusión [difu'sjon] nf (RADIO, TV) broadcasting

diga etc vb ver **decir**

digerir [dixe'rir] vt to digest; (fig) to absorb; **digestión** nf digestion; **digestivo, a** adj digestive

digital [dixi'tal] adj digital

dignarse [diɣ'narse] vr to deign to

dignatario, a [diɣna'tarjo, a] nm/f dignitary

dignidad [diɣni'ðað] nf dignity

digno, a ['diɣno, a] adj worthy

digo etc vb ver **decir**

dije etc vb ver **decir**

dilapidar [dilapi'ðar] vt (dinero, herencia) to squander, waste

dilatar [dila'tar] vt (cuerpo) to dilate; (prolongar) to prolong

dilema [di'lema] nm dilemma

diligencia [dili'xenθja] nf diligence; (ocupación) errand, job; **~s** nfpl (JUR) formalities; **diligente** adj diligent

diluir [dilu'ir] vt to dilute

diluvio [di'luβjo] nm deluge, flood

dimensión [dimen'sjon] nf dimension

diminuto, a [dimi'nuto, a] adj tiny, diminutive

dimitir [dimi'tir] vi to resign

dimos vb ver **dar**

Dinamarca [dina'marka] nf Denmark

dinámico, a [di'namiko, a] adj dynamic

dinamita [dina'mita] nf dynamite

dinamo ['dinamo] nf dynamo

dineral [dine'ral] nm large sum of money, fortune

dinero [di'nero] nm money; **~ contante, ~ efectivo** (ready) cash; **~ suelto** (loose) change

dio vb ver **dar**

dios [djos] nm god; **¡D~ mío!** (oh,

my God!

diosa ['djosa] nf goddess

diploma [di'ploma] nm diploma

diplomacia [diplo'maθja] nf diplomacy; (fig) tact

diplomado, a [diplo'maðo, a] adj qualified

diplomático, a [diplo'matiko, a] adj diplomatic ♦ nm/f diplomat

diputación [diputa'θjon] nf (tb: ~ provincial) ≈ county council

diputado, a [dipu'taðo, a] nm/f delegate; (POL) ≈ member of parliament (BRIT), ≈ representative (US)

dique ['dike] nm dyke

diré etc vb ver **decir**

dirección [direk'θjon] nf direction; (señas) address; (AUTO) steering; (gerencia) management; (POL) leadership; **~ única/prohibida** one-way street/no entry

directa [di'rekta] nf (AUT) top gear

directiva [direk'tiβa] nf (DEP, tb: junta ~) board of directors

directo, a [di'rekto, a] adj direct; (RADIO, TV) live; **transmitir en ~** to broadcast live

director, a [direk'tor, a] adj leading ♦ nm/f director; (ESCOL) head(teacher) (BRIT), principal (US); (gerente) manager(ess); (PRENSA) editor; **~ de cine** film director; **~ general** managing director

dirigente [diri'xente] nm/f (POL) leader

dirigir [diri'xir] vt to direct; (carta) to address; (obra de teatro, film) to direct; (MUS) to conduct; (negocio) to manage; **~se vr: ~se a** to go towards, make one's way towards; (hablar con) to speak to

dirija etc vb ver **dirigir**

discernir [disθer'nir] vt to discern

disciplina [disθi'plina] nf discipline

discípulo, a [dis'θipulo, a] nm/f disciple

disco ['disko] nm disc; (DEPORTE)

discus (TEL) dial; (AUTO: semáforo)
light; (MUS) record; (INFORM):
~ flexible/rígido floppy/hard disk;
~ compacto/de larga duración
compact disc/long-playing record;
~ de freno brake disc

disconforme [diskon'forme] adj
differing; **estar ~ (con)** to be in
disagreement (with)

discordia [dis'korðja] nf discord

discoteca [disko'teka] nf
disco(theque)

discreción [diskre'θjon] nf discretion;
(reserva) prudence; **comer a ~** to eat
as much as one wishes; **discrecional**
adj (facultativo) discretionary

discrepancia [diskre'panθja] nf
(diferencia) discrepancy; (desacuerdo)
disagreement

discreto, a [dis'kreto, a] adj discreet

discriminación [diskrimina'θjon] nf
discrimination

disculpa [dis'kulpa] nf excuse; (pedir
perdón) apology; **pedir ~s a/por** to
apologize to/for; **disculpar** vt to
excuse, pardon; **disculparse** vr to
excuse o.s.; to apologize

discurrir [disku'rrir] vi (pensar,
reflexionar) to think, meditate; (el
tiempo) to pass, go by

discurso [dis'kurso] nm speech

discusión [disku'sjon] nf (diálogo)
discussion; (riña) argument

discutir [disku'tir] vt (debatir) to
discuss; (pelear) to argue about; vi
(contradecir) to argue against ♦ vi
(debatir) to discuss; (pelearse) to argue

disecar [dise'kar] vt (conservar: animal)
to stuff; (: planta) to dry

diseminar [disemi'nar] vt to
disseminate, spread

diseñar [dise'nar] vt, vi to design

diseño [di'seno] nm design

disfraz [dis'fraθ] nm (máscara)
disguise; (excusa) pretext; **~ar** vt to
disguise; **~arse** vr: **~arse de** to
disguise o.s. as

disfrutar [disfru'tar] vt to enjoy ♦ vi to
enjoy o.s.; **~ de** to enjoy, possess

disgregarse [disvre'varse] vr
(muchedumbre) to disperse

disgustar [disvus'tar] vt (no gustar) to
displease; (contrariar, enojar) to annoy,
upset; **~se** vr (enfadarse) to get upset;
(dos personas) to fall out

disgusto [dis'vusto] nm (contrariedad)
annoyance; (tristeza) grief; (riña)
quarrel

disidente [disi'ðente] nm dissident

disimular [disimu'lar] vt (ocultar) to
hide, conceal ♦ vi to dissemble

disipar [disi'par] vt to dispel; (fortuna)
to squander; **~se** vr (nubes) to vanish;
(indisciplinarse) to dissipate

dislocarse [dislo'karse] vr
(articulación) to sprain, dislocate

disminución [disminu'θjon] nf
decrease, reduction

disminuido, a [disminu'iðo, a] nm/f:
~ mental/físico mentally/physically
handicapped person

disminuir [disminu'ir] vt to decrease,
diminish

disociarse [diso'θjarse] vr: **~ (de)** to
dissociate o.s. (from)

disolver [disol'ßer] vt (gen) to
dissolve; **~se** vr to dissolve; (COM) to
go into liquidation

dispar [dis'par] adj different

disparar [dispa'rar] vt, vi to shoot, fire

disparate [dispa'rate] nm (tontería)
foolish remark; (error) blunder; **decir
~s** to talk nonsense

disparo [dis'paro] nm shot

dispensar [dispen'sar] vt to dispense;
(disculpar) to excuse

dispersar [disper'sar] vt to disperse;
~se vr to scatter

disponer [dispo'ner] vt (arreglar) to
arrange; (ordenar) to put in order;
(preparar) to prepare, get ready ♦ vi:
~ de to have, own; **~se** vr: **~se a o
para hacer** to prepare to do

disponible [dispo'nißle] adj available

disposición [disposi'θjon] nf
arrangement, disposition; (INFORM)
layout; **a la ~ de** at the disposal of;
~ de animo state of mind

dispositivo [disposi'tiβo] nm device,
mechanism

dispuesto, a [dis'pwesto, a] pp de
disponer ♦ adj (arreglado) arranged;
(preparado) disposed

disputar [dispu'tar] vt (carrera) to
compete in

disquete [dis'kete] nm floppy disk,
diskette

distancia [dis'tanθja] nf distance

distanciar [distan'θjar] vt to space
out; **~se** vr to become estranged

distante [dis'tante] adj distant

distar [dis'tar] vi: **dista 5km de aquí**
it is 5km from here

diste vb ver **dar**

disteis ['disteis] vb ver **dar**

distensión [disten'sjon] nf (en las
relaciones) relaxation; (POL) détente;
(muscular) strain

distinción [distin'θjon] nf distinction;
(elegancia) elegance; (honor) honour

distinguido, a [distin'giðo, a] adj
distinguished

distinguir [distin'gir] vt to distinguish;
(escoger) to single out; **~se** vr to be
distinguished

distintivo [distin'tiβo] nm badge; (fig)
characteristic

distinto, a [dis'tinto, a] adj different;
(claro) clear

distracción [distrak'θjon] nf
distraction; (pasatiempo) hobby,
pastime; (olvido) absent-mindedness,
distraction

distraer [distra'er] vt (atención) to
distract; (divertir) to amuse; (fondos) to
embezzle; **~se** vr (entretenerse) to
amuse o.s.; (perder la concentración) to
allow one's attention to wander

distraído, a [distra'iðo, a] adj (gen)
absent-minded; (entretenido) amusing

distribuidor, a [distriβui'ðor, a] nm/f

distributor; **distribuidora** nf (COM)
dealer, agent; (CINE) distributor

distribuir [distriβu'ir] vt to distribute

distrito [dis'trito] nm (sector, territorio)
region; (barrio) district

disturbio [dis'turβjo] nm disturbance;
(desorden) riot

disuadir [diswa'ðir] vt to dissuade

disuelto [di'swelto] pp de **disolver**

disyuntiva [disjun'tiβa] nf dilemma

DIU nm abr (= dispositivo intrauterino)
IUD

diurno, a ['djurno, a] adj day cpd

divagar [diβa'var] vi (desviarse) to
digress

diván [di'βan] nm divan

divergencia [diβer'xenθja] nf
divergence

diversidad [diβersi'ðað] nf diversity,
variety

diversificar [diβersifi'kar] vt to
diversify

diversión [diβer'sjon] nf (gen)
entertainment; (actividad) hobby,
pastime

diverso, a [di'βerso, a] adj diverse; **~s
libros** several books; **~s** nmpl sundries

divertido, a [diβer'tiðo, a] adj (chiste)
amusing; (fiesta etc) enjoyable

divertir [diβer'tir] vt (entretener,
recrear) to amuse; **~se** vr (pasarlo bien)
to have a good time; (distraerse) to
amuse o.s.

dividendos [diβi'ðendos] nmpl (COM)
dividends

dividir [diβi'ðir] vt (gen) to divide;
(distribuir) to distribute, share out

divierta etc vb ver **divertir**

divino, a [di'βino, a] adj divine

divirtiendo etc vb ver **divertir**

divisa [di'βisa] nf (emblema) emblem,
badge; **~s** nfpl foreign exchange sg

divisar [diβi'sar] vt to make out,
distinguish

división [diβi'sjon] nf (gen) division;
(de partido) split; (de país) partition

divorciar [diβor'θjar] vt to divorce;

~se vr to get divorced; **divorcio** nm divorce

divulgar [diβul'ɣar] vt (ideas) to spread; (secreto) to divulge

DNI (ESP) nm abr (= Documento Nacional de Identidad) national identity card

DNI

The **Documento Nacional de Identidad** is a Spanish ID card which must be carried at all times and produced on request for the police. It contains the holder's photo, fingerprints and personal details. It is also known as the DNI or "carnet de identidad".

Dña. abr (= doña) Mrs

do [do] nm (MUS) do, C

dobladillo [doβla'ðiʎo] nm (de vestido) hem; (de pantalón: vuelta) turn-up (BRIT), cuff (US)

doblar [do'βlar] vt to double; (papel) to fold; (caño) to bend; (la esquina) to turn, go round; (film) to dub ♦ vi to turn; (campana) to toll; **~se** vr (plegarse) to fold (up), crease; (encorvarse) to bend

doble ['doβle] adj double; (de dos aspectos) dual; (fig) two-faced ♦ nm double ♦ nm/f (TEATRO) double, stand-in; **~s** nmpl (DEPORTE) doubles sg; **con sentido ~** with a double meaning

doblegar [doβle'ɣar] vt to bend, crease; **~se** vr to yield

doblez [do'βleθ] nm fold, hem ♦ nf insincerity, duplicity

doce ['doθe] num twelve; **~na** nf dozen

docente [do'θente] adj: **centro/personal ~** teaching establishment/staff

dócil ['doθil] adj (pasivo) docile; (obediente) obedient

docto, a ['dokto, a] adj: **~ en** instructed in

doctor, a [dok'tor, a] nm/f doctor

doctorado [dokto'raðo] nm doctorate

doctrina [dok'trina] nf doctrine, teaching

documentación [dokumenta'θjon] nf documentation, papers pl

documental [dokumen'tal] adj, nm documentary

documento [doku'mento] nm (certificado) document; **~ national de identidad** identity card

dólar ['dolar] nm dollar

doler [do'ler] vt, vi to hurt; (fig) to grieve; **~se** vr (de su situación) to grieve, feel sorry; (de las desgracias ajenas) to sympathize; **me duele el brazo** my arm hurts

dolor [do'lor] nm pain; (fig) grief, sorrow; **~ de cabeza** headache; **~ de estómago** stomachache

domar [do'mar] vt to tame

domesticar [domesti'kar] vt = **domar**

doméstico, a [do'mestiko, a] adj (vida, servicio) home; (tareas) household; (animal) tame, pet

domiciliación [domiθilja'θjon] nf: **~ de pagos** (COM) standing order

domicilio [domi'θiljo] nm home; **~ particular** private residence; **~ social** (COM) head office; **sin ~ fijo** of no fixed abode

dominante [domi'nante] adj dominant; (persona) domineering

dominar [domi'nar] vt (gen) to dominate; (idiomas) to be fluent in ♦ vi to dominate, prevail; **~se** vr to control o.s.

domingo [do'mingo] nm Sunday

dominio [do'minjo] nm (tierras) domain; (autoridad) power, authority; (de las pasiones) grip, hold; (de idiomas) command

don [don] nm (talento) gift; **~ Juan Gómez** Mr Juan Gómez, Juan Gómez Esq (BRIT)

donaire [do'naire] nm charm

donaire [do'naire] nm charm
donar [do'nar] vt to donate
donativo [dona'tiβo] nm donation
doncella [don'θeʎa] nf (criada) maid
donde ['donde] adv where ♦ prep: **el
coche está allí ~ el farol** the car is
over there by the lamppost o where
the lamppost is; **en ~** where, in which
dónde ['donde] adv interrogativo
where?; **¿a ~ vas?** where are you
going (to)?; **¿de ~ vienes?** where
have you been?; **¿por ~?** where?,
whereabouts?
dondequiera [donde'kjera] adv
anywhere; **por ~** everywhere, all over
the place ♦ conj: **~ que** wherever
doña ['dona] nf: **~ Alicia** Alicia;
~ Victoria Benito Mrs Victoria Benito
dorado, a [do'raðo, a] adj (color)
golden; (TEC) gilt
dormir [dor'mir] vt: **~ la siesta** to
have an afternoon nap ♦ vi to sleep;
~se vr to fall asleep
dormitar [dormi'tar] vi to doze
dormitorio [dormi'torjo] nm
bedroom; **~ común** dormitory
dorsal [dor'sal] nm (DEPORTE) number
dorso ['dorso] nm (de mano) back; (de
hoja) other side
dos [dos] num two
dosis ['dosis] nf inv dose, dosage
dotado, a [do'taðo, a] adj gifted; **~ de**
endowed with

dotar [do'tar] vt to endow; **dote** nf
dowry; **dotes** nfpl (talentos) gifts
doy vb ver **dar**
dragar [dra'xar] vt (río) to dredge;
(minas) to sweep
drama ['drama] nm drama
dramaturgo [drama'turxo] nm
dramatist, playwright
drástico, a ['drastiko, a] adj drastic
drenaje [dre'naxe] nm drainage
droga ['droxa] nf drug
drogadicto, a [droxa'ðikto, a] nm/f
drug addict
droguería [droxe'ria] nf hardware
shop (BRIT) o store (US)
ducha ['dutʃa] nf (baño) shower; (MED)
douche; **ducharse** vr to take a shower
duda ['duða] nf doubt; **dudar** vt, vi to
doubt; **dudoso, a** [du'ðoso, a] adj
(incierto) hesitant; (sospechoso)
doubtful
duela etc vb ver **doler**
duelo ['dwelo] vb ver **doler** ♦ nm
(combate) duel; (luto) mourning
duende ['dwende] nm imp, goblin
dueño, a ['dweɲo, a] nm/f (propietario)
owner; (de pensión, taberna) landlord/
lady; (empresario) employer
duermo etc vb ver **dormir**
dulce ['dulθe] adj sweet ♦ adv gently,
softly ♦ nm sweet
dulzura [dul'θura] nf sweetness;
(ternura) gentleness
duna ['duna] nf (GEO) dune
dúo ['duo] nm duet
duplicar [dupli'kar] vt (hacer el doble
de) to duplicate; **~se** vr to double
duque ['duke] nm duke; **~sa** nf
duchess
duración [dura'θjon] nf (de película,
disco etc) length; (de pila etc) life;
(curso: de acontecimientos etc) duration
duradero, a [dura'ðero, a] adj (tela
etc) hard-wearing; (fe, paz) lasting
durante [du'rante] prep during
durar [du'rar] vt to last; (recuerdo) to
remain

durazno [du'raθno] (AM) nm (fruta) peach; (árbol) peach tree

durex ['dureks] (AM) nm (tira adhesiva) Sellotape ® (BRIT), Scotch tape ® (US)

dureza [du'reθa] nf (calidad) hardness

duro, a ['duro, a] adj hard; (carácter) tough ♦ adv hard ♦ nm (moneda) five peseta coin o piece

DVD nm abr (= disco de vídeo digital) DVD

E, e

E abr (= este) E

e [e] conj and

ebanista [eßa'nista] nm/f cabinetmaker

ébano ['eßano] nm ebony

ebrio, a ['eßrjo, a] adj drunk

ebullición [eßuʎi'θjon] nf boiling

eccema [ek'θema] nf (MED) eczema

echar [e'tʃar] vt to throw; (agua, vino) to pour (out); (empleado: despedir) to fire, sack; (hojas) to sprout; (cartas) to post; (humo) to emit, give out ♦ vi: **~ a correr/llorar** to run off/burst into tears; **~se** vr to lie down; **~ llave a** to lock (up); **~ abajo** (gobierno) to overthrow; (edificio) to demolish; **~ mano a** to lay hands on; **~ una mano a uno** (ayudar) to give sb a hand; **~ de menos** to miss

eclesiástico, a [ekle'sjastiko, a] adj ecclesiastical

eco ['eko] nm echo; **tener ~** to catch on

ecología [ekolo'xia] nf ecology; **ecológico, a** adj (producto, método) environmentally-friendly; (agricultura) organic; **ecologista** adj ecological, environmental ♦ nm/f environmentalist

economato [ekono'mato] nm cooperative store

economía [ekono'mia] nf (sistema) economy; (carrera) economics

económico, a [eko'nomiko, a] adj (barato) cheap, economical; (ahorrativo) thrifty; (COM: año etc) financial; (: situación) economic

economista [ekono'mista] nm/f economist

ECU [eku] nm ECU

ecuador [ekwa'ðor] nm equator; **(el) E~** Ecuador

ecuánime [e'kwanime] adj (carácter) level-headed; (estado) calm

ecuatoriano, a [ekwato'rjano, a] adj, nm/f Ecuadorian

ecuestre [e'kwestre] adj equestrian

eczema [ek'θema] nm = **eccema**

edad [e'ðað] nf age; **¿qué ~ tienes?** how old are you?; **tiene ocho años de ~** he is eight (years old); **de ~ mediana/avanzada** middle-aged/advanced in years; **la E~ Media** the Middle Ages

edición [eði'θjon] nf (acto) publication; (ejemplar) edition

edificar [eðifi'kar] vt, vi to build

edificio [eði'fiθjo] nm building; (fig) edifice, structure

Edimburgo [eðim'burɣo] nm Edinburgh

editar [eði'tar] vt (publicar) to publish; (preparar textos) to edit

editor, a [eði'tor, a] nm/f (que publica) publisher; (redactor) editor ♦ adj: **casa ~a** a publishing house, publisher; **~ial** adj editorial ♦ nm leading article, editorial; **casa ~ial** publisher

edredón [eðre'ðon] nm duvet

educación [eðuka'θjon] nf education; (crianza) upbringing; (modales) (good) manners pl

educado, a [eðu'kaðo, a] adj: **bien/mal ~** well/badly behaved

educar [eðu'kar] vt to educate; (criar) to bring up; (voz) to train

EE. UU. nmpl abr (= Estados Unidos) US(A)

efectista [efek'tista] adj sensationalist

efectivamente [efectißa'mente] adv (como respuesta) exactly, precisely;

(*verdaderamente*) really; (*de hecho*) in fact

efectivo, a [efek'tiβo, a] adj effective; (*real*) actual, real ♦ nm: **pagar en ~** to pay (in) cash; **hacer ~ un cheque** to cash a cheque

efecto [e'fekto] nm effect, result; **~s** nmpl (~s personales) effects; (*bienes*) goods; (COM) assets; **en ~** in fact; (*respuesta*) exactly, indeed; **~ 2000** millennium bug; **~ invernadero** greenhouse effect

efectuar [efek'twar] vt to carry out; (*viaje*) to make

eficacia [efi'kaθja] nf (*de persona*) efficiency; (*de medicamento etc*) effectiveness

eficaz [efi'kaθ] adj (*persona*) efficient; (*acción*) effective

eficiente [efi'θjente] adj efficient

efusivo, a [efu'siβo, a] adj effusive; **mis más efusivas gracias** my warmest thanks

EGB (ESP) nf abr (ESCOL) = Educación General Básica

egipcio, a [e'xipθjo, a] adj, nm/f Egyptian

Egipto [e'xipto] nm Egypt

egoísmo [exo'ismo] nm egoism

egoísta [exo'ista] adj egoistical, selfish ♦ nm/f egoist

egregio, a [e'vrexjo, a] adj eminent, distinguished

Eire ['eire] nm Eire

ej. abr (= ejemplo) eg

eje ['exe] nm (GEO, MAT) axis; (*de rueda*) axle; (*de máquina*) shaft, spindle

ejecución [exeku'θjon] nf execution; (*cumplimiento*) fulfilment; (MUS) performance; (JUR: embargo de deudor) attachment

ejecutar [exeku'tar] vt to execute, carry out; (*matar*) to execute; (*cumplir*) to fulfil; (MUS) to perform; (JUR: embargar) to attach, distrain (on)

ejecutivo, a [exeku'tiβo, a] adj executive; **el (poder) ~** the executive

(*power*)

ejemplar [exem'plar] adj exemplary ♦ nm example; (ZOOL) specimen; (*de libro*) copy; (*de periódico*) number, issue

ejemplo [e'xemplo] nm example; **por ~** for example

ejercer [exer'θer] vt to exercise; (*influencia*) to exert; (*un oficio*) to practise ♦ vi (*practicar*): **~ (de)** to practise (as)

ejercicio [exer'θiθjo] nm exercise; (*período*) tenure; **~ comercial** financial year

ejército [e'xerθito] nm army; **entrar en el ~** to join the army, join up

ejote [e'xote] (AM) nm green bean

PALABRA CLAVE

---

el [el] (f **la**, pl **los, las**, neutro **lo**) art def 1 the; **el libro/la mesa/los estudiantes** the book/table/students

2 (*con n abstracto: no se traduce*): **el amor/la juventud** love/youth

3 (*posesión: se traduce a menudo por adj posesivo*): **romperse el brazo** to break one's arm; **levantó la mano** he put his hand up; **se puso el sombrero** she put her hat on

4 (*valor descriptivo*): **tener la boca grande/los ojos azules** to have a big mouth/blue eyes

5 (*con días*) on; **me iré el viernes** I'll leave on Friday; **los domingos suelo ir a nadar** on Sundays I generally go swimming

6 (*lo + adj*): **lo difícil/caro** what is difficult/expensive; (= *cuán*): **no se da cuenta de lo pesado que es** he doesn't realise how boring he is

♦ pron demos 1: **mi libro y el de usted** my book and yours; **las de Pepe son mejores** Pepe's are better; **no la(s) blanca(s) sino la(s) gris(es)** not the white ones but the grey one(s)

2: **lo: lo de ayer** what happened yesterday; **lo de las facturas** that business about the invoices

♦ pron relativo: **el que** etc 1 (indef): **el (los) que quiera(n) que se vaya(n)** anyone who wants to can leave; **llévese el que más le guste** take the one you like best

2 (def): **el que compré ayer** the one I bought yesterday; **los que se van** those who leave

3: **lo que: lo que pienso yo/más me gusta** what I think/like most

♦ conj: **el que: el que lo diga** the fact that he says so; **el que sea tan vago me molesta** his being so lazy bothers me

♦ excl: **¡el susto que me diste!** what a fright you gave me!

♦ pron personal 1 (persona: m) him; (: f) her; (: pl) them; **lo/las veo** I can see him/them

2 (animal, cosa: sg) it; (: pl) them; **lo (o la) veo** I can see it; **los (o las) veo** I can see them

3: **lo** (como sustituto de frase): **no lo sabía** I didn't know; **ya lo entiendo** I understand now

---

él [el] pron (persona) he; (cosa) it; (después de prep: persona) him; (: cosa) it; **de ~** his

elaborar [elaβo'rar] vt (producto) to make, manufacture; (preparar) to prepare; (madera, metal etc) to work; (proyecto etc) to work on o out

elasticidad [elastiθi'ðað] nf elasticity

elástico, a [e'lastiko, a] adj elastic; (flexible) flexible ♦ nm elastic; (un ~) elastic band

elección [elek'θjon] nf election; (selección) choice, selection

electorado [elekto'raðo] nm electorate, voters pl

electricidad [elektriθi'ðað] nf electricity

electricista [elektri'θista] nm/f electrician

eléctrico, a [e'lektriko, a] adj electric

electro... [elektro] prefijo electro...;

~**cardiograma** nm electrocardiogram; ~**cutar** vt to electrocute; ~**do** nm electrode; ~**domésticos** nmpl (electrical) household appliances; ~**magnético, a** adj electromagnetic

electrónica [elek'tronika] nf electronics sg

electrónico, a [elek'troniko, a] adj electronic

elefante [ele'fante] nm elephant

elegancia [ele'ganθja] nf elegance, grace; (estilo) stylishness

elegante [ele'vante] adj elegant, graceful; (estiloso) stylish, fashionable

elegir [ele'xir] vt (escoger) to choose, select; (optar) to opt for; (presidente) to elect

elemental [elemen'tal] adj (claro, obvio) elementary; (fundamental) elemental, fundamental

elemento [ele'mento] nm element; (fig) ingredient; ~**s** nmpl elements, rudiments

elepé [ele'pe] (pl: **elepés**) nm L.P.

elevación [eleβa'θjon] nf elevation; (acto) raising, lifting; (de precios) rise; (GEO etc) height, altitude

elevar [ele'βar] vt to raise, lift (up); (precio) to put up; ~**se** vr (edificio) to rise; (precios) to go up

eligiendo etc vb ver **elegir**

elija etc vb ver **elegir**

eliminar [elimi'nar] vt to eliminate, remove

eliminatoria [elimina'torja] nf heat, preliminary (round)

elite [e'lite] nf elite

ella ['eʎa] pron (persona) she; (cosa) it; (después de prep: persona) her; (: cosa) it; **de ~** hers

ellas ['eʎas] pron (personas y cosas) they; (después de prep) them; **de ~** theirs

ello ['eʎo] pron it

ellos ['eʎos] pron they; (después de prep) them; **de ~** theirs

elocuencia [elo'kwenθja] nf

eloquence

elogiar [elo'xjar] vt to praise; **elogio** nm praise

elote [e'lote] (AM) nm corn on the cob

eludir [elu'ðir] vt to avoid

emanar [ema'nar] vi: ~ **de** to emanate from, come from; (derivar de) to originate in

emancipar [emanθi'par] vt to emancipate; ~**se** vr to become emancipated, free o.s.

embadurnar [embaður'nar] vt to smear

embajada [emba'xaða] nf embassy

embajador, a [embaxa'ðor, a] nm/f ambassador/ambassadress

embalaje [emba'laxe] nm packing

embalar [emba'lar] vt to parcel, wrap (up); ~**se** vr to go fast

embalsamar [embalsa'mar] vt to embalm

embalse [em'balse] nm (presa) dam; (lago) reservoir

embarazada [embara'θaða] adj pregnant ♦ nf pregnant woman

embarazo [emba'raθo] nm (de mujer) pregnancy; (impedimento) obstacle, obstruction; (timidez) embarrassment; **embarazoso, a** adj awkward, embarrassing

embarcación [embarka'θjon] nf (barco) boat, craft; (acto) embarkation, boarding

embarcadero [embarka'ðero] nm pier, landing stage

embarcar [embar'kar] vt (cargamento) to ship, stow; (persona) to embark, put on board; ~**se** vr to embark, go on board

embargar [embar'var] vt (JUR) to seize, impound

embargo [em'barvo] nm (JUR) seizure; (COM, POL) embargo

embargue [em'barve] etc vb ver **embargar**

embarque etc [em'barke] vb ver **embarcar** ♦ nm shipment, loading

embaucar [embau'kar] vt to trick, fool

embeber [embe'βer] vt (absorber) to absorb, soak up; (empapar) to saturate ♦ vi to shrink; ~**se** vr: ~**se en un libro** to be engrossed o absorbed in a book

embellecer [embeʎe'θer] vt to embellish, beautify

embestida [embes'tiða] nf attack, onslaught; (carga) charge

embestir [embes'tir] vt to attack, assault; to charge, attack ♦ vi to attack

emblema [em'blema] nm emblem

embobado, a [embo'βaðo, a] adj (atontado) stunned, bewildered

embolia [em'bolja] nf (MED) clot

émbolo [em'bolo] nm (AUTO) piston

embolsar [embol'sar] vt to pocket, put in one's pocket

emborrachar [emborra'tʃar] vt to make drunk, intoxicate; ~**se** vr to get drunk

emboscada [embos'kaða] nf ambush

embotar [embo'tar] vt to blunt, dull; ~**se** vr (adormecerse) to go numb

embotellamiento [emboteʎa'mjento] nm (AUTO) traffic jam

embotellar [embote'ʎar] vt to bottle

embrague [em'braƔe] nm (tb: pedal de ~) clutch

embriagar [embrja'Ɣar] vt (emborrachar) to make drunk; ~**se** vr (emborracharse) to get drunk

embrión [em'brjon] nm embryo

embrollar [embro'ʎar] vt (el asunto) to confuse, complicate; (implicar) to involve, embroil; ~**se** vr (confundirse) to get into a muddle o mess

embrollo [em'broʎo] nm (enredo) muddle, confusion; (aprieto) fix, jam

embrujado, a [embru'xaðo, a] adj bewitched; **casa embrujada** haunted house

embrutecer [embrute'θer] vt (atontar) to stupefy; ~**se** vr to be stupefied

embudo [em'buðo] nm funnel

embuste [em'buste] nm (mentira) lie;

~ro, a *adj* lying, deceitful ♦ *nm/f* (*mentiroso*) liar

embutido [embu'tiðo] *nm* (*CULIN*) sausage; (*TEC*) inlay

emergencia [emer'xenθja] *nf* emergency; (*surgimiento*) emergence

emerger [emer'xer] *vi* to emerge, appear

emigración [emiɣra'θjon] *nf* emigration; (*de pájaros*) migration

emigrar [emi'ɣrar] *vi* (*personas*) to emigrate; (*pájaros*) to migrate

eminencia [emi'nenθja] *nf* eminence; **eminente** *adj* eminent, distinguished; (*elevado*) high

emisario [emi'sarjo] *nm* emissary

emisión [emi'sjon] *nf* (*acto*) emission; (*COM etc*) issue; (*RADIO, TV*: *acto*) broadcasting; (: *programa*) broadcast, programme (*BRIT*), program (*US*)

emisora [emi'sora] *nf* radio o broadcasting station

emitir [emi'tir] *vt* (*olor etc*) to emit, give off; (*moneda etc*) to issue; (*opinión*) to express; (*RADIO*) to broadcast

emoción [emo'θjon] *nf* emotion; (*excitación*) excitement; (*sentimiento*) feeling

emocionante [emoθjo'nante] *adj* (*excitante*) exciting, thrilling

emocionar [emoθjo'nar] *vt* (*excitar*) to excite, thrill; (*conmover*) to move, touch; (*impresionar*) to impress

emotivo, a [emo'tiβo, a] *adj* emotional

empacar [empa'kar] *vt* (*gen*) to pack; (*en caja*) to bale, crate

empacho [em'patʃo] *nm* (*MED*) indigestion; (*fig*) embarrassment

empadronarse [empaðro'narse] *vr* (*POL*: *como elector*) to register

empalagoso, a [empala'ɣoso, a] *adj* cloying; (*fig*) tiresome

empalmar [empal'mar] *vt* to join, connect ♦ *vi* (*dos caminos*) to meet, join; **empalme** *nm* joint, connection;

junction; (*de trenes*) connection

empanada *nf* pie, pasty

empantanarse [empanta'narse] *vr* to get swamped; (*fig*) to get bogged down

empañarse [empa'ɲarse] *vr* (*cristales etc*) to steam up

empapar [empa'par] *vt* (*mojar*) to soak, saturate; (*absorber*) to soak up, absorb; **~se** *vr*: **~se de** to soak up

empapelar [empape'lar] *vt* (*paredes*) to paper

empaquetar [empake'tar] *vt* to pack, parcel up

empastar [empas'tar] *vt* (*embadurnar*) to paste; (*diente*) to fill

empaste [em'paste] *nm* (*de diente*) filling

empatar [empa'tar] *vi* to draw, tie; **empate** *nm* draw, tie

empecé *etc vb ver* **empezar**

empedernido, a [empeðer'niðo, a] *adj* heartless; (*fumador*) inveterate

empedrado, a [empe'ðraðo, a] *adj* paved ♦ *nm* paving

empeine [em'peine] *nm* (*de pie*, *zapato*) instep

empellón [empe'ʎon] *nm* push, shove

empeñado, a [empe'ɲaðo, a] *adj* (*persona*) determined; (*objeto*) pawned

empeñar [empe'ɲar] *vt* (*objeto*) to pawn, pledge; (*persona*) to compel; **~se** *vr* (*endeudarse*) to get into debt; **~se en** to be set on, be determined to

empeño [em'peɲo] *nm* (*determinación*, *insistencia*) determination, insistence; **casa de ~s** pawnshop

empeorar [empeo'rar] *vt* to make worse, worsen ♦ *vi* to get worse, deteriorate

empequeñecer [empekeɲe'θer] *vt* to dwarf; (*minusvalorar*) to belittle

emperador [empera'ðor] *nm* emperor; **emperatriz** *nf* empress

empezar [empe'θar] *vt*, *vi* to begin, start

empiece *etc vb ver* **empezar**

empiezo etc vb ver **empezar**

empinar [empi'nar] vt to raise; **~se** (persona) to stand on tiptoe; (animal) to rear up; (camino) to climb steeply

empírico, a [em'piriko, a] adj empirical

emplasto [em'plasto] nm (MED) plaster

emplazamiento [emplaθa'mjento] nm site, location; (JUR) summons

emplazar [empla'θar] vt (ubicar) to site, place, locate; (JUR) to summons; (convocar) to summon

empleado, a [emple'aðo, a] nm/f (gen) employee; (de banco etc) clerk

emplear [emple'ar] vt (usar) to use, employ; (dar trabajo a) to employ; **~se** vr (conseguir trabajo) to be employed; (ocuparse) to occupy o.s.

empleo [em'pleo] nm (puesto) job; (puestos: colectivamente) employment; (uso) use, employment

empobrecer [empoβre'θer] vt to impoverish; **~se** vr to become poor o impoverished

empollar [empo'ʎar] (fam) vt, vi to swot (up); **empollón, ona** (fam) nm/f swot

emporio [em'porjo] nm (AM: gran almacén) department store

empotrado, a [empo'traðo, a] adj (armario etc) built-in

emprender [empren'der] vt (empezar) to begin, embark on; (acometer) to tackle, take on

empresa [em'presa] nf (de espíritu etc) enterprise; (COM) company, firm; **~rio, a** nm/f (COM) businessman/woman

empréstito [em'prestito] nm (public) loan

empujar [empu'xar] vt to push, shove

empujón [empu'xon] nm push, shove

empuñar [empu'ɲar] vt (asir) to grasp, take (firm) hold of

emular [emu'lar] vt to emulate; (rivalizar) to rival

en [en] prep **1** (posición) in; (: sobre) on; **está ~ el cajón** it's in the drawer; **~ Argentina/La Paz** in Argentina/La Paz; **~ la oficina/el colegio** at the office/school; **está ~ el suelo/quinto piso** it's on the floor/the fifth floor

2 (dirección) into; **entró ~ el aula** she went into the classroom; **meter algo ~ el bolso** to put sth into one's bag

3 (tiempo) in; on; **~ 1605/3 semanas/invierno** in 1605/3 weeks/ winter; **~ (el mes de) enero** in (the month of) January; **~ aquella ocasión/época** on that occasion/at that time

4 (precio) for; **lo vendió ~ 20 dólares** he sold it for 20 dollars

5 (diferencia) by; **reducir/aumentar ~ una tercera parte/un 20 por ciento** to reduce/increase by a third/ 20 per cent

6 (manera): **~ avión/autobús** by plane/bus; **escrito ~ inglés** written in English

7 (después de vb que indica gastar etc) on; **han cobrado demasiado ~ dietas** they've charged too much to expenses; **se le va la mitad del sueldo ~ comida** he spends half his salary on food

8 (tema, ocupación): **experto ~ la materia** expert on the subject; **trabaja ~ la construcción** he works in the building industry

9 (adj + ~ + infin): **lento ~ reaccionar** slow to react

enaguas [e'naɣwas] nfpl petticoat sg, underskirt sg

enajenación [enaxena'θjon] nf: **~ mental** mental derangement

enajenar [enaxe'nar] vt (volver loco) to drive mad

enamorado, a [enamo'raðo, a] adj in love ♦ nm/f lover

enamorar [enamo'rar] *vt* to win the love of; **~se de alguien** to fall in love with sb

enano, a [e'nano, a] *adj* tiny ♦ *nm/f* dwarf

enardecer [enarðe'θer] *vt* (*pasiones*) to fire, inflame; (*persona*) to fill with enthusiasm; **~se** *vr*: **~se por** to get excited about; (*entusiasmarse*) to get enthusiastic about

encabezamiento [enkaβeθa'mjento] *nm* (*de carta*) heading; (*de periódico*) headline

encabezar [enkaβe'θar] *vt* (*movimiento, revolución*) to lead, head; (*lista*) to head, be at the top of; (*carta*) to put a heading to

encadenar [enkaðe'nar] *vt* to chain (together); (*poner grilletes a*) to shackle

encajar [enka'xar] *vt* (*ajustar*): **~ (en)** to fit (into); (*fam: golpe*) to take ♦ *vi* to fit (well); (*fig: corresponder a*) to match; **~se** *vr*: **~se en un sillón** to squeeze into a chair

encaje [en'kaxe] *nm* (*labor*) lace

encalar [enka'lar] *vt* (*pared*) to whitewash

encallar [enka'ʎar] *vi* (*NAUT*) to run aground

encaminar [enkami'nar] *vt* to direct, send; **~se** *vr*: **~se a** to set out for

encantado, a [enkan'taðo, a] *adj* (*hechizado*) bewitched; (*muy contento*) delighted; **¡~!** how do you do, pleased to meet you

encantador, a [enkanta'ðor, a] *adj* charming, lovely ♦ *nm/f* magician, enchanter/enchantress

encantar [enkan'tar] *vt* (*agradar*) to charm, delight; (*hechizar*) to bewitch, cast a spell on; **me encanta eso** I love that; **encanto** (*hechizo*) spell, charm; (*fig*) charm, delight

encarcelar [enkarθe'lar] *vt* to imprison, jail

encarecer [enkare'θer] *vt* to put up the price of; **~se** *vr* to get dearer

encarecimiento [enkareθi'mjento] *nm* price increase

encargado, a [enkar'ɣaðo, a] *adj* in charge ♦ *nm/f* agent, representative; (*responsable*) person in charge

encargar [enkar'ɣar] *vt* to entrust; (*recomendar*) to urge, recommend; **~se de** to look after, take charge of

encargo [en'karɣo] *nm* (*tarea*) assignment, job; (*responsabilidad*) responsibility; (*COM*) order

encariñarse [enkari'narse] *vr*: **~ con** to grow fond of, get attached to

encarnación [enkarna'θjon] *nf* incarnation, embodiment

encarnizado, a [enkarni'θaðo, a] *adj* (*lucha*) bloody, fierce

encarrilar [enkarri'lar] *vt* (*tren*) to put back on the rails; (*fig*) to correct, put on the right track

encasillar [enkasi'ʎar] *vt* (*tb fig*) to pigeonhole; (*actor*) to typecast

encauzar [enkau'θar] *vt* to channel

encendedor [enθende'ðor] *nm* lighter

encender [enθen'der] *vt* (*con fuego*) to light; (*luz, radio*) to put on, switch on; (*avivar: pasiones*) to inflame; **~se** *vr* to catch fire; (*excitarse*) to get excited; (*el rostro*) to blush

encendido [enθen'diðo] *nm* (*AUTO*) ignition

encerado [enθe'raðo] *nm* (*ESCOL*) blackboard

encerar [enθe'rar] *vt* (*suelo*) to wax, polish

encerrar [enθe'rrar] *vt* (*confinar*) to shut in, shut up; (*comprender, incluir*) to include, contain

encharcado, a [entʃar'kaðo, a] *adj* (*terreno*) flooded

encharcarse [entʃar'karse] *vr* to get flooded

enchufado, a [entʃu'faðo, a] (*fam*) *nm/f* well-connected person

enchufar [entʃu'far] *vt* (*ELEC*) to plug in; (*TEC*) to connect, fit together; **enchufe** *nm* (*ELEC*: *clavija*) plug;

(: *toma*) socket; (*de dos tubos*) joint,
connection; (*fam: influencia*) contact,
connection; (*puesto*) cushy job

encía [en'θia] *nf* gum

encienda *etc vb ver* **encender**

encierro *etc* [en'θjerro] *vb ver*
encerrar ♦ *nm* shutting in, shutting
up; (*calabozo*) prison

encima [en'θima] *adv* (*sobre*) above,
over; (*además*) besides; **~ de** (*en*) on,
on top of; (*sobre*) above, over; (*además
de*) besides, on top of; **por ~ de** over;
¿llevas dinero ~? have you (got) any
money on you?; **se me vino ~** it took
me by surprise

encina [en'θina] *nf* holm oak

encinta [en'θinta] *adj* pregnant

enclenque [en'klenke] *adj* weak, sickly

encoger [enko'xer] *vt* (*tela*) to shrink,
contract; **~se** *vr* to shrink, contract;
(*fig*) to cringe; **~se de hombros** to
shrug one's shoulders

encolar [enko'lar] *vt* (*engomar*) to
glue, paste; (*pegar*) to stick down

encolerizar [enkoleri'θar] *vt* to anger,
provoke; **~se** *vr* to get angry

encomendar [enkomen'dar] *vt* to
entrust, commend; **~se** *vr*: **~se a** to
put one's trust in

encomiar [enko'mjar] *vt* to praise, pay
tribute to

encomienda *etc* [enko'mjenda] *vb ver*
encomendar ♦ *nf* (*encargo*) charge,
commission; (*elogio*) tribute; **~ postal**
(*AM*) parcel post

encontrado, a [enkon'traðo, a] *adj*
(*contrario*) contrary, conflicting

encontrar [enkon'trar] *vt* (*hallar*) to
find; (*inesperadamente*) to meet, run
into; **~se** *vr* to meet (each other);
(*situarse*) to be (situated); **~se con** to
meet; **~se bien** (*de salud*) to feel
well

encrespar [enkres'par] *vt* (*cabellos*) to
curl; (*fig*) to anger, irritate; **~se** *vr* (*el
mar*) to get rough; (*fig*) to get cross,
get irritated

encrucijada [enkruθi'xaða] *nf*
crossroads *sg*

encuadernación [enkwaðerna'θjon]
nf binding

encuadernador, a [enkwaðerna'ðor,
a] *nm/f* bookbinder

encuadrar [enkwa'ðrar] *vt* (*retrato*) to
frame; (*ajustar*) to fit, insert; (*contener*)
to contain

encubrir [enku'ßrir] *vt* (*ocultar*) to
hide, conceal; (*criminal*) to harbour,
shelter

encuentro *etc* [en'kwentro] *vb ver*
encontrar ♦ *nm* (*de personas*)
meeting; (*AUTO etc*) collision, crash;
(*DEPORTE*) match, game; (*MIL.*)
encounter

encuesta [en'kwesta] *nf* inquiry,
investigation; (*sondeo*) (public) opinion
poll; **~ judicial** post mortem

encumbrar [enkum'brar] *vt* (*persona*)
to exalt

endeble [en'deßle] *adj* (*argumento,
excusa, persona*) weak

endémico, a [en'demiko, a] *adj* (*MED*)
endemic; (*fig*) rife, chronic

endemoniado, a [endemo'njaðo, a]
adj possessed (of the devil); (*travieso*)
devilish

enderezar [endere'θar] *vt* (*poner
derecho*) to straighten (out);
(*: verticalmente*) to set upright;
(*situación*) to straighten o sort out;
(*dirigir*) to direct; **~se** *vr* (*persona
sentada*) to straighten up

endeudarse [endeu'ðarse] *vr* to get
into debt

endiablado, a [endja'ßlaðo, a] *adj*
devilish, diabolical; (*travieso*)
mischievous

endilgar [endil'gar] (*fam*) *vt*: **~le algo
a uno** to lumber sb with sth; **~le un
sermón a uno** to lecture sb

endiñar [endi'nar] (*fam*) *vt* (*bofetón*)
to land, belt

endosar [endo'sar] *vt* (*cheque etc*) to
endorse

endulzar [endul'θar] vt to sweeten; (suavizar) to soften

endurecer [endure'θer] vt to harden; **~se** vr to harden, grow hard

enema [e'nema] nm (MED) enema

enemigo, a [ene'miɣo, a] adj enemy, hostile ♦ nm/f enemy

enemistad [enemis'taθ] nf enmity

enemistar [enemis'tar] vt to make enemies of, cause a rift between; **~se** vr to become enemies; (amigos) to fall out

energía [ener'xia] nf (vigor) energy, drive; (empuje) push; (TEC, ELEC) energy, power; **~ eólica** wind power; **~ solar** solar energy/power

enérgico, a [e'nerxiko, a] adj (gen) energetic; (voz, modales) forceful

energúmeno, a [ener'yumeno, a] (fam) nm/f (fig) madman/woman

enero [e'nero] nm January

enfadado, a [enfa'ðaðo, a] adj angry, annoyed

enfadar [enfa'ðar] vt to anger, annoy; **~se** vr to get angry o annoyed

enfado [en'faðo] nm (enojo) anger, annoyance; (disgusto) trouble, bother

énfasis ['enfasis] nm emphasis, stress

enfático, a [en'fatiko, a] adj emphatic

enfermar [enfer'mar] vt to make ill ♦ vi to fall ill, be taken ill

enfermedad [enferme'ðaθ] nf illness; **~ venérea** venereal disease

enfermera [enfer'mera] nf nurse

enfermería [enferme'ria] nf infirmary; (de colegio etc) sick bay

enfermero [enfer'mero] nm (male) nurse

enfermizo, a [enfer'miθo, a] adj (persona) sickly, unhealthy; (fig) unhealthy

enfermo, a [en'fermo, a] adj ill, sick ♦ nm/f invalid, sick person; (en hospital) patient

enflaquecer [enflake'θer] vt (adelgazar) to make thin; (debilitar) to weaken

enfocar [enfo'kar] vt (foto etc) to focus; (problema etc) to approach

enfoque etc [en'foke] vb ver **enfocar** ♦ nm focus.

enfrascarse [enfras'karse] vr: **~ en algo** to bury o.s. in sth

enfrentar [enfren'tar] vt (peligro) to face (up to), confront; (oponer) to bring face to face; **~se** vr (dos personas) to face o confront each other; (DEPORTE: dos equipos) to meet; **~se a** o **con** to face up to, confront

enfrente [en'frente] adv opposite; **la casa de ~** the house opposite, the house across the street; **~ de** opposite, facing

enfriamiento [enfria'mjento] nm chilling, refrigeration; (MED) cold, chill

enfriar [enfri'ar] vt (alimentos) to cool, chill; (algo caliente) to cool down; **~se** vr to cool down; (MED) to catch a chill; (amistad) to cool

enfurecer [enfure'θer] vt to enrage, madden; **~se** vr to become furious, fly into a rage; (mar) to get rough

engalanar [engala'nar] vt (adornar) to adorn; (ciudad) to decorate; **~se** vr to get dressed up

enganchar [engan'tʃar] vt to hook; (dos vagones) to hitch up; (TEC) to couple, connect; (MIL) to recruit; **~se** vr (MIL) to enlist, join up

enganche [en'gantʃe] nm hook; (TEC) coupling, connection; (acto) hooking (up); (MIL) recruitment, enlistment; (AM: depósito) deposit

engañar [enga'ɲar] vt to deceive; (estafar) to cheat, swindle; **~se** vr (equivocarse) to be wrong; (disimular la verdad) to deceive o.s.

engaño [en'gaɲo] nm deceit; (estafa) trick, swindle; (error) mistake, misunderstanding; (ilusión) delusion; **~so, a** adj (tramposo) crooked; (mentiroso) dishonest, deceitful; (aspecto) deceptive; (consejo) misleading

engarzar [engar'θar] vt (joya) to set, mount; (fig) to link, connect

engatusar [engatu'sar] vt (fam) to coax

engendrar [enxen'drar] vt to breed; (procrear) to beget; (causar) to cause, produce; **engendro** nm (BIO) foetus; (fig) monstrosity

englobar [englo'βar] vt to include, comprise

engordar [engor'ðar] vt to fatten ♦ vi to get fat, put on weight

engorroso, a [engo'rroso, a] adj bothersome, trying

engranaje [engra'naxe] nm (AUTO) gear

engrandecer [engrande'θer] vt to enlarge, magnify; (alabar) to praise, speak highly of; (exagerar) to exaggerate

engrasar [engra'sar] vt (TEC: poner grasa) to grease; (: lubricar) to lubricate, oil; (manchar) to make greasy

engreído, a [engre'iðo, a] adj vain, conceited

engrosar [engro'sar] vt (ensanchar) to enlarge; (aumentar) to increase; (hinchar) to swell

enhebrar [ene'βrar] vt to thread

enhorabuena [enora'βwena] excl ¡~! congratulations! ♦ nf: **dar la ~ a** to congratulate

enigma [e'niɣma] nm enigma; (problema) puzzle; (misterio) mystery

enjabonar [enxaβo'nar] vt to soap; (fam: adular) to soft-soap

enjambre [en'xambre] nm swarm

enjaular [enxau'lar] vt to (put in a) cage; (fam) to jail, lock up

enjuagar [enxwa'ɣar] vt (ropa) to rinse (out)

enjuague etc [en'xwaɣe] vb ver **enjuagar** ♦ nm (MED) mouthwash; (de ropa) rinse, rinsing

enjugar [enxu'ɣar] vt to wipe (off); (lágrimas) to dry; (déficit) to wipe out

enjuiciar [enxwi'θjar] vt (JUR: procesar) to prosecute, try; (fig) to judge

enjuto, a [en'xuto, a] adj (flaco) lean, skinny

enlace [en'laθe] nm link, connection; (relación) relationship; (tb: ~ matrimonial) marriage; (de carretera, trenes) connection; **~ sindical** shop steward

enlatado, a [enla'taðo, a] adj (comida, productos) tinned, canned

enlazar [enla'θar] vt (unir con lazos) to bind together; (atar) to tie; (conectar) to link, connect; (AM) to lasso

enlodar [enlo'ðar] vt to cover in mud; (fig: manchar) to stain; (: rebajar) to debase

enloquecer [enloke'θer] vt to drive mad ♦ vi to go mad; **~se** vr to go mad

enlutado, a [enlu'taðo, a] adj (persona) in mourning

enmarañar [enmara'ɲar] vt (enredar) to tangle (up), entangle; (complicar) to complicate; (confundir) to confuse; **~se** vr (enredarse) to become entangled; (confundirse) to get confused

enmarcar [enmar'kar] vt (cuadro) to frame

enmendar [enmen'dar] vt to emend, correct; (constitución etc) to amend; (comportamiento) to reform; **~se** vr to reform, mend one's ways; **enmienda** nf correction; amendment; reform

enmohecerse [enmoe'θerse] vr (metal) to rust, go rusty; (muro, plantas) to get mouldy

enmudecer [enmuðe'θer] vi (perder el habla) to fall silent; (guardar silencio) to remain silent

ennegrecer [enneɣre'θer] vt (poner negro) to blacken; (oscurecer) to darken; **~se** vr to turn black; (oscurecerse) to get dark, darken

ennoblecer [ennoβle'θer] vt to ennoble

enojar [eno'xar] vt (encolerizar) to

enojo [e'noxo] nm (*cólera*) anger; (*irritación*) annoyance; **~so, a** adj annoying

enorgullecerse [enorɣuʎe'θerse] vr to be proud; **~ de** to pride o.s. on, be proud of

enorme [e'norme] adj enormous, huge; (*fig*) monstrous; **enormidad** nf hugeness, immensity

enrarecido, a [enrare'θiðo, a] adj (*atmósfera, aire*) rarefied

enredadera [enreða'ðera] nf (*BOT*) creeper, climbing plant

enredar [enre'ðar] vt (*cables, hilos etc*) to tangle (up), entangle; (*situación*) to complicate, confuse; (*meter cizaña*) to sow discord among o between; (*implicar*) to embroil, implicate; **~se** vr to get entangled, get tangled (up); (*situación*) to get complicated; (*persona*) to get embroiled; (*AM: fam*) to meddle

enredo [en'reðo] nm (*maraña*) tangle; (*confusión*) mix-up, confusion; (*intriga*) intrigue

enrejado [enre'xaðo] nm fence, railings pl

enrevesado, a [enreβe'saðo, a] adj (*asunto*) complicated, involved

enriquecer [enrike'θer] vt to make rich, enrich; **~se** vr to get rich

enrojecer [enroxe'θer] vt to redden ♦ vi (*persona*) to blush; **~se** vr to redden

enrolar [enro'lar] vt (*MIL*) to enlist; (*reclutar*) to recruit; **~se** vr (*MIL*) to join up; (*afiliarse*) to enrol

enrollar [enro'ʎar] vt to roll (up), wind (up)

enroscar [enros'kar] vt (*torcer, doblar*) to coil (round), wind; (*tornillo, rosca*) to screw in; **~se** vr to coil, wind

ensalada [ensa'laða] nf salad; **ensaladilla (rusa)** nf Russian salad

ensalzar [ensal'θar] vt (*alabar*) to praise, extol; (*exaltar*) to exalt

ensamblaje [ensam'blaxe] nm assembly; (*TEC*) joint

ensanchar [ensan'tʃar] vt (*hacer más ancho*) to widen; (*agrandar*) to enlarge, expand; (*COSTURA*) to let out; **~se** vr to get wider, expand; **ensanche** nm (*de calle*) widening

ensangrentar [ensangren'tar] vt to stain with blood

ensañar [ensa'ɲar] vt to enrage; **~se con** to treat brutally

ensartar [ensar'tar] vt (*cuentas, perlas etc*) to string (together)

ensayar [ensa'jar] vt to test, try (out); (*TEATRO*) to rehearse

ensayo [en'sajo] nm test, trial; (*QUÍM*) experiment; (*TEATRO*) rehearsal; (*DEPORTE*) try; (*ESCOL, LITERATURA*) essay

enseguida [ense'βiða] adv at once, right away

ensenada [ense'naða] nf inlet, cove

enseñanza [ense'naɲθa] nf (*educación*) education; (*acción*) teaching; (*doctrina*) teaching, doctrine

enseñar [ense'par] vt (*educar*) to teach; (*mostrar, señalar*) to show

enseres [en'seres] nmpl belongings

ensillar [ensi'ʎar] vt to saddle

ensimismarse [ensimis'marse] vr (*abstraerse*) to become lost in thought; (*AM*) to become conceited

ensombrecer [ensombre'θer] vt to darken, cast a shadow over; (*fig*) to overshadow, put in the shade

ensordecer [ensorðe'θer] vt to deafen ♦ vi to go deaf

ensortijado, a [ensorti'xaðo, a] adj (*pelo*) curly

ensuciar [ensu'θjar] vt (*manchar*) to dirty, soil; (*fig*) to defile; **~se** vr to get dirty; (*niño*) to wet o.s.

ensueño [en'sweɲo] nm (*sueño*) dream, fantasy; (*ilusión*) illusion; (*soñando despierto*) daydream

entablar [enta'βlar] vt (*recubrir*) to board (up); (*AJEDREZ, DAMAS*) to set up; (*conversación*) to strike up; (*JUR*) to file

♦ *vi* to draw

entablillar |entaβliˈʎar| *vt* (MED) to (put in a) splint

entallar |entaˈʎar| *vt* (traje) to tailor ♦ *vi*: **el traje entalla bien** the suit fits well

ente |ˈente| *nm* (organización) body, organization; (fam: persona) odd character

entender |entenˈder| *vt* (comprender) to understand; (darse cuenta) to realize ♦ *vi* to understand; (creer) to think, believe; **~se** *vr* (comprenderse) to be understood; (2 personas) to get on together; (ponerse de acuerdo) to agree, reach an agreement; **~ de** to know all about; **~ algo de** to know a little about; **~ en** to deal with, have to do with; **~se mal** (2 personas) to get on badly

entendido, a |entenˈdiðo, a| *adj* (comprendido) understood; (hábil) skilled; (inteligente) knowledgeable ♦ *nm/f* (experto) expert ♦ *excl* agreed!; **entendimiento** *nm* (comprensión) understanding; (inteligencia) mind, intellect; (juicio) judgement

enterado, a |enteˈraðo, a| *adj* well-informed; **estar ~** to know about, be aware of

enteramente |enteraˈmente| *adv* entirely, completely

enterar |enteˈrar| *vt* (informar) to inform, tell; **~se** *vr* to find out, get to know

entereza |enteˈreθa| *nf* (totalidad) entirety; (fig: carácter) strength of mind; (: honradez) integrity

enternecer |enterneˈθer| *vt* (ablandar) to soften; (apiadar) to touch, move; **~se** *vr* to be touched, be moved

entero, a |enˈtero, a| *adj* (total) whole, entire; (fig: honesto) honest; (: firme) firm, resolute ♦ *nm* (COM: punto) point; (AM: pago) payment

enterrador |enterraˈðor| *nm* gravedigger

enterrar |enteˈrrar| *vt* to bury

entibiar |entiˈβjar| *vt* (enfriar) to cool; (calentar) to warm; **~se** *vr* (fig) to cool

entidad |entiˈðað| *nf* (empresa) firm, company; (organismo) body; (sociedad) society; (FILOSOFÍA) entity

entiendo *etc vb ver* **entender**

entierro |enˈtjerro| *nm* (acción) burial; (funeral) funeral

entonación |entonaˈθjon| *nf* (LING) intonation

entonar |entoˈnar| *vt* (canción) to intone; (colores) to tone; (MED) to tone up ♦ *vi* to be in tune

entonces |enˈtonθes| *adv* then, at that time; **desde ~** since then; **en aquel ~** at that time; **(pues) ~** and so

entornar |entorˈnar| *vt* (puerta, ventana) to half close, leave ajar; (los ojos) to screw up

entorpecer |entorpeˈθer| *vt* (entendimiento) to dull; (impedir) to obstruct, hinder; (: tránsito) to slow down, delay

entrada |enˈtraða| *nf* (acción) entry, access; (sitio) entrance, way in; (INFORM) input; (COM) receipts *pl*, takings *pl*; (CULIN) starter; (DEPORTE) innings *sg*; (TEATRO) house, audience; (billete) ticket; (COM): **~s y salidas** income and expenditure; (TEC): **~ de aire** air intake o inlet; **de ~** from the outset

entrado, a |enˈtraðo, a| *adj*: **~ en años** elderly; **una vez ~ el verano** in the summer(time), when summer comes

entramparse |entramˈparse| *vr* to get into debt

entrante |enˈtrante| *adj* next, coming; **mes/año ~** next month/year; **~s** *nmpl* starters

entraña |enˈtraɲa| *nf* (fig: centro) heart, core; (raíz) root; **~s** *nfpl* (ANAT) entrails; (fig) heart *sg*; **sin ~s** heartless; **entrañable** *adj* close, intimate; **entrañar** *vt* to entail

entrar [en'trar] vt (introducir) to bring in; (INFORM) to input ♦ vi (meterse) to go in, come in, enter; (comenzar):
~ **diciendo** to begin by saying; **hacer** ~ to show in; **no me entra** I can't get the hang of it

entre ['entre] prep (dos) between; (más de dos) among(st)

entreabrir [entrea'ßrir] vt to half-open, open halfway

entrecejo [entre'θexo] nm: **fruncir el** ~ to frown

entrecortado, a [entrekor'taðo, a] adj (respiración) difficult; (habla) faltering

entredicho [entre'ðitʃo] nm (JUR) injunction; **poner en** ~ to cast doubt on; **estar en** ~ to be in doubt

entrega [en'treγa] nf (de mercancías) delivery; (de novela etc) instalment

entregar [entre'γar] vt (dar) to hand (over), deliver; ~**se** vr (rendirse) to surrender, give in, submit; (dedicarse) to devote o.s.

entrelazar [entrela'θar] vt to entwine

entremeses [entre'meses] nmpl hors d'œuvres

entremeter [entreme'ter] vt to insert, put in; ~**se** vr to meddle, interfere; **entremetido, a** adj meddling, interfering

entremezclar [entremeθ'klar] vt to intermingle; ~**se** vr to intermingle

entrenador, a [entrena'ðor, a] nm/f trainer, coach

entrenarse [entre'narse] vr to train

entrepierna [entre'pjerna] nf crotch

entresacar [entresa'kar] vt to pick out, select

entresuelo [entre'swelo] nm mezzanine

entretanto [entre'tanto] adv meanwhile, meantime

entretejer [entrete'xer] vt to interweave

entretener [entrete'ner] vt (divertir) to entertain, amuse; (detener) to hold up, delay; ~**se** vr (divertirse) to amuse o.s.; (retrasarse) to delay, linger;
entretenido, a adj entertaining, amusing; **entretenimiento** nm entertainment, amusement

entrever [entre'ßer] vt to glimpse, catch a glimpse of

entrevista [entre'ßista] nf interview;
entrevistar vt to interview;
entrevistarse vr to have an interview

entristecer [entriste'θer] vt to sadden, grieve; ~**se** vr to grow sad

entrometerse [entrome'terse] vr: ~ **(en)** to interfere (in o with)

entroncar [entron'kar] vi to be connected o related

entumecer [entume'θer] vt to numb, benumb; ~**se** vr (por el frío) to go o become numb; **entumecido, a** adj numb, stiff

enturbiar [entur'ßjar] vt (el agua) to make cloudy; (fig) to confuse; ~**se** vr (oscurecerse) to become cloudy; (fig) to get confused, become obscure

entusiasmar [entusjas'mar] vt to excite, fill with enthusiasm; (gustar mucho) to delight; ~**se** vr: ~**se con** o **por** to get enthusiastic o excited about

entusiasmo [entu'sjasmo] nm enthusiasm; (excitación) excitement

entusiasta [entu'sjasta] adj enthusiastic ♦ nm/f enthusiast

enumerar [enume'rar] vt to enumerate

enunciación [enunθja'θjon] nf enunciation

enunciado [enun'θjaðo] nm enunciation

envainar [embai'nar] vt to sheathe

envalentonar [embalento'nar] vt to give courage to; ~**se** vr (pey: jactarse) to boast, brag

envanecer [embane'θer] vt to make conceited; ~**se** vr to grow conceited

envasar [emba'sar] vt (empaquetar) to pack, wrap; (enfrascar) to bottle; (enlatar) to can; (embolsar) to pocket

envase [em'base] nm (en paquete) packing, wrapping; (en botella) bottling; (en lata) canning; (recipiente) container; (paquete) package; (botella) bottle; (lata) tin (BRIT), can

envejecer [embexe'θer] vt to make old, age ♦ vi (volverse viejo) to grow old; (parecer viejo) to age; **~se** vr to grow old; to age

envenenar [embene'nar] vt to poison; (fig) to embitter

envergadura [emberγa'ðura] nf (fig) scope, compass

envés [em'bes] nm (de tela) back, wrong side

enviar [em'bjar] vt to send

enviciarse [embi'θjarse] vr: **~ (con)** to get addicted to

envidia [em'biðja] nf envy; **tener ~ a** to envy, be jealous of; **envidiar** vt to envy

envío [em'bio] nm (acción) sending; (de mercancías) consignment; (de dinero) remittance

enviudar [embju'ðar] vi to be widowed

envoltura [embol'tura] nf (cobertura) cover; (embalaje) wrapper, wrapping; **envoltorio** nm package

envolver [embol'βer] vt to wrap (up); (cubrir) to cover; (enemigo) to surround; (implicar) to involve, implicate

envuelto [em'bwelto] pp de **envolver**

enyesar [enje'sar] vt (pared) to plaster; (MED) to put in plaster

enzarzarse [enθar'θarse] vr: **~ en** (pelea) to get mixed up in; (disputa) to get involved in

épica ['epika] nf epic

épico, a ['epiko, a] adj epic

epidemia [epi'ðemja] nf epidemic

epilepsia [epi'lepsja] nf epilepsy

epílogo [e'piloγo] nm epilogue

episodio [epi'soðjo] nm episode

epístola [e'pistola] nf epistle

época ['epoka] nf period, time;

(HISTORIA) age, epoch; **hacer ~** to be epoch-making

equilibrar [ekili'βrar] vt to balance; **equilibrio** nm balance, equilibrium; **equilibrista** nm/f (funámbulo) tightrope walker; (acróbata) acrobat

equipaje [eki'paxe] nm luggage; (avíos): **~ de mano** hand luggage

equipar [eki'par] vt (proveer) to equip

equipararse [ekipa'rarse] vr: **~ con** to be on a level with

equipo [e'kipo] nm (conjunto de cosas) equipment; (DEPORTE) team; (de obreros) squad

equis ['ekis] nf inv (the letter) X

equitación [ekita'θjon] nf horse riding

equitativo, a [ekita'tiβo, a] adj equitable, fair

equivalente [ekiβa'lente] adj, nm equivalent

equivaler [ekiβa'ler] vi to be equivalent o equal

equivocación [ekiβoka'θjon] nf mistake, error

equivocado, a [ekiβo'kaðo, a] adj wrong, mistaken

equivocarse [ekiβo'karse] vr to be wrong, make a mistake; **~ de camino** to take the wrong road

equívoco, a [e'kiβoko, a] adj (dudoso) suspect; (ambiguo) ambiguous ♦ nm ambiguity; (malentendido) misunderstanding

era ['era] vb ver **ser** ♦ nf era, age

erais vb ver **ser**

éramos vb ver **ser**

eran vb ver **ser**

erario [e'rarjo] nm exchequer (BRIT), treasury

eras vb ver **ser**

erección [erek'θjon] nf erection

eres vb ver **ser**

erguir [er'xir] vt to raise, lift; (poner derecho) to straighten; **~se** vr to straighten up

erigir [eri'xir] vt to erect, build; **~se** vr: **~se en** to set o.s. up as

erizarse [eri'θarse] vr (pelo: de perro) to bristle; (: de persona) to stand on end

erizo [e'riθo] nm (ZOOL) hedgehog; **~ de mar** sea-urchin

ermita [er'mita] nf hermitage

ermitaño, a [ermi'taɲo, a] nm/f hermit

erosión [ero'sjon] nf erosion

erosionar [erosjo'nar] vt to erode

erótico, a [e'rotiko, a] adj erotic; **erotismo** nm eroticism

erradicar [erraði'kar] vt to eradicate

errante [e'rrante] adj wandering, errant

errar [e'rrar] vi (vagar) to wander, roam; (equivocarse) to be mistaken ♦ vt: **~ el camino** to take the wrong road; **~ el tiro** to miss

erróneo, a [e'rroneo, a] adj (equivocado) wrong, mistaken

error [e'rror] nm error, mistake; (INFORM) bug; **~ de imprenta** misprint

eructar [eruk'tar] vt to belch, burp

erudito, a [eru'ðito, a] adj erudite, learned

erupción [erup'θjon] nf eruption; (MED) rash

es vb ver **ser**

esa ['esa] (pl **esas**) adj demos ver **ese**

ésa ['esa] (pl **ésas**) pron ver **ése**

esbelto, a [es'βelto, a] adj slim, slender

esbozo [es'βoθo] nm sketch, outline

escabeche [eska'βetʃe] nm brine; (de aceitunas etc) pickle; **en ~** pickled

escabroso, a [eska'βroso, a] adj (accidentado) rough, uneven; (fig) tough, difficult; (: atrevido) risqué

escabullirse [eskaβu'ʎirse] vr to slip away, to clear out

escafandra [eska'fandra] nf (buzo) diving suit; (~ espacial) space suit

escala [es'kala] nf (proporción, MUS) scale; (de mano) ladder; (AVIAT) stopover; **hacer ~ en** to stop o call in at

escalafón [eskala'fon] nm (escala de salarios) salary scale, wage scale

escalar [eska'lar] vt to climb, scale

escalera [eska'lera] nf stairs pl, staircase; (escala) ladder; (NAIPES) run; **~ mecánica** escalator; **~ de caracol** spiral staircase

escalfar [eskal'far] vt (huevos) to poach

escalinata [eskali'nata] nf staircase

escalofriante [eskalo'frjante] adj chilling

escalofrío [eskalo'frio] nm (MED) chill; **~s** nmpl (fig) shivers

escalón [eska'lon] nm step, stair; (de escalera) rung

escalope [eska'lope] nm (CULIN) escalope

escama [es'kama] nf (de pez, serpiente) scale; (de jabón) flake; (fig) resentment

escamar [eska'mar] vt (fig) to make wary o suspicious

escamotear [eskamote'ar] vt (robar) to lift, swipe; (hacer desaparecer) to make disappear

escampar [eskam'par] vb impers to stop raining

escandalizar [eskandali'θar] vt to scandalize, shock; **~se** vr to be shocked; (ofenderse) to be offended

escándalo [es'kandalo] nm scandal; (alboroto, tumulto) row, uproar; **escandaloso, a** adj scandalous, shocking

escandinavo, a [eskandi'naβo, a] adj, nm/f Scandinavian

escaño [es'kaɲo] nm bench; (POL) seat

escapar [eska'par] vi (gen) to escape, run away; (DEPORTE) to break away; **~se** vr to escape, get away; (agua, gas) to leak (out)

escaparate [eskapa'rate] nm shop window

escape [es'kape] nm (de agua, gas) leak; (de motor) exhaust

escarabajo [eskara'βaxo] nm beetle

escaramuza [eskara'muθa] nf skirmish

escarbar [eskar'βar] vt (tierra) to scratch

escarceos [eskar'θeos] nmpl (fig): **en mis ~ con la política ...** in my dealings with politics ...; **~ amorosos** love affairs

escarcha [es'kartʃa] nf frost

escarchado, a [eskar'tʃaðo, a] adj (CULIN: fruta) crystallized

escarlata [eskar'lata] adj inv scarlet; **escarlatina** nf scarlet fever

escarmentar [eskarmen'tar] vt to punish severely ♦ vi to learn one's lesson

escarmiento etc [eskar'mjento] vb ver **escarmentar** ♦ nm (ejemplo) lesson; (castigo) punishment

escarnio [es'karnjo] nm mockery; (injuria) insult

escarola [eska'rola] nf endive

escarpado, a [eskar'paðo, a] adj (pendiente) sheer, steep; (rocas) craggy

escasear [eskase'ar] vi to be scarce

escasez [eska'seθ] nf (falta) shortage, scarcity; (pobreza) poverty

escaso, a [es'kaso, a] adj (poco) scarce; (raro) rare; (ralo) thin, sparse; (limitado) limited

escatimar [eskati'mar] vt to skimp (on), be sparing with

escayola [eska'jola] nf plaster

escena [es'θena] nf scene

escenario [esθe'narjo] nm (TEATRO) stage; (CINE) set; (fig) scene; **escenografía** nf set design

escepticismo [esθepti'θismo] nm scepticism; **escéptico, a** adj sceptical ♦ nm/f sceptic

escisión [esθi'sjon] nf (de partido, secta) split

esclarecer [esklare'θer] vt (misterio, problema) to shed light on

esclavitud [esklaβi'tuð] nf slavery

esclavizar [esklaβi'θar] vt to enslave

esclavo, a [es'klaβo, a] nm/f slave

esclusa [es'klusa] nf (de canal) lock; (compuerta) floodgate

escoba [es'koβa] nf broom; **escobilla** nf brush

escocer [esko'θer] vi to burn, sting; **~se** vr to chafe, get chafed

escocés, esa [esko'θes, esa] adj Scottish ♦ nm/f Scotsman/woman, Scot

Escocia [es'koθja] nf Scotland

escoger [esko'xer] vt to choose, pick, select; **escogido, a** adj chosen, selected

escolar [esko'lar] adj school cpd ♦ nm/f schoolboy/girl, pupil

escollo [es'koʎo] nm (obstáculo) pitfall

escolta [es'kolta] nf escort; **escoltar** vt to escort

escombros [es'kombros] nmpl (basura) rubbish sg; (restos) debris sg

esconder [eskon'der] vt to hide, conceal; **~se** vr to hide; **escondidas** (AM) nfpl: **a escondidas** secretly; **escondite** nm hiding place; (juego) hide-and-seek; **escondrijo** nm hiding place, hideout

escopeta [esko'peta] nf shotgun

escoria [es'korja] nf (de alto horno) slag; (fig) scum, dregs pl

Escorpio [es'korpjo] nm Scorpio

escorpión [eskor'pjon] nm scorpion

escotado, a [esko'taðo, a] adj low-cut

escote [es'kote] nm (de vestido) low neck; **pagar a ~** to share the expenses

escotilla [esko'tiʎa] nf (NAUT) hatch(way)

escozor [esko'θor] nm (dolor) sting(ing)

escribir [eskri'βir] vt, vi to write; **~ a máquina** to type; **¿cómo se escribe?** how do you spell it?

escrito, a [es'krito, a] pp de **escribir** ♦ nm (documento) document; (manuscrito) text, manuscript; **por ~** in writing

escritor, a [eskri'tor, a] nm/f writer

escritorio [eskri'torjo] nm desk

escritura [eskri'tura] nf (acción) writing; (caligrafía) (hand)writing; (JUR: documento) deed

escrúpulo [es'krupulo] nm scruple; (minuciosidad) scrupulousness; **escrupuloso, a** adj scrupulous

escrutar [eskru'tar] vt to scrutinize, examine; (votos) to count

escrutinio [eskru'tinjo] nm (examen atento) scrutiny; (POL: recuento de votos) count(ing)

escuadra [es'kwaðra] nf (MIL etc) squad; (NAUT) squadron; (de coches etc) fleet; **escuadrilla** nf (de aviones) squadron; (AM: de obreros) gang

escuadrón [eskwa'ðron] nm squadron

escuálido, a [es'kwaliðo, a] adj skinny, scraggy; (sucio) squalid

escuchar [esku'tʃar] vt to listen to ♦ vi to listen

escudilla [esku'ðiʎa] nf bowl, basin

escudo [es'kuðo] nm shield

escudriñar [eskuðri'nar] vt (examinar) to investigate, scrutinize; (mirar de lejos) to scan

escuela [es'kwela] nf school; ~ de artes y oficios (ESP) ≈ technical college; ~ normal teacher training college

escueto, a [es'kweto, a] adj plain; (estilo) simple

escuincle [es'kwinkle] (AM: fam) nm/f kid

esculpir [eskul'pir] vt to sculpt; (grabar) to engrave; (tallar) to carve; **escultor, a** nm/f sculptor/tress; **escultura** nf sculpture

escupidera [eskupi'ðera] nf spittoon

escupir [esku'pir] vt, vi to spit (out)

escurreplatos [eskurre'platos] nm inv plate rack

escurridizo, a [eskurri'ðiθo, a] adj slippery

escurridor [eskurri'ðor] nm colander

escurrir [esku'rrir] vt (ropa) to wring out; (verduras, platos) to drain ♦ vi (líquidos) to drip; **~se** vr (secarse) to drain; (resbalarse) to slip, slide; (escaparse) to slip away

ese [ese] (f **esa**, pl **esos, esas**) adj

demos (sg) that; (pl) those

ése [ese] (f **ésa**, pl **ésos, ésas**) pron (sg) that (one); (pl) those (ones); ~ ... **éste** ... the former ... the latter ...; **no me vengas con ésas** don't give me any more of that nonsense

esencia [e'senθja] nf essence; **esencial** adj essential

esfera [es'fera] nf sphere; (de reloj) face; **esférico, a** adj spherical

esforzarse [esfor'θarse] vr to exert o.s., make an effort

esfuerzo [es'fwerθo] vb ver **esforzar** ♦ nm effort

esfumarse [esfu'marse] vr (apoyo, esperanzas) to fade away

esgrima [es'xrima] nf fencing

esgrimir [esxri'mir] vt (arma) to brandish; (argumento) to use

esguince [es'xinθe] nm (MED) sprain

eslabón [esla'ßon] nm link

eslip [ez'lip] nm pants pl (BRIT), briefs pl

eslovaco, a [eslo'ßako, a] adj, nm/f Slovak, Slovakian ♦ nm (LING) Slovak, Slovakian

Eslovaquia [eslo'ßakja] nf Slovakia

esmaltar [esmal'tar] vt to enamel; **esmalte** nm enamel; **esmalte de uñas** nail varnish o polish

esmerado, a [esme'raðo, a] adj careful, neat

esmeralda [esme'ralda] nf emerald

esmerarse [esme'rarse] vr (aplicarse) to take great pains, exercise great care; (afanarse) to work hard

esmero [es'mero] nm (great) care

esnob [es'nob] (pl **~s**) adj (persona) snobbish ♦ nm/f snob; **~ismo** nm snobbery

eso [eso] pron that, that thing o matter; **~ de su coche** that business about his car; **~ de ir al cine** all that about going to the cinema; **a ~ de las cinco** at about five o'clock; **en ~** thereupon, at that point; **~ es** that's it; **¡~ sí que es vida!** now that is really living!; **por ~ te lo dije** that's why I told you; **y ~ que llovía** in spite of the fact it was raining

esos ['esos] adj demos ver **ese**

ésos ['esos] pron ver **ése**

espabilar etc [espaβi'lar] = **despabilar** etc

espacial [espa'θjal] adj (del espacio) space cpd

espaciar [espa'θjar] vt to space (out)

espacio [es'paθjo] nm space; (MUS) interval; (RADIO, TV) programme (BRIT), program (US); **el ~** space; **~so, a** adj spacious, roomy

espada [es'paða] nf sword; **~s** nfpl (NAIPES) spades

espaguetis [espa'vetis] nmpl spaghetti sg

espalda [es'palda] nf back; **~s** nfpl (hombros) shoulders; **a ~s de uno** behind sb's back; **tenderse de ~s** to lie (down) on one's back; **volver la ~ a alguien** to cold-shoulder sb

espantajo [espan'taxo] nm = **espantapájaros**

espantapájaros [espanta'paxaros] nm inv scarecrow

espantar [espan'tar] vt (asustar) to frighten, scare; (ahuyentar) to frighten off; (asombrar) to horrify, appal; **~se** vr to get frightened o scared; to be appalled

espanto [es'panto] nm (susto) fright; (terror) terror; (asombro) astonishment; **~so, a** adj frightening; terrifying; astonishing

España [es'paɲa] nf Spain; **español, a** adj Spanish ♦ nm/f Spaniard ♦ nm (LING) Spanish

esparadrapo [espara'ðrapo] nm (sticking) plaster (BRIT), adhesive tape (US)

esparcimiento [esparθi'mjento] nm (dispersión) spreading; (diseminación) scattering; (fig) cheerfulness

esparcir [espar'θir] vt to spread; (diseminar) to scatter; **~se** vr to spread (out); to scatter; (divertirse) to enjoy

o.s.

espárrago [es'parraxo] nm asparagus

esparto [es'parto] nm esparto (grass)

espasmo [es'pasmo] nm spasm

espátula [es'patula] nf spatula

especia [es'peθja] nf spice

especial [espe'θjal] adj special; **~idad** nf speciality (BRIT), specialty (US)

especie [es'peθje] nf (BIO) species; (clase) kind, sort; **en ~** in kind

especificar [espeθifi'kar] vt to specify; **específico, a** adj specific

espécimen [es'peθimen] (pl **especímenes**) nm specimen

espectáculo [espek'takulo] nm (gen) spectacle; (TEATRO etc) show

espectador, a [espekta'ðor, a] nm/f spectator

espectro [es'pektro] nm ghost; (fig) spectre

especular [espeku'lar] vt, vi to speculate

espejismo [espe'xismo] nm mirage

espejo [es'pexo] nm mirror; **~ retrovisor** rear-view mirror

espeluznante [espeluθ'nante] adj horrifying, hair-raising

espera [es'pera] nf (pausa, intervalo) wait; (JUR: plazo) respite; **en ~ de** waiting for; (con expectativa) expecting

esperanza [espe'ranθa] nf (confianza) hope; (expectativa) expectation; **hay pocas ~s de que venga** there is little prospect of his coming

esperar [espe'rar] vt (aguardar) to wait for; (tener expectativa de) to expect; (desear) to hope for ♦ vi to wait; to expect; to hope

esperma [es'perma] nf sperm

espesar [espe'sar] vt to thicken; **~se** vr to thicken, get thicker

espeso, a [es'peso, a] adj thick; **espesor** nm thickness

espía [es'pia] nmf spy; **espiar** (observar) to spy on

espiga [es'pixa] nf (BOT: de trigo etc) ear

espigón [espi'γon] nm (BOT) ear; (NAUT) breakwater

espina [es'pina] nf thorn; (de pez) bone; **~ dorsal** (ANAT) spine

espinaca [espi'naka] nf spinach

espinazo [espi'naθo] nm spine, backbone

espinilla [espi'niʎa] nf (ANAT: tibia) shin(bone); (grano) blackhead

espinoso, a [espi'noso, a] adj (planta) thorny, prickly; (asunto) difficult

espionaje [espjo'naxe] nm spying, espionage

espiral [espi'ral] adj, nf spiral

espirar [espi'rar] vt to breathe out, exhale

espiritista [espiri'tista] adj, nm/f spiritualist

espíritu [es'piritu] nm spirit; **espiritual** adj spiritual

espita [es'pita] nf tap

espléndido, a [es'plendiðo, a] adj (magnífico) magnificent, splendid; (generoso) generous

esplendor [esplen'dor] nm splendour

espolear [espole'ar] vt to spur on

espoleta [espo'leta] nf (de bomba) fuse

espolón [espo'lon] nm sea wall

espolvorear [espolβore'ar] vt to dust, sprinkle

esponja [es'ponxa] nf sponge; (fig) sponger; **esponjoso, a** adj spongy

espontaneidad [espontanei'ðað] nf spontaneity; **espontáneo, a** adj spontaneous

esposa [es'posa] nf wife; **~s** nfpl handcuffs; **esposar** vt to handcuff

esposo [es'poso] nm husband

espray [es'prai] nm spray

espuela [es'pwela] nf spur

espuma [es'puma] nf foam; (de cerveza) froth, head; (de jabón) lather; **espumadera** nf (utensilio) skimmer; **espumoso, a** adj frothy, foamy; (vino) sparkling

esqueleto [eske'leto] nm skeleton

esquema [es'kema] nm (diagrama)

diagram; (dibujo) plan; (FILOSOFÍA) schema

esquí [es'ki] (pl **~s**) nm (objeto) ski; (DEPORTE) skiing; **~ acuático** water-skiing; **esquiar** vi to ski

esquilar [eski'lar] vt to shear

esquimal [eski'mal] adj, nm/f Eskimo

esquina [es'kina] nf corner

esquinazo [eski'naθo] nm: **dar ~ a algn** to give sb the slip

esquirol [eski'rol] nm blackleg

esquivar [eski'βar] vt to avoid

esquivo, a [es'kiβo, a] adj evasive; (tímido) reserved; (huraño) unsociable

esta ['esta] adj demos ver **este²**

está vb ver **estar**

ésta ['esta] pron ver **éste**

estabilidad [estaβili'ðað] nf stability; **estable** adj stable

establecer [estaβle'θer] vt to establish; **~se** vr to establish o.s.; (echar raíces) to settle (down); **establecimiento** nm establishment

establo [es'taβlo] nm (AGR) stable

estaca [es'taka] nf stake, post; (de tienda de campaña) peg

estacada [esta'kaða] nf (cerca) fence, fencing; (palenque) stockade

estación [esta'θjon] nf station; (del año) season; **~ de autobuses** bus station; **~ balnearia** seaside resort; **~ de servicio** service station

estacionamiento [estaθjona'mjento] nm (AUTO) parking; (MIL) stationing

estacionar [estaθjo'nar] vt (AUTO) to park; (MIL) to station; **~io, a** adj stationary; (COM: mercado) slack

estadio [es'taðjo] nm (fase) stage, phase; (DEPORTE) stadium

estadista [esta'ðista] nm (POL) statesman; (ESTADÍSTICA) statistician

estadística [esta'ðistika] nf figure, statistic; (ciencia) statistics sg

estado [es'taðo] nm (POL: condición) state; **~ de ánimo** state of mind; **~ de cuenta** bank statement; **~ de sitio** state of siege; **~ civil** marital status;

~ mayor staff; **estar en ~** to be pregnant; **(los) E~s Unidos** nmpl the United States (of America) sg

estadounidense [estaðouniˈðense] adj United States cpd, American ♦ nm/f American

estafa [esˈtafa] nf swindle, trick;

estafar vt to swindle, defraud

estafeta [estaˈfeta] nf (oficina de correos) post office; **~ diplomática** diplomatic bag

estáis vb ver **estar**

estallar [estaˈʎar] vi to burst; (bomba) to explode, go off; (epidemia, guerra, rebelión) to break out; **~ en llanto** to burst into tears; **estallido** nm explosion; (fig) outbreak

estampa [esˈtampa] nf print, engraving

estampado, a [estamˈpaðo, a] adj printed ♦ nm (impresión: acción) printing; (: efecto) print; (marca) stamping

estampar [estamˈpar] vt (imprimir) to print; (marcar) to stamp; (metal) to engrave; (poner sello en) to stamp; (fig) to stamp, imprint

estampida [estamˈpiða] nf stampede

estampido [estamˈpiðo] nm bang, report

están vb ver **estar**

estancado, a [estanˈkaðo, a] adj stagnant

estancar [estanˈkar] vt (aguas) to hold up, hold back; (COM) to monopolize; (fig) to block, hold up; **~se** vr to stagnate

estancia [esˈtanθja] nf (permanencia) stay; (sala) room; (AM) farm, ranch; **estanciero** (AM) nm farmer, rancher

estanco, a [esˈtanko, a] adj watertight ♦ nm tobacconist's (shop), cigar store (US)

Estanco

Cigarettes, tobacco, postage stamps and official forms are all sold under

state monopoly in shops called an estanco. Although tobacco products can also be bought in bars and quioscos they are generally more expensive.

estándar [esˈtandar] adj, nm standard;

estandarizar vt to standardize

estandarte [estanˈdarte] nm banner, standard

estanque [esˈtanke] nm (lago) pool, pond; (AGR) reservoir

estanquero, a [estanˈkero, a] nm/f tobacconist

estante [esˈtante] nm (armario) rack, stand; (biblioteca) bookcase; (anaquel) shelf; (AM) prop; **estantería** nf shelving, shelves pl

estaño [esˈtaɲo] nm tin

PALABRA CLAVE

estar [esˈtar] vi **1** (posición) to be; **está en la plaza** it's in the square; **¿está Juan?** is Juan in?; **estamos a 30 km de Junín** we're 30 kms from Junín

2 (+ adj: estado) to be; **~ enfermo** to be ill; **está muy elegante** he's looking very smart; **¿cómo estás?** how are you keeping?

3 (+ gerundio): **estoy leyendo** I'm reading

4 (uso pasivo): **está condenado a muerte** he's been condemned to death; **está envasado en ...** it's packed in ...

5 (con fechas): **¿a cuántos estamos?** what's the date today?; **estamos a 5 de mayo** it's the 5th of May

6 (locuciones): **¿estamos?** (¿de acuerdo?) okay?; (¿listo?) ready?; **¡ya está bien!** that's enough!

7: ~ de: ~ de vacaciones/viaje to be on holiday/away o on a trip; **está de camarero** he's working as a waiter

8: ~ para: está para salir he's about to leave; **no estoy para bromas** I'm not in the mood for jokes

9: ~ **por** (*propuesta etc*) to be in favour of; (*persona etc*) to support, side with; **está por limpiar** it still has to be cleaned

10: ~ **sin:** ~ **sin dinero** to have no money; **está sin terminar** it isn't finished yet

♦ ~**se** *vr:* **se estuvo en la cama toda la tarde** he stayed in bed all afternoon

estas ['estas] *adj demos ver* **este²**
éstas ['estas] *pron ver* **éste**
estatal [esta'tal] *adj* state *cpd*
estático, a [es'tatiko, a] *adj* static
estatua [es'tatwa] *nf* statue
estatura [esta'tura] *nf* stature, height
estatuto [esta'tuto] *nm* (*JUR*) statute; (*de ciudad*) bye-law; (*de comité*) rule
este¹ ['este] *nm* east
este² ['este] (*f* **esta**, *pl* **estos, estas**) *adj demos* (*sg*) this; (*pl*) these
esté *etc vb ver* **estar**
éste ['este] (*f* **ésta**, *pl* **éstos, éstas**) *pron* (*sg*) this (one); (*pl*) these (ones); **ése** ... ~ ... the former ... the latter ....
estelar [este'lar] *adj* (*ASTRO*) stellar; (*actuación, reparto*) star (*atr*)
estén *etc vb ver* **estar**
estepa [es'tepa] *nf* (*GEO*) steppe
estera [es'tera] *nf* mat(ting)
estéreo [es'tereo] *adj inv, nm* stereo; **estereotipo** *nm* stereotype
estéril [es'teril] *adj* sterile, barren; (*fig*) vain, futile; **esterilizar** *vt* to sterilize
esterlina [ester'lina] *adj:* **libra** ~ pound sterling
estés *etc vb ver* **estar**
estética [es'tetika] *nf* aesthetics *sg*
estético, a [es'tetiko, a] *adj* aesthetic
estibador [estiβa'ðor] *nm* stevedore, docker
estiércol [es'tjerkol] *nm* dung, manure
estigma [es'tixma] *nm* stigma
estilarse [esti'larse] *vr* to be in fashion
estilo [es'tilo] *nm* style; (*TEC*) stylus; (*NATACIÓN*) stroke; **algo por el** ~

something along those lines

estima [es'tima] *nf* esteem, respect
estimación [estima'θjon] *nf* (*evaluación*) estimation; (*aprecio, afecto*) esteem, regard
estimar [esti'mar] *vt* (*evaluar*) to estimate; (*valorar*) to value; (*apreciar*) to esteem, respect; (*pensar, considerar*) to think, reckon
estimulante [estimu'lante] *adj* stimulating ♦ *nm* stimulant
estimular [estimu'lar] *vt* to stimulate; (*excitar*) to excite
estímulo [es'timulo] *nm* stimulus; (*ánimo*) encouragement
estipulación [estipula'θjon] *nf* stipulation, condition
estipular [estipu'lar] *vt* to stipulate
estirado, a [esti'raðo, a] *adj* (*tenso*) (stretched *o* drawn) tight; (*fig: persona*) stiff, pompous
estirar [esti'rar] *vt* to stretch; (*dinero, suma etc*) to stretch out; ~**se** *vr* to stretch
estirón [esti'ron] *nm* pull, tug; (*crecimiento*) spurt, sudden growth; **dar un** ~ (*niño*) to shoot up
estirpe [es'tirpe] *nf* stock, lineage
estival [esti'βal] *adj* summer *cpd*
esto ['esto] *pron* this, this thing *o* matter; ~ **de la boda** this business about the wedding
Estocolmo [esto'kolmo] *nm* Stockholm
estofado [esto'faðo] *nm* stew
estofar [esto'far] *vt* to stew
estómago [es'tomaxo] *nm* stomach; **tener** ~ to be thick-skinned
estorbar [estor'βar] *vt* to hinder, obstruct; (*molestar*) to bother, disturb ♦ *vi* to be in the way; **estorbo** *nm* (*molestia*) bother, nuisance; (*obstáculo*) hindrance, obstacle
estornudar [estornu'ðar] *vi* to sneeze
estos ['estos] *adj demos ver* **este²**
éstos ['estos] *pron ver* **éste**
estoy *vb ver* **estar**

estrado [es'traðo] nm platform

estrafalario, a [estrafa'larjo, a] adj odd, eccentric

estrago [es'travo] nm ruin, destruction; **hacer ~s en** to wreak havoc among

estragón [estra'von] nm tarragon

estrambótico, a [estram'botiko, a] adj (persona) eccentric; (peinado, ropa) outlandish

estrangulador, a [estrangula'ðor, a] nm/f strangler ♦ nm (TEC) throttle; (AUTO) choke

estrangular [estrangu'lar] vt (persona) to strangle; (MED) to strangulate

estratagema [estrata'xema] nf (MIL) stratagem; (astucia) cunning

estrategia [estra'texja] nf strategy; **estratégico, a** adj strategic

estrato [es'trato] nm stratum, layer

estrechamente [estretʃa'mente] adv (íntimamente) closely, intimately; (pobremente: vivir) poorly

estrechar [estre'tʃar] vt (reducir) to narrow; (COSTURA) to take in; (abrazar) to hug, embrace; **~se** vr (reducirse) to narrow, grow narrow; (abrazarse) to embrace; **~ la mano** to shake hands

estrechez [estre'tʃeθ] nf narrowness; (de ropa) tightness; **estrecheces** nfpl (dificultades económicas) financial difficulties

estrecho, a [es'tretʃo, a] adj narrow; (apretado) tight; (íntimo) close, intimate; (miserable) mean ♦ nm strait; **~ de miras** narrow-minded

estrella [es'treʎa] nf star; **~ de mar** (ZOOL) starfish; **~ fugaz** shooting star; **estrellado, a** adj (forma) star-shaped; (cielo) starry

estrellar [estre'ʎar] vt (hacer añicos) to smash (to pieces); (huevos) to fry; **~se** vr to smash; (chocarse) to crash; (fracasar) to fail

estremecer [estreme'θer] vt to shake; **~se** vr to shake, tremble; **estremecimiento** nm (temblor)

trembling, shaking

estrenar [estre'nar] vt (vestido) to wear for the first time; (casa) to move into; (película, obra de teatro) to premiere; **~se** vr (persona) to make one's début; **estreno** nm (CINE etc) première

estreñido, a [estre'niðo, a] adj constipated

estreñimiento [estreni'mjento] nm constipation

estrépito [es'trepito] nm noise, racket; (fig) fuss; **estrepitoso, a** adj noisy; (fiesta) rowdy

estría [es'tria] nf groove

estribación [estriβa'θjon] nf (GEO) spur, foothill

estribar [estri'βar] vi: **~ en** to lie on

estribillo [estri'βiʎo] nm (LITERATURA) refrain; (MUS) chorus

estribo [es'triβo] nm (de jinete) stirrup; (de coche, tren) step; (de puente) support; (GEO) spur; **perder los ~s** to fly off the handle

estribor [estri'βor] nm (NAUT) starboard

estricto, a [es'trikto, a] adj (riguroso) strict; (severo) severe

estridente [estri'ðente] adj (color) loud; (voz) raucous

estropajo [estro'paxo] nm scourer

estropear [estrope'ar] vt to spoil; (dañar) to damage; **~se** vr (objeto) to get damaged; (persona: la piel etc) to be ruined

estructura [estruk'tura] nf structure

estruendo [es'trwendo] nm (ruido) racket, din; (fig: alboroto) uproar, turmoil

estrujar [estru'xar] vt (apretar) to squeeze; (aplastar) to crush; (fig) to drain, bleed

estuario [es'twarjo] nm estuary

estuche [es'tutʃe] nm box, case

estudiante [estu'ðjante] nm/f student; **estudiantil** adj student cpd

estudiar [estu'ðjar] vt to study

estudio [es'tuðjo] nm study; (CINE,

ARTE, RADIO) studio; **~s** nmpl studies; (erudición) learning sg; **~so, a** adj studious

estufa [es'tufa] nf heater, fire

estupefaciente [estupefa'θjente] nm drug, narcotic

estupefacto, a [estupe'fakto, a] adj speechless, thunderstruck

estupendo, a [estu'pendo, a] adj wonderful, terrific; (fam) great; ¡~! that's great!, fantastic!

estupidez [estupi'ðeθ] nf (torpeza) stupidity; (acto) stupid thing (to do)

estúpido, a [es'tupiðo, a] adj stupid, silly

estupor [estu'por] nm stupor; (fig) astonishment, amazement

estuve etc vb ver **estar**

esvástica [es'βastika] nf swastika

ETA ['eta] (ESP) nf abr (= Euskadi ta Askatasuna) ETA

etapa [e'tapa] nf (de viaje) stage; (DEPORTE) leg; (parada) stopping place; (fase) stage, phase

etarra [e'tarra] nm/f member of ETA

etc. abr (= etcétera) etc

etcétera [et'θetera] adv etcetera

eternidad [eterni'ðað] nf eternity;

eterno, a [e'terno, a] adj eternal, everlasting

ética ['etika] nf ethics pl

ético, a ['etiko, a] adj ethical

etiqueta [eti'keta] nf (modales) etiquette; (rótulo) label, tag

Eucaristía [eukaris'tia] nf Eucharist

eufemismo [eufe'mismo] nm euphemism

euforia [eu'forja] nf euphoria

euro ['euro] sm (moneda) euro.

eurodiputado, a [euroðipu'taðo, a] nm/f Euro MP, MEP

Europa [eu'ropa] nf Europe; **europeo, a** adj, nm/f European

Euskadi [eus'kaði] nm the Basque Country o Provinces pl

euskera [eus'kera] nm (LING) Basque

evacuación [eβakwa'θjon] nf evacuation

evacuar [eβa'kwar] vt to evacuate

evadir [eβa'ðir] vt to evade, avoid; **~se** vr to escape

evaluar [eβa'lwar] vt to evaluate

evangelio [eβan'xeljo] nm gospel

evaporar [eβapo'rar] vt to evaporate; **~se** vr to vanish

evasión [eβa'sjon] nf escape, flight; (fig) evasion; **~ de capitales** flight of capital

evasiva [eβa'siβa] nf (pretexto) excuse

evasivo, a [eβa'siβo, a] adj evasive, non-committal

evento [e'βento] nm event

eventual [eβen'twal] adj possible, conditional (upon circumstances); (trabajador) casual, temporary

evidencia [eβi'ðenθja] nf evidence, proof; **evidenciar** vt (hacer patente) to make evident; (probar) to prove, show; **evidenciarse** vr to be evident

evidente [eβi'ðente] adj obvious, clear, evident

evitar [eβi'tar] vt (evadir) to avoid; (impedir) to prevent

evocar [eβo'kar] vt to evoke, call forth

evolución [eβolu'θjon] nf (desarrollo) evolution, development; (cambio) change; (MIL) manoeuvre; **evolucionar** vi to evolve; to manoeuvre

ex [eks] adj ex-; **el ~ ministro** the former minister, the ex-minister

exacerbar [eksaθer'βar] vt to irritate, annoy

exactamente [eksakta'mente] adv exactly

exactitud [eksakti'tuð] nf exactness; (precisión) accuracy; (puntualidad) punctuality; **exacto, a** adj exact; accurate; punctual; ¡**exacto!** exactly!

exageración [eksaxera'θjon] nf exaggeration

exagerar [eksaxe'rar] vt, vi to exaggerate

exaltado, a [eksal'taðo, a] adj (apasionado) over-excited, worked-up; (POL) extreme

exaltar [eksal'tar] vt to exalt, glorify; **~se** vr (excitarse) to get excited o worked-up

examen [ek'samen] nm examination

examinar [eksami'nar] vt to examine; **~se** vr to be examined, take an examination

exasperar [eksaspe'rar] vt to exasperate; **~se** vr to get exasperated, lose patience

Exca. abr = **Excelencia**

excavadora [ekskaßa'ðora] nf excavator

excavar [ekska'ßar] vt to excavate

excedencia [eksθe'ðenθja] nf: **estar en ~** to be on leave; **pedir** o **solicitar la ~** to ask for leave

excedente [eksθe'ðente] adj, nm excess, surplus

exceder [eksθe'ðer] vt to exceed, surpass; **~se** vr (extralimitarse) to go too far

excelencia [eksθe'lenθja] nf excellence; **E~** Excellency; **excelente** adj excellent

excentricidad [eksθentriθi'ðað] nf eccentricity; **excéntrico, a** adj, nm/f eccentric

excepción [eksθep'θjon] nf exception; **excepcional** adj exceptional

excepto [eks'θepto] adv excepting, except (for)

exceptuar [eksθep'twar] vt to except, exclude

excesivo, a [eksθe'sißo, a] adj excessive

exceso [eks'θeso] nm (gen) excess; (COM) surplus; **~ de equipaje/peso** excess luggage/weight

excitación [eksθita'θjon] nf (sensación) excitement; (acción) excitation

excitado, a [eksθi'taðo, a] adj excited; (emociones) aroused

excitar [eksθi'tar] vt to excite; (incitar) to urge; **~se** vr to get excited

exclamación [eksklama'θjon] nf exclamation

exclamar [ekskla'mar] vi to exclaim

excluir [eksklu'ir] vt to exclude; (dejar fuera) to shut out; (descartar) to reject; **exclusión** nf exclusion

exclusiva [eksklu'sißa] nf (PRENSA) exclusive, scoop; (COM) sole right

exclusivo, a [eksklu'sißo, a] adj exclusive; **derecho ~** sole o exclusive right

Excmo. abr = **excelentísimo**

excomulgar [ekskomul'var] vt (REL) to excommunicate

excomunión [ekskomu'njon] nf excommunication

excursión [ekskur'sjon] nf excursion, outing; **excursionista** nm/f (turista) sightseer

excusa [eks'kusa] nf excuse; (disculpa) apology

excusar [eksku'sar] vt to excuse; **~se** vr (disculparse) to apologize

exhalar [eksa'lar] vt to exhale, breathe out; (olor etc) to give off; (suspiro) to breathe, heave

exhaustivo, a [eksaus'tißo, a] adj (análisis) thorough; (estudio) exhaustive

exhausto, a [ek'sausto, a] adj exhausted

exhibición [eksißi'θjon] nf exhibition, display, show

exhibir [eksi'ßir] vt to exhibit, display, show

exhortar [eksor'tar] vt: **~ a** to exhort to

exigencia [eksi'xenθja] nf demand, requirement; **exigente** adj demanding

exigir [eksi'xir] vt (gen) to demand, require; **~ el pago** to demand payment

exiliado, a [eksi'ljaðo, a] adj exiled ♦ nm/f exile

exilio [ek'siljo] nm exile

eximir [eksi'mir] vt to exempt

existencia [eksis'tenθja] nf existence; **~s** nfpl stock(s) (pl)

existir [eksis'tir] vi to exist, be

éxito ['eksito] *nm* (*triunfo*) success; (*MUS etc*) hit; **tener ~** to be successful

exonerar [eksone'rar] *vt* to exonerate; **~ de una obligación** to free from an obligation

exorbitante [eksorßi'tante] *adj* (*precio*) exorbitant; (*cantidad*) excessive

exorcizar [eksorθi'θar] *vt* to exorcize

exótico, a [ek'sotiko, a] *adj* exotic

expandir [ekspan'dir] *vt* to expand

expansión [ekspan'sjon] *nf* expansion

expansivo, a [ekspan'sißo, a] *adj*: **onda ~a** shock wave

expatriarse [ekspa'trjarse] *vr* to emigrate; (*POL*) to go into exile

expectativa [ekspekta'tißa] *nf* (*espera*) expectation; (*perspectiva*) prospect

expedición [ekspeði'θjon] *nf* (*excursión*) expedition

expediente [ekspe'ðjente] *nm* expedient; (*JUR: procedimiento*) action, proceedings *pl*; (: *papeles*) dossier, file, record

expedir [ekspe'ðir] *vt* (*despachar*) to send, forward; (*pasaporte*) to issue

expendedor, a [ekspende'ðor, a] *nm/f* (*vendedor*) dealer

expensas [eks'pensas] *nfpl*: **a ~ de** at the expense of

experiencia [ekspe'rjenθja] *nf* experience

experimentado, a [eksperimen'taðo, a] *adj* experienced

experimentar [eksperimen'tar] *vt* (*en laboratorio*) to experiment with; (*probar*) to test, try out; (*notar, observar*) to experience; (*deterioro, pérdida*) to suffer; **experimento** *nm* experiment

experto, a [eks'perto, a] *adj* expert, skilled ♦ *nm/f* expert

expiar [ekspi'ar] *vt* to atone for

expirar [ekspi'rar] *vi* to expire

explanada [ekspla'naða] *nf* (*llano*) plain

explayarse [ekspla'jarse] *vr* (*en discurso*) to speak at length; **~ con**

uno to confide in sb

explicación [eksplika'θjon] *nf* explanation

explicar [ekspli'kar] *vt* to explain; **~se** *vr* to explain (o.s.)

explícito, a [eks'pliθito, a] *adj* explicit

explique *etc vb ver* **explicar**

explorador, a [eksplora'ðor, a] *nm/f* (*pionero*) explorer; (*MIL*) scout ♦ *nm* (*MED*) probe; (*TEC*) (radar) scanner

explorar [eksplo'rar] *vt* to explore; (*MED*) to probe; (*radar*) to scan

explosión [eksplo'sjon] *nf* explosion

explosivo, a *adj* explosive

explotación [eksplota'θjon] *nf* exploitation; (*de planta etc*) running

explotar [eksplo'tar] *vt* to exploit; to run, operate ♦ *vi* to explode

exponer [ekspo'ner] *vt* to expose; (*cuadro*) to display; (*vida*) to risk; (*idea*) to explain; **~se** *vr*: **~se a (hacer) algo** to run the risk of (doing) sth

exportación [eksporta'θjon] *nf* (*acción*) export; (*mercancías*) exports *pl*

exportar [ekspor'tar] *vt* to export

exposición [eksposi'θjon] *nf* (*gen*) exposure; (*de arte*) show, exhibition; (*explicación*) explanation; (*declaración*) account, statement

expresamente [ekspresa'mente] *adv* (*decir*) clearly; (*a propósito*) expressly

expresar [ekspre'sar] *vt* to express; **expresión** *nf* expression

expresivo, a [ekspre'sißo, a] *adj* (*persona, gesto, palabras*) expressive; (*cariñoso*) affectionate

expreso, a [eks'preso, a] *pp de* **expresar** ♦ *adj* (*explícito*) express; (*claro*) specific, clear; (*tren*) fast ♦ *adv*: **mandar ~** to send by express (delivery)

express [eks'pres] (*AM*) *adv*: **enviar algo ~** to send sth special delivery

exprimidor [eksprimi'ðor] *nm* squeezer

exprimir [ekspri'mir] *vt* (*fruta*) to squeeze; (*zumo*) to squeeze out

expropiar [ekspro'pjar] vt to expropriate

expuesto, a [eks'pwesto, a] pp de **exponer** ♦ adj exposed; (cuadro etc) on show, on display

expulsar [ekspul'sar] vt (echar) to eject, throw out; (alumno) to expel; (despedir) to sack, fire; (DEPORTE) to send off; **expulsión** nf expulsion; sending-off

exquisito, a [ekski'sito, a] adj exquisite; (comida) delicious

éxtasis ['ekstasis] nm ecstasy

extender [eksten'der] vt to extend; (los brazos) to stretch out, hold out; (mapa, tela) to spread (out), open (out); (mantequilla) to spread; (certificado) to issue; (cheque, recibo) to make out; (documento) to draw up; **~se** vr (gen) to extend; (persona: en el suelo) to stretch out; (epidemia) to spread; **extendido, a** adj (abierto) spread out, open; (brazos) outstretched; (costumbre) widespread

extensión [eksten'sjon] nf (de terreno, mar) expanse, stretch; (de tiempo) length, duration; (TEL) extension; **en toda la ~ de la palabra** in every sense of the word

extenso, a [eks'tenso, a] adj extensive

extenuar [ekste'nwar] vt (debilitar) to weaken

exterior [ekste'rjor] adj (de fuera) external; (afuera) outside, exterior; (apariencia) outward; (deuda, relaciones) foreign ♦ nm (gen) exterior, outside; (aspecto) outward appearance; (DEPORTE) wing(er); (países extranjeros) abroad; **en el ~** abroad; **al ~** outwardly, on the surface

exterminar [ekstermi'nar] vt to exterminate; **exterminio** nm extermination

externo, a [eks'terno, a] adj (exterior) external, outside; (superficial) outward ♦ nm/f day pupil

extinguir [ekstin'gir] vt (fuego) to

extinguish, put out; (raza, población) to wipe out; **~se** vr (fuego) to go out; (BIO) to die out, become extinct

extinto, a [eks'tinto, a] adj extinct

extintor [ekstin'tor] nm (fire) extinguisher

extirpar [ekstir'par] vt (MED) to remove (surgically)

extorsión [ekstor'sjon] nf extorsion

extra ['ekstra] adj inv (tiempo) extra; (chocolate, vino) good-quality ♦ nm/f extra ♦ nm extra; (bono) bonus

extracción [ekstrak'θjon] nf extraction; (en lotería) draw

extracto [eks'trakto] nm extract

extradición [ekstraði'θjon] nf extradition

extraer [ekstra'er] vt to extract, take out

extraescolar [ekstraesko'lar] adj: **actividad ~** extracurricular activity

extralimitarse [ekstralimi'tarse] vr to go too far

extranjero, a [ekstran'xero, a] adj foreign ♦ nm/f foreigner ♦ nm foreign countries pl; **en el ~** abroad

extrañar [ekstra'ɲar] vt (sorprender) to find strange o odd; (echar de menos) to miss; **~se** vr (sorprenderse) to be amazed, be surprised

extrañeza [ekstra'ɲeθa] nf (rareza) strangeness, oddness; (asombro) amazement, surprise

extraño, a [eks'traɲo, a] adj (extranjero) foreign; (raro, sorprendente) strange, odd

extraordinario, a [ekstraorði'narjo, a] adj extraordinary; (edición, número) special ♦ nm (de periódico) special edition; **horas extraordinarias** overtime sg

extrarradio [ekstra'rraðjo] nm suburbs

extravagancia [ekstraßa'xanθja] nf oddness; outlandishness

extravagante [ekstraßa'xante] adj (excéntrico) eccentric; (estrafalario) outlandish

extraviado, a [ekstra'ßjaðo, a] adj

lost, missing

extraviar [ekstra'βjar] *vt* (*persona*: *desorientar*) to mislead, misdirect; (*perder*) to lose, misplace; **~se** *vr* to lose one's way, get lost; **extravío** *nm* loss; (*fig*) deviation

extremar [ekstre'mar] *vt* to carry to extremes; **~se** *vr* to do one's utmost, make every effort

extremaunción [ekstremaun'θjon] *nf* extreme unction

extremidad [ekstremi'ðað] *nf* (*de punta*) extremity; **~es** *nfpl* (*ANAT*) extremities

extremo, a [eks'tremo, a] *adj* extreme; (*último*) last ♦ *nm* end; (*límite*, *grado sumo*) extreme; **en último ~** as a last resort

extrovertido, a [ekstroβer'tiðo, a] *adj*, *nm/f* extrovert

exuberancia [eksuβe'ranθja] *nf* exuberance; **exuberante** *adj* exuberant; (*fig*) luxuriant, lush

eyacular [ejaku'lar] *vt*, *vi* to ejaculate

F, f

f.a.b. *abr* (= *franco a bordo*) f.o.b.

fabada [fa'βaða] *nf* bean and sausage stew

fábrica [ˈfaβrika] *nf* factory; **marca de ~** trademark; **precio de ~** factory price

fabricación [faβrika'θjon] *nf* (*manufactura*) manufacture; (*producción*) production; **de ~ casera** home-made; **~ en serie** mass production

fabricante [faβri'kante] *nm/f* manufacturer

fabricar [faβri'kar] *vt* (*manufacturar*) to manufacture, make; (*construir*) to build; (*cuento*) to fabricate, devise

fábula [ˈfaβula] *nf* (*cuento*) fable; (*chisme*) rumour; (*mentira*) fib

fabuloso, a [faβu'loso, a] *adj* (*oportunidad*, *tiempo*) fabulous, great

facción [fak'θjon] *nf* (*POL*) faction;

facciones *nfpl* (*del rostro*) features

faceta [fa'θeta] *nf* facet

facha [ˈfatʃa] (*fam*) *nf* (*aspecto*) look; (*cara*) face

fachada [fa'tʃaða] *nf* (*ARQ*) façade, front

fácil [ˈfaθil] *adj* (*simple*) easy; (*probable*) likely

facilidad [faθili'ðað] *nf* (*capacidad*) ease; (*sencillez*) simplicity; (*de palabra*) fluency; **~es** *nfpl* facilities

facilitar [faθili'tar] *vt* (*hacer fácil*) to make easy; (*proporcionar*) to provide

fácilmente [ˈfaθilmente] *adv* easily

facsímil [fak'simil] *nm* facsimile, fax

factible [fak'tiβle] *adj* feasible

factor [fak'tor] *nm* factor

factura [fak'tura] *nf* (*cuenta*) bill; **facturación** *nf* (*de equipaje*) check-in; **facturar** *vt* (*COM*) to invoice, charge for; (*equipaje*) to check in

facultad [fakul'tað] *nf* (*aptitud*, *ESCOL* etc) faculty; (*poder*) power

faena [fa'ena] *nf* (*trabajo*) work; (*quehacer*) task, job

faisán [fai'san] *nm* pheasant

faja [ˈfaxa] *nf* (*para la cintura*) sash; (*de mujer*) corset; (*de tierra*) strip

fajo [ˈfaxo] *nm* (*de papeles*) bundle; (*de billetes*) wad

falacia [fa'laθja] *nf* fallacy

falda [ˈfalda] *nf* (*prenda de vestir*) skirt

falla [ˈfaʎa] *nf* (*defecto*) fault, flaw

fallar [fa'ʎar] *vt* (*JUR*) to pronounce sentence on ♦ *vi* (*memoria*) to fail; (*motor*) to miss

---

Fallas

In the week of 19 March (the feast of San José), Valencia honours its patron saint with a spectacular fiesta called **Las Fallas**. *The Fallas are huge papier-mâché, cardboard and wooden sculptures which are built by competing teams throughout the year. They depict politicians and well-known public figures and are thrown* *onto bonfires and set alight once a jury has judged them - only their sheer sculpture escapes the flames.*

fallecer [faʎe'θer] *vi* to pass away, die; **fallecimiento** *nm* decease, demise

fallido, a [fa'ʎiðo, a] *adj* (*gen*) frustrated, unsuccessful

fallo ['faʎo] *nm* (*JUR*) verdict, ruling; (*fracaso*) failure; ~ **cardíaco** heart failure

falsedad [false'ðað] *nf* falseness; (*hipocresía*) hypocrisy; (*mentira*) falsehood

falsificar [falsifi'kar] *vt* (*firma etc*) to forge; (*moneda*) to counterfeit

falso, a ['falso, a] *adj* false; (*documento, moneda etc*) fake; **en** ~ falsely

falta ['falta] *nf* (*defecto*) fault, flaw; (*privación*) lack, want; (*ausencia*) absence; (*carencia*) shortage; (*equivocación*) mistake; (*DEPORTE*) foul; **echar en** ~ to miss; **hacer** ~ **hacer algo** to be necessary to do sth; **me hace** ~ **una pluma** I need a pen; ~ **de educación** bad manners *pl*

faltar [fal'tar] *vi* (*escasear*) to be lacking, be wanting; (*ausentarse*) to be absent, be missing; **faltan 2 horas para llegar** there are 2 hours to go till arrival; ~ **al respeto a uno** to be disrespectful to sb; **¡no faltaba más!** (*no hay de qué*) don't mention it!

fama ['fama] *nf* (*renombre*) fame; (*reputación*) reputation

famélico, a [fa'meliko, a] *adj* starving

familia [fa'milja] *nf* family; ~ **política** in-laws *pl*

familiar [fami'ljar] *adj* (*relativo a la familia*) family *cpd*; (*conocido, informal*) familiar ♦ *nm* relative, relation; ~**idad** *nf* (*informalidad*) familiarity; (*informalidad*) homeliness; ~**izarse** *vr*: ~**izarse con** to familiarize o.s. with

famoso, a [fa'moso, a] *adj* (*renombrado*) famous

fanático, a [fa'natiko, a] *adj* fanatical ♦ *nm/f* fanatic; (*CINE, DEPORTE*) fan; **fanatismo** *nm* fanaticism

fanfarrón, ona [fanfa'rron, ona] *adj* boastful

fango ['fango] *nm* mud; ~**so, a** *adj* muddy

fantasía [fanta'sia] *nf* fantasy, imagination; **joyas de** ~ imitation jewellery *sg*

fantasma [fan'tasma] *nm* (*espectro*) ghost, apparition; (*fanfarrón*) show-off

fantástico, a [fan'tastiko, a] *adj* fantastic

farmacéutico, a [farma'θeutiko, a] *adj* pharmaceutical ♦ *nm/f* chemist (*BRIT*), pharmacist

farmacia [far'maθja] *nf* chemist's (shop) (*BRIT*), pharmacy; ~ **de guardia** all-night chemist

fármaco ['farmako] *nm* drug

faro ['faro] *nm* (*NAUT: torre*) lighthouse; (*AUTO*) headlamp; ~**s antiniebla** fog lamps; ~**s delanteros/traseros** headlights/rear lights

farol [fa'rol] *nm* lantern, lamp

farola [fa'rola] *nf* street lamp (*BRIT*) o light (*US*)

farsa [farsa] *nf* (*gen*) farce

farsante [far'sante] *nm/f* fraud, fake

fascículo [fasθikulo] *nm* (*de revista*) part, instalment

fascinar [fasθi'nar] *vt* (*gen*) to fascinate

fascismo [fasθismo] *nm* fascism; **fascista** *adj*, *nm/f* fascist

fase ['fase] *nf* phase

fastidiar [fasti'ðjar] *vt* (*molestar*) to annoy, bother; (*estropear*) to spoil; ~**se** *vr*: **¡que se fastidie!** (*fam*) he'll just have to put up with it!

fastidio [fas'tiðjo] *nm* (*molestia*) annoyance; ~**so, a** *adj* (*molesto*) annoying

fastuoso, a [fas'twoso, a] *adj* (*banquete, boda*) lavish; (*acto*) pompous

fatal [fa'tal] adj (gen) fatal;
(desgraciado) ill-fated; (fam: malo,
pésimo) awful; **~idad** nf (destino) fate;
(mala suerte) misfortune

fatiga [fa'tiɣa] nf (cansancio) fatigue,
weariness

fatigar [fati'ɣar] vt to tire, weary; **~se**
vr to get tired

fatigoso, a [fati'ɣoso, a] adj (cansador)
tiring

fatuo, a [ˈfatwo, a] adj (vano) fatuous;
(presuntuoso) conceited

favor [faˈβor] nm favour; **estar a ~ de**
to be in favour of; **haga el ~ de...**
would you be so good as to...,
kindly...; **por ~** please; **~able** adj
favourable

favorecer [faβoreˈθer] vt to favour;
(vestido etc) to become, flatter; **este
peinado le favorece** this hairstyle
suits him

favorito, a [faβoˈrito, a] adj, nm/f
favourite

fax [faks] nm inv fax; **mandar por ~** to
fax

faz [faθ] nf face; **la ~ de la tierra** the
face of the earth

fe [fe] nf (REL) faith; (documento)
certificate; **prestar ~ a** to believe,
credit; **actuar con buena/mala ~** to
act in good/bad faith; **dar ~ de** to
bear witness to

fealdad [fealˈdad] nf ugliness

febrero [feˈβrero] nm February

febril [feˈβril] adj (fig: actividad) hectic;
(mente, mirada) feverish

fecha [ˈfetʃa] nf date; **~ de caducidad**
(de producto alimenticio) sell-by date;
(de contrato etc) expiry date; **con
~ adelantada** postdated; **en
~ próxima** soon; **hasta la ~** to date,
so far; **poner ~ a** to date; **fechar** vt to
date

fecundar [fekunˈdar] vt (generar) to
fertilize, make fertile; **fecundo, a** adj
(fértil) fertile; (fig) prolific; (productivo)
productive

federación [feðeraˈθjon] nf federation

felicidad [feliθiˈdad] nf happiness; **~es**
nfpl (felicitaciones) best wishes,
congratulations

felicitación [feliθitaˈθjon] nf:
¡felicitaciones! congratulations!

felicitar [feliθiˈtar] vt to congratulate

feligrés, esa [feliˈɣres, esa] nm/f
parishioner

feliz [feˈliθ] adj happy

felpudo [felˈpuðo] nm doormat

femenino, a [femeˈnino, a] adj, nm
feminine

feminista [femiˈnista] adj, nm/f
feminist

fenómeno [feˈnomeno] nm
phenomenon; (fig) freak, accident
♦ adj great ♦ excl great!, marvellous!

fenomenal adj = **fenómeno**

feo, a [ˈfeo, a] adj (gen) ugly;
(desagradable) bad, nasty

féretro [ˈferetro] nm (ataúd) coffin;
(sarcófago) bier

feria [ˈferja] nf (gen) fair; (descanso)
holiday, rest day; (AM: mercado) village
market; (: cambio) loose o small
change

fermentar [fermenˈtar] vi to ferment

ferocidad [feroθiˈdad] nf fierceness,
ferocity

feroz [feˈroθ] adj (cruel) cruel; (salvaje)
fierce

férreo, a [ˈferreo, a] adj iron

ferretería [ferreteˈria] nf (tienda)
ironmonger's (shop) (BRIT), hardware
store

ferrocarril [ferrokaˈrril] nm railway

ferroviario, a [ferroˈβjarjo, a] adj rail
cpd

fértil [ˈfertil] adj (productivo) fertile;
(rico) rich; **fertilidad** nf (gen) fertility;
(productividad) fruitfulness

ferviente [ferˈβjente] adj fervent

fervor [ferˈβor] nm fervour; **~oso, a**
adj fervent

festejar [festeˈxar] vt (celebrar) to

celebrate

festejo [fes'texo] *nm* celebration;
 festejos *nmpl (fiestas)* festivals

festín [fes'tin] *nm* feast, banquet

festival [festi'βal] *nm* festival

festividad [festiβi'ðað] *nf* festivity

festivo, a [fes'tiβo, a] *adj (de fiesta)*
 festive; *(CINE, LITERATURA)* humorous;
 día ~ holiday

fétido, a ['fetiðo, a] *adj* foul-smelling

feto ['feto] *nm* foetus

fiable ['fjaβle] *adj (persona)*
 trustworthy; *(máquina)* reliable

fiador, a [fja'ðor, a] *nm/f (JUR)* surety,
 guarantor; *(COM)* backer; **salir ~ por
 uno** to stand bail for sb

fiambre ['fjambre] *nm* cold meat

fianza ['fjanθa] *nf* surety; *(JUR):*
 libertad bajo ~ release on bail

fiar [fi'ar] *vt (salir garante de)* to
 guarantee; *(vender a crédito)* to sell on
 credit; *(secreto):* **~ a** to confide (to) ♦ *vi*
 to trust; **~se** *vr* to trust (in), rely on;
 ~se de uno to rely on sb

fibra ['fiβra] *nf* fibre; **~ óptica** optical
 fibre

ficción [fik'θjon] *nf* fiction

ficha ['fitʃa] *nf (TEL)* token; *(en juegos)*
 counter, marker; *(tarjeta)* (index) card;
 fichar *vt (archivar)* to file, index;
 (DEPORTE) to sign; **estar fichado** to
 have a record; **fichero** *nm* box file;
 (INFORM) file

ficticio, a [fik'tiθjo, a] *adj (imaginario)*
 fictitious; *(falso)* fabricated

fidelidad [fiðeli'ðað] *nf (lealtad)*
 fidelity, loyalty; **alta ~** high fidelity, hi-
 fi

fideos [fi'ðeos] *nmpl* noodles

fiebre ['fjeβre] *nf (MED)* fever; *(fig)*
 fever, excitement; **~ amarilla/del
 heno** yellow/hay fever; **~ palúdica**
 malaria; **tener ~** to have a
 temperature

fiel [fjel] *adj (leal)* faithful, loyal; *(fiable)*
 reliable; *(exacto)* accurate, faithful
 ♦ *nm:* **los ~es** the faithful

fieltro ['fjeltro] *nm* felt

fiera ['fjera] *nf (animal feroz)* wild
 animal o beast; *(fig)* dragon; *ver tb*
 fiero

fiero, a ['fjero, a] *adj (cruel)* cruel;
 (feroz) fierce; *(duro)* harsh

fiesta ['fjesta] *nf* party; *(de pueblo)*
 festival; *(vacaciones, tb: ~s)* holiday *sg;*
 (REL): **~ de guardar** day of obligation

> ### Fiestas
>
> **Fiestas** *can be official public holidays
> or holidays set by each autonomous
> region, many of which coincide with
> religious festivals. There are also
> many* **fiestas** *all over Spain for a
> local patron saint or the Virgin Mary.
> These often last several days and can
> include religious processions, carnival
> parades, bullfights and dancing.*

figura [fi'xura] *nf (gen)* figure; *(forma,
 imagen)* shape, form; *(NAIPES)* face card

figurar [fixu'rar] *vt (representar)* to
 represent; *(fingir)* to figure ♦ *vi* to
 figure; **~se** *vr (imaginarse)* to imagine;
 (suponer) to suppose

fijador [fixa'ðor] *nm (FOTO etc)* fixative;
 (de pelo) gel

fijar [fi'xar] *vt (gen)* to fix; *(estampilla)*
 to affix, stick (on); **~se** *vr:* **~se en** to
 notice

fijo, a ['fixo, a] *adj (gen)* fixed; *(firme)*
 firm; *(permanente)* permanent ♦ *adv:*
 mirar ~ to stare

fila ['fila] *nf* row; *(MIL)* rank; **ponerse
 en ~** to line up, get into line

filántropo, a [fi'lantropo, a] *nm/f*
 philanthropist

filatelia [fila'telja] *nf* philately, stamp
 collecting

filete [fi'lete] *nm (carne)* fillet steak;
 (pescado) fillet

filiación [filja'θjon] *nf (POL)* affiliation

filial [fi'ljal] *adj* filial ♦ *nf* subsidiary

Filipinas [fili'pinas] *nfpl:* **las ~** the
 Philippines; **filipino, a** *adj, nm/f*

Philippine

filmar [fil'mar] vt to film, shoot

filo ['filo] nm (gen) edge; **sacar ~ a** to sharpen; **al ~ del mediodía** at about midday; **de doble ~** double-edged

filón [fi'lon] nm (MINERÍA) vein, lode; (fig) goldmine

filosofía [filoso'fia] nf philosophy; **filósofo, a** nm/f philosopher

filtrar [fil'trar] vt, vi to filter, strain; **~se** vr to filter; **filtro** nm (TEC, utensilio) filter

fin [fin] nm end; (objetivo) aim, purpose; **al ~ y al cabo** when all's said and done; **a ~ de** in order to; **por ~** finally; **en ~** in short; **~ de semana** weekend

final [fi'nal] adj final ♦ nm end, conclusion ♦ nf final; **~idad** nf (propósito) purpose, intention; **~ista** nm/f finalist; **~izar** vt to end, finish; (INFORM) to log out o off ♦ vi to end, come to an end

financiar [finan'θjar] vt to finance; **financiero, a** adj financial ♦ nm/f financier

finca ['finka] nf (bien inmueble) property, land; (casa de campo) country house; (AM) farm

fingir [fin'xir] vt (simular) to simulate, feign ♦ vi (aparentar) to pretend

finlandés, esa [finlan'des, esa] adj Finnish ♦ nm/f Finn ♦ nm (LING) Finnish

Finlandia [fin'landja] nf Finland

fino, a ['fino, a] adj fine; (delgado) slender; (de buenas maneras) polite, refined; (jerez) fino, dry

firma ['firma] nf signature; (COM) firm, company

firmamento [firma'mento] nm firmament

firmar [fir'mar] vt to sign

firme ['firme] adj firm; (estable) stable; (sólido) solid; (constante) steady; (decidido) resolute ♦ nm road surface); **~mente** adv firmly; **~za** nf firmness; (constancia) steadiness; (solidez) solidity

fiscal [fis'kal] adj fiscal ♦ nm/f public prosecutor; **año ~** tax o fiscal year

fisco ['fisko] nm (hacienda) treasury, exchequer (BRIT)

fisgar [fis'ɣar] vt to pry into

fisgonear [fisɣone'ar] vt to poke one's nose into ♦ vi to pry, spy

física ['fisika] nf physics sg; ver tb **físico**

físico, a ['fisiko, a] adj physical ♦ nm physique ♦ nm/f physicist

fisura [fi'sura] nf crack; (MED) fracture

flác(c)ido, a ['flak(θ)iðo, a] adj flabby

flaco, a ['flako, a] adj (muy delgado) skinny, thin; (débil) weak, feeble

flagrante [fla'ɣrante] adj flagrant

flamante [fla'mante] (fam) adj brilliant; (nuevo) brand-new

flamenco, a [fla'menko, a] adj (de Flandes) Flemish; (baile, música) flamenco ♦ nm (baile, música) flamenco

flan [flan] nm creme caramel

flaqueza [fla'keθa] nf (delgadez) thinness, leanness; (fig) weakness

flash [flaʃ] (pl ~s o ~es) nm (FOTO) flash

flauta ['flauta] nf (MUS) flute

flecha ['fletʃa] nf arrow

flechazo [fle'tʃaθo] nm love at first sight

fleco ['fleko] nm fringe

flema ['flema] nm phlegm

flequillo [fle'kiʎo] nm (en pelo) fringe

flexible [flek'sißle] adj flexible

flexión [flek'sjon] nf press-up

flexo ['flekso] nm adjustable table-lamp

flojera [flo'xera] (AM: fam) nf: **me da ~** I can't be bothered

flojo, a ['floxo, a] adj (gen) loose; (sin fuerzas) limp; (débil) weak

flor [flor] nf flower; **a ~ de** on the surface of; **~ecer** vi (BOT) to flower, bloom; (fig) to flourish; **~eciente** adj (BOT) in flower, flowering; (fig) thriving; **~ero** nm vase; **~istería** nf florist's (shop)

flota ['flota] *nf* fleet

flotador [flota'ðor] *nm* (*gen*) float; (*para nadar*) rubber ring

flotar [flo'tar] *vi* (*gen*) to float; **flote** *nm*: **a flote** afloat; **salir a flote** (*fig*) to get back on one's feet

fluctuar [fluk'twar] *vi* (*oscilar*) to fluctuate

fluidez [flui'ðeθ] *nf* fluidity; (*fig*) fluency

flúido, a ['fluiðo, a] *adj, nm* fluid

fluir [flu'ir] *vi* to flow

flujo ['fluxo] *nm* flow; **~ y reflujo** ebb and flow

flúor ['fluor] *nm* fluoride

fluvial [flu'βi'al] *adj* (*navegación, cuenca*) fluvial, river *cpd*

foca ['foka] *nf* seal

foco ['foko] *nm* focus; (*ELEC*) floodlight; (*AM*) (light) bulb

fofo, a ['fofo, a] *adj* soft, spongy; (*carnes*) flabby

fogata [fo'yata] *nf* bonfire

fogón [fo'yon] *nm* (*de cocina*) ring, burner

fogoso, a [fo'yoso, a] *adj* spirited

folio ['foljo] *nm* folio, page

follaje [fo'λaxe] *nm* foliage

folletín [foλe'tin] *nm* newspaper serial

folleto [fo'λeto] *nm* (*POL*) pamphlet

follón [fo'λon] (*fam*) *nm* (*lío*) mess; (*conmoción*) fuss; **armar un ~** to kick up a row

fomentar [fomen'tar] *vt* (*MED*) to foment; **fomento** *nm* (*promoción*) promotion

fonda ['fonda] *nf* inn

fondo ['fondo] *nm* (*de mar*) bottom; (*de coche, sala*) back; (*ARTE etc*) background; (*reserva*) fund; **~s** *nmpl* (*COM*) funds, resources; **una investigación a ~** a thorough investigation; **en el ~** at bottom, deep down

fonobuzón [fonoβu'θon] *nm* voice mail

fontanería [fontane'ria] *nf* plumbing; **fontanero, a** *nm/f* plumber

footing ['futin] *nm* jogging; **hacer ~**

to jog, go jogging

forastero, a [foras'tero, a] *nm/f* stranger

forcejear [forθexe'ar] *vi* (*luchar*) to struggle

forense [fo'rense] *nm/f* pathologist

forjar [for'xar] *vt* to forge

forma ['forma] *nf* (*figura*) form, shape; (*MED*) fitness; (*método*) way, means; **las ~s** the conventions; **estar en ~** to be fit

formación [forma'θjon] *nf* (*gen*) formation; (*educación*) education; **~ profesional** vocational training

formal [for'mal] *adj* (*gen*) formal; (*fig: serio*) serious; (: *de fiar*) reliable; **~idad** *nf* formality; seriousness; **~izar** *vt* (*JUR*) to formalize; (*situación*) to put in order, regularize; **~izarse** *vr* (*situación*) to be put in order, be regularized

formar [for'mar] *vt* (*componer*) to form, shape; (*constituir*) to make up, constitute; (*ESCOL*) to train, educate; **~se** *vr* (*ESCOL*) to be trained, educated; (*cobrar forma*) to form, take form; (*desarrollarse*) to develop

formatear [formate'ar] *vt* to format

formativo, a [forma'tiβo, a] *adj* (*lecturas, años*) formative

formato [for'mato] *nm* format

formidable [formi'ðaβle] *adj* (*temible*) formidable; (*estupendo*) tremendous

fórmula ['formula] *nf* formula

formular [formu'lar] *vt* (*queja*) to make, lodge; (*petición*) to draw up; (*pregunta*) to pose

formulario [formu'larjo] *nm* form

fornido, a [for'niðo, a] *adj* well-built

forrar [fo'rrar] *vt* (*abrigo*) to line; (*libro*) to cover; **forro** *nm* (*de cuaderno*) cover; (*COSTURA*) lining; (*de sillón*) upholstery

fortalecer [fortale'θer] *vt* to strengthen

fortaleza [forta'leθa] *nf* (*MIL*) fortress, stronghold; (*fuerza*) strength; (*determinación*) resolution

fortuito, a [for'twito, a] adj accidental

fortuna [for'tuna] nf (suerte) fortune, (good) luck; (riqueza) fortune, wealth

forzar [for'θar] vt (puerta) to force (open); (compeler) to compel

forzoso, a [for'θoso, a] adj necessary

fosa ['fosa] nf (sepultura) grave; (en tierra) pit; **~s nasales** nostrils

fósforo ['fosforo] nm (QUÍM) phosphorus; (cerilla) match

foso ['foso] nm ditch; (TEATRO) pit; (AUTO): **~ de reconocimiento** inspection pit

foto ['foto] nf photo, snap(shot); **sacar una ~** to take a photo o picture

fotocopia [foto'kopja] nf photocopy; **fotocopiadora** nf photocopier; **fotocopiar** vt to photocopy

fotografía [fotoɣra'fia] nf (ARTE) photography; (una ~) photograph; **fotografiar** vt to photograph

fotógrafo, a [fo'toɣrafo, a] nm/f photographer

fracasar [fraka'sar] vi (gen) to fail

fracaso [fra'kaso] nm failure

fracción [frak'θjon] nf fraction; **fraccionamiento** (AM) nm housing estate

fractura [frak'tura] nf fracture, break

fragancia [fra'ɣanθja] nf (olor) fragrance, perfume

frágil ['fraxil] adj (débil) fragile, (COM) breakable

fragmento [fraɣ'mento] nm (pedazo) fragment

fragua ['fraɣwa] nf forge; **fraguar** vt to forge; (fig) to concoct ♦ vi to harden

fraile ['fraile] nm (REL) friar; (: monje) monk

frambuesa [fram'bwesa] nf raspberry

francamente adv (hablar, decir) frankly; (realmente) really

francés, esa [fran'θes, esa] adj French ♦ nm/f Frenchman/woman ♦ nm (LING) French

Francia ['franθja] nf France

franco, a ['franko, a] adj (cándido)

frank, open; (COM: exento) free ♦ nm (moneda) franc

francotirador, a [frankotira'ðor, a] nm/f sniper

franela [fra'nela] nf flannel

franja ['franxa] nf fringe

franquear [franke'ar] vt (camino) to clear; (carta, paquete postal) to frank, stamp; (obstáculo) to overcome

franqueo [fran'keo] nm postage

franqueza [fran'keθa] nf (candor) frankness

frasco ['frasko] nm bottle, flask; **~ al vacío** (vacuum) flask

frase ['frase] nf sentence; **~ hecha** set phrase; (pey) stock phrase

fraterno, a [fra'terno, a] adj brotherly, fraternal

fraude ['frauðe] nm (cualidad) dishonesty; (acto) fraud; **fraudulento, a** adj fraudulent

frazada [fra'saða] (AM) nf blanket

frecuencia [fre'kwenθja] nf frequency; **con ~** frequently, often

frecuentar [frekwen'tar] vt to frequent

fregadero [freɣa'ðero] nm (kitchen) sink

fregar [fre'ɣar] vt (frotar) to scrub; (platos) to wash (up); (AM) to annoy

fregona [fre'ɣona] nf mop

freír [fre'ir] vt to fry

frenar [fre'nar] vt to brake; (fig) to check

frenazo [fre'naθo] nm: **dar un ~** to brake sharply

frenesí [frene'si] nm frenzy; **frenético, a** adj frantic

freno ['freno] nm (TEC, AUTO) brake; (de cabalgadura) bit; (fig) check

frente ['frente] nm (ARQ, POL) front; (de objeto) front part ♦ nf forehead; brow; **~ a** in front of; (en situación opuesta de) opposite; **al ~ de** (fig) at the head of; **chocar de ~** to crash head-on; **hacer ~ a** to face up to

fresa ['fresa] (ESP) nf strawberry

fresco, a ['fresko, a] adj (nuevo) fresh;

frío) cool; (*descarado*) cheeky ♦ *nm* (*aire*) fresh air; (*ARTE*) fresco; (*AM: jugo*) fruit drink ♦ *nm/f* (*fam*): **ser un ~** to have a nerve; **tomar el ~** to get some fresh air; **frescura** (*f*) freshness; (*descaro*) cheek, nerve

frialdad [frial'daθ] *nf* (*gen*) coldness; (*indiferencia*) indifference

fricción [frik'θjon] *nf* (*gen*) friction; (*acto*) rub(bing); (*MED*) massage

frigidez [frixi'ðeθ] *nf* frigidity

frigorífico [friγo'rifiko] *nm* refrigerator

frijol [fri'xol] *nm* kidney bean

frío, a etc [ˈfrio, a] *vb ver* **freír** ♦ *adj* cold; (*indiferente*) indifferent ♦ *nm* cold; indifference; **hace** ~ it's cold; **tener** ~ to be cold

frito, a [ˈfrito, a] *adj* fried; **me trae ~ ese hombre** I'm sick and tired of that man; **fritos** *nmpl* fried food

frívolo, a [ˈfriβolo, a] *adj* frivolous

frontal [fron'tal] *adj* frontal; **choque ~** head-on collision

frontera [fron'tera] *nf* frontier; **fronterizo, a** *adj* frontier *cpd*; (*contiguo*) bordering

frontón [fron'ton] *nm* (*DEPORTE: cancha*) pelota court; (*: juego*) pelota

frotar [fro'tar] *vt* to rub; **~se** *vr*: **~se las manos** to rub one's hands

fructífero, a [fruk'tifero, a] *adj* fruitful

fruncir [frun'θir] *vt* to pucker; (*COSTURA*) to pleat; **~ el ceño** to knit one's brow

frustrar [frus'trar] *vt* to frustrate

fruta [ˈfruta] *nf* fruit; **frutería** *nf* fruit shop; **frutero, a** *adj* fruit *cpd* ♦ *nm/f* fruiterer ♦ *nm* fruit bowl

frutilla [fru'tiʎa] (*AM*) *nf* strawberry

fruto [ˈfruto] *nm* fruit; (*fig: resultado*) result; (*: beneficio*) benefit; **~s secos** nuts; (*pasas etc*) dried fruit *sg*

fue *vb ver* **ser; ir**

fuego [ˈfweγo] *nm* (*gen*) fire; **a ~ lento** on a low heat; **¿tienes ~?** have you (got) a light?; **~s artificiales** *o* **de artificio** fireworks

fuente [ˈfwente] *nf* fountain; (*manantial, fig*) spring; (*origen*) source; (*plato*) large dish

fuera etc [ˈfwera] *vb ver* **ser, ir** ♦ *adv* out(side); (*en otra parte*) away; (*excepto, salvo*) except, save ♦ *prep*: **~ de** outside; (*fig*) besides; **~ de sí** beside o.s.; **por ~** (on the) outside

fuera-borda [fwera'βorða] *nm* speedboat

fuerte [ˈfwerte] *adj* strong; (*golpe*) hard; (*ruido*) loud; (*comida*) rich; (*lluvia*) heavy; (*dolor*) intense ♦ *adv* strongly; hard; loud(ly)

fuerza etc [ˈfwerθa] *vb ver* **forzar** ♦ *nf* (*fortaleza*) strength; (*TEC, ELEC*) power; (*coacción*) force; (*MIL: tb*: **~s**) forces *pl*; **a ~ de** by dint of; **cobrar ~s** to recover one's strength; **tener ~s para** to have the strength to; **a la ~** forcibly, by force; **por ~** of necessity; **~ de voluntad** willpower

fuga [ˈfuxa] *nf* (*huida*) flight, escape; (*de gas etc*) leak

fugarse [fu'xarse] *vr* to flee, escape

fugaz [fu'xaθ] *adj* fleeting

fugitivo, a [fuxi'tiβo, a] *adj, nm/f* fugitive

fui *vb ver* **ser; ir**

fulano, a [fu'lano, a] *nm/f* so-and-so, what's-his-name/what's-her-name

fulminante [fulmi'nante] *adj* (*fig: mirada*) fierce; (*MED: enfermedad, ataque*) sudden; (*fam: éxito, golpe*) sudden

fumador, a [fuma'ðor, a] *nm/f* smoker

fumar [fu'mar] *vt, vi* to smoke; **~ en pipa** to smoke a pipe

función [fun'θjon] *nf* function; (*de trabajo*) duties *pl*; (*espectáculo*) show; **entrar en funciones** to take up one's duties

funcionar [funθjo'nar] *vi* (*gen*) to function; (*máquina*) to work; **"no funciona"** "out of order"

funcionario, a [funθjo'narjo, a] *nm/f* civil servant

funda ['funda] nf (gen) cover; (de almohada) pillowcase

fundación [funda'θjon] nf foundation

fundamental [fundamen'tal] adj fundamental, basic

fundamentar [fundamen'tar] vt (poner base) to lay the foundations of; (establecer) to found; (fig) to base; **fundamento** nm (base) foundation

fundar [fun'dar] vt to found; **~se** vr: **~ se en** to be founded on

fundición [fundi'θjon] nf fusing; (fábrica) foundry

fundir [fun'dir] vt (gen) to fuse; (metal) to smelt, melt down; (nieve etc) to melt; (COM) to merge; (estatua) to cast; **~se** vr (colores etc) to merge, blend; (unirse) to fuse together; (ELEC: fusible, lámpara etc) to fuse, blow; (nieve etc) to melt

fúnebre ['funeβre] adj funeral cpd, funereal

funeral [fune'ral] nm funeral; **funeraria** nf undertaker's

funesto, a [fu'nesto, a] adj (día) ill-fated; (decisión) fatal

furgón [fur'xon] nm wagon; **furgoneta** nf (AUTO, COM) (transit) van (BRIT), pick-up (truck) (US)

furia ['furja] nf (ira) fury; (violencia) violence; **furibundo, a** adj furious; **furioso, a** adj (iracundo) furious; (violento) violent; **furor** nm (cólera) rage

furtivo, a [fur'tiβo, a] adj furtive ♦ nm poacher

fusible [fu'siβle] nm fuse

fusil [fu'sil] nm rifle; **~ar** vt to shoot

fusión [fu'sjon] nf (gen) melting; (unión) fusion; (COM) merger

fútbol ['futβol] nm football; **futbolín** nm table football; **futbolista** nm footballer

futuro, a [fu'turo, a] adj, nm future

G, g

gabardina [gaβar'ðina] nf raincoat, gabardine

gabinete [gaβi'nete] nm (POL) cabinet; (estudio) study; (de abogados etc) office

gaceta [ga'θeta] nf gazette

gachas ['gatʃas] nfpl porridge sg

gafas ['gafas] nfpl glasses; **~ de sol** sunglasses

gafe [gafe] nm jinx

gaita ['gaita] nf bagpipes pl

gajes ['gaxes] nmpl: **los ~ del oficio** occupational hazards

gajo ['gaxo] nm (de naranja) segment

gala ['gala] nf (traje de etiqueta) full dress; **~s** nfpl (ropa) finery sg; **estar de ~** to be in one's best clothes; **hacer ~ de** to display

galante [ga'lante] adj gallant; **galantería** nf (caballerosidad) gallantry; (cumplido) politeness; (comentario) compliment

galápago [ga'lapaɣo] nm (ZOOL) turtle

galardón [galar'ðon] nm award, prize

galaxia [ga'laksja] nf galaxy

galera [ga'lera] nf (nave) galley; (carro) wagon; (IMPRENTA) galley

galería [gale'ria] nf (gen) gallery; (balcón) veranda(h); (pasillo) corridor

Gales ['gales] nm (tb: País de ~) Wales; **galés, esa** adj Welsh ♦ nm/f Welshman/woman ♦ nm (LING) Welsh

galgo [ga'lɣo, a] nm/f greyhound

galimatías [galima'tias] nmpl (lenguaje) gibberish sg, nonsense sg

gallardía [gaʎar'ðia] nf (valor) bravery

gallego, a [ga'ʎeɣo, a] adj, nm/f Galician

galleta [ga'ʎeta] nf biscuit (BRIT), cookie (US)

gallina [ga'ʎina] nf hen ♦ nm/f (fam: cobarde) chicken; **gallinero** nm henhouse; (TEATRO) top gallery

gallo ['gaʎo] nm cock, rooster

galón [ga'lon] *nm* (MIL) stripe; (COSTURA) braid; (*medida*) gallon

galopar [galo'par] *vi* to gallop

gama ['gama] *nf* (fig) range

gamba ['gamba] *nf* prawn (BRIT), shrimp (US)

gamberro, a [gam'berro, a] *nm/f* hooligan, lout

gamuza [ga'muθa] *nf* chamois

gana ['gana] *nf* (*deseo*) desire, wish; (*apetito*) appetite; (*voluntad*) will; (*añoranza*) longing; **de buena ~** willingly; **de mala ~** reluctantly; **me da ~s de** I want to, I want to; **no me da la ~** I don't feel like it; **tener ~s de** to feel like

ganadería [ganaðe'ria] *nf* (*ganado*) livestock; (*ganado vacuno*) cattle *pl*; (*cría, comercio*) cattle raising

ganado [ga'naðo] *nm* livestock; **~ lanar** sheep *pl*; **~ mayor** cattle *pl*; **~ porcino** pigs *pl*

ganador, a [gana'ðor, a] *adj* winning ♦ *nm/f* winner

ganancia [ga'nanθja] *nf* (*lo ganado*) gain; (*aumento*) increase; (*beneficio*) profit; **~s** *nfpl* (*ingresos*) earnings; (*beneficios*) profit *sg*, winnings

ganar [ga'nar] *vt* (*obtener*) to get, obtain; (*sacar ventaja*) to gain; (*salario etc*) to earn; (DEPORTE: *premio*) to win; (*derrotar a*) to beat; (*alcanzar*) to reach ♦ *vi* (DEPORTE) to win; **~se** *vr*: **~se la vida** to earn one's living

ganchillo [gan't∫iʎo] *nm* crochet

gancho ['gant∫o] *nm* (*gen*) hook; (*colgador*) hanger

gandul, a [gan'dul, a] *adj*, *nm/f* good-for-nothing, layabout

ganga ['ganga] *nf* bargain

gangrena [gan'grena] *nf* gangrene

ganso, a ['ganso, a] *nm/f* (ZOOL) goose; (*fam*) idiot

ganzúa [gan'θua] *nf* skeleton key

garabatear [garaβate'ar] *vi*, *vt* (*al escribir*) to scribble, scrawl

garabato [gara'βato] *nm* (*escritura*) scrawl, scribble

garaje [ga'raxe] *nm* garage

garante [ga'rante] *adj* responsible ♦ *nm/f* guarantor

garantía [garan'tia] *nf* guarantee

garantizar [garanti'θar] *vt* to guarantee

garbanzo [gar'βanθo] *nm* chickpea (BRIT), garbanzo (US)

garbo ['garβo] *nm* grace, elegance

garfio ['garfjo] *nm* grappling iron

garganta [gar'γanta] *nf* (ANAT) throat; (*de botella*) neck; **gargantilla** *nf* necklace

gárgaras ['garγaras] *nfpl*: **hacer ~** to gargle

garita [ga'rita] *nf* cabin, hut; (MIL) sentry box

garra ['garra] *nf* (*de gato, TEC*) claw; (*de ave*) talon; (*fam: mano*) hand, paw

garrafa [ga'rrafa] *nf* carafe, decanter

garrapata [garra'pata] *nf* tick

garrote [ga'rrote] *nm* (*palo*) stick; (*porra*) cudgel; (*suplicio*) garrotte

garza [ˈgarθa] *nf* heron

gas [gas] *nm* gas

gasa ['gasa] *nf* gauze

gaseosa [gase'osa] *nf* lemonade

gaseoso, a [gase'oso, a] *adj* gassy, fizzy

gasoil [ga'soil] *nm* diesel (oil)

gasóleo [ga'soleo] *nm* = **gasoil**

gasolina [gaso'lina] *nf* petrol, gas(oline) (US); **gasolinera** *nf* petrol (BRIT) o gas (US) station

gastado, a [gas'taðo, a] *adj* (*dinero*) spent; (*ropa*) worn out; (*usado: frase etc*) trite

gastar [gas'tar] *vt* (*dinero, tiempo*) to spend; (*fuerzas*) to use up; (*desperdiciar*) to waste; (*llevar*) to wear; **~se** *vr* to wear out; (*estropearse*) to waste; **~ en** to spend on; **~ bromas** to crack jokes; **¿qué número gastas?** what size (shoe) do you take?

gasto ['gasto] *nm* (*desembolso*) expenditure, spending; (*consumo, uso*) use; **~s** nmpl (desembolsos) expenses; (cargos) charges, costs

gastronomía [ɣastrono'mia] nf gastronomy

gatear [gate'ar] vi (andar a gatas) to go on all fours

gatillo [ga'tiʎo] nm (de arma de fuego) trigger; (de dentista) forceps

gato, a ['ɣato, a] nm/f cat ♦ nm (TEC) jack; **andar a gatas** to go on all fours

gaviota [ɣa'βjota] nf seagull

gay [ge] adj inv, nm gay, homosexual

gazpacho [ɣaθ'patʃo] nm gazpacho

gel [xel] nm (tb: ~ de baño/ducha) gel

gelatina [xela'tina] nf jelly; (polvos etc) gelatine

gema ['xema] nf gem

gemelo, a [xe'melo, a] adj, nm/f twin; **~s** nmpl (de camisa) cufflinks; (prismáticos) field glasses, binoculars

gemido [xe'miðo] nm (quejido) moan, groan; (aullido) howl

Géminis ['xeminis] nm Gemini

gemir [xe'mir] vi (quejarse) to moan, groan; (aullar) to howl

generación [xenera'θjon] nf generation

general [xene'ral] adj general ♦ nm general; **por lo o en ~** in general; **G~itat** nf Catalan parliament; **~izar** vt to generalize; **~izarse** vr to become generalized, spread; **~mente** adv generally

generar [xene'rar] vt to generate

género ['xenero] nm (clase) kind, sort; (tipo) type; (BIO) genus; (LING) gender; (COM) material; **~ humano** human race

generosidad [xenerosi'ðað] nf generosity; **generoso, a** adj generous

genial [xe'njal] adj inspired; (idea) brilliant; (afable) genial

genio ['xenjo] nm (carácter) nature, disposition; (humor) temper; (facultad creadora) genius; **de mal ~** bad-tempered

genital [xeni'tal] adj genital; **genitales** nmpl genitals

gente ['xente] nf (personas) people pl; (parientes) relatives pl

gentil [xen'til] adj (elegante) graceful; (encantador) charming; **~eza** nf grace; charm; (cortesía) courtesy

gentío [xen'tio] nm crowd, throng

genuino, a [xe'nwino, a] adj genuine

geografía [xeoɣra'fia] nf geography

geología [xeolo'xia] nf geology

geometría [xeome'tria] nf geometry

gerencia [xe'renθja] nf management; **gerente** nm/f (supervisor) manager; (jefe) director

geriatría [xeria'tria] nf (MED) geriatrics sg

germen ['xermen] nm germ

germinar [xermi'nar] vi to germinate

gesticular [xestiku'lar] vi to gesticulate; (hacer muecas) to grimace; **gesticulación** nf gesticulation; (mueca) grimace

gestión [xes'tjon] nf management; (diligencia, acción) negotiation; **gestionar** vt (lograr) to try to arrange; (dirigir) to manage

gesto ['xesto] nm (mueca) grimace; (ademán) gesture

Gibraltar [xißral'tar] nm Gibraltar; **gibraltareño, a** adj, nm/f Gibraltarian

gigante [xi'ɣante] adj, nm/f giant; **gigantesco, a** adj gigantic

gilipollas [xili'poʎas] (fam) adj inv daft ♦ nm/f inv wally

gimnasia [xim'nasja] nf gymnastics pl; **gimnasio** nm gymnasium; **gimnasta** nm/f gymnast

gimotear [ximote'ar] vi to whine, whimper

ginebra [xi'neßra] nf gin

ginecólogo, a [xine'koloɣo, a] nm/f gynaecologist

gira ['xira] nf tour, trip

girar [xi'rar] vt (darla vuelta) to turn (around); (: rápidamente) to spin; (COM: giro postal) to draw; (: letra de cambio) to issue ♦ *vi* to turn (round); (*rápido*) to spin

girasol [xira'sol] *nm* sunflower

giratorio, a [xira'torjo, a] *adj* revolving

giro ['xiro] *nm* (*movimiento*) turn, revolution; (*LING*) expression; (*COM*) draft; ~ **bancario/postal** bank giro/ postal order

gis [xis] (*AM*) *nm* chalk

gitano, a [xi'tano, a] *adj, nm/f* gypsy

glacial [gla'θjal] *adj* icy, freezing

glaciar [gla'θjar] *nm* glacier

glándula ['glandula] *nf* gland

global [glo'βal] *adj* global

globo ['gloβo] *nm* (*esfera*) globe, sphere; (*aerostato, juguete*) balloon

glóbulo ['gloβulo] *nm* globule; (*ANAT*) corpuscle

gloria ['glorja] *nf* glory

glorieta [glo'rjeta] *nf* (*de jardín*) bower, arbour; (*plazoleta*) roundabout (*BRIT*), traffic circle (*US*)

glorificar [glorifi'kar] *vt* (*enaltecer*) to glorify, praise

glorioso, a [glo'rjoso, a] *adj* glorious

glotón, ona [glo'ton, ona] *adj* gluttonous, greedy ♦ *nm/f* glutton

glucosa [glu'kosa] *nf* glucose

gobernador, a [goβerna'ðor, a] *adj* governing ♦ *nm/f* governor

gobernante *adj* governing

gobernar [goβer'nar] *vt* (*dirigir*) to guide, direct; (*POL*) to rule, govern ♦ *vi* to govern; (*NAUT*) to steer

gobierno *etc* [go'βjerno] *vb ver* **gobernar** ♦ *nm* (*POL*) government; (*dirección*) guidance, direction; (*NAUT*) steering

goce *etc* [go'θe] *vb ver* **gozar** ♦ *nm* enjoyment

gol [gol] *nm* goal

golf [golf] *nm* golf

golfa ['golfa] (*fam!*) *nf* (*mujer*) slut, whore

golfo, a ['golfo, a] *nm* (*GEO*) gulf ♦ *nm/f* (*fam: niño*) urchin; (*gamberro*)

lout

golondrina [golon'drina] *nf* swallow

golosina [golo'sina] *nf* (*dulce*) sweet; **goloso, a** *adj* sweet-toothed

golpe ['golpe] *nm* blow; (*de puño*) punch; (*de mano*) smack; (*de remo*) stroke; (*fig: choque*) clash; **no dar** ~ to be bone idle; **de un** ~ with one blow; **de** ~ suddenly; ~ **(de estado)** coup (d'état); **golpear** *vt, vi* to strike, knock; (*asestar*) to beat; (*de puño*) to punch; (*golpetear*) to tap

goma ['goma] *nf* (*caucho*) rubber; (*elástico*) elastic; (*una* ~) elastic band; ~ **espuma** foam rubber; ~ **de pegar** gum, glue; ~ **de borrar** eraser, rubber (*BRIT*)

gomina [go'mina] *nf* hair gel

gordo, a [ˈgorðo, a] *adj* fat; (*fam*) enormous; **el (premio)** ~ (*en lotería*) first prize; **gordura** *nf* fat; (*corpulencia*) fatness, stoutness

gorila [go'rila] *nm* gorilla

gorjear [gorxe'ar] *vi* to twitter, chirp

gorra ['gorra] *nf* cap; (*de niño*) bonnet; (*militar*) bearskin; **entrar de** ~ (*fam*) to gatecrash; **ir de** ~ to sponge

gorrión [go'rrjon] *nm* sparrow

gorro ['gorro] *nm* (*gen*) cap; (*de niño, mujer*) bonnet

gorrón, ona [go'rron, ona] *nm/f* scrounger; **gorronear** *vi* to scrounge

gota ['gota] *nf* (*gen*) drop; (*de sudor*) bead; (*MED*) gout; **gotear** *vi* to drip; (*lloviznar*) to drizzle; **gotera** *nf* leak

gozar [go'θar] *vi* to enjoy o.s.; ~ **de** (*disfrutar*) to enjoy; (*poseer*) to possess

gozne [go'θne] *nm* hinge

gozo ['goθo] *nm* (*alegría*) joy; (*placer*) pleasure

gr. *abr* (= *gramo, gramos*) g

grabación [graßa'θjon] *nf* recording

grabado [gra'βaðo] *nm* print, engraving

grabadora [graßa'ðora] *nf* tape-recorder

grabar [gra'ßar] vt to engrave; (discos, cintas) to record

gracia ['graθja] nf (encanto) grace, gracefulness; (humor) humour, wit; ¡(muchas) ~s! thanks (very much)!; ~s a thanks to; tener ~ (chiste etc) to be funny; **no me hace ~** I am not keen; **gracioso, a** adj (divertido) funny, amusing; (cómico) comical ♦ nm/f (TEATRO) comic character

grada ['graða] nf (de escalera) step; (de anfiteatro) tier, row; ~s nfpl (DEPORTE: de estadio) terraces

gradería [graðe'ria] nf (gradas) (flight of) steps pl; (de anfiteatro) tiers pl, rows pl; (DEPORTE: de estadio) terraces pl; ~ **cubierta** covered stand

grado ['graðo] nm degree; (de aceite, vino) grade; (etapa) step; (MIL) rank; **de buen ~** willingly

graduación [graðwa'θjon] nf (del alcohol) proof, strength; (ESCOL) graduation; (MIL) rank

gradual [gra'ðwal] adj gradual

graduar [gra'ðwar] vt (gen) to graduate; (MIL) to commission; ~**se** vr to graduate; ~**se la vista** to have one's eyes tested

gráfica ['grafika] nf graph

gráfico, a ['grafiko, a] adj graphic ♦ nm diagram; ~**s** nmpl (INFORM) graphics

grajo ['graxo] nm rook

Gral abr (= General) Gen.

gramática [gra'matika] nf grammar

gramo ['gramo] nm gramme (BRIT), gram (US)

gran [gran] adj ver **grande**

grana ['grana] nf (color, tela) scarlet

granada [gra'naða] nf pomegranate; (MIL) grenade

granate [gra'nate] adj deep red

Gran Bretaña [-bre'taɲa] nf Great Britain

grande ['grande] (antes de nmsg: **gran**) adj (de tamaño) big, large; (alto) tall; (distinguido) great; (impresionante)

grand ♦ nm grandee; **grandeza** nf greatness

grandioso, a [gran'djoso, a] adj magnificent, grand

granel [gra'nel]: **a ~** adv (COM) in bulk

granero [gra'nero] nm granary, barn

granito [gra'nito] nm (AGR) small grain; (roca) granite

granizado [grani'θaðo] nm iced drink

granizar [grani'θar] vi to hail; **granizo** nm hail

granja ['granxa] nf (gen) farm;

granjear [granxe'ar] vt to win, gain; **granjearse** vr to win, gain; **granjero, a** nm/f farmer

grano ['grano] nm grain; (semilla) seed; (de café) bean; (MED) pimple, spot

granuja [gra'nuxa] nm/f rogue; (golfillo) urchin

grapa ['grapa] nf staple; (TEC) clamp; **grapadora** nf stapler

grasa ['grasa] nf (gen) grease; (de cocinar) fat, lard; (sebo) suet; (mugre) filth; **grasiento, a** adj greasy; (de aceite) oily; **graso, a** adj (leche, queso, carne) fatty; (pelo, piel) greasy

gratificación [gratifika'θjon] nf (bono) bonus; (recompensa) reward

gratificar [gratifi'kar] vt to reward

gratinar [grati'nar] vt to cook au gratin

gratis ['gratis] adv free

gratitud [grati'tuð] nf gratitude

grato, a ['grato, a] adj (agradable) pleasant, agreeable

gratuito, a [gra'twito, a] adj (gratis) free; (sin razón) gratuitous

gravamen [gra'ßamen] nm (impuesto) tax

gravar [gra'ßar] vt to tax

grave ['graße] adj heavy; (serio) grave, serious; ~**dad** nf gravity

gravilla [gra'ßiʎa] nf gravel

gravitar [graßi'tar] vi to gravitate; ~ **sobre** to rest on

graznar [graθ'nar] vi (cuervo) to squawk; (pato) to quack; (hablar ronco) to croak

Grecia ['greθja] nf Greece

gremio ['gremjo] nm trade, industry

greña ['greɲa] nf (cabellos) shock of hair

gresca ['greska] nf uproar

griego, a ['grjeɣo, a] adj, nm/f Greek

grieta ['grjeta] nf crack

grifo ['grifo] nm tap; (AM: AUTO) petrol (BRIT) o gas (US) station

grilletes [gri'ʎetes] nmpl fetters

grillo ['griʎo] nm (ZOOL) cricket

gripe ['gripe] nf flu, influenza

gris [gris] adj (color) grey

gritar [gri'tar] vt, vi to shout, yell; **grito** nm shout, yell; (de horror) scream

grosella [gro'seʎa] nf (red)currant; ~ **negra** blackcurrant

grosería [grose'ria] nf (actitud) rudeness; (comentario) vulgar comment; **grosero, a** adj (poco cortés) rude, bad-mannered; (ordinario) vulgar, crude

grosor [gro'sor] nm thickness

grotesco, a [gro'tesko, a] adj grotesque

grúa ['grua] nf (TEC) crane; (de petróleo) derrick

grueso, a ['grweso, a] adj thick; (persona) stout ♦ nm bulk; **el ~ de** the bulk of

grulla ['gruʎa] nf crane

grumo ['grumo] nm clot, lump

gruñido [gru'niðo] nm grunt; (de persona) grumble

gruñir [gru'nir] vi (animal) to growl; (persona) to grumble

grupa ['grupa] nf (ZOOL) rump

grupo ['grupo] nm group; (TEC) unit, set

gruta ['gruta] nf grotto

guadaña [gwa'ðaɲa] nf scythe

guagua ['gwaxwa] nf (AM) nf (niño) baby; (bus) bus

guante ['gwante] nm glove; ~**ra** nf glove compartment

guapo, a ['gwapo, a] adj good-looking, attractive; (elegante) smart

guarda ['gwarða] nm/f (persona) guard, keeper ♦ nf (acto) guarding; (custodia) custody; ~**bosques** nm inv gamekeeper; ~**costas** nm inv coastguard vessel ♦ nm/f guardian, protector; ~**espaldas** nm/f inv bodyguard; ~**meta** nm/f goalkeeper; **guardar** vt (gen) to keep; (vigilar) to guard, watch over; (dinero: ahorrar) to save; **guardarse** vr (preservarse) to protect o.s.; (evitar) to avoid; **guardar cama** to stay in bed; ~**rropa** nm (armario) wardrobe; (en establecimiento público) cloakroom

guardería [gwarðe'ria] nf nursery

guardia ['gwarðja] nf (MIL) guard; (cuidado) care, custody ♦ nm/f guard; (policía) policeman/woman; **estar de** ~ to be on guard; **montar** ~ to mount guard; **G~ Civil** Civil Guard; **G~ Nacional** National Guard

guardián, ana [gwar'ðjan, ana] nm/f (gen) guardian, keeper

guarecer [gware'θer] vt (proteger) to protect; (abrigar) to shelter; ~**se** vr to take refuge

guarida [gwa'riða] nf (de animal) den, lair; (refugio) refuge

guarnecer [gwarne'θer] vt (equipar) to provide; (adornar) to adorn; (TEC) to reinforce; **guarnición** nf (de vestimenta) trimming; (de piedra) mount; (CULIN) garnish; (arneses) harness; (MIL) garrison

guarro, a ['gwarro, a] nm/f pig

guasa ['gwasa] nf joke; **guasón, ona** adj (bromista) joking ♦ nm/f wit; (bromista)

Guatemala [gwate'mala] nf Guatemala

guay [gwai] (fam) adj super, great

gubernativo, a [guβerna'tiβo, a] adj governmental

guerra ['gerra] nf war; ~ **civil** civil war; ~ **fría** cold war; **dar** ~ to annoy; **guerrear** vi to wage war; **guerrero, a**

adj fighting; (*carácter*) warlike ♦ *nm/f* warrior

guerrilla [geˈrriʎa] *nf* guerrilla warfare; (*tropas*) guerrilla band o group

guía *etc* [ˈgia] *vb ver* **guiar** ♦ *nm/f* (*persona*) guide ♦ *nf* (*libro*) guidebook; **~ de ferrocarriles** railway timetable; **~ telefónica** telephone directory

guiar [giˈar] *vt* to guide, direct; (*AUTO*) to steer; **~se** *vr*: **~se por** to be guided by

guijarro [giˈxarro] *nm* pebble

guillotina [giʎoˈtina] *nf* guillotine

guinda [ˈginda] *nf* morello cherry

guindilla [ginˈdiʎa] *nf* chilli pepper

guiñapo [giˈɲapo] *nm* (*harapo*) rag; (*persona*) reprobate, rogue

guiñar [giˈɲar] *vt* to wink

guión [giˈon] *nm* (*LING*) hyphen, dash; (*CINE*) script; **guionista** *nm/f* scriptwriter

guiri [ˈgiri] (*fam: pey*) *nm/f* foreigner

guirnalda [girˈnalda] *nf* garland

guisado [giˈsaðo] *nm* stew

guisante [giˈsante] *nm* pea

guisar [giˈsar] *vt, vi* to cook; **guiso** *nm* cooked dish

guitarra [giˈtarra] *nf* guitar

gula [ˈgula] *nf* gluttony, greed

gusano [guˈsano] *nm* worm; (*lombriz*) earthworm

gustar [gusˈtar] *vt* to taste, sample ♦ *vi* to please, be pleasing; **~ de algo** to like o enjoy sth; **me gustan las uvas** I like grapes; **le gusta nadar** she likes o enjoys swimming

gusto [ˈgusto] *nm* (*sentido, sabor*) taste; (*placer*) pleasure; **tiene ~ a menta** it tastes of mint; **tener buen ~** to have good taste; **sentirse a ~** to feel at ease; **mucho ~ (en conocerle)** pleased to meet you; **el ~ es mío** the pleasure is mine; **con ~** willingly, gladly; **por ~** voluntarily; **~so**, *adj* (*sabroso*) tasty; (*agradable*) pleasant

H, h

ha *vb ver* **haber**

haba [ˈaβa] *nf* bean

Habana [aˈβana] *nf*: **la ~** Havana

habano [aˈβano] *nm* Havana cigar

habéis *vb ver* **haber**

PALABRA CLAVE
---

haber [aˈβer] *vb aux* **1** (*tiempos compuestos*) to have; **había comido** I had eaten; **antes/después de ~lo visto** before seeing/after seeing o having seen it

2: **¡~lo dicho antes!** you should have said so before!

3: **~ de**: **he de hacerlo** I have to do it; **ha de llegar mañana** it should arrive tomorrow

♦ *vb impers* **1** (*existencia: sg*) there is; (*pl*) there are; **hay un hermano/dos hermanos** there is one brother/there are two brothers; **¿cuánto hay de aquí a Sucre?** how far is it from here to Sucre?

2 (*obligación*): **hay que hacer algo** something must be done; **hay que apuntarlo o acordarse** you have to write it down to remember

3: **¡hay que ver!** well I never!

4: **¡no hay de o por (AM) qué!** don't mention it!, not at all!

5: **¿qué hay?** (*¿qué pasa?*) what's up?, what's the matter?; (*¿qué tal?*) how's it going?

♦ **~se** *vr*: **habérselas con uno** to have it out with sb

♦ *vt*: **he aquí unas sugerencias** here are some suggestions; **no hay cintas blancas pero sí las hay rojas** there aren't any white ribbons but there are some red ones

♦ *nm* (*en cuenta*) credit side; **~es** *nmpl* assets; **¿cuánto tengo en el ~?** how much do I have in my account?; **tiene**

varias novelas en su ~ he has several novels to his credit

habichuela [aβi'tʃwela] nf kidney bean

hábil ['aβil] adj (listo) clever, smart; (capaz) fit, capable; (experto) expert; **día ~** working day; **habilidad** nf skill, ability

habilitar [aβili'tar] vt (capacitar) to enable; (dar instrumentos) to equip; (financiar) to finance

hábilmente [aβil'mente] adv skilfully, expertly

habitación [aβita'θjon] nf (cuarto) room; (BIO: morada) habitat; **~ sencilla** o **individual** single room; **~ doble** o **de matrimonio** double room

habitante [aβi'tante] nm/f inhabitant

habitar [aβi'tar] vt (residir en) to inhabit; (ocupar) to occupy ♦ vi to live

hábito ['aβito] nm habit

habitual [aβi'twal] adj usual

habituar [aβi'twar] vt to accustom; **~se** vr: **~se a** to get used to

habla ['aβla] nf (capacidad de hablar) speech; (idioma) language; (dialecto) dialect; **perder el ~** to become speechless; **de ~ francesa** French-speaking; **estar al ~** to be on the line; **¡González al ~!** (TEL) González speaking!

hablador, a [aβla'ðor, a] adj talkative ♦ nm/f chatterbox

habladuría [aβlaðu'ria] nf rumour; **~s** nfpl gossip sg

hablante [a'βlante] adj speaking ♦ nm/f speaker

hablar [a'βlar] vt to speak, talk ♦ vi to speak; **~se** vr to speak to each other; **~ con** to speak to; **~ de** to speak o talk of o about; **"se habla inglés"** "English spoken here"; **¡ni ~!** it's out of the question!

habré etc vb ver **haber**

hacendoso, a [aθen'doso, a] adj industrious

hacer [a'θer] vt **1** (fabricar, producir) to make; (construir) to build; **~ una película/un ruido** to make a film/noise; **el guisado lo hice yo** I made o cooked the stew

2 (ejecutar: trabajo etc) to do; **~ la colada** to do the washing; **~ la comida** to do the cooking; **¿qué haces?** what are you doing?; **~ el malo** o **el papel del malo** (TEATRO) to play the villain

3 (estudios, algunos deportes) to do; **~ español/económicas** to do o study Spanish/economics; **~ yoga/gimnasia** to do yoga/go to gym

4 (transformar, incidir en): **esto lo hará más difícil** this will make it more difficult; **salir te hará sentir mejor** going out will make you feel better

5 (cálculo): **2 y 2 hacen 4** 2 and 2 make 4; **éste hace 100** this one makes 100

6 (+ sub): **esto hará que ganemos** this will make us win; **harás que no quiera venir** you'll stop him wanting to come

7 (como sustituto de vb) to do; **él bebió y yo hice lo mismo** he drank and I did likewise

8: **no hace más que criticar** all he does is criticize

♦ vb semi-aux: **hacer** + infin **1** (directo): **les hice venir** I made o had them come; **~ trabajar a los demás** to get others to work

2 (por intermedio de otros): **~ reparar algo** to get sth repaired

♦ vi **1**: **haz como que no lo sabes** act as if you don't know

2 (ser apropiado): **si os hace** if it's alright with you

3: **~ de: ~ de madre para uno** to be like a mother to sb; (TEATRO): **~ de Otelo** to play Othello

♦ vb impers 1: hace calor/frío it's hot/cold; ver tb **bueno; sol; tiempo**
2 (*tiempo*): **hace 3 años** 3 years ago; **hace un mes que no/no voy** I've been going/I haven't been for a month
3: ¿cómo has hecho para llegar tan rápido? how did you manage to get here so quickly?
♦ ~se vr 1 (*volverse*) to become; **se hicieron amigos** they became friends
2 (*acostumbrarse*): **~se a** to get used to
3: se hace con huevos y leche it's made out of eggs and milk; **eso no se hace** that's not done
4 (*obtener*): **~se de o con algo** to get hold of sth
5 (*fingirse*): **~se el sueco** to turn a deaf ear

hacha [a'tʃa] *nf* axe; (*antorcha*) torch
hachís [a'tʃis] *nm* hashish
hacia ['aθja] *prep* (*en dirección de*) towards; (*cerca de*) near; (*actitud*) towards; **~ arriba/abajo** up(wards)/down(wards); **~ mediodía** about noon
hacienda [a'θjenda] *nf* (*propiedad*) property; (*finca*) farm; (*AM*) ranch; **~ pública** public finance; **(Ministerio de) H~** Exchequer (*BRIT*), Treasury Department (*US*)
hada ['aða] *nf* fairy
Haití [ai'ti] *nm* Haiti
hago *etc vb ver* **hacer**
halagar [ala'xar] *vt* to flatter
halago [a'laxo] *nm* flattery; **halagüeño, a** *adj* flattering
halcón [al'kon] *nm* falcon, hawk
hallar [a'ʎar] *vt* (*gen*) to find; (*descubrir*) to discover; (*toparse con*) to run into; **~se vr** to be (situated); **hallazgo** *nm* discovery; (*cosa*) find
halterofilia [altero'filja] *nf* weightlifting
hamaca [a'maka] *nf* hammock
hambre ['ambre] *nf* hunger; (*plaga*) famine; (*deseo*) longing; **tener ~** to be

hungry; **hambriento, a** *adj* hungry, starving
hamburguesa [ambur'xesa] *nf* hamburger; **hamburguesería** *nf* burger bar
han *vb ver* **haber**
harapiento, a [ara'pjento, a] *adj* tattered, in rags
harapos [a'rapos] *nmpl* rags
haré *etc vb ver* **hacer**
harina [a'rina] *nf* flour
hartar [ar'tar] *vt* to satiate, glut; (*fig*) to tire, sicken; **~se vr** (*de comida*) to fill o.s., gorge o.s.; (*cansarse*) to get fed up (*de with*); **hartazgo** *nm* surfeit, glut; **harto, a** *adj* (*lleno*) full; (*cansado*) fed up **♦** *adv* (*bastante*) enough; (*muy*) very; **estar harto de** to be fed up with
has *vb ver* **haber**
hasta ['asta] *adv* even **♦** *prep* (*alcanzando a*) as far as; up to; down to; (*de tiempo: a tal hora*) till, until; (*antes de*) before **♦** *conj*: **~ que** until; **~ luego/el sábado** see you soon/on Saturday
hastiar [as'tjar] *vt* (*gen*) to weary; (*aburrir*) to bore; **~se vr**: **~se de** to get fed up with; **hastío** *nm* weariness; boredom
hatillo [a'tiʎo] *nm* belongings *pl*, kit; (*montón*) bundle, heap
hay *vb ver* **haber**
Haya ['aja] *nf*: **la ~** The Hague
haya *etc* ['aja] *vb ver* **haber** **♦** *nf* beech tree
haz [aθ] *vb ver* **hacer** **♦** *nm* (*de luz*) beam
hazaña [a'θaɲa] *nf* feat, exploit
hazmerreír [aθmerre'ir] *nm inv* laughing stock
he *vb ver* **haber**
hebilla [e'ßiʎa] *nf* buckle, clasp
hebra ['eßra] *nf* thread; (*BOT: fibra*) fibre, grain
hebreo, a [e'ßreo, a] *adj, nm/f* Hebrew **♦** *nm* (*LING*) Hebrew

hechizar [etʃi'θar] vt to cast a spell on, bewitch

hechizo [e'tʃiθo] nm witchcraft, magic; (acto de magia) spell, charm

hecho, a ['etʃo, a] pp de **hacer** ♦ adj (carne) done; (COSTURA) ready-to-wear ♦ nm deed, act; (dato) fact; (cuestión) matter; (suceso) event ♦ excl agreed!, done!; **¡bien ~!** well done!; **de ~** in fact, as a matter of fact

hechura [e'tʃura] nf (forma) form, shape; (de persona) build

hectárea [ek'tarea] nf hectare

heder [e'ðer] vi to stink, smell

hediondo, a [e'ðjondo, a] adj stinking

hedor [e'ðor] nm stench

helada [e'laða] nf frost

heladera [ela'ðera] (AM) nf (refrigerador) refrigerator

helado, a [e'laðo, a] adj frozen; (glacial) icy; (fig) chilly, cold ♦ nm ice cream

helar [e'lar] vt to freeze, ice (up); (dejar atónito) to amaze; (desalentar) to discourage ♦ vi to freeze; **~se** vr to freeze

helecho [e'letʃo] nm fern

hélice ['eliθe] nf (TEC) propeller

helicóptero [eli'koptero] nm helicopter

hembra ['embra] nf (BOT, ZOOL) female; (mujer) woman; (TEC) nut

hemorragia [emo'rraxja] nf haemorrhage

hemorroides [emo'rroiðes] nfpl haemorrhoids, piles

hemos vb ver **haber**

hendidura [endi'ðura] nf crack, split

heno ['eno] nm hay

herbicida [erβi'θiða] nm weedkiller

heredad [ere'ðað] nf landed property; (granja) farm

heredar [ere'ðar] vt to inherit; **heredero, a** nm/f heir(ess)

hereje [e'rexe] nm/f heretic

herencia [e'renθja] nf inheritance

herida [e'riða] nf wound, injury; ver tb

herido

herido, a [e'riðo, a] adj injured, wounded ♦ nm/f casualty

herir [e'rir] vt to wound, injure; (fig) to offend

hermanastro, a [erma'nastro, a] nm/f stepbrother/sister

hermandad [erman'dað] nf brotherhood

hermano, a [er'mano, a] nm/f brother/sister; **~ gemelo** twin brother; **hermana gemela** twin sister; **~ político** brother-in-law; **hermana política** sister-in-law

hermético, a [er'metiko, a] adj hermetic; (fig) watertight

hermoso, a [er'moso, a] adj beautiful, lovely; (estupendo) splendid; (guapo) handsome; **hermosura** nf beauty

hernia ['ernja] nf hernia

héroe ['eroe] nm hero

heroína [ero'ina] nf (mujer) heroine; (droga) heroin

heroísmo [ero'ismo] nm heroism

herradura [erra'ðura] nf horseshoe

herramienta [erra'mjenta] nf tool

herrero [e'rrero] nm blacksmith

herrumbre [e'rrumbre] nf rust

hervidero [erβi'ðero] nm (fig) swarm; (POL etc) hotbed

hervir [er'βir] vi to boil; (burbujear) to bubble; (fig): **~ de** to teem with; **~ a fuego lento** to simmer; **hervor** nm boiling; (fig) ardour, fervour

heterosexual [eterosek'swal] adj heterosexual

hice etc vb ver **hacer**

hidratante [iðra'tante] adj: **crema ~** moisturizing cream, moisturizer; **hidratar** vt (piel) to moisturize; **hidrato** nm: **hidratos de carbono** carbohydrates

hidráulica [i'ðraulika] nf hydraulics s

hidráulico, a [i'ðrauliko, a] adj hydraulic

hidro... [iðro] prefijo hydro..., water-...; **~eléctrico, a** adj hydroelectric

~fobia nf hydrophobia, rabies; **hidrógeno** nm hydrogen

hiedra ['jeðra] nf ivy

hiel [jel] nf gall, bile; (fig) bitterness

hiela etc vb ver **helar**

hielo ['jelo] nm (gen) ice; (escarcha) frost; (fig) coldness, reserve

hiena ['jena] nf hyena

hierba ['jerβa] nf (pasto) grass; (CULIN, MED: planta) herb; **mala ~** weed; (fig) evil influence; **~buena** nf mint

hierro ['jerro] nm (metal) iron; (objeto) iron object

hígado ['iɣaðo] nm liver

higiene [i'xjene] nf hygiene; **higiénico, a** adj hygienic

higo ['iɣo] nm fig; **higuera** nf fig tree

hijastro, a [i'xastro, a] nm/f stepson/daughter

hijo, a ['ixo, a] nm/f son/daughter, child; **~s** nmpl children, sons and daughters; **~ de papá/mamá** daddy's/mummy's boy; **~ de puta** (fam!) bastard (!), son of a bitch (!)

hilar [i'lar] vt to spin; **~ fino** to split hairs

hilera [i'lera] nf row, file

hilo ['ilo] nm thread; (BOT) fibre; (metal) wire; (de agua) trickle, thin stream

hilvanar [ilβa'nar] vt (COSTURA) to tack (BRIT), baste (US); (fig) to do hurriedly

himno ['imno] nm hymn; **~ nacional** national anthem

hincapié [inka'pje] nm: **hacer ~ en** to emphasize

hincar [in'kar] vt to drive (in), thrust (in); **~se** vr: **~se de rodillas** to kneel down

hincha ['intʃa] (fam) nm/f fan

hinchado, a [in'tʃaðo, a] adj (gen) swollen; (persona) pompous

hinchar [in'tʃar] vt (gen) to swell; (inflar) to blow up, inflate; (fig) to exaggerate; **~se** vr (inflarse) to swell up; (fam: de comer) to stuff o.s.

hinchazón nf (MED) swelling; (altivez) arrogance

hinojo [i'noxo] nm fennel

hipermercado [ipermer'kaðo] nm hypermarket, superstore

hípico, a ['ipiko, a] adj horse cpd

hipnotismo [ipno'tismo] nm hypnotism; **hipnotizar** vt to hypnotize

hipo ['ipo] nm hiccups pl

hipocresía [ipokre'sia] nf hypocrisy; **hipócrita** adj hypocritical ♦ nm/f hypocrite

hipódromo [i'poðromo] nm racetrack

hipopótamo [ipo'potamo] nm hippopotamus

hipoteca [ipo'teka] nf mortgage

hipótesis [i'potesis] nf inv hypothesis

hiriente [i'rjente] adj offensive, wounding

hispánico, a [is'paniko, a] adj Hispanic

hispano, a [is'pano, a] adj Hispanic, Spanish, Hispano- ♦ nm/f Spaniard; **H~américa** nf Latin America; **~americano, a** adj, nm/f Latin American

histeria [is'terja] nf hysteria

historia [is'torja] nf history; (cuento) story, tale; **~s** nfpl (chismes) gossip sg; **dejarse de ~s** to come to the point; **pasar a la ~** to go down in history; **~dor, a** nm/f historian; **historial** nm (profesional) curriculum vitae, C.V.; (MED) case history; **histórico, a** adj historical; (memorable) historic

historieta [isto'rjeta] nf tale, anecdote; (dibujos) comic strip

hito ['ito] nm (fig) landmark

hizo vb ver **hacer**

Hnos abr (= Hermanos) Bros.

hocico [o'θiko] nm snout

hockey ['xoki] nm hockey; **~ sobre hielo** ice hockey

hogar [o'ɣar] nm fireplace, hearth; (casa) home; (vida familiar) home life; **~eño, a** adj home cpd; (persona) home-loving

hoguera [o'ɣera] nf (gen) bonfire

hoja ['oxa] nf (gen) leaf; (de flor) petal; (de papel) sheet; (página) page; **~ de afeitar** razor blade

hojalata [oxa'lata] nf tin(plate)

hojaldre [o'xaldre] nm (CULIN) puff pastry

hojear [oxe'ar] vt to leaf through, turn the pages of

hola ['ola] excl hello!

Holanda [o'landa] nf Holland; **holandés, esa** adj Dutch ♦ nm/f Dutchman/woman ♦ nm (LING) Dutch

holgado, a [ol'yaðo, a] adj (ropa) loose, baggy; (rico) comfortable

holgar [ol'yar] vi (descansar) to rest; (sobrar) to be superfluous; **huelga decir que** it goes without saying that

holgazán, ana [olya'θan, ana] adj idle, lazy ♦ nm/f loafer

holgura [ol'yura] nf looseness, bagginess; (TEC) play, free movement; (vida) comfortable living

hollín [o'ʎin] nm soot

hombre ['ombre] nm (gen) man; (raza humana): **el ~** man(kind) ♦ excl ¡sí ~! (claro) of course!; (para énfasis) man, old boy; **~ de negocios** businessman; **~ de pro** honest man; **~-rana** frogman

hombrera [om'brera] nf shoulder strap

hombro ['ombro] nm shoulder

hombruno, a [om'bruno, a] adj mannish

homenaje [ome'naxe] nm (gen) homage; (tributo) tribute

homicida [omi'θiða] adj homicidal ♦ nm/f murderer; **homicidio** nm murder, homicide

homologar [omolo'ɣar] vt (COM: productos, tamaños) to standardize; **homólogo, a** nm/f: **su etc homólogo** his etc counterpart o opposite number

homosexual [omosek'swal] adj, nm/f homosexual

hondo, a ['ondo, a] adj deep; **lo ~** the depth(s) (pl), the bottom; **~nada** nf

hollow, depression; (cañón) ravine

Honduras [on'duras] nf Honduras

hondureño, a [ondu'reɲo, a] adj, nm/f Honduran

honestidad [onesti'ðað] nf purity, chastity; (decencia) decency; **honesto, a** adj chaste; decent, honest; (justo) just

hongo ['oŋgo] nm (BOT: gen) fungus; (: comestible) mushroom; (: venenoso) toadstool

honor [o'nor] nm (gen) honour; **en ~ a la verdad** to be fair; **~able** adj honourable

honorario, a [ono'rarjo, a] adj honorary; **~s** nmpl fees

honra ['onra] nf (gen) honour; (renombre) good name; **~dez** nf honesty; (de persona) integrity; **~do, a** adj honest, upright

honrar [on'rar] vt to honour; **~se** vr: **~se con algo/de hacer algo** to be honoured by sth/to do sth

honroso, a [on'roso, a] adj (honrado) honourable; (respetado) respectable

hora ['ora] nf (una ~) hour; (tiempo) time; ¿qué ~ es? what time is it?; ¿a qué ~? at what time?; **media ~** half an hour; **a la ~ de recreo** at playtime; **a primera ~** first thing (in the morning); **a última ~** at the last moment; **a altas ~s** in the small hours; ¡a buena ~! about time, too!; **dar la ~** to strike the hour; **~s de oficina/de trabajo** office/working hours; **~s de visita** visiting times; **~s extras** o **extraordinarias** overtime sg; **~s punta** rush hours

horadar [ora'ðar] vt to drill, bore

horario, a [o'rarjo, a] adj hourly, hour cpd ♦ nm timetable; **~ comercial** business hours pl

horca ['orka] nf gallows sg

horcajadas [orka'xaðas]: **a ~** adv astride

horchata [or'tʃata] nf cold drink made from tiger nuts and water, tiger nut milk

horizontal [oriθon'tal] *adj* horizontal

horizonte [ori'θonte] *nm* horizon

horma ['orma] *nf* mould

hormiga [or'miɣa] *nf* ant; **~s** *nfpl* (MED) pins and needles

hormigón [ormi'ɣon] *nm* concrete; **~ armado/pretensado** reinforced/prestressed concrete

hormigueo [ormi'ɣeo] *nm* (comezón) itch

hormona [or'mona] *nf* hormone

hornada [or'naða] *nf* batch (of loaves etc)

hornillo [or'niʎo] *nm* (cocina) portable stove

horno ['orno] *nm* (CULIN) oven; (TEC) furnace; **alto ~** blast furnace

horóscopo [o'roskopo] *nm* horoscope

horquilla [or'kiʎa] *nf* hairpin; (AGR) pitchfork

horrendo, a [o'rrendo, a] *adj* horrendous, frightful

horrible [o'rriβle] *adj* horrible, dreadful

horripilante [orripi'lante] *adj* hair-raising, horrifying

horror [o'rror] *nm* horror, dread; (atrocidad) atrocity; **¡qué ~!** (fam) how awful!; **~izar** *vt* to horrify, frighten; **~izarse** *vr* to be horrified; **~oso, a** *adj* horrifying, ghastly

hortaliza [orta'liθa] *nf* vegetable

hortelano, a [orte'lano, a] *nm/f* (market) gardener

hortera [or'tera] (fam) *adj* tacky

hosco, a ['osko, a] *adj* sullen, gloomy

hospedar [ospe'ðar] *vt* to put up; **~se** *vr* to stay, lodge

hospital [ospi'tal] *nm* hospital

hospitalario, a [ospita'larjo, a] *adj* (acogedor) hospitable; **hospitalidad** *nf* hospitality

hostal [os'tal] *nm* small hotel

hostelería [ostele'ria] *nf* hotel business o trade

hostia ['ostja] *nf* (REL) host, consecrated wafer; (fam!: golpe) whack, punch ♦ *excl* (fam!): **¡~(s)!** damn!

hostigar [osti'ɣar] *vt* to whip; (fig) to harass, pester

hostil [os'til] *adj* hostile; **~idad** *nf* hostility

hotel [o'tel] *nm* hotel; **~ero, a** *adj* hotel *cpd* ♦ *nm/f* hotelier

---

Hotel

*In Spain you can choose from the following categories of accommodation, in descending order of quality and price: **hotel** (from 5 stars to 1), **hostal**, **pensión**, **casa de huéspedes**, **fonda**. The State also runs luxury hotels called **paradores**, which are usually sited in places of particular historical interest and are often historic buildings themselves.*

---

hoy [oi] *adv* (este día) today; (la actualidad) now(adays) ♦ *nm* present time; **~ (en) día** now(adays)

hoyo ['ojo] *nm* hole, pit; **hoyuelo** *nm* dimple

hoz [oθ] *nf* sickle

hube *etc* *vb ver* **haber**

hucha ['utʃa] *nf* money box

hueco, a ['weko, a] *adj* (vacío) hollow, empty; (resonante) booming ♦ *nm* hollow, cavity

huelga *etc* ['welɣa] *vb ver* **holgar** ♦ *nf* strike; **declararse en ~** to go on strike, come out on strike; **~ de hambre** hunger strike

huelguista [wel'vista] *nm/f* striker

huella ['weʎa] *nf* (pisada) tread; (marca del paso) footprint, footstep; (: de animal, máquina) track; **~ digital** fingerprint

huelo *etc* *vb ver* **oler**

huérfano, a ['werfano, a] *adj* orphan(ed) ♦ *nm/f* orphan

huerta ['werta] *nf* market garden; (en Murcia y Valencia) irrigated region

huerto ['werto] *nm* kitchen garden; (de árboles frutales) orchard

hueso ['weso] nm (ANAT) bone; (de fruta) stone

huésped, a ['wespeð, a] nm/f guest

huesudo, a [we'suðo, a] adj bony, big-boned

hueva ['weßa] nf roe

huevera [we'ßera] nf eggcup

huevo [u'eßo] nm egg; ~ **duro/ escalfado/frito** (ESP) **o estrellado** (AM)**/pasado por agua** hard-boiled/ poached/fried/soft-boiled egg; ~s **revueltos** scrambled eggs

huida [u'iða] nf escape, flight

huidizo, a [ui'ðiθo, a] adj shy

huir [u'ir] vi (escapar) to flee, escape; (evitar) to avoid; ~se vr (escaparse) to escape

hule ['ule] nm oilskin

humanidad [umani'ðað] nf (género humano) man(kind); (cualidad) humanity

humanitario, a [umani'tarjo, a] adj humanitarian

humano, a [u'mano, a] adj (gen) human; (humanitario) humane ♦ nm human; **ser** ~ nm human being

humareda [uma'reða] nf cloud of smoke

humedad [ume'ðað] nf (del clima) humidity; (de pared etc) dampness; a **prueba de** ~ damp-proof;

humedecer vt to moisten, wet; **humedecerse** vr to get wet

húmedo, a ['umeðo, a] adj (mojado) damp, wet; (tiempo etc) humid

humildad [umil'ðað] nf humility, humbleness; **humilde** adj humble, modest

humillación [umiʎa'θjon] nf humiliation; **humillante** adj humiliating

humillar [umi'ʎar] vt to humiliate; ~se vr to humble o.s., grovel

humo ['umo] nm (de fuego) smoke; (gas nocivo) fumes pl; (vapor) steam, vapour; ~s nmpl (fig) conceit sg

humor [u'mor] nm (disposición) mood,

temper; (lo que divierte) humour; **de buen/mal** ~ in a good/bad mood; ~**ista** nm/f comic; ~**ístico, a** adj funny, humorous

hundimiento [undi'mjento] nm (gen) sinking; (colapso) collapse

hundir [un'dir] vt to sink; (edificio, plan) to ruin, destroy; ~se vr to sink, collapse

húngaro, a ['ungaro, a] adj, nm/f Hungarian

Hungría [un'gria] nf Hungary

huracán [ura'kan] nm hurricane

huraño, a [u'raɲo, a] adj (antisocial) unsociable

hurgar [ur'var] vt to poke, jab; (remover) to stir (up); ~se vr: ~se **(las narices)** to pick one's nose

hurón, ona [u'ron, ona] nm (ZOOL) ferret

hurtadillas [urta'ðiʎas]: a ~ adv stealthily, on the sly

hurtar [ur'tar] vt to steal; **hurto** nm theft, stealing

husmear [usme'ar] vt (oler) to sniff out, scent; (fam) to pry into

huyo etc vb ver **huir**

I, i

iba etc vb ver **ir**

ibérico, a [i'ßeriko, a] adj Iberian

iberoamericano, a [ißeroameri'kano, a] adj, nm/f Latin American

Ibiza [i'ßiθa] nf Ibiza

iceberg [iθe'ßer] nm iceberg

icono [i'kono] nm ikon, icon

iconoclasta [ikono'klasta] adj iconoclastic ♦ nm/f iconoclast

ictericia [ikte'riθja] nf jaundice

I + D abr (= Investigación y Desarrollo) R & D

ida ['iða] nf going, departure; ~ **y vuelta** round trip, return

idea [i'ðea] nf idea; **no tengo la menor** ~ I haven't a clue

ideal [iðe'al] *adj, nm* ideal; **~ista** *nm/f* idealist; **~izar** *vt* to idealize

idear [iðe'ar] *vt* to think up; *(aparato)* to invent; *(viaje)* to plan

ídem ['iðem] *pron* ditto

idéntico, a [i'ðentiko, a] *adj* identical

identidad [iðenti'ðað] *nf* identity

identificación [iðentifika'θjon] *nf* identification

identificar [iðentifi'kar] *vt* to identify; **~se**: **~se con** to identify with

ideología [iðeolo'xia] *nf* ideology

idilio [i'ðiljo] *nm* love-affair

idioma [i'ðjoma] *nm (gen)* language

idiota [i'ðjota] *adj* idiotic ♦ *nm/f* idiot; **idiotez** *nf* idiocy

ídolo ['iðolo] *nm (tb: fig)* idol

idóneo, a [i'ðoneo, a] *adj* suitable

iglesia [i'ɣlesja] *nf* church

ignorancia [iɣno'ranθja] *nf* ignorance; **ignorante** *adj* ignorant, uninformed ♦ *nm/f* ignoramus

ignorar [iɣno'rar] *vt* not to know, be ignorant of; *(no hacer caso a)* to ignore

igual [i'ɣwal] *adj (gen)* equal; *(similar)* like, similar; *(mismo)* the same; *(constante)* constant; *(temperatura)* even ♦ *nm/f* equal; **~ que** like, the same as; **me da o es ~** I don't care; **son ~es** they're the same; **al ~ que** *prep, conj* like, just like

igualada [iɣwa'laða] *nf* equaliser

igualar [iɣwa'lar] *vt (gen)* to equalize, make equal; *(allanar, nivelar)* to level (off), even (out); **~se** *vr (platos de balanza)* to balance out

igualdad [iɣwal'dað] *nf* equality; *(similaridad)* sameness; *(uniformidad)* uniformity

igualmente [iɣwal'mente] *adv* equally; *(también)* also, likewise ♦ *excl* the same to you!

ikurriña [iku'rriɲa] *nf* Basque flag

ilegal [ile'ɣal] *adj* illegal

ilegítimo, a [ile'xitimo, a] *adj* illegitimate

ileso, a [i'leso, a] *adj* unhurt

ilícito, a [i'liθito] *adj* illicit

ilimitado, a [ilimi'taðo, a] *adj* unlimited

ilógico, a [i'loxiko, a] *adj* illogical

iluminación [ilumina'θjon] *nf* illumination; *(alumbrado)* lighting

iluminar [ilumi'nar] *vt* to illuminate, light (up); *(fig)* to enlighten

ilusión [ilu'sjon] *nf* illusion; *(quimera)* delusion; *(esperanza)* hope; **hacerse ilusiones** to build up one's hopes; **ilusionado, a** *adj* excited; **ilusionar** *vt*: **le ilusiona ir de vacaciones** he's looking forward to going on holiday; **ilusionarse** *vr*: **ilusionarse (con)** to get excited (about)

ilusionista [ilusjo'nista] *nm/f* conjurer

iluso, a [i'luso, a] *adj* easily deceived ♦ *nm/f* dreamer

ilusorio, a [ilu'sorjo, a] *adj (de ilusión)* illusory, deceptive; *(esperanza)* vain

ilustración [ilustra'θjon] *nf* illustration; *(saber)* learning, erudition; **la I~** the Enlightenment; **ilustrado, a** *adj* illustrated; learned

ilustrar [ilus'trar] *vt* to illustrate; *(instruir)* to instruct; *(explicar)* to explain, make clear; **~se** *vr* to acquire knowledge

ilustre [i'lustre] *adj* famous, illustrious

imagen [i'maxen] *nf* image; *(dibujo)* picture

imaginación [imaxina'θjon] *nf* imagination

imaginar [imaxi'nar] *vt (gen)* to imagine; *(idear)* to think up; *(suponer)* to suppose; **~se** *vr* to imagine; **~io, a** *adj* imaginary; **imaginativo, a** *adj* imaginative

imán [i'man] *nm* magnet

imbécil [im'beθil] *nm/f* imbecile, idiot

imitación [imita'θjon] *nf* imitation

imitar [imi'tar] *vt* to imitate; *(parodiar, remedar)* to mimic, ape

impaciencia [impa'θjenθja] *nf* impatience; **impaciente** *adj* impatient; *(nervioso)* anxious

impacto [im'pakto] *nm* impact

impar [im'par] *adj* odd

imparcial [impar'θjal] *adj* impartial, fair

impartir [impar'tir] *vt* to impart, give

impasible [impa'siβle] *adj* impassive

impecable [impe'kaβle] *adj* impeccable

impedimento [impeði'mento] *nm* impediment, obstacle

impedir [impe'ðir] *vt* (*obstruir*) to impede, obstruct; (*estorbar*) to prevent

impenetrable [impene'traβle] *adj* impenetrable; (*fig*) incomprehensible

imperar [impe'rar] *vi* (*reinar*) to rule, reign; (*fig*) to prevail, reign; (*precio*) to be current

imperativo, a [impera'tiβo, a] *adj* (*urgente*, LING) imperative

imperceptible [imperθep'tiβle] *adj* imperceptible

imperdible [imper'ðiβle] *nm* safety pin

imperdonable [imperðo'naβle] *adj* unforgivable, inexcusable

imperfección [imperfek'θjon] *nf* imperfection

imperfecto, a [imper'fekto, a] *adj* imperfect

imperial [impe'rjal] *adj* imperial; **~ismo** *nm* imperialism

imperio [im'perjo] *nm* empire; (*autoridad*) rule, authority; (*fig*) pride, haughtiness; **~so, a** *adj* imperious; (*urgente*) urgent; (*imperativo*) imperative

impermeable [imperme'aβle] *adj* waterproof ♦ *nm* raincoat, mac (*BRIT*)

impersonal [imperso'nal] *adj* impersonal

impertinencia [imperti'nenθja] *nf* impertinence; **impertinente** *adj* impertinent

imperturbable [impertur'βaβle] *adj* imperturbable

ímpetu ['impetu] *nm* (*impulso*) impetus, impulse; (*impetuosidad*)

impetuosity; (*violencia*) violence

impetuoso, a [impe'twoso, a] *adj* impetuous; (*río*) rushing; (*acto*) hasty

impío, a [im'pio, a] *adj* impious, ungodly

implacable [impla'kaβle] *adj* implacable

implantar [implan'tar] *vt* to introduce

implicar [impli'kar] *vt* to involve; (*entrañar*) to imply

implícito, a [im'pliθito, a] *adj* (*tácito*) implicit; (*sobreentendido*) implied

implorar [implo'rar] *vt* to beg, implore

imponente [impo'nente] *adj* (*impresionante*) impressive, imposing; (*solemne*) grand

imponer [impo'ner] *vt* (*gen*) to impose; (*exigir*) to exact; **~se** *vr* to assert o.s.; (*prevalecer*) to prevail; **imponible** (*COM*) taxable

impopular [impopu'lar] *adj* unpopular

importación [importa'θjon] *nf* (*acto*) importing; (*mercancías*) imports *pl*

importancia [impor'tanθja] *nf* importance; (*valor*) value, significance; (*extensión*) size, magnitude

importante *adj* important; valuable, significant

importar [impor'tar] *vt* (*del extranjero*) to import; (*costar*) to amount to ♦ *vi* to be important, matter; **me importa un rábano** I couldn't care less; **no importa** it doesn't matter; **¿le importa que fume?** do you mind if I smoke?

importe [im'porte] *nm* (*total*) amount; (*valor*) value

importunar [importu'nar] *vt* to bother, pester

imposibilidad [imposiβili'ðað] *nf* impossibility; **imposibilitar** *vt* to make impossible, prevent

imposible [impo'siβle] *adj* (*gen*) impossible; (*insoportable*) unbearable, intolerable

imposición [imposi'θjon] *nf*

imposition; (COM: *impuesto*) tax;
(: *inversión*) deposit
impostor, a [impos'tor, a] nm/f
impostor
impotencia [impoten'θja] nf
impotence; **impotente** adj impotent
impracticable [imprakti'kaβle] adj
(*irrealizable*) impracticable;
(*intransitable*) impassable
impreciso, a [impre'θiso, a] adj
imprecise, vague
impregnar [impreγ'nar] vt to
impregnate; **~se** vr to become
impregnated
imprenta [im'prenta] nf (*acto*)
printing; (*aparato*) press; (*casa*)
printer's; (*letra*) print
imprescindible [impresθin'diβle] adj
essential, vital
impresión [impre'sjon] nf (*gen*)
impression; (*IMPRENTA*) printing;
(*edición*) edition; (*FOTO*) print; (*marca*)
imprint; **~ digital** fingerprint
impresionable [impresjo'naβle] adj
(*sensible*) impressionable
impresionante [impresjo'nante] adj
impressive; (*tremendo*) tremendous;
(*maravilloso*) great, marvellous
impresionar [impresjo'nar] vt
(*conmover*) to move; (*afectar*) to
impress, strike; (*película fotográfica*) to
expose; **~se** vr to be impressed;
(*conmoverse*) to be moved
impreso, a [im'preso, a] pp de
imprimir ♦ adj printed; **~s** nmpl
printed matter; **impresora** nf printer
imprevisto, a [impre'βisto, a] adj
(*gen*) unforeseen; (*inesperado*)
unexpected
imprimir [impri'mir] vt to imprint,
impress, stamp; (*textos*) to print;
(*INFORM*) to output, print out
improbable [impro'βaβle] adj
improbable; (*inverosímil*) unlikely
improcedente [improθe'ðente] adj
inappropriate
improductivo, a [improðuk'tiβo, a]

adj unproductive
improperio [impro'perjo] nm insult
impropio, a [im'propjo, a] adj
improper
improvisado, a [improβi'saðo, a] adj
improvised
improvisar [improβi'sar] vt to
improvise
improviso, a [impro'βiso, a] adj: **de
~** unexpectedly, suddenly
imprudencia [impru'ðenθja] nf
imprudence; (*indiscreción*) indiscretion;
(*descuido*) carelessness; **imprudente**
adj unwise, imprudent; (*indiscreto*)
indiscreet
impúdico, a [im'puðiko, a] adj
shameless; (*lujurioso*) lecherous
impuesto, a [im'pwesto, a] adj
imposed ♦ nm tax; **~ sobre el valor
añadido** value added tax
impugnar [impuγ'nar] vt to oppose,
contest; (*refutar*) to refute, impugn
impulsar [impul'sar] vt to drive; (*
promover*) to promote, stimulate
impulsivo, a [impul'siβo, a] adj
impulsive; **impulso** nm impulse;
(*fuerza, empuje*) thrust, drive; (*fig:
sentimiento*) urge, impulse
impune [im'pune] adj unpunished
impureza [impu're θa] nf impurity;
impuro, a [im'puro, a] adj impure
imputar [impu'tar] vt to attribute
inacabable [inaka'βaβle] adj (*infinito*)
endless; (*interminable*) interminable
inaccesible [inakθe'siβle] adj
inaccessible
inacción [inak'θjon] nf inactivity
inaceptable [inaθep'taβle] adj
unacceptable
inactividad [inaktiβi'ðað] nf inactivity;
(*COM*) dullness; **inactivo, a** [inak'tiβo, a] adj
inactive
inadecuado, a [inaðe'kwaðo, a] adj
(*insuficiente*) inadequate; (*inapto*)
unsuitable
inadmisible [inaðmi'siβle] adj
inadmissible

inadvertido, a [inaðßer'tiðo, a] *adj*
(*no visto*) unnoticed

inagotable [inayo'taßle] *adj*
inexhaustible

inaguantable [inaywan'taßle] *adj*
unbearable

inalterable [inalte'raßle] *adj*
immutable, unchangeable

inanición [inani'θjon] *nf* starvation

inanimado, a [inani'maðo, a] *adj*
inanimate

inapreciable [inapre'θjaßle] *adj*
(*cantidad, diferencia*) imperceptible;
(*ayuda, servicio*) invaluable

inaudito, a [inau'ðito, a] *adj*
unheard-of

inauguración [inauxura'θjon] *nf*
inauguration; opening

inaugurar [inauxu'rar] *vt* to
inaugurate; (*exposición*) to open

inca ['inka] *nm/f* Inca

incalculable [inkalku'laßle] *adj*
incalculable

incandescente [inkandes'θente] *adj*
incandescent

incansable [inkan'saßle] *adj* tireless,
untiring

incapacidad [inkapaθi'ðað] *nf*
incapacity; (*incompetencia*)
incompetence; **~ física/mental**
physical/mental disability

incapacitar [inkapaθi'tar] *vt*
(*inhabilitar*) to incapacitate, render
unfit; (*descalificar*) to disqualify

incapaz [inka'paθ] *adj* incapable

incautación [inkauta'θjon] *nf*
confiscation

incautarse [inkau'tarse] *vr*: **~ de** to
seize, confiscate

incauto, a [in'kauto, a] *adj*
(*imprudente*) incautious, unwary

incendiar [inθen'djar] *vt* to set fire to;
(*fig*) to inflame; **~se** *vr* to catch fire;
~io, a *adj* incendiary

incendio [in'θendjo] *nm* fire

incentivo [inθen'tißo] *nm* incentive

incertidumbre [inθerti'ðumbre] *nf*

(*inseguridad*) uncertainty; (*duda*) doubt

incesante [inθe'sante] *adj* incessant

incesto [in'θesto] *nm* incest

incidencia [inθi'ðenθja] *nf* (*MAT*)
incidence

incidente [inθi'ðente] *nm* incident

incidir [inθi'ðir] *vi* (*influir*) to influence;
(*afectar*) to affect; **~ en un error** to
fall into error

incienso [in'θjenso] *nm* incense

incierto, a [in'θjerto, a] *adj* uncertain

incineración [inθinera'θjon] *nf*
incineration; (*de cadáveres*) cremation

incinerar [inθine'rar] *vt* to burn;
(*cadáveres*) to cremate

incipiente [inθi'pjente] *adj* incipient

incisión [inθi'sjon] *nf* incision

incisivo, a [inθi'sißo, a] *adj* sharp,
cutting; (*fig*) incisive

incitar [inθi'tar] *vt* to incite, rouse

inclemencia [inkle'menθja] *nf*
(*severidad*) harshness, severity; (*del
tiempo*) inclemency

inclinación [inklina'θjon] *nf* (*gen*)
inclination; (*de tierras*) slope, incline;
(*de cabeza*) nod, bow; (*fig*) leaning,
bent

inclinar [inkli'nar] *vt* to incline;
(*cabeza*) to nod, bow, ♦ *vi* to lean,
slope; **~se** *vr* to bow; (*encorvarse*) to
stoop; **~se a** (*parecerse a*) to take after,
resemble; **~se ante** to bow down to;
me inclino a pensar que I'm
inclined to think that

incluir [inklu'ir] *vt* to include;
(*incorporar*) to incorporate; (*meter*) to
enclose

inclusive [inklu'siße] *adv* inclusive
♦ *prep* including

incluso [in'kluso] *adv* even

incógnita [in'koɣnita] *nf* (*MAT*)
unknown quantity

incógnito [in'koɣnito] *nm*: **de ~**
incognito

incoherente [inkoe'rente] *adj*
incoherent

incoloro, a [inko'loro, a] *adj*

colourless
incólume [in'kolume] adj unhurt, unharmed
incomodar [inkomo'ðar] vt to inconvenience; (molestar) to bother, trouble; (fastidiar) to annoy; ~se vr to put o.s. out; (fastidiarse) to get annoyed
incomodidad [inkomoði'ðað] nf inconvenience; (fastidio, enojo) annoyance; (de vivienda) discomfort
incómodo, a [in'komoðo, a] adj (incómfortable) uncomfortable; (molesto) annoying; (inconveniente) inconvenient
incomparable [inkompa'raßle] adj incomparable
incompatible [inkompa'tißle] adj incompatible
incompetencia [inkompe'tenθja] nf incompetence; **incompetente** adj incompetent
incompleto, a [inkom'pleto, a] adj incomplete, unfinished
incomprensible [inkompren'sißle] adj incomprehensible
incomunicado, a [inkomuni'kaðo, a] adj (aislado) cut off, isolated; (confinado) in solitary confinement
inconcebible [inkonθe'ßißle] adj inconceivable
incondicional [inkondiθjo'nal] adj unconditional; (apoyo) wholehearted; (partidario) staunch
inconexo, a [inko'nekso, a] adj (gen) unconnected; (desunido) disconnected
inconfundible [inkonfun'dißle] adj unmistakable
incongruente [inkon'grwente] adj incongruous
inconsciencia [inkons'θjenθja] nf unconsciousness; (fig) thoughtlessness; **inconsciente** adj unconscious; thoughtless
inconsecuente [inkonse'kwente] adj inconsistent
inconsiderado, a [inkonsiðe'raðo, a] adj inconsiderate

inconsistente [inkonsis'tente] adj weak; (tela) flimsy
inconstancia [inkon'stanθja] nf inconstancy; (inestabilidad) unsteadiness; **inconstante** adj inconstant
incontable [inkon'taßle] adj countless, innumerable
incontestable [inkontes'taßle] adj unanswerable; (innegable) undeniable
incontinencia [inkonti'nenθja] nf incontinence
inconveniencia [inkombe'njenθja] nf unsuitability, inappropriateness; (descortesía) impoliteness; **inconveniente** adj unsuitable; impolite ♦ nm obstacle; (desventaja) disadvantage; **el inconveniente es que ...** the trouble is that ...
incordiar [inkor'ðjar] (fam) vt to bug, annoy
incorporación [inkorpora'θjon] nf incorporation
incorporar [inkorpo'rar] vt to incorporate; ~se vr to sit up
incorrección [inkorrek'θjon] nf (gen) incorrectness, inaccuracy; (descortesía) bad-mannered behaviour; **incorrecto, a** adj (gen) incorrect, wrong; (comportamiento) bad-mannered
incorregible [inkorre'xißle] adj incorrigible
incredulidad [inkreðuli'ðað] nf incredulity; (escepticismo) scepticism; **incrédulo, a** adj incredulous, unbelieving; sceptical
increíble [inkre'ißle] adj incredible
incremento [inkre'mento] nm increment; (aumento) rise, increase
increpar [inkre'par] vt to reprimand
incruento, a [in'krwento, a] adj bloodless
incrustar [inkrus'tar] vt to incrust; (piedras: en joya) to inlay
incubar [inku'ßar] vt to incubate
inculcar [inkul'kar] vt to inculcate
inculpar [inkul'par] vt (acusar) to

accuse; (*achacar, atribuir*) to charge, blame

inculto, a [in'kulto, a] *adj* (*persona*) uneducated; (*grosero*) uncouth ♦ *nm/f* ignoramus

incumplimiento [inkumpli'mjento] *nm* non-fulfilment; **~ de contrato** breach of contract

incurrir [inku'rrir] *vi*: **~ en** to incur; (*crimen*) to commit; **~ en un error** to make a mistake

indagación [indaɣa'θjon] *nf* investigation; (*búsqueda*) search; (*JUR*) inquest

indagar [inda'ɣar] *vt* to investigate; to search; (*averiguar*) to ascertain

indecente [inde'θente] *adj* indecent, improper; (*lascivo*) obscene

indecible [inde'θiβle] *adj* unspeakable; (*indescriptible*) indescribable

indeciso, a [inde'θiso, a] *adj* (*por decidir*) undecided; (*vacilante*) hesitant

indefenso, a [inde'fenso, a] *adj* defenceless

indefinido, a [indefi'niðo, a] *adj* indefinite; (*vago*) vague, undefined

indeleble [inde'leβle] *adj* indelible

indemne [in'demne] *adj* (*objeto*) undamaged; (*persona*) unharmed, unhurt

indemnizar [indemni'θar] *vt* to indemnify; (*compensar*) to compensate

independencia [indepen'denθja] *nf* independence

independiente [indepen'djente] *adj* (*libre*) independent; (*autónomo*) self-sufficient

indeterminado, a [indetermi'naðo, a] *adj* indefinite; (*desconocido*) indeterminate

India ['indja] *nf*: **la ~** India

indicación [indika'θjon] *nf* indication; (*señal*) sign; (*sugerencia*) suggestion, hint

indicado, a [indi'kaðo, a] *adj* (*momento, método*) right; (*tratamiento*) appropriate; (*solución*) likely

indicador [indika'ðor] *nm* indicator; (*TEC*) gauge, meter

indicar [indi'kar] *vt* (*mostrar*) to indicate, show; (*termómetro etc*) to read, register; (*señalar*) to point to

índice ['indiθe] *nm* index; (*catálogo*) catalogue; (*ANAT*) index finger, forefinger

indicio [in'diθjo] *nm* indication, sign; (*en pesquisa etc*) clue

indiferencia [indife'renθja] *nf* indifference; (*apatía*) apathy; **indiferente** *adj* indifferent

indígena [in'dixena] *adj* indigenous, native ♦ *nm/f* native

indigencia [indi'xenθja] *nf* poverty, need

indigestión [indixes'tjon] *nf* indigestion

indigesto, a [indi'xesto, a] *adj* (*alimento*) indigestible; (*fig*) turgid

indignación [indiɣna'θjon] *nf* indignation

indignar [indiɣ'nar] *vt* to anger, make indignant; **~se** *vr*: **~se por** to get indignant about

indigno, a [in'diɣno, a] *adj* (*despreciable*) low, contemptible; (*inmerecido*) unworthy

indio, a ['indjo, a] *adj*, *nm/f* Indian

indirecta [indi'rekta] *nf* insinuation, innuendo; (*sugerencia*) hint

indirecto, a [indi'rekto, a] *adj* indirect

indiscreción [indiskre'θjon] *nf* (*imprudencia*) indiscretion; (*irreflexión*) tactlessness; (*acto*) gaffe, faux pas

indiscreto, a [indis'kreto, a] *adj* indiscreet

indiscriminado, a [indiskrimi'naðo, a] *adj* indiscriminate

indiscutible [indisku'tiβle] *adj* indisputable, unquestionable

indispensable [indispen'saβle] *adj* indispensable, essential

indisponer [indispo'ner] *vt* to spoil, upset; (*salud*) to make ill; **~se** *vr* to fall ill; **~se con uno** to fall out with sb

indisposición [indisposi'θjon] nf indisposition

indispuesto, a [indis'pwesto, a] adj (*enfermo*) unwell, indisposed

indistinto, a [indis'tinto, a] adj indistinct; (*vago*) vague

individual [indiβi'δwal] adj individual; (*habitación*) single ♦ nm (DEPORTE) singles sg

individuo, a [indi'βiδwo, a] adj, nm individual

índole ['indole] nf (*naturaleza*) nature; (*clase*) sort, kind

indómito, a [in'domito, a] adj indomitable

inducir [indu'θir] vt to induce; (*inferir*) to infer; (*persuadir*) to persuade

indudable [indu'δaβle] adj undoubted; (*incuestionable*) unquestionable

indulgencia [indul'xenθja] nf indulgence

indultar [indul'tar] vt (*perdonar*) to pardon, reprieve; (*librar de pago*) to exempt; **indulto** nm pardon; exemption

industria [in'dustrja] nf industry; (*habilidad*) skill; **industrial** adj industrial ♦ nm industrialist

inédito, a [in'eδito, a] adj (*texto*) unpublished; (*nuevo*) new

inefable [ine'faβle] adj ineffable, indescribable

ineficaz [inefi'kaθ] adj (*inútil*) ineffective; (*ineficiente*) inefficient

ineludible [inelu'δiβle] adj inescapable, unavoidable

ineptitud [inepti'tuδ] nf ineptitude, incompetence; **inepto, a** adj inept, incompetent

inequívoco, a [ine'kiβoko, a] adj unequivocal; (*inconfundible*) unmistakable

inercia [in'erθja] nf inertia; (*pasividad*) passivity

inerme [in'erme] adj (*sin armas*) unarmed; (*indefenso*) defenceless

inerte [in'erte] adj inert; (*inmóvil*) motionless

inesperado, a [inespe'raδo, a] adj unexpected, unforeseen

inestable [ines'taβle] adj unstable

inevitable [ineβi'taβle] adj inevitable

inexactitud [ineksakti'tuδ] nf inaccuracy; **inexacto, a** adj inaccurate; (*falso*) untrue

inexperto, a [inek'sperto, a] adj (*novato*) inexperienced

infalible [infa'liβle] adj infallible; (*plan*) foolproof

infame [in'fame] adj infamous; (*horrible*) dreadful; **infamia** nf infamy; (*deshonra*) disgrace

infancia [in'fanθja] nf infancy, childhood

infantería [infante'ria] nf infantry

infantil [infan'til] adj (*pueril, aniñado*) infantile; (*cándido*) childlike; (*literatura, ropa* etc) children's

infarto [in'farto] nm (tb: ~ de miocardio) heart attack

infatigable [infati'xaβle] adj tireless, untiring

infección [infek'θjon] nf infection; **infeccioso, a** adj infectious

infectar [infek'tar] vt to infect; **~se** vr to become infected

infeliz [infe'liθ] adj unhappy, wretched ♦ nm/f wretch

inferior [infe'rjor] adj inferior; (*situación*) lower ♦ nm/f inferior, subordinate

inferir [infe'rir] vt (*deducir*) to infer, deduce; (*causar*) to cause

infestar [infes'tar] vt to infest

infidelidad [infiδeli'δaδ] nf (*gen*) infidelity, unfaithfulness

infiel [in'fjel] adj unfaithful, disloyal; (*erróneo*) inaccurate ♦ nm/f infidel, unbeliever

infierno [in'fjerno] nm hell

infiltrarse [infil'trarse] vr: ~ en to infiltrate in(to); (*persona*) to work one's way in(to)

ínfimo, a ['infimo, a] *adj (más bajo)*
lowest; *(despreciable)* vile, mean

infinidad [infini'ðað] *nf* infinity;
(abundancia) great quantity

infinito, a [infi'nito, a] *adj, nm* infinite

inflación [infla'θjon] *nf (hinchazón)*
swelling; *(monetaria)* inflation; *(fig)*
conceit; **inflacionario, a** *adj*
inflationary

inflamar [infla'mar] *vt (MED, fig)* to
inflame; **~se** *vr* to catch fire; to
become inflamed

inflar [in'flar] *vt (hinchar)* to inflate,
blow up; *(fig)* to exaggerate; **~se** *vr* to
swell (up); *(fig)* to get conceited

inflexible [inflek'siβle] *adj* inflexible;
(fig) unbending

infligir [infli'xir] *vt* to inflict

influencia [influ'enθja] *nf* influence;
influenciar *vt* to influence

influir [influ'ir] *vt* to influence

influjo [in'fluxo] *nm* influence

influya *etc vb ver* **influir**

influyente [influ'jente] *adj* influential

información [informa'θjon] *nf*
information; *(noticias)* news *sg; (JUR)*
inquiry; **I~** *(oficina)* Information Office;
(mostrador) Information Desk; *(TEL)*
Directory Enquiries

informal [infor'mal] *adj* informal

informar [infor'mar] *vt (gen)* to
inform; *(revelar)* to reveal, make known
♦ *vi (JUR)* to plead; *(denunciar)* to
inform; *(dar cuenta de)* to report on;
~se *vr* to find out; **~se de** to inquire
into

informática [infor'matika] *nf*
computer science, information
technology

informe [in'forme] *adj* shapeless ♦ *nm*
report

infortunio [infor'tunjo] *nm* misfortune

infracción [infrak'θjon] *nf* infraction,
infringement

infranqueable [infranke'aβle] *adj*
impassable; *(fig)* insurmountable

infravalorar [infraβalo'rar] *vt* to
undervalue, underestimate

infringir [infrin'xir] *vt* to infringe,
contravene

infructuoso, a [infruk'twoso, a] *adj*
fruitless, unsuccessful

infundado, a [infun'daðo, a] *adj*
groundless, unfounded

infundir [infun'dir] *vt* to infuse, instil

infusión [infu'sjon] *nf* infusion; **~ de
manzanilla** camomile tea

ingeniar [inxe'njar] *vt* to think up,
devise; **~se** *vr*: **~se para** to manage to

ingeniería [inxenje'ria] *nf*
engineering; **~ genética** genetic
engineering; **ingeniero, a** *nm/f*
engineer; **ingeniero de caminos/de
sonido** civil engineer/sound engineer

ingenio [in'xenjo] *nm (talento)* talent;
(agudeza) wit; *(habilidad)* ingenuity,
inventiveness; **~ azucarero** *(AM)* sugar
refinery

ingenioso, a [inxe'njoso, a] *adj*
ingenious, clever; *(divertido)* witty

ingenuidad [inxenwi'ðað] *nf*
ingenuousness; *(sencillez)* simplicity;
ingenuo, a *adj* ingenuous

ingerir [inxe'rir] *vt* to ingest; *(tragar)*
to swallow; *(consumir)* to consume

Inglaterra [ingla'terra] *nf* England

ingle ['ingle] *nf* groin

inglés, esa [in'gles, esa] *adj* English
♦ *nm/f* Englishman/woman ♦ *nm
(LING)* English

ingratitud [ingrati'tuð] *nf* ingratitude;
ingrato, a *adj (gen)* ungrateful

ingrediente [ingre'ðjente] *nm*
ingredient

ingresar [ingre'sar] *vt (dinero)* to
deposit ♦ *vi (entrar)* to enter; **~ en un club**
to join a club; **~ en el hospital** to go
into hospital

ingreso [in'greso] *nm (entrada)* entry;
(: en hospital etc) admission; **~s** *nmpl
(dinero)* income *sg; (: COM)* takings *pl*

inhabitable [inaβi'taβle] *adj*
uninhabitable

inhalar [ina'lar] *vt* to inhale

inherente [ine'rente] *adj* inherent

inhibir [ini'βir] *vt* to inhibit

inhóspito, a [i'nospito, a] *adj (región, paisaje)* inhospitable

inhumano, a [inu'mano, a] *adj* inhuman

inicial [ini'θjal] *adj, nf* initial

iniciar [ini'θjar] *vt (persona)* to initiate; *(empezar)* to begin, commence; *(conversación)* to start up

iniciativa [iniθja'tiβa] *nf* initiative; **la ~ privada** private enterprise

ininterrumpido, a [ininterrum'piðo, a] *adj* uninterrupted

injerencia [inxe'renθja] *nf* interference

injertar [inxer'tar] *vt* to graft; **injerto** *nm* graft

injuria [in'xurja] *nf (agravio, ofensa)* offence; *(insulto)* insult; **injuriar** *vt* to insult; **injurioso, a** *adj* offensive, insulting

injusticia [inxus'tiθja] *nf* injustice

injusto, a [in'xusto, a] *adj* unjust, unfair

inmadurez [inmaðu'reθ] *nf* immaturity

inmediaciones [inmeðja'θjones] *nfpl* neighbourhood *sg*, environs

inmediato, a [inme'ðjato, a] *adj* immediate; *(contiguo)* adjoining; *(rápido)* prompt; *(próximo)* neighbouring, next; **de ~** immediately

inmejorable [inmexo'raβle] *adj* unsurpassable; *(precio)* unbeatable

inmenso, a [in'menso, a] *adj* immense, huge

inmerecido, a [inmere'θiðo, a] *adj* undeserved

inmigración [inmiɣra'θjon] *nf* immigration

inmiscuirse [inmisku'irse] *vr* to interfere, meddle

inmobiliaria [inmoβi'ljarja] *nf* estate agency

inmobiliario, a [inmoβi'ljarjo, a] *adj* real-estate *cpd*, property *cpd*

inmolar [inmo'lar] *vt* to immolate,

sacrifice

inmoral [inmo'ral] *adj* immoral

inmortal [inmor'tal] *adj* immortal; **~izar** *vt* to immortalize

inmóvil [in'moβil] *adj* immobile

inmueble [in'mweβle] *adj*: **bienes ~s** real estate, landed property ♦ *nm* property

inmundicia [inmun'diθja] *nf* filth; **inmundo, a** *adj* filthy

inmune [in'mune] *adj*: **~ (a)** *(MED)* immune (to)

inmunidad [inmuni'ðað] *nf* immunity

inmutarse [inmu'tarse] *vr* to turn pale; **no se inmutó** he didn't turn a hair

innato, a [in'nato, a] *adj* innate

innecesario, a [inneθe'sarjo, a] *adj* unnecessary

innoble [in'noβle] *adj* ignoble

innovación [innoβa'θjon] *nf* innovation

innovar [inno'βar] *vt* to introduce

inocencia [ino'θenθja] *nf* innocence

inocentada [inoθen'taða] *nf* practical joke

inocente [ino'θente] *adj (ingenuo)* naive, innocent; *(inculpable)* innocent; *(sin malicia)* harmless ♦ *nm/f* simpleton

Día de los Santos Inocentes

The 28th December, **el día de los (Santos) Inocentes**, *is when the Church commemorates the story of Herod's slaughter of the innocent children of Judaea. On this day Spaniards play* **inocentadas** *(practical jokes) on each other, much like our April Fool's Day pranks.*

inodoro [ino'ðoro] *nm* toilet, lavatory *(BRIT)*

inofensivo, a [inofen'siβo, a] *adj* inoffensive, harmless

inolvidable [inolβi'ðaβle] *adj* unforgettable

inopinado, a [inopi'naðo, a] *adj*

unexpected

inoportuno, a [inopor'tuno, a] adj untimely; (molesto) inconvenient

inoxidable [inoksi'ðaßle] adj: **acero ~** stainless steel

inquebrantable [inkeßran'taßle] adj unbreakable

inquietar [inkje'tar] vt to worry, trouble; **~se** vr to worry, get upset; **inquieto, a** adj anxious, worried; **inquietud** nf anxiety, worry

inquilino, a [inki'lino, a] nm/f tenant

inquirir [inki'rir] vt to enquire into, investigate

insaciable [insa'θjaßle] adj insatiable

insalubre [insa'lußre] adj unhealthy

inscribir [inskri'ßir] vt to inscribe; **~ a uno en** (lista) to put sb on; (censo) to register sb on

inscripción [inskrip'θjon] nf inscription; (ESCOL etc) enrolment; (censo) registration

insecticida [insekti'θiða] nm insecticide

insecto [in'sekto] nm insect

inseguridad [inseyuri'ðað] nf insecurity

inseguro, a [inse'yuro, a] adj insecure; (inconstante) unsteady; (incierto) uncertain

insensato, a [insen'sato, a] adj foolish, stupid

insensibilidad [insensißili'ðað] nf (gen) insensitivity; (dureza de corazón) callousness

insensible [insen'sißle] adj (gen) insensitive; (movimiento) imperceptible; (sin sentido) numb

insertar [inser'tar] vt to insert

inservible [inser'ßißle] adj useless

insidioso, a [insi'ðjoso, a] adj insidious

insignia [in'siynja] nf (señal distintiva) badge; (estandarte) flag

insignificante [insiynifi'kante] adj insignificant

insinuar [insi'nwar] vt to insinuate,

imply

insípido, a [in'sipiðo, a] adj insipid

insistencia [insis'tenθja] nf insistence

insistir [insis'tir] vi to insist; **~ en algo** to insist on sth; (enfatizar) to stress sth

insolación [insola'θjon] nf (MED) sunstroke

insolencia [inso'lenθja] nf insolence; **insolente** adj insolent

insólito, a [in'solito, a] adj unusual

insoluble [inso'lußle] adj insoluble

insolvencia [insol'ßenθja] nf insolvency

insomnio [in'somnjo] nm insomnia

insondable [inson'daßle] adj bottomless; (fig) impenetrable

insonorizado, a [insonori'θaðo, a] adj (cuarto etc) soundproof

insoportable [insopor'taßle] adj unbearable

insospechado, a [insospe'tʃaðo, a] adj (inesperado) unexpected

inspección [inspek'θjon] nf inspection, check; **inspeccionar** vt (examinar) to inspect, examine; (controlar) to control

inspector, a [inspek'tor, a] nm/f inspector

inspiración [inspira'θjon] nf inspiration

inspirar [inspi'rar] vt to inspire; (MED) to inhale; **~se** vr: **~se en** to be inspired by

instalación [instala'θjon] nf (equipo) fittings pl, equipment; **~ eléctrica** wiring

instalar [insta'lar] vt (establecer) to instal; (erguir) to set up, erect; **~se** vr to establish o.s.; (en una vivienda) to move into

instancia [ins'tanθja] nf (JUR) petition; (ruego) request; **en última ~** as a last resort

instantánea [instan'tanea] nf snap(shot)

instantáneo, a [instan'taneo, a] adj instantaneous; **café ~** instant coffee

instante [ins'tante] *nm* instant, moment

instar [ins'tar] *vt* to press, urge

instaurar [instau'rar] *vt* (*costumbre*) to establish; (*normas, sistema*) to bring in, introduce; (*gobierno*) to instal

instigar [insti'ɣar] *vt* to instigate

instinto [ins'tinto] *nm* instinct; **por ~** instinctively

institución [institu'θjon] *nf* institution, establishment

instituir [institu'ir] *vt* to found; (*fundar*) to found; **instituto** *nm* (*gen*) institute; (*ESP: ESCOL*) ≈ comprehensive (*BRIT*) o high (*US*) school

institutriz [institu'triθ] *nf* governess

instrucción [instruk'θjon] *nf* instruction

instructivo, a [instruk'tiβo, a] *adj* instructive

instruir [instru'ir] *vt* (*gen*) to instruct; (*enseñar*) to teach, educate

instrumento [instru'mento] *nm* (*gen*) instrument; (*herramienta*) tool, implement

insubordinarse [insuβorði'narse] *vr* to rebel

insuficiencia [insufi'θjenθja] *nf* (*carencia*) lack; (*inadecuación*) inadequacy; **insuficiente** *adj* (*gen*) insufficient; (*ESCOL: calificación*) unsatisfactory

insufrible [insu'friβle] *adj* insufferable

insular [insu'lar] *adj* insular

insultar [insul'tar] *vt* to insult; **insulto** *nm* insult

insumiso, a [insu'miso, a] *nm/f* (*POL*) *person who refuses to do military service or its substitute, community service*

insuperable [insupe'raβle] *adj* (*excelente*) unsurpassable; (*problema etc*) insurmountable

insurgente [insur'xente] *adj, nm/f* insurgent

insurrección [insurrek'θjon] *nf* insurrection, rebellion

intachable [inta'tʃaβle] *adj* irreproachable

intacto, a [in'takto, a] *adj* intact

integral [inte'ɣral] *adj* integral; (*completo*) complete; **pan ~** wholemeal (*BRIT*) o wholewheat (*US*) bread

integrar [inte'ɣrar] *vt* to make up, compose; (*MAT, fig*) to integrate

integridad [inteɣri'ðað] *nf* wholeness; (*carácter*) integrity; **íntegro, a** *adj* whole, entire; (*honrado*) honest

intelectual [intelek'twal] *adj, nm/f* intellectual

inteligencia [inteli'xenθja] *nf* intelligence; (*ingenio*) ability; **inteligente** *adj* intelligent

inteligible [inteli'xiβle] *adj* intelligible

intemperie [intem'perje] *nf*: **a la ~** out in the open, exposed to the elements

intempestivo, a [intempes'tiβo, a] *adj* untimely

intención [inten'θjon] *nf* (*gen*) intention, purpose; **con segundas intenciones** maliciously; **con ~** deliberately

intencionado, a [intenθjo'naðo, a] *adj* deliberate; **bien ~** well-meaning; **mal ~** ill-disposed, hostile

intensidad [intensi'ðað] *nf* (*gen*) intensity; (*ELEC, TEC*) strength; **llover con ~** to rain hard

intenso, a [in'tenso, a] *adj* intense; (*sentimiento*) profound, deep

intentar [inten'tar] *vt* (*tratar*) to try, attempt; **intento** *nm* attempt

interactivo, a [interak'tiβo, a] *adj* (*INFORM*) interactive

intercalar [interka'lar] *vt* to insert

intercambio [inter'kambjo] *nm* exchange, swap

interceder [interθe'ðer] *vi* to intercede

interceptar [interθep'tar] *vt* to intercept

intercesión [interθe'sjon] *nf* intercession

interés [inte'res] *nm* (*gen*) interest; (*parte*) share, part; (*pey*) self-interest;

intereses creados vested interests

interesado, a [intere'saðo, a] *adj* interested; *(prejuiciado)* prejudiced; *(pey)* mercenary, self-seeking

interesante [intere'sante] *adj* interesting

interesar [intere'sar] *vt, vi* to interest, be of interest to; **~se** *vr*: **~se en** *o* **por** to take an interest in

interferir [interfe'rir] *vt* to interfere with; *(TEL)* to jam ♦ *vi* to interfere

interfono [inter'fono] *nm* intercom

interino, a [inte'rino, a] *adj* temporary ♦ *nm/f* temporary holder of a post; *(MED)* locum; *(ESCOL)* supply teacher

interior [inte'rjor] *adj* inner, inside; *(COM)* domestic, internal ♦ *nm* interior, inside; *(fig)* soul, mind; **Ministerio del I~** ≈ Home Office *(BRIT)*, ≈ Department of the Interior *(US)*

interjección [interxek'θjon] *nf* interjection

interlocutor, a [interloku'tor, a] *nm/f* speaker

intermedio, a [inter'meðjo, a] *adj* intermediate ♦ *nm* interval

interminable [intermi'naßle] *adj* endless

intermitente [intermi'tente] *adj* intermittent ♦ *nm* (*AUTO*) indicator

internacional [internaθjo'nal] *adj* international

internado [inter'naðo] *nm* boarding school

internar [inter'nar] *vt* to intern; *(en un manicomio)* to commit; **~se** *vr* *(penetrar)* to penetrate

Internet [inter'net] *nm* o *nf*: **el** o **la ~** the Internet

interno, a [in'terno, a] *adj* internal, interior; *(POL etc)* domestic ♦ *nm/f* *(alumno)* boarder

interponer [interpo'ner] *vt* to interpose, put in; **~se** *vr* to intervene

interpretación [interpreta'θjon] *nf* interpretation

interpretar [interpre'tar] *vt* to interpret; *(TEATRO, MUS)* to perform, play; **intérprete** *nm/f* (*LING*) interpreter, translator; *(MUS, TEATRO)* performer, artist(e)

interrogación [interroɣa'θjon] *nf* interrogation; *(LING: tb: signo de ~)* question mark

interrogar [interro'ɣar] *vt* to interrogate, question

interrumpir [interrum'pir] *vt* to interrupt

interrupción [interrup'θjon] *nf* interruption

interruptor [interrup'tor] *nm* (*ELEC*) switch

intersección [intersek'θjon] *nf* intersection

interurbano, a [interur'ßano, a] *adj*: **llamada interurbana** long-distance call

intervalo [inter'ßalo] *nm* interval; *(descanso)* break; **a ~s** at intervals, every now and then

intervenir [interße'nir] *vt (controlar)* to control, supervise; *(MED)* to operate on ♦ *vi (participar)* to take part, participate; *(mediar)* to intervene

interventor, a [interßen'tor, a] *nm/f* inspector; *(COM)* auditor

intestino [intes'tino] *nm* (*MED*) intestine

intimar [inti'mar] *vi* to become friendly

intimidad [intimi'ðað] *nf* intimacy; *(familiaridad)* familiarity; *(vida privada)* private life; *(JUR)* privacy

íntimo, a ['intimo, a] *adj* intimate

intolerable [intole'raßle] *adj* intolerable, unbearable

intoxicación [intoksika'θjon] *nf* poisoning

intranet [intra'net] *nf* intranet

intranquilizarse [intrankili'θarse] *vr* to get worried o anxious; **intranquilo, a** *adj* worried

intransitable [intransi'taßle] *adj*

impassable

intrépido, a [in'trepiðo, a] adj
intrepid

intriga [in'triɣa] nf intrigue; (plan)
plot; **intrigar** vt, vi to intrigue

intrincado, a [intriŋ'kaðo, a] adj
intricate

intrínseco, a [in'trinseko, a] adj
intrinsic

introducción [introðuk'θjon] nf
introduction

introducir [introðu'θir] vt (gen) to
introduce; (moneda etc) to insert;
(INFORM) to input, enter

intromisión [intromi'sjon] nf
interference, meddling

introvertido, a [introβer'tiðo, a] adj,
nm/f introvert

intruso, a [in'truso, a] adj intrusive
♦ nm/f intruder

intuición [intwi'θjon] nf intuition

inundación [inunda'θjon] nf
flood(ing); **inundar** vt to flood; (fig) to
swamp, inundate

inusitado, a [inusi'taðo, a] adj
unusual, rare

inútil [in'util] adj useless; (esfuerzo)
vain, fruitless; **inutilidad** nf uselessness

inutilizar [inutili'θar] vt to make o
render useless; **~se** vr to become
useless

invadir [inβa'ðir] vt to invade

inválido, a [im'baliðo, a] adj invalid
♦ nm/f invalid

invariable [imba'rjaβle] adj invariable

invasión [imba'sjon] nf invasion

invasor, a [imba'sor, a] adj invading
♦ nm/f invader

invención [imben'θjon] nf invention

inventar [imben'tar] vt to invent

inventario [imben'tarjo] nm inventory

inventiva [imben'tiβa] nf
inventiveness

invento [im'bento] nm invention

inventor, a [imben'tor, a] nm/f
inventor

invernadero [imberna'ðero] nm
greenhouse

inverosímil [imbero'simil] adj
implausible

inversión [imber'sjon] nf (COM)
investment

inverso, a [im'berso, a] adj inverse,
opposite; **en el orden ~** in reverse
order; **a la inversa** inversely, the other
way round

inversor, a [imber'sor, a] nm/f (COM)
investor

invertir [imber'tir] vt (COM) to invest;
(volcar) to turn upside down; (tiempo
etc) to spend

investigación [imbestiɣa'θjon] nf
investigation; (ESCOL) research; **~ de
mercado** market research

investigar [imbesti'ɣar] vt to
investigate; (ESCOL) to do research into

invierno [im'bjerno] nm winter

invisible [imbi'siβle] adj invisible

invitado, a [imbi'taðo, a] nm/f guest

invitar [imbi'tar] vt to invite; (incitar)
to entice; (pagar) to buy, pay for

invocar [imbo'kar] vt to invoke, call on

involucrar [imbolu'krar] vt: **~ en** to
involve in; **~se** vr (persona): **~ en** to
get mixed up in

involuntario, a [imbolun'tarjo, a] adj
(movimiento, gesto) involuntary; (error)
unintentional

inyección [injek'θjon] nf injection

inyectar [injek'tar] vt to inject

PALABRA CLAVE

---

ir [ir] vi **1** to go; (a pie) to walk; (viajar)
to travel; **~ caminando** to walk; **fui
en tren** I went o travelled by train;
¡(ahora) voy! (I'm just) coming!

2: **~ (a) por**: **~ (a) por el médico** to
fetch the doctor

3 (progresar: persona, cosa) to go; **el
trabajo va muy bien** work is going
very well; **¿cómo te va?** how are
things going?; **me va muy bien** I'm
getting on very well; **le fue fatal** it
went awfully badly for him

4 (*funcionar*): **el coche no va muy bien** the car isn't running very well
5: **te va estupendamente ese color** that colour suits you fantastically well
6 (*locuciones*): **¿vino? – ¡que va!** did he come? – of course not!; **vamos, no llores** come on, don't cry; **¡vaya coche!** what a car!, that's some car!
7: **no vaya a ser**: **tienes que correr, no vaya a ser que pierdas el tren** you'll have to run so as not to miss the train
8 (+ *pp*): **iba vestido muy bien** he was very well dressed
9: **me vi ira no me viene I** etc don't care

♦ *vb aux* **1**: **~ se**: **a**: **voy/iba a hacerlo hoy** I am/was going to do it today
2 (+ *gerundio*): **iba anocheciendo** it was getting dark; **todo se me iba aclarando** everything was gradually becoming clearer to me
3 (+ *pp* = *pasivo*): **van vendidos 300 ejemplares** 300 copies have been sold so far

♦ *se vr* **1**: **¿por dónde se va al zoológico?** which is the way to the zoo?
2 (*marcharse*) to leave; **ya se habrán ido** they must already have left *o* gone

ira [ˈira] *nf* anger, rage
Irak [iˈrak] *nm* = **Iraq**
Irán [iˈran] *nm* Iran; **iraní** *adj*, *nm/f* Iranian
Iraq [iˈrak] *nm* Iraq; **iraquí** *adj*, *nm/f* Iraqui
iris [ˈiris] *nm inv* (*tb*: **arco ~**) rainbow; (*ANAT*) iris
Irlanda [irˈlanda] *nf* Ireland; **irlandés, esa** *adj* Irish ♦ *nm/f* Irishman/woman; **los irlandeses** the Irish
ironía [iroˈnia] *nf* irony; **irónico, a** *adj* ironic(al)
IRPF [ˈi ˈerre ˈpe ˈefe] *n abr* (= *Impuesto sobre la Renta de las Personas Físicas*) (personal) income tax

irreal [irreˈal] *adj* unreal
irrecuperable [irrekupeˈraßle] *adj* irrecoverable, irretrievable
irreflexión [irreflekˈsjon] *nf* thoughtlessness
irregular [irrexuˈlar] *adj* (*gen*) irregular; (*situación*) abnormal
irremediable [irremeˈðjaßle] *adj* irremediable; (*vicio*) incurable
irreparable [irrepaˈraßle] *adj* (*daños*) irreparable; (*pérdida*) irrecoverable
irresoluto, a [irresoˈluto, a] *adj* irresolute, hesitant
irrespetuoso, a [irrespeˈtwoso, a] *adj* disrespectful
irresponsable [irresponˈsaßle] *adj* irresponsible
irreversible [irreßerˈsible] *adj* irreversible
irrigar [irriˈɣar] *vt* to irrigate
irrisorio, a [irriˈsorjo, a] *adj* derisory, ridiculous
irritar [irriˈtar] *vt* to irritate, annoy
irrupción [irrupˈθjon] *nf* irruption; (*invasión*) invasion
isla [ˈisla] *nf* island
islandés, esa [islanˈdes, esa] *adj* Icelandic ♦ *nm/f* Icelander
Islandia [isˈlandja] *nf* Iceland
isleño, a [isˈleɲo, a] *adj* island *cpd* ♦ *nm/f* islander
Israel [israˈel] *nm* Israel; **israelí** *adj*, *nm/f* Israeli
istmo [ˈistmo] *nm* isthmus
Italia [iˈtalja] *nf* Italy; **italiano, a** *adj*, *nm/f* Italian
itinerario [itineˈrarjo] *nm* itinerary, route
IVA [ˈißa] *nm abr* (= *impuesto sobre el valor añadido*) VAT
izar [iˈθar] *vt* to hoist
izdo, a *abr* (= *izquierdo, a*) l.
izquierda [iθˈkjerða] *nf* left; (*POL*) left (wing); **a la ~** (*estar*) on the left; (*torcer etc*) to the left
izquierdista [iθkjerˈðista] *nm/f* left-winger, leftist

izquierdo, a [iθˈkjerðo, a] adj left

J, j

jabalí [xaβaˈli] nm wild boar
jabalina [xaβaˈlina] nf javelin
jabón [xaˈβon] nm soap; **jabonar** vt to soap
jaca [ˈxaka] nf pony
jacinto [xaˈθinto] nm hyacinth
jactarse [xakˈtarse] vr to boast, brag
jadear [xaðeˈar] vi to pant, gasp for breath; **jadeo** nm panting, gasping
jaguar [xaˈɣwar] nm jaguar
jalea [xaˈlea] nf jelly
jaleo [xaˈleo] nm racket, uproar; **armar un ~** to kick up a racket
jalón [xaˈlon] (AM) nm tug
jamás [xaˈmas] adv never
jamón [xaˈmon] nm ham; **~ dulce, ~ de York** cooked ham; **~ serrano** cured ham
Japón [xaˈpon] nm: **el ~** Japan; **japonés, esa** adj, nm/f Japanese ♦ nm (LING) Japanese
jaque [ˈxake] nm: **~ mate** checkmate
jaqueca [xaˈkeka] nf (very bad) headache, migraine
jarabe [xaˈraβe] nm syrup
jarcia [ˈxarθja] nf (NAUT) ropes pl, rigging
jardín [xarˈðin] nm garden; **~ de infancia** (ESP) o **de niños** (AM) nursery (school); **jardinería** nf gardening; **jardinero, a** nm/f gardener
jarra [ˈxarra] nf jar; (jarro) jug
jarro [ˈxarro] nm jug
jarrón [xaˈrron] nm vase
jaula [ˈxaula] nf cage
jauría [xauˈria] nf pack of hounds
jazmín [xaθˈmin] nm jasmine
J. C. abr (= Jesucristo) J.C.
jefa [ˈxefa] nf ver jefe
jefatura [xefaˈtura] nf: **~ de policía** police headquarters sg

jefe, a [ˈxefe, a] nm/f (gen) chief, head; (patrón) boss; **~ de cocina** chef; **~ de estación** stationmaster; **~ de estado** head of state
jengibre [xenˈxiβre] nm ginger
jeque [ˈxeke] nm sheik
jerarquía [xerarˈkia] nf (orden) hierarchy; (rango) rank; **jerárquico, a** adj hierarchic(al)
jerez [xeˈreθ] nm sherry
jerga [ˈxerɣa] nf jargon
jeringa [xeˈrinɡa] nf syringe; (AM) annoyance, bother; **~ de engrase** grease gun; **jeringar** vt (fam) to annoy, bother; **jeringuilla** nf syringe
jeroglífico [xeroˈɣlifiko] nm hieroglyphic
jersey [xerˈsei] (pl ~s) nm jersey, pullover, jumper
Jerusalén [xerusaˈlen] n Jerusalem
Jesucristo [xesuˈkristo] nm Jesus Christ
jesuita [xeˈswita] adj, nm Jesuit
Jesús [xeˈsus] nm Jesus; **¡~!** good heavens!; (al estornudar) bless you!
jinete, a [xiˈnete, a] nm/f horseman/ woman, rider
jipijapa [xipiˈxapa] (AM) nm straw hat
jirafa [xiˈrafa] nf giraffe
jirón [xiˈron] nm rag, shred
jocoso, a [xoˈkoso, a] adj humorous, jocular
joder [xoˈðer] (fam!) vt, vi to fuck(!)
jofaina [xoˈfaina] nf washbasin
jornada [xorˈnaða] nf (viaje de un día) day's journey; (camino o viaje entero) journey; (día de trabajo) working day
jornal [xorˈnal] nm (day's wage); **~ero** nm (day) labourer
joroba [xoˈroβa] nf hump, hunched back; **~do, a** adj hunchbacked ♦ nm/f hunchback
jota [ˈxota] nf (the letter) J; (danza) Aragonese dance; **no saber ni ~** to have no idea
joven [ˈxoβen] (pl jóvenes) adj young

♦ nm young man, youth ♦ nf young woman, girl

jovial [xo'ßjal] adj cheerful, jolly

joya ['xoja] nf jewel, gem; (fig: persona) gem; **joyería** nf (joyas) jewellery; (tienda) jeweller's (shop); **joyero** nm (persona) jeweller; (caja) jewel case

juanete [xwa'nete] nm (del pie) bunion

jubilación [xußila'θjon] nf (retiro) retirement

jubilado, a [xußi'lað̃o, a] adj retired ♦ nm/f pensioner (BRIT), senior citizen

jubilar [xußi'lar] vt to pension off, retire; (fam) to discard; **~se** vr to retire

júbilo ['xußilo] nm joy, rejoicing; **jubiloso, a** adj jubilant

judía [xu'ðia] nf (CULIN) bean; **~ verde** French bean; ver tb **judío**

judicial [xuði'θjal] adj judicial

judío, a [xu'ðio, a] adj Jewish ♦ nm/f Jew(ess)

judo ['xuðo] nm judo

juego etc ['xwexo] vb ver **jugar** ♦ nm (gen) play; (pasatiempo, partido) game; (en casino) gambling; (conjunto) set; **fuera de ~** (DEPORTE: persona) offside; (: pelota) out of play; **J~s Olímpicos** Olympic Games

juerga ['xwerxa] nf binge; (fiesta) party; **ir de ~** to go out on a binge

jueves ['xweßes] nm inv Thursday

juez [xweθ] nm/f judge; **~ de línea** linesman; **~ de salida** starter

jugada [xu'xaða] nf play; **buena ~** good move/shot/stroke etc

jugador, a [xuxa'ð̃or, a] nm/f player; (en casino) gambler

jugar [xu'xar] vt, vi to play; (en casino) to gamble; (apostar) to bet; **~ al fútbol** to play football

juglar [xu'xlar] nm minstrel

jugo ['xuxo] nm (BOT) juice; (fig) essence, substance; **~ de fruta** (AM) fruit juice; **~so, a** adj juicy; (fig) substantial, important

juguete [xu'xete] nm toy; **~ar** vi to play; **~ría** nf toyshop

juguetón, ona [xuxe'ton, ona] adj playful

juicio ['xwiθjo] nm judgement; (razón) sanity, reason; (opinión) opinion; **~so, a** adj wise, sensible

julio ['xuljo] nm July

junco ['xunko] nm rush, reed

jungla ['xuŋgla] nf jungle

junio ['xunjo] nm June

junta ['xunta] nf (asamblea) meeting, assembly; (comité, consejo) board, council, committee; (TEC) joint

juntar [xun'tar] vt to join, unite; (maquinaria) to assemble, put together; (dinero) to collect; **~se** vr to join, meet; (reunirse: personas) to meet, assemble; (arrimarse) to approach, draw closer; **~se con uno** to join sb

junto, a ['xunto, a] adj joined; (unido) united; (anexo) near, close; (contiguo, próximo) next, adjacent ♦ adv: **todo ~** all at once; **~s** together; **~ a** near (to), next to

jurado [xu'raðo] nm (JUR: individuo) juror; (: grupo) jury; (de concurso: grupo) panel of judges; (: individuo) member of a panel

juramento [xura'mento] nm oath; (maldición) oath, curse; **prestar ~** to take the oath; **tomar ~ a** to swear in, administer the oath to

jurar [xu'rar] vt, vi to swear; **~ en falso** to commit perjury; **jurárselas a uno** to have it in for sb

jurídico, a [xu'riðiko, a] adj legal

jurisdicción [xurisð̃ik'θjon] nf (poder, autoridad) jurisdiction; (territorio) district

jurisprudencia [xurispru'ð̃enθja] nf jurisprudence

jurista [xu'rista] nm/f jurist

justamente [xusta'mente] adv justly, fairly; (precisamente) just, exactly

justicia [xus'tiθja] nf justice; (equidad) fairness, justice; **justiciero, a** adj just, righteous

justificación [xustifika'θjon] nf justification; **justificar** vt to justify

justo, a ['xusto, a] adj (equitativo) just, fair, right; (preciso) exact, correct; (ajustado) tight ♦ adv (precisamente) exactly, precisely; (AM: apenas a tiempo) just in time

juvenil [xuβe'nil] adj youthful

juventud [xuβen'tuð] nf (adolescencia) youth; (jóvenes) young people pl

juzgado [xuθ'γaðo] nm tribunal; (JUR) court

juzgar [xuθ'γar] vt to judge; **a ~ por** ... to judge by ..., judging by ...

K, k

kg abr (= kilogramo) l

kilo ['kilo] nm kilo ♦ pref: **~gramo** nm kilogramme; **~metraje** nm distance in kilometres, ≈ mileage; **kilómetro** nm kilometre; **~vatio** nm kilowatt

kiosco ['kjosko] nm = **quiosco**

Kosovo [ko'soβo] nm Kosovo

km abr (= kilómetro) km

kv abr (= kilovatio) kw

L, l

l abr (= litro) l

la [la] art def the ♦ pron her; (Ud.) you; (cosa) it ♦ nm (MUS) la; **~ del sombrero rojo** the girl in the red hat; tb ver **el**

laberinto [laβe'rinto] nm labyrinth

labia ['laβja] nf fluency; (pey) glib tongue

labio ['laβjo] nm lip

labor [la'βor] nf labour; (AGR) farm work; (tarea) job, task; (COSTURA) needlework; **~able** adj (AGR) workable; **día ~able** working day; **~al** adj (accidente) at work; (jornada) working

laboratorio [laβora'torjo] nm laboratory

laborioso, a [laβo'rjoso, a] adj (persona) hard-working; (trabajo) tough

laborista [laβo'rista] adj: **Partido L~** Labour Party

labrado, a [la'βraðo, a] adj worked; (madera) carved; (metal) wrought

labrador, a [laβra'ðor, a] adj farming cpd ♦ nm/f farmer

labranza [la'βranθa] nf (AGR) cultivation

labrar [la'βrar] vt (gen) to work; (madera etc) to carve; (fig) to cause, bring about

labriego, a [la'βrjeγo, a] nm/f peasant

laca ['laka] nf lacquer

lacayo [la'kajo] nm lackey

lacio, a ['laθjo, a] adj (pelo) straight

lacón [la'kon] nm shoulder of pork

lacónico, a [la'koniko, a] adj laconic

lacra ['lakra] nf (fig) blot; **lacrar** vt (cerrar) to seal (with sealing wax); **lacre** nm sealing wax

lactancia [lak'tanθja] nf lactation

lactar [lak'tar] vt, vi to suckle

lácteo, a ['lakteo, a] adj: **productos ~s** dairy products

ladear [laðe'ar] vt to tip, tilt ♦ vi to tilt; **~se** vr to lean

ladera [la'ðera] nf slope

lado ['laðo] nm (gen) side; (fig) protection; (MIL) flank; **al ~ de** beside; **poner de ~** to put on its side; **poner a un ~** to put aside; **por todos ~s** on all sides, all round (BRIT)

ladrar [la'ðrar] vi to bark; **ladrido** nm bark, barking

ladrillo [la'ðriʎo] nm (gen) brick; (azulejo) tile

ladrón, ona [la'ðron, ona] nm/f thief

lagartija [laγar'tixa] nf (ZOOL) (small) lizard

lagarto [la'γarto] nm (ZOOL) lizard

lago ['laγo] nm lake

lágrima ['laγrima] nf tear

laguna [la'γuna] nf (lago) lagoon; (hueco) gap

laico, a ['laiko, a] adj lay

lamentable [lamen'taβle] adj

lamentable, regrettable; (*miserable*) pitiful

lamentar [lamen'tar] vt (*sentir*) to regret; (*deplorar*) to lament; **lo lamento mucho** I'm very sorry; **~se** vr to lament; **lamento** nm lament

lamer [la'mer] vt to lick

lámina ['lamina] nf (*plancha delgada*) sheet; (*para estampar, estampa*) plate

lámpara ['lampara] nf lamp; **~ de alcohol/gas** spirit/gas lamp; **~ de pie** standard lamp

lamparón [lampa'ron] nm grease spot

lana ['lana] nf wool

lancha ['lantʃa] nf launch; **~ de pesca** fishing boat; **~ salvavidas/torpedera** lifeboat/torpedo boat

langosta [lan'gosta] nf (*crustáceo*) lobster; (: *de río*) crayfish; **langostino** nm Dublin Bay prawn

languidecer [langiðe'θer] vi to languish; **languidez** nf languor; **lánguido, a** adj (*gen*) languid; (*sin energía*) listless

lanilla [la'niʎa] nf nap

lanza ['lanθa] nf (*arma*) lance, spear

lanzamiento [lanθa'mjento] nm (*gen*) throwing; (*NAUT, COM*) launch, launching; **~ de peso** putting the shot

lanzar [lan'θar] vt (*gen*) to throw; (*DEPORTE: pelota*) to bowl; (*NAUT, COM*) to launch; (*JUR*) to evict; **~se** vr to throw o.s.

lapa ['lapa] nf limpet

lapicero [lapi'θero] nm pencil; (*AM: bolígrafo*) Biro ®

lápida ['lapiða] nf stone; **~ mortuoria** headstone; **~ conmemorativa** memorial stone; **lapidario, a** adj, nm lapidary

lápiz ['lapiθ] nm pencil; **~ de color** coloured pencil; **~ de labios** lipstick

lapón, ona [la'pon, ona] nm/f Laplander, Lapp

lapso ['lapso] nm (*de tiempo*) interval; (*error*) error

lapsus ['lapsus] nm inv error, mistake

largar [lar'xar] vt (*soltar*) to release; (*aflojar*) to loosen; (*lanzar*) to launch; (*fam*) to let fly; (*velas*) to unfurl; (*AM*) to throw; **~se** vr (*fam*) to beat it; **~se a** (*AM*) to start to

largo, a ['larxo, a] adj (*longitud*) long; (*tiempo*) lengthy; (*fig*) generous ♦ nm length; (*MUS*) largo; **dos años ~s** two long years; **tiene 9 metros de ~** it is 9 metres long; **a lo ~ de** along; (*tiempo*) all through, throughout; **~metraje** nm feature film

laringe [la'rinxe] nf larynx; **laringitis** nf laryngitis

larva ['larβa] nf larva

las [las] art def the ♦ pron them; **~ que canten** the ones/women/girls who sing; tb ver **el**

lascivo, a [las'θiβo, a] adj lewd

láser ['laser] nm laser

lástima ['lastima] nf (*pena*) pity; **dar ~** to be pitiful; **es una ~ que** it's a pity that; **¡qué ~!** what a pity!; **ella está hecha una ~** she looks pitiful

lastimar [lasti'mar] vt (*herir*) to wound; (*ofender*) to offend; **~se** vr to hurt o.s.; **lastimero, a** adj pitiful, pathetic

lastre ['lastre] nm (*TEC, NAUT*) ballast; (*fig*) dead weight

lata ['lata] nf (*metal*) tin; (*caja*) tin (*BRIT*), can; (*fam*) nuisance; **en ~** tinned (*BRIT*), canned; **dar (la) ~** to be a nuisance

latente [la'tente] adj latent

lateral [late'ral] adj side cpd, lateral ♦ nm (*TEATRO*) wings

latido [la'tiðo] nm (*del corazón*) beat

latifundio [lati'fundjo] nm large estate; **latifundista** nm/f owner of a large estate

latigazo [lati'xaθo] nm (*golpe*) lash; (*sonido*) crack

látigo ['latixo] nm whip

latín [la'tin] nm Latin

latino, a [la'tino, a] adj Latin; **~americano, a** adj, nm/f Latin-

American

latir [la'tir] vi (corazón, pulso) to beat
latitud [lati'tuð] nf (GEO) latitude
latón [la'ton] nm brass
latoso, a [la'toso, a] adj (molesto) annoying; (aburrido) boring
laúd [la'uð] nm lute
laurel [lau'rel] nm (BOT) laurel; (CULIN) bay
lava ['laßa] nf lava
lavabo [la'ßaßo] nm (pila) washbasin; (tb: ~s) toilet
lavado [la'ßaðo] nm washing; (de ropa) laundry; (ARTE) wash; ~ **de cerebro** brainwashing; ~ **en seco** dry-cleaning
lavadora [laßa'ðora] nf washing machine
lavanda [la'ßanda] nf lavender
lavandería [laßande'ria] nf laundry; (automática) launderette
lavaplatos [laßa'platos] nm inv dishwasher
lavar [la'ßar] vt to wash; (borrar) to wipe away; ~**se** vr to wash o.s.; ~**se las manos** to wash one's hands; ~**se los dientes** to brush one's teeth; ~ **y marcar** (pelo) to shampoo and set; ~ **en seco** to dry-clean; ~ **los platos** to wash the dishes
lavavajillas [laßaßa'xiʎas] nm inv dishwasher
laxante [lak'sante] nm laxative
lazada [la'θaða] nf bow
lazarillo [laθa'riʎo] nm: **perro** ~ guide dog
lazo ['laθo] nm knot; (lazada) bow; (para animales) lasso; (trampa) snare; (vínculo) tie
le [le] pron (directo) him (o her); (: usted) you; (indirecto) to him (o her o it); (: usted) to you
leal [le'al] adj loyal; ~**tad** nf loyalty
lección [lek'θjon] nf lesson
leche ['letʃe] nf milk; **tiene mala ~** (fam!) he's a swine (!); ~ **conden- sada/en polvo** condensed/powdered milk; ~ **desnatada** skimmed milk; ~**ra**

nf (vendedora) milkmaid; (recipiente) (milk) churn; (AM) cow; ~**ro, a** adj dairy
lecho ['letʃo] nm (cama, de río) bed; (GEO) layer
lechón [le'tʃon] nm sucking (BRIT) o suckling (US) pig
lechoso, a [le'tʃoso, a] adj milky
lechuga [le'tʃuɣa] nf lettuce
lechuza [le'tʃuθa] nf owl
lector, a [lek'tor, a] nm/f reader ♦ nm: ~ **de discos compactos** CD player
lectura [lek'tura] nf reading
leer [le'er] vt to read
legado [le'ɣaðo] nm (don) bequest; (herencia) legacy; (enviado) legate
legajo [le'ɣaxo] nm file
legal [le'ɣal] adj (gen) legal; (persona) trustworthy; ~**idad** nf legality
legalizar [leɣali'θar] vt to legalize; (documento) to authenticate
legaña [le'ɣaɲa] nf sleep (in eyes)
legar [le'ɣar] vt to bequeath, leave
legendario, a [lexen'darjo, a] adj legendary
legión [le'xjon] nf legion; **legionario, a** adj legionary ♦ nm legionnaire
legislación [lexisla'θjon] nf legislation
legislar [lexis'lar] vi to legislate
legislatura [lexisla'tura] nf (POL) period of office
legitimar [lexiti'mar] vt to legitimize; **legítimo, a** adj (genuino) authentic; (legal) legitimate
lego, a ['leɣo, a] adj (REL) secular; (ignorante) ignorant ♦ nm layman
legua ['leɣwa] nf league
legumbres [le'ɣumbres] nfpl pulses
leído, a [le'iðo, a] adj well-read
lejanía [lexa'nia] nf distance; **lejano, a** adj far-off; (en el tiempo) distant; (fig) remote
lejía [le'xia] nf bleach
lejos ['lexos] adv far, far away; **a lo ~** in the distance; **de o desde ~** from afar; ~ **de** far from
lelo, a ['lelo, a] adj silly ♦ nm/f idiot

lema ['lema] nm motto; (POL) slogan
lencería [lenθe'ria] nf linen, drapery
lengua ['lengwa] nf tongue; (LING) language; **morderse la ~** to hold one's tongue
lenguado [len'gwaðo] nm sole
lenguaje [len'gwaxe] nm language
lengüeta [len'gweta] nf (ANAT) epiglottis; (zapatos) tongue, (MUS) reed
lente ['lente] nf lens; (lupa) magnifying glass; **~s** nfpl (gafas) glasses; **~s de contacto** contact lenses
lenteja [len'texa] nf lentil; **lentejuela** nf sequin
lentilla [len'tiʎa] nf contact lens
lentitud [lenti'tuð] nf slowness; **con ~** slowly
lento, a ['lento, a] adj slow
leña ['leɲa] nf firewood; **~dor, a** nm/f woodcutter
leño ['leɲo] nm (trozo de árbol) log; (madera) timber; (fig) blockhead
Leo ['leo] nm Leo
león [le'on] nm lion; **~ marino** sea lion
leopardo [leo'parðo] nm leopard
leotardos [leo'tarðos] nmpl tights
lepra ['lepra] nf leprosy; **leproso, a** nm/f leper
lerdo, a ['lerðo, a] adj (lento) slow; (patoso) clumsy
les [les] pron (directo) them; (: ustedes) you; (indirecto) to them; (: ustedes) to you
lesbiana [les'βjana] adj, nf lesbian
lesión [le'sjon] nf wound, lesion; (DEPORTE) injury; **lesionado, a** adj injured ♦ nm/f injured person
letal [le'tal] adj lethal
letanía [leta'nia] nf litany
letargo [le'tarxo] nm lethargy
letra ['letra] nf letter; (escritura) handwriting; (MUS) lyrics pl; **~ de cambio** bill of exchange; **~ de imprenta** print; **~do, a** adj learned ♦ nm/f lawyer; **letrero** nm (cartel) sign; (etiqueta) label
letrina [le'trina] nf latrine

leucemia [leu'θemja] nf leukaemia
levadizo [leβa'ðiθo] adj: **puente ~** drawbridge
levadura [leβa'ðura] nf (para el pan) yeast; (de la cerveza) brewer's yeast
levantamiento [leβanta'mjento] nm raising, lifting; (rebelión) revolt, uprising; **~ de pesos** weight-lifting
levantar [leβan'tar] vt (gen) to raise; (del suelo) to pick up; (hacia arriba) to lift (up); (plan) to make, draw up; (mesa) to clear; (campamento) to strike; (fig) to cheer up, hearten; **~se** vr to get up; (enderezarse) to straighten up; (rebelarse) to rebel; **~ el ánimo** to cheer up
levante [le'βante] nm east coast; **el L~** region of Spain extending from Castellón to Murcia
levar [le'βar] vt to weigh
leve ['leβe] adj light; (fig) trivial; **~dad** nf lightness
levita [le'βita] nf frock coat
léxico ['leksiko] nm (vocabulario) vocabulary
ley [lei] nf (gen) law; (metal) standard
leyenda [le'jenda] nf legend
leyó etc vb ver **leer**
liar [li'ar] vt to tie (up); (unir) to bind; (envolver) to wrap up; (enredar) to confuse; (cigarrillo) to roll; **~se** vr (fam) to get involved; **~se a palos** to get involved in a fight
Líbano ['liβano] nm: **el ~** (the) Lebanon
libelo [li'βelo] nm satire, lampoon
libélula [li'βelula] nf dragonfly
liberación [liβera'θjon] nf liberation; (de la cárcel) release
liberal [liβe'ral] adj, nm/f liberal; **~idad** nf liberality, generosity
liberar [liβe'rar] vt to liberate
libertad [liβer'tað] nf liberty, freedom; **~ de culto/de prensa/de comercio** freedom of worship/of the press/of trade; **~ condicional** probation; **~ bajo palabra** parole; **~ bajo fianza**

bail

libertar [liβer'tar] *vt (preso)* to set free; *(de una obligación)* to release; *(eximir)* to exempt

libertino, a [liβer'tino, a] *adj* permissive ♦ *nm/f* permissive person

libra ['liβra] *nf* pound; *(ASTROLOGÍA)*: **L~** Libra; **~ esterlina** pound sterling

librar [li'βrar] *vt (de peligro)* to save; *(batalla)* to wage, fight; *(de impuestos)* to exempt; *(cheque)* to make out; *(JUR)* to exempt; **~se** *vr*: **~se de** to escape from, free o.s. from

libre ['liβre] *adj* free; *(lugar)* unoccupied; *(asiento)* vacant; *(de deudas)* free of debts; **~ de impuestos** free of tax; **tiro ~** free kick; **los 100 metros ~** the 100 metres free-style (race); **al aire ~** in the open air

librería [liβre'ria] *nf (tienda)* bookshop; **librero, a** *nm/f* bookseller

libreta [li'βreta] *nf* notebook; **~ de ahorros** savings book

libro ['liβro] *nm* book; **~ de bolsillo** paperback; **~ de caja** cashbook; **~ de cheques** chequebook *(BRIT)*, checkbook *(US)*; **~ de texto** textbook

Lic. *abr* = **licenciado, a**

licencia [li'θenθja] *nf (gen)* licence; *(permiso)* permission; **~ por enfermedad** sick leave; **~ de caza** game licence; **~do, a** *adj* licensed ♦ *nm/f* graduate; **licenciar** *vt (empleado)* to dismiss; *(permitir)* to permit, allow; *(soldado)* to discharge; *(estudiante)* to confer a degree upon; **licenciarse** *vr*: **licenciarse en letras** to graduate in arts

licencioso, a [liθen'θjoso, a] *adj* licentious

licitar [liθi'tar] *vt* to bid for; *(AM)* to sell by auction

lícito, a ['liθito, a] *adj (legal)* lawful; *(justo)* fair, just; *(permisible)* permissible

licor [li'kor] *nm* spirits *pl (BRIT)*, liquor *(US)*; *(de frutas etc)* liqueur

licuadora [likwa'ðora] *nf* blender

licuar [li'kwar] *vt* to liquidize

líder ['liðer] *nm/f* leader; **liderato** *nm* leadership; **liderazgo** *nm* leadership

lidia ['liðja] *nf* bullfighting; *(una ~)* bullfight; **toros de ~** fighting bulls; **lidiar** *vt, vi* to fight

liebre ['ljeβre] *nf* hare

lienzo ['ljenθo] *nm* linen; *(ARTE)* canvas; *(ARQ)* wall

liga ['liɣa] *nf (de medias)* garter, suspender; *(AM: gomita)* rubber band; *(confederación)* league

ligadura [liɣa'ðura] *nf* bond, tie; *(MED, MUS)* ligature

ligamento [liɣa'mento] *nm* ligament

ligar [li'ɣar] *vt (atar)* to tie; *(unir)* to join; *(MED)* to bind up; *(MUS)* to slur ♦ *vi* to mix, blend; *(fam)*: **(él) liga mucho** he pulls a lot of women; **~se** *vr* to commit o.s.

ligereza [lixe'reθa] *nf* lightness; *(rapidez)* swiftness; *(agilidad)* agility; *(superficialidad)* flippancy

ligero, a [li'xero, a] *adj (de peso)* light; *(tela)* thin; *(rápido)* swift, quick; *(ágil)* agile, nimble; *(de importancia)* slight; *(de carácter)* flippant, superficial ♦ *adv*: **a la ligera** superficially

liguero [li'ɣero] *nm* suspender *(BRIT)* o garter *(US)* belt

lija ['lixa] *nf (ZOOL)* dogfish; *(tb: papel de ~)* sandpaper

lila ['lila] *nf* lilac

lima ['lima] *nf* file; *(BOT)* lime; **~ de uñas** nailfile; **limar** *vt* to file

limitación [limita'θjon] *nf* limitation, limit; **~ de velocidad** speed limit

limitar [limi'tar] *vt* to limit; *(reducir)* to reduce, cut down ♦ *vi*: **~ con** to border on; **~se** *vr*: **~se a** to limit o.s. to

límite ['limite] *nm (gen)* limit; *(fin)* end; *(frontera)* border; **~ de velocidad** speed limit

limítrofe [li'mitrofe] *adj* neighbouring

limón [li'mon] *nm* lemon ♦ *adj*:

amarillo ~ lemon-yellow; **limonada**
nf lemonade

limosna [li'mosna] *nf* alms *pl*; **vivir de**
~ to live on charity

limpiaparabrisas [limpjapara'βrisas]
nm inv windscreen (*BRIT*) o windshield
(*US*) wiper

limpiar [lim'pjar] *vt* to clean; (*con
trapo*) to wipe; (*quitar*) to wipe away;
(*zapatos*) to shine, polish; (*fig*) to clean
up

limpieza [lim'pjeθa] *nf* (*estado*)
cleanliness; (*acto*) cleaning; (: *de las
calles*) cleansing; (: *de zapatos*)
polishing; (*habilidad*) skill; (*fig: POLICÍA*)
clean-up; (*pureza*) purity; (*MIL*):
operación de ~ mopping-up
operation; ~ **en seco** dry cleaning

limpio, a [ˈlimpjo, a] *adj* clean;
(*moralmente*) pure; (*COM*) clear, net;
(*fam*) honest ♦ *adv*: **jugar** ~ to play
fair; **pasar a** (*ESP*) o **en** (*AM*) ~ to
make a clean copy

linaje [li'naxe] *nm* lineage, family

lince [ˈlinθe] *nm* lynx

linchar [lin'tʃar] *vt* to lynch

lindar [lin'dar] *vi* to adjoin; ~ **con** to
border on; **linde** *nm* o *f* boundary;
lindero, a *adj* adjoining ♦ *nm*
boundary

lindo, a [ˈlindo, a] *adj* pretty, lovely
♦ *adv*: **nos divertimos de lo** ~ we
had a marvellous time; **canta muy** ~
(*AM*) he sings beautifully

línea [ˈlinea] *nf* (*gen*) line; **en** ~
(*INFORM*) on line; ~ **aérea** airline; ~ **de
meta** goal line; (*de carrera*) finishing
line; ~ **recta** straight line

lingote [linˈgote] *nm* ingot

lingüista [linˈgwista] *nm/f* linguist;
lingüística *nf* linguistics *sg*

lino [ˈlino] *nm* linen; (*BOT*) flax

linóleo [liˈnoleo] *nm* lino, linoleum

linterna [linˈterna] *nf* torch (*BRIT*),
flashlight (*US*)

lío [ˈlio] *nm* bundle; (*fam*) fuss;
(*desorden*) muddle, mess; **armar un** ~

to make a fuss

liquen [ˈliken] *nm* lichen

liquidación [likiða'θjon] *nf*
liquidation; **venta de** ~ clearance sale

liquidar [likiˈðar] *vt* (*mercancías*) to
liquidate; (*deudas*) to pay off; (*empresa*)
to wind up

líquido, a [ˈlikiðo, a] *adj* liquid;
(*ganancia*) net ♦ *nm* liquid; ~
imponible net taxable income

lira [ˈlira] *nf* (*MUS*) lyre; (*moneda*) lira

lírico, a [ˈliriko, a] *adj* lyrical

lirio [ˈlirjo] *nm* (*BOT*) iris

lirón [liˈron] *nm* (*ZOOL*) dormouse; (*fig*)
sleepyhead

Lisboa [lisˈβoa] *n* Lisbon

lisiado, a [liˈsjaðo, a] *adj* injured
♦ *nm/f* cripple

lisiar [liˈsjar] *vt* to maim; ~**se** *vr* to
injure o.s.

liso, a [ˈliso, a] *adj* (*terreno*) flat;
(*cabello*) straight; (*superficie*) even;
(*tela*) plain

lisonja [liˈsonxa] *nf* flattery

lista [ˈlista] *nf* list; (*de alumnos*) school
register; (*de libros*) catalogue; (*de
platos*) menu; (*de precios*) price list;
pasar ~ to call the roll; ~ **de correos**
poste restante; ~ **de espera** waiting
list; **tela de** ~ striped material; **listín**
nm: ~ (*telefónico*) telephone directory

listo, a [ˈlisto, a] *adj* (*perspicaz*) smart,
clever; (*preparado*) ready

listón [lisˈton] *nm* (*de madera, metal*)
strip

litera [liˈtera] *nf* (*en barco, tren*) berth;
(*en dormitorio*) bunk, bunk bed

literal [liteˈral] *adj* literal

literario, a [liteˈrarjo, a] *adj* literary

literato, a [liteˈrato, a] *adj* literary
♦ *nm/f* writer

literatura [literaˈtura] *nf* literature

litigar [litiˈxar] *vt* to fight ♦ *vi* (*JUR*) to
go to law; (*fig*) to dispute, argue

litigio [liˈtixjo] *nm* (*JUR*) lawsuit; (*fig*):
en ~ **con** in dispute with

litografía [litoɣraˈfia] *nf* lithography.

(una ~) lithograph

litoral [lito'ral] *adj* coastal ♦ *nm* coast, seaboard

litro ['litro] *nm* litre

liviano, a [li'βjano, a] *adj* (*cosa, objeto*) trivial

lívido, a ['liβiðo, a] *adj* livid

llaga ['ʎaɣa] *nf* wound

llama ['ʎama] *nf* flame; (*ZOOL*) llama

llamada [ʎa'maða] *nf* call; ~ **al orden** call to order; ~ **a pie de página** reference note

llamamiento [ʎama'mjento] *nm* call

llamar [ʎa'mar] *vt* to call; (*atención*) to attract ♦ *vi* (*por teléfono*) to telephone; (*a la puerta*) to knock (*o* ring); (*por señas*) to beckon; (*MIL*) to call up; ~**se** *vr* to be called, be named; **¿cómo se llama usted?** what's your name?

llamarada [ʎama'raða] *nf* (*llamas*) blaze; (*rubor*) flush

llamativo, a [ʎama'tiβo, a] *adj* showy; (*color*) loud

llano, a ['ʎano, a] *adj* (*superficie*) flat; (*persona*) straightforward; (*estilo*) clear ♦ *nm* plain, flat ground

llanta ['ʎanta] *nf* (wheel) rim; (*AM*): ~ **(de goma)** tyre; (: *cámara*) inner (tube)

llanto ['ʎanto] *nm* weeping

llanura [ʎa'nura] *nf* plain

llave ['ʎaβe] *nf* key; (*del agua*) tap; (*MECÁNICA*) spanner; (*de la luz*) switch; (*MUS*) key; ~ **inglesa** monkey wrench; ~ **maestra** master key; ~ **de contacto** (*AUTO*) ignition key; ~ **de paso** stopcock; **echar la** ~ to lock up; ~**ro** *nm* keyring

llegada [ʎe'ɣaða] *nf* arrival

llegar [ʎe'ɣar] *vi* to arrive; (*alcanzar*) to reach; (*bastar*) to be enough; ~**se** *vr*: ~**se a** to approach; ~ **a** to manage to, succeed in; ~ **a saber** to find out; ~ **a ser** to become; ~ **a las manos de** to come into the hands of

llenar [ʎe'nar] *vt* to fill; (*espacio*) to cover; (*formulario*) to fill in *o* up; (*fig*)

to heap

lleno, a ['ʎeno, a] *adj* full, filled; (*repleto*) full up ♦ *nm* (*TEATRO*) full house; **dar de ~ contra un muro** to hit a wall head-on

llevadero, a [ʎeβa'ðero, a] *adj* bearable, tolerable

llevar [ʎe'βar] *vt* to take; (*ropa*) to wear; (*cargar*) to carry; (*quitar*) to take away; (*en coche*) to drive; (*transportar*) to transport; (*traer: dinero*) to carry; (*conducir*) to lead; (*MAT*) to carry ♦ *vi* (*suj: camino etc*): ~ **a** to lead to; ~**se** *vr* to carry off, take away; **llevamos dos días aquí** we have been here for two days; **él me lleva 2 años** he's 2 years older than me; (*COM*): ~ **los libros** to keep the books; ~**se bien** to get on well (together)

llorar [ʎo'rar] *vt, vi* to cry, weep; ~ **de risa** to cry with laughter

lloriquear [ʎorike'ar] *vi* to snivel, whimper

lloro ['ʎoro] *nm* crying, weeping; **llorón, ona** *adj* tearful ♦ *nm/f* cry-baby; ~**so, a** *adj* (*gen*) weeping, tearful; (*triste*) sad, sorrowful

llover [ʎo'βer] *vi* to rain

llovizna [ʎo'βiθna] *nf* drizzle; **lloviznar** *vi* to drizzle

llueve *etc vb ver* **llover**

lluvia ['ʎuβja] *nf* rain; ~ **radioactiva** (radioactive) fallout; **lluvioso, a** *adj* rainy

lo [lo] *art def*: ~ **bello** the beautiful, what is beautiful, that which is beautiful ♦ *pron* (*persona*) him; (*cosa*) it; *tb ver* **el**

loable [lo'aβle] *adj* praiseworthy; **loar** *vt* to praise

lobo ['loβo] *nm* wolf; ~ **de mar** (*fig*) sea dog; ~ **marino** seal

lóbrego, a ['loβreɣo, a] *adj* dark; (*fig*) gloomy

lóbulo ['loβulo] *nm* lobe

local [lo'kal] *adj* local ♦ *nm* place, site; (*oficinas*) premises *pl*; ~**idad** *nf* (*barrio*) locality; (*lugar*) location; (*TEATRO*) seat, ticket; ~**izar** *vt* (*ubicar*) to locate; find; (*restringir*) to localize; (*situar*) to place

loción [lo'θjon] *nf* lotion

loco, a ['loko, a] *adj* mad ♦ *nm/f* lunatic, mad person

locomotora [lokomo'tora] *nf* engine, locomotive

locuaz [lo'kwaθ] *adj* loquacious

locución [loku'θjon] *nf* expression

locura [lo'kura] *nf* madness; (*acto*) crazy act

locutor, a [loku'tor, a] *nm/f* (*RADIO*) announcer; (*comentarista*) commentator; (*TV*) newsreader

locutorio [loku'torjo] *nm* (*en telefónica*) telephone booth

lodo ['loðo] *nm* mud

lógica ['loxika] *nf* logic

lógico, a ['loxiko, a] *adj* logical

logística [lo'xistika] *nf* logistics *sg*

logotipo [loɣo'tipo] *nm* logo

logrado, a [lo'ɣraðo, a] *adj* (*interpretación, reproducción*) polished, excellent

lograr [lo'vrar] *vt* to achieve; (*obtener*) to get, obtain; ~ **hacer** to manage to do; ~ **que uno venga** to manage to get sb to come

logro ['loɣro] *nm* achievement, success

loma ['loma] *nf* hillock (*BRIT*), small hill

lombriz [lom'briθ] *nf* worm

lomo ['lomo] *nm* (*de animal*) back; (*CULIN: de cerdo*) pork loin; (: *de vaca*) rib steak; (*de libro*) spine

lona ['lona] *nf* canvas

loncha ['lontʃa] *nf* = **lonja**

lonche ['lontʃe] (*AM*) *nm* lunch; ~**ría** (*AM*) *nf* snack bar, diner (*US*)

Londres ['londres] *n* London

longaniza [longa'niθa] *nf* pork sausage

longitud [lonxi'tuð] *nf* length; (*GEO*) longitude; **tener 3 metros de** ~ to be 3 metres long; ~ **de onda** wavelength

lonja ['lonxa] *nf* slice; (*de tocino*) rasher; ~ **de pescado** fish market

loro ['loro] *nm* parrot

los [los] *art def* the ♦ *pron* them; (*ustedes*) you; **mis libros y** ~ **tuyos** my books and yours; **tb** *ver* **el**

losa ['losa] *nf* stone; ~ **sepulcral** gravestone

lote ['lote] *nm* portion; (*COM*) lot

lotería [lote'ria] *nf* lottery; (*juego*) lotto

loza ['loθa] *nf* crockery

lubina [lu'ßina] *nf* sea bass

lubricante [lußri'kante] *nm* lubricant

lubricar [lußri'kar] *vt* to lubricate

lucha ['lutʃa] *nf* fight, struggle; ~ **de clases** class struggle; ~ **libre** wrestling; **luchar** *vi* to fight

lucidez [luθi'ðeθ] *nf* lucidity

lúcido, a ['luθiðo, a] *adj* (*persona*) lucid; (*mente*) logical; (*idea*) crystal-clear

luciérnaga [lu'θjernaxa] *nf* glow-worm

lucir [lu'θir] *vt* to illuminate, light (up); (*ostentar*) to show off ♦ *vi* (*brillar*) to shine; ~**se** *vr* (*irónico*) to make a fool of o.s.

lucro ['lukro] *nm* profit, gain

lúdico, a ['luðiko, a] *adj* (*aspecto, actividad*) play *cpd*

luego [lu'weɣo] *adv* (*después*) next; (*más tarde*) later, afterwards

lugar [lu'ɣar] *nm* place; (*sitio*) spot; **en** ~ **de** instead of; **hacer** ~ to make room; **fuera de** ~ out of place; **tener** ~ to take place; ~ **común** commonplace

lugareño, a [luɣa'reɲo, a] *adj* village *cpd* ♦ *nm/f* villager

lugarteniente [luɣarte'njente] *nm* deputy

lúgubre ['luɣuβre] *adj* mournful

lujo ['luxo] *nm* luxury; (*fig*) profusion, abundance; **~so, a** *adj* luxurious

lujuria [lu'xurja] *nf* lust

lumbre ['lumbre] *nf* fire; (*para cigarrillo*) light

lumbrera [lum'brera] *nf* luminary

luminoso, a [lumi'noso, a] *adj* luminous, shining

luna ['luna] *nf* moon; (*de un espejo*) glass; (*de gafas*) lens; (*fig*) crescent; **~ llena/nueva** full/new moon; **estar en la ~** to have one's head in the clouds; **~ de miel** honeymoon

lunar [lu'nar] *adj* lunar ♦ *nm* (ANAT) mole; **tela de ~es** spotted material

lunes ['lunes] *nm inv* Monday

lupa ['lupa] *nf* magnifying glass

lustrar [lus'trar] *vt* (*mueble*) to polish; (*zapatos*) to shine; **lustre** *nm* polish; (*fig*) lustre; **dar lustre a** to polish; **lustroso, a** *adj* shining

luto ['luto] *nm* mourning; **llevar el** *o* **vestirse de ~** to be in mourning

Luxemburgo [luksem'burɣo] *nm* Luxembourg

luz [luθ] (*pl* **luces**) *nf* light; **dar a ~ un niño** to give birth to a child; **sacar a la ~** to bring to light; **dar** *o* **encender** (*ESP*) *o* **prender** (*AM*)/**apagar la ~** to switch the light on/off; **a todas luces** by any reckoning; **tener pocas luces** to be dim *o* stupid; **~ roja/verde** red/ green light; **~ de freno** brake light; **luces de tráfico** traffic lights; **traje de luces** bullfighter's costume

M, m

m *abr* (= *metro*) m; (= *minuto*) m

macarrones [maka'rrones] *nmpl* macaroni *sg*

macedonia [maθe'ðonja] *nf*: **~ de frutas** fruit salad

macerar [maθe'rar] *vt* to macerate

maceta [ma'θeta] *nf* (*de flores*) pot of flowers; (*para plantas*) flowerpot

machacar [matʃa'kar] *vt* to crush, pound ♦ *vi* (*insistir*) to go on, keep on

machete [ma'tʃete] (*AM*) *nm* machete, (large) knife

machismo [ma'tʃismo] *nm* male chauvinism; **machista** *adj*, *nm* sexist

macho ['matʃo] *adj* male; (*fig*) virile ♦ *nm* male; (*fig*) he-man

macizo, a [ma'θiθo, a] *adj* (*grande*) massive; (*fuerte*, *sólido*) solid ♦ *nm* mass, chunk

madeja [ma'ðexa] *nf* (*de lana*) skein, hank; (*de pelo*) mass, mop

madera [ma'ðera] *nf* wood; (*fig*) nature, character; **una ~** a piece of wood

madero [ma'ðero] *nm* beam

madrastra [ma'ðrastra] *nf* stepmother

madre ['maðre] *adj* mother *cpd*; (*AM*) tremendous ♦ *nf* mother; (*de vino etc*) dregs *pl*; **~ política/soltera** mother-in-law/unmarried mother

Madrid [ma'ðrið] *n* Madrid

madriguera [maðri'ɣera] *nf* burrow

madrileño, a [maðri'leɲo, a] *adj* of from Madrid ♦ *nm/f* native of Madrid

madrina [ma'ðrina] *nf* godmother; (*ARQ*) prop, shore; (*TEC*) brace; (*de boda*) bridesmaid

madrugada [maðru'ɣaða] *nf* early morning; (*alba*) dawn, daybreak

madrugador, a [maðruɣa'ðor, a] *adj* early-rising

madrugar [maðru'ɣar] *vi* to get up early; (*fig*) to get ahead

madurar [maðu'rar] *vt*, *vi* (*fruta*) to ripen; (*fig*) to mature; **madurez** *nf* ripeness; maturity; **maduro, a** *adj* ripe; mature

maestra [ma'estra] *nf ver* maestro

maestría [maes'tria] *nf* mastery; (*habilidad*) skill, expertise

maestro, a [ma'estro, a] *adj* masterly; (*principal*) main ♦ *nm/f* master/mistress; (*profesor*) teacher ♦ *nm* (*autoridad*) authority; (*MUS*) maestro; (*AM*) skilled workman; **~ albañil** master mason

magdalena [mavða'lena] *nf* fairy cake

magia ['maxja] *nf* magic; **mágico, a** *adj* magic(al) ♦ *nm/f* magician

magisterio [maxis'terjo] *nm* (*enseñanza*) teaching; (*profesión*) teaching profession; (*maestros*) teachers *pl*

magistrado [maxis'traðo] *nm* magistrate

magistral [maxis'tral] *adj* magisterial; (*fig*) masterly

magnánimo, a [mav'nanimo, a] *adj* magnanimous

magnate [mav'nate] *nm* magnate, tycoon

magnético, a [mav'netiko, a] *adj* magnetic; **magnetizar** *vt* to magnetize

magnetófon [mavneto'fon] *nm* tape recorder; **magnetofónico, a** *adj*: **cinta magnetofónica** recording tape

magnetófono [mav'netofono] *nm* = **magnetófon**

magnífico, a [mav'nifiko, a] *adj* splendid, magnificent

magnitud [mavni'tuð] *nf* magnitude

mago, a ['mavo, a] *nm/f* magician; **los Reyes M~s** the Magi, the Three Wise Men

magro, a ['mavro, a] *adj* (*carne*) lean

maguey [ma'xei] *nm* agave

magullar [mavu'ʎar] *vt* (*amoratar*) to bruise; (*dañar*) to damage

mahometano, a [maome'tano, a] *adj* Mohammedan

mahonesa [mao'nesa] *nf* mayonnaise

maíz [ma'iθ] *nm* maize (*BRIT*), corn (*US*); sweet corn

majadero, a [maxa'ðero, a] *adj* silly, stupid

majestad [maxes'taθ] *nf* majesty; **majestuoso, a** *adj* majestic

majo, a ['maxo, a] *adj* nice; (*guapo*) attractive, good-looking; (*elegante*) smart

mal [mal] *adv* badly; (*equivocadamente*) wrongly ♦ *adj* = **malo** ♦ *nm* evil; (*desgracia*) misfortune; (*daño*) harm, damage; (*MED*) illness; **~ que bien** rightly or wrongly; **ir de ~ en peor** to get worse and worse

malabarismo [malaβa'rismo] *nm* juggling; **malabarista** *nm/f* juggler

malaria [ma'larja] *nf* malaria

malcriado, a [mal'krjaðo, a] *adj* spoiled

maldad [mal'daθ] *nf* evil, wickedness

maldecir [malde'θir] *vt* to curse ♦ *vi*: **~ de** to speak ill of

maldición [maldi'θjon] *nf* curse

maldito, a [mal'dito, a] *adj* (*condenado*) damned; (*perverso*) wicked; **¡~ sea!** damn it!

maleante [male'ante] *nm/f* criminal, crook

maledicencia [maleði'θenθja] *nf* slander, scandal

maleducado, a [maleðu'kaðo, a] *adj* bad-mannered, rude

malentendido [malenten'diðo] *nm* misunderstanding

malestar [males'tar] *nm* (*gen*) discomfort; (*fig*: *inquietud*) uneasiness; (*POL*) unrest

maleta [ma'leta] *nf* case, suitcase; (*AUTO*) boot (*BRIT*), trunk (*US*); **hacer las ~s** to pack; **maletera** (*AM*) *nf*, **maletero** *nm* (*AUTO*) boot (*BRIT*), trunk (*US*); **maletín** *nm* small case, bag

malévolo, a [ma'leβolo, a] *adj* malicious, spiteful

maleza [ma'leθa] *nf* (*hierbas malas*) weeds *pl*; (*arbustos*) thicket

malgastar [malvas'tar] *vt* (*tiempo*, *dinero*) to waste; (*salud*) to ruin

malhechor [male'tʃor, a] *nm/f* delinquent

malhumorado, a [malumo'raðo, a] *adj* bad-tempered

malicia [ma'liθja] nf (maldad)
wickedness; (astucia) slyness, guile;
(mala intención) malice, spite; (carácter
travieso) mischievousness; **malicioso,
a** adj wicked, evil; sly, crafty; malicious,
spiteful; mischievous

maligno, a [ma'livno, a] adj evil;
(malévolo) malicious; (MED) malignant

malla ['maʎa] nf mesh; (de baño)
swimsuit; (de ballet, gimnasia) leotard;
~s nfpl tights; ~ **de alambre** wire
mesh

Mallorca [ma'ʎorka] nf Majorca

malo, a ['malo, a] adj bad; (falso) false
♦ nm/f villain; **estar** ~ to be ill

malograr [malo'vrar] vt to spoil; (plan)
to upset; (ocasión) to waste; ~**se** vr
(plan etc) to fail, come to grief;
(persona) to die before one's time

malparado, a [malpa'raðo, a] adj:
salir ~ to come off badly

malpensado, a [malpen'saðo, a] adj
nasty

malsano, a [mal'sano, a] adj
unhealthy

malteada [malte'aða] (AM) nf milk
shake

maltratar [maltra'tar] vt to ill-treat,
mistreat

maltrecho, a [mal'tretʃo, a] adj
battered, damaged

malvado, a [mal'ɓaðo, a] adj evil,
villainous

malversar [malɓer'sar] vt to
embezzle, misappropriate

Malvinas [mal'ɓinas]: **Islas** ~ nfpl
Falkland Islands

malvivir [malɓi'ɓir] vi to live poorly

mama ['mama] nf (de animal) teat; (de
mujer) breast

mamá [ma'ma] (pl ~**s**) (fam) nf mum,
mummy

mamar [ma'mar] vt, vi to suck

mamarracho [mama'rratʃo] nm sight,
mess

mamífero [ma'mifero] nm mammal

mampara [mam'para] nf (entre

habitaciones) partition; (biombo) screen

mampostería [mamposte'ria] nf
masonry

manada [ma'naða] nf (ZOOL) herd;
(: de leones) pride; (: de lobos) pack

manantial [manan'tjal] nm spring

manar [ma'nar] vi to run, flow

mancha [mantʃa] nf stain, mark;
(ZOOL) patch; **manchar** vt (gen) to
stain, mark; (ensuciar) to soil, dirty

manchego, a [man'tʃevo, a] adj of o
from La Mancha

manco, a ['manko, a] adj (de un
brazo) one-armed; (de una mano) one-
handed; (fig) defective, faulty

mancomunar [mankomu'nar] vt to
unite, bring together; (recursos) to
pool; (JUR) to make jointly responsible;
mancomunidad nf union,
association; (comunidad) community;
(JUR) joint responsibility

mandamiento [manda'mjento] nm
(orden) order, command; (REL)
commandment; ~ **judicial** warrant

mandar [man'dar] vt (ordenar) to
order; (dirigir) to lead, command;
(enviar) to send; (pedir) to order, ask
for ♦ vi to be in charge; (pey) to be
bossy; **¿mande?** pardon?, excuse me?;
~ **hacer un traje** to have a suit made

mandarina [manda'rina] nf tangerine,
mandarin (orange)

mandato [man'dato] nm (orden)
order; (POL: período) term of office;
(: territorio) mandate; ~ **judicial**
(search) warrant

mandíbula [man'diɓula] nf jaw

mandil [man'dil] nm apron

mando [man'do] nm (MIL) command;
(de país) rule; (el primer lugar) lead;
(POL) term of office; (TEC) control; ~ **a
la izquierda** left-hand drive

mandón, ona [man'don, ona] adj
bossy, domineering

manejable [mane'xaɓle] adj
manageable

manejar [mane'xar] vt to manage;

(*máquina*) to work, operate; (*caballo etc*) to handle; (*casa*) to run, manage; (*AM: AUTO*) to drive; **~se** *vr* (*comportarse*) to act, behave; (*arreglárselas*) to manage; **manejo** *nm* management; handling; running; driving; (*facilidad de trato*) ease, confidence; **manejos** *nmpl* (*intrigas*) intrigues

manera [ma'nera] *nf* way, manner, fashion; **~s** *nfpl* (*modales*) manners; **su ~ de ser** the way he is; (*aire*) his manner; **de ninguna ~** no way, by no means; **de otra ~** otherwise; **de todas ~s** at any rate; **no hay ~ de persuadirle** there's no way of convincing him

manga ['manga] *nf* (*de camisa*) sleeve; (*de riego*) hose

mangar [man'gar] (*fam*) *vt* to pinch, nick

mango ['mango] *nm* handle; (*BOT*) mango

mangonear [mangone'ar] *vi* (*meterse*) to meddle, interfere; (*ser mandón*) to boss people about

manguera [man'gera] *nf* hose

manía [ma'nia] *nf* (*MED*) mania; (*fig: moda*) rage, craze; (*disgusto*) dislike; (*malicia*) spite; **maníaco, a** *adj* maniac(al) ♦ *nm/f* maniac

maniatar [manja'tar] *vt* to tie the hands of

maniático, a [ma'njatiko, a] *adj* maniac(al) ♦ *nm/f* maniac

manicomio [mani'komjo] *nm* mental hospital (*BRIT*), insane asylum (*US*)

manifestación [manifesta'θjon] *nf* (*declaración*) statement, declaration; (*de emoción*) show, display; (*POL: desfile*) demonstration; (*: concentración*) mass meeting

manifestar [manifes'tar] *vt* to show, manifest; (*declarar*) to state, declare; **manifiesto, a** *adj* clear, manifest ♦ *nm* manifesto

manillar [mani'ʎar] *nm* handlebars *pl*

maniobra [ma'njoβra] *nf* manoeuvre; **~s** *nfpl* (*MIL*) manoeuvres; **maniobrar** *vt* to manoeuvre

manipulación [manipula'θjon] *nf* manipulation

manipular [manipu'lar] *vt* to manipulate; (*manejar*) to handle

maniquí [mani'ki] *nm* dummy ♦ *nm/f* model

manirroto, a [mani'rroto, a] *adj* lavish, extravagant ♦ *nm/f* spendthrift

manivela [mani'βela] *nf* crank

manjar [man'xar] *nm* (tasty) dish

mano ['mano] *nf* hand; (*ZOOL*) foot, paw; (*de pintura*) coat; (*serie*) lot, series; **a ~** by hand; **a ~ derecha/izquierda** on the right(-hand side)/left(-hand side); **de primera ~** (at) first hand; **de segunda ~** (at) second hand; **robo a ~ armada** armed robbery; **~ de obra** labour, manpower; **estrechar la ~ a uno** to shake sb's hand

manojo [ma'noxo] *nm* handful, bunch; **~ de llaves** bunch of keys

manopla [ma'nopla] *nf* mitten

manoseado, a [manose'aðo, a] *adj* well-worn

manosear [manose'ar] *vt* (*tocar*) to handle, touch; (*desordenar*) to mess up, rumple; (*insistir en*) to overwork; (*AM*) to caress, fondle

manotazo [mano'taθo] *nm* slap, smack

mansalva [man'salβa]: **a ~** *adv* indiscriminately

mansedumbre [manse'ðumbre] *nf* gentleness, meekness

mansión [man'sjon] *nf* mansion

manso, a ['manso, a] *adj* gentle, mild; (*animal*) tame

manta ['manta] *nf* blanket; (*AM: poncho*) poncho

manteca [man'teka] *nf* fat; (*AM*) butter; **~ de cacahuete/cacao** peanut/cocoa butter; **~ de cerdo** lard

mantecado [mante'kaðo] (*AM*) *nm* ice

cream

mantel [man'tel] *nm* tablecloth

mantendré *etc vb ver* **mantener**

mantener [mante'ner] *vt* to support, maintain; (*alimentar*) to sustain; (*conservar*) to keep; (*TEC*) to maintain, service; **~se** *vr* (*seguir de pie*) to be still standing; (*no ceder*) to hold one's ground; (*subsistir*) to sustain o.s., keep going; **mantenimiento** *nm* maintenance; sustenance; (*apoyo*) support

mantequilla [mante'kiʎa] *nf* butter

mantilla [man'tiʎa] *nf* mantilla; **~s** *nfpl* (*de bebé*) baby clothes

manto ['manto] *nm* (*capa*) cloak; (*de ceremonia*) robe, gown

mantuve *etc vb ver* **mantener**

manual [ma'nwal] *adj* manual ♦ *nm* manual, handbook

manufactura [manufak'tura] *nf* manufacture; (*fábrica*) factory; **manufacturado, a** *adj* (*producto*) manufactured

manuscrito, a [manus'krito, a] *adj* handwritten ♦ *nm* manuscript

manutención [manuten'θjon] *nf* maintenance; (*sustento*) support

manzana [man'θana] *nf* apple; (*ARQ*) block (of houses)

manzanilla [manθa'niʎa] *nf* (*planta*) camomile; (*infusión*) camomile tea

manzano [man'θano] *nm* apple tree

maña ['maɲa] *nf* (*gen*) skill, dexterity; (*pey*) guile; (*destreza*) trick, knack

mañana [ma'ɲana] *adv* tomorrow ♦ *nm* future ♦ *nf* morning; **de** *o* **por la ~** in the morning; **¡hasta ~!** see you tomorrow!; **~ por la ~** tomorrow morning

mañoso, a [ma'ɲoso, a] *adj* (*hábil*) skilful; (*astuto*) smart, clever

mapa ['mapa] *nm* map

maqueta [ma'keta] *nf* (*scale*) model

maquillaje [maki'ʎaxe] *nm* make-up; (*acto*) making up

maquillar [maki'ʎar] *vt* to make up;

~se *vr* to put on (some) make-up

máquina ['makina] *nf* machine; (*de tren*) locomotive, engine; (*FOTO*) camera; (*AM: coche*) car; (*fig*) machinery; **escrito a ~** typewritten; **~ de escribir** typewriter; **~ de coser/lavar** sewing/washing machine

maquinación [makina'θjon] *nf* machination, plot

maquinal [maki'nal] *adj* (*fig*) mechanical, automatic

maquinaria [maki'narja] *nf* (*máquinas*) machinery; (*mecanismo*) mechanism, works *pl*

maquinilla [maki'niʎa] *nf*: **~ de afeitar** razor

maquinista [maki'nista] *nm/f* (*de tren*) engine driver; (*TEC*) operator; (*NAUT*) engineer

mar [mar] *nm o f* sea; **~ adentro** *o* **afuera** out at sea; **en alta ~** on the high seas; **la ~ de** (*fam*) lots of; **el M~ Negro/Báltico** the Black/Baltic Sea

maraña [ma'raɲa] *nf* (*maleza*) thicket; (*confusión*) tangle

maravilla [mara'βiʎa] *nf* marvel, wonder; (*BOT*) marigold; **maravillar** *vt* to astonish, amaze; **maravillarse** *vr* to be astonished, be amazed; **maravilloso, a** *adj* wonderful, marvellous

marca ['marka] *nf* (*gen*) mark; (*sello*) stamp; (*COM*) make, brand; **de ~** excellent, outstanding; **~ de fábrica** trademark; **~ registrada** registered trademark

marcado, a [mar'kaðo, a] *adj* marked, strong

marcador [marka'ðor] *nm* (*DEPORTE*) scoreboard; (: *persona*) scorer

marcapasos [marka'pasos] *nm inv* pacemaker

marcar [mar'kar] *vt* (*gen*) to mark; (*número de teléfono*) to dial; (*gol*) to score; (*números*) to record, keep a tally of; (*pelo*) to set ♦ *vi* (*DEPORTE*) to score;

(*TEL*) to dial

marcha ['martʃa] nf march; (*TEC*) running, working; (*AUTO*) gear; (*velocidad*) speed; (*fig*) progress; (*dirección*) course; **poner en ~** to put into gear; (*fig*) to set in motion, get going; **dar ~ atrás** to reverse, put into reverse; **estar en ~** to be under way, be in motion

marchar [mar'tʃar] vi (*ir*) to go; (*funcionar*) to work, go; **~se** vr to go (away), leave

marchitar [martʃi'tar] vt to wither, dry up; **~se** vr (*BOT*) to wither; (*fig*) to fade away; **marchito, a** adj withered, faded; (*fig*) in decline

marcial [mar'θjal] adj martial, military

marciano, a [mar'θjano, a] adj, nm/f Martian

marco ['marko] nm frame; (*moneda*) mark; (*fig*) framework

marea [ma'rea] nf tide

marear [mare'ar] vt (*fig*) to annoy, upset; (*MED*): **~ a uno** to make sb feel sick; **~se** vr (*tener náuseas*) to feel sick; (*desvanecerse*) to feel faint; (*aturdirse*) to feel dizzy; (*fam: emborracharse*) to get tipsy

maremoto [mare'moto] nm tidal wave

mareo [ma'reo] nm (*náusea*) sick feeling; (*en viaje*) travel sickness; (*aturdimiento*) dizziness; (*fam: lata*) nuisance

marfil [mar'fil] nm ivory

margarina [marva'rina] nf margarine

margarita [marva'rita] nf (*BOT*) daisy; (*rueda*) ~ daisywheel

margen ['marxen] nm (*borde*) edge, border; (*fig*) margin, space ♦ nf (*de río etc*) bank; **dar ~ para** to give an opportunity for; **mantenerse al ~** to keep out (of things)

marginar [marxi'nar] vt (*socialmente*) to marginalize, ostracize

marica [ma'rika] (*fam*) nm sissy

maricón [mari'kon] (*fam*) nm queer

marido [ma'riðo] nm husband

marihuana [mari'wana] nf marijuana, cannabis

marina [ma'rina] nf navy; **~ mercante** merchant navy

marinero, a [mari'nero, a] adj sea cpd ♦ nm sailor, seaman

marino, a [ma'rino, a] adj sea cpd, marine ♦ nm sailor

marioneta [marjo'neta] nf puppet

mariposa [mari'posa] nf butterfly

mariquita [mari'kita] nf ladybird (*BRIT*), ladybug (*US*)

mariscos [ma'riskos] nmpl shellfish inv, seafood(s)

marítimo, a [ma'ritimo, a] adj sea cpd, maritime

mármol ['marmol] nm marble

marqués, esa [mar'kes, esa] nm/f marquis/marchioness

marrón [ma'rron] adj brown

marroquí [marro'ki] adj, nm/f Moroccan ♦ nm Morocco (leather)

Marruecos [ma'rrwekos] nm Morocco

martes ['martes] nm inv Tuesday

Martes y Trece

According to Spanish superstition Tuesday is an unlucky day, even more so if it falls on the 13th of the month.

martillo [mar'tiʎo] nm hammer; **~ neumático** pneumatic drill (*BRIT*), jackhammer

mártir ['martir] nm/f martyr; **martirio** nm martyrdom; (*fig*) torture, torment

marxismo [mark'sismo] nm Marxism; **marxista** adj, nm/f Marxist

marzo [mar'θo] nm March

PALABRA CLAVE
---

más [mas] adj, adv 1: **~ (que, de)** (*compar*) more (than), ...+ er (than); **~ grande/inteligente** bigger/more intelligent; **trabaja ~ (que yo)** he

works more (than me); ver tb **cada**
2 (superl): **el ~** the most, ...**+** est; **el
~ grande/inteligente (de)** the
biggest/most intelligent (in)
3 (negativo): **no tengo ~ dinero** I
haven't got any more money; **no
viene ~ por aquí** he doesn't come
round here any more
4 (adicional): **no le veo ~ solución
que ...** I see no other solution than to
...; **¿quién ~?** anybody else?
5 (+ adj: valor intensivo): **¡qué perro
~ sucio!** what a filthy dog!; **¡es
~ tonto!** he's so stupid!
6 (locuciones): **~ o menos** more or
less; **los ~** most people; **es ~**
furthermore; **~ bien** rather; **¡qué
~ da!** what does it matter!; ver tb **da**
7: por ~: **por ~ que te esfuerces** no
matter how hard you try; **por ~ que
quisiera ...** much as I should like to ...
8: de ~: **veo que aquí estoy de ~** I
can see I'm not needed here;
tenemos uno de ~ we've got one
extra
♦ prep: **2 ~ 2 son 4** 2 and 2 plus 2
are 4
♦ nm inv: **este trabajo tiene sus ~ y
sus menos** this job's got its good
points and its bad points

mas |mas| conj but
masa |'masa| nf (mezcla) dough;
(volumen) volume, mass; (física) mass;
en ~ en masse; **las ~s** (POL) the
masses
masacre |ma'sakre| nf massacre
masaje |ma'saxe| nm massage
máscara |'maskara| nf mask;
mascarilla nf (de belleza, MED) mask
masculino, a |masku'lino, a| adj
masculine; (BIO) male
masía |ma'sia| nf farmhouse
masificación |masifika'θjon| nf
overcrowding
masivo, a |ma'siβo, a| adj mass cpd
masón |ma'son| nm (free)mason

masoquista |maso'kista| nm/f
masochist
masticar |masti'kar| vt to chew
mástil |'mastil| nm (de navío) mast; (de
guitarra) neck
mastín |mas'tin| nm mastiff
masturbación |masturβa'θjon| nf
masturbation
masturbarse |mastur'βarse| vr to
masturbate
mata |'mata| nf (arbusto) bush, shrub;
(de hierba) tuft
matadero |mata'ðero| nm
slaughterhouse, abattoir
matador, a |mata'ðor, a| adj killing
♦ nm/f killer ♦ nm (TAUR) matador,
bullfighter
matamoscas |mata'moskas| nm inv
(palo) fly swat
matanza |ma'tanθa| nf slaughter
matar |ma'tar| vt, vi to kill; **~se** vr
(suicidarse) to kill o.s., commit suicide;
(morir) to be o get killed; **~ el hambre**
to stave off hunger
matasellos |mata'seʎos| nm inv
postmark
mate |'mate| adj matt ♦ nm (en
ajedrez) (check)mate; (AM: hierba)
maté; (: vasija) gourd
matemáticas |mate'matikas| nfpl
mathematics; **matemático, a** adj
mathematical ♦ nm/f mathematician
materia |ma'terja| nf (gen) matter;
(TEC) material; (ESCOL) subject; **en
~ de** on the subject of; **~ prima** raw
material; **material** adj material ♦ nm
material; (TEC) equipment;
materialismo nm materialism;
materialista adj materialist(ic);
materialmente adv materially; (fig)
absolutely
maternal |mater'nal| adj motherly,
maternal
maternidad |materni'ðað| nf
motherhood, maternity; **materno, a**
adj maternal; (lengua) mother cpd
matinal |mati'nal| adj morning cpd

matiz [ma'tiθ] *nm* shade; **~ar** *vt* (*variar*) to vary; (*ARTE*) to blend; **~ar de** to tinge with

matón [ma'ton] *nm* bully

matorral [mato'rral] *nm* thicket

matraca [ma'traka] *nf* rattle

matrícula [ma'trikula] *nf* (*registro*) register; (*AUTO*) registration number; (: *placa*) number plate; **matricular** *vt* to register, enrol

matrimonial [matrimo'njal] *adj* matrimonial

matrimonio [matri'monjo] *nm* (*pareja*) (married) couple; (*unión*) marriage

matriz [ma'triθ] *nf* (*ANAT*) womb; (*TEC*) mould; **casa ~** (*COM*) head office

matrona [ma'trona] *nf* (*persona de edad*) matron; (*comadrona*) midwife

maxilar [maksi'lar] *nm* jaw(bone)

máxima ['maksima] *nf* maxim

máxime ['maksime] *adv* especially

máximo, a ['maksimo, a] *adj* maximum; (*más alto*) highest; (*más grande*) greatest ♦ *nm* maximum

mayo ['majo] *nm* May

mayonesa [majo'nesa] *nf* mayonnaise

mayor [ma'jor] *adj* main, chief; (*adulto*) adult; (*de edad avanzada*) elderly; (*MUS*) major; (*compar: de tamaño*) bigger; (: *de edad*) older; (*superl: de tamaño*) biggest; (: *de edad*) oldest ♦ *nm* (*adulto*) adult; **al por ~** wholesale; **~ de edad** adult; **~es** *nmpl* (*antepasados*) ancestors

mayoral [majo'ral] *nm* foreman

mayordomo [major'ðomo] *nm* butler

mayoría [majo'ria] *nf* majority, greater part

mayorista [majo'rista] *nm/f* wholesaler

mayoritario, a [majori'tarjo, a] *adj* majority *cpd*

mayúscula [ma'juskula] *nf* capital letter

mayúsculo, a [ma'juskulo, a] *adj* (*fig*) big, tremendous

mazapán [maθa'pan] *nm* marzipan

mazo ['maθo] *nm* (*martillo*) mallet; (*de flores*) bunch; (*DEPORTE*) bat

me [me] *pron* (*directo*) me; (*indirecto*) (to) me; (*reflexivo*) (to) myself; **¡dámelo!** give it to me!

mear [me'ar] (*fam*) *vi* to pee, piss (!)

mecánica [me'kanika] *nf* (*ESCOL*) mechanics *sg*; (*mecanismo*) mechanism; *ver tb* **mecánico**

mecánico, a [me'kaniko, a] *adj* mechanical ♦ *nm/f* mechanic

mecanismo [meka'nismo] *nm* mechanism; (*marcha*) gear

mecanografía [mekanoɣra'fia] *nf* typewriting; **mecanógrafo, a** *nm/f* typist

mecate [me'kate] (*AM*) *nm* rope

mecedora [meθe'ðora] *nf* rocking chair

mecer [me'θer] *vt* (*cuna*) to rock; **~se** *vr* to rock; (*ramo*) to sway

mecha ['metʃa] *nf* (*de vela*) wick; (*de bomba*) fuse

mechero [me'tʃero] *nm* (*cigarette*) lighter

mechón [me'tʃon] *nm* (*gen*) tuft; (*de pelo*) lock

medalla [me'ðaʎa] *nf* medal

media ['meðja] *nf* (*ESP*) stocking; (*AM*) sock; (*promedio*) average

mediado, a [me'ðjaðo, a] *adj* half-full; (*trabajo*) half-completed; **a ~s de** in the middle of, halfway through

mediano, a [me'ðjano, a] *adj* (*regular*) medium, average; (*mediocre*) mediocre

medianoche [meðja'notʃe] *nf* midnight

mediante [me'ðjante] *adv* by (means of), through

mediar [me'ðjar] *vi* (*interceder*) to mediate, intervene

medicación [meðika'θjon] *nf* medication, treatment

medicamento [meðika'mento] *nm* medicine, drug

medicina [meði'θina] nf medicine
medición [meði'θjon] nf
measurement
médico, a ['meðiko, a] adj medical
♦ nm/f doctor
medida [me'ðiða] nf measure;
(medición) measurement; (prudencia)
moderation, prudence; **en cierta/
gran ~** up to a point/to a great
extent; **un traje a la ~** made-to-
measure suit; **~ de cuello** collar size;
a ~ de in proportion to; (de acuerdo con)
in keeping with; **a ~ que** (conforme) as
medio, a ['meðjo, a] adj half (a);
(punto) mid, middle; (promedio)
average ♦ adv half ♦ nm (centro)
middle, centre; (promedio) average;
(método) means, way; (ambiente)
environment; **~s** nmpl means,
resources; **~ litro** half a litre; **las tres
y media** half past three; **medio
ambiente** environment; **M~ Oriente**
Middle East; **a ~ terminar** half
finished; **pagar a medias** to share the
cost; **~ambiental** adj (política, efectos)
environmental
mediocre [me'ðjokre] adj mediocre
mediodía [meðjo'ðia] nm midday,
noon
medir [me'ðir] vt, vi (gen) to measure
meditar [meði'tar] vt to ponder, think
over, meditate on; (planear) to think
out
mediterráneo, a [meðite'rraneo, a]
adj Mediterranean ♦ nm: **el M~** the
Mediterranean (Sea)
médula ['meðula] nf (ANAT) marrow;
~ espinal spinal cord
medusa [me'ðusa] (ESP) nf jellyfish
megafonía [meɣafo'nia] nf public
address system, PA system; **megáfono**
nm megaphone
megalómano, a [meɣa'lomano, a]
nm/f megalomaniac
mejicano, a [mexi'kano, a] adj, nm/f
Mexican
Méjico ['mexiko] nm Mexico

mejilla [me'xiʎa] nf cheek
mejillón [mexi'ʎon] nm mussel
mejor [me'xor] adj, adv (compar)
better; (superl) best; **a lo ~** probably;
(quizá) maybe; **~ dicho** rather; **tanto
~** so much the better
mejora [me'xora] nf improvement;
mejorar vt to improve, make better
♦ vi to improve, get better; **mejorarse**
vr to improve, get better
melancólico, a [melan'koliko, a] adj
(triste) sad, melancholy; (soñador)
dreamy
melena [me'lena] nf (de persona) long
hair; (ZOOL) mane
mellizo, a [me'ʎiθo, a] adj, nm/f twin;
~s nmpl (AM) cufflinks
melocotón [meloko'ton] (ESP) nm
peach
melodía [melo'ðia] nf melody, tune
melodrama [melo'ðrama] nm
melodrama; **melodramático, a** adj
melodramatic
melón [me'lon] nm melon
membrete [mem'brete] nm letterhead
membrillo [mem'briʎo] nm quince;
carne de ~ quince jelly
memorable [memo'raßle] adj
memorable
memoria [me'morja] nf (gen)
memory; **~s** nfpl (de autor) memoirs;
memorizar vt to memorize
menaje [me'naxe] nm: **~ de cocina**
kitchenware
mencionar [menθjo'nar] vt to
mention
mendigar [mendi'ɣar] vt to beg (for)
mendigo, a [men'diɣo, a] nm/f
beggar
mendrugo [men'druɣo] nm crust
menear [mene'ar] vt to move; **~se** vr
to shake; (balancearse) to sway;
(moverse) to move; (fig) to get a move
on
menestra [me'nestra] nf: **~ de
verduras** vegetable stew
menguante [men'gwante] adj

decreasing, diminishing

menguar [meŋ'gwar] vt to lessen, diminish ♦ vi to diminish, decrease

menopausia [meno'pausja] nf menopause

menor [me'nor] adj (más pequeño: compar) smaller; (: superl) smallest; (más joven: compar) younger; (: superl) youngest; (MUS) minor ♦ nm/f (joven) young person, juvenile; **no tengo la ~ idea** I haven't the faintest idea; **al por ~** retail; **~ de edad** person under age

Menorca [me'norka] nf Minorca

PALABRA CLAVE

---

menos [menos] adj 1: **~ (que, de)** (compar: cantidad) less (than); (: número) fewer (than); **con ~ entusiasmo** with less enthusiasm; **~ gente** fewer people; ver tb **cada**
2 (superl): **es el que ~ culpa tiene** is the least to blame
♦ adv 1 (compar): **~ (que, de)** less (than); **me gusta ~ que el otro** I like it less than the other one
2 (superl): **es el ~ listo (de su clase)** he's the least bright in his class; **de todas ellas es la que ~ me agrada** out of all of them she's the one I like least; **(por) lo ~** the (very) least
3 (locuciones): **no quiero verle y ~ visitarle** I don't want to see him let alone visit him; **tenemos 7 de ~** we're seven short
♦ prep except; (cifras) minus; **todos ~ él** everyone except (for) him; **5 ~ 2** 5 minus 2
♦ conj: **a ~ que: a ~ que venga mañana** unless he comes tomorrow

---

menospreciar [menospre'θjar] vt to underrate, undervalue; (despreciar) to scorn, despise

mensaje [men'saxe] nm message; **~ro, a** nm/f messenger

menstruación [menstrua'θjon] nf

menstruation

menstruar [mens'trwar] vi to menstruate

mensual [men'swal] adj monthly; **1000 ptas ~es** 1000 ptas a month; **~idad** nf (salario) monthly salary; (COM) monthly payment, monthly instalment

menta ['menta] nf mint

mental [men'tal] adj mental; **~idad** nf mentality; **~izar** vt (sensibilizar) to make aware; (convencer) to convince; (padres) to prepare (mentally); **~izarse** vr (concienciarse) to become aware; **~izarse (de)** to get used to the idea (of); **~izarse de que ...** (convencerse) to get it into one's head that ...

mentar [men'tar] vt to mention, name

mente ['mente] nf mind

mentir [men'tir] vi to lie

mentira [men'tira] nf (una ~) lie; (acto) lying; (invención) fiction; **parece ~ que ...** it seems incredible that ..., I can't believe that ...

mentiroso, a [menti'roso, a] adj lying ♦ nm/f liar

menú [me'nu] (pl ~s) nm menu; (AM) set meal; **~ del día** set menu

menudo, a [me'nuðo, a] adj (pequeño) small, tiny; (sin importancia) petty, insignificant; **¡~ negocio!** (fam) some deal!; **a ~** often, frequently

meñique [me'ɲike] nm little finger

meollo [me'oλo] nm (fig) core

mercado [mer'kaðo] nm market

mercancía [merkan'θia] nf commodity; **~s** nfpl goods, merchandise sg

mercantil [merkan'til] adj mercantile, commercial

mercenario, a [merθe'narjo, a] adj, nm mercenary

mercería [merθe'ria] nf haberdashery (BRIT), notions (US); (tienda) haberdasher's (BRIT), notions store (US); (AM) drapery

mercurio [mer'kurjo] nm mercury

merecer [mere'θer] vt to deserve, merit ♦ vi to be deserving, be worthy; **merece la pena** it's worthwhile; **merecido, a** adj (well) deserved; **llevar su merecido** to get one's deserts

merendar [meren'dar] vt to have for tea ♦ vi to have tea; (en el campo) to have a picnic; **merendero** nm open-air cafe

merengue [me'renge] nm meringue

meridiano [meri'ðjano] nm (GEO) meridian

merienda [me'rjenda] nf (light) tea, afternoon snack; (de campo) picnic

mérito ['merito] nm merit; (valor) worth, value

merluza [mer'luθa] nf hake

merma ['merma] nf decrease; (pérdida) wastage; **mermar** vt to reduce, lessen ♦ vi to decrease, dwindle

mermelada [merme'laða] nf jam

mero, a ['mero, a] adj mere; (AM: fam) very

merodear [meroðe'ar] vi: ~ **por** to prowl about

mes [mes] nm month

mesa ['mesa] nf table; (de trabajo) desk; (GEO) plateau; ~ **directiva** board; ~ **redonda** (reunión) round table; **poner/quitar la** ~ to lay/clear the table; **mesero, a** (AM) nm/f waiter/waitress

meseta [me'seta] nf (GEO) meseta, tableland

mesilla [me'siʎa] nf: ~ **(de noche)** bedside table

mesón [me'son] nm inn

mestizo, a [mes'tiθo, a] adj half-caste, of mixed race ♦ nm/f half-caste

mesura [me'sura] nf moderation, restraint

meta ['meta] nf goal; (de carrera) finish

metabolismo [metaβo'lismo] nm metabolism

metáfora [me'tafora] nf metaphor

metal [me'tal] nm (materia) metal; (MUS) brass; **metálico, a** adj metallic; (de metal) metal ♦ nm (dinero contante) cash

metalurgia [meta'lurxja] nf metallurgy

meteoro [mete'oro] nm meteor; **~logía** nf meteorology

meter [me'ter] vt (colocar) to put, place; (introducir) to put in, insert; (involucrar) to involve; (causar) to make, cause; ~**se** vr: ~**se en** to go into, enter; (fig) to interfere in, meddle in; ~**se a** to start; ~**se a escritor** to become a writer; ~**se con uno** to provoke sb, pick a quarrel with sb

meticuloso, a [metiku'loso, a] adj meticulous, thorough

metódico, a [me'toðiko, a] adj methodical

método [me'toðo] nm method

metralleta [metra'ʎeta] nf sub-machine-gun

métrico, a ['metriko, a] adj metric

metro ['metro] nm metre; (tren) underground (BRIT), subway (US)

México ['mexiko] nm Mexico; **Ciudad de ~** Mexico City

mezcla [me'θkla] nf mixture; **mezclar** vt to mix (up); **mezclarse** vr to mix, mingle; **mezclarse en** to get mixed up in, get involved in

mezquino, a [meθ'kino, a] adj mean

mezquita [meθ'kita] nf mosque

mg. abr (= miligramo) mg

mi [mi] adj pos my ♦ nm (MUS) E

mí [mi] pron me; myself

mía ['mia] pron ver **mío**

miaja ['mjaxa] nf crumb

michelín [mitʃe'lin] (fam) nm (de grasa) spare tyre

micro ['mikro] (AM) nm minibus

microbio [mi'kroβjo] nm microbe

micrófono [mi'krofono] nm microphone

microondas [mikro'ondas] nm inv (tb: horno ~) microwave (oven)

microscopio [mikro'skopjo] nm

microscope

miedo ['mjeðo] nm fear; (nerviosismo) apprehension, nervousness; **tener ~ to be afraid; de ~** wonderful, marvellous; **hace un frío de ~** (fam) it's terribly cold; **~so, a** adj fearful, timid

miel [mjel] nf honey

miembro ['mjembro] nm limb; (socio) member; **~ viril** penis

mientras ['mjentras] conj while; (duración) as long as ♦ adv meanwhile; **~ tanto** meanwhile; **~ más tiene, más quiere** the more he has, the more he wants

miércoles ['mjerkoles] nm inv Wednesday

mierda ['mjerða] (fam!) nf shit; (fig: meollo) essence; **hacer buenas ~s** (fam) to get on well

miga ['miɣa] nf crumb; (fig: meollo) essence; **hacer buenas ~s** (fam) to get on well

mil [mil] num thousand; **dos ~ libras** two thousand pounds

milagro [mi'laɣro] nm miracle; **~so, a** adj miraculous

milésima [mi'lesima] nf (de segundo) thousandth

mili ['mili] (fam) nf: **hacer la ~ to do** one's military service

milicia [mi'liθja] nf militia; (servicio militar) military service

milímetro [mi'limetro] nm millimetre

militante [mili'tante] adj militant

militar [mili'tar] adj military ♦ nm/f soldier ♦ vi (MIL) to serve; (en un partido) to be a member

milla ['miʎa] nf mile

millar [mi'ʎar] nm thousand

millón [mi'ʎon] num million; **millonario, a** nm/f millionaire

mimar [mi'mar] vt to spoil, pamper

mimbre ['mimbre] nm wicker

mímica ['mimika] nf (para comunicarse) sign language; (imitación) mimicry

mimo ['mimo] nm (caricia) caress; (de niño) spoiling; (TEATRO) mime; (: actor) mime artist

mina ['mina] nf mine; **minar** vt to mine; (fig) to undermine

mineral [mine'ral] adj mineral ♦ nm (GEO) mineral; (mena) ore

minero, a [mi'nero, a] adj mining cpd ♦ nm/f miner

miniatura [minja'tura] adj inv, nf miniature

minidisco [mini'disko] nm MiniDisc®

minifalda [mini'falda] nf miniskirt

mínimo, a ['minimo, a] adj, nm minimum

minino, a [mi'nino, a] (fam) nm/f puss, pussy

ministerio [minis'terjo] nm Ministry; **M~ de Hacienda/de Asuntos Exteriores** Treasury (BRIT), Treasury Department (US)/Foreign Office (BRIT), State Department (US)

ministro, a [mi'nistro, a] nm/f minister

minoría [mino'ria] nf minority

minucioso, a [minu'θjoso, a] adj thorough, meticulous; (prolijo) very detailed

minúscula [mi'nuskula] nf small letter

minúsculo, a [mi'nuskulo, a] adj tiny, minute

minusválido, a [minus'βaliðo, a] adj (physically) handicapped ♦ nm/f (physically) handicapped person

minuta [mi'nuta] nf (de comida) menu

minutero [minu'tero] nm minute hand

minuto [mi'nuto] nm minute

mío, a ['mio, a] pron: **el ~/la mía** mine; **un amigo ~** a friend of mine; **lo ~** what is mine

miope [mi'ope] adj short-sighted

mira ['mira] nf (de arma) sight(s) (pl); (fig) aim, intention

mirada [mi'raða] nf look, glance; (expresión) look, expression; **clavar la ~ en** to stare at; **echar una ~** to glance at

mirado, a [mi'raðo, a] adj (sensato) sensible; (considerado) considerate;

. **bien/mal ~** well/not well thought of;
. **bien ~** all things considered
mirador [mira'ðor] *nm* viewpoint,
vantage point
mirar [mi'rar] *vt* to look at; (*observar*)
to watch; (*considerar*) to consider,
think over; (*vigilar, cuidar*) to watch,
look after ♦ *vi* to look; (*ARQ*) to face;
~se *vr* (*dos personas*) to look at each
other; **~ bien/mal** to think highly of/
have a poor opinion of; **~se al espejo**
to look at o.s. in the mirror
mirilla [mi'riʎa] *nf* spyhole, peephole
mirlo ['mirlo] *nm* blackbird
misa ['misa] *nf* mass
miserable [mise'raßle] *adj* (*avaro*)
mean, stingy; (*nimio*) miserable, paltry;
(*lugar*) squalid; (*fam*) vile, despicable
♦ *nm/f* (*malvado*) rogue
miseria [mi'serja] *nf* (*pobreza*) poverty;
(*tacañería*) meanness, stinginess;
(*condiciones*) squalor; **una ~** a pittance
misericordia [miseri'korðja] *nf*
(*compasión*) compassion, pity; (*piedad*)
mercy
misil [mi'sil] *nm* missile
misión [mi'sjon] *nf* mission;
misionero, a *nm/f* missionary
mismo, a ['mismo, a] *adj* (*semejante*)
same; (*después de pron*) -self; (*para
énfasis*) very ♦ *adv*: **aquí/hoy ~** right
here/this very day; **ahora ~** right now
♦ *conj*: **lo ~ que** just like, just as; **el
~ traje** the same suit; **en ese
~ momento** at that very moment;
vino el ~ Ministro the minister
himself came; **yo ~ lo vi** I saw it
myself; **lo ~** the same (thing); **da lo ~**
it's all the same; **quedamos en las
mismas** we're no further forward; **por
lo ~** for the same reason
misterio [mis'terjo] *nm* mystery; **~so,
a** *adj* mysterious
mitad [mi'tað] *nf* (*medio*) half; (*centro*)
middle; **a ~ de precio** (a) half-price;
en o a ~ del camino halfway along
the road; **cortar por la ~** to cut

through the middle
mitigar [miti'var] *vt* to mitigate;
(*dolor*) to ease; (*sed*) to quench
mitin ['mitin] (*pl* **mítines**) *nm*
meeting
mito ['mito] *nm* myth
mixto, a ['miksto, a] *adj* mixed
ml. *abr* (= *mililitro*) ml
mm. *abr* (= *milímetro*) mm
mobiliario [moßi'ljarjo] *nm* furniture
mochila [mo'tʃila] *nf* rucksack (*BRIT*),
back-pack
moción [mo'θjon] *nf* motion
moco ['moko] *nm* mucus; **~s** *nmpl*
(*fam*) snot; **limpiarse los ~s de la
nariz** (*fam*) to wipe one's nose
moda ['moða] *nf* fashion; (*estilo*) style;
a la o de ~ in fashion, fashionable;
pasado de ~ out of fashion
modales [mo'ðales] *nmpl* manners
modalidad [moðali'ðað] *nf* kind,
variety
modelar [moðe'lar] *vt* to model
modelo [mo'ðelo] *adj inv, nm/f* model
módem ['moðem] *nm* (*INFORM*)
modem
moderado, a [moðe'raðo, a] *adj*
moderate
moderar [moðe'rar] *vt* to moderate;
(*violencia*) to restrain, control;
(*velocidad*) to reduce; **~se** *vr* to restrain
o.s., control o.s.
modernizar [moðerni'θar] *vt* to
modernize
moderno, a [mo'ðerno, a] *adj*
modern; (*actual*) present-day
modestia [mo'ðestja] *nf* modesty;
modesto, a *adj* modest
módico, a ['moðiko, a] *adj* moderate,
reasonable
modificar [moðifi'kar] *vt* to modify
modisto, a [mo'ðisto, a] *nm/f*
(*diseñador*) couturier, designer; (*que
confecciona*) dressmaker
modo ['moðo] *nm* way, manner; (*MUS*)
mode; **~s** *nmpl* manners; **de ningún ~**
in no way; **de todos ~s** at any rate;

~ de empleo directions pl (for use)

modorra [mo'ðorra] nf drowsiness

mofa ['mofa] nf: **hacer ~ de** to mock; **mofarse** vr: **mofarse de** to mock, scoff at

mogollón [moɣo'ʎon] (fam) adv a hell of a lot

moho ['moo] nm mould, mildew; (en metal) rust; **~so, a** adj mouldy; rusty

mojar [mo'xar] vt to wet; (humedecer) to damp(en), moisten; (calar) to soak; **~se** vr to get wet

mojón [mo'xon] nm boundary stone

molde ['molde] nm mould; (COSTURA) pattern; (fig) model; **~ado** nm soft perm; **~ar** vt to mould

mole ['mole] nf mass, bulk; (edificio) pile

moler [mo'ler] vt to grind, crush

molestar [moles'tar] vt to bother; (fastidiar) to annoy; (incomodar) to inconvenience, put out ♦ vi to be a nuisance; **~se** vr to bother; (incomodarse) to go to trouble; (ofenderse) to take offence; **¿(no) te molesta si ...?** do you mind if ...?

molestia [mo'lestja] nf bother, trouble; (incomodidad) inconvenience; (MED) discomfort; **es una ~** it's a nuisance; **molesto, a** adj (que fastidia) annoying; (incómodo) inconvenient; (inquieto) uncomfortable, ill at ease; (enfadado) annoyed

molido, a [mo'liðo, a] adj: **estar ~** (fig) to be exhausted o dead beat

molinillo [moli'niʎo] nm: **~ de carne/café** mincer/coffee grinder

molino [mo'lino] nm (edificio) mill; (máquina) grinder

momentáneo, a [momen'taneo, a] adj momentary

momento [mo'mento] nm moment; **de ~** at the moment, for the moment

momia ['momja] nf mummy

monarca [mo'narka] nm/f monarch, ruler; **monarquía** nf monarchy; **monárquico, a** nm/f royalist;

monarchist

monasterio [monas'terjo] nm monastery

mondar [mon'dar] vt to peel; **~se** vr: **~se de risa** (fam) to split one's sides laughing

moneda [mo'neða] nf (tipo de dinero) currency, money; (pieza) coin; **una ~ de 5 pesetas** a 5 peseta piece; **monedero** nm purse; **monetario, a** adj monetary, financial

monitor, a [moni'tor, a] nm/f instructor, coach ♦ nm (TV) set; (INFORM) monitor

monja ['monxa] nf nun

monje ['monxe] nm monk

mono, a ['mono, a] adj (bonito) lovely, pretty; (gracioso) nice, charming ♦ nm/f monkey, ape ♦ nm dungarees pl; (overoles) overalls pl

monopatín [monopa'tin] nm skateboard

monopolio [mono'poljo] nm monopoly; **monopolizar** vt to monopolize

monotonía [monoto'nia] nf (sonido) monotone; (fig) monotony

monótono, a [mo'notono, a] adj monotonous

monstruo ['monstrwo] nm monster ♦ adj inv fantastic; **~so, a** adj monstrous

montaje [mon'taxe] nm assembly; (TEATRO) décor; (CINE) montage

montaña [mon'taɲa] nf (monte) mountain; (sierra) mountains pl, mountainous area; (AM: selva) forest; **~ rusa** roller coaster; **montañero, a** nm/f mountaineer; **montañés, esa** nm/f highlander; **montañismo** nm mountaineering

montar [mon'tar] vt (subir a) to mount, get on; (TEC) to assemble, put together; (negocio) to set up; (arma) to cock; (colocar) to lift on to; (CULIN) to beat ♦ vi to mount, get on; (sobresalir) to overlap; **~ en cólera** to get angry;

~ a caballo to ride, go horseriding

monte ['monte] nm (montaña) mountain; (bosque) woodland; (área sin cultivar) wild area, wild country; **M~ de Piedad** pawnshop

montón [mon'ton] nm heap, pile; (fig): **un ~ de** heaps of, lots of

monumento [monu'mento] nm monument

monzón [mon'θon] nm monsoon

moño ['mopo] nm bun

moqueta [mo'keta] nf fitted carpet

mora ['mora] nf blackberry; ver tb **moro**

morada [mo'raða] nf (casa) dwelling, abode

morado, a [mo'raðo, a] adj purple, violet ♦ nm bruise

moral [mo'ral] adj moral ♦ nf (ética) ethics pl; (moralidad) morals pl, morality; (ánimo) morale

moraleja [mora'lexa] nf moral

moralidad [morali'ðað] nf morals pl, morality

morboso, a [mor'βoso, a] adj morbid

morcilla [mor'θiʎa] nf blood sausage, ≈ black pudding (BRIT)

mordaz [mor'ðaθ] adj (crítica) biting, scathing

mordaza [mor'ðaθa] nf (para la boca) gag; (TEC) clamp

morder [mor'ðer] vt to bite; (fig: consumir) to eat away, eat into; **mordisco** nm bite

moreno, a [mo'reno, a] adj (color) (dark) brown; (de tez) dark; (de pelo ~) dark-haired; (negro) black

morfina [mor'fina] nf morphine

moribundo, a [mori'βundo, a] adj dying

morir [mo'rir] vi to die; (fuego) to die down; (luz) to go out; **~se** vr to die; (fig) to be dying; **murió en un accidente** he was killed in an accident; **~se por algo** to be dying for sth

moro, a ['moro, a] adj Moorish ♦ nm/f

Moor

moroso, a [mo'roso, a] nm/f bad debtor, defaulter

morral [mo'rral] nm haversack

morro ['morro] nm (ZOOL) snout, nose; (AUTO, AVIAT) nose

morsa ['morsa] nf walrus

mortadela [morta'ðela] nf mortadella

mortaja [mor'taxa] nf shroud

mortal [mor'tal] adj mortal; (golpe) deadly; **~idad** nf mortality

mortero [mor'tero] nm mortar

mortífero, a [mor'tifero, a] adj deadly, lethal

mortificar [mortifi'kar] vt to mortify

mosca ['moska] nf fly

Moscú [mos'ku] n Moscow

mosquearse [moske'arse] (fam) vr (enojarse) to get cross; (ofenderse) to take offence

mosquitero [moski'tero] nm mosquito net

mosquito [mos'kito] nm mosquito

mostaza [mos'taθa] nf mustard

mosto ['mosto] nm (unfermented) grape juice

mostrador [mostra'ðor] nm (de tienda) counter; (de café) bar

mostrar [mos'trar] vt to show; (exhibir) to display, exhibit; (explicar) to explain; **~se** vr: **~se amable** to be kind; to prove to be kind; **no se muestra muy inteligente** he doesn't seem (to be) very intelligent

mota ['mota] nf speck, tiny piece; (en diseño) dot

mote ['mote] nm nickname

motín [mo'tin] nm (del pueblo) revolt, rising; (del ejército) mutiny

motivar [moti'βar] vt (causar) to cause, motivate; (explicar) to explain, justify; **motivo** nm motive, reason

moto ['moto] (fam) nf = **motocicleta**

motocicleta [motoθi'kleta] nf motorbike (BRIT), motorcycle

motor [mo'tor] nm motor, engine; **~ a chorro** o **de reacción/de explosión**

jet engine/internal combustion engine

motora [mo'tora] nf motorboat

movedizo, a [moße'ðiθo, a] adj ver **arena**

mover [mo'ßer] vt to move; (cabeza) to shake; (accionar) to drive; (fig) to cause, provoke; ~se vr to move; (fig) to get a move on

móvil ['moßil] adj mobile; (pieza de máquina) moving; (mueble) movable ♦ nm motive; **movilidad** nf mobility; **movilizar** vt to mobilize

movimiento [moßi'mjento] nm movement; (TEC) motion; (actividad) activity

mozo, a ['moθo, a] adj (joven) young ♦ nm/f youth, young man/girl

muchacho, a [mu'tʃatʃo, a] nm/f (niño) boy/girl; (criado) servant; (criada) maid

muchedumbre [mutʃe'ðumbre] nf crowd

PALABRA CLAVE
---

mucho, a ['mutʃo, a] adj **1** (cantidad) a lot of, much; (número) lots of, a lot of, many; ~ **dinero** a lot of money; **muchas amigas** lots o a lot of friends

2 (sg: grande): **ésta es mucha casa para él** this house is much too big for him

♦ pron: **tengo ~ que hacer** I've got a lot to do; ~**s dicen que ...** lots of people say that ...; ver tb **tener**

♦ adv **1**: **me gusta** ~ I like it a lot; **lo siento** ~ I'm very sorry; **come** ~ he eats a lot; **¿te vas a quedar** ~? are you going to be staying long?

2 (respuesta): **como** ~ at (the most); **¿estás cansado? –** ¡~! are you tired? – very!

3 (locuciones): **como** ~ at (the most); **con** ~: **el mejor con** ~ by far the best; **ni** ~ **menos**: **no es rico ni** ~ **menos** it's far from being rich

4: **por** ~ **que**: **por** ~ **que le creas** no

---

matter how o however much you believe her

---

muda ['muða] nf change of clothes

mudanza [mu'ðanθa] nf (de casa) move

mudar [mu'ðar] vt to change; (ZOOL) to shed ♦ vi to change; ~se vr (la ropa) to change; ~**se de casa** to move house

mudo, a ['muðo, a] adj dumb; (callado, CINE) silent

mueble ['mweβle] nm piece of furniture; ~**s** nmpl furniture sg

mueca ['mweka] nf face, grimace; **hacer** ~**s a** to make faces at

muela ['mwela] nf (back) tooth

muelle ['mweʎe]nm spring; (NAUT) wharf; (malecón) pier

muero etc vb ver **morir**

muerte ['mwerte] nf death; (homicidio) murder; **dar** ~ **a** to kill

muerto, a ['mwerto, a] pp de **morir** ♦ adj dead ♦ nm/f dead man/woman; (difunto) deceased; (cadáver) corpse; **estar** ~ **de cansancio** to be dead tired

muestra ['mwestra] nf (señal) indication, sign; (demostración) demonstration; (prueba) proof; (estadística) sample; (modelo) model, pattern; (testimonio) sample

muestreo [mwes'treo] nm sample, sampling

muestro etc vb ver **mostrar**

muevo etc vb ver **mover**

mugir [mu'xir] vi (vaca) to moo

mugre ['muxre] nf dirt, filth; **mugriento, a** adj dirty, filthy

mujer [mu'xer] nf woman; (esposa) wife; ~**iego** nm womanizer

mula ['mula] nf mule

muleta [mu'leta] nf (para andar) crutch; (TAUR) stick with red cape attached

mullido, a [mu'ʎiðo, a] adj (cama) soft; (hierba) soft, springy

multa ['multa] nf fine; **poner una ~ a** to fine; **multar** vt to fine

multicines [multi'θines] nmpl multiscreen cinema

multinacional [multinaθjo'nal] nf multinational

múltiple ['multiple] adj multiple; (pl) many, numerous

multiplicar [multipli'kar] vt (MAT) to multiply; (fig) to increase; **~se** vr (BIO) to multiply; (fig) to be everywhere at once

multitud [multi'tuð] nf (muchedumbre) crowd; **~ de** lots of

mundano, a [mun'dano, a] adj worldly

mundial [mun'djal] adj world-wide, universal; (guerra, récord) world cpd

mundo ['mundo] nm world; **todo el ~** everybody; **tener ~** to be experienced, know one's way around

munición [muni'θjon] nf ammunition

municipal [muniθi'pal] adj municipal, local

municipio [muni'θipjo] nm (ayuntamiento) town council, corporation; (territorio administrativo) town, municipality

muñeca [mu'ɲeka] nf (ANAT) wrist; (juguete) doll

muñeco [mu'ɲeko] nm (figura) figure; (marioneta) puppet; (fig) puppet, pawn

mural [mu'ral] adj mural, wall cpd
♦ nm mural

muralla [mu'raʎa] nf (city) wall(s) (pl)

murciélago [mur'θjelaɣo] nm bat

murmullo [mur'muʎo] nm murmur(ing); (cuchicheo) whispering

murmuración [murmura'θjon] nf gossip; **murmurar** vi to murmur, whisper; (cotillear) to gossip

muro ['muro] nm wall

muscular [musku'lar] adj muscular

músculo ['muskulo] nm muscle

museo [mu'seo] nm museum; **~ de arte** art gallery

musgo ['musɣo] nm moss

música ['musika] nf music; ver tb músico

músico, a ['musiko, a] adj musical
♦ nm/f musician

muslo ['muslo] nm thigh

mustio, a ['mustjo, a] adj (persona) depressed, gloomy; (planta) faded, withered

musulmán, ana [musul'man, ana] nm/f Moslem

mutación [muta'θjon] nf (BIO) mutation; (cambio) (sudden) change

mutilar [muti'lar] vt to mutilate; (a una persona) to maim

mutismo [mu'tismo] nm (de persona) uncommunicativeness; (de autoridades) silence

mutuamente [mutwa'mente] adv mutually

mutuo, a ['mutwo, a] adj mutual

muy [mwi] adv very; (demasiado) too; **M~ Señor mío** Dear Sir; **~ de noche** very late at night; **eso es ~ de él** that's just like him

N, n

N abr (= norte) N

nabo ['naβo] nm turnip

nácar ['nakar] nm mother-of-pearl

nacer [na'θer] vi to be born; (de huevo) to hatch; (vegetal) to sprout; (río) to rise; **nací en Barcelona** I was born in Barcelona; **nació una sospecha en su mente** a suspicion formed in her mind; **nacido, a** adj born; **recién nacido** newborn; **naciente** adj new, emerging; (sol) rising; **nacimiento** nm birth; (de Navidad) Nativity; (de río) source

nación [na'θjon] nf nation; **nacional** adj national; **nacionalismo** nm nationalism; **nacionalista** nm/f nationalist; **nacionalizar** vt to nationalize; **nacionalizarse** vr (persona) to become naturalized

nada ['naða] *pron* nothing ♦ *adv* not at all, in no way; **no decir ~** to say nothing, not to say anything; **~ más** nothing else; **de ~** don't mention it

nadador, a [naða'ðor, a] *nm/f* swimmer

nadar [na'ðar] *vi* to swim

nadie ['naðje] *pron* nobody, no-one; **~ habló** nobody spoke; **no había ~** there was nobody there, there wasn't anybody there

nado ['naðo]: **a ~** *adv*: **pasar a ~** to swim across

nafta ['nafta] (*AM*) *nf* petrol (*BRIT*), gas (*US*)

naipe ['naipe] *nm* (playing) card; **~s** *nmpl* cards

nalgas ['nalɣas] *nfpl* buttocks

nana ['nana] *nf* lullaby

naranja [na'ranxa] *adj inv, nf* orange; **media ~** (*fam*) better half; **naranjada** *nf* orangeade; **naranjo** *nm* orange tree

narciso [nar'θiso] *nm* narcissus

narcótico, a [nar'kotiko, a] *adj, nm* narcotic; **narcotizar** *vt* to drug; **narcotráfico** *nm* drug trafficking *o* running

nardo ['narðo] *nm* lily

narigudo, a [nari'ɣuðo, a] *adj* big-nosed

nariz [na'riθ] *nf* nose

narración [narra'θjon] *nf* narration; **narrador, a** *nm/f* narrator

narrar [na'rrar] *vt* to narrate, recount; **narrativa** *nf* narrative

nata ['nata] *nf* cream

natación [nata'θjon] *nf* swimming

natal [na'tal] *adj*: **ciudad ~** home town; **~idad** *nf* birth rate

natillas [na'tiʎas] *nfpl* custard *sg*

nativo, a [na'tiβo, a] *adj, nm/f* native

nato, a ['nato, a] *adj* born; **un músico ~** a born musician

natural [natu'ral] *adj* natural; (*fruta etc*) fresh ♦ *nm/f* native ♦ *nm* (*disposición*) nature

naturaleza [natura'leθa] *nf* nature;

(*género*) nature, kind; **~ muerta** still life

naturalidad [naturali'ðað] *nf* naturalness

naturalmente [natural'mente] *adv* (*de modo natural*) in a natural way; **¡~!** of course!

naufragar [naufra'ɣar] *vi* to sink; **naufragio** *nm* shipwreck; **náufrago, a** *nm/f* castaway, shipwrecked person

nauseabundo, a [nausea'βundo, a] *adj* nauseating, sickening

náuseas ['nauseas] *nfpl* nausea *sg*; **me da ~** it makes me feel sick

náutico, a ['nautiko, a] *adj* nautical

navaja [na'βaxa] *nf* knife; (*de barbero, peluquero*) razor

naval [na'βal] *adj* naval

Navarra [na'βarra] *n* Navarre

nave ['naβe] *nf* (*barco*) ship, vessel; (*ARQ*) nave; **~ espacial** spaceship

navegación [naβeɣa'θjon] *nf* navigation; (*viaje*) sea journey; **~ aérea** air traffic; **~ costera** coastal shipping; **navegador** *nm* (*INFORM*) browser; **navegante** *nm/f* navigator; **navegar** *vi* (*barco*) to sail; (*avión*) to fly

navidad [naβi'ðað] *nf* Christmas; **~es** *nfpl* Christmas time; **Feliz N~** Merry Christmas; **navideño, a** *adj* Christmas *cpd*

navío [na'βio] *nm* ship

nazca *etc vb ver* **nacer**

nazi ['naθi] *adj, nm/f* Nazi

NE *abr* (= *nor(d)este*) NE

neblina [ne'βlina] *nf* mist

nebulosa [neβu'losa] *nf* nebula

necesario, a [neθe'sarjo, a] *adj* necessary

neceser [neθe'ser] *nm* toilet bag; (*bolsa grande*) holdall

necesidad [neθesi'ðað] *nf* need; (*lo inevitable*) necessity; (*miseria*) poverty; **en caso de ~** in case of need *o* emergency; **hacer sus ~es** to relieve o.s.

necesitado, a [neθesi'taðo, a] *adj* needy, poor; **~ de** in need of

necesitar [neθesi'tar] vt to need, require

necio, a ['neθjo, a] adj foolish

necrópolis [ne'kropolis] nf inv cemetery

nectarina [nekta'rina] nf nectarine

nefasto, a [ne'fasto, a] adj ill-fated, unlucky

negación [neɣa'θjon] nf negation; *(rechazo)* refusal, denial

negar [ne'ɣar] vt *(renegar, rechazar)* to refuse; *(prohibir)* to refuse, deny; *(desmentir)* to deny; **~se** vr: **~se a** to refuse to

negativa [neɣa'tiβa] nf negative; *(rechazo)* refusal, denial

negativo, a [neɣa'tiβo, a] adj, nm negative

negligencia [neɣli'xenθja] nf negligence; **negligente** adj negligent

negociado [neɣo'θjaðo] nm department, section

negociante [neɣo'θjante] nm/f businessman/woman

negociar [neɣo'θjar] vt, vi to negotiate; **~ en** to deal in, trade in

negocio [ne'ɣoθjo] nm *(COM)* business; *(asunto)* affair, business; *(operación comercial)* deal, transaction; *(AM)* firm; *(lugar)* place of business; **los ~s** business sg; **hacer ~** to do business

negra ['neɣra] nf *(MUS)* crotchet; *ver tb* **negro**

negro, a ['neɣro, a] adj black; *(suerte)* awful ♦ nm black ♦ nm/f black man/woman

nene, a ['nene, a] nm/f baby, small child

nenúfar [ne'nufar] nm water lily

neologismo [neolo'xismo] nm neologism

neón [ne'on] nm: **luces/lámpara de ~** neon lights/lamp

neoyorquino, a [neojor'kino, a] adj (of) New York

nervio ['nerβjo] nm nerve

nerviosismo nm nervousness, nerves

pl; **~so, a** adj nervous

neto, a ['neto, a] adj net

neumático, a [neu'matiko, a] adj pneumatic ♦ nm *(ESP)* tyre *(BRIT)*, tire *(US)*; **~ de recambio** spare tyre

neurastenia, a [neuras'teniko, a] adj *(fig)* hysterical

neurólogo, a [neu'rolovo, a] nm/f neurologist

neurona [neu'rona] nf nerve cell

neutral [neu'tral] adj neutral; **~izar** to neutralize; *(contrarrestar)* to counteract

neutro, a ['neutro, a] adj *(BIO, LING)* neuter

neutrón [neu'tron] nm neutron

nevada [ne'βaða] nf snowstorm; *(caída de nieve)* snowfall

nevar [ne'βar] vi to snow

nevera [ne'βera] *(ESP)* nf refrigerator *(BRIT)*, icebox *(US)*

nevería [neβe'ria] *(AM)* nf ice-cream parlour

nexo ['nekso] nm link, connection

ni [ni] conj nor, neither; *(tb: ~ siquiera)* not ... even; **~ aunque que** not even if; **~ blanco ~ negro** neither white nor black

Nicaragua [nika'raɣwa] nf Nicaragua; **nicaragüense** adj, nm/f Nicaraguan

nicho ['nitʃo] nm niche

nicotina [niko'tina] nf nicotine

nido ['niðo] nm nest

niebla ['njeβla] nf fog; *(neblina)* mist

niego etc vb ver **negar**

nieto, a ['njeto, a] nm/f grandson/daughter; **~s** nmpl grandchildren

nieve etc ['njeβe] vb ver **nevar** ♦ nf snow; *(AM)* icecream

N.I.F. nm abr (= *Número de Identificación Fiscal*) personal identification number used for financial and tax purposes

nimiedad [nimje'ðað] nf triviality

nimio, a ['nimjo, a] adj trivial, insignificant

ninfa ['ninfa] nf nymph

ningún [nin'gun] adj ver **ninguno**

ninguno, a [nin'guno, a] (delante de nm: **ningún**) adj no ♦ pron (nadie) nobody; (ni uno) none, not one; (ni uno ni otro) neither; **de ninguna manera** by no means, not at all

niña ['niɲa] nf (ANAT) pupil; ver tb **niño**

niñera [ni'ɲera] nf nursemaid, nanny; **niñería** nf childish act

niñez [ni'ɲeθ] nf childhood; (infancia) infancy

niño, a ['niɲo, a] adj (joven) young; (inmaduro) immature ♦ nm/f child, boy/girl

nipón, ona [ni'pon, ona] adj, nm/f Japanese

níquel ['nikel] nm nickel; **niquelar** vt (TEC) to nickel-plate

níspero ['nispero] nm medlar

nitidez [niti'ðeθ] nf (claridad) clarity; (: de imagen) sharpness; **nítido, a** adj clear; sharp

nitrato [ni'trato] nm nitrate

nitrógeno [ni'troxeno] nm nitrogen

nivel [ni'ßel] nm (GEO) level; (norma) level, standard; (altura) height; **~ de aceite** oil level; **~ de aire** spirit level; **~ de vida** standard of living; **~ar** vt to level out; (fig) to even up; (COM) to balance

NN. UU. nfpl abr (= Naciones Unidas) UN sg

no [no] adv no; not; (con verbo) non ♦ excl no!; **~ tengo nada** I don't have anything, I have nothing; **~ es mío** it's not mine; **ahora ~** not now; **¿~ lo sabes?** don't you know?; **~ mucho** not much; **¡bien termine!** lo entregaré as soon as I finish I'll hand it over; **~ más: ayer ~ más** just yesterday; **¡pase ~ más!** come in!; **¡a que ~ lo sabes!** I bet you don't know!; **¡cómo ~!** of course!; **los países ~ alineados** the non-aligned countries; **la ~ intervención** non-intervention

noble ['noßle] adj, nm/f noble; **~za** nf nobility

noche ['notʃe] nf night, night-time; (la tarde) evening; **de ~, por la ~** at night; **es de ~** it's dark

---

Noche de San Juan

The **Noche de San Juan** on the 24th June is a **fiesta** coinciding with the summer solstice and which has taken the place of other ancient pagan festivals. Traditionally fire plays a major part in these festivities with celebrations and dancing taking place around bonfires in towns and villages across the country.

---

nochebuena [notʃe'ßwena] nf Christmas Eve

Nochebuena

Traditional Christmas celebrations in Spanish-speaking countries mainly take place on the night of **Nochebuena**, Christmas Eve. Families gather together for a large meal and the more religiously inclined attend Midnight Mass. While presents are traditionally given by **los Reyes Magos** on the 6th January, more and more people are exchanging gifts on Christmas Eve.

---

nochevieja [notʃe'ßjexa] nf New Year's Eve

noción [no'θjon] nf notion

nocivo, a [no'θißo, a] adj harmful

noctámbulo, a [nok'tambulo, a] nm/f sleepwalker

nocturno, a [nok'turno, a] adj (de la noche) nocturnal, night cpd; (de la tarde) evening cpd ♦ nm nocturne

nodriza [no'ðriθa] nf wet nurse; **buque** o **nave ~** supply ship

nogal [no'ɣal] nm walnut tree

nómada ['nomaða] adj nomadic ♦ nm/f nomad

nombramiento [nombra'mjento] nm naming; (a un empleo) appointment

nombrar [nom'brar] vt (designar) to name; (mencionar) to mention; (dar puesto a) to appoint

nombre ['nombre] nm name; (sustantivo) noun; ~ **y apellidos** name in full; ~ **común/propio** common/proper noun; ~ **de pila/de soltera** Christian/maiden name; **poner** ~ **a** to call, name

nómina ['nomina] nf (lista) payroll; (hoja) payslip

nominal [nomi'nal] adj nominal

nominar [nomi'nar] vt to nominate

nominativo, a [nomina'tiβo, a] adj (COM): **cheque** ~ **a X** cheque made out to X

nono, a ['nono, a] adj ninth

nordeste [nor'ðeste] adj north-east, north-eastern, north-easterly ♦ nm north-east

nórdico, a ['norðiko, a] adj Nordic

noreste [no'reste] adj, nm = **nordeste**

noria ['norja] nf (AGR) waterwheel; (de carnaval) big (BRIT) o Ferris (US) wheel

norma ['norma] nf rule (of thumb)

normal [nor'mal] adj (corriente) normal; (habitual) usual, natural; ~**idad** nf normality; **restablecer la** ~**idad** to restore order; ~**izar** vt (reglamentar) to normalize; (TEC) to standardize; ~**izarse** vr to return to normal; ~**mente** adv normally

normando, a [nor'mando, a] adj, nm/f Norman

normativa [norma'tiβa] nf (set of) rules pl, regulations pl

noroeste [noro'este] adj north-west, north-western, north-westerly ♦ nm north-west

norte ['norte] adj north, northern, northerly ♦ nm north; (fig) guide

norteamericano, a [norteameri'kano, a] adj, nm/f (North) American

Noruega [no'rweɣa] nf Norway

noruego, a [no'rweɣo, a] adj, nm/f Norwegian

nos [nos] pron (directo) us; (indirecto) us; to us; for us; from us; (reflexivo) (to) ourselves; (recíproco) (to) each other; ~ **levantamos a las 7** we get up at 7

nosotros, as [no'sotros, as] pron (sujeto) we; (después de prep) us

nostalgia [nos'talxja] nf nostalgia

nota ['nota] nf note; (ESCOL) mark

notable [no'taβle] adj notable; (ESCOL) outstanding

notar [no'tar] vt to notice, note; ~**se** vr to be obvious; **se nota que** ... one observes that ...

notarial [nota'rjal] adj: **acta** ~ affidavit

notario [no'tarjo] nm notary

noticia [no'tiθja] nf (información) piece of news; **las** ~**s** the news sg; **tener** ~**s de alguien** to hear from sb

noticiero [noti'θjero] (AM) nm news bulletin

notificación [notifika'θjon] nf notification; **notificar** vt to notify, inform

notoriedad [notorje'ðað] nf fame, renown; **notorio, a** adj (público) well-known; (evidente) obvious

novato, a [no'βato, a] adj inexperienced ♦ nm/f beginner, novice

novecientos, as [noβe'θjentos, as] num nine hundred

novedad [noβe'ðað] nf (calidad de nuevo) newness; (noticia) piece of news; (cambio) change, (new) development

novel [no'βel] adj new; (inexperto) inexperienced ♦ nm/f beginner

novela [no'βela] nf novel

noveno, a [no'βeno, a] adj ninth

noventa [no'βenta] num ninety

novia ['noβja] nf ver **novio**

noviazgo [no'βjaθɣo] nm engagement

novicio, a [no'βiθjo, a] nm/f novice

noviembre [no'βjembre] nm November

novillada [noβi'ʎaða] nf (TAUR) bullfight with young bulls; **novillero** nm novice bullfighter; **novillo** nm young bull, bullock; **hacer novillos** (fam) to play truant

novio, a ['noβjo, a] nm/f boyfriend/ girlfriend; (prometido) fiancé/fiancée; (recién casado) bridegroom/bride; **los ~s** the newly-weds

nubarrón [nuβa'rron] nm storm cloud

nube ['nuβe] nf cloud

nublado, a [nu'βlaðo, a] adj cloudy; **nublarse** vr to grow dark

nubosidad [nuβosi'ðað] nf cloudiness; **había mucha ~** it was very cloudy

nuca ['nuka] nf nape of the neck

nuclear [nukle'ar] adj nuclear

núcleo ['nukleo] nm (centro) core; (FÍSICA) nucleus

nudillo [nu'ðiʎo] nm knuckle

nudista [nu'ðista] adj nudist

nudo ['nuðo] nm knot; **~so, a** adj knotty

nuera ['nwera] nf daughter-in-law

nuestro, a ['nwestro, a] adj pos our ♦ pron ours; **padre** ~ our father; **un amigo ~** a friend of ours; **es el ~** it's ours

nueva ['nweβa] nf piece of news

nuevamente [nweβa'mente] adv (otra vez) again; (de nuevo) anew

Nueva York [-'jɔrk] n New York

Nueva Zelanda [-θe'landa] nf New Zealand

nueve ['nweβe] num nine

nuevo, a ['nweβo, a] adj (gen) new; **de ~** again

nuez [nweθ] nf walnut; **~ de Adán** Adam's apple; **~ moscada** nutmeg

nulidad [nuli'ðað] nf (incapacidad) incompetence; (abolición) nullity

nulo, a ['nulo, a] adj (inepto, torpe) useless; (inválido) (null and) void; (DEPORTE) drawn, tied

núm. abr (= número) no

numeración [numera'θjon] nf (cifras) numbers pl; (arábiga, romana etc) numerals pl

numeral [nume'ral] nm numeral

numerar [nume'rar] vt to number

número ['numero] nm (gen) number; (tamaño: de zapato) size; (ejemplar: de diario) number, issue; **sin ~** numberless, unnumbered; **~ de matrícula/de teléfono** registration/ telephone number; **~ atrasado** back number

numeroso, a [nume'roso, a] adj numerous

nunca ['nunka] adv (jamás) never; **~ lo pensé** I never thought it; **no viene ~** he never comes; **~ más** never again; **más que ~** more than ever

nupcias ['nupθjas] nfpl wedding sg, nuptials

nutria ['nutrja] nf otter

nutrición [nutri'θjon] nf nutrition

nutrido, a [nu'triðo, a] adj (alimentado) nourished; (fig: grande) large; (abundante) abundant

nutrir [nu'trir] vt (alimentar) to nourish; (dar de comer) to feed; (fig) to strengthen; **nutritivo, a** adj nourishing, nutritious

nylon [ni'lon] nm nylon

Ñ ñ

ñato, a ['ɲato, a] (AM) adj snub-nosed

ñoñería [ɲoɲe'ria] nf insipidness

ñoño, a ['ɲoɲo, a] adj (AM: tonto) silly, stupid; (soso) insipid; (persona) spineless

O, o

O abr (= oeste) W

o [o] conj or

o/ abr (= orden) o.

oasis [o'asis] nm inv oasis

obcecarse [oßθe'karse] vr to get o

become stubborn

obedecer [oßeðe'θer] *vt* to obey;
  obediencia *nf* obedience; **obediente**
  adj obedient

obertura [oßer'tura] *nf* overture

obesidad [oßesi'ðað] *nf* obesity;
  obeso, a *adj* obese

obispo [o'ßispo] *nm* bishop

objeción [oßxe'θjon] *nf* objection;
  poner objeciones to raise objections

objetar [oßxe'tar] *vt*, *vi* to object

objetivo, a [oßxe'tißo, a] *adj*, *nm*
  objective

objeto [oß'xeto] *nm* (*cosa*) object; (*fin*)
  aim

objetor, a [oßxe'tor, a] *nm/f* objector

oblicuo, a [o'ßlikwo, a] *adj* oblique;
  (*mirada*) sidelong

obligación [oßliɣa'θjon] *nf* obligation;
  (*COM*) bond

obligar [oßli'ßar] *vt* to force; **~se** *vr* to
  bind o.s.; **obligatorio, a** *adj*
  compulsory, obligatory

oboe [o'ßoe] *nm* oboe

obra ['oßra] *nf* work; (*ARQ*)
  construction, building; (*TEATRO*) play;
  ~ maestra masterpiece; **~s públicas**
  public works; **por ~ de** thanks to (the
  efforts of); **obrar** *vt* to work; (*tener
  efecto*) to have an effect on ♦ *vi* to
  behave; (*tener efecto*) to have an effect;
  la carta obra en su poder the letter
  is in his/her possession

obrero, a [o'ßrero, a] *adj* (*clase*)
  working; (*movimiento*) labour *cpd*
  ♦ *nm/f* (*gen*) worker; (*sin oficio*)
  labourer

obscenidad [oßsθeni'ðað] *nf*
  obscenity; **obsceno, a** *adj* obscene

obscu... = oscu...

obsequiar [oßse'kjar] *vt* (*ofrecer*) to
  present with; (*agasajar*) to make a fuss
  of, lavish attention on; **obsequio** *nm*
  (*regalo*) gift; (*cortesía*) courtesy,
  attention

observación [oßserßa'θjon] *nf*
  observation; (*reflexión*) remark

observador, a [oßserßa'ðor, a] *nm/f*
  observer

observar [oßser'ßar] *vt* to observe;
  (*anotar*) to notice; **~se** *vr* to keep to,
  observe

obsesión [oßse'sjon] *nf* obsession;
  obsesivo, a *adj* obsessive

obsoleto, a [oßso'leto, a] *adj* obsolete

obstáculo [oßs'takulo] *nm* obstacle;
  (*impedimento*) hindrance, drawback

obstante [oßs'tante]: **no ~** *adv*
  nevertheless

obstinado, a [oßsti'naðo, a] *adj*
  obstinate, stubborn

obstinarse [oßsti'narse] *vr* to be
  obstinate; **~ en** to persist in

obstrucción [oßstruk'θjon] *nf*
  obstruction; **obstruir** *vt* to obstruct

obtener [oßte'ner] *vt* (*gen*) to obtain;
  (*premio*) to win

obturador [oßtura'ðor] *nm* (*FOTO*)
  shutter

obvio, a ['oßßjo, a] *adj* obvious

oca ['oka] *nf* (*animal*) goose; (*juego*)
  ≈ snakes and ladders

ocasión [oka'sjon] *nf* (*oportunidad*)
  opportunity, chance; (*momento*)
  occasion, time; (*causa*) cause; **de ~**
  secondhand; **ocasionar** *vt* to cause

ocaso [o'kaso] *nm* (*fig*) decline

occidente [okθi'ðente] *nm* west

OCDE *nf abr* (= Organización de
  Cooperación y Desarrollo Económico)
  OECD

océano [o'θeano] *nm* ocean; **el
  ~ Índico** the Indian Ocean

ochenta [o'tʃenta] *num* eighty

ocho ['otʃo] *num* eight; **~ días** a week

ocio [o'θjo] *nm* (*tiempo*) leisure; (*pey*)
  idleness; **~so, a** *adj* (*inactivo*) idle;
  (*inútil*) useless

octavilla [okta'viʎa] *nf* leaflet,
  pamphlet

octavo, a [ok'taßo, a] *adj* eighth

octubre [ok'tußre] *nm* October

ocular [oku'lar] *adj* ocular, eye *cpd*;
  testigo ~ eyewitness

oculista [oku'lista] nm/f oculist

ocultar [okul'tar] vt (esconder) to hide; (callar) to conceal; **oculto, a** adj hidden; (fig) secret

ocupación [okupa'θjon] nf occupation

ocupado, a [oku'paðo, a] adj (persona) busy; (plaza) occupied, taken; (teléfono) engaged; **ocupar** vt (gen) to occupy; **ocuparse** vr: **ocuparse de o en** (gen) to concern o.s. with; (cuidar) to look after

ocurrencia [oku'rrenθja] nf (idea) bright idea

ocurrir [oku'rrir] vi to happen; **~se** vr: **se me ocurrió que ...** it occurred to me that ...

odiar [o'ðjar] vt to hate; **odio** nm hate, hatred; **odioso, a** adj (gen) hateful; (malo) nasty

odontólogo, a [oðon'toloxo, a] nm/f dentist, dental surgeon

OEA nf abr (= Organización de Estados Americanos) OAS

oeste [o'este] nm west; **una película del ~** a western

ofender [ofen'der] vt (agraviar) to offend; (insultar) to insult; **~se** vr to take offence; **ofensa** nf offence; **ofensiva** nf offensive; **ofensivo, a** adj offensive

oferta [o'ferta] nf offer; (propuesta) proposal; **la ~ y la demanda** supply and demand; **artículos en ~** goods on offer

oficial [ofi'θjal] adj official ♦ nm (MIL) officer

oficina [ofi'θina] nf office; **~ de correos** post office; **~ de turismo** tourist office; **oficinista** nm/f clerk

oficio [o'fiθjo] nm (profesión) profession; (puesto) post; (REL) service; **ser del ~** to be an old hand; **tener mucho ~** to have a lot of experience; **~ de difuntos** funeral service

oficioso, a [ofi'θjoso, a] adj (pey) officious; (no oficial) unofficial, informal

ofimática [ofi'matika] nf office

automation

ofrecer [ofre'θer] vt (dar) to offer; (proponer) to propose; **~se** vr (persona) to offer o.s., volunteer; (situación) to present itself; **¿qué se le ofrece?, ¿se le ofrece algo?** what can I do for you?, can I get you anything?

ofrecimiento [ofreθi'mjento] nm offer

oftalmólogo, a [oftal'molovo, a] nm/f ophthalmologist

ofuscar [ofus'kar] vt (por pasión) to blind; (por luz) to dazzle

oída [o'iða] nf: **de ~s** by hearsay

oído [o'iðo] nm (ANAT) ear; (sentido) hearing

oiga etc vb ver **oir**

oir [o'ir] vt (gen) to hear; (atender a) to listen to; **¡oiga!** listen!; **~ misa** to attend mass

OIT nf abr (= Organización Internacional del Trabajo) ILO

ojal [o'xal] nm buttonhole

ojalá [oxa'la] excl if only (it were so)!, some hope! ♦ conj if only ...!, would that ...!; **~ (que) venga hoy** I hope he comes today

ojeada [oxe'aða] nf glance

ojera [o'xera] nf: **tener ~s** to have bags under one's eyes

ojeriza [oxe'riθa] nf ill-will

ojeroso, a [oxe'roso, a] adj haggard

ojo ['oxo] nm eye; (de puente) span; (de cerradura) keyhole ♦ excl careful!; **tener ~ para** to have an eye for; **~ de buey** porthole

okupa [o'kupa] (fam) nm/f squatter

ola ['ola] nf wave

olé [o'le] excl bravo!, olé!

oleada [ole'aða] nf big wave, swell; (fig) wave

oleaje [ole'axe] nm swell

óleo ['oleo] nm oil; **oleoducto** [oleo'ðukto] nm (oil) pipeline

oler [o'ler] vt (gen) to smell; (inquirir) to pry into; (fig: sospechar) to sniff out ♦ vi to smell; **~ a** to smell of

olfatear [olfate'ar] vt to smell; (inquirir)

to pry into; **olfato** nm sense of smell

oligarquía [oliɣar'kia] nf oligarchy

olimpíada [olim'piaða] nf: **las O~s** the Olympics; **olímpico, a** [o'limpiko, a] adj Olympic

oliva [o'liβa] nf (aceituna) olive; **aceite de ~** olive oil; **olivo** [o'liβo] nm olive tree

olla ['oʎa] nf pan; (comida) stew; **~ a presión** o **exprés** pressure cooker; **~ podrida** type of Spanish stew

olmo ['olmo] nm elm (tree)

olor [o'lor] nm smell; **~oso, a** adj scented

olvidar [olβi'ðar] vt to forget; (omitir) to omit; **~se** vr (fig) to forget o.s.; **se me olvidó** I forgot

olvido [ol'βiðo] nm oblivion; (despiste) forgetfulness

ombligo [om'bliɣo] nm navel

omisión [omi'sjon] nf (abstención) omission; (descuido) neglect

omiso, a [o'miso, a] adj: **hacer caso ~ de** to ignore, pass over

omitir [omi'tir] vt to omit

omnipotente [omnipo'tente] adj omnipotent

omóplato [o'moplato] nm shoulder blade

OMS nf abr (= Organización Mundial de la Salud) WHO

once ['onθe] num eleven; **~s** (AM) nfpl tea break

onda ['onda] nf wave; **~ corta/larga/ media** short/long/medium wave; **ondear** vt, vi to wave; (tener ondas) to be wavy; (agua) to ripple; **ondearse** vr to swing, sway

ondulación [ondula'θjon] nf undulation; **ondulado, a** adj wavy

ondular [ondu'lar] vt (el pelo) to wave ♦ vi to undulate; **~se** vr to undulate

ONG nf abr (= organización no gubernamental) NGO

ONU ['onu] nf abr (= Organización de las Naciones Unidas) UNO

opaco, a [o'pako, a] adj opaque

opción [op'θjon] nf (gen) option;

(derecho) right, option

OPEP ['opep] nf abr (= Organización de Países Exportadores de Petróleo) OPEC

ópera ['opera] nf opera; **~ bufa** o **cómica** comic opera

operación [opera'θjon] nf (gen) operation; (COM) transaction, deal

operador, a [opera'ðor, a] nm/f operator; (CINE: proyección) projectionist; (: rodaje) cameraman

operar [ope'rar] vt (producir) to produce, bring about; (MED) to operate on ♦ vi (COM) to operate, deal; **~se** vr to occur; (MED) to have an operation

opereta [ope'reta] nf operetta

opinar [opi'nar] vt to think ♦ vi to think one's opinion; **opinión** [opi'njon] nf (creencia) belief; (criterio) opinion

opio ['opjo] nm opium

oponente [opo'nente] nm/f opponent

oponer [opo'ner] vt (resistencia) to put up, offer; **~se** vr (objetar) to object; (estar frente a frente) to be opposed; (dos personas) to oppose each other; **~ A a B** to set A against B; **me opongo a pensar que ...** I refuse to believe o think that ...

oportunidad [oportuni'ðað] nf (ocasión) opportunity; (posibilidad) chance

oportuno, a [opor'tuno, a] adj (en su tiempo) opportune, timely; (respuesta) suitable; **en el momento ~** at the right moment

oposición [oposi'θjon] nf opposition; **oposiciones** nfpl (ESCOL) public examinations

opositor, a [oposi'tor, a] nm/f (adversario) opponent; (candidato): **~ (a)** candidate (for)

opresión [opre'sjon] nf oppression; **opresivo, a** adj oppressive; **opresor, a** nm/f oppressor

oprimir [opri'mir] vt to squeeze; (fig) to oppress

optar [op'tar] vi (elegir) to choose; **~**

por to opt for; **optativo, a** *adj* optional

óptico, a [ˈoptiko, a] *adj* optic(al) ♦ *nm/f* optician; **óptica** *nf* optician's (shop); **desde esta óptica** from this point of view

optimismo [optiˈmismo] *nm* optimism; **optimista** *nm/f* optimist

óptimo, a [ˈoptimo, a] *adj* (el mejor) very best

opuesto, a [oˈpwesto, a] *adj* (contrario) opposite; (antagónico) opposing

opulencia [opuˈlenθja] *nf* opulence; **opulento, a** *adj* opulent

oración [oraˈθjon] *nf* (REL) prayer; (LING) sentence

orador, a [oraˈðor, a] *nm/f* (conferenciante) speaker, orator

oral [oˈral] *adj* oral

orangután [oranguˈtan] *nm* orangután

orar [oˈrar] *vi* to pray

oratoria [oraˈtorja] *nf* oratory

órbita [ˈorβita] *nf* orbit

orden [ˈorðen] *nm* (gen) order ♦ *nf* (gen) order; (INFORM) command; **~ del día** agenda; **de primer ~** first-rate; **en ~ de prioridad** in order of priority

ordenado, a [orðeˈnaðo, a] *adj* (metódico) methodical; (arreglado) orderly

ordenador [orðenaˈðor] *nm* computer; **~ central** mainframe computer

ordenanza [orðeˈnanθa] *nf* ordinance

ordenar [orðeˈnar] *vt* (mandar) to order; (poner orden) to put in order, arrange; **~se** *vr* (REL) to be ordained

ordeñar [orðeˈɲar] *vt* to milk

ordinario, a [orðiˈnarjo, a] *adj* (común) ordinary, usual; (vulgar) vulgar, common

orégano [oˈreɣano] *nm* oregano

oreja [oˈrexa] *nf* ear; (MECÁNICA) lug, flange

orfanato [orfaˈnato] *nm* orphanage

orfandad [orfanˈdað] *nf* orphanhood

orfebrería [orfeβreˈria] *nf* gold/silver work

orgánico, a [orˈɣaniko, a] *adj* organic

organigrama [orɣaniˈɣrama] *nm* flow chart

organismo [orɣaˈnismo] *nm* (BIO) organism; (POL) organization

organización [orɣaniθaˈθjon] *nf* organization; **organizar** *vt* to organize

órgano [ˈorɣano] *nm* organ

orgasmo [orˈɣasmo] *nm* orgasm

orgía [orˈxia] *nf* orgy

orgullo [orˈɣuʎo] *nm* pride; **orgulloso, a** *adj* (gen) proud; (altanero) haughty

orientación [orjentaˈθjon] *nf* (posición) position; (dirección) direction

oriental [orjenˈtal] *adj* eastern; (del Lejano Oriente) oriental

orientar [orjenˈtar] *vt* (situar) to orientate; (señalar) to point; (dirigir) to direct; (guiar) to guide; **~se** *vr* to get one's bearings

oriente [oˈrjente] *nm* east; **Cercano/Medio/Lejano O~** Near/Middle/Far East

origen [oˈrixen] *nm* origin

original [orixiˈnal] *adj* (nuevo) original; (extraño) odd, strange; **~idad** *nf* originality

originar [orixiˈnar] *vt* to start, cause; **~se** *vr* to originate; **~io, a** *adj* original; **~io de** native of

orilla [oˈriʎa] *nf* (borde) border; (de río) bank; (de bosque, tela) edge; (de mar) shore

orina [oˈrina] *nf* urine; **orinal** *nm* (chamber) pot; **orinar** *vi* to urinate; **orinarse** *vr* to wet o.s.; **orines** *nmpl* urine

oriundo, a [oˈrjundo, a] *adj*: **~ de** native of

ornitología [ornitoloˈxia] *nf* ornithology, bird-watching

oro [ˈoro] *nm* gold; **~s** *nmpl* (NAIPES) hearts

oropel [oro'pel] nm tinsel

orquesta [or'kesta] nf orchestra; **~ de cámara/sinfónica** chamber/ symphony orchestra

orquídea [or'kiðea] nf orchid

ortiga [or'tixa] nf nettle

ortodoxo, a [orto'ðokso, a] adj orthodox

ortografía [ortovra'fia] nf spelling

ortopedia [orto'peðja] nf orthopaedics sg; **ortopédico, a** adj orthopaedic

oruga [o'ruva] nf caterpillar

orzuelo [or'θwelo] nm stye

os [os] pron (gen) you; (a vosotros) to you

osa ['osa] nf (she-)bear; **O~ Mayor/ Menor** Great/Little Bear

osadía [osa'ðia] nf daring

osar [o'sar] vi to dare

oscilación [osθila'θjon] nf (movimiento) oscillation; (fluctuación) fluctuation

oscilar [osθi'lar] vi to oscillate; to fluctuate

oscurecer [oskure'θer] vt to darken ♦ vi to grow dark; **~se** vr to grow o get dark

oscuridad [oskuri'ðað] nf obscurity; (tinieblas) darkness

oscuro, a [os'kuro, a] adj dark; (fig) obscure; **a oscuras** in the dark

óseo, a ['oseo, a] adj bone cpd

oso ['oso] nm bear; **~ de peluche** teddy bear; **~ hormiguero** anteater

ostentación [ostenta'θjon] nf (gen) ostentation; (acto) display

ostentar [osten'tar] vt (gen) to show; (pey) to flaunt, show off; (poseer) to have, possess

ostra ['ostra] nf oyster

OTAN ['otan] nf abr (= Organización del Tratado del Atlántico Norte) NATO

otear [ote'ar] vt to observe; (fig) to look into

otitis [o'titis] nf earache

otoñal [oto'ɲal] adj autumnal

otoño [o'toɲo] nm autumn

otorgar [otor'xar] vt (conceder) to concede; (dar) to grant

otorrino, a [oto'rrino, a], **otorrinolaringólogo, a** [otorrinolarin'golovo, a] nm/f ear, nose and throat specialist

---
PALABRA CLAVE
---

otro, a ['otro, a] adj 1 (distinto: sg) another; (: pl) other; **con ~s amigos** with other o different friends

2 (adicional): **tráigame ~ café (más), por favor** can I have another coffee please; **~s 10 días más** another ten days

♦ pron 1: **el ~** the other one; **(los) ~s** (the) others; **de ~** somebody else's; **que lo haga ~** let somebody else do it

2 (recíproco): **se odian (la) una a (la) otra** they hate one another o each other

3: **~ tanto: comer ~ tanto** to eat the same o as much again; **recibió una decena de telegramas y otras tantas llamadas** he got about ten telegrams and as many calls

---

ovación [oßa'θjon] nf ovation

oval [o'ßal] adj oval; **~ado, a** adj oval; **óvalo** nm oval

ovario [o'ßarjo] nm ovary

oveja [o'ßexa] nf sheep

overol [oße'rol] (AM) nm overalls pl

ovillo [o'ßiʎo] nm (de lana) ball of wool; **hacerse un ~** to curl up

OVNI ['oßni] nm abr (= objeto volante no identificado) UFO

ovulación [oßula'θjon] nf ovulation; **óvulo** nm ovum

oxidación [oksiða'θjon] nf rusting

oxidar [oksi'ðar] vt to rust; **~se** vr to go rusty

óxido ['oksiðo] nm oxide

oxigenado, a [oksixe'naðo, a] adj (QUIM) oxygenated; (pelo) bleached

oxígeno [ok'sixeno] nm oxygen

oyente [o'jente] nm/f listener
oyes etc vb ver **oír**
ozono [o'θono] nm ozone

P, p

P abr (= **padre**) Fr.

pabellón [paβe'ʎon] nm bell tent; (ARQ) pavilion; (de hospital etc) block, section; (bandera) flag
pacer [pa'θer] vi to graze
paciencia [pa'θjenθja] nf patience
paciente [pa'θjente] adj, nm/f patient
pacificación [paθifika'θjon] nf pacification
pacificar [paθifi'kar] vt to pacify; (tranquilizar) to calm
pacífico, a [pa'θifiko, a] adj (persona) peaceable; (existencia) peaceful; **el (océano) P~** the Pacific (Ocean)
pacifismo [paθi'fismo] nm pacifism; **pacifista** nm/f pacifist
pacotilla [pako'tiʎa] nf: **de ~** (actor, escritor) third-rate; (mueble etc) cheap
pactar [pak'tar] vt to agree to o con ♦ vi to come to an agreement
pacto ['pakto] nm (tratado) pact; (acuerdo) agreement
padecer [paðe'θer] vt (sufrir) to suffer; (soportar) to endure, put up with; **padecimiento** nm suffering
padrastro [pa'ðrastro] nm stepfather
padre ['paðre] nm father ♦ adj (fam): **un éxito ~** a tremendous success; **~s** nmpl parents
padrino [pa'ðrino] nm (REL) godfather; (tb: **~ de boda**) best man; (fig) sponsor, patron; **~s** nmpl godparents
padrón [pa'ðron] nm (censo) census, roll
paella [pa'eʎa] nf paella, dish of rice with meat, shellfish etc
paga ['paɣa] nf (pago) payment; (sueldo) pay, wages pl
pagano, a [pa'ɣano, a] adj, nm/f

pagan, heathen
pagar [pa'ɣar] vt to pay; (las compras, crimen) to pay for; (fig: favor) to repay ♦ vi to pay; **~ al contado/a plazos** to pay (in) cash/in instalments
pagaré [paɣa're] nm I.O.U.
página ['paxina] nf page; **~ de inicio** (INFORM) home page
pago ['paɣo] nm (dinero) payment; **~ anticipado/a cuenta/contra reembolso/en especie** advance payment/payment on account/cash on delivery/payment in kind; **en ~ de** in return for
pág(s). abr (= **página(s)**) p(p).
pague etc vb ver **pagar**
país [pa'is] nm (gen) country; (región) land; **los P~es Bajos** the Low Countries; **el P~ Vasco** the Basque Country
paisaje [pai'saxe] nm landscape, scenery
paisano, a [pai'sano, a] adj of the same country ♦ nm/f (compatriota) fellow countryman/woman; **vestir de ~** (soldado) to be in civvies; (guardia) to be in plain clothes
paja ['paxa] nf straw; (fig) rubbish (BRIT), trash (US)
pajarita [paxa'rita] nf (corbata) bow tie
pájaro [paxaro] nm bird; **~ carpintero** woodpecker
pajita [pa'xita] nf (drinking) straw
pala ['pala] nf spade, shovel; (raqueta etc) bat; (: de tenis) racquet; (CULIN) slice; **~ matamoscas** fly swat
palabra [pa'laβra] nf word; (facultad) (power of) speech; (derecho de hablar) right to speak; **tomar la ~** (en mitin) to take the floor
palabrota [pala'βrota] nf swearword
palacio [pa'laθjo] nm palace; (mansión) mansion, large house; **~ de justicia** courthouse; **~ municipal** town/city hall
paladar [pala'ðar] nm palate; **paladear** vt to taste

palanca [pa'lanka] nf lever; (fig) pull, influence

palangana [palaŋ'gana] nf washbasin

palco ['palko] nm box

Palestina [pales'tina] nf Palestine; **palestino, a** nm/f Palestinian

paleta [pa'leta] nf (de pintor) palette; (de albañil) trowel; (de ping-pong) bat; (AM) ice lolly

paleto, a [pa'leto, a] (fam, pey) nm/f yokel

paliar [pa'ljar] vt (mitigar) to mitigate, alleviate; **paliativo** nm palliative

palidecer [paliðe'θer] vi to turn pale; **palidez** nf paleness; **pálido, a** adj pale

palillo [pa'liʎo] nm (mondadientes) toothpick; (para comer) chopstick

paliza [pa'liθa] nf beating, thrashing

palma ['palma] nf (ANAT) palm; (árbol) palm tree; **batir** o **dar ~s** to clap, applaud; **~da** nf slap; **~das** nfpl clapping sg, applause sg

palmar [pal'mar] (fam) vi (tb: ~la) to die, kick the bucket

palmear [palme'ar] vi to clap

palmera [pal'mera] nf (BOT) palm tree

palmo ['palmo] nm (medida) span; (fig) small amount; **~ a ~** inch by inch

palo ['palo] nm stick; (poste) post; (de tienda de campaña) pole; (mango) handle, shaft; (golpe) blow, hit; (de golf) club; (de béisbol) bat; (NAUT) mast; (NAIPES) suit

paloma [pa'loma] nf dove, pigeon

palomitas [palo'mitas] nfpl popcorn sg

palpar [pal'par] vt to touch, feel

palpitación [palpita'θjon] nf palpitation

palpitante [palpi'tante] adj palpitating; (fig) burning

palpitar [palpi'tar] vi to palpitate; (latir) to beat

palta ['palta] (AM) nf avocado (pear)

paludismo [palu'ðismo] nm malaria

pamela [pa'mela] nf picture hat, sun hat

pampa ['pampa] (AM) nf pampas, prairie

pan [pan] nm bread; (una barra) loaf; **~ integral** wholemeal (BRIT) o wholewheat (US) bread; **~ rallado** breadcrumbs pl

pana ['pana] nf corduroy

panadería [panaðe'ria] nf baker's (shop); **panadero, a** nm/f baker

Panamá [pana'ma] nm Panama; **panameño, a** adj Panamanian

pancarta [pan'karta] nf placard, banner

panda ['panda] nm (ZOOL) panda

pandereta [pande'reta] nf tambourine

pandilla [pan'diʎa] nf set, group; (de criminales) gang; (pey: camarilla) clique

panecillo [pane'θiʎo] nm (bread) roll

panel [pa'nel] nm panel; **~ solar** solar panel

panfleto [pan'fleto] nm pamphlet

pánico ['paniko] nm panic

panorama [pano'rama] nm panorama; (vista) view

pantalla [pan'taʎa] nf (de cine) screen; (de lámpara) lampshade

pantalón [panta'lon] nm trousers; **pantalones** nmpl trousers

pantano [pan'tano] nm (ciénaga) marsh, swamp; (depósito: de agua) reservoir; (fig) jam, difficulty

panteón [pante'on] nm: **~ familiar** family tomb

pantera [pan'tera] nf panther

panti(e)s [pantis] nmpl tights

pantomima [panto'mima] nf pantomime

pantorrilla [panto'rriʎa] nf calf (of the leg)

pantufla [pan'tufla] nf slipper

panty(s) ['pantis] nm(pl) tights

panza ['panθa] nf belly, paunch

pañal [pa'ɲal] nm nappy (BRIT), diaper (US); **~es** nmpl (fig) early stages, infancy sg

paño ['paɲo] nm (tela) cloth; (pedazo

de tela (piece of) cloth; (*trapo*) duster, rag; (*higiénico* sanitary towel; **~s menores** underclothes

pañuelo [pa'nwelo] *nm* handkerchief, hanky (*fam*); (*para la cabeza*) (head)scarf

papa ['papa] *nm*: **el P~** the Pope ♦ *nf* (AM) potato

papá [pa'pa] (*pl* **~s**) (*fam*) *nm* dad(dy), pa (US)

papada [pa'paða] *nf* double chin

papagayo [papa'vajo] *nm* parrot

papanatas [papa'natas] (*fam*) *nm inv* simpleton

paparrucha [papa'rrutʃa] *nf* piece of nonsense

papaya [pa'paja] *nf* papaya

papear [pape'ar] (*fam*) *vt, vi* to scoff

papel [pa'pel] *nm* paper; (*hoja de ~*) sheet of paper; (*TEATRO, fig*) role; **~ de calco/carbón/de cartas** tracing paper/carbon paper/stationery; **~ de envolver/pintado** wrapping paper/ wallpaper; **~ de aluminio/higiénico** aluminium (BRIT) o aluminum (US) foil/ toilet paper; **~ de estaño** o **plata** tinfoil; **~ de lija** sandpaper; **~ moneda** paper money; **~ secante** blotting paper

papeleo [pape'leo] *nm* red tape

papelera [pape'lera] *nf* wastepaper basket; (*en la calle*) litter bin

papelería [papele'ria] *nf* stationer's (shop)

papeleta [pape'leta] *nf* (*POL*) ballot paper; (*ESCOL*) report

paperas [pa'peras] *nfpl* mumps *sg*

papilla [pa'piʎa] *nf* (*para niños*) baby food

paquete [pa'kete] *nm* (*de cigarrillos etc*) packet; (*CORREOS etc*) parcel; (*AM*) package tour; (: *fam*) nuisance

par [par] *adj* (*igual*) like, equal; (*MAT*) even ♦ *nm* equal; (*de guantes*) pair; (*de veces*) couple; (*POL*) peer; (*GOLF, COM*) par; **abrir de ~ en ~** to open wide

para ['para] *prep* for; **no es ~ comer**

it's not for eating; **decir ~ sí** to say to o.s.; **¿~ qué lo quieres?** what do you want it for?; **se casaron ~ separarse otra vez** they married only to separate again; **lo tendré ~ mañana** I'll have it (for) tomorrow; **ir ~ casa** to go home, head for home; **~ profesor es muy estúpido** he's very stupid for a teacher; **¿quién es usted ~ gritar así?** who are you to shout like that?; **tengo bastante ~ vivir** I have enough to live on; *ver tb* **con**

parabién [para'βjen] *nm* congratulations *pl*

parábola [pa'raβola] *nf* parable; (*MAT*) parabola; **parabólica** *nf* (*tb: antena ~*) satellite dish

parabrisas [para'βrisas] *nm inv* windscreen (BRIT), windshield (US)

paracaídas [paraka'iðas] *nm inv* parachute; **paracaidista** *nm/f* parachutist; (*MIL*) paratrooper

parachoques [para'tʃokes] *nm inv* (*AUTO*) bumper; (*MECÁNICA etc*) shock absorber

parada [pa'raða] *nf* stop; (*acto*) stopping; (*de industria*) shutdown, stoppage; (*lugar*) stopping place; **~ de autobús** bus stop

paradero [para'ðero] *nm* stopping-place; (*situación*) whereabouts

parado, a [pa'raðo, a] *adj* (*persona*) motionless, standing still; (*fábrica*) closed, at a standstill; (*coche*) stopped; (*AM*) standing (up); (*sin empleo*) unemployed, idle

paradoja [para'ðoxa] *nf* paradox

parador [para'ðor] *nm* parador, state-run hotel

paráfrasis [pa'rafrasis] *nf inv* paraphrase

paraguas [pa'raɣwas] *nm inv* umbrella

Paraguay [para'ɣwai] *nm*: **el ~** Paraguay; **paraguayo, a** *adj, nm/f* Paraguayan

paraíso [para'iso] *nm* paradise, heaven

paraje [pa'raxe] *nm* place, spot

paralelo, a [para'lelo, a] *adj* parallel

parálisis [pa'ralisis] *nf inv* paralysis; **paralítico, a** *adj, nm/f* paralytic

paralizar [parali'θar] *vt* to paralyse; **~se** *vr* to become paralysed; (*fig*) to come to a standstill

paramilitar [paramili'tar] *adj* paramilitary

páramo ['paramo] *nm* bleak plateau

parangón [paran'gon] *nm*: **sin ~** incomparable

paranoico, a [para'noiko, a] *nm/f* paranoiac

parapente [para'pente] *nm* (*deporte*) paragliding; (*aparato*) paraglider

parapléjico, a [para'plexiko, a] *adj, nm/f* paraplegic

parar [pa'rar] *vt* to stop; (*golpe*) to ward off ♦ *vi* to stop; **~se** *vr* to stop; (*AM*) to stand up; **ha parado de llover** it has stopped raining; **van a ir a ~ a comisaría** they're going to end up in the police station; **~se en** to pay attention to

pararrayos [para'rrajos] *nm inv* lightning conductor

parásito, a [pa'rasito, a] *nm/f* parasite

parcela [par'θela] *nf* plot, piece of ground

parche ['partʃe] *nm* (*gen*) patch

parchís [par'tʃis] *nm* ludo

parcial [par'θjal] *adj* (*pago*) part-; (*eclipse*) partial; (*JUR*) prejudiced, biased; (*POL*) partisan; **~idad** *nf* prejudice, bias

pardillo, a [par'ðiʎo, a] (*pey*) *adj* yokel

parecer [pare'θer] *nm* (*opinión*) opinion, view; (*aspecto*) looks *pl* ♦ *vi* (*tener apariencia*) to seem, to look; (*asemejarse*) to seem o seem like; (*aparecer, llegar*) to appear; **~se** *vr* to look alike, resemble each other; **~se a** to look like, resemble; **según parece** evidently, apparently; **me parece que** I think (that), it seems to me

parecido, a [pare'θiðo, a] *adj* similar ♦ *nm* similarity, likeness, resemblance;

bien ~ good-looking, nice-looking

pared [pa'reð] *nf* wall

pareja [pa'rexa] *nf* (*par*) pair; (*dos personas*) couple; (*otro: de un par*) other one (of a pair); (*persona*) partner

parentela [paren'tela] *nf* relations *pl*

parentesco [paren'tesko] *nm* relationship

paréntesis [pa'rentesis] *nm inv* parenthesis; (*en escrito*) bracket

parezco *etc vb ver* **parecer**

pariente, a [pa'rjente, a] *nm/f* relative, relation

parir [pa'rir] *vt* to give birth to ♦ *vi* (*mujer*) to give birth, have a baby

París [pa'ris] *n* Paris

parking ['parkin] *nm* car park (*BRIT*), parking lot (*US*)

parlamentar [parlamen'tar] *vi* to parley

parlamentario, a [parlamen'tarjo, a] *adj* parliamentary ♦ *nm/f* member of parliament

parlamento [parla'mento] *nm* parliament

parlanchín, ina [parlan'tʃin, ina] *adj* indiscreet ♦ *nm/f* chatterbox

parlar [par'lar] *vi* to chatter (away)

paro ['paro] *nm* (*huelga*) stoppage of work), strike; (*desempleo*) unemployment; **subsidio de ~** unemployment benefit

parodia [pa'roðja] *nf* parody

parodiar *vt* to parody

parpadear [parpaðe'ar] *vi* (*ojos*) to blink; (*luz*) to flicker

párpado [par'paðo] *nm* eyelid

parque ['parke] *nm* (*lugar verde*) park; **~ de atracciones/infantil/zoológico** fairground/playground/zoo

parqué [par'ke] *nm* parquet (flooring)

parquímetro [par'kimetro] *nm* parking meter

parra ['parra] *nf* (grape)vine

párrafo ['parrafo] *nm* paragraph; **echar un ~** (*fam*) to have a chat

parranda [pa'rranda] (*fam*) *nf* spree,

binge

parrilla [pa'rriʎa] nf (CULIN:) grill; (de coche) grille; (**carne a la**) **~** barbecue; **~da** nf barbecue

párroco ['parroko] nm parish priest

parroquia [pa'rrokja] nf parish; (iglesia) parish church; (COM) clientele, customers pl; **~no, a** nm/f parishioner; client, customer

parsimonia [parsi'monja] nf calmness, level-headedness

parte ['parte] nm message; (informe) report ♦ nf (gen) part; (lado, cara) side; (de reparto) share; (JUR) party; **en alguna ~ de Europa** somewhere in Europe; **en/por todas ~s** everywhere; **en gran ~** to a large extent; **la mayor ~ de los españoles** most Spaniards; **de un tiempo a esta ~** for some time past; **de ~ de alguien** on sb's behalf; **¿de ~ de quién?** (TEL) who is speaking?; **por ~ de** on the part of; **yo por mí ~** I for my part; **por otra ~** on the other hand; **dar ~** to inform; **tomar ~** to take part

partición [parti'θjon] nf division, sharing-out; (POL) partition

participación [partiθipa'θjon] nf (acto) participation, taking part; (parte, COM) share; (de lotería) shared prize; (aviso) notice, notification

participante [partiθi'pante] nm/f participant

participar [partiθi'par] vt to notify, inform ♦ vi to take part, participate

partícipe [par'tiθipe] nm/f participant

particular [partiku'lar] adj (especial) particular, special; (individual, personal) private, personal ♦ nm (punto, asunto) particular, point; (individuo) individual; **tiene coche** ~ he has a car of his own

partida [par'tiða] nf (salida) departure; (COM) entry, item; (juego) game; (grupo de personas) band, group; **mala ~** dirty trick; **~ de nacimiento/ matrimonio/ defunción** birth/ marriage/ death certificate

partidario, a [parti'ðarjo, a] adj partisan ♦ nm/f supporter, follower

partido [par'tiðo] nm (POL) party; (DEPORTE) game, match; **sacar ~ de** to profit o benefit from; **tomar ~** to take sides

partir [par'tir] vt (dividir) to split, divide; (compartir, distribuir) to share (out), distribute; (romper) to break open, split open; (rebanada) to cut (off) ♦ vi (ponerse en camino) to set off o out; (comenzar) to start (off o out); **~se** vr to crack o split o break (in two etc); **a ~ de** (starting) from

partitura [parti'tura] nf (MUS) score

parto ['parto] nm birth; (fig) product, creation; **estar de ~** to be in labour

pasa ['pasa] nf raisin; **~ de Corinto/ Esmirna** currant/sultana

pasada [pa'saða] nf passing, passage; **de ~** in passing, incidentally; **una mala ~** a dirty trick

pasadizo [pasa'ðiθo] nm (pasillo) passage, corridor; (callejuela) alley

pasado, a [pa'saðo, a] adj past; (malo: comida, fruta) bad; (muy cocido) overdone; (anticuado) out of date ♦ nm past; **~ mañana** the day after tomorrow; **el mes ~** last month

pasador [pasa'ðor] nm (cerrojo) bolt; (de pelo) hair slide; (horquilla) grip

pasaje [pa'saxe] nm passage; (pago de viaje) fare; (los pasajeros) passengers pl; (pasillo) passageway

pasajero, a [pasa'xero, a] adj passing; (situación, estado) temporary; (amor, enfermedad) brief ♦ nm/f passenger

pasamontañas [pasamon'taɲas] nm inv balaclava helmet

pasaporte [pasa'porte] nm passport

pasar [pa'sar] vt to pass; (tiempo) to spend; (desgracias) to suffer, endure; (noticia) to give, pass on; (río) to cross; (barrera) to pass through; (falta) to overlook, tolerate; (contrincante) to surpass, do better than; (coche) to overtake; (CINE) to show; (enfermedad) to give, infect with ♦ vi (gen) to pass; (terminarse) to be over; (ocurrir) to happen; ~se vr (flores) to fade; (comida) to go bad o off; (fig) to overdo it, go too far; ~ de to go beyond, exceed; ~ por (AM) to fetch; ~lo bien/mal to have a good/bad time; ¡pase! come in!; hacer ~ to show in; ~se al enemigo to go over to the enemy; se me pasó I forgot; no se le pasa nada he misses nothing; pase lo que pase come what may; ¿qué pasa? what's going on?; what's up?; ¿qué te pasa? what's wrong?

pasarela [pasa'rela] nf footbridge; (en barco) gangway

pasatiempo [pasa'tjempo] nm pastime, hobby

Pascua ['paskwa] nf: ~ (de Resurrección) Easter; ~ de Navidad Christmas; ~s nfpl Christmas (time); ¡felices ~s! Merry Christmas!

pase ['pase] nm pass; (CINE) performance, showing

pasear [pase'ar] vt to take for a walk, (exhibir) to parade, show off ♦ vi to walk, go for a walk; ~se vr to walk, go for a walk; ~ en coche to go for a drive; **paseo** nm (avenida) avenue; (distancia corta) walk, stroll; **dar un** o **ir de paseo** to go for a walk

pasillo [pa'siʎo] nm passage, corridor

pasión [pa'sjon] nf passion

pasivo, a [pa'siβo, a] adj passive; (inactivo) inactive ♦ nm (COM) liabilities pl, debts pl

pasmar [pas'mar] vt (asombrar) to amaze, astonish; **pasmo** nm amazement, astonishment; (resfriado) chill; (fig) wonder, marvel; **pasmoso, a** adj amazing, astonishing

paso, a ['paso, a] adj dried ♦ nm step; (modo de andar) walk; (huella) footprint; (rapidez) speed, pace, rate; (camino accesible) way through, passage; (cruce) crossing; (pasaje)

passing, passage; (GEO) pass; (estrecho) strait; ~ a nivel (FERRO) level-crossing; ~ de peatones pedestrian crossing; a ese ~ (fig) at that rate; salir al ~ de o a to waylay; estar de ~ to be passing through; ~ elevado flyover; **prohibido el** ~ no entry; **ceda el** ~ give way

pasota [pa'sota] (fam) adj, nm/f ≈ dropout; **ser un (tipo)** ~ to be a bit of a dropout; (ser indiferente) not to care about anything

pasta ['pasta] nf paste; (CULIN: masa) dough; (: de bizcochos etc) pastry; (fam) dough; ~s nfpl (bizcochos) pastries, small cakes; (fideos, espaguetis etc) pasta; ~ de dientes o dentífrica toothpaste

pastar [pas'tar] vt, vi to graze

pastel [pas'tel] nm (dulce) cake; (ARTE) pastel; ~ de carne meat pie; ~ería nf cake shop

pasteurizado, a [pasteuri'θaðo, a] adj pasteurized

pastilla [pas'tiʎa] nf (de jabón, chocolate) bar; (píldora) tablet, pill

pasto ['pasto] nm (hierba) grass; (lugar) pasture, field

pastor, a [pas'tor, a] nm/f shepherd/ess ♦ nm (REL) clergyman, pastor; ~ alemán Alsatian

pata ['pata] nf (pierna) leg; (pie) foot; (de muebles) leg; ~s arriba upside down; **meterá de** ~ (fam) gaffe; **meter la** ~ (fam) to put one's foot in it; (TEC): ~ de cabra crowbar; **tener buena/mala** ~ to be lucky/unlucky; ~da nf kick; (en el suelo) stamp

patalear [patale'ar] vi (en el suelo) to stamp one's feet

patata [pa'tata] nf potato; ~s fritas chips, French fries; (de bolsa) crisps

paté [pa'te] nm pâté

patear [pate'ar] vt (pisar) to stamp on, trample on; (pegar con el pie) to kick ♦ vi to stamp (with rage), stamp one's feet

patentar [paten'tar] vt to patent

patente [pa'tente] adj obvious, evident; (COM) patent ♦ nf patent

paternal [pater'nal] adj fatherly, paternal; **paterno, a** adj paternal

patético, a [pa'tetiko, a] adj pathetic, moving

patilla [pa'tiʎa] nf (de gafas) side(piece); **~s** nfpl sideburns

patín [pa'tin] nm skate; (de trineo) runner; **patinaje** nm skating; **patinar** vi to skate; (resbalarse) to skid, slip; (fam) to slip up, blunder

patio ['patjo] nm (de casa) patio, courtyard; **~ de recreo** playground

pato ['pato] nm duck; **pagar el ~** (fam) to take the blame, carry the can

patológico, a [pato'loxiko, a] adj pathological

patoso, a [pa'toso, a] (fam) adj clumsy

patraña [pa'traɲa] nf story, fib

patria ['patrja] nf native land, mother country

patrimonio [patri'monjo] nm inheritance; (fig) heritage

patriota [pa'trjota] nm/f patriot; **patriotismo** nm patriotism

patrocinar [patroθi'nar] vt to sponsor; **patrocinio** nm sponsorship

patrón, ona [pa'tron, ona] nm/f (jefe) boss, chief, master/mistress; (propietario) landlord/lady; (REL) patron saint ♦ nm (TEC, COSTURA) pattern

patronal [patro'nal] adj: **la clase ~** management

patronato [patro'nato] nm sponsorship; (acto) patronage; (fundación benéfica) trust, foundation

patrulla [pa'truʎa] nf patrol

pausa ['pausa] nf pause, break

pausado, a [pau'saðo, a] adj slow, deliberate

pauta ['pauta] nf line, guide line

pavimento [paβi'mento] nm (con losas) pavement, paving

pavo ['paβo] nm turkey; **~ real** peacock

pavor [pa'βor] nm dread, terror

payaso, a [pa'jaso, a] nm/f clown

payo, a ['pajo, a] nm/f non-gipsy

paz [paθ] nf peace; (tranquilidad) peacefulness, tranquillity; **hacer las paces** to make peace; (fig) to make up

pazo ['paθo] nm country house

P.D. abr (= posdata) P.S., p.s.

peaje [pe'axe] nm toll

peatón [pea'ton] nm pedestrian

peca ['peka] nf freckle

pecado [pe'kaðo] nm sin; **pecador, a** adj sinful ♦ nm/f sinner

pecaminoso, a [pekami'noso, a] adj sinful

pecar [pe'kar] vi (REL) to sin; **peca de generoso** he is generous to a fault

pecera [pe'θera] nf fish tank; (redondo) goldfish bowl

pecho ['petʃo] nm (ANAT) chest; (de mujer) breast; **dar el ~ a** to breast-feed; **tomar algo a ~** to take sth to heart

pechuga [pe'tʃuɣa] nf breast

peculiar [peku'ljar] adj special, peculiar; (característico) typical, characteristic; **~idad** nf peculiarity; special feature, characteristic

pedal [pe'ðal] nm pedal; **~ear** vi to pedal

pedante [pe'ðante] adj pedantic ♦ nm/f pedant; **~ría** nf pedantry

pedazo [pe'ðaθo] nm piece, bit; **hacerse ~s** to smash, shatter

pedernal [peðer'nal] nm flint

pediatra [pe'ðjatra] nm/f paediatrician

pedido [pe'ðiðo] nm (COM) order; (petición) request

pedir [pe'ðir] vt to ask for, request; (comida, COM: mandar) to order; (necesitar) to need, demand, require ♦ vi to ask; **me pidió que cerrara la puerta** he asked me to shut the door; **¿cuánto piden por el coche?** how much are they asking for the car?

pedo ['peðo] (fam!) nm fart

pega ['peɣa] nf snag; **poner ~s (a)** to

complain (about)

pegadizo, a [peɣa'ðiθo, a] adj (MUS) catchy

pegajoso, a [peɣa'xoso, a] adj sticky, adhesive

pegamento [peɣa'mento] nm gum, glue

pegar [pe'ɣar] vt (papel, sellos) to stick (on); (cartel) to stick up; (coser) to sew (on); (unir: partes) to join, fix together; (MED) to give, infect with; (dar: golpe) to give, deal ♦ vi (adherirse) to stick, adhere; (ir juntos: colores) to match, go together; (golpear) to hit; (quemar: el sol) to strike hot, burn (fig); **~se** vr (gen) to stick; (dos personas) to hit each other, fight; (fam): **~ un grito** to let out a yell; **~ un salto** to jump (with fright); **~ en** to touch; **~se un tiro** to shoot o.s.

pegatina [peɣa'tina] nf sticker

pegote [pe'ɣote] (fam) nm eyesore, sight

peinado [pei'naðo] nm hairstyle

peinar [pei'nar] vt to comb; (hacer estilo) to style; **~se** vr to comb one's hair

peine ['peine] nm comb; **~ta** nf ornamental comb

p.ej. abr (= por ejemplo) e.g.

Pekín [pe'kin] n Peking(g)

pelado, a [pe'laðo, a] adj (fruta, patata etc) peeled; (cabeza) shorn; (campo, fig) bare; (fam: sin dinero) broke

pelaje [pe'laxe] nm (ZOOL) fur, coat; (fig) appearance

pelar [pe'lar] vt (fruta, patatas etc) to peel; (cortar el pelo a) to cut the hair of; (quitar la piel: animal) to skin; **~se** vr (la piel) to peel off; **voy a ~me** I'm going to get my hair cut

peldaño [pel'daɲo] nm step

pelea [pe'lea] nf (lucha) fight; (discusión) quarrel, row

peleado, a [pele'aðo, a] adj: **estar ~ (con uno)** to have fallen out (with sb)

pelear [pele'ar] vi to fight; **~se** vr (reñirse) to fight; (enemistarse) to fall out, quarrel

peletería [pelete'ria] nf furrier's, fur shop

pelícano [pe'likano] nm pelican

película [pe'likula] nf film; (cobertura ligera) thin covering; (FOTO: rollo) roll o reel of film

peligro [pe'liɣro] nm danger; (riesgo) risk; **correr ~ de** to run the risk of; **~so, a** adj dangerous; risky

pelirrojo, a [peli'rroxo, a] adj red-haired, red-headed ♦ nm/f redhead

pellejo [pe'ʎexo] nm (de animal) skin, hide

pellizcar [peʎiθ'kar] vt to pinch, nip

pelma ['pelma] (fam) nm/f pain (in the neck)

pelmazo [pel'maθo] (fam) nm = **pelma**

pelo ['pelo] nm (cabellos) hair; (de barba, bigote) whisker; (de animal: pellejo) hair, fur, coat; **al ~** just right; **venir al ~** to be exactly what one needs; **un hombre de ~ en pecho** a brave man; **por los ~s** by the skin of one's teeth; **no tener ~s en la lengua** to be outspoken, not mince words; **tomar el ~ a uno** to pull sb's leg

pelota [pe'lota] nf ball; **en ~** stark naked; **hacer la ~ (a uno)** (fam) to creep (to sb); **~ vasca** pelota

pelotari [pelo'tari] nm pelota player

pelotón [pelo'ton] nm (MIL) squad, detachment

peluca [pe'luka] nf wig

peluche [pe'lutʃe] nm: **oso/muñeco de ~** teddy bear/soft toy

peludo, a [pe'luðo, a] adj hairy, shaggy

peluquería [peluke'ria] nf hairdresser's; **peluquero, a** nm/f hairdresser

pelusa [pe'lusa] nf (BOT) down; (en tela) fluff

pena ['pena] nf (congoja) grief,

sadness; (*remordimiento*) regret; (*dificultad*) trouble; (*dolor*) pain; (*JUR*) sentence; **merecer** o **valer la ~** to be worthwhile; **a duras ~s** with great difficulty; **~ de muerte** death penalty; **~ pecuniaria** fine; **¡qué ~!** what a shame!

penal [pe'nal] *adj* penal ♦ *nm* (*cárcel*) prison

penalidad |penali'ðað| *nf* (*problema, dificultad*) trouble, hardship; (*JUR*) penalty, punishment; **~es** *nfpl* trouble, hardship

penalti, penalty [pe'nalti] (*pl* **~s** o **~es**) *nm* penalty kick

pendiente |pen'djente| *adj* pending, unsettled ♦ *nf* earring ♦ *nf* hill, slope

pene ['pene] *nm* penis

penetración |penetra'θjon| *nf* (*acto*) penetration; (*agudeza*) sharpness, insight

penetrante |pene'trante| *adj* (*herida*) deep; (*persona, arma*) sharp; (*sonido*) penetrating, piercing; (*mirada*) searching; (*viento, ironía*) biting

penetrar |pene'trar| *vt* to penetrate, pierce; (*entender*) to grasp ♦ *vi* to penetrate, go in; (*entrar*) to enter, go in; (*líquido*) to soak in; (*fig*) to pierce

penicilina |peniθi'lina| *nf* penicillin

península |pe'ninsula| *nf* peninsula; **peninsular** *adj* peninsular

penique |pe'nike| *nm* penny

penitencia |peni'tenθja| *nf* penance

penoso, a |pe'noso, a| *adj* (*doloroso*) (*lamentable*) distressing; (*difícil*) arduous, difficult

pensador, a |pensa'ðor, a| *nm/f* thinker

pensamiento |pensa'mjento| *nm* thought; (*mente*) mind; (*idea*) idea

pensar |pen'sar| *vt* to think; (*considerar*) to think over, think out; (*proponerse*) to intend, plan; (*imaginarse*) to think up, invent ♦ *vi* to think; **~ en** to aim at, aspire to; **pensativo, a** *adj* thoughtful, pensive

pensión |pen'sjon| *nf* (*casa*) boarding o guest house; (*dinero*) pension; (*cama y comida*) board and lodging; **~ completa** full board; **media ~** half-board; **pensionista** *nm/f* (*jubilado*) (old-age) pensioner; (*huésped*) lodger

penúltimo, a |pe'nultimo, a| *adj* penultimate, last but one

penumbra |pe'numbra| *nf* half-light

penuria |pe'nurja| *nf* shortage, want

peña |'pena| *nf* (*roca*) rock; (*cuesta*) cliff, crag; (*grupo*) group, circle; (*AM: club*) folk club

peñasco |pe'nasco| *nm* large rock, boulder

peñón |pe'non| *nm* wall of rock; **el P~** the Rock (of Gibraltar)

peón |pe'on| *nm* labourer; (*AM*) farm labourer, farmhand; (*AJEDREZ*) pawn

peonza |pe'onθa| *nf* spinning top

peor |pe'or| *adj* (*comparativo*) worse; (*superlativo*) worst ♦ *adv* worse; worst; **de mal en ~** from bad to worse

pepinillo |pepi'niʎo| *nm* gherkin

pepino |pe'pino| *nm* cucumber; (no) **me importa un ~** I don't care one bit

pepita |pe'pita| *nf* (*BOT*) pip; (*MINERÍA*) nugget

pepito |pe'pito| *nm*: **~ (de ternera)** steak sandwich

pequeñez |peke'neθ| *nf* smallness, littleness; (*trivialidad*) trifle, triviality

pequeño, a |pe'keno, a| *adj* small, little

pera |'pera| *nf* pear; **peral** *nm* pear tree

percance |per'kanθe| *nm* setback, misfortune

percatarse |perka'tarse| *vr*: **~ de** to notice, take note of

percebe |per'θeβe| *nm* barnacle

percepción |perθep'θjon| *nf* (*vista*) perception; (*idea*) notion, idea

percha |'pertʃa| *nf* (*coat*)hanger; (*ganchos*) coat hooks *pl*; (*de ave*) perch

percibir |perθi'ßir| *vt* to perceive, notice; (*COM*) to earn, get

percusión [perku'sjon] nf percussion

perdedor, a [perðe'ðor, a] adj losing
♦ nm/f loser

perder [per'ðer] vt to lose; (tiempo, palabras) to waste; (oportunidad) to lose, miss; (tren) to miss ♦ vi to lose; **~se** vr (extraviarse) to get lost; (desaparecer) to disappear, be lost to view; (arruinarse) to be ruined; **echar a ~** (comida) to spoil, ruin; (oportunidad) to waste

perdición [perði'θjon] nf perdition, ruin

pérdida ['perðiða] nf loss; (de tiempo) waste; **~s** nfpl (COM) losses

perdido, a [per'ðiðo, a] adj lost

perdiz [per'ðiθ] nf partridge

perdón [per'ðon] nm (disculpa) pardon, forgiveness; (clemencia) mercy; **¡~!** sorry!, I beg your pardon!;

perdonar vt to pardon, forgive; (la vida) to spare; (excusar) to exempt, excuse; **¡perdone (usted)!** sorry!, I beg your pardon!

perdurar [perðu'rar] vi (resistir) to last, endure; (seguir existiendo) to stand, still exist

perecedero, a [pereθe'ðero, a] adj perishable

perecer [pere'θer] vi to perish, die

peregrinación [peregrina'θjon] nf (REL) pilgrimage

peregrino, a [pere'yrino, a] adj (idea) strange, absurd ♦ nm/f pilgrim

perejil [pere'xil] nm parsley

perenne [pe'renne] adj everlasting, perennial

pereza [pe'reθa] nf laziness, idleness; **perezoso, a** adj lazy, idle

perfección [perfek'θjon] nf perfection; **perfeccionar** vt to perfect; (mejorar) to improve; (acabar) to complete, finish

perfectamente [perfekta'mente] adv perfectly

perfecto, a [per'fekto, a] adj perfect; (total) complete

perfil [per'fil] nm profile; (contorno) silhouette, outline; (ARQ) (cross) section; **~es** nmpl features; **~ar** vt (trazar) to outline; (fig) to shape, give character to

perforación [perfora'θjon] nf perforation; (con taladro) drilling; **perforadora** nf punch

perforar [perfo'rar] vt to perforate; (agujero) to drill, bore; (papel) to punch a hole in ♦ vi to drill, bore

perfume [per'fume] nm perfume, scent

pericia [pe'riθja] nf skill, expertise

periferia [peri'ferja] nf periphery; (de ciudad) outskirts pl

periférico [peri'feriko] (AM) nm ring road (BRIT), beltway (US)

perímetro [pe'rimetro] nm perimeter

periódico, a [pe'rjoðiko, a] adj periodic(al) ♦ nm newspaper

periodismo [perjo'ðismo] nm journalism; **periodista** nm/f journalist

periodo [pe'rjoðo] nm period

período [pe'rioðo] nm = **periodo**

periquito [peri'kito] nm budgerigar, budgie

perito, a [pe'rito, a] adj (experto) expert; (diestro) skilled, skilful ♦ nm/f expert; skilled worker; (técnico) technician

perjudicar [perxuði'kar] vt (gen) to damage, harm; **perjudicial** adj damaging, harmful; (en detrimento) detrimental; **perjuicio** nm damage, harm

perjurar [perxu'rar] vi to commit perjury

perla ['perla] nf pearl; **me viene de ~s** it suits me fine

permanecer [permane'θer] vi (quedarse) to stay, remain; (seguir) to continue to be

permanencia [perma'nenθja] nf permanence; (estancia) stay

permanente [perma'nente] adj permanent, constant ♦ nf perm

permiso [per'miso] nm permission; (*licencia*) permit, licence; **con ~** excuse me; **estar de ~** (MIL) to be on leave; **~ de conducir** driving licence (BRIT), driver's license (US)

permitir [permi'tir] vt to permit, allow

pernera [per'nera] nf trouser leg

pernicioso, a [perni'θjoso, a] adj pernicious

pero ['pero] conj but; (*aún*) yet ♦ nm (*defecto*) flaw, defect; (*reparo*) objection

perpendicular [perpendiku'lar] adj perpendicular

perpetrar [perpe'trar] vt to perpetrate

perpetuar [perpe'twar] vt to perpetuate; **perpetuo, a** [per'petwo, a] adj perpetual

perplejo, a [per'plexo, a] adj perplexed, bewildered

perra ['perra] nf (ZOOL) bitch; **estar sin una ~** to be flat broke

perrera [pe'rrera] nf kennel

perrito [pe'rrito] nm: **~ caliente** hot dog

perro ['perro] nm dog

persa ['persa] adj, nm/f Persian

persecución [perseku'θjon] nf pursuit, chase; (REL, POL) persecution

perseguir [perse'vir] vt to pursue, hunt; (*cortejar*) to chase after; (*molestar*) to pester, annoy; (REL, POL) to persecute

perseverante [perseβe'rante] adj persevering, persistent

perseverar [perseβe'rar] vi to persevere, persist

persiana [per'sjana] nf (Venetian) blind

persignarse [persiv'narse] vr to cross o.s.

persistente [persis'tente] adj persistent

persistir [persis'tir] vi to persist

persona [per'sona] nf person; **~ mayor** elderly person

personaje [perso'naxe] nm important person, celebrity; (TEATRO etc)

character

personal [perso'nal] adj (*particular*) personal; (*para una persona*) single, for one person ♦ nm personnel, staff; **~idad** nf personality

personarse [perso'narse] vr to appear in person

personificar [personifi'kar] vt to personify

perspectiva [perspek'tiβa] nf perspective; (*vista, panorama*) view, panorama; (*posibilidad futura*) outlook, prospect

perspicacia [perspi'kaθja] nf discernment, perspicacity

perspicaz [perspi'kaθ] adj shrewd

persuadir [perswa'ðir] vt (*gen*) to persuade; (*convencer*) to convince; **~se** vr to become convinced; **persuasión** nf persuasion; **persuasivo, a** adj persuasive, convincing

pertenecer [pertene'θer] vi to belong; (*fig*) to concern; **perteneciente** adj: **perteneciente a** belonging to; **pertenencia** nf ownership; **pertenencias** nfpl (*bienes*) possessions, property sg

pertenezca etc vb ver **pertenecer**

pértiga ['pertixa] nf: **salto de ~** pole vault

pertinente [perti'nente] adj relevant, pertinent; (*apropiado*) appropriate; **~ a** concerning, relevant to

perturbación [perturβa'θjon] nf (POL) disturbance; (MED) upset, disturbance

perturbado, a [pertur'βaðo, a] adj mentally unbalanced

perturbar [pertur'βar] vt (*el orden*) to disturb; (MED) to upset, disturb; (*mentalmente*) to perturb

Perú [pe'ru] nm: **el ~** Peru; **peruano, a** adj, nm/f Peruvian

perversión [perβer'sjon] nf perversion; **perverso, a** adj perverse; (*depravado*) depraved

pervertido, a [perβer'tiðo, a] adj perverted ♦ nm/f pervert

pervertir [perβer'tir] vt to pervert, corrupt

pesa ['pesa] nf weight; (DEPORTE) shot

pesadez [pesa'ðeθ] nf (peso) heaviness; (lentitud) slowness; (aburrimiento) tediousness

pesadilla [pesa'ðiʎa] nf nightmare, bad dream

pesado, a [pe'saðo, a] adj heavy; (lento) slow; (difícil, duro) tough, hard; (aburrido) boring, tedious; (tiempo) sultry

pésame ['pesame] nm expression of condolence, message of sympathy; **dar el ~** to express one's condolences

pesar [pe'sar] vt to weigh ♦ vi to weigh; (ser pesado) to weigh a lot, be heavy; (fig: opinión) to carry weight; **no pesa mucho** it is not very heavy ♦ nm (arrepentimiento) regret; (pena) grief, sorrow; **a ~ de o pese a (que)** in spite of, despite

pesca ['peska] nf (acto) fishing; (lo pescado) catch; **ir de ~** to go fishing

pescadería [peskaðe'ria] nf fish shop, fishmonger's

pescadilla [peska'ðiʎa] nf whiting

pescado [pes'kaðo] nm fish

pescador, a [peska'ðor, a] nm/f fisherman/woman

pescar [pes'kar] vt (tomar) to catch; (intentar tomar) to fish for; (conseguir: trabajo) to manage to get ♦ vi to fish, go fishing

pescuezo [pes'kweθo] nm neck

pesebre [pe'seβre] nm manger

peseta [pe'seta] nf peseta

pesimista [pesi'mista] adj pessimistic ♦ nm/f pessimist

pésimo, a ['pesimo, a] adj awful, dreadful

peso ['peso] nm weight; (balanza) scales pl; (moneda) peso; ~ **bruto/ neto** gross/net weight; **vender al ~** to sell by weight

pesquero, a [pes'kero, a] adj fishing cpd

pesquisa [pes'kisa] nf inquiry, investigation

pestaña [pes'taɲa] nf (ANAT) eyelash; (borde) rim; **pestañear** vi to blink

peste ['peste] nf plague; (mal olor) stink, stench

pesticida [pesti'θiða] nm pesticide

pestillo [pes'tiʎo] nm (cerrojo) bolt; (picaporte) doorhandle

petaca [pe'taka] nf (de cigarros) cigarette case; (de pipa) tobacco pouch; (AM: maleta) suitcase

pétalo ['petalo] nm petal

petardo [pe'tarðo] nm firework, firecracker

petición [peti'θjon] nf (pedido) request, plea; (memorial) petition; (JUR) plea

petrificar [petrifi'kar] vt to petrify

petróleo [pe'troleo] nm oil, petroleum; **petrolero, a** adj petroleum cpd ♦ nm (oil) tanker

peyorativo, a [pejora'tiβo, a] adj pejorative

pez [peθ] nm fish

pezón [pe'θon] nm teat, nipple

pezuña [pe'θuɲa] nf hoof

piadoso, a [pja'ðoso, a] adj (devoto) pious, devout; (misericordioso) kind, merciful

pianista [pja'nista] nm/f pianist

piano ['pjano] nm piano

piar [pjar] vi to cheep

pibe, a ['piβe, a] (AM) nm/f boy/girl

picadero [pika'ðero] nm riding school

picadillo [pika'ðiʎo] nm mince, minced meat

picado, a [pi'kaðo, a] adj pricked, punctured; (CULIN) minced, chopped; (mar) choppy; (diente) bad; (tabaco) cut; (enfadado) cross

picador [pika'ðor] nm (TAUR) picador; (minero) faceworker

picadura [pika'ðura] nf (pinchazo) puncture; (de abeja) sting; (de mosquito) bite; (tabaco picado) cut tobacco

picante [pi'kante] *adj* hot; (*comentario*) racy, spicy

picaporte [pika'porte] *nm* (*manija*) doorhandle; (*pestillo*) latch

picar [pi'kar] *vt* (*agujerear, perforar*) to prick, puncture; (*abeja*) to sting; (*mosquito, serpiente*) to bite; (*CULIN*) to mince, chop; (*incitar*) to incite, goad; (*dañar, irritar*) to annoy, bother; (*quemar: lengua*) to burn, sting ♦ *vi* (*pez*) to bite, take the bait; (*sol*) to burn, scorch; (*abeja, MED*) to sting; (*mosquito*) to bite; **~se** *vr* (*agriarse*) to turn sour, go off; (*ofenderse*) to take offence

picardía [pikar'ðia] *nf* villainy; (*astucia*) slyness, craftiness; (*travesura*) rude/bad word o expression

pícaro, a [pikaro, a] *adj* (*malicioso*) villainous; (*travieso*) mischievous ♦ *nm* (*astuto*) crafty sort; (*sinvergüenza*) rascal, scoundrel

pichón [pi'tʃon] *nm* young pigeon

pico [piko] *nm* (*de ave*) beak; (*punta*) sharp point; (*TEC*) pick, pickaxe; (*GEO*) peak, summit; **y ~** and a bit

picor [pi'kor] *nm* itch

picotear [pikote'ar] *vt* to peck ♦ *vi* to nibble, pick

picudo, a [pi'kuðo, a] *adj* pointed, with a point

pidió *etc vb ver* **pedir**

pido *etc vb ver* **pedir**

pie [pje] (*pl* **~s**) *nm* foot; (*fig: motivo*) motive, basis; (*: fundamento*) foothold; **ir a ~** to go on foot, walk; **estar de ~** to be standing (up); **ponerse de ~** to stand up; **de ~s a cabeza** from top to bottom; **al ~ de la letra** (*citar*) literally, verbatim; (*copiar*) exactly, word for word; **en ~ de guerra** on a war footing; **dar ~ a** to give cause for; **hacer ~** (*en el agua*) to touch (the) bottom

piedad [pje'ðað] *nf* (*lástima*) pity, compassion; (*clemencia*) mercy; (*devoción*) piety, devotion

piedra ['pjeðra] *nf* stone; (*roca*) rock; (*de mechero*) flint; (*METEOROLOGÍA*) hailstone

piel [pjel] *nf* (*ANAT*) skin; (*ZOOL*) skin, hide, fur; (*cuero*) leather; (*BOT*) skin, peel

pienso *etc vb ver* **pensar**

pierdo *etc vb ver* **perder**

pierna ['pjerna] *nf* leg

pieza ['pjeθa] *nf* piece; (*habitación*) room; **~ de recambio** o **repuesto** spare (part)

pigmeo, a [piɣ'meo, a] *adj, nm/f* pigmy

pijama [pi'xama] *nm* pyjamas *pl*

pila ['pila] *nf* (*ELEC*) battery; (*montón*) heap, pile; (*lavabo*) sink

píldora ['pildora] *nf* pill; **la ~** (*anticonceptiva*) (the contraceptive) pill

pileta [pi'leta] *nf* basin, bowl; (*AM*) swimming pool

pillaje [pi'ʎaxe] *nm* pillage, plunder

pillar [pi'ʎar] *vt* (*saquear*) to pillage, plunder; (*fam: coger*) to catch; (*: agarrar*) to grasp, seize; (*: entender*) to grasp, catch on to; **~se** *vr*: **~se un dedo con la puerta** to catch one's finger in the door

pillo, a [piʎo, a] *adj* villainous; (*astuto*) sly, crafty ♦ *nm/f* rascal, rogue, scoundrel

piloto [pi'loto] *nm* pilot; (*de aparato*) (pilot) light; (*AUTO: luz*) tail o rear light; (*: conductor*) driver

pimentón [pimen'ton] *nm* paprika

pimienta [pi'mjenta] *nf* pepper

pimiento [pi'mjento] *nm* pepper, pimiento

pin [pin] (*pl* **pins**) *nm* badge

pinacoteca [pinako'teka] *nf* art gallery

pinar [pi'nar] *nm* pine forest (*BRIT*), pine grove (*US*)

pincel [pin'θel] *nm* paintbrush

pinchadiscos [pintʃa'ðiskos] *nm/f inv* disc-jockey, DJ

pinchar [pin'tʃar] *vt* (*perforar*) to prick,

pierce; (*neumático*) to puncture; (*fig*) to prod

pinchazo [pin't∫aθo] *nm* (*perforación*) prick; (*de neumático*) puncture; (*fig*) prod

pincho ['pint∫o] *nm* savoury (snack); ~ **moruno** shish kebab; ~ **de tortilla** small slice of omelette

ping-pong [pin'pon] *nm* table tennis

pingüino [pin'gwino] *nm* penguin

pino ['pino] *nm* pine (tree)

pinta ['pinta] *nf* spot; (*de líquidos*) spot, drop; (*aspecto*) appearance, look(s) (*pl*); ~**do, a** *adj* spotted; (*de colores*) colourful; ~**das** *nfpl* graffiti *sg*

pintar [pin'tar] *vt* to paint ♦ *vi* to paint; (*fam*) to count, be important; ~**se** *vr* to put on make-up

pintor, a [pin'tor, a] *nm/f* painter

pintoresco, a [pinto'resko, a] *adj* picturesque

pintura [pin'tura] *nf* painting; ~ **a la acuarela** watercolour; ~ **al óleo** oil painting

pinza ['pinθa] *nf* (*ZOOL*) claw; (*para colgar ropa*) clothes peg; (*TEC*) pincers *pl*; ~**s** *nfpl* (*para depilar etc*) tweezers *pl*

piña ['pina] *nf* (*fruto del pino*) pine cone; (*fruta*) pineapple; (*fig*) group

piñón [pi'non] *nm* (*fruto*) pine nut; (*TEC*) pinion

pío, a ['pio, a] *adj* (*devoto*) pious, devout; (*misericordioso*) merciful

piojo ['pioxo] *nm* louse

pionero, a [pio'nero, a] *adj* pioneering ♦ *nm/f* pioneer

pipa ['pipa] *nf* pipe; ~**s** *nfpl* (*BOT*) (edible) sunflower seeds

pipí [pi'pi] (*fam*) *nm*: **hacer** ~ to have a wee-(wee) (*BRIT*), to go (wee-wee) (*US*)

pique ['pike] *nm* (*resentimiento*) pique, resentment; (*rivalidad*) rivalry, competition; **irse a** ~ to sink; (*esperanza, familia*) to be ruined

piqueta [pi'keta] *nf* pick(axe)

piquete [pi'kete] *nm* (*MIL*) squad,

party; (*de obreros*) picket

pirado, a [pi'raðo, a] (*fam*) *adj* round the bend ♦ *nm/f* nutter

piragua [pi'raɣwa] *nf* canoe; **piragüismo** *nm* canoeing

pirámide [pi'ramiðe] *nf* pyramid

pirata [pi'rata] *adj, nm* pirate ♦ *nm/f*: ~ **informático/a** hacker

Pirineo(s) [piri'neo(s)] *nm(pl)* Pyrenees *pl*

pirómano, a [pi'romano, a] *nm/f* (*MED, JUR*) arsonist

piropo [pi'ropo] *nm* compliment, (piece of) flattery

pirueta [pi'rweta] *nf* pirouette

pis [pis] (*fam*) *nm* pee, piss; **hacer** ~ to have a pee; (*para niños*) to wee-wee

pisada [pi'saða] *nf* (*paso*) footstep; (*huella*) footprint

pisar [pi'sar] *vt* (*caminar sobre*) to walk on, tread on; (*apretar con el pie*) to press; (*fig*) to trample on, walk all over ♦ *vi* to tread, step, walk

piscina [pis'θina] *nf* swimming pool

Piscis ['pisθis] *nm* Pisces

piso ['piso] *nm* (*suelo, planta*) floor; (*apartamento*) flat (*BRIT*), apartment; **primer** ~ (*ESP*) first floor; (*AM*) ground floor

pisotear [pisote'ar] *vt* to trample (on o underfoot)

pisotón [piso'ton] *nm* (*con el pie*) stamp (of the foot)

pista ['pista] *nf* track, trail; (*indicio*) clue; ~ **de aterrizaje** runway; ~ **de baile** dance floor; ~ **de hielo** ice rink; ~ **de tenis** tennis court

pistola [pis'tola] *nf* pistol; (*TEC*) spray-gun; **pistolero, a** *nm/f* gunman/woman, gangster

pistón [pis'ton] *nm* (*TEC*) piston; (*MUS*) key

pitar [pi'tar] *vt* (*silbato*) to blow; (*rechiflar*) to whistle o boo ♦ *vi* to whistle; (*AUTO*) to sound o toot one's horn; (*AM*) to smoke

pitillo [pi'tiʎo] *nm* cigarette

pito ['pito] *nm* whistle; (*de coche*) horn

pitón [pi'ton] *nm* (*ZOOL*) python

pitonisa [pito'nisa] *nf* fortune-teller

pitorreo [pito'rreo] *nm* joke; **estar de ~** to be joking

pizarra [pi'θarra] *nf* (*piedra*) slate; (*encerado*) blackboard

pizca ['piθka] *nf* pinch, spot; (*fig*) spot, speck; **ni ~** not a bit

placa ['plaka] *nf* plate; (*distintivo*) badge, insignia; **~ de matrícula** number plate

placentero, a [plaθen'tero, a] *adj* pleasant, agreeable

placer [pla'θer] *nm* pleasure ♦ *vt* to please

plácido, a ['plaθiðo, a] *adj* placid

plaga ['plaɣa] *nf* pest; (*MED*) plague; (*abundancia*) abundance; **plagar** *vt* to infest, plague; (*llenar*) to fill

plagio ['plaxjo] *nm* plagiarism

plan [plan] *nm* (*esquema, proyecto*) plan; (*idea, intento*) idea, intention; **tener ~** (*fam*) to have a date; **tener un ~** (*fam*) to have an affair; **en ~ económico** (*fam*) on the cheap; **vamos en ~ de turismo** we're going as tourists; **si te pones en ese ~** ... if that's your attitude

plana ['plana] *nf* sheet (of paper), page; (*TEC*) trowel; **en primera ~** on the front page; **~ mayor** staff

plancha ['plantʃa] *nf* (*para planchar*) iron; (*rótulo*) plate, sheet; (*NAUT*) gangway; **a la** (*CULIN*) grilled; **~do** *nm* ironing; **planchar** *vt* to iron ♦ *vi* to do the ironing

planeador [planea'ðor] *nm* glider

planear [plane'ar] *vt* to plan ♦ *vi* to glide

planeta [pla'neta] *nm* planet

planicie [pla'niθje] *nf* plain

planificación [planifika'θjon] *nf* planning; **~ familiar** family planning

plano, a ['plano, a] *adj* flat, level, even ♦ *nm* (*MAT, TEC*) plane; (*FOTO*) shot; (*ARQ*) plane; (*GEO*) map; (*de ciudad*) map, street plan; **primer ~** close-up; **caer de ~** to fall flat

planta ['planta] *nf* (*BOT, TEC*) plant; (*ANAT*) sole of the foot, foot; (*piso*) floor; (*AM: personal*) staff; **~ baja** ground floor

plantación [planta'θjon] *nf* (*AGR*) plantation; (*acto*) planting

plantar [plan'tar] *vt* (*BOT*) to plant; (*levantar*) to erect, set up; **~se** *vr* to stand firm; **~ a uno en la calle** to throw sb out; **dejar plantado a uno** (*fam*) to stand sb up

plantear [plante'ar] *vt* (*problema*) to pose; (*dificultad*) to raise

plantilla [plan'tiʎa] *nf* (*de zapato*) insole; (*personal*) personnel; **ser de ~** to be on the staff

plantón [plan'ton] *nm* (*MIL*) guard, sentry; (*fam*) long wait; **dar (un) ~ a uno** to stand sb up

plasmar [plas'mar] *vt* (*dar forma*) to mould, shape; (*representar*) to represent; **~se vr**: **~se en** to take the form of

plasta ['plasta] (*fam*) *adj inv* boring ♦ *nm/f* bore

plástico, a ['plastiko, a] *adj* plastic ♦ *nm* plastic

Plastilina ® [plasti'lina] *nf* Plasticine ®

plata ['plata] *nf* (*metal*) silver; (*cosas hechas de ~*) silverware; (*AM*) cash, dough; **hablar en ~** to speak bluntly o frankly

plataforma [plata'forma] *nf* platform; **~ de lanzamiento/perforación** launch(ing) pad/drilling rig

plátano ['platano] *nm* (*fruta*) banana; (*árbol*) plane tree; banana tree

platea [pla'tea] *nf* (*TEATRO*) pit

plateado, a [plate'aðo, a] *adj* silver; (*TEC*) silver-plated

plática ['platika] *nf* talk, chat; **platicar** *vi* to talk, chat

platillo [pla'tiʎo] *nm* saucer; **~s** *nmpl* (*MUS*) cymbals; **~ volador o volante** flying saucer

platino [pla'tino] *nm* platinum; **~s**

nmpl (AUTO) contact points

plato ['plato] *nm* plate, dish; *(parte de comida)* course; *(comida)* dish; **~ combinado** set main course *(served on one plate)*; **~ fuerte** main course; **primer ~** first course

playa ['plaja] *nf* beach; *(costa)* seaside; **~ de estacionamiento** *(AM)* car park

playera [pla'jera] *nf (AM: camiseta)* T-shirt; **~s** *nfpl (zapatos)* canvas shoes

plaza ['plaθa] *nf* square; *(mercado)* market(place); *(sitio)* room, space; *(en vehículo)* seat, place; *(colocación)* post, job; **~ de toros** bullring

plazo ['plaθo] *nm (lapso de tiempo)* time, period; *(fecha de vencimiento)* expiry date; *(pago parcial)* instalment; **a corto/largo ~** short-/long-term; **comprar algo a ~s** to buy sth on hire purchase *(BRIT)* o on time *(US)*

plazoleta [plaθo'leta] *nf* small square

pleamar [plea'mar] *nf* high tide

plebe ['pleβe] *nf*: **la ~** the common people *pl*, the masses *pl*; *(pey)* the plebs *pl*; **~yo, a** *adj* plebeian; *(pey)* coarse, common

plebiscito [pleβis'θito] *nm* plebiscite

plegable [ple'βaβle] *adj* collapsible; *(silla)* folding

plegar [ple'ɣar] *vt (doblar)* to fold, bend; *(COSTURA)* to pleat; **~se** *vr* to yield, submit

pleito ['pleito] *nm (JUR)* lawsuit, case; *(fig)* dispute, feud

plenilunio [pleni'lunjo] *nm* full moon

plenitud [pleni'tuð] *nf* plenitude, fullness; *(abundancia)* abundance

pleno, a ['pleno, a] *adj* full; *(completo)* complete ♦ *nm* plenum; **en ~ día** in broad daylight; **en ~ verano** at the height of summer; **en plena cara** full in the face

pliego etc ['pljeɣo] *vb ver* **plegar** ♦ *nm (hoja)* sheet (of paper); *(carta)* sealed letter/document; **~ de condiciones** details *pl*, specifications *pl*

pliegue etc ['pljeɣe] *vb ver* **plegar**

♦ *nm* fold, crease; *(de vestido)* pleat

plomero [plo'mero] *nm (AM)* plumber

plomo ['plomo] *nm (metal)* lead; *(ELEC)* fuse; **sin ~** unleaded

pluma ['pluma] *nf* feather; *(para escribir)*: **~ (estilográfica)** ink pen; **~ fuente** *(AM)* fountain pen

plumero [plu'mero] *nm (para el polvo)* feather duster

plumón [plu'mon] *nm (de ave)* down; *(AM: fino)* felt-tip pen; (: *ancho*) marker

plural [plu'ral] *adj* plural; **~idad** *nf* plurality

pluriempleo [pluriem'pleo] *nm* having more than one job

plus [plus] *nm* bonus; **~valía** *nf (COM)* appreciation

población [poβla'θjon] *nf* population; *(pueblo, ciudad)* town, city

poblado, a [po'βlaðo, a] *adj* inhabited ♦ *nm (aldea)* village; *(pueblo)* (small) town; **densamente ~** densely populated

poblador, a [poβla'ðor, a] *nm/f* settler, colonist

poblar [po'βlar] *vt (colonizar)* to colonize; *(fundar)* to found; *(habitar)* to inhabit

pobre ['poβre] *adj* poor ♦ *nm/f* poor person; **~za** *nf* poverty

pocilga [po'θilɣa] *nf* pigsty

pócima ['poθima] *nf* = **poción**

PALABRA CLAVE

poco, a ['poko, a] *adj* 1 *(sg)* little, not much; **~ tiempo** little o not much time; **de ~ interés** of little interest, not very interesting; **poca cosa** not much

2 *(pl)* few, not many; **unos ~s** a few, some; **~s niños comen lo que les conviene** few children eat what they should

♦ *adv* 1 little, not much; **cuesta ~** it doesn't cost much

2 (+ *adj:* = *negativo, antónimo*): **~ amable/inteligente** not very nice/

intelligent
3: por ~ me caigo I almost fell
4: a ~: a ~ de haberse casado
shortly after getting married
5: ~ a ~ little by little
♦ *nm* a little, a bit; **un ~ triste/de
dinero** a little sad/money

---

podar [po'ðar] *vt* to prune

PALABRA CLAVE

poder [po'ðer] *vi* **1** (*capacidad*) can, be
able to; **no puedo hacerlo** I can't do
it, I'm unable to do it
2 (*permiso*) can, may, be allowed to;
¿se puede? may I (o we)?; **puedes
irte ahora** you can go now; **no se
puede fumar en este hospital**
smoking is not allowed in this hospital
3 (*posibilidad*) may, might, could;
puede llegar mañana he may o
might arrive tomorrow; **pudiste
haberte hecho daño** you might o
could have hurt yourself; **¡podías
habérmelo dicho antes!** you might
have told me before!
4: puede ser: puede ser perhaps;
puede ser que lo sepa Tomás
Tomás may o might know
5: ¡no puedo más! I've had enough!;
no pude menos que dejarlo I
couldn't help but leave it; **es tonto a
más no ~** he's as stupid as they come
6: ~ con: no puedo con este crío
this kid's too much for me
♦ *nm* power; **~ adquisitivo**
purchasing power; **detentar** o **ocupar**
o **estar en el ~** to be in power

poderoso, a [poðe'roso, a] *adj*
(*político, país*) powerful
podio ['poðjo] *nm* (DEPORTE) podium
podium ['poðjum] = **podio**
podrido, a [po'ðriðo, a] *adj* rotten,
bad; (*fig*) rotten, corrupt
podrir [po'ðrir] = **pudrir**
poema [po'ema] *nm* poem

poesía [poe'sia] *nf* poetry
poeta [po'eta] *nm/f* poet; **poético, a**
adj poetic(al)
poetisa [poe'tisa] *nf* (woman) poet
póker ['poker] *nm* poker
polaco, a [po'lako, a] *adj* Polish
♦ *nm/f* Pole
polar [po'lar] *adj* polar; **~idad** *nf*
polarity; **~izarse** *vr* to polarize
polea [po'lea] *nf* pulley
polémica [po'lemika] *nf* polemics *sg*;
(*una ~*) controversy, polemic
polen ['polen] *nm* pollen
policía [poli'θia] *nm/f* policeman/
woman ♦ *nf* police; **~co, a** *adj* police
cpd; **novela policíaca** detective story;
policial *adj* police *cpd*
polideportivo [poliðepor'tiβo] *nm*
sports centre o complex
poligamia [poli'γamja] *nf* polygamy
polígono [po'liγono] *nm* (MAT)
polygon; **~ industrial** industrial estate
polilla [po'liλa] *nf* moth
polio ['poljo] *nf* polio
política [po'litika] *nf* politics *sg*;
(*económica, agraria etc*) policy; *ver tb*
político
político, a [po'litiko, a] *adj* political;
(*discreto*) tactful; (*de familia*) -in-law
♦ *nm/f* politician; **padre ~** father-in-
law
póliza ['poliθa] *nf* certificate, voucher;
(*impuesto*) tax stamp; **~ de seguros**
insurance policy
polizón [poli'θon] *nm* stowaway
pollera [po'λera] (AM) *nf* skirt
pollería [poλe'ria] *nf* poulterer's (shop)
pollo ['poλo] *nm* chicken
polo ['polo] *nm* (GEO, ELEC) pole;
(*helado*) ice lolly; (DEPORTE) polo;
(*suéter*) polo-neck; **~ Norte/Sur**
North/South Pole
Polonia [po'lonja] *nf* Poland
poltrona [pol'trona] *nf* easy chair
polución [polu'θjon] *nf* pollution
polvera [pol'βera] *nf* powder compact
polvo ['polβo] *nm* dust; (QUÍM, CULIN,

MED) powder; **~s** nmpl (maquillaje) powder sg; **quitar el ~** to dust; **~ de talco** talcum powder; **estar hecho ~** (fam) to be worn out o exhausted

pólvora [ˈpolβora] nf gunpowder; (fuegos artificiales) fireworks pl

polvoriento, a [polβoˈrjento, a] adj (superficie) dusty; (sustancia) powdery

pomada [poˈmaða] nf cream, ointment

pomelo [poˈmelo] nm grapefruit

pómez [ˈpomeθ] nf: **piedra ~** pumice stone

pomo [ˈpomo] nm doorknob

pompa [ˈpompa] nf (burbuja) bubble; (bomba) pump; (esplendor) pomp, splendour; **pomposo, a** adj splendid, magnificent; (pey) pompous

pómulo [ˈpomulo] nm cheekbone

pon [pon] vb ver **poner**

ponche [ˈpontʃe] nm punch

poncho [ˈpontʃo] nm poncho

ponderar [pondeˈrar] vt (considerar) to weigh up, consider; (elogiar) to praise highly, speak in praise of

pondré etc vb ver **poner**

PALABRA CLAVE

poner [poˈner] vt **1** (colocar) to put; (telegrama) to send; (obra de teatro) to put on; (película) to show; **ponlo más fuerte** turn it up; **¿qué ponen en el Excelsior?** what's on at the Excelsior?
2 (tienda) to open; (instalar: gas etc) to put in; (radio, TV) to switch o turn on
3 (suponer): **pongamos que ...** let's suppose that ...
4 (contribuir): **el gobierno ha puesto otro millón** the government has contributed another million
5 (TELEC): **póngame con el Sr. López** can you put me through to Mr. López?
6: **~ de**: **le han puesto de director general** they've appointed him general manager
7 (+ adj) to make; **me estás**

poniendo nerviosa you're making me nervous
8 (dar nombre): **al hijo le pusieron Diego** they called their son Diego
♦ vi (gallina) to lay
♦ **~se** vr **1** (colocarse): **se puso a mi lado** he came and stood beside me; **tú ponte en esa silla** you go and sit on that chair
2 (vestido, cosméticos) to put on; **¿por qué no te pones el vestido nuevo?** why don't you put on o wear your new dress?
3 (+ adj) to turn; to get, become: **se puso muy serio** he got very serious; **después de lavarla la tela se puso azul** after washing it the material turned blue
4: **~se a**: **se puso a llorar** he started to cry; **tienes que ~te a estudiar** you must get down to studying
5: **~se bien con uno** to make it up with sb; **~se mal con uno** to get on the wrong side of sb

---

pongo etc vb ver **poner**

poniente [poˈnjente] nm (occidente) west; (viento) west wind

pontífice [ponˈtifiθe] nm pope, pontiff

popa [ˈpopa] nf stern

popular [popuˈlar] adj popular; (cultura) of the people, folk cpd; **~idad** nf popularity; **~izarse** vr to become popular

---

PALABRA CLAVE

por [por] prep **1** (objetivo) for; **luchar ~ la patria** to fight for one's country
2 (+ infin): **no llegar tarde** so as not to arrive late; **~ citar unos ejemplos** to give a few examples
3 (causa) out of, because of; **~ escasez de fondos** through o for lack of funds
4 (tiempo): **~ la mañana/noche** in the morning/at night; **se queda ~ una semana** she's staying (for) a

week

5 (*lugar*): **pasar ~ Madrid** to pass through Madrid; **ir a Guayaquil ~ Quito** to go to Guayaquil via Quito; **caminar ~ la calle** to walk along the street; *ver tb* **bajo**

6 (*cambio, precio*): **te doy uno nuevo ~ el que tienes** I'll give you a new one (in return) for the one you've got

7 (*valor distributivo*): **550 pesetas ~ hora/cabeza** 550 pesetas an o per hour/a o per head

8 (*modo, medio*) by; **~ correo/avión** by post/air; **día ~ día** day by day; **entrar ~ la entrada principal** to go in through the main entrance

9: **10 ~ 10 son 100** 10 times 10 is 100

10 (*en lugar de*): **vino él ~ su jefe** he came instead of his boss

11: **~ mí que revienten** as far as I'm concerned they can drop dead

12: **¿~ qué?** why?; **¿~ qué no?** why not?

porcelana [porθe'lana] *nf* porcelain; (*china*) china

porcentaje [porθen'taxe] *nm* percentage

porción [por'θjon] *nf* (*parte*) portion, share; (*cantidad*) quantity, amount

pordiosero, a [porðjo'sero, a] *nm/f* beggar

porfiar [por'fjar] *vi* to persist, insist; (*disputar*) to argue stubbornly

pormenor [porme'nor] *nm* detail, particular

pornografía [pornovra'fia] *nf* pornography

poro ['poro] *nm* pore; **~so, a** *adj* porous

porque ['porke] *conj* (*a causa de*) because; (*ya que*) since; (*con el fin de*) so that, in order that

porqué [por'ke] *nm* reason, cause

porquería [porke'ria] *nf* (*suciedad*) filth, dirt; (*acción*) dirty trick; (*objeto*) small thing, trifle; (*fig*) rubbish

porra ['porra] *nf* (*arma*) stick, club

porrazo [po'rraθo] *nm* blow, bump

porro ['porro] (*fam*) *nm* (*droga*) joint (*fam*)

porrón [po'rron] *nm* glass wine jar with a long spout

portaaviones [porta(a)'βjones] *nm inv* aircraft carrier

portada [por'taða] *nf* (*de revista*) cover

portador, a [porta'ðor, a] *nm/f* carrier, bearer; (*COM*) bearer, payee

portaequipajes [portaeki'paxes] *nm inv* (*AUTO: maletero*) boot; (*: baca*) luggage rack

portal [por'tal] *nm* (*entrada*) vestibule, hall; (*portada*) porch, doorway; (*puerta de entrada*) main door

portamaletas [portama'letas] *nm inv* (*AUTO: maletero*) boot; (*: baca*) roof rack

portarse [por'tarse] *vr* to behave, conduct o.s.

portátil [por'tatil] *adj* portable

portavoz [porta'βoθ] *nm/f* spokesman/woman

portazo [por'taθo] *nm*: **dar un ~** to slam the door

porte ['porte] *nm* (*COM*) transport; (*precio*) transport charges *pl*

portento [por'tento] *nm* marvel, wonder; **~so, a** *adj* marvellous, extraordinary

porteño, a [por'teño, a] *adj* of o from Buenos Aires

portería [porte'ria] *nf* (*oficina*) porter's office; (*DEPORTE*) goal

portero, a [por'tero, a] *nm/f* porter; (*conserje*) caretaker; (*ujier*) doorman; (*DEPORTE*) goalkeeper; **~ automático** intercom

pórtico ['portiko] *nm* (*patio*) portico, porch; (*fig*) gateway; (*arcada*) arcade

portorriqueño, a [portorri'keño, a] *adj* Puerto Rican

Portugal [portu'val] *nm* Portugal; **portugués, esa** *adj, nm/f* Portuguese

♦ *nm* (*LING*) Portuguese

porvenir [porße'nir] *nm* future

pos [pos] *prep*: **en ~ de** after, in pursuit of

posada [po'saða] *nf* (*refugio*) shelter, lodging; (*mesón*) guest house; **dar ~ a** to give shelter to, take in

posaderas [posa'ðeras] *nfpl* backside *sg*, buttocks

posar [po'sar] *vt* (*en el suelo*) to lay down, put down; (*la mano*) to place, put gently ♦ *vi* (*modelo*) to sit, pose; **~se** *vr* to settle; (*pájaro*) to perch; (*avión*) to land, come down

posavasos [posa'βasos] *nm inv* coaster; (*para cerveza*) beermat

posdata [pos'ðata] *nf* postscript

pose ['pose] *nf* pose

poseedor, a [posee'ðor, a] *nm/f* owner, possessor; (*de récord, puesto*) holder

poseer [pose'er] *vt* to possess, own; (*ventaja*) to enjoy; (*récord, puesto*) to hold

posesión [pose'sjon] *nf* possession; **posesionarse** *vr*: **posesionarse de** to take possession of, take over

posesivo, a [pose'siβo, a] *adj* possessive

posgrado [pos'graðo] *nm*: **curso de ~** postgraduate course

posibilidad [posiβili'ðað] *nf* possibility; (*oportunidad*) chance; **posibilitar** *vt* to make possible; (*hacer realizable*) to make feasible

posible [po'siβle] *adj* possible; (*realizable*) feasible; **de ser ~** if possible; **en lo ~** as far as possible

posición [posi'θjon] *nf* position; (*rango social*) status

positivo, a [posi'tiβo, a] *adj* positive

poso ['poso] *nm* sediment; (*heces*) dregs *pl*

posponer [pospo'ner] *vt* (*relegar*) to put behind/below; (*aplazar*) to postpone

posta ['posta] *nf*: **a ~** deliberately, on purpose

postal [pos'tal] *adj* postal ♦ *nf* postcard

poste ['poste] *nm* (*de telégrafos etc*) post, pole; (*columna*) pillar

póster ['poster] (*pl* **pósteres, pósters**) *nm* poster

postergar [poster'var] *vt* to postpone, delay

posteridad [posteri'ðað] *nf* posterity

posterior [poste'rjor] *adj* back, rear; (*siguiente*) following, subsequent; (*más tarde*) later; **~idad** *nf*: **con ~idad** later, subsequently

postgrado [post'graðo] *nm* = **posgrado**

postizo, a [pos'tiθo, a] *adj* false, artificial ♦ *nm* hairpiece

postor [pos'tor, a] *nm/f* bidder

postre ['postre] *nm* sweet, dessert

postrero, a [pos'trero, a] (*delante de nmsg*: **postrer**) *adj* (*último*) last; (*que viene detrás*) rear

postulado [postu'laðo] *nm* postulate

póstumo, a ['postumo, a] *adj* posthumous

postura [pos'tura] *nf* (*del cuerpo*) posture, position; (*fig*) attitude, position

potable [po'taßle] *adj* drinkable; **agua ~** drinking water

potaje [po'taxe] *nm* thick vegetable soup

pote ['pote] *nm* pot, jar

potencia [po'tenθja] *nf* power; **~l** [poten'θjal] *adj, nm* potential; **~r** *vt* to boost

potente [po'tente] *adj* powerful

potro, a ['potro, a] *nm/f* (*ZOOL.*) colt/filly ♦ *nm* (*de gimnasia*) vaulting horse

pozo ['poθo] *nm* well; (*de río*) deep pool; (*de mina*) shaft

P.P. *abr* (= *porte pagado*) CP

práctica ['praktika] *nf* practice; (*método*) method; (*arte, capacidad*) skill; **en la ~** in practice

practicable [prakti'kaßle] *adj*

practicable; (*camino*) passable

practicante |prakti'kante| *nm/f* (*MED: ayudante de doctor*) medical assistant; (: *enfermero*) nurse; (*quien practica algo*) practitioner ♦ *adj* practising

practicar |prakti'kar| *vt* to practise; (*DEPORTE*) to play; (*realizar*) to carry out, perform

práctico, a |'praktiko, a| *adj* practical; (*instruido: persona*) skilled, expert

practique *etc vb ver* **practicar**

pradera |pra'ðera| *nf* meadow; (*US etc*) prairie

prado |'praðo| *nm* (*campo*) meadow, field; (*pastizal*) pasture

Praga |'praxa| *n* Prague

pragmático, a |prax'matiko, a| *adj* pragmatic

preámbulo |pre'ambulo| *nm* preamble, introduction

precario, a |pre'karjo, a| *adj* precarious

precaución |prekau'θjon| *nf* (*medida preventiva*) preventive measure, precaution; (*prudencia*) caution, wariness

precaver |preka'βer| *vt* to guard against; (*impedir*) to forestall; **~se** *vr*: **~se de** o **contra algo** to (be on one's) guard against sth; **precavido, a** *adj* cautious, wary

precedente |preθe'ðente| *adj* preceding; (*anterior*) former ♦ *nm* precedent

preceder |preθe'ðer| *vt, vi* to precede, go before, come before

precepto |pre'θepto| *nm* precept

preciado, a |pre'θjaðo, a| *adj* (*estimado*) esteemed, valuable

preciarse |pre'θjarse| *vr* to boast; **~se de** to pride o.s. on, boast of being

precinto |pre'θinto| *nm* (*tb:* **~ de garantía**) seal

precio |'preθjo| *nm* price; (*costo*) cost; (*valor*) value, worth; (*de viaje*) fare; **~ al contado/de coste/de oportunidad** cash/cost/bargain price; **~ al detalle** o

al por menor retail price; **~ tope** top price

preciosidad |preθjosi'ðað| *nf* (*valor*) (high) value, (great) worth; (*encanto*) charm; (*cosa bonita*) beautiful thing; **es una ~** it's lovely, it's really beautiful

precioso, a |pre'θjoso, a| *adj* precious; (*de mucho valor*) valuable; (*fam*) lovely, beautiful

precipicio |preθi'piθjo| *nm* cliff, precipice; (*fig*) abyss

precipitación |preθipita'θjon| *nf* haste; (*lluvia*) rainfall

precipitado, a |preθipi'taðo, a| *adj* (*conducta*) hasty, rash; (*salida*) hasty, sudden

precipitar |preθipi'tar| *vt* (*arrojar*) to hurl down, throw; (*apresurar*) to hasten; (*acelerar*) to speed up, accelerate; **~se** *vr* to throw o.s.; (*apresurarse*) to rush; (*actuar sin pensar*) to act rashly

precisamente |preθisa'mente| *adv* precisely; (*exactamente*) precisely, exactly

precisar |preθi'sar| *vt* (*necesitar*) to need, require; (*fijar*) to determine exactly, fix; (*especificar*) to specify

precisión |preθi'sjon| *nf* (*exactitud*) precision

preciso, a |pre'θiso, a| *adj* (*exacto*) precise; (*necesario*) necessary, essential

preconcebido, a |prekonθe'βiðo, a| *adj* preconceived

precoz |pre'koθ| *adj* (*persona*) precocious; (*calvicie etc*) premature

precursor, a |prekur'sor, a| *nm/f* predecessor, forerunner

predecir |preðe'θir| *vt* to predict, forecast

predestinado, a |preðesti'naðo, a| *adj* predestined

predicar |preði'kar| *vt, vi* to preach

predicción |preðik'θjon| *nf* prediction

predilecto, a |preði'lekto, a| *adj* favourite

predisponer |preðispo'ner| *vt* to

predispose; (*pey*) to prejudice;
predisposición *nf* inclination;
prejudice, bias

predominante [preðomi'nante] *adj*
predominant

predominar [preðomi'nar] *vt* to
dominate ♦ *vi* to predominate;
(*prevalecer*) to prevail; **predominio**
nm predominance; prevalence

preescolar [pre(e)sko'lar] *adj*
preschool

prefabricado, a [prefaβri'kaðo, a] *adj*
prefabricated

prefacio [pre'faθjo] *nm* preface

preferencia [prefe'renθja] *nf*
preference; **de ~** preferably, for
preference

preferible [prefe'riβle] *adj* preferable

preferir [prefe'rir] *vt* to prefer

prefiero *etc vb ver* **preferir**

prefijo [pre'fixo] *nm* (*TELEC*) (dialling)
code

pregonar [prego'nar] *vt* to proclaim,
announce

pregunta [pre'ɣunta] *nf* question;
hacer una ~ to ask a question

preguntar [preɣun'tar] *vt* to ask;
(*cuestionar*) to question ♦ *vi* to ask; **~se**
vr to wonder; **~ por alguien** to ask for
sb

preguntón, ona [preɣun'ton, ona]
adj inquisitive

prehistórico, a [preis'toriko, a] *adj*
prehistoric

prejuicio [pre'xwiθjo] *nm* (*acto*)
prejudgement; (*idea preconcebida*)
preconception; (*parcialidad*) prejudice,
bias

preliminar [prelimi'nar] *adj*
preliminary

preludio [pre'luðjo] *nm* prelude

prematuro, a [prema'turo, a] *adj*
premature

premeditación [premeðita'θjon] *nf*
premeditation

premeditar [premeði'tar] *vt* to
premeditate

premiar [pre'mjar] *vt* to reward; (*en
un concurso*) to give a prize to

premio ['premjo] *nm* reward; prize;
(*COM*) premium

premonición [premoni'θjon] *nf*
premonition

prenatal [prena'tal] *adj* antenatal,
prenatal

prenda ['prenda] *nf* (*ropa*) garment,
article of clothing; (*garantía*) pledge;
~s *nfpl* (*talentos*) talents, gifts

prendedor [prende'ðor] *nm* brooch

prender [pren'der] *vt* (*captar*) to catch,
capture; (*detener*) to arrest; (*COSTURA*)
to pin, attach; (*sujetar*) to fasten ♦ *vi* to
catch; (*arraigar*) to take root; **~se** *vr*
(*encenderse*) to catch fire

prendido, a [pren'diðo, a] (*AM*) *adj*
(*luz etc*) on

prensa ['prensa] *nf* press; **la ~** the
press; **prensar** *vt* to press

preñado, a [pre'ɲaðo, a] *adj*
pregnant; **~ de** pregnant with, full of

preocupación [preokupa'θjon] *nf*
worry, concern; (*ansiedad*) anxiety

preocupado, a [preoku'paðo, a] *adj*
worried, concerned; (*ansioso*) anxious

preocupar [preoku'par] *vt* to worry;
~se *vr* to worry; **~se de algo** (*hacerse
cargo*) to take care of sth

preparación [prepara'θjon] *nf* (*acto*)
preparation; (*estado*) readiness;
(*entrenamiento*) training

preparado, a [prepa'raðo, a] *adj*
(*dispuesto*) prepared; (*CULIN*) ready (to
serve) ♦ *nm* preparation

preparar [prepa'rar] *vt* (*disponer*) to
prepare, get ready; (*TEC*: *tratar*) to
prepare, process; (*entrenar*) to teach,
train; **~se** *vr*: **~se a o para** to prepare
to o for, get ready to o for;
preparativo, a *adj* preparatory,
preliminary; **preparativos** *nmpl*
preparations; **preparatoria** (*AM*) *nf*
sixth-form college (*BRIT*), senior high
school (*US*)

prerrogativa [prerroɣa'tiβa] *nf*

prerogative, privilege

presa ['presa] nf (cosa apresada) catch; (víctima) victim; (de animal) prey; (de agua) dam

presagiar [presa'xjar] vt to presage, forebode; **presagio** nm omen

prescindir [presθin'dir] vi: ~ de (privarse de) to do without, go without; (descartar) to dispense with

prescribir [preskri'βir] vt to prescribe; **prescripción** nf prescription

presencia [pre'senθja] nf presence; **presencial** adj: **testigo presencial** eyewitness; **presenciar** vt to be present at; (asistir a) to attend; (ver) to see, witness

presentación [presenta'θjon] nf presentation; (introducción) introduction

presentador, a [presenta'ðor, a] nm/f presenter, compère

presentar [presen'tar] vt to present; (ofrecer) to offer; (mostrar) to show, display; (a una persona) to introduce; **~se** vr (llegar inesperadamente) to appear, turn up; (ofrecerse como candidato) to run, stand; (aparecer) to show, appear; (solicitar empleo) to apply

presente [pre'sente] adj present ♦ nm present; **hacer ~** to state, declare; **tener ~** to remember, bear in mind

presentimiento [presenti'mjento] nm premonition, presentiment

presentir [presen'tir] vt to have a premonition of

preservación [preserßa'θjon] nf protection, preservation

preservar [preser'ßar] vt to protect, preserve; **preservativo** nm sheath, condom

presidencia [presi'ðenθja] nf presidency; (de comité) chairmanship

presidente [presi'ðente] nm/f president; (de comité) chairman/woman

presidiario [presi'ðjarjo] nm convict

presidio [pre'sidjo] nm prison, penitentiary

presidir [presi'ðir] vt (dirigir) to preside at, preside over; (: comité) to take the chair at; (dominar) to dominate, rule ♦ vi to preside; to take the chair

presión [pre'sjon] nf pressure; **presionar** vt to press; (fig) to press, put pressure on ♦ vi: **presionar para** to press for

preso, a ['preso, a] nm/f prisoner; **tomar o llevar ~ a uno** to arrest sb, take sb prisoner

prestación [presta'θjon] nf service; (subsidio) benefit; **prestaciones** nfpl (TEC, AUT) performance features

prestado, a [pres'taðo, a] adj on loan; **pedir ~** to borrow

prestamista [presta'mista] nm/f moneylender

préstamo ['prestamo] nm loan; **~ hipotecario** mortgage

prestar [pres'tar] vt to lend, loan; (atención) to pay; (ayuda) to give

presteza [pres'teθa] nf speed, promptness

prestigio [pres'tixjo] nm prestige; **~so, a** adj (honorable) prestigious; (famoso, renombrado) renowned, famous

presumido, a [presu'miðo, a] adj (persona) vain

presumir [presu'mir] vt to presume ♦ vi (tener aires) to be conceited; **según cabe ~** as may be presumed, presumably; **presunción** nf presumption; **presunto, a** adj (supuesto) supposed, presumed; (así llamado) so-called; **presuntuoso, a** adj conceited, presumptuous

presuponer [presupo'ner] vt to presuppose

presupuesto [presu'pwesto] pp de **presuponer** ♦ nm (FINANZAS) budget; (estimación: de costo) estimate

pretencioso, a [preten'θjoso, a] pretentious

pretender [preten'der] *vt* (*intentar*) to try to, seek to; (*reivindicar*) to claim; (*buscar*) to seek, try for; (*cortejar*) to woo, court; **~ que** to expect that; **pretendiente** *nm/f* (*amante*) suitor; (*al trono*) pretender; **pretensión** *nf* (*aspiración*) aspiration; (*reivindicación*) claim; (*orgullo*) pretension

pretexto [pre'teksto] *nm* pretext; (*excusa*) excuse

prevalecer [preβaleˈθer] *vi* to prevail

prevención [preβenˈθjon] *nf* prevention; (*precaución*) precaution

prevenido, a [preβeˈniðo, a] *adj* prepared, ready; (*cauteloso*) cautious

prevenir [preβeˈnir] *vt* (*impedir*) to prevent; (*predisponer*) to prejudice, bias; (*avisar*) to warn; (*preparar*) to prepare, get ready; **~se** *vr* to get ready, prepare; **~se contra** to take precautions against; **preventivo, a** *adj* preventive, precautionary

prever [pre'βer] *vt* to foresee

previo, a [ˈpreβjo, a] *adj* (*anterior*) previous; (*preliminar*) preliminary ♦ *prep*: **~ acuerdo de los otros** subject to the agreement of the others

previsión [preβiˈsjon] *nf* (*perspicacia*) foresight; (*predicción*) forecast; **previsto, a** *adj* anticipated, forecast

prima [ˈprima] *nf* (*COM*) bonus; **~ de seguro** insurance premium; *ver tb* **primo**

primacía [primaˈθia] *nf* primacy

primario, a [priˈmarjo, a] *adj* primary

primavera [primaˈβera] *nf* spring(-time)

primera [priˈmera] *nf* (*AUTO*) first gear; (*FERRO*: *tb*: **~ clase**) first class ♦ *adj* (*fam*) first-class, first-rate

primero, a [priˈmero, a] *adj* (*delante de nmsg*: **primer**) first; (*principal*) prime ♦ *adv* first; (*más bien*) sooner, rather; **primera plana** front page

primicia [priˈmiθja] *nf* (*tb*: **~ informativa**) scoop

primitivo, a [primiˈtiβo, a] *adj*

primitive; (*original*) original

primo, a [ˈprimo, a] *adj* prime ♦ *nm/f* cousin; (*fam*) fool, idiot; **~ hermano** first cousin; **materias primas** raw materials

primogénito, a [primoˈxenito, a] *adj* first-born

primordial [primorˈðjal] *adj* basic, fundamental

primoroso, a [primoˈroso, a] *adj* exquisite, delicate

princesa [prinˈθesa] *nf* princess

principal [prinθiˈpal] *adj* principal, main ♦ *nm* (*jefe*) chief, principal

príncipe [ˈprinθipe] *nm* prince

principiante [prinθiˈpjante] *nm/f* beginner

principio [prinˈθipjo] *nm* (*comienzo*) beginning, start; (*origen*) origin; (*primera etapa*) rudiment, basic idea; (*moral*) principle; **a ~s de** at the beginning of

pringoso, a [prinˈɣoso, a] *adj* (*grasiento*) greasy; (*pegajoso*) sticky

pringue [ˈpringe] *nm* (*grasa*) grease, fat, dripping

prioridad [prioriˈðað] *nf* priority

prisa [ˈprisa] *nf* (*apresuramiento*) hurry, haste; (*rapidez*) speed; (*urgencia*) (sense of) urgency; **a o de ~** quickly; **darse ~** to hurry up; **estar de o tener ~** to be in a hurry

prisión [priˈsjon] *nf* (*cárcel*) prison; (*período de cárcel*) imprisonment; **prisionero, a** *nm/f* prisoner

prismáticos [prisˈmatikos] *nmpl* binoculars

privación [priβaˈθjon] *nf* deprivation; (*falta*) want, privation

privado, a [priˈβaðo, a] *adj* private

privar [priˈβar] *vt* to deprive; **privativo, a** *adj* exclusive

privilegiado, a [priβileˈxjaðo, a] *adj* privileged; (*memoria*) very good

privilegiar [priβileˈxjar] *vt* to grant a privilege to; (*favorecer*) to favour

privilegio [priβiˈlexjo] *nm* privilege;

(concesión) concession

pro [pro] *nm o f* profit, advantage
♦ *prep:* **asociación ~ ciegos**
association for the blind ♦ *prefijo:*
~ soviético/americano pro-Soviet/
American; **en ~ de** on behalf of, for;
los ~s y los contras the pros and
cons

proa ['proa] *nf* bow, prow; **de ~** bow
cpd, fore

probabilidad [proβaβili'ðað] *nf*
probability, likelihood; (*oportunidad,
posibilidad*) chance, prospect;

probable *adj* probable, likely

probador [proβa'ðor] *nm* (*en tienda*)
fitting room

probar [pro'βar] *vt* (*demostrar*) to
prove; (*someter a prueba*) to test, try
out; (*ropa*) to try on; (*comida*) to taste
♦ *vi* to try; **~se un traje** to try on a
suit

probeta [pro'βeta] *nf* test tube

problema [pro'βlema] *nm* problem

procedente [proθe'ðente] *adj*
(*razonable*) reasonable; (*conforme a
derecho*) proper, fitting; **~ de** coming
from, originating in

proceder [proθe'ðer] *vi* (*avanzar*) to
proceed; (*actuar*) to act; (*ser correcto*)
to be right (and proper), be fitting
♦ *nm* (*comportamiento*) behaviour,
conduct; **~ de** to come from, originate
in; **procedimiento** *nm* procedure;
(*proceso*) process; (*método*) means *pl*,
method

procesado, a [proθe'saðo, a] *nm/f*
accused

procesador [proθesa'ðor] *nm:* **~ de
textos** word processor

procesar [proθe'sar] *vt* to try, put on
trial

procesión [proθe'sjon] *nf* procession

proceso [pro'θeso] *nm* process; (*JUR*)
trial

proclamar [prokla'mar] *vt* to proclaim

procreación [prokrea'θjon] *nf*
procreation

procrear [prokre'ar] *vt, vi* to procreate

procurador, a [prokura'ðor, a] *nm/f*
attorney

procurar [proku'rar] *vt* (*intentar*) to
try, endeavour; (*conseguir*) to get,
obtain; (*asegurar*) to secure; (*producir*)
to produce

prodigio [pro'ðixjo] *nm* prodigy;
(*milagro*) wonder, marvel; **~so, a** *adj*
prodigious, marvellous

pródigo, a ['proðiɣo, a] *adj:* **hijo ~**
prodigal son

producción [proðuk'θjon] *nf* (*gen*)
production; (*producto*) output; **~ en
serie** mass production

producir [proðu'θir] *vt* to produce;
(*causar*) to cause, bring about; **~se** *vr*
(*cambio*) to come about; (*accidente*) to
take place; (*problema etc*) to arise;
(*hacerse*) to be produced, be made;
(*estallar*) to break out

productividad [proðuktiβi'ðað] *nf*
productivity; **productivo, a** *adj*
productive; (*provechoso*) profitable

producto [pro'ðukto] *nm* product

productor, a [proðuk'tor, a] *adj*
productive, producing ♦ *nm/f* producer

proeza [pro'eθa] *nf* exploit, feat

profanar [profa'nar] *vt* to desecrate,
profane; **profano, a** *adj* profane
♦ *nm/f* layman/woman

profecía [profe'θia] *nf* prophecy

proferir [profe'rir] *vt* (*palabra, sonido*)
to utter; (*injuria*) to hurl, let fly

profesión [profe'sjon] *nf* profession;
profesional *adj* professional

profesor, a [profe'sor, a] *nm/f*
teacher; **~ado** *nm* teaching profession

profeta [pro'feta] *nm/f* prophet;
profetizar *vt, vi* to prophesy

prófugo, a ['profuɣo, a] *nm/f* fugitive;
(*MIL: desertor*) deserter

profundidad [profundi'ðað] *nf* depth;
profundizar *vi:* **profundizar en** to
go deeply into; **profundo, a** *adj* deep;
(*misterio, pensador*) profound

progenitor [proxeni'tor] *nm* ancestor;

~es nmpl (padres) parents
programa [proˈɣrama] nm
programme (BRIT), program (US);
~ción nf programming; **~dor, a** nm/f
programmer; **programar** vt to
program
progresar [proɣreˈsar] vi to progress,
make progress; **progresista** adj, nm/f
progressive; **progresivo, a** adj
progressive; (gradual) gradual;
(continuo) continuous; **progreso** nm
progress
prohibición [proiβiˈθjon] nf
prohibition, ban
prohibir [proiˈβir] vt to prohibit, ban,
forbid; **se prohibe fumar, prohibido
fumar** no smoking; **"prohibido el
paso"** "no entry"
prójimo, a [ˈproximo, a] nm/f fellow
man; (vecino) neighbour
proletariado [proletaˈrjaðo] nm
proletariat
proletario, a [proleˈtarjo, a] adj, nm/f
proletarian
proliferación [proliferaˈθjon] nf
proliferation
proliferar [proliferar] vi to proliferate;
prolífico, a adj prolific
prólogo [ˈproloɣo] nm prologue
prolongación [prolongaˈθjon] nf
extension; **prolongado, a** adj (largo)
long; (alargado) lengthy
prolongar [prolonˈɣar] vt to extend;
(reunión etc) to prolong; (calle, tubo) to
extend
promedio [proˈmeðjo] nm average;
(de distancia) middle, mid-point
promesa [proˈmesa] nf promise
prometer [promeˈter] vt to promise
♦ vi to show promise; **~se** vr (novios)
to get engaged; **prometido, a** adj
promised; engaged ♦ nm/f fiancé/
fiancée
prominente [promiˈnente] adj
prominent
promiscuo, a [proˈmiskwo, a] adj
promiscuous

promoción [promoˈθjon] nf
promotion
promotor [promoˈtor] nm promoter;
(instigador) instigator
promover [promoˈβer] vt to promote;
(causar) to cause; (instigar) to instigate,
stir up
promulgar [promulˈɣar] vt to
promulgate; (anunciar) to proclaim
pronombre [proˈnombre] nm
pronoun
pronosticar [pronostiˈkar] vt to
predict, foretell, forecast; **pronóstico**
nm prediction, forecast; **pronóstico
del tiempo** weather forecast
pronto, a [ˈpronto, a] adj (rápido)
prompt, quick; (preparado) ready ♦ adv
quickly, promptly; (en seguida) at once,
right away; (dentro de poco) soon;
(temprano) early ♦ nm: **tener ~s de
enojo** to be quick-tempered; **de ~**
suddenly; **por lo ~** meanwhile, for the
present
pronunciación [pronunθjaˈθjon] nf
pronunciation
pronunciar [pronunˈθjar] vt to
pronounce; (discurso) to make, deliver;
~se vr to revolt, rebel; (declararse) to
declare o.s.
propagación [propaɣaˈθjon] nf
propagation
propaganda [propaˈɣanda] nf
(política) propaganda; (comercial)
advertising
propagar [propaˈɣar] vt to propagate
propensión [propenˈsjon] nf
inclination, propensity; **propenso, a**
adj inclined to; **ser propenso a** to be
inclined to, have a tendency to
propicio, a [proˈpiθjo, a] adj
favourable, propitious
propiedad [propjeˈðað] nf property;
(posesión) possession, ownership;
~ particular private property
propietario, a [propjeˈtarjo, a] nm/f
owner, proprietor
propina [proˈpina] nf tip

propio, a ['propjo, a] adj own, of one's own; (característico) characteristic, typical; (debido) proper; (mismo) selfsame, very; **el ~ ministro** the minister himself; **¿tienes casa propia?** have you a house of your own?

proponer [propo'ner] vt to propose, put forward; (problema) to pose; **~se** vr to propose, intend

proporción [propor'θjon] nf proportion; (MAT) ratio; **proporciones** nfpl (dimensiones) dimensions; (fig) size sg; **proporcionado, a** adj proportionate; (regular) medium, middling; (justo) just right; **proporcionar** vt (dar) to give, supply, provide

proposición [proposi'θjon] nf proposition; (propuesta) proposal

propósito [pro'posito] nm purpose; (intento) aim, intention ♦ adv: **a ~ by** the way, incidentally; (a posta) on purpose, deliberately; **~ de** about, with regard to

propuesta [pro'pwesta] vb ver **proponer** ♦ nf proposal

propulsar [propul'sar] vt to drive, propel; (fig) to promote, encourage; **propulsión** nf propulsion; **propulsión a chorro o por reacción** jet propulsion

prórroga ['prorroxa] nf extension; (JUR) stay; (COM) deferment; (DEPORTE) extra time; **prorrogar** vt (período) to extend; (decisión) to defer, postpone

prorrumpir [prorrum'pir] vi to burst forth, break out

prosa ['prosa] nf prose

proscrito, a [pro'skrito, a] adj banned

proseguir [prose'xir] vt to continue, carry on ♦ vi to continue, go on

prospección [prospek'θjon] nf exploration; (del oro) prospecting

prospecto [pro'spekto] nm prospectus

prosperar [prospe'rar] vi to prosper, thrive, flourish; **prosperidad** nf

prosperity; (éxito) success; **próspero, a** adj prosperous, flourishing; (que tiene éxito) successful

prostíbulo [pros'tiβulo] nm brothel (BRIT), house of prostitution (US)

prostitución [prostitu'θjon] nf prostitution

prostituir [prosti'twir] vt to prostitute; **~se** vr to prostitute o.s., become a prostitute

prostituta [prosti'tuta] nf prostitute

protagonista [protaxo'nista] nm/f protagonist

protagonizar [protaxoni'θar] vt to take the chief rôle in

protección [protek'θjon] nf protection

protector, a [protek'tor, a] adj protective, protecting ♦ nm/f protector

proteger [prote'xer] vt to protect; **protegido, a** nm/f protégé/protégée

proteína [prote'ina] nf protein

protesta [pro'testa] nf protest; (declaración) protestation

protestante [protes'tante] adj Protestant

protestar [protes'tar] vt to protest, declare ♦ vi to protest

protocolo [proto'kolo] nm protocol

prototipo [proto'tipo] nm prototype

prov. abr (= provincia) prov

provecho [pro'βetʃo] nm advantage, benefit; (FINANZAS) profit; **¡buen ~!** bon appétit!; **en ~ de** to the benefit of; **sacar ~ de** to benefit from, profit by

proveer [proβe'er] vt to provide, supply ♦ vi: **~ a** to provide for

provenir [proβe'nir] vi: **~ de** to come from, stem from

proverbio [pro'βerβjo] nm proverb

providencia [proβi'δenθja] nf providence

provincia [pro'βinθja] nf province; **~no, a** adj provincial; (del campo) country cpd

provisión [proβi'sjon] nf provision; (abastecimiento) provision, supply;

(*medida*) measure, step
provisional [proβisjoˈnal] *adj* provisional
provocación [proβokaˈθjon] *nf* provocation
provocar [proβoˈkar] *vt* to provoke; (*alentar*) to tempt, invite; (*causar*) to bring about, lead to; (*promover*) to promote; (*estimular*) to rouse, stimulate; ¿**te provoca un café?** (*AM*) would you like a coffee?;
provocativo, a *adj* provocative
próximamente [proksimaˈmente] *adv* shortly, soon
proximidad [proksimiˈðað] *nf* closeness, proximity; **próximo, a** *adj* near, close; (*vecino*) neighbouring; (*siguiente*) next
proyectar [projekˈtar] *vt* (*objeto*) to hurl, throw; (*luz*) to cast, shed; (*CINE*) to screen, show; (*planear*) to plan
proyectil [projekˈtil] *nm* projectile, missile
proyecto [proˈjekto] *nm* plan; (*estimación de costo*) detailed estimate
proyector [projekˈtor] *nm* (*CINE*) projector
prudencia [pruˈðenθja] *nf* (*sabiduría*) wisdom; (*cuidado*) care; **prudente** *adj* sensible, wise; (*conductor*) careful
prueba *etc* [ˈprweβa] *vb ver* **probar** ♦ *nf* proof; (*ensayo*) test, trial; (*degustación*) tasting, sampling; (*de ropa*) fitting; **a ~** on trial; **a ~ de** proof against; **a ~ de agua/fuego** waterproof/fireproof; **someter a ~** to put to the test
prurito [pruˈrito] *nm* itch; (*de bebé*) nappy (*BRIT*) o diaper (*US*) rash
psico... [siko] *prefijo* psycho...; **~análisis** *nm inv* psychoanalysis; **~logía** *nf* psychology; **~lógico, a** *adj* psychological; **psicólogo, a** *nm/f* psychologist; **psicópata** *nm/f* psychopath; **~sis** *nf inv* psychosis
psiquiatra [siˈkjatra] *nm/f* psychiatrist; **psiquiátrico, a** *adj* psychiatric

psíquico, a [ˈsikiko, a] *adj* psychic(al)
PSOE [peˈsoe] *nm* = **Partido Socialista Obrero Español**
pta(s) *abr* = **peseta(s)**
pts *abr* = **pesetas**
púa [ˈpua] *nf* (*BOT, ZOOL*) prickle, spine; (*para guitarra*) plectrum (*BRIT*), pick (*US*); **alambre de ~** barbed wire
pubertad [puβerˈtað] *nf* puberty
publicación [puβlikaˈθjon] *nf* publication
publicar [puβliˈkar] *vt* (*editar*) to publish; (*hacer público*) to publicize; (*divulgar*) to make public, divulge
publicidad [puβliθiˈðað] *nf* publicity; (*COM: propaganda*) advertising; **publicitario, a** *adj* publicity *cpd*; advertising *cpd*
público, a [ˈpuβliko, a] *adj* public ♦ *nm* public; (*TEATRO etc*) audience
puchero [puˈtʃero] *nm* (*CULIN: guiso*) stew; (: *olla*) cooking pot; **hacer ~s** to pout
pude *etc vb ver* **poder**
púdico, a [ˈpuðiko, a] *adj* modest
pudiente [puˈðjente] *adj* (*rico*) wealthy, well-to-do
pudiera *etc vb ver* **poder**
pudor [puˈðor] *nm* modesty
pudrir [puˈðrir] *vt* to rot; **~se** *vr* to rot, decay
pueblo [ˈpweβlo] *nm* people; (*nación*) nation; (*aldea*) village
puedo *etc vb ver* **poder**
puente [ˈpwente] *nm* bridge; **hacer ~** (*inf*) to take extra days off work between 2 public holidays; to take a long weekend; **~ aéreo** shuttle service; **~ colgante** suspension bridge

| hacer puente |

When a public holiday in Spain falls on a Tuesday or Thursday it is common practice for employers to make the Monday or Friday a holiday as well and to give everyone a four-day weekend. This is known as hacer puente. *When a named public holiday such as the* **Día de la Constitución** *falls on a Tuesday or Thursday, people refer to the whole holiday period as e.g. the* **puente de la Constitución**.

puerco, a ['pwerko, a] *nm/f* pig/sow
♦ *adj* (*sucio*) dirty, filthy; (*obsceno*) disgusting; **~ de mar** porpoise; **~ marino** dolphin
pueril [pwe'ril] *adj* childish
puerro ['pwerro] *nm* leek
puerta ['pwerta] *nf* door; (*de jardín*) gate; (*portal*) doorway; (*fig*) gateway; (*portería*) goal; **a la ~** at the door; **a ~ cerrada** behind closed doors; **~ giratoria** revolving door
puerto ['pwerto] *nm* port; (*paso*) pass; (*fig*) haven, refuge
Puerto Rico [pwerto'riko] *nm* Puerto Rico; **puertorriqueño, a** *adj, nm/f* Puerto Rican
pues [pwes] *adv* (*entonces*) then; (*bueno*) well, well then; (*así que*) so
♦ *conj* (*ya que*) since; **¡~!** (*sí*) yes!, certainly!
puesta ['pwesta] *nf* (*apuesta*) bet, stake; **~ en marcha** starting; **~ del sol** sunset
puesto, a ['pwesto, a] *pp de* **poner**
♦ *adj*: **tener algo ~** to have sth on, be wearing sth ♦ *nm* (*lugar, posición*) place; (*trabajo*) post, job; (*COM*) stall
♦ *conj*: **~ que** since, as
púgil ['puxil] *nm* boxer
pugna ['puɣna] *nf* battle, conflict; **pugnar** *vi* (*luchar*) to struggle, fight; (*pelear*) to fight
pujar [pu'xar] *vi* (*en subasta*) to bid; (*esforzarse*) to struggle, strain
pulcro, a ['pulkro, a] *adj* neat, tidy
pulga ['pulɣa] *nf* flea
pulgada [pul'ɣaða] *nf* inch
pulgar [pul'ɣar] *nm* thumb
pulir [pu'lir] *vt* (*bruñir*) to smooth; (*alisar*) to smooth; (*fig*) to polish up, touch up

pulla ['puʎa] *nf* cutting remark
pulmón [pul'mon] *nm* lung; **pulmonía** *nf* pneumonia
pulpa ['pulpa] *nf* pulp; (*de fruta*) flesh, soft part
pulpería [pulpe'ria] (*AM*) *nf* (*tienda*) small grocery store
púlpito ['pulpito] *nm* pulpit
pulpo ['pulpo] *nm* octopus
pulsación [pulsa'θjon] *nf* beat; **pulsaciones** pulse rate
pulsar [pul'sar] *vt* (*tecla*) to touch, tap; (*MUS*) to play; (*botón*) to press, push ♦ *vi* to pulsate; (*latir*) to beat, throb; (*MED*): **~ a uno** to take sb's pulse
pulsera [pul'sera] *nf* bracelet
pulso ['pulso] *nm* (*ANAT*) pulse; (*fuerza*) strength; (*firmeza*) steadiness, steady hand
pulverizador [pulßeriθa'ðor] *nm* spray, spray gun
pulverizar [pulßeri'θar] *vt* to pulverize; (*líquido*) to spray
puna ['puna] (*AM*) *nf* mountain sickness
punitivo, a [puni'tißo, a] *adj* punitive
punta ['punta] *nf* point, tip; (*extremidad*) end; (*fig*) touch, trace; **horas ~s** peak hours, rush hours; **sacar ~ a** to sharpen
puntada [pun'taða] *nf* (*COSTURA*) stitch
puntal [pun'tal] *nm* prop, support
puntapié [punta'pje] *nm* kick
puntear [punte'ar] *vt* to tick, mark
puntería [punte'ria] *nf* (*de arma*) aim, aiming; (*destreza*) marksmanship
puntero, a [pun'tero, a] *adj* leading ♦ *nm* (*palo*) pointer
puntiagudo, a [puntja'ɣuðo, a] *adj* sharp, pointed
puntilla [pun'tiʎa] *nf* (*encaje*) lace edging o trim; (**andar) de ~s** (to walk) on tiptoe
punto ['punto] *nm* (*gen*) point; (*señal diminuta*) spot, dot; (*COSTURA, MED*) stitch; (*lugar*) spot, place; (*momento*) point, moment; **a ~** ready; **estar a ~ de** to be on the point of o about to;

en ~ on the dot; **~ muerto** dead centre; (AUTO) neutral (gear); **~ final** full stop (BRIT), period (US); **~ y coma** semicolon; **~ de interrogación** question mark; **~ de vista** point of view, viewpoint; **hacer ~** (tejer) to knit

puntuación [puntwa'θjon] nf punctuation; (puntos: en examen) mark(s) (pl); (: DEPORTE) score

puntual [pun'twal] adj (a tiempo) punctual; (exacto) exact, accurate; **~idad** nf punctuality; exactness, accuracy; **~izar** vt to fix, specify

puntuar [pun'twar] vi (DEPORTE) to score, count

punzada [pun'θaða] nf (de dolor) twinge

punzante [pun'θante] adj (dolor) shooting, sharp; (instrumento) sharp; **punzar** vt to prick, pierce ♦ vi to shoot, stab

puñado [pu'ɲaðo] nm handful

puñal [pu'ɲal] nm dagger; **~ada** nf stab

puñetazo [puɲe'taθo] nm punch

puño [ˈpuɲo] nm (ANAT) fist; (cantidad) fistful, handful; (COSTURA) cuff; (de herramienta) handle

pupila [pu'pila] nf pupil

pupitre [pu'pitre] nm desk

puré [pu're] nm puree; (sopa) (thick) soup; **~ de patatas** mashed potatoes

pureza [pu'reθa] nf purity

purga [ˈpurxa] nf purge; **purgante** adj nm purgative; **purgar** vt to purge

purgatorio [purxa'torjo] nm purgatory

purificar [purifi'kar] vt to purify; (refinar) to refine

puritano, a [puri'tano, a] adj (actitud) puritanical; (iglesia, tradición) puritan ♦ nm/f puritan

puro, a [ˈpuro, a] adj pure; (verdad) simple, plain ♦ adv: **de ~ cansado** out of sheer tiredness ♦ nm cigar

púrpura [ˈpurpura] nf purple; **purpúreo, a** adj purple

pus [pus] nm pus

puse etc vb ver **poner**

pusiera etc vb ver **poner**

pústula [ˈpustula] nf pimple, sore

puta [ˈputa] (fam!) nf whore, prostitute

putrefacción [putrefak'θjon] nf rotting, putrefaction

PVP abr (ESP: = precio venta al público) RRP

pyme, PYME [ˈpime] nf abr (= Pequeña y Mediana Empresa) SME

Q, q

PALABRA CLAVE

---

que [ke] conj **1** (con oración subordinada): muchas veces no se traduce): **dijo ~ vendría** he said (that) he would come; **espero ~ lo encuentres** I hope (that) you find it; ver tb **el**

2 (en oración independiente): **¡~ entre!** send him in; **¡~ se mejore tu padre!** I hope your father gets better

3 (enfático): **¿me quieres? – ¡~ sí!** do you love me? – of course!

4 (consecutivo: muchas veces no se traduce): **es tan grande ~ no lo puedo levantar** it's so big (that) I can't lift it

5 (comparaciones) than; **yo ~ tú/él** if I were you/him; ver tb **más**; **menos**; **mismo**

6 (valor disyuntivo): **~ le guste o no** whether he likes it or not; **~ venga o ~ no venga** whether he comes or not

7 (porque): **no puedo, ~ tengo ~ quedarme en casa** I can't, I've got to stay in

♦ pron **1** (cosa) that, which; (+ prep) which; **el sombrero ~ te compraste** the hat (that o which) you bought; **la cama en ~ ~ dormí** the bed (that o which) I slept in

2 (persona: suj) that, who; (: objeto)

that, whom; **el amigo ~ me
acompañó al museo** the friend that
o who went to the museum with me:
la chica ~ invité the girl (that o
whom) I invited

qué [ke] *adj* what?, which? ♦ *pron*
what?; **¡~ divertido!** how funny!;
¿~ edad tienes? how old are you?;
¿de ~ me hablas? what are you
saying to me?; **¿~ tal?** how are you?,
how are things?; **¿~ hay (de nuevo)?**
what's new?

quebradizo, a [keβra'ðiθo, a] *adj*
fragile; (*persona*) frail

quebrado, a [ke'βraðo, a] *adj* (*roto*)
broken ♦ *nm/f* bankrupt ♦ *nm* (*MAT*)
fraction

quebrantar [keβran'tar] *vt* (*infringir*)
to violate, transgress; **~se** *vr* (*persona*)
to fail in health

quebranto [ke'βranto] *nm* damage,
harm; (*dolor*) grief, pain

quebrar [ke'βrar] *vt* to break, smash
♦ *vi* to go bankrupt; **~se** *vr* to break,
get broken; (*MED*) to be ruptured

quedar [ke'ðar] *vi* to stay, remain; (*encontrarse: sitio*) to be; (*haber aún*) to
remain, be left; **~se** *vr* to remain, stay
(behind); **~se (con) algo** to keep sth;
~ en (*acordar*) to agree on/to; **~ en
nada** to come to nothing; **~ por
hacer** to be still to be done; **~ ciego/
mudo** to be left blind/dumb; **no te
queda bien** ese vestido that dress
doesn't suit you; **eso queda muy
lejos** that's a long way (away);
quedamos a las seis we agreed to
meet at six

quedo, a [ˈkeðo, a] *adj* still ♦ *adv*
softly, gently

quehacer [keaˈθer] *nm* task, job; **~es
(domésticos)** *nmpl* household chores

queja [ˈkexa] *nf* complaint; **quejarse**
vr (*enfermo*) to moan, groan; (*protestar*)
to complain; **quejarse de que** to
complain (about the fact) that;

quejido *nm* moan

quemado, a [keˈmaðo, a] *adj* burnt

quemadura [kemaˈðura] *nf* burn,
scald

quemar [keˈmar] *vt* to burn; (*fig:
malgastar*) to burn up, squander ♦ *vi* to
be burning hot; **~se** *vr* (*consumirse*) to
burn (up); (*del sol*) to get sunburnt

quemarropa [kemaˈrropa]: **a ~** *adv*
point-blank

quepo *etc vb ver* **caber**

querella [keˈreʎa] *nf* (*JUR*) charge;
(*disputa*) dispute; **~rse** *vr* (*JUR*) to file a
complaint

PALABRA CLAVE

querer [keˈrer] *vt* **1** (*desear*) to want;
quiero más dinero I want more
money; **quisiera o querría un té** I'd
like a tea; **sin ~** unintentionally;
quiero ayudar/que vayas I want to
help/you to go

2 (*preguntas: para pedir algo*): **¿quiere
abrir la ventana?** could you open the
window?; **¿quieres echarme una
mano?** can you give me a hand?

3 (*amar*) to love; (*tener cariño a*) to be
fond of; **quiere mucho a sus hijos**
he's very fond of his children

4 (*requerir*): **esta planta quiere más
luz** this plant needs more light

**5: le pedí que me dejara ir pero no
quiso** I asked him to let me go but he
refused

---

querido, a [keˈriðo, a] *adj* dear ♦ *nm/f*
darling; (*amante*) lover

queso [ˈkeso] *nm* cheese

quicio [ˈkiθjo] *nm* hinge; **sacar a uno
de ~** to get on sb's nerves

quiebra [ˈkjeβra] *nf* break, split; (*COM*)
bankruptcy; (*ECON*) slump

quiebro [ˈkjeβro] *nm* (*del cuerpo*)
swerve

quien [kjen] *pron who*; **hay ~ piensa
que** there are those who think that;
no hay ~ lo haga no-one will do it

quién [kjen] *pron* who, whom; **¿~ es?** who's there?

quienquiera [kjen'kjera] (*pl* **quienesquiera**) *pron* whoever

quiero *etc vb ver* **querer**

quieto, a [ˈkjeto, a] *adj* still; (*carácter*) placid; **quietud** *nf* stillness

quilate [kiˈlate] *nm* carat

quilla [ˈkiʎa] *nf* keel

quimera [kiˈmera] *nf* chimera; **quimérico, a** *adj* fantastic

químico, a [ˈkimiko, a] *adj* chemical ♦ *nm/f* chemist ♦ *nf* chemistry

quincalla [kinˈkaʎa] *nf* hardware, ironmongery (*BRIT*)

quince [ˈkinθe] *num* fifteen; **~ días** a fortnight; **~añero, a** *nm/f* teenager; **~na** *nf* fortnight; (*pago*) fortnightly pay; **~nal** *adj* fortnightly

quiniela [kiˈnjela] *nf* football pools *pl*; **~s** *nfpl* (*impreso*) pools coupon *sg*

quinientos, as [kiˈnjentos, as] *adj*, *num* five hundred

quinina [kiˈnina] *nf* quinine

quinto, a [ˈkinto, a] *adj* fifth ♦ *nm* country house; (*MIL*) call-up, draft

quiosco [ˈkjosko] *nm* (*de música*) bandstand; (*de periódicos*) news stand

quirófano [kiˈrofano] *nm* operating theatre

quirúrgico, a [kiˈrurxiko, a] *adj* surgical

quise *etc vb ver* **querer**

quisiera *etc vb ver* **querer**

quisquilloso, a [kiskiˈʎoso, a] *adj* (*susceptible*) touchy; (*meticuloso*) pernickety

quiste [ˈkiste] *nm* cyst

quitaesmalte [kitaesˈmalte] *nm* nail-polish remover

quitamanchas [kitaˈmantʃas] *nm inv* stain remover

quitanieves [kitaˈnjeβes] *nm inv* snowplough (*BRIT*), snowplow (*US*)

quitar [kiˈtar] *vt* to remove, take away; (*ropa*) to take off; (*dolor*) to relieve; **¡quita de ahí!** get away!; **~se** *vr* to

withdraw; (*ropa*) to take off; **se quitó el sombrero** he took off his hat

quite [ˈkite] *nm* (*esgrima*) parry; (*evasión*) dodge

Quito [ˈkito] *n* Quito

quizá(s) [kiˈθa(s)] *adv* perhaps, maybe

R, r

rábano [ˈraβano] *nm* radish; **me importa un ~** I don't give a damn

rabia [ˈraβja] *nf* (*MED*) rabies *sg*; (*ira*) fury, rage; **rabiar** *vi* to have rabies; to rage, be furious; **rabiar por algo** to long for sth

rabieta [raˈβjeta] *nf* tantrum, fit of temper

rabino [raˈβino] *nm* rabbi

rabioso, a [raˈβjoso, a] *adj* rabid; (*fig*) furious

rabo [ˈraβo] *nm* tail

racha [ˈratʃa] *nf* gust of wind; **buena/ mala ~** spell of good/bad luck

racial [raˈθjal] *adj* racial, race *cpd*

racimo [raˈθimo] *nm* bunch

raciocinio [raθjoˈθinjo] *nm* reason

ración [raˈθjon] *nf* portion; **raciones** *nfpl* rations

racional [raθjoˈnal] *adj* (*razonable*) reasonable; (*lógico*) rational; **~izar** *vt* to rationalize

racionar [raθjoˈnar] *vt* to ration (out)

racismo [raˈθismo] *nm* racism; **racista** *adj*, *nm/f* racist

radar [raˈðar] *nm* radar

radiactivo, a [raðiakˈtiβo, a] *adj* = **radioactivo**

radiador [raðjaˈðor] *nm* radiator

radiante [raˈðjante] *adj* radiant

radical [raðiˈkal] *adj*, *nm/f* radical

radicar [raðiˈkar] *vi*: **~ en** (*dificultad*, *problema*) to lie in; (*solución*) to consist in; **~se** *vr* to establish o.s., put down (one's) roots

radio [ˈraðjo] *nf* radio; (*aparato*) radio (set) ♦ *nm* (*MAT*) radius; (*QUÍM*) radium;

~actividad nf radioactivity; **~activo, a** adj radioactive; **~difusión** nf broadcasting; **~emisora** nf transmitter, radio station; **~escucha** nm/f listener; **~grafía** nf X-ray; **~grafiar** vt to X-ray; **~terapia** nf radiotherapy; **~yente** nm/f listener

ráfaga ['rafaxa] nf gust; (de luz) flash; (de tiros) burst

raído, a [ra'iðo, a] adj (ropa) threadbare

raigambre [rai'xambre] nf (BOT) roots pl; (fig) tradition

raíz [ra'iθ] nf root; ~ **cuadrada** square root; **a ~ de** as a result of

raja ['raxa] nf (de melón etc) slice; (grieta) crack; **rajar** vt to split; (fam) to slash; **rajarse** vr to split, crack; **rajarse de** to back out of

rajatabla [raxa'taßla]: **a ~** adv (estrictamente) strictly, to the letter

rallador [raʎa'ðor] nm grater

rallar [ra'ʎar] vt to grate

rama ['rama] nf branch; **~je** nm branches pl, foliage; **ramal** nm (de cuerda) strand; (FERRO) branch line (BRIT); (AUTO) branch (road) (BRIT)

rambla ['rambla] nf (avenida) avenue

ramificación [ramifika'θjon] nf ramification

ramificarse [ramifi'karse] vr to branch out

ramillete [rami'ʎete] nm bouquet

ramo ['ramo] nm branch; (sección) department, section

rampa ['rampa] nf ramp

ramplón, ona [ram'plon, ona] adj uncouth, coarse

rana ['rana] nf frog; **salto de ~** leapfrog

ranchero [ran'tʃero] nm (AM) rancher; smallholder

rancho ['rantʃo] nm (grande) ranch; (pequeño) small farm

rancio, a ['ranθjo, a] adj (comestibles) rancid; (vino) aged, mellow; (fig) ancient

rango ['rango] nm rank, standing

ranura [ra'nura] nf groove; (de teléfono etc) slot

rapar [ra'par] vt to shave; (los cabellos) to crop

rapaz [ra'paθ] (nf: **rapaza**) nm/f young boy/girl ♦ adj (ZOOL) predatory

rape ['rape] nm (pez) monkfish; **al ~** cropped

rapé [ra'pe] nm snuff

rapidez [rapi'ðeθ] nf speed, rapidity; **rápido, a** adj fast, quick ♦ adv quickly ♦ nm (FERRO) express; **rápidos** nmpl rapids

rapiña [ra'piɲa] nf robbery; **ave de ~** bird of prey

raptar [rap'tar] vt to kidnap; **rapto** nm kidnapping; (impulso) sudden impulse; (éxtasis) ecstasy, rapture

raqueta [ra'keta] nf racquet

raquítico, a [ra'kitiko, a] adj stunted; (fig) poor, inadequate; **raquitismo** nm rickets sg

rareza [ra'reθa] nf rarity; (fig) eccentricity

raro, a ['raro, a] adj (poco común) rare; (extraño) odd, strange; (excepcional) remarkable

ras [ras] nm: **a ~ de** level with; **a ~ de tierra** at ground level

rasar [ra'sar] vt (igualar) to level

rascacielos [raska'θjelos] nm inv skyscraper

rascar [ras'kar] vt (con las uñas etc) to scratch; (raspar) to scrape; **~se** vr to scratch (o.s.)

rasgar [ras'xar] vt to tear, rip (up)

rasgo ['rasxo] nm (con pluma) stroke; **~s** nmpl (facciones) features, characteristics; **a grandes ~s** in outline, broadly

rasguñar [rasxu'ɲar] vt to scratch; **rasguño** nm scratch

raso, a ['raso, a] adj (liso) flat, level; (a baja altura) very low ♦ nm satin; **cielo ~** clear sky

raspadura [raspa'ðura] nf (acto)

scrape, scraping; (*marca*) scratch; **~s** *nfpl* (*de papel etc*) scrapings

raspar [ras'par] *vt* to scrape; (*arañar*) to scratch; (*limar*) to file

rastra ['rastra] *nf* (*AGR*) rake; **a ~s** by dragging; (*fig*) unwillingly

rastreador [rastrea'ðor] *nm* tracker; **~ de minas** minesweeper

rastrear [rastre'ar] *vt* (*seguir*) to track

rastrero, a [ras'trero, a] *adj* (*BOT, ZOOL*) creeping; (*fig*) despicable, mean

rastrillo [ras'triʎo] *nm* rake

rastro ['rastro] *nm* (*AGR*) rake; (*pista*) track, trail; (*vestigio*) trace; **el R~** the Madrid fleamarket

rastrojo [ras'troxo] *nm* stubble

rasurador [rasura'ðor] *nm* (*AM*) **rasuradora** [rasura'ðora] (*AM*) *nf* = **rasurador**

rasurarse [rasu'rarse] *vr* to shave

rata ['rata] *nf* rat

ratear [rate'ar] *vt* (*robar*) to steal

ratero, a [ra'tero, a] *adj* light-fingered
♦ *nm/f* (*carterista*) pickpocket; (*AM: de casas*) burglar

ratificar [ratifi'kar] *vt* to ratify

rato ['rato] *nm* while, short time; **a ~s** from time to time; **hay para ~** there's still a long way to go; **al poco ~** soon afterwards; **pasar el ~** to kill time; **pasar un buen/mal ~** to have a good/rough time; **en mis ~s libres** in my spare time

ratón [ra'ton] *nm* mouse; **ratonera** [rato'nera] *nf* mousetrap

raudal [rau'ðal] *nm* torrent; **a ~es** in abundance

raya ['raja] *nf* line; (*marca*) scratch; (*en tela*) stripe; (*de pelo*) parting; (*límite*) boundary; (*pez*) ray; (*puntuación*) dash; **a ~s** striped; **pasarse de la ~** to go too far; **tener a ~** to keep in check; **rayar** *vt* to line; to scratch; (*subrayar*) to underline ♦ *vi*: **rayar en** *o* **con** to border on

rayo ['rajo] *nm* (*del sol*) ray, beam; (*de luz*) shaft; (*en una tormenta*) (flash of) lightning; **~s X** X-rays

raza ['raθa] *nf* race; **~ humana** human race

razón [ra'θon] *nf* reason; (*justicia*) right, justice; (*razonamiento*) reasoning; (*motivo*) reason, motive; (*MAT*) ratio; **a ~ de 10 cada día** at the rate of 10 a day; **"~: ..."** "inquiries to ..."; **en ~ de** with regard to; **dar o una** to agree that sb is right; **tener ~** to be right; **~ directa/inversa** direct/inverse proportion; **de ser** raison d'être; **razonable** *adj* reasonable; (*justo, moderado*) fair; **razonamiento** *nm* (*juicio*) judg(e)ment; (*argumento*) reasoning; **razonar** *vt, vi* to reason, argue

reacción [reak'θjon] *nf* reaction; **avión a ~** jet plane; **~ en cadena** chain reaction; **reaccionar** *vi* to react; **reaccionario, a** *adj* reactionary

reacio, a [re'aθjo, a] *adj* stubborn

reactivar [reakti'ßar] *vt* to revitalize

reactor [reak'tor] *nm* reactor

readaptación [reaðapta'θjon] *nf*: **~ profesional** industrial retraining

reajuste [rea'xuste] *nm* readjustment

real [re'al] *adj* real; (*del rey, fig*) royal

realce [re'alθe] *nm* (*lustre, fig*) splendour; **poner de ~** to emphasize

realidad [reali'ðað] *nf* reality, fact; (*verdad*) truth

realista [rea'lista] *nm/f* realist

realización [realiθa'θjon] *nf* fulfilment

realizador, a [realiθa'ðor, a] *nm/f* film-maker

realizar [reali'θar] *vt* (*objetivo*) to achieve; (*plan*) to carry out; (*viaje*) to make, undertake; **~se** *vr* to come about, come true

realmente [real'mente] *adv* really, actually

realquilar [realki'lar] *vt* to sublet

realzar [real'θar] *vt* to enhance; (*acentuar*) to highlight

reanimar [reani'mar] *vt* to revive;

(*alentar*) to encourage; **~se** *vr* to revive

reanudar [reanu'ðar] *vt* (*renovar*) to renew; (*historia, viaje*) to resume

reaparición [reapari'θjon] *nf* reappearance

rearme [re'arme] *nm* rearmament

rebaja [re'βaxa] *nf* (COM) reduction; (: *descuento*) discount; **~s** *nfpl* (COM) sale; **rebajar** *vt* (*bajar*) to lower; (*reducir*) to reduce; (*disminuir*) to lessen; (*humillar*) to humble

rebanada [reβa'naða] *nf* slice

rebañar [reβa'nar] *vt* (*comida*) to scrape up; (*plato*) to scrape clean

rebaño [re'βaɲo] *nm* herd; (*de ovejas*) flock

rebasar [reβa'sar] *vt* (*tb: ~ de*) to exceed

rebatir [reβa'tir] *vt* to refute

rebeca [re'βeka] *nf* cardigan

rebelarse [reβe'larse] *vr* to rebel, revolt

rebelde [re'βelde] *adj* rebellious; (*niño*) unruly ♦ *nm/f* rebel; **rebeldía** *nf* rebelliousness; (*desobediencia*) disobedience

rebelión [reβe'ljon] *nf* rebellion

reblandecer [reβlande'θer] *vt* to soften

rebobinar [reβoβi'nar] *vt* (*cinta, película de vídeo*) to rewind

rebosante [reβo'sante] *adj* overflowing

rebosar [reβo'sar] *vi* (*líquido, recipiente*) to overflow; (*abundar*) to abound, be plentiful

rebotar [reβo'tar] *vt* to bounce; (*rechazar*) to repel ♦ *vi* (*pelota*) to bounce; (*bala*) to ricochet; **rebote** *nm* rebound; **de rebote** on the rebound

rebozado, a [reβo'θaðo, a] *adj* fried in batter o breadcrumbs

rebozar [reβo'θar] *vt* to wrap up; (CULIN) to fry in batter o breadcrumbs

rebuscado, a [reβus'kaðo, a] *adj* (*amanerado*) affected; (*palabra*) recherché; (*idea*) far-fetched

rebuscar [reβus'kar] *vi*: **~ (en/por)** to search carefully (in/for)

rebuznar [reβuθ'nar] *vi* to bray

recado [re'kaðo] *nm* (*mensaje*) message; (*encargo*) errand; **tomar un ~** (TEL) to take a message

recaer [reka'er] *vi* to relapse; **~ en** to fall to o on; (*criminal etc*) to fall back into, relapse into; **recaída** *nf* relapse

recalcar [rekal'kar] *vt* (*fig*) to stress, emphasize

recalcitrante [rekalθi'trante] *adj* recalcitrant

recalentar [rekalen'tar] *vt* (*volver a calentar*) to reheat; (*calentar demasiado*) to overheat

recámara [re'kamara] *nf* (AM) nf bedroom

recambio [re'kambjo] *nm* spare; (*de pluma*) refill

recapacitar [rekapaθi'tar] *vi* to reflect

recargado, a [rekar'ɣaðo, a] *adj* overloaded

recargar [rekar'ɣar] *vt* to overload; (*batería*) to recharge; **recargo** *nm* surcharge; (*aumento*) increase

recatado, a [reka'taðo, a] *adj* (*modesto*) modest, demure; (*prudente*) cautious

recato [re'kato] *nm* (*modestia*) modesty, demureness; (*cautela*) caution

recaudación [rekauða'θjon] *nf* (*acción*) collection; (*cantidad*) takings *pl*; (*en depósito*) gate; **recaudador, a** *nm/f* tax collector

recelar [reθe'lar] *vt*: **~ que** (*sospechar*) to suspect that; (*temer*) to fear that ♦ *vi*: **~ de** to distrust; **recelo** *nm* distrust, suspicion; **receloso, a** *adj* distrustful, suspicious

recepción [reθep'θjon] *nf* reception; **recepcionista** *nm/f* receptionist

receptáculo [reθep'takulo] *nm* receptacle

receptivo, a [reθep'tiβo, a] *adj* receptive

receptor, a [reθep'tor, a] *nm/f*

recipient *nm* (TEL) receiver

recesión [reθe'sjon] *nf* (COM) recession

receta [re'θeta] *nf* (CULIN) recipe; (MED) prescription

rechazar [retʃa'θar] *vt* to reject; (oferta) to turn down; (ataque) to repel

rechazo [re'tʃaθo] *nm* rejection

rechifla [re'tʃifla] *nf* hissing, booing; (fig) derision

rechinar [retʃi'nar] *vi* to creak; (dientes) to grind

rechistar [retʃis'tar] *vi*: **sin ~** without a murmur

rechoncho, a [re'tʃontʃo, a] (fam) adj thickset (BRIT), heavy-set (US)

rechupete [retʃu'pete]: **de ~** (comida) delicious, scrumptious

recibidor, a [reθiβi'ðor, a] *nm* entrance hall

recibimiento [reθiβi'mjento] *nm* reception, welcome

recibir [reθi'βir] *vt* to receive; (dar la bienvenida) to welcome ♦ *vi* to entertain; **~se** *vr*: **~se de** to qualify as; **recibo** *nm* receipt

reciclar [reθi'klar] *vt* to recycle

recién [re'θjen] *adv* recently, newly; **los ~ casados** the newly-weds; **el ~ llegado** the newcomer; **el ~ nacido** the newborn child

reciente [re'θjente] *adj* recent; (fresco) fresh; **~mente** *adv* recently

recinto [re'θinto] *nm* enclosure; (área) area, place

recio, a ['reθjo, a] *adj* strong, tough; (voz) loud ♦ *adv* hard; loud(ly)

recipiente [reθi'pjente] *nm* receptacle

reciprocidad [reθiproθi'ðað] *nf* reciprocity; **recíproco, a** adj reciprocal

recital [reθi'tal] *nm* (MUS) recital; (LITERATURA) reading

recitar [reθi'tar] *vt* to recite

reclamación [reklama'θjon] *nf* claim, demand; (queja) complaint

reclamar [rekla'mar] *vt* to claim, demand ♦ *vi*: **~ contra** to complain about; **~ a uno en justicia** to take sb

to court; **reclamo** *nm* (anuncio) advertisement; (tentación) attraction

reclinar [rekli'nar] *vt* to recline, lean; **~se** *vr* to lean back

recluir [reklu'ir] *vt* to intern, confine

reclusión [reklu'sjon] *nf* (prisión) prison; (refugio) seclusion; **~ perpetua** life imprisonment

recluta [re'kluta] *nm/f* recruit ♦ *nf* recruitment; **reclutar** *vt* (datos) to collect; (dinero) to collect up; **~miento** [rekluta'mjento] *nm* recruitment

recobrar [reko'βrar] *vt* (salud) to recover; (rescatar) to get back; **~se** *vr* to recover

recodo [re'koðo] *nm* (de río, camino) bend

recogedor [rekoxe'ðor] *nm* dustpan

recoger [reko'xer] *vt* to collect; (AGR) to harvest; (levantar) to pick up; (juntar) to gather; (pasar a buscar) to come for, get; (dar asilo) to give shelter to; (faldas) to gather up; (pelo) to put up; **~se** *vr* (retirarse) to retire; **recogido, a** adj (lugar) quiet, secluded; (pequeño) small ♦ *nf* (CORREOS) collection; (AGR) harvest

recolección [rekolek'θjon] *nf* (AGR) harvesting; (colecta) collection

recomendación [rekomenda'θjon] *nf* (sugerencia) suggestion, recommendation; (referencia) reference

recomendar [rekomen'dar] *vt* to suggest, recommend; (confiar) to entrust

recompensa [rekom'pensa] *nf* reward, recompense; **recompensar** *vt* to reward, recompense

recomponer [rekompo'ner] *vt* to mend

reconciliación [rekonθilja'θjon] *nf* reconciliation

reconciliar [rekonθi'ljar] *vt* to reconcile; **~se** *vr* to become reconciled

recóndito, a [re'kondito, a] *adj* (lugar) hidden, secret

reconfortar [rekonfor'tar] *vt* to

comfort

reconocer [rekono'θer] vt to recognize; (registrar) to search; (MED) to examine; **reconocido, a** adj recognized; (agradecido) grateful; **reconocimiento** nm recognition; search; examination; gratitude; (confesión) admission

reconquista [rekon'kista] nf reconquest; **la R~** the Reconquest (of Spain)

reconstituyente [rekonstitu'jente] nm tonic

reconstruir [rekonstru'ir] vt to reconstruct

reconversión [rekonβer'sjon] nf: **~ industrial** industrial rationalization

recopilación [rekopila'θjon] nf (resumen) summary; (compilación) compilation; **recopilar** vt to compile

récord ['rekorð] (pl **~s**) adj inv, nm record

recordar [rekor'ðar] vt (acordarse de) to remember; (acordar a otro) to remind ♦ vi to remember

recorrer [reko'rrer] vt (país) to cross, travel through; (distancia) to cover; (registrar) to search; (repasar) to look over; **recorrido** nm run, journey; **tren de largo recorrido** main-line train

recortado, a [rekor'taðo, a] adj uneven, irregular

recortar [rekor'tar] vt to cut out; **recorte** nm (acción, de prensa) cutting; (de telas, chapas) trimming; **recorte presupuestario** budget cut

recostado, a [rekos'taðo, a] adj leaning; **estar ~** to be lying down

recostar [rekos'tar] vt to lean; **~se** vr to lie down

recoveco [reko'βeko] nm (de camino, río etc) bend; (en casa) cubby hole

recreación [rekrea'θjon] nf recreation

recrear [rekre'ar] vt (entretener) to entertain; (volver a crear) to recreate; **recreativo, a** adj recreational; **recreo** nm recreation; (ESCOL) break, playtime

recriminar [rekrimi'nar] vt to reproach ♦ vi to recriminate; **~se** vr to reproach each other

recrudecer [rekruðe'θer] vt, vi to worsen; **~se** vr to worsen

recrudecimiento [rekruðeθi'mjento] nm upsurge

recta ['rekta] nf straight line

rectángulo, á [rek'tangulo, a] adj rectangular ♦ nm rectangle

rectificar [rektifi'kar] vt to rectify; (volverse recto) to straighten ♦ vi to correct o.s.

rectitud [rekti'tuð] nf straightness

recto, a ['rekto, a] adj straight; (persona) honest, upright ♦ nm rectum

rector, a [rek'tor, a] adj governing

recuadro [re'kwaðro] nm box; (TIPOGRAFÍA) inset

recubrir [reku'βrir] vt: **~ (con)** (pintura, crema) to cover (with)

recuento [re'kwento] nm inventory; **hacer el ~ de** to count o reckon up

recuerdo [re'kwerðo] nm souvenir; **~s** nmpl (memorias) memories; **¡~s a tu madre!** give my regards to your mother!

recular [reku'lar] vi to back down

recuperable [rekupe'raβle] adj recoverable

recuperación [rekupera'θjon] nf recovery

recuperar [rekupe'rar] vt to recover; (tiempo) to make up; **~se** vr to recuperate

recurrir [reku'rrir] vi (JUR) to appeal; **~ a** to resort to; (persona) to turn to; **recurso** nm resort; (medios) means pl, resources pl; (JUR) appeal

recusar [reku'sar] vt to reject, refuse

red [reð] nf net, mesh; (FERRO etc) network; (trampa) trap; **la R~** (Internet) the Net

redacción [reðak'θjon] nf (acción) editing; (personal) editorial staff; (ESCOL) essay, composition

redactar [reðak'tar] vt to draw up,

draft; (*periódico*) to edit

redactor, a [reðak'tor, a] *nm/f* editor

redada [re'ðaða] *nf*: **~ policial** police raid, round-up

rededor [reðe'ðor] *nm*: **al o en ~** around, round about

redención [reðen'θjon] *nf* redemption

redicho, a [re'ðitʃo, a] *adj* affected

redil [re'ðil] *nm* sheepfold

redimir [reði'mir] *vt* to redeem

rédito ['reðito] *nm* interest, yield

redoblar [reðo'βlar] *vt* to redouble ♦ *vi* (*tambor*) to roll

redomado, a [reðo'maðo, a] *adj* (*astuto*) sly, crafty; (*perfecto*) utter

redonda [re'ðonda] *nf*: **a la ~** around, round about

redondear [reðonde'ar] *vt* to round, round off

redondel [reðon'del] *nm* (*círculo*) circle; (*TAUR*) bullring, arena

redondo, a [re'ðondo, a] *adj* (*circular*) round; (*completo*) complete

reducción [reðuk'θjon] *nf* reduction

reducido, a [reðu'θiðo, a] *adj* reduced; (*limitado*) limited; (*pequeño*) small

reducir [reðu'θir] *vt* to reduce; to limit; **~se** *vr* to diminish

redundancia [reðun'danθja] *nf* redundancy

reembolsar [re(e)mbol'sar] *vt* (*persona*) to reimburse; (*dinero*) to repay, pay back; (*depósito*) to refund; **reembolso** *nm* reimbursement; refund

reemplazar [re(e)mpla'θar] *vt* to replace; **reemplazo** *nm* replacement; **de reemplazo** (*MIL*) reserve

reencuentro [re(e)n'kwentro] *nm* reunion

referencia [refe'renθja] *nf* reference; **con ~ a** with reference to

referéndum [refe'rendum] (*pl* **~s**) *nm* referendum

referente [refe'rente] *adj*: **~ a** concerning, relating to

referir [refe'rir] *vt* (*contar*) to tell, recount; (*relacionar*) to refer, relate; **~se** *vr*: **~se a** to refer to

refilón [refi'lon]: **de ~** *adv* obliquely

refinado, a [refi'naðo, a] *adj* refined

refinamiento [refina'mjento] *nm* refinement

refinar [refi'nar] *vt* to refine; **refinería** *nf* refinery

reflejar [refle'xar] *vt* to reflect; **reflejo, a** *adj* reflected; (*movimiento*) reflex ♦ *nm* reflection; (*ANAT*) reflex

reflexión [reflek'sjon] *nf* reflection; **reflexionar** *vt* to reflect on ♦ *vi* to reflect; (*detenerse*) to pause (to think)

reflexivo, a [reflek'siβo, a] *adj* thoughtful; (*LING*) reflexive

reflujo [re'fluxo] *nm* ebb

reforma [re'forma] *nf* reform; (*ARQ etc*) repair; **~ agraria** agrarian reform

reformar [refor'mar] *vt* to reform; (*modificar*) to change, alter; (*ARQ*) to repair; **~se** *vr* to mend one's ways

reformatorio [reforma'torjo] *nm* reformatory

reforzar [refor'θar] *vt* to strengthen; (*ARQ*) to reinforce; (*fig*) to encourage

refractario, a [refrak'tarjo, a] *adj* (*TEC*) heat-resistant

refrán [re'fran] *nm* proverb, saying

refregar [refre'xar] *vt* to scrub

refrenar [refre'nar] *vt* to check, restrain

refrendar [refren'dar] *vt* (*firma*) to endorse, countersign; (*ley*) to approve

refrescante [refres'kante] *adj* refreshing, cooling

refrescar [refres'kar] *vt* to refresh ♦ *vi* to cool down; **~se** *vr* to get cooler; (*tomar aire fresco*) to go out for a breath of fresh air; (*beber*) to have a drink

refresco [re'fresko] *nm* soft drink, cool drink; **"~s"** "refreshments"

refriega [re'frjexa] *nf* scuffle, brawl

refrigeración [refrixera'θjon] *nf* refrigeration; (*de sala*) air-conditioning

refrigerador |refrixera'ðor| nm refrigerator (BRIT), icebox (US)

refrigerar |refrixe'rar| vt to refrigerate; (sala) to air-condition

refuerzo |re'fwerθo| nm reinforcement; (TEC) support

refugiado, a |refu'xjaðo, a| nm/f refugee

refugiarse |refu'xjarse| vr to take refuge, shelter

refugio |re'fuxjo| nm refuge; (protección) shelter

refunfuñar |refunfu'ɲar| vi to grunt, growl; (quejarse) to grumble

refutar |refu'tar| vt to refute

regadera |reɣa'ðera| nf watering can

regadío |reɣa'ðio| nm irrigated land

regalado, a |reɣa'laðo, a| adj comfortable, luxurious; (gratis) free, for nothing

regalar |reɣa'lar| vt (dar) to give (as a present); (entregar) to give away; (mimar) to pamper, make a fuss of

regaliz |reɣa'liθ| nm liquorice

regalo |re'ɣalo| nm (obsequio) gift, present; (gusto) pleasure

regañadientes |reɣaɲa'ðjentes|: a ~ adv reluctantly

regañar |reɣa'ɲar| vt to scold ♦ vi to grumble; **regañón, ona** adj nagging

regar |re'ɣar| vt to water, irrigate; (fig) to scatter, sprinkle

regatear |reɣate'ar| vt (COM) to bargain over; (escatimar) to be mean with ♦ vi to bargain, haggle; (DEPORTE) to dribble; **regateo** nm bargaining; dribbling; (del cuerpo) swerve, dodge

regazo |re'ɣaθo| nm lap

regeneración |rexenera'θjon| nf regeneration

regenerar |rexene'rar| vt to regenerate

regentar |rexen'tar| vt to direct, manage; **regente** nm (COM) manager; (POL) regent

régimen |'reximen| (pl **regímenes**) nm regime; (MED) diet

regimiento |rexi'mjento| nm regiment

regio, a |'rexjo, a| adj royal, regal; (fig: suntuoso) splendid; (AM: fam) great, terrific

región |re'xjon| nf region

regir |re'xir| vt to govern, rule; (dirigir) to manage, run ♦ vi to apply, be in force

registrar |rexis'trar| vt (buscar) to search; (: en cajón) to look through; (inspeccionar) to inspect; (anotar) to register, record; (INFORM) to log; **~se** vr to register; (ocurrir) to happen

registro |re'xistro| nm (acto) registration; (MUS, libro) register; (inspección) inspection, search; **~ civil** registry office

regla |'reɣla| nf (ley) rule, regulation; (de medir) ruler, rule; (MED: período) period

reglamentación |reɣlamenta'θjon| nf (acto) regulation; (lista) rules pl

reglamentar |reɣlamen'tar| vt to regulate; **reglamentario, a** adj statutory; **reglamento** nm rules pl, regulations pl

regocijarse |reɣoθi'xarse| vr: **~ de** to rejoice at, be happy about; **regocijo** nm joy, happiness

regodearse |reɣoðe'arse| vr to be glad, be delighted; **regodeo** nm delight

regresar |reɣre'sar| vi to come back, go back, return; **regresivo, a** adj backward; (fig) regressive; **regreso** nm return

reguero |re'ɣero| nm (de sangre etc) trickle; (de humo) trail

regulador |reɣula'ðor| nm regulator; (de radio etc) knob, control

regular |reɣu'lar| adj regular; (normal) normal, usual; (común) ordinary; (organizado) regular, orderly; (mediano) average; (fam) not bad, so-so ♦ adv so-so, alright ♦ vt (controlar) to control, regulate; (TEC) to adjust; **por lo ~** as a rule; **~idad** nf regularity; **~izar** vt to regularize

regusto [re'γusto] nm aftertaste

rehabilitación [reaβilita'θjon] nf rehabilitation; (ARQ) restoration

rehabilitar [reaβili'tar] vt to rehabilitate; (ARQ) to restore; (reintegrar) to reinstate

rehacer [rea'θer] vt (reparar) to mend, repair; (volver a hacer) to redo, repeat; **~se** vr (MED) to recover

rehén [re'en] nm hostage

rehuir [reu'ir] vt to avoid, shun

rehusar [reu'sar] vt, vi to refuse

reina ['reina] nf queen; **~do** nm reign

reinante [rei'nante] adj (fig) prevailing

reinar [rei'nar] vi to reign

reincidir [reinθi'ðir] vi to relapse

reincorporarse [reinkorpo'rarse] vr: **~ a** to rejoin

reino ['reino] nm kingdom; **el R~ Unido** the United Kingdom

reintegrar [reinte'γrar] vt (reconstituir) to reconstruct; (persona) to reinstate; (dinero) to refund, pay back; **~se** vr: **~se a** to return to

reír [re'ir] vi to laugh; **~se** vr to laugh; **~se de** to laugh at

reiterar [reite'rar] vt to reiterate

reivindicación [reiβindika'θjon] nf (demanda) claim, demand; (justificación) vindication

reivindicar [reiβindi'kar] vt to claim

reja ['rexa] nf (de ventana) grille, bars pl; (en la calle) grating

rejilla [re'xiʎa] nf grating, grille; (muebles) wickerwork; (de ventilación) vent; (de coche etc) luggage rack

rejoneador [rexonea'ðor] nm mounted bullfighter

rejuvenecer [rexuβene'θer] vt, vi to rejuvenate

relación [rela'θjon] nf relation, relationship; (MAT) ratio; (narración) report; **relaciones públicas** public relations; **con ~ a, en ~ con** in relation to; **relacionar** vt to relate,

connect; **relacionarse** vr to be connected, be linked

relajación [relaxa'θjon] nf relaxation

relajado, a [rela'xaðo, a] adj (disoluto) loose; (cómodo) relaxed; (MED) ruptured

relajar [rela'xar] vt to relax; **~se** vr to relax

relamerse [rela'merse] vr to lick one's lips

relamido, a [rela'miðo, a] adj (pulcro) overdressed; (afectado) affected

relámpago [re'lampaγo] nm flash of lightning; **visita/huelga ~** lightning visit/strike; **relampaguear** vi to flash

relatar [rela'tar] vt to tell, relate

relativo, a [rela'tiβo, a] adj relative; **en lo ~ a** concerning

relato [re'lato] nm (narración) story, tale

relegar [rele'γar] vt to relegate

relevante [rele'βante] adj eminent, outstanding

relevar [rele'βar] vt (sustituir) to relieve; **~se** vr to relay; **~ a uno de un cargo** to relieve sb of his post

relevo [re'leβo] nm relief; **carrera de ~s** relay race

relieve [re'ljeβe] nm (ARTE, TEC) relief; (fig) prominence, importance; **bajo ~** bas-relief

religión [reli'xjon] nf religion; **religioso, a** adj religious ♦ nm/f monk/nun

relinchar [relin'tʃar] vi to neigh; **relincho** nm neigh; (acto) neighing

reliquia [re'likja] nf relic; **~ de familia** heirloom

rellano [re'ʎano] nm (ARQ) landing

rellenar [reʎe'nar] vt (llenar) to fill up; (CULIN) to stuff; (COSTURA) to pad; **relleno, a** adj full up; stuffed ♦ nm stuffing; (de tapicería) padding

reloj [re'lo(x)] nm clock; **~ (de pulsera)** wristwatch; **~ (despertador)** alarm (clock); **poner el ~** to set one's watch (o the clock); **~ero, a** nm/f clockmaker; watchmaker

reluciente [relu'θjente] adj brilliant, shining

relucir [relu'θir] vi to shine; (fig) to excel

relumbrar [relum'brar] vi to dazzle, shine brilliantly

remachar [rema'tʃar] vt to rivet; (fig) to hammer home, drive home; **remache** nm rivet

remanente [rema'nente] nm remainder; (COM) balance; (de producto) surplus

remangar [reman'gar] vt to roll up

remanso [re'manso] nm pool

remar [re'mar] vi to row

rematado, a [rema'taðo, a] adj complete, utter

rematar [rema'tar] vt to finish off; (COM) to sell off cheap ♦ vi to end, finish off; (DEPORTE) to shoot

remate [re'mate] nm end, finish; (punta: DEPORTE) tip; **de o para** to crown it all (BRIT), to top it off

remedar [reme'ðar] vt to imitate

remediar [reme'ðjar] vt to remedy; (subsanar) to make good, repair; (evitar) to avoid

remedio [re'meðjo] nm remedy; (alivio) relief, help; (JUR) recourse, remedy; **poner ~ a** to correct, stop; **no tener más ~** to have no alternative; **¡qué ~!** there's no choice!; **sin ~** hopeless

remedo [re'meðo] nm imitation; (pey) parody

remendar [remen'dar] vt to repair; (con parche) to patch

remesa [re'mesa] nf remittance; (COM) shipment

remiendo [re'mjendo] nm mend; (con parche) patch; (cosido) darn

remilgado, a [remil'gaðo, a] adj prim; (afectado) affected

remilgo [re'milɣo] nm primness; (afectación) affectation

reminiscencia [reminis'θenθja] nf reminiscence

remiso, a [re'miso, a] adj slack, slow

remite [re'mite] nm (en sobre) name and address of sender

remitir [remi'tir] vt to remit, send ♦ vi to slacken; (en carta): **remite: X** sender: **X**; **remitente** nm/f sender

remo ['remo] nm (de barco) oar; (DEPORTE) rowing

remojar [remo'xar] vt to steep, soak; (galleta etc) to dip, dunk

remojo [re'moxo] nm: **dejar la ropa en ~** to leave clothes to soak

remolacha [remo'latʃa] nf beet, beetroot

remolcador [remolka'ðor] nm (NAUT) tug; (AUTO) breakdown lorry

remolcar [remol'kar] vt to tow

remolino [remo'lino] nm eddy; (de agua) whirlpool; (de viento) whirlwind; (de gente) crowd

remolque [re'molke] nm tow, towing; (cuerda) towrope; **llevar a ~** to tow

remontar [remon'tar] vt to mend; **~se** vr to soar; **~se a** (COM) to amount to; **~ el vuelo** to soar

remorder [remor'ðer] vt to distress, disturb; **~le la conciencia a uno** to have a guilty conscience; **remordimiento** nm remorse

remoto, a [re'moto, a] adj remote

remover [remo'ßer] vt to stir; (tierra) to turn over; (objetos) to move round

remozar [remo'θar] vt (ARQ) to refurbish

remuneración [remunera'θjon] nf remuneration

remunerar [remune'rar] vt to remunerate; (premiar) to reward

renacer [rena'θer] vi to be reborn; (fig) to revive; **renacimiento** nm rebirth; **el Renacimiento** the Renaissance

renacuajo [rena'kwaxo] nm (ZOOL) tadpole

renal [re'nal] adj renal, kidney cpd

rencilla [ren'θiʎa] nf quarrel

rencor [ren'kor] nm rancour,
bitterness; **~oso, a** adj spiteful
rendición [rendi'θjon] nf surrender
rendido, a [ren'diðo, a] adj (sumiso)
submissive; (cansado) worn-out,
exhausted
rendija [ren'dixa] nf (hendedura) crack,
cleft
rendimiento [rendi'mjento] nm
(producción) output; (TEC, COM)
efficiency
rendir [ren'dir] vt (vencer) to defeat;
(producir) to produce; (dar beneficio) to
yield; (agotar) to exhaust ♦ vi to pay;
~se vr (someterse) to surrender;
(cansarse) to wear o.s. out;
~ homenaje o **culto a** to pay
homage to
renegar [rene'var] vt (renunciar) to
renounce; (blasfemar) to blaspheme;
(quejarse) to complain
RENFE ['renfe] nf abr (= Red Nacional
de los Ferrocarriles Españoles) ≈ BR
(BRIT)
renglón [ren'glon] nm (línea) line;
(COM) item, article; **a ~ seguido**
immediately after
renombrado, a [renom'braðo, a] adj
renowned
renombre [re'nombre] nm renown
renovación [renoßa'θjon] nf (de
contrato) renewal; (ARQ) renovation
renovar [reno'ßar] vt to renew; (ARQ)
to renovate
renta ['renta] nf (ingresos) income;
(beneficio) profit; (alquiler) rent;
~ vitalicia annuity; **rentable** adj
profitable; **rentar** vt to produce, yield
renuncia [re'nunθja] nf resignation
renunciar [renun'θjar] vt to renounce;
(tabaco, alcohol etc): **~ a** to give up;
(oferta, oportunidad) to turn down;
(puesto) to resign ♦ vi to resign
reñido, a [re'ɲiðo, a] adj (batalla)
bitter, hard-fought; **estar ~ con uno**
to be on bad terms with sb
reñir [re'ɲir] vt (regañar) to scold ♦ vi

(estar peleado) to quarrel, fall out;
(combatir) to fight
reo ['reo] nm/f culprit, offender; **~ de
muerte** prisoner condemned to death
reojo [re'oxo]: **de ~** adv out of the
corner of one's eye
reparación [repara'θjon] nf (acto)
mending, repairing; (TEC) repair; (fig)
amends, reparation
reparar [repa'rar] vt to repair; (fig) to
make amends for; (observar) to observe
♦ vi: **~ en** (darse cuenta de) to notice;
(prestar atención a) to pay attention to
reparo [re'paro] nm (advertencia)
observation; (duda) doubt; (dificultad)
difficulty; **poner ~s (a)** to raise
objections (to)
repartición [reparti'θjon] nf
distribution; (división) division;
repartidor, a nm/f distributor
repartir [repar'tir] vt to distribute,
share out; (CORREOS) to deliver;
reparto nm distribution; delivery;
(TEATRO, CINE) cast; (AM: urbanización)
housing estate (BRIT), real estate
development (US)
repasar [repa'sar] vt (ESCOL) to revise;
(MECÁNICA) to check, overhaul;
(COSTURA) to mend; **repaso** nm
revision; overhaul, check; mending
repatriar [repa'trjar] vt to repatriate
repecho [re'petʃo] nm steep incline
repelente [repe'lente] adj repellent,
repulsive
repeler [repe'ler] vt to repel
repensar [repen'sar] vt to reconsider
repente [re'pente] nm: **de ~** suddenly;
~ de ira fit of anger
repentino, a [repen'tino, a] adj
sudden
repercusión [reperku'sjon] nf
repercussion
repercutir [reperku'tir] vi (objeto) to
rebound; (sonido) to echo; **~ en** (fig)
to have repercussions on
repertorio [reper'torjo] nm list;
(TEATRO) repertoire

repetición [repeti'θjon] nf repetition

repetir [repe'tir] vt to repeat; (*plato*) to have a second helping of ♦ vi to repeat; (*sabor*) to come back; **~se** vr (*volver sobre un tema*) to repeat o.s.

repetitivo, a [repeti'tiβo, a] adj repetitive, repetitious

repicar [repi'kar] vt (*campanas*) to ring

repique [re'pike] nm pealing, ringing; **~teo** nm pealing; (*de tambor*) drumming

repisa [re'pisa] nf ledge, shelf; (*de ventana*) windowsill; **~ de chimenea** mantelpiece

repito etc vb ver **repetir**

replantearse [replante'arse] vr: **~ un problema** to reconsider a problem

replegarse [reple'varse] vr to fall back, retreat

repleto, a [re'pleto, a] adj replete, full up

réplica ['replika] nf answer; (*ARTE*) replica

replicar [repli'kar] vi to answer; (*objetar*) to argue, answer back

repliegue [re'pljeve] nm (*MIL*) withdrawal

repoblación [repoβla'θjon] nf repopulation; (*de río*) restocking; **~ forestal** reafforestation

repoblar [repo'βlar] vt to repopulate; (*con árboles*) to reafforest

repollo [re'poλo] nm cabbage

reponer [repo'ner] vt to replace, put back; (*TEATRO*) to revive; **~se** vr to recover; **~ que** to reply that

reportaje [repor'taxe] nm report, article

reportero, a [repor'tero, a] nm/f reporter

reposacabezas [reposaka'βeθas] nm inv headrest

reposado, a [repo'saðo, a] adj (*descansado*) restful; (*tranquilo*) calm

reposar [repo'sar] vi to rest, repose

reposición [reposi'θjon] nf replacement; (*CINE*) remake

reposo [re'poso] nm rest

repostar [repos'tar] vt to replenish; (*AUTO*) to fill up (with petrol (*BRIT*) o gasoline (*US*))

repostería [reposte'ria] nf confectioner's (shop); **repostero, a** nm/f confectioner

reprender [repren'der] vt to reprimand

represa [re'presa] nf dam; (*lago artificial*) lake, pool

represalia [repre'salja] nf reprisal

representación [representa'θjon] nf representation; (*TEATRO*) performance; **representante** nm/f representative; performer

representar [represen'tar] vt to represent; (*TEATRO*) to perform; (*edad*) to look; **~se** vr to imagine; **representativo, a** adj representative

represión [repre'sjon] nf repression

reprimenda [repri'menda] nf reprimand, rebuke

reprimir [repri'mir] vt to repress

reprobar [repro'βar] vt to censure, reprove

reprochar [repro'tʃar] vt to reproach; **reproche** nm reproach

reproducción [reproðuk'θjon] nf reproduction

reproducir [reproðu'θir] vt to reproduce; **~se** vr to breed; (*situación*) to recur

reproductor, a [reproðuk'tor, a] adj reproductive

reptil [rep'til] nm reptile

república [re'puβlika] nf republic; **R~ Dominicana** Dominican Republic; **republicano, a** adj, nm/f republican

repudiar [repu'ðjar] vt to repudiate; (*fe*) to renounce

repuesto [re'pwesto] nm (*pieza de recambio*) spare (part); (*abastecimiento*) supply; **rueda de ~** spare wheel

repugnancia [repuɣ'nanθja] nf repugnance; **repugnante** adj repugnant, repulsive

repugnar [repuɣˈnar] vt to disgust

repulsa [reˈpulsa] nf rebuff

repulsión [repulˈsjon] nf repulsion, aversion; **repulsivo, a** adj repulsive

reputación [reputaˈθjon] nf reputation

requemado, a [rekeˈmaðo, a] adj (quemado) scorched; (bronceado) tanned

requerimiento [rekeriˈmjento] nm request; (JUR) summons

requerir [rekeˈrir] vt (pedir) to ask, request; (exigir) to require; (llamar) to send for, summon

requesón [rekeˈson] nm cottage cheese

requete... [reˈkete] prefijo extremely

réquiem [ˈrekjem] (pl **~s**) nm requiem

requisito [rekiˈsito] nm requirement, requisite

res [res] nf beast, animal

resaca [reˈsaka] nf (en el mar) undertow, undercurrent; (fam) hangover

resaltar [resalˈtar] vi to project, stick out; (fig) to stand out

resarcir [resarˈθir] vt to compensate; **~se** vr to make up for

resbaladizo, a [resβalaˈðiθo, a] adj slippery

resbalar [resβaˈlar] vi to slip, slide; (fig) to slip (up); **~se** vr: to slip, slide; to slip (up); **resbalón** nm (acción) slip

rescatar [reskaˈtar] vt (salvar) to save, rescue; (objeto) to get back, recover; (cautivos) to ransom

rescate [resˈkate] nm rescue; (de objeto) recovery; **pagar un ~** to pay a ransom

rescindir [resθinˈdir] vt to rescind

rescisión [resθiˈsjon] nf cancellation

rescoldo [resˈkoldo] nm embers pl

resecar [reseˈkar] vt to dry thoroughly; (MED) to cut out, remove; **~se** vr to dry up

reseco, a [reˈseko, a] adj very dry; (fig) skinny

resentido, a [resenˈtiðo, a] adj resentful

resentimiento [resentiˈmjento] nm resentment, bitterness

resentirse [resenˈtirse] vr (debilitarse: persona) to suffer; **~ de** (consecuencias) to feel the effects of; **~ de** (o por) **algo** to resent sth, be bitter about sth

reseña [reˈseɲa] nf (cuenta) account; (informe) report; (LITERATURA) review

reseñar [reseˈɲar] vt to describe; (LITERATURA) to review

reserva [reˈserβa] nf reserve; (reservación) reservation; **a ~ de que ...** unless ...; **con toda ~** in strictest confidence

reservado, a [reserˈβaðo, a] adj reserved; (retraído) cold, distant ♦ nm private room

reservar [reserˈβar] vt (guardar) to keep; (habitación, entrada) to reserve; **~se** vr to save o.s.; (callar) to keep to o.s.

resfriado [resfriˈaðo] nm cold; **resfriarse** vr to cool; (MED) to catch (a) cold

resguardar [resɣwarˈðar] vt to protect, shield; **~se** vr: **~se de** to guard against; **resguardo** nm defence; (vale) voucher; (recibo) receipt, slip

residencia [resiˈðenθja] nf residence; **~l** (urbanización) housing estate

residente [resiˈðente] adj, nm/f resident

residir [resiˈðir] vi to reside, live; **~ en** to reside in, lie in

residuo [reˈsiðwo] nm residue

resignación [resiɣnaˈθjon] nf resignation; **resignarse** vr: **resignarse a** o **con** to resign o.s. to, be resigned to

resina [reˈsina] nf resin

resistencia [resisˈtenθja] nf (dureza) endurance, strength; (oposición, ELEC) resistance; **resistente** adj strong, hardy; resistant

resistir [resisˈtir] vt (soportar) to bear,

(*oponerse a*) to resist, oppose; (*aguantar*) to put up with ♦ *vi* to resist; (*aguantar*) to last, endure; **~se** *vr*: **~se a** to refuse to, resist

resolución [resolu'θjon] *nf* resolution; (*decisión*) decision; **resoluto, a** *adj* resolute

resolver [resol'βer] *vt* to resolve; (*solucionar*) to solve, resolve; (*decidir*) to decide, settle; **~se** *vr* to make up one's mind

resonancia [reso'nanθja] *nf* (*del sonido*) resonance; (*repercusión*) repercussion

resonar [reso'nar] *vi* to ring, echo

resoplar [reso'plar] *vi* to snort; **resoplido** *nm* heavy breathing

resorte [re'sorte] *nm* spring; (*fig*) lever

respaldar [respal'dar] *vt* to back (up), support; **~se** *vr* to lean back; **~se con** o **en** (*fig*) to take one's stand on; **respaldo** *nm* (*de sillón*) back; (*fig*) support, backing

respectivo, a [respek'tiβo, a] *adj* respective; **en lo ~ a** with regard to

respecto [res'pekto] *nm*: **al ~** on this matter; **con ~ a**, **~ de** with regard to, in relation to

respetable [respe'taβle] *adj* respectable

respetar [respe'tar] *vt* to respect; **respeto** *nm* respect; (*acatamiento*) deference; **respetos** *nmpl* respects; **respetuoso, a** *adj* respectful

respingo [res'pingo] *nm* start, jump

respiración [respira'θjon] *nf* breathing; (*MED*) respiration; (*ventilación*) ventilation

respirar [respi'rar] *vi* to breathe; **respiratorio, a** *adj* respiratory; **respiro** *nm* breathing; (*fig: descanso*) respite

resplandecer [resplande'θer] *vi* to shine; **resplandeciente** *adj* resplendent, shining; **resplandor** *nm* brilliance, brightness; (*de luz, fuego*) blaze

responder [respon'der] *vt* to answer ♦ *vi* to answer; (*fig*) to respond; (*pey*) to answer back; **~ de** o **por** to answer for; **respondón, ona** *adj* cheeky

responsabilidad [responsaβili'ðað] *nf* responsibility

responsabilizarse [responsaβili-'θarse] *vr* to make o.s. responsible, take charge

responsable [respon'saβle] *adj* responsible

respuesta [res'pwesta] *nf* answer, reply

resquebrajar [reskeβra'xar] *vt* to crack, split; **~se** *vr* to crack, split

resquemor [reske'mor] *nm* resentment

resquicio [res'kiθjo] *nm* chink; (*hendedura*) crack

resta ['resta] *nf* (*MAT*) remainder

restablecer [restaβle'θer] *vt* to re-establish, restore; **~se** *vr* to recover

restallar [resta'λar] *vi* to crack

restante [res'tante] *adj* remaining; **lo ~** the remainder

restar [res'tar] *vt* (*MAT*) to subtract; (*fig*) to take away ♦ *vi* to remain, be left

restauración [restaura'θjon] *nf* restoration

restaurante [restau'rante] *nm* restaurant

restaurar [restau'rar] *vt* to restore

restitución [restitu'θjon] *nf* return, restitution

restituir [restitu'ir] *vt* (*devolver*) to return, give back; (*rehabilitar*) to restore

resto ['resto] *nm* (*residuo*) rest, remainder; (*apuesta*) stake; **~s** *nmpl* remains

restregar [restre'var] *vt* to scrub, rub

restricción [restrik'θjon] *nf* restriction

restrictivo, a [restrik'tiβo, a] *adj* restrictive

restringir [restrin'xir] *vt* to restrict, limit

resucitar [resuθi'tar] vt, vi to resuscitate, revive

resuello [re'sweλo] nm (aliento) breath; **estar sin ~** to be breathless

resuelto, a [re'swelto, a] pp de **resolver** ♦ adj resolute, determined

resultado [resul'taðo] nm result; (conclusión) outcome; **resultante** adj resulting, resultant

resultar [resul'tar] vi (ser) to be; (llegar a ser) to turn out to be; (salir bien) to turn out well; (COM) to amount to; **~ de** to stem from; **me resulta difícil hacerlo** it's difficult for me to do it

resumen [re'sumen] (pl resúmenes) nm summary, résumé; **en ~** in short

resumir [resu'mir] vt to sum up; (cortar) to abridge, cut down; (condensar) to summarize

resurgir [resur'xir] vi (reaparecer) to reappear

resurrección [resurre(k)'θjon] nf resurrection

retablo [re'taβlo] nm altarpiece

retaguardia [reta'ɣwarðja] nf rearguard

retahíla [reta'ila] nf series, string

retal [re'tal] nm remnant

retar [re'tar] vt to challenge; (desafiar) to defy, dare

retardar [retar'ðar] vt (demorar) to delay; (hacer más lento) to slow down; (retener) to hold back

retazo [re'taθo] nm snippet (BRIT), fragment

retener [rete'ner] vt (intereses) to withhold

reticente [reti'θente] adj (tono) insinuating; (postura) reluctant; **ser ~ a hacer algo** to be reluctant o unwilling to do sth

retina [re'tina] nf retina

retintín [retin'tin] nm jangle, jingle

retirada [reti'raða] nf (MIL, refugio) retreat; (de dinero) withdrawal; (de embajador) recall; **retirado, a** adj (lugar) remote; (vida) quiet; (jubilado) retired

retirar [reti'rar] vt to withdraw; (quitar) to remove; (jubilar) to retire, pension off; **~se** vr to retreat, withdraw; to retire; (acostarse) to retire, go to bed; **retiro** nm retreat; retirement; (pago) pension

reto ['reto] nm dare, challenge

retocar [reto'kar] vt (fotografía) to touch up, retouch

retoño [re'toɲo] nm sprout, shoot; (fig) offspring, child

retoque [re'toke] nm retouching

retorcer [retor'θer] vt to twist; (manos, lavado) to wring; **~se** vr to become twisted; (mover el cuerpo) to writhe

retorcido, a [retor'θiðo, a] adj (persona) devious

retórica [re'torika] nf rhetoric; (pey) affectedness; **retórico, a** adj rhetorical

retornar [retor'nar] vt to return, give back ♦ vi to return, go/come back; **retorno** nm return

retortijón [retorti'xon] nm twist, twisting

retozar [reto'θar] vi (juguetear) to frolic, romp; (saltar) to gambol; **retozón, ona** adj playful

retracción [retrak'θjon] nf retraction

retractarse [retrak'tarse] vr to retract; **me retracto** I take that back

retraerse [retra'erse] vr to retreat, withdraw; **retraído, a** adj shy, retiring; **retraimiento** nm retirement; (timidez) shyness

retransmisión [retransmi'sjon] nf repeat (broadcast)

retransmitir [retransmi'tir] vt (mensaje) to relay; (TV etc) to repeat, retransmit; (: en vivo) to broadcast live

retrasado, a [retra'saðo, a] adj late; (MED) mentally retarded; (país etc) backward, underdeveloped

retrasar [retra'sar] vt (demorar) to postpone, put off; (retardar) to slow down ♦ vi (atrasarse) to be late; (reloj) to be slow; (producción) to fall off;

(*quedarse atrás*) to lag behind; **~se** *vr* to be late; to be slow; to fall (off); to lag behind

retraso [re'traso] *nm* (*demora*) delay; (*lentitud*) slowness; (*tardanza*) lateness; (*atraso*) backwardness; **~s** (*FINANZAS*) *nmpl* arrears; **llegar con ~** to arrive late; **~ mental** mental deficiency

retratar [retra'tar] *vt* (*ARTE*) to paint the portrait of; (*fotografiar*) to photograph; (*fig*) to depict, describe; **~se** *vr* to have one's portrait painted; to have one's photograph taken; **retrato** *nm* portrait; (*fig*) likeness; **retrato-robot** *nm* Identikit ® picture

retreta [re'treta] *nf* retreat

retrete [re'trete] *nm* toilet

retribución [retriβu'θjon] *nf* (*recompensa*) reward; (*pago*) pay, payment

retribuir [retri'βwir] *vt* (*recompensar*) to reward; (*pagar*) to pay

retro... ['retro] *prefijo* retro...

retroactivo, a [retroak'tiβo, a] *adj* retroactive, retrospective

retroceder [retroθe'ðer] *vi* (*echarse atrás*) to move back(wards); (*fig*) to back down

retroceso [retro'θeso] *nm* backward movement; (*MED*) relapse; (*fig*) backing down

retrógrado, a [re'troγraðo, a] *adj* retrograde, retrogressive; (*POL*) reactionary

retrospectivo, a [retrospek'tiβo, a] *adj* retrospective

retrovisor [retroβi'sor] *nm* (*tb: espejo ~*) rear-view mirror

retumbar [retum'bar] *vi* to echo, resound

reúma [re'uma], **reuma** ['reuma] *nm* rheumatism

reumatismo [reuma'tismo] *nm* = **reúma**

reunificar [reunifi'kar] *vt* to reunify

reunión [reu'njon] *nf* (*asamblea*) meeting; (*fiesta*) party

reunir [reu'nir] *vt* (*juntar*) to reunite, join (together); (*recoger*) to gather (together); (*personas*) to get together; (*cualidades*) to combine; **~se** *vr* (*personas: en asamblea*) to meet, gather

revalidar [reβali'ðar] *vt* (*ratificar*) to confirm, ratify

revalorizar [reβalori'θar] *vt* to revalue, reassess

revancha [re'βantʃa] *nf* revenge

revelación [reβela'θjon] *nf* revelation

revelado [reβe'laðo] *nm* developing

revelar [reβe'lar] *vt* to reveal; (*FOTO*) to develop

reventa [re'βenta] *nf* (*de entradas: para concierto*) touting

reventar [reβen'tar] *vt* to burst, explode

reventón [reβen'ton] *nm* (*AUTO*) blow-out (*BRIT*), flat (*US*)

reverencia [reβe'renθja] *nf* reverence; **reverenciar** *vt* to revere

reverendo, a [reβe'rendo, a] *adj* reverend

reverente [reβe'rente] *adj* reverent

reversible [reβer'siβle] *adj* (*prenda*) reversible

reverso [re'βerso] *nm* back, other side; (*de moneda*) reverse

revertir [reβer'tir] *vi* to revert

revés [re'βes] *nm* back, wrong side; (*fig*) reverse, setback; (*DEPORTE*) backhand; **al ~** the wrong way round; (*de arriba abajo*) upside down; (*ropa*) inside out; **volver algo del ~** to turn sth round; (*ropa*) to turn sth inside out

revestir [reβes'tir] *vt* (*cubrir*) to cover, coat

revisar [reβi'sar] *vt* (*examinar*) to check; (*texto etc*) to revise; **revisión** *nf* revision

revisor, a [reβi'sor, a] *nm/f* inspector; (*FERRO*) ticket collector

revista [re'βista] *nf* magazine, review; (*TEATRO*) revue; (*inspección*) inspection; **pasar ~ a** to review, inspect

revivir [reβi'βir] *vi* to revive

revocación [reβoka'θjon] *nf* repeal

revocar [reβo'kar] *vt* to revoke

revolcarse [reβol'karse] *vr* to roll about

revolotear [reβolote'ar] *vi* to flutter

revoltijo [reβol'tixo] *nm* mess, jumble

revoltoso, a [reβol'toso, a] *adj* (*travieso*) naughty, unruly

revolución [reβolu'θjon] *nf* revolution; **revolucionar** *vt* to revolutionize; **revolucionario, a** *adj, nm/f* revolutionary

revolver [reβol'βer] *vt* (*desordenar*) to disturb, mess up; (*mover*) to move about ♦ *vi*: ~ **en** to go through, rummage (about) in; **~se** *vr* (*volver contra*) to turn on *o* against

revólver [re'βolßer] *nm* revolver

revuelo [re'ßwelo] *nm* fluttering; (*fig*) commotion

revuelta [re'ßwelta] *nf* (*motín*) revolt; (*agitación*) commotion

revuelto, a [re'ßwelto, a] *pp de* **revolver** ♦ *adj* (*mezclado*) mixed-up, in disorder

rey [rei] *nm* king; **Día de R~es** Twelfth Night

reyerta [re'jerta] *nf* quarrel, brawl

rezagado, a [reθa'vaðo, a] *nm/f* straggler

rezagar [reθa'var] *vt* (*dejar atrás*) to leave behind; (*retrasar*) to delay, postpone

rezar [re'θar] *vi* to pray; ~ **con** (*fam*) to concern, have to do with; **rezo** *nm* prayer

rezongar [reθon'gar] *vi* to grumble

rezumar [reθu'mar] *vt* to ooze

ría ['ria] *nf* estuary

riada [ri'aða] *nf* flood

ribera [ri'ßera] *nf* (*de río*) bank; (: *área*) riverside

ribete [ri'ßete] *nm* (*de vestido*) border; (*fig*) addition; **~ar** *vt* to edge, border

ricino [ri'θino] *nm*: **aceite de ~** castor oil

rico, a ['riko, a] *adj* rich; (*adinerado*) wealthy, rich; (*lujoso*) luxurious; (*comida*) delicious; (*niño*) lovely, cute ♦ *nm/f* rich person

rictus ['riktus] *nm* (*mueca*) sneer, grin

ridículez [riðiku'leθ] *nf* absurdity

ridiculizar [riðikuli'θar] *vt* to ridicule

ridículo, a [ri'ðikulo, a] *adj* ridiculous; **hacer el ~** to make a fool of o.s.; **poner a uno en ~** to make a fool of sb

riego ['rjevo] *nm* (*aspersión*) watering; (*irrigación*) irrigation

riel [rjel] *nm* rail

rienda ['rjenda] *nf* rein; **dar ~ suelta a** to give free rein to

riesgo ['rjesvo] *nm* risk; **correr el ~ de** to run the risk of

rifa ['rifa] *nf* (*lotería*) raffle; **rifar** *vt* to raffle

rifle ['rifle] *nm* rifle

rigidez [rixi'ðeθ] *nf* rigidity, stiffness; (*fig*) strictness; **rígido, a** *adj* rigid, stiff; strict, inflexible

rigor [ri'vor] *nm* strictness, rigour; (*inclemencia*) harshness; **de ~** de rigueur, essential; **riguroso, a** *adj* rigorous; harsh; (*severo*) severe

rimar [ri'mar] *vi* to rhyme

rimbombante [rimbom'bante] *adj* pompous

rímel ['rimel] *nm* mascara

rímmel ['rimel] *nm* = **rímel**

rincón [rin'kon] *nm* corner (*inside*)

rinoceronte [rinoθe'ronte] nm rhinoceros

riña ['riɲa] nf (disputa) argument; (pelea) brawl

riñón [ri'ɲon] nm kidney

río etc ['rio] vb ver **reír** ♦ nm river; (fig) torrent; stream; ~ **abajo/arriba** downstream/upstream; ~ **de la Plata** River Plate

rioja [ri'oxa] nm (vino) rioja (wine)

rioplatense [riopla'tense] adj de o from the River Plate region

riqueza [ri'keθa] nf wealth, riches pl; (cualidad) richness

risa ['risa] nf laughter; (una ~) laugh; **¡qué ~!** what a laugh!

risco ['risko] nm crag, cliff

risible [ri'siβle] adj ludicrous, laughable

risotada [riso'taða] nf guffaw, loud laugh

ristra ['ristra] nf string

risueño, a [ri'sweɲo, a] adj (sonriente) smiling; (contento) cheerful

ritmo ['ritmo] nm rhythm; **a ~ lento** slowly; **trabajar a ~ lento** to go slow

rito ['rito] nm rite

ritual [ri'twal] adj, nm ritual

rival [ri'βal] adj, nm/f rival; **~idad** nf rivalry; **~izar** vi: **~izar con** to rival, vie with

rizado, a [ri'θaðo, a] adj curly ♦ nm curls pl

rizar [ri'θar] vt to curl; **~se** vr (pelo) to curl; (agua) to ripple; **rizo** nm curl; ripple

RNE nf abr = **Radio Nacional de España**

robar [ro'βar] vt to rob; (objeto) to steal; (casa etc) to break into; (NAIPES) to draw

roble ['roβle] nm oak; **~dal** nm oakwood

robo ['roβo] nm robbery, theft

robot [ro'βot] nm robot; ~ **(de cocina)** food processor

robustecer [roβuste'θer] vt to strengthen

robusto, a [ro'βusto, a] adj robust, strong

roca ['roka] nf rock

roce ['roθe] nm (caricia) brush; (TEC) friction; (en la piel) graze; **tener ~ con** to be in close contact with

rociar [ro'θjar] vt to spray

rocín [ro'θin] nm nag, hack

rocío [ro'θio] nm dew

rocoso, a [ro'koso, a] adj rocky

rodaballo [roða'βaʎo] nm turbot

rodado, a [ro'ðaðo, a] adj (con ruedas) wheeled

rodaja [ro'ðaxa] nf slice

rodaje [ro'ðaxe] nm (CINE) shooting, filming; (AUTO): **en ~** running in

rodar [ro'ðar] vt (vehículo) to wheel (along); (escalera) to roll down; (viajar por) to travel (over) ♦ vi (coche) to go, run; (CINE) to shoot, film

rodear [roðe'ar] vt to surround ♦ vi to go round; **~se** vr: **~se de amigos** to surround o.s. with friends

rodeo [ro'ðeo] nm (ruta indirecta) detour; (evasión) evasion; (AM) rodeo; **hablar sin ~s** to come to the point, speak plainly

rodilla [ro'ðiʎa] nf knee; **de ~s** kneeling; **ponerse de ~s** to kneel (down)

rodillo [ro'ðiʎo] nm roller; (CULIN) rolling-pin

roedor, a [roe'ðor, a] adj gnawing ♦ nm rodent

roer [ro'er] vt (masticar) to gnaw; (corroer, fig) to corrode

rogar [ro'ɣar] vt, vi (pedir) to ask for; (suplicar) to beg, plead; **se ruega no fumar** please do not smoke

rojizo, a [ro'xiθo, a] adj reddish

rojo, a ['roxo, a] adj, nm red; **al ~ vivo** red-hot

rol [rol] nm list, roll; (papel) role

rollito [ro'ʎito] nm: ~ **de primavera** spring roll

rollizo, a [ro'ʎiθo, a] adj (objeto) cylindrical; (persona) plump

rollo ['roʎo] nm roll; (de cuerda) coil; (madera) log; (fam) bore; ¡qué ~! what a carry-on!

Roma ['roma] n Rome

romance [ro'manθe] nm (amoroso) romance; (LITERATURA) ballad

romano, a [ro'mano, a] adj, nm/f Roman; **a la romana** in batter

romanticismo [romanti'θismo] nm romanticism

romántico, a [ro'mantiko, a] adj romantic

rombo ['rombo] nm (GEOM) rhombus

romería [rome'ria] nf (REL) pilgrimage; (excursión) trip, outing

---
Romería

Originally a pilgrimage to a shrine or church to express devotion to the Virgin Mary or a local Saint, the **romería** has also become a rural festival which accompanies the pilgrimage. People come from all over to attend, bringing their own food and drink, and spend the day in celebration.

---

romero, a [ro'mero, a] nm/f pilgrim ♦ nm rosemary

romo, a ['romo, a] adj blunt; (fig) dull

rompecabezas [rompeka'beθas] nm inv riddle, puzzle; (juego) jigsaw (puzzle)

rompeolas [rompe'olas] nm inv breakwater

romper [rom'per] vt to break; (hacer pedazos) to smash; (papel, tela etc) to tear, rip ♦ vi (olas) to break; (sol, diente) to break through; ~ **un contrato** to break a contract; ~ **a** (empezar a) to start (suddenly) to; ~ **a llorar** to burst into tears; ~ **con uno** to fall out with sb

ron [ron] nm rum

roncar [ron'kar] vi to snore

ronco, a ['ronko, a] adj (afónico) hoarse; (áspero) raucous

ronda ['ronda] nf (gen) round; (patrulla) patrol; **rondar** vt to patrol ♦ vi to patrol; (fig) to prowl round

ronquido [ron'kiðo] nm snore, snoring

ronronear [ronrone'ar] vi to purr; **ronroneo** nm purr

roña ['roɲa] nf (VETERINARIA) mange; (mugre) dirt, grime; (óxido) rust

roñoso, a [ro'ɲoso, a] adj (mugriento) filthy; (tacaño) mean

ropa ['ropa] nf clothes pl, clothing; ~ **blanca** linen; ~ **de cama** bed linen; ~ **interior** underwear; ~ **para lavar** washing; **~je** nm gown, robes pl

ropero [ro'pero] nm linen cupboard; (guardarropa) wardrobe

rosa ['rosa] adj pink ♦ nf rose; ~ **de los vientos** the compass

rosado, a [ro'saðo, a] adj pink ♦ nm rosé

rosal [ro'sal] nm rosebush

rosario [ro'sarjo] nm (REL) rosary; **rezar el** ~ to say the rosary

rosca ['roska] nf (de tornillo) thread; (de humo) coil, spiral; (pan, postre) ring-shaped roll/pastry

rosetón [rose'ton] nm rosette; (ARQ) rose window

rosquilla [ros'kiʎa] nf doughnut-shaped fritter

rostro ['rostro] nm (cara) face

rotación [rota'θjon] nf rotation; ~ **de cultivos** crop rotation

rotativo, a [rota'tiβa, a] adj rotary

roto, a ['roto, a] pp de **romper** ♦ adj broken

rotonda [ro'tonda] nf roundabout

rótula ['rotula] nf kneecap; (TEC) ball-and-socket joint

rotulador [rotula'ðor] nm felt-tip pen

rotular [rotu'lar] vt (carta, documento) to head, entitle; (objeto) to label; **rótulo** nm heading, title; label; (letrero) sign

rotundamente [rotunda'mente] adv (negar) flatly; (responder, afirmar) emphatically; **rotundo, a** adj round;

(*enfático*) emphatic

rotura [ro'tura] nf (*acto*) breaking; (*MED*) fracture

roturar [rotu'rar] vt to plough

rozadura [roθa'ðura] nf abrasion, graze

rozar [ro'θar] vt (*frotar*) to rub; (*arañar*) to scratch; (*tocar ligeramente*) to shave, touch lightly; **~se** vr to rub (together); **~se con** (*fam*) to rub shoulders with

rte. abr (= *remite, remitente*) sender

RTVE nf abr = **Radiotelevisión Española**

rubí [ru'βi] nm ruby; (*de reloj*) jewel

rubio, a ['ruβjo, a] adj fair-haired, blond(e) ♦ nm/f blond/blonde; **tabaco** ~ Virginia tobacco

rubor [ru'βor] nm (*sonrojo*) blush; (*timidez*) bashfulness; **~izarse** vr to blush

rúbrica [ru'βrika] nf (*de la firma*) flourish; **rubricar** vt (*firmar*) to sign with a flourish; (*concluir*) to sign and seal

rudimentario, a [ruðimen'tarjo, a] adj rudimentary; **rudimento** nm rudiment

rudo, a ['ruðo, a] adj (*sin pulir*) unpolished; (*grosero*) coarse; (*violento*) violent; (*sencillo*) simple

rueda ['rweða] nf wheel; (*círculo*) ring, circle; (*rodaja*) slice, round; ~ **delantera/trasera/de repuesto** front/back/spare wheel; ~ **de prensa** press conference

ruedo ['rweðo] nm (*círculo*) circle; (*TAUR*) arena, bullring

ruego etc ['rweγo] vb ver **rogar** ♦ nm request

rufián [ru'fjan] nm scoundrel

rugby ['ruγβi] nm rugby

rugido [ru'xiðo] nm roar

rugir [ru'xir] vi to roar

rugoso, a [ru'γoso, a] adj (*arrugado*) wrinkled; (*áspero*) rough; (*desigual*) ridged

ruido ['rwiðo] nm noise; (*sonido*)

sound; (*alboroto*) racket, row; (*escándalo*) commotion, rumpus; **~so, a** adj noisy, loud; (*fig*) sensational

ruin [rwin] adj contemptible, mean

ruina ['rwina] nf ruin; (*colapso*) collapse; (*de persona*) ruin, downfall

ruindad [rwin'dað] nf lowness, meanness; (*acto*) low o mean act

ruinoso, a [rwi'noso, a] adj ruinous; (*destartalado*) dilapidated, tumbledown; (*COM*) disastrous

ruiseñor [rwise'ɲor] nm nightingale

ruleta [ru'leta] nf roulette

rulo ['rulo] nm (*para el pelo*) curler

Rumanía [ruma'nia] nf Rumania

rumba ['rumba] nf rumba

rumbo ['rumbo] nm (*ruta*) route, direction; (*ángulo de dirección*) course, bearing; (*fig*) course of events; **ir con** ~ **a** to be heading for

rumboso, a [rum'boso, a] adj generous

rumiante [ru'mjante] nm ruminant

rumiar [ru'mjar] vt to chew; (*fig*) to chew over ♦ vi to chew the cud

rumor [ru'mor] nm (*ruido sordo*) low sound; (*murmuración*) murmur, buzz

rumorearse vr: **se rumorea que** it is rumoured that

runrún [run'run] nm (*voces*) murmur, sound of voices; (*fig*) rumour

rupestre [ru'pestre] adj rock cpd

ruptura [rup'tura] nf rupture

rural [ru'ral] adj rural

Rusia ['rusja] nf Russia; **ruso, a** adj, nm/f Russian

rústica ['rustika] nf: **libro en** ~ paperback (book); ver tb **rústico**

rústico, a ['rustiko, a] adj rustic; (*ordinario*) coarse, uncouth ♦ nm/f yokel

ruta ['ruta] nf route

rutina [ru'tina] nf routine; **~rio, a** adj routine

S, s

S *abr* (= *santo, a*) St; (= *sur*) S
s. *abr* (= *siglo*) C.; (= *siguiente*) foll
S.A. *abr* (= *Sociedad Anónima*) Ltd. (*BRIT*), Inc. (*US*)
sábado ['saβaðo] *nm* Saturday
sábana ['saβana] *nf* sheet
sabandija [saβan'dixa] *nf* bug, insect
sabañón [saβa'ɲon] *nm* chilblain
saber [sa'βer] *vt* to know (*llegar a conocer*) to find out, learn; (*tener capacidad de*) to know how to ♦ *vi*: ~ a to taste of, taste like ♦ *nm* knowledge, learning; a ~ namely; *¿sabes conducir/nadar?* can you drive/swim?; *¿sabes francés?* do you speak French?; ~ **de memoria** to know by heart; **hacer ~ algo a uno** to inform sb of sth, let sb know sth
sabiduría [saβiðu'ria] *nf* (*conocimientos*) wisdom; (*instrucción*) learning
sabiendas [sa'βjendas]: a ~ *adv* knowingly
sabio, a ['saβjo,a] *adj* (*docto*) learned; (*prudente*) wise, sensible
sabor [sa'βor] *nm* taste, flavour; **~ear** *vt* to taste, savour; (*fig*) to relish
sabotaje [saβo'taxe] *nm* sabotage
saboteador, a [saβotea'ðor, a] *nm/f* saboteur
sabotear [saβote'ar] *vt* to sabotage
sabré *etc vb ver* **saber**
sabroso, a [sa'βroso, a] *adj* tasty; (*fig: fam*) racy, salty
sacacorchos [saka'kortʃos] *nm inv* corkscrew
sacapuntas [saka'puntas] *nm inv* pencil sharpener
sacar [sa'kar] *vt* to take out; (*fig: extraer*) to get (out); (*quitar*) to remove, get out; (*hacer salir*) to bring out; (*conclusión*) to draw; (*novela etc*) to publish, bring out; (*ropa*) to take off;

(*obra*) to make; (*premio*) to receive; (*entradas*) to get; (*TENIS*) to serve; ~ **adelante** (*niño*) to bring up; (*negocio*) to carry on, go on with; ~ **uno a bailar** to get sb up to dance; ~ **una foto** to take a photo; ~ **la lengua** to stick out one's tongue; ~ **buenas/malas notas** to get good/bad marks
sacarina [saka'rina] *nf* saccharin(e)
sacerdote [saθer'ðote] *nm* priest
saciar [sa'θjar] *vt* (*hambre, sed*) to satisfy; ~**se** *vr* (*de comida*) to get full up; **comer hasta ~se** to eat one's fill
saco ['sako] *nm* bag; (*grande*) sack; (*su contenido*) bagful; (*AM*) jacket; ~ **de dormir** sleeping bag
sacramento [sakra'mento] *nm* sacrament
sacrificar [sakrifi'kar] *vt* to sacrifice; **sacrificio** *nm* sacrifice
sacrilegio [sakri'lexjo] *nm* sacrilege; **sacrílego, a** *adj* sacrilegious
sacristía [sakris'tia] *nf* sacristy
sacro, a ['sakro, a] *adj* sacred
sacudida [saku'ðiða] *nf* (*agitación*) shake, shaking; (*sacudimiento*) jolt, bump; ~ **eléctrica** electric shock
sacudir [saku'ðir] *vt* to shake; (*golpear*) to hit
sádico, a ['saðiko, a] *adj* sadistic ♦ *nm/f* sadist; **sadismo** *nm* sadism
saeta [sa'eta] *nf* (*flecha*) arrow
sagacidad [saɣaθi'ðað] *nf* shrewdness, cleverness; **sagaz** *adj* shrewd, clever
sagitario [saxi'tarjo] *nm* Sagittarius
sagrado, a [sa'ɣraðo, a] *adj* sacred, holy
Sáhara ['saara] *nm*: **el** ~ the Sahara (desert)
sal [sal] *vb ver* **salir** ♦ *nf* salt
sala ['sala] *nf* room; (~ **de estar**) living room; (*TEATRO*) house, auditorium; (*de hospital*) ward; ~ **de apelación** court; ~ **de espera** waiting room; ~ **de estar** living room; ~ **de fiestas** dance hall

salado, a [sa'laðo, a] adj salty; (fig) witty, amusing; **agua salada** salt water

salar [sa'lar] vt to salt, add salt to

salarial [sala'rjal] adj (aumento, revisión) wage cpd, salary cpd

salario [sa'larjo] nm wage, pay

salchicha [sal'tʃitʃa] nf (pork) sausage; **salchichón** nm (salami-type) sausage

saldar [sal'dar] vt to pay; (vender) to sell off; (fig) to settle, resolve; **saldo** nm (pago) settlement; (de una cuenta) balance; (lo restante) remnant(s) (pl), remainder; **saldos** nmpl (en tienda) sale

saldré etc vb ver **salir**

salero [sa'lero] nm salt cellar

salgo etc vb ver **salir**

salida [sa'liða] nf (puerta etc) exit, way out; (acto) leaving, going out; (de tren, AVIAT) departure; (TEC) output, production; (fig) way out; (COM) opening; (GEO, válvula) outlet; (de gas) leak; **calle sin ~** cul-de-sac; **~ de incendios** fire escape

saliente [sa'ljente] adj (ARQ) projecting; (sol) rising; (fig) outstanding

---

PALABRA CLAVE

salir [sa'lir] vi **1** (partir: tb: ~ **de**) to leave; **Juan ha salido** Juan is out; **salió de la cocina** he came out of the kitchen

2 (aparecer) to appear; (disco, libro) to come out; **anoche salió en la tele** she appeared o was on TV last night; **salió en todos los periódicos** it was in all the papers

3 (resultar): **la muchacha nos salió muy trabajadora** the girl turned out to be a very hard worker; **la comida te ha salido exquisita** the food was delicious; **sale muy caro** it's very expensive

4: **~le a uno algo: la entrevista que hice me salió bien/mal** the interview I did went o turned out well/ badly

5: **~ adelante: no sé como haré para ~ adelante** I don't know how I'll get by

♦ **~se** vr (líquido) to spill; (animal) to escape

---

saliva [sa'liβa] nf saliva

salmo ['salmo] nm psalm

salmón [sal'mon] nm salmon

salmonete [salmo'nete] nm red mullet

salmuera [sal'mwera] nf pickle, brine

salón [sa'lon] nm (de casa) living room, lounge; (muebles) lounge suite; **~ de belleza** beauty parlour; **~ de baile** dance hall

salpicadero [salpika'ðero] nm (AUTO) dashboard

salpicar [salpi'kar] vt (rociar) to sprinkle, spatter; (esparcir) to scatter

salpicón [salpi'kon] nm: **~ de mariscos** seafood salad

salsa ['salsa] nf sauce; (con carne asada) gravy; (fig) savoir faire

saltamontes [salta'montes] nm inv grasshopper

saltar [sal'tar] vt to jump (over), leap (over); (dejar de lado) to skip, miss out ♦ vi to jump, leap; (pelota) to bounce; (al aire) to fly up; (quebrarse) to break; (al agua) to dive; (fig) to explode, blow up

salto ['salto] nm jump, leap; (al agua) dive; **~ de agua** waterfall; **~ de altura** high jump

saltón, ona [sal'ton, ona] adj (ojos) bulging, popping; (dientes) protruding

salud [sa'luð] nf health; **¡(a su) ~!** cheers!, good health!; **~able** adj (de buena ~) healthy; (provechoso) good, beneficial

saludar [salu'ðar] vt to greet; (MIL) to salute; **saludo** nm greeting; **"saludos"** (en carta) best wishes", "regards"

salva ['salβa] *nf*: ~ **de aplausos** ovation

salvación [salβa'θjon] *nf* salvation; (*rescate*) rescue

salvado [sal'βaðo] *nm* bran

salvaguardar [salβaɣwar'ðar] *vt* to safeguard

salvajada [salβa'xaða] *nf* atrocity

salvaje [sal'βaxe] *adj* wild; (*tribu*) savage; **salvajismo** *nm* savagery

salvamento [salβa'mento] *nm* rescue

salvar [sal'βar] *vt* (*rescatar*) to save, rescue; (*resolver*) to overcome, resolve; (*cubrir distancias*) to cover, travel; (*hacer excepción*) to except, exclude; (*barco*) to salvage

salvavidas [salβa'βiðas] *adj inv*: **bote/chaleco/cinturón** ~ lifeboat/life jacket/life belt

salvo, a ['salβo, a] *adj* safe ♦ *adv* except (for), save; **a** ~ out of danger; ~ **que** unless; ~**conducto** *nm* safe-conduct

san [san] *adj* saint; **S~ Juan** St John

sanar [sa'nar] *vt* (*herida*) to heal; (*persona*) to cure ♦ *vi* (*persona*) to get well, recover; (*herida*) to heal

sanatorio [sana'torjo] *nm* sanatorium

sanción [san'θjon] *nf* sanction; **sancionar** *vt* to sanction

sandalia [san'dalja] *nf* sandal

sandez [san'deθ] *nf* foolishness

sandía [san'dia] *nf* watermelon

sandwich ['sandwitʃ] (*pl* ~s, ~es) *nm* sandwich

saneamiento [sanea'mjento] *nm* sanitation

sanear [sane'ar] *vt* to clean up; (*terreno*) to drain

Sanfermines

The **Sanfermines** is a week-long festival in Pamplona made famous by Ernest Hemingway. From the 7th July, the feast of "San Fermín", crowds of mainly young people take to the streets drinking, singing and
dancing. Early in the morning bulls are released along the narrow streets leading to the bullring, and young men risk serious injury to show their bravery by running out in front of them, a custom which is also typical of many Spanish villages.

---

sangrar [san'grar] *vt, vi* to bleed; **sangre** *nf* blood

sangría [san'gria] *nf* sangria, sweetened drink of red wine with fruit

sangriento, a [san'grjento, a] *adj* bloody

sanguijuela [sangi'xwela] *nf* (*ZOOL, fig*) leech

sanguinario, a [sangi'narjo, a] *adj* bloodthirsty

sanguíneo, a [san'gineo, a] *adj* blood *cpd*

sanidad [sani'ðað] *nf*: ~ (**pública**) public health

San Isidro

San Isidro is the patron saint of Madrid, and gives his name to the week-long festivities which take place around the 15th May. Originally an 18th-century trade fair, the **San Isidro** celebrations now include music, dance, a famous **romería**, theatre and bullfighting.

---

sanitario, a [sani'tarjo, a] *adj* health *cpd*; ~**s** *nmpl* toilets (*BRIT*), washroom (*US*)

sano, a ['sano, a] *adj* healthy; (*sin daños*) sound; (*comida*) wholesome; (*entero*) whole, intact; **y salvo** safe and sound

Santiago [san'tjaxo] *nm*: ~ (**de Chile**) Santiago

santiamén [santja'men] *nm*: **en un** ~ in no time at all

santidad [santi'ðað] *nf* holiness, sanctity

santiguarse [santi'ɣwarse] *vr* to make

the sign of the cross

santo, a ['santo, a] *adj* holy; *(fig)* wonderful, miraculous ♦ *nm/f* saint ♦ *nm* saint's day; **~ y seña** password

santuario [san'twarjo] *nm* sanctuary, shrine

saña ['saɲa] *nf* rage, fury

sapo ['sapo] *nm* toad

saque ['sake] *nm* (TENIS) service, serve; (FÚTBOL) throw-in; **~ de esquina** corner (kick)

saquear [sake'ar] *vt* (MIL.) to sack; *(robar)* to loot, plunder; *(fig)* to ransack; **saqueo** *nm* sacking; looting, plundering; ransacking

sarampión [saram'pjon] *nm* measles *sg*

sarcasmo [sar'kasmo] *nm* sarcasm; **sarcástico, a** *adj* sarcastic

sardina [sar'ðina] *nf* sardine

sargento [sar'xento] *nm* sergeant

sarmiento [sar'mjento] *nm* (BOT) vine shoot

sarna ['sarna] *nf* itch; (MED) scabies

sarpullido [sarpu'ʎiðo] *nm* (MED) rash

sarro ['sarro] *nm* (en dientes) tartar, plaque

sartén [sar'ten] *nf* frying pan

sastre ['sastre] *nm* tailor; **-ría** *nf* (arte) tailoring; *(tienda)* tailor's (shop)

Satanás [sata'nas] *nm* Satan

satélite [sa'telite] *nm* satellite

sátira ['satira] *nf* satire

satisfacción [satisfak'θjon] *nf* satisfaction

satisfacer [satisfa'θer] *vt* to satisfy; *(gastos)* to meet; *(pérdida)* to make good; **~se** *vr* to satisfy o.s., be satisfied; *(vengarse)* to take revenge; **satisfecho, a** *adj* satisfied; *(contento)* content(ed), happy; *(tb: satisfecho de sí mismo)* self-satisfied, smug

saturar [satu'rar] *vt* to saturate; **~se** *vr* (mercado, aeropuerto) to reach saturation point

sauce ['sauθe] *nm* willow; **~ llorón** weeping willow

sauna ['sauna] *nf* sauna

savia ['saβja] *nf* sap

saxofón [sakso'fon] *nm* saxophone

sazonar [saθo'nar] *vt* to ripen; *(CULIN)* to flavour, season

SE *abr* (= *sudeste*) SE

PALABRA CLAVE

se [se] *pron* **1** *(reflexivo: sg: m)* himself; *(: f)* herself; *(: pl)* themselves; *(: cosa)* itself; *(: de Vd)* yourself; *(: de Vds)* yourselves; **está preparando** she's preparing herself; *para usos léxicos del pron ver el vb en cuestión, p.ej.* **arrepentirse**

2 *(con complemento indirecto)* to him; to her; to them; to it; to you; **a usted ~ lo dije ayer** I told you yesterday; **~ compró un sombrero** he bought himself a hat; **~ rompió la pierna** he broke his leg

3 *(uso recíproco)* each other, one another; **~ miraron (el uno al otro)** they looked at each other o one another

4 *(en oraciones pasivas)*: **se han vendido muchos libros** a lot of books have been sold

5 *(impers)*: **~ dice que** people say that, it is said that; **allí ~ come muy bien** the food there is very good, you can eat very well there

---

sé *vb ver* **saber; ser**

sea *etc vb ver* **ser**

sebo ['seβo] *nm* fat, grease

secador [seka'ðor] *nm*: **~ de pelo** hair-dryer

secadora [seka'ðora] *nf* tumble dryer

secar [se'kar] *vt* to dry; **~se** *vr* to dry (off); *(río, planta)* to dry up

sección [sek'θjon] *nf* section

seco, a ['seko, a] *adj* dry; *(carácter)* cold; *(respuesta)* sharp, curt; **habrá pan a secas** there will be just bread; **decir algo a secas** to say sth curtly; **parar en ~** to stop dead

secretaría [sekreta'ria] nf secretariat
secretario, a [sekre'tarjo, a] nm/f secretary
secreto, a [se'kreto, a] adj secret; (persona) secretive ♦ nm secret; (calidad) secrecy
secta ['sekta] nf sect; **~rio, a** adj sectarian
sector [sek'tor] nm sector
secuela [se'kwela] nf consequence
secuencia [se'kwenθja] nf sequence
secuestrar [sekwes'trar] vt to kidnap; (bienes) to seize, confiscate; **secuestro** nm kidnapping; seizure, confiscation
secular [seku'lar] adj secular
secundar [sekun'dar] vt to second, support
secundario, a [sekun'darjo, a] adj secondary
sed [seð] nf thirst; **tener ~** to be thirsty
seda ['seða] nf silk
sedal [se'ðal] nm fishing line
sedante [se'ðante] nm sedative
sede ['seðe] nf (de gobierno) seat; (de compañía) headquarters pl; **Santa S~** Holy See
sedentario, a [seðen'tarjo, a] adj sedentary
sediento, a [se'ðjento, a] adj thirsty
sedimento [seði'mento] nm sediment
sedoso, a [se'ðoso, a] adj silky, silken
seducción [seðuk'θjon] nf seduction
seducir [seðu'θir] vt to seduce; (cautivar) to charm, fascinate; (atraer) to attract; **seductor, a** adj seductive, charming, fascinating ♦ nm/f seducer
segar [se'ɣar] vt (mies) to reap, cut; (hierba) to mow, cut
seglar [se'ɣlar] adj secular, lay
segregación [seɣreɣa'θjon] nf segregation. **~ racial** racial segregation
segregar [seɣre'ɣar] vt to segregate, separate
seguida [se'ɣiða] nf: **en ~** at once, right away
seguido, a [se'ɣiðo, a] adj (continuo)

continuous, unbroken; (recto) straight ♦ adv (directo) straight (on); (después) after; (AM: a menudo) often; **~s** consecutive, successive; **5 días ~s** 5 days running, 5 days in a row
seguimiento [seɣi'mjento] nm chase, pursuit; (continuación) continuation
seguir [se'ɣir] vt to follow; (venir después) to follow on, come after; (proseguir) to continue; (perseguir) to chase, pursue ♦ vi (gen) to follow; (continuar) to continue, carry o go on; **~se** vr to follow; **sigo sin comprender** I still don't understand; **sigue lloviendo** it's still raining
según [se'ɣun] prep according to ♦ adv: **¿irás?** — are you going? — it all depends ♦ conj as; **~ caminamos** while we walk
segundo, a [se'ɣundo, a] adj second ♦ nm second ♦ nf second meaning; **de ~a mano** second-hand; **segunda (clase)** second class; **segunda enseñanza** secondary education; **segunda (marcha)** (AUT) second (gear)
seguramente [seɣura'mente] adv surely; (con certeza) for sure, with certainty
seguridad [seɣuri'ðað] nf safety; (del estado, de casa etc) security; (certidumbre) certainty; (confianza) confidence; (estabilidad) stability; **~ social** social security
seguro, a [se'ɣuro, a] adj (cierto) sure, certain; (fiel) trustworthy; (libre de peligro) safe; (bien defendido, firme) secure ♦ adv for sure, certainly ♦ nm (COM) insurance; **~ contra terceros/a todo riesgo** third party/ comprehensive insurance; **~s sociales** social security sg
seis [seis] num six
seísmo [se'ismo] nm tremor, earthquake
selección [selek'θjon] nf selection;
seleccionar vt to pick, choose, select

selectividad [selekti&i'ðað] (*ESP*) *nf* university entrance examination

selecto, a [se'lekto, a] *adj* select, choice; (*escogido*) selected

sellar [se'ʎar] *vt* (*documento oficial*) to seal; (*pasaporte, visado*) to stamp

sello ['seʎo] *nm* stamp; (*precinto*) seal

selva ['selβa] *nf* (*bosque*) forest, woods *pl*; (*jungla*) jungle

semáforo [se'maforo] *nm* (*AUTO*) traffic lights *pl*; (*FERRO*) signal

semana [se'mana] *nf* week; **entre ~** during the week; **S~ Santa** Holy Week; **semanal** *adj* weekly; **~rio** weekly magazine

---

Semana Santa

In Spain celebrations for **Semana Santa** *(Holy Week) are often spectacular. "Viernes Santo", "Sábado Santo" and "Domingo de Resurrección" (Good Friday, Holy Saturday, Easter Sunday) are all national holidays, with additional days being given as local holidays. There are fabulous* **procesiones** *all over the country, with members of "cofradías" (brotherhoods) dressing in hooded robes and parading their "pasos" (religious floats and sculptures) through the streets. Seville has the most famous Holy Week processions.*

---

semblante [sem'blante] *nm* face; (*fig*) look

sembrar [sem'brar] *vt* to sow; (*objetos*) to sprinkle, scatter about; (*noticias etc*) to spread

semejante [seme'xante] *adj* (*parecido*) similar ♦ *nm* fellow man, fellow creature; **~s** alike, similar; **nunca hizo cosa ~** he never did any such thing; **semejanza** *nf* similarity, resemblance

semejar [seme'xar] *vi* to seem like, resemble; **~se** *vr* to look alike, be similar

semen ['semen] *nm* semen

semestral [semes'tral] *adj* half-yearly, bi-annual

semicírculo [semi'θirkulo] *nm* semicircle

semidesnatado, a [semiðesna'taðo, a] *adj* semi-skimmed

semifinal [semifi'nal] *nf* semifinal

semilla [se'miʎa] *nf* seed

seminario [semi'narjo] *nm* (*REL*) seminary; (*ESCOL*) seminar

sémola ['semola] *nf* semolina

Sena ['sena] *nm*: **el ~** the (river) Seine

senado [se'naðo] *nm* senate; **senador, a** *nm/f* senator

sencillez [senθi'ʎeθ] *nf* simplicity; (*de persona*) naturalness; **sencillo, a** *adj* simple; natural, unaffected

senda ['senda] *nf* path, track

senderismo [sende'rismo] *nm* hiking

sendero [sen'dero] *nm* path, track

sendos, as ['sendos, as] *adj pl*: **les dio ~ golpes** he hit both of them

senil [se'nil] *adj* senile

seno ['seno] *nm* (*ANAT*) bosom, bust; (*fig*) bosom; **~s** breasts

sensación [sensa'θjon] *nf* sensation; (*sentido*) sense; (*sentimiento*) feeling; **sensacional** *adj* sensational

sensato, a [sen'sato, a] *adj* sensible

sensible [sen'sible] *adj* sensitive; (*apreciable*) perceptible, appreciable; (*pérdida*) considerable; **~ro, a** *adj* sentimental

sensitivo, a [sensi'tiβo, a] *adj* sense *cpd*

sensorial [senso'rjal] *adj* sensory

sensual [sen'swal] *adj* sensual

sentada [sen'taða] *nf* sitting; (*protesta*) sit-in

sentado, a [sen'taðo, a] *adj*: **estar ~** to sit, be sitting (down); **dar por ~** to take for granted, assume

sentar [sen'tar] *vt* to sit, seat; (*fig*) to establish ♦ *vi* (*vestido*) to suit; (*alimento*): **bien/mal a** to agree/disagree with; **~se** *vr* (*persona*) to sit, sit down; (*los depósitos*) to settle

sentencia [sen'tenθja] nf (máxima) maxim, saying; (JUR) sentence; **sentenciar** vt to sentence

sentido, a [sen'tiðo, a] adj (pérdida) regrettable; (carácter) sensitive ♦ nm sense; (sentimiento) feeling; (significado) sense, meaning; (dirección) direction; **mi ~ pésame** my deepest sympathy; **~ del humor** sense of humour; **~ único** one-way (street); **tener ~** to make sense

sentimental [sentimen'tal] adj sentimental; **vida ~** love life

sentimiento [senti'mjento] nm feeling

sentir [sen'tir] vt to feel; (percibir) to perceive, sense; (lamentar) to regret, be sorry for ♦ vi (tener la sensación) to feel; (lamentarse) to feel sorry ♦ nm opinion, judgement; **~se bien/mal** to feel well/ill; **lo siento** I'm sorry

seña ['seɲa] nf sign; (MIL) password; **~s** nfpl (dirección) address sg; **~s personales** personal description sg

señal [se'ɲal] nf sign; (síntoma) symptom; (FERRO, TELEC) signal; (marca) mark; (COM) deposit; **en ~ de** as a token of, as a sign of; **~ar** vt to mark; (indicar) to point out, indicate

señor [se'ɲor] nm (hombre) man; (caballero) gentleman; (dueño) owner, master; (trato: antes de nombre propio) Mr; (: hablando directamente) sir; **muy ~ mío** Dear Sir; **el ~ alcalde/ presidente** the mayor/president

señora [se'ɲora] nf (dama) lady; (trato: antes de nombre propio) Mrs; (: hablando directamente) madam; (esposa) wife; **Nuestra S~** Our Lady

señorita [seɲo'rita] nf (con nombre y/o apellido) Miss; (mujer joven) young lady

señorito [seɲo'rito] nm young gentleman; (pey) rich kid

señuelo [se'ɲwelo] nm decoy

sepa etc vb ver **saber**

separación [separa'θjon] nf separation; (división) division; (hueco)

gap

separar [sepa'rar] vt to separate; (dividir) to divide; **~se** vr (parte) to come away; (partes) to come apart; (persona) to leave, go away; (matrimonio) to separate

separatismo nm separatism

sepia ['sepja] nf cuttlefish

septentrional [septentrjo'nal] adj northern

septiembre [sep'tjembre] nm September

séptimo, a ['septimo, a] adj, nm seventh

sepulcral [sepul'kral] adj (fig: silencio, atmósfera) deadly; **sepulcro** nm tomb, grave

sepultar [sepul'tar] vt to bury; **sepultura** nf (acto) burial; (tumba) grave, tomb

sequedad [seke'ðað] nf dryness; (fig) brusqueness, curtness

sequía [se'kia] nf drought

séquito ['sekito] nm (de rey etc) retinue; (seguidores) followers pl

---
| PALABRA CLAVE |
---

ser [ser] vi **1** (descripción) to be; **es médica/muy alta** she's a doctor/very tall; **la familia es de Cuzco** his (o her etc) family is from Cuzco; **soy Ana** (TELEC) Ana speaking o here

2 (propiedad): **es de Joaquín** it's Joaquín's, it belongs to Joaquín

3 (horas, fechas, números): **es la una** it's one o'clock; **son las seis y media** it's half-past six; **es el 1 de junio** it's the first of June; **somos/son seis** there are six of us/them

4 (en oraciones pasivas): **ha sido descubierto ya** it's already been discovered

5: **es de esperar que ...** it is to be hoped o I etc hope that ...

6 (locuciones con sub): **o sea** that is to say; **sea él sea su hermana** either him or his sister

7: **a no ~ por él** ... but for him ...

8: **a no ~ que: a no ~ que tenga uno ya** unless he's got one already
♦ *nm* being; **~ humano** human being

serenarse [sere'narse] *vr* to calm down

sereno, a [se'reno, a] *adj* (*persona*) calm, unruffled; (*el tiempo*) fine, settled; (*ambiente*) calm, peaceful ♦ *nm* night watchman

serial [ser'jal] *nm* serial

serie |'serje| *nf* series; (*cadena*) sequence, succession; **fuera de ~** out of order; (*fig*) special, out of the ordinary; **fabricación en ~** mass production

seriedad [serje'ðað] *nf* seriousness; (*formalidad*) reliability; **serio, a** *adj* serious; reliable, dependable; grave, serious; **en serio** *adv* seriously

serigrafía [serixra'fia] *nf* silk-screen printing

sermón [ser'mon] *nm* (*REL*) sermon

seropositivo, a [seroposi'tißo] *adj* HIV positive

serpentear [serpente'ar] *vi* to wriggle; (*camino, río*) to wind, snake

serpentina [serpen'tina] *nf* streamer

serpiente [ser'pjente] *nf* snake; **~ de cascabel** rattlesnake

serranía [serra'nia] *nf* mountainous area

serrar [se'rrar] *vt* = **aserrar**

serrín [se'rrin] *nm* = **aserrín**

serrucho [se'rrutʃo] *nm* saw

servicio [ser'ßiθjo] *nm* service; **~s** *nmpl* toilet(s); **~ incluido** service charge included; **~ militar** military service

servidumbre [serßi'ðumbre] *nf* (*sujeción*) servitude; (*criados*) servants *pl*, staff

servil [ser'ßil] *adj* servile

servilleta [serßi'Áeta] *nf* serviette, napkin

servir [ser'ßir] *vt* to serve ♦ *vi* to serve;

(*tener utilidad*) to be of use, be useful; **~se** *vr* to serve o help o.s.; **~se de algo** to make use of sth, use sth; **sírvase pasar** please come in

sesenta [se'senta] *num* sixty

sesgo ['sesxo] *nm* slant; (*fig*) slant, twist

sesión [se'sjon] *nf* (*POL*) session, sitting; (*CINE*) showing

seso ['seso] *nm* brain; **sesudo, a** *adj* sensible, wise

seta ['seta] *nf* mushroom; **~ venenosa** toadstool

setecientos, as [sete'θjentos, as] *adj*, *num* seven hundred

setenta [se'tenta] *num* seventy

seto ['seto] *nm* hedge

seudónimo [seu'ðonimo] *nm* pseudonym

severidad [seßeri'ðað] *nf* severity; **severo, a** *adj* severe

Sevilla [se'ßiÁa] *n* Seville; **sevillano, a** *adj* of o from Seville ♦ *nm/f* native o inhabitant of Seville

sexo ['sekso] *nm* sex

sexto, a [a 'seksto, a] *adj*, *nm* sixth

sexual [sek'swal] *adj* sexual; **vida ~** sex life

si [si] *conj* if; **me pregunto ~** ... I wonder if o whether ...

sí [si] *adv* yes ♦ *nm* consent ♦ *pron* (*uso impersonal*) oneself; (*sg: m*) himself; (*: f*) herself; (*: de cosa*) itself; (*de usted*) yourself; (*pl*) themselves; (*de ustedes*) yourselves; (*recíproco*) each other; **él no quiere pero yo ~** he doesn't want to but I do; **ella ~ vendrá** she will certainly come, she is sure to come; **claro que ~** of course; **creo que ~** I think so

siamés, esa [sja'mes, esa] *adj, nm/f* Siamese

SIDA ['siða] *nm abr* (= *Síndrome de Inmunodeficiencia Adquirida*) AIDS

siderúrgico, a [siðe'rurxico, a] *adj* iron and steel *cpd*

sidra ['siðra] *nf* cider

siembra ['sjembra] nf sowing

siempre ['sjempre] adv always; (todo el tiempo) all the time; ~ **que** (cada vez) whenever; (dado que) provided that; **como** ~ as usual; **para** ~ for ever

sien [sjen] nf temple

siento etc vb ver **sentar**; **sentir**

sierra ['sjerra] nf (TEC) saw; (cadena de montañas) mountain range

siervo, a ['sjerßo, a] nm/f slave

siesta ['sjesta] nf siesta, nap; **echar la** ~ to have an afternoon nap o a siesta

siete ['sjete] num seven

sífilis ['sifilis] nf syphilis

sifón [si'fon] nm syphon; **whisky con** ~ whisky and soda

sigla ['siɣla] nf abbreviation; acronym

siglo ['siɣlo] nm century; (fig) age

significación [siɣnifika'θjon] nf significance

significado [siɣnifi'kaðo] nm (de palabra etc) meaning

significar [siɣnifi'kar] vt to mean, signify; (notificar) to make known, express; **significativo, a** adj significant

signo ['siɣno] nm sign; ~ **de admiración** o **exclamación** exclamation mark; ~ **de interrogación** question mark

sigo etc vb ver **seguir**

siguiente [si'ɣjente] adj next, following

siguió etc vb ver **seguir**

sílaba ['silaßa] nf syllable

silbar [sil'ßar] vt, vi to whistle; **silbato** nm whistle; **silbido** nm whistle, whistling

silenciador [silenθja'ðor] nm silencer

silenciar [silen'θjar] vt (persona) to silence; (escándalo) to hush up; **silencio** nm silence, quiet; **silencioso, a** adj silent, quiet

silla ['siʎa] nf (asiento) chair; (tb: ~ de montar) saddle; ~ **de ruedas** wheelchair

sillón [si'ʎon] nm armchair, easy chair

silueta [si'lweta] nf silhouette; (de edificio) outline; (figura) figure

silvestre [sil'ßestre] adj wild

simbólico, a [sim'boliko, a] adj symbolic(al)

simbolizar [simboli'θar] vt to symbolize

símbolo ['simbolo] nm symbol

simetría [sime'tria] nf symmetry

simiente [si'mjente] nf seed

similar [simi'lar] adj similar

simio ['simjo] nm ape

simpatía [simpa'tia] nf liking; (afecto) affection; (amabilidad) kindness; **simpático, a** adj nice, pleasant; kind

simpatizante [simpati'θante] nm/f sympathizer

simpatizar [simpati'θar] vi: ~ **con** to get on well with

simple ['simple] adj simple; (elemental) simple, easy; (mero) mere; (puro) pure, sheer ♦ nm/f simpleton; **~za** nf simpleness; (necedad) silly thing; **simplificar** vt to simplify

simposio [sim'posjo] nm symposium

simular [simu'lar] vt to simulate

simultáneo, a [simul'taneo, a] adj simultaneous

sin [sin] prep without; **la ropa está** ~ **lavar** the clothes are unwashed; ~ **que** without; ~ **embargo** however, still

sinagoga [sina'ɣoɣa] nf synagogue

sinceridad [sinθeri'ðað] nf sincerity; **sincero, a** adj sincere

sincronizar [sinkroni'θar] vt to synchronize

sindical [sindi'kal] adj union cpd, trade-union cpd; **~ista** adj, nm/f trade unionist

sindicato [sindi'kato] nm (de trabajadores) trade(s) union; (de negociantes) syndicate

síndrome ['sindrome] nm (MED) syndrome; ~ **de abstinencia** (MED) withdrawal symptoms

sinfín [sin'fin] nm: **un** ~ **de** a great

many, no end of

sinfonía [sinfo'nia] nf symphony

singular [singu'lar] adj singular; (fig) outstanding, exceptional; (raro) peculiar, odd; **~idad** nf singularity, peculiarity; **~izarse** vr to distinguish o.s., stand out

siniestro, a [si'njestro, a] adj sinister ♦ nm (accidente) accident

sinnúmero [sin'numero] nm = **sinfín**

sino ['sino] nm fate, destiny ♦ conj (pero) but; (salvo) except, save

sinónimo, a [si'nonimo, a] adj synonymous ♦ nm synonym

síntesis ['sintesis] nf synthesis; **sintético, a** adj synthetic

sintetizar [sinteti'θar] vt to synthesize

sintió vb ver **sentir**

síntoma ['sintoma] nm symptom

sintonía [sinto'nia] nf (RADIO, MUS: de programa) tuning; **sintonizar** vt (RADIO: emisora) to tune (in)

sinvergüenza [simber'xwenθa] nm/f rogue, scoundrel; **¡es un ~!** he's got a nerve!

siquiera [si'kjera] conj even if, even though ♦ adv at least; **ni ~** not even

Siria ['sirja] nf Syria

sirviente, a [sir'βjente, a] nm/f servant

sirvo etc vb ver **servir**

sisear [sise'ar] vt, vi to hiss

sistema [sis'tema] nm system; (método) method; **sistemático, a** adj systematic

---

Sistema educativo

*The reform of the Spanish **sistema educativo** (education system) begun in the early 90s has replaced the courses EGB, BUP and COU with the following: "Primaria" a compulsory 6 years; "Secundaria" a compulsory 4 years and "Bachillerato" an optional 2-year secondary school course, essential for those wishing to go on to higher education.*

---

sitiar [si'tjar] vt to besiege, lay siege to

sitio ['sitjo] nm (lugar) place; (espacio) room, space; (MIL) siege; **~ Web** (INFORM) website

situación [sitwa'θjon] nf situation, position; (estatus) position, standing

situado, a [situ'aðo] adj situated, placed

situar [situ'ar] vt to place, put; (edificio) to locate, situate

slip [slip] nm pants pl, briefs pl

smoking ['smokin, es'mokin] (pl **~s**) nm dinner jacket (BRIT), tuxedo (US)

snob [es'nob] = **esnob**

SO abr (= suroeste) SW

sobaco [so'βako] nm armpit

sobar [so'βar] vt (ropa) to rumple; (comida) to play around with

soberanía [soβera'nia] nf sovereignty; **soberano, a** adj sovereign; (fig) supreme ♦ nm/f sovereign

soberbia [so'βerβja] nf pride; haughtiness, arrogance; magnificence

soberbio, a [so'βerβjo, a] adj (orgulloso) proud; (altivo) arrogant; (estupendo) magnificent, superb

sobornar [soβor'nar] vt to bribe; **soborno** nm bribe

sobra ['soβra] nf excess, surplus; **~s** nfpl left-overs, scraps; **de ~** surplus, extra; **tengo de ~** I've more than enough; **~do, a** adj (más que suficiente) more than enough; (superfluo) excessive; **sobrante** adj remaining, extra ♦ nm surplus, remainder

sobrar [so'βrar] vt to exceed, surpass ♦ vi (tener de más) to be more than enough; (quedar) to remain, be left (over)

sobrasada [soβra'saða] nf pork sausage spread

sobre ['soβre] prep (gen) on; (encima) on (top of); (por encima de, arriba de) over, above; (*más que*) more than; (*además*) in addition to, besides; (*alrededor de*) about ♦ *nm* envelope; **~ todo** above all

sobrecama [soβre'kama] *nf* bedspread

sobrecargar [soβrekar'ɣar] *vt* (*camión*) to overload; (*COM*) to surcharge

sobredosis [soβre'ðosis] *nf inv* overdose

sobreentender [soβre(e)nten'der] *vt* to deduce, infer; **~se** *vr*: **se sobreentiende que ...** it is implied that ...

sobrehumano, a [soβreu'mano, a] *adj* superhuman

sobrellevar [soβreʎe'βar] *vt* to bear, endure

sobremesa [soβre'mesa] *nf*: **durante la ~** after dinner; **ordenador de ~** desktop computer

sobrenatural [soβrenatu'ral] *adj* supernatural

sobrenombre [soβre'nombre] *nm* nickname

sobrepasar [soβrepa'sar] *vt* to exceed, surpass

sobreponerse [soβrepo'nerse] *vr*: **~ a** to overcome

sobresaliente [soβresa'ljente] *adj* outstanding, excellent

sobresalir [soβresa'lir] *vi* to project, jut out; (*fig*) to stand out, excel

sobresaltar [soβresal'tar] *vt* (*asustar*) to scare, frighten; (*sobrecoger*) to startle; **sobresalto** *nm* (*movimiento*) start; (*susto*) scare; (*turbación*) sudden shock

sobretodo [soβre'toðo] *nm* overcoat

sobrevenir [soβreβe'nir] *vi* (*ocurrir*) to happen (unexpectedly); (*resultar*) to follow, ensue

sobreviviente [soβreβi'βjente] *adj* surviving ♦ *nm/f* survivor

sobrevivir [soβreβi'βir] *vi* to survive

sobrevolar [soβreβo'lar] *vt* to fly over

sobriedad [soβrje'ðað] *nf* sobriety, soberness; (*moderación*) moderation, restraint

sobrino, a [so'βrino, a] *nm/f* nephew/niece

sobrio, a ['soβrjo, a] *adj* sober; (*moderado*) moderate, restrained

socarrón, ona [soka'rron, ona] *adj* (*sarcástico*) sarcastic, ironic(al)

socavar [soka'βar] *vt* (*tb fig*) to undermine

socavón [soka'βon] *nm* (*hoyo*) hole

sociable [so'θjaβle] *adj* (*persona*) sociable, friendly; (*animal*) social

social [so'θjal] *adj* social; (*COM*) company *cpd*

socialdemócrata [soθjalde'mokrata] *nm/f* social democrat

socialista [soθja'lista] *adj*, *nm/f* socialist

socializar [soθjali'θar] *vt* to socialize

sociedad [soθje'ðað] *nf* society; (*COM*) company; **~ anónima** limited company; **~ de consumo** consumer society

socio, a ['soθjo, a] *nm/f* (*miembro*) member; (*COM*) partner

sociología [soθjoloˈxia] *nf* sociology; **sociólogo, a** *nm/f* sociologist

socorrer [soko'rrer] *vt* to help; **socorrista** *nm/f* first aider; (*en piscina, playa*) lifeguard; **socorro** *nm* (*ayuda*) help, aid; (*MIL*) relief; **¡socorro!** help!

soda ['soða] *nf* (*sosa*) soda; (*bebida*) soda (water)

sofá [so'fa] (*pl* **~s**) *nm* sofa, settee; **~-cama** *nm* studio couch; sofa bed

sofisticación [sofistika'θjon] *nf* sophistication

sofocar [sofo'kar] *vt* to suffocate; (*apagar*) to smother, put out; **~se** *vr* to suffocate; (*fig*) to blush, feel embarrassed; **sofoco** *nm* suffocation; embarrassment

sofreír [sofre'ir] *vt* (*CULIN*) to fry lightly

soga ['soɣa] *nf* rope

sois *vb ver* **ser**

soja ['soxa] nf soya

sol [sol] nm sun; (luz) sunshine, sunlight; **hace ~** it is sunny

solamente [sola'mente] adv only, just

solapa [so'lapa] nf (de chaqueta) lapel; (de libro) jacket

solapado, a [sola'paðo, a] adj (intenciones) underhand; (gestos, movimiento) sly

solar [so'lar] adj solar, sun cpd

solaz [so'laθ] nm recreation, relaxation; **~ar** vt (divertir) to amuse

soldado [sol'daðo] nm soldier; **~ raso** private

soldador [solda'ðor] nm soldering iron; (persona) welder

soldar [sol'dar] vt to solder, weld

soleado, a [sole'aðo, a] adj sunny

soledad [sole'ðað] nf solitude; (estado infeliz) loneliness

solemne [so'lemne] adj solemn; **solemnidad** nf solemnity

soler [so'ler] vi to be in the habit of, be accustomed to; **suele salir a las ocho** she usually goes out at 8 o'clock

solfeo [sol'feo] nm solfa

solicitar [soliθi'tar] vt (permiso) to ask for, seek; (puesto) to apply for; (votos) to canvass for; (atención) to attract

solícito, a [so'liθito, a] adj (diligente) diligent; (cuidadoso) careful; **solicitud** nf (calidad) great care; (petición) request; (a un puesto) application

solidaridad [soliðari'ðað] nf solidarity; **solidario, a** adj (participación) joint, common; (compromiso) mutually binding

solidez [soli'ðeθ] nf solidity; **sólido, a** adj solid

soliloquio [soli'lokjo] nm soliloquy

solista [so'lista] nm/f soloist

solitario, a [soli'tarjo, a] adj (persona) lonely, solitary; (lugar) lonely, desolate ♦ nm/f (recluso) recluse; (en la sociedad) loner ♦ nm solitaire

sollozar [soλo'θar] vi to sob; **sollozo** nm sob

solo, a ['solo, a] adj (único) single, sole; (sin compañía) alone; (solitario) lonely; **hay una sola dificultad** there is just one difficulty; **a solas** alone, by oneself

sólo ['solo] adv only, just

solomillo [solo'miλo] nm sirloin

soltar [sol'tar] vt (dejar ir) to let go of; (desprender) to unfasten, loosen; (librar) to release, set free; (risa etc) to let out

soltero, a [sol'tero, a] adj single, unmarried ♦ nm/f bachelor/single woman; **solterón, ona** nm/f old bachelor/spinster

soltura [sol'tura] nf looseness, slackness; (de los miembros) agility, ease of movement; (en el hablar) fluency, ease

soluble [so'luβle] adj (QUÍM) soluble; (problema) solvable; **~ en agua** soluble in water

solución [solu'θjon] nf solution; **solucionar** vt (problema) to solve; (asunto) to settle, resolve

solventar [solβen'tar] vt (pagar) to settle, pay; (resolver) to resolve; **solvente** adj (ECON: empresa, persona) solvent

sombra ['sombra] nf shadow; (como protección) shade; **~s** nfpl (oscuridad) darkness sg, shadows; **tener buena/mala ~** to be lucky/unlucky

sombrero [som'brero] nm hat

sombrilla [som'briλa] nf parasol, sunshade

sombrío, a [som'brio, a] adj (oscuro) dark; (triste) sombre, sad; (persona) gloomy

somero, a [so'mero, a] adj superficial

someter [some'ter] vt (país) to conquer; (persona) to subject to one's will; (informe) to present, submit; **~se** vr to give in, yield, submit; **~ a** to subject to

somier [so'mjer] (pl **somiers**) n spring mattress

somnífero [som'nifero] nm sleeping

pill
somnolencia [somno'lenθja] nf
sleepiness, drowsiness
somos vb ver **ser**
son [son] vb ver **ser** ♦ nm sound; **en
~ de broma** as a joke
sonajero [sona'xero] nm (baby's)
rattle
sonambulismo [sonambu'lismo] nm
sleepwalking; **sonámbulo, a** nm/f
sleepwalker
sonar [so'nar] vt to ring ♦ vi to sound;
(hacer ruido) to make a noise;
(pronunciarse) to be sounded, be
pronounced; (ser conocido) to sound
familiar; (campana) to ring; (reloj) to
strike, chime; **~se** vr: **~se (las
narices)** to blow one's nose; **me
suena ese nombre** that name rings a
bell
sonda ['sonda] nf (NAUT) sounding;
(TEC) bore, drill; (MED) probe
sondear [sonde'ar] vt to sound; to
bore (into), drill; to probe, sound; (fig)
to sound out; **sondeo** nm sounding,
boring, drilling; (fig) poll, enquiry
sonido [so'niðo] nm sound
sonoro, a [so'noro, a] adj sonorous;
(resonante) loud, resonant
sonreír [sonre'ir] vi to smile; **~se** vr to
smile; **sonriente** adj smiling; **sonrisa**
nf smile
sonrojarse [sonro'xarse] vr to blush,
go red; **sonrojo** nm blush
soñador, a [soɲa'ðor, a] nm/f dreamer
soñar [so'ɲar] vt, vi to dream; **~ con**
to dream about o of
soñoliento, a [soɲo'ljento, a] adj
sleepy, drowsy
sopa ['sopa] nf soup
sopesar [sope'sar] vt to consider,
weigh up
soplar [so'plar] vt (polvo) to blow
away, blow off; (inflar) to blow up;
(vela) to blow out ♦ vi to blow; **soplo**
nm blow, puff; (de viento) puff, gust
soplón, ona [so'plon, ona] (fam),

nm/f (niño) telltale; (de policía) grass
(fam)
sopor [so'por] nm drowsiness
soporífero [sopo'rifero] nm sleeping
pill
soportable [sopor'taßle] adj bearable
soportar [sopor'tar] vt to bear, carry;
(fig) to bear, put up with; **soporte** nm
support; (fig) pillar, support
soprano [so'prano] nf soprano
sorber [sor'ßer] vt (chupar) to sip;
(absorber) to soak up, absorb
sorbete [sor'ßete] nm iced fruit drink
sorbo ['sorßo] nm (trago: grande) gulp,
swallow; (: pequeño) sip
sordera [sor'ðera] nf deafness
sórdido, a [sor'ðiðo, a] adj dirty,
squalid
sordo, a [sor'ðo, a] adj (persona) deaf
♦ nm/f deaf person; **~mudo, a** adj
deaf and dumb
sorna ['sorna] nf sarcastic tone
soroche [so'rotʃe] (AM) nm mountain
sickness
sorprendente [sorpren'dente] adj
surprising
sorprender [sorpren'der] vt to
surprise; **sorpresa** nf surprise
sortear [sorte'ar] vt to draw lots for;
(rifar) to raffle; (dificultad) to avoid;
sorteo nm (en lotería) draw; (rifa)
raffle
sortija [sor'tixa] nf ring; (rizo) ringlet,
curl
sosegado, a [sose'ɣaðo, a] adj quiet,
calm
sosegar [sose'ɣar] vt to quieten, calm;
(el ánimo) to reassure ♦ vi to rest;
sosiego nm quiet(ness), calm(ness)
soslayo [sos'lajo]: **de ~** adv obliquely,
sideways
soso, a ['soso, a] adj (CULIN) tasteless;
(aburrido) dull, uninteresting
sospecha [sos'petʃa] nf suspicion;
sospechar vt to suspect;
sospechoso, a adj suspicious;
(testimonio, opinión) suspect ♦ nm/f

suspect

sostén [sos'ten] nm (apoyo) support; (sujetador) bra; (alimentación) sustenance, food

sostener [soste'ner] vt to support; (mantener) to keep up, maintain; (alimentar) to sustain, keep going; **~se** vr to support o.s.; (seguir) to continue, remain; **sostenido, a** adj continuous, sustained; (prolongado) prolonged

sotana [so'tana] nf (REL) cassock

sótano ['sotano] nm basement

soviético, a [so'βjetiko, a] adj Soviet; **los ~s** the Soviets

soy vb ver **ser**

Sr. abr (= Señor) Mr

Sra. abr (= Señora) Mrs

S.R.C. abr (= se ruega contestación) R.S.V.P.

Sres. abr (= Señores) Messrs

Srta. abr (= Señorita) Miss

Sta. abr (= Santa) St

status ['status, e'status] nm inv status

Sto. abr (= Santo) St

su [su] pron (de él) his; (de ella) her; (de una cosa) its; (de ellos, ellas) their; (de usted, ustedes) your

suave ['swaβe] adj gentle; (superficie) smooth; (trabajo) easy; (música, voz) soft, sweet; **suavidad** nf gentleness; smoothness; softness, sweetness; **suavizante** nm (de ropa) softener; (del pelo) conditioner; **suavizar** vt to soften; (quitar la aspereza) to smooth (out)

subalimentado, a [suβalimen'taðo, a] adj undernourished

subasta [su'βasta] nf auction; **subastar** vt to auction (off)

subcampeón, ona [suβkampe'on, ona] nm/f runner-up

subconsciente [suβkon'sθjente] adj, nm subconscious

subdesarrollado, a [suβðesarro'ʎaðo, a] adj underdeveloped

subdesarrollo [suβðesa'rroʎo] nm underdevelopment

subdirector, a [suβðirek'tor, a] nm/f assistant director

súbdito, a ['suβðito, a] nm/f subject

subestimar [suβesti'mar] vt to underestimate, underrate

subida [su'βiða] nf (de montaña etc) ascent, climb; (de precio) rise, increase; (pendiente) slope, hill

subir [su'βir] vt (objeto) to raise, lift up; (cuesta, calle) to go up; (colina, montaña) to climb; (precio) to raise, put up ♦ vi to go up, come up; (a un coche) to get in; (a un autobús, tren o avión) to get on, board; (precio) to rise, go up; (río, marea) to rise; **~se** vr to get up, climb

súbito, a ['suβito, a] adj (repentino) sudden; (imprevisto) unexpected

subjetivo, a [suβxe'tiβo, a] adj subjective

sublevación [suβleβa'θjon] nf revolt, rising

sublevar [suβle'βar] vt to rouse to revolt; **~se** vr to revolt, rise

sublime [su'βlime] adj sublime

submarinismo [suβmari'nismo] nm scuba diving

submarino, a [suβma'rino, a] adj underwater ♦ nm submarine

subnormal [suβnor'mal] adj subnormal ♦ nm/f subnormal person

subordinado, a [suβorði'naðo, a] adj, nm/f subordinate

subrayar [suβra'jar] vt to underline

subsanar [suβsa'nar] vt to rectify

subscribir [suβskri'βir] vt = **suscribir**

subsidio [suβ'siðjo] nm (ayuda) aid, financial help; (subvención) subsidy, grant; (de enfermedad, paro etc) benefit, allowance

subsistencia [suβsis'tenθja] nf subsistence

subsistir [suβsis'tir] vi to subsist; (sobrevivir) to survive, endure

subterráneo, a [suβte'rraneo, a] adj underground, subterranean ♦ nm

underpass, underground passage
subtítulo [suß'titulo] nm (CINE) subtitle
suburbano, a [sußur'ßano, a] adj suburban
suburbio [su'ßurßjo] nm (barrio) slum quarter
subvención [sußßen'θjon] nf (ECON) subsidy, grant; **subvencionar** vt to subsidize
subversión [sußßer'sjon] nf subversion; **subversivo, a** adj subversive
subyugar [sußju'ɣar] vt (país) to subjugate, subdue; (enemigo) to overpower; (voluntad) to dominate
sucedáneo, a [suθe'ðaneo, a] adj substitute ♦ nm substitute (food)
suceder [suθe'ðer] vt, vi to happen; (seguir) to succeed, follow; **lo que sucede es que ...** the fact is that ...; **sucesión** nf succession; (serie) sequence, series
sucesivamente [suθesißa'mente] adv: **y así ~** and so on
sucesivo, a [suθe'sißo, a] adj successive, following; **en lo ~** in future, from now on
suceso [su'θeso] nm (hecho) event, happening; (incidente) incident
suciedad [suθje'ðað] nf (estado) dirtiness; (mugre) dirt, filth
sucinto, a [su'θinto, a] adj (conciso) succinct, concise
sucio, a ['suθjo, a] adj dirty
suculento, a [suku'lento, a] adj succulent
sucumbir [sukum'bir] vi to succumb
sucursal [sukur'sal] nf branch (office)
sudadera [suða'ðera] nf sweatshirt
Sudáfrica [suð'afrika] nf South Africa
Sudamérica [suða'merika] nf South America; **sudamericano, a** adj, nm/f South American
sudar [su'ðar] vt, vi to sweat
sudeste [su'ðeste] nm south-east
sudoeste [suðo'este] nm south-west

sudor [su'ðor] nm sweat; **~oso, a** adj sweaty, sweating
Suecia ['sweθja] nf Sweden; **sueco, a** adj Swedish ♦ nm/f Swede
suegro, a ['sweɣro, a] nm/f father-/mother-in-law
suela ['swela] nf sole
sueldo ['sweldo] nm pay, wage(s) (pl)
suele etc vb ver **soler**
suelo ['swelo] nm (tierra) ground; (de casa) floor
suelto, a ['swelto, a] adj loose; (libre) free; (separado) detached; (ágil) quick, agile ♦ nm (loose) change, small change
sueño etc ['sweɲo] vb ver **soñar** ♦ nm sleep; (somnolencia) sleepiness, drowsiness; (lo soñado, fig) dream; **tener ~** to be sleepy
suero ['swero] nm (MED) serum; (de leche) whey
suerte ['swerte] nf (fortuna) luck; (azar) chance; (destino) fate, destiny; (especie) sort, kind; **tener ~** to be lucky; **de otra ~** otherwise, if not; **de ~ que** so that, in such a way that
suéter ['sweter] nm sweater
suficiente [sufi'θjente] adj enough, sufficient ♦ nm (ESCOL) pass
sufragio [su'fraxjo] nm (voto) vote; (derecho de voto) suffrage
sufrido, a [su'friðo, a] adj (persona) tough; (paciente) long-suffering, patient
sufrimiento [sufri'mjento] nm (dolor) suffering
sufrir [su'frir] vt (padecer) to suffer; (soportar) to bear, put up with; (apoyar) to hold up, support ♦ vi to suffer
sugerencia [suxe'renθja] nf suggestion
sugerir [suxe'rir] vt to suggest; (sutilmente) to hint
sugestión [suxes'tjon] nf suggestion; (sutil) hint; **sugestionar** vt to influence

sugestivo, a [suxes'tiβo, a] *adj* stimulating; (*fascinante*) fascinating

suicida [sui'θiða] *adj* suicidal ♦ *nm/f* suicidal person; (*muerto*) suicide, person who has committed suicide; **suicidarse** *vr* to commit suicide, kill o.s.; **suicidio** *nm* suicide

Suiza ['swiθa] *nf* Switzerland; **suizo, a** *adj, nm/f* Swiss

sujeción [suxe'θjon] *nf* subjection

sujetador [suxeta'ðor] *nm* (*sostén*) bra

sujetar [suxe'tar] *vt* (*fijar*) to fasten; (*detener*) to hold down; **~se** *vr* to subject o.s.; **sujeto, a** *adj* fastened, secure ♦ *nm* subject; (*individuo*) individual; **sujeto a** subject to

suma ['suma] *nf* (*cantidad*) total, sum; (*de dinero*) sum; (*acto*) adding (up), addition; **en ~** in short

sumamente [suma'mente] *adv* extremely, exceedingly

sumar [su'mar] *vt* to add (up) ♦ *vi* to add up

sumario, a [su'marjo, a] *adj* brief, concise ♦ *nm* summary

sumergir [sumer'xir] *vt* to submerge; (*hundir*) to sink

suministrar [suminis'trar] *vt* to supply, provide; **suministro** *nm* supply; (*acto*) supplying, providing

sumir [su'mir] *vt* to sink, submerge; (*fig*) to plunge

sumisión [sumi'sjon] *nf* (*acto*) submission; (*calidad*) submissiveness, docility; **sumiso, a** *adj* submissive, docile

sumo, a ['sumo, a] *adj* great, extreme; (*autoridad*) highest, supreme

suntuoso, a [sun'twoso, a] *adj* sumptuous, magnificent

supe *etc vb ver* **saber**

supeditar [supeði'tar] *vt*: ~ **algo a algo** to subordinate sth to sth

super... ['super] *prefijo* super..., over...; **~bueno** *adj* great, fantastic

súper ['super] *nf* (*gasolina*) three-star (petrol)

superar [supe'rar] *vt* (*sobreponerse a*) to overcome; (*rebasar*) to surpass, do better than; (*pasar*) to go beyond; **~se** *vr* to excel o.s.

superávit [supe'raβit] *nm inv* surplus

superficial [superfi'θjal] *adj* superficial; (*medida*) surface *cpd*, of the surface

superficie [super'fiθje] *nf* surface; (*área*) area

superfluo, a [su'perflwo, a] *adj* superfluous

superior [supe'rjor] *adj* (*piso, clase*) upper; (*temperatura, número, nivel*) higher; (*mejor: calidad, producto*) superior, better ♦ *nm/f* superior; **~idad** *nf* superiority

supermercado [supermer'kaðo] *nm* supermarket

superponer [superpo'ner] *vt* to superimpose

supersónico, a [super'soniko, a] *adj* supersonic

superstición [supersti'θjon] *nf* superstition; **supersticioso, a** *adj* superstitious

supervisar [superβi'sar] *vt* to supervise

supervivencia [superβi'βenθja] *nf* survival

superviviente [superβi'βjente] *adj* surviving

supiera *etc vb ver* **saber**

suplantar [suplan'tar] *vt* to supplant

suplemento [suple'mento] *nm* supplement

suplente [su'plente] *adj, nm/f* substitute

supletorio, a [suple'torjo, a] *adj* supplementary ♦ *nm* supplement; **teléfono ~** extension

súplica ['suplika] *nf* request; (*JUR*) petition

suplicar [supli'kar] *vt* (*cosa*) to beg (for), plead for; (*persona*) to beg, plead with

suplicio [su'pliθjo] *nm* torture

suplir [su'plir] vt (compensar) to make good, make up for; (reemplazar) to replace, substitute ♦ vi: ~ a to take the place of, substitute for

supo etc vb ver **saber**

suponer [supo'ner] vt to suppose; **suposición** nf supposition

supremacía [suprema'θia] nf supremacy

supremo, a [su'premo, a] adj supreme

supresión [supre'sjon] nf suppression; (de derecho) abolition; (de palabra etc) deletion; (de restricción) cancellation, lifting

suprimir [supri'mir] vt to suppress; (derecho, costumbre) to abolish; (palabra etc) to delete; (restricción) to cancel, lift

supuesto, a [su'pwesto, a] pp de **suponer** ♦ adj (hipotético) supposed ♦ nm assumption, hypothesis; **~ que** since; **por ~** of course

sur [sur] nm south

surcar [sur'kar] vt to plough; **surco** nm (en metal, disco) groove; (AGR) furrow

surgir [sur'xir] vi to arise, emerge; (dificultad) to come up, crop up

suroeste [suro'este] nm south-west

surtido, a [sur'tiðo, a] adj mixed, assorted ♦ nm (selección) selection, assortment; (abastecimiento) supply, stock; **~r nm** (also: **~ de gasolina**) petrol pump (BRIT), gas pump (US)

surtir [sur'tir] vt to supply, provide ♦ vi to spout, spurt

susceptible [susθep'tißle] adj susceptible; (sensible) sensitive; **~ de** capable of

suscitar [susθi'tar] vt to cause, provoke; (interés, sospechas) to arouse

suscribir [suskri'ßir] vt (firmar) to sign; (respaldar) to subscribe to, endorse; **~se a** vt to subscribe; **suscripción** nf subscription

susodicho, a [suso'ðitʃo, a] adj

above-mentioned

suspender [suspen'der] vt (objeto) to hang (up), suspend; (trabajo) to stop, suspend; (ESCOL) to fail; (interrumpir) to adjourn; (atrasar) to postpone; **suspensión** nf suspension; (fig) stoppage, suspension

suspenso, a [sus'penso, a] adj hanging, suspended; (ESCOL) failed ♦ nm (ESCOL) fail; **quedar o estar en ~** to be pending

suspicacia [suspi'kaθja] nf suspicion, mistrust; **suspicaz** adj suspicious, distrustful

suspirar [suspi'rar] vi to sigh; **suspiro** nm sigh

sustancia [sus'tanθja] nf substance

sustentar [susten'tar] vt (alimentar) to sustain, nourish; (objeto) to hold up, support; (idea, teoría) to maintain, uphold; (fig) to sustain, keep going; **sustento** nm support; (alimento) sustenance, food

sustituir [sustitu'ir] vt to substitute, replace; **sustituto, a** nm/f substitute, replacement

susto ['susto] nm fright, scare

sustraer [sustra'er] vt to remove, take away; (MAT) to subtract

susurrar [susu'rrar] vi to whisper; **susurro** nm whisper

sutil [su'til] adj (aroma, diferencia) subtle; (tenue) thin; (inteligencia, persona) sharp; **~eza** nf subtlety; thinness

suyo, a ['sujo, a] (con artículo o después del verbo ser) adj (de él) his; (de ella) hers; (de ellos, ellas) theirs; (de Ud, Uds) yours; **un amigo ~** a friend of his (o hers o theirs o yours)

T, t

tabacalera [taßaka'lera] nf: **T~** Spanish state tobacco monopoly

tabaco [ta'ßako] nm tobacco; (fam)

cigarettes pl

taberna [ta'βerna] nf bar, pub (BRIT)

tabique [ta'βike] nm partition (wall)

tabla [ta'βla] nf (de madera) plank; (estante) shelf; (de vestido) pleat; (ARTE) panel; ~s nfpl: estar o quedar en ~s to draw; ~do nm (plataforma) platform; (TEATRO) stage

tablao [ta'βlao] nm (tb: ~ flamenco) flamenco show

tablero [ta'βlero] nm (de madera) plank, board; (de ajedrez, damas) board; ~ de anuncios notice o bulletin board (US)

tableta [ta'βleta] nf (MED) tablet; (de chocolate) bar

tablón [ta'βlon] nm (de suelo) plank; (de techo) beam; ~ de anuncios notice board (BRIT), bulletin board (US)

tabú [ta'βu] nm taboo

tabular [taβu'lar] vt to tabulate

taburete [taβu'rete] nm stool

tacaño, a [ta'kaɲo, a] adj mean

tacha [ˈtatʃa] nf flaw; (TEC) stud; **tachar** vt (borrar) to cross out; **tachar de** to accuse of

tácito, a [ˈtaθito, a] adj tacit

taciturno, a [taθiˈturno, a] adj silent

taco [ˈtako] nm (BILLAR) cue; (libro de billetes) book; (AM: de zapato) heel; (tarugo) peg; (palabrota) swear word

tacón [taˈkon] nm heel; **de ~ alto** high-heeled; **taconeo** nm (heel) stamping

táctica [ˈtaktika] nf tactics pl

táctico, a [ˈtaktiko, a] adj tactical

tacto [ˈtakto] nm touch; (fig) tact

taimado, a [taiˈmaðo, a] adj (astuto) sly

tajada [taˈxaða] nf slice

tajante [taˈxante] adj sharp

tajo [ˈtaxo] nm (corte) cut; (GEO) cleft

tal [tal] adj such; ~ vez perhaps ♦ pron (persona) someone, a one; (cosa) something, such a thing; ~ como such as; ~ para cual (dos iguales) two of a kind ♦ adv: ~ como (igual) just as;

~ **cual** (como es) just as it is; ¿qué ~? how are things?; ¿qué ~ te gusta? how do you like it? ♦ conj: **con ~ de que** provided that

taladrar [talaˈðrar] vt to drill; **taladro** nm drill

talante [taˈlante] nm (humor) mood; (voluntad) will, willingness

talar [taˈlar] vt to fell, cut down; (devastar) to devastate

talco [ˈtalko] nm (polvos) talcum powder

talego [taˈlexo] nm sack

talento [taˈlento] nm talent; (capacidad) ability

TALGO [ˈtalvo] (ESP) nm abr (= tren articulado ligero Goicoechea-Oriol) ≈ HST (BRIT)

talismán [talisˈman] nm talisman

talla [ˈtaʎa] nf (estatura, fig, MED) height, stature; (palo) measuring rod; (ARTE) carving; (medida) size

tallado, a [taˈʎaðo, a] adj carved ♦ nm carving

tallar [taˈʎar] vt (madera) to carve; (metal etc) to engrave; (medir) to measure

tallarines [taʎaˈrines] nmpl noodles

talle [ˈtaʎe] nm (ANAT) waist; (fig) appearance

taller [taˈʎer] nm (TEC) workshop; (de artista) studio

tallo [ˈtaʎo] nm (de planta) stem; (de hierba) blade; (brote) shoot

talón [taˈlon] nm (ANAT) heel; (COM) counterfoil; (cheque) cheque (BRIT), check (US)

talonario [taloˈnarjo] nm (de cheques) chequebook (BRIT), checkbook (US); (de recibos) receipt book

tamaño, a [taˈmaɲo, a] adj (tan grande) such a big; (tan pequeño) such a small ♦ nm size; **de ~ natural** full-size

tamarindo [tamaˈrindo] nm tamarind

tambalearse [tambaleˈarse] vr (persona) to stagger; (vehículo) to sway

también [tam'bjen] adv (igualmente) also, too, as well; (además) besides

tambor [tam'bor] nm drum; (ANAT) eardrum; ~ **del freno** brake drum

tamiz [ta'miθ] nm sieve; ~**ar** vt to sieve

tampoco [tam'poko] adv nor, neither; **yo ~ lo compré** I didn't buy it either

tampón [tam'pon] nm tampon

tan [tan] adv so; ~ **es así que** ... so much so that ....

tanda ['tanda] nf (gen) series; (turno) shift

tangente [tan'xente] nf tangent

Tánger ['tanxer] n Tangier

tangible [tan'xiβle] adj tangible

tanque ['tanke] nm (cisterna, MIL) tank; (AUTO) tanker

tantear [tante'ar] vt (calcular) to reckon (up); (medir) to take the measure of; (probar) to test, try out; (tomar la medida: persona) to take the measurements of; (situación) to weigh up; (persona: opinión) to sound out ♦ vi (DEPORTE) to score; **tanteo** nm (cálculo) (rough) calculation; (prueba) test, trial; (DEPORTE) scoring

tanto, a ['tanto, a] adj (cantidad) so much, as much; ~**s** so many, as many; **20 y ~s** 20-odd ♦ adv (cantidad) so much, as much; (tiempo) so long, as long ♦ conj: **en ~ que** while; **hasta ~ (que)** until such time as ♦ nm (suma) certain amount; (proporción) so much; (punto) point; (gol) goal; **un ~ perezoso** somewhat lazy ♦ pron: **cada uno paga ~** each one pays so much; **~ tú como yo** both you and I; **~ como eso** as much as that; **~ más ... cuanto que** all the more ...; **~ mejor/peor** so much the better/the worse; **~ si viene como si va** whether he comes or whether he goes; **~ es así que** so much so that; **por ~ o por lo ~** therefore; **me ha vuelto ronco de o con ~ hablar** I have become hoarse with so much

talking; **a ~s de agosto** on such and such a day in August

tapa ['tapa] nf (de caja, olla) lid; (de botella) top; (de libro) cover; (comida) snack

tapadera [tapa'ðera] nf lid, cover

tapar [ta'par] vt (cubrir) to cover; (envolver) to wrap o cover up; (la vista) to obstruct; (persona, falta) to conceal; (AM) to fill; ~**se** vr to wrap o.s. up

taparrabo [tapa'rraβo] nm loincloth

tapete [ta'pete] nm table cover

tapia ['tapja] nf (garden) wall; **tapiar** vt to wall in

tapicería [tapiθe'ria] nf tapestry; (para muebles) upholstery; (tienda) upholsterer's (shop)

tapiz [ta'piθ] nm (alfombra) carpet; (tela tejida) tapestry; ~**ar** vt (muebles) to upholster

tapón [ta'pon] nm (de botella) top; (de lavabo) plug; ~ **de rosca** screw-top

taquigrafía [takixra'fia] nf shorthand; **taquígrafo, a** nm/f shorthand writer, stenographer

taquilla [ta'kiʎa] nf (donde se compra) booking office; (suma recogida) takings pl; **taquillero, a** adj: **función taquillera** box office success ♦ nm/f ticket clerk

tara ['tara] nf (defecto) defect; (COM) tare

tarántula [ta'rantula] nf tarantula

tararear [tarare'ar] vt to hum

tardar [tar'ðar] vi (tomar tiempo) to take a long time; (llegar tarde) to be late; (demorar) to delay; **¿tarda mucho el tren?** does the train take (very) long?; **a más ~** at the latest; **no tardes en venir** come soon

tarde ['tarðe] adv late ♦ nf (de día) afternoon; (al anochecer) evening; **de ~ en ~** from time to time; **¡buenas ~s!** good afternoon!; **a o por la ~** in the afternoon, in the evening

tardío, a [tar'ðio, a] adj (retrasado) late; (lento) slow (to arrive)

tarea [ta'rea] nf task; (faena) chore; (ESCOL) homework

tarifa [ta'rifa] nf (lista de precios) price list; (precio) tariff

tarima [ta'rima] nf (plataforma) platform

tarjeta [tar'xeta] nf card; ~ postal/de crédito/de Navidad postcard/credit card/Christmas card

tarro ['tarro] nm jar, pot

tarta ['tarta] nf (pastel) cake; (de base dura) tart

tartamudear [tartamuðe'ar] vi to stammer; **tartamudo, a** adj stammering ♦ nm/f stammerer

tártaro, a ['tartaro, a] adj: **salsa tártara** tartar(e) sauce

tasa ['tasa] nf (precio) (fixed) price, rate; (valoración) valuation; (medida, norma) measure, standard; ~ **de cambio/interés** exchange/interest rate; ~**s universitarias** university fees; ~**s de aeropuerto** airport tax; ~**ción** nf valuation; ~**dor, a** nm/f valuer

tasar [ta'sar] vt (arreglar el precio) to fix a price for; (valorar) to value, assess

tasca ['taska] (fam) nf pub

tatarabuelo, a [tatara'ßwelo, a] nm/f great-great-grandfather/mother

tatuaje [ta'twaxe] nm (dibujo) tattoo; (acto) tattooing

tatuar [ta'twar] vt to tattoo

taurino, a [tau'rino, a] adj bullfighting cpd

Tauro ['tauro] nm Taurus

tauromaquia [tauro'makja] nf tauromachy, (art of) bullfighting

taxi ['taksi] nm taxi

taxista [tak'sista] nm/f taxi driver

taza ['taθa] nf cup; (de retrete) bowl; ~ **para café** coffee cup; **tazón** nm (taza grande) mug, large cup; (de lavabo) basin

te [te] pron (complemento de objeto) you; (complemento indirecto) (to) you; (reflexivo) (to) yourself; ¿~ **duele mucho el brazo?** does your arm hurt

a lot?; ~ **equivocas** you're wrong; ¡**cálma**~! calm down!

té [te] nm tea

tea ['tea] nf torch

teatral [tea'tral] adj theatre cpd; (fig) theatrical

teatro [te'atro] nm theatre; (LITERATURA) plays pl, drama

tebeo [te'ßeo] nm comic

techo ['tetʃo] nm (externo) roof; (interno) ceiling; ~ **corredizo** sunroof

tecla ['tekla] nf key; ~**do** nm keyboard; **teclear** vi (MUS) to drum; (con los dedos) to tap ♦ vt (INFORM) to key in

técnica ['teknika] nf technique; (tecnología) technology; ver tb **técnico**

técnico, a ['tekniko, a] adj technical ♦ nm/f technician; (experto) expert

tecnología [teknolo'xia] nf technology; **tecnológico, a** adj technological

tedio ['teðjo] nm boredom, tedium; ~**so, a** adj boring, tedious

teja ['texa] nf tile; (BOT) lime (tree); ~**do** nm (tiled) roof

tejemaneje [texema'nexe] nm (lío) fuss; (intriga) intrigue

tejer [te'xer] vt to weave; (hacer punto) to knit; (fig) to fabricate; **tejido** nm (tela) material, fabric; (telaraña) web; (ANAT) tissue

tel [tel] abr (= teléfono) tel

tela ['tela] nf (tejido) material; (telaraña) web; (en líquido) skin; **telar** nm (máquina) loom

telaraña [tela'raɲa] nf cobweb

tele ['tele] (fam) nf telly (BRIT), tube (US)

tele... ['tele] pref tele...; ~**comunicación** nf telecommunication; ~**control** nm remote control; ~**diario** nm television news; ~**difusión** nf (television) broadcast; ~**dirigido, a** adj remote-controlled

teléf abr (= teléfono) tel

teleférico [tele'feriko] nm (de esquí)

ski-lift

telefonear [telefone'ar] vi to
telephone

telefónico, a [tele'foniko, a] adj
telephone cpd

telefonillo [telefo'niʎo] nm (de puerta)
intercom

telefonista [telefo'nista] nm/f
telephonist

teléfono [te'lefono] nm (tele)phone;
estar hablando al ~ to be on the
phone; **llamar a uno por ~** to ring sb
(up) o phone sb (up); **~ móvil** car
phone; **~ portátil** mobile phone

telegrafía [teleɣra'fia] nf telegraphy

telégrafo [te'leɣrafo] nm telegraph

telegrama [tele'ɣrama] nm telegram

tele: **~impresor** nm teleprinter (BRIT),
teletype (US); **~novela** nf soap (opera);
~objetivo, **a** nm telephoto lens; **~patía**
nf telepathy; **~pático, a** adj telepathic;
~scópico, a adj telescopic; **~scopio**
nm telescope; **~silla** nm chairlift;
~spectador, a nm/f viewer; **~squí**
nm ski-lift; **~tarjeta** nf phonecard;
~tipo nm teletype; **~ventas** nfpl
telesales

televidente [teleßi'ðente] nm/f viewer

televisar [teleßi'sar] vt to televise

televisión [teleßi'sjon] nf television;
~ digital digital television

televisor [teleßi'sor] nm television set

télex ['teleks] nm inv telex

telón [te'lon] nm curtain; **~ de acero**
(POL) iron curtain; **~ de fondo**
backcloth, background

tema ['tema] nm (asunto) subject,
topic; (MUS) theme; **temática** nf
(social, histórica, artística) range of
topics; **temático, a** adj thematic

temblar [tem'blar] vi to shake,
tremble; (de frío) to shiver; **temblón,
ona** adj shaking; **temblor** nm
trembling; (de tierra) earthquake;
tembloroso, a adj trembling

temer [te'mer] vt to fear ♦ vi to be
afraid; **temo que llegue tarde** I am

afraid he may be late

temerario, a [teme'rarjo, a] adj
(descuidado) reckless; (irreflexivo) hasty;
temeridad nf (imprudencia) rashness;
(audacia) boldness

temeroso, a [teme'roso, a] adj
(miedoso) fearful; (que inspira temor)
frightful

temible [te'mißle] adj fearsome

temor [te'mor] nm (miedo) fear; (duda)
suspicion

témpano ['tempano] nm: **~ de hielo**
ice-floe

temperamento [tempera'mento] nm
temperament

temperatura [tempera'tura] nf
temperature

tempestad [tempes'taθ] nf storm;
tempestuoso, a adj stormy

templado, a [tem'plaðo, a] adj
(moderado) moderate; (frugal) frugal;
(agua) lukewarm; (clima) mild; (MUS)
well-tuned; **templanza** nf moderation;
mildness

templar [tem'plar] vt (moderar) to
moderate; (furia) to restrain; (calor) to
reduce; (afinar) to tune (up); (acero)
temper; (tuerca) to tighten up; **temple**
nm (ajuste) tempering; (afinación)
tuning; (pintura) tempera

templo ['templo] nm (iglesia) church;
(pagano etc) temple

temporada [tempo'raða] nf time,
period; (estación) season

temporal [tempo'ral] adj (no
permanente) temporary ♦ nm storm

tempranero, a [tempra'nero, a] adj
(BOT) early; (persona) early-rising

temprano, a [tem'prano, a] adj early;
(demasiado pronto) too soon, too early

ten vb ver **tener**

tenaces [te'naθes] adj pl ver **tenaz**

tenacidad [tenaθi'ðaθ] nf tenacity;
(dureza) toughness; (terquedad)
stubbornness

tenacillas [tena'θiʎas] nfpl tongs;
(para el pelo) curling tongs (BRIT) o tongs

sg (US); (MED) forceps

tenaz [te'naθ] *adj* (*material*) tough; (*persona*) tenacious; (*creencia, resistencia*) stubborn

tenaza(s) [te'naθa(s)] *nf(pl)* (MED) forceps; (TEC) pliers; (ZOOL) pincers

tendedero [tende'ðero] *nm* (*para ropa*) drying place; (*cuerda*) clothes line

tendencia [ten'denθja] *nf* tendency; **tener ~ a** to tend to, have a tendency to; **tendencioso, a** *adj* tendentious

tender [ten'der] *vt* (*extender*) to spread out; (*colgar*) to hang out; (*vía férrea, cable*) to lay; (*estirar*) to stretch ♦ *vi*: **~ a** to tend to, have a tendency towards; **~se** *vr* to lie down; **~ la cama/la mesa** (AM) to make the bed/lay (BRIT) o set (US) the table

tenderete [tende'rete] *nm* (*puesto*) stall; (*exposición*) display of goods

tendero, a [ten'dero, a] *nm/f* shopkeeper

tendido, a [ten'diðo, a] *adj* (*acostado*) lying down, flat; (*colgado*) hanging ♦ *nm* (TAUR) front rows of seats; **a galope ~** flat out

tendón [ten'don] *nm* tendon

tendré *etc vb ver* **tener**

tenebroso, a [tene'βroso, a] *adj* (*oscuro*) dark; (*fig*) gloomy

tenedor [tene'ðor] *nm* (CULIN) fork; **~ de libros** book-keeper

tenencia [te'nenθja] *nf* (*de casa*) tenancy; (*de oficio*) tenure; (*de propiedad*) possession

---

PALABRA CLAVE

tener [te'ner] *vt* **1** (*poseer, gen*) to have; (*en la mano*) to hold; **¿tienes un boli?** have you got a pen?; **va a ~ un niño** she's going to have a baby; **¡ten** (o **tenga**)!, **¡aquí tienes** (o **tiene**)! here you are!

2 (*edad, medidas*) to be; **tiene 7 años** she's 7 (years old); **tiene 15 cm de largo** it's 15 cm long; *ver* **calor**; **hambre** *etc*

3 (*considerar*): **lo tengo por brillante** I consider him to be brilliant; **~ en mucho a uno** to think very highly of sb

4 (+ *pp*: = *pretérito*): **tengo terminada ya la mitad del trabajo** I've done half the work already

5: **~ que hacer algo** to have to do sth; **tengo que acabar este trabajo hoy** I have to finish this job today

6: **¿qué tienes, estás enfermo?** what's the matter with you, are you ill?

~se *vr* **1**: **~se en pie** to stand up

2: **~se por** to think o.s.; **se tiene por muy listo** he thinks himself very clever

---

tengo *etc vb ver* **tener**

tenia ['tenja] *nf* tapeworm

teniente [te'njente] *nm* (*rango*) lieutenant; (*ayudante*) deputy

tenis ['tenis] *nm* tennis; **~ de mesa** table tennis; **~ta** *nm/f* tennis player

tenor [te'nor] *nm* (*sentido*) meaning; (MUS) tenor; **a ~ de** on the lines of

tensar [ten'sar] *vt* to tighten; (*arco*) to draw

tensión [ten'sjon] *nf* tension; (TEC) stress; (MED): **~ arterial** blood pressure; **tener la ~ alta** to have high blood pressure

tenso, a ['tenso, a] *adj* tense

tentación [tenta'θjon] *nf* temptation

tentáculo [ten'takulo] *nm* tentacle

tentador, a [tenta'ðor, a] *adj* tempting

tentar [ten'tar] *vt* (*seducir*) to tempt; (*atraer*) to attract; **tentativa** *nf* attempt; **tentativa de asesinato** attempted murder

tentempié [tentem'pje] *nm* snack

tenue ['tenwe] *adj* (*delgado*) thin, slender; (*neblina*) light; (*lazo, vínculo*) slight

teñir [te'ɲir] *vt* to dye; (*fig*) to tinge; **~se** *vr* to dye; **~se el pelo** to dye one's hair

teología [teolo'xia] *nf* theology

teoría [teo'ria] nf theory; **en ~** in theory; **teóricamente** adv theoretically; **teórico, a** adj theoretic(al) ♦ nm/f theoretician, theorist; **teorizar** vi to theorize

terapéutico, a [tera'peutiko, a] adj therapeutic

terapia [te'rapja] nf therapy

tercer [ter'θer] adj ver **tercero**

tercermundista [terθermun'dista] adj Third World cpd

tercero, a [ter'θero, a] adj (delante de nmsg: **tercer**) third ♦ nm (JUR) third party

terceto [ter'θeto] nm trio

terciar [ter'θjar] vi (participar) to take part; (hacer de árbitro) to mediate; **~se** vr to come up; **~io, a** adj tertiary

tercio ['terθjo] nm third

terciopelo [terθjo'pelo] nm velvet

terco, a ['terko, a] adj obstinate

tergal ® [ter'val] nm type of polyester

tergiversar [terxißer'sar] vt to distort

termal [ter'mal] adj thermal

termas ['termas] nfpl hot springs

térmico, a ['termiko, a] adj thermal

terminación [termina'θjon] nf (final) end; (conclusión) conclusion, ending

terminal [termi'nal] adj, nm, nf terminal

terminante [termi'nante] adj (final) final, definitive; (tajante) categorical; **~mente** adv: **~mente prohibido** strictly forbidden

terminar [termi'nar] vt (completar) to complete, finish; (concluir) to end ♦ vi (llegar a su fin) to end; (parar) to stop; (acabar) to finish; **~se** vr to come to an end; **~ por hacer algo** to end up (by) doing sth

término ['termino] nm end, conclusion; (parada) terminus; (límite) boundary; **~ medio** average; (fig) middle way; **en último ~** (a fin de cuentas) in the last analysis; (como último recurso) as a last resort

terminología [terminolo'xia] nf terminology

termodinámico, a [termoði'namiko, a] adj thermodynamic

termómetro [ter'mometro] nm thermometer

termonuclear [termonukle'ar] adj thermonuclear

termo(s) ® ['termo(s)] nm Thermos ® (flask)

termostato [termo'stato] nm thermostat

ternero, a [ter'nero, a] nm/f (animal) calf ♦ nf (carne) veal

ternura [ter'nura] nf (trato) tenderness; (palabra) endearment; (cariño) fondness

terquedad [terke'ðað] nf obstinacy

terraado [te'rraðo] nm terrace

terraplén [terra'plen] nm embankment

terrateniente [terrate'njente] nm/f landowner

terraza [te'rraθa] nf (balcón) balcony; (tejado) (flat) roof; (AGR) terrace

terremoto [terre'moto] nm earthquake

terrenal [terre'nal] adj earthly

terreno, a [te'rreno] nm (tierra) land; (parcela) plot; (suelo) soil; (fig) field; **un ~ a piece of land**

terrestre [te'rrestre] adj terrestrial; (ruta) land cpd

terrible [te'rrißle] adj terrible, awful

territorio [terri'torjo] nm territory

terrón [te'rron] nm (de azúcar) lump; (de tierra) clod, lump

terror [te'rror] nm terror; **~ífico, a** adj terrifying; **~ista** adj, nm/f terrorist

terso, a ['terso, a] adj (liso) smooth; (pulido) polished; **tersura** nf smoothness

tertulia [ter'tulja] nf (reunión informal) social gathering; (grupo) group, circle

tesis ['tesis] nf inv thesis

tesón [te'son] nm (firmeza) firmness; (tenacidad) tenacity

tesorero, a [teso'rero, a] nm/f

treasurer

tesoro [te'soro] nm treasure; (COM, POL) treasury

testaferro [testa'ferro] nm figurehead

testamentario, a [testamen'tarjo, a] adj testamentary ♦ nm/f executor/executrix

testamento [testa'mento] nm will

testar [tes'tar] vi to make a will

testarudo, a [testa'ruðo, a] adj stubborn

testículo [tes'tikulo] nm testicle

testificar [testifi'kar] vt to testify; (fig) to attest ♦ vi to give evidence

testigo [tes'tixo] nm/f witness; ~ de cargo/descargo witness for the prosecution/defence; ~ ocular eye witness

testimoniar [testimo'njar] vt to testify to; (fig) to show; **testimonio** nm testimony

teta ['teta] nf (de biberón) teat; (ANAT: fam) breast

tétanos ['tetanos] nm tetanus

tetera [te'tera] nf teapot

tétrico, a ['tetriko, a] adj gloomy, dismal

textil [teks'til] adj textile

texto ['teksto] nm text; **textual** adj textual

textura [teks'tura] nf (de tejido) texture

tez [teθ] nf (cutis) complexion

ti [ti] pron you; (reflexivo) yourself

tía ['tia] nf (pariente) aunt; (fam) chick, bird

tibieza [ti'βjeθa] nf (temperatura) tepidness; (actitud) coolness; **tibio, a** adj lukewarm

tiburón [tiβu'ron] nm shark

tic [tik] nm (ruido) click; (de reloj) tick; (MED): ~ nervioso nervous tic

tictac [tik'tak] nm (de reloj) tick tock

tiempo ['tjempo] nm time; (época, período) age, period; (METEOROLOGÍA) weather; (LING) tense; (DEPORTE) half; a ~ in time; a un o al mismo ~ at the same time; al poco ~ very soon

(after); **se quedó poco** ~ he didn't stay very long; **hace poco** ~ not long ago; **mucho** ~ a long time; **de** ~ **en** ~ from time to time; **hace buen/mal** ~ the weather is fine/bad; **estar a** ~ to be in time; **hace** ~ some time ago; **hacer** ~ to while away the time; **motor de 2** ~**s** two-stroke engine; **primer** ~ first half

tienda ['tjenda] nf shop, store; ~ (de campaña) tent; ~ de alimentación o comestibles grocer's (BRIT), grocery store (US)

tienes etc vb ver **tener**

tienta etc [tjenta] vb ver **tentar** ♦ nf: **andar a** ~**s** to grope one's way along

tiento ['tjento] vb ver **tentar** ♦ nm (tacto) touch; (precaución) wariness

tierno, a ['tjerno, a] adj (blando) tender; (fresco) fresh; (amable) sweet

tierra ['tjerra] nf (gen) land; (suelo) soil; (mundo) earth, world; (país) country, land; ~ adentro inland

tieso, a ['tjeso, a] adj (rígido) rigid; (duro) stiff; (fam: orgulloso) conceited

tiesto ['tjesto] nm flowerpot

tifoidea [tifoi'ðea] nf typhoid

tifón [ti'fon] nm typhoon

tifus ['tifus] nm typhus

tigre ['tixre] nm tiger

tijera [ti'xera] nf scissors pl; (ZOOL) claw; ~**s** nfpl scissors; (para plantas) shears

tijeretear [tixerete'ar] vt to snip

tila ['tila] nf lime blossom tea

tildar [til'dar] vt: ~ **de** to brand as

tilde ['tilde] nf (TIP) tilde

tilín [ti'lin] nm tinkle

tilo ['tilo] nm lime tree

timar [ti'mar] vt (estafar) to swindle

timbal [tim'bal] nm small drum

timbrar [tim'brar] vt to stamp

timbre ['timbre] nm (sello) stamp; (campanilla) bell; (tono) timbre; (COM) stamp duty

timidez [timi'ðeθ] nf shyness; **tímido, a** adj shy

timo ['timo] nm swindle

timón [ti'mon] nm helm, rudder; **timonel** nm helmsman

tímpano ['timpano] nm (ANAT) eardrum; (MUS) small drum

tina ['tina] nf tub; (baño) bath(tub); **tinaja** nf large jar

tinglado [tin'glaðo] nm (cobertizo) shed; (fig: truco) trick; (intriga) intrigue

tinieblas [ti'njeβlas] nfpl darkness sg; (sombras) shadows

tino ['tino] nm (habilidad) skill; (juicio) insight

tinta ['tinta] nf ink; (TEC) dye; (ARTE) colour

tinte ['tinte] nm dye

tintero [tin'tero] nm inkwell

tintinear [tintine'ar] vt to tinkle

tinto ['tinto] nm red wine

tintorería [tintore'ria] nf dry cleaner's

tintura [tin'tura] nf (QUÍM) dye; (farmacéutico) tincture

tío ['tio] nm (pariente) uncle; (fam: individuo) bloke (BRIT), guy

tiovivo [tio'βiβo] nm merry-go-round

típico, a ['tipiko, a] adj typical

tipo ['tipo] nm (clase) type, kind; (hombre) fellow; (ANAT: de hombre) build; (: de mujer) figure; (IMPRENTA) type; **~ bancario/de descuento/de interés/de cambio** bank/discount/interest/exchange rate

tipografía [tipoγra'fia] nf printing cpd; **tipográfico, a** adj printing cpd

tiquet ['tiket] (pl **~s**) nm ticket; (en tienda) cash slip

tiquismiquis [tikis'mikis] nm inv fussy person ♦ nmpl (querellas) squabbling sg; (escrúpulos) silly scruples

tira ['tira] nf strip; (fig) abundance; **~ y afloja** give and take

tirabuzón [tiraβu'θon] nm (rizo) curl

tirachinas [tira'tʃinas] nm inv catapult

tirada [ti'raða] nf (acto) cast, throw; (serie) series; (TIP) printing, edition; **de una** ~ at one go

tirado, a [ti'raðo, a] adj (barato) dirt-cheap; (fam: fácil) very easy

tirador [tira'ðor] nm (mango) handle

tiranía [tira'nia] nf tyranny; **tirano, a** adj tyrannical ♦ nm/f tyrant

tirante [ti'rante] adj (cuerda etc) tight, taut; (relaciones) strained ♦ nm (ARQ) brace; (TEC) stay; **~s** nmpl (de pantalón) braces (BRIT), suspenders (US); **tirantez** nf tightness; (fig) tension

tirar [ti'rar] vt to throw; (dejar caer) to drop; (volcar) to upset; (derribar) to knock down o over; (desechar) to throw out o away; (dinero) to squander; (imprimir) to print ♦ vi (disparar) to shoot; (de la puerta etc) to pull; (fam: andar) to go; (tender a, buscar realizar) to tend to; (DEPORTE) to shoot; **~se** vr to throw o.s.; **~ abajo** to bring down, destroy; **tira más a su padre** he takes more after his father; **ir tirando** to manage; **a todo** ~ at the most

tirita [ti'rita] nf (sticking) plaster (BRIT), bandaid (US)

tiritar [tiri'tar] vi to shiver

tiro ['tiro] nm (lanzamiento) throw; (disparo) shot; (DEPORTE) shot; (GOLF, TENIS) drive; (alcance) range; **~ al blanco** target practice; **caballo de ~** cart-horse; **andar de ~s largos** to be all dressed up; **al ~** (AM) at once

tirón [ti'ron] nm (sacudida) pull, tug; **de un** ~ in one go, all at once

tiroteo [tiro'teo] nm exchange of shots, shooting

tísico, a ['tisiko, a] adj consumptive

tisis ['tisis] nf inv consumption, tuberculosis

títere ['titere] nm puppet

titiritero, a [titiri'tero, a] nm/f puppeteer

titubeante [tituβe'ante] adj (al andar) shaky, tottering; (al hablar) stammering; (dudoso) hesitant

titubear [tituβe'ar] vi to stagger; to stammer; (fig) to hesitate; **titubeo** nm staggering; stammering; hesitation

titulado, a [titu'laðo, a] *adj* (*libro*)
entitled; (*persona*) titled

titular [titu'lar] *adj* titular ♦ *nm/f*
holder ♦ *vt* to headline; (*de diario*) headline; (*certificado*) professional qualification; (*universitario*) (university) degree; **a título de** in the capacity of

tiza ['tiθa] *nf* chalk

tiznar [tiθ'nar] *vt* to blacken

tizón [ti'θon] *nm* brand

toalla [to'aʎa] *nf* towel

tobillo [to'βiʎo] *nm* ankle

tobogán [toβo'van] *nm* (*montaña rusa*) roller-coaster; (*de niños*) chute, slide

tocadiscos [toka'ðiskos] *nm inv* record player

tocado, a [to'kaðo, a] *adj* (*fam*) touched ♦ *nm* headdress

tocador [toka'ðor] *nm* (*mueble*) dressing table; (*cuarto*) boudoir; (*fam*) ladies' toilet (*BRIT*) o room (*US*)

tocante [to'kante]: **~ a** *prep* with regard to

tocar [to'kar] *vt* to touch; (*MUS*) to play; (*referirse a*) to allude to; (*timbre*) to ring ♦ *vi* (*a la puerta*) to knock (on o at the door); (*ser de turno*) to fall to, be the turn of; (*ser hora*) to be due; **~se** *vr* (*cubrirse la cabeza*) to cover one's head; (*tener contacto*) to touch (each other); **por lo que a mí me toca** as far as I am concerned; **te toca a ti** it's your turn

tocayo, a [to'kajo, a] *nm/f* namesake

tocino [to'θino] *nm* bacon

todavía [toða'βia] *adv* (*aun*) even; (*aún*) still, yet; **~ más** yet more; **~ no** not yet

PALABRA CLAVE

todo, a ['toðo, a] *adj* **1** (*con artículo sg*) all; **toda la carne** all the meat; **toda la noche** all night, the whole night; **~ el libro** the whole book; **toda una**

botella a whole bottle; **~ lo contrario** quite the opposite; **está toda sucia** she's all dirty; **por ~ el país** throughout the whole country

2 (*con artículo pl*) all; every; **~ los libros** all the books; **todas las noches** every night; **~s los que quieran salir** all those who want to leave

♦ *pron* **1** everything, all; **~s** everyone, everybody; **lo sabemos ~** we know everything; **~s querían más tiempo** everybody o everyone wanted more time; **nos marchamos ~s** all of us left

2: con ~: con ~ él me sigue gustando even so I still like him

♦ *adv* all; **vaya ~ seguido** keep straight on o ahead

♦ *nm*: **como un ~** as a whole; **del ~: no me agrada del ~** I don't entirely like it

todopoderoso, a [toðopoðe'roso, a] *adj* all powerful; (*REL*) almighty

toga ['tova] *nf* toga; (*ESCOL*) gown

Tokio ['tokjo] *n* Tokyo

toldo ['toldo] *nm* (*para el sol*) sunshade (*BRIT*), parasol; (*tienda*) marquee

tolerancia [tole'ranθja] *nf* tolerance;
tolerante *adj* (*sociedad*) liberal; (*persona*) open-minded

tolerar [tole'rar] *vt* to tolerate; (*resistir*) to endure

toma ['toma] *nf* (*acto*) taking; (*MED*) dose; **~ (de corriente)** socket

tomar [to'mar] *vt* to take; (*aspecto*) to take on; (*beber*) to drink ♦ *vi* to take; (*AM*) to drink; **~se** *vr* to take; **~se por** to consider o.s. to be; **~ a bien/a mal** to take well/badly; **~ en serio** to take seriously; **~ el pelo a alguien** to pull sb's leg; **~la con uno** to pick a quarrel with sb; **¡tome!** here you are!; **~ el sol** to sunbathe

tomate [to'mate] *nm* tomato

tomillo [to'miʎo] *nm* thyme

tomo ['tomo] *nm* (*libro*) volume

ton [ton] *abr* = **tonelada** ♦ *nm*: **sin ~ ni son** without rhyme or reason

tonada [to'naða] *nf* tune

tonalidad [tonali'ðað] *nf* tone

tonel [to'nel] *nm* barrel

tonelada [tone'laða] *nf* ton; **tonelaje** *nm* tonnage

tónica ['tonika] *nf* (*MUS*) tonic; (*fig*) keynote

tónico, a ['toniko, a] *adj* tonic ♦ *nm* (*MED*) tonic

tonificar [tonifi'kar] *vt* to tone up

tono ['tono] *nm* tone; **fuera de ~** inappropriate; **darse ~** to put on airs

tontería [tonte'ria] *nf* (*estupidez*) foolishness; (*cosa*) stupid thing; (*acto*) foolish act; **~s** *nfpl* (*disparates*) rubbish *sg*, nonsense *sg*

tonto, a ['tonto, a] *adj* stupid, silly ♦ *nm/f* fool

topar [to'par] *vi*: **~ contra** *o* **en** to run into; **~ con** to run up against

tope ['tope] *adj* maximum ♦ *nm* (*fin*) end; (*límite*) limit; (*FERRO*) buffer; (*AUTO*) bumper; **al ~** to end to end

tópico, a ['topiko, a] *adj* topical ♦ *nm* platitude

topo ['topo] *nm* (*ZOOL*) mole; (*fig*) blunderer

topografía [topoɣra'fia] *nf* topography; **topógrafo, a** *nm/f* topographer

toque *etc* ['toke] *vb ver* **tocar** ♦ *nm* touch; (*MUS*) beat; (*de campana*) peal; **dar un ~ a** to warn; **~ de queda** curfew

toqué *vb ver* **tocar**

toquetear [tokete'ar] *vt* to finger

toquilla [to'kiʎa] *nf* (*pañuelo*) headscarf; (*chal*) shawl

tórax ['toraks] *nm* thorax

torbellino [torbe'ʎino] *nm* whirlwind; (*fig*) whirl

torcedura [torθe'ðura] *nf* twist; (*MED*) sprain

torcer [tor'θer] *vt* to twist; (*la esquina*)

to turn; (*MED*) to sprain ♦ *vi* (*desviar*) to turn off; **~se** *vr* (*ladearse*) to bend; (*desviarse*) to go astray; (*fracasar*) to go wrong; **torcido, a** *adj* twisted; (*fig*) crooked ♦ *nm* curl

tordo, a ['torðo, a] *adj* dappled ♦ *nm* thrush

torear [tore'ar] *vt* (*fig: evadir*) to avoid; (*jugar con*) to tease ♦ *vi* to fight bulls; **toreo** *nm* bullfighting; **torero, a** *nm/f* bullfighter

tormenta [tor'menta] *nf* storm; (*fig: confusión*) turmoil

tormento [tor'mento] *nm* torture; (*fig*) anguish

tornar [tor'nar] *vt* (*devolver*) to return, give back; (*transformar*) to transform ♦ *vi* to go back; **~se** *vr* (*ponerse*) to become

tornasolado, a [tornaso'laðo, a] *adj* (*brillante*) iridescent; (*reluciente*) shimmering

torneo [tor'neo] *nm* tournament

tornillo [tor'niʎo] *nm* screw

torniquete [torni'kete] *nm* (*MED*) tourniquet

torno ['torno] *nm* (*TEC*) winch; (*tambor*) drum; **en ~ (a)** round, about

toro ['toro] *nm* bull; (*fam*) he-man; **los ~s** bullfighting

toronja [to'ronxa] *nf* grapefruit

torpe ['torpe] *adj* (*poco hábil*) clumsy, awkward; (*necio*) dim; (*lento*) slow

torpedo [tor'peðo] *nm* torpedo

torpeza [tor'peθa] *nf* (*falta de agilidad*) clumsiness; (*lentitud*) slowness; (*error*) mistake

torre ['torre] *nf* tower; (*de petróleo*) derrick

torrefacto, a [torre'fakto, a] *adj* roasted

torrente [to'rrente] *nm* torrent

tórrido, a ['torriðo, a] *adj* torrid

torrija [to'rrixa] *nf* French toast

torsión [tor'sjon] *nf* twisting

torso ['torso] *nm* torso

torta ['torta] *nf* cake; (*fam*) slap

torticolis [tor'tikolis] nm inv stiff neck

tortilla [tor'tiʎa] nf omelette; (AM) maize pancake; ~ **francesa/española** plain/potato omelette

tórtola ['tortola] nf turtledove

tortuga [tor'tuɣa] nf tortoise

tortuoso, a [tor'twoso, a] adj winding

tortura [tor'tura] nf torture; **torturar** vt to torture

tos [tos] nf cough; ~ **ferina** whooping cough

tosco, a ['tosko, a] adj coarse

toser [to'ser] vi to cough

tostada [tos'taða] nf piece of toast;

tostado, a adj toasted; (por el sol) dark brown; (piel) tanned

tostador [tosta'ðor] nm toaster

tostar [tos'tar] vt to toast; (café) to roast; (persona) to tan; ~**se** vr to get brown

total [to'tal] adj total ♦ adv in short; (al fin y al cabo) when all is said and done ♦ nm total; ~ **que** to cut (BRIT) o make (US) a long story short

totalidad [totali'ðað] nf whole

totalitario, a [totali'tarjo, a] adj totalitarian

tóxico, a ['toksiko, a] adj toxic ♦ nm poison; **toxicómano, a** nm/f drug addict

toxina [to'ksina] nf toxin

tozudo, a [to'θuðo, a] adj obstinate

traba ['traβa] nf bond, tie; (cadena) shackle

trabajador, a [traβaxa'ðor, a] adj hard-working ♦ nm/f worker

trabajar [traβa'xar] vt to work; (AGR) to till; (empeñarse en) to work at; (convencer) to persuade ♦ vi to work; (esforzarse) to strive; **trabajo** nm work; (tarea) task; (POL) labour; (fig) effort; **tomarse el trabajo** de to take the trouble to; **trabajo por turno/a destajo** shift work/piecework; **trabajoso, a** adj hard

trabalenguas [traβa'lengwas] nm inv tongue twister

trabar [tra'βar] vt (juntar) to join, unite; (atar) to tie down, fetter; (agarrar) to seize; (amistad) to strike up; ~**se** vr to become entangled; **trabársele a uno la lengua** to be tongue-tied

tracción [trak'θjon] nf traction; ~ **delantera/trasera** front-wheel/rear-wheel drive

tractor [trak'tor] nm tractor

tradición [traði'θjon] nf tradition; **tradicional** adj traditional

traducción [traðuk'θjon] nf translation

traducir [traðu'θir] vt to translate; **traductor, a** nm/f translator

traer [tra'er] vt to bring; (llevar) to carry; (llevar puesto) to wear; (incluir) to carry; (causar) to cause; ~**se** vr: ~**se algo** to be up to sth

traficar [trafi'kar] vi to trade

tráfico ['trafiko] nm (COM) trade; (AUTO) traffic

tragaluz [traɣa'luθ] nm skylight

tragaperras [traɣa'perras] nm o f inv slot machine

tragar [tra'ɣar] vt to swallow; (devorar) to devour, bolt down; ~**se** vr to swallow

tragedia [tra'xeðja] nf tragedy; **trágico, a** adj tragic

trago ['traɣo] nm (líquido) drink; (bocado) gulp; (fam: de bebida) swig; (desgracia) blow

traición [trai'θjon] nf treachery; (JUR) treason; (una ~) act of treachery; **traicionar** vt to betray

traicionero, a [traiθjo'nero, a] adj treacherous

traidor, a [trai'ðor, a] adj treacherous ♦ nm/f traitor

traigo etc vb ver **traer**

traje ['traxe] vb ver **traer** ♦ nm (de hombre) suit; (de mujer) dress; (vestido típico) costume; ~ **de baño** swimsuit; ~ **de luces** bullfighter's costume

trajera etc vb ver **traer**

trajín [tra'xin] nm (fam: movimiento) bustle; **trajinar** vi (moverse) to bustle about

trama ['trama] nf (intriga) plot; (de tejido) weft (BRIT), woof (US); **tramar** vt to plot; (TEC) to weave

tramitar [trami'tar] vt (asunto) to transact; (negociar) to negotiate

trámite ['tramite] nm (paso) step; (JUR) transaction; **~s** nmpl (burocracia) procedure sg; (JUR) proceedings

tramo ['tramo] nm (de tierra) plot; (de escalera) flight; (de vía) section

tramoya [tra'moja] nf (TEATRO) piece of stage machinery; **tramoyista** nm/f scene shifter; (fig) trickster

trampa ['trampa] nf trap; (en el suelo) trapdoor; (truco) trick; (engaño) fiddle; **trampear** vt, vi to cheat

trampolín [trampo'lin] nm (de piscina etc) diving board

tramposo, a [tram'poso, a] adj crooked, cheating ♦ nm/f crook, cheat

tranca ['tranka] nf (palo) stick; (de puerta, ventana) bar; **trancar** vt to bar

trance ['tranθe] nm (momento difícil) difficult moment o juncture; (estado hipnotizado) trance

tranquilidad [trankili'ðað] nf (calma) calmness, stillness; (paz) peacefulness

tranquilizar [trankili'θar] vt (calmar) to calm (down); (asegurar) to reassure; **~se** vr to calm down; **tranquilo, a** adj (calmado) calm; (apacible) peaceful; (mar) calm; (mente) untroubled

transacción [transak'θjon] nf transaction

transbordador [transβorða'ðor] nm ferry

transbordar [transβor'ðar] vt to transfer; **transbordo** nm transfer; **hacer transbordo** to change (trains etc)

transcurrir [transku'rrir] vi (tiempo) to pass; (hecho) to take place

transcurso [trans'kurso] nm: **~ del tiempo** lapse (of time)

transeúnte [transe'unte] nm/f passer-by

transferencia [transfe'renθja] nf transference; (COM) transfer

transferir [transfe'rir] vt to transfer

transformador [transforma'ðor] nm (ELEC) transformer

transformar [transfor'mar] vt to transform; (convertir) to convert

tránsfuga ['transfuɣa] nm/f (MIL) deserter; (POL) turncoat

transfusión [transfu'sjon] nf transfusion

transgénico, a [trans'xeniko, a] adj genetically modified, GM

transición [transi'θjon] nf transition

transigir [transi'xir] vi to compromise, make concessions

transitar [transi'tar] vi to go (from place to place); **tránsito** nm transit; (AUTO) traffic; **transitorio, a** adj transitory

transmisión [transmi'sjon] nf (TEC) transmission; (transferencia) transfer; **~ en directo/exterior** live/outside broadcast

transmitir [transmi'tir] vt to transmit; (RADIO, TV) to broadcast

transparencia [transpa'renθja] nf transparency; (claridad) clearness, clarity; (foto) slide

transparentar [transparen'tar] vt to reveal ♦ vi to be transparent; **transparente** adj transparent; (claro) clear

transpirar [transpi'rar] vi to perspire

transportar [transpor'tar] vt to transport; (llevar) to carry; **transporte** nm transport; (COM) haulage

transversal [transβer'sal] adj transverse, cross

tranvía [tram'bia] nm tram

trapecio [tra'peθjo] nm trapeze; **trapecista** nm/f trapeze artist

trapero, a [tra'pero, a] nm/f ragman

trapicheo [trapi'tʃeo] (fam) nm scheme, fiddle

trapo ['trapo] nm (tela) rag; (de cocina)

cloth

tráquea [ˈtrakea] nf windpipe

traqueteo [trakeˈteo] nm rattling

tras [tras] prep (detrás) behind; (después) after

trasatlántico [trasatˈlantiko] nm (barco) (cabin) cruiser

trascendencia [trasθenˈdenθja] nf (importancia) importance; (FILOSOFÍA) transcendence

trascendental [trasθendenˈtal] adj important; (FILOSOFÍA) transcendental

trascender [trasθenˈder] vi (noticias) to come out; (suceso) to have a wide effect

trasero, a [traˈsero, a] adj back, rear ♦ nm (ANAT) bottom

trasfondo [trasˈfondo] nm background

trasgredir [trasɣreˈðir] vt to contravene

trashumante [trasuˈmante] adj (animales) migrating

trasladar [traslaˈðar] vt to move; (persona) to transfer; (empleado: de puesto) to move; (copiar) to copy; **~se** vr (mudarse) to move; **traslado** nm move; (mudanza) move, removal

traslucir [trasluˈθir] vt to show; **~se** vr to be translucent; (fig) to be revealed

trasluz [trasˈluθ] nm reflected light; **al ~** against o up to the light

trasnochador, a [trasnotʃaˈðor, a] nm/f night owl

trasnochar [trasnoˈtʃar] vi (acostarse tarde) to stay up late

traspapelar [traspapeˈlar] vt (documento, carta) to mislay, misplace

traspasar [traspaˈsar] vt (suj: bala etc) to pierce, go through; (propiedad) to sell, transfer; (calle) to cross over; (límites) to go beyond; (ley) to break; **traspaso** nm (venta) transfer, sale

traspié [trasˈpje] nm (tropezón) trip; (error) blunder

trasplantar [trasplanˈtar] vt to transplant

traste [ˈtraste] nm (MÚS) fret; **dar al ~ con algo** to ruin sth

trastero [trasˈtero] nm storage room

trastienda [trasˈtjenda] nf back of shop

trasto [ˈtrasto] nm (pey) (cosa) piece of junk; (persona) dead loss

trastornado, a [trastorˈnaðo, a] adj (loco) mad, crazy

trastornar [trastorˈnar] vt (fig: planes) to disrupt; (: nervios) to shatter; (: persona) to drive crazy; **~se** vr (volverse loco) to go mad o crazy; **trastorno** nm (acto) overturning; (confusión) confusion

tratable [traˈtaβle] adj friendly

tratado [traˈtaðo] nm (POL) treaty; (COM) agreement

tratamiento [trataˈmjento] nm treatment; **~ de textos** (INFORM) word processing cpd

tratar [traˈtar] vt (ocuparse de) to treat; (manejar, TEC) to handle; (MED) to treat; (dirigirse a: persona) to address ♦ vi: **~ de** (hablar sobre) to deal with, be about; (intentar) to try to; **~se** vr to treat each other; **~ con** (COM) to trade in; (negociar) to negotiate with; (tener contactos) to have dealings with; **¿de qué se trata?** what's it about?; **trato** nm dealings pl; (relaciones) relationship; (comportamiento) manner; (COM) agreement

trauma [ˈtrauma] nm trauma

través [traˈβes] nm (fig) reverse; **al ~** across, crossways; **a ~ de** across; (sobre) over; (por) through

travesaño [traβeˈsaɲo] nm (ARQ) crossbeam; (DEPORTE) crossbar

travesía [traβeˈsia] nf (calle) cross-street; (NAUT) crossing

travesura [traβeˈsura] nf (broma) prank; (ingenio) wit

traviesa [traˈβjesa] nf (ARQ) crossbeam

travieso, a [traˈβjeso, a] adj (niño) naughty

trayecto [traˈjekto] nm (ruta) road,

way; (*viaje*) journey; (*tramo*) stretch;
~ria nf trajectory; (*fig*) path
traza ['traθa] nf (*aspecto*) looks pl;
(*señal*) sign; (*fig*) **bien ~do**
shapely, well-formed ♦ nm (*ARQ*) plan,
design; (*fig*) outline
trazar [tra'θar] vt (*ARQ*) to plan; (*ARTE*)
to sketch; (*fig*) to trace; (*plan*) to draw
up; **trazo** nm (*línea*) line; (*bosquejo*)
sketch
trébol ['treβol] nm (*BOT*) clover
trece ['treθe] num thirteen
trecho ['tretʃo] nm (*distancia*) distance;
(*de tiempo*) while; **de ~ en ~** at
intervals
tregua ['treɣwa] nf (*MIL*) truce; (*fig*)
respite
treinta ['treinta] num thirty
tremendo, a [tre'mendo, a] adj
(*terrible*) terrible; (*imponente: cosa*)
imposing; (*fam: fabuloso*) tremendous
trémulo, a ['tremulo, a] adj quiver-
ing
tren [tren] nm train; **~ de aterrizaje**
undercarriage
trenca ['trenka] nf duffel coat
trenza ['trenθa] nf (*de pelo*) plait
(*BRIT*), braid (*US*); **trenzar** vt (*pelo*) to
plait, braid; **trenzarse** vr (*AM*) to
become involved
trepadora [trepa'ðora] nf (*BOT*)
climber
trepar [tre'par] vt, vi to climb
trepidante [trepi'ðante] adj (*acción*)
fast; (*ritmo*) hectic
tres [tres] num three
tresillo [tre'siʎo] nm three-piece suite;
(*MUS*) triplet
treta ['treta] nf trick
triángulo ['trjangulo] nm triangle
tribu ['triβu] nf tribe
tribuna [tri'βuna] nf (*plataforma*)
platform; (*DEPORTE*) (grand)stand
tribunal [triβu'nal] nm (*JUR*) court;
(*comisión, fig*) tribunal
tributar [triβu'tar] vt (*gen*) to pay;
tributo nm (*COM*) tax

tricotar [triko'tar] vi to knit
trigal [tri'ɣal] nm wheat field
trigo ['triɣo] nm wheat
trigueño, a [tri'ɣeɲo, a] adj (*pelo*)
corn-coloured
trillado, a [tri'ʎaðo, a] adj threshed;
(*asunto*) trite, hackneyed; **trilladora** nf
threshing machine
trillar [tri'ʎar] vt (*AGR*) to thresh
trimestral [trimes'tral] adj quarterly;
(*ESCOL*) termly
trimestre [tri'mestre] nm (*ESCOL*) term
trinar [tri'nar] vi (*pájaros*) to sing;
(*rabiar*) to fume, be angry
trinchar [trin'tʃar] vt to carve
trinchera [trin'tʃera] nf (*fosa*) trench
trineo [tri'neo] nm sledge
trinidad [trini'ðað] nf trio; (*REL*): **la T~**
the Trinity
trino ['trino] nm trill
tripa ['tripa] nf (*ANAT*) intestine; (*fam:
tb:* **~s**) insides pl
triple ['triple] adj triple
triplicado, a [tripli'kaðo, a] adj: **por ~**
in triplicate
tripulación [tripula'θjon] nf crew
tripulante [tripu'lante] nm/f
crewman/woman
tripular [tripu'lar] vt (*barco*) to man;
(*AUTO*) to drive
triquiñuela [triki'ɲwela] nf trick
tris [tris] nm inv crack; **en un ~** in an
instant
triste ['triste] adj (*gen*); (*lamentable*)
sorry, miserable; **~za** nf (*aflicción*)
sadness; (*melancolía*) melancholy
triturar [tritu'rar] vt (*moler*) to grind;
(*mascar*) to chew
triunfar [trjun'far] vi (*tener éxito*) to
triumph; (*ganar*) to win; **triunfo** nm
triumph
trivial [tri'βjal] adj trivial; **~izar** vt to
minimize, play down
triza ['triθa] nf: **hacer ~s** to smash to
bits; (*papel*) to tear to shreds
trocar [tro'kar] vt to exchange
trocear [troθe'ar] vt (*carne, manzana*)

to cut up, cut into pieces

trocha ['trotʃa] nf short cut

troche ['trotʃe]: **a ~ y moche** adv helter-skelter, pell-mell

trofeo [tro'feo] nm (premio) trophy; (éxito) success

tromba ['tromba] nf downpour

trombón [trom'bon] nm trombone

trombosis [trom'bosis] nf inv thrombosis

trompa ['trompa] nf horn; (trompo) humming top; (hocico) snout; (fam): **cogerse una ~** to get tight

trompazo [trom'paθo] nm bump, bang

trompeta [trom'peta] nf trumpet; (clarín) bugle

trompicón [trompi'kon]: **a ~es** adv in fits and starts

trompo ['trompo] nm spinning top

trompón [trom'pon] nm bump

tronar [tro'nar] vt (AM) to shoot ♦ vi to thunder; (fig) to rage

tronchar [tron'tʃar] vt (árbol) to chop down; (fig: vida) to cut short; (: esperanza) to shatter; (persona) to tire out; **~se** vr to fall down

tronco ['tronko] nm (de árbol, ANAT) trunk

trono ['trono] nm throne

tropa ['tropa] nf (MIL) troop; (soldados) soldiers pl

tropel [tro'pel] nm (muchedumbre) crowd

tropezar [trope'θar] vi to trip, stumble; (errar) to slip up; **~ con** to run into; (topar con) to bump into; **tropezón** nm trip; (fig) blunder

tropical [tropi'kal] adj tropical

trópico ['tropiko] nm tropic

tropiezo [tro'pjeθo] vb ver **tropezar** ♦ nm (error) slip, blunder; (desgracia) misfortune; (obstáculo) snag

trotamundos [trota'mundos] nm inv globetrotter

trotar [tro'tar] vi to trot; **trote** nm trot; (fam) travelling; **de mucho trote**

hard-wearing

trozo ['troθo] nm bit, piece

trucha ['trutʃa] nf trout

truco ['truko] nm (habilidad) knack; (engaño) trick

trueno ['trweno] nm thunder; (estampido) bang

trueque etc ['trweke] vb ver **trocar** ♦ nm exchange; (COM) barter

trufa ['trufa] nf (BOT) truffle

truhán, ana [tru'an, ana] nm/f rogue

truncar [trun'kar] vt (cortar) to truncate; (fig: la vida etc) to cut short; (: el desarrollo) to stunt

tu [tu] adj your

tú [tu] pron you

tubérculo [tu'βerkulo] nm (BOT) tuber

tuberculosis [tußerku'losis] nf inv tuberculosis

tubería [tuße'ria] nf pipes pl; (conducto) pipeline

tubo ['tußo] nm tube, pipe; **~ de ensayo** test tube; **~ de escape** exhaust (pipe)

tuerca ['twerka] nf nut

tuerto, a ['twerto, a] adj blind in one eye ♦ nm/f one-eyed person

tuerza etc vb ver **torcer**

tuétano ['twetano] nm marrow; (BOT) pith

tufo ['tufo] nm (hedor) stench

tul [tul] nm tulle

tulipán [tuli'pan] nm tulip

tullido, a [tu'λiðo, a] adj crippled

tumba ['tumba] nf (sepultura) tomb

tumbar [tum'bar] vt to knock down; **~se** vr (echarse) to lie down; (extenderse) to stretch out

tumbo ['tumbo] nm: **dar ~s** to stagger

tumbona [tum'bona] nf (butaca) easy chair; (de playa) deckchair (BRIT), beach chair (US)

tumor [tu'mor] nm tumour

tumulto [tu'multo] nm turmoil

tuna ['tuna] nf (MUS) student music group; ver tb **tuno**

Tuna

A **tuna** *is a musical group made up of university students or former students who dress up in costumes from the "Edad de Oro", the Spanish Golden Age. These groups go through the town playing their guitars, lutes and tambourines and serenade the young ladies in the halls of residence or make impromptu appearances at weddings or parties singing traditional Spanish songs for a few* **pesetas.**

---

tunante [tu'nante] *nm/f* rascal

tunda ['tunda] *nf (golpeo)* beating

túnel ['tunel] *nm* tunnel

Túnez ['tuneθ] *nm* Tunisia; *(ciudad)* Tunis

tuno, a ['tuno, a] *nm/f (fam)* rogue ♦ *nm member of student music group*

tupido, a [tu'piðo, a] *adj (denso)* dense; *(tela)* close-woven

turba ['turβa] *nf* crowd

turbante [tur'βante] *nm* turban

turbar [tur'βar] *vt (molestar)* to disturb; *(incomodar)* to upset; **~se** *vr* to be disturbed

turbina [tur'βina] *nf* turbine

turbio, a ['turβjo, a] *adj* cloudy; *(tema etc)* confused

turbulencia [turβu'lenθja] *nf* turbulence; *(fig)* restlessness;
turbulento, a *adj* turbulent; *(fig: intranquilo)* restless; *(: ruidoso)* noisy

turco, a ['turko, a] *adj* Turkish ♦ *nm/f* Turk

turismo [tu'rismo] *nm* tourism; *(coche)* car; **turista** *nm/f* tourist; **turístico, a** *adj* tourist *cpd*

turnar [tur'nar] *vi* to take (it in) turns; **~se** *vr* to take (it in) turns; **turno** *nm (de trabajo)* shift; *(juegos etc)* turn

turquesa [tur'kesa] *nf* turquoise

Turquía [tur'kia] *nf* Turkey

turrón [tu'rron] *nm (dulce)* nougat

tutear [tute'ar] *vt* to address as familiar

"tú"; **~se** *vr* to be on familiar terms

tutela [tu'tela] *nf (legal)* guardianship;
tutelar *adj* tutelary ♦ *vt* to protect

tutor, a [tu'tor, a] *nm/f (legal)* guardian; *(ESCOL)* tutor

tuve *etc vb ver* **tener**

tuviera *etc vb ver* **tener**

tuyo, a [tujo, a] *adj* yours, of yours ♦ *pron* yours; **un amigo ~** a friend of yours; **los ~s** *(fam)* your relations, your family

TV ['te'βe] *nf abr (= televisión)* TV

TVE *nf abr =* **Televisión Española**

U, u

u [u] *conj* or

ubicar [uβi'kar] *vt* to place, situate; *(AM: encontrar)* to find; **~se** *vr* to lie, be located

ubre ['uβre] *nf* udder

UCI *nf abr (= Unidad de Cuidados Intensivos)* ICU

Ud(s) *abr =* **usted(es)**

UE *nf abr (= Unión Europea)* EU

ufanarse [ufa'narse] *vr* to boast; **~ de** to pride o.s. on; **ufano, a** *adj (arrogante)* arrogant; *(presumido)* conceited

UGT *nf abr =* **Unión General de Trabajadores**

ujier [u'xjer] *nm* usher; *(portero)* doorkeeper

úlcera ['ulθera] *nf* ulcer

ulcerar [ulθe'rar] *vt* to make sore; **~se** *vr* to ulcerate

ulterior [ulte'rjor] *adj (más allá)* farther, further; *(subsecuente, siguiente)* subsequent

últimamente ['ultimamente] *adv (recientemente)* lately, recently

ultimar [ulti'mar] *vt* to finish; *(finalizar)* to finalize; *(AM: rematar)* to finish off

ultimátum [ulti'matum] *(pl* **~s)** *nm* ultimatum

último   291   uña

último, a ['ultimo, a] *adj* last; (*más reciente*) latest, most recent; (*más bajo*) bottom; (*más alto*) top; **en las últimas** on one's last legs; **por ~** finally

ultra ['ultra] *adj* ultra ♦ *nm/f* extreme right-winger

ultrajar [ultra'xar] *vt* (*ofender*) to outrage; (*insultar*) to insult, abuse; **ultraje** *nm* outrage; insult

ultramar [ultra'mar] *nm*: **de o en ~** abroad, overseas

ultramarinos [ultrama'rinos] *nmpl* groceries; **tienda de ~** grocer's (shop)

ultranza [ul'tranθa]: **a ~** *adv* (*a todo trance*) at all costs; (*completo*) outright

ultratumba [ultra'tumba] *nf*: **la vida de ~** the next life

umbral [um'bral] *nm* (*gen*) threshold

umbrío, a [um'brio, a] *adj* shady

PALABRA CLAVE
---

un, una [un, 'una] *art indef* a; (*antes de vocal*) an; **una mujer/naranja** a woman/an orange
♦ *adj*: **unos** (*o* **unas**): **hay unos regalos para ti** there are some presents for you; **hay unas cervezas en la nevera** there are some beers in the fridge

unánime [u'nanime] *adj* unanimous; **unanimidad** *nf* unanimity

undécimo, a [un'deθimo, a] *adj* eleventh

ungir [un'xir] *vt* to anoint

ungüento [un'gwento] *nm* ointment

únicamente ['unikamente] *adv* solely, only

único, a ['uniko, a] *adj* only, sole; (*sin par*) unique

unidad [uni'ðað] *nf* unity; (*COM, TEC etc*) unit

unido, a [u'niðo, a] *adj* joined, linked; (*fig*) united

unificar [unifi'kar] *vt* to unite, unify

uniformar [unifor'mar] *vt* to make uniform, level up; (*persona*) to put into uniform

uniforme [uni'forme] *adj* uniform, equal; (*superficie*) even ♦ *nm* uniform; **uniformidad** *nf* uniformity; (*de terreno*) levelness, evenness

unilateral [unilate'ral] *adj* unilateral

unión [u'njon] *nf* union; (*acto*) uniting, joining; (*unidad*) unity; (*TEC*) joint; **la U~ Europea** the European Union; **la U~ Soviética** the Soviet Union

unir [u'nir] *vt* (*juntar*) to join, unite; (*atar*) to tie, fasten; (*combinar*) to combine; **~se** *vr* to join together, unite; (*empresas*) to merge

unísono [u'nisono] *nm*: **al ~** in unison

universal [unißer'sal] *adj* universal; (*mundial*) world *cpd*

universidad [unißersi'ðað] *nf* university

universitario, a [unißersi'tarjo, a] *adj* university *cpd* ♦ *nm/f* (*profesor*) lecturer; (*estudiante*) (university) student; (*graduado*) graduate

universo [uni'ßerso] *nm* universe

PALABRA CLAVE
---

uno, a ['uno, a] *adj* one; **es todo ~** it's all one and the same; **~s pocos** a few; **~s cien** about a hundred
♦ *pron* **1** one; **quiero sólo ~** I only want one; **~ de ellos** one of them
2 (*alguien*) somebody, someone; **conozco a ~ que se te parece** I know somebody *o* someone who looks like you; **~ mismo** oneself; **~s querían quedarse** some (people) wanted to stay
3: (**los**) **~s ...** (**los**) **otros ...** some ... others; **una y otra son muy agradables** they're both very nice
♦ *nf* one; **es la una** it's one o'clock
♦ *nm* (number) one

untar [un'tar] *vt* (*mantequilla*) to spread; (*engrasar*) to grease, oil

uña ['uɲa] *nf* (*ANAT*) nail; (*garra*) claw;

(*casco*) hoof; (*arrancaclavos*) claw

uranio [u'ranjo] *nm* uranium

urbanidad [urβani'ðað] *nf* courtesy, politeness

urbanismo [urβa'nismo] *nm* town planning

urbanización [urβaniθa'θjon] *nf* (*barrio, colonia*) housing estate

urbanizar [urβani'θar] *vt* (*zona*) to develop, urbanize

urbano, a [ur'βano, a] *adj* (*de ciudad*) urban; (*cortés*) courteous, polite

urbe ['urβe] *nf* large city

urdimbre [ur'ðimbre] *nf* (*de tejido*) warp; (*intriga*) intrigue

urdir [ur'ðir] *vt* to warp; (*complot*) to plot, contrive

urgencia [ur'xenθja] *nf* urgency; (*prisa*) haste, rush; (*emergencia*) emergency; **servicios de ~** emergency services; **"Urgencias"** "Casualty"; **urgente** *adj* urgent

urgir [ur'xir] *vi* to be urgent; **me urge** I'm in a hurry for it

urinario, a [uri'narjo, a] *adj* urinary ♦ *nm* urinal

urna ['urna] *nf* urn; (*POL*) ballot box

urraca [u'rraka] *nf* magpie

URSS *nf*: **la ~** the USSR

Uruguay [uru'ɣwai] *nm*: **el ~** Uruguay; **uruguayo, a** *adj, nm/f* Uruguayan

usado, a [u'saðo, a] *adj* used; (*de segunda mano*) secondhand

usar [u'sar] *vt* to use; (*ropa*) to wear; (*tener costumbre*) to be in the habit of; **~se** *vr* to be used; **uso** *nm* use; wear; (*costumbre*) usage, custom; (*moda*) fashion; **al uso** in keeping with custom; **al uso de** in the style of

usted [us'teð] *pron* (*sg*) you *sg*; (*pl*): **~es** you *pl*

usual [u'swal] *adj* usual

usuario, a [usu'arjo, a] *nm/f* user

usura [u'sura] *nf* usury; **usurero, a** *nm/f* usurer

usurpar [usur'par] *vt* to usurp

utensilio [uten'siljo] *nm* tool; (*CULIN*) utensil

útero ['utero] *nm* uterus, womb

útil ['util] *adj* useful ♦ *nm* tool; **utilidad** *nf* usefulness; (*COM*) profit; **utilizar** *vt* to use, utilize

utopía [uto'pia] *nf* Utopia; **utópico, a** *adj* Utopian

uva ['uβa] *nf* grape

Las Uvas

In Spain Las **uvas** play a big part on New Year's Eve (**Nochevieja**), when on the stroke of midnight people gather at home, in restaurants or in the plaza mayor and eat a grape for each stroke of the clock of the Puerta del Sol in Madrid. It is said to bring luck for the following year.

V, v

v *abr* (= *voltio*) v

va *vb ver* **ir**

vaca ['baka] *nf* (*animal*) cow; **carne de ~** beef

vacaciones [baka'θjones] *nfpl* holidays

vacante [ba'kante] *adj* vacant, empty ♦ *nf* vacancy

vaciar [ba'θjar] *vt* to empty out; (*ahuecar*) to hollow out; (*moldear*) to cast; **~se** *vr* to empty

vacilante [baθi'lante] *adj* unsteady; (*habla*) faltering; (*dudoso*) hesitant

vacilar [baθi'lar] *vi* to be unsteady; (*al hablar*) to falter; (*dudar*) to hesitate, waver; (*memoria*) to fail

vacío, a [ba'θio, a] *adj* empty; (*puesto*) vacant; (*desocupado*) idle; (*vano*) vain ♦ *nm* emptiness; (*FÍSICA*) vacuum; (*un ~*) (empty) space

vacuna [ba'kuna] *nf* vaccine; **vacunar** *vt* to vaccinate

vacuno, a [ba'kuno, a] *adj* cow *cpd*; **ganado ~** cattle

vacuo, a ['bakwo, a] *adj* empty

vadear [baðe'ar] *vt (río)* to ford; **vado**
nm ford

vagabundo, a [baɣa'βundo, a] *adj*
wandering ♦ *nm* tramp

vagamente [baɣa'mente] *adv* vaguely

vagancia [ba'ɣanθja] *nf (pereza)*
idleness, laziness

vagar [ba'ɣar] *vi* to wander; *(no hacer
nada)* to idle

vagina [ba'xina] *nf* vagina

vago, a [ba'ɣo, a] *adj* vague; *(perezoso)*
lazy ♦ *nm/f (vagabundo)* tramp; *(flojo)*
lazybones *sg*, idler

vagón [ba'ɣon] *nm (FERRO: de
pasajeros)* carriage; *(: de mercancías)*
wagon

vaguedad [baɣe'ðað] *nf* vagueness

vaho ['bao] *nm (vapor)* vapour, steam;
(respiración) breath

vaina ['baina] *nf* sheath

vainilla [bai'niʎa] *nf* vanilla

vainita [bai'nita] *(AM) nf* green o
French bean

vais *vb ver* **ir**

vaivén [bai'βen] *nm* to-and-fro
movement; *(de tránsito)* coming and
going; **vaivenes** *nmpl (fig)* ups and
downs

vajilla [ba'xiʎa] *nf* crockery, dishes *pl*;
lavar la ~ to do the washing-up
(BRIT), wash the dishes *(US)*

valdré *etc vb ver* **valer**

vale ['bale] *nm* voucher; *(recibo)*
receipt; *(pagaré)* IOU

valedero, a [bale'ðero, a] *adj* valid

valenciano, a [balen'θjano, a] *adj*
Valencian

valentía [balen'tia] *nf* courage, bravery

valer [ba'ler] *vt* to be worth; *(MAT)* to
equal; *(costar)* to cost ♦ *vi (ser útil)* to
be useful; *(ser válido)* to be valid; **~se**
vr to take care of oneself; **~se de** to
make use of, take advantage of; **~ la
pena** to be worthwhile; **¿vale?** *(ESP)*
OK?

valeroso, a [bale'roso, a] *adj* brave,
valiant

valgo *etc vb ver* **valer**

valía [ba'lia] *nf* worth, value

validar [bali'ðar] *vt* to validate;
validez *nf* validity; **válido, a** *adj* valid

valiente [ba'ljente] *adj* brave, valiant
♦ *nm* hero

valioso, a [ba'ljoso, a] *adj* valuable

valla ['baʎa] *nf* fence; *(DEPORTE)* hurdle;
~ publicitaria hoarding; **vallar** *vt* to
fence in

valle ['baʎe] *nm* valley

valor [ba'lor] *nm* value, worth; *(precio)*
price; *(valentía)* valour, courage;
(importancia) importance; **~es** *nmpl*
(COM) securities; **~ar** *vt* to value

vals [bals] *nm inv* waltz

válvula ['balβula] *nf* valve

vamos *vb ver* **ir**

vampiro, resa [bam'piro, 'resa] *nm/f*
vampire

van *vb ver* **ir**

vanagloriarse [banaɣlo'rjarse] *vr* to
boast

vandalismo [banda'lismo] *nm*
vandalism; **vándalo, a** *nm/f* vandal

vanguardia [ban'gwarðja] *nf*
vanguard; *(ARTE etc)* avant-garde

vanidad [bani'ðað] *nf* vanity;
vanidoso, a *adj* vain, conceited

vano, a ['bano, a] *adj* vain

vapor [ba'por] *nm* vapour; *(vaho)*
steam; **al ~** *(CULIN)* steamed; **~izador**
nm atomizer; **~izar** *vt* to vaporize;
~oso, a *adj* vaporous

vapulear [bapule'ar] *vt* to beat, thrash

vaquero, a [ba'kero, a] *adj* cattle *cpd*
♦ *nm* cowboy; **~s** *nmpl (pantalones)*
jeans

vaquilla [ba'kiʎa] *nf (ZOOL)* heifer

vara ['bara] *nf* stick; *(TEC)* rod;
~ mágica magic wand

variable [ba'rjaβle] *adj*, *nf* variable

variación [barja'θjon] *nf* variation

variar [bar'jar] *vt* to vary; *(modificar)* to
modify; *(cambiar de posición)* to switch
around ♦ *vi* to vary

varicela [bari'θela] *nf* chickenpox

varices [ba'riθes] *nfpl* varicose veins

variedad [barje'ðað] *nf* variety

varilla [ba'riʎa] *nf* stick; (BOT) twig; (TEC) rod; (de rueda) spoke

vario, a ['barjo, a] *adj* varied; **~s** various, several

varita [ba'rita] *nf*: **~ mágica** magic wand

varón [ba'ron] *nm* male, man; **varonil** *adj* manly, virile

Varsovia [bar'soβja] *n* Warsaw

vas *vb ver* **ir**

vasco, a ['basko, a] *adj, nm/f* Basque

vascongado, a [baskon'gaðo, a] *adj* Basque; **las Vascongadas** the Basque Country

vascuence [bas'kwenθe] *adj* = **vascongado**

vaselina [base'lina] *nf* Vaseline ®

vasija [ba'sixa] *nf* container, vessel

vaso ['baso] *nm* glass, tumbler; (ANAT) vessel

vástago ['bastaɣo] *nm* (BOT) shoot; (TEC) rod; (fig) offspring

vasto, a ['basto, a] *adj* vast, huge

Vaticano [bati'kano] *nm*: **el ~ the** Vatican

vatio ['batjo] *nm* (ELEC.) watt

vaya *etc vb ver* **ir**

Vd(s) *abr* = **usted(es)**

ve *vb ver* **ir; ver**

vecindad [beθin'dað] *nf* neighbourhood; (habitantes) residents *pl*

vecindario [beθin'darjo] *nm* neighbourhood; residents *pl*

vecino, a [be'θino, a] *adj* neighbouring ♦ *nm/f* neighbour; (residente) resident

veda ['beða] *nf* prohibition

vedar [be'ðar] *vt* (prohibir) to ban, prohibit; (impedir) to stop, prevent

vegetación [bexeta'θjon] *nf* vegetation

vegetal [bexe'tal] *adj, nm* vegetable

vegetariano, a [bexeta'rjano, a] *adj, nm/f* vegetarian

vehemencia [be(e)'menθja] *nf* vehemence; **vehemente** *adj* vehement

vehículo [be'ikulo] *nm* vehicle; (MED) carrier

veía *etc vb ver* **ver**

veinte ['beinte] *num* twenty

vejación [bexa'θjon] *nf* vexation; (humillación) humiliation

vejar [be'xar] *vt* (irritar) to annoy, vex; (humillar) to humiliate

vejez [be'xeθ] *nf* old age

vejiga [be'xixa] *nf* (ANAT) bladder

vela ['bela] *nf* (de cera) candle; (NAUT) sail; (insomnio) sleeplessness; (vigilia) vigil; (MIL) sentry duty; **estar a dos ~s** (fam: sin dinero) to be skint

velado, a [be'laðo, a] *adj* veiled; (sonido) muffled; (FOTO) blurred ♦ *nf* soirée

velar [be'lar] *vt* (vigilar) to keep watch over ♦ *vi* to stay awake; **~ por** to watch over, look after

velatorio [bela'torjo] *nm* (funeral) wake

veleidad [belei'ðað] *nf* (ligereza) fickleness; (capricho) whim

velero [be'lero] *nm* (NAUT) sailing ship; (AVIAT) glider

veleta [be'leta] *nf* weather vane

veliz [be'lis] (AM) *nm* suitcase

vello ['beλo] *nm* down, fuzz

velo ['belo] *nm* veil

velocidad [beloθi'ðað] *nf* speed; (TEC, AUTO) gear

velocímetro [belo'θimetro] *nm* speedometer

veloz [be'loθ] *adj* fast

ven *vb ver* **venir**

vena ['bena] *nf* vein

venado [be'naðo] *nm* deer

vencedor, a [benθe'ðor, a] *adj* victorious ♦ *nm/f* victor, winner

vencer [ben'θer] *vt* (dominar) to defeat, beat; (derrotar) to vanquish; (superar, controlar) to overcome, master ♦ *vi* (triunfar) to win (through),

triumph; (*plazo*) to expire; **vencido, a**
adj (*derrotado*) defeated, beaten; (COM)
due ♦ *adv:* **pagar vencido** to pay in
arrears; **vencimiento** *nm* (COM)
maturity

venda ['benda] *nf* bandage; **vendaje**
nm bandage, dressing; **vendar** *vt* to
bandage; **vendar los ojos** to
blindfold

vendaval [benda'βal] *nm* (*viento*) gale

vendedor, a [bende'ðor, a] *nm/f* seller

vender [ben'der] *vt* to sell; ~ **al**
contado/al por mayor/al por
menor to sell for cash/wholesale/retail

vendimia [ben'dimja] *nf* grape harvest

vendré *etc vb ver* **venir**

veneno [be'neno] *nm* poison; (*de*
serpiente) venom; ~**so, a** *adj*
poisonous; venomous

venerable [bene'raßle] *adj* venerable;
venerar *vt* (*respetar*) to revere;
(*adorar*) to worship

venéreo, a [be'nereo, a] *adj:*
enfermedad venérea venereal
disease

venezolano, a [beneθo'lano, a] *adj*
Venezuelan

Venezuela [bene'θwela] *nf* Venezuela

venganza [ben'ganθa] *nf* vengeance,
revenge; **vengar** *vt* to avenge;
vengarse *vr* to take revenge;
vengativo, a *adj* (*persona*) vindictive

vengo *etc vb ver* **venir**

venia ['benja] *nf* (*perdón*) pardon;
(*permiso*) consent

venial [be'njal] *adj* venial

venida [be'niða] *nf* (*llegada*) arrival;
(*regreso*) return

venidero, a [beni'ðero, a] *adj* coming,
future

venir [be'nir] *vi* to come; (*llegar*) to
arrive; (*ocurrir*) to happen; (*fig*): ~ **de**
to stem from; ~ **bien/mal** to be
suitable/unsuitable; **el año que viene**
next year; ~**se abajo** to collapse

venta ['benta] *nf* (COM) sale; ~ **a**
plazos hire purchase; ~ **al contado/**
al por mayor/al por menor o **al**
detalle cash sale/wholesale/retail;
~ **con derecho a retorno** sale or
return; "**en** ~" "for sale"

ventaja [ben'taxa] *nf* advantage;
ventajoso, a *adj* advantageous

ventana [ben'tana] *nf* window;
ventanilla (*de taquilla*) window (*of*
booking office etc)

ventilación [bentila'θjon] *nf*
ventilation; (*corriente*) draught

ventilador [bentila'ðor] *nm* fan

ventilar [benti'lar] *vt* to ventilate;
(*para secar*) to put out to dry; (*asunto*)
to air, discuss

ventisca [ben'tiska] *nf* blizzard

ventrílocuo, a [ben'trilokwo, a] *nm/f*
ventriloquist

ventura [ben'tura] *nf* (*felicidad*)
happiness; (*buena suerte*) luck; (*destino*)
fortune; **a la** (**buena**) ~ at random;
venturoso, a *adj* happy; (*afortunado*)
lucky, fortunate

veo *etc vb ver* **ver**

ver [ber] *vt* to see; (*mirar*) to look at,
watch; (*entender*) to understand;
(*investigar*) to look into; ♦ *vi* to see; to
understand; ~**se** *vr* (*encontrarse*) to
meet; (*dejarse* ~) to be seen; (*hallarse:*
en un apuro) to find o.s., be; ~ **let's**
see; **no tener nada que** ~ **con** to
have nothing to do with; **a mi modo**
de ~ as I see it

vera ['bera] *nf* edge, verge; (*de río*) bank

veracidad [beraθi'ðað] *nf* truthfulness

veranear [berane'ar] *vi* to spend the
summer; **veraneo** *nm* summer
holiday; **veraniego, a** *adj* summer *cpd*

verano [be'rano] *nm* summer

veras ['beras] *nfpl* truth *sg*; **de** ~ really,
truly

veraz [be'raθ] *adj* truthful

verbal [ber'βal] *adj* verbal

verbena [ber'βena] *nf* (*baile*) open-air
dance

verbo ['berβo] *nm* verb; ~**so, a** *adj*
verbose

verdad [ber'ðað] *nf* truth; *(fiabilidad)* reliability; **de ~ real**, proper; **a decir ~** to tell the truth; **~ero, a** *adj (veraz)* true, truthful; *(fiable)* reliable; *(fig)* real

verde ['berðe] *adj* green; *(chiste)* blue, dirty ♦ *nm* green; **viejo ~** dirty old man; **~ar** *vi* to turn green; **verdor** *nm* greenness

verdugo [ber'ðuɣo] *nm* executioner

verdulero, a [berðu'lero, a] *nm/f* greengrocer

verduras [ber'ðuras] *nfpl (CULIN)* greens

vereda [be'reða] *nf* path; *(AM)* pavement *(BRIT)*, sidewalk *(US)*

veredicto [bere'ðikto] *nm* verdict

vergonzoso, a [berɣon'θoso, a] *adj* shameful; *(tímido)* timid, bashful

vergüenza [ber'ɣwenθa] *nf* shame, sense of shame; *(timidez)* bashfulness; *(pudor)* modesty; **me da ~** I'm ashamed

verídico, a [be'riðiko, a] *adj* true, truthful

verificar [berifi'kar] *vt* to check; *(corroborar)* to verify; *(llevar a cabo)* to carry out; **~se** *vr (predicción)* to prove to be true

verja ['berxa] *nf (cancela)* iron gate; *(valla)* iron railings *pl*; *(de ventana)* grille

vermut [ber'mut] *(pl* **~s)** *nm* vermouth

verosímil [bero'simil] *adj* likely, probable; *(relato)* credible

verruga [be'rruɣa] *nf* wart

versado, a [ber'saðo, a] *adj*: **~ en** versed in

versátil [ber'satil] *adj* versatile

versión [ber'sjon] *nf* version

verso ['berso] *nm* verse; **un ~** a line of poetry

vértebra ['berteβra] *nf* vertebra

verter [ber'ter] *vt (líquido: adrede)* to empty, pour (out); *(: sin querer)* to spill; *(basura)* to dump ♦ *vi* to flow

vertical [berti'kal] *adj* vertical

vértice ['bertiθe] *nm* vertex, apex

vertidos [ber'tiðos] *nmpl* waste *sg*

vertiente [ber'tjente] *nf* slope; *(fig)* aspect

vertiginoso, a [bertixi'noso, a] *adj* giddy, dizzy

vértigo ['bertixo] *nm* vertigo; *(mareo)* dizziness

vesícula [be'sikula] *nf* blister

vespino ® [bes'pino] *nm o nf* moped

vestíbulo [bes'tiβulo] *nm* hall; *(de teatro)* foyer

vestido [bes'tiðo] *pp de* **vestir; ~ de azul/marinero** dressed in blue/as a sailor ♦ *nm (ropa)* clothes *pl*, clothing; *(de mujer)* dress, frock

vestigio [bes'tixjo] *nm (huella)* trace; **~s** *nmpl (restos)* remains

vestimenta [besti'menta] *nf* clothing

vestir [bes'tir] *vt (poner: ropa)* to put on; *(llevar: ropa)* to wear; *(proveer de ropa a)* to clothe; *(suj: sastre)* to make clothes for ♦ *vi* to dress; *(verse bien)* to look good; **~se** *vr* to get dressed, dress o.s.

vestuario [bes'twarjo] *nm* clothes *pl*, wardrobe; *(TEATRO: cuarto)* dressing room; *(DEPORTE)* changing room

veta ['beta] *nf (vena)* vein, seam; *(en carne)* streak; *(de madera)* grain

vetar [be'tar] *vt* to veto

veterano, a [bete'rano, a] *adj, nm* veteran

veterinaria [beteri'narja] *nf* veterinary science; *ver tb* **veterinario**

veterinario, a [beteri'narjo, a] *nm/f* vet(erinary surgeon)

veto ['beto] *nm* veto

vez [beθ] *nf* time; *(turno)* turn; **a la ~ que** at the same time as; **a su ~** in its turn; **otra ~** again; **una ~** once; **de una ~** in one go; **de una ~ para siempre** once and for all; **en ~ de** instead of; **a o algunas veces** sometimes; **una y otra ~** repeatedly; **de ~ en cuando** from time to time; **7 veces 9** 7 times 9; **hacer las veces de** to stand in for; **tal ~** perhaps

vía ['bia] nf track, route; (FERRO) line; (fig) way; (ANAT) passage, tube ♦ prep via, by way of; **por ~ judicial** by legal means; **por ~ oficial** through official channels; **en ~s de** in the process of; **~ aérea** airway; **V~ Láctea** Milky Way; **~ pública** public road o thoroughfare

viable ['bjaβle] adj (solución, plan, alternativa) feasible

viaducto [bja'δukto] nm viaduct

viajante [bja'xante] nm commercial traveller

viajar [bja'xar] vi to travel; **viaje** nm journey, trip; (gira) tour; **estar de viaje** to be on a trip; **viaje de ida y vuelta** round trip; **viaje de novios** honeymoon; **viajero, a** adj travelling; (ZOOL) migratory ♦ nm/f (quien viaja) traveller; (pasajero) passenger

vial [bjal] adj road cpd, traffic cpd

víbora ['biβora] nf viper; (AM) poisonous snake

vibración [biβra'θjon] nf vibration

vibrar [bi'βrar] vt, vi to vibrate

vicario [bi'karjo] nm curate

vicepresidente [biθepresi'δente] nm/f vice-president

viceversa [biθe'βersa] adv vice versa

viciado, a [bi'θjaδo, a] adj (corrompido) corrupt; (contaminado) foul, contaminated; **viciar** vt (pervertir) to pervert; (estropear) to nullify; (estropear) to spoil; **viciarse** vr to become corrupted

vicio ['biθjo] nm vice; (mala costumbre) bad habit; **~so, a** adj (muy malo) vicious; (corrompido) depraved ♦ nm/f depraved person

vicisitud [biθisi'tuδ] nf vicissitude

víctima ['biktima] nf victim

victoria [bik'torja] nf victory; **victorioso, a** adj victorious

vid [biδ] nf vine

vida ['biδa] nf (gen) life; (duración) lifetime; **de por ~** for life; **en la/mi**

never; **estar con ~** to be still alive; **ganarse la ~** to earn one's living

vídeo ['biδeo] nm video ♦ adj inv: **película ~** video film; **~cámara** nf camcorder; **~casete** nm video cassette, videotape; **~club** nm video club; **~juego** nm video game

vidriero, a [bi'δrjero, a] nm/f glazier ♦ nf (ventana) stained-glass window; (AM: de tienda) shop window; (puerta) glass door

vidrio ['biδrjo] nm glass

vieira ['bjeira] nf scallop

viejo, a ['bjexo, a] adj old ♦ nm/f old man/woman; **hacerse ~** to get old

Viena ['bjena] n Vienna

vienes etc vb ver **venir**

vienés, esa [bje'nes, esa] adj Viennese

viento ['bjento] nm wind; **hacer ~** to be windy

vientre ['bjentre] nm belly; (matriz) womb

viernes ['bjernes] nm inv Friday; **V~ Santo** Good Friday

Vietnam [bjet'nam] nm: **el ~** Vietnam; **vietnamita** adj Vietnamese

viga ['biɣa] nf beam, rafter; (de metal) girder

vigencia [bi'xenθja] nf validity; **estar en ~** to be in force; **vigente** adj valid, in force; (imperante) prevailing

vigésimo, a [bi'xesimo, a] adj twentieth

vigía [bi'xia] nm look-out

vigilancia [bixi'lanθja] nf: **tener a uno bajo ~** to keep watch on sb

vigilar [bixi'lar] vt to watch over ♦ vi (gen) to be vigilant; (hacer guardia) to keep watch; **~ por** to take care of

vigilia [bi'xilja] nf wakefulness, being awake; (REL) fast

vigor [bi'ɣor] nm vigour, vitality; **en ~** in force; **entrar/poner en ~** to come/put into effect; **~oso, a** adj vigorous

VIH nm abr (= virus de la inmunodeficiencia humana) HIV;

~ positivo/negativo HIV-positive/-negative

vil [bil] adj vile, low; **~eza** nf vileness; (acto) base deed

vilipendiar [bilipen'djar] vt to vilify, revile

villa ['biʎa] nf (casa) villa; (pueblo) small town; (municipalidad) municipality; **~ miseria** (AM) shantytown

villancico [biʎan'θiko] nm (Christmas) carol

villorrio [bi'ʎorrjo] nm shantytown

vilo ['bilo]: **en ~** adv in the air, suspended; (fig) on tenterhooks, in suspense

vinagre [bi'naɣre] nm vinegar

vinagreta [bina'ɣreta] nf vinaigrette, French dressing

vinculación [binkula'θjon] nf (lazo) link, bond; (acción) linking

vincular [binku'lar] vt to link, bind; **vínculo** nm link, bond

vine etc vb ver **venir**

vinicultura [binikul'tura] nf wine growing

viniera etc vb ver **venir**

vino ['bino] vb ver **venir** ♦ nm wine; **~ blanco/tinto** white/red wine

viña ['biɲa] nf vineyard; **viñedo** nm vineyard

viola ['bjola] nf viola

violación [bjola'θjon] nf violation; **~ (sexual)** rape

violar [bjo'lar] vt to violate; (sexualmente) to rape

violencia [bjo'lenθja] nf violence, force; (incomodidad) embarrassment; (acto injusto) unjust act; **violentar** vt to force; (casa) to break into; (agredir) to assault; (violar) to violate; **violento, a** adj violent; (furioso) furious; (situación) embarrassing; (acto) forced, unnatural

violeta [bjo'leta] nf violet

violín [bjo'lin] nm violin

violón [bjo'lon] nm double bass

viraje [bi'raxe] nm turn; (de vehículo) swerve; (fig) change of direction; **virar** vi to change direction

virgen ['birxen] adj, nf virgin

Virgo ['birɣo] nm Virgo

viril [bi'ril] adj virile; **~idad** nf virility

virtud [bir'tuð] nf virtue; **en ~ de** by virtue of; **virtuoso, a** adj virtuous ♦ nm/f virtuoso

viruela [bi'rwela] nf smallpox

virulento, a [biru'lento, a] adj virulent

virus ['birus] nm inv virus

visa ['bisa] (AM) nf = **visado**

visado [bi'saðo] nm visa

víscera ['bisθera] nf (ANAT, ZOOL) gut, bowel; **~s** nfpl entrails

visceral [bisθe'ral] adj (odio) intense; **reacción ~** gut reaction

viscoso, a [bis'koso, a] adj viscous

visera [bi'sera] nf visor

visibilidad [bisiβili'ðað] nf visibility; **visible** adj visible; (fig) obvious

visillos [bi'siʎos] nmpl lace curtains

visión [bi'sjon] nf (ANAT) vision, (eye)sight; (fantasía) vision, fantasy

visita [bi'sita] nf call, visit; (persona) visitor; **hacer una ~** to pay a visit

visitar [bisi'tar] vt to visit, call on

vislumbrar [bislum'brar] vt to glimpse, catch a glimpse of

viso ['biso] nm (del metal) glint, gleam; (de tela) sheen; (aspecto) appearance

visón [bi'son] nm mink

visor [bi'sor] nm (FOTO) viewfinder

víspera ['bispera] nf: **la ~ de ...** the day before ...

vista ['bista] nf sight, vision; (capacidad de ver) (eye)sight; (mirada) look(s) (pl); **a primera ~** at first glance; **hacer la ~ gorda** to turn a blind eye; **volver la ~** to look back; **está a la ~ que** it's obvious that; **en ~ de** in view of; **en ~ de que** in view of the fact that; **¡hasta la ~!** so long!, see you!; **con ~s a** with a view to; **~zo** nm glance; **dar o echar un ~zo a** to glance at

visto, a ['bisto, a] pp de ver ♦ vb ver **visto**

tb **vestir ♦** *adj* seen; (*considerado*) considered **♦** *nm*: **~ bueno** approval; **"~ bueno" "approved"; por lo ~** apparently; **está ~ que** it's clear that; **está bien/mal ~** it's acceptable/ unacceptable; **~ que** since, considering that

vistoso, a [bis'toso, a] *adj* colourful

visual [bi'swal] *adj* visual

vital [bi'tal] *adj* life *cpd*, living *cpd*; vital; (*persona*) lively, vivacious; **~icio, a** *adj* for life; **~idad** *nf* (*de persona, negocio*) energy; (*de ciudad*) liveliness

vitamina [bita'mina] *nf* vitamin

viticultor, a [bitikul'tor, a] *nm/f* wine grower; **viticultura** *nf* wine growing

vitorear [bitore'ar] *vt* to cheer, acclaim

vitrina [bi'trina] *nf* show case; (*AM*) shop window

viudez *nf* widowhood

viudo, a [ˈbjuðo, a] *nm/f* widower/ widow

viva [ˈbiβa] *excl* hurrah!; **¡~ el rey!** long live the king!

vivacidad [biβaθiˈðað] *nf* (*vigor*) vigour; (*vida*) liveliness

vivaracho, a [biβaˈratʃo, a] *adj* jaunty, lively; (*ojos*) bright, twinkling

vivaz [biˈβaθ] *adj* lively

víveres [ˈbiβeres] *nmpl* provisions

vivero [biˈβero] *nm* (*para plantas*) nursery; (*para peces*) fish farm; (*fig*) hotbed

viveza [biˈβeθa] *nf* liveliness; (*agudeza mental*) sharpness

vivienda [biˈβjenda] *nf* housing; (*una ~*) house; (*piso*) flat (*BRIT*), apartment (*US*)

viviente [biˈβjente] *adj* living

vivir [biˈβir] *vt, vi* to live **♦** *nm* life, living

vivo, a [ˈbiβo, a] *adj* living, alive; (*fig: descripción*) vivid; (*persona: astuto*) smart, clever; **en ~** (*transmisión etc*) live

vocablo [boˈkaβlo] *nm* (*palabra*) word; (*término*) term

vocabulario [bokaβuˈlarjo] *nm* vocabulary

vocación [bokaˈθjon] *nf* vocation; **vocacional** (*AM*) *nf* ≈ technical college

vocal [boˈkal] *adj* vocal **♦** *nf* vowel; **~izar** *vt* to vocalize

vocear [boθeˈar] *vt* (*para vender*) to cry; (*aclamar*) to acclaim; (*fig*) to proclaim **♦** *vi* to yell; **vocerío** *nm* shouting

vocero [boˈθero] *nm/f* spokesman/ woman

voces [ˈboθes] *pl de* **voz**

vociferar [boθifeˈrar] *vt* to shout **♦** *vi* to yell

vodka [ˈboðka] *nm o f* vodka

vol *abr* = **volumen**

volador, a [bolaˈðor, a] *adj* flying

volandas [boˈlandas]: **en ~** *adv* in the air

volante [boˈlante] *adj* flying **♦** *nm* (*de coche*) steering wheel; (*de reloj*) balance

volar [boˈlar] *vt* (*edificio*) to blow up **♦** *vi* to fly

volátil [boˈlatil] *adj* volatile

volcán [bolˈkan] *nm* volcano; **~ico, a** *adj* volcanic

volcar [bolˈkar] *vt* to upset, overturn; (*tumbar, derribar*) to knock over; (*vaciar*) to empty out **♦** *vi* to overturn; **~se** *vr* to tip over

voleibol [boleiˈβol] *nm* volleyball

volqué *etc vb ver* **volcar**

voltaje [bolˈtaxe] *nm* voltage

voltear [bolteˈar] *vt* to turn over; (*volcar*) to turn upside down

voltereta [bolteˈreta] *nf* somersault

voltio [ˈboltjo] *nm* volt

voluble [boˈluβle] *adj* fickle

volumen [boˈlumen] (*pl* **volúmenes**) *nm* volume; **voluminoso, a** *adj* voluminous; (*enorme*) massive

voluntad [bolunˈtað] *nf* will; (*resolución*) willpower; (*deseo*) desire, wish

voluntario, a [bolunˈtarjo, a] *adj*

voluntary ♦ nm/f volunteer

voluntarioso, a [bolunta'rjoso, a] adj headstrong

voluptuoso, a [bolup'twoso, a] adj voluptuous

volver [bol'ßer] vt (gen) to turn; (dar vuelta a) to turn (over); (voltear) to turn round, turn upside down; (poner al revés) to turn inside out; (devolver) to return ♦ vi to turn, go back, come back; ~se vr to turn round; ~ la espalda to turn one's back; ~ triste etc a uno to make sb sad etc; ~ a hacer to do again; ~ en sí to come to; ~se insoportable/muy caro to get o become unbearable/very expensive; ~se loco to go mad

vomitar [bomi'tar] vt, vi to vomit; **vómito** nm vomit

voraz [bo'raθ] adj voracious

vos [bos] (AM) pron you

vosotros, as [bo'sotros, as] pron you; (reflexivo): **entre/para** ~ among/for yourselves

votación [bota'θjon] nf (acto) voting; (voto) vote

votar [bo'tar] vi to vote; **voto** nm vote; (promesa) vow; **votos** (good) wishes

voy vb ver **ir**

voz [boθ] nf voice; (grito) shout; (rumor) rumour; (LING) word; **dar voces** to shout, yell; **a media** ~ in a low voice; **a** ~ **en cuello** o **en grito** at the top of one's voice; **de viva** ~ verbally; **en** ~ **alta** aloud; ~ **de mando** command

vuelco ['bwelko] vb ver **volcar** ♦ nm spill, overturning

vuelo ['bwelo] vb ver **volar** ♦ nm flight; (encaje) lace, frill; **coger al** ~ to catch in flight; ~ **charter/regular** charter/scheduled flight; ~ **libre** (DEPORTE) hang-gliding

vuelque etc vb ver **volcar**

vuelta ['bwelta] nf (gen) turn; (curva) bend, curve; (regreso) return;

(revolución) revolution; (de circuito) lap; (de papel, tela) reverse; (cambio) change; **a la** ~ on one's return; **a** ~ **de correo** by return of post; **dar** ~s (suj: cabeza) to spin; **dar** ~s **a una idea** to turn over an idea (in one's head); **estar de** ~ to be back; **dar una** ~ to go for a walk; (en coche) to go for a drive; ~ **ciclista** (DEPORTE) (cycle) tour

vuelto pp de **volver**

vuelvo etc vb ver **volver**

vuestro, a ['bwestro, a] adj your; **un amigo** ~ a friend of yours ♦ pron: **el** ~/**la vuestra, los** ~s/**las vuestras** yours

vulgar [bul'xar] adj (ordinario) vulgar; (común) common; ~**idad** nf commonness; (acto) vulgarity; (expresión) coarse expression; ~**izar** vt to popularize

vulgo ['bulxo] nm common people

vulnerable [bulne'raßle] adj vulnerable

vulnerar [bulne'rar] vt (ley, acuerdo) to violate, breach; (derechos, intimidad) to violate; (reputación) to damage

W, w

Walkman ® [wak'man] nm Walkman ®

wáter ['bater] nm toilet

whisky ['wiski] nm whisky, whiskey

X, x

xenofobia [kseno'foßja] nf xenophobia

xilófono [ksi'lofono] nm xylophone

Y, y

y [i] conj and

ya [ja] adv (gen) already; (ahora) now;

(en seguida) at once; (pronto) soon ♦ excl all right! ♦ conj (ahora que) now that; **~ lo sé** I know; **~ que** since

yacer [ja'θer] vi to lie

yacimiento [jaθi'mjento] nm (de mineral) deposit; (arqueológico) site

yanqui ['janki] adj, nm/f Yankee

yate ['jate] nm yacht

yazco etc vb ver **yacer**

yedra ['jeðra] nf ivy

yegua ['jeɣwa] nf mare

yema ['jema] nf (del huevo) yolk; (BOT) leaf bud; (fig) best part; **~ del dedo** fingertip

yergo etc vb ver **erguir**

yermo, a ['jermo, a] adj (estéril, fig) barren ♦ nm wasteland

yerno ['jerno] nm son-in-law

yerro etc vb ver **errar**

yeso ['jeso] nm plaster

yo [jo] pron I; **soy ~** it's me, it is I

yodo ['joðo] nm iodine

yoga ['joxa] nm yoga

yogur(t) [jo'ɣur(t)] nm yoghurt

yugo ['juxo] nm yoke

Yugoslavia [juvos'laßja] nf Yugoslavia

yugular [juvu'lar] adj jugular

yunque ['junke] nm anvil

yunta ['junta] nf yoke

yuxtaponer [jukstapo'ner] vt to juxtapose; **yuxtaposición** nf juxtaposition

Z, z

zafar [θa'far] vt (soltar) to untie; (superficie) to clear; **~se** vr (escaparse) to escape; (TEC) to slip off

zafio, a ['θafjo, a] adj coarse

zafiro [θa'firo] nm sapphire

zaga ['θaɣa] nf: **a la ~** behind, in the rear

zaguán [θa'ɣwan] nm hallway

zaherir [θae'rir] vt (criticar) to criticize

zaino, a ['θaino, a] adj (caballo) chestnut

zalamería [θalame'ria] nf flattery; **zalamero, a** adj flattering; (cobista) suave

zamarra [θa'marra] nf (chaqueta) sheepskin jacket

zambullirse [θambu'ʎirse] vr to dive

zampar [θam'par] vt to gobble down

zanahoria [θana'orja] nf carrot

zancada [θan'kaða] nf stride

zancadilla [θanka'ðiʎa] nf trip

zanco ['θanko] nm stilt

zancudo, a [θan'kuðo, a] adj long-legged ♦ nm (AM) mosquito

zángano ['θangano] nm drone

zanja ['θanxa] nf ditch; (para resolver) to resolve

zapata [θa'pata] nf (MECÁNICA) shoe

zapatear [θapate'ar] vi to tap with one's feet

zapatería [θapate'ria] nf (oficio) shoemaking; (tienda) shoe shop; (fábrica) shoe factory; **zapatero, a** nm/f shoemaker

zapatilla [θapa'tiʎa] nf slipper; **~ de deporte** training shoe

zapato [θa'pato] nm shoe

zapping ['θapin] nm channel-hopping; **hacer ~** to flick through the channels

zar [θar] nm tsar, czar

zarandear [θarande'ar] vt (fam) to shake vigorously

zarpa ['θarpa] nf (garra) claw

zarpar [θar'par] vi to weigh anchor

zarza ['θarθa] nf (BOT) bramble; **zarzal** nm (matorral) bramble patch

zarzamora [θarθa'mora] nf blackberry

zarzuela [θar'θwela] nf Spanish light opera

zigzag [θiɣ'θax] nm zigzag; **zigzaguear** vi to zigzag

zinc [θink] nm zinc

zócalo ['θokalo] nm (ARQ) plinth, base

zodíaco [θo'ðiako] nm (ASTRO) zodiac

zona ['θona] nf zone; **~ fronteriza** border area

zoo ['θoo] nm zoo

zoología [θoolo'xia] nf zoology

zoológico, a adj zoological ♦ nm (tb: parque ~) zoo; **zoólogo, a** nm/f zoologist

zoom [θum] nm zoom lens

zopilote [θopi'lote] (AM) nm buzzard

zoquete [θo'kete] nm (fam) blockhead

zorro, a ['θorro, a] adj crafty ♦ nm/f fox/vixen

zozobra [θo'θoβra] nf (fig) anxiety; **zozobrar** vi (hundirse) to capsize; (fig) to fail

zueco ['θweko] nm clog

zumbar [θum'bar] vt (golpear) to hit ♦ vi to buzz; **zumbido** nm buzzing

zumo ['θumo] nm juice

zurcir [θur'θir] vt (coser) to darn

zurdo, a ['θurðo, a] adj (persona) left-handed

zurrar [θu'rrar] (fam) vt to wallop

ENGLISH • SPANISH
INGLÉS • ESPAÑOL

ENGLISH-SPANISH
INGLÉS-ESPAÑOL

A, a

A [eɪ] n (MUS) la m

> **KEYWORD**

a [ə] indef art (before vowel or silent h: **an**) **1** un(a); **~ book** un libro; **an apple** una manzana; **she's ~ doctor** (ella) es médica

2 (instead of the number "one") un(a); **~ year ago** hace un año; **~ hundred/thousand etc pounds** cien/mil etc libras

3 (in expressing rations, prices etc): **3 ~ day/week** 3 al día/a la semana; **10 km an hour** 10 km por hora; **£5 ~ person** £5 por persona; **30p ~ kilo** 30p el kilo

A.A. n abbr (= Automobile Association: BRIT) ≈ RACE m (SP); (= Alcoholics Anonymous) Alcohólicos Anónimos

A.A.A. n (US) = American Automobile Association) ≈ RACE m (SP)

aback [ə'bæk] adv: **to be taken ~** quedar desconcertado

abandon [ə'bændən] vt abandonar; (give up) renunciar a

abate [ə'beɪt] vi (storm) amainar; (anger) aplacarse; (terror) disminuir

abattoir ['æbətwɑ:*] (BRIT) n matadero

abbey ['æbɪ] n abadía

abbot ['æbət] n abad m

abbreviation [əbri:vɪ'eɪʃən] n (short form) abreviatura

abdicate ['æbdɪkeɪt] vt renunciar a ♦ vi abdicar

abdomen ['æbdəmən] n abdomen m

abduct [æb'dʌkt] vt raptar, secuestrar

abeyance [ə'beɪəns] n: **in ~** (law) en

desuso; (matter) en suspenso

abide [ə'baɪd] vt: **I can't ~ it/him** no lo/le puedo ver; **~ by** vt fus atenerse a

ability [ə'bɪlɪtɪ] n habilidad f, capacidad f; (talent) talento

abject ['æbdʒekt] adj (poverty) miserable; (apology) rastrero

ablaze [ə'bleɪz] adj en llamas, ardiendo

able ['eɪbl] adj capaz; (skilled) hábil; **to be ~ to do sth** poder hacer algo; **~-bodied** adj sano; **ably** adv hábilmente

abnormal [æb'nɔ:məl] adj anormal

aboard [ə'bɔ:d] adv a bordo ♦ prep a bordo de

abode [ə'bəud] n: **of no fixed ~** sin domicilio fijo

abolish [ə'bɒlɪʃ] vt suprimir, abolir

aborigine [æbə'rɪdʒɪnɪ] n aborigen m/f

abort [ə'bɔ:t] vt, vi abortar; **~ion** [ə'bɔ:ʃən] n aborto; **to have an ~ion** abortar, hacerse abortar; **~ive** adj malogrado

> **KEYWORD**

about [ə'baut] adv **1** (approximately) más o menos, aproximadamente; **~ a hundred/thousand etc** unos(unas) cien/mil etc; **it takes ~ 10 hours** se tarda unas 10 horas; **at ~ 2 o'clock** sobre las dos; **I've just finished** casi he terminado

2 (referring to place) por todas partes; **to leave things lying ~** dejar las cosas (tiradas) por ahí; **to run ~** correr por todas partes; **to walk ~** pasearse, ir y venir

3: to be ~ to do sth estar a punto de hacer algo

above ♦ prep 1 (*relating to*) de, sobre, acerca de; **a book ~ London** un libro sobre or acerca de Londres; **what is it ~?** ¿de qué se trata?, ¿qué pasa?; **we talked ~ it** hablamos de eso or ello; **what or how ~ doing this?** ¿qué tal si hacemos esto?
2 (*referring to place*) por; **to walk ~ the town** caminar por la ciudad

above [ə'bʌv] *adv* encima, por encima, arriba ♦ *prep* encima de; (*greater than: in number*) más de; (*: in rank*) superior a; **mentioned ~** susodicho; **~ all** sobre todo; **~ board** legítimo

abrasive [ə'breızıv] *adj* abrasivo; (*manner*) brusco

abreast [ə'brest] *adv* de frente; **to keep ~ of** (*fig*) mantenerse al corriente de

abroad [ə'brɔːd] *adv* (*to be*) en el extranjero; (*to go*) al extranjero

abrupt [ə'brʌpt] *adj* (*sudden*) brusco; (*curt*) áspero

abruptly [ə'brʌptlı] *adv* (*leave*) repentinamente; (*speak*) bruscamente

abscess ['æbsıs] *n* absceso

abscond [əb'skɒnd] *vi* (*thief*): **to ~ with** fugarse con; (*prisoner*): **to ~ (from)** escaparse (de)

absence ['æbsəns] *n* ausencia

absent ['æbsənt] *adj* ausente; **~ee** [-'tiː] *n* ausente m/f; **~-minded** *adj* distraído

absolute ['æbsəluːt] *adj* absoluto; **~ly** [-'luːtlı] *adv* (*totally*) totalmente; (*certainly*) ¡por supuesto (que sí)!

absolve [əb'zɒlv] *vt*: **to ~ sb (from)** absolver a alguien (de)

absorb [əb'zɔːb] *vt* absorber; **to be ~ed in a book** estar absorto en un libro; **~ent cotton** (*US*) *n* algodón m hidrófilo; **~ing** *adj* absorbente

absorption [əb'zɔːpʃən] *n* absorción f

abstain [əb'steın] *vi*: **to ~ (from)** abstenerse (de)

abstinence ['æbstınəns] *n* abstinencia

abstract ['æbstrækt] *adj* abstracto

absurd [əb'sɜːd] *adj* absurdo

abundance [ə'bʌndəns] *n* abundancia

abuse [*n* ə'bjuːs, *vb* ə'bjuːz] *n* (*insults*) insultos mpl, injurias fpl; (*ill-treatment*) malos tratos mpl; (*misuse*) abuso ♦ *vt* insultar; maltratar; abusar de; **abusive** *adj* ofensivo

abysmal [ə'bızml] *adj* pésimo; (*failure*) garrafal; (*ignorance*) supino

abyss [ə'bıs] *n* abismo

AC *abbr* (= *alternating current*) corriente f alterna

academic [ækə'demık] *adj* académico, universitario; (*pej: theoretical*) puramente teórico ♦ *n* estudioso/a; profesor(a) m/f

academy [ə'kædəmı] *n* (*learned body*) academia; (*school*) instituto, colegio; **~ of music** conservatorio

accelerate [æk'seləreıt] *vt, vi* acelerar; **accelerator** (*BRIT*) *n* acelerador m

accent ['æksent] *n* acento; (*fig*) énfasis m

accept [ək'sept] *vt* aceptar; (*responsibility, blame*) admitir; **~able** *adj* aceptable; **~ance** *n* aceptación f

access ['ækses] *n* acceso; **to have ~ to** tener libre acceso a; **~ible** [-'sesəbl] *adj* (*place, person*) accesible; (*knowledge etc*) asequible

accessory [æk'sesərı] *n* accesorio; (*LAW*): **~ to** cómplice de

accident ['æksıdənt] *n* accidente m; (*chance event*) casualidad f; **by ~** (*unintentionally*) sin querer; (*by chance*) por casualidad; **~al** [-'dentl] *adj* accidental, fortuito; **~ally** [-'dentəlı] *adv* sin querer; por casualidad; **~ insurance** *n* seguro contra accidentes; **~-prone** *adj* propenso a los accidentes

acclaim [ə'kleım] *vt* aclamar, aplaudir ♦ *n* aclamación f, aplausos mpl

acclimatize [ə'klaımətaız] *vt* (*US*: **acclimate**) *vt*: **to become ~d** aclimatarse

accommodate [ə'kɒmədeɪt] vt (subj: person) alojar, hospedar; (: car, hotel etc) tener cabida para; (oblige, help) complacer; **accommodating** adj servicial, complaciente

accommodation [əkɒmə'deɪʃən] n (US **accommodations** npl) alojamiento

accompany [ə'kʌmpənɪ] vt acompañar

accomplice [ə'kʌmplɪs] n cómplice m/f

accomplish [ə'kʌmplɪʃ] vt (finish) concluir; (achieve) lograr; ~ed adj experto, hábil; ~ment n (skill: gen pl) talento; (completion) realización f

accord [ə'kɔːd] n acuerdo ♦ vt conceder; of his own ~ espontáneamente; ~ance n: in ~ance with de acuerdo con; ~ing: ~ing to prep según; (in accordance with) conforme a; ~ingly adv (appropriately) de acuerdo con esto; (as a result) en consecuencia

accordion [ə'kɔːdɪən] n acordeón m

accost [ə'kɒst] vt abordar, dirigirse a

account [ə'kaʊnt] n (comm) cuenta; (report) informe m; ~s npl (comm) cuentas fpl; of no ~ de ninguna importancia; on ~ a cuenta; on no ~ bajo ningún concepto; on ~ of a causa de, por motivo de; to take into ~, take ~ of tener en cuenta; ~ for vt fus (explain) explicar; (represent) representar; ~able adj: ~able (to) responsable (ante); ~ancy n contabilidad f; ~ant n contable m/f, contador(a) m/f; ~ number n (at bank etc) número de cuenta

accrued interest [ə'kruːd-] n interés m acumulado

accumulate [ə'kjuːmjʊleɪt] vt acumular ♦ vi acumularse

accuracy ['ækjʊrəsɪ] n (of total) exactitud f; (of description etc) precisión f

accurate ['ækjʊrɪt] adj (total) exacto;

(description) preciso; (person) cuidadoso; (device) de precisión; ~ly adv con precisión

accusation [ækju'zeɪʃən] n acusación f

accuse [ə'kjuːz] vt: to ~ sb (of sth) acusar a uno (de algo); ~d n (law) acusado/a

accustom [ə'kʌstəm] vt acostumbrar; ~ed adj: ~ed to acostumbrado a

ace [eɪs] n as m

ache [eɪk] n dolor m ♦ vi doler; my head ~s me duele la cabeza

achieve [ə'tʃiːv] vt (aim, result) alcanzar; (success) lograr, conseguir; ~ment n (completion) realización f; (success) éxito

acid ['æsɪd] adj ácido; (taste) agrio ♦ n (chem, inf: LSD) ácido; ~ rain n lluvia ácida

acknowledge [ək'nɒlɪdʒ] vt (letter: also: ~ receipt of) acusar recibo de; (fact, situation, person) reconocer; ~ment n acuse m de recibo

acne ['æknɪ] n acné m

acorn ['eɪkɔːn] n bellota

acoustic [ə'kuːstɪk] adj acústico; ~s n, npl acústica sg

acquaint [ə'kweɪnt] vt: to ~ sb with sth (inform) poner a uno al corriente de algo; to be ~ed with conocer; ~ance n (person) conocido/a; (with person, subject) conocimiento

acquire [ə'kwaɪə*] vt adquirir; **acquisition** [ækwɪ'zɪʃən] n adquisición f

acquit [ə'kwɪt] vt absolver, exculpar; to ~ o.s. well salir con éxito

acre ['eɪkə*] n acre m

acrid ['ækrɪd] adj acre

acrobat ['ækrəbæt] n acróbata m/f

across [ə'krɒs] prep (on the other side of) al otro lado de, al otro lado de; (crosswise) a través de ♦ adv de un lado a otro, de una parte a otra; a través, al través; (measurement): the road is 10m ~ la carretera tiene 10m de ancho; to run/swim ~ atravesar corriendo/nadando; **~ from** enfrente de

acrylic [ə'krɪlɪk] *adj* acrílico ♦ *n* acrílica

act [ækt] *n* acto, acción *f*; (*of play*) acto; (*in music hall etc*) número; (LAW) decreto, ley *f* ♦ *vi* (*behave*) comportarse; (*have effect: drug, chemical*) hacer efecto; (THEATRE) actuar; (*pretend*) fingir; (*take action*) obrar ♦ *vt* (*part*) hacer el papel de; **in the ~ of: to catch sb in the ~ of ...** pillar a uno en el momento en que ...; **to ~ as** actuar de; hacer de; **~ing** *adj* suplente ♦ *n* (*activity*) actuación *f*; (*profession*) profesión *f* de actor

action [ækʃən] *n* acción *f*, acto; (MIL) acción *f*, batalla; (LAW) proceso, demanda; **out of ~** (*person*) fuera de combate; (*thing*) estropeado; **to take ~** tomar medidas; **~ replay** *n* (TV) repetición *f*

activate [æktɪveɪt] *vt* activar

active [æktɪv] *adj* activo, enérgico; (*volcano*) en actividad; **~ly** *adv* (*participate*) activamente; (*discourage, dislike*) enérgicamente; **activity** ['tɪvɪtɪ] *n* actividad *f*; **activity holiday** *n* vacaciones *fpl* con actividades organizadas

actor [æktə*] *n* actor *m*

actress [æktrɪs] *n* actriz *f*

actual [æktjuəl] *adj* verdadero, real; (*emphatic use*) propiamente dicho; **~ly** *adv* realmente, en realidad; (*even*) incluso

acumen [ækjumən] *n* perspicacia

acute [ə'kju:t] *adj* agudo

ad [æd] *n abbr* = **advertisement**

A.D. *adv abbr* (= *anno Domini*) A.C.

adamant [ædəmənt] *adj* firme, inflexible

adapt [ə'dæpt] *vt* adaptar ♦ *vi*: **to ~ (to)** adaptarse (a), ajustarse (a); **~able** *adj* adaptable; **~er, ~or** *n* (ELEC) adaptador *m*

add [æd] *vt* añadir, agregar; (*figures: also:* **~ up**) sumar ♦ *vi*: **to ~ to** (*increase*) aumentar, acrecentar; **it doesn't ~ up** (*fig*) no tiene sentido

adder [ædə*] *n* víbora

addict [ædɪkt] *n* adicto/a; (*enthusiast*) entusiasta *m/f*; **~ed** [ə'dɪktɪd] *adj*: **to be ~ed to** ser adicto a; (*football etc*) ser fanático de; **~ion** [ə'dɪkʃən] *n* (*to drugs etc*) adicción *f*; **~ive** [ə'dɪktɪv] *adj* que causa adicción

addition [ə'dɪʃən] *n* (*adding up*) adición *f*; (*thing added*) añadidura, añadido; **in ~** además, por añadidura; **in ~ to** además de; **~al** *adj* adicional

additive [ædɪtɪv] *n* aditivo

address [ə'dres] *n* dirección *f*, señas *fpl*; (*speech*) discurso ♦ *vt* (*letter*) dirigir; (*speak to*) dirigirse a, dirigir la palabra a; (*problem*) tratar

adept [ædept] *adj*: **~ at** experto o hábil en

adequate [ædɪkwɪt] *adj* (*satisfactory*) adecuado; (*enough*) suficiente

adhere [əd'hɪə*] *vi*: **to ~ to** (*stick to*) pegarse a; (*fig: abide by*) observar; (: *belief etc*) ser partidario de

adhesive [əd'hi:zɪv] *adj* adhesivo; **~ tape** *n* (BRIT) cinta adhesiva; (US: MED) esparadrapo

ad hoc [æd'hɔk] *adj* ad hoc

adjacent [ə'dʒeɪsənt] *adj*: **~ to** contiguo a, inmediato a

adjective [ædʒektɪv] *n* adjetivo

adjoining [ə'dʒɔɪnɪŋ] *adj* contiguo, vecino

adjourn [ə'dʒɜ:n] *vt* aplazar ♦ *vi* suspenderse

adjudicate [ə'dʒu:dɪkeɪt] *vi* sentenciar

adjust [ə'dʒʌst] *vt* (*change*) modificar; (*clothing*) arreglar; (*machine*) ajustar ♦ *vi*: **to ~ (to)** adaptarse (a); **~able** *adj* ajustable; **~ment** *n* adaptación *f*; (*to machine, prices*) ajuste *m*

ad-lib [æd'lɪb] *vt, vi* improvisar; **ad lib** *adv* de forma improvisada

administer [əd'mɪnɪstə*] *vt* administrar; **administration** ['treɪʃən] *n* (*management*)

administración f; (government)
gobierno; **administrative** [-trətɪv] adj
administrativo

admiral [ˈædmərəl] n almirante m;
A~ty (BRIT) n Ministerio de Marina,
Almirantazgo

admiration [ædməˈreɪʃən] n
admiración f

admire [ədˈmaɪə*] vt admirar; **~r** n
(fan) admirador(a) m/f

admission [ədˈmɪʃən] n (to university,
club) ingreso; (entry fee) entrada;
(confession) confesión f

admit [ədˈmɪt] vt (confess) confesar;
(permit to enter) dejar entrar, dar
entrada a; (to club, organization)
admitir; (accept: defeat) reconocer; **to
be ~ted to hospital** ingresar en el
hospital; **~ to** vt fus confesarse
culpable de; **~tance** n entrada; **~tedly**
adv es cierto or verdad que

admonish [ədˈmɒnɪʃ] vt amonestar

ad nauseam [æd ˈnɔːsɪæm] adv hasta
el cansancio

ado [əˈduː] n: **without (any) more ~**
sin más (ni más)

adolescent [ædəˈlɛsnt] adj, n
adolescente m/f

adopt [əˈdɒpt] vt adoptar; **~ed** adj
adoptivo; **~ion** [əˈdɒpʃən] n adopción f

adore [əˈdɔː*] vt adorar

Adriatic [eɪdrɪˈætɪk] n: **the ~ (Sea)** el
(Mar) Adriático

adrift [əˈdrɪft] adv a la deriva

adult [ˈædʌlt] n adulto ♦ adj (grown-
up) adulto; (for adults) para adultos

adultery [əˈdʌltərɪ] n adulterio

advance [ədˈvɑːns] n (progress)
adelanto, progreso; (money) anticipo,
préstamo; (MIL) avance m ♦ adj:
~ booking venta anticipada;
~ notice, ~ warning previo aviso ♦ vt
(money) anticipar; (theory, idea)
proponer (para la discusión) ♦ vi
avanzar, adelantarse; **to make ~s (to
sb)** hacer proposiciones (a alguien); **in**

~ por adelantado; **~d** adj avanzado;
(SCOL: studies) adelantado

advantage [ədˈvɑːntɪdʒ] n (also
TENNIS) ventaja; **to take ~ of** (person)
aprovecharse de; (opportunity)
aprovechar

Advent [ˈædvənt] n (REL) Adviento

adventure [ədˈvɛntʃə*] n aventura;
adventurous [-tʃərəs] adj atrevido;
aventurero

adverb [ˈædvəːb] n adverbio

adverse [ˈædvəːs] adj adverso,
contrario

adversity [ədˈvəːsɪtɪ] n infortunio

advert [ˈædvəːt] (BRIT) n abbr =
advertisement

advertise [ˈædvətaɪz] vi (in newspaper
etc) anunciar, hacer publicidad; **to
~ for** (staff, accommodation etc) buscar
por medio de anuncios ♦ vt anunciar;
~ment [ədˈvəːtɪsmənt] n (COMM)
anuncio; **~r** n anunciante m/f

advertising n publicidad f, anuncios
mpl; (industry) industria publicitaria

advice [ədˈvaɪs] n consejo, consejos
mpl; (notification) aviso; **a piece of ~**
un consejo; **to take legal ~** consultar
con un abogado

advisable [ədˈvaɪzəbl] adj aconsejable,
conveniente

advise [ədˈvaɪz] vt aconsejar; (inform):
to ~ sb of sth informar a uno de
algo; **to ~ sb against sth/doing sth**
desaconsejar algo a uno/aconsejar a
uno que no haga algo; **~dly**
[ədˈvaɪzɪdlɪ] adv (deliberately)
deliberadamente; **~r** n = **advisor**

advisor n consejero/a; (consultant)
asesor(a) m/f; **advisory** adj consultivo

advocate [ˈædvəkeɪt] vt abogar por
♦ n [-kɪt] (lawyer) abogado/a;
(supporter): **~ of defensor/a** m/f de

Aegean [iːˈdʒiːən] n: **the ~ (Sea)** el
(Mar) Egeo

aerial [ˈɛərɪəl] n antena ♦ adj aéreo

aerobics [ɛəˈrəubɪks] n aerobic m

aeroplane [ˈɛərəpleɪn] (BRIT) n

avión m

aerosol ['ɛərəsɒl] n aerosol m

aesthetic [iːs'θetɪk] adj estético

afar [ə'fɑː*] adv: **from ~** desde lejos

affair [ə'fɛə*] n asunto; (also: **love ~**) aventura (amorosa)

affect [ə'fekt] vt (influence) afectar, influir en; (afflict, concern) afectar; (move) conmover; **~ed** adj afectado

affection [ə'fekʃən] n afecto, cariño; **~ate** adj afectuoso, cariñoso

affinity [ə'fɪnɪtɪ] n (bond, rapport): **to feel an ~ with** sentirse identificado con; (resemblance) afinidad f

afflict [ə'flɪkt] vt afligir

affluence ['æfluəns] n opulencia, riqueza

affluent ['æfluənt] adj (wealthy) acomodado; **the ~ society** la sociedad opulenta

afford [ə'fɔːd] vt (provide) proporcionar; **can we ~ (to buy) it?** ¿tenemos bastante dinero para comprarlo?

Afghanistan [æf'gænɪstæn] n Afganistán m

afield [ə'fiːld] adv: **far ~** muy lejos

afloat [ə'fləut] adv (floating) a flote

afoot [ə'fut] adv: **there is something ~** algo se está tramando

afraid [ə'freɪd] adj: **to be ~ of** (person) tener miedo a; (thing) tener miedo de; **to be ~ to** tener miedo de, temer; **I am ~ that** me temo que; **I am ~ not/so** lo siento, pero no/es así

afresh [ə'freʃ] adv de nuevo, otra vez

Africa ['æfrɪkə] n África; **~n** adj, n africano/a m/f

after ['ɑːftə*] prep (time) después de; (place, order) detrás de, tras ♦ adv después ♦ conj después (de) que; **what/who are you ~?** ¿qué/a quién busca usted?; **~ having done/he left** después de haber hecho/después de que se marchó; **to name sb ~ sb** llamar a uno por uno; **it's twenty ~ eight** (US) son las ocho y veinte; **to ask ~ sb** preguntar por alguien; **~ all** después de todo, al fin y al cabo; **~ you!** ¡pase usted!; **~-effects** npl consecuencias fpl, efectos mpl; **~math** n consecuencias fpl, resultados mpl; **~noon** n tarde f; **~s** (inf) n (dessert) postre m; **~-sales service** (BRIT) n servicio de asistencia pos-venta; **~-shave (lotion)** n aftershave m; **~sun (lotion/cream)** n loción f/crema para después del sol, aftersun m; **~thought** n ocurrencia (tardía); **~ward** (US **~wards**) adv después, más tarde

again [ə'gen] adv otra vez, de nuevo; **to do sth ~** volver a hacer algo; **~ and ~** una y otra vez

against [ə'genst] prep (in opposition to) en contra de; (leaning on, touching) contra, junto a

age [eɪdʒ] n edad f; (period) época ♦ vi envejecer(se) ♦ vt envejecer; **she is 20 years of ~** tiene 20 años; **to come of ~** llegar a la mayoría de edad; **it's been ~s since I saw you** hace siglos que no te veo; **~d 10** de 10 años de edad; **the ~d** ['eɪdʒɪd] npl los ancianos; **~ group** n: **to be in the same ~ group** tener la misma edad; **~ limit** n edad f mínima (or máxima)

agency ['eɪdʒənsɪ] n agencia

agenda [ə'dʒendə] n orden m del día

agent ['eɪdʒənt] n agente m/f; (COMM: holding concession) representante m/f, delegado/a; (CHEM, fig) agente m

aggravate ['ægrəveɪt] vt (situation) agravar; (person) irritar

aggregate ['ægrɪgət] n conjunto

aggressive [ə'gresɪv] adj (belligerent) agresivo; (assertive) enérgico

aggrieved [ə'griːvd] adj ofendido, agraviado

aghast [ə'gɑːst] adj horrorizado

agile ['ædʒaɪl] adj ágil

agitate ['ædʒɪteɪt] vt (trouble) inquietar ♦ vi: **to ~ for/against** hacer campaña pro o en favor de/en contra de

AGM n abbr (= annual general meeting)

asamblea anual

ago [ə'gəʊ] adv: **2 days ~** hace 2 días; **not long ~** hace poco; **how long ~?** ¿hace cuánto tiempo?

agog [ə'gɒg] adj (eager) ansioso; (excited) emocionado

agonizing ['ægənaɪzɪŋ] adj (pain) atroz; (decision, wait) angustioso

agony ['ægənɪ] n (pain) dolor m agudo; (distress) angustia; **to be in ~** retorcerse de dolor

agree [ə'griː] vt (price, date) acordar, quedar en ♦ vi (have same opinion) estar de acuerdo; **to ~ (with/that)** estar de acuerdo (con/que); (correspond) coincidir, concordar; (consent) acceder; **to ~ with** (subj: person) estar de acuerdo con, ponerse de acuerdo con, (: food) sentar bien a; (LING) concordar con; **to ~ to sth/to do sth** consentir en algo/aceptar hacer algo; **to ~ that** (admit) estar de acuerdo en que; **~able** adj (sensation) agradable; (person) simpático; (willing) de acuerdo, conforme; **~d** adj (time, place) convenido; **~ment** n acuerdo; (contract) contrato; **in ~ment** de acuerdo, conforme

agricultural [ægrɪ'kʌltʃərəl] adj agrícola

agriculture ['ægrɪkʌltʃə*] n agricultura m/f

aground [ə'graʊnd] adv: **to run ~** (NAUT) encallar, embarrancar

ahead [ə'hed] adv (in front) delante; (into the future): **she had no time to think ~** no tenía tiempo de hacer planes para el futuro; **~ of** delante de; (in advance of) antes de; **~ of time** antes de la hora; **go right** or **straight ~** (direction) siga adelante; (permission) hazlo (or hágalo)

aid [eɪd] n ayuda, auxilio; (device) aparato ♦ vt ayudar, auxiliar; **in ~ of** a beneficio de

aide [eɪd] n (person, also: MIL) ayudante m/f

AIDS [eɪdz] n abbr (= acquired immune deficiency syndrome) SIDA m

ailment ['eɪlmənt] n enfermedad f, achaque m

aim [eɪm] vt (gun, camera) apuntar; (missile, remark) dirigir; (blow) asestar ♦ vi (also: take ~) apuntar ♦ n (in shooting: skill) puntería; (objective) propósito, meta; **to ~ at** (with weapon) apuntar a; (objective) aspirar a, pretender; **to ~ to do** tener la intención de hacer; **~less** adj sin propósito, sin objeto

ain't [eɪnt] (inf) = **am not; aren't; isn't**

air [ɛə*] n aire m; (appearance) aspecto ♦ vt (room) ventilar; (clothes, ideas) airear ♦ cpd aéreo; **to throw sth into the ~** (ball etc) lanzar algo al aire; **by ~** (travel) en avión; **to be on the ~** (RADIO, TV) estar en antena; **~bed** (BRIT) n colchón m neumático; **~conditioned** adj climatizado; **~ conditioning** n aire acondicionado; **~craft** n inv avión m; **~craft carrier** n porta(a)viones m inv; **~field** n campo de aviación; **A~ Force** n fuerzas fpl aéreas, aviación f; **~ freshener** n ambientador m; **~gun** n escopeta de aire comprimido; **~ hostess** (BRIT) n azafata; **~ letter** (BRIT) n carta aérea; **~lift** n puente m aéreo; **~line** n línea aérea; **~liner** n avión m de pasajeros; **~mail** n: **by ~mail** por avión; **~plane** (US) n avión m; **~port** n aeropuerto; **~ raid** n ataque m aéreo; **~sick** adj: **to be ~sick** marearse (en avión); **~space** n espacio aéreo; **~tight** adj hermético; **~traffic controller** n controlador(a) m/f aéreo/a; **~y** adj (room) bien ventilado; (fig: manner) desenfadado

aisle [aɪl] n (of church) nave f; (of theatre, supermarket) pasillo; **~ seat** n (on plane) asiento de pasillo

ajar [ə'dʒɑː*] adj entreabierto

alarm [ə'lɑːm] n (in shop, bank) alarma; (anxiety) inquietud f ♦ vt asustar, inquietar; **~ call** n (in hotel etc) alarma; **~ clock** n despertador m

alas [ə'læs] adv desgraciadamente

albeit [ɔːl'biːıt] conj aunque

album ['ælbəm] n álbum m; (L.P.) elepé m

alcohol ['ælkəhɔl] n alcohol m; **~ic** [-'hɔlɪk] adj, n alcohólico/a m/f

ale [eɪl] n cerveza

alert [ə'lɜːt] adj (attentive) atento; (to danger, opportunity) alerta ♦ n alerta m, alarma ♦ vt poner sobre aviso; **to be on the ~** (also MIL) estar alerta or sobre aviso

algebra ['ældʒıbrə] n álgebra

Algeria [æl'dʒıərıə] n Argelia

alias ['eɪlɪəs] adv alias, conocido por ♦ n (of criminal) apodo; (of writer) seudónimo

alibi ['ælɪbaɪ] n coartada

alien ['eɪlɪən] n (foreigner) extranjero/a m/f; (extraterrestrial) extraterrestre m/f ♦ adj: **~ to** ajeno a; **~ate** vt enajenar, alejar

alight [ə'laɪt] adj ardiendo; (eyes) brillante ♦ vi (person) apearse, bajar; (bird) posarse

align [ə'laɪn] vt alinear

alike [ə'laɪk] adj semejantes, iguales ♦ adv igualmente, del mismo modo; **to look ~** parecerse

alimony ['ælɪmənɪ] n manutención f

alive [ə'laɪv] adj vivo; (lively) alegre

KEYWORD

all [ɔːl] adj (sg) todo/a; (pl) todos/as; **~ day** todo el día; **~ night** toda la noche; **~ men** todos los hombres; **~ five came** vinieron los cinco; **~ the books** todos los libros; **~ his life** toda su vida

♦ pron 1 todo; **I ate it ~**, **I ate ~ of it** me lo comí todo; **~ of us went** fuimos todos, **~ the boys went** fueron todos los chicos; **is that ~?** ¿eso es todo?, ¿algo más?; (in shop) ¿algo más?, ¿alguna cosa más?

2 (in phrases): **above ~** sobre todo; por encima de todo; **after ~** después

de todo; **at ~: not at ~** (in answer to question) en absoluto; (in answer to thanks) ¡de nada!, no hay de qué!; **I'm not at ~ tired** no estoy nada cansado/a; **anything at ~ will do** cualquier cosa viene bien; **~ in ~** a fin de cuentas

♦ adv: **~ alone** completamente solo/a; **it's not as hard as ~ that** no es tan difícil como lo pintas; **the more the better** tanto más/mejor; **but ~** casi; **the score is 2 ~** están empatados a 2

---

all clear n (after attack etc) fin m de la alerta; (fig) luz f verde

allege [ə'ledʒ] vt pretender; **~dly** [ə'ledʒıdlı] adv supuestamente, según se afirma

allegiance [ə'liːdʒəns] n lealtad f

allergy ['ælədʒı] n alergia

alleviate [ə'liːvıeıt] vt aliviar

alley ['ælı] n callejuela

alliance [ə'laıəns] n alianza

allied ['ælaıd] adj aliado

alligator ['ælıgeıtə*] n (ZOOL) caimán m

all-in (BRIT) adj, adv (charge) todo incluido

all-night adj (café, shop) abierto toda la noche; (party) que dura toda la noche

allocate ['æləkeıt] vt (money etc) asignar

allot [ə'lɔt] vt asignar; **~ment** n ración f; (garden) parcela

all-out adj (effort etc) supremo; **all out** adv con todas las fuerzas

allow [ə'lau] vt permitir, dejar; (a claim) admitir; (sum, time etc) dar, conceder; (concede): **to ~ that** reconocer que; **to ~ sb to do** permitir a alguien hacer; **he is ~ed to ...** se le permite ...; **~ for** vt fus tener en cuenta; **~ance** n subvención f; (welfare payment) subsidio, pensión f; (pocket money) dinero de bolsillo; (tax ~ance) desgravación f; **to make ~ances for** (person) disculpar a; (thing) tener en cuenta

alloy ['ælɔɪ] n mezcla
all: ~ **right** adv bien; (as answer)
¡conforme!, ¡está bien!; ~**rounder** n:
he's a good ~**rounder** se le da bien
todo; ~-**time** adj (record) de todos los
tiempos
alluring [ə'ljuərɪŋ] adj atractivo,
tentador(a)
ally ['ælaɪ] n aliado/a ♦ vt: **to** ~ **o.s.**
with aliarse con
almighty [ɔ:l'maɪtɪ] adj todopoderoso;
(row etc) imponente
almond ['ɑ:mənd] n almendra
almost ['ɔ:lməust] adv casi
alone [ə'ləun] adj, adv solo; **to leave**
sb ~ dejar a uno en paz; **to leave sth**
~ no tocar algo, dejar algo sin tocar;
let ~ ... y mucho menos ...
along [ə'lɔŋ] prep a lo largo de, por
♦ adv: **is he coming** ~ **with us?**
¿viene con nosotros?; **he was**
limping ~ iba cojeando; ~ **with** junto
con; **all** ~ (all the time) desde el
principio; ~**side** prep al lado de ♦ adv
al lado
aloof [ə'lu:f] adj reservado ♦ adv: **to**
stand ~ mantenerse apartado
aloud [ə'laud] adv en voz alta
alphabet ['ælfəbet] n alfabeto
Alps [ælps] npl: **the** ~ los Alpes
already [ɔ:l'redɪ] adv ya
alright ['ɔ:l'raɪt] (BRIT) adv = **all right**
Alsatian [æl'seɪʃən] n (dog) pastor m
alemán
also ['ɔ:lsəu] adv también, además
altar ['ɔltə*] n altar m
alter ['ɔltə*] vt cambiar, modificar ♦ vi
cambiar; ~**ation** [ɔltə'reɪʃən] n
cambio; (to clothes) arreglo; (to
building) arreglos mpl
alternate [adj ɔl'tə:nɪt, vb 'ɔltə:neɪt]
adj (actions etc) alternativo; (events)
alterno; (US) = **alternative** ♦ vi: **to**
~ **(with)** alternar (con); **on** ~ **days** un
día sí y otro no; **alternating current**
[-neɪtɪŋ] n corriente f alterna
alternative [ɔl'tə:nətɪv] adj alternativo

♦ n alternativa; ~ **medicine** medicina
alternativa; ~**ly** adv: ~**ly one could** ...
por otra parte se podría ...
although [ɔ:l'ðəu] conj aunque
altitude ['æltɪtju:d] n altura
alto ['æltəu] n (female) contralto f;
(male) alto
altogether [ɔ:ltə'geðə*] adv
completamente, del todo; (on the
whole) en total, en conjunto
aluminium [ælju'mɪnɪəm] (BRIT),
aluminum [ə'lu:mɪnəm] (US) n
aluminio
always ['ɔ:lweɪz] adv siempre
Alzheimer's (disease) ['æltshaɪməz-]
n enfermedad f de Alzheimer
AM n abbr (= Assembly Member)
parlamentario/a m/f
am [æm] vb see **be**
a.m. adv abbr (= ante meridiem) de la
mañana
amalgamate [ə'mælgəmeɪt] vi
amalgamarse ♦ vt amalgamar, unir
amateur ['æmətə*] n aficionado/a,
amateur m/f; ~**ish** adj inexperto
amaze [ə'meɪz] vt asombrar, pasmar;
to be ~**d (at)** quedar pasmado (de);
~**ment** n asombro, sorpresa; **amazing**
adj extraordinario; (fantastic) increíble
Amazon ['æməzən] n (GEO) Amazonas
m
ambassador [æm'bæsədə*] n
embajador(a) m/f
amber ['æmbə*] n ámbar m; **at** ~
(BRIT: AUT) en el amarillo
ambiguous [æm'bɪgjuəs] adj ambiguo
ambition [æm'bɪʃən] n ambición f;
ambitious [-ʃəs] adj ambicioso
ambulance ['æmbjuləns] n
ambulancia
ambush ['æmbuʃ] n emboscada ♦ vt
tender una emboscada a
amenable [ə'mi:nəbl] adj: **to be** ~ **to**
dejarse influir por
amend [ə'mend] vt enmendar; **to**
make ~**s** dar cumplida satisfacción
amenities [ə'mi:nɪtɪz] npl

comodidades fpl

America [ə'merɪkə] n (USA) Estados mpl Unidos; **~n** adj, n norteamericano/a m/f; estadounidense m/f

amiable ['eɪmɪəbl] adj amable, simpático

amicable ['æmɪkəbl] adj amistoso, amigable

amid(st) [ə'mɪd(st)] prep entre, en medio de

amiss [ə'mɪs] adv: **to take sth ~** tomar algo a mal; **there's something ~** pasa algo

ammonia [ə'məunɪə] n amoníaco

ammunition [æmju'nɪʃən] n municiones fpl

amnesty ['æmnɪstɪ] n amnistía

amok [ə'mɔk] adv: **to run ~** enloquecerse, desbocarse

among(st) [ə'mʌŋ(st)] prep entre, en medio de

amorous ['æmərəs] adj amoroso

amount [ə'maunt] n (gen) cantidad f; (of bill etc) suma, importe m ♦ vi: **to ~ to** sumar; (be same as) equivaler a, significar

amp(ère) ['æmp(ɛə*)] n amperio

ample ['æmpl] adj (large) grande; (abundant) abundante; (enough) bastante, suficiente

amplifier ['æmplɪfaɪə*] n amplificador m

amuse [ə'mju:z] vt divertir; (distract) distraer, entretener; **~ment** n diversión f; (pastime) pasatiempo; (laughter) risa; **~ment arcade** n salón m de juegos; **~ment park** n parque m de atracciones

an [æn] indef art see **a**

anaemic [ə'ni:mɪk] (US **anemic**) adj anémico; (fig) soso, insípido

anaesthetic [ænɪs'θetɪk] n (US **anesthetic**) anestesia

analog(ue) ['ænəlɔg] adj (computer, watch) analógico

analyse ['ænəlaɪz] vt

analizar; **analysis** [ə'næləsɪs] (pl **analyses**) n análisis m inv; **analyst** [-lɪst] n (political analyst, psychoanalyst) analista m/f

analyze ['ænəlaɪz] (US) vt = **analyse**

anarchist ['ænəkɪst] n anarquista m/f

anatomy [ə'nætəmɪ] n anatomía

ancestor ['ænsɪstə*] n antepasado

anchor ['æŋkə*] n ancla, áncora ♦ vi (also: **to drop ~**) anclar ♦ vt anclar; **to weigh ~** levar anclas

anchovy ['æntʃəvɪ] n anchoa

ancient ['eɪnʃənt] adj antiguo

ancillary [æn'sɪlərɪ] adj auxiliar

and [ænd] conj y; (before i-, hi- + consonant) e; **men ~ women** hombres y mujeres; **father ~ son** padre e hijo; **trees ~ grass** árboles y hierba; **~ so on** etcétera, y así sucesivamente; **try ~ come** procura venir; **he talked ~ talked** habló sin parar; **better ~ better** cada vez mejor

Andes ['ændi:z] npl: **the ~** los Andes

anemic etc [ə'ni:mɪk] (US) = **anaemic** etc

anesthetic etc [ænɪs'θetɪk] (US) = **anaesthetic** etc

anew [ə'nju:] adv de nuevo, otra vez

angel ['eɪndʒəl] n ángel m

anger ['æŋgə*] n cólera

angina [æn'dʒaɪnə] n angina (del pecho)

angle ['æŋgl] n ángulo; **from their ~** desde su punto de vista

angler ['æŋglə*] n pescador(a) m/f (de caña)

Anglican ['æŋglɪkən] adj, n anglicano/a m/f

angling ['æŋglɪŋ] n pesca con caña

Anglo... ['æŋgləu] prefix anglo...

angrily ['æŋgrɪlɪ] adv coléricamente, airadamente

angry ['æŋgrɪ] adj enfadado, airado; (wound) inflamado; **to be ~ with sb/ at sth** estar enfadado con alguien/por algo; **to get ~** enfadarse, enojarse

anguish ['æŋgwɪʃ] n (physical)

tormentos *mpl*; (*mental*) angustia
animal ['ænɪml] *n* animal *m*; (*pej: person*) bestia ♦ *adj* animal
animate ['ænɪmeɪt] *adj* vivo; **~d** [-meɪtɪd] *adj* animado
aniseed ['ænɪsiːd] *n* anís *m*
ankle ['æŋkl] *n* tobillo *m*; **~ sock** *n* calcetín *m* corto
annex [*n* 'æneks, *vb* æ'neks] *n* (*also:* BRIT: *annexe*) (*building*) edificio anexo ♦ *vt* (*territory*) anexionar
annihilate [ə'naɪəleɪt] *vt* aniquilar
anniversary [ænɪ'vɜːsərɪ] *n* aniversario
announce [ə'naʊns] *vt* anunciar; **~ment** *n* anuncio; (*official*) declaración *f*; **~r** *n* (RADIO) locutor(a) *m/f*; (TV) presentador(a) *m/f*
annoy [ə'nɔɪ] *vt* molestar, fastidiar; **don't get ~ed!** no se enfade!; **~ance** *n* enojo; **~ing** *adj* molesto, fastidioso; (*person*) pesado
annual ['ænjuəl] *adj* anual ♦ *n* (BOT) anual *m*; (*book*) anuario; **~ly** *adv* anualmente, cada año
annul [ə'nʌl] *vt* anular
annum ['ænəm] *n see* **per**
anonymous [ə'nɒnɪməs] *adj* anónimo
anorak ['ænəræk] *n* anorak *m*
anorexia [ænə'reksɪə] *n* (MED: *also:* **~ nervosa**) anorexia
another [ə'nʌðə*] *adj* (*one more, a different one*) otro ♦ *pron* otro; otra
answer ['ɑːnsə*] *n* contestación *f*, respuesta; (*to problem*) solución *f* ♦ *vi* contestar, responder ♦ *vt* (*reply to*) contestar a, responder a; (*problem*) resolver; (*prayer*) escuchar; **in ~ to your letter** en contestación a su carta; **to ~ the phone** contestar *or* coger el teléfono; **to ~ the bell** *or* **the door** acudir a la puerta; **~ back** *vi* replicar, ser respondón/ona; **~ for** *vt fus* responder de *or* por; **~ to** *vt fus* (*description*) corresponder a; **~able** *adj*: **~able to sb for sth** responsable ante uno de algo; **~ing machine** *n* contestador *m*

automático
ant [ænt] *n* hormiga
antagonism [æn'tæɡənɪzm] *n* antagonismo, hostilidad *f*
antagonize [æn'tæɡənaɪz] *vt* provocar la enemistad de
Antarctic [ænt'ɑːktɪk] *n*: **the ~** el Antártico
antelope ['æntɪləʊp] *n* antílope *m*
antenatal ['æntɪ'neɪtl] *adj* antenatal, prenatal; **~ clinic** *n* clínica prenatal
anthem ['ænθəm] *n*: **national ~** himno nacional
anthropology [ænθrə'pɒlədʒɪ] *n* antropología
anti... [æntɪ] *prefix* anti...; **~-aircraft** [-'eəkrɑːft] *adj* antiaéreo; **~biotic** [-baɪ'ɒtɪk] *n* antibiótico; **~body** ['æntɪbɒdɪ] *n* anticuerpo
anticipate [æn'tɪsɪpeɪt] *vt* prever; (*expect*) esperar, contar con; (*look forward to*) esperar con ilusión; (*do first*) anticiparse a, adelantarse a; **anticipation** [-'peɪʃən] *n* (*expectation*) previsión *f*; (*eagerness*) ilusión *f*, expectación *f*
anticlimax [æntɪ'klaɪmæks] *n* decepción *f*
anticlockwise [æntɪ'klɒkwaɪz] (BRIT) *adv* en dirección contraria a la de las agujas del reloj
antics ['æntɪks] *npl* gracias *fpl*
anticyclone [æntɪ'saɪkləʊn] *n* anticiclón *m*
antidepressant ['æntɪdɪ'presnt] *n* antidepresivo
antidote ['æntɪdəʊt] *n* antídoto *m*
antifreeze ['æntɪfriːz] *n* anticongelante *m*
antihistamine [æntɪ'hɪstəmiːn] *n* antihistamínico
antiquated ['æntɪkweɪtɪd] *adj* anticuado
antique [æn'tiːk] *n* antigüedad *f* ♦ *adj* antiguo; **~ dealer** *n* anticuario/a; **~ shop** *n* tienda de antigüedades
antiquity [æn'tɪkwɪtɪ] *n* antigüedad *f*

antiseptic [ˌæntɪˈseptɪk] *adj, n*
antiséptico

antlers [ˈæntləz] *npl* cuernas *fpl*,
cornamenta *sg*

anus [ˈeɪnəs] *n* ano

anvil [ˈænvɪl] *n* yunque *m*

anxiety [æŋˈzaɪətɪ] *n* inquietud *f*; (MED)
ansiedad *f*; ~ **to do** deseo de hacer

anxious [ˈæŋkʃəs] *adj* inquieto,
preocupado; (worrying) preocupante;
(keen): **to be ~ to do** tener muchas
ganas de hacer

KEYWORD

any [ˈenɪ] *adj* **1** (in questions etc)
algún/alguna; **have you ~ butter/
children?** ¿tienes mantequilla/hijos?; **if
there are ~ tickets left** si quedan
billetes, si queda algún billete

2 (with negative): **I haven't ~
money/books** no tengo dinero/
libros

3 (no matter which) cualquier;
~ **excuse will do** valdrá or servirá
cualquier excusa; **choose ~ book you
like** escoge el libro que quieras;
~ **teacher you ask will tell you**
cualquier profesor al que preguntes te
lo dirá

4 (in phrases): **in ~ case** de todas
formas, en cualquier caso; ~ **day now**
cualquier día (de estos); **at ~ moment**
en cualquier momento, de un
momento a otro; **at ~ rate** en todo
caso; ~ **time: come (at) ~ time** ven
cuando quieras; **he might come (at)
~ time** podría llegar en un momento a
otro

♦ *pron* **1** (in questions etc): **have you
got ~?** ¿tienes alguno(s)/a(s)?; **can
~ of you sing?** ¿sabe cantar alguno
de vosotros/ustedes?

2 (with negative): **I haven't ~ (of
them)** no tengo ninguno

3 (no matter which one(s)): **take ~ of
those books (you like)** toma el libro
que quieras de ésos

♦ *adv* **1** (in questions etc): **do you
want ~ more soup/sandwiches?**
¿quieres más sopa/bocadillos?; **are
you feeling ~ better?** ¿te sientes
algo mejor?

2 (with negative): **I can't hear him
~ more** ya no le oigo; **don't wait
~ longer** no esperes más

anybody [ˈenɪbɒdɪ] *pron* cualquiera; (in
interrogative sentences) alguien; (in
negative sentences): **I don't see ~** no
veo a nadie; **if ~ should phone ...** si
llama alguien ...

anyhow [ˈenɪhau] *adv* (at any rate) de
todos modos, de todas formas; (haphazard): **do it ~ you like** hazlo
como quieras; **she leaves things just ~**
deja las cosas como quiera or de
cualquier modo; **I shall go ~** de todos
modos iré

anyone [ˈenɪwʌn] *pron* = **anybody**

anything [ˈenɪθɪŋ] *pron* (in questions
etc) algo, alguna cosa; (with negative)
nada; **can you see ~?** ¿ves algo?; **if
~ happens to me ...** si algo me
ocurre ...; (no matter what): **you can
say ~ you like** puedes decir lo que
quieras; ~ **will do** vale todo or
cualquier cosa; **he'll eat ~** come de
todo o lo que sea

anyway [ˈenɪweɪ] *adv* (at any rate) de
todos modos, de todas formas; **I shall
go ~** iré de todos modos; (besides): ~,
**I couldn't come even if I wanted
to** además, no podría venir aunque
quisiera; **why are you phoning, ~?**
¿entonces, por qué llamas?, ¿por qué
llamas, pues?

anywhere [ˈenɪweə*] *adv* (in questions
etc): **can you see him ~?** ¿le ves por
algún lado?; **are you going ~?** ¿vas a
algún sitio?; (with negative): **I can't
see him ~** no le veo por ninguna
parte; ~ **in the world** (no matter
where) en cualquier parte (del mundo);
put the books down ~ deja los

apart [ə'pɑːt] adv (aside) aparte; (situation): ~ **(from)** separado (de); (movement): ~ **to pull** ~ separar; **10 miles** ~ separados por 10 millas; **to take** ~ desmontar; ~ **from** prep aparte de

apartheid [ə'pɑːteɪt] n apartheid m

apartment [ə'pɑːtmənt] n (US) piso (SP), departamento (AM), apartamento; (room) cuarto; ~ **building** (US) edificio de apartamentos

apathetic [æpə'θetɪk] adj apático, indiferente

ape [eɪp] n mono ♦ vt imitar, remedar

aperitif [ə'perɪtɪf] n aperitivo

aperture ['æpətʃjuə*] n rendija, resquicio; (PHOT) abertura

APEX ['eɪpeks] n abbr (= Advanced Purchase Excursion Fare) tarifa APEX f

apex ['eɪpeks] n ápice m; (fig) cumbre f

apiece [ə'piːs] adv cada uno

aplomb [ə'plɔm] n aplomo

apologetic [əpɔlə'dʒetɪk] adj de disculpa; (person) arrepentido

apologize [ə'pɔlədʒaɪz] vi: **to** ~ **(for sth to sb)** disculparse (con alguien de algo)

apology [ə'pɔlədʒɪ] n disculpa, excusa

apostrophe [ə'pɔstrəfɪ] n apóstrofo m

appal [ə'pɔːl] vt horrorizar, espantar; ~**ling** [ə'pɔːlɪŋ] adj espantoso; (awful) pésimo

apparatus [æpə'reɪtəs] n (equipment) equipo; (organization) aparato; (in gymnasium) aparatos mpl

apparel [ə'pærl] n (US) n ropa

apparent [ə'pærənt] adj aparente; (obvious) evidente; ~**ly** adv por lo visto, al parecer

appeal [ə'piːl] vi (LAW) apelar ♦ n (LAW) apelación f; (request) llamamiento, petición f; (plea) súplica; (charm) atractivo; **to** ~ **for** reclamar; **to** ~ **to** (be attractive to) atraer; **it doesn't** ~ **to me** no me atrae, no me llama la atención; ~**ing** adj (attractive) atractivo

appear [ə'pɪə*] vi aparecer,

presentarse; (LAW) comparecer; (publication) salir (a luz), publicarse; (seem) parecer; **to** ~ **on TV/in "Hamlet"** salir por la tele/hacer un papel en "Hamlet"; **it would** ~ **that** parecería que; ~**ance** n aparición f; (look) apariencia, aspecto

appease [ə'piːz] vt (pacify) apaciguar; (satisfy) satisfacer

appendices [ə'pendɪsiːz] npl of appendix

appendicitis [əpendɪ'saɪtɪs] n apendicitis f

appendix [ə'pendɪks] (pl appendices) n apéndice m

appetite ['æpɪtaɪt] n apetito; (fig) deseo, anhelo

appetizer ['æpɪtaɪzə*] n (drink) aperitivo; (food) tapas fpl (SP)

applaud [ə'plɔːd] vt, vi aplaudir

applause [ə'plɔːz] n aplausos mpl

apple ['æpl] n manzana; ~ **tree** n manzano

appliance [ə'plaɪəns] n aparato

applicable [ə'plɪkəbl] adj (relevant): **to be** ~ **(to)** referirse a

applicant [ə'plɪkənt] n candidato/a; solicitante m/f

application [æplɪ'keɪʃən] n aplicación f; (for a job etc) solicitud f, petición f; ~ **form** n solicitud f

applied [ə'plaɪd] adj aplicado

apply [ə'plaɪ] vt (paint etc) poner; (law etc: put into practice) poner en vigor ♦ vi: **to** ~ **(to)** dirigirse a; (be applicable) ser aplicable a; **to** ~ **for** (permit, grant, job) solicitar; **to** ~ **o.s. to** aplicarse a, dedicarse a

appoint [ə'pɔɪnt] vt (to post) nombrar; ~**ed** adj: **at the** ~**ed time** a la hora señalada; ~**ment** n (with client) cita; (act) nombramiento; (post) puesto; (at hairdresser etc): **to have an** ~**ment** tener hora; **to make an** ~**ment (with sb)** citarse (con uno)

appraisal [ə'preɪzl] n valoración f

appreciate [ə'priːʃɪeɪt] vt apreciar,

tener en mucho; (be grateful for) agradecer; (be aware of) comprender ♦ vi (COMM) aumentar(se) m

appreciation [ə'priːʃɪ'eɪʃən] n apreciación f; (gratitude) reconocimiento, agradecimiento; (COMM) aumento en valor

appreciative [ə'priːʃɪətɪv] adj apreciativo; (comment) agradecido

apprehensive [æprɪ'hensɪv] adj aprensivo

apprentice [ə'prentɪs] n aprendiz a m/f; ~ship n aprendizaje m

approach [ə'prəutʃ] vi acercarse ♦ vt acercarse a; (ask, apply to) dirigirse a; (situation, problem) abordar ♦ n acercamiento; (access) acceso; (to problem, situation): ~ (to) actitud f (ante); ~able adj (person) abordable; (place) accesible

appropriate [adj ə'prəupriːt, vb ə'prəupriːeɪt] adj apropiado, conveniente ♦ vt (take) apropiarse de

approval [ə'pruːvəl] n aprobación f, visto bueno f; (permission) consentimiento; **on ~** (COMM) a prueba

approve [ə'pruːv] vt aprobar; ~ of vt fus (thing) aprobar; (person): **they don't ~ of her** (ella) no les parece bien

approximate [ə'prɒksɪmɪt] adj aproximado; ~**ly** adv aproximadamente, más o menos

apricot ['eɪprɪkɒt] n albaricoque m (SP), damasco (AM)

April ['eɪprəl] n abril m; ~ **Fools' Day** n el primero de abril; ≈ día m de los Inocentes (28 December)

apron ['eɪprən] n delantal m

apt [æpt] adj acertado, apropiado; (likely): ~ **to do** propenso a hacer

aquarium [ə'kweərɪəm] n acuario

Aquarius [ə'kweərɪəs] n Acuario

Arab ['ærəb] n, adj árabe m/f

Arabian [ə'reɪbɪən] adj árabe

Arabic ['ærəbɪk] adj árabe; (numerals) arábigo ♦ n árabe m

arable ['ærəbl] adj cultivable

Aragon ['ærəgən] n Aragón m

arbitrary ['ɑːbɪtrərɪ] adj arbitrario

arbitration [ɑːbɪ'treɪʃən] n arbitraje m

arcade [ɑː'keɪd] n (round a square) soportales mpl; (shopping mall) galería comercial

arch [ɑːtʃ] n arco; (of foot) arco del pie ♦ vt arquear

archaeologist [ɑːkɪ'ɒlədʒɪst] (US archeologist) n arqueólogo/a

archaeology [ɑːkɪ'ɒlədʒɪ] (US archeology) n arqueología

archbishop [ɑːtʃ'bɪʃəp] n arzobispo

archeology etc [ɑːkɪ'ɒlədʒɪ] (US) = **archaeology** etc

archery ['ɑːtʃərɪ] n tiro al arco

architect ['ɑːkɪtɛkt] n arquitecto/a; ~**ure** n arquitectura

archives ['ɑːkaɪvz] npl archivo

Arctic ['ɑːktɪk] adj ártico ♦ n: **the ~** el Ártico

ardent ['ɑːdənt] adj ardiente, apasionado

arduous ['ɑːdjuəs] adj (task) arduo; (journey) agotador(a)

are [ɑː*] vb see **be**

area ['ɛərɪə] n área, región f; (part of place) zona; (MATH etc) área, superficie f; (in room: e.g. dining ~) parte f; (of knowledge, experience) campo

arena [ə'riːnə] n estadio; (of circus) pista

aren't [ɑːnt] = **are not**

Argentina [ɑːdʒən'tiːnə] n Argentina; **Argentinian** [-'tɪnɪən] adj, n argentino/a m/f

arguably ['ɑːgjuəblɪ] adv posiblemente

argue ['ɑːgjuː] vi (quarrel) discutir, pelearse; (reason) razonar, argumentar; **to ~ that** sostener que

argument ['ɑːgjumənt] n discusión f, pelea; (reasons) argumento; ~**ative** [-'mɛntətɪv] adj discutidor(a)

Aries ['ɛərɪz] n Aries m

arise [ə'raɪz] (pt arose, pp arisen) vi surgir, presentarse

arisen [əˈrɪzn] pp of **arise**

aristocrat [ˈærɪstəkræt] n aristócrata m/f

arithmetic [əˈrɪθmətɪk] n aritmética f

ark [ɑːk] n: Noah's A~ el Arca f de Noé

arm [ɑːm] n brazo ♦ vt armar; ~s npl armas fpl; ~ **in** ~ cogidos del brazo

armaments [ˈɑːməmənts] npl armamento

armchair [ˈɑːmtʃeəʳ] n sillón m, butaca

armed [ɑːmd] adj armado; ~ **robbery** n robo a mano armada

armour [ˈɑːməʳ] (US **armor**) n armadura; (MIL: tanks) blindaje m; ~**ed car** n coche m (SP) or carro (AM) blindado

armpit [ˈɑːmpɪt] n sobaco, axila

armrest [ˈɑːmrest] n apoyabrazos m inv

army [ˈɑːmɪ] n ejército m, (fig) multitud f

aroma [əˈrəumə] n aroma m, fragancia; ~**therapy** n aromaterapia

arose [əˈrəuz] pt of **arise**

around [əˈraund] adv alrededor; (in the area): **there is no one else** ~ no hay nadie más por aquí ♦ prep alrededor de

arouse [əˈrauz] vt despertar; (anger) provocar

arrange [əˈreɪndʒ] vt arreglar, ordenar; (organize) organizar; **to** ~ **to do sth** quedar en hacer algo; ~**ment** n arreglo; (agreement) acuerdo; ~**ments** npl (preparations) preparativos mpl

array [əˈreɪ] n: ~ **of** (things) serie f de; (people) conjunto de

arrears [əˈrɪəz] npl atrasos mpl; **to be in** ~ **with one's rent** estar retrasado en el pago del alquiler

arrest [əˈrest] vt detener; (sb's attention) llamar ♦ n detención f; **under** ~ detenido

arrival [əˈraɪvl] n llegada; **new** ~ recién nacido

arrive [əˈraɪv] vi llegar; (baby) nacer

arrogant [ˈærəgənt] adj arrogante

arrow [ˈærəu] n flecha

arse [ɑːs] (BRIT: inf!) n culo, trasero

arson [ˈɑːsn] n incendio premeditado

art [ɑːt] n arte m; (skill) destreza; **A~s** npl (SCOL) Letras fpl

artery [ˈɑːtərɪ] n arteria

art gallery n pinacoteca; (saleroom) galería de arte

arthritis [ɑːˈθraɪtɪs] n artritis f

artichoke [ˈɑːtɪtʃəuk] n alcachofa; **Jerusalem** ~ aguaturma

article [ˈɑːtɪkl] n artículo; (BRIT: LAW: training) ~**s** npl contrato de aprendizaje; ~ **of clothing** prenda de vestir

articulate [adj ɑːˈtɪkjulɪt, vb ɑːˈtɪkjuleɪt] adj claro, bien expresado ♦ vt expresar; ~**d lorry** (BRIT) n trailer m

artificial [ɑːtɪˈfɪʃl] adj artificial; (affected) afectado

artillery [ɑːˈtɪlərɪ] n artillería

artisan [ˈɑːtɪzæn] n artesano

artist [ˈɑːtɪst] n artista m/f; (MUS) intérprete m/f; ~**ic** [ɑːˈtɪstɪk] adj artístico; ~**ry** n arte m, habilidad f (artística)

art school n escuela de bellas artes

KEYWORD

as [æz] conj 1 (referring to time) cuando, mientras; a medida que; ~ **the years went by** con el paso de los años; **he came in** ~ **I was leaving** entró cuando me marchaba; ~ **from tomorrow** desde o a partir de mañana

2 (in comparisons): ~ **big** ~ tan grande como; **twice** ~ **big** ~ el doble de grande que; ~ **much money/many books** ~ tanto dinero/tantos libros como; ~ **soon** ~ en cuanto

3 (since, because) como, ya que; **he left early** ~ **he had to be home by 10** se fue temprano ya que tenía que estar en casa a las 10

4 (referring to manner, way): **do** ~ **you**

wish haz lo que quieras; **~ she said** como dijo; **he gave it to me ~ a present** me lo dio de regalo

5 (*in the capacity of*): **he works ~ a barman** trabaja de barman; **~ chairman of the company, he ...** como presidente de la compañía, ...

6 (*concerning*): **~ for** or **to that** por or en lo que respecta a eso

7: **~ if** or **though** como si; **he looked ~ if he was ill** parecía como si estuviera enfermo, tenía aspecto de enfermo; *see also* **long**; **such**; **well**

a.s.a.p. *abbr* (= *as soon as possible*) cuanto antes

asbestos [æz'bestəs] *n* asbesto, amianto

ascend [ə'sɛnd] *vt* subir; (*throne*) ascender or subir a

ascent [ə'sɛnt] *n* subida; (*slope*) cuesta, pendiente *f*

ascertain [æsə'tɛɪn] *vt* averiguar

ash [æʃ] *n* ceniza; (*tree*) fresno

ashamed [ə'feɪmd] *adj* avergonzado, apenado (*AM*); **to be ~ of** avergonzarse de

ashore [ə'ʃɔ:*] *adv* en tierra; (*swim etc*) a tierra

ashtray ['æʃtreɪ] *n* cenicero

Ash Wednesday *n* miércoles *m* de Ceniza

Asia ['eɪʃə] *n* Asia; **~n** *adj*, *n* asiático/a *m/f*

aside [ə'saɪd] *adv* a un lado ♦ *n* aparte *m*

ask [ɑ:sk] *vt* (*question*) preguntar; (*invite*) invitar; **to ~ sb/to do sth** preguntar algo a uno/pedir a alguien que haga algo; **to ~ sb about sth** preguntar algo a alguien; **to ~ (sb) a question** hacer una pregunta (a alguien); **to ~ sb out to dinner** invitar a cenar a uno; **~ after** *vt fus* preguntar por; **~ for** *vt fus* pedir; (*trouble*) buscar

asking price *n* precio inicial

asleep [ə'sli:p] *adj* dormido; **to fall ~** dormirse, quedarse dormido

asparagus [əs'pærəgəs] *n* (*plant*) espárrago; (*food*) espárragos *mpl*

aspect ['æspekt] *n* aspecto, apariencia; (*direction in which a building etc faces*) orientación *f*

aspersions [əs'pə:ʃənz] *npl*: **to cast ~ on** difamar a, calumniar a

asphyxiation [æsfɪksɪ'eɪʃən] *n* asfixia

aspire [əs'paɪə*] *vi*: **to ~** aspirar a, ambicionar

aspirin ['æsprɪn] *n* aspirina

ass [æs] *n* asno, burro; (*inf*: *idiot*) imbécil *m/f*; (*US*: *inf!*) culo, trasero

assailant [ə'seɪlənt] *n* asaltador(a) *m/f*, agresor(a) *m/f*

assassinate [ə'sæsɪneɪt] *vt* asesinar; **assassination** [əsæsɪ'neɪʃən] *n* asesinato

assault [ə'sɔ:lt] *n* asalto; (*LAW*) agresión ♦ *vt* asaltar, atacar; (*sexually*) violar

assemble [ə'sɛmbl] *vt* reunir, juntar; (*TECH*) montar ♦ *vi* reunirse, juntarse

assembly [ə'sɛmblɪ] *n* reunión *f*, asamblea; (*parliament*) parlamento *f*, (*construction*) montaje *m*; **~ line** cadena de montaje

assent [ə'sɛnt] *n* asentimiento, aprobación *f*

assert [ə'sə:t] *vt* afirmar; (*authority*) hacer valer; **~ion** [-ʃən] *n* afirmación *f*

assess [ə'sɛs] *vt* valorar, calcular; (*for tax*) gravar; **~ment** *n* valoración *f*; (*for tax*) gravamen *m*; **~or** *n* asesor/a *m/f*

asset ['æsɛt] *n* ventaja; **~s** *npl* (*COMM*) activo; (*property*, *funds*) fondos *mpl*

assign [ə'saɪn] *vt*: **to ~ (to)** (*date*) fijar (para); (*task*) asignar (a); (*resources*) destinar (a); **~ment** *n* tarea

assist [ə'sɪst] *vt* ayudar; **~ance** *n* ayuda, auxilio; **~ant** *n* ayudante *m/f*; (*BRIT*: *also*: **shop ~ant**) dependiente/a *m/f*

associate [*adj*, *n* ə'səuʃɪt, *vb*

əˈsəuɪerat] adj asociado ♦ n (at work)
colega m/f ♦ vt asociar; (connect)
relacionar ♦ vi: to ~ with sb tratar
con alguien

association [əsəusɪˈeɪʃən] n asociación
f

assorted [əˈsɔːtɪd] adj surtido, variado
assortment [əˈsɔːtmənt] n (of shapes,
colours) surtido; (of books) colección f;
(of people) mezcla
assume [əˈsjuːm] vt suponer;
(responsibilities) asumir; (attitude)
adoptar, tomar
assumption [əˈsʌmpʃən] n suposición
f, presunción f; (of power etc) toma
assurance [əˈʃuərəns] n garantía,
promesa; (confidence) confianza,
aplomo; (insurance) seguro
assure [əˈʃuə*] vt asegurar
asthma [ˈæsmə] n asma
astonish [əˈstɔnɪʃ] vt asombrar,
pasmar; ~ment n asombro, sorpresa
astound [əˈstaund] vt asombrar,
pasmar
astray [əˈstreɪ] adv: to go ~
extraviarse; to lead ~ (morally) llevar
por mal camino
astride [əˈstraɪd] prep a caballo or
horcajadas sobre
astrology [əsˈtrɔlədʒɪ] n astrología
astronaut [ˈæstrənɔːt] n astronauta
m/f
astronomy [əsˈtrɔnəmɪ] n astronomía
asylum [əˈsaɪləm] n (refuge) asilo;
(mental hospital) manicomio

KEYWORD
---

at [æt] prep **1** (referring to position):
(in direction) a; ~ the top en lo alto;
~ home/school en casa/la escuela; to
look ~ sth/sb mirar algo/a uno
2 (referring to time): ~ 4 o'clock a las
4; ~ night por la noche; ~ Christmas
en Navidad; ~ times a veces
3 (referring to rates, speed etc): ~ £1 a
kilo a una libra el kilo; two ~ a time
de dos en dos; ~ 50 km/h a 50 km/h

4 (referring to manner): ~ a stroke de
un golpe; ~ peace en paz
5 (referring to activity): to be ~ work
estar trabajando; (in the office etc) estar
en el trabajo; to play ~ cowboys
jugar a los vaqueros; to be good ~
sth ser bueno en algo
6 (referring to cause): shocked/
surprised/annoyed ~ sth
asombrado/sorprendido/fastidiado por
algo; I went ~ his suggestion fui a
instancias suyas

ate [eɪt] pt of **eat**
atheist [ˈeɪθɪɪst] n ateo/a
Athens [ˈæθɪnz] n Atenas
athlete [ˈæθliːt] n atleta m/f
athletic [æθˈletɪk] adj atlético; ~s n
atletismo
Atlantic [ətˈlæntɪk] adj atlántico ♦ n:
the ~ (Ocean) el (Océano) Atlántico
atlas [ˈætləs] n atlas m
A.T.M. n abbr (= automated telling
machine) cajero automático
atmosphere [ˈætməsfɪə*] n atmósfera;
(of place) ambiente m
atom [ˈætəm] n átomo; ~ic [əˈtɔmɪk]
adj atómico; ~(ic) bomb n bomba
atómica; ~izer [ˈætəmaɪzə*] n
atomizador m
atone [əˈtəun] vi: to ~ for expiar
atrocious [əˈtrəuʃəs] adj atroz
attach [əˈtætʃ] vt (fasten) atar; (join)
unir, sujetar; (document, letter)
adjuntar; (importance etc) dar,
conceder; to be ~ed to sb/sth (to
like) tener cariño a alguien/a algo
attaché case [əˈtæʃeɪ-] n maletín m
attachment [əˈtætʃmənt] n (tool)
accesorio; (love): ~ (to) apego (a)
attack [əˈtæk] vt atacar; (sub:
criminal) agredir, asaltar; (criticize)
criticar; (task) emprender ♦ n ataque
m, asalto; (on sb's life) atentado; (fig:
criticism) crítica; (of illness) ataque m;
heart ~ infarto (de miocardio); ~er n
agresor(a) m/f, asaltante m/f

attain [ə'teɪn] vt (also: ~ to) alcanzar; (achieve) lograr, conseguir

attempt [ə'tempt] n tentativa, intento; (attack) atentado ♦ vt intentar; ~ed adj: ~ed burglary/murder/suicide tentativa or intento de robo/asesinato/suicidio

attend [ə'tend] vt asistir a; (patient) atender; ~ to vt fus ocuparse de; (customer, patient) atender a; ~ance n asistencia, presencia; (people present) concurrencia; ~ant n ayudante m/f; (in garage etc) encargado/a ♦ adj (dangers) concomitante

attention [ə'tenʃən] n atención f; (care) atenciones fpl ♦ excl (MIL) ¡firme(s)!; for the ~ of ... (ADMIN) atención ...

attentive [ə'tentɪv] adj atento

attic ['ætɪk] n desván m

attitude ['ætɪtjuːd] n actitud f; (disposition) disposición f

attorney [ə'tɜːnɪ] n (lawyer) abogado/a; A~ General (BRIT) n Presidente m del Consejo del Poder Judicial (SP); (US) n ministro de justicia

attract [ə'trækt] vt atraer; (sb's attention) llamar; ~ion [ə'trækʃən] n encanto; (gen pl: amusements) diversiones fpl; (PHYSICS) atracción f; (fig: towards sb, sth) atractivo; ~ive adj guapo; (interesting) atrayente

attribute [n 'ætrɪbjuːt, vb ə'trɪbjuːt] n atributo ♦ vt: to ~ sth to atribuir algo a

attrition [ə'trɪʃən] n: war of ~ guerra de agotamiento

aubergine ['əʊbəʒiːn] (BRIT) n berenjena f; (colour) morado

auburn ['ɔːbən] adj color castaño rojizo

auction ['ɔːkʃən] n (also: sale by ~) subasta ♦ vt subastar; ~eer [-'nɪə*] n subastador/a m/f

audible ['ɔːdɪbl] adj audible, que se puede oír

audience ['ɔːdɪəns] n público; (RADIO,

radioescuchas mpl; (TV) telespectadores mpl; (interview) audiencia

audio-visual ['ɔːdɪəʊ'vɪzjuəl] adj audiovisual; ~ aid n ayuda audiovisual

audit ['ɔːdɪt] vt revisar, intervenir

audition [ɔː'dɪʃən] n audición f

auditor ['ɔːdɪtə*] n interventor(a) m/f, censor(a) m/f de cuentas

augment [ɔːg'ment] vt aumentar

augur ['ɔːgə*] vi: it ~s well es un buen augurio

August ['ɔːgəst] n agosto

aunt [ɑːnt] n tía; ~ie n diminutive of aunt; ~y n diminutive of aunt

au pair ['əʊ'peə*] n (also: ~ girl) (chica) au pair f

auspicious [ɔːs'pɪʃəs] adj propicio, de buen augurio

Australia [ɔs'treɪlɪə] n Australia; ~n adj, n australiano/a m/f

Austria ['ɒstrɪə] n Austria; ~n adj, n austríaco/a m/f

authentic [ɔː'θentɪk] adj auténtico

author ['ɔːθə*] n autor(a) m/f

authoritarian [ɔːθɒrɪ'teərɪən] adj autoritario

authoritative [ɔː'θɒrɪtətɪv] adj autorizado; (manner) autoritario

authority [ɔː'θɒrɪtɪ] n autoridad f; (official permission) autorización f; the authorities npl las autoridades

authorize ['ɔːθəraɪz] vt autorizar

auto ['ɔːtəʊ] (US) n coche m (SP), carro (AM), automóvil m

auto: ~biography [ɔːtəbaɪ'ɒgrəfɪ] n autobiografía; ~graph ['ɔːtəgraːf] n autógrafo ♦ vt (photo etc) dedicar; (programme) firmar; ~mated ['ɔːtəmeɪtɪd] adj automatizado; ~matic [ɔːtə'mætɪk] adj automático ♦ n (gun) pistola automática; (car) coche m automático; ~matically adv automáticamente; ~mation [ɔːtə'meɪʃən] n reconversión f; ~mobile [ɔːtəmə'biːl] (US) n coche m (SP), carro (AM), automóvil m; ~nomy [ɔː'tɒnəmɪ] n autonomía

autumn ['ɔ:təm] n otoño
auxiliary [ɔ:g'zɪlɪərɪ] adj, n auxiliar m/f
avail [ə'veɪl] vt: to ~ o.s. of aprovechar(se) de ♦ n: to no ~ en vano, sin resultado
available [ə'veɪləbl] adj disponible; (unoccupied) libre; (person: unattached) soltero y sin compromiso
avalanche ['ævəlɑ:nʃ] n alud m, avalancha
avant-garde ['ævɑ̃'gɑ:d] adj de vanguardia
Ave. abbr = **avenue**
avenge [ə'vendʒ] vt vengar
avenue ['ævənju:] n avenida; (fig) camino
average ['ævərɪdʒ] n promedio, término medio ♦ adj medio, de término medio; (ordinary) regular, corriente ♦ vt sacar un promedio de; **on ~** por regla general; **~ out** vi: to **~ out at** salir en un promedio de
averse [ə'vɜ:s] adj: **to be ~ to sth/doing** sentir aversión o antipatía por algo/por hacer
avert [ə'vɜ:t] vt prevenir; (blow) desviar; (one's eyes) apartar
aviary ['eɪvɪərɪ] n pajarera, avería
avocado [ævə'kɑ:dəu] n (also: BRIT: ~ pear) aguacate m (SP), palta (AM)
avoid [ə'vɔɪd] vt evitar, eludir
await [ə'weɪt] vt esperar, aguardar
awake [ə'weɪk] (pt awoke, pp awoken or awaked) adj despierto ♦ vt despertar ♦ vi despertarse; **to be ~** estar despierto; **~ning** n el despertar
award [ə'wɔ:d] n premio; (LAW: damages) indemnización f ♦ vt otorgar, conceder; (LAW: damages) adjudicar
aware [ə'weə*] adj: ~ (of) consciente (de); **to become ~ of/that** (realize) darse cuenta de/de que; (learn) enterarse de/de que; (learn) **~ness** n conciencia; (knowledge) conocimiento
awash [ə'wɒʃ] adj ~ (with) inundado (de)
away [ə'weɪ] adv fuera; (movement): **she went ~** se marchó; (far ~) lejos; **two kilometres ~** a dos kilómetros

de distancia; **two hours ~ by car** a dos horas en coche; **the holiday was two weeks ~** faltaban dos semanas para las vacaciones; **he's ~ for a week** estará ausente una semana; **to take ~ (from)** quitar a(x); (subtract) substraer (de); **to work/pedal ~** seguir trabajando/pedaleando; **to fade ~** (colour) desvanecerse; (sound) apagarse; **~ game** n (SPORT) partido de fuera
awe [ɔ:] n admiración f respetuosa; **~-inspiring** adj imponente
awful ['ɔ:fəl] adj horroroso; (quantity): **an ~ lot (of)** cantidad (de); **~ly** adv (very) terriblemente
awkward ['ɔ:kwəd] adj desmañado, torpe; (shape) incómodo; (embarrassing) delicado, difícil
awning ['ɔ:nɪŋ] n (of tent, caravan, shop) toldo
awoke [ə'wəuk] pt of awake
awoken [ə'wəukən] pp of awake
awry [ə'raɪ] adv: **to be ~** estar descolocado o mal puesto
axe [æks] (US **ax**) n hacha ♦ vt (project) cortar; (jobs) reducir
axes ['æksi:z] npl of axis
axis ['æksɪs] (pl axes) n eje m
axle ['æksl] n eje m, árbol m
ay(e) [aɪ] excl sí

B, b

B [bi:] n (MUS) si m
B.A. abbr = **Bachelor of Arts**
baby ['beɪbɪ] n bebé m/f; (US: inf: darling) mi amor; **~ carriage** n (US) cochecito; **~-sit** vi hacer de canguro; **~-sitter** n canguro/a; **~ wipe** n toallita húmeda (para bebés)
bachelor ['bætʃələ*] n soltero; **B~ of Arts/Science** licenciado/a en Filosofía y Letras/Ciencias
back [bæk] n (of person) espalda; (of animal) lomo; (of hand) dorso; (as

opposed to front) parte f de atrás; (*of chair*) respaldo; (*of page*) reverso; (*of book*) final m; (FOOTBALL) defensa m; (*of crowd*): **the ones at the ~** los del fondo ♦ vt (*candidate: also: ~ up*) respaldar, apoyar; (*horse: at races*) apostar a; (*car*) dar marcha atrás a or con ♦ vi (*car etc*) ir (or salir or entrar) marcha atrás ♦ adj (*payment, rent*) atrasado; (*seats, wheels*) de atrás ♦ adv (*not forward*) (hacia) atrás; (*returned*): **he's ~** está de vuelta, ha vuelto; **he ran ~** volvió corriendo; (*restitution*): **throw the ball ~** devuelve la pelota; **can I have it ~?** ¿me lo devuelve?; (*again*): **he called ~** llamó de nuevo; **~ down** vi echarse atrás; **~ out** vi (*of promise*) volverse atrás; **~ up** vt (*person*) apoyar, respaldar; (*theory*) defender; (COMPUT) hacer una copia preventiva or de reserva; **~bencher** n (BRIT) miembro del parlamento sin cargo relevante; **~bone** n columna vertebral; **~date** vt (*pay rise*) dar efecto retroactivo a; (*letter*) poner fecha atrasada a; **~drop** n telón m de fondo; **~fire** vi (AUT) petardear; (*plans*) fallar, salir mal; **~ground** n fondo; (*of events*) antecedentes mpl; (*basic knowledge*) bases fpl; (*experience*) conocimientos mpl, educación f; **~ family ~ground** origen m, antecedentes mpl; **~hand** n (TENNIS: also: **~hand stroke**) revés m; **~hander** n (BRIT) (*bribe*) soborno; **~ing** n (*fig*) apoyo, respaldo; **~lash** n reacción f; **~log** n: **~log of work** trabajo atrasado; **~ number** n (*of magazine etc*) número atrasado; **~pack** n mochila; **~packer** n mochilero(a); **~ pay** n pago atrasado; **~side** (*inf*) n trasero, culo; **~stage** adv entre bastidores; **~stroke** n espalda; **~up** adj suplementario; (*support*) de reserva ♦ n (*support*) apoyo; (*also: ~up file*) copia preventiva or de reserva; **~ward** adj (*person, country*) atrasado; **~wards** adv hacia atrás; (*read a list*) al revés;

(*fall*) de espaldas; **~yard** n traspatio

bacon ['beɪkən] n tocino, beicon m

bad [bæd] adj malo; (*mistake, accident*) grave; (*food*) podrido, pasado; **his ~ leg** su pierna lisiada; **to go ~** (*food*) pasarse

badge [bædʒ] n insignia; (*policeman's*) chapa, placa

badger ['bædʒə*] n tejón m

badly ['bædlɪ] adv mal; **to reflect ~ on sb** influir negativamente en la reputación de uno; **~ wounded** gravemente herido; **he needs it ~** le hace gran falta; **to be ~ off (for money)** andar mal de dinero

badminton ['bædmɪntn] n bádminton m

bad-tempered adj de mal genio o carácter; (*temporarily*) de mal humor

bag [bæg] n bolsa; (*handbag*) bolso; (*satchel*) mochila; (*case*) maleta; **~s of** (*inf*) un montón de; **~gage** n equipaje m; **~gage allowance** n límite m de equipaje; **~gage reclaim** n recogida de equipajes; **~gy** adj amplio; **~pipes** npl gaita

Bahamas [bə'hɑːməz] npl: **the ~** las Islas Bahamas

bail [beɪl] n fianza ♦ vt (*prisoner: gen: grant ~ to*) poner en libertad bajo fianza; (*boat: also: ~ out*) achicar; **on ~** (*prisoner*) bajo fianza; **to ~ sb out** obtener la libertad de uno bajo fianza; *see also* **bale**

bailiff ['beɪlɪf] n alguacil m

bait [beɪt] n cebo ♦ vt poner cebo en; (*tease*) tomar el pelo a

bake [beɪk] vt cocer (al horno) ♦ vi cocerse; **~d beans** npl judías fpl en salsa de tomate; **~d potato** n patata al horno; **~r** n panadero; **~ry** n panadería; (*for cakes*) pastelería; **baking** (COMPUT) al amasar m; (*batch*) hornada; **baking powder** n levadura (en polvo)

balance ['bæləns] n equilibrio; (COMM: *sum*) balance m; (*remainder*) resto;

balcony ['bælkənɪ] n (open) balcón m ▸ (closed) galería; (in theatre) anfiteatro
bald [bɔːld] adj calvo; (tyre) liso
bale [beɪl] n (AGR) paca, fardo; (of papers etc) fajo; ~ **out** vi lanzarse en paracaídas
Balearics [bælɪˈærɪks] npl: the ~ las Baleares
ball [bɔːl] n pelota; (football) balón m; (of wool, string) ovillo; (dance) baile m; **to play** ~ (fig) cooperar
ballast ['bæləst] n lastre m
ballerina [bælə'riːnə] n bailarina
ballet ['bæleɪ] n ballet m; ~ **dancer** n bailarín/ina m/f
balloon [bə'luːn] n globo
ballot ['bælət] n votación f; ~ **paper** n papeleta (para votar)
ballpoint (pen) ['bɔːlpɔɪnt-] n bolígrafo
ballroom ['bɔːlrʊm] n salón m de baile
Baltic ['bɔːltɪk] n: the ~ (Sea) el (Mar) Báltico
ban [bæn] n prohibición f, proscripción f ▸ vt prohibir, proscribir
banal [bə'nɑːl] adj banal, vulgar
banana [bə'nɑːnə] n plátano (SP), banana (AM)
band [bænd] n grupo; (strip) faja, tira; (stripe) lista; (MUS: jazz) orquesta; (: rock) grupo; (: MIL) banda; ~ **together** vi juntarse, asociarse
bandage ['bændɪdʒ] n venda, vendaje m ▸ vt vendar
Bandaid ® ['bændeɪd] n (US) n tirita
bandit ['bændɪt] n bandido
bandy-legged ['bændɪ'legd] adj estevado
bang [bæŋ] n (of gun, exhaust)

estallido, detonación f; (of door) portazo; (blow) golpe m ▸ vt (door) cerrar de golpe; (one's head) golpear ▸ vi estallar; (door) cerrar de golpe
Bangladesh [bɑːŋglə'deʃ] n Bangladesh m
bangs [bæŋz] n (US) npl flequillo
banish ['bænɪʃ] vt desterrar
banister(s) ['bænɪstə(z)] n(pl) barandilla, pasamanos m inv
bank [bæŋk] n (COMM) banco; (of river, lake) ribera, orilla; (of earth) terraplén m ▸ vi (AVIAT) ladearse; ~ **on** vt fus contar con; ~ **account** n cuenta de banco; ~ **card** n tarjeta bancaria; ~**er** n banquero; ~**er's card** (BRIT) n = ~ **card**; **B~ holiday** (BRIT) n día m festivo; ~**ing** n banca; ~**note** n billete m de banco; ~ **rate** n tipo de interés bancario

---

| **bank holiday** |

En el término bank holiday se aplica en el Reino Unido a todo día festivo oficial en el que cierran bancos y comercios. Los más importantes son en Navidad, Semana Santa, finales de mayo y finales de agosto y, al contrario que en los países de tradición católica, no coinciden necesariamente con una celebración religiosa.

---

bankrupt ['bæŋkrʌpt] adj quebrado, insolvente; **to go** ~ hacer bancarrota; **to be** ~ estar en quiebra; ~**cy** n quiebra
bank statement n balance m or detalle m de cuenta
banner ['bænə*] n pancarta
bannister(s) ['bænɪstə(z)] n(pl) = **banister(s)**
baptism ['bæptɪzəm] n bautismo; (act) bautizo
bar [bɑː*] n (pub) bar m; (counter) mostrador m; (rod) barra; (of window, cage) reja; (of soap) pastilla; (of

chocolate) tableta; (fig: hindrance)
obstáculo; (prohibition) proscripción f;
(MUS) barra ♦ vt (road) excluir;
(person) excluir; (activity) prohibir; the
B~ (LAW) la abogacía; behind ~s
entre rejas; ~ none sin excepción

barbaric [baː'bærɪk] adj bárbaro

barbecue ['baːbɪkjuː] n barbacoa

barbed wire ['baːbd-] n alambre m de
púas

barber ['baːbə*] n peluquero, barbero

bar code n código de barras

bare [bɛə*] adj (trees) sin
hojas; (necessities etc) básico ♦ vt
desnudar; (teeth) enseñar; **~back** adv a
pelo, sin silla; **~faced** adj descarado;
~foot adj, adv descalzo; **~ly** adv
apenas

bargain ['baːgɪn] n pacto, negocio;
(good buy) ganga ♦ vi negociar;
(haggle) regatear; **into the** ~ además,
por añadidura; ~ **for** vt fus: **he got
more than he ~ed for** le resultó peor
de lo que esperaba

barge [baːdʒ] n barcaza; ~ **in** vi
irrumpir; (interrupt: conversation)
interrumpir

bark [baːk] n (of tree) corteza; (of dog)
ladrido ♦ vi ladrar

barley ['baːlɪ] n cebada

barmaid ['baːmeɪd] n camarera

barman ['baːmən] n camarero,
barman m

barn [baːn] n granero

barometer [bə'rɒmɪtə*] n barómetro

baron ['bærən] n barón m; (press - etc)
magnate m; **~ess** n baronesa

barracks ['bærəks] npl cuartel m

barrage ['bæraːʒ] n (MIL) descarga,
bombardeo; (dam) presa; (of criticism)
lluvia, aluvión m

barrel ['bærəl] n barril m; (of gun)
cañón m

barren ['bærən] adj estéril

barricade [bærɪ'keɪd] n barricada

barrier ['bærɪə*] n barrera

barring ['baːrɪŋ] prep excepto, salvo

barrister ['bærɪstə*] (BRIT) n abogado/
a

barrow ['bærəu] n (cart) carretilla (de
mano)

bartender ['baːtendə*] (US) n
camarero, barman m

barter ['baːtə*] vt: **to ~ sth for sth**
trocar algo por algo

base [beɪs] n base ♦ vt: **to ~ sth on**
basar o fundar algo en ♦ adj bajo,
infame

baseball ['beɪsbɔːl] n béisbol m

basement ['beɪsmənt] n sótano

bases¹ ['beɪsiːz] npl of **basis**

bases² ['beɪsɪz] npl of **base**

bash [bæʃ] (inf) vt golpear

bashful ['bæʃful] adj tímido,
vergonzoso

basic ['beɪsɪk] adj básico; **~ally** adv
fundamentalmente, en el fondo;
(simply) sencillamente; **~s** npl: **the ~s**
los fundamentos

basil ['bæzl] n albahaca

basin ['beɪsn] n cuenco, tazón m; (GEO)
cuenca; (also: wash~) lavabo

basis ['beɪsɪs] (pl **bases**) n base f; **on a
part-time/trial** ~ a tiempo parcial/a
prueba

bask [baːsk] vi: **to ~ in the sun** tomar
el sol

basket ['baːskɪt] n cesta, cesto;
canasta; **~ball** n baloncesto

Basque [bæsk] adj, n vasco/a m/f;
~ Country n Euskadi m, País m Vasco

bass [beɪs] n (MUS: instrument) bajo;
(double ~) contrabajo; (singer) bajo

bassoon [bə'suːn] n fagot m

bastard ['baːstəd] n bastardo; (inf!)
hijo de puta (!)

bat [bæt] n (ZOOL) murciélago; (for ball
games) palo; (BRIT: for table tennis) pala
♦ vt: **he didn't ~ an eyelid** ni
pestañeó

batch [bætʃ] n (of bread) hornada; (of
letters etc) lote m

bated ['beɪtɪd] adj: **with ~ breath** sin
respirar

bath [bɑːθ, pl bɑːðz] n (action) baño;
(~tub) baño (SP), bañera (AM) ♦ vt bañar; **to have a ~** bañarse,
tomar un baño; see also **baths**

bathe [beɪð] vi bañarse ♦ vt (wound)
lavar; **~r** n bañista m/f

bathing ['beɪðɪŋ] n el bañarse;
~ costume (US = **suit**) n traje m de
baño

bath: ~robe n (man's) batín m;
(woman's) bata; **~room** n (cuarto de)
baño; **~s** [bɑːðz] npl (also: **swimming
~s**) piscina; **~ towel** n toalla de baño

baton ['bætən] n (MUS) batuta;
(ATHLETICS) testigo; (weapon) porra

batter ['bætə*] vt maltratar; (subj: rain
etc) azotar ♦ n masa (para rebozar);
~ed adj (hat, pan) estropeado

battery ['bætərɪ] n (AUT) batería; (of
torch) pila

battle ['bætl] n batalla, (fig) lucha ♦ vi
luchar; **~ship** n acorazado

bawl [bɔːl] vi chillar, gritar; (child)
berrear

bay [beɪ] n (GEO) bahía; **B~ of Biscay**
n mar Cantábrico; **to hold sb at ~**
mantener a alguien a raya; **~ leaf** n
hoja de laurel

bay window n ventana salediza

bazaar [bə'zɑː*] n bazar m; (fete) venta
con fines benéficos

B. & B. n abbr (= bed and breakfast)
cama y desayuno

BBC n abbr (= British Broadcasting
Corporation) cadena de radio y televisión
estatal británica

B.C. adv abbr (= before Christ) a. de C.

KEYWORD

be [biː] (pt was, were, pp been) aux
vb 1 (with present participle: forming
continuous tenses): **what are you
doing?** ¿qué estás haciendo?; **they're
coming tomorrow** vienen mañana; **I've
been waiting for you for hours** llevo horas
esperándote

2 (with pp: forming passives) ser (but
often replaced by active or reflective
constructions); **to ~ murdered** ser
asesinado; **the box had been
opened** habían abierto la caja; **the
thief was nowhere to ~ seen** no se
veía al ladrón por ninguna parte

3 (in tag questions): **it was fun,
wasn't it?** fue divertido, ¿no? or
¿verdad?; **he's good-looking, isn't
he?** es guapo, ¿no te parece?; **she's
back again, is she?** entonces, ¿ha
vuelto?

4 (+ to + infin): **the house is to
~ sold** (necessity) hay que vender la
casa; (future) van a vender la casa;
he's not to open it no tiene que
abrirlo

♦ vb + complement 1 (with n or num
complement, but see also 3, 4, 5 and
impers vb below) ser; **I'm a doctor** es
médico; **2 and 2 are 4** 2 y 2 son 4

2 (with adj complement: expressing
permanent or inherent quality) ser;
(: expressing state seen as temporary or
reversible) estar; **I'm English** soy
inglés/esa; **she's tall/pretty** es alta/
bonita; **he's young** es joven;
~ careful/good/quiet ten cuidado/
pórtate bien/cállate; **I'm tired** estoy
cansado/a; **it's dirty** está sucio/a

3 (of health) estar; **how are you?**
¿cómo estás?; **he's very ill** está muy
enfermo; **I'm better now** ya estoy
mejor

4 (of age) tener; **how old are you?**
¿cuántos años tienes?; **I'm sixteen
(years old)** tengo dieciséis años

5 (cost) costar; ser; **how much was
the meal?** ¿cuánto fue or costó la
comida?; **that'll ~ £5.75, please** son
£5.75, por favor; **this shirt is £17**
esta camisa cuesta £17

♦ vi 1 (exist, occur etc) existir, haber;
the best singer that ever was el
mejor cantante que existió jamás; **is
there a God?** ¿hay un Dios?; ¿existe

Dios?; ~ **that as it may** sea como sea; **so** ~ **it** así sea

2 (*referring to place*) estar; **I won't** ~ **here tomorrow** no estaré aquí mañana

3 (*referring to movement*): **where have you been?** ¿dónde has estado?

4 *impers vb* **1** (*referring to time*): **it's 5 o'clock** son las 5; **it's the 28th of April** estamos a 28 de abril

2 (*referring to distance*): **it's 10 km to the village** el pueblo está a 10 km

3 (*referring to the weather*): **it's too hot/cold** hace demasiado calor/frío; **it's windy today** hace viento hoy

4 (*emphatic*): **it's me** soy yo; **it was Maria who paid the bill** fue María la que pagó la cuenta

beach [biːtʃ] *n* playa ♦ *vt* varar
beacon ['biːkən] *n* (*lighthouse*) faro; (*marker*) guía
bead [biːd] *n* cuenta; (*of sweat etc*) gota
beak [biːk] *n* pico
beaker ['biːkə*] *n* vaso de plástico
beam [biːm] *n* (*ARCH*) viga, travesaño ♦ (*of light*) rayo, haz *m* de luz ♦ *vi* brillar; (*smile*) sonreír
bean [biːn] *n* judía; **runner/broad ~** habichuela/haba; **coffee ~** grano de café; **~sprouts** *npl* brotes *mpl* de soja
bear [bɛə*] (*pt* **bore**, *pp* **borne**) *n* oso ♦ *vt* (*weight etc*) llevar; (*cost*) pagar; (*responsibility*) tener; (*endure*) soportar, aguantar; (*children*) parir, tener; (*fruit*) dar ♦ *vi*: **to ~ right/left** torcer a la derecha/izquierda; **~ out** *vt* (*suspicions*) corroborar, confirmar; (*person*) dar la razón a; **~ up** *vi* (*remain cheerful*) mantenerse animado
beard [bɪəd] *n* barba; **~ed** *adj* con barba, barbudo
bearer ['bɛərə*] *n* portador/a *m/f*
bearing ['bɛərɪŋ] *n* porte *m*, comportamiento; (*connection*) relación

f; **~s** *npl* (*also*: **ball ~s**) cojinetes *mpl* a bolas; **to take a ~** tomar marcaciones; **to find one's ~s** orientarse
beast [biːst] *n* bestia; (*inf*) bruto, salvaje *m*; **~ly** (*inf*) *adj* horrible
beat [biːt] (*pt* **beat**, *pp* **beaten**) *n* (*of heart*) latido; (*MUS*) ritmo, compás *m*; (*of policeman*) ronda ♦ *vt* pegar, golpear; (*eggs*) batir; (*defeat: opponent*) vencer, derrotar; (*: record*) sobrepasar ♦ *vi* (*heart*) latir; (*drum*) redoblar; (*rain, wind*) azotar; **off the ~en track** aislado; **to ~ it** (*inf*) largarse; **~ off** *vt* rechazar; **~ up** *vt* (*attack*) dar una paliza a; **~ing** *n* paliza
beautiful ['bjuːtɪful] *adj* precioso, hermoso, bello; **~ly** *adv* maravillosamente
beauty ['bjuːtɪ] *n* belleza; **~ salon** *n* salón *m* de belleza; **~ spot** *n* (*TOURISM*) lugar *m* pintoresco
beaver ['biːvə*] *n* castor *m*
became [bɪ'keɪm] *pt of* **become**
because [bɪ'kɒz] *conj* porque; **~ of** debido a, a causa de
beckon ['bɛkən] *vt* (*also*: **~ to**) llamar con señas
become [bɪ'kʌm] (*irreg*: *like* **come**) *vt* (*suit*) favorecer, sentar bien a ♦ *vi* (+ *n*) hacerse, llegar a ser; (+ *adj*) ponerse, volverse; **~ fat** engordar
becoming [bɪ'kʌmɪŋ] *adj* (*behaviour*) decoroso; (*clothes*) favorecedor/a
bed [bɛd] *n* cama; (*of flowers*) macizo; (*of coal, clay*) capa; (*of river*) lecho; (*of sea*) fondo; **to go to ~** acostarse; **~ and breakfast** *n* (*place*) pensión *f*; (*terms*) cama y desayuno; **~clothes** *npl* ropa de cama; **~ding** *n* ropa de cama

Bed and Breakfast

Se llama Bed and Breakfast a una forma de alojamiento, en el campo o la ciudad, que ofrece cama y desayuno a precios inferiores a los de un hotel. El servicio se suele anunciar

con carteles en los que a menudo se usa
únicamente la abreviatura B. & B.

bedraggled [br'drægld] adj (untidy:
person) desastrado; (clothes, hair)
desordenado

bed: ~ridden adj postrado (en cama);
~**room** n dormitorio; ~**side** n: at the
~**side of** a la cabecera de; ~**sit(ter)**
(BRIT) n estudio (SP), suite m (AM);
~**spread** n cubrecama m, colcha;
~**time** n hora de acostarse

bee [bi:] n abeja

beech [bi:tʃ] n haya

beef [bi:f] n carne f de vaca; **roast** ~
rosbif m; ~**burger** n hamburguesa;
B~eater n alabardero de la Torre de
Londres

beehive ['bi:haɪv] n colmena

beeline ['bi:laɪn] n: to make a ~ for
ir derecho a

been [bi:n] pp of **be**

beer [bɪə*] n cerveza

beet [bi:t] (US) n (also: red ~)
remolacha

beetle ['bi:tl] n escarabajo

beetroot ['bi:tru:t] (BRIT) n remolacha

before [bɪ'fɔ:*] prep (of time) antes de;
(of space) delante de ♦ conj antes (de)
que ♦ adv antes, anteriormente;
delante, adelante; ~ **going** antes de
marcharse; ~ **she goes** antes de que
se vaya; **the week** ~ la semana
anterior; **I've never seen it** ~ no lo
he visto nunca; ~**hand** adv de
antemano, con anticipación

beg [beg] vi pedir limosna ♦ vt pedir,
rogar; (entreat) suplicar; **to ~ sb to do
sth** rogar a uno que haga algo; see
also **pardon**

began [bɪ'gæn] pt of **begin**

beggar ['begə*] n mendigo/a

begin [bɪ'gɪn] (pt **began**, pp **begun**)
vt, vi empezar, comenzar; **to ~ doing
or to do sth** empezar a hacer algo;
~**ner** n principiante m/f; ~**ning** n
principio, comienzo

begun [bɪ'gʌn] pp of **begin**

behalf [bɪ'hɑ:f] n: on ~ of en nombre
de, por; (for benefit of) en beneficio de;
on my/his ~ por mí/él

behave [bɪ'heɪv] vi (person) portarse,
comportarse; (well: also: ~ o.s.)
portarse bien; **behaviour** (US
behavior) n comportamiento,
conducta

behind [bɪ'haɪnd] prep detrás de;
(supporting): **to be ~ sb** apoyar a
alguien ♦ adv detrás, por detrás, atrás
♦ n trasero; **to be ~ (schedule)** ir
retrasado; ~ **the scenes** (fig) entre
bastidores

behold [bɪ'həuld] (irreg: like **hold**) vt
contemplar

beige [beɪʒ] adj color beige

Beijing [beɪ'dʒɪŋ] n Pekín m

being ['bi:ɪŋ] n ser m; (existence): **in ~**
existente; **to come into ~** aparecer

Beirut [beɪ'ru:t] n Beirut m

Belarus [bɛlə'rus] n Bielorrusia

belated [bɪ'leɪtɪd] adj atrasado, tardío

belch [bɛltʃ] vi eructar ♦ vt (gen: ~ out:
smoke etc) arrojar

Belgian ['bɛldʒən] adj, n belga m/f

Belgium ['bɛldʒəm] n Bélgica

belief [bɪ'li:f] n opinión f; (faith) fe f

believe [bɪ'li:v] vt, vi creer; **to ~ in**
creer en; ~**r** n partidario/a; (REL)
creyente m/f, fiel m/f

belittle [bɪ'lɪtl] vt quitar importancia a

bell [bɛl] n campana; (small)
campanilla; (on door) timbre m

belligerent [bɪ'lɪdʒərənt] adj agresivo

bellow ['bɛləu] vi bramar; (person)
rugir

belly ['bɛlɪ] n barriga, panza

belong [bɪ'lɒŋ] vi: **to ~ to** pertenecer
a; (club etc) ser socio de; **this book ~s
here** este libro va aquí; ~**ings** npl
pertenencias fpl

beloved [bɪ'lʌvɪd] adj querido/a

below [bɪ'ləu] prep bajo, debajo de;
(less than) inferior a ♦ adv abajo, (por)
debajo; see ~ véase más abajo

belt [bɛlt] n cinturón m; (TECH) correa, cinta ♦ vt (thrash) pegar con correa; **~way** (US) n (AUT) carretera de circunvalación

bench [bɛntʃ] n banco; (BRIT: POL): **the Government/Opposition ~es** (los asientos de) los miembros del Gobierno/de la Oposición; **the B~** (LAW: judges) magistratura

bend [bɛnd] (pt, pp bent) vt doblar ♦ vi inclinarse ♦ n (BRIT: in road, river) curva; (in pipe) codo; **~ down** vi inclinarse, doblarse; **~ over** vi inclinarse

beneath [bɪ'niːθ] prep bajo, debajo de; (unworthy of) indigno de ♦ adv abajo, (por) debajo

benefactor ['bɛnɪfæktə*] n bienhechor m

beneficial [bɛnɪ'fɪʃəl] adj beneficioso

benefit ['bɛnɪfɪt] n beneficio; (allowance of money) subsidio ♦ vt beneficiar ♦ vi: **he'll ~ from it** le sacará provecho

benevolent [bɪ'nɛvələnt] adj (person) benévolo

benign [bɪ'naɪn] adj benigno; (smile) afable

bent [bɛnt] pt, pp of **bend** ♦ n inclinación f ♦ adj: **to be ~ on** estar empeñado en

bequest [bɪ'kwɛst] n legado

bereaved [bɪ'riːvd] npl: **the ~** los íntimos de una persona afligidos por su muerte

beret ['bɛreɪ] n boina

Berlin [bəː'lɪn] n Berlín

berm [bəːm] (US) n (AUT) arcén m

Bermuda [bəː'mjuːdə] n las Bermudas

berry ['bɛrɪ] n baya

berserk [bə'səːk] adj: **to go ~** perder los estribos

berth [bəːθ] n (bed) litera; (cabin) camarote m; (for ship) amarradero ♦ vi atracar, amarrar

beseech [bɪ'siːtʃ] (pt, pp besought) vt suplicar

beset [bɪ'sɛt] (pt, pp beset) vt (person) acosar

beside [bɪ'saɪd] prep junto a, al lado de; **to be ~ o.s. with anger** estar fuera de sí; **that's ~ the point** eso no tiene nada que ver; **~s** adv además ♦ prep además de

besiege [bɪ'siːdʒ] vt sitiar; (fig) asediar

best [bɛst] adj (el/la) mejor ♦ adv (lo) mejor; **the ~ part of** (quantity) la mayor parte de los; **at ~** en el mejor de los casos; **to make the ~ of sth** sacar el mejor partido de algo; **to do one's ~** hacer todo lo posible; **to the ~ of my knowledge** que yo sepa; **to the ~ of my ability** como mejor puedo; **~-before date** n fecha de consumo preferente; **~ man** n padrino de boda

bestow [bɪ'stəʊ] vt (title) otorgar

bestseller [bɛst'sɛlə*] n éxito de librería, bestseller m

bet [bɛt] (pt, pp bet or betted) n apuesta ♦ vt: **to ~ money on** apostar dinero por; **to ~ sb sth** apostar algo a uno ♦ vi apostar

betray [bɪ'treɪ] vt traicionar; (trust) faltar a; **~al** n traición f

better ['bɛtə*] adj, adv mejor ♦ vt superar ♦ n: **to get the ~ of sb** quedar por encima de alguien; **you had ~ do it** más vale que lo hagas; **he thought ~ of it** cambió de parecer; **to get ~** (MED) mejorar(se); **~ off** adj (wealthier) más acomodado

betting ['bɛtɪŋ] n juego, el apostar; **~ shop** (BRIT) n agencia de apuestas

between [bɪ'twiːn] prep entre ♦ adv (time) mientras tanto; (place) en medio

beverage ['bɛvərɪdʒ] n bebida

beware [bɪ'wɛə*] vt, vi: **to ~ (of)** tener cuidado (con); **"~ of the dog"** "perro peligroso"

bewildered [bɪ'wɪldəd] adj aturdido, perplejo

beyond [bɪ'jɔnd] prep más allá de; (past: understanding) fuera de; (after:

date) después de, más allá de; *(above)* superior a ♦ *adv (in space)* más allá; *(in time)* posteriormente; **~ doubt** fuera de toda duda; **~ repair** irreparable

bias ['baɪəs] *n (prejudice)* prejuicio, pasión *f; (preference)* predisposición *f;* **~(s)ed** *adj* parcial

bib [bɪb] *n* babero

Bible ['baɪbl] *n* Biblia

bicarbonate of soda [baɪ'kɑ:bənɪt-] *n* bicarbonato sódico

bicker ['bɪkə*] *vi* pelearse

bicycle ['baɪsɪkl] *n* bicicleta

bid [bɪd] *(pt bade or bid, pp bidden or bid) n* oferta, postura; *(in tender)* licitación *f; (attempt)* tentativa, conato ♦ *vi* hacer una oferta ♦ *vt (offer)* ofrecer; **to ~ sb good day** dar a uno los buenos días; **~der** *n:* **the highest ~der** el mejor postor; **~ding** *n (at auction)* ofertas *fpl*

bide [baɪd] *vt:* **to ~ one's time** esperar el momento adecuado

bifocals [baɪ'fəʊklz] *npl* gafas *fpl (SP)* or anteojos *mpl (AM)* bifocales

big [bɪg] *adj* grande; *(brother, sister)* mayor

bigheaded ['bɪg'hedɪd] *adj* engreído

bigot ['bɪgət] *n* fanático/a, intolerante *m/f;* **~ed** *adj* fanático, intolerante; **~ry** *n* fanatismo, intolerancia

big top *n (at circus)* carpa

bike [baɪk] *n* bici *f*

bikini [bɪ'ki:nɪ] *n* bikini *m*

bilingual [baɪ'lɪŋgwəl] *adj* bilingüe

bill [bɪl] *n* cuenta; *(invoice)* factura; *(POL)* proyecto de ley; *(US: banknote)* billete *m; (of bird)* pico; *(of show)* programa *m;* **"post no ~s"** "prohibido fijar carteles"; **to fit** or **fill the ~** *(fig)* cumplir con los requisitos; **~board** *(US) n* cartelera

billet ['bɪlɪt] *n* alojamiento

billfold ['bɪlfəʊld] *(US) n* cartera

billiards ['bɪljədz] *n* billar *m*

billion ['bɪljən] *n (BRIT)* billón *m (millón de millones); (US)* mil millones *mpl*

bimbo ['bɪmbəʊ] *(inf) n* tía buena sin seso

bin [bɪn] *n (for rubbish)* cubo *(SP)* or bote *m (AM)* de la basura; *(container)* recipiente *m*

bind [baɪnd] *(pt, pp bound) vt* atar; *(book)* encuadernar; *(oblige)* obligar ♦ *n (inf: nuisance)* lata; **~ing** *adj (contract)* obligatorio

binge [bɪndʒ] *(inf) n:* **to go on a ~** ir de juerga

bingo ['bɪŋgəʊ] *n* bingo *m*

binoculars [bɪ'nɔkjuləz] *npl* prismáticos *m*

bio... [baɪə] *prefix:* **~chemistry** *n* bioquímica; **~degradable** [baɪəʊdɪ'greɪdəbl] *adj* biodegradable; **~graphy** [baɪ'ɔgrəfɪ] *n* biografía; **~logical** [baɪə'lɔdʒɪkl] *adj* biológico; **~logy** [baɪ'ɔlədʒɪ] *n* biología

birch [bə:tʃ] *n (tree)* abedul *m*

bird [bə:d] *n* ave *f,* pájaro; *(BRIT: inf: girl)* chica; **~'s eye view** *n (aerial view)* vista de pájaro; *(overview)* visión de conjunto; **~ watcher** *n* ornitólogo/a

Biro ® ['baɪrəʊ] *n* bolígrafo

birth [bə:θ] *n* nacimiento; **to give ~ to** parir, dar a luz; **~ certificate** *n* partida de nacimiento; **~ control** *n (policy)* control *m* de natalidad; *(methods)* métodos *mpl* anticonceptivos; **~day** *n* cumpleaños *m inv* ♦ *cpd (cake, card etc)* de cumpleaños; **~place** *n* lugar *m* de nacimiento; **~ rate** *n (tasa de)* natalidad *f*

biscuit ['bɪskɪt] *(BRIT) n* galleta, bizcocho *(AM)*

bisect [baɪ'sɛkt] *vt* bisecar

bishop ['bɪʃəp] *n* obispo; *(CHESS)* alfil *m*

bit [bɪt] *pt of* **bite** ♦ *n* trozo, pedazo, pedacito; *(COMPUT)* bit *m,* bitio; *(for horse)* freno, bocado; **a ~ of** un poco de; **a ~ mad** un poco loco; **~ by ~** poco a poco

bitch [bɪtʃ] *n* perra; *(inf!: woman)* zorra *(!)*

bite [baɪt] (pt **bit**, pp **bitten**) vt, vi morder; (insect etc) picar ♦ n (insect ~) picadura; (mouthful) bocado; **to ~ one's nails** comerse las uñas; **let's have a ~ (to eat)** (inf) vamos a comer algo

bitter ['bɪtə*] adj amargo; (wind) cortante, penetrante; (battle) encarnizado ♦ n (BRIT: beer) cerveza típica británica a base de lúpulos; **~ness** n lo amargo, amargura; (anger) rencor m

bizarre [bɪ'zɑ:*] adj raro, extraño

black [blæk] adj negro; (tea, coffee) solo ♦ n color m negro; (person): **B~** Negro/a ♦ vt (BRIT: INDUSTRY) boicotear; **to give sb a ~ eye** ponerle a uno el ojo morado; **~ and blue** (bruised) amoratado; **to be in the ~** (bank account) estar en números negros; **~berry** n zarzamora; **~bird** n mirlo; **~board** n pizarra; **~ coffee** n café m solo; **~currant** n grosella negra; **~en** vt (fig) desacreditar; **~ ice** n hielo invisible en la carretera; **~leg** (BRIT) n esquirol m, rompehuelgas m inv; **~list** n lista negra; **~mail** n chantaje m ♦ vt chantajear; **~ market** n mercado negro; **~out** n (MIL) oscurecimiento; (power cut) apagón m; (TV, RADIO) interrupción f de programas; (fainting) desvanecimiento; **B~ Sea** n: **the B~ Sea** el Mar Negro; **~ sheep** n (fig) oveja negra; **~smith** n herrero; **~ spot** n (AUT) lugar m peligroso; (for unemployment etc) punto negro

bladder ['blædə*] n vejiga

blade [bleɪd] n hoja; (of propeller) paleta; **a ~ of grass** una brizna de hierba

blame [bleɪm] n culpa ♦ vt: **to ~ sb for sth** echar a uno la culpa de algo; **to be to ~** tener la culpa de

bland [blænd] adj (music, taste) soso

blank [blæŋk] adj en blanco; (look) sin expresión ♦ n (of memory): **my mind is a ~** no puedo recordar nada; (on form) blanco, espacio en blanco;

(cartridge) cartucho sin bala or de fogueo; **~ cheque** n cheque m en blanco

blanket ['blæŋkɪt] n manta (SP), cobija (AM); (of snow) capa; (of fog) manto

blare [blɛə*] vi sonar estrepitosamente

blasé ['blɑ:zeɪ] adj hastiado

blast [blɑ:st] n (of wind) ráfaga, soplo; (of explosive) explosión f ♦ vt (blow up) volar; **~-off** n (SPACE) lanzamiento

blatant ['bleɪtənt] adj descarado

blaze [bleɪz] n (fire) fuego; (fig: of colour) despliegue m; (: of glory) esplendor m ♦ vi arder en llamas; (fig) brillar ♦ vt: **to ~ a trail** (fig) abrir (un) camino; **in a ~ of publicity** con gran publicidad

blazer ['bleɪzə*] n chaqueta de uniforme de colegial o de socio de club

bleach [bli:tʃ] n (also: household ~) lejía ♦ vt blanquear; **~ed** adj (hair) teñido (de rubio); **~ers** (US) npl (SPORT) gradas fpl al sol

bleak [bli:k] adj (countryside) desierto; (prospect) poco prometedor(a); (weather) crudo; (smile) triste

bleat [bli:t] vi balar

bleed [bli:d] (pt, pp **bled**) vt, vi sangrar; **my nose is ~ing** me está sangrando la nariz

bleeper ['bli:pə*] n busca m

blemish ['blemɪʃ] n marca, mancha; (on reputation) tacha

blend [blend] n mezcla ♦ vt mezclar; (colours etc) combinar, mezclar ♦ vi (colours etc: also: ~ in) combinarse, mezclarse

bless [bles] (pt, pp **blessed** or **blest**) vt bendecir; **~ you!** (after sneeze) ¡Jesús!; **~ing** n (approval) aprobación f; (godsend) don m del cielo, bendición f; (advantage) beneficio, ventaja

blew [blu:] pt of **blow**

blind [blaɪnd] adj ciego; (fig): **(to)** ciego (a) ♦ n (for window) persiana ♦ vt cegar; (dazzle) deslumbrar; (deceive): **to ~ sb to ...** cegar a uno a ...; **the ~**

npl los ciegos; **~ alley** *n* callejón *m* sin
salida; **~ corner** *n* (BRIT) *n* esquina
escondida; **~fold** *n* venda ♦ *adv* con
los ojos vendados ♦ *vt* vendar los ojos
a; **~ly** *adv* a ciegas, ciegamente;
~ness *n* ceguera; **~ spot** *n* (AUT)
ángulo ciego

blink [blɪŋk] *vi* parpadear, pestañear;
(light) oscilar; **~ers** *npl* anteojeras *fpl*

bliss [blɪs] *n* felicidad *f*

blister ['blɪstə*] *n* ampolla ♦ *vi* (paint)
ampollarse

blizzard ['blɪzəd] *n* ventisca

bloated ['bləʊtɪd] *adj* hinchado;
(person: full) ahíto

blob [blɒb] *n* (drop) gota; (indistinct
object) bulto

bloc [blɒk] *n* (POL) bloque *m*

block [blɒk] *n* bloque *m*; (in pipes)
obstáculo; (of buildings) manzana (SP),
cuadra (AM) ♦ *vt* obstruir, cerrar;
(progress) estorbar; **~ of flats** (BRIT)
bloque *m* de pisos; **mental ~** bloqueo
mental; **~ade** [-'keɪd] *n* bloqueo ♦ *vt*
bloquear; **~age** *n* estorbo, obstrucción
f; **~buster** *n* (book) bestseller *m*; (film)
éxito de público; **~ letters** *npl* letras
fpl de molde

bloke [bləʊk] (BRIT: inf) *n* tipo, tío

blond(e) [blɒnd] *adj, n* rubio/a *m/f*

blood [blʌd] *n* sangre *f*; **~ donor** *n*
donante *m* de sangre; **~ group** *n*
grupo sanguíneo; **~hound** *n* sabueso;
~ poisoning *n* envenenamiento de la
sangre; **~ pressure** *n* presión *f*
sanguínea; **~shed** *n* derramamiento de
sangre; **~shot** *adj* inyectado en
sangre; **~stream** *n* corriente *f*
sanguínea; **~ test** *n* análisis *m inv* de
sangre; **~thirsty** *adj* sanguinario;
~ vessel *n* vaso sanguíneo; **~y** *adj*
sangriento; (nose etc) lleno de sangre;
(BRIT: inf!) **this ~y...** este ~ condenado *e*
puñetero ... (!) ♦ *adv*: **~y strong/**
good (BRIT: inf!) terriblemente fuerte/
bueno; **~y-minded** *adj* (BRIT: inf)
puñetero (!)

bloom [bluːm] *n* flor *f* ♦ *vi* florecer

blossom ['blɒsəm] *n* flor *f* ♦ *vi* (also
fig) florecer

blot [blɒt] *n* borrón *m*; (fig) mancha
♦ *vt* (stain) manchar; **~ out** *vt* (view)
tapar

blotchy ['blɒtʃɪ] *adj* (complexion) lleno
de manchas

blotting paper ['blɒtɪŋ-] *n* papel *m*
secante

blouse [blaʊz] *n* blusa

blow [bləʊ] (pt **blew**, pp **blown**) *n*
golpe *m*; (with sword) espadazo ♦ *vi*
soplar; (dust, sand etc) volar; (fuse)
fundirse ♦ *vt* (subj: wind) llevarse; (fuse)
quemar; (instrument) tocar; **to ~ one's**
nose sonarse; **~ away** *vt* llevarse,
arrancar; **~ down** *vt* derribar; **~ off** *vt*
arrebatar; **~ out** *vi* apagarse; **~ over** *vi*
amainar; **~ up** *vi* estallar ♦ *vt* volar;
(tyre) inflar; (PHOT) ampliar; **~-dry** *n*
moldeado (con secador) *m*; **~lamp** (BRIT)
n soplete *m*, lámpara de soldar; **~out**
n (of tyre) pinchazo; **~torch** *n* =
~lamp

blue [bluː] *adj* azul; (depressed)
deprimido; **~ film/joke** película/chiste
m verde; **out of the ~** (fig) de
repente; **~bell** *n* campanilla,
campánula azul; **~bottle** *n* moscarda,
mosca azul; **~print** *n* (fig)
anteproyecto

bluff [blʌf] *vi* tirarse un farol, farolear
♦ *n* farol *m*; **to call sb's ~** coger a
uno la palabra

blunder ['blʌndə*] *n* patinazo,
metedura de pata ♦ *vi* cometer un
error, meter la pata

blunt [blʌnt] *adj* (pencil) despuntado;
(knife) desafilado, romo; (person)
franco, directo

blur [bləː*] *n* (shape): **to become a ~**
hacerse borroso ♦ *vt* (vision) enturbiar;
(distinction) borrar

blush [blʌʃ] *vi* ruborizarse, ponerse
colorado ♦ *n* rubor *m*

blustery ['blʌstərɪ] *adj* (weather)

tempestuoso, tormentoso

boar [bɔ:*] n verraco, cerdo

board [bɔ:d] n (card~) cartón m; (wooden) tabla, tablero; (on wall) tablón m; (for chess etc) tablero; (committee) junta, consejo; (pres mesa or junta directiva; (NAUT, AVIAT): **on ~** a bordo ♦ vt (ship) embarcarse en; (train) subir a; **full ~** (BRIT) pensión completa; **half ~** (BRIT) media pensión; **to go by the ~** (fig) ser abandonado or olvidado; **~ up** vt (door) tapiar; **~ and lodging** n casa y comida; **~er** n (SCOL) interno/a; **~ing card** (BRIT) n tarjeta de embarque; **~ing house** n casa de huéspedes; **~ing pass** (US) n = **~ing card**; **~ing school** n internado; **~ room** n sala de juntas

boast [bəust] vi: **to ~ (about or of)** alardear (de)

boat [bəut] n barco, buque m; (small) barca, bote m

bob [bɔb] vi (also: **~ up and down**) menearse, balancearse; **~ up** vi (re)aparecer de repente

bobby [bɔbi] (BRIT: inf) n poli m

bobsleigh [bɔbslei] n bob m

bode [bəud] vi: **to ~ well/ill (for)** ser prometedor/poco prometedor (para)

bodily [bɔdili] adj corporal ♦ adv (move: person) en peso

body [bɔdi] n cuerpo; (corpse) cadáver m; (of car) caja, carrocería; (fig: group) grupo; (: organization) organismo; **~-building** n culturismo; **~guard** n guardaespaldas m inv; **~work** n carrocería

bog [bɔg] n pantano, ciénaga ♦ vt: **to get ~ged down** (fig) empantanarse, atascarse

bogus [bəugəs] adj falso, fraudulento

boil [bɔil] vt (water) hervir; (eggs) pasar por agua, cocer ♦ vi hervir; (fig: with anger) estar furioso; (: with heat) asfixiarse ♦ n (MED) furúnculo, divieso; **to come to the ~, to come to a ~** (US) comenzar a hervir; **to ~ down to**

(fig) reducirse a; **~ over** vi salirse, rebosar; (anger etc) llegar al colmo; **~ed egg** n huevo cocido (SP) or pasado (AM); **~ed potatoes** npl patatas fpl (SP) or papas fpl (AM) hervidas; **~er** n caldera; **~er suit** (BRIT) n mono; **~ing point** n punto de ebullición

boisterous [bɔistərəs] adj (noisy) bullicioso; (excitable) exuberante; (crowd) tumultuoso

bold [bəuld] adj valiente, audaz; (pej) descarado; (colour) llamativo

Bolivia [bəliviə] n Bolivia; **~n** adj, n boliviano/a m/f

bollard [bɔləd] (BRIT) n (AUT) poste m

bolt [bəult] n (lock) cerrojo; (with nut) perno, tornillo ♦ adv: **~ upright** rígido, erguido ♦ vt (door) echar el cerrojo a; (also: **~ together**) sujetar con tornillos; (food) engullir ♦ vi fugarse; (horse) desbocarse

bomb [bɔm] n bomba ♦ vt bombardear; **~ disposal** n desmontaje m de explosivos; **~er** n (AVIAT) bombardero; **~shell** n (fig) bomba

bond [bɔnd] n (promise) fianza; (FINANCE) bono; (link) vínculo, lazo; (COMM): **in ~** en depósito bajo fianza

bondage [bɔndidʒ] n esclavitud f

bone [bəun] n hueso; (of fish) espina ♦ vt deshuesar; quitar las espinas a; **~ idle** adj gandul; **~ marrow** n médula

bonfire [bɔnfaiə*] n hoguera, fogata

bonnet [bɔnit] n gorra; (BRIT: of car) capó m

bonus [bəunəs] n (payment) paga extraordinaria, plus m; (fig) bendición f

bony [bəuni] adj (arm, face) huesudo; (MED: tissue) óseo; (meat) lleno de huesos; (fish) lleno de espinas

boo [bu:] excl ¡uh! ♦ vt abuchear, rechiflar

booby trap [bu:bi-] n trampa explosiva

book [buk] n libro; (of tickets) taco; (of

burocracia

burglar ['bɜːglə*] n ladrón/ona m/f;
~ alarm n alarma f antirrobo; **~y** n
robo con allanamiento, robo de una
casa

burial ['bɛrɪəl] n entierro

burly ['bɜːlɪ] adj fornido, membrudo

Burma ['bɜːmə] n Birmania

burn [bɜːn] (pt, pp **burned** or **burnt**)
vt quemar; (house) incendiar ♦ vi
quemarse, arder; incendiarse; (sting)
escocer ♦ n quemadura f; **~ down** vt
incendiar; **~er** n (on cooker etc)
quemador m; **~ing** adj (building) en
llamas; (hot: sand etc) abrasador(a);
(ambition) ardiente

burrow ['bʌrəʊ] n madriguera f ♦ vi
hacer una madriguera; (rummage)
hurgar

bursary ['bɜːsərɪ] (BRIT) n beca

burst [bɜːst] (pt, pp **burst**) vt reventar;
(subj: river: banks etc) romper ♦ vi
reventarse; (tyre) pincharse ♦ n (of
gunfire) ráfaga; (also: ~ pipe) reventón
m; a ~ of energy/speed/
enthusiasm una explosión de
energía/un ímpetu de velocidad/un
arranque de entusiasmo; **to ~ into
flames** estallar en llamas; **to ~ into
tears** deshacerse en lágrimas; **to
~ out laughing** soltar la carcajada; **to
~ open** abrirse de golpe; **to be ~ing
with** (subj: container) estar lleno a
rebosar de; (person) reventar por or de;
~ into vt fus (room etc) irrumpir en

bury ['bɛrɪ] vt enterrar; (body) enterrar,
sepultar

bus [bʌs] (pl **~es**) n autobús m

bush [buʃ] n arbusto; (scrub land)
monte m; **to beat about the ~**
andar(se) con rodeos

bushy [buʃɪ] adj (thick) espeso,
poblado

busily ['bɪzɪlɪ] adv afanosamente

business ['bɪznɪs] n (matter) asunto;
(trading) comercio, negocios mpl; (firm)
empresa, casa; (occupation) oficio; **to**

be away on ~ estar en viaje de
negocios; **it's my ~ to ...** me toca or
corresponde a mí ...; **it's none of my ~** yo
no tengo nada que ver; **he means ~**
habla en serio; **~like** adj eficiente;
~man n hombre m de negocios; **~
trip** n viaje m de negocios;
~woman n mujer f de negocios

busker ['bʌskə*] (BRIT) n músico/a
ambulante

bus: ~ shelter n parada cubierta;
~ station n estación f de autobuses;
~stop n parada de autobús

bust [bʌst] n (ANAT) pecho; (sculpture)
busto ♦ adj (inf: broken) roto,
estropeado; **to go ~** quebrar

bustle ['bʌsl] n bullicio, movimiento
♦ vi menearse, apresurarse; **bustling**
adj (town) animado, bullicioso

busy ['bɪzɪ] adj ocupado, atareado;
(shop, street) concurrido, animado;
(TEL: line) comunicando ♦ vt: **to ~ o.s.
with** ocuparse en; **~body** n
entrometido/a; **~ signal** (US) n (TEL)
señal f de comunicando

but [bʌt] conj **1** pero; **he's not very
bright, ~ he's hard-working** no es
muy inteligente, pero es trabajador
2 (in direct contradiction) sino; **he's
not English ~ French** no es inglés
sino francés; **he didn't sing ~ he
shouted** no cantó sino que gritó
3 (showing disagreement, surprise etc):
~ that's far too expensive! ¡pero
eso es carísimo!; **~ it does work!**
¡(pero) sí que funciona!

♦ prep (apart from, except) menos,
salvo; **we've had nothing ~ trouble**
no hemos tenido más que problemas;
no-one ~ him can do it nadie más
que él puede hacerlo; **who ~ a
lunatic would do such a thing?**
¡sólo un loco haría una cosa así!; **~ for
you/your help** si no fuera por ti/tu
ayuda; **anything ~ that** cualquier

cosa menos eso
♦ adv (just, only): **she's ~ a child** no es más que una niña; **had I ~ known** si lo hubiera sabido; **I can ~ try** al menos lo puedo intentar; **it's all ~ finished** está casi acabado

butcher ['butʃə*] n carnicero ♦ vt hacer una carnicería con; (cattle etc) matar; **~'s (shop)** n carnicería

butler ['bʌtlə*] n mayordomo

butt [bʌt] n (barrel) tonel m; (of gun) culata; (of cigarette) colilla; (BRIT: fig: target) blanco ♦ vt dar cabezadas contra, top(et)ar; **~ in** vi (interrupt) interrumpir

butter ['bʌtə*] n mantequilla ♦ vt untar con mantequilla; **~cup** n botón m de oro

butterfly ['bʌtəflaɪ] n mariposa; (SWIMMING: also: **~ stroke**) braza de mariposa

buttocks ['bʌtəks] npl nalgas fpl

button ['bʌtn] n botón m; (US) placa, chapa ♦ vt (also: **~ up**) abotonar, abrochar ♦ vi abrocharse

buttress ['bʌtrɪs] n contrafuerte m

buy [baɪ] (pt, pp **bought**) vt comprar ♦ n compra; **to ~ sb sth/sth from sb** comprarle algo a alguien; **to ~ sb a drink** invitar a alguien a tomar algo; **~er** n comprador(a) m/f

buzz [bʌz] n zumbido; (inf: phone call) llamada (por teléfono) ♦ vi zumbar; **~er** n timbre m; **~ word** n palabra que está de moda

---

KEYWORD

---

by [baɪ] prep 1 (referring to cause, agent) por; **killed ~ lightning** muerto por un relámpago; **a painting ~ Picasso** un cuadro de Picasso
2 (referring to method, manner, means): **~ bus/car/train** en autobús/coche/tren; **to pay ~ cheque** pagar con un cheque; **~ moonlight/candlelight** a la luz de la luna/una vela; **~ saving**

hard, he ... ahorrando, ...
3 (via, through) por; **we came ~ Dover** vinimos por Dover
4 (close to, past) por; **the house ~ the river** la casa junto al río; **she rushed ~ me** pasó a mi lado como una exhalación; **I go ~ the post office every day** paso por delante de Correos todos los días
5 (time: not later than) para; (: during): **~ daylight** de día; **~ 4 o'clock** para las cuatro; **~ this time tomorrow** mañana a estas horas; **~ the time I got here it was too late** cuando llegué ya era demasiado tarde
6 (amount): **~ the metre/kilo** por metro/kilo; **paid ~ the hour** pagado por hora
7 (MATH, measure): **to divide/multiply ~ 3** dividir/multiplicar por 3; **a room 3 metres ~ 4** una habitación de 3 metros por 4; **it's broader ~ a metre** es un metro más ancho
8 (according to) según, de acuerdo con; **it's 3 o'clock ~ my watch** según mi reloj, son las tres; **it's all right ~ me** por mí, está bien
9: **(all) ~ oneself** etc todo solo; **he did it (all) ~ himself** lo hizo él solo; **he was standing (all) ~ himself in a corner** estaba de pie solo en un rincón
10: **~ the way** a propósito, por cierto; **this wasn't my idea, ~ the way** pues, no fue idea mía
♦ adv 1 see **go**; pass etc
2: **~ and ~** finalmente; **they'll come back ~ and ~** acabarán volviendo; **~ and large** en líneas generales, en general

bye(-bye) ['baɪ('baɪ)] excl adiós, hasta luego

by(e)-law n ordenanza municipal

by-: ~election (BRIT) n elección f parcial; **~gone** ['baɪgɔn] adj pasado, del pasado ♦ n: **let ~gones be**

~gones lo pasado, pasado está;
~pass ['baɪpɑːs] n carretera de circunvalación (MED) (operación f de) by-pass m ♦ vt evitar; **~product** n subproducto, derivado; (of situation) consecuencia; **~stander** ['baɪstændə*] n espectador(a) m/f

byte [baɪt] n (COMPUT) byte m, octeto

byword ['baɪwɜːd] n: **to be a ~ for** ser conocidísimo por

C, c

C [siː] n (MUS) do m

C. abbr (= centigrade) C.

C.A. abbr = **chartered accountant**

cab [kæb] n taxi m; (of truck) cabina

cabbage ['kæbɪdʒ] n col f, berza

cabin ['kæbɪn] n cabaña; (on ship) camarote m; (on plane) cabina; **~ crew** n tripulación f de cabina; **~ cruiser** n yate m de motor

cabinet ['kæbɪnɪt] n (POL) consejo de ministros; (furniture) armario; (also: display ~) vitrina

cable ['keɪbl] n cable m ♦ vt cablegrafiar; **~-car** n teleférico; **~ television** n televisión f por cable

cache [kæʃ] n (of arms, drugs etc) alijo

cackle ['kækl] vi lanzar risotadas; (hen) cacarear

cactus ['kæktəs] (pl **cacti**) n cacto

cadge [kædʒ] (inf) vt gorronear

Caesarean [siːˈzɛəriən] adj: **~ (section)** cesárea

café ['kæfeɪ] n café m

cafeteria [kæfɪˈtɪəriə] n cafetería

cage [keɪdʒ] n jaula

cagey ['keɪdʒɪ] (inf) adj cauteloso, reservado

cagoule [kəˈguːl] n chubasquero

cajole [kəˈdʒəʊl] vt engatusar

cake [keɪk] n (CULIN: large) tarta; (: small) pastel m; (of soap) pastilla; **~d adj: ~d with** cubierto de

calculate ['kælkjʊleɪt] vt calcular;

calculation [-'leɪʃən] n cálculo, cómputo; **calculator** n calculadora

calendar ['kæləndə*] n calendario; **~ month/year** n mes m/año civil

calf [kɑːf] (pl **calves**) n (of cow) ternero, becerro; (of other animals) cría; (also: ~skin) piel f de becerro; (ANAT) pantorrilla

calibre ['kælɪbə*] (US **caliber**) n calibre m

call [kɔːl] vt llamar; (meeting) convocar ♦ vi (shout) llamar; (TEL) llamar (por teléfono), telefonear (esp AM); (visit: also: ~ in, ~ round) hacer una visita ♦ n llamada; (of bird) canto; **to be ~ed** llamarse; **on ~** (on duty) de guardia; **~ back** vi (return) volver; (TEL) volver a llamar; **~ for** vt fus (demand) pedir, exigir; (fetch) venir por (SP), pasar por (AM); **~ off** vt (cancel: meeting, race) cancelar; (: deal) anular; (: strike) desconvocar; **~ on** vt fus (visit) visitar; (turn to) acudir a; **~ out** vi gritar; **~ up** vt (MIL) llamar al servicio militar; (TEL) llamar; **~box** n (BRIT) cabina telefónica; **~ centre** n (BRIT) centro de atención al cliente; **~er** n visita; (TEL) usuario/a; **~ girl** n prostituta; **~-in** n (US) (programa m) coloquio (por teléfono); **~ing** n vocación f; (occupation) profesión f; **~ing card** n (US) tarjeta de visita

callous ['kæləs] adj insensible, cruel

calm [kɑːm] adj tranquilo; (sea) liso, en calma ♦ n calma, tranquilidad f ♦ vt calmar, tranquilizar; **~ down** vi calmarse, tranquilizarse ♦ vt calmar, tranquilizar

Calor gas ® ['kælə*-] n butano

calorie ['kælərɪ] n caloría

calves [kɑːvz] npl of **calf**

Cambodia [kæmˈbəʊdɪə] n Camboya

camcorder ['kæmkɔːdə*] n videocámara

came [keɪm] pt of **come**

camel ['kæməl] n camello

camera ['kæmərə] n máquina fotográfica; (CINEMA, TV) cámara; **in ~** (LAW) a puerta cerrada; **~man** n cámara m

camouflage ['kæməflɑːʒ] n camuflaje m ♦ vt camuflar

camp [kæmp] n campamento, camping m; (MIL) campamento; (for prisoners) campo; (fig: faction) bando ♦ vi acampar ♦ adj afectado, afeminado

campaign [kæm'peɪn] n (MIL, POL etc) campaña ♦ vi hacer campaña

camp: **~bed** (BRIT) n cama de campaña; **~er** n campista m/f; (vehicle) caravana; **~ing** n camping m; **to go ~ing** hacer camping; **~site** n camping m

campus ['kæmpəs] n ciudad f universitaria

can¹ [kæn] n (of oil, water) bidón m; (tin) lata, bote m ♦ vt enlatar

KEYWORD

can² [kæn] (negative **cannot, can't;** conditional and pt **could**) aux vb **1** (be able to) poder; **you ~ do it if you try** puedes hacerlo si lo intentas; **I ~'t see you** no te veo

2 (know how to) saber; **I ~ swim/play tennis/drive** sé nadar/jugar al tenis/ conducir; **~ you speak French?** ¿hablas or sabes hablar francés?

3 (may) poder; **~ I use your phone?** ¿me dejas or puedo usar tu teléfono?

4 (expressing disbelief, puzzlement etc): **it ~'t be true!** ¡no puede ser (verdad)!; **what CAN he want?** ¿qué querrá?

5 (expressing possibility, suggestion etc): **he could be in the library** podría estar en la biblioteca; **she could have been delayed** pudo haberse retrasado

Canada ['kænədə] n (el) Canadá; **Canadian** [kə'neɪdɪən] adj, n canadiense m/f

canal [kə'næl] n canal m

canary [kə'neərɪ] n canario; **the C~ Islands** npl las (Islas) Canarias

cancel ['kænsəl] vt cancelar; (train) suprimir; (cross out) tachar, borrar; **~lation** [-'leɪʃən] n cancelación f; supresión f

cancer ['kænsə*] n cáncer m; **C~** (ASTROLOGY) Cáncer m

candid ['kændɪd] adj franco, abierto

candidate ['kændɪdeɪt] n candidato/a

candle ['kændl] n vela; (in church) cirio; **~light** n: **by ~light** a la luz de una vela; **~stick** n (single) candelero; (low) palmatoria; (bigger, ornate) candelabro

candour ['kændə*] (US **candor**) n franqueza

candy ['kændɪ] n azúcar m cande; (US) caramelo; **~floss** n (BRIT) algodón m (azucarado)

cane [keɪn] n (BOT) caña; (stick) vara, palmeta; (for furniture) mimbre f ♦ (BRIT) vt (SCOL) castigar (con vara)

canister ['kænɪstə*] n bote m, lata; (of gas) bombona

cannabis ['kænəbɪs] n marijuana

canned [kænd] adj en lata, de lata

cannon ['kænən] (pl ~ or ~s) n cañón m

cannot ['kænɒt] = **can not**

canoe [kə'nuː] n canoa; (SPORT) piragua; **~ing** n piragüismo

canon ['kænən] n (clergyman) canónigo; (standard) canon m

can-opener n abrelatas m inv

canopy ['kænəpɪ] n dosel m; toldo

can't [kænt] = **can not**

canteen [kæn'tiːn] n (eating place) cantina; (BRIT: of cutlery) juego

canter ['kæntə*] vi a medio galope

canvas ['kænvəs] n (material) lona; (painting) lienzo; (NAUT) velas fpl

canvass ['kænvəs] vi (POL): **to ~ for** solicitar votos por ♦ vt (COMM) sondear

canyon ['kænjən] n cañón m

cap [kæp] n (hat) gorra; (of pen) capuchón m; (of bottle) tapa, tapón m; (contraceptive) diafragma m; (for toy gun) cápsula ♦ vt (outdo) superar;

(*limit*) recortar
capability [keɪpəˈbɪlɪtɪ] *n* capacidad *f*
capable [ˈkeɪpəbl] *adj* capaz
capacity [kəˈpæsɪtɪ] *n* capacidad *f*; (*position*) calidad *f*
cape [keɪp] *n* capa; *f* (GEO) cabo *m*
caper [ˈkeɪpə*] *n* (CULIN: *gen*: ~s) alcaparra; (*prank*) broma
capital [ˈkæpɪtl] *n* (*also*: ~ *city*) capital *f*; (*money*) capital *m*; (*also*: ~ *letter*) mayúscula; ~ **gains tax** *n* impuesto sobre las ganancias de capital; **~ism** *n* capitalismo *m*; **~ist** *adj*, capitalista *m/f*; **~ize** *vt fus* aprovechar; **~ punishment** *n* pena de muerte

<table><tr><td>Capitol</td></tr></table>

El Capitolio (**Capitol**) *es el edificio del Congreso* (**Congress**) *de los Estados Unidos, situado en la ciudad de Washington. Por extensión, también se suele llamar así al edificio en el que tienen lugar las sesiones parlamentarias de la cámara de representantes de muchos de los estados.*

Capricorn [ˈkæprɪkɔːn] *n* (ASTROLOGY) Capricornio
capsize [kæpˈsaɪz] *vt* volcar, hacer zozobrar ♦ *vi* volcarse, zozobrar
capsule [ˈkæpsjuːl] *n* cápsula
captain [ˈkæptɪn] *n* capitán *m*
caption [ˈkæpʃən] *n* (*heading*) título; (*to picture*) leyenda
captive [ˈkæptɪv] *adj*, *n* cautivo/a *m/f*
capture [ˈkæptʃə*] *vt* prender, apresar; (*animal*, COMPUT) capturar; (*place*) tomar; (*attention*) captar, llamar ♦ *n* apresamiento; captura; toma; (*data* →) formulación *f* de datos
car [kɑː*] *n* coche *m*, carro (AM), automóvil *m*; (US: RAIL) vagón *m*
carafe [kəˈræf] *n* jarra
carat [ˈkærət] *n* quilate *m*
caravan [ˈkærəvæn] *n* (BRIT) caravana, ruló *f*; (*in desert*) caravana; **~ning** *n*: **to**

go ~ning ir de vacaciones en caravana, viajar en caravana; **~ site** (BRIT) *n* camping *m* para caravanas
carbohydrate [kɑːbəʊˈhaɪdreɪt] *n* hidrato de carbono; (*food*) fécula
carbon [ˈkɑːbən] *n* carbono; **~ paper** *n* papel *m* carbón
car boot sale *n* mercadillo organizado en un aparcamiento, en el que se exponen las mercancías en el maletero del coche
carburettor [kɑːbjuˈretə*] (US **carburetor**) *n* carburador *m*
card [kɑːd] *n* (*material*) cartulina; (*index* ~ *etc*) ficha; (*playing* ~) carta, naipe *m*; (*visiting* ~, *greetings* ~ *etc*) tarjeta; **~board** *n* cartón *m*, cartulina
cardiac [ˈkɑːdɪæk] *adj* cardíaco
cardigan [ˈkɑːdɪgən] *n* rebeca
cardinal [ˈkɑːdɪnl] *adj* cardinal; (*importance, principal*) esencial ♦ *n* cardenal *m*
card index *n* fichero
care [keə*] *n* cuidado; (*worry*) inquietud *f*; (*charge*) cargo, custodia ♦ *vi*: **to ~ about** (*person, animal*) tener cariño a; (*thing, idea*) preocuparse por; **to ~** **en casa de**, al cuidado de; **in sb's ~** a cargo de uno; **to take ~ to** cuidarse de, tener cuidado de; **to take ~ of** cuidar; (*problem etc*) ocuparse de; **I don't ~** no me importa; **I couldn't ~ less** eso me trae sin cuidado; **~ for** *vt fus* cuidar a; (*like*) querer
career [kəˈrɪə*] *n* profesión *f*; (*in work, school*) carrera ♦ *vi* (*also*: ~ *along*) correr a toda velocidad; **~ woman** *n* mujer *f* dedicada a su profesión
care: ~free *adj* despreocupado; **~ful** *adj* cuidadoso; (*cautious*) cauteloso; (**be**) **~ful!** ¡tenga cuidado!; **~fully** *adv* con cuidado, cuidadosamente; con cautela; **~less** *adj* descuidado; (*heedless*) poco atento; **~lessness** *n* descuido; falta de atención; **~r** [ˈkeərə*] *n* enfermero/a *m/f* (*official*); (*unpaid*) persona que cuida a un pariente o vecino

caress [kə'rɛs] n caricia ♦ vt acariciar

caretaker ['kɛəteɪkə*] n portero/a, conserje m/f

car-ferry n transbordador m para coches

cargo ['kɑ:gəu] (pl ~es) n cargamento, carga

car hire n alquiler m de automóviles

Caribbean [kærɪ'bi:ən] n: the ~ (Sea) el (Mar) Caribe

caring ['kɛərɪŋ] adj humanitario; (behaviour) afectuoso

carnation [kɑ:'neɪʃən] n clavel m

carnival ['kɑ:nɪvəl] n carnaval m; (US: funfair) parque m de atracciones

carol ['kærəl] n: (Christmas) ~ villancico

carp [kɑ:p] n (fish) carpa

car park (BRIT) n aparcamiento, parking m

carpenter ['kɑ:pɪntə*] n carpintero/a

carpet ['kɑ:pɪt] n alfombra; (fitted) moqueta ♦ vt alfombrar

car phone n teléfono móvil

car rental (US) n alquiler m de coches

carriage ['kærɪdʒ] n (BRIT: RAIL) vagón m; (horse-drawn) coche m; (of goods) transporte m; (: cost) porte m, flete m; ~way (BRIT) n (part of road) calzada

carrier ['kærɪə*] n (transport company) transportista, empresa de transportes; (MED) portador m; ~ bag (BRIT) n bolsa de papel or plástico

carrot ['kærət] n zanahoria

carry ['kærɪ] vt (subj: person) llevar; (transport) transportar; (involve: responsibilities etc) entrañar, implicar; (MED) ser portador de ♦ vi (sound) oírse; **to get carried away** (fig) entusiasmarse; ~ **on** vi (continue) seguir (adelante), continuar ♦ vt proseguir, continuar; ~ **out** vt (orders) cumplir; (investigation) llevar a cabo, realizar; ~ **cot** (BRIT) n cuna portátil; ~**on** n (inf) fuss) lío

cart [kɑ:t] n carro, carreta ♦ vt (inf: transport) acarrear

carton ['kɑ:tən] n (box) caja (de cartón); (of milk etc) bote m; (of yogurt) tarrina

cartoon [kɑ:'tu:n] n (PRESS) caricatura; (comic strip) tira cómica; (film) dibujos mpl animados

cartridge ['kɑ:trɪdʒ] n cartucho; (of pen) recambio; (of record player) cápsula

carve [kɑ:v] vt (meat) trinchar; (wood, stone) cincelar, esculpir; (initials etc) grabar; ~ **up** vt dividir, repartir; **carving** n (object) escultura; (design) talla; (art) tallado; **carving knife** n trinchante m

car wash n lavado de coches

case [keɪs] n (container) caja; (MED) caso; (for jewels etc) estuche m; (LAW) causa, proceso; (also: suit~) maleta; **in ~ of** en caso de; **in any ~** en todo caso; **just in ~** por si acaso

cash [kæʃ] n dinero en efectivo, dinero contante ♦ vt cobrar, hacer efectivo; **to pay (in) ~** pagar al contado; ~ **on delivery** cóbrese al entregar; ~**book** n libro de caja; ~ **card** n tarjeta f dinero; ~ **desk** (BRIT) n caja; ~ **dispenser** n cajero automático

cashew [kæ'ʃu:] n (also: ~ nut) anacardo

cash flow n flujo de fondos, cash-flow m

cashier [kæ'ʃɪə*] n cajero/a

cashmere ['kæʃmɪə*] n cachemira

cash register n caja

casing ['keɪsɪŋ] n revestimiento

casino [kə'si:nəu] n casino

casket ['kɑ:skɪt] n cofre m, estuche m; (US: coffin) ataúd m

casserole ['kæsərəul] n (food, pot) cazuela

cassette [kæ'sɛt] n cassette f; ~ **player/recorder** n tocacassettes m inv, cassette m

cast [kɑ:st] (pt, pp **cast**) vt (throw) echar, arrojar, lanzar; (glance, eyes) dirigir; (THEATRE): **to ~ sb as Othello**

dar a uno el papel de Otelo ♦ vi
(FISHING) lanzar ♦ n (THEATRE) reparto;
(also: plaster ~) vaciado; **to ~ one's
vote** votar; **to ~ doubt on** suscitar
dudas acerca de; **~ off** vi (NAUT)
desamarrar; (KNITTING) cerrar (los
puntos); **~ on** vi (KNITTING) poner los
puntos

castanets [kæstə'nɛts] npl castañuelas
fpl

castaway ['kɑ:stəweɪ] n náufrago/a m

caster sugar ['kɑ:stə*-] (BRIT) n azúcar
m extrafino

Castile [kæs'ti:l] n Castilla; **Castilian**
adj, n castellano/a m/f

casting vote ['kɑ:stɪŋ-] (BRIT) n voto
decisivo

cast iron n hierro fundido

castle ['kɑ:sl] n castillo; (CHESS) torre f

castor oil ['kɑ:stə*-] n aceite m de
ricino

casual ['kæʒjul] adj fortuito; (irregular:
work etc) temporero; (unconcerned)
despreocupado; (clothes) de sport; **~ly**
adv de manera despreocupada; (dress) de sport

casualty ['kæʒjultɪ] n víctima, herido;
(dead) muerto; (MED: department)
urgencias fpl

cat [kæt] n gato; (big ~) felino

Catalan ['kætələn] adj, n catalán/ana
m/f

catalogue ['kætəlɔg] (US catalog) n
catálogo ♦ vt catalogar

Catalonia [kætə'ləʊnɪə] n Cataluña

catalyst ['kætəlɪst] n catalizador m

catalytic convertor [kætə'lɪtɪk
kən'vɜ:tə*] n catalizador m

catapult ['kætəpʌlt] n tirachinas m inv

catarrh [kə'tɑ:*] n catarro

catastrophe [kə'tæstrəfɪ] n catástrofe f

catch [kætʃ] (pt, pp caught) vt coger
(SP), agarrar (AM); (arrest) detener;
(grasp) asir; (breath) contener; (surprise:
person) sorprender; (attract: attention)
captar; (hear) oír; (MED) contagiarse de,
coger; (also: ~ up) alcanzar ♦ vi (fire)

encenderse; (in branches etc) enredarse
♦ n (fish etc) pesca; (act of catching)
cogida; (hidden problem) dificultad f;
(game) pilla-pilla; (of lock) pestillo,
cerradura; **to ~ fire** encenderse; **to
~ sight of** divisar; **~ on** vi
(understand) caer en la cuenta; (grow
popular) hacerse popular; **~ up** vi (fig)
ponerse al día; **~ing** ['kætʃɪŋ] adj
(MED) contagioso; **~ment area**
['kætʃmənt-] (BRIT) n zona de
captación; **~phrase** ['kætʃfreɪz] n lema
m, eslogan m; **~y** ['kætʃɪ] adj (tune)
pegadizo

category ['kætɪgərɪ] n categoría, clase
f

cater ['keɪtə*] vi: **to ~ for** (BRIT)
abastecer a; (needs) atender a; (COMM:
parties etc) proveer comida a; **~er** n
abastecedor(a) m/f, proveedor(a) m/f;
~ing n (trade) hostelería

caterpillar ['kætəpɪlə*] n oruga,
gusano

cathedral [kə'θi:drəl] n catedral f

catholic ['kæθəlɪk] adj (tastes etc)
amplio; **C~** adj, n (REL) católico/a m/f

CAT scan [kæt-] n TAC f, tomografía

Cat'seye ® ['kæts'aɪ] (BRIT) n (AUT)
catafoto

cattle ['kætl] npl ganado

catty ['kætɪ] adj malicioso, rencoroso

caucus ['kɔ:kəs] n (POL) camarilla
política; (: US: to elect candidates)
comité m electoral

caught [kɔ:t] pt, pp of **catch**

cauliflower ['kɒlɪflaʊə*] n coliflor f

cause [kɔ:z] n causa, motivo, razón f;
(principle: also: POL) causa ♦ vt causar

caution ['kɔ:ʃən] n cautela, prudencia;
(warning) advertencia, amonestación f
♦ vt amonestar; **cautious** adj
cauteloso, prudente, precavido

cavalry ['kævəlrɪ] n caballería

cave [keɪv] n cueva, caverna; **~ in** vi
(roof etc) derrumbarse, hundirse

caviar(e) ['kævɪɑ:*] n caviar m

CB n abbr (= Citizens' Band (Radio))

banda ciudadana

CBI n abbr (= Confederation of British Industry) ≈ C.E.O.E. f (SP)

cc abbr = **cubic centimetres**; = **carbon copy**

CCTV n abbr (= closed-circuit television) circuito cerrado de televisión

CD n abbr (= compact disc) DC m; (player) (reproductor m de) disco compacto; ~ **player** n lector m de discos compactos; **~-ROM** [si:di:'rɔm] n abbr CD-ROM m

cease [si:s] vt, vi cesar; **~fire** n alto m el fuego; **~less** adj incesante

cedar ['si:də*] n cedro

ceiling ['si:lɪŋ] n techo; (fig) límite m

celebrate ['selɪbreɪt] vt celebrar ♦ vi divertirse; **~d** adj célebre; **celebration** [-'breɪʃən] n fiesta, celebración f

celery ['selərɪ] n apio

cell [sel] n celda; (BIOL) célula; (ELEC) elemento

cellar ['selə*] n sótano; (for wine) bodega

cello ['tʃeləu] n violoncelo

Cellophane ® ['seləfeɪn] n celofán m

cellphone ['selfəun] n teléfono celular

Celt [kelt, selt] adj, n celta m/f; **~ic** adj celta

cement [sə'ment] n cemento; ~ **mixer** n hormigonera

cemetery ['semɪtrɪ] n cementerio

censor ['sensə*] n censor m ♦ vt (cut) censurar; **~ship** n censura

censure ['senʃə*] vt censurar

census ['sensəs] n censo

cent [sent] n (unit of dollar) centavo, céntimo; (unit of euro) céntimo; see also **per**

centenary [sen'ti:nərɪ] n centenario

center ['sentə*] n (US) = **centre**

centi... [sentɪ] prefix: **~grade** adj centígrado; **~litre** (US **~liter**) n centilitro; **~metre** (US **~meter**) n centímetro

centipede ['sentɪpi:d] n ciempiés m inv

central ['sentrəl] adj central; (of house etc) céntrico; **C~ America** n Centroamérica; ~ **heating** n calefacción f central; **~ize** vt centralizar

centre ['sentə*] (US **center**) n centro; (fig) núcleo ♦ vt centrar; **~-forward** n (SPORT) delantero centro; **~-half** n (SPORT) medio centro

century ['sentjurɪ] n siglo; **20th ~** siglo veinte

ceramic [sɪ'ræmɪk] adj cerámico; **~s** n cerámica

cereal ['si:rɪəl] n cereal m

ceremony ['serɪmənɪ] n ceremonia; **to stand on ~** hacer ceremonias, estar de cumplido

certain ['sɜ:tən] adj seguro; (person): **a ~ Mr Smith** un tal Sr Smith; (particular, some) cierto; **for ~** a ciencia cierta; **~ly** adv (undoubtedly) ciertamente; (of course) desde luego, por supuesto; **~ty** n certeza, certidumbre f, seguridad f; (inevitability) certeza

certificate [sə'tɪfɪkɪt] n certificado

certified ['sɜ:tɪfaɪd] n: ~ **mail** (US) n correo certificado; ~ **public accountant** (US) n contable m/f diplomado/a

certify ['sɜ:tɪfaɪ] vt certificar; (award diploma to) conceder un diploma a; (declare insane) declarar loco

cervical ['sɜ:vɪkl] adj cervical

cervix ['sɜ:vɪks] n cuello del útero

cf. abbr (= compare) cfr

CFC n abbr (= chlorofluorocarbon) CFC m

ch. abbr (= chapter) cap

chain [tʃeɪn] n cadena; (of mountains) cordillera; (of events) sucesión f ♦ vt (also: ~ up) encadenar; **~ reaction** n reacción f en cadena; **~-smoke** vi fumar un cigarrillo tras otro; **~ store** n tienda de una cadena; **≈ gran almacén**

chair [tʃeə*] n silla; (armchair) sillón m, butaca; (of university) cátedra; (of meeting etc) presidencia ♦ vt (meeting)

chalk [tʃɔːk] n (GEO) creta; (for writing) tiza (SP), gis m (AM)

challenge ['tʃælɪndʒ] n desafío, reto ♦ vt desafiar, retar; (statement, right) poner en duda; **to ~ sb to do sth** retar a uno a que haga algo; **challenging** adj exigente; (tone) de desafío

chamber ['tʃeɪmbə*] n cámara, sala; (POL) cámara; (BRIT: LAW: gen pl) despacho; **~ of commerce** cámara de comercio; **~maid** n camarera

chamois ['ʃæmwɑ:] n gamuza

champagne [ʃæm'peɪn] n champaña m, champán m

champion ['tʃæmpɪən] n campeón/ona m/f; (of cause) defensor(a) m/f; **~ship** n campeonato

chance [tʃɑːns] n (opportunity) ocasión f, oportunidad f; (likelihood) posibilidad f; (risk) riesgo ♦ vt arriesgar, probar ♦ adj fortuito, casual; **to ~ it** arriesgarse, intentarlo; **to take a ~** arriesgarse; **by ~** por casualidad

chancellor ['tʃɑːnsələ*] n canciller m; **C~ of the Exchequer** (BRIT) n Ministro de Hacienda

chandelier [ʃændə'lɪə*] n araña (de luces)

change [tʃeɪndʒ] vt cambiar; (replace) cambiar, reemplazar; (gear, clothes, job) cambiar de; (transform) transformar ♦ vi cambiar(se); (trains) hacer transbordo; (traffic lights) cambiar de color; (be transformed): **to ~ into** transformarse en ♦ n cambio; (alteration) modificación f, transformación f; (of clothes) muda; (coins) suelto, sencillo; (money returned) vuelta; **to ~ gear** (AUT) cambiar de marcha; **to ~ one's mind** cambiar de opinión o idea; **for a ~** para variar; **~able** adj (weather) cambiable; **~ machine** n máquina de cambio; **~over** n (to new system) cambio; **changing** adj cambiante; **changing**

room (BRIT) n vestuario

channel ['tʃænl] n (TV) canal m; (of river) cauce m; (groove) conducto; (fig: medium) medio ♦ vt (river etc) encauzar; **the (English) C~** el Canal (de la Mancha); **the C~ Islands** las Islas Normandas; **the C~ Tunnel** el túnel del Canal de la Mancha, el Eurotúnel; **~-hopping** n (TV) zapping m

chant [tʃɑːnt] n (of crowd) gritos mpl; (REL) canto ♦ vt (slogan, word) repetir a gritos

chaos ['keɪɔs] n caos m

chap [tʃæp] (BRIT: inf) n (man) tío, tipo

chapel ['tʃæpl] n capilla

chaperone ['ʃæpərəʊn] n carabina

chaplain ['tʃæplɪn] n capellán m

chapped [tʃæpt] adj agrietado

chapter ['tʃæptə*] n capítulo

char [tʃɑː*] vt (burn) carbonizar, chamuscar

character ['kærɪktə*] n carácter m, naturaleza, índole f; (moral strength, personality) carácter; (in novel, film) personaje m; **~istic** ['-rɪstɪk] adj característico ♦ n característica

charcoal ['tʃɑːkəʊl] n carbón m vegetal; (ART) carboncillo

charge [tʃɑːdʒ] n (LAW) cargo, acusación f; (cost) precio, coste m; (responsibility) cargo ♦ vt (LAW): **to ~ (with)** acusar de; (battery) cargar; (price) pedir; (customer) cobrar ♦ vi precipitarse; (MIL) cargar, atacar; **~s** npl: **to reverse the ~s** (BRIT: TEL) revertir el cobro; **to take ~ of** hacerse cargo de, encargarse de; **to be in ~ of** estar encargado de; (business) mandar; **how much do you ~?** ¿cuánto cobra usted?; **to ~ an expense (up) to sb's account** cargar algo a cuenta de alguien; **~ card** n tarjeta de cuenta

charity ['tʃærɪtɪ] n caridad f; (organization) sociedad f benéfica; (money, gifts) limosnas fpl

charm [tʃɑːm] n encanto, atractivo; (talisman) hechizo; (on bracelet) dije n

chart 348 chestnut

♦ vt encantar; **~ing** adj encantador(a)

chart [tʃɑːt] n (diagram) cuadro; (graph) gráfica; (map) carta de navegación f; (progress) seguir; **~s** npl (Top 40): **the ~s** = los 40 principales

charter [ˈtʃɑːtə*] vt (plane) alquilar; (ship) fletar ♦ n (document) carta; (of university, company) estatutos mpl; **~ed accountant** (BRIT) n contable m/f diplomado/a; **~ flight** n vuelo chárter

chase [tʃeɪs] vt (pursue) perseguir ♦ n persecución f

chasm [ˈkæzəm] n sima

chassis [ˈʃæsɪ] n chasis m

chat [tʃæt] vi (also: **have a ~**) charlar ♦ n charla; **~ show** (BRIT) n programa m de entrevistas

chatter [ˈtʃætə*] vi (person) charlar; (teeth) castañetear ♦ n (of birds) parloteo; (of people) charla, cháchara; **~box** (inf) n parlanchín/ina m/f

chatty [ˈtʃætɪ] adj (style) informal; (person) hablador(a)

chauffeur [ˈʃəʊfə*] n chófer m

chauvinist [ˈʃəʊvɪnɪst] n (male ~) machista m; (nationalist) chovinista m/f

cheap [tʃiːp] adj barato; (joke) de mal gusto; (poor quality) de mala calidad ♦ adv barato; **~ day return** n billete m de día y vuelta al mismo día; **~er** adj más barato; **~ly** adv barato, a bajo precio

cheat [tʃiːt] vi hacer trampa ♦ vt: **to ~ sb (out of sth)** estafar (algo) a uno ♦ n (person) tramposo/a

check [tʃek] vt (examine) controlar; (facts) comprobar; (halt) parar, detener; (restrain) refrenar, restringir ♦ n (inspection) control m, inspección f; (curb) freno; (US: bill) nota, cuenta; (US) = **cheque**; (pattern: gen pl) cuadro ♦ adj (also: **~ed**: pattern, cloth) a cuadros; **~ in** vi (at hotel) firmar el registro, (at airport) facturar el equipaje ♦ vt (luggage) facturar; **~ out** vi (of hotel) marcharse; **~ up** vi: **to ~ up on** sth comprobar algo; **to ~ up on sb** investigar a alguien; **~ered** (US) adj = **check; chequered; ~ers** (US) n juego de damas; **~-in** (desk) n mostrador m de facturación; **~ing account** (US) n cuenta corriente; **~mate** n jaque m mate; **~out** n caja; **~point** n (punto de) control m; **~room** (US) n consigna; **~up** n (MED) reconocimiento general

cheek [tʃiːk] n mejilla; (impudence) descaro; **what a ~!** ¡qué caral; **~bone** n pómulo; **~y** adj fresco, descarado

cheep [tʃiːp] vi piar

cheer [tʃɪə*] vt vitorear, aplaudir; (gladden) alegrar, animar ♦ vi dar vivas ♦ n viva m; **~s** npl aplausos mpl; **~s!** ¡salud!; **~ up** vi animarse ♦ vt alegrar, animar; **~ful** adj alegre

cheerio [tʃɪərɪˈəʊ] (BRIT) excl ¡hasta luego!

cheese [tʃiːz] n queso; **~board** n tabla de quesos

cheetah [ˈtʃiːtə] n leopardo cazador

chef [ʃef] n jefe/a m/f de cocina

chemical [ˈkemɪkəl] adj químico ♦ n producto químico

chemist [ˈkemɪst] n (BRIT: pharmacist) farmacéutico/a; (scientist) químico/a; **~ry** n química; **~'s (shop)** (BRIT) n farmacia

cheque [tʃek] (US check) n cheque m; **~book** n talonario de cheques (SP), chequera (AM); **~ card** n tarjeta de cheque

chequered [ˈtʃekəd] (US checkered) adj (fig) accidentado

cherish [ˈtʃerɪʃ] vt (love) querer, apreciar; (protect) cuidar; (hope etc) abrigar

cherry [ˈtʃerɪ] n cereza; (also: **~ tree**) cerezo

chess [tʃes] n ajedrez m; **~board** n tablero de ajedrez

chest [tʃest] n (ANAT) pecho; (box) cofre m, cajón m; **~ of drawers** n cómoda

chestnut [ˈtʃesnʌt] n castaña; **~ (tree)**

n castaño

chew [tʃuː] vt mascar, masticar; **~ing gum** n chicle m

chic [ʃiːk] adj elegante

chick [tʃɪk] n pollito, polluelo; (inf: girl) chica

chicken ['tʃɪkɪn] n gallina, pollo; (food) pollo; (inf: coward) gallina m/f; **~ out** (inf) vi rajarse; **~pox** n varicela

chicory ['tʃɪkərɪ] n (for coffee) achicoria; (salad) escarola

chief [tʃiːf] n jefe/a m/f ♦ adj principal; **~ executive** n director(a) m/f general; **~ly** adv principalmente

chilblain ['tʃɪlbleɪn] n sabañón m

child [tʃaɪld] (pl **children**) n niño/a; (offspring) hijo/a; **~birth** n parto; **~hood** n niñez f, infancia; **~ish** adj pueril, aniñado; **~like** adj de niño; **~ minder** (BRIT) n madre f de día; **~ren** ['tʃɪldrən] npl of child

Chile ['tʃɪlɪ] n Chile m; **~an** adj, n chileno/a m/f

chill [tʃɪl] n frío; (MED) resfriado ♦ vt enfriar; (CULIN) congelar

chil(l)i ['tʃɪlɪ] (BRIT) n chile m (SP), ají m (AM)

chilly ['tʃɪlɪ] adj frío

chime [tʃaɪm] n repique m; (of clock) campanada ♦ vi repicar; sonar

chimney ['tʃɪmnɪ] n chimenea; **~ sweep** n deshollinador m

chimpanzee [tʃɪmpæn'ziː] n chimpancé m

chin [tʃɪn] n mentón m, barbilla

china ['tʃaɪnə] n porcelana; (crockery) loza

China ['tʃaɪnə] n China; **Chinese** [tʃaɪ'niːz] adj chino ♦ n inv chino/a; (LING) chino

chink [tʃɪŋk] n (opening) grieta, hendedura; (noise) tintineo

chip [tʃɪp] n (gen pl: CULIN: BRIT) patata (SP) or papa (AM) frita; (: US: also: potato ~) patata or papa frita; (of wood) astilla; (of glass, stone) lasca; (at poker) ficha; (COMPUT) chip m ♦ vt (cup, plate)

desconchar

chip shop

Se denomina chip shop o "fish-and-chip shop" a un establecimiento en el que se sirven algunas especialidades de comida rápida, muy populares entre los británicos, sobre todo pescado rebozado y patatas fritas.

chiropodist [kɪ'rɔpədɪst] (BRIT) n pedicuro/a, callista m/f

chirp [tʃəːp] vi (bird) gorjear, piar

chisel ['tʃɪzl] n (for wood) escoplo; (for stone) cincel m

chit [tʃɪt] n nota

chitchat ['tʃɪttʃæt] n chismes mpl, habladurías fpl

chivalry ['ʃɪvəlrɪ] n caballerosidad f

chives [tʃaɪvz] npl cebollinos mpl

chlorine ['klɔːriːn] n cloro

chock-a-block ['tʃɔkə'blɔk] adj atestado

chock-full ['tʃɔk'ful] adj atestado

chocolate ['tʃɔklɪt] n chocolate m; (sweet) bombón m

choice [tʃɔɪs] n elección, selección f; (option) opción f; (preference) preferencia ♦ adj escogido

choir ['kwaɪə*] n coro; **~boy** n niño de coro

choke [tʃəuk] vi ahogarse; (on food) atragantarse ♦ vt estrangular, ahogar; (block): **to be ~d with** estar atascado de ♦ n (AUT) estárter m

cholesterol [kə'lɛstərɔl] n colesterol m

choose [tʃuːz] (pt **chose**, pp **chosen**) vt escoger, elegir; (select): **to ~ to do sth** optar por hacer algo

choosy ['tʃuːzɪ] adj delicado

chop [tʃɔp] vt (wood) cortar, tajar; (CULIN: also: **~ up**) picar ♦ n (CULIN) chuleta; **~s** npl (jaws) boca, labios mpl

chopper ['tʃɔpə*] n (helicopter) helicóptero

choppy ['tʃɔpɪ] adj (sea) picado, agitado

chopsticks ['tʃɔpstɪks] npl palillos mpl

chord [kɔːd] n (MUS) acorde m

chore [tʃɔː*] n faena, tarea; (routine task) trabajo rutinario

chorus ['kɔːrəs] n coro; (repeated part of song) estribillo

chose [tʃəuz] pt of **choose**

chosen ['tʃəuzn] pp of **choose**

chowder ['tʃaudə*] n (esp US) sopa de pescado

Christ [kraɪst] n Cristo

christen ['krɪsn] vt bautizar

Christian ['krɪstɪən] adj, n cristiano/a m/f; **~ity** [-'ænɪtɪ] n cristianismo; **~ name** n nombre m de pila

Christmas ['krɪsməs] n Navidad f; **Merry ~!** ¡Felices Pascuas!; **~ card** n tarjeta de Navidad, crismas m inv, tarjeta de Navidad; **~ Day** n día m de Navidad; **~ Eve** n Nochebuena; **~ tree** n árbol m de Navidad

chrome [krəum] n cromo

chronic ['krɔnɪk] adj crónico

chronological [krɔnə'lɔdʒɪkəl] adj cronológica

chubby ['tʃʌbɪ] adj regordete

chuck [tʃʌk] (inf) vt lanzar, arrojar; (BRIT: also: ~ up) abandonar; **~ out** (person) echar (fuera); (rubbish etc) tirar

chuckle ['tʃʌkl] vi reírse entre dientes

chug [tʃʌg] vi resoplar; (car, boat: also: ~ along) avanzar traqueteando

chum [tʃʌm] n compañero/a

chunk [tʃʌŋk] n pedazo, trozo

church [tʃəːtʃ] n iglesia; **~yard** n cementerio

churn [tʃəːn] n (for butter) mantequera; (for milk) lechera; **~ out** vt producir en serie

chute [ʃuːt] n (also: rubbish ~) vertedero; (for coal etc) rampa de caída

chutney ['tʃʌtnɪ] n condimento a base de frutas de la India

CIA (US) n abbr (= Central Intelligence Agency) CIA f

CID (BRIT) n abbr (= Criminal Investigation Department) ≈ B.I.C. f (SP)

cider ['saɪdə*] n sidra

cigar [sɪ'gɑː*] n puro

cigarette [sɪgə'ret] n cigarrillo (SP), cigarro (AM); pitillo; **~ case** n pitillera; **~ end** n colilla

Cinderella [sɪndə'relə] n Cenicienta

cine camera ['sɪnɪ-] (BRIT) n cámara cinematográfica

cinema ['sɪnəmə] n cine m

cinnamon ['sɪnəmən] n canela

circle ['səːkl] n círculo; (in theatre) anfiteatro ♦ vi dar vueltas ♦ vt (surround) rodear, cercar; (move round) dar la vuelta a

circuit ['səːkɪt] n circuito; (tour) gira; (track) pista; (lap) vuelta; **~ous** [səː'kjuɪtəs] adj indirecto

circular ['səːkjulə*] adj circular ♦ n circular f

circulate ['səːkjuleɪt] vi circular; (person: at party etc) hablar con los invitados ♦ vt poner en circulación; **~ion** [-'leɪʃən] n circulación f; (of newspaper) tirada

circumstances ['səːkəmstənsɪz] npl circunstancias fpl; (financial condition) situación f económica

circus ['səːkəs] n circo

CIS n abbr (= Commonwealth of Independent States) CEI f

cistern ['sɪstən] n tanque m, depósito; (in toilet) cisterna

citizen ['sɪtɪzn] n (POL) ciudadano/a; (of city) vecino/a, habitante m/f; **~ship** n ciudadanía

citrus fruits ['sɪtrəs-] npl agrios mpl

city ['sɪtɪ] n ciudad f; **the C~** centro financiero de Londres

civic ['sɪvɪk] adj cívico; (authorities) municipal; **~ centre** (BRIT) n centro público

civil ['sɪvɪl] adj civil; (polite) atento, cortés; **~ engineer** n ingeniero de caminos, canales y puertos); **~ian** [sɪ'vɪlɪən] adj civil (no militar) ♦ n civil m/f, paisano/a

civilization [sɪvɪlaɪ'zeɪʃən] *n* civilización *f*

civilized ['sɪvɪlaɪzd] *adj* civilizado

civil: ~ **law** *n* derecho civil; ~ **servant** *n* funcionario/a del Estado; **C~ Service** *n* administración *f* pública; ~ **war** *n* guerra civil

claim [kleɪm] *vt* exigir, reclamar; (*rights etc*) reivindicar; (*assert*) pretender ♦ *vi* (*for insurance*) reclamar ♦ *n* reclamación *f*; pretensión *f*; ~**ant** *n* demandante *m/f*

clairvoyant [kleə'vɔɪənt] *n* clarividente *m/f*

clam [klæm] *n* almeja

clamber ['klæmbə*] *vi* trepar

clammy ['klæmɪ] *adj* frío y húmedo

clamour ['klæmə*] (US **clamor**) *vi:* **to** ~ **for** clamar por, pedir a voces

clamp [klæmp] *n* abrazadera, grapa ♦ *vt* (*2 things together*) cerrar fuertemente; (*one thing on another*) afianzar (con abrazadera); (AUT: *wheel*) poner el cepo a; ~ **down on** *vt fus* (*subj: government, police*) reforzar la lucha contra

clang [klæŋ] *vi* sonar, hacer estruendo

clap [klæp] *vi* aplaudir; ~**ping** *n* aplausos *mpl*

claret ['klærət] *n* burdeos *m inv*

clarify ['klærɪfaɪ] *vt* aclarar

clarinet [klærɪ'net] *n* clarinete *m*

clash [klæʃ] *n* enfrentamiento; choque *m*; desacuerdo; estruendo ♦ *vi* (*in fight*) enfrentarse; (*beliefs*) chocar; (*disagree*) estar en desacuerdo; (*colours*) desentonar; (*two events*) coincidir

clasp [klɑːsp] *n* (*hold*) apretón *m*; (*of necklace, bag*) cierre *m* ♦ *vt* apretar; abrazar

class [klɑːs] *n* clase *f* ♦ *vt* clasificar

classic ['klæsɪk] *adj*, *n* clásico; ~**al** *adj* clásico

classified ['klæsɪfaɪd] *adj* (*information*) reservado; ~ **advertisement** *n* anuncio por palabras

classmate ['klɑːsmeɪt] *n* compañero/a de clase

classroom ['klɑːsrʊm] *n* aula

clatter ['klætə*] *n* estrépito ♦ *vi* hacer ruido o estrépito

clause [klɔːz] *n* cláusula; (LING) oración *f*

claw [klɔː] *n* (*of cat*) uña; (*of bird of prey*) garra; (*of lobster*) pinza

clay [kleɪ] *n* arcilla

clean [kliːn] *adj* limpio; (*record, reputation*) bueno, intachable; (*joke*) decente ♦ *vt* limpiar; (*hands etc*) lavar; ~ **out** *vt* limpiar; ~ **up** *vt* limpiar, asear; ~**-cut** *adj* (*person*) bien parecido; ~**er** *n* (*person*) asistenta; (*substance*) producto para la limpieza; ~**er's** *n* tintorería; ~**ing** *n* limpieza; ~**liness** *n* ['klenlɪnɪs] *n* limpieza

cleanse [klenz] *vt* limpiar; ~**r** *n* (*for face*) crema limpiadora

clean-shaven *adj* sin barba, afeitado

cleansing department (BRIT) *n* departamento de limpieza

clear [klɪə*] *adj* claro; (*road, way*) libre; (*conscience*) limpio, tranquilo; (*skin*) terso; (*sky*) despejado ♦ *vt* (*space*) despejar, limpiar; (LAW: *suspect*) absolver; (*obstacle*) salvar, saltar por encima de; (*cheque*) aceptar ♦ *vi* (*fog etc*) despejarse ♦ *adv*: ~ **of** a distancia de; **to** ~ **the table** recoger o levantar la mesa; ~ **up** *vt* limpiar; (*mystery*) aclarar, resolver; ~**ance** *n* (*removal*) despeje *m*; (*permission*) acreditación *f*; ~**-cut** *adj* bien definido, nítido; ~**ing** *n* (*in wood*) claro; ~**ing bank** (BRIT) *n* cámara de compensación; ~**ly** *adv* claramente; (*evidently*) sin duda; ~**way** (BRIT) *n* carretera donde no se puede parar

clef [klef] *n* (MUS) clave *f*

cleft [kleft] *n* (*in rock*) grieta, hendedura

clench [klentʃ] *vt* apretar, cerrar

clergy ['klɜːdʒɪ] *n* clero; ~**man** *n* clérigo

clerical ['klerɪkəl] *adj* de oficina; (REL)

clerical

clerk [klɑːk, (US) klɜːrk] n (BRIT)
oficinista m/f; (US) dependiente/a m/f

clever ['klevəʳ] adj (intelligent)
inteligente, listo; (skilful) hábil; (device,
arrangement) ingenioso

click [klɪk] vt (tongue) chasquear;
(heels) taconear ♦ vi (COMPUT) hacer
clic; **to ~ on an icon** hacer clic en un
icono

client ['klaɪənt] n cliente m/f

cliff [klɪf] n acantilado

climate ['klaɪmɪt] n clima m

climax ['klaɪmæks] n (of battle, career)
apogeo; (of film, book) punto
culminante; (sexual) orgasmo

climb [klaɪm] vi subir; (plant) trepar;
(move with effort): **to ~ over a wall/
into a car** trepar a una tapia/subir a
un coche ♦ vt (stairs) subir; (tree)
trepar a; (mountain) escalar ♦ n subida;
~down n vuelta atrás; **~er** n alpinista
m/f (SP), andinista m/f (AM); **~ing**
n alpinismo (SP), andinismo (AM)

clinch [klɪntʃ] vt (deal) cerrar;
(argument) rematar

cling [klɪŋ] (pt, pp clung) vi: **to ~ to**
agarrarse a; (clothes) pegarse a

clinic ['klɪnɪk] n clínica; **~al** adj clínico;
(fig) frío

clink [klɪŋk] vi tintinar

clip [klɪp] n (for hair) horquilla; (also:
paper ~) sujetapapeles m inv, clip m;
(TV, CINEMA) fragmento ♦ vt (cut)
cortar; (also: ~ together) unir; **~pers**
npl (for gardening) tijeras fpl; **~ping**
n (newspaper) recorte m

cloak [kləuk] n capa, manto ♦ vt (fig)
encubrir, disimular; **~room** n
guardarropa; (BRIT: WC) lavabo (SP),
aseos mpl (SP), baño (AM)

clock [klɔk] n reloj m; **~ in** or **on** vi
fichar, picar; **~ off** or **out** vi fichar or
picar la salida; **~wise** adv en el sentido
de las agujas del reloj; **~work** n
aparato de relojería ♦ adj (toy) de
cuerda

clog [klɔg] n zueco, chanclo ♦ vt
atascar ♦ vi (also: ~ up) atascarse

cloister ['klɔɪstəʳ] n claustro

clone [kləun] n clon m ♦ vt clonar

close¹ [kləus] adj (near): **~ (to)** cerca
(de); (friend) íntimo; (connection)
estrecho; (examination) detallado,
minucioso; (weather) bochornoso; **to
have a ~ shave** (fig) escaparse por un
pelo ♦ adv cerca; **~ by, ~ at hand**
muy cerca; **~ to** prep cerca de

close² [kləuz] vt (shut) cerrar; (end)
concluir, terminar ♦ vi (shop etc)
cerrarse; (end) concluirse, terminarse
♦ n (end) fin m, final m, conclusión f;
~ down vi cerrarse definitivamente;
~d adj (shop etc) cerrado; **~d shop** n
taller m gremial

close-knit [kləus'nɪt] adj (fig) muy
unido

closely ['kləuslɪ] adv (study) con
detalle; (watch) de cerca; (resemble)
estrechamente

closet ['klɔzɪt] n armario

close-up ['kləusʌp] n primer plano

closure ['kləuʒəʳ] n cierre m

clot [klɔt] n (gen) coágulo; (inf: idiot)
imbécil m/f ♦ vi (blood) coagularse

cloth [klɔθ] n (material) tela, paño;
(rag) trapo

clothe [kləuð] vt vestir; **~s** npl ropa; **~s
brush** n cepillo (para la ropa); **~s line**
n cuerda (para tender la ropa); **~s peg**
(US **~s pin**) n pinza

clothing ['kləuðɪŋ] n = **clothes**

cloud [klaud] n nube f; **~burst** n
aguacero; **~y** adj nublado, nubloso;
(liquid) turbio

clout [klaut] vt dar un tortazo a

clove [kləuv] n clavo; **~ of garlic**
diente m de ajo

clover ['kləuvəʳ] n trébol m

clown [klaun] n payaso ♦ vi (also:
~ about, ~ around) hacer el payaso

cloying ['klɔɪɪŋ] adj empalagoso

club [klʌb] n (society) club m; (weapon)
porra, cachiporra; (also: golf ~) palo

♦ vt aporrear ♦ vi: **to ~ together** (for gift) comprar entre todos; **~s** npl (CARDS) tréboles mpl; **~ class** n (AVIAT) clase f preferente; **~house** n local social, sobre todo en clubs deportivos

cluck [klʌk] vi cloquear

clue [kluː] n pista; (in crosswords) indicación f; **I haven't a ~** no tengo ni idea

clump [klʌmp] n (of trees) grupo

clumsy ['klʌmzɪ] adj (person) torpe, desmañado; (tool) difícil de manejar; (movement) desgarbado

clung [klʌŋ] pt, pp of **cling**

cluster ['klʌstə*] n grupo ♦ vi agruparse, apiñarse

clutch [klʌtʃ] n (AUT) embrague m; (grasp): **~es** garras fpl ♦ vt asir; agarrar

clutter ['klʌtə*] vt atestar

cm abbr (= centimetre) cm

CND n abbr (= Campaign for Nuclear Disarmament) plataforma pro desarme nuclear

Co. abbr = **county; company**

c/o abbr (= care of) c/a, a/c

coach [kəutʃ] n autocar m (SP), coche m de línea; (horse-drawn) coche m; (of train) vagón m, coche m; (SPORT) entrenador(a) m/f, instructor(a) m/f; (tutor) profesor(a) m/f particular ♦ vt (SPORT) entrenar; (student) preparar, enseñar; **~ trip** n excursión f en autocar

coal [kəul] n carbón m; **~ face** n frente m de carbón; **~field** n yacimiento de carbón

coalition [kəuə'lɪʃən] n coalición f

coalman ['kəulmən] (irreg) n carbonero

coalmine ['kəulmaɪn] n mina de carbón

coarse [kɔːs] adj basto, burdo; (vulgar) grosero, ordinario

coast [kəust] n costa, litoral m ♦ vi (AUT) ir en punto muerto; **~al** adj costero, costanero; **~guard** n guardacostas m inv; **~line** n litoral m

coat [kəut] n abrigo; (of animal) pelaje m, lana; (of paint) mano f, capa ♦ vt cubrir, revestir; **~ of arms** n escudo de armas; **~ hanger** n percha (SP), gancho (AM); **~ing** n capa, baño

coax [kəuks] vt engatusar

cobbler ['kɔblə] n zapatero (remendón)

cobbles ['kɔblz] npl, **cobblestones** ['kɔblstəunz] npl adoquines mpl

cobweb ['kɔbweb] n telaraña

cocaine [kə'keɪn] n cocaína

cock [kɔk] n (rooster) gallo; (male bird) macho ♦ vt (gun) amartillar; **~erel** n gallito

cockle ['kɔkl] n berberecho

cockney ['kɔknɪ] n habitante de ciertos barrios de Londres

cockpit ['kɔkpɪt] n cabina

cockroach ['kɔkrəutʃ] n cucaracha

cocktail ['kɔkteɪl] n coctel m, cóctel m; **~ cabinet** n mueble-bar m; **~ party** n coctel m, cóctel m

cocoa ['kəukau] n cacao; (drink) chocolate m

coconut ['kəukənʌt] n coco

cod [kɔd] n bacalao

C.O.D. abbr (= cash on delivery) C.A.E.

code [kəud] n código; (cipher) clave f; (dialling ~) prefijo; (post ~) código postal

cod-liver oil ['kɔdlɪvər-] n aceite m de hígado de bacalao

coercion [kəu'əːʃən] n coacción f

coffee ['kɔfɪ] n café m; **~ bar** (BRIT) n cafetería; **~ bean** n grano de café; **~ break** n descanso (para tomar café); **~pot** n cafetera; **~ table** n mesita (para servir el café)

coffin ['kɔfɪn] n ataúd m

cog [kɔg] n (wheel) rueda dentada; (tooth) diente m

cogent ['kəudʒənt] adj convincente

cognac ['kɔnjæk] n coñac m

coil [kɔɪl] n rollo; (ELEC) bobina, carrete m; (contraceptive) espiral f ♦ vt enrollar

coin [kɔɪn] n moneda ♦ vt (word)

inventar, idear; **~age** n moneda; **~box** n cabina telefónica

coincide [kəʊn'saɪd] vi coincidir; (agree) estar de acuerdo; **coincidence** [kəʊ'ɪnsɪdəns] n casualidad f

Coke ® [kəʊk] n Coca-Cola ®

coke [kəʊk] n (coal) coque m

colander ['kɒləndə*] n colador m, escurridor m

cold [kəʊld] adj frío ♦ n frío; (MED) resfriado; **it's ~** hace frío; **to be ~** (person) tener frío; **to catch ~**, **to catch a ~** resfriarse, acatarrarse; **in ~ blood** a sangre fría; **~-shoulder** vt dar or volver la espalda a; **~ sore** n herpes mpl o fpl

coleslaw ['kəʊlslɔː] n especie de ensalada de col

colic ['kɒlɪk] n cólico

collapse [kə'læps] vi hundirse, derrumbarse; (MED) sufrir un colapso ♦ n hundimiento, derrumbamiento; (MED) colapso; **collapsible** adj plegable

collar ['kɒlə*] n (of coat, shirt) cuello; (of dog etc) collar; **~bone** n clavícula

collateral [kɒ'lætərəl] n garantía colateral

colleague ['kɒliːg] n colega m/f; (at work) compañero, a

collect [kə'lekt] vt (litter, mail etc) recoger; (as a hobby) coleccionar; (BRIT: call and pick up) recoger; (debts, subscriptions etc) recaudar ♦ vi reunirse; (dust) acumularse; **to call ~** (US: TEL) llamar a cobro revertido; **~ion** [kə'lekʃən] n colección f; (of mail, for charity) recogida; **~or** n coleccionista m/f

college ['kɒlɪdʒ] n colegio mayor; (of agriculture, technology) escuela universitaria

collide [kə'laɪd] vi chocar

colliery ['kɒliəri] (BRIT) n mina de carbón

collision [kə'lɪʒən] n choque m

colloquial [kə'ləʊkwɪəl] adj familiar,

coloquial

Colombia [kə'lɒmbiə] n Colombia; **~n** adj, n colombiano/a

colon ['kəʊlən] n (sign) dos puntos; (MED) colon m

colonel ['kɜːnl] n coronel m

colonial [kə'ləʊniəl] adj colonial

colony ['kɒləni] n colonia

colour ['kʌlə*] (US **color**) n color m ♦ vt color(e)ar; (dye) teñir; (fig: account) adornar; (: judgement) distorsionar ♦ vi (blush) sonrojarse; **~s** npl (of party, club) colores mpl; **in ~** en color; **~ in** vt colorear; **~ bar** n segregación f racial; **~-blind** adj daltónico; **~ed** adj de color; (photo) en color; **~ film** n película en color; **~ful** adj lleno de color; (story) fantástico; (person) excéntrico; **~ing** n (complexion) tez f; (in food) colorante m; **~ scheme** n combinación f de colores; **~ television** n televisión f en color

colt [kəʊlt] n potro

column ['kɒləm] n columna; **~ist** ['kɒləmnɪst] n columnista m/f

coma ['kəʊmə] n coma m

comb [kəʊm] n peine m; (ornamental) peineta ♦ vt (hair) peinar; (area) registrar a fondo

combat ['kɒmbæt] n combate m ♦ vt combatir

combination [kɒmbɪ'neɪʃən] n combinación f

combine [vb kəm'baɪn, n 'kɒmbaɪn] vt combinar; (qualities) reunir ♦ vi combinarse; (ECON) cartel m; **~ (harvester)** n cosechadora

KEYWORD

come [kʌm] (pt **came**, pp **come**) vi **1** (movement towards) venir; **to ~ running** venir corriendo **2** (arrive) llegar; **he's ~ here to work** ha venido aquí para trabajar; **to ~ home** volver a casa **3** (reach): **to ~ to** llegar a; **the bill**

came to £40 la cuenta ascendía a cuarenta libras

4 (occur): **an idea came to me** se me ocurrió una idea

5 (be, become): **to ~ loose/undone** etc aflojarse/desabrocharse, desatarse etc; **I've ~ to like him** por fin ha llegado a gustarme

come about vi suceder, ocurrir

come across vt fus (person) topar con; (thing) dar con

come away vi (leave) marcharse; (become detached) desprenderse

come back vi (return) volver

come by vt fus (acquire) conseguir

come down vi (price) bajar; (tree, building) ser derribado

come forward vi presentarse

come from vt fus (place, source) ser de

come in vi (visitor) entrar; (train, report) llegar; (fashion) ponerse de moda; (on deal etc) entrar

come in for vt fus (criticism etc) recibir

come into vt fus (money) heredar; (be involved) tener que ver con; **to ~ into fashion** ponerse de moda

come off vi (button) soltarse, desprenderse; (attempt) salir bien

come on vi (pupil) progresar; (work, project) desarrollarse; (lights) encenderse; (electricity) volver; **~ on!** ¡vamos!

come out vi (fact) salir a la luz; (book, sun) salir; (stain) quitarse

come round vi (after faint, operation) volver en sí

come to vi (wake) volver en sí

come up vi (sun) salir; (problem) surgir; (event) aproximarse; (in conversation) mencionarse

come up against vt fus (resistance etc) tropezar con

come up with vt fus (idea) sugerir; (money) conseguir

come upon vt fus (find) dar con

comeback ['kʌmbæk] n: **to make a ~** (THEATRE) volver a las tablas

comedian [kə'mi:dɪən] n cómico; **comedienne** ['-ɛn] n cómica

comedy ['kɒmɪdɪ] n comedia; (humour) comicidad f

comet ['kɒmɪt] n cometa m

comeuppance [kʌm'ʌpəns] n: **to get one's ~** llevar su merecido

comfort ['kʌmfət] n bienestar m; (relief) alivio ♦ vt consolar; **~s** npl (of home etc) comodidades fpl; **~able** adj cómodo; (financially) acomodado; (easy) fácil; **~ably** adv (sit) cómodamente; (live) holgadamente; **~ station** (US) n servicios mpl

comic ['kɒmɪk] adj (also: **~al**) cómico ♦ n (comedian) cómico; (BRIT: for children) tebeo; (BRIT: for adults) comic m; **~ strip** n tira cómica

coming ['kʌmɪŋ] n venida, llegada ♦ adj que viene; **~(s) and going(s)** n(pl) ir y venir m, ajetreo

comma ['kɒmə] n coma

command [kə'mɑ:nd] n orden f, mandato; (MIL: authority) mando; (mastery) dominio ♦ vt (troops) mandar; (give orders to): **to ~ sb to do** mandar u ordenar a uno hacer; **~eer** [kɒmən'dɪə*] vt requisar; **~er** n (MIL) comandante m/f, jefe/a m/f

commemorate [kə'mɛməreɪt] vt conmemorar

commence [kə'mɛns] vt, vi comenzar, empezar

commend [kə'mɛnd] vt elogiar, alabar; (recommend) recomendar

commensurate [kə'mɛnʃərɪt] adj: **~ with** en proporción a, que corresponde a

comment ['kɒmɛnt] n comentario ♦ vi: **to ~ on** hacer comentarios sobre; **"no ~"** (written) "sin comentarios"; (spoken) "no tengo nada que decir"; **~ary** ['kɒməntərɪ] n comentario; **~ator** ['kɒməntˌeɪtə*] n comentarista m/f

commerce ['kɔmə:s] n comercio

commercial [kə'mə:ʃəl] adj comercial
♦ n (TV, RADIO) anuncio

commiserate [kə'mɪzəreɪt] vi: **to ~ with** compadecerse de, condolerse de

commission [kə'mɪʃən] n (committee, fee) comisión f ♦ vt (work of art) encargar; **out of ~** fuera de servicio; **~aire** [kəmɪʃə'nɛə*] (BRIT) n portero; **~er** n (POLICE) comisario de policía

commit [kə'mɪt] vt (act) cometer; (resources) dedicar; (to sb's care) entregar; **to ~ o.s. (to do)** comprometerse (a hacer); **to ~ suicide** suicidarse; **~ment** n compromiso; (to ideology etc) entrega

committee [kə'mɪtɪ] n comité m

commodity [kə'mɔdɪtɪ] n mercancía

common ['kɔmən] adj común; (pej) ordinario ♦ n campo común; **the C~s** npl (BRIT) (la Cámara de) los Comunes mpl; **in ~** en común; **~er** n plebeyo; **~ law** n ley f consuetudinaria; **~ly** adv comúnmente; **C~ Market** n Mercado Común; **~place** adj de lo más común; **~room** n sala común; **~ sense** n sentido común; **the C~wealth** n la Commonwealth

commotion [kə'məuʃən] n tumulto, confusión f

commune [n 'kɔmju:n, vb kə'mju:n] n (group) comuna ♦ vi: **to ~ with** comulgar o conversar con

communicate [kə'mju:nɪkeɪt] vt comunicar ♦ vi: **to ~ (with)** comunicarse (con); (in writing) estar en contacto (con)

communication [kəmju:nɪ'keɪʃən] n comunicación f; **~ cord** (BRIT) n timbre m de alarma

communion [kə'mju:nɪən] n (also: Holy C~) comunión f

communiqué [kə'mju:nɪkeɪ] n comunicado, parte f

communism ['kɔmjunɪzəm] n comunismo; **communist** adj, n

comunista m/f

community [kə'mju:nɪtɪ] n comunidad f; (large group) colectividad f; **~ centre** n centro social; **~ chest** (US) n arca comunitaria, fondo común

commutation ticket [kɔmju'teɪʃən-] (US) n billete m de abono

commute [kə'mju:t] vi viajar a diario de la casa al trabajo ♦ vt conmutar; **~r** n persona (que viaja ... see vi)

compact [adj kəm'pækt, n 'kɔmpækt] adj compacto ♦ n (also: powder ~) polvera; **~ disc** n compact disc m; **~ disc player** n reproductor m de disco compacto, compact disc m

companion [kəm'pænɪən] n compañero/a; **~ship** n compañerismo

company ['kʌmpənɪ] n compañía; (COMM) sociedad f, compañía; **to keep sb ~** acompañar a uno; **~ secretary** (BRIT) n secretario/a de compañía

comparative [kəm'pærətɪv] adj relativo; (study) comparativo; **~ly** adv (relatively) relativamente

compare [kəm'pɛə*] vt: **to ~ sth/sb with/to** comparar algo/a uno con ♦ vi: **to ~ (with)** compararse (con); **comparison** [-'pærɪsn] n comparación f

compartment [kəm'pɑ:tmənt] n (also: RAIL.) compartim(i)ento

compass ['kʌmpəs] n brújula; **~es** npl (MATH) compás m

compassion [kəm'pæʃən] n compasión f; **~ate** adj compasivo

compatible [kəm'pætɪbl] adj compatible

compel [kəm'pel] vt obligar

compensate ['kɔmpənseɪt] vt compensar ♦ vi: **to ~ for** compensar; **compensation** [-'seɪʃən] n (for loss) indemnización f

compère ['kɔmpɛə*] n presentador m

compete [kəm'pi:t] vi (take part) tomar parte, concurrir; (vie with): **to ~ with** competir con, hacer competencia a

competent ['kɒmpɪtənt] adj
competente, capaz

competition [kɒmpɪ'tɪʃən] n (contest)
concurso; (rivalry) competencia

competitive [kəm'petɪtɪv] adj (ECON,
SPORT) competitivo

competitor [kəm'petɪtə*] n (rival)
competidor(a) m/f; (participant)
concursante m/f

complacency [kəm'pleɪsnsɪ] n
autosatisfacción f

complacent [kəm'pleɪsənt] adj
autocomplaciente

complain [kəm'pleɪn] vi quejarse;
(COMM) reclamar; **~t** n queja;
reclamación f; (MED) enfermedad f

complement [n 'kɒmplɪmənt, vb
'kɒmplɪmɛnt] n complemento; (esp of
ship's crew) dotación f ♦ vt (enhance)
complementar; **~ary** [kɒmplɪ'mɛntərɪ]
adj complementario

complete [kəm'pliːt] adj (full)
completo; (finished) acabado ♦ vt
(fulfil) completar; (finish) acabar; (a
form) llenar; **~ly** adv completamente;
completion [-'pliːʃən] n terminación
f; (of contract) realización f

complex ['kɒmplɛks] adj, n complejo

complexion [kəm'plɛkʃən] n (of face)
tez f, cutis m

compliance [kəm'plaɪəns] n
(submission) sumisión f; (agreement)
conformidad f; **in ~ with** de acuerdo
con

complicate ['kɒmplɪkeɪt] vt complicar;
~d adj complicado; **complication**
[-'keɪʃən] n complicación f

compliment ['kɒmplɪmənt] n (formal)
cumplido ♦ vt felicitar; **~s** npl (regards)
saludos mpl; **to pay sb a ~** hacer
cumplidos a uno; **~ary** [-'mɛntərɪ] adj
lisonjero; (free) de favor

comply [kəm'plaɪ] vi: **to ~ with**
cumplir con

component [kəm'pəʊnənt] adj
componente ♦ n (TECH) pieza

compose [kəm'pəʊz] vt: **to be ~d of**

componerse de; (music etc) componer;
to ~ o.s. tranquilizarse; **~d** adj
sosegado; **~r** n (MUS) compositor(a)
m/f; **composition** [kɒmpə'zɪʃən] n
composición f

compost ['kɒmpɒst] n abono (vegetal)

composure [kəm'pəʊʒə*] n serenidad
f, calma

compound ['kɒmpaʊnd] n (CHEM)
compuesto; (LING) palabra compuesta;
(enclosure) recinto ♦ adj compuesto;
(fracture) complicado

comprehend [kɒmprɪ'hɛnd] vt
comprender; **comprehension**
[-'hɛnʃən] n comprensión f

comprehensive [kɒmprɪ'hɛnsɪv] adj
exhaustivo; (INSURANCE) contra todo
riesgo; **~ (school)** n centro estatal de
enseñanza secundaria; ≈ Instituto
Nacional de Bachillerato (SP)

compress [vb kəm'prɛs, n 'kɒmprɛs]
vt comprimir; (information) condensar
♦ n (MED) compresa

comprise [kəm'praɪz] vt (also: be ~d
of) comprender, constar de; (constitute)
constituir

compromise ['kɒmprəmaɪz] n
(agreement) arreglo ♦ vt comprometer
♦ vi transigir

compulsion [kəm'pʌlʃən] n
compulsión f; (force) obligación f

compulsive [kəm'pʌlsɪv] adj
compulsivo; (viewing, reading) obligado

compulsory [kəm'pʌlsərɪ] adj
obligatorio

computer [kəm'pjuːtə*] n ordenador
m, computador m, computadora;
~ game n juego para ordenador; **~-
generated** adj realizado por
ordenador, creado por ordenador; **~-
ize** vt (data) computerizar; (system)
informatizar; **~ programmer** n
programador(a) m/f; **~ programming**
n programación f; **~ science** n
informática; **computing** [kəm'pjuːtɪŋ]
n (activity, science) informática

comrade ['kɒmrɪd] n (POL, MIL)

camarada; (*friend*) compañero/a;
~**ship** *n* camaradería, compañerismo

con [kɔn] *vt* (*deceive*) engañar; (*cheat*)
estafar ♦ *n* estafa

conceal [kən'si:l] *vt* ocultar

conceit [kən'si:t] *n* presunción *f*; ~**ed**
adj presumido

conceive [kən'si:v] *vt*, *vi* concebir

concentrate ['kɔnsəntreɪt] *vi*
concentrarse ♦ *vt* concentrar

concentration [kɔnsən'treɪʃən] *n*
concentración *f*

concept ['kɔnsept] *n* concepto

concern [kən'sə:n] *n* (*matter*) asunto;
(COMM) empresa; (*anxiety*)
preocupación *f* ♦ *vt* (*worry*) preocupar;
(*involve*) afectar; (*relate to*) tener que
ver con; **to be ~ed** (**about**)
interesarse (por), preocuparse (por);
~**ing** *prep* sobre, acerca de

concert ['kɔnsət] *n* concierto; ~**ed**
[kən'sə:təd] *adj* (*efforts etc*)
concertado; ~ **hall** *n* sala de conciertos

concerto [kən'tʃɜːtəu] *n* concierto

concession [kən'seʃən] *n* concesión *f*;
tax ~ *n* privilegio fiscal

conclude [kən'klu:d] *vt* concluir;
(*treaty etc*) firmar; (*agreement*) llegar a;
(*decide*) llegar a la conclusión de;
conclusion [-'klu:ʒən] *n* conclusión *f*,
firma; **conclusive** [-'klu:sɪv] *adj*
decisivo, concluyente

concoct [kən'kɔkt] *vt* confeccionar;
(*plot*) tramar; ~**ion** [-'kɔkʃən] *n* mezcla

concourse ['kɔŋkɔ:s] *n* vestíbulo

concrete ['kɔnkri:t] *n* hormigón *m*
♦ *adj* de hormigón; (*fig*) concreto

concur [kən'kə:*] *vi* estar de acuerdo,
asentir

concurrently [kən'kʌrntlɪ] *adv* al
mismo tiempo

concussion [kən'kʌʃən] *n* conmoción
f cerebral

condemn [kən'dem] *vt* condenar;
(*building*) declarar en ruina

condense [kən'dens] *vi* condensarse
♦ *vt* condensar, abreviar; ~**d milk** *n*

leche *f* condensada

condition [kən'dɪʃən] *n* condición *f*,
estado; (*requirement*) condición *f* ♦ *vt*
condicionar; **on ~ that** a condición
(de) que; ~**er** *n* suavizante

condolences [kən'dəulənsɪz] *npl*
pésame *m*

condom ['kɔndəm] *n* condón *m*

condone [kən'dəun] *vt* condonar

conducive [kən'dju:sɪv] *adj*: ~ **to**
conducente a

conduct [*n* 'kɔndʌkt, *vb* kən'dʌkt] *n*
conducta, comportamiento ♦ *vt* (*lead*)
conducir; (*manage*) llevar a cabo,
dirigir; (MUS) dirigir; **to** ~ **o.s.**
comportarse; ~**ed tour** (BRIT) *n* visita
acompañada; ~**or** *n* (*of orchestra*)
director *m*; (US: *on train*) revisor(a) *m/f*;
(*on bus*) cobrador *m*; (ELEC) conductor
m; ~**ress** *n* (*on bus*) cobradora

cone [kəun] *n* cono; (*pine*) piña; (*on
road*) pivote *m*; (*for ice-cream*)
cucurucho

confectioner [kən'fekʃənə*] *n*
repostero/a; ~**'s (shop)** *n* confitería;
~**y** *n* dulces *mpl*

confer [kən'fə:*] *vt*: **to** ~ **sth on**
otorgar algo a ♦ *vi* conferenciar

conference ['kɔnfərns] *n* (*meeting*)
reunión *f*; (*convention*) congreso

confess [kən'fes] *vt* confesar ♦ *vi*
admitir; ~**ion** [-'feʃən] *n* confesión *f*

confetti [kən'fetɪ] *n* confeti *m*

confide [kən'faɪd] *vi*: **to** ~ **in** confiar
en

confidence ['kɔnfɪdns] *n* (*also: self-~*)
confianza; (*secret*) confidencia; **in** ~
(*speak, write*) en confianza; ~ **trick** *n*
timo; **confident** *adj* seguro de sí
mismo; (*certain*) seguro; **confidential**
[kɔnfɪ'denʃəl] *adj* confidencial

confine [kən'faɪn] *vt* (*limit*) limitar;
(*shut up*) encerrar; ~**d** *adj* (*space*)
reducido; ~**ment** *n* (*prison*) prisión *f*;
~**s** ['kɔnfaɪnz] *npl* confines *mpl*

confirm [kən'fə:m] *vt* confirmar;
~**ation** [kɔnfə'meɪʃən] *n* confirmación

f; **~ed** adj empedernido

confiscate ['kɒnfɪskeɪt] vt confiscar

conflict [n 'kɒnflɪkt, vb kən'flɪkt] n conflicto ♦ vi (opinions) chocar; ~ing adj contradictorio

conform [kən'fɔːm] vi conformarse; **to ~ to** ajustarse a

confound [kən'faʊnd] vt confundir

confront [kən'frʌnt] vt (problems) hacer frente a; (enemy, danger) enfrentarse con; **~ation** [kɒnfrən'teɪʃən] n enfrentamiento

confuse [kən'fjuːz] vt (perplex) aturdir, desconcertar; (mix up) confundir; (complicate) complicar; **~d** adj confuso; (person) perplejo; **confusing** adj confuso; **confusion** [-'fjuːʒən] n confusión f

congeal [kən'dʒiːl] vi (blood) coagularse; (sauce etc) cuajarse

congested [kən'dʒestɪd] adj congestionado; **congestion** n congestión f

congratulate [kən'grætjʊleɪt] vt: **to ~ sb (on)** felicitar a uno (por); **congratulations** [-'leɪʃənz] npl felicitaciones fpl; **congratulations!** ¡enhorabuena!

congregate ['kɒŋgrɪgeɪt] vi congregarse; **congregation** [-'geɪʃən] n (of a church) feligreses mpl

congress ['kɒŋgres] n congreso; (US): **C~** Congreso; **C~man** (irreg) (US) n miembro del Congreso

conifer ['kɒnɪfəʳ] n conífera

conjunctivitis [kəndʒʌŋktɪ'vaɪtɪs] n conjuntivitis f

conjure ['kʌndʒəʳ] vi hacer juegos de manos; **~ up** vt (ghost, spirit) hacer aparecer; (memories) evocar; **~r** n ilusionista m f

con man ['kɒn-] n estafador m

connect [kə'nekt] vt juntar, unir; (ELEC) conectar; (TEL: subscriber) poner; (: caller) poner al habla; (fig) relacionar, asociar ♦ vi: **to ~ with** (train) enlazar con; **to be ~ed with** (associated) estar

relacionado con; **~ion** n juntura, unión f; (ELEC) conexión f; (RAIL) enlace m; (TEL) comunicación f; (fig) relación f

connive [kə'naɪv] vi: **to ~ at** hacer la vista gorda a

connoisseur [kɒnɪ'səːʳ] n experto/a, entendido/a

conquer ['kɒŋkəʳ] vt (territory) conquistar; (enemy, feelings) vencer; **~or** n conquistador m

conquest ['kɒŋkwest] n conquista

cons [kɒnz] npl see **convenience**; **pro**

conscience ['kɒnʃəns] n conciencia

conscientious [kɒnʃɪ'enʃəs] adj concienzudo; (objection) de conciencia

conscious ['kɒnʃəs] adj (deliberate) deliberado; (awake, aware) consciente; **~ness** n conciencia; (MED) conocimiento

conscript ['kɒnskrɪpt] n recluta m; **~ion** [kən'skrɪpʃən] n servicio militar (obligatorio)

consensus [kən'sensəs] n consenso

consent [kən'sent] n consentimiento ♦ vi: **to ~ (to)** consentir (en)

consequence ['kɒnsɪkwəns] n consecuencia; (significance) importancia

consequently ['kɒnsɪkwəntlɪ] adv por consiguiente

conservation [kɒnsə'veɪʃən] n conservación f

conservative [kən'səːvətɪv] adj conservador(a); (estimate etc) cauteloso; **C~** (BRIT) adj, n (POL) conservador/a m f

conservatory [kən'səːvətrɪ] n invernadero; (MUS) conservatorio

conserve [kən'səːv] vt conservar ♦ n conserva

consider [kən'sɪdəʳ] vt considerar; (take into account) tener en cuenta; (study) estudiar, examinar; **to ~ doing sth** pensar en (la posibilidad de) hacer algo; **~able** adj considerable; **~ably** adv notablemente; **~ate** adj considerado; **consideration** [-'reɪʃən] n consideración f; (factor) factor m; (fee

give sth further consideration
estudiar algo más a fondo; **~ing** prep
teniendo en cuenta

consign [kən'saɪn] vt: **to ~ to** (sth
unwanted) relegar a; (person) destinar
a; **~ment** n envío

consist [kən'sɪst] vi: **to ~ of** consistir
en

consistency [kən'sɪstənsɪ] n (of
argument etc) coherencia;
consecuencia; (thickness) consistencia

consistent [kən'sɪstənt] adj (person)
consecuente; (argument etc) coherente

consolation [kɒnsə'leɪʃən] n consuelo

console[1] [kən'səul] vt consolar

console[2] ['kɒnsəul] n consola

consonant ['kɒnsənənt] n consonante
f

consortium [kən'sɔːtɪəm] n consorcio

conspicuous [kən'spɪkjuəs] adj
(visible) visible

conspiracy [kən'spɪrəsɪ] n conjura,
complot m

constable ['kʌnstəbl] (BRIT) n policía
m/f; **chief ~** ≈ jefe m de policía

constabulary [kən'stæbjulərɪ] n ≈
policía

constant ['kɒnstənt] adj constante;
~ly adv constantemente

constipated ['kɒnstɪpeɪtəd] adj
estreñido; **constipation**
[kɒnstɪ'peɪʃən] n estreñimiento

constituency [kən'stɪtjuənsɪ] n (POL:
area) distrito electoral; (: electors)
electorado; **constituent** [-ənt] n (POL)
elector(a) m/f; (part) componente m

constitution [kɒnstɪ'tjuːʃən] n
constitución f; **~al** adj constitucional

constraint [kən'streɪnt] n obligación f;
(limit) restricción f

construct [kən'strʌkt] vt construir;
~ion [-ʃən] n construcción f; **~ive** adj
constructivo

consul ['kɒnsl] n cónsul m/f; **~ate**
['kɒnsjulɪt] n consulado

consult [kən'sʌlt] vt consultar; **~ant** n
(BRIT: MED) especialista m/f; (other

specialist) asesor(a) m/f; **~ation**
[kɒnsəl'teɪʃən] n consulta; **~ing room**
(BRIT) n consultorio

consume [kən'sjuːm] vt (eat) comerse;
(drink) beberse; (fire etc, COMM)
consumir; **~r** n consumidor(a) m/f; **~r
goods** npl bienes mpl de consumo

consummate ['kɒnsəmeɪt] vt
consumar

consumption [kən'sʌmpʃən] n
consumo

cont. abbr (= continued) sigue

contact ['kɒntækt] n contacto; (person)
contacto; (: pej) enchufe m ♦ vt
ponerse en contacto con; **~ lenses** npl
lentes fpl de contacto

contagious [kən'teɪdʒəs] adj
contagioso

contain [kən'teɪn] vt contener; **to
~ o.s.** contenerse; **~er** n recipiente m;
(for shipping etc) contenedor m

contaminate [kən'tæmɪneɪt] vt
contaminar

cont'd abbr (= continued) sigue

contemplate ['kɒntəmpleɪt] vt
contemplar; (reflect upon) considerar

contemporary [kən'tempərərɪ] adj,
n contemporáneo/a m/f

contempt [kən'tempt] n desprecio;
~ of court (LAW) desacato a (los
tribunales); **~ible** adj despreciable;
~uous adj desdeñoso

contend [kən'tend] vt (argue) afirmar
♦ vi: **to ~ with/for** luchar contra/por;
~er n (SPORT) contendiente m/f

content [adj, vb kən'tent, n 'kɒntent]
adj (happy) contento; (satisfied)
satisfecho ♦ vt contentar; satisfacer ♦
n contenido; **~s** npl contenido; (table
of) **~s** n índice m de materias; **~ed** adj
contento; satisfecho

contention [kən'tenʃən] n (assertion)
aseveración f; (disagreement) discusión f

contest [n 'kɒntest, vb kən'test] n
lucha; (competition) concurso ♦ vt
(dispute) impugnar; (POL) presentarse
como candidato/a en; **~ant**

[kən'testənt] n concursante m/f; (in fight) contendiente m/f

context ['kɔntekst] n contexto

continent ['kɔntɪnənt] n continente m; **the C~** (BRIT) el continente europeo; **~al** [-'nentl] adj continental; **~al breakfast** n desayuno estilo europeo; **~al quilt** (BRIT) n edredón m

contingency [kən'tɪndʒənsɪ] n contingencia

continual [kən'tɪnjuəl] adj continuo; **~ly** adv constantemente

continuation [kəntɪnju'eɪʃən] n prolongación f; (after interruption) reanudación f

continue [kən'tɪnju:] vi, vt seguir, continuar

continuous [kən'tɪnjuəs] adj continuo

contort [kən'tɔ:t] vt retorcer

contour ['kɔntuə*] n contorno; (also: ~ line) curva de nivel

contraband ['kɔntrəbænd] n contrabando

contraceptive [kɔntrə'septɪv] adj, n anticonceptivo

contract [n 'kɔntrækt, vb kən'trækt] n contrato ♦ vi **to ~ to do sth** comprometerse por contrato a hacer algo; (become smaller) contraerse, encogerse ♦ vt contraer; **~ion** [kən'trækʃən] n contracción f; **~or** n contratista m/f

contradict [kɔntrə'dɪkt] vt contradecir; **~ion** [-ʃən] n contradicción f

contraption [kən'træpʃən] (pej) n artilugio m

contrary¹ ['kɔntrərɪ] adj contrario ♦ n lo contrario; **on the ~** al contrario; **unless you hear to the ~** a no ser que le digan lo contrario

contrary² [kən'treərɪ] adj (perverse) terco

contrast [n 'kɔntrɑːst, vt kən'trɑːst] n contraste m ♦ vt comparar; **in ~ to** en contraste con

contravene [kɔntrə'viːn] vt infringir

contribute [kən'trɪbjuːt] vi contribuir

♦ vt: **to ~ £10/an article to** contribuir con 10 libras/un artículo a; **to ~ to** (charity) donar a; (newspaper) escribir para; (discussion) intervenir en; **contribution** [kɔntrɪ'bjuːʃən] n (donation) donativo; (BRIT: for social security) cotización f; (to debate) intervención f; (to journal) colaboración f; **contributor** n contribuyente m/f; (to newspaper) colaborador/a m/f

contrive [kən'traɪv] vt (invent) idear ♦ vi: **to ~ to do** lograr hacer

control [kən'trəul] vt controlar; (process etc) dirigir; (machinery) manejar; (temper) dominar; (disease) contener ♦ n control m; **~s** npl (of vehicle) instrumentos mpl de mando; (of radio) controles mpl; (governmental) medidas fpl de control; **under ~** bajo control; **to be in ~ of** tener el mando de; **the car went out of ~** se perdió el control del coche; **~led substance** n sustancia controlada; **~ panel** n tablero de instrumentos; **~ room** n sala de mando; **~ tower** n (AVIAT) torre f de control

controversial [kɔntrə'vəːʃl] adj polémico

controversy ['kɔntrəvəːsɪ] n polémica

convalesce [kɔnvə'les] vi convalecer

convector [kən'vektə*] n calentador m de aire

convene [kən'viːn] vt convocar ♦ vi reunirse

convenience [kən'viːnɪəns] n (easiness) comodidad f; (suitability) idoneidad f; (advantage) ventaja; **at your ~** cuando le sea conveniente; **all modern ~s, all mod cons** (BRIT) todo confort

convenient [kən'viːnɪənt] adj (useful) útil; (place, time) conveniente

convent ['kɔnvənt] n convento

convention [kən'venʃən] n convención f; (meeting) asamblea; (agreement) convenio; **~al** adj convencional

converge [kən'vɜːdʒ] vi convergir; (people): **to ~ on** dirigirse todos a

conversant [kən'vɜːsnt] adj: **to be ~ with** estar al tanto de

conversation [kɒnvə'seɪʃən] n conversación f; **~al** adj familiar; **~al skill** facilidad f de palabra

converse [n 'kɒnvɜːs, vb kən'vɜːs] n inversa ♦ vi conversar; **~ly** [-'vɜːslɪ] adv a la inversa

conversion [kən'vɜːʃən] n conversión f

convert [vb kən'vɜːt, n 'kɒnvɜːt] vt (REL, COMM) convertir; (alter): **to ~ sth into/to** convertir algo en/convertir algo a ♦ n converso/a; **~ible** adj convertible ♦ n descapotable m

convey [kən'veɪ] vt llevar; (thanks) comunicar; (idea) expresar; **~or belt** n cinta transportadora

convict [vb kən'vɪkt, n 'kɒnvɪkt] vt (find guilty) declarar culpable a ♦ n presidiario/a; **~ion** [-ʃən] n condena; (belief, certainty) convicción f

convince [kən'vɪns] vt convencer; **~d** adj: **~d of/that** convencido de/de que; **convincing** adj convincente

convoluted ['kɒnvəluːtɪd] adj (argument etc) enrevesado

convoy ['kɒnvɔɪ] n convoy m

convulse [kən'vʌls] vt: **to be ~d with laughter** desternillarse de risa; **convulsion** [-'vʌlʃən] n convulsión f

cook [kuk] vt (stew etc) guisar; preparar ♦ vi cocer; (person) cocinar ♦ n cocinero/a; **~ book** n libro de cocina; **~er** n cocina; **~ery** n cocina; **~ery book** (BRIT) n = **book**; **~ie** (US) n galleta; **~ing** n cocina

cool [kuːl] adj fresco; (not afraid) tranquilo; (unfriendly) frío ♦ vt enfriar ♦ vi enfriarse; **~ness** n frescura; tranquilidad f; (indifference) falta de entusiasmo

coop [kuːp] n gallinero ♦ vt: **to ~ up** (fig) encerrar

cooperate [kəu'ɒpəreɪt] vi cooperar,

colaborar; **cooperation** [-'reɪʃən] n cooperación f, colaboración f

cooperative [-rətɪv] adj (business) cooperativo; (person) servicial ♦ n cooperativa

coordinate [vb kəu'ɔːdɪneɪt, n kəu'ɔːdɪnət] vt coordinar ♦ n (MATH) coordenada; **~s** npl (clothes) coordinados mpl; **coordination** [-'neɪʃən] n coordinación f

co-ownership [kəu'əunəʃɪp] n co-propiedad f

cop [kɒp] (inf) n poli m (SP), tira m (AM)

cope [kəup] vi: **to ~ with** (problem) hacer frente a

copper ['kɒpə*] n (metal) cobre m; (BRIT: inf) poli m; **~s** npl (money) calderilla (SP), centavos mpl (AM)

copulate ['kɒpjuleɪt] vi copularse

copy ['kɒpɪ] n copia; (of book etc) ejemplar m ♦ vt copiar; **~right** n derechos mpl de autor

coral ['kɒrəl] n coral m

cord [kɔːd] n cuerda; (ELEC) cable m; (fabric) pana

cordial ['kɔːdɪəl] adj cordial ♦ n cordial m

cordon ['kɔːdn] n cordón m; **~ off** vt acordonar

corduroy ['kɔːdərɔɪ] n pana

core [kɔː*] n centro, núcleo; (of fruit) corazón m; (of problem) meollo ♦ vt quitar el corazón de

coriander [kɒrɪ'ændə*] n culantro

cork [kɔːk] n corcho; (tree) alcornoque m; **~screw** n sacacorchos m inv

corn [kɔːn] n (BRIT: cereal crop) trigo; (US: maize) maíz; (on foot) callo; **~ on the cob** (CULIN) maíz en la mazorca (SP), choclo (AM)

corned beef ['kɔːnd-] n carne f acecinada (en lata)

corner ['kɔːnə*] n (outside) esquina; (inside) rincón m; (in road) curva; (FOOTBALL) córner m; (BOXING) esquina ♦ vt (trap) arrinconar; (COMM) acaparar ♦ vi (in car) tomar las curvas; **~stone** n

(also fig) piedra angular
cornet ['kɔ:nɪt] n (MUS) corneta; (BRIT: of ice-cream) cucurucho
cornflakes ['kɔ:nfleɪks] npl copos mpl de maíz, cornflakes mpl
cornflour ['kɔ:nflaʊə*] (BRIT), **cornstarch** ['kɔ:nstɑ:tʃ] (US) n harina de maíz
Cornwall ['kɔ:nwəl] n Cornualles m
corny ['kɔ:nɪ] (inf) adj gastado
coronary ['kɔrənərɪ] n (also: ~ thrombosis) infarto
coronation [kɔrə'neɪʃən] n coronación f
coroner ['kɔrənə*] n juez m (de instrucción)
corporal ['kɔ:pərl] n cabo ♦ adj: ~ **punishment** castigo corporal
corporate ['kɔ:pərɪt] adj (action, ownership) colectivo; (finance, image) corporativo
corporation [kɔ:pə'reɪʃən] n (of town) ayuntamiento m; (COMM) corporación f
corps [kɔ:*, pl kɔ:z] n inv cuerpo; diplomatic ~ cuerpo diplomático; press ~ gabinete m de prensa
corpse [kɔ:ps] n cadáver m
correct [kə'rɛkt] adj justo, exacto; (proper) correcto ♦ vt corregir; (exam) corregir, calificar; **~ion** [-ʃən] n (act) corrección f; (instance) rectificación f
correspond [kɔrɪs'pɔnd] vi (write): to ~ **(with)** escribirse (con); (be equivalent to): to ~ **(to)** corresponder (a); (be in accordance): to ~ **(with)** corresponder (con); **~ence** n correspondencia; **~ence course** n curso por correspondencia; **~ent** n corresponsal m/f
corridor ['kɔrɪdɔ:*] n pasillo
corrode [kə'rəud] vt corroer ♦ vi corroerse
corrugated ['kɔrəgeɪtɪd] adj ondulado; **~ iron** n chapa ondulada
corrupt [kə'rʌpt] adj (person) corrupto; (COMPUT) corrompido ♦ vt corromper; (COMPUT) degradar

Corsica ['kɔ:sɪkə] n Córcega
cosmetic [kɔz'mɛtɪk] adj, n cosmético
cosmopolitan [kɔzmə'pɔlɪtn] adj cosmopolita
cost [kɔst] (pt, pp cost) n (price) precio; ~s npl (COMM) costes mpl; (LAW) costas fpl ♦ vi costar, valer ♦ vt preparar el presupuesto de; **how much does it ~?** ¿cuánto cuesta?; to ~ **sb time/effort** costarle a uno tiempo/esfuerzo; **it ~ him his life** le costó la vida; **at all ~s** cueste lo que cueste
co-star ['kəustɑ:*] n coprotagonista m/f
Costa Rica ['kɔstə'ri:kə] n Costa Rica; ~n adj, n costarriqueño/a m/f
cost-effective [kɔstɪ'fɛktɪv] adj rentable
costly ['kɔstlɪ] adj costoso
cost-of-living [kɔstəv'lɪvɪŋ] adj: **~ allowance** plus m de carestía de vida; **~ index** índice m del costo de vida
cost price (BRIT) n precio de coste
costume ['kɔstju:m] n traje m; (BRIT: also: swimming ~) traje de baño; **~ jewellery** n bisutería
cosy ['kəuzɪ] (US **cozy**) adj (person) cómodo; (room) acogedor(a)
cot [kɔt] n (BRIT: child's) cuna; (US: campbed) cama de campaña
cottage ['kɔtɪdʒ] n casita de campo; (rustic) barraca; **~ cheese** n requesón m
cotton ['kɔtn] n algodón m; (thread) hilo; **~ on to** (inf) vt fus caer en la cuenta de; **~ candy** (US) n algodón m (azucarado); **~ wool** (BRIT) n algodón m (hidrófilo)
couch [kautʃ] n sofá m; (doctor's etc) diván m
couchette [ku:'ʃɛt] n litera
cough [kɔf] vi toser ♦ n tos f; **~ drop** n pastilla para la tos
could [kud] pt of can²; **~n't** = could not

council ['kaʊnsl] n consejo; **city** or **town ~** consejo municipal; **~ estate** (BRIT) n urbanización f de viviendas municipales de alquiler; **~ house** (BRIT) n vivienda municipal de alquiler; **~lor** n concejal(a) m/f

counsel ['kaʊnsl] n (advice) consejo; (lawyer) abogado/a ♦ vt aconsejar; **~lor** n consejero/a; **~or** (US) n abogado/a

count [kaʊnt] vt contar; (include) incluir ♦ vi contar ♦ n cuenta; (of votes) escrutinio; (level) nivel m; (nobleman) conde m; **~ on** vt fus contar con; **~down** n cuenta atrás

countenance ['kaʊntɪnəns] n semblante m, rostro ♦ vt (tolerate) aprobar, tolerar

counter ['kaʊntə*] n (in shop) mostrador m; (in games) ficha ♦ vt contrarrestar ♦ adv: **to run ~ to** ser contrario a, ir en contra de; **~act** vt contrarrestar

counterfeit ['kaʊntəfɪt] n falsificación f, simulación f ♦ vt falsificar ♦ adj falso, falsificado

counterfoil ['kaʊntəfɔɪl] n talón m

counterpart ['kaʊntəpɑːt] n homólogo/a

counter-productive [kaʊntəprə'-dʌktɪv] adj contraproducente

countersign ['kaʊntəsaɪn] vt refrendar

countess ['kaʊntɪs] n condesa

countless ['kaʊntlɪs] adj innumerable

country ['kʌntrɪ] n país m; (native land) patria; (as opposed to town) campo; (region) región f, tierra; **~ dancing** (BRIT) n baile m regional; **~ house** n casa de campo; **~man** (irreg) (compatriot) compatriota m; (rural) campesino, paisano; **~side** n campo

county ['kaʊntɪ] n condado

coup [kuː] (pl **~s**) n (also: **~ d'état**) golpe m (de estado); (achievement) éxito

couple ['kʌpl] n (of things) par m; (of people) pareja; (married **~**) matrimonio; **a ~ of** un par de

coupon ['kuːpɔn] n cupón m; (voucher) valé m

courage ['kʌrɪdʒ] n valor m, valentía; **~ous** [kə'reɪdʒəs] adj valiente

courgette [kʊə'ʒet] (BRIT) n calabacín m (SP), calabacita (AM)

courier ['kʊərɪə*] n mensajero/a; (for tourists) guía m/f de turismo

course [kɔːs] n (direction) dirección f; (of river, SCOL) curso; (process) transcurso; (MED): **~ of treatment** tratamiento; (of ship) rumbo; (part of meal) plato; (GOLF) campo; **of ~** desde luego, naturalmente; **of ~!** ¡claro!

court [kɔːt] n (royal) corte f; (LAW) tribunal m, juzgado; (TENNIS etc) pista, cancha ♦ vt (woman) cortejar a; **to take to ~** demandar

courteous ['kɜːtɪəs] adj cortés

courtesy ['kɜːtəsɪ] n cortesía; **(by) ~ of** por cortesía de; **~ bus, ~ coach** n autobús m gratuito

court-house ['kɔːthaʊs] (US) n palacio de justicia

courtier ['kɔːtɪə*] n cortesano

court-martial (pl **courts-martial**) n consejo de guerra

courtroom ['kɔːtrum] n sala de justicia

courtyard ['kɔːtjɑːd] n patio

cousin ['kʌzn] n primo/a; **first ~** primo/a carnal, primo/a hermano/a

cove [kəʊv] n cala, ensenada

covenant ['kʌvənənt] n pacto

cover ['kʌvə*] vt cubrir; (feelings, mistake) ocultar; (with lid) tapar; (book etc) forrar; (distance) recorrer; (include) abarcar; (protect: also: INSURANCE) cubrir; (PRESS) investigar; (discuss) tratar ♦ n cubierta; (lid) tapa; (for chair etc) funda; (envelope) sobre m; (for book) forro; (of magazine) portada; (shelter) abrigo; (INSURANCE) cobertura; (of spy) cobertura; **~s** npl (on bed) sábanas; mantas; **to take to ~** (shelter) protegerse, resguardarse; **under ~** (indoors) bajo techo; **under ~ of darkness** al amparo de la oscuridad; **under separate ~** (COMM) por separado; **~ up** vi: **to ~ up for sb** encubrir a uno; **~age** n (TV, PRESS) cobertura; **~alls** (US) npl mono; **~ charge** n precio del cubierto; **~ing** n capa; **~ing letter** (= **letter**) n carta de explicación; **~ note** (INSURANCE) póliza provisional

covert ['kʌvət] adj secreto, encubierto

cover-up n encubrimiento

cow [kau] n vaca; (inf: woman) bruja ♦ vt intimidar

coward ['kauəd] n cobarde m/f; **~ice** [-ɪs] n cobardía; **~ly** adj cobarde

cowboy ['kaubɔɪ] n vaquero

cower ['kauə*] vi encogerse (de miedo)

coy [kɔɪ] adj tímido

cozy ['kəuzɪ] (US) adj = **cosy**

CPA (US) n abbr = **certified public accountant**

crab [kræb] n cangrejo; **~ apple** n manzana silvestre

crack [kræk] n grieta; (noise) crujido; (drug) crack m ♦ vt agrietar, romper; (nut) cascar; (solve: problem) resolver; (: code) descifrar; (whip etc) chasquear; (knuckles) crujir; (joke) contar ♦ adj (expert) de primera; **~ down on** vt fus adoptar fuertes medidas contra; **~ up** vi (MED) sufrir una crisis nerviosa; **~er** n (biscuit) cráquer m; (Christmas **~er**) petardo sorpresa

crackle ['krækl] vi crepitar

cradle ['kreɪdl] n cuna

craft [krɑːft] n (skill) arte m; (trade) oficio; (cunning) astucia; (boat: pl inv) barco; (plane: pl inv) avión m

craftsman ['krɑːftsmən] n artesano; **~ship** n (quality) destreza

crafty ['krɑːftɪ] adj astuto

crag [kræg] n peñasco

cram [kræm] vt: **to ~ sth with** llenar algo a (reventar) de; (put): **to ~ sth into** meter algo a la fuerza en

♦ vi (for exams) empollar

cramp [kræmp] n (MED) calambre m; **~ed** adj apretado, estrecho

cranberry ['krænbərɪ] n arándano agrio

crane [kreɪn] n (TECH) grúa; (bird) grulla

crank [kræŋk] n manivela; (person) chiflado

cranny ['krænɪ] n see **nook**

crash [kræʃ] n (noise) estrépito; (of cars etc) choque m; (of plane) accidente m de aviación; (COMM) quiebra ♦ vt (car, plane) estrellar ♦ vi (car, plane) estrellarse; (two cars) chocar; (COMM) quebrar; **~ course** n curso acelerado; **~ helmet** n casco (protector); **~ landing** n aterrizaje m forzado

crass [kræs] adj grosero, maleducado

crate [kreɪt] n cajón m de embalaje; (for bottles) caja

cravat(e) [krə'væt] n pañuelo

crave [kreɪv] vt, vi: **to ~ (for)** ansiar, anhelar

crawl [krɔːl] vi (drag o.s.) arrastrarse; (child) andar a gatas, gatear; (vehicle) avanzar (lentamente) ♦ n (SWIMMING) crol m

crayfish ['kreɪfɪʃ] n inv (freshwater) cangrejo de río; (saltwater) cigala

crayon ['kreɪən] n lápiz m de color

craze [kreɪz] n (fashion) moda

crazy ['kreɪzɪ] adj (person) loco; (idea) disparatado; (inf: keen): **~ about sb/ sth** loco por uno/algo

creak [kriːk] vi (floorboard) crujir; (hinge etc) chirriar, rechinar

cream [kriːm] n (of milk) nata, crema; (lotion) crema; (fig) flor f y nata ♦ adj (colour) color crema; **~ cake** n pastel m de nata; **~ cheese** n queso blanco; **~y** adj cremoso; (colour) color crema

crease [kriːs] n (fold) pliegue m; (in trousers) raya; (wrinkle) arruga ♦ vt (wrinkle) arrugar ♦ vi (wrinkle up) arrugarse

create [kriː'eɪt] vt crear; **creation**

[-ʃən] n creación f; **creative** adj
creativo; **creator** n creador(a) m/f
creature ['kri:tʃə*] n (animal) animal
m, bicho; (person) criatura
crèche [krɛʃ] n guardería (infantil)
credence ['kri:dəns] n: **to lend** or
give ~ to creer en, dar crédito a
credentials [krɪ'dɛnʃlz] npl (references)
referencias fpl; (identity papers)
documentos mpl de identidad
credible ['krɛdɪbl] adj creíble;
(trustworthy) digno de confianza
credit ['krɛdɪt] n crédito m; (merit) honor
m, mérito ♦ vt (COMM) abonar; (believe:
also: **give ~ to**) creer, prestar fe a ♦ adj
crediticio; **~s** npl (CINEMA) fichas fpl
técnicas; **to be in ~** (person) tener
saldo a favor; **to ~ sb with** (fig)
reconocer a uno el mérito de; **~ card**
n tarjeta de crédito; **~or** n acreedor(a)
m/f
creed [kri:d] n credo m
creek [kri:k] n cala, ensenada; (US)
riachuelo
creep [kri:p] (pt, pp **crept**) vi
arrastrarse; **~er** n enredadera; **~y** adj
(frightening) horripilante
cremate [krɪ'meɪt] vt incinerar
crematorium [krɛmə'tɔ:rɪəm] (pl
crematoria) n crematorio
crêpe [kreɪp] n (fabric) crespón m;
(also: **~ rubber**) crepé m; **~ bandage**
(BRIT) n venda de crepé
crept [krɛpt] pt, pp of **creep**
crescent ['krɛsnt] n media luna;
(street) calle f (en forma de semicírculo)
cress [krɛs] n berro
crest [krɛst] n (of bird) cresta; (of hill)
cima, cumbre f; (of coat of arms)
blasón m; **~fallen** adj alicaído
crevice ['krɛvɪs] n grieta, hendedura
crew [kru:] n (of ship etc) tripulación f;
(TV, CINEMA) equipo; **~cut** n corte m
al rape; **~-neck** n cuello a la caja
crib [krɪb] n cuna ♦ vt (inf) plagiar
crick [krɪk] n (in neck) tortícolis f
cricket ['krɪkɪt] n (insect) grillo; (game)

críquet m
crime [kraɪm] n (no pl: illegal activities)
crimen m; (illegal action) delito;
criminal ['krɪmɪnl] n criminal m/f,
delincuente m/f ♦ adj criminal; (illegal)
delictivo; (law) penal
crimson ['krɪmzn] adj carmesí
cringe [krɪndʒ] vi agacharse, encogerse
cripple ['krɪpl] n lisiado/a, cojo/a ♦ vt
lisiar, mutilar
crisis ['kraɪsɪs] (pl **crises**) n crisis f inv
crisp [krɪsp] adj fresco; (vegetables etc)
crujiente; (manner) seco; **~s** (BRIT) npl
patatas fpl (SP) or papas fpl (AM) fritas
crisscross ['krɪskrɔs] adj entrelazado
criterion [kraɪ'tɪərɪən] (pl **criteria**) n
criterio
critic ['krɪtɪk] n crítico/a; **~al** adj
crítico; (illness) grave; **~ally** adv (speak
etc) en tono crítico; (ill) gravemente;
~ism ['krɪtɪsɪzm] n crítica; **~ize**
['krɪtɪsaɪz] vt criticar
croak [krəuk] vi (frog) croar; (raven)
graznar; (person) gruñir
Croatia [krəu'eɪʃə] n Croacia
crochet ['krəuʃeɪ] n ganchillo
crockery ['krɔkərɪ] n loza, vajilla
crocodile ['krɔkədaɪl] n cocodrilo
crocus ['krəukəs] n croco, crocus m
croft [krɔft] n granja pequeña
crony ['krəunɪ] (inf: pej) n compinche
m/f
crook [kruk] n ladrón/ona m/f; (of
shepherd) cayado; **~ed** ['krukɪd] adj
torcido; (dishonest) nada honrado
crop [krɔp] n (produce) cultivo; (amount
produced) cosecha; (riding) ~ látigo de
montar ♦ vt cortar, recortar; **~ up** vi
surgir, presentarse
cross [krɔs] n cruz f; (hybrid) cruce m
♦ vt (street etc) cruzar, atravesar ♦ adj
de mal humor, enojado; **~ out** vt
tachar; **~ over** vi cruzar; **~bar** n
travesaño; **~country (race)** n carrera
a campo traviesa, cross m; **~-examine**
vt interrogar; **~-eyed** adj bizco; **~fire**

n fuego cruzado; **~ing** *n* (*sea passage*) travesía; (*also*: *pedestrian ~ing*) paso para peatones; **~ing guard** (*US*) *n* persona encargada de ayudar a los niños a cruzar la calle; **~ purposes** *npl*: **to be at ~ purposes** no comprenderse uno a otro; **~reference** *n* referencia, llamada; **~roads** *n* cruce *m*, encrucijada; (*of* population) muestra (*representativa*); **~walk** (*US*) *n* paso de peatones; **~wind** *n* viento de costado; **~word** *n* crucigrama *m*

crotch [krɔtʃ] *n* (*ANAT*, *of garment*) entrepierna

crotchet ['krɔtʃit] *n* (*MUS*) negra

crouch [krautʃ] *vi* agacharse, acurrucarse

crow [krəu] *n* (*bird*) cuervo; (*of cock*) canto, cacareo ♦ *vi* (*cock*) cantar

crowbar ['krəubɑ:*] *n* palanca

crowd [kraud] *n* muchedumbre *f*, multitud *f* ♦ *vt* (*fill*) llenar ♦ *vi* (*gather*): **to ~ round** reunirse en torno a; (*cram*): **to ~ in** entrar en tropel; **~ed** *adj* (*full*) atestado; (*densely populated*) superpoblado

crown [kraun] *n* corona; (*of head*) coronilla; (*for tooth*) funda; (*of hill*) cumbre *f* ♦ *vt* coronar; (*tooth*) rematar; **~ jewels** *npl* joyas *fpl* reales; **~ prince** *n* príncipe *m* heredero

crow's feet *npl* patas *fpl* de gallo

crucial ['kru:ʃl] *adj* decisivo

crucifix ['kru:sɪfɪks] *n* crucifijo; **~ion** [-'fɪkʃən] *n* crucifixión *f*

crude [kru:d] *adj* (*materials*) bruto; (*fig*: *basic*) tosco; (: *vulgar*) ordinario; **~ (oil)** *n* (petróleo) crudo

cruel ['kruəl] *adj* cruel; **~ty** *n* crueldad *f*

cruise [kru:z] *n* crucero ♦ *vi* (*ship*) hacer un crucero; (*car*) ir a velocidad de crucero; **~r** *n* (*motorboat*) yate *m* de motor; (*warship*) crucero

crumb [krʌm] *n* miga, migaja

crumble ['krʌmbl] *vt* desmenuzar ♦ *vi*

(*building*, *also fig*) desmoronarse; **crumbly** *adj* que se desmigaja fácilmente

crumpet ['krʌmpit] *n* ≈ bollo para tostar

crumple ['krʌmpl] *vt* (*paper*) estrujar; (*material*) arrugar

crunch [krʌntʃ] *vt* (*with teeth*) mascar; (*underfoot*) hacer crujir ♦ *n* (*fig*) hora o momento de la verdad; **~y** *adj* crujiente

crusade [kru:'seid] *n* cruzada

crush [krʌʃ] *n* (*crowd*) aglomeración *f*; (*infatuation*): **to have a ~ on sb** estar loco por uno; (*drink*): **lemon ~** limonada ♦ *vt* aplastar; (*paper*) estrujar; (*cloth*) arrugar; (*fruit*) exprimir; (*opposition*) aplastar; (*hopes*) destruir

crust [krʌst] *n* corteza; (*of snow, ice*) costra

crutch [krʌtʃ] *n* muleta

crux [krʌks] *n*: **the ~ of** lo esencial de, el quid de

cry [krai] *vi* llorar; (*shout*: *also*: **~ out**) gritar ♦ *n* (*shriek*) chillido; (*shout*) grito; **~ off** *vi* echarse atrás

cryptic ['krɪptik] *adj* enigmático, secreto

crystal ['krɪstl] *n* cristal *m*; **~-clear** *adj* claro como el agua

cub [kʌb] *n* cachorro; (*also*: **~ scout**) niño explorador

Cuba ['kju:bə] *n* Cuba; **~n** *adj*, *n* cubano/a *m/f*

cube [kju:b] *n* cubo ♦ *vt* (*MATH*) cubicar; **cubic** *adj* cúbico

cubicle ['kju:bɪkl] *n* (*at pool*) caseta; (*for bed*) cubículo

cuckoo ['kuku:] *n* cuco; **~ clock** *n* reloj *m* de cucú

cucumber ['kju:kʌmbə*] *n* pepino

cuddle ['kʌdl] *vt* abrazar ♦ *vi* abrazarse

cue [kju:] *n* (*snooker* ~) taco; (*THEATRE etc*) señal *f*

cuff [kʌf] *n* (*of sleeve*) puño; (*US*: *of trousers*) vuelta; (*blow*) bofetada; **off the ~** *adv* de improviso; **~links** *npl* gemelos *mpl*

cuisine [kwɪ'ziːn] *n* cocina

cul-de-sac ['kʌldəsæk] *n* callejón *m* sin salida

cull [kʌl] *vt* (*idea*) sacar ♦ *n* (*of animals*) matanza selectiva

culminate ['kʌlmɪneɪt] *vi*: **to ~ in** terminar en; **culmination** [-'neɪʃən] *n* culminación *f*, colmo

culottes [kuː'lɒts] *npl* falda pantalón *f*

culprit ['kʌlprɪt] *n* culpable *m/f*

cult [kʌlt] *n* culto

cultivate ['kʌltɪveɪt] *vt* (*also fig*) cultivar; **~d** *adj* culto; **cultivation** [-'veɪʃən] *n* cultivo

cultural ['kʌltʃərəl] *adj* cultural

culture ['kʌltʃə*] *n* (*also fig*) cultura; (*BIO*) cultivo; **~d** *adj* culto

cumbersome ['kʌmbəsəm] *adj* de mucho bulto, voluminoso; (*process*) enrevesado

cunning ['kʌnɪŋ] *n* astucia ♦ *adj* astuto

cup [kʌp] *n* taza; (*as prize*) copa

cupboard ['kʌbəd] *n* armario; (*kitchen*) alacena

cup tie (*BRIT*) *n* partido de copa

curate ['kjuərɪt] *n* cura *m*

curator [kjuə'reɪtə*] *n* director(a) *m/f*

curb [kɜːb] *vt* refrenar; (*person*) reprimir ♦ *n* freno; (*US*) bordillo

curdle ['kɜːdl] *vi* cuajarse

cure [kjuə*] *vt* curar ♦ *n* cura, curación *f*; (*fig: solution*) remedio

curfew ['kɜːfjuː] *n* toque *m* de queda

curiosity [kjuərɪ'ɒsɪti] *n* curiosidad *f*

curious ['kjuərɪəs] *adj* curioso; (*person: interested*): **to be ~** sentir curiosidad

curl [kɜːl] *n* rizo ♦ *vt* (*hair*) rizar ♦ *vi* rizarse; **~ up** (*person*) hacerse un ovillo; **~er** *n* rulo; **~y** *adj* rizado

currant ['kʌrnt] *n* pasa (de Corinto); (*black~, red~*) grosella

currency ['kʌrnsɪ] *n* moneda; **to gain ~** (*fig*) difundirse

current ['kʌrnt] *n* corriente *f* ♦ *adj* (*accepted*) corriente; (*present*) actual; **~ account** (*BRIT*) *n* cuenta corriente;

~ affairs *npl* noticias *fpl* de actualidad;

~ly *adv* actualmente

curriculum [kə'rɪkjuləm] (*pl* **~s** or **curricula**) *n* plan *m* de estudios; **~ vitae** *n* currículum *m*

curry ['kʌrɪ] *n* curry *m* ♦ *vt*: **to ~ favour with** buscar favores con; **~ powder** *n* curry *m* en polvo

curse [kɜːs] *vi* soltar tacos ♦ *vt* maldecir ♦ *n* maldición *f*; (*swearword*) palabrota, taco

cursor ['kɜːsə*] *n* (*COMPUT*) cursor *m*

cursory ['kɜːsərɪ] *adj* rápido, superficial

curt [kɜːt] *adj* corto, seco

curtail [kɜː'teɪl] *vt* (*visit etc*) acortar; (*freedom*) restringir; (*expenses etc*) reducir

curtain ['kɜːtn] *n* cortina; (*THEATRE*) telón *m*

curts(e)y ['kɜːtsɪ] *vi* hacer una reverencia

curve [kɜːv] *n* curva ♦ *vi* (*road*) hacer una curva; (*line etc*) curvarse

cushion ['kuʃən] *n* cojín *m*; (*of air*) colchón *m* ♦ *vt* (*shock*) amortiguar

custard ['kʌstəd] *n* natillas *fpl*

custody ['kʌstədɪ] *n* custodia; **to take into ~** detener

custom ['kʌstəm] *n* costumbre *f*; (*COMM*) clientela; **~ary** *adj* acostumbrado

customer ['kʌstəmə*] *n* cliente *m/f*

customized ['kʌstəmaɪzd] *adj* (*car etc*) hecho a encargo

custom-made *adj* hecho a la medida

customs ['kʌstəmz] *npl* aduana; **~ officer** *n* aduanero/a

cut [kʌt] (*pt, pp* **cut**) *vt* cortar; (*price*) rebajar; (*text, programme*) acortar; (*reduce*) reducir ♦ *vi* cortar ♦ *n* (*in garment*) corte *m*; (*in skin*) cortadura; (*in salary etc*) rebaja; (*in spending*) reducción *f*, recorte *m*; (*slice of meat*) tajada; **to ~ a tooth** echar un diente; **~ down** *vt* (*tree*) derribar; (*reduce*) reducir; **~ off** *vt* cortar; (*person, place*) aislar; (*TEL*) desconectar; **~ out** *vt* (*shape*) recortar; (*stop: activity etc*)

cute dejar; (*remove*) quitar; **~ up** *vt* cortar (en pedazos); **~back** *n* reducción *f*

cute [kju:t] *adj* mono

cuticle ['kju:tɪkl] *n* cutícula

cutlery ['kʌtlərɪ] *n* cubiertos *mpl*

cutlet ['kʌtlɪt] *n* chuleta; (*pork etc* ~) plato vegetariano hecho con nueces y verdura en forma de chuleta

cut: **~out** *n* (*switch*) dispositivo de seguridad, disyuntor *m*; (*cardboard ~out*) recortable *m*; **~-price** (*US* **~-rate**) *adj* a precio reducido; **~throat** *n* asesino/a ♦ *adj* feroz

cutting ['kʌtɪŋ] *adj* (*remark*) mordaz ♦ *n* (*BRIT: from newspaper*) recorte *m*; (*from plant*) esqueje *m*

CV *n abbr* = **curriculum vitae**

cwt *abbr* = **hundredweight(s)**

cyanide ['saɪənaɪd] *n* cianuro

cybercafé ['saɪbəkæfeɪ] *n* cibercafé *m*

cycle ['saɪkl] *n* ciclo; (*bicycle*) bicicleta ♦ *vi* ir en bicicleta; **~ lane** *n* carril-bici *m*; **~ path** *n* carril-bici *m*; **cycling** *n* ciclismo; **cyclist** *n* ciclista *m/f*

cyclone ['saɪkləun] *n* ciclón *m*

cygnet ['sɪgnɪt] *n* pollo de cisne

cylinder ['sɪlɪndə*] *n* cilindro; (*of gas*) bombona; **~-head gasket** *n* junta de culata

cymbals ['sɪmblz] *npl* platillos *mpl*

cynic ['sɪnɪk] *n* cínico/a *f*; **~al** *adj* cínico; **~ism** ['sɪnɪsɪzəm] *n* cinismo

Cyprus ['saɪprəs] *n* Chipre *f*

cyst [sɪst] *n* quiste *m*; **~itis** [-'taɪtɪs] *n* cistitis *f*

czar [zɑ:*] *n* zar *m*

Czech [tʃek] *adj, n* checo/a *m/f*; **~ Republic** *n* la República Checa

D, d

D [di:] *n* (*MUS*) re *m*

dab [dæb] *vt* (*eyes, wound*) tocar (ligeramente); (*paint, cream*) poner un poco de

dabble ['dæbl] *vi*: **to ~ in** ser algo

aficionado a

dad [dæd] *n* = **daddy**

daddy ['dædɪ] *n* papá *m*

daffodil ['dæfədɪl] *n* narciso

daft [dɑ:ft] *adj* tonto

dagger ['dægə*] *n* puñal *m*, daga

daily ['deɪlɪ] *adj* diario, cotidiano ♦ *adv* todos los días, cada día

dainty ['deɪntɪ] *adj* delicado

dairy ['dɛərɪ] *n* (*shop*) lechería; (*on farm*) vaquería; **~ farm** *n* granja; **~ products** *npl* productos *mpl* lácteos; **~ store** (*US*) *n* lechería

daisy ['deɪzɪ] *n* margarita

dale [deɪl] *n* valle *m*

dam [dæm] *n* presa ♦ *vt* construir una presa sobre, represar

damage ['dæmɪdʒ] *n* lesión *f*; daño; (*dents etc*) desperfectos *mpl*; (*fig*) perjuicio ♦ *vt* dañar, perjudicar; (*spoil, break*) estropear; **~s** *npl* (*LAW*) daños *mpl* y perjuicios

damn [dæm] *vt* condenar; (*curse*) maldecir ♦ *n* (*inf*): **I don't give a ~** me importa un pito ♦ *adj* (*inf: also: ~ed*) maldito; **~ (it)!** ¡maldito sea!; **~ing** *adj* (*evidence*) irrecusable

damp [dæmp] *adj* húmedo, mojado ♦ *n* humedad *f* ♦ *vt* (*also: ~en*) (*cloth, rag*) mojar; (: *enthusiasm*) enfriar

damson ['dæmzən] *n* ciruela damascena

dance [dɑ:ns] *n* baile *m* ♦ *vi* bailar; **~ hall** *n* salón *m* de baile; **~r** *n* bailador(a) *m/f*; (*professional*) bailarín/ina *m/f*; **dancing** *n* baile *m*

dandelion ['dændɪlaɪən] *n* diente de león

dandruff ['dændrəf] *n* caspa

Dane [deɪn] *n* danés/esa *m/f*

danger ['deɪndʒə*] *n* peligro; (*risk*) riesgo; **~!** (*on sign*) ¡peligro de muerte!; **to be in ~ of** correr riesgo de; **~ous** *adj* peligroso; **~ously** *adv* peligrosamente

dangle ['dæŋgl] *vt* colgar ♦ *vi* pender, colgar

Danish ['deɪnɪʃ] adj danés/esa ♦ n (LING) danés m

dare [dɛə*] vt: to ~ sb to do desafiar a uno a hacer ♦ vi: to ~ (to) do sth atreverse a hacer algo; I ~ say (I suppose) puede ser (que); **daring** adj atrevido, osado ♦ n atrevimiento, osadía

dark [dɑ:k] adj oscuro; (hair, complexion) moreno ♦ n: in the ~ a oscuras; to be in the ~ about (fig) no saber nada de; after ~ después del anochecer; ~en vt (colour) hacer más oscuro ♦ vi oscurecerse; ~ glasses npl gafas fpl negras (SP), anteojos mpl negros (AM); ~ness n oscuridad f; ~room n cuarto oscuro

darling ['dɑ:lɪŋ] adj, n querido/a m/f

darn [dɑ:n] vt zurcir

dart [dɑ:t] n dardo; (in sewing) sisa ♦ vi precipitarse; ~ away/along vi salir/marchar disparado; ~board n diana; ~s n dardos mpl

dash [dæʃ] n (small quantity: of liquid) gota, chorrito; (: of solid) pizca; (sign) raya ♦ vt (throw) tirar; (hopes) defraudar ♦ vi precipitarse, ir de prisa; ~ away or off vi marcharse apresuradamente

dashboard ['dæʃbɔ:d] n (AUT) salpicadero

dashing ['dæʃɪŋ] adj gallardo

data ['deɪtə] npl datos mpl; ~base n base f de datos; ~ processing n proceso de datos

date [deɪt] n (day) fecha; (with friend) cita; (fruit) dátil m ♦ vt fechar; (person) salir con; ~ of birth fecha de nacimiento; to ~ ad hasta la fecha; ~d adj anticuado; ~ rape n violación ocurrida durante una cita con un conocido

daub [dɔ:b] vt embadurnar

daughter ['dɔ:tə*] n hija; ~-in-law n nuera, hija política

daunting ['dɔ:ntɪŋ] adj desalentador(a)

dawdle ['dɔ:dl] vi (go slowly) andar muy despacio

dawn [dɔ:n] n alba, amanecer m; (fig) nacimiento ♦ vi (day) amanecer; (fig): it ~ed on him that ... cayó en la cuenta de que ...

day [deɪ] n día m; (working ~) jornada; (hey~) tiempos mpl, auge m; the ~ before/after el día anterior/siguiente; the ~ after tomorrow pasado mañana; the ~ before yesterday anteayer; the following ~ el día siguiente; by ~ de día; ~break n amanecer m; ~dream vi soñar despierto; ~light n luz f del (día); ~ return (BRIT) n billete m de ida y vuelta (en un día); ~time n día m; ~to~ adj cotidiano

daze [deɪz] vt (stun) aturdir ♦ n: in a ~ aturdido

dazzle ['dæzl] vt deslumbrar

DC abbr (= direct current) corriente f continua

dead [dɛd] adj muerto; (limb) dormido; (telephone) cortado; (battery) agotado ♦ adv (completely) totalmente; (exactly) exactamente; to shoot sb ~ matar a uno a tiros; ~ tired muerto (de cansancio); to stop ~ pararse en seco; the ~ npl los muertos; to be a ~ loss (inf: person) ser un inútil; ~en vt (blow, sound) amortiguar; (pain etc) aliviar; ~ end n callejón m sin salida; ~ heat n (SPORT) empate m; ~line n fecha (or hora) tope; ~lock n to reach ~lock llegar a un punto muerto; ~ly adj mortal, fatal; ~pan adj sin expresión; the D~ Sea n el Mar Muerto

deaf [dɛf] adj sordo; ~en vt ensordecer; ~ness n sordera

deal [di:l] n (pt, pp dealt) n (agreement) pacto, convenio; (business ~) trato ♦ vt dar; (card) repartir; a great ~ (of) bastante, mucho; ~ in vt fus tratar en, comerciar en; ~ with vt fus (people) tratar con; (problem) ocuparse de; (subject) tratar de; ~ings npl (COMM) transacciones *fpl*; (*relations*) relaciones *fpl*

dealt [delt] *pt, pp of* **deal**

dean [di:n] *n* (REL) deán *m*; (SCOL: BRIT) decano; (: US) decano *m*, rector *m*

dear [dɪə*] *adj* querido; (*expensive*) caro ♦ *n*: **my** ~ mi querido/a ♦ *excl*: ~ **me**! ¡Dios mío!; **D~ Sir/Madam** (*in letter*) Muy Señor Mío, Estimado Señor/ Estimada Señora; **D~ Mr/Mrs X** Estimado/a Señor/a X; ~**ly** *adv* (*love*) mucho; (*pay*) caro

death [deθ] *n* muerte *f*; ~ **certificate** *n* partida de defunción; ~**ly** *adj* (*white*) como un muerto; (*silence*) sepulcral; ~ **penalty** *n* pena de muerte; ~ **rate** *n* mortalidad *f*; ~ **toll** *n* número de víctimas

debacle [deɪ'bɑːkl] *n* desastre *m*

debase [dɪ'beɪs] *vt* degradar

debatable [dɪ'beɪtəbl] *adj* discutible

debate [dɪ'beɪt] *n* debate *m* ♦ *vt* discutir

debit ['debɪt] *n* debe *m* ♦ *vt*: **to ~ a sum to sb** or **to sb's account** cargar una suma en cuenta a alguien

debris ['debriː] *n* escombros *mpl*

debt [det] *n* deuda; **to be in** ~ tener deudas; ~**or** *n* deudor(a) *m/f*

début ['deɪbjuː] *n* presentación *f*

decade ['dekeɪd] *n* decenio, década

decadence ['dekədəns] *n* decadencia *f*

decaff ['diː'kæf] (*inf*) descafeinado

decaffeinated [diː'kæfɪneɪtɪd] *adj* descafeinado

decanter [dɪ'kæntə*] *n* garrafa

decay [dɪ'keɪ] *n* (*of building*) desmoronamiento; (*of tooth*) caries *f inv* ♦ *vi* (*rot*) pudrirse

deceased [dɪ'siːst] *n*: **the** ~ el/la difunto/a

deceit [dɪ'siːt] *n* engaño; ~**ful** *adj* engañoso; **deceive** [dɪ'siːv] *vt* engañar

December [dɪ'sembə*] *n* diciembre *m*

decent ['diːsənt] *adj* (*proper*) decente; (*person: kind*) amable, bueno

deception [dɪ'sepʃən] *n* engaño

deceptive [dɪ'septɪv] *adj* engañoso

decibel ['desɪbel] *n* decibel(io) *m*

decide [dɪ'saɪd] *vt* (*person*) decidir; (*question, argument*) resolver ♦ *vi* decidir; **to ~ to do/that** decidir hacer/que; **to ~ on sth** decidirse por algo; ~**d** *adj* (*resolute*) decidido; (*clear, definite*) indudable; ~**dly** [-dɪdlɪ] *adv* decididamente; (*emphatically*) con resolución

deciduous [dɪ'sɪdjuəs] *adj* de hoja caduca

decimal ['desɪməl] *adj* decimal ♦ *n* decimal *m*; ~ **point** *n* coma decimal

decipher [dɪ'saɪfə*] *vt* descifrar

decision [dɪ'sɪʒən] *n* decisión *f*

decisive [dɪ'saɪsɪv] *adj* decisivo; (*person*) decidido

deck [dek] *n* (NAUT) cubierta; (*of bus*) piso; (*record* ~) platina; (*of cards*) baraja; ~**chair** *n* tumbona

declaration [deklə'reɪʃən] *n* declaración *f*

declare [dɪ'kleə*] *vt* declarar

decline [dɪ'klaɪn] *n* disminución *f*, descenso ♦ *vt* rehusar ♦ *vi* (*person, business*) decaer; (*strength*) disminuir

decoder [diː'kəʊdə*] *n* (TV) decodificador *m*

décor ['deɪkɔː*] *n* decoración *f*; (THEATRE) decorado

decorate ['dekəreɪt] *vt* (*adorn*): **to ~ (with)** adornar (de), decorar (de); (*paint*) pintar; (*paper*) empapelar; **decoration** [-'reɪʃən] *n* adorno; (*act*) decoración *f*; (*medal*) condecoración *f*; **decorator** (*workman*) pintor *m* (decorador)

decorum [dɪ'kɔːrəm] *n* decoro

decoy ['diːkɔɪ] *n* señuelo

decrease [*n* 'diːkriːs, *vb* diː'kriːs] *n*: ~ (**in**) disminución *f* (de) ♦ *vt* disminuir, reducir ♦ *vi* reducirse

decree [dɪ'kriː] *n* decreto; ~ **nisi** *n* sentencia provisional de divorcio

dedicate ['dedɪkeɪt] *vt* dedicar; **dedication** [-'keɪʃən] *n* (*devotion*) dedicación f; (in book) dedicatoria

deduce [dɪ'dju:s] vt deducir

deduct [dɪ'dʌkt] vt restar; descontar; **~ion** [dɪ'dʌkʃən] n (amount deducted) descuento; (conclusion) deducción f, conclusión f

deed [di:d] n hecho, acto; (feat) hazaña; (LAW) escritura

deep [di:p] adj profundo; (expressing measurements) de profundidad; (voice) bajo; (breath) profundo; (colour) intenso ♦ adv: **the spectators stood 20 ~** los espectadores se formaron en 20 en fondo; **to be 4 metres ~** tener 4 metros de profundidad; **~en** vt ahondar, profundizar ♦ vi aumentar, crecer; **~freeze** n congelador m; **~fry** vt freír en aceite abundante; **~ly** adv (breathe) a pleno pulmón; (interested, moved, grateful) profundamente, hondamente; **~sea diving** n buceo de altura; **~seated** adj (beliefs) (profundamente) arraigado

deer [dɪə*] n inv ciervo

deface [dɪ'feɪs] vt (wall, surface) estropear, pintarrajear

default [dɪ'fɔ:lt] n: **by ~** (win) por incomparecencia; (COMPUT) por defecto

defeat [dɪ'fi:t] n derrota ♦ vt derrotar, vencer; **~ist** adj, n derrotista m/f

defect [n 'di:fɛkt, vb dɪ'fɛkt] n defecto ♦ vi: **to ~ to the enemy** pasarse al enemigo; **~ive** [dɪ'fɛktɪv] adj defectuoso

defence [dɪ'fɛns] (US **defense**) n defensa; **~less** adj indefenso

defend [dɪ'fɛnd] vt defender; **~ant** n acusado/a; (in civil case) demandado/a; **~er** n defensor(a) m/f; (SPORT) defensa m/f

defense [dɪ'fɛns] (US) n = **defence**

defensive [dɪ'fɛnsɪv] adj defensivo ♦ n: **on the ~** a la defensiva

defer [dɪ'fə:*] vt aplazar

defiance [dɪ'faɪəns] n desafío; **in ~ of** en contra de; **defiant** [dɪ'faɪənt] adj

(challenging) desafiante, retador(a)

deficiency [dɪ'fɪʃənsɪ] n (lack) falta; (defect) defecto m; **deficient** [dɪ'fɪʃənt] adj deficiente

deficit ['dɛfɪsɪt] n déficit m

define [dɪ'faɪn] vt (word etc) definir; (limits etc) determinar

definite ['dɛfɪnɪt] adj (fixed) determinado; (obvious) claro; (certain) indudable; **he was ~ about it** no dejó lugar a dudas (sobre ello); **~ly** adv desde luego, por supuesto

definition [dɛfɪ'nɪʃən] n definición f; (clearness) nitidez f

deflate [di:'fleɪt] vt desinflar

deflect [dɪ'flɛkt] vt desviar

defraud [dɪ'frɔ:d] vt: **to ~ sb of sth** estafar algo a uno

defrost [di:'frɔst] vt descongelar; **~er** (US) n (demister) eliminador m de vaho

deft [dɛft] adj diestro, hábil

defunct [dɪ'fʌŋkt] adj difunto; (organization etc) ya que no existe

defuse [di:'fju:z] vt desactivar; (situation) calmar

defy [dɪ'faɪ] vt (resist) oponerse a; (challenge) desafiar; (fig): **it defies description** resulta imposible describirlo

degenerate [vb dɪ'dʒɛnəreɪt, adj dɪ'dʒɛnərɪt] vi degenerar ♦ adj degenerado

degree [dɪ'gri:] n grado; (SCOL) título; **to have a ~ in maths** tener una licenciatura en matemáticas; **by ~s** (gradually) poco a poco, por etapas; **to some ~** hasta cierto punto

dehydrated [di:haɪ'dreɪtɪd] adj deshidratado; (milk) en polvo

de-ice [di:'aɪs] vt deshelar

deign [deɪn] vi: **to ~ to do** dignarse hacer

dejected [dɪ'dʒɛktɪd] adj abatido, desanimado

delay [dɪ'leɪ] vt demorar, aplazar; (person) entretener; (train) retrasar ♦ vi tardar ♦ n demora, retraso; **to be ~ed**

retrasarse; **without ~** en seguida, sin
tardar

delectable [dɪ'lektəbl] adj (person)
encantador(a); (food) delicioso

delegate [n 'delɪgɪt, vb 'delɪgeɪt] n
delegado/a ♦ vt (person) delegar en;
(task) delegar

delete [dɪ'liːt] vt suprimir, tachar

deliberate [adj dɪ'lɪbərɪt, vb
dɪ'lɪbəreɪt] adj (intentional)
intencionado; (slow) pausado, lento
♦ vi deliberar; **~ly** adv (on purpose) a
propósito

delicacy ['delɪkəsɪ] n delicadeza;
(choice food) manjar m

delicate ['delɪkɪt] adj delicado; (fragile)
frágil

delicatessen [delɪkə'tesn] n
ultramarinos mpl finos

delicious [dɪ'lɪʃəs] adj delicioso

delight [dɪ'laɪt] n (feeling) placer m,
deleite m; (person, experience etc)
encanto, delicia ♦ vt encantar, deleitar;
to take ~ in deleitarse en; **~ed** adj:
~ed (at or with/to do) encantado
(con/de hacer); **~ful** adj encantador(a),
delicioso

delinquent [dɪ'lɪŋkwənt] adj, n
delincuente m/f

delirious [dɪ'lɪrɪəs] adj: **to be ~**
delirar, desvariar; **to be ~ with** estar
loco de

deliver [dɪ'lɪvə*] vt (distribute) repartir;
(hand over) entregar; (message)
comunicar; (speech) pronunciar; (MED)
asistir al parto de; **~y** n reparto;
entrega; (of speaker) modo de
expresarse; (MED) parto,
alumbramiento; **to take ~y of** recibir

delude [dɪ'luːd] vt engañar

deluge ['deljuːdʒ] n diluvio

delusion [dɪ'luːʒən] n ilusión f, engaño

de luxe [də'lʌks] adj de lujo

demand [dɪ'mɑːnd] vt (gen) exigir;
(rights) reclamar ♦ n exigencia; (claim)
reclamación f; (ECON) demanda; **to be
in ~** ser muy solicitado; **on ~** a

solicitud; **~ing** adj (boss) exigente;
(work) absorbente

demean [dɪ'miːn] vt: **to ~ o.s.**
rebajarse

demeanour [dɪ'miːnə*] (US
demeanor) n porte m, conducta

demented [dɪ'mentɪd] adj demente

demise [dɪ'maɪz] n (death)
fallecimiento

demister [diː'mɪstə*] n (AUT)
eliminador m de vaho

demo ['deməu] (inf) n abbr
(= demonstration) manifestación f

democracy [dɪ'mɔkrəsɪ] n democracia;
democrat ['deməkræt] n demócrata
m/f; **democratic** [demə'krætɪk] adj
democrático; (US) demócrata

demolish [dɪ'mɔlɪʃ] vt derribar,
demoler; (fig: argument) destruir

demon ['diːmən] n (evil spirit)
demonio

demonstrate ['demənstreɪt] vt
demostrar; (skill, appliance) mostrar ♦ vi
manifestarse; **demonstration**
[-'streɪʃən] n (POL) manifestación f;
(proof, exhibition) demostración f;
demonstrator n (POL) manifestante
m/f; (COMM) demostrador/a m/f;
vendedor/a m/f

demote [dɪ'məut] vt degradar

demure [dɪ'mjuə*] adj recatado

den [den] n (of animal) guarida; (room)
habitación f

denial [dɪ'naɪəl] n (refusal) negativa; (of
report etc) negación f

denim ['denɪm] n tela vaquera; **~s** npl
vaqueros mpl

Denmark ['denmɑːk] n Dinamarca

denomination [dɪnɔmɪ'neɪʃən] n
valor m; (REL) confesión f

denounce [dɪ'nauns] vt denunciar

dense [dens] adj (crowd) denso; (thick)
espeso; (: foliage etc) tupido; (inf:
stupid) torpe; **~ly** adv: **~ly populated**
con una alta densidad de población

density ['densɪtɪ] n densidad f;
single/double-~ disk n (COMPUT)

disco de densidad sencilla/doble densidad

dent [dent] n abolladura ♦ vt (also: **make a ~ in**) abollar

dental ['dentl] adj dental; **~ surgeon** n odontólogo/a

dentist ['dentɪst] n dentista m/f

dentures ['dentʃəz] npl dentadura (postiza)

deny [dɪ'naɪ] vt negar; (charge) rechazar

deodorant [diː'əʊdərənt] n desodorante m

depart [dɪ'pɑːt] vi irse, marcharse; (train) salir; **to ~ from** (fig: differ from) apartarse de

department [dɪ'pɑːtmənt] n (COMM) sección f; (SCOL) departamento; (POL) ministerio; **~ store** n gran almacén m

departure [dɪ'pɑːtʃə*] n partida, ida; (of train) salida; (of employee) marcha; **a new ~** un nuevo rumbo; **~ lounge** n (at airport) sala de embarque

depend [dɪ'pend] vi: **to ~ on** depender de; (rely on) contar con; **it ~s** depende, según; **~ing on the result** según el resultado; **~able** adj (person) formal, serio; (watch) exacto; (car) seguro; **~ant** n dependiente m/f; **~ent** adj: **to be ~ent on** depender de ♦ n = **dependant**

depict [dɪ'pɪkt] vt (in picture) pintar; (describe) representar

depleted [dɪ'pliːtɪd] adj reducido

deploy [dɪ'plɔɪ] vt desplegar

deport [dɪ'pɔːt] vt deportar

deposit [dɪ'pɔzɪt] n depósito; (CHEM) sedimento; (of ore, oil) yacimiento m ♦ (gen) depositar; **~ account** (BRIT) n cuenta de ahorros

depot ['depəʊ] n (storehouse) depósito; (for vehicles) parque m; (US) estación f

depreciate [dɪ'priːʃɪeɪt] vi depreciarse, perder valor

depress [dɪ'pres] vt deprimir; (wages etc) hacer bajar; (press down) apretar; **~ed** adj deprimido; **~ing** adj

deprimente; **~ion** [dɪ'preʃən] n depresión f

deprivation [deprɪ'veɪʃən] n privación f

deprive [dɪ'praɪv] vt: **to ~ sb of** privar a uno de; **~d** adj necesitado

depth [depθ] n profundidad f; (of cupboard) fondo; **to be in the ~s of despair** sentir la mayor desesperación; **to be out of one's ~** (in water) no hacer pie; (fig) sentirse totalmente perdido

deputize ['depjutaɪz] vi: **to ~ for sb** suplir a uno

deputy ['depjutɪ] adj: **~ head** subdirector(a) m/f ♦ n sustituto/a, suplente m/f; (US: POL) diputado/a; (US: also: **~ sheriff**) agente m (del sheriff)

derail [dɪ'reɪl] vt: **to be ~ed** descarrilarse

deranged [dɪ'reɪndʒd] adj trastornado

derby ['dɑːbɪ] (US) n (hat) hongo

derelict ['derɪlɪkt] adj abandonado

derisory [dɪ'raɪzərɪ] adj (sum) irrisorio

derive [dɪ'raɪv] vt (benefit etc) obtener ♦ vi: **to ~ from** derivarse de

derogatory [dɪ'rɒgətərɪ] adj despectivo

descend [dɪ'send] vt, vi descender, bajar; **to ~ from** descender de; **to ~ to** rebajarse a; **~ant** n descendiente m/f

descent [dɪ'sent] n descenso; (origin) descendencia

describe [dɪs'kraɪb] vt describir; **description** [-'krɪpʃən] n descripción f; (sort) clase f, género

desecrate ['desɪkreɪt] vt profanar

desert [n 'dezət, vb dɪ'zɜːt] n desierto ♦ vt abandonar ♦ vi (MIL) desertar; **~er** [dɪ'zɜːtə*] n desertor(a) m/f; **~ion** [dɪ'zɜːʃən] n deserción f; (LAW) abandono; **~ island** n isla desierta; **~s** [dɪ'zɜːts] npl: **to get one's just ~s** llevar su merecido

deserve [dɪ'zɜːv] vt merecer, ser digno de; **deserving** adj (person) digno, (action, cause) meritorio

design [dɪˈzaɪn] n (sketch) bosquejo; (layout, shape) diseño; (pattern) intención f ♦ vt diseñar

designate [vb ˈdezɪɡneɪt, adj ˈdezɪɡnɪt] (appoint) nombrar; (destine) designar ♦ adj designado

designer [dɪˈzaɪnə*] n/f (fashion ~) modisto/a, diseñador/a m/f de moda

desirable [dɪˈzaɪərəbl] adj (proper) deseable; (attractive) atractivo

desire [dɪˈzaɪə*] n deseo ♦ vt desear

desk [desk] n (in office) escritorio; (for pupil) pupitre m; (in hotel, at airport) recepción f; (BRIT: in shop, restaurant) caja

desk-top publishing [ˈdesktɒp-] n autoedición f

desolate [ˈdesəlɪt] adj (place) desierto; (person) afligido

despair [dɪsˈpeə*] n desesperación f ♦ vi: to ~ of perder la esperanza de

despatch [dɪsˈpætʃ] n, vt = dispatch

desperate [ˈdespərɪt] adj desesperado; (fugitive) peligroso; to be ~ for sth/to do necesitar urgentemente algo/hacer; ~ly adv desesperadamente; (very) terriblemente, gravemente

desperation [despəˈreɪʃən] n desesperación f; in (sheer) ~ (absolutamente) desesperado

despicable [dɪsˈpɪkəbl] adj vil, despreciable

despise [dɪsˈpaɪz] vt despreciar

despite [dɪsˈpaɪt] prep a pesar de, pese a

despondent [dɪsˈpɒndənt] adj deprimido, abatido

dessert [dɪˈzɜːt] n postre m; ~spoon n cuchara (de postre)

destination [destɪˈneɪʃən] n destino

destiny [ˈdestɪnɪ] n destino

destitute [ˈdestɪtjuːt] adj desamparado, indigente

destroy [dɪsˈtrɔɪ] vt destruir; (animal) sacrificar; ~er n (NAUT) destructor m

destruction [dɪsˈtrʌkʃən] n destrucción f

detach [dɪˈtætʃ] vt separar; (unstick) despegar; ~ed adj (attitude) objetivo, imparcial; ~ed house n ≈ chalé m, ≈ chalet m; ~ment n (aloofness) frialdad f; (MIL) destacamento

detail [ˈdiːteɪl] n detalle m; (no pl: in picture etc) detalles mpl; (trifle) pequeñez f ♦ vt detallar; (MIL) destacar; in ~ detalladamente; ~ed adj detallado

detain [dɪˈteɪn] vt retener; (in captivity) detener

detect [dɪˈtekt] vt descubrir; (MED, POLICE) identificar; (MIL, RADAR, TECH) detectar; ~ion [dɪˈtekʃən] n descubrimiento; (identification f; ~ive n detective m/f; ~ive story n novela policíaca; ~or n detector m

detention [dɪˈtenʃən] n detención f, arresto; (SCOL) castigo

deter [dɪˈtɜː*] vt (dissuade) disuadir

detergent [dɪˈtɜːdʒənt] n detergente m

deteriorate [dɪˈtɪərɪəreɪt] vi deteriorarse; **deterioration** [-ˈreɪʃən] n deterioro

determination [dɪtɜːmɪˈneɪʃən] n resolución f

determine [dɪˈtɜːmɪn] vt determinar; ~d adj (person) resuelto, decidido; ~d to do resuelto a hacer

deterrent [dɪˈterənt] n (MIL) fuerza de disuasión

detest [dɪˈtest] vt aborrecer

detonate [ˈdetəneɪt] vi estallar ♦ vt hacer detonar

detour [ˈdiːtuə*] n (gen, US: AUT) desviación f

detract [dɪˈtrækt] vt: to ~ from quitar mérito a, desvirtuar

detriment [ˈdetrɪmənt] n: to the ~ of en perjuicio de; ~al [detrɪˈmentl] adj: ~al (to) perjudicial (a)

devaluation [dɪvæljuˈeɪʃən] n devaluación f

devalue [di:'vælju:] vt (currency) devaluar; (fig) quitar mérito a

devastate ['dɛvəsteɪt] vt devastar; (fig): **to be ~d by** quedar destrozado por; **devastating** adj devastador(a); (fig) arrollador(a)

develop [dɪ'vɛləp] vt desarrollar; (PHOT) revelar; (disease) coger; (habit) adquirir; (fault) empezar a tener ♦ vi desarrollarse; (advance) progresar; (facts, symptoms) aparecer; ~**er** n promotor m; ~**ing country** n país m en (vías de) desarrollo; ~**ment** n desarrollo; (advance) progreso; (of affair, case) desenvolvimiento; (of land) urbanización f

deviation [di:vɪ'eɪʃən] n desviación f

device [dɪ'vaɪs] n (apparatus) aparato, mecanismo

devil ['dɛvl] n diablo, demonio

devious ['di:vɪəs] adj taimado

devise [dɪ'vaɪz] vt idear, inventar

devoid [dɪ'vɔɪd] adj: ~ **of** desprovisto de

devolution [di:və'lu:ʃən] n (POL) descentralización f

devote [dɪ'vəʊt] vt: **to ~ sth to** dedicar algo a; ~**d** adj (loyal) leal, fiel; **to be ~d to sb** querer con devoción a alguien; **the book is ~d to politics** el libro trata de la política; ~**e** [dɛvəʊ'ti:] n entusiasta m/f; (REL) devoto/a; **devotion** n dedicación f; (REL) devoción f

devour [dɪ'vaʊə*] vt devorar

devout [dɪ'vaʊt] adj devoto

dew [dju:] n rocío

diabetes [daɪə'bi:ti:z] n diabetes f;

diabetic [-'bɛtɪk] adj, n diabético/a m/f

diabolical [daɪə'bɔlɪkl] (inf) adj (weather, behaviour) pésimo

diagnosis [daɪəg'nəʊsɪs] (pl -ses) n diagnóstico

diagonal [daɪ'ægənl] n, adj diagonal f

diagram ['daɪəgræm] n diagrama m, esquema m

dial ['daɪəl] n esfera, cuadrante m, cara f (AM); (on radio etc) selector m; (of phone) disco ♦ vt (number) marcar

dialling ['daɪəlɪŋ]: ~ **code** n prefijo; ~ **tone** (US **dial tone**) n (BRIT) señal f or tono de marcar

dialogue ['daɪəlɔg] (US **dialog**) n diálogo

diameter [daɪ'æmɪtə*] n diámetro

diamond ['daɪəmənd] n diamante m; (shape) rombo; ~**s** npl (CARDS) diamantes mpl

diaper ['daɪəpə*] (US) n pañal m

diaphragm ['daɪəfræm] n diafragma m

diarrhoea [daɪə'ri:ə] (US **diarrhea**) n diarrea

diary ['daɪərɪ] n (daily account) diario; (book) agenda

dice [daɪs] n inv dados mpl ♦ vt (CULIN) cortar en cuadritos

Dictaphone ® ['dɪktəfəʊn] n dictáfono ®

dictate [dɪk'teɪt] vt dictar; (conditions) imponer; **dictation** [-'teɪʃən] n dictado; (giving of orders) órdenes fpl

dictator [dɪk'teɪtə*] n dictador m; ~**ship** n dictadura

dictionary ['dɪkʃənrɪ] n diccionario

did [dɪd] pt of **do**

didn't ['dɪdənt] = **did not**

die [daɪ] vi morir; (fig: fade) desvanecerse, desaparecer; **to be dying for sth/to do sth** morirse por algo/de ganas de hacer algo; ~ **away** vi (sound, light) perderse; ~ **down** vi apagarse; (wind) amainar; ~ **out** vi desaparecer

diesel ['di:zl] n vehículo con motor Diesel; ~ **engine** n motor m Diesel; ~ **(oil)** n gasoil m

diet ['daɪət] n dieta; (restricted food) régimen m ♦ vi (also: **be on a ~**) estar a dieta, hacer régimen

differ ['dɪfə*] vi: **to ~ (from)** (be different) ser distinto (a), diferenciarse (de); (disagree) discrepar (de); ~**ence** n diferencia; (disagreement) desacuerdo

~ent adj diferente, distinto; ~entiate [-'renʃɪeɪt] vi: to ~entiate (between) distinguir (entre); ~ently adv de otro modo, en forma distinta

difficult ['dɪfɪkəlt] adj difícil; ~y n dificultad f

diffident ['dɪfɪdənt] adj tímido

dig [dɪg] (pt, pp dug) vt (hole, ground) cavar ♦ n (prod) empujón m; (archaeological) excavación f; (remark) indirecta; to ~ one's nails into clavar las uñas en; ~ into vt fus (savings) consumir; ~ up vt (information) desenterrar; (plant) desarraigar

digest [vb daɪ'dʒest, n 'daɪdʒest] vt (food) digerir; (facts) asimilar ♦ n resumen m, compendio m; ~ion [dɪ'dʒestʃən] n digestión f

digit ['dɪdʒɪt] n (number) dígito; (finger) dedo; ~al adj digital; ~al camera n cámara digital; ~al TV n televisión f digital

dignified ['dɪgnɪfaɪd] adj grave, solemne

dignity ['dɪgnɪtɪ] n dignidad f

digress [daɪ'gres] vi: to ~ from apartarse de

digs [dɪgz] (BRIT: inf) npl pensión f, alojamiento m

dilapidated [dɪ'læpɪdeɪtɪd] adj desmoronado, ruinoso

dilemma [daɪ'lemə] n dilema m

diligent ['dɪlɪdʒənt] adj diligente

dilute [daɪ'lu:t] vt diluir

dim [dɪm] adj (light) débil; (outline) indistinto; (room) oscuro; (inf: stupid) lerdo ♦ vt (light) bajar

dime [daɪm] (US) n moneda de diez centavos

dimension [dɪ'menʃən] n dimensión f

diminish [dɪ'mɪnɪʃ] vt, vi disminuir

diminutive [dɪ'mɪnjutɪv] adj diminuto ♦ n (LING) diminutivo

dimmers ['dɪməz] (US) npl (AUT: dipped headlights) luces fpl cortas; (: parking lights) luces fpl de posición

dimple ['dɪmpl] n hoyuelo

din [dɪn] n estruendo, estrépito

dine [daɪn] vi cenar; ~r n (person) comensal m/f

dinghy ['dɪŋgɪ] n bote m; (also: rubber ~) lancha (neumática)

dingy ['dɪndʒɪ] adj (room) sombrío; (colour) sucio

dining car ['daɪnɪŋ-] (BRIT) n (RAIL) coche-comedor m

dining room n comedor m

dinner ['dɪnə*] n (evening meal) cena; (lunch) comida; (public) cena, banquete m; ~ jacket n smoking m; ~ party n cena; ~ time n (evening) hora de cenar; (midday) hora de comer

dinosaur ['daɪnəsɔ:*] n dinosaurio

dip [dɪp] n (slope) pendiente m; (in sea) baño; (CULIN) salsa ♦ vt (in water) mojar; (ladle etc) meter; (BRIT: AUT): to ~ one's lights poner luces de cruce ♦ vi (road etc) descender, bajar

diploma [dɪ'pləumə] n diploma m

diplomacy [dɪ'pləuməsɪ] n diplomacia

diplomat ['dɪpləmæt] n diplomático/a; ~ic [dɪplə'mætɪk] adj diplomático

diprod ['dɪprɒd] (US) n = dipstick

dipstick ['dɪpstɪk] (BRIT) n (AUT) varilla de nivel (del aceite)

dipswitch ['dɪpswɪtʃ] (BRIT) n (AUT) interruptor m

dire [daɪə*] adj calamitoso

direct [daɪ'rekt] adj directo; (challenge) claro; (person) franco ♦ vt dirigir; (order): to ~ sb to do sth mandar a uno hacer algo ♦ adv derecho; can you ~ me to...? ¿puede indicarme dónde está...?; ~ debit (BRIT) n domiciliación f bancaria de recibos

direction [dɪ'rekʃən] n dirección f; sense of ~ sentido de la dirección; ~s npl (instructions) instrucciones fpl; ~s for use modo de empleo

directly [dɪ'rektlɪ] adv (in straight line) directamente; (at once) en seguida

director [dɪ'rektə*] n director(a) m/f

directory [dɪ'rektərɪ] n (TEL) guía (telefónica); (COMPUT) directorio;

~ enquiries, ~ assistance (US) n (servicio de) información f

dirt [dɜːt] n suciedad f; (earth) tierra; **~-cheap** adj baratísimo; **~y** adj sucio; (joke) verde (SP), colorado (AM) ♦ vt ensuciar; (stain) manchar; **~y trick** n juego sucio

disability [dɪsə'bɪlɪtɪ] n incapacidad f

disabled [dɪs'eɪbld] adj: **to be physically ~** ser minusválido/a; **to be mentally ~** ser deficiente mental

disadvantage [dɪsəd'vɑːntɪdʒ] n desventaja, inconveniente m

disagree [dɪsə'griː] vi (differ) discrepar; **to ~ (with)** no estar de acuerdo (con); **~able** adj desagradable; (person) antipático; **~ment** n desacuerdo

disallow [dɪsə'lau] vt (goal) anular; (claim) rechazar

disappear [dɪsə'pɪə*] vi desaparecer; **~ance** n desaparición f

disappoint [dɪsə'pɔɪnt] vt decepcionar, defraudar; **~ed** adj decepcionado; **~ing** adj decepcionante; **~ment** n decepción f

disapproval [dɪsə'pruːvəl] n desaprobación f

disapprove [dɪsə'pruːv] vi: **to ~ of** ver mal

disarmament [dɪs'ɑːməmənt] n desarme m

disarray [dɪsə'reɪ] n: **in ~** (army, organization) desorganizado; (hair, clothes) desarreglado

disaster [dɪ'zɑːstə*] n desastre m

disband [dɪs'bænd] vt disolver ♦ vi desbandarse

disbelief [dɪsbə'liːf] n incredulidad f

disc [dɪsk] n disco; (COMPUT) = **disk**

discard [dɪs'kɑːd] vt (old things) tirar; (fig) descartar

discern [dɪ'sɜːn] vt percibir, discernir; (understand) comprender; **~ing** adj perspicaz

discharge [vb dɪs'tʃɑːdʒ, n 'dɪstʃɑːdʒ] vt (task, duty) cumplir; (waste) verter; (patient) dar de alta; (employee)

despedir; (soldier) licenciar; (defendant) poner en libertad ♦ n (ELEC) descarga; (MED) supuración f; (dismissal) despedida; (of duty) desempeño; (of debt) pago, descargo

discipline ['dɪsɪplɪn] n disciplina ♦ vt disciplinar; (punish) castigar

disc jockey [dɪsk 'dʒɒkɪ] n pinchadiscos m/f inv

disclaim [dɪs'kleɪm] vt negar

disclose [dɪs'kləuz] vt revelar; **disclosure** [-'kləuʒə*] n revelación f

disco ['dɪskəu] n abbr = **discothèque**

discomfort [dɪs'kʌmfət] n incomodidad f; (unease) inquietud f; (physical) malestar m

disconcert [dɪskən'sɜːt] vt desconcertar

disconnect [dɪskə'nɛkt] vt separar; (ELEC etc) desconectar

discontent [dɪskən'tɛnt] n descontento; **~ed** adj descontento

discontinue [dɪskən'tɪnjuː] vt interrumpir; (payments) suspender; **"~d"** (COMM) "ya no se fabrica"

discord ['dɪskɔːd] n discordia; (MUS) disonancia

discothèque [dɪskəu'tɛk] n discoteca

discount [n 'dɪskaunt, vb dɪs'kaunt] n descuento ♦ vt descontar

discourage [dɪs'kʌrɪdʒ] vt desalentar; (advise against): **to ~ sb from doing** disuadir a uno de hacer

discover [dɪs'kʌvə*] vt descubrir; (error) darse cuenta de; **~y** n descubrimiento

discredit [dɪs'krɛdɪt] vt desacreditar

discreet [dɪs'kriːt] adj (tactful) discreto; (careful) circunspecto, prudente

discrepancy [dɪs'krɛpənsɪ] n diferencia

discretion [dɪs'krɛʃən] n (tact) discreción f; **at the ~ of** a criterio de

discriminate [dɪs'krɪmɪneɪt] vi: **to ~ between** distinguir entre; **to ~ against** discriminar contra; **discriminating** adj entendido; **discrimination** [-'neɪʃən] n (*discernment*) perspicacia; (*bias*) discriminación f

discuss [dɪs'kʌs] vt discutir; (*a theme*) tratar; **~ion** [dɪ'skʌʃən] n discusión f

disdain [dɪs'deɪn] n desdén m

disease [dɪ'ziːz] n enfermedad f

disembark [dɪsɪm'bɑːk] vt, vi desembarcar

disentangle [dɪsɪn'tæŋgl] vt soltar; (*wire, thread*) desenredar

disfigure [dɪs'fɪgə*] vt (*person*) desfigurar; (*face*) afear

disgrace [dɪs'greɪs] n ignominia; (*shame*) vergüenza, escándalo ♦ vt deshonrar; **~ful** adj vergonzoso

disgruntled [dɪs'grʌntld] adj disgustado, descontento

disguise [dɪs'gaɪz] n disfraz m ♦ vt disfrazar; **in ~** disfrazado

disgust [dɪs'gʌst] n repugnancia ♦ vt repugnar, dar asco a; **~ing** adj repugnante, asqueroso; (*behaviour*) vergonzoso

dish [dɪʃ] n (*gen*) plato; **to do** or **wash the ~es** fregar los platos; **~ out** vt repartir; **~ up** vt servir; **~cloth** n estropajo

dishearten [dɪs'hɑːtn] vt desalentar

dishevelled [dɪ'ʃevəld] (*US* **disheveled**) adj (*hair*) despeinado; (*appearance*) desarreglado

dishonest [dɪs'ɔnɪst] adj (*person*) poco honrado, tramposo; (*means*) fraudulento; **~y** n falta de honradez

dishonour [dɪs'ɔnə*] (*US* **dishonor**) n deshonra; **~able** adj deshonroso

dishtowel [dɪʃtauəl] (*US*) n estropajo

dishwasher [dɪʃwɔʃə*] n lavaplatos m inv

disillusion [dɪsɪ'luːʒən] vt desilusionar

disinfect [dɪsɪn'fekt] vt desinfectar; **~ant** n desinfectante m

disintegrate [dɪs'ɪntɪgreɪt] vi disgregarse, desintegrarse

disinterested [dɪs'ɪntrəstɪd] adj desinteresado

disjointed [dɪs'dʒɔɪntɪd] adj inconexo

disk [dɪsk] n (*esp US*) = **disc**; (*COMPUT*) disco, disquete m; **single-/double-sided ~** disco de una cara/dos caras; **~ drive** n disc drive m; **~ette** [-'et] n = **disk**

dislike [dɪs'laɪk] n antipatía, aversión f ♦ vt tener antipatía a

dislocate ['dɪsləkeɪt] vt dislocar

dislodge [dɪs'lɔdʒ] vt sacar

disloyal [dɪs'lɔɪəl] adj desleal

dismal ['dɪzml] adj (*gloomy*) deprimente, triste; (*very bad*) malísimo, fatal

dismantle [dɪs'mæntl] vt desmontar, desarmar

dismay [dɪs'meɪ] n consternación f ♦ vt consternar

dismiss [dɪs'mɪs] vt (*worker*) despedir; (*pupils*) dejar marchar; (*soldiers*) dar permiso para irse; (*idea, LAW*) rechazar; (*possibility*) descartar; **~al** n despido

dismount [dɪs'maunt] vi apearse

disobedient [dɪsə'biːdɪənt] adj desobediente

disobey [dɪsə'beɪ] vt desobedecer

disorder [dɪs'ɔːdə*] n desorden m; (*rioting*) disturbios mpl; (*MED*) trastorno; **~ly** adj desordenado; (*meeting*) alborotado; (*conduct*) escandaloso

disorientated [dɪs'ɔːrɪənteɪtəd] adj desorientado

disown [dɪs'əun] vt (*action*) renegar de; (*person*) negar cualquier tipo de relación con

disparaging [dɪs'pærɪdʒɪŋ] adj despreciativo

dispassionate [dɪs'pæʃənɪt] adj (*unbiased*) imparcial

dispatch [dɪs'pætʃ] vt enviar ♦ n (*sending*) envío; (*PRESS*) informe m; (*MIL*) parte m

dispel [dɪs'pel] vt disipar

dispense [dɪs'pens] vt (*medicines*) preparar; **~ with** vt fus prescindir de; **~r** n (*container*) distribuidor m automático; **dispensing chemist** (*BRIT*) n farmacia

disperse [dɪs'pəːs] vt dispersar ♦ vi dispersarse

dispirited [dɪ'spɪrɪtɪd] adj desanimado, desalentado

displace [dɪs'pleɪs] vt desplazar, reemplazar; **~d person** n (POL) desplazado/a

display [dɪs'pleɪ] n (in shop window) escaparate m; (exhibition) exposición f; (COMPUT) visualización f; (of feeling) manifestación f ♦ vt exponer; manifestar; (ostentatiously) lucir

displease [dɪs'pliːz] vt (offend) ofender; (annoy) fastidiar; **~d** adj: **~d with** disgustado con; **displeasure** [-'plɛʒə*] n disgusto

disposable [dɪs'pəuzəbl] adj desechable; (income) disponible; **~ nappy** n pañal m desechable

disposal [dɪs'pəuzl] n (of rubbish) destrucción f; **at one's ~** a su disposición

dispose [dɪs'pəuz] vi: **to ~ of** (unwanted goods) deshacerse de; (problem etc) resolver; **~d** adj: **~d to do** dispuesto a hacer; **to be well-~d towards sb** estar bien dispuesto hacia uno; **disposition** [dɪspə'zɪʃən] n (nature) temperamento; (inclination) propensión f

disprove [dɪs'pruːv] vt refutar

dispute [dɪs'pjuːt] n (argument, also: industrial ~) conflicto (laboral) ♦ vt (argue) disputar, discutir; (question) cuestionar

disqualify [dɪs'kwɒlɪfaɪ] vt (SPORT) desclasificar; **to ~ sb for sth/from doing sth** incapacitar a alguien para algo/hacer algo

disquiet [dɪs'kwaɪət] n preocupación f, inquietud f

disregard [dɪsrɪ'gɑːd] vt (ignore) no hacer caso de

disrepair [dɪsrɪ'pɛə*] n: **to fall into ~** (building) desmoronarse

disreputable [dɪs'rɛpjutəbl] adj (person) de mala fama; (behaviour) vergonzoso

disrespectful [dɪsrɪ'spɛktfʊl] adj irrespetuoso

disrupt [dɪs'rʌpt] vt (plans) desbaratar, trastornar; (conversation) interrumpir

dissatisfaction [dɪssætɪs'fækʃən] n disgusto, descontento

dissect [dɪ'sɛkt] vt disecar

dissent [dɪ'sɛnt] n disensión f

dissertation [dɪsə'teɪʃən] n tesina

disservice [dɪs'səːvɪs] n: **to do sb a ~** perjudicar a alguien

dissimilar [dɪ'sɪmɪlə*] adj distinto

dissipate ['dɪsɪpeɪt] vt disipar; (waste) desperdiciar

dissolve [dɪ'zɒlv] vt disolver ♦ vi disolverse; **to ~ in(to) tears** deshacerse en lágrimas

dissuade [dɪ'sweɪd] vt: **to ~ sb (from)** disuadir a uno (de)

distance ['dɪstəns] n distancia; **in the ~** a lo lejos

distant ['dɪstənt] adj lejano; (manner) reservado, frío

distaste [dɪs'teɪst] n repugnancia; **~ful** adj repugnante, desagradable

distended [dɪs'tɛndɪd] adj (stomach) hinchado

distil [dɪs'tɪl] (US **distill**) vt destilar; **~lery** n destilería

distinct [dɪs'tɪŋkt] adj (different) distinto; (clear) claro; (unmistakeable) inequívoco; **as ~ from** a diferencia de; **~ion** [dɪs'tɪŋkʃən] n (difference) f; (honour) honor m; (in exam) sobresaliente m; **~ive** adj distintivo

distinguish [dɪs'tɪŋgwɪʃ] vt distinguir; **to ~ o.s.** destacarse; **~ed** adj (eminent) distinguido; **~ing** adj (feature) distintivo

distort [dɪs'tɔːt] vt distorsionar; (shape, image) deformar; **~ion** [dɪs'tɔːʃən] n distorsión f; deformación f

distract [dɪs'trækt] vt distraer; **~ed** adj distraído; **~ion** [dɪs'trækʃən] n distracción f; (confusion) aturdimiento

distraught [dɪs'trɔːt] adj loco de

inquietud

distress [dɪs'trɛs] n (*anguish*) angustia, aflicción f ♦ vt afligir; **~ing** adj angustioso; doloroso; ~ **signal** n señal f de socorro

distribute [dɪs'trɪbju:t] vt distribuir; (*share out*) repartir; **distribution** [-'bju:ʃən] n reparto, distribución f, reparto; **distributor** n (AUT) distribuidor m; (COMM) distribuidora

district [ˈdɪstrɪkt] n (*of country*) zona, región f; (*of town*) barrio; (ADMIN) distrito; ~ **attorney** n (US) fiscal m/f; ~ **nurse** (BRIT) n enfermera que atiende a pacientes a domicilio

distrust [dɪs'trʌst] n desconfianza ♦ vt desconfiar de

disturb [dɪs'tə:b] vt (*person: bother, interrupt*) molestar; (*: upset*) perturbar, inquietar; (*disorganize*) alterar; **~ance** n (*upheaval*) perturbación f; (*political etc: gen pl*) disturbio; (*of mind*) trastorno; **~ed** adj (*worried, upset*) preocupado, angustiado; **emotionally ~ed** trastornado; (*childhood*) inseguro; **~ing** adj inquietante, perturbador(a)

disuse [dɪs'ju:s] n: **to fall into ~** caer en desuso

disused [dɪs'ju:zd] adj abandonado

ditch [dɪtʃ] n zanja; (*irrigation ~*) acequia ♦ vt (inf: *partner*) deshacerse de; (*: plan, car etc*) deshacerse de

dither [ˈdɪðə*] (pej) vi vacilar

ditto [ˈdɪtəu] adv ídem, lo mismo

divan [dɪ'væn] n (*also: ~ bed*) cama turca

dive [daɪv] n (*from board*) salto; (*underwater*) buceo; (*of submarine*) sumersión f ♦ vi (*swimmer: into water*) saltar; (*: under water*) zambullirse, bucear; (*fish, submarine*) sumergirse; (*bird*) lanzarse en picado; **to ~ into** (*bag etc*) meter la mano en; (*shop*) meterse de prisa en; **~r** n (*underwater*) buzo

diverse [daɪ'və:s] adj diversos/as, varios/as

diversion [daɪ'və:ʃən] n (BRIT: AUT) desviación f; (*distraction, MIL*) diversión f; (*of funds*) distracción f

divert [daɪ'və:t] vt (*turn aside*) desviar

divide [dɪ'vaɪd] vt dividir; (*separate*) separar ♦ vi dividirse; (*road*) bifurcarse; **~d highway** (US) n carretera de doble calzada

dividend [ˈdɪvɪdɛnd] n dividendo, (fig): **to pay ~s** proporcionar beneficios

divine [dɪ'vaɪn] adj (*also fig*) divino

diving [ˈdaɪvɪŋ] n (SPORT) salto; (*underwater*) buceo; ~ **board** n trampolín m

divinity [dɪ'vɪnɪtɪ] n divinidad f; (SCOL) teología

division [dɪ'vɪʒən] n división f; (*sharing out*) reparto; (*disagreement*) diferencias fpl; (COMM) sección f

divorce [dɪ'vɔːs] n divorcio ♦ vt divorciarse de; **~d** adj divorciado; **~e** [-'si:] n divorciado/a

divulge [daɪ'vʌldʒ] vt divulgar, revelar

D.I.Y. (BRIT) adj, n abbr = **do-it-yourself**

dizzy [ˈdɪzɪ] adj (*spell*) de mareo; **to feel ~** marearse

DJ n abbr = **disc jockey**

KEYWORD

do [du:] (pt **did**, pp **done**) n (inf: *party etc*): **we're having a little ~ on Saturday** damos una fiestecita el sábado; **it was rather a grand ~** fue un acontecimiento a lo grande
♦ aux vb 1 (*in negative constructions: not translated*) **I don't understand** no entiendo

2 (*to form questions: not translated*) **didn't you know?** ¿no lo sabías?; **what ~ you think?** ¿qué opinas?

3 (*for emphasis, in polite expressions*): **people ~ make mistakes sometimes** sí que se cometen errores a veces; **she does seem rather late** a mí también me parece que se ha

retrasado; ~ **sit down/help yourself** siéntate/sírvete por favor; ~ **take care!** ¡ten cuidado/(, te pido)!

4 (used to avoid repeating vb): **she sings better than I** ~ canta mejor que yo; ~ **you agree?** — yes, I ~/**no, I don't** ¿estás de acuerdo? — sí (lo estoy)/no (lo estoy); **she lives in Glasgow** — **so** ~ **I** vive en Glasgow — yo también; **he didn't like it and neither did we** no le gustó a él ni a nosotros tampoco; **who made this mess?** — **I did** ¿quién hizo esta chapuza? — yo; **he asked me to help him and I did** me pidió que le ayudara y lo hice

5 (in question tags): **you like him, don't you?** te gusta, ¿verdad? or ¿no?; **I don't know him, ~ I?** creo que no le conozco

♦ **vt 1** (gen, carry out, perform etc): **what are you ~ing tonight?** ¿qué haces esta noche?; **what can I ~ for you?** ¿en qué puedo servirle?; **to ~ the washing-up/cooking** fregar los platos/cocinar; **to ~ one's teeth/hair/nails** lavarse los dientes/arreglarse el pelo/arreglarse las uñas

2 (AUT etc): **the car was ~ing 100** el coche iba a 100; **we've done 200 km already** ya hemos hecho 200 km; **he can ~ 100 in that car** puede ir a 100 en ese coche

♦ **vi 1** (act, behave) hacer; ~ **as I ~** haz como yo

2 (get on, fare): **he's ~ing well/badly at school** va bien/mal en la escuela; **the firm is ~ing well** la empresa anda or va bien; **how ~ you ~?** mucho gusto; (less formal) ¿qué tal?

3 (suit): **will it ~?** ¿sirve?, ¿está or va bien?

4 (be sufficient) bastar; **will £10 ~?** ¿será bastante con £10?; **that'll ~** así está bien; **that'll ~!** (in annoyance) ¡ya está bien!, ¡basta ya!; **to make ~ (with)** arreglárselas (con)

do away with vt fus (kill, disease) eliminar; (abolish: law etc) abolir; (withdraw) retirar

do up vt (laces) atar; (zip, dress, shirt) abrochar; (renovate: room, house) renovar

do with vt fus (need): **I could ~ with a drink/some help** no me vendría mal un trago/un poco de ayuda; (be connected) tener que ver con; **what has it got to ~ with you?** ¿qué tiene que ver contigo?

do without vi pasar sin; **if you're late for tea you'll ~ without** si llegas tarde tendrás que quedarte sin cenar ♦ vt fus pasar sin; **I can ~ without a car** puedo pasar sin coche

dock [dɔk] n (NAUT) muelle m; (LAW) banquillo (de los acusados); ~s npl (NAUT) muelles mpl, puerto sg ♦ vi (enter: ~ to a) atracar (la) muelle; (SPACE) acoplarse; ~**er** n trabajador m portuario, estibador m; ~**yard** n astillero

doctor ['dɔktə*] n médico/a m; (Ph.D. etc) doctor(a) m/f ♦ vt (drink etc) adulterar; **D~ of Philosophy** n Doctor en Filosofía y Letras

document ['dɔkjumənt] n documento; ~**ary** [-'mɛntərɪ] adj documental ♦ n documental m

dodge [dɔdʒ] n (fig) truco ♦ vt evadir; (blow) esquivar

dodgems ['dɔdʒəmz] npl (BRIT) coches mpl de choque

doe [dəu] n (deer) cierva, gama; (rabbit) coneja

does [dʌz] vb see **do**; ~**n't = does not**

dog [dɔg] n perro ♦ vt seguir los pasos de; (subj: bad luck) perseguir; ~ **collar** n collar m de perro; (fig) alzacuellos m inv; ~~**eared** adj sobado

dogged ['dɔgɪd] adj tenaz, obstinado

dogsbody ['dɔgzbɔdɪ] n (BRIT: inf)

burro de carga

doings ['duːɪŋz] npl (activities)
actividades fpl

do-it-yourself n bricolaje m

doldrums ['dɔldrəmz] npl: to be in
the ~ (person) estar abatido; (business)
estar estancado

dole (BRIT) n (payment) subsidio
de paro; **on the ~** parado; **~ out** vt
repartir

doll [dɔl] n muñeca; (US: inf: woman)
muñeca, gachí f

dollar ['dɔlə*] n dólar m

dolled up (inf) adj arreglado

dolphin ['dɔlfɪn] n delfín m

domain [də'meɪn] n (fig) campo,
competencia; (land) dominios mpl

dome [dəum] n (ARCH) cúpula

domestic [də'mɛstɪk] adj (animal,
duty) doméstico; (flight, policy)
nacional; **~ated** adj domesticado;
(home-loving) casero, hogareño

dominate ['dɔmɪneɪt] vt dominar

domineering [dɔmɪ'nɪərɪŋ] adj
dominante

dominion [də'mɪnɪən] n dominio

domino ['dɔmɪnəu] (pl **~es**) n ficha de
dominó; **~es** (game) dominó

don [dɔn] (BRIT) n profesor(a) m/f
universitario/a

donate [də'neɪt] vt donar; **donation**
[də'neɪʃən] n donativo

done [dʌn] pp of **do**

donkey ['dɔŋkɪ] n burro

donor ['dəunə*] n donante m/f;
~ card n carnet m de donante

don't [dəunt] = **do not**

donut ['dəunʌt] (US) n = **doughnut**

doodle ['duːdl] vi hacer dibujitos or
garabatos

doom [duːm] n (fate) suerte f ♦ vt: to
be **~ed to failure** estar condenado al
fracaso

door [dɔː*] n puerta; **~bell** n timbre m;
~handle n tirador m; (of car) manija;
~man (irreg) n (in hotel) portero;
~mat n felpudo, estera; **~step**

peldaño; **~-to-** adj de puerta en
puerta; **~way** n entrada, puerta

dope [dəup] n (inf: illegal drug) droga;
(: person) imbécil m/f ♦ vt (horse etc)
drogar

dormant ['dɔːmənt] adj inactivo

dormitory ['dɔːmɪtrɪ] n (BRIT)
dormitorio; (US) colegio mayor

dormouse ['dɔːmaus] (pl **-mice**) n
lirón m

DOS n abbr (= disk operating system)
DOS m

dosage ['dəusɪdʒ] n dosis f inv

dose [dəus] n dosis f inv

doss house ['dɔss-] (BRIT) n pensión f
de mala muerte

dossier ['dɔsɪeɪ] n expediente m,
dosier m

dot [dɔt] n punto ♦ vi: **~ted with**
salpicado de; **on the ~** en punto

double ['dʌbl] adj doble ♦ adv (twice):
to cost ~ costar el doble ♦ n doble m
♦ vt doblar ♦ vi doblarse; **on the ~**, at
the ~ (BRIT) corriendo; **~ bass** n
contrabajo; **~ bed** n cama de
matrimonio; **~ bend** (BRIT) n doble
curva; **~-breasted** adj cruzado;
~-click vi (COMPUT) hacer doble clic;
~-cross vt (trick) engañar; (betray)
traicionar; **~-decker** n autobús m de
dos pisos; **~ glazing** (BRIT) n doble
acristalamiento; **~ room** n habitación f
doble; **~s** n (TENNIS) juego de dobles;
doubly adv doblemente

doubt [daut] n duda ♦ vt dudar;
(suspect) dudar de; **to ~ that** dudar
que; **~ful** adj dudoso; (person): **to be
~ful about sth** tener dudas sobre
algo; **~less** adv sin duda

dough [dəu] n masa, pasta; **~nut** (US
donut) n = rosquilla

dove [dʌv] n paloma

dovetail ['dʌvteɪl] vi (fig) encajar

dowdy ['daudɪ] adj (person) mal
vestido; (clothes) pasado de moda

down [daun] n (feathers) plumón m,
flojel ♦ adv (~wards) abajo, hacia

abajo; *(on the ground)* por o en tierra ♦ *prep* abajo ♦ *vt (inf: drink)* beberse; ~ **with X!** ¡abajo X!; ~**-and-out** *adj* vagabundo/a; ~**-at-heel** *adj* venido a menos; *(appearance)* desaliñado; ~**cast** *adj* abatido; ~**fall** *n* caída, ruina; ~**hearted** *adj* desanimado; ~**hill** *adv*: **to go** ~**hill** *(also fig)* ir cuesta abajo; ~**load** *vt (COMPUT)* bajar; ~ **payment** *n* entrada, pago al contado; ~**pour** *n* aguacero; ~**right** *adj (nonsense, lie)* manifiesto; *(refusal)* terminante; ~**size** *vi (ECON: company)* reducir la plantilla de

Downing Street

Downing Street es la calle de Londres en la que están las residencias oficiales del Presidente del Gobierno *(Prime Minister)*, tradicionalmente en el No. 10, y del Ministro de Economía *(Chancellor of the Exchequer)*. La calle está situada en el céntrico barrio londinense de Westminster y está cerrada al tráfico de peatones y vehículos. En lenguaje periodístico, se usa también Downing Street para referirse al primer ministro o al Gobierno.

Down's syndrome ['daunz-] *n* síndrome *m* de Down
down: ~**stairs** *adv (below)* (en la casa de) abajo; *(downwards)* escaleras abajo; ~**stream** *adv* aguas o río abajo; ~**-to-earth** *adj* práctico; ~**town** *adv* en el centro de la ciudad; *(US)* en Australia (o Nueva Zelanda); ~**ward** [-wəd] *adj, adv* hacia abajo; ~**wards** [-wədz] *adv* hacia abajo
dowry ['dauri] *n* dote *f*
doz. *abbr* = **dozen**
doze [dəuz] *vi* dormitar; ~ **off** *vi* quedarse medio dormido
dozen ['dʌzn] *n* docena; **a** ~ **books** una docena de libros; ~**s of** cantidad de

Dr. *abbr* = **doctor**; **drive**
drab [dræb] *adj* gris, monótono
draft [drɑːft] *n (first copy)* borrador *m*; *(POL: of bill)* anteproyecto; *(US: call-up)* quinta ♦ *vt (plan)* preparar; *(write roughly)* hacer un borrador de; *see also* **draught**
draftsman ['drɑːftsmən] *(US)* *n* = **draughtsman**
drag [dræg] *vt* arrastrar; *(river)* dragar, rastrear ♦ *vi (time)* pasar despacio; *(play, film etc)* hacerse pesado ♦ *n (inf)* lata; *(women's clothing)*: **in** ~ vestido de travestí; ~ **on** *vi* ser interminable; ~ **and drop** *vt (COMPUT)* arrastrar y soltar
dragonfly ['drægənflaɪ] *n* libélula
drain [dreɪn] *n* desaguadero; *(in street)* sumidero; *(source of loss)*: **to be a** ~ **on** consumir, agotar ♦ *vt (land, marshes)* desaguar; *(reservoir)* desecar; *(vegetables)* escurrir ♦ *vi* escurrirse; ~**age** *n (act)* desagüe *m*; *(MED, AGR)* drenaje *m*; *(sewage)* alcantarillado; ~**ing board** *(US* ~**board)** *n* escurridera, escurridor *m*; ~**pipe** *n* tubo de desagüe
drama ['drɑːmə] *n (art)* teatro; *(play)* drama *m*; *(excitement)* emoción *f*; ~**tic** [drə'mætɪk] *adj* dramático; *(sudden, marked)* espectacular; ~**tist** ['dræmətɪst] *n* dramaturgo/a; ~**tize** ['dræmətaɪz] *vt (events)* dramatizar
drank [dræŋk] *pt of* **drink**
drape [dreɪp] *vt (cloth)* colocar; *(flag)* colgar; ~**s** *npl* cortinas *fpl*
drastic ['dræstɪk] *adj (measure)* severo; *(change)* radical, drástico
draught [drɑːft] *(US* **draft**) *n (of air)* corriente *f* de aire; *(NAUT)* calado; **on** ~ *(beer)* de barril; ~ **beer** *n* cerveza de barril; ~**board** *(BRIT)* *n* tablero de damas; ~**s** *(BRIT)* *n (game)* juego de damas
draughtsman ['drɑːftsmən] *(US* **draftsman**) *(irreg)* *n* delineante *m*
draw [drɔː] *(pt* **drew**, *pp* **drawn**) *n*

(picture) dibujar; (cart) tirar de; (curtain) correr; (take out) sacar; (attract) atraer; (money) retirar ♦ vi (SPORT) empatar ♦ n (SPORT) empate m; (lottery) sorteo; ~ **near** vi acercarse; ~ **out** vi (stop) pararse ♦ vt sacar; ~ **up** vi (stop) pararse ♦ vt (chair) acercar; (document) redactar; ~**back** n inconveniente m, desventaja f; ~**bridge** n puente m levadizo

drawer [drɔ:*] n cajón m

drawing ['drɔ:ɪŋ] n dibujo; ~ **board** n tablero (de dibujante); ~ **pin** n (BRIT) chincheta f; ~ **room** n salón m

drawl [drɔ:l] n habla lenta y cansina

drawn [drɔ:n] pp of **draw**

dread [drɛd] n pavor m, terror m ♦ vt temer, tener miedo or pavor a; ~**ful** adj horroroso

dream [dri:m] n (pt, pp **dreamed** or **dreamt**) ♦ n sueño ♦ vt, vi soñar; (distracted) soñador(a), distraído; ~**y** adj (distracted) soñador(a), distraído; (music) suave

dreary ['drɪərɪ] adj monótono

dredge [drɛdʒ] vt dragar

dregs [drɛgz] npl posos mpl; (of humanity) hez f

drench [drɛntʃ] vt empapar

dress [drɛs] n vestido; (clothing) ropa ♦ vt vestir; (wound) vendar ♦ vi vestirse; **to get ~ed** vestirse; ~ **up** vi vestirse de etiqueta; (in fancy dress) disfrazarse; ~ **circle** n (BRIT) principal m; ~**er** n (furniture) aparador m; (: US cómoda (con espejo)); ~**ing** n (MED) vendaje m; (CULIN) aliño; ~**ing gown** n (BRIT) bata f; ~**ing room** n (THEATRE) camarín m; (SPORT) vestuario; ~**ing table** n tocador m; ~**maker** n modista, costurera; ~ **rehearsal** n ensayo general

drew [dru:] pt of **draw**

dribble ['drɪbl] vi (baby) babear ♦ vt (ball) regatear

dried [draɪd] adj (fruit) seco; (milk) en polvo

drier ['draɪə*] n = **dryer**

drift [drɪft] n (of current etc) flujo; (of snow) ventisquero; (meaning) significado ♦ vi (boat) ir a la deriva; (sand, snow) amontonarse; ~**wood** n madera de deriva

drill [drɪl] n (~ bit) broca; (tool for DIY etc) taladro; (of dentist) fresa; (for mining etc) perforadora, barrena; (MIL) instrucción f ♦ vt perforar, taladrar; (troops) enseñar la instrucción a ♦ vi (for oil) perforar

drink [drɪŋk] (pt **drank**, pp **drunk**) n bebida; (sip) trago ♦ vt, vi beber; **to have a ~** tomar algo; tomar una copa or un trago; **a ~ of water** un trago de agua; ~**er** n bebedor(a) m/f; ~**ing water** n agua potable

drip [drɪp] n (act) goteo; (one ~) gota; (MED) gota a gota m ♦ vi gotear; ~**-dry** adj (shirt) inarrugable; ~**ping** n (animal fat) pringue m

drive [draɪv] (pt **drove**, pp **driven**) n (journey) viaje m (en coche); (also: ~way) entrada; (energy) energía, vigor m; (COMPUT: also: disk ~) drive m ♦ vt (car) conducir (SP), manejar (AM); (nail) clavar; (push) empujar; (TECH: motor) impulsar ♦ vi (AUT: at controls) conducir; (: travel) pasearse en coche; **left-/right-hand** ~ conducción f a la izquierda/derecha; **to ~ sb mad** volverle loco a uno

drivel ['drɪvl] (inf) n tonterías fpl

driven ['drɪvn] pp of **drive**

driver ['draɪvə*] n conductor(a) m/f (SP), chofer m (AM); (of taxi, bus) chofer; ~'**s license** n (US) carnet m de conducir

driveway ['draɪvweɪ] n entrada

driving ['draɪvɪŋ] n el conducir (SP), el manejar (AM); ~ **instructor** n instructor(a) m/f de conducción or manejo; ~ **lesson** n clase f de conducción or manejo; ~ **licence** n (BRIT) n permiso de conducir; ~ **school** n autoescuela; ~ **test** n examen m de conducción or manejo

drizzle ['drɪzl] *n* llovizna

drool [druːl] *vi* babear

droop [druːp] *vi* (*flower*) marchitarse; (*shoulders*) encorvarse; (*head*) inclinarse

drop [drɔp] *n* (*of water*) gota; (*lessening*) baja; (*fall*) caída ♦ *vt* dejar caer; (*voice, eyes, price*) bajar; (*passenger*) dejar; (*omit*) omitir ♦ *vi* (*object*) caer; (*wind*) amainar; **~s** *npl* (*MED*) gotas *fpl*; **~ off** *vi* (*sleep*) dormirse ♦ *vt* (*passenger*) dejar; **~ out** *vi* (*withdraw*) retirarse; **~-out** *n* marginado/a; (*SCOL*) estudiante que abandona los estudios; **~per** *n* cuentagotas *m inv*; **~pings** *npl* excremento

drought [draut] *n* sequía

drove [drəuv] *pt of* **drive**

drown [draun] *vt* ahogar ♦ *vi* ahogarse

drowsy ['drauzɪ] *adj* soñoliento; **to be ~** tener sueño

drug [drʌg] *n* medicamento; (*narcotic*) droga ♦ *vt* drogar; **to be on ~s** drogarse; **~ addict** *n* drogadicto/a; **~gist** (*US*) *n* farmacéutico; **~store** (*US*) *n* farmacia

drum [drʌm] *n* tambor *m*; (*for oil, petrol*) bidón *m*; **~s** *npl* batería; **~mer** *n* tambor *m*

drunk [drʌŋk] *pp of* **drink** ♦ *adj* borracho ♦ *n* (*also*: **~ard**) borracho/a; **~en** *adj* borracho; (*laughter, party*) de borrachos

dry [draɪ] *adj* seco; (*day*) sin lluvia; (*climate*) árido, seco ♦ *vt* secar; (*tears*) enjugarse ♦ *vi* secarse; **~ up** *vi* (*river*) secarse; **~-cleaner's** *n* tintorería; **~-cleaning** *n* lavado en seco; **~er** *n* (*for hair*) secador *m*; (*US*: *for clothes*) secadora; **~ rot** *n* putrefacción *f* fungoide

DSS *n abbr* = **Department of Social Security**

DTP *n abbr* (= **desk-top publishing**) autoedición *f*

dual ['djuəl] *adj* doble; **~ carriageway** (*BRIT*) *n* carretera de

doble calzada; **~-purpose** *adj* de doble uso

dubbed [dʌbd] *adj* (*CINEMA*) doblado

dubious ['djuːbɪəs] *adj* indeciso; (*reputation, company*) sospechoso

duchess ['dʌtʃɪs] *n* duquesa

duck [dʌk] *n* pato ♦ *vi* agacharse; **~ling** *n* patito

duct [dʌkt] *n* conducto, canal *m*

dud [dʌd] *n* (*object, tool*) engaño, engañifa ♦ *adj*: **~ cheque** (*BRIT*) cheque *m* sin fondos

due [djuː] *adj* (*owed*): **he is ~ £10** se le deben 10 libras; (*expected*: *event*): **the meeting is ~ on Wednesday** la reunión tendrá lugar el miércoles; (*: arrival*) **the train is ~ at 8am** el tren tiene su llegada para las 8; (*proper*) debido ♦ *n*: **to give sb his** (*or her*) **~** ser justo con alguien ♦ *adv*: **~ north** derecho al norte; **~s** *npl* (*for club, union*) cuota; (*in harbour*) derechos *mpl*; **in ~ course** a su debido tiempo; **~ to** debido a; **to be ~ to** deberse a

duet [djuː'et] *n* dúo

duffel bag ['dʌfəl-] *n* bolsa de lona

duffel coat *n* trenca, abrigo de tres cuartos

dug [dʌg] *pt, pp of* **dig**

duke [djuːk] *n* duque *m*

dull [dʌl] *adj* (*light*) débil; (*stupid*) torpe; (*boring*) pesado; (*sound, pain*) sordo; (*weather, day*) gris ♦ *vt* (*pain, grief*) aliviar; (*mind, senses*) entorpecer

duly ['djuːlɪ] *adv* debidamente; (*on time*) a su debido tiempo

dumb [dʌm] *adj* mudo; (*pej*: *stupid*) estúpido; **~founded** [dʌm'faundid] *adj* pasmado

dummy ['dʌmɪ] *n* (*tailor's ~*) maniquí *m*; (*mock-up*) maqueta; (*BRIT*: *for baby*) chupete *m* ♦ *adj* falso, postizo

dump [dʌmp] *n* (*also*: **rubbish ~**) basurero, vertedero; (*inf*: *place*) cuchitril *m* ♦ *vt* (*put down*) dejar; (*get rid of*) deshacerse de; (*COMPUT*: *data*) transferir

dumpling ['dʌmplɪŋ] n bola de masa hervida

dumpy ['dʌmpɪ] adj regordete/a

dunce [dʌns] n zopenco

dung [dʌŋ] n estiércol m

dungarees [dʌŋgə'riːz] npl mono m

dungeon ['dʌndʒən] n calabozo

duplex ['djuːpleks] n dúplex m

duplicate n ['djuːplɪkət, vb 'djuːplɪkeɪt] n duplicado ♦ vt duplicar; *(photocopy)* fotocopiar; *(repeat)* repetir; **in ~** por duplicado

durable ['djuərəbl] adj duradero/a

duration [djuə'reɪʃən] n duración f

during ['djuərɪŋ] prep durante

dusk [dʌsk] n crepúsculo, anochecer m

dust [dʌst] n polvo ♦ vt quitar el polvo a, desempolvar; **~ to ~** vt (tax etc): **~ to** vt quitar el polvo a, desempolvar; *(cake etc)*: **~ to** espolvorear de; **~bin** (BRIT) n cubo de la basura (SP), balde m (LAM); **~er** n paño, trapo; **~man** (BRIT irreg) n basurero; **~y** adj polvoriento

Dutch [dʌtʃ] adj holandés/esa ♦ n *(LING)* holandés m; **the ~** npl los holandeses; **to go ~** (inf) pagar cada uno lo suyo; **~man/woman** (irreg) n holandés/esa m/f

duty ['djuːtɪ] n deber m; *(tax)* derechos mpl de aduana; **on ~** de servicio; *(at night etc)* de guardia; **off ~** libre (de servicio); **~-free** adj libre de impuestos

duvet ['duːveɪ] (BRIT) n edredón m

DVD n abbr (= *digital versatile or video disc*) DVD m

dwarf [dwɔːf] (pl **dwarves**) n enano/a ♦ vt empequeñecer

dwell [dwel] (pt, pp **dwelt**) vi morar; **~ on** vt fus explayarse en

dwindle ['dwɪndl] vi disminuir

dye [daɪ] n tinte m ♦ vt teñir

dying ['daɪɪŋ] adj moribundo

dyke [daɪk] (BRIT) n dique m

dynamic [daɪ'næmɪk] adj dinámico

dynamite ['daɪnəmaɪt] n dinamita

dynamo ['daɪnəməʊ] n dínamo f

dynasty ['dɪnəstɪ] n dinastía f

E, e

E [iː] n *(MUS)* mi m

each [iːtʃ] adj cada inv ♦ pron cada uno; **~ other** el uno al otro; **they hate ~ other** se odian (entre ellos or mutuamente); **they have 2 books ~** tienen 2 libros por persona

eager ['iːgər] adj *(keen)* entusiasmado; **to be ~ to do sth** tener muchas ganas de hacer algo, impacientarse por hacer algo; **to be ~ for** tener muchas ganas de

eagle ['iːgl] n águila

ear [ɪər] n oreja; oído; *(of corn)* espiga; **~ache** n dolor m de oídos; **~drum** n tímpano

earl [əːl] n conde m

earlier ['əːlɪər] adj anterior ♦ adv antes

early ['əːlɪ] adv temprano; *(before time)* con tiempo, con anticipación ♦ adj temprano; *(settlers etc)* primitivo; *(death, departure)* prematuro; *(reply)* pronto; **to have an ~ night** acostarse temprano; **in the ~ or ~ in the spring/19th century** a principios de primavera/del siglo diecinueve; **~ retirement** n jubilación f anticipada

earmark ['ɪəmɑːk] vt: **to ~ (for)** reservar (para), destinar (a)

earn [əːn] vt *(salary)* percibir; *(interest)* devengar; *(praise)* merecerse

earnest ['əːnɪst] adj *(wish)* fervoroso; *(person)* serio, formal; **in ~** in serio

earnings ['əːnɪŋz] npl *(personal)* sueldo, ingresos mpl; *(company)* ganancias fpl

ear: ~phones npl auriculares mpl; **~ring** n pendiente m, arete m; **~shot** n: **within ~shot** al alcance del oído

earth [əːθ] n tierra; (BRIT: ELEC) cable m de toma de tierra ♦ vt (BRIT: ELEC) conectar a tierra; **~enware** n loza (de barro); **~quake** n terremoto; **~y** adj *(fig: vulgar)* grosero

ease [iːz] n facilidad f; (comfort) comodidad f ♦ vt (lessen: problem) mitigar; (: pain) aliviar; (: tension) reducir; **to ~ sth in/out** meter/sacar algo con cuidado; **at ~!** (MIL) ¡descansen!; **~ off** or **up** vi (wind, rain) amainar; (slow down) aflojar la marcha

easel ['iːzl] n caballete m

easily ['iːzɪlɪ] adv fácilmente

east [iːst] n este m ♦ adj del este, oriental; (wind) este ♦ adv al este, hacia el este; **the E~** el Oriente; (POL) los países del Este

Easter ['iːstə*] n Pascua (de Resurrección) f

east: ~erly ['iːstəlɪ] adj (to the east) al este; (wind) este; **~ern** ['iːstən] adj del este, oriental; (oriental) oriental; **~ward(s)** ['iːstwəd(z)] adv hacia el este

easy ['iːzɪ] adj fácil; (simple) sencillo; (comfortable) holgado, cómodo; (relaxed) tranquilo ♦ adv: **to take it** or **things** ~ (not worry) tomarlo con calma; (rest) descansar; **~ chair** n sillón m; **~-going** adj acomodadizo

eat [iːt] (pt **ate**, pp **eaten**) vt comer; **~ away** at vt fus corroer; mermar; **~ into** vt fus corroer; (savings) mermar

eaves [iːvz] npl alero

eavesdrop ['iːvzdrɔp] vi: **to ~ (on)** escuchar a escondidas

ebb [eb] n reflujo ♦ vi bajar; (fig: also: **~ away**) decaer

ebony ['ebənɪ] n ébano

EC n abbr (= European Community) CE f

ECB n abbr (= European Central Bank) BCE m

eccentric [ɪk'sentrɪk] adj, n excéntrico/a m/f

echo ['ekəu] (pl **~es**) n eco m ♦ vt (sound) repetir ♦ vi resonar, hacer eco

éclair [ɪ'klɛə*] n pastelito relleno de crema y con chocolate por encima

eclipse [ɪ'klɪps] n eclipse m

ecology [ɪ'kɔlədʒɪ] n ecología f

e-commerce n abbr (= electronic commerce) comercio electrónico

economic [iːkə'nɔmɪk] adj económico; (business etc) rentable; **~al** adj económico; **~s** npl (of project etc) rentabilidad f

economize [ɪ'kɔnəmaɪz] vi economizar, ahorrar

economy [ɪ'kɔnəmɪ] n economía f; **~ class** n (AVIAT) clase f económica; **~ size** n tamaño económico

ecstasy ['ekstəsɪ] n éxtasis m inv; (drug) éxtasis m inv; **ecstatic** [eks'tætɪk] adj extático

ECU ['eɪkjuː] n (= European Currency Unit) ECU m

Ecuador ['ekwədɔː*] n Ecuador m; **~ian** adj n ecuatoriano/a m/f

eczema ['eksɪmə] n eczema m

edge [edʒ] n (of knife) filo; (of object) borde m; (of lake) orilla f ♦ vt (SEWING) ribetear; **on ~** (fig) = **edgy**; **to ~ away from** alejarse poco a poco de; **~ways** adv: **he couldn't get a word in ~ways** no pudo meter ni baza

edgy ['edʒɪ] adj nervioso, inquieto

edible ['edɪbl] adj comestible

Edinburgh ['edɪnbərə] n Edimburgo

edit ['edɪt] vt (be editor of) dirigir; (text, report) corregir, preparar; **~ion** [ɪ'dɪʃən] n edición f; **~or** n (of newspaper) director(a) m/f; (of column): **foreign/political ~or** encargado de la sección de extranjero/política; (of book) redactor(a) m/f; **~orial** [-'tɔːrɪəl] adj editorial ♦ n editorial m

educate ['edjukeɪt] vt (gen) educar; (instruct) instruir

education [edju'keɪʃən] n (gen) educación f; (schooling) enseñanza; (SCOL) pedagogía; **~al** adj (policy etc) educacional; (teaching) docente; (toy) educativo

EEC n abbr (= European Economic Community) CEE f

eel [iːl] n anguila

eerie ['ɪərɪ] adj misterioso

effect [ɪ'fekt] n efecto ♦ vt efectuar, llevar a cabo; **to take ~** (law) entrar

effeminate en vigor o vigencia; *(drug)* surtir efecto; **in** ~ en realidad; **~ive** *adj* eficaz; *(actual)* verdadero; **~ively** *adv* eficazmente; *(in reality)* efectivamente; **~iveness** *n* eficacia

effeminate [ɪˈfemɪnɪt] *adj* afeminado

efficiency [ɪˈfɪʃənsɪ] *n* eficiencia; rendimiento

efficient [ɪˈfɪʃənt] *adj* eficiente; *(machine)* de buen rendimiento

effort [ˈefət] *n* esfuerzo; **~less** *adj* sin ningún esfuerzo; *(style)* natural

effusive [ɪˈfjuːsɪv] *adj* efusivo

e.g. *adv abbr* (= *exempli gratia*) p. ej.

egg [eg] *n* huevo; **hard-boiled/soft-boiled ~** huevo duro/pasado por agua; **to ~ on** incitar; **~cup** *n* huevera; **~ plant** *(esp US)* *n* berenjena; **~shell** *n* cáscara de huevo

ego [ˈiːgəu] *n* ego; **~tism** *n* egoísmo; **~tist** *n* egoísta *m/f*

Egypt [ˈiːdʒɪpt] *n* Egipto; **~ian** [ɪˈdʒɪpʃən] *adj, n* egipcio/a *m/f*

eiderdown [ˈaɪdədaun] *n* edredón *m*

eight [eɪt] *num* ocho; **~een** *num* diez y ocho, dieciocho; **~h** [eɪtθ] *num* octavo; **~y** *num* ochenta

Eire [ˈeərə] *n* Eire *m*

either [ˈaɪðə*] *adj* cualquiera de los dos; *(both, each)* cada; **~** *pron*: **~ (of them)** cualquiera (de los dos) ♦ *adv* tampoco; **on ~ side** en ambos lados; **I don't like ~** no me gusta ninguno/a de los/las dos; **no, I don't ~** no, yo tampoco ♦ *conj*: **~ yes or no** o sí o no

eject [ɪˈdʒekt] *vt* echar, expulsar; *(tenant)* desahuciar; **~or seat** *n* asiento proyectable

elaborate *[adj* ɪˈlæbərɪt, *vb* ɪˈlæbəreɪt] *adj (complex)* complejo ♦ *vt (expand)* ampliar; *(refine)* refinar ♦ *vi* explicar con más detalles

elastic [ɪˈlæstɪk] *n* elástico ♦ *adj* elástico; *(fig)* flexible; **~ band** *(BRIT)* *n* gomita

elated [ɪˈleɪtɪd] *adj*: **to be ~** regocijarse

elbow [ˈelbəu] *n* codo

elder [ˈeldə*] *adj* mayor ♦ *n (tree)* saúco; *(person)* mayor; **~ly** *adj* de edad, mayor ♦ *npl*: **the ~ly** los mayores

eldest [ˈeldɪst] *adj, n* el/la mayor

elect [ɪˈlekt] *vt* elegir ♦ *adj*: **the president ~** el presidente electo; **to ~ to do** optar por hacer; **~ion** [ɪˈlekʃən] *n* elección *f*; **~ioneering** [ɪlekʃəˈnɪərɪŋ] *n* campaña electoral; **~or** *n* elector(a) *m/f*; **~oral** *adj* electoral; **~orate** *n* electorado

electric [ɪˈlektrɪk] *adj* eléctrico; **~al** *adj* eléctrico; **~ blanket** *n* manta eléctrica; **~ fire** *n* estufa eléctrica; **~ian** [ɪlekˈtrɪʃən] *n* electricista *m/f*; **~ity** [ɪlekˈtrɪsɪtɪ] *n* electricidad *f*; **electrify** [ɪˈlektrɪfaɪ] *vt (RAIL)* electrificar; *(fig: audience)* electrizar

electronic [ɪlekˈtrɒnɪk] *adj* electrónico; **~ mail** *n* correo electrónico; **~s** *n* electrónica

elegant [ˈelɪgənt] *adj* elegante

element [ˈelɪmənt] *n* elemento; *(of kettle etc)* resistencia; **~ary** [ɪˈmentərɪ] *adj* elemental; *(primitive)* rudimentario; *(school)* primario

elephant [ˈelɪfənt] *n* elefante *m*

elevation [elɪˈveɪʃən] *n* elevación *f*; *(height)* altura

elevator [ˈelɪveɪtə*] *n (US)* ascensor *m*; *(in warehouse etc)* montacargas *m inv*

eleven [ɪˈlevn] *num* once; **~ses** *(BRIT)* *npl* café *m* de las once; **~th** *num* undécimo

elicit [ɪˈlɪsɪt] *vt*: **to ~ (from)** sacar (de)

eligible [ˈelɪdʒəbl] *adj*: **an ~ young man/woman** un buen partido; **to be ~ for sth** llenar los requisitos para algo

elm [elm] *n* olmo

elongated [ˈiːlɒŋgeɪtɪd] *adj* alargado

elope [ɪˈləup] *vi* fugarse (para casarse)

eloquent [ˈeləkwənt] *adj* elocuente

else [els] *adv*: **something ~** otra cosa; **somewhere ~** en otra parte; **everywhere ~** en todas partes menos aquí; **where ~?** ¿dónde más?; **~an**

otra parte?; **there was little ~ to do**
apenas quedaba otra cosa que hacer;
nobody ~ spoke no habló nadie más;
~where adv (be) en otra parte; (go) a
otra parte

elude [ɪ'luːd] vt (subj: idea etc)
escapar a; (capture) esquivar
elusive [ɪ'luːsɪv] adj esquivo; (quality)
difícil de encontrar
emaciated [ɪ'meɪsɪeɪtɪd] adj
demacrado
E-mail, e-mail ['iːmeɪl] n abbr
(= electronic mail) correo electrónico,
e-mail m
emancipate [ɪ'mænsɪpeɪt] vt
emancipar
embankment [ɪm'bæŋkmənt] n
terraplén m
embark [ɪm'bɑːk] vi embarcarse ♦ vt
embarcar; **to ~ on** (journey)
emprender; (course of action) lanzarse
a; **~ation** [embaː'keɪʃən] n (people)
embarco; (goods) embarque m
embarrass [ɪm'bærəs] vt avergonzar;
(government etc) dejar en mal lugar;
~ed adj (laugh, silence) embarazoso;
~ing adj (situation) violento; (question)
embarazoso; **~ment** n (shame)
vergüenza; (problem): **to be an
~ment for sb** poner en un aprieto a
uno
embassy ['embəsɪ] n embajada
embedded [ɪm'bedɪd] adj (object)
empotrado; (thorn etc) clavado
embellish [ɪm'belɪʃ] vt embellecer;
(story) adornar
embers ['embəz] npl rescoldo, ascua
embezzle [ɪm'bezl] vt desfalcar,
malversar
embitter [ɪm'bɪtə*] vt (fig: sour)
amargar
embody [ɪm'bɒdɪ] vt (spirit) encarnar;
(include) incorporar
embossed [ɪm'bɒst] adj realzado
embrace [ɪm'breɪs] vt abrazar, dar un
abrazo a; (include) abarcar ♦ vi
abrazarse ♦ n abrazo

embroider [ɪm'brɔɪdə*] vt bordar; **~y**
n bordado
embryo ['embrɪəu] n embrión m
emerald ['emərəld] n esmeralda
emerge [ɪ'mɜːdʒ] vi salir; (arise) surgir
emergency [ɪ'mɜːdʒənsɪ] n crisis f inv;
in an ~ en caso de urgencia; **state of
~** estado de emergencia; **~ cord** (US) n
timbre m de alarma; **~ exit** n salida de
emergencia; **~ landing** n aterrizaje m
forzoso; **~ services** npl (fire, police,
ambulance) servicios mpl de urgencia or
emergencia
emery board ['emərɪ-] n lima de uñas
emigrate ['emɪgreɪt] vi emigrar
emissions [ɪ'mɪʃənz] npl emisión f
emit [ɪ'mɪt] vt (heat) emitir; (smoke) arrojar;
(smell) despedir; (sound) producir
emotion [ɪ'məuʃən] n emoción f; **~al**
adj (needs) emocional; (person)
sentimental; (scene) conmovedor(a),
emocionante; (speech) emocionado
emperor ['empərə*] n emperador m
emphasis ['emfəsɪs] (pl **-ses**) n énfasis
m inv
emphasize ['emfəsaɪz] vt (word, point)
subrayar, recalcar; (feature) hacer
resaltar
emphatic [em'fætɪk] adj (reply)
categórico; (person) insistente
empire ['empaɪə*] n (also fig) imperio
employ [ɪm'plɔɪ] vt emplear; **~ee** [-'iː]
n empleado/a; **~er** n patrón/ona m/f;
empresario; **~ment** n (work) trabajo;
~ment agency n agencia de
colocaciones
empower [ɪm'pauə*] vt: **to ~ sb to
do sth** autorizar a uno para hacer algo
empress ['empris] n emperatriz f
emptiness ['emptɪnɪs] n vacío m; (of life
etc) vaciedad f
empty ['emptɪ] adj vacío; (place)
desierto; (house) desocupado; (threat)
vano ♦ vt vaciar; (place) dejar vacío ♦ vi
vaciarse; (house etc) quedar
desocupado; **~-handed** adj con las
manos vacías

EMU n abbr (= European Monetary Union) UME f

emulate ['ɛmjʊleɪt] n emular

emulsion [ɪ'mʌlʃən] n emulsión f; (also: ~ paint) pintura emulsión

enable [ɪ'neɪbl] vt: to ~ sb to do sth permitir a uno hacer algo

enamel [ɪ'næməl] n esmalte m; (also: ~ paint) pintura esmaltada

enchant [ɪn'tʃɑːnt] vt encantar; **~ing** adj encantador(a)

encl. abbr (= enclosed) adj

enclose [ɪn'kləʊz] vt (land) cercar; (letter etc) adjuntar; **please find ~d** le mandamos adjunto

enclosure [ɪn'kləʊʒə*] n cercado, recinto

encompass [ɪn'kʌmpəs] vt abarcar

encore [ɔŋ'kɔː*] excl ¡otra!, ¡bis! ♦ n bis m

encounter [ɪn'kaʊntə*] n encuentro ♦ vt encontrar, encontrarse con; (difficulty) tropezar con

encourage [ɪn'kʌrɪdʒ] vt alentar, animar; (activity) fomentar; (growth) estimular; **~ment** n estímulo, (of industry) fomento

encroach [ɪn'krəʊtʃ] vi: to ~ (up)on invadir; (rights) usurpar; (time) adueñarse de

encyclop(a)edia [ɛnsaɪkləʊ'piːdɪə] n enciclopedia

end [ɛnd] n (gen, also aim) fin m; (of table) extremo; (of street) final m; (SPORT) lado ♦ vt terminar, acabar; (also: bring to an ~, put an ~ to) acabar con ♦ vi terminar, acabar; **in the ~** al fin; to ~ (object) de punta, de cabeza; **to stand on ~** (hair) erizarse; **for hours on ~** hora tras hora; **~ up** vi: to ~ up in terminar en; (place) ir a parar en

endanger [ɪn'deɪndʒə*] vt poner en peligro; **an ~ed species** una especie en peligro de extinción

endearing [ɪn'dɪərɪŋ] adj simpático, atractivo

endeavour [ɪn'devə*] (US **endeavor**) n esfuerzo; (attempt) tentativa ♦ vi: to ~ to do esforzarse por hacer; (try) procurar hacer

ending ['endɪŋ] n (of book) desenlace m; (LING) terminación f

endive ['endaɪv] n (chicory) endibia; (curly) escarola

endless ['endlɪs] adj interminable, inacabable

endorse [ɪn'dɔːs] vt (cheque) endosar; (approve) aprobar; **~ment** n (on driving licence) nota de inhabilitación

endure [ɪn'djʊə*] vt (bear) aguantar, soportar ♦ vi (last) durar

enemy ['enəmɪ] adj, n enemigo m/f

energetic [enə'dʒetɪk] adj enérgico

energy ['enədʒɪ] n energía

enforce [ɪn'fɔːs] vt (LAW) hacer cumplir

engage [ɪn'geɪdʒ] vt (attention) llamar; (interest) ocupar; (in conversation) abordar; (worker) contratar; (AUT): to ~ **the clutch** embragar ♦ vi (TECH) engranar; to ~ in dedicarse a, ocuparse en; **~d** adj (BRIT: busy, in use) ocupado; (betrothed) prometido; to **get ~d** prometerse; **~d tone** n (TEL) señal f de comunicando; **~ment** n (appointment) compromiso, cita; (booking) contratación f; (to marry) compromiso; (period) noviazgo; **~ment ring** n anillo de prometida

engaging [ɪn'geɪdʒɪŋ] adj atractivo

engine ['endʒɪn] n (AUT) motor m; (RAIL) locomotora f; **~ driver** n (RAIL) maquinista m/f

engineer [endʒɪ'nɪə*] n ingeniero; (BRIT: for repairs) mecánico; (on ship, US: RAIL) maquinista m/f; **~ing** n ingeniería

England ['ɪŋglənd] n Inglaterra

English ['ɪŋglɪʃ] adj inglés/esa ♦ n (LING) inglés m; **the ~** npl los ingleses mpl; **the ~ Channel** n (el Canal de) la Mancha; **~man/woman** (irreg) n inglés/esa m/f

engraving [ɪn'greɪvɪŋ] n grabado

engrossed [ɪn'grəʊst] adj: ~ **in** absorto en

engulf [ɪn'gʌlf] vt (subj: water) sumergir, hundir; (: fire) prender; (: fear) apoderarse de

enhance [ɪn'hɑːns] vt (gen) aumentar; (beauty) realzar

enjoy [ɪn'dʒɔɪ] vt (health, fortune) disfrutar de, gozar de; (like) gustarle a uno; **to ~ o.s.** divertirse; **~able** adj agradable; (amusing) divertido; **~ment** n (joy) placer m; (activity) diversión f

enlarge [ɪn'lɑːdʒ] vt aumentar; (broaden) extender; (PHOT) ampliar ♦ vi: aumentar; (subject) tratar con más detalles; **~ment** n (PHOT) ampliación f

enlighten [ɪn'laɪtn] vt (inform) informar; **~ed** adj comprensivo; **the E~ment** n (HISTORY) ≈ la Ilustración, ≈ el Siglo de las Luces

enlist [ɪn'lɪst] vt alistar; (support) conseguir ♦ vi alistarse

enmity ['enmɪtɪ] n enemistad f

enormous [ɪ'nɔːməs] adj enorme

enough [ɪ'nʌf] adj: ~ **time/books** bastante tiempo/bastantes libros ♦ pron bastante(s) ♦ adv: **big ~** bastante grande; **he has not worked ~** no ha trabajado bastante; **have you got ~?** ¿tiene usted bastante(s)?; **~ to eat** (lo) suficiente or (lo) bastante para comer; **~!** ¡basta ya!; **that's ~, thanks** con eso basta, gracias; **I've had ~ of him** estoy harto de él; ... **which, funnily** or **oddly ~** ... ... lo que, por extraño que parezca ...

enquire [ɪn'kwaɪə*] vt, vi = **inquire**

enrage [ɪn'reɪdʒ] vt enfurecer

enrol [ɪn'rəʊl] (US **enroll**) vt (members) inscribir; (SCOL) matricular ♦ vi inscribirse; matricularse; **~ment** (US **enrollment**) n inscripción f; matriculación f

en route [ɒn'ruːt] adv durante el viaje

en suite [ɒn'swiːt] adj: **with ~ bathroom** con baño

ensure [ɪn'ʃʊə*] vt asegurar

entail [ɪn'teɪl] vt suponer

entangled [ɪn'tæŋgld] adj: **to become ~ (in)** quedarse enredado (en) or enmarañado (en)

enter ['entə*] vt (room) entrar en; (club) hacerse socio de; (army) alistarse en; (sb for a competition) inscribir; (write down) anotar, apuntar; (COMPUT) meter ♦ vi entrar; **~ for** vt fus presentarse para; **~ into** vt fus (discussion etc) entablar; (agreement) llegar a, firmar

enterprise ['entəpraɪz] n empresa; (spirit) iniciativa; **free ~** la libre empresa; **private ~** la iniciativa privada; **enterprising** adj emprendedor(a)

entertain [entə'teɪn] vt (amuse) divertir; (invite: guest) invitar (a casa); (idea) abrigar; **~er** n artista m/f; **~ing** adj divertido, entretenido; **~ment** n (amusement) diversión f; (show) espectáculo

enthralled [ɪn'θrɔːld] adj encantado

enthusiasm [ɪn'θuːzɪæzəm] n entusiasmo

enthusiast [ɪn'θuːzɪæst] n entusiasta m/f; **~ic** [-'æstɪk] adj entusiasta; **to be ~ic about** entusiasmarse por

entire [ɪn'taɪə*] adj entero; **~ly** adv totalmente, en su totalidad; **~ty** [ɪn'taɪərətɪ] n: **in its ~ty** en su totalidad

entitle [ɪn'taɪtl] vt: **to ~ sb to sth** dar a uno derecho a algo; **~d** adj (book) titulado; **to be ~d to do** tener derecho a hacer

entrance [n 'entrəns, vb ɪn'trɑːns] n entrada ♦ vt encantar, hechizar; **to gain ~ to** (university etc) ingresar en; **~ examination** n examen m de ingreso; **~ fee** n cuota; **~ ramp** (US) n (AUT) rampa de acceso

entrant ['entrənt] n (in race, competition) participante m/f; (in examination) candidato/a

entrenched [en'trentʃd] adj inamovible

entrepreneur [ɔntrəprə'nə:] n empresario

entrust [in'trʌst] vt: to ~ sth to sb confiar algo a uno

entry ['entri] n entrada; (in competition) participación f; (in register) apunte m; (in account) partida; (in reference book) artículo; "no ~" "prohibido el paso"; (AUT) "dirección prohibida"; ~ form n hoja de inscripción; ~ phone n portero automático

envelop [in'veləp] vt envolver

envelope ['envələʊp] n sobre m

envious ['enviəs] adj envidioso; (look) de envidia

environment [in'vaiərnmənt] n (surroundings) entorno; (natural world): the ~ el medio ambiente; ~al [-'mentl] adj ambiental; medioambiental; ~friendly adj no perjudicial para el medio ambiente

envisage [in'vizidʒ] vt prever

envoy ['envɔi] n enviado

envy ['envi] n envidia ♦ vt tener envidia a; to ~ sb sth envidiar algo a uno

epic ['epik] n épica ♦ adj épico

epidemic [epi'demik] n epidemia

epilepsy ['epilepsi] n epilepsia

episode ['episəʊd] n episodio

epitomize [i'pitəmaiz] vt epitomar, resumir

equal ['i:kwl] adj igual; (treatment) equitativo ♦ n igual m/f ♦ vt ser igual a; (fig) igualar; to be ~ to (task) estar a la altura de; ~ity [i:'kwɔliti] n igualdad f; ~ize vi (SPORT) empatar; ~ly adv igualmente; (share etc) a partes iguales

equate [i'kweit] vt: to ~ sth with equiparar algo con; **equation** [i'kweiʒən] n (MATH) ecuación f

equator [i'kweitə*] n ecuador m

equilibrium [i:kwi'libriəm] n equilibrio

equip [i'kwip] vt equipar; (person) proveer; to be well ~ped estar bien

equipado; ~**ment** n equipo; (tools) avíos mpl

equities ['ekwitiz] (BRIT) npl (COMM) derechos mpl sobre or en el activo

equivalent [i'kwivələnt] adj: ~ (to) equivalente a ♦ n equivalente m

era ['iərə] n era, época

eradicate [i'rædikeit] vt erradicar

erase [i'reiz] vt borrar; ~r n goma de borrar

erect [i'rekt] adj erguido ♦ vt erigir, levantar; (assemble) montar; ~ion [-ʃən] n construcción f; (assembly) montaje m; (PHYSIOL) erección f

ERM n abbr (= Exchange Rate Mechanism) tipo de cambio europeo

erode [i'rəʊd] vt (GEO) erosionar; (metal) corroer, desgastar; (fig) desgastar

erotic [i'rɔtik] adj erótico

errand ['ernd] n recado (SP), mandado (AM)

erratic [i'rætik] adj desigual, poco uniforme

error ['erə*] n error m, equivocación f

erupt [i'rʌpt] vi entrar en erupción; (fig) estallar; ~ion [i'rʌpʃən] n erupción f; (of war) estallido

escalate ['eskəleit] vi extenderse, intensificarse

escalator ['eskəleitə*] n escalera móvil

escapade [eskə'peid] n travesura

escape [i'skeip] n fuga ♦ vi escaparse; (flee) huir, evadirse; (leak) fugarse ♦ vt (responsibility etc) evitar, eludir; (consequences) escapar a; (elude): his name ~s me no me sale su nombre; to ~ from (place) escaparse de; (person) escaparse a

escort [n 'eskɔ:t, vb i'skɔ:t] n acompañante m/f; (MIL) escolta ♦ vt acompañar

Eskimo ['eskiməʊ] n esquimal m/f

especially [i'speʃli] adv (above all) sobre todo; (particularly) en particular, especialmente

espionage ['espiənɑ:ʒ] n espionaje m

esplanade [ɛspləˈneɪd] n (by sea) paseo marítimo

Esquire [ɪˈskwaɪə] n (abbr **Esq.**) n: J. Brown, ~ Sr. D. J. Brown

essay [ˈeseɪ] n (LITERATURE) ensayo m, (SCOL: short) redacción f; (: long) trabajo

essence [ˈesns] n esencia

essential [ɪˈsenʃl] adj (necessary) imprescindible; (basic) esencial; ~s npl lo imprescindible, lo esencial; ~ly adv esencialmente

establish [ɪˈstæblɪʃ] vt establecer; (prove) demostrar; (relations) entablar; (reputation) ganarse; (practice) arraigado; ~ment n establecimiento; the E~ment n la clase dirigente

estate [ɪˈsteɪt] n (land) finca, hacienda; (inheritance) herencia; (BRIT: also: housing ~) urbanización f; ~ agent (BRIT) n agente m/f inmobiliario/a; ~ car (BRIT) n furgoneta f

esteem [ɪˈstiːm] n: to hold sb in high ~ estimar en mucho a uno

esthetic [ɪsˈθetɪk] (US) adj = aesthetic

estimate [n ˈestɪmət, vb ˈestɪmeɪt] n estimación f, apreciación f; (assessment) tasa, cálculo; (COMM) presupuesto ♦ vt estimar, tasar; calcular; **estimation** [-ˈmeɪʃən] n opinión f, juicio; cálculo

estranged [ɪˈstreɪndʒd] adj separado

estuary [ˈestjuərɪ] n estuario, ría

etc abbr (= et cetera) etc

eternal [ɪˈtɜːnl] adj eterno

eternity [ɪˈtɜːnɪtɪ] n eternidad f

ethical [ˈeθɪkl] adj ético, **ethics** [ˈeθɪks] n ética ♦ npl moralidad f

Ethiopia [iːˈθɪəupɪə] n Etiopía

ethnic [ˈeθnɪk] adj étnico; ~ **minority** n minoría étnica

ethos [ˈiːθɒs] n genio, carácter m

EU n abbr (= European Union) UE f

euro n euro

Eurocheque [ˈjuərəutʃek] n Eurocheque m

Euroland [ˈjuərəulænd] n zona (del)

euro

Europe [ˈjuərəp] n Europa; ~**an** [-ˈpiːən] adj, n europeo/a m/f; ~**an Community** n Comunidad f Europea; ~**an Union** n Unión f Europea

evacuate [ɪˈvækjueɪt] vt (people) evacuar; (place) desocupar

evade [ɪˈveɪd] vt evadir, eludir

evaporate [ɪˈvæpəreɪt] vi evaporarse; (fig) desvanecerse; ~**d milk** n leche f evaporada

evasion [ɪˈveɪʒən] n evasión f

eve [iːv] n: **on the** ~ **of** en vísperas de

even [ˈiːvn] adj (level) llano; (smooth) liso; (speed, temperature) uniforme; (number) par ♦ adv hasta, incluso; (introducing a comparison) aún, todavía; ~ **if**, ~ **though** aunque + subj; ~ **more** aún más; ~ **so** aun así; **not** ~ ni siquiera; ~ **he was there** hasta él estuvo allí; ~ **on Sundays** incluso los domingos; **to get** ~ **with sb** ajustar cuentas con uno

evening [ˈiːvnɪŋ] n tarde f; (late) noche f; **in the** ~ por la tarde; ~ **class** n clase f nocturna; ~ **dress** n (no pl: formal clothes) traje m de etiqueta; (woman's) traje m de noche

event [ɪˈvent] n suceso, acontecimiento; (SPORT) prueba; **in the** ~ **of** en caso de; ~**ful** adj (life) activo; (day) ajetreado

eventual [ɪˈventʃuəl] adj final; ~**ity** [-ˈælɪtɪ] n eventualidad f; ~**ly** adv (finally) finalmente; (in time) con el tiempo

ever [ˈevə*] adv (at any time) nunca, jamás; (at all times) siempre; (in question) **why** ~ **not?** ¿y por qué no?; **the best** ~ lo mejor que jamás; **have you** ~ **seen it?** ¿lo ha visto usted alguna vez?; **better than** ~ mejor que nunca; ~ **since** adv desde entonces ♦ conj después de que; ~**green** n árbol m de hoja perenne; ~**lasting** adj eterno, perpetuo

KEYWORD

every ['ɛvrɪ] adj **1** (each) cada; ~ **one of them** (persons) todos ellos/as; (objects) cada uno de ellos/as; ~ **shop in the town was closed** todas las tiendas de la ciudad estaban cerradas **2** (all possible) todo; **I gave you ~ assistance** te di toda la ayuda posible; **I have ~ confidence in him** tiene toda mi confianza; **we wish you ~ success** te deseamos toda suerte de éxitos **3** (showing recurrence) todo/a; ~ **day/ week** todos los días/todas las semanas; ~ **other car had been broken into** habían forzado uno de cada dos coches; **she visits me ~ other/third day** me visita cada dos/tres días; ~ **now and then** de vez en cuando

every: ~body pron = **everyone**; **~day** adj (daily) cotidiano, de todos los días; (usual) acostumbrado; **~one** pron todos/as, todo el mundo; **~thing** pron todo; **this shop sells ~thing** esta tienda vende de todo; **~where** adv: **I've been looking for you ~where** te he estado buscando por todas partes; **~where you go you meet ...** en todas partes encuentra ...

evict [ɪ'vɪkt] vt desahuciar; **~ion** [ɪ'vɪkʃən] n desahucio

evidence ['ɛvɪdəns] n (proof) prueba, (of witness) testimonio; (sign) indicios mpl; **to give ~** prestar declaración, dar testimonio

evident ['ɛvɪdənt] adj evidente, manifiesto; **~ly** adv por lo visto

evil ['iːvl] adj malo; (influence) funesto ♦ n mal m

evoke [ɪ'vəuk] vt evocar

evolution [iːvə'luːʃən] n evolución f

evolve [ɪ'vɔlv] vt desarrollar ♦ vi evolucionar, desarrollarse

ewe [juː] n oveja

ex- [ɛks] prefix ex

exact [ɪg'zækt] adj exacto; (person) meticuloso ♦ vt: **to ~ sth (from)** exigir algo (de); **~ing** adj exigente; (conditions) arduo; **~ly** adv exactamente; (indicating agreement) exacto

exaggerate [ɪg'zædʒəreɪt] vt, vi exagerar; **exaggeration** [-'reɪʃən] n exageración f

exalted [ɪg'zɔːltɪd] adj eminente

exam [ɪg'zæm] n abbr (SCOL) = **examination**

examination [ɪgzæmɪ'neɪʃən] n examen m; (MED) reconocimiento

examine [ɪg'zæmɪn] vt examinar; (inspect) inspeccionar, escudriñar; (MED) reconocer; **~r** n examinador(a) m/f

example [ɪg'zɑːmpl] n ejemplo; **for ~** por ejemplo

exasperate [ɪg'zɑːspəreɪt] vt exasperar, irritar; **exasperation** [-'ʃən] n exasperación f, irritación f

excavate ['ɛkskəveɪt] vt excavar

exceed [ɪk'siːd] vt (amount) exceder; (number) pasar de; (speed limit) sobrepasar; (powers) excederse en; (hopes) superar; **~ingly** adv sumamente, sobremanera

excellent ['ɛksələnt] adj excelente

except [ɪk'sɛpt] prep (also: ~ **for**, ~**ing**) excepto, salvo ♦ vt exceptuar, excluir; ~ **if/when** excepto si/cuando; ~ **that** salvo que; **~ion** [ɪk'sɛpʃən] n excepción f; **to take ~ion to** ofenderse por; **~ional** [ɪk'sɛpʃənl] adj excepcional

excerpt ['ɛksəːpt] n extracto

excess [ɪk'sɛs] n exceso; **~es** npl (of cruelty etc) atrocidades fpl; ~ **baggage** n exceso de equipaje; ~ **fare** n suplemento; **~ive** adj excesivo

exchange [ɪks'tʃeɪndʒ] n intercambio; (conversation) diálogo; (also: telephone ~) central f (telefónica) ♦ vt: **to ~ (for)** cambiar (por); ~ **rate** n tipo de cambio

exchequer [ɪks'tʃekə*] (BRIT) n: **the E~** la Hacienda del Fisco

excise ['eksaɪz] n impuestos mpl sobre el alcohol y el tabaco

excite [ɪk'saɪt] vt (stimulate) estimular; (arouse) excitar; **~d** adj: **to get ~d** emocionarse; **~ment** n (agitation) excitación f; (exhilaration) emoción f; **exciting** adj emocionante

exclaim [ɪks'kleɪm] vi exclamar; **exclamation** [eksklə'meɪʃən] n exclamación f; **exclamation mark** n punto de admiración

exclude [ɪks'kluːd] vt excluir; exceptuar

exclusive [ɪks'kluːsɪv] adj exclusivo; (club, district) selecto; **~ of tax** excluyendo impuestos; **~ly** adv únicamente

excruciating [ɪks'kruːʃɪeɪtɪŋ] adj (pain) agudísimo, atroz; (noise, embarrassment) horrible

excursion [ɪks'kɜːʃən] n (tourist ~) excursión f

excuse [n ɪk'skjuːs, vb ɪk'skjuːz] n disculpa, excusa; (pretext) pretexto ♦ vt (justify) justificar; (forgive) disculpar, perdonar; **to ~ sb from doing sth** dispensar a uno de hacer algo; **~ me!** (attracting attention) ¡por favor!; (apologizing) ¡perdón!; **if you will ~ me** con su permiso

ex-directory ['eksdɪ'rektərɪ] (BRIT) adj que no consta en la guía

execute ['eksɪkjuːt] vt (plan) realizar; (order) cumplir; (person) ajusticiar, ejecutar; **execution** [-'kjuːʃən] n realización f; cumplimiento; ejecución f

executive [ɪg'zekjʊtɪv] n (person, committee) ejecutivo; (POL: committee) poder m ejecutivo ♦ adj ejecutivo

exemplify [ɪg'zemplɪfaɪ] vt ejemplificar; (illustrate) ilustrar

exempt [ɪg'zempt] adj: **~ from** exento de ♦ vt: **to ~ sb from doing sth** eximir a uno de; **~ion** [-ʃən] n exención f

exercise ['eksəsaɪz] n ejercicio ♦ vt (patience) usar de; (right) valerse de; (dog) llevar de paseo; (mind) preocupar ♦ vi (also: to take ~) hacer ejercicio(s); **~ bike** n ciclostátic ® m, bicicleta estática; **~ book** n cuaderno

exert [ɪg'zɜːt] vt ejercer; **to ~ o.s.** esforzarse; **~ion** [-ʃən] n esfuerzo

exhale [eks'heɪl] vt despedir ♦ vi exhalar

exhaust [ɪg'zɔːst] n (AUT: also: ~ pipe) escape m; (: fumes) gases mpl de escape ♦ vt agotar; **~ed** adj agotado; **~ion** [ɪg'zɔːstʃən] n agotamiento; **nervous ~ion** postración f nerviosa; **~ive** adj exhaustivo

exhibit [ɪg'zɪbɪt] n (ART) obra expuesta; (LAW) objeto expuesto ♦ vt (show: emotions) manifestar; (: courage, skill) demostrar; (paintings) exponer; **~ion** [eksɪ'bɪʃən] n exposición f; (of talent etc) demostración f

exhilarating [ɪg'zɪləreɪtɪŋ] adj estimulante, tónico

exile ['eksaɪl] n exilio; (person) exiliado/a ♦ vt desterrar, exiliar

exist [ɪg'zɪst] vi existir; (live) vivir; **~ence** n existencia; **~ing** adj existente, actual

exit ['eksɪt] n salida ♦ vi (THEATRE) hacer mutis; (COMPUT) salir (al sistema); **~ poll** n encuesta a la salida de los colegios electorales; **~ ramp** (US) n (AUT) vía de acceso

exodus ['eksədəs] n éxodo

exonerate [ɪg'zɔnəreɪt] vt: **to ~ from** exculpar de

exotic [ɪg'zɔtɪk] adj exótico

expand [ɪk'spænd] vt ampliar; (number) aumentar ♦ vi (population) aumentar; (trade etc) expandirse; (gas, metal) dilatarse

expanse [ɪk'spæns] n extensión f

expansion [ɪk'spænʃən] n (of population) aumento; (of trade) expansión f

expect [ɪk'spekt] vt esperar; (require)

contar con; (*suppose*) suponer ♦ *vi*: **to be ~ing** (*pregnant woman*) estar embarazada; **~ancy** *n* (*anticipation*) esperanza; **life ~ancy** esperanza de vida; **~ant mother** *n* futura madre *f*; **~ation** [ɛkspɛkˈteɪʃən] *n* (*hope*) esperanza; (*belief*) expectativa

expedient [ɪkˈspiːdɪənt] *adj* conveniente, oportuno ♦ *n* recurso, expediente *m*

expedition [ɛkspəˈdɪʃən] *n* expedición *f*

expel [ɪkˈspɛl] *vt* arrojar; (*from place*) expulsar

expend [ɪkˈspɛnd] *vt* (*money*) gastar; (*time, energy*) consumir; **~iture** *n* gastos *mpl*, desembolso; consumo

expense [ɪkˈspɛns] *n* gasto, gastos *mpl*; (*high cost*) costa; **~s** *npl* (*COMM*) gastos *mpl*; **at the ~ of** a costa de; **~ account** *n* cuenta de gastos

expensive [ɪkˈspɛnsɪv] *adj* caro, costoso

experience [ɪkˈspɪərɪəns] *n* experiencia ♦ *vt* experimentar; (*suffer*) sufrir; **~d** *adj* experimentado

experiment [ɪkˈspɛrɪmənt] *n* experimento ♦ *vi* hacer experimentos

expert [ˈɛkspəːt] *adj* experto, perito ♦ *n* experto/a, perito/a; (*specialist*) especialista *m/f*; **~ise** [-ˈtiːz] *n* pericia

expire [ɪkˈspaɪə*] *vi* caducar, vencer; **expiry** *n* vencimiento

explain [ɪkˈspleɪn] *vt* explicar; **explanation** [ɛkspləˈneɪʃən] *n* explicación *f*; **explanatory** [ɪkˈsplænətrɪ] *adj* explicativo; aclaratorio

explicit [ɪkˈsplɪsɪt] *adj* explícito

explode [ɪkˈspləud] *vi* estallar, explotar; (*population*) crecer rápidamente; (*with anger*) reventar

exploit [*n* ˈɛkspləɪt, *vb* ɪkˈspləɪt] *n* hazaña ♦ *vt* explotar; **~ation** [-ˈteɪʃən] *n* explotación *f*

exploratory [ɪkˈsplɔrətrɪ] *adj* de exploración, (*fig: talks*) exploratorio,

preliminar

explore [ɪkˈsplɔː*] *vt* explorar; (*fig*) examinar; investigar; **~r** *n* explorador(a) *m/f*

explosion [ɪkˈspləuʒən] *n* (*also fig*) explosión *f*; **explosive** [ɪksˈpləusɪv] *adj, n* explosivo

exponent [ɪkˈspəunənt] *n* (*of theory etc*) partidario/a; (*of skill etc*) exponente *m/f*

export [*vb* ɛkˈspɔːt, *n* ˈɛkspɔːt] *vt* exportar ♦ *n* (*process*) exportación *f*; (*product*) producto de exportación ♦ *cpd* de exportación; **~er** *n* exportador *m*

expose [ɪkˈspəuz] *vt* exponer; (*unmask*) desenmascarar; **~d** *adj* expuesto

exposure [ɪkˈspəuʒə*] *n* exposición *f*; (*publicity*) publicidad *f*; (*PHOT: speed*) velocidad *f* de obturación; (: *shot*) fotografía; **to die from ~** (*MED*) morir de frío; **~ meter** *n* fotómetro

express [ɪkˈsprɛs] *adj* (*definite*) expreso, explícito; (*BRIT: letter etc*) urgente ♦ *n* (*train*) rápido ♦ *vt* expresar; **~ion** [ɪkˈsprɛʃən] *n* expresión *f*; (*of actor etc*) sentimiento; **~ly** *adv* expresamente; **~way** (*US*) *n* (*urban motorway*) autopista

exquisite [ɛkˈskwɪzɪt] *adj* exquisito

extend [ɪkˈstɛnd] *vt* (*visit, street*) prolongar; (*building*) ampliar; (*invitation*) ofrecer ♦ *vi* (*land*) extenderse; (*period of time*) prolongarse

extension [ɪkˈstɛnʃən] *n* extensión *f*; (*building*) ampliación *f*; (*of time*) prolongación *f*; (*TEL: in private house*) línea derivada; (: *in office*) extensión *f*

extensive [ɪkˈstɛnsɪv] *adj* extenso; (*damage*) importante; (*knowledge*) amplio; **~ly** *adv*: **he's travelled ~ly** ha viajado por muchos países

extent [ɪkˈstɛnt] *n* (*breadth*) extensión *f*; (*scope*) alcance *m*; **to some ~** hasta cierto punto; **to the ~ of...** hasta el punto de...; **to such an ~ that...** hasta tal punto que...; **to what ~?**

¿hasta qué punto?
extenuating [ɪkˈstenjueɪtɪŋ] adj:
~ **circumstances** circunstancias fpl
atenuantes
exterior [ekˈstɪərɪəʳ] adj exterior,
externo ♦ n exterior m
external [ekˈstɜːnl] adj externo
extinct [ɪkˈstɪŋkt] adj (volcano)
extinguido; (race) extinto
extinguish [ɪkˈstɪŋgwɪʃ] vt extinguir,
apagar; ~**er** n extintor m
extort [ɪkˈstɔːt] vt obtener por fuerza;
~**ionate** adj excesivo, exorbitante
extra [ˈekstrə] adj adicional ♦ adv (in
addition) de más ♦ n (luxury, addition)
extra m; (CINEMA, THEATRE) extra m/f,
comparsa m/f
extra... [ˈekstrə] prefix extra...
extract [vb ɪkˈstrækt, n ˈekstrækt] vt
sacar; (tooth) extraer; (money, promise)
obtener ♦ n extracto
extracurricular [ekstrəkəˈrɪkjuləʳ] adj
extraescolar, extra-académico
extradite [ˈekstrədaɪt] vt extraditar
extra- [ˈekstrə] : ~**marital** adj extramatrimonial;
~**mural** [ekstrəˈmjuərl] adj
extraescolar; **ordinary** [ɪkˈstrɔːdnrɪ]
adj extraordinario; (odd) raro
extravagance [ɪkˈstrævəgəns] n
derroche m, despilfarro; (thing bought)
extravagancia
extravagant [ɪkˈstrævəgənt] adj
(lavish: person) pródigo, (: gift)
(demasiado) caro; (wasteful)
despilfarrador
extreme [ɪkˈstriːm] adj extremo,
extremado ♦ n extremo; ~**ly** adv
sumamente, extremadamente
extricate [ˈekstrɪkeɪt] vt: **to** ~ **sth/sb**
from librar algo/a uno de
extrovert [ˈekstrəvɜːt] n extrovertido/a
eye [aɪ] n ojo ♦ vt mirar de soslayo,
ojear; **to keep an** ~ **on** vigilar; ~**bath**
n ojera; ~**brow** n ceja; ~**drops** npl
gotas fpl para los ojos, colirio; ~**lash** n
pestaña; ~**lid** n párpado; ~**liner** n lápiz
m de ojos; ~**-opener** n revelación f,

gran sorpresa; ~**shadow** n
sombreador m de ojos; ~**sight** n vista;
~**sore** n monstruosidad f; ~ **witness**
n testigo m/f presencial

F, f

F [ef] n (MUS) fa m
F. abbr = **Fahrenheit**
fable [ˈfeɪbl] n fábula
fabric [ˈfæbrɪk] n tejido, tela
fabulous [ˈfæbjuləs] adj fabuloso
façade [fəˈsɑːd] n fachada
face [feɪs] n (ANAT) cara, rostro; (of
clock) esfera (SP), cara (AM); (of
mountain) cara, ladera; (of building)
fachada ♦ vt (direction) estar de cara a;
(situation) hacer frente a; (facts)
aceptar; ~ **down** (person, card) boca
abajo; **to lose** ~ desprestigiarse; **to**
make or **pull a** ~ hacer muecas; **in**
the ~ **of** (difficulties etc) ante; **on the**
~ **of it** a primera vista; **to** ~ **cara a**
cara; ~ **up to** vt fus hacer frente a,
arrostrar; ~ **cloth** (BRIT) n manopla;
~ **cream** n crema (de belleza); ~ **lift**
n estirado facial; (of building) renovación
f; ~ **powder** n polvos mpl; ~**-saving**
adj para salvar las apariencias; ~ **value**
n (of stamp) valor m nominal; **to take**
sth at ~ **value** (fig) tomar algo en
sentido literal
facilities [fəˈsɪlɪtɪz] npl (buildings)
instalaciones fpl; (equipment) servicios
mpl; **credit** ~ facilidades fpl de crédito
facing [ˈfeɪsɪŋ] prep frente a
facsimile [fækˈsɪmɪlɪ] n (replica)
facsímil(e); (machine) telefax m; (fax)
fax m
fact [fækt] n hecho; **in** ~ en realidad
factor [ˈfæktəʳ] n factor m
factory [ˈfæktərɪ] n fábrica
factual [ˈfæktjuəl] adj basado en los
hechos
faculty [ˈfækltɪ] n facultad f; (US:
teaching staff) personal m docente

fad [fæd] n novedad f, moda

fade [feɪd] vi desteñirse; (sound, smile) desvanecerse; (light) apagarse; (flower) marchitarse; (hope, memory) perderse

fag [fæg] n (BRIT: inf) n (cigarette) pitillo (SP), cigarro

fail [feɪl] vt (candidate) suspender; (exam) no aprobar (SP), reprobar (AM); (subj: memory etc) fallar a ♦ vi suspender; (be unsuccessful) fracasar; (strength, brakes) fallar; (light) acabarse; **to ~ to do sth** (neglect) dejar de hacer algo; (be unable) no poder hacer algo; **without ~** sin falta; **~ing** n falta, defecto ♦ prep a falta de; **~ure** ['feɪljə*] n fracaso; (person) fracasado/a; (mechanical etc) fallo

faint [feɪnt] adj débil; (recollection) vago; (mark) apenas visible ♦ n desmayo ♦ vi desmayarse; **to feel ~** estar mareado, marearse

fair [fɛə*] adj justo; (hair, person) rubio; (weather) bueno; (good enough) regular; (considerable) considerable ♦ adv (play) limpio ♦ n feria; (BRIT: funfair) parque m de atracciones; **~ly** adv (justly) con justicia; (quite) bastante; **~ness** n justicia, imparcialidad f; **~ play** n juego limpio

fairy ['fɛərɪ] n hada; **~ tale** n cuento de hadas

faith [feɪθ] n fe f; (trust) confianza; (sect) religión f; **~ful** adj (loyal: troops etc) leal; (spouse) fiel; (account) exacto; **~fully** adv fielmente; **yours ~fully** (BRIT: in letters) le saluda atentamente

fake [feɪk] n (painting etc) falsificación f; (person) impostor(a) m/f ♦ adj falso ♦ vt fingir; (painting etc) falsificar

falcon ['fɔːlkən] n halcón m

fall [fɔːl] (pt **fell**, pp **fallen**) n caída; (in price etc) descenso; (US) otoño ♦ vi caer(se); (price) bajar, descender; **~s** npl (water~) cascada, salto de agua; **to ~ flat** (on one's face) caerse (boca abajo); (plan) fracasar; (joke, story) no hacer gracia; **~ back** vi retroceder;

~ back on vt fus (remedy etc) recurrir a; **~ behind** vi quedarse atrás; **~ down** vi (person) caerse; (building, hopes) derrumbarse; **~ for** vt fus (trick) dejarse engañar por; (person) enamorarse de; **~ in** vi (roof) hundirse; (MIL) alinearse; **~ off** vi caerse; (diminish) disminuir; **~ out** vi (friends etc) reñir; (hair, teeth) caerse; **~ through** vi (plan, project) fracasar

fallacy ['fæləsɪ] n error m

fallen ['fɔːlən] pp of **fall**

fallout ['fɔːlaut] n lluvia radioactiva

fallow ['fæləu] adj en barbecho

false [fɔːls] adj falso; **under ~ pretences** con engaños; **~ alarm** n falsa alarma; **~ teeth** (BRIT) npl dentadura postiza

falter ['fɔːltə*] vi vacilar; (engine) fallar

fame [feɪm] n fama

familiar [fə'mɪlɪə*] adj conocido, familiar; (tone) de confianza; **to be ~ with** (subject) conocer (bien)

family ['fæmɪlɪ] n familia; **~ business** n negocio familiar; **~ doctor** n médico/a de cabecera

famine ['fæmɪn] n hambre f, hambruna

famished ['fæmɪʃt] adj hambriento

famous ['feɪməs] adj famoso, célebre; **~ly** adv (get on) estupendamente

fan [fæn] n abanico; (ELEC) ventilador m; (of pop star) fan m/f; (SPORT) hincha m/f ♦ vt abanicar; (fire, quarrel) avivar

fanatic [fə'nætɪk] n fanático/a

fan belt n correa del ventilador

fanciful ['fænsɪful] adj (design, name) fantástico

fancy ['fænsɪ] n (whim) capricho, antojo; (imagination) imaginación f ♦ adj (luxury) lujoso, de lujo ♦ vt (feel like, want) tener ganas de; (imagine) imaginarse; (think) creer; **to take a ~ to sb** tomar cariño a uno; **he fancies her** (inf) le gusta (ella) mucho; **~ dress** n disfraz m; **~-dress ball** n baile m de disfraces

fanfare ['fænfeə*] n fanfarria (de trompeta)

fang [fæŋ] n colmillo

fantastic [fæn'tæstɪk] adj (enormous) enorme; (strange, wonderful) fantástico

fantasy ['fæntəzɪ] n (dream) sueño; (unreality) fantasía

far [fɑː*] adj (distant) lejano ♦ adv lejos; (much, greatly) mucho; ~ **away**, ~ **off** (a lo) lejos; ~ **better** mucho mejor; ~ **from** lejos de; **by** ~ con mucho; **go as** ~ **as the farm** vaya hasta la granja; **as** ~ **as I know** que yo sepa; **how** ~? ¿hasta dónde?; (fig) ¿hasta qué punto?; ~**away** adj remoto; (look) distraído

farce [fɑːs] n farsa

fare [feə*] n (on trains, buses) precio (del billete); (in taxi: cost) tarifa; (food) comida; **half** ~ medio pasaje m; **full** ~ pasaje completo

Far East n: **the** ~ el Extremo Oriente

farewell [feə'wel] excl, n adiós m

farm [fɑːm] n granja (SP), finca (AM), estancia (AM) ♦ vt cultivar; ~**er** n granjero (SP), estanciero (AM); ~**hand** n peón m; ~**house** n granja, casa de hacienda (AM); ~**ing** n agricultura; (of crops) cultivo; (of animals) cría; ~**land** n tierra de cultivo; ~ **worker** n = ~**hand**; ~**yard** n corral m

far-reaching [fɑː'riːtʃɪŋ] adj (reform, effect) de gran alcance

fart [fɑːt] (inf!) vi tirarse un pedo (!)

farther ['fɑːðə*] adv más lejos, más allá ♦ adj más lejano

farthest ['fɑːðɪst] superlative of **far**

fascinate ['fæsɪneɪt] vt fascinar

fascination [-'neɪʃən] n fascinación f

fascism ['fæʃɪzəm] n fascismo

fashion ['fæʃən] n moda; (~ industry) industria de la moda; (manner) manera ♦ vt formar; **in** ~ a la moda; **out of** ~ pasado de moda; ~**able** adj de moda; ~ **show** n desfile m de modelos

fast [fɑːst] adj (quick) rápido; (dye, colour) resistente; (clock): **to be** ~ estar adelantado ♦ adv rápidamente, de

prisa; (stuck, held) firmemente ♦ n ayuno ♦ vi ayunar; ~ **asleep** profundamente dormido

fasten ['fɑːsn] vt atar, sujetar; (coat, belt) abrochar ♦ vi atarse; abrocharse; ~**er**, ~**ing** n cierre m; (of door etc) cerrojo

fast food n comida rápida, platos mpl preparados

fastidious [fæs'tɪdɪəs] adj (fussy) quisquilloso

fat [fæt] adj gordo; (book) grueso; (profit) grande, pingüe ♦ n grasa; (on person) carnes fpl; (lard) manteca

fatal ['feɪtl] adj (mistake) fatal; (injury) mortal; ~**ity** [fə'tælɪtɪ] n (road death etc) víctima; ~**ly** adv fatalmente, mortalmente

fate [feɪt] n destino; (of person) suerte f; ~**ful** adj fatídico

father ['fɑːðə*] n padre m; ~**-in-law** n suegro; ~**ly** adj paternal

fathom ['fæðəm] n braza ♦ vt (mystery) desentrañar; (understand) lograr comprender

fatigue [fə'tiːg] n fatiga, cansancio

fatten ['fætn] vt, vi engordar

fatty ['fætɪ] adj (food) graso ♦ n (inf) gordito/a, gordinflón/ona m/f

fatuous ['fætjuəs] adj fatuo, necio

faucet ['fɔːsɪt] (US) n grifo (SP), llave f (AM)

fault [fɔːlt] n (blame) culpa; (defect: in person, machine) defecto; (GEO) falla ♦ vt criticar; **it's my** ~ es culpa mía; **to find** ~ **with** criticar, poner peros a; **at** ~ culpable; ~**y** adj defectuoso

fauna ['fɔːnə] n fauna

favour ['feɪvə*] (US **favor**) n favor m; (approval) aprobación f ♦ vt (proposition) estar a favor de, aprobar; (assist) ser propicio a; **to do sb a** ~ hacer un favor a uno; **to find** ~ **with sb** caer en gracia a uno; **in** ~ **of** a favor de; ~**able** adj favorable; ~**ite** ['feɪvrɪt] adj, n favorito, preferido

fawn [fɔːn] n cervato ♦ adj (also: ~

coloured) color de cervato, leonado
♦ vi: to ~ (up)on adular

fax [fæks] n (document) fax m; (machine) telefax m ♦ vt mandar por telefax

FBI (US) n abbr (= Federal Bureau of Investigation) ≈ BIC f (SP)

fear [fɪə*] n miedo, temor m ♦ vt tener miedo de, temer; **for ~ of** por si; **~ful** adj temeroso, miedoso; (awful) terrible; **~less** adj audaz

feasible ['fiːzəbl] adj factible

feast [fiːst] n banquete m; (REL: also: ~ day) fiesta ♦ vi festejar

feat [fiːt] n hazaña

feather ['feðə*] n pluma

feature ['fiːtʃə*] n característica; (article) artículo de fondo ♦ vt (subj: film) presentar ♦ vi: to ~ in tener un papel destacado en; ~s npl (of face) facciones fpl; ~ **film** n largometraje m

February ['februərɪ] n febrero

fed [fed] pt, pp of **feed**

federal ['fedərəl] adj federal

fed up [fed'ʌp] adj: **to be ~ (with)** estar harto de

fee [fiː] n pago; (professional) derechos mpl, honorarios mpl; (of club) cuota; **school ~** n matrícula

feeble ['fiːbl] adj débil; (joke) flojo

feed [fiːd] (pt, pp **fed**) n comida; (of animal) pienso; (on printer) dispositivo de alimentación ♦ vt alimentar; (BRIT: baby: breast~) dar el pecho a; (animal) dar de comer a; (data, information): **to ~ into** meter en; **~ on** vt fus alimentarse de; **~back** n reacción f, feedback m

feel [fiːl] (pt, pp **felt**) n (sensation) sensación f; (sense of touch) tacto; (impression): **to have the ~ of** parecerse a ♦ vt tocar; (pain etc) sentir; (think, believe) creer; **to ~ hungry/ cold** tener hambre/frío; **to ~ lonely/ better** sentirse solo/mejor; **I don't ~ well** no me siento bien; **it ~s soft** es suave al tacto; **to ~ like** (want)

tener ganas de; **~ about** or **around** vi tantear; **~er** n (of insect) antena; **~ing** n (physical) sensación f; (foreboding) presentimiento; (emotion) sentimiento

feet [fiːt] npl of **foot**

feign [feɪn] vt fingir

fell [fel] pt of **fall** ♦ vt (tree) talar

fellow ['feləu] n tipo, tío (SP); (comrade) compañero; (of learned society) socio/a ♦ cpd: ~ **citizen** n conciudadano/a; ~ **countryman** (irreg) n compatriota m; ~ **men** npl semejantes mpl; ~**ship** n compañerismo; (grant) beca

felony ['feləni] n crimen m

felt [felt] pt, pp of **feel** ♦ n fieltro; ~**-tip pen** n rotulador m

female ['fiːmeɪl] n (pej: woman) mujer f, tía; (ZOOL) hembra ♦ adj femenino; hembra

feminine ['feminin] adj femenino

feminist ['feminist] n feminista

fence [fens] n valla, cerca ♦ vt (also: ~ **in**) cercar ♦ vi (SPORT) hacer esgrima; **fencing** n esgrima

fend [fend] vi: **to ~ for o.s.** valerse por sí mismo; ~ **off** vt (attack) rechazar; (questions) evadir

fender ['fendə*] n guardafuego; (US: AUT) parachoques m inv

ferment [vb fə'mɛnt, n 'fəːmɛnt] vi fermentar ♦ n (fig) agitación f

fern [fəːn] n helecho

ferocious [fə'rəuʃəs] adj feroz

ferret ['ferit] n hurón m

ferry ['feri] n (small) barca (de pasaje), balsa; (large: also: ~**boat**) transbordador m (SP), embarcadero (AM) ♦ vt transportar

fertile ['fəːtail] adj fértil; (BIOL) fecundo; **fertilize** ['fəːtilaiz] vt (BIOL) fecundar; (AGR) abonar; **fertilizer** n abono

fester ['festə*] vi ulcerarse

festival ['festivəl] n (REL) fiesta; (ART, MUS) festival m

festive ['festiv] adj festivo; **the**

~ season (BRIT: Christmas) las Navidades

festivities [fes'tɪvɪtɪz] npl fiestas fpl

festoon [fes'tuːn] vt: **to ~ with** engalanar de

fetch [fetʃ] vt ir a buscar; (sell for) venderse por

fête [feɪt] n fiesta

fetus [ˈfiːtəs] (US) n = **foetus**

feud [fjuːd] n (hostility) enemistad f; (quarrel) disputa

fever [ˈfiːvə*] n fiebre f; **~ish** adj febril

few [fjuː] adj (not many) pocos ♦ pron pocos; **a ~** adj unos pocos, algunos; **~er** adj menos; **~est** adj los/ las menos

fiancé [fɪ'ɑːŋseɪ] n novio, prometido; **~e** n novia, prometida

fib [fɪb] n mentirilla

fibre [ˈfaɪbə*] (US **fiber**) n fibra; **~glass** (Fiberglass ® US) n fibra de vidrio

fickle [ˈfɪkl] adj inconstante

fiction [ˈfɪkʃən] n ficción f; **~al** adj novelesco; **fictitious** [fɪk'tɪʃəs] adj ficticio

fiddle [ˈfɪdl] n (MUS) violín m; (cheating) trampa ♦ vt (BRIT: accounts) falsificar; **~ with** vt fus juguetear con

fidget [ˈfɪdʒɪt] vi enredar; **stop ~ing!** ¡estáte quieto!

field [fiːld] n campo; (fig) esfera; (SPORT) campo, cancha (AM); **~ marshal** n mariscal m; **~work** n trabajo de campo

fiend [fiːnd] n demonio

fierce [fɪəs] adj feroz; (wind, heat) fuerte; (fighting, enemy) encarnizado

fiery [ˈfaɪərɪ] adj (burning) ardiente; (temperament) apasionado

fifteen [fɪf'tiːn] num quince

fifth [fɪfθ] num quinto

fifty [ˈfɪftɪ] num cincuenta; **~-~** adj (deal, split) a medias ♦ adv a medias, mitad por mitad

fig [fɪg] n higo

fight [faɪt] (pt, pp **fought**) n (gen) pelea; (MIL) combate m; (struggle)

lucha ♦ vt luchar contra; (cancer, alcoholism) combatir; (election) intentar ganar; (emotion) resistir ♦ vi pelear, luchar; **~er** n combatiente m/f; (plane) caza m; **~ing** n combate m, pelea

figment [ˈfɪgmənt] n: **a ~ of the imagination** una quimera

figurative [ˈfɪgjʊrətɪv] adj (meaning) figurado; (style) figurativo

figure [ˈfɪgə*] n (DRAWING, GEOM) figura, dibujo; (number, cipher) cifra; (body, outline) tipo; (personality) figura ♦ vt (esp US) imaginar ♦ vi (appear) figurar; **~ out** vt (work out) resolver; **~head** n (NAUT) mascarón m de proa; (pej: leader) figura decorativa; **~ of speech** n figura retórica

file [faɪl] n (tool) lima; (dossier) expediente m; (folder) carpeta; (COMPUT) fichero; (row) fila ♦ vt limar; (LAW: claim) presentar; (store) archivar; **~ in/out** vi entrar/salir en fila; **filing cabinet** n fichero, archivador m

fill [fɪl] vt (space): **to ~ (with)** llenar (de); (vacancy, need) cubrir ♦ n: **to eat one's ~** llenarse; **~ in** vt rellenar; **~ up** vt llenar (hasta el borde) ♦ vi (AUT) poner gasolina

fillet [ˈfɪlɪt] n filete m; **~ steak** filete m de ternera

filling [ˈfɪlɪŋ] n (CULIN) relleno; (for tooth) empaste m; **~ station** n estación f de servicio

film [fɪlm] n película; vt (scene) filmar ♦ vi rodar (una película); **~ star** n astro, estrella de cine

filter [ˈfɪltə*] n filtro ♦ vt filtrar; **~ lane** (BRIT) n carril m de selección; **~-tipped** adj con filtro

filth [fɪlθ] n suciedad f; **~y** adj sucio; (language) obsceno

fin [fɪn] n (of fish) aleta

final [ˈfaɪnl] adj (last) final, último; (definitive) definitivo, terminante ♦ n (BRIT: SPORT) final f; **~s** npl (SCOL) examen m final; (US: SPORT) final f

finale [fɪ'nɑːlɪ] n final m

final: ~**ist** n (SPORT) finalista m/f; ~**ize**
vt concluir, completar; ~**ly** adv (lastly)
por último, finalmente; (eventually) por
fin

finance [faɪˈnæns] n (money) fondos
mpl, ~**s** npl finanzas fpl; (personal ~s)
situación f económica ♦ vt financiar;
financial [-ˈnænʃəl] adj financiero

find [faɪnd] (pt, pp **found**) vt
encontrar, hallar; (come upon)
descubrir ♦ n hallazgo; descubrimiento;
to ~ sb guilty (LAW) declarar culpable
a uno; (truth,
secret) descubrir; **to ~ out** averiguar; (truth,
secret) descubrir; **to ~ out about**
(subject) informarse sobre; (by chance)
enterarse de; ~**ings** npl (LAW)
veredicto, fallo; (of report)
recomendaciones fpl

fine [faɪn] adj excelente; (thin) fino
♦ adv (well) bien ♦ n (LAW) multa ♦ vt
(LAW) multar; **to be ~** (person) estar
bien; (weather) hacer buen tiempo;
~ **arts** npl bellas artes fpl

finery [ˈfaɪnərɪ] n adornos mpl

finger [ˈfɪŋgə*] n dedo ♦ vt (touch)
manosear; **little/index ~** dedo
meñique m/índice m; ~**nail** n uña;
~**print** n huella dactilar; ~**tip** n yema
del dedo

finish [ˈfɪnɪʃ] n (end) fin m; (SPORT)
meta; (polish etc) acabado ♦ vt, vi
terminar; **to ~ doing sth** acabar de
hacer algo; **to ~ third** llegar el tercero;
~ **off** vt acabar, terminar; (kill) acabar
con; ~ **up** vt acabar, terminar ♦ vi ir a
parar, terminar; ~**ing line** n línea de
llegada o meta

finite [ˈfaɪnaɪt] adj finito; (verb)
conjugado

Finland [ˈfɪnlənd] n Finlandia

Finn [fɪn] n finlandés/esa m/f; ~**ish** adj
finlandés/esa ♦ n (LING) finlandés m

fir [fɜ:*] n abeto

fire [faɪə*] n fuego; (in hearth) lumbre
f; (accidental) incendio; (heater) estufa
♦ vt (gun) disparar; (interest) despertar;
(inf: dismiss) despedir ♦ vi (shoot)

disparar; **on ~** ardiendo, en llamas;
~ **alarm** n alarma de incendios; ~**arm**
n arma de fuego; ~ **brigade** (US
~ **department**) n (cuerpo de)
bomberos mpl; ~ **engine** n coche m
de bomberos; ~ **escape** n escalera de
incendios; ~ **extinguisher** n extintor
m (de incendios); ~**guard** n rejilla de
protección; ~**man** (irreg) n bombero;
~**place** n chimenea; ~**side** n: **by the
~side** al lado de la chimenea; ~
station n parque m de bomberos;
~**wood** n leña; ~**works** npl fuegos
mpl artificiales

firing squad [ˈfaɪərɪŋ-] n pelotón m de
ejecución

firm [fɜ:m] adj firme; (look, voice)
resuelto ♦ n firma, empresa; ~**ly** adv
firmemente, resueltamente

first [fɜ:st] adj primero ♦ adv (before
others) primero; (when listing reasons
etc) en primer lugar, primeramente ♦ n
(person: in race) primero/a; (AUT)
primera; (BRIT: SCOL) título de licenciado
con calificación de sobresaliente; **at ~** al
principio; ~ **of all** ante todo; ~ **aid** n
primera ayuda, primeros auxilios mpl;
~**aid kit** n botiquín m; ~**-class** adj
(excellent) de primera (categoría);
(ticket etc) de primera clase; ~**hand**
adj de primera mano; **F~ Lady** (esp
US) n primera dama; ~**ly** adv en primer
lugar; ~ **name** n nombre m (de pila);
~**-rate** adj estupendo

fish [fɪʃ] n inv pez m; (food) pescado
♦ vt, vi pescar; **to go ~ing** ir de pesca;
~**erman** (irreg) n pescador m; ~ **farm**
n criadero de peces; ~ **fingers** (BRIT)
npl croquetas fpl de pescado; ~**ing
boat** n barca de pesca; ~**ing line** n
sedal m; ~**ing rod** n caña (de pescar);
~**monger's (shop)** (BRIT) n
pescadería; ~ **sticks** (US) npl =
~ **fingers**; ~**y** (inf) adj sospechoso

fist [fɪst] n puño

fit [fɪt] adj (healthy) en (buena) forma;
(proper) adecuado, apropiado ♦ vt

(subj: clothes) estar or sentar bien a; (instal) poner; (equip) proveer, dotar; (facts) cuadrar or corresponder con ♦ vi (clothes) sentar bien; (in space, gap) caber; (facts) coincidir ♦ n (MED) ataque m; ~ **to** (ready) a punto de; ~ **for** apropiado para; **a ~ of** anger/pride un arranque de cólera/orgullo; **this dress is a good ~** este vestido me sienta bien; **by ~s and starts** a rachas; ~ **in** vi (fig: person) llevarse bien (con todos); **~ful** adj espasmódico, intermitente; **~ment** n módulo adosable; **~ness** n (MED) salud f; **~ted carpet** n moqueta; **~ted kitchen** n cocina amueblada; **~ter** n ajustador m; **~ting** adj apropiado ♦ n (of dress) prueba; (of piece of equipment) instalación f; **~ting room** n probador m; **~tings** npl instalaciones fpl

five [faɪv] num cinco; ~**r** n (BRIT) billete m de cinco libras; (US) billete m de cinco dólares

fix [fɪks] vt (secure) fijar, asegurar; (mend) arreglar; (prepare) preparar ♦ n: **to be in a ~** estar en un aprieto; ~ **up** vt (meeting) arreglar; **to ~ sb up with sth** proveer a uno de algo; **~ation** [fɪk'seɪʃən] n obsesión f; **~ed** adj (prices etc) fijo; **~ture** n (SPORT) encuentro; **~tures** npl (cupboards etc) instalaciones fpl

fizzy [ˈfɪzɪ] adj (drink) gaseoso

fjord [fjɔːd] n fiordo

flabbergasted [ˈflæbəgɑːstɪd] adj pasmado, alucinado

flabby [ˈflæbɪ] adj gordo

flag [flæg] n bandera; (stone) losa ♦ vi decaer; **to ~ sb down** hacer señas a uno para que se pare; **~pole** n asta de bandera; **~ship** n buque m insignia; (fig) bandera

flair [flεə*] n aptitud f especial

flak [flæk] n (MIL) fuego antiaéreo; (inf: criticism) lluvia de críticas

flake [fleɪk] n (of rust, paint) escama; (of snow, soap powder) copo ♦ vi (also:

~ off) desconcharse

flamboyant [flæmˈbɔɪənt] adj (dress) vistoso; (person) extravagante

flame [fleɪm] n llama

flamingo [fləˈmɪŋgəʊ] n flamenco

flammable [ˈflæməbl] adj inflamable

flan [flæn] n (BRIT) tarta

flank [flæŋk] n (of animal) ijar m; (of army) flanco ♦ vt flanquear

flannel [ˈflænl] n (BRIT: also: face ~) manopla; (fabric) franela

flap [flæp] n (of pocket, envelope) solapa ♦ vt (wings, arms) agitar ♦ vi (sail, flag) ondear

flare [flεə*] n llamarada; (MIL) bengala; (in skirt etc) vuelo; ~ **up** vi encenderse; (fig: person) encolerizarse; (: revolt) estallar

flash [flæʃ] n relámpago; (also: news ~) noticias fpl de última hora; (PHOT) flash m ♦ vt (light, headlights) lanzar un destello por; (news, message) transmitir; (smile) lanzar ♦ vi brillar; (hazard light etc) lanzar destellos; **in a ~** en un instante; **he ~ed by** or **past** pasó como un rayo; **~back** n (CINEMA) flashback m; **~bulb** n bombilla fusible; **~ cube** n cubo de flash; **~light** n linterna

flashy [ˈflæʃɪ] (pej) adj ostentoso

flask [flɑːsk] n frasco; (also: vacuum ~) termo

flat [flæt] adj llano; (smooth) liso; (tyre) desinflado; (battery) descargado; (beer) muerto; (refusal etc) rotundo; (MUS) desafinado; (rate) fijo ♦ n (BRIT: apartment) piso (SP), departamento (AM), apartamento (AUT) pinchazo; (MUS) bemol m; **to work ~ out** trabajar a toda mecha; **~ly** adv terminantemente, de plano; **~ten** vt (also: ~ten out) allanar; (smooth out) alisar; (building, plants) arrasar

flatter [ˈflætə*] vt adular, halagar; **~ing** adj halagüeño; (dress) que favorece; **~y** n adulación f

flaunt [flɔːnt] vt ostentar, lucir

flavour ['fleɪvə*] (*US* **flavor**) *n* sabor *m*, gusto ♦ *vt* sazonar, condimentar; **strawberry-~ed** con sabor a fresa; **~ing** *n* (*in product*) aromatizante *m*

flaw [flɔː] *n* defecto *m*; **~less** *adj* impecable

flax [flæks] *n* lino

flea [fliː] *n* pulga

fleck [flek] *n* (*mark*) mota

flee [fliː] (*pt, pp* **fled**) *vt* huir de ♦ *vi* huir, fugarse

fleece [fliːs] *n* vellón *m*; (*wool*) lana ♦ *vt* (*inf*) desplumar

fleet [fliːt] *n* flota; (*of lorries etc*) escuadra

fleeting ['fliːtɪŋ] *adj* fugaz

Flemish ['flemɪʃ] *adj* flamenco

flesh [fleʃ] *n* carne *f*; (*skin*) piel *f*; (*of fruit*) pulpa; **~ wound** *n* herida superficial

flew [fluː] *pt of* **fly**

flex [fleks] *n* cordón *m* ♦ *vt* (*muscles*) tensar; **~ible** *adj* flexible

flick [flɪk] *n* capirotazo; chasquido ♦ *vt* (*with hand*) dar un capirotazo a; (*whip etc*) chasquear; (*switch*) accionar; **~ through** *vt fus* hojear

flicker ['flɪkə*] *vi* (*light*) parpadear; (*flame*) vacilar

flier ['flaɪə*] *n* aviador(a) *m/f*

flight [flaɪt] *n* vuelo; (*escape*) huida, fuga; (*also: ~ of steps*) tramo (de escaleras); **~ attendant** (*US*) *n* camarero/azafata; **~ deck** *n* (*AVIAT*) cabina de mandos; (*NAUT*) cubierta de aterrizaje

flimsy ['flɪmzɪ] *adj* (*thin*) muy ligero; (*building*) endeble; (*excuse*) flojo

flinch [flɪntʃ] *vi* encogerse; **to ~ from** retroceder ante

fling [flɪŋ] (*pt, pp* **flung**) *vt* arrojar

flint [flɪnt] *n* pedernal *m*; (*in lighter*) piedra

flip [flɪp] *vt* dar la vuelta a; (*switch: turn on*) encender; (*: turn off*) apagar; (*coin*) echar a cara o cruz

flippant ['flɪpənt] *adj* poco serio

flipper ['flɪpə*] *n* aleta

flirt [flɜːt] *vi* coquetear, flirtear ♦ *n* coqueta

float [fləut] *n* flotador *m*; (*in procession*) carroza; (*money*) reserva ♦ *vi* flotar; (*swimmer*) hacer la plancha

flock [flɒk] *n* (*of sheep*) rebaño; (*of birds*) bandada ♦ *vi*: **to ~** acudir en tropel a

flog [flɒg] *vt* azotar

flood [flʌd] *n* inundación *f*; (*of letters, imports etc*) avalancha ♦ *vt* inundar ♦ *vi* (*place*) inundarse; (*people*): **to ~ into** inundar; **~ing** *n* inundaciones *fpl*; **~light** *n* foco

floor [flɔː*] *n* suelo; (*storey*) piso; (*of sea*) fondo ♦ *vt* (*subj: question*) dejar sin respuesta; (*: blow*) derribar; **ground ~, first ~** (*US*) planta baja; **first ~, second ~** (*US*) primer piso; **~board** *n* tabla; **~ show** *n* cabaret *m*

flop [flɒp] *n* fracaso ♦ *vi* (*fail*) fracasar; (*fall*) derrumbarse; **~py** *adj* flojo ♦ *n* (*COMPUT: also: ~py disk*) floppy *m*

flora ['flɔːrə] *n* flora

floral ['flɔːrl] *adj* (*pattern*) floreado

florid ['flɒrɪd] *adj* (*complexion*) rubicundo

florist ['flɒrɪst] *n* florista *m/f*; **~'s (shop)** *n* florería

flounder ['flaundə*] *vi* (*swimmer*) patalear; (*fig: economy*) estar en dificultades ♦ *n* (*ZOOL*) platija

flour ['flauə*] *n* harina

flourish ['flʌrɪʃ] *vi* florecer ♦ *n* ademán *m*, movimiento (ostentoso)

flout [flaut] *vt* burlarse de

flow [fləu] *n* (*movement*) flujo; (*of traffic*) circulación *f*; (*tide*) corriente *f* ♦ *vi* (*river, blood*) fluir; (*traffic*) circular; **~ chart** *n* organigrama *m*

flower ['flauə*] *n* flor *f* ♦ *vi* florecer; **~ bed** *n* macizo; **~pot** *n* tiesto; **~y** *adj* (*fragrance*) floral; (*pattern*) floreado; (*speech*) florido

flown [fləun] *pp of* **fly**

flu [fluː] *n*: **to have ~** tener la gripe

fluctuate ['flʌktjueɪt] vi fluctuar

fluent ['fluːənt] adj (linguist) que habla perfectamente; (speech) elocuente; **he speaks ~ French, he's ~ in French** domina el francés; **~ly** adv con fluidez

fluff [flʌf] n pelusa; **~y** adj de pelo suave

fluid ['fluːɪd] adj (movement) fluido, líquido; (situation) inestable ♦ n fluido, líquido

fluke [fluːk] (inf) n chiripa

flung [flʌŋ] pt, pp of **fling**

fluoride ['fluəraɪd] n fluoruro

flurry ['flʌrɪ] n (of snow) temporal n; **~ of activity** frenesí m de actividad

flush [flʌʃ] n rubor m; (fig: of youth etc) resplandor m ♦ vt limpiar con agua ♦ vi ruborizarse ♦ adj: **~ with** a ras de; **to ~ the toilet** hacer funcionar la cisterna; **~ed** adj ruborizado

flustered ['flʌstəd] adj aturdido

flute [fluːt] n flauta

flutter ['flʌtə*] n (of wings) revoloteo, aleteo; **a ~ of panic/excitement** una oleada de pánico/excitación ♦ vi revolotear

flux [flʌks] n: **to be in a state of ~** estar continuamente cambiando

fly [flaɪ] (pt flew, pp flown) n mosca; (on trousers: also: flies) bragueta ♦ vt (plane) pilot(e)ar; (cargo) transportar (en avión); (distances) recorrer (en avión) ♦ vi volar; (passengers) ir en avión; (escape) evadirse; (flag) ondear; **~ away** or **off** vi emprender el vuelo; **~-drive** n **~-drive holiday** vacaciones que incluyen vuelo y alquiler de coche; **~ing** n (activity) (el) volar; (action) vuelo ♦ adj: **~ing visit** visita relámpago; **with ~ing colours** con lucimiento; **~ing saucer** n platillo volante; **~ing start** n: **to get off to a ~ing start** empezar con buen pie; **~over** (BRIT) n paso a desnivel or superior; **~sheet** n (for tent) doble techo

foal [fəul] n potro

foam [fəum] n espuma ♦ vi hacer espuma; **~ rubber** n goma espuma

fob [fɔb] vt: **to ~ sb off with sth** despachar a uno con algo

focal point ['fəukl-] n (fig) centro de atención

focus ['fəukəs] (pl ~es) n foco; (centre) centro ♦ vt (field glasses etc) enfocar ♦ vi: **to ~ (on)** enfocar (a); (issue etc) centrarse en; **in/out of ~** enfocado/desenfocado

fodder ['fɔdə*] n pienso

foetus ['fiːtəs] (US fetus) n feto

fog [fɔg] n niebla; **~gy** adj: **it's ~gy** hay niebla, está brumoso; **~ lamp** (US **~ light**) n (AUT) faro de niebla

foil [fɔɪl] vt frustrar ♦ n hoja; (kitchen ~) papel m de aluminio; (complement) complemento; (FENCING) florete m

fold [fəuld] n (bend, crease) pliegue m; (AGR) redil m ♦ vt doblar; (arms) cruzar; **~ up** vi plegarse, doblarse; (business) quebrar ♦ vt (map etc) plegar; **~er** n (for papers) carpeta; (COMPUT) directorio; **~ing** adj (chair, bed) plegable

foliage ['fəulɪɪdʒ] n follaje m

folk [fəuk] n gente f ♦ adj popular, folklórico; **~s** npl (family) familia sg, parientes mpl; **~lore** ['fəuklɔː*] n folklore m; **~ song** n canción f popular

follow ['fɔləu] vt seguir ♦ vi seguir; (result) resultar; **to ~ suit** hacer lo mismo; **~ up** vt (letter, offer) responder a; (case) investigar; **~er** n (of person, belief) partidario/a, **~ing** adj siguiente ♦ n afición f, partidarios mpl

folly ['fɔlɪ] n locura

fond [fɔnd] adj (memory, smile etc) cariñoso; (hopes) ilusorio; **to be ~ of** tener cariño a; (pastime, food) ser aficionado a

fondle ['fɔndl] vt acariciar

font [fɔnt] n pila bautismal; (TYP) fundición f

food [fuːd] n comida; **~ mixer** n batidora; **~ poisoning** n intoxicación f

alimenticia; **~ processor** n robot m de cocina; **~stuffs** npl comestibles mpl
fool [fuːl] n tonto/a; (CULIN) puré m de frutas con nata ♦ vt engañar ♦ vi: **~ around**) bromear; **~hardy** adj temerario; **~ish** adj (careless) imprudente; **~proof** adj (plan etc) infalible
foot [fut] (pl **feet**) n pie m; (measure) pie m (= 304 mm); (of animal) pata f ♦ vt (bill) pagar; **on ~** a pie; **~age** n (CINEMA) imágenes fpl; **~ball** n balón m; (game: BRIT) fútbol m; (: US) fútbol m americano; **~ball player** n (BRIT: also: **~baller**) futbolista m; (US) jugador m de fútbol americano; **~brake** n freno de pie; **~bridge** n puente m para peatones; **~hills** npl estribaciones fpl; **~hold** n pie m firme; (fig) posición f; **to lose one's ~ing** perder el pie; **~lights** npl candilejas fpl; **~note** n nota (al pie de la página); **~path** n sendero; **~print** n huella, pisada; **~step** n paso; **~wear** n calzado

---

KEYWORD

for [fɔː] prep **1** (indicating destination, intention) para; **the train ~ London** el tren con destino a or de Londres; **he left ~ Rome** marchó para Roma; **he went ~ the paper** fue por or el periódico; **is this ~ me?** ¿es esto para mí?; **it's time ~ lunch** es la hora de comer
2 (indicating purpose) para; **what's it ~?** ¿para qué (es)?; **to pray ~ peace** rezar por la paz
3 (on behalf of, representing): **the MP ~ Hove** el diputado por Hove; **he works ~ the government/a local firm** trabaja para el gobierno/en una empresa local; **I'll ask him ~ you** se lo pediré por ti; **G ~ George** G de Gerona
4 (because of) por esta razón; **~ fear of being criticized** por temor a ser

criticado
5 (with regard to) para; **it's cold ~ July** hace frío para julio; **he has a gift ~ languages** tiene don de lenguas
6 (in exchange for) por; **I sold it ~ £5** lo vendí por £5; **to pay 50 pence ~ a ticket** pagar 50 peniques por un billete
7 (in favour of): **are you ~ or against us?** ¿estás con nosotros o contra nosotros?; **I'm all ~ it** estoy totalmente a favor; **vote ~ X** vote (a) X
8 (referring to distance): **there are roadworks ~ 5 km** hay obras en 5 km; **we walked ~ miles** caminamos kilómetros y kilómetros
9 (referring to time): **he was away ~ 2 years** estuvo fuera (durante) dos años; **it hasn't rained ~ 3 weeks** no ha llovido durante or en 3 semanas; **I have known her ~ years** la conozco desde hace años; **can you do it ~ tomorrow?** ¿lo podrás hacer para mañana?
10 (with infinitive clauses): **it is not ~ me to decide** la decisión no es cosa mía; **it would be best ~ you to leave** sería mejor que te fueras; **there is still time ~ you to do it** todavía te queda tiempo para hacerlo; **~ this to be possible ...** para que esto sea posible ...
11 (in spite of) a pesar de; **~ all his complaints** a pesar de sus quejas ♦ conj (since, as: rather formal) puesto que

---

forage ['fɔrɪdʒ] vi (animal) forrajear; (person): **to ~ for** hurgar en busca de
foray ['fɔreɪ] n incursión f
forbid [fə'bɪd] (pt **forbad(e)**, pp **forbidden**) vt prohibir; **to ~ sb to do sth** prohibir a uno hacer algo; **~ding** adj amenazador(a)
force [fɔːs] n fuerza ♦ vt forzar; (push)

forcibly meter a la fuerza; **to ~ o.s. to do** hacer un esfuerzo por hacer; **the F~s** npl (BRIT) las Fuerzas Armadas; **in ~** en vigor; **~d** [fɔːst] adj forzado; **~-feed** vt alimentar a la fuerza; **~ful** adj enérgico

forcibly ['fɔːsəblɪ] adv a la fuerza; (speak) enérgicamente

ford [fɔːd] n vado

fore [fɔː*] n: **to come to the ~** empezar a destacar

fore: **~arm** n antebrazo; **~boding** n presentimiento; **~cast** n pronóstico ♦ vt (irreg: like cast) pronosticar; **~court** n (BRIT) patio; **~finger** n (dedo) índice m; **~front** n: **in the ~front of** en la vanguardia de

forego [fɔː'gəʊ] = **forgo**

foregone ['fɔːgɒn] pp of **forego** ♦ adj: **it's a ~ conclusion** es una conclusión evidente

foreground ['fɔːgraʊnd] n primer plano

forehead ['fɒrɪd] n frente f

foreign ['fɒrɪn] adj extranjero; (trade) exterior; (object) extraño; **~er** n extranjero/a; **~ exchange** n divisas fpl; **F~ Office** (BRIT) n Ministerio de Asuntos Exteriores; **F~ Secretary** (BRIT) n Ministro de Asuntos Exteriores

fore: **~leg** n pata delantera; **~man** (irreg) n capataz m; (in construction) maestro de obras; **~most** adj principal ♦ adv: **first and ~most** ante todo

forensic [fə'rɛnsɪk] adj forense

fore: **~runner** n precursor/a m/f; **~see** (pt foresaw, pp foreseen) vt prever; **~seeable** adj previsible; **~shadow** vt prefigurar, anunciar; **~sight** n previsión f

forest ['fɒrɪst] n bosque m

forestry ['fɒrɪstrɪ] n silvicultura

foretaste ['fɔːteɪst] n muestra

foretell [fɔː'tɛl] (pt, pp **foretold**) vt predecir, pronosticar

forever [fə'rɛvə*] adv para siempre; (endlessly) constantemente

foreword ['fɔːwəːd] n prefacio

forfeit ['fɔːfɪt] vt perder

forgave [fə'geɪv] pt of **forgive**

forge [fɔːdʒ] n herrería ♦ vt (signature, money) falsificar; (metal) forjar; **~ ahead** vi avanzar mucho; **~ry** n falsificación f

forget [fə'gɛt] (pt forgot, pp forgotten) vt olvidar ♦ vi olvidarse; **~ful** adj despistado; **~-me-not** n nomeolvides f inv

forgive [fə'gɪv] (pt forgave, pp forgiven) vt perdonar; **to ~ sb for sth** perdonar algo a uno; **~ness** n perdón m

forgo [fɔː'gəʊ] (pt forwent, pp forgone) vt (give up) renunciar a; (go without) privarse de

forgot [fə'gɒt] pt of **forget**

forgotten [fə'gɒtn] pp of **forget**

fork [fɔːk] n (for eating) tenedor m; (for gardening) horca; (of roads) bifurcación f ♦ vi (road) bifurcarse; **~ out** (inf) vt (pay) desembolsar; **~-lift truck** n máquina elevadora

forlorn [fə'lɔːn] adj (person) triste, melancólico; (place) abandonado; (attempt, hope) desesperado

form [fɔːm] n forma; (BRIT: SCOL) clase f; (document) formulario ♦ vt formar; (idea) concebir; (habit) adquirir; **in top ~** en plena forma; **to ~ a queue** hacer cola

formal ['fɔːməl] adj (offer, receipt) por escrito; (person etc) correcto; (occasion, dinner) de etiqueta; (dress) correcto; (garden) de estilo) clásico; **~ity** [-'mælɪtɪ] n (of procedure) trámite m, corrección f; etiqueta; **~ly** adv oficialmente

format ['fɔːmæt] n formato ♦ vt (COMPUT) formatear

formative ['fɔːmətɪv] adj (years) de formación; (influence) formativo

former ['fɔːmə*] adj anterior; (earlier) antiguo; (ex) ex; **the ~ ... the latter ...** aquél ... éste ...; **~ly** adv antes

formula ['fɔːmjʊlə] n fórmula

forsake [fə'seɪk] (pt **forsook**, pp **forsaken**) vt (gen) abandonar; (plan) renunciar a

fort [fɔ:t] n fuerte m

forte ['fɔ:tɪ] n fuerte m

forth [fɔ:θ] adv: **back and ~** de acá para allá; **and so ~** y así sucesivamente; **~coming** adj próximo, venidero; (help, information) disponible; (character) comunicativo; **~right** adj franco; **~with** adv en el acto

fortify ['fɔ:tɪfaɪ] vt (city) fortificar; (person) fortalecer

fortitude ['fɔ:tɪtju:d] n fortaleza f

fortnight ['fɔ:tnaɪt] (BRIT) n quince días mpl; quincena f; **~ly** adj de cada quince días, quincenal ♦ adv cada quince días, quincenalmente

fortress ['fɔ:trɪs] n fortaleza f

fortunate ['fɔ:tʃənɪt] adj afortunado; **it is ~ that ...** (es una) suerte que ...; **~ly** adv afortunadamente

fortune ['fɔ:tʃən] n suerte f; (wealth) fortuna f; **~-teller** n adivino/a

forty ['fɔ:tɪ] num cuarenta

forum ['fɔ:rəm] n foro m

forward ['fɔ:wəd] adj (movement, position) avanzado; (front) delantero; (in time) adelantado; (not shy) atrevido ♦ n (SPORT) delantero ♦ vt (letter) remitir; (career) promocionar; **to move ~** avanzar; **~(s)** adv (hacia) adelante

fossil ['fɔsl] n fósil m

foster ['fɔstə*] vt (child) acoger en una familia; fomentar; **~ child** n hijo/a adoptivo/a

fought [fɔ:t] pt, pp of **fight**

foul [faul] adj sucio, puerco; (weather, smell etc) asqueroso; (language) grosero; (temper) malísimo ♦ n (SPORT) falta ♦ vt (dirty) ensuciar; **~ play** n (LAW) muerte f violenta

found [faund] pt, pp of **find** ♦ vt fundar; **~ation** [-'deɪʃən] n (act) fundación f; (basis) base f; (also: **~ation cream**) crema base; **~ations** npl (of building) cimientos mpl

founder ['faundə*] n fundador(a) m/f ♦ vi hundirse

foundry ['faundrɪ] n fundición f

fountain ['fauntɪn] n fuente f; **~ pen** n pluma (estilográfica) (SP), pluma-fuente f (AM)

four [fɔ:*] num cuatro; **on all ~s** a gatas; **~-poster (bed)** n cama de dosel; **~teen** num catorce; **~th** num cuarto

fowl [faul] n ave f (de corral)

fox [fɔks] n zorro ♦ vt confundir

foyer ['fɔɪeɪ] n vestíbulo

fraction ['frækʃən] n fracción f

fracture ['fræktʃə*] n fractura f

fragile ['frædʒaɪl] adj frágil

fragment ['frægmənt] n fragmento

fragrant ['freɪgrənt] adj fragante, oloroso

frail [freɪl] adj frágil; (person) débil

frame [freɪm] n (TECH) armazón m; (of person) cuerpo; (of picture, door etc) marco; (of spectacles: also: **~s**) montura ♦ vt enmarcar; **~ of mind** n estado de ánimo; **~work** n marco

France [frɑ:ns] n Francia

franchise ['fræntʃaɪz] n (POL) derecho de votar, sufragio; (COMM) licencia, concesión f

frank [fræŋk] adj franco ♦ vt (letter) franquear; **~ly** adv francamente

frantic ['fræntɪk] adj (distraught) desesperado; (hectic) frenético

fraternity [frə'tə:nɪtɪ] n (feeling) fraternidad f; (group of people) círculos mpl

fraud [frɔ:d] n fraude m; (person) impostor/a m/f

fraught [frɔ:t] adj: **~ with** lleno de

fray [freɪ] vi deshilacharse

freak [fri:k] n (person) fenómeno; (event) suceso anormal

freckle ['frekl] n peca

free [fri:] adj libre; (gratis) gratuito ♦ vt (prisoner etc) poner en libertad; (jammed object) soltar; **~ (of charge)**, **for ~** gratis; **~dom** ['fri:dəm] n

libertad f; **F~fone** ® ['fri:fəun] n
número gratuito; **~-for-all** n riña
general; **~ gift** n prima; **~hold** n
propiedad f vitalicia; **~ kick** n tiro libre;
~lance adj independiente ♦ adv por
cuenta propia; **~ly** adv libremente;
(liberally) generosamente; **F~mason** n
francmasón m; **F~post** ® n porte
pagado; **~range** adj (hen, eggs) de
granja; **~ trade** n comercio;
~way (US) n autopista; **~ will** n libre
albedrío; **of one's own ~** por su
propia voluntad

freeze [fri:z] (pt **froze**, pp **frozen**) vi
(weather) helar; (liquid, pipe, person)
helarse, congelarse ♦ vt helar; (food,
prices, salaries) congelar ♦ n helada;
(on arms, wages) congelación f; **~-
dried** adj liofilizado; **~r** n congelador
m (SP), congeladora (AM)

freezing ['fri:zɪŋ] adj helado; **3
degrees below ~** tres grados bajo
cero; **~ point** n punto de congelación

freight [freɪt] n (goods) carga; (money
charged) flete m; **~ train** (US) n tren m
de mercancías

French [frɛntʃ] adj francés/esa ♦ n
(LING) francés m; **the ~** npl los
franceses; **~ bean** n judía verde;
~ fried potatoes npl patatas fpl (SP)
or papas fpl (AM) fritas; **~ fries** (US) npl
= **~ fried potatoes**; **~man/woman**
(irreg) n francés/esa m/f; **~ window** n
puerta de cristal

frenzy ['frɛnzɪ] n frenesí m

frequent [adj 'fri:kwənt, vb frɪ'kwɛnt]
adj frecuente ♦ vt frecuentar; **~ly**
[-əntlɪ] adv frecuentemente, a menudo

fresh [frɛʃ] adj fresco; (bread) tierno;
(new) nuevo; **~en** vi (wind, air) soplar
más recio; **~en up** vi (person)
arreglarse, lavarse; **~er** (BRIT: inf) n
(UNIV) estudiante m/f de primer año;
~ly adv (made, painted) recién; **~-
man** (US irreg) n = **~er**; **~ness** n
frescura; **~water** adj (fish) de agua
dulce

fret [frɛt] vi inquietarse

friar ['fraɪə*] n fraile m; (before name)
fray m

friction ['frɪkʃən] n fricción f

Friday ['fraɪdɪ] n viernes m inv

fridge [frɪdʒ] (BRIT) n nevera (SP),
refrigerador m (AM)

fried [fraɪd] adj frito

friend [frɛnd] n amigo/a; **~ly** adj
simpático; (government) amigo; (place)
acogedor(a); (match) amistoso; **~ly-
fire** fuego amigo, disparos mpl del
propio bando; **~ship** n amistad f

frieze [fri:z] n friso

fright [fraɪt] n (terror) terror m; (scare)
susto; **to take ~** asustarse; **~en** vt
asustar; **~ened** adj asustado; **~ening**
adj espantoso; **~ful** adj espantoso,
horrible

frill [frɪl] n volante m

fringe [frɪndʒ] n (BRIT: of hair) flequillo;
(on lampshade etc) flecos mpl; (of forest
etc) borde m, margen m; **~ benefits**
npl beneficios mpl marginales

frisk [frɪsk] vt cachear, registrar

frisky ['frɪskɪ] adj juguetón/ona

fritter ['frɪtə*] n buñuelo; **~ away** vt
desperdiciar

frivolous ['frɪvələs] adj frívolo

frizzy ['frɪzɪ] adj rizado

fro [frəu] see **to**

frock [frɔk] n vestido

frog [frɔg] n rana; **~man** n hombre-
rana m

frolic ['frɔlɪk] vi juguetear

KEYWORD

from [frɔm] prep **1** (indicating starting
place) de, desde; **where do you
come ~?** ¿de dónde eres?; **~ London
to Glasgow** de Londres a Glasgow;
to escape ~ sth/sb escaparse de
algo/alguien

2 (indicating origin etc) de; **a letter/
telephone call** una carta/llamada de mi hermana; **tell
him ~ me that ...** dígale de mi

parte que ...
3 (*indicating time*): ~ **one o'clock** to or **until** or **till two** (de)(sde) la una a or hasta las dos; ~ **January** (**on**) a partir de enero
4 (*indicating distance*) de; **the hotel is 1 km** ~ **the beach** el hotel está a 1 km de la playa
5 (*indicating price, number etc*) de; **prices range** ~ **£10** to **£50** los precios van desde £10 a or hasta £50; **the interest rate was increased** ~ **9%** to **10%** el tipo de interés fue incrementado de un 9% a un 10%
6 (*indicating difference*) de; **he can't tell red** ~ **green** no sabe distinguir el rojo del verde; **to be different** ~ **sb/ sth** ser diferente a algo/alguien
7 (*because of, on the basis of*): ~ **what he says** por lo que dice; **weak** ~ **hunger** debilitado por el hambre

front [frʌnt] n (*foremost part*) parte f delantera; (*of house*) fachada; (*of dress*) delantero; (*promenade*: *also*: **sea** ~) paseo marítimo; (MIL, POL, METEOROLOGY) frente m; (*fig*: *appearances*) apariencias fpl ♦ adj (*wheel, leg*) delantero; (*row, line*) primero; **in** ~ (**of**) delante (de); ~ **door** n puerta principal; ~**ier** ['frʌntɪə*] n frontera; ~ **page** n primera plana; ~ **room** n (BRIT) salón m, sala; ~**wheel drive** n tracción f delantera

frost [frɔst] n helada; (*also*: **hoar**~) escarcha; ~**bite** n congelación f; ~**ed** adj (*glass*) deslustrado; ~**y** adj (*weather*) de helada; (*welcome etc*) glacial

froth [frɔθ] n espuma

frown [fraun] vi fruncir el ceño

froze [frəuz] pt of **freeze**

frozen ['frəuzn] pp of **freeze**

fruit [fru:t] n inv fruta; fruto; (*fig*) fruto; resultados mpl; ~**erer** n frutero/a; ~**erer's** (**shop**) n frutería; ~**ful** adj

provechoso; ~**ion** [fru:'ɪʃən] n to **come to** or **bring to** ~ realizar; ~ **juice** n zumo (SP) or jugo (AM) de fruta; ~ **machine** n (BRIT) máquina f tragaperras; ~ **salad** n macedonia (SP) or ensalada (AM) de frutas

frustrate [frʌs'treɪt] vt frustrar

fry [fraɪ] (*pt, pp* **fried**) vt freír; **small** ~ gente f menuda; ~**ing pan** n sartén f

ft. abbr = **foot**; **feet**

fudge [fʌdʒ] n (CULIN) caramelo blando

fuel [fjuəl] n (*for heating*) combustible m; (*coal*) carbón m; (*wood*) leña; (*for engine*) carburante m; ~ **oil** n fuel oil m; ~ **tank** n depósito de combustible

fugitive ['fju:dʒɪtɪv] n fugitivo/a

fulfil [ful'fɪl] vt (*function*) cumplir con; (*condition*) satisfacer; (*wish, desire*) realizar; ~**ment** (US **fulfillment**) n satisfacción f; (*of promise, desire*) realización f

full [ful] adj lleno; (*fig*) pleno; (*complete*) completo; (*maximum*) máximo; (*information*) detallado; (*price*) íntegro; (*skirt*) amplio ♦ adv: **to know** ~ **well** that sabe perfectamente que; **I'm** ~ (**up**) no puedo más; ~ **employment** n pleno empleo; **a** ~ **two hours** dos horas completas; **at** ~ **speed** a máxima velocidad; **in** ~ (*reproduce, quote*) íntegramente; ~ **length** adj (*novel etc*) entero; (*coat*) largo; (*portrait*) de cuerpo entero; ~ **moon** n luna llena; ~**scale** adj (*attack, war*) en gran escala; (*model*) de tamaño natural; ~ **stop** n punto; ~ **time** adj (*work*) de tiempo completo ♦ adv: **to work** ~**time** trabajar a tiempo completo; ~**y** adv completamente; (*at least*) por lo menos; ~**y-fledged** adj (*teacher, barrister*) diplomado

fumble ['fʌmbl] vi: **to** ~ **with** manejar torpemente

fume [fju:m] vi (*rage*) estar furioso; ~**s** npl humo, gases mpl

fun [fʌn] n (*amusement*) diversión f; **to**

have ~ divertirse; **for ~** en broma; **to make ~ of** burlarse de

function ['fʌŋkʃən] n función f ♦ vi funcionar; **~al** adj (operational) en buen estado; (practical) funcional

fund [fʌnd] n (money) reserva; (reserve) reserva; **~s** npl (money) fondos mpl

fundamental [fʌndə'mentl] adj fundamental

funeral ['fju:nərəl] n (burial) entierro; (ceremony) funerales mpl; **~ parlour** (BRIT) n funeraria; **~ service** n misa de difuntos, funeral m

funfair ['fʌnfɛə*] (BRIT) n parque m de atracciones

fungus ['fʌŋgəs] (pl fungi) n hongo; (mould) moho m

funnel ['fʌnl] n embudo; (of ship) chimenea

funny ['fʌnɪ] adj gracioso, divertido; (strange) curioso, raro

fur [fə:*] n piel f; (BRIT: in kettle etc) sarro; **~ coat** n abrigo de pieles

furious ['fjʊərɪəs] adj furioso; (effort) violento

furlong ['fə:lɒŋ] n octava parte de una milla, = 201.17 m

furnace ['fə:nɪs] n horno

furnish ['fə:nɪʃ] vt amueblar; (supply) suministrar; (information) facilitar; **~ings** npl muebles mpl

furniture ['fə:nɪtʃə*] n muebles mpl; **piece of ~** mueble m

furrow ['fʌrəʊ] n surco

furry ['fə:rɪ] adj peludo

further ['fə:ðə*] adj (new) nuevo, adicional ♦ adv más lejos; (more) más; (moreover) además ♦ vt promover, adelantar; **~ education** n educación f superior; **~more** [fə:ðə'mɔ:*] adv además

furthest ['fə:ðɪst] superlative of **far**

fury ['fjʊərɪ] n furia

fuse [fju:z] (US **fuze**) n fusible m; (for bomb etc) mecha ♦ vt (metal) fundir; (fig) fusionar ♦ vi fundirse; fusionarse; (BRIT: ELEC): **to ~ the lights** fundir los plomos; **~ box** n caja de fusibles

fuss [fʌs] n (excitement) conmoción f; (trouble) alboroto; **to make a ~** armar un lío or jaleo; **to make a ~ of sb** mimar a uno; **~y** adj (person) exigente; (too ornate) recargado

futile ['fju:taɪl] adj vano

future ['fju:tʃə*] adj futuro; (coming) venidero ♦ n futuro; (prospects) porvenir m; **in ~** de ahora en adelante

fuze [fju:z] (US) = **fuse**

fuzzy ['fʌzɪ] adj (PHOT) borroso; (hair) muy rizado

G, g

G [dʒi:] n (MUS) sol m

g. abbr (= gram(s)) gr.

G7 abbr (= Group of Seven) el grupo de los 7

gabble ['gæbl] vi hablar atropelladamente

gable ['geɪbl] n aguilón m

gadget ['gædʒɪt] n aparato

Gaelic ['geɪlɪk] adj, n (LING) gaélico

gag [gæg] n (on mouth) mordaza; (joke) chiste m ♦ vt amordazar

gaiety ['geɪɪtɪ] n alegría

gaily ['geɪlɪ] adv alegremente

gain [geɪn] n: **~ (in)** aumento (de); (profit) ganancia ♦ vt ganar ♦ vi (watch) adelantarse; **to ~ from/by sth** sacar provecho de algo; **to ~ on sb** ganar terreno a uno; **to ~ 3 lbs (in weight)** engordar 3 libras

gal. abbr = **gallon**

gala ['gɑ:lə] n fiesta

gale [geɪl] n (wind) vendaval m

gallant ['gælənt] adj valiente; (towards ladies) atento

gall bladder ['gɔ:l-] n vesícula biliar

gallery ['gælərɪ] n (also: art ~: public) pinacoteca; (: private) galería de arte; (for spectators) tribuna

gallon ['gælən] n galón m (BRIT = 4,546 litros, US = 3,785 litros)

gallop ['gæləp] n galope m ♦ vi galopar

gallows ['gæləuz] n horca

gallstone ['gɔ:lstəun] n cálculo biliario

galore [gə'lɔ:*] adv en cantidad, en abundancia

gambit ['gæmbɪt] n (fig): **(opening) ~** estrategia (inicial)

gamble ['gæmbl] n (risk) riesgo ♦ vt jugar, apostar ♦ vi (take a risk) jugárselas; (bet) apostar; **to ~ on** apostar a; (success etc) contar con; **~r** n jugador(a) m/f; **gambling** n juego

game [geɪm] n juego; (match) partido; (of cards) partida; (HUNTING) caza ♦ adj (willing): **to be ~ for anything** atreverse a todo; **big ~** caza mayor; **~keeper** n guardabosques m inv

gammon ['gæmən] n (bacon) tocino ahumado; (ham) jamón m ahumado

gamut ['gæmət] n gama

gang [gæŋ] n (of criminals) pandilla; (of friends etc) grupo; (of workmen) brigada; **~ up** vi: **to ~ up on sb** aliarse contra uno

gangster ['gæŋstə*] n gángster m

gangway ['gæŋweɪ] n (in theatre, bus etc) pasarela; (BRIT) pasillo

gaol [dʒeɪl] (BRIT) n, vt = **jail**

gap [gæp] n vacío, hueco (AM); (in trees, traffic) claro; (in time) intervalo; (difference): **~ (between)** diferencia (entre)

gape [geɪp] vi mirar boquiabierto; (shirt etc) abrirse (completamente); **gaping** adj (completamente) abierto

garage ['gærɑ:ʒ] n garaje m; (for repairs) taller m

garbage ['gɑ:bɪdʒ] (US) n basura; (inf: nonsense) tonterías fpl; **~ can** n cubo (SP) or bote m (AM) de la basura

garbled ['gɑ:bld] adj (distorted) falsificado, amañado

garden ['gɑ:dn] n jardín m; **~s** npl (park) parque m; **~er** n jardinero/a; **~ing** n jardinería

gargle ['gɑ:gl] vi hacer gárgaras, gargarear (AM)

garish ['gɛərɪʃ] adj chillón/ona

garland ['gɑ:lənd] n guirnalda

garlic ['gɑ:lɪk] n ajo

garment ['gɑ:mənt] n prenda (de vestir)

garnish ['gɑ:nɪʃ] vt (CULIN) aderezar

garrison ['gærɪsn] n guarnición f

garter ['gɑ:tə*] n (for sock) liga; (US) liguero

gas [gæs] n gas m; (fuel) combustible m; (US: gasoline) gasolina ♦ vt asfixiar con gas; **~ cooker** (BRIT) n cocina de gas; **~ cylinder** n bombona de gas; **~ fire** n estufa de gas

gash [gæʃ] n raja; (wound) cuchillada ♦ vt rajar; acuchillar

gasket ['gæskɪt] n (AUT) junta de culata

gas mask n careta antigás

gas meter n contador m de gas

gasoline ['gæsəli:n] (US) n gasolina

gasp [gɑ:sp] n boqueada; (of shock etc) grito sofocado ♦ vi (pant) jadear

gas station (US) n gasolinera

gastric ['gæstrɪk] adj gástrico

gate [geɪt] n puerta; (iron ~) verja; **~crash** (BRIT) vt colarse en; **~way** n (also fig) puerta

gather ['gæðə*] vt (flowers, fruit) coger (SP), recoger; (assemble) reunir; (pick up) recoger; (SEWING) fruncir; (understand) entender ♦ vi (assemble) reunirse; **to ~ speed** ganar velocidad; **~ing** n reunión f, asamblea

gaudy ['gɔ:dɪ] adj chillón/ona

gauge [geɪdʒ] n (instrument) indicador m ♦ vt medir; (fig) juzgar

gaunt [gɔ:nt] adj (haggard) demacrado; (stark) desolado

gauntlet ['gɔ:ntlɪt] n (fig): **to run the ~ of** exponerse a; **to throw down the ~** arrojar el guante

gauze [gɔ:z] n gasa

gave [geɪv] pt of **give**

gay [geɪ] adj (homosexual) gay; (joyful)

alegre; (colour) vivo

gaze [geɪz] n mirada fija ♦ vi: **to ~ at sth** mirar algo fijamente

gazelle [gəˈzɛl] n gacela

gazumping [gəˈzʌmpɪŋ] (BRIT) n la subida del precio de una casa una vez que ya ha sido apalabrado

GB abbr = **Great Britain**

GCE n abbr (BRIT) = **General Certificate of Education**

GCSE (BRIT) n abbr (= General Certificate of Secondary Education) examen de reválida que se hace a los 16 años

gear [gɪə*] n equipo, herramientas fpl; (TECH) engranaje m; (AUT) velocidad f, marcha ♦ vt (fig: adapt): **to ~ sth to** adaptar or ajustar algo a; **top** or **high** (US)/**low** ~ cuarta/primera velocidad; **in** ~ en marcha; ~ **box** n caja de cambios; ~ **lever** n palanca de cambio; ~ **shift** (US) n = ~ **lever**

geese [giːs] npl of **goose**

gel [dʒɛl] n gel m

gem [dʒɛm] n piedra preciosa

Gemini [ˈdʒɛmɪnaɪ] n Géminis m, Gemelos mpl

gender [ˈdʒɛndə*] n género

gene [dʒiːn] n gen(e) m

general [ˈdʒɛnərl] n general m ♦ adj general; **in** ~ en general; ~ **delivery** (US) n lista de correos; ~ **election** n elecciones fpl generales; ~**ly** adv generalmente, en general; ~ **practitioner** n médico general

generate [ˈdʒɛnəreɪt] vt (ELEC) generar; (jobs, profits) producir

generation [dʒɛnəˈreɪʃən] n generación f

generator [ˈdʒɛnəreɪtə*] n generador m

generosity [dʒɛnəˈrɔsɪtɪ] n generosidad f

generous [ˈdʒɛnərəs] adj generoso

genetic [dʒɪˈnɛtɪk] adj: ~ **engineering** ingeniería f genética; ~ **fingerprinting** identificación f genética

Geneva [dʒɪˈniːvə] n Ginebra

genial [ˈdʒiːnɪəl] adj afable, simpático

genitals [ˈdʒɛnɪtlz] npl (órganos mpl) genitales mpl

genius [ˈdʒiːnɪəs] n genio

genteel [dʒɛnˈtiːl] adj fino, elegante

gentle [ˈdʒɛntl] adj apacible, dulce; (animal) manso; (breeze, curve etc) suave

gentleman [ˈdʒɛntlmən] (irreg) n señor m; (well-bred man) caballero

gently [ˈdʒɛntlɪ] adv dulcemente, suavemente

gentry [ˈdʒɛntrɪ] n alta burguesía

gents [dʒɛnts] n aseos mpl (de caballeros)

genuine [ˈdʒɛnjuɪn] adj auténtico; (person) sincero

geography [dʒɪˈɔɡrəfɪ] n geografía

geology [dʒɪˈɔlədʒɪ] n geología

geometric(al) [dʒɪəˈmɛtrɪk(l)] adj geométrico

geranium [dʒɪˈreɪnjəm] n geranio

geriatric [dʒɛrɪˈætrɪk] adj, n geriátrico/a m/f

germ [dʒəːm] n (microbe) microbio, bacteria; (seed, fig) germen m

German [ˈdʒəːmən] adj alemán/ana ♦ n alemán/ana m/f; (LING) alemán m; ~ **measles** n rubéola

Germany [ˈdʒəːmənɪ] n Alemania

gesture [ˈdʒɛstjə*] n gesto; (symbol) muestra

┌─────────────────────┐
│ **KEYWORD** │
└─────────────────────┘

get [gɛt] (pt, pp **got**, pp **gotten** (US)) vi
1 (become, be) ponerse, volverse; **to ~ old/tired** envejecer/cansarse; **to ~ drunk** emborracharse; **to ~ dirty** ensuciarse; **to ~ married** casarse; **when do I ~ paid?** ¿cuándo me pagan or se me paga?; **it's ~ting late** se está haciendo tarde
2 (go): **to ~ to/from** llegar a/de; **to ~ home** llegar a casa
3 (begin) empezar a; **to ~ to know sb** (llegar a) conocer a uno; **I'm ~ting to**

like him me está empezando a gustar; **let's ~ going** or **started** ¡vamos (a empezar)!

4 (modal aux vb): **you've got to do it** tienes que hacerlo

♦ vt **1: to ~ sth done** (finish) terminar algo; (have done) mandar hacer algo; **to ~ one's hair cut** cortarse el pelo; **to ~ the car going** or **to go** arrancar el coche; **to ~ sb to do sth** conseguir or hacer que alguien haga algo; **to ~ sth/sb ready** preparar algo/a alguien

2 (obtain: money, permission, results) conseguir; (find: job, flat) encontrar; (fetch: person, doctor) buscar; (object) ir a buscar, traer; **to ~ sth for sb** conseguir algo para alguien; **~ me Mr Jones, please** (TEL) póngame or comuníqueme (AM) con el Sr. Jones, por favor; **can I ~ you a drink?** ¿quieres algo de beber?

3 (receive: present, letter) recibir; (acquire: reputation) alcanzar; (: prize) ganar; **what did you ~ for your birthday?** ¿qué te regalaron por tu cumpleaños?; **how much did you ~ for the painting?** ¿cuánto sacaste por el cuadro?

4 (catch) coger (SP), agarrar (AM); (hit: target etc) dar en; **to ~ sb by the arm/throat** coger or agarrar a uno por el brazo/cuello; **~ him!** ¡cógelo! (SP), ¡atrápalo! (AM); **the bullet got him in the leg** la bala le dio en la pierna

5 (take, move) llevar; **to ~ sth to sb** hacer llegar algo a alguien; **do you think we'll ~ it through the door?** ¿crees que lo podremos meter por la puerta?

6 (catch, take: plane, bus etc) coger (SP), tomar (AM); **where do I ~ the train for Birmingham?** ¿dónde se coge or se toma el tren para Birmingham?

7 (understand) entender; (hear) oír;

I've got it! ¡ya lo tengo!, ¡eureka!; **I don't ~ your meaning** no te entiendo; **I'm sorry, I didn't ~ your name** lo siento, no cogí tu nombre

8 (have, possess): **to have got** tener

get about vi salir mucho; (news) divulgarse

get along vi (agree) llevarse bien; (depart) marcharse; (manage) = **get by**

get at vt fus (attack) atacar; (reach) alcanzar

get away vi marcharse; (escape) escaparse

get away with vt fus hacer impunemente

get back vi (return) volver ♦ vt recobrar

get by vi (pass) lograr pasar; (manage) arreglárselas

get down vi ♦ vt fus bajar ♦ vt bajar; (depress) deprimir

get down to vt fus (work) ponerse a

get in vi entrar; (train) llegar; (arrive home) volver a casa, regresar

get into vt fus entrar en; (vehicle) subir a; **to ~ into a rage** enfadarse

get off vi (from train etc) bajar; (depart: person, car) marcharse ♦ vt (remove) quitar ♦ vt fus (train, bus) bajar de

get on vi (at exam etc): **how are you ~ting on?** ¿cómo te va?; (agree): **to ~ on (with)** llevarse bien (con) ♦ vt fus subir a

get out vi salir; (of vehicle) bajar ♦ vt sacar

get out of vt fus salir de; (duty etc) escaparse de

get over vt fus (illness) recobrarse de

get round vt fus rodear; (fig: person) engatusar a

get through vi (TEL) (lograr) comunicarse

get through to vt fus (TEL) comunicar con

get together vi reunirse ♦ vt reunir,

juntar

get up vi (rise) levantarse ♦ vt fus subir
get up to vt fus (reach) llegar a; (prank) hacer

geyser ['giːzə*] n (water heater) calentador m de agua; (GEO) géiser m
ghastly ['gɑːstlɪ] adj horrible
gherkin ['gəːkɪn] n pepinillo
ghetto blaster ['getəʊblɑːstə*] n cassette m portátil de gran tamaño
ghost [gəʊst] n fantasma m
giant ['dʒaɪənt] n gigante m/f ♦ adj gigantesco, gigante
gibberish ['dʒɪbərɪʃ] n galimatías m
giblets ['dʒɪblɪts] npl menudillos mpl
Gibraltar [dʒɪ'brɔːltə*] n Gibraltar m
giddy ['gɪdɪ] adj mareado
gift [gɪft] n regalo; (ability) talento; **~ed** adj dotado; **~ token** or **voucher** n vale m canjeable por un regalo
gigantic [dʒaɪ'gæntɪk] adj gigantesco
giggle ['gɪgl] vi reírse tontamente
gill [dʒɪl] n (measure) = 0.25 pints (BRIT = 0.148l, US = 0.118l)
gills [gɪlz] npl (of fish) branquias fpl, agallas fpl
gilt [gɪlt] adj, n dorado; **~-edged** adj (COMM) de máxima garantía
gimmick ['gɪmɪk] n truco
gin [dʒɪn] n ginebra
ginger ['dʒɪndʒə*] n jengibre m; **~ ale** = **~ beer**; **~ beer** (BRIT) n gaseosa de jengibre; **~bread** n pan m (or galleta) de jengibre
gingerly ['dʒɪndʒəlɪ] adv con cautela
gipsy ['dʒɪpsɪ] n = **gypsy**
giraffe [dʒɪ'rɑːf] n jirafa
girder ['gəːdə*] n viga
girl [gəːl] n (small) niña; (young woman) chica, joven f, muchacha; (daughter) hija; **an English ~** una (chica) inglesa; **~friend** n (of girl) amiga; (of boy) novia; **~ish** adj de niña
giro ['dʒaɪrəʊ] n (BRIT: bank ~) giro bancario; (post office ~) giro postal; (state benefit) cheque quincenal del

subsidio de desempleo
gist [dʒɪst] n lo esencial
give [gɪv] (pt **gave**, pp **given**) vt dar; (deliver) entregar; (as gift) regalar ♦ vi (break) romperse; (stretch: fabric) dar de sí; **to ~ sb sth**, **~ sth to sb** dar algo a uno; **~ away** vt (give free) regalar; (betray) traicionar; (disclose) revelar; **~ back** vt devolver; **~ in** vi ceder ♦ vt entregar; **~ off** vt despedir; **~ out** vt distribuir; **~ up** vi rendirse, darse por vencido ♦ vt renunciar a; **to ~ up smoking** dejar de fumar; **to o.s. up** entregarse; **~ way** vi ceder; (BRIT: AUT) ceder el paso
glacier ['glæsɪə*] n glaciar m
glad [glæd] adj contento
gladly ['glædlɪ] adv con mucho gusto
glamorous ['glæmərəs] adj encantador(a), atractivo; **glamour** ['glæmə*] n encanto, atractivo
glance [glɑːns] n ojeada, mirada ♦ vi: **to ~** at echar una ojeada a; **glancing** adj (blow) oblicuo
gland [glænd] n glándula
glare [glɛə*] n (of anger) mirada feroz; (of light) deslumbramiento, brillo; **to be in the ~ of publicity** estar en el foco de la atención pública ♦ vi deslumbrar; **to ~** at mirar con odio a; **glaring** adj (mistake) manifiesto
glass [glɑːs] n vidrio, cristal m; (for drinking) vaso; (: with stem) copa; **~es** npl (spectacles) gafas fpl; **~house** n invernadero; **~ware** n cristalería
glaze [gleɪz] vt (window) poner cristales a; (pottery) vidriar ♦ n vidriado; **glazier** ['gleɪzɪə*] n vidriero
gleam [gliːm] vi brillar
glean [gliːn] vt (information) recoger
glee [gliː] n alegría, regocijo
glen [glen] n cañada
glib [glɪb] adj de mucha labia; (promise, response) poco sincero
glide [glaɪd] vi deslizarse; (AVIAT) planear; **~r** n (AVIAT) planeador m; **gliding** n (AVIAT) vuelo sin motor

glimmer ['glɪmə*] n luz f tenue; (of interest) muestra; (of hope) rayo

glimpse [glɪmps] n vislumbre m ♦ vt vislumbrar, entrever

glint [glɪnt] vi centellear

glisten ['glɪsn] vi relucir, brillar

glitter ['glɪtə*] vi relucir, brillar

gloat [gləʊt] vi: to ~ over recrearse en

global ['gləʊbl] adj mundial; ~ **warming** (re)calentamiento global

globe [gləʊb] n globo; (model) globo terráqueo

gloom [gluːm] n oscuridad f; (sadness) tristeza; **~y** adj (dark) oscuro; (sad) triste; (pessimistic) pesimista

glorious ['glɔːrɪəs] adj glorioso; (weather etc) magnífico

glory ['glɔːrɪ] n gloria

gloss [glɒs] n (shine) brillo; (paint) pintura de aceite; ~ **over** vt fus disimular

glossary ['glɒsərɪ] n glosario

glossy ['glɒsɪ] adj lustroso; (magazine) de lujo

glove [glʌv] n guante m; ~ **compartment** n (AUT) guantera

glow [gləʊ] vi brillar

glower ['glaʊə*] vi: to ~ at mirar con ceño

glue [gluː] n goma (de pegar), cemento ♦ vt pegar

glum [glʌm] adj (person, tone) melancólico

glut [glʌt] n superabundancia

glutton ['glʌtn] n glotón/ona m/f; a ~ **for work** un(a) trabajador(a) incansable

GM adj abbr (= genetically modified) transgénico

GMO n abbr (= genetically-modified organism) organismo transgénico

gnat [næt] n mosquito

gnaw [nɔː] vt roer

gnome [nəʊm] n gnomo

go [gəʊ] (pt went, pp gone; pl ~es) vi ir; (travel) viajar; (depart) irse, marcharse; (work) funcionar, marchar; (be sold) venderse; (time) pasar; (fit, suit): **to ~ with** hacer juego con; (become) ponerse; (break etc) estropearse, romperse ♦ n: **to have a ~ (at)** probar suerte (con); **to be on the ~** no parar; **whose ~ is it?** ¿a quién le toca?; **he's going to do it** va a hacerlo; **to ~ for a walk** ir de paseo; **to ~ dancing** ir a bailar; **how did it ~?** ¿qué tal salió or resultó?, ¿cómo ha ido?; **to ~ round the back** pasar por detrás; ~ **about** vi (rumour) propagarse ♦ vt fus: **how do I ~ about this?** ¿cómo me las arreglo para hacer esto?; ~ **ahead** vi seguir adelante; ~ **along** vi ir ♦ vt fus bordear; **to ~ along with** (agree) estar de acuerdo con; ~ **away** vi irse, marcharse; ~ **back** vi volver; ~ **back on** vt fus (promise) faltar a; ~ **by** (time) pasar ♦ vt fus guiarse por; ~ **down** vi bajar; (ship) hundirse; (sun) ponerse ♦ vt fus bajar; ~ **for** vt fus (fetch) ir por; (like) gustar; (attack) atacar; ~ **in** vi entrar; ~ **in for** vt fus (competition) presentarse a; ~ **into** vt fus entrar en; (investigate) investigar; (embark on) dedicarse a; ~ **off** vi irse, marcharse; (food) pasarse; (explode) estallar; (event) realizarse ♦ vt fus dejar de gustar; **I'm going off him/the idea** ya no me gusta tanto él/la idea; ~ **on** vi (continue) seguir, continuar; (happen) pasar, ocurrir; **to ~ on doing sth** seguir haciendo algo; ~ **out** vi salir; (fire, light) apagarse; ~ **over** vi (ship) zozobrar ♦ vt fus (check) revisar; ~ **through** vt fus (town etc) atravesar; ~ **up** vi, vt fus subir; ~ **without** vt fus pasarse sin

goad [gəʊd] vt aguijonear

go-ahead ['gəʊəhed] adj (person) dinámico; (firm) innovador/a ♦ n luz f verde

goal [gəʊl] n meta; (score) gol m; **~keeper** n portero; **~-post** n poste m (de la portería)

goat [gəʊt] n cabra

gobble ['gɒbl] vt (also: ~ down, ~ up) tragarse, engullir

go-between n intermediario/a
god [gɔd] n dios m; **G~** n Dios m;
~child n ahijado/a; **~daughter** n
ahijada; **~dess** n diosa; **~father** n
padrino; **~forsaken** adj dejado de la
mano de Dios; **~mother** n madrina;
~send n don m del cielo; **~son** n
ahijado
goggles [ˈgɔglz] npl gafas fpl
going [ˈgəʊɪŋ] n (conditions) estado del
terreno ♦ adj: **the ~ rate** la tarifa
corriente or en vigor
gold [gəʊld] n oro ♦ adj de oro; **~en**
adj (made of ~) de oro; (~ in colour)
dorado; **~fish** n pez m de colores;
~mine n (also fig) mina de oro; **~-
plated** adj chapado en oro; **~smith** n
orfebre m/f
golf [gɔlf] n golf m; **~ ball** n (for game)
pelota de golf; (on typewriter) esfera;
~ club n club m de golf; (stick) palo
(de golf); **~ course** n campo de golf;
~er n golfista m/f
gone [gɔn] pp of **go**
good [gud] adj bueno; (pleasant)
agradable; (kind) bueno, amable;
(well-behaved) educado ♦ n bien m,
provecho; **~s** npl (COMM) mercancías
fpl; **~!** ¡qué bien!; **to be ~ at** tener
aptitud para; **to be ~ for** servir para;
it's ~ for you te hace bien; **would
you be ~ enough to ...?** ¿podría
hacerme el favor de ...?; ¿sería tan
amable de ...?; **a ~ deal (of)** mucho; **a
~ many** muchos; **to make ~** reparar;
it's no ~ complaining no vale la
pena (de) quejarse; **for ~** para siempre,
definitivamente; **~ morning/
afternoon!** ¡buenos días/buenas
tardes!; **~ evening!** ¡buenas noches!;
~ night! ¡buenas noches!; **~-bye!**
¡adiós!; **to say ~bye** despedirse;
G~ Friday n Viernes m Santo; **~-
looking** adj guapo; **~-natured** adj
amable, simpático; **~ness** n (of person)
bondad f; **for ~ness sake!** ¡por Dios!;
~ness gracious! ¡Dios mío!; **~s train**

(BRIT) n tren m de mercancías; **~will** n
buena voluntad f
goose [guːs] n (pl **geese**) n ganso, oca
gooseberry [ˈguzbərɪ] n grosella
espinosa; **to play ~** hacer de carabina
gooseflesh [ˈguːsfleʃ] n = **goose
pimples**
goose pimples npl carne f de gallina
gore [gɔː*] vt cornear ♦ n sangre f
gorge [gɔːdʒ] n barranco ♦ vr: **to
~ o.s. (on)** atracarse (de)
gorgeous [ˈgɔːdʒəs] adj (thing)
precioso; (weather) espléndido; (person)
guapísimo
gorilla [gəˈrɪlə] n gorila m
gorse [gɔːs] n tojo
gory [ˈgɔːrɪ] adj sangriento
go-slow (BRIT) n huelga de manos
caídas
gospel [ˈgɔspl] n evangelio
gossip [ˈgɔsɪp] n (scandal) cotilleo,
chismes mpl; (chat) charla;
(scandalmonger) cotilla m/f, chismoso/a
♦ vi cotillear
got [gɔt] pt, pp of **get**; **~ten** (US) pp of
get
gout [gaut] n gota
govern [ˈgʌvən] vt gobernar;
(influence) dominar; **~ess** n institutriz f;
~ment n gobierno; **~or** n
gobernador(a) m/f; (of school etc)
miembro del consejo; (of jail)
director(a) m/f
gown [gaun] n traje m; (of teacher,
BRIT: of judge) toga
G.P. n abbr = **general practitioner**
grab [græb] vt coger (SP) or agarrar
(AM), arrebatar ♦ vi: **to ~ at** intentar
agarrar
grace [greɪs] n gracia ♦ vt honrar;
(adorn) adornar; **5 days' ~** un plazo
de 5 días; **~ful** adj grácil, ágil; (style,
shape) elegante, gracioso; **gracious**
[ˈgreɪʃəs] adj amable
grade [greɪd] n (quality) clase f, calidad
f; (in hierarchy) grado; (SCOL: mark)
nota; (US: school class) curso ♦ adj

clasificar; **~ crossing** (US) n paso a
nivel; **~ school** (US) n escuela primaria
gradient ['greidiənt] n pendiente f
gradual ['grædjuəl] adj paulatino; **~ly**
adv paulatinamente
graduate [n 'grædjuit, vb 'grædjueit]
n (US: of high school) graduado/a; (of
university) licenciado/a ♦ vi graduarse;
licenciarse; **graduation** [-'eɪʃən] n
(ceremony) entrega del título
graffiti [grə'fi:ti] n pintadas fpl
graft [grɑ:ft] n (AGR, MED) injerto;
(BRIT: inf) trabajo duro; (bribery)
corrupción f ♦ vt injertar
grain [grein] n (single particle) grano;
(corn) granos mpl, cereales mpl; (of
wood) fibra
gram [græm] n gramo
grammar ['græmə*] n gramática;
~ school (BRIT) n ≈ instituto de
segunda enseñanza, liceo (SP)
grammatical [grə'mætikl] adj
gramatical
gramme [græm] n = **gram**
gramophone ['græməfəun] (BRIT) n
tocadiscos m inv
grand [grænd] adj magnífico,
imponente; (wonderful) estupendo;
(gesture etc) grandioso; **~children** npl
nietos mpl; **~dad** (inf) n yayo, abuelito
~daughter n nieta; **~eur** ['grændjə*]
n magnificencia, lo grandioso; **~father**
n abuelo; **~ma** (inf) n yaya, abuelita;
~mother n abuela; **~pa** (inf) n =
~dad; **~parents** npl abuelos mpl;
~ piano n piano de cola; **~son** n
nieto; **~stand** n (SPORT) tribuna
granite ['grænit] n granito
granny ['græni] (inf) n abuelita, yaya
grant [grɑ:nt] vt (concede) conceder;
(admit) reconocer ♦ n (SCOL) beca;
(ADMIN) subvención f; **to take sth/sb
for ~ed** dar algo por sentado/no hacer
ningún caso a uno
granulated sugar ['grænju:leitid-]
(BRIT) n azúcar m blanquilla
grape [greip] n uva

grapefruit ['greipfru:t] n pomelo (SP),
toronja (AM)
graph [grɑ:f] n gráfica; **~ic** ['græfik]
adj gráfico; **~ics** n artes fpl gráficas
♦ npl (drawings) dibujos mpl
grapple ['græpl] vi: **to ~ with sth/sb**
agarrar a algo/uno
grasp [grɑ:sp] vt agarrar, asir;
(understand) comprender ♦ n (grip)
asimiento; (understanding)
comprensión f; **~ing** adj (mean) avaro
grass [grɑ:s] n hierba; (lawn) césped
m; **~hopper** n saltamontes m inv; **~
roots** adj (fig) popular
grate [greit] n parrilla de chimenea
♦ vi: **to ~ (on)** chirriar (sobre) ♦ vt
(CULIN) rallar
grateful ['greitful] adj agradecido
grater ['greitə*] n rallador m
gratifying ['grætifaiiŋ] adj grato
grating ['greitiŋ] n (iron bars) reja
♦ adj (noise) áspero
gratitude ['grætitju:d] n
agradecimiento
gratuity [grə'tju:iti] n gratificación f
grave [greiv] n tumba ♦ adj serio,
grave
gravel ['grævl] n grava
gravestone ['greivstəun] n lápida
graveyard ['greivjɑ:d] n cementerio
gravity ['græviti] n gravedad f
gravy ['greivi] n salsa de carne
gray [grei] adj = **grey**
graze [greiz] vi pacer ♦ vt (touch
lightly) rozar; (scrape) raspar ♦ n (MED)
abrasión f
grease [gri:s] n (fat) grasa; (lubricant)
lubricante m ♦ vt engrasar; lubrificar;
~proof paper (BRIT) n papel m
apergaminado; **greasy** adj grasiento
great [greit] adj grande; (inf)
magnífico, estupendo; **G~ Britain** n
Gran Bretaña; **~-grandfather** n
bisabuelo; **~-grandmother** n
bisabuela; **~ly** adv muy; (with verb)
mucho; **~ness** n grandeza
Greece [gri:s] n Grecia

greed [griːd] n (also: ~iness) codicia,
avaricia; (for food) gula; (for power etc)
avidez f; **~y** adj avaro; (for food)
glotón/ona

Greek [griːk] adj griego ♦ n griego/a;
(LING) griego

green [griːn] adj (also POL) verde;
(inexperienced) novato ♦ n verde m;
(stretch of grass) césped m; (GOLF)
green m; **~s** npl (vegetables) verduras
fpl; **~ belt** n zona verde; **~ card** n
(AUT) carta verde; (US: work permit)
permiso de trabajo para los extranjeros
en EE. UU.; **~ery** n verdura; **~grocer**
(BRIT) n verdulero/a; **~house** n
invernadero; **~house effect** n efecto
invernadero; **~house gas** n gases mpl
de invernadero; **~ish** adj verdoso

Greenland ['griːnlənd] n Groenlandia

greet [griːt] vt (welcome) dar la
bienvenida a; (receive: news) recibir;
~ing (welcome) bienvenida; **~ing(s)
card** n tarjeta de felicitación

grenade [grə'neɪd] n granada

grew [gruː] pt of **grow**

grey [greɪ] adj gris; (weather) sombrío;
~-haired adj canoso; **~hound** n galgo

grid [grɪd] n reja; (ELEC) red f;
(traffic jam) retención f

grief [griːf] n dolor m, pena

grievance ['griːvəns] n motivo de
queja, agravio

grieve [griːv] vi afligirse, acongojarse
♦ vt dar pena a; **to ~ for** llorar por

grievous ['griːvəs] adj: **~ bodily
harm** (LAW) daños mpl corporales
graves

grill [grɪl] n (on cooker) parrilla; (also:
mixed ~) parrillada ♦ vt (BRIT) asar a la
parrilla; (inf: question) interrogar

grille [grɪl] n reja; (AUT) rejilla

grim [grɪm] adj (place) sombrío;
(situation) triste; (person) ceñudo

grimace [grɪ'meɪs] n mueca ♦ vi hacer
muecas

grime [graɪm] n mugre f, suciedad f

grin [grɪn] n sonrisa abierta ♦ vi sonreír

abiertamente

grind [graɪnd] (pt, pp **ground**) vt
(coffee, pepper etc) moler; (US: meat)
picar; (make sharp) afilar ♦ n (work)
rutina

grip [grɪp] n (hold) asimiento; (control)
control m, dominio; (of tyre etc): **to
have a good/bad ~** agarrarse bien/
mal; (handle) asidero; (holdall) maletín
m ♦ vt agarrar; (viewer, reader) fascinar;
to get to ~s with enfrentarse con;
~ping adj absorbente

grisly ['grɪzlɪ] adj horripilante, horrible

gristle ['grɪsl] n ternilla

grit [grɪt] n gravilla; (courage) valor m
♦ vt (road) poner gravilla en; **to
~ one's teeth** apretar los dientes

groan [grəun] n gemido; quejido ♦ vi
gemir; quejarse

grocer ['grəusə*] n tendero (de
ultramarinos (SP)); **~ies** npl comestibles
mpl; **~'s (shop)** n tienda de
ultramarinos or de abarrotes (AM)

groin [grɔɪn] n ingle f

groom [gruːm] n mozo/a de cuadra;
(also: bride~) novio ♦ vt (horse)
almohazar; (fig): **to ~ sb for** preparar
a uno para; **well-~ed** de buena
presencia

groove [gruːv] n ranura, surco

grope [grəup] : **to ~ for** vt fus bu[...]
tientas

gross [grəus] adj (neglect, injustic[...]
grave; (vulgar: behaviour) groser[...]
(: appearance) de mal gusto; (COMM[...]
bruto; **~ly** adv (greatly) enormement[...]

grotto ['grɔtəu] n gruta

grotty ['grɔtɪ] adj (inf) asq horrible

ground [graund] pt, pp of **grind** ♦ n
suelo, tierra; (SPORT) campo, terreno;
(reason: gen pl) causa, razón f; (US: also:
~ wire) tierra ♦ vt (plane) mantener en
tierra; (US: ELEC) conectar con tierra; **~s**
npl (of coffee etc) poso; (gardens etc)
jardines mpl, parque m; **on the ~** en el
suelo; **to the ~** al suelo; **to gain/lose
~** ganar/perder terreno; **~ cloth** (US)

= **~sheet**; **~ing** n (in education)
conocimientos mpl básicos; **~less** adj
infundado; **~sheet** (BRIT) n tela
impermeable; suelo; **~ staff** n personal
m de tierra; **~work** n preparación f

group [gru:p] n grupo; (musical)
conjunto ♦ vt (also: **~ together**) agrupar
♦ vi (also: **~ together**) agruparse

grouse [graus] n inv (bird) urogallo ♦ vi
(complain) quejarse

grove [grəuv] n arboleda

grovel ['grɔvl] vi (fig): **to ~ before**
humillarse ante

grow [grəu] (pt grew, pp grown) vi
crecer; (increase) aumentar; (expand)
desarrollarse; (become) volverse; **to
~ rich/weak** enriquecerse/debilitarse
♦ vt cultivar; (hair, beard) dejar crecer;
~ up vi crecer, hacerse hombre/mujer;
~er n cultivador/a m/f, productor/a
m/f; **~ing** adj creciente

growl [graul] vi gruñir

grown [grəun] pp of **grow**; **~-up** n
adulto, mayor m/f

growth [grəuθ] n crecimiento,
desarrollo; (what has grown) brote m;
(MED) tumor m

grub [grʌb] n larva, gusano; (inf: food)
comida

grubby ['grʌbɪ] adj sucio, mugriento

grudge [grʌdʒ] n (motivo de) rencor m
♦ vt: **to ~ sb sth** dar algo a uno de
mala gana; **to bear sb a ~** guardar
rencor a uno

gruelling ['gruəlɪŋ] (US **grueling**) adj
penoso, duro

gruesome ['gru:səm] adj horrible

gruff [grʌf] adj (voice) ronco; (manner)
brusco

grumble ['grʌmbl] vi refunfuñar,
quejarse

grumpy ['grʌmpɪ] adj gruñón/ona

grunt [grʌnt] vi gruñir

G-string ['dʒi:strɪŋ] n taparrabo

guarantee [gærən'ti:] n garantía f ♦ vt
garantizar

guard [gɑ:d] n (squad) guardia; (one

man) guardia m; (BRIT: RAIL) jefe m de
tren; (on machine) dispositivo de
seguridad; (also: fire-) rejilla de
protección ♦ vt guardar; (prisoner)
vigilar; **to be on one's ~** estar alerta;
~ against vt fus (prevent) protegerse
de; **~ed** adj (fig) cauteloso; **~ian** n
guardián/ana m/f; (of minor) tutor(a)
m/f; **~'s van** (BRIT: RAIL) furgón m

Guatemala [gwætɪ'mɑ:lə] n
Guatemala; **~n** adj, n guatemalteco/a
m/f

guerrilla [gə'rɪlə] n guerrillero/a

guess [gɛs] vi adivinar; (US) suponer
♦ vt adivinar; suponer n suposición f,
conjetura; **to take** o **have a ~** tratar
de adivinar; **~work** n conjeturas fpl

guest [gɛst] n invitado/a; (in hotel)
huésped a) m/f; **~ house** n casa de
huéspedes, pensión f; **~ room** n
cuarto de huéspedes

guffaw [gʌ'fɔ:] vi reírse a carcajadas

guidance ['gaɪdəns] n (advice)
consejos mpl

guide [gaɪd] n (person) guía m/f; (book,
fig) guía f ♦ vt (round museum etc) guiar;
(lead) conducir; (direct) orientar; (girl)
~ n exploradora; **~book** n guía; **dog**
n perro m guía; **~lines** npl (advice)
directrices fpl

guild [gɪld] n gremio

guilt [gɪlt] n culpabilidad f; **~y** adj
culpable

guinea pig ['gɪnɪ-] n cobaya; (fig)
conejillo m de Indias

guise [gaɪz] n: **in** o **under the ~** of
bajo apariencia f

guitar [gɪ'tɑ:'] n guitarra

gulf [gʌlf] n golfo; (abyss) abismo

gull [gʌl] n gaviota

gullible ['gʌlɪbl] adj crédulo

gully ['gʌlɪ] n barranco

gulp [gʌlp] vi tragar saliva ♦ vt (also:
~ down) tragarse

gum [gʌm] n (ANAT) encía; (glue)
goma, cemento; (sweet) caramelo de
goma; (also: chewing-~) chicle m ♦ vt

pegar con goma; **~boots** (BRIT) npl botas fpl de goma

gun [gʌn] n (small) pistola, revólver m; (shotgun) escopeta; (rifle) fusil m; (cannon) cañón m; **~boat** n cañonero; **~fire** n disparos mpl; **~man** n pistolero; **~point** n: **at ~point** a mano armada; **~powder** n pólvora; **~shot** n escopetazo

gurgle ['gɔːgl] vi (baby) gorgojear; (water) borbotear

gush [gʌʃ] vi salir a raudales; (person) deshacerse en efusiones

gust [gʌst] n (of wind) ráfaga

gusto ['gʌstəu] n entusiasmo

gut [gʌt] n intestino; **~s** npl (ANAT) tripas fpl; (courage) valor m

gutter ['gʌtə*] n (of roof) canalón m; (in street) cuneta

guy [gaɪ] n (also: **~rope**) cuerda; (inf: man) tío m, tipo; (figure) monigote m

Guy Fawkes' Night

La noche del cinco de noviembre, Guy Fawkes' Night, se celebra en el Reino Unido el fracaso de una conspiración de la pólvora ("Gunpowder Plot"), un intento fallido de volar el parlamento de Jaime I en 1605. Esa noche se lanzan fuegos artificiales y se hacen hogueras en las que se queman unos muñecos de trapo que representan a Guy Fawkes, uno de las cabecillas de la revuelta. Días antes, los niños tienen por costumbre pedir a los transeúntes "a penny for the guy", dinero que emplean en comprar cohetes y petardos.

guzzle ['gʌzl] vi tragar ♦ vt engullir

gym [dʒɪm] n (also: **gymnasium**) gimnasio; (also: **gymnastics**) gimnasia; **~nast** n gimnasta m/f; **~ shoes** npl zapatillas fpl (de deporte); **~ slip** (BRIT) n túnica de colegiala

gynaecologist [gaɪnɪ'kɒlədʒɪst] (US

gynecologist) n ginecólogo/a

gypsy ['dʒɪpsɪ] n gitano/a

H, h

haberdashery [hæbə'dæʃərɪ] (BRIT) n mercería

habit ['hæbɪt] n hábito, costumbre f; (drug ~) adicción f; (costume) hábito

habitual [hə'bɪtjuəl] adj acostumbrado, habitual; (drinker, liar) empedernido

hack [hæk] vt (cut) cortar; (slice) tajar ♦ n (pej: writer) escritor/a m/f a sueldo; **~er** n (COMPUT) pirata m/f informático/a

hackneyed ['hæknɪd] adj trillado

had [hæd] pt, pp of **have**

haddock ['hædək] (pl **~** or **~s**) n especie de merluza

hadn't ['hædnt] = **had not**

haemorrhage ['hemərɪdʒ] (US **hemorrhage**) n hemorragia

haemorrhoids ['hemərɔɪdz] (US **hemorrhoids**) npl hemorroides fpl

haggle ['hægl] vi regatear

Hague [heɪg] n: **The ~** La Haya

hail [heɪl] n granizo; (fig) lluvia ♦ vt saludar; (taxi) llamar a; (acclaim) aclamar ♦ vi granizar; **~stone** n (piedra del) granizo

hair [hɛə*] n pelo, cabellos mpl; (one ~) pelo, cabello; (on legs etc) vello; **to do one's ~** arreglarse el pelo; **to have grey ~** tener canas fpl; **~brush** n cepillo (para el pelo); **~cut** n corte m (de pelo); **~do** n peinado; **~dresser** n peluquero/a; **~dresser's** n peluquería; **~ dryer** n secador m de pelo; **~grip** n horquilla; **~net** n redecilla; **~piece** n postizo; **~pin** n horquilla, **~pin bend** (US **~pin curve**) n curva de horquilla; **~raising** adj espeluznante; **~ removing cream** n crema depilatoria; **~ spray** n laca, **~style** n peinado; **~y** adj peludo; velludo; (inf:

frightening) espeluznante

hake [heɪk] (pl inv or **~s**) n merluza

half [hɑːf] (pl **halves**) n mitad f; (of beer) → caña (SP), media pinta; (RAIL, BUS) billete m de niño ♦ adj medio ♦ adv medio, a medias; **two and a ~** dos y media; **~ a dozen** media docena; **~ a pound** media libra; **to cut sth in ~** cortar algo por la mitad; **~caste** ['hɑːfkɑːst] n mestizo/a; **~hearted** adj indiferente, poco entusiasta; **~hour** n media hora; **~mast** n: **at ~mast** (flag) a media asta; **~price** adj, adv a mitad de precio; **~ term** (BRIT) n (SCOL) vacaciones de mediados del trimestre; **~time** n descanso; **~way** adv a medio camino; (in period of time) a mitad de

hall [hɔːl] n (for concerts) sala; (entrance way) hall m; vestíbulo; **~ of residence** (BRIT) n residencia

hallmark ['hɔːlmɑːk] n sello

hallo [hʌ'ləu] excl = **hello**

Hallowe'en [hæləuˈiːn] n víspera de Todos los Santos

Hallowe'en

La tradición anglosajona dice que en la noche del 31 de octubre, Hallowe'en, víspera de Todos los Santos, es posible ver a brujas y fantasmas. En este día los niños se disfrazan y van de puerta en puerta llevando un farol hecho con una calabaza en forma de cabeza humana. Cuando se les abre la puerta gritan "trick or treat", amenazando con gastar una broma a quien no les dé golosinas o algo de calderilla.

---

hallucination [həluːsɪˈneɪʃən] n alucinación f

hallway ['hɔːlweɪ] n hall m

halo ['heɪləu] n (of saint) halo, aureola

halt [hɔːlt] n (stop) alto, parada ♦ vt parar; interrumpir ♦ vi pararse

halve [hɑːv] vt partir por la mitad

halves [hɑːvz] npl of **half**

ham [hæm] n jamón m (cocido)

hamburger ['hæmbɜːgə*] n hamburguesa

hamlet ['hæmlɪt] n aldea

hammer ['hæmə*] n martillo ♦ vt (nail) clavar; (force): **to ~ an idea into sb/a message across** meter una idea en la cabeza a uno/machacar una idea ♦ vi dar golpes

hammock ['hæmək] n hamaca

hamper ['hæmpə*] vt estorbar ♦ n cesto

hand [hænd] n mano f; (of clock) aguja; (writing) letra; (worker) obrero ♦ vt (give): **to give** o **lend sb a ~** echar una mano a uno, ayudar a uno; **at ~** a mano; **in ~** (time) libre; (job etc) entre manos; **on ~** (person, services) a mano, al alcance; **to ~** (information etc) a mano; **on the one ~ ..., on the other ~ ...** por una parte ... por otra (parte) ...; **~ in** vt entregar; **~ out** vt distribuir; **~ over** vt (deliver) entregar; **~bag** n bolso (SP), cartera (AM); **~book** n manual m; **~brake** n freno de mano; **~cuffs** npl esposas fpl; **~ful** n puñado

handicap ['hændɪkæp] n minusvalía f (disadvantage) desventaja; (SPORT) handicap m ♦ vt estorbar; **mentally/physically ~ped** deficiente m/f (mental)/minusválido/a (físico/a)

handicraft ['hændɪkrɑːft] n artesanía; (object) objeto de artesanía

handiwork ['hændɪwɜːk] n obra

handkerchief ['hæŋkətʃɪf] n pañuelo

handle ['hændl] n (of door etc) tirador m; (of cup etc) asa; (of knife etc) mango; (for winding) manivela ♦ vt (touch) tocar; (deal with) encargarse de; (treat: people) manejar; **"~ with care"** "(manéjese) con cuidado"; **to fly off the ~** perder los estribos; **~bar(s)** n(pl) manillar m

hand: ~ luggage n equipaje m de

mano; **~made** adj hecho a mano;
~out n (money etc) limosna; (leaflet)
folleto; **~rail** n pasamanos m inv;
~shake n apretón m de manos

handsome ['hænsəm] adj guapo;
(building) bello; (fig: profit) considerable

handwriting ['hændraıtıŋ] n letra

handy ['hændı] adj (close at hand) a la
mano; (tool etc) práctico; (skilful) hábil,
diestro

hang [hæŋ] (pt, pp hung) vt colgar;
(criminal: pt, pp hanged) ahorcar ♦ vi
(painting, coat etc) colgar; (hair,
drapery) caer; **to get the ~ of sth**
(inf) lograr dominar algo; **~ about** or
around vi haraganear; **~ on** vi (wait)
esperar; **~ up** vi (TEL) colgar ♦ vt
colgar

hanger ['hæŋə*] n percha; **~-on** n
parásito

hang: ~-gliding ['-glaıdıŋ] n vuelo
libre; **~over** n (after drinking) resaca;
~-up n complejo

hanker ['hæŋkə*] vi: **to ~ after** añorar

hankie, hanky ['hæŋkı] n
abbr = **handkerchief**

haphazard [hæp'hæzəd] adj fortuito

happen ['hæpən] vi suceder, ocurrir;
(chance): **he ~ed to hear/see** dió la
casualidad de que oyó/vió; **as it ~s** da
la casualidad de que; **~ing** n suceso,
acontecimiento

happily ['hæpılı] adv (luckily)
afortunadamente; (cheerfully)
alegremente

happiness ['hæpınıs] n felicidad f;
(cheerfulness) alegría

happy ['hæpı] adj feliz; (cheerful)
alegre; **to be ~ (with)** estar contento
(con); **to be ~ to do** estar encantado
de hacer; **~ birthday!** ¡feliz
cumpleaños!; **~-go-lucky** adj
despreocupado; **~ hour** n horas en las
que la bebida es más barata, happy
hour f

harass ['hærəs] vt acosar, hostigar;
~ment n persecución f

harbour ['hɑːbə*] (US **harbor**) n
puerto ♦ vt (fugitive) dar abrigo a;
(hope etc) abrigar

hard [hɑːd] adj (work): (difficult) difícil;
(work) arduo; (person) severo; (fact)
innegable ♦ adv (work) mucho, duro;
(think) profundamente; **to look ~ at**
clavar los ojos en; **to try ~** esforzarse;
no ~ feelings! ¡sin rencor(es)!; **to be
~ of hearing** ser duro de oído; **to be
~ done by** ser tratado injustamente;
~back n libro en cartoné; **~ cash** n
dinero contante; **~ disk** n (COMPUT)
disco duro or rígido; **~en** vt endurecer;
(fig) curtir ♦ vi endurecerse; curtirse;
~-headed adj realista; **~ labour** n
trabajos mpl forzados

hardly ['hɑːdlı] adv apenas; **~ ever**
casi nunca

hard: ~ship n privación f; **~ shoulder**
(BRIT) n (AUT) arcén m; **~-up** (inf) adj
sin un duro (SP), sin plata (AM); **~ware**
n ferretería; (COMPUT) hardware m;
(MIL) armamento; **~ware shop** n
ferretería; **~-wearing** adj resistente,
duradero; **~-working** adj trabajador(a)

hardy ['hɑːdı] adj fuerte; (plant)
resistente

hare [hɛə*] n liebre f; **~-brained** adj
descabellado

harm [hɑːm] n daño, mal m ♦ vt
(person) hacer daño a; (health,
interests) perjudicar; (thing) dañar; **out
of ~'s way** a salvo; **~ful** adj dañino;
~less adj (person) inofensivo; (joke etc)
inocente

harmony ['hɑːmənı] n armonía

harness ['hɑːnıs] n arreos mpl; (for
child) arnés m; (safety ~) arneses mpl
♦ vt (horse) enjaezar; (resources)
aprovechar

harp [hɑːp] n arpa ♦ vi: **to ~ on
(about)** machacar (con)

harrowing ['hærəuıŋ] adj angustioso

harsh [hɑːʃ] adj (cruel) duro, cruel;
(severe) severo; (sound) áspero; (light)
deslumbrador(a)

harvest ['hɑːvɪst] n (~ time) siega; (of cereals etc) cosecha; (of grapes) vendimia ♦ vt cosechar

has [hæz] vb see have

hash [hæʃ] n (CULIN) picadillo; (fig: mess) lío

hashish ['hæʃɪʃ] n hachís m

hasn't ['hæznt] = has not

hassle ['hæsl] (inf) n lata

haste [heɪst] n prisa; ~n ['heɪsn] vt acelerar ♦ vi darse prisa; **hastily** adv de prisa; precipitadamente; **hasty** adj apresurado; (rash) precipitado

hat [hæt] n sombrero

hatch [hætʃ] n (NAUT: also: ~way) escotilla; (also: service ~) ventanilla ♦ vi (bird) salir del cascarón ♦ vt incubar; (plot) tramar; **5 eggs have ~ed** han salido 5 pollos

hatchback ['hætʃbæk] n (AUT) tres or cinco puertas m

hatchet ['hætʃɪt] n hacha

hate [heɪt] vt odiar, aborrecer ♦ n odio; **~ful** adj odioso; **hatred** ['heɪtrɪd] n odio

haughty ['hɔːtɪ] adj altanero

haul [hɔːl] vt tirar ♦ n (of fish) redada; (of stolen goods etc) botín m; **~age** (BRIT) n transporte m; (costs) gastos mpl de transporte; **~ier** (US **~er**) n transportista m/f

haunch [hɔːntʃ] n anca; (of meat) pierna

haunt [hɔːnt] vt (subj: ghost) aparecerse en; (obsess) obsesionar ♦ n guarida

---

KEYWORD

---

have [hæv] (pt, pp had) aux vb 1 (gen) haber; **to ~ arrived/eaten** haber llegado/comido; **having finished** or **when he had finished,** **he left** cuando hubo acabado, se fue

2 (in tag questions): **you've done it,** **~n't you?** lo has hecho, ¿verdad? or ¿no?

3 (in short answers and questions): **I**

~n't no; **so I ~** pues, es verdad; **we** **~n't paid — ~ we!** no hemos pagado — ¡sí que hemos pagado!; **I've** **been there before, ~ you?** he estado allí antes, ¿y tú?

♦ modal aux vb (be obliged): **to ~ (got)** **to do sth** tener que hacer algo; **you** **~n't to tell her** no hay que or no debes decírselo

♦ vt 1 (possess): **he has (got) blue** **eyes/dark hair** tiene los ojos azules/el pelo negro

2 (referring to meals etc): **to ~ breakfast/lunch/dinner** desayunar/comer/cenar; **to ~ a** **drink/a cigarette** tomar algo/fumar un cigarrillo

3 (receive): recibir; (obtain): obtener; **may I ~ your address?** ¿puedes darme tu dirección?; **you can ~ it for** **£5** te lo puedes quedar por £5; **I must** **~ it by tomorrow** lo necesito para mañana; **to ~ a baby** tener un niño or bebé

4 (maintain, allow): **I won't ~ it/this** **nonsense!** ¡no lo permitiré!/¡no permitiré estas tonterías!; **we can't** **~ that** no podemos permitir eso

5: **to ~ sth done** hacer or mandar hacer algo; **to ~ one's hair cut** cortarse el pelo; **to ~ sb do sth** hacer que alguien haga algo

6 (experience, suffer): **to ~ a cold/flu** tener un resfriado/la gripe; **she had** **her bag stolen/her arm broken** le robaron el bolso/se rompió un brazo; **to** **~ an operation** operarse

7 (+ noun): **to ~ a swim/walk/** **bath/rest** nadar/dar un paseo/darse un baño/descansar; **let's ~ a** **look** vamos a ver; **to ~ a meeting/party** celebrar una reunión/una fiesta; **let** **me ~ a try** déjame intentarlo

have out vt: **to ~ it out with sb** (settle a problem etc) dejar las cosas en claro con alguien

haven ['heɪvn] n puerto; (fig) refugio
haven't ['hævnt] = have not
havoc ['hævək] n estragos mpl
hawk [hɔ:k] n halcón m
hay [heɪ] n heno; ~ **fever** n fiebre f del heno; ~**stack** n almiar m
haywire ['heɪwaɪə*] (inf) adj: **to go** ~ (plan) embrollarse
hazard ['hæzəd] n peligro ♦ vt aventurar; ~**ous** adj peligroso; ~ **warning lights** npl (AUT) señales fpl de emergencia
haze [heɪz] n neblina
hazelnut ['heɪzlnʌt] n avellana
hazy ['heɪzɪ] adj brumoso; (idea) vago
he [hi:] pron él; ~ **who ...** él que ..., quien ...
head [hɛd] n cabeza; (leader) jefe/a m/f; (of school) director(a) m/f ♦ vt (list) encabezar; (group) capitanear; (company) dirigir; ~**s (or tails)** cara (o cruz); ~ **first** de cabeza; ~ **over heels** (in love) perdidamente; **to ~ the ball** cabecear (la pelota); ~ **for** vt fus dirigirse a; (disaster) ir camino de; ~**ache** n dolor m de cabeza; ~**dress** n tocado; ~**ing** n título; ~**lamp** (BRIT) n = ~**light**; ~**land** n promontorio; ~**light** n faro; ~**line** n titular m; ~**long** adv (fall) de cabeza; (rush) precipitadamente; ~**master/mistress** n director(a) m/f (de escuela); ~**office** n oficina central, central f; ~**-on** adj (collision) de frente; ~**phones** npl auriculares mpl; ~**quarters** npl sede f central; (MIL) cuartel m general; ~**rest** n reposa-cabezas m inv; ~**room** n (in car) altura interior; (under bridge) (límite m de) altura; ~**scarf** n pañuelo; ~**strong** adj testarudo; ~ **waiter** n maître m; ~ **way** n: **to make** ~**way** (fig) hacer progresos; ~**wind** n viento contrario; ~**y** adj (experience, period) apasionante; (wine) cabezón; (atmosphere) embriagador/a
heal [hi:l] vt curar ♦ vi cicatrizarse
health [hɛlθ] n salud f; ~ **food** n

alimentos mpl orgánicos; **the H~ Service** (BRIT) n el servicio de salud pública; = el Insalud (SP); ~**y** adj sano, saludable
heap [hi:p] n montón m ♦ vt: **to ~ (up)** amontonar; **to ~ sth with** llenar algo hasta arriba de; ~**s of** un montón de
hear [hɪə*] (pt, pp **heard**) vt (also LAW) oír; (news) saber ♦ vi oír; **to ~ about** oír hablar de; **to ~ from sb** tener noticias de uno; ~**ing** n (sense) oído; (LAW) vista; ~**ing aid** n audífono; ~**say** n rumores mpl, hablillas f
hearse [hɜ:s] n coche m fúnebre
heart [hɑ:t] n corazón m; (fig) valor m; (of lettuce) cogollo; ~**s** npl (CARDS) corazones m; **to lose/take ~** descorazonarse/cobrar ánimo; **at ~** en el fondo; **by ~** (learn, know) de memoria; ~ **attack** n infarto de miocardio; ~**beat** n latido (del corazón); ~**breaking** adj desgarrador(a); ~**broken** adj: **she was ~broken about it** esto le partió el corazón; ~**burn** n acedía; ~ **failure** n fallo cardíaco; ~**felt** adj (deeply felt) más sentido
hearth [hɑ:θ] n (fireplace) chimenea
hearty ['hɑ:tɪ] adj (person) campechano; (laugh) sano; (dislike, support) absoluto
heat [hi:t] n calor m; (SPORT: also: qualifying ~) prueba eliminatoria ♦ vt calentar; ~ **up** vi calentarse ♦ vt calentar; ~**ed** adj caliente; (fig) acalorado; ~**er** n estufa; (in car) calefacción f
heath [hi:θ] (BRIT) n brezal m
heather ['hɛðə*] n brezo
heating ['hi:tɪŋ] n calefacción f
heatstroke ['hi:tstrəuk] n insolación f
heatwave ['hi:tweɪv] n ola de calor
heave [hi:v] vt (pull) tirar; (push) empujar con esfuerzo; (lift) levantar (con esfuerzo) ♦ vi (chest) palpitar; (retch) tener náuseas ♦ n tirón m;

empujón *m*; **to ~ a sigh** suspirar

heaven ['hɛvn] *n* cielo; (*fig*) una maravilla; **~ly** *adj* celestial; (*fig*) maravilloso

heavily ['hɛvɪlɪ] *adv* pesadamente; (*drink, smoke*) con exceso; (*sleep, sigh*) profundamente; (*depend*) mucho

heavy ['hɛvɪ] *adj* pesado; (*work, blow*) duro; (*sea, rain, meal*) fuerte; (*drinker, smoker*) grande; (*responsibility*) grave; (*schedule*) ocupado; (*weather*) bochornoso; **~ goods vehicle** *n* vehículo pesado; **~weight** *n* (*SPORT*) peso pesado

Hebrew ['hiːbruː] *adj, n* (*LING*) hebreo

heckle ['hɛkl] *vt* interrumpir

hectic ['hɛktɪk] *adj* agitado

he'd [hiːd] = **he would**; **he had**

hedge [hɛdʒ] *n* seto ♦ *vi* contestar con evasivas; **to ~ one's bets** (*fig*) cubrirse

hedgehog ['hɛdʒhɒg] *n* erizo

heed [hiːd] *vt* (*also*: **take ~ of**) (*pay attention to*) hacer caso de; **~less** *adj*: **to be ~less (of)** no hacer caso de

heel [hiːl] *n* talón *m*; (*of shoe*) tacón *m* ♦ *vt* (*shoe*) poner tacón a

hefty ['hɛftɪ] *adj* (*person*) fornido; (*parcel, profit*) gordo

heifer ['hɛfə*] *n* novilla, ternera

height [haɪt] *n* (*of person*) estatura; (*of building*) altura; (*high ground*) cerro; (*altitude*) altura *f*; (*fig*: *of season*): **at the ~ of summer** en los días más calurosos del verano; (: *of power etc*) cúspide *f*; (: *of stupidity etc*) colmo; **~en** *vt* elevar; (*fig*) aumentar

heir [ɛə*] *n* heredero; **~ess** *n* heredera; **~loom** *n* reliquia de familia

held [hɛld] *pt, pp* of **hold**

helicopter ['hɛlɪkɒptə*] *n* helicóptero

hell [hɛl] *n* infierno; **~!** (*inf*) ¡demonios!

he'll [hiːl] = **he will**; **he shall**

hello [hə'ləu] *excl* ¡hola!; (*to attract attention*) ¡oiga!; (*surprise*) ¡caramba!

helm [hɛlm] *n* (*NAUT*) timón *m*

helmet ['hɛlmɪt] *n* casco

help [hɛlp] *n* ayuda; (*cleaner etc*)

criada, asistenta ♦ *vt* ayudar; **~!** ¡socorro!; **~ yourself** sírvete; **he can't ~ it** no es culpa suya; **~er** *n* ayudante *m/f*; **~ful** *adj* útil; (*person*) servicial; (*advice*) útil; **~ing** *n* ración *f*; **~less** *adj* (*incapable*) incapaz; (*defenceless*) indefenso

hem [hɛm] *n* dobladillo ♦ *vt* poner or coser el dobladillo; **~ in** *vt* cercar

hemorrhage ['hɛmərɪdʒ] (*US*) *n* = **haemorrhage**

hemorrhoids ['hɛmərɔɪdz] (*US*) *npl* = **haemorrhoids**

hen [hɛn] *n* gallina; (*female bird*) hembra

hence [hɛns] *adv* (*therefore*) por lo tanto; **2 years ~** de aquí a 2 años; **~forth** *adv* de hoy en adelante

hepatitis [hɛpə'taɪtɪs] *n* hepatitis *f*

her [həː*] *pron* (*direct*) la; (*indirect*) le; (*stressed, after prep*) ella ♦ *adj* su; *see also* **me**; **my**

herald ['hɛrəld] *n* heraldo ♦ *vt* anunciar; **~ry** *n* heráldica

herb [həːb] *n* hierba

herd [həːd] *n* rebaño

here [hɪə*] *adv* aquí; (*at this point*) en este punto; **~!** (*present*) ¡presente!; **~ is/are** aquí está/están; **~ she is** aquí está; **~after** *adv* en el futuro; **~by** *adv* (*in letter*) por la presente

heritage ['hɛrɪtɪdʒ] *n* patrimonio

hermit ['həːmɪt] *n* ermitaño/a

hernia ['həːnɪə] *n* hernia

hero ['hɪərəu] (*pl* **~es**) *n* héroe *m*; (*in book, film*) protagonista *m*

heroin ['hɛrəuɪn] *n* heroína

heroine ['hɛrəuɪn] *n* heroína; (*in book, film*) protagonista

heron ['hɛrən] *n* garza

herring ['hɛrɪŋ] *n* arenque *m*

hers [həːz] *pron* (*el*) suyo/(la) suya *etc*; *see also* **mine**[1]

herself [həː'sɛlf] *pron* (*reflexive*) se; (*emphatic*) ella misma; (*after prep*) sí (misma); *see also* **oneself**

he's [hiːz] = **he is**; **he has**

hesitant ['hezɪtənt] adj vacilante

hesitate ['hezɪteɪt] vi vacilar; (in speech) titubear; (be unwilling) resistirse a; **hesitation** ['-'teɪʃən] n indecisión f; titubeo; dudas fpl

heterosexual [hetərəu'seksjuəl] adj heterosexual

heyday ['heɪdeɪ] n: **the ~ of** el apogeo de

HGV n abbr = **heavy goods vehicle**

hi [haɪ] excl ¡hola!; (to attract attention) ¡oiga!

hiatus [haɪ'eɪtəs] n vacío

hibernate ['haɪbəneɪt] vi invernar

hiccough ['hɪkʌp] n = **hiccup**

hiccup ['hɪkʌp] vi hipar; **~s** npl hipo

hide [haɪd] (pt **hid**, pp **hidden**) n (skin) piel f ♦ vt esconder, ocultar ♦ vi: **to ~ (from sb)** esconderse or ocultarse (de uno); **~-and-seek** n escondite m

hideous ['hɪdɪəs] adj horrible

hiding ['haɪdɪŋ] n (beating) paliza; **to be in ~** (concealed) estar escondido

hierarchy ['haɪərɑːkɪ] n jerarquía

hi-fi ['haɪfaɪ] n estéreo, hifi m ♦ adj de alta fidelidad

high [haɪ] adj alto; (speed, number) grande; (price) elevado; (wind) fuerte; (voice) agudo ♦ adv alto, a gran altura; **it is 20 m ~** tiene 20 m de altura; **~ in the air** en las alturas; **~brow** adj intelectual; **~chair** n silla alta; **~ education** n educación f or enseñanza superior; **~-handed** adj despótico; **~-heeled** adj de tacón alto; **~ jump** n (SPORT) salto de altura; **the H~lands** npl las tierras altas de Escocia; **~light** n (fig: of event) punto culminante; (: in hair) reflejo ♦ vt subrayar; **~ly** adv (paid) muy bien; (critical, confidential) sumamente; (a lot): **to speak/think ~ly of** hablar muy bien de/tener en mucho a; **~ly strung** adj hipertenso; **~ness** n altura; **Her** or **His H~ness** Su Alteza; **~-pitched** adj agudo; **~-rise block** n torre f de pisos; **~ school** n Instituto Nacional de Bachillerato (SP);

~ season (BRIT) n temporada alta; **~ street** (BRIT) n calle f mayor; **~way** n carretera; (US) carretera nacional; autopista; **H~way Code** (BRIT) n código de la circulación

hijack ['haɪdʒæk] vt secuestrar; **~er** n secuestrador/a m/f

hike [haɪk] vi (go walking) ir de excursión (a pie) ♦ n caminata; **~r** n excursionista m/f; **hiking** n senderismo

hilarious [hɪ'leərɪəs] adj divertidísimo

hill [hɪl] n colina, cerro m; montaña; (slope) cuesta; **~side** n ladera; **~ walking** n senderismo de (montaña); **~y** adj montañoso

hilt [hɪlt] n (of sword) empuñadura; **to the ~** (fig: support) incondicionalmente

him [hɪm] pron (direct) le, lo; (indirect) le; (stressed, after prep) él; see also **me**; **~self** pron (reflexive) se; (emphatic) él mismo; (after prep) sí (mismo); see also **oneself**

hinder ['hɪndə*] vt estorbar, impedir; **hindrance** ['hɪndrəns] n estorbo

hindsight ['haɪndsaɪt] n: **with ~** en retrospectiva

Hindu ['hɪnduː] n hindú m/f

hinge [hɪndʒ] n bisagra, gozne m ♦ vi (fig): **to ~ on** depender de

hint [hɪnt] n indirecta; (advice) consejo; (sign) dejo ♦ vt: **to ~ that** insinuar que ♦ vi: **to ~ at** hacer alusión a

hip [hɪp] n cadera

hippopotamus [hɪpə'pɒtəməs] (pl **~es** or **hippopotami**) n hipopótamo

hire ['haɪə*] vt (BRIT: car, equipment) alquilar; (worker) contratar ♦ n alquiler m; **for ~** se alquila; (taxi) libre; **~(d) car** (BRIT) n coche m de alquiler; **~ purchase** (BRIT) n compra a plazos

his [hɪz] pron (el) suyo/(la) suya etc ♦ adj su; see also **mine**[1]; **my**

Hispanic [hɪs'pænɪk] adj hispánico

hiss [hɪs] vi silbar

historian [hɪ'stɔːrɪən] n historiador/a m/f

historic(al) [hɪ'stɒrɪk(l)] adj histórico

history ['hɪstərɪ] *n* historia
hit [hɪt] (*pt, pp* **hit**) *vt* (*strike*) golpear,
pegar; (*reach: target*) alcanzar; (*collide
with: car*) chocar contra; (*fig: affect*)
afectar ♦ *n* golpe *m*; (*success*) éxito; **to
~ it off with sb** llevarse bien con uno;
~-and-run driver *n* conductor(a) que
atropella y huye
hitch [hɪtʃ] *vt* (*fasten*) atar, amarrar;
(*also: ~ up*) remangar ♦ *n* (*difficulty*)
dificultad *f*; **to ~ a lift** hacer autostop
hitch-hike *vi* hacer autostop; **~hiking**
n autostop *m*
hi-tech [haɪˈtek] *adj* de alta tecnología
hitherto [ˈhɪðəˈtuː] *adv* hasta ahora
HIV *n abbr* (= *human immunodeficiency
virus*) VIH *m*; **~-negative/positive** *adj*
VIH negativo/positivo
hive [haɪv] *n* colmena
HMS *abbr* = **His (Her) Majesty's
Ship**
hoard [hɔːd] *n* (*treasure*) tesoro;
(*stockpile*) provisión *f* ♦ *vt* acumular;
(*goods in short supply*) acaparar; **~ing** *n*
(*for posters*) cartelera
hoarse [hɔːs] *adj* ronco
hoax [həʊks] *n* trampa
hob [hɔb] *n* quemador *m*
hobble [ˈhɔbl] *vi* cojear
hobby [ˈhɔbɪ] *n* pasatiempo, afición *f*
hobo [ˈhəʊbəʊ] (*US*) *n* vagabundo
hockey [ˈhɔkɪ] *n* hockey *m*
hog [hɔg] *n* cerdo, puerco ♦ *vt* (*fig*)
acaparar; **to go the whole ~** poner
toda la carne en el asador
hoist [hɔɪst] *n* (*crane*) grúa ♦ *vt*
levantar, alzar; (*flag, sail*) izar
hold [həʊld] (*pt, pp* **held**) *vt* sostener;
(*contain*) contener; (*have: power,
qualification*) tener; (*keep back*) retener;
(*believe*) sostener; (*consider*) considerar;
(*keep in position*): **to ~ one's head up**
mantener la cabeza alta; (*meeting*)
celebrar ♦ *vi* (*withstand pressure*)
resistir; (*be valid*) valer ♦ *n* (*grasp*)
asimiento; (*fig*) dominio; **~ the line!**
(*TEL*) ¡no cuelgue!; **to ~ one's own**

(*fig*) defenderse; **to catch** *or* **get** (a)
~ of agarrarse *or* asirse de; **~ back** *vt*
retener; (*secret*) ocultar; **~ down** *vt*
(*person*) sujetar; (*job*) mantener; **~ off**
vt (*enemy*) rechazar; **~ on** *vi* agarrarse
bien; (*wait*) esperar; **~ on!** (*TEL*)
¡espere) un momento!; **~ on to** *vt fus*
agarrarse a; (*keep*) guardar; **~ out** *vt*
ofrecer ♦ *vi* (*resist*) resistir; **~ up** *vt*
(*raise*) levantar; (*support*) apoyar;
(*delay*) retrasar; (*rob*) asaltar; **~all** (*BRIT*)
n bolsa; **~er** *n* (*container*) receptáculo;
(*of ticket, record*) poseedor(a) *m/f*; (*of
office, title etc*) titular *m/f*; **~ing** *n*
(*share*) interés *m*; (*farmland*) parcela;
~up *n* (*robbery*) atraco; (*delay*) retraso;
(*BRIT: in traffic*) embotellamiento *m*
hole [həʊl] *n* agujero
holiday [ˈhɔlədɪ] *n* vacaciones *fpl*;
(*public ~*) (día *m* de) fiesta, día *m*
feriado; **on ~** de vacaciones; **~ camp**
n (*BRIT: also: ~ centre*) centro de
vacaciones; **~-maker** (*BRIT*) *n* turista
m/f; **~ resort** *n* centro turístico
holiness [ˈhəʊlɪnɪs] *n* santidad *f*
Holland [ˈhɔlənd] *n* Holanda
hollow [ˈhɔləʊ] *adj* hueco; (*claim*)
vacío; (*eyes*) hundido; (*sound*) sordo
♦ *n* hueco; (*in ground*) hoyo ♦ *vt*:
~ out excavar
holly [ˈhɔlɪ] *n* acebo
holocaust [ˈhɔləkɔːst] *n* holocausto
holy [ˈhəʊlɪ] *adj* santo, sagrado; (*water*)
bendito
homage [ˈhɔmɪdʒ] *n* homenaje *m*
home [həʊm] *n* casa; (*country*) patria;
(*institution*) asilo ♦ *cpd* (*domestic*)
casero, de casa; (*ECON, POL*) nacional
♦ *adv* (*direction*) a casa; (*right in: nail
etc*) a fondo; **at ~** en casa; (*in country*)
en el país; (*fig*) como pez en el agua;
to go/come ~ ir/volver a casa; **make
yourself at ~** ¡estás en tu casa!;
~ address *n* domicilio; **~land** *n* tierra
natal; **~less** *adj* sin hogar, sin casa;
~ly *adj* (*simple*) sencillo; **~-made** *adj*
casero; **H~ Office** (*BRIT*) *n* Ministerio

del Interior; ~ **page** n página de inicio; ~ **rule** n autonomía; **H~ Secretary** (BRIT) n Ministro del Interior; **~sick** adj: **to be ~sick** tener morriña, sentir nostalgia; ~ **town** n ciudad f natal; **~ward** ['həumwəd] adj (journey) hacia casa; **~work** n deberes mpl

homoeopathic ['həumɪəu'pæθɪk] (US **homeopathic**) adj homeopático

homosexual [hɔməu'sɛksjuəl] adj, n homosexual m/f

Honduran [hɔn'djuərən] adj, n hondureño/a m/f

Honduras [hɔn'djuərəs] n Honduras f

honest ['ɔnɪst] adj honrado; (sincere) franco, sincero; **~ly** adv honradamente; francamente; **~y** n honradez f

honey ['hʌnɪ] n miel f; **~comb** n panal m; **~moon** n luna de miel; **~suckle** n madreselva

honk [hɔŋk] vi (AUT) tocar el pito, pitar

honorary ['ɔnərərɪ] adj (member, president) de honor; (title) honorífico; ~ **degree** n doctorado honoris causa

honour ['ɔnə*] (US **honor**) vt honrar; (commitment, promise) cumplir con ♦ n honor m, honra; **~able** adj honorable; **~s degree** n (SCOL) título de licenciado con calificación alta

hood [hud] n capucha f; (BRIT: AUT) capota; (US: AUT) capó m; (of cooker) campana de humos

hoof [hu:f] (pl **hooves**) n pezuña

hook [huk] n gancho; (on dress) corchete m, broche m; (for fishing) anzuelo ♦ vt enganchar; (fish) pescar

hooligan ['hu:lɪgən] n gamberro

hoop [hu:p] n aro

hooray [hu:'reɪ] excl = **hurray**

hoot [hu:t] (BRIT) vi (AUT) tocar el pito, pitar; (siren) sonar la sirena; (owl) ulular; **~er** (BRIT) n (AUT) pito, claxon m; (NAUT) sirena

Hoover ℗ ['hu:və*] (BRIT) n aspiradora ♦ vt: **h~** pasar la aspiradora por

hooves [hu:vz] npl of **hoof**

hop [hɔp] vi saltar, brincar; (on one

foot) saltar con un pie

hope [həup] vt, vi esperar ♦ n esperanza; I ~ **so/not** espero que sí/ no; **~ful** adj (person) optimista; (situation) prometedor(a); **~fully** adv con esperanza; (one hopes) **~fully he will recover** esperamos que se recupere; **~less** adj desesperado; (person): **to be ~less** ser un desastre

hops [hɔps] npl lúpulo

horizon [hə'raɪzn] n horizonte m; **~tal** [hɔrɪ'zɔntl] adj horizontal

hormone ['hɔ:məun] n hormona

horn [hɔ:n] n cuerno; (MUS: also: French ~) trompa; (AUT) pito, claxon m

hornet ['hɔ:nɪt] n avispón m

horoscope ['hɔrəskəup] n horóscopo

horrible ['hɔrɪbl] adj horrible

horrid ['hɔrɪd] adj horrible, horroroso

horrify ['hɔrɪfaɪ] vt horrorizar

horror ['hɔrə*] n horror m; ~ **film** n película de horror

hors d'œuvre [ɔ:'də:vrə] n entremeses mpl

horse [hɔ:s] n caballo; **~back**: **on ~back** a caballo; ~ **chestnut** n (tree) castaño de Indias; (nut) castaña de Indias; **~man/woman** (irreg) n jinete a m/f; **~power** n caballo de (fuerza); **~racing** n carreras fpl de caballos; **~radish** n rábano picante; **~shoe** n herradura

hose [həuz] n (also: ~pipe) manguera

hospitable ['hɔspɪtəbl] adj hospitalario

hospital ['hɔspɪtl] n hospital m

hospitality [hɔspɪ'tælɪtɪ] n hospitalidad f

host [həust] n anfitrión m; (TV, RADIO) presentador m; (REL) hostia; (large number): **a ~ of** multitud de

hostage ['hɔstɪdʒ] n rehén m

hostel ['hɔstl] n hostal m; **(youth) ~** n albergue m juvenil

hostess ['həustɪs] n anfitriona f; (BRIT: air ~) azafata; (TV, RADIO) presentadora

hostile ['hɔstaɪl] adj hostil

hot [hɔt] adj caliente; (weather)

caluroso, de calor; (as opposed to warm) muy caliente; (spicy) picante; **to be** ~ (person) tener calor; (object) estar caliente; (weather) hacer calor; ~**bed** n (fig) semillero; ~ **dog** n perro caliente

hotel [hau'tel] n hotel m

hot: ~**house** n invernadero; ~ **line** n (POL) teléfono rojo; ~**ly** adv con pasión, apasionadamente; ~**water bottle** n bolsa de agua caliente

hound [haund] vt acosar ♦ n perro (de caza)

hour ['auə*] n hora; ~**ly** adj (de) cada hora

house [n haus, pl 'hauziz, vb hauz] n (gen, firm) casa; (POL) cámara; (THEATRE) sala ♦ vt (person) alojar; (collection) albergar; **on the** ~ (fig) la casa invita; ~ **arrest** n arresto domiciliario; ~**boat** n casa flotante; ~**bound** adj confinado en casa; ~**breaking** n allanamiento de morada; ~**hold** n familia; (home) casa; ~**keeper** n ama de llaves; ~**keeping** n (work) trabajos mpl domésticos; ~**keeping** (money) n dinero para gastos domésticos; ~**warming party** n fiesta de estreno de una casa; ~**wife** (irreg) n ama de casa; ~**work** n faenas fpl (de la casa)

housing ['hauziŋ] n (act) alojamiento; (houses) viviendas fpl; ~ **development**, ~ **estate** (BRIT) n urbanización f

hovel ['hɔvl] n casucha

hover ['hɔvə*] vi flotar (en el aire); ~**craft** n aerodeslizador m

how [hau] adv (in what way) cómo; ~ **are you?** ¿cómo estás?; ~ **much milk/many people?** ¿cuánta leche/gente?; ~ **much does it cost?** ¿cuánto cuesta?; ~ **long have you been here?** ¿cuánto hace que estás aquí?; ~ **old are you?** ¿cuántos años tienes?; ~ **tall is he?** ¿cómo es de alto?; ~ **is school?** ¿cómo (te) va (en) la escuela?; ~ **was the film?** ¿qué tal la película?; ~ **lovely/awful!** ¡qué

bonito/horror!

however [hau'ɛvə*] adv: ~ **I do it** lo haga como lo haga; ~ **cold it is** por mucho frío que haga; ~ **fast he runs** por muy rápido que corra; ~ **did you do it?** ¿cómo lo hiciste? ♦ conj sin embargo, no obstante

howl [haul] n aullido ♦ vi aullar; (person) dar alaridos; (wind) ulular

H.P. n abbr = **hire purchase**

h.p. abbr = **horse power**

HQ n abbr = **headquarters**

HTML n abbr (= hypertext markup language) lenguaje m de hipertexto

hub [hʌb] n (of wheel) cubo; (fig) centro

hubcap ['hʌbkæp] n tapacubos m inv

huddle ['hʌdl] vi: **to** ~ **together** acurrucarse

hue [hju:] n color m, matiz m

huff [hʌf] n: **in a** ~ enojado

hug [hʌg] vt abrazar; (thing) apretar con los brazos

huge [hju:dʒ] adj enorme

hull [hʌl] n (of ship) casco

hullo [hə'ləu] excl = **hello**

hum [hʌm] vt tararear, canturrear ♦ vi tararear, canturrear; (insect) zumbar

human ['hju:mən] adj, n humano; ~**e** [hju:'meɪn] adj humano, humanitario; ~**itarian** [hju:mænɪ'tɛəriən] adj humanitario; ~**ity** [hju:'mænɪtɪ] n humanidad f

humble ['hʌmbl] adj humilde

humdrum ['hʌmdrʌm] adj (boring) monótono, aburrido

humid ['hju:mɪd] adj húmedo

humiliate [hju:'mɪlɪeɪt] vt humillar

humorous ['hju:mərəs] adj gracioso, divertido

humour ['hju:mə*] (US **humor**) n humorismo, sentido del humor; (mood) humor m ♦ vt (person) complacer

hump [hʌmp] n (in ground) montículo; (camel's) giba

hunch [hʌntʃ] n (premonition) presentimiento; ~**back** n joroba m/f; ~**ed** adj jorobado

hundred ['hʌndrəd] num ciento;
  (before n) cien; **~s of** centenares de;
  ~weight n (BRIT) = 50.8 kg; 112 lb;
  (US) = 45.3 kg; 100 lb
hung [hʌŋ] pt, pp of **hang**
Hungarian [hʌŋˈgeəriən] adj, n
  húngaro/a m/f
Hungary ['hʌŋgəri] n Hungría
hunger ['hʌŋgə*] n hambre f ♦ vi: **to
  ~ for** (fig) tener hambre de, anhelar;
  ~ strike n huelga de hambre
hungry ['hʌŋgri] adj: **~ (for)**
  hambriento, **to be ~** tener
  hambre
hunk [hʌŋk] n (of bread etc) trozo,
  pedazo
hunt [hʌnt] vt (seek) buscar; (SPORT)
  cazar ♦ vi (search): **to ~ (for)** buscar;
  (SPORT) cazar ♦ n búsqueda; caza,
  cacería; **~er** n cazador(a) m/f; **~ing**
  n caza
hurdle ['hɜ:dl] n (SPORT) valla; (fig)
  obstáculo
hurl [hɜ:l] vt lanzar, arrojar
hurrah [hu'rɑ:] excl = **hurray**
hurray [hu'reɪ] excl ¡viva!
hurricane ['hʌrɪkən] n huracán m
hurried ['hʌrɪd] adj (rushed) hecho de
  prisa; **~ly** adv con prisa,
  apresuradamente
hurry ['hʌrɪ] n prisa ♦ vi (also: **~ up**)
  apresurarse, darse prisa ♦ vt (also: **~ up:**
  person) dar prisa a; (: work) apresurar,
  hacer de prisa; **to be in a ~** tener
  prisa
hurt [hɜ:t] (pt, pp **hurt**) vt hacer daño
  a ♦ vi doler ♦ adj lastimado; **~ful** adj
  (remark etc) hiriente
hurtle ['hɜ:tl] vi: **to ~ past** pasar
  como un rayo; **to ~ down** ir a toda
  velocidad
husband ['hʌzbənd] n marido
hush [hʌʃ] n silencio ♦ vt hacer callar;
  ~! ¡chitón!, ¡cállate!; **~ up** vt encubrir
husk [hʌsk] n (of wheat) cáscara
husky ['hʌskɪ] adj ronco ♦ n perro
  esquimal

hustle ['hʌsl] vt (hurry) dar prisa a ♦ n:
  ~ and bustle ajetreo
hut [hʌt] n cabaña; (shed) cobertizo
hutch [hʌtʃ] n conejera
hyacinth ['haɪəsɪnθ] n jacinto
hydrant ['haɪdrənt] n (also: **fire ~**)
  boca de incendios
hydraulic [haɪ'drɔ:lɪk] adj hidráulico
hydroelectric [haɪdrəu'lektrɪk] adj
  hidroeléctrico
hydrofoil ['haɪdrəfɔɪl] n aerodeslizador
  m
hydrogen ['haɪdrədʒən] n hidrógeno
hygiene ['haɪdʒi:n] n higiene f;
  hygienic [-'dʒi:nɪk] adj higiénico
hymn [hɪm] n himno
hype [haɪp] (inf) n bombardeo
  publicitario
hypermarket ['haɪpəmɑːkɪt] n
  hipermercado
hyphen ['haɪfn] n guión m
hypnotize ['hɪpnətaɪz] vt hipnotizar
hypocrisy [hɪ'pɒkrɪsɪ] n hipocresía;
  hypocrite ['hɪpəkrɪt] n hipócrita m/f;
  hypocritical [hɪpə'krɪtɪkl] adj
  hipócrita
hypothesis [haɪ'pɒθɪsɪs] n (pl
  hypotheses) n hipótesis f inv
hysteria [hɪ'stɪərɪə] n histeria;
  hysterical [-'sterɪkl] adj histérico
  (funny) para morirse de risa; **hysterics**
  [-'sterɪks] npl histeria; **to be in
  hysterics** (fig) morirse de risa

I, i

I [aɪ] pron yo
ice [aɪs] n hielo; (~ cream) helado ♦ vt
  (cake) alcorzar ♦ vi (also: **~ over**, **~ up**)
  helarse; **~berg** n iceberg m; **~box** n
  (BRIT) congelador m; (US) nevera (SP),
  refrigeradora (AM); **~ cream** n helado;
  ~ cube n cubito de hielo; **~d** adj
  (cake) escarchado; (drink) helado;
  ~ hockey n hockey m sobre hielo
Iceland ['aɪslənd] n Islandia

ice: ~ **lolly** (BRIT) n polo; ~ **rink** n pista de hielo; ~ **skating** n patinaje m sobre hielo

icicle ['aɪsɪkl] n carámbano

icing ['aɪsɪŋ] n (CULIN) alcorza; ~ **sugar** (BRIT) n azúcar m glas(eado)

icon ['aɪkɒn] n icono

icy ['aɪsɪ] adj helado

I'd [aɪd] = **I would; I had**

idea [aɪ'dɪə] n idea

ideal [aɪ'dɪəl] n ideal m ♦ adj ideal

identical [aɪ'dentɪkl] adj idéntico

identification [aɪdentɪfɪ'keɪʃən] n identificación f; **(means of)** ~ documentos mpl personales

identify [aɪ'dentɪfaɪ] vt identificar

Identikit ® [aɪ'dentɪkɪt] n: ~ **(picture)** retrato-robot m

identity [aɪ'dentɪtɪ] n identidad f; ~ **card** n carnet m de identidad

ideology [aɪdɪ'ɔlədʒɪ] n ideología

idiom ['ɪdɪəm] n modismo; **(style of speaking)** lenguaje m

idiosyncrasy [ɪdɪəʊ'sɪŋkrəsɪ] n idiosincrasia

idiot ['ɪdɪət] n idiota m/f; ~**ic** [-'ɔtɪk] adj tonto

idle ['aɪdl] adj (inactive) ocioso; (lazy) holgazán/ana; (unemployed) parado, desocupado; (machinery etc) parado; (talk etc) frívolo ♦ vi (machine) marchar en vacío

idol ['aɪdl] n ídolo; ~**ize** vt idolatrar

i.e. abbr (= that is) esto es

if [ɪf] conj si; ~ **necessary** si fuera necesario, si hiciese falta; ~ **I were you** yo en tu lugar; ~ **so/not** de ser así/si no; ~ **only I could!** ¡ojalá pudiera!; see also **as; even**

igloo ['ɪɡluː] n iglú m

ignite [ɪɡ'naɪt] vt (set fire to) encender ♦ vi encenderse

ignition [ɪɡ'nɪʃən] n (AUT: process) ignición f; (: mechanism) encendido; **to switch on/off the** ~ arrancar/apagar el motor; ~ **key** n (AUT) llave f de contacto

ignorant ['ɪɡnərənt] adj ignorante; **to be** ~ **of** ignorar

ignore [ɪɡ'nɔː*] vt (person, advice) no hacer caso de; (fact) pasar por alto

I'll [aɪl] = **I will; I shall**

ill [ɪl] adj enfermo, malo ♦ n mal m ♦ adv mal; **to be taken** ~ ponerse enfermo; ~**-advised** adj (decision) imprudente; ~**-at-ease** adj incómodo

illegal [ɪ'liːɡl] adj ilegal

illegible [ɪ'ledʒɪbl] adj ilegible

illegitimate [ɪlɪ'dʒɪtɪmət] adj ilegítimo

ill-fated adj malogrado

ill feeling n rencor m

illiterate [ɪ'lɪtərət] adj analfabeto

ill: ~**-mannered** adj mal educado; ~**ness** n enfermedad f; ~**-treat** vt maltratar

illuminate [ɪ'luːmɪneɪt] vt (room, street) iluminar, alumbrar; **illumination** [-'neɪʃən] n alumbrado; **illuminations** npl (decorative lights) iluminaciones fpl, luces fpl

illusion [ɪ'luːʒən] n ilusión f; (trick) truco

illustrate ['ɪləstreɪt] vt ilustrar

illustration [ɪlə'streɪʃən] n (act of illustrating) ilustración f; (example) ejemplo, ilustración f; (in book) lámina

illustrious [ɪ'lʌstrɪəs] adj ilustre

I'm [aɪm] = **I am**

image ['ɪmɪdʒ] n imagen f; ~**ry** [-ərɪ] n imágenes fpl

imaginary [ɪ'mædʒɪnərɪ] adj imaginario

imagination [ɪmædʒɪ'neɪʃən] n imaginación f; (inventiveness) inventiva

imaginative [ɪ'mædʒɪnətɪv] adj imaginativo

imagine [ɪ'mædʒɪn] vt imaginarse

imbalance [ɪm'bæləns] n desequilibrio

imitate ['ɪmɪteɪt] vt imitar; **imitation** [ɪmɪ'teɪʃən] n imitación f; (copy) copia

immaculate [ɪ'mækjulət] adj inmaculado

immaterial [ɪmə'tɪərɪəl] adj (unimportant) sin importancia

immature [ɪmə'tjuə*] adj (person)
inmaduro

immediate [ɪ'miːdɪət] adj inmediato;
(pressing) urgente, apremiante;
(nearest: family) próximo;
(: neighbourhood) inmediato; **~ly** adv
(at once) en seguida; (directly)
inmediatamente; **~ly next to** muy
junto a

immense [ɪ'mɛns] adj inmenso,
enorme; (importance) enorme

immerse [ɪ'mɜːs] vt (submerge)
sumergir; **to be ~d in** (fig) estar
absorto en

immersion heater [ɪ'mɜːʃən-] (BRIT)
n calentador m de inmersión

immigrant ['ɪmɪɡrənt] n inmigrante
m/f; **immigration** [ɪmɪ'ɡreɪʃən] n
inmigración f

imminent ['ɪmɪnənt] adj inminente

immobile [ɪ'məʊbaɪl] adj inmóvil

immoral [ɪ'mɒrl] adj inmoral

immortal [ɪ'mɔːtl] adj inmortal

immune [ɪ'mjuːn] adj: **~ (to)** inmune
(a); **immunity** n (MED, of diplomat)
inmunidad f

immunize [ɪ'mjuːnaɪz] vt inmunizar

impact ['ɪmpækt] n impacto

impair [ɪm'pɛə*] vt perjudicar

impart [ɪm'pɑːt] vt comunicar;
(flavour) proporcionar

impartial [ɪm'pɑːʃl] adj imparcial

impassable [ɪm'pɑːsəbl] adj (barrier)
infranqueable; (river, road) intransitable

impassive [ɪm'pæsɪv] adj impasible

impatience [ɪm'peɪʃəns] n impaciencia

impatient [ɪm'peɪʃənt] adj impaciente;
to get or **grow ~** impacientarse

impeccable [ɪm'pekəbl] adj impecable

impede [ɪm'piːd] vt estorbar

impediment [ɪm'pedɪmənt] n
obstáculo, estorbo; (also: speech ~)
defecto (del habla)

impending [ɪm'pendɪŋ] adj inminente

imperative [ɪm'perətɪv] adj (tone)
imperioso; (need) imprescindible ♦ n
(LING) imperativo

imperfect [ɪm'pɜːfɪkt] adj (goods etc)

defectuoso ♦ n (LING: also: ~ tense)
imperfecto

imperial [ɪm'pɪərɪəl] adj imperial

impersonal [ɪm'pɜːsənl] adj
impersonal

impersonate [ɪm'pɜːsəneɪt] vt hacerse
pasar por; (THEATRE) imitar

impertinent [ɪm'pɜːtɪnənt] adj
impertinente, insolente

impervious [ɪm'pɜːvɪəs] adj
impermeable; (fig): **~ to** insensible a

impetuous [ɪm'petjuəs] adj impetuoso

impetus ['ɪmpətəs] n ímpetu m; (fig)
impulso

impinge [ɪm'pɪndʒ]: **to ~ on** vt fus
(affect) afectar a

implement [n 'ɪmplɪmənt, vb
'ɪmplɪment] n herramienta; (for
cooking) utensilio ♦ vt (regulation)
hacer efectivo; (plan) realizar

implicit [ɪm'plɪsɪt] adj implícito; (belief,
trust) absoluto

imply [ɪm'plaɪ] vt (involve) suponer;
(hint) dar a entender que

impolite [ɪmpə'laɪt] adj mal educado

import [vb ɪm'pɔːt, n 'ɪmpɔːt] vt
importar ♦ n (COMM) importación f;
(: article) producto importado;
(meaning) significado, sentido

importance [ɪm'pɔːtəns] n
importancia

important [ɪm'pɔːtənt] adj
importante; **it's not ~** no importa, no
tiene importancia

importer [ɪm'pɔːtə*] n importador(a)
m/f

impose [ɪm'pəʊz] vt imponer ♦ vi: **to
~ on sb** abusar de uno; **imposing**
adj imponente, impresionante

imposition [ɪmpə'zɪʃn] n (of tax etc)
imposición f; **to be an ~ on** (person)
molestar a

impossible [ɪm'pɒsɪbl] adj imposible;
(person) insoportable

impotent ['ɪmpətənt] adj impotente

impound [ɪm'paʊnd] vt embargar

impoverished [ɪm'pɒvərɪʃt] adj

necesitado

impractical [ɪm'præktɪkl] *adj* (*person, plan*) poco práctico

imprecise [ɪmprɪ'saɪs] *adj* impreciso

impregnable [ɪm'prɛgnəbl] *adj* (*castle*) inexpugnable

impress [ɪm'prɛs] *vt* impresionar; (*mark*) estampar; **to ~ sth on sb** hacer entender algo a uno

impression [ɪm'prɛʃən] *n* impresión *f*; (*imitation*) imitación *f*; **to be under the ~ that** tener la impresión de que; **~ist** *n* impresionista *m/f*

impressive [ɪm'prɛsɪv] *adj* impresionante

imprint ['ɪmprɪnt] *n* (*outline*) huella, (*PUBLISHING*) pie *m* de imprenta

imprison [ɪm'prɪzn] *vt* encarcelar; **~ment** *n* encarcelamiento; (*term of ~ment*) cárcel *f*

improbable [ɪm'prɔbəbl] *adj* improbable, inverosímil

improper [ɪm'prɔpə*] *adj* (*unsuitable: conduct etc*) incorrecto; (*: activities*) deshonesto

improve [ɪm'pruːv] *vt* mejorar; (*foreign language*) perfeccionar ♦ *vi* mejorarse; **~ment** *n* mejoramiento; perfección *f*, progreso

improvise ['ɪmprəvaɪz] *vt, vi* improvisar

impulse ['ɪmpʌls] *n* impulso; **to act on ~** obrar sin reflexión; **impulsive** [-'pʌlsɪv] *adj* irreflexivo

impure [ɪm'pjuə*] *adj* (*adulterated*) adulterado; (*morally*) impuro; **impurity** *n* impureza

─ KEYWORD ─

in [ɪn] *prep* **1** (*indicating place, position, with place names*) en; **~ the house/ garden** en (la) casa/el jardín; **~ here/ there** aquí/ahí o allí dentro; **~ London/England** en Londres/ Inglaterra

2 (*indicating time*) en; **~ spring** en (la) primavera; **~ the afternoon** por la tarde; **at 4 o'clock ~ the afternoon** a las 4 de la tarde; **I did it ~ 3 hours/days** lo hice en 3 horas/días; **I'll see you ~ 2 weeks** *or* **~ 2 weeks' time** te veré dentro de 2 semanas

3 (*indicating manner etc*) en; **~ a loud/soft voice** en voz alta/baja; **~ pencil/ink** a lápiz/bolígrafo; **the boy ~ the blue shirt** el chico de la camisa azul

4 (*indicating circumstances*): **~ the sun/shade/rain** al sol/a la sombra/ bajo la lluvia; **a change ~ policy** un cambio de política

5 (*indicating mood, state*): **~ tears** en lágrimas, llorando; **~ anger/despair** enfadado/desesperado; **to live ~ luxury** vivir lujosamente

6 (*with ratios, numbers*): **1 ~ 10 households, 1 household ~ 10** una de cada 10 familias; **20 pence ~ the pound** 20 peniques por libra; **they lined up ~ twos** se alinearon de dos en dos

7 (*referring to people, works*) en; entre; **the disease is common ~ children** la enfermedad es común entre los niños; **~ (the works of) Dickens** en (las obras de) Dickens

8 (*indicating profession etc*): **to be ~ teaching** estar en la enseñanza

9 (*after superlative*) de; **the best pupil ~ the class** el/la mejor alumno/a de la clase

10 (*with present participle*): **~ saying this** al decir esto

♦ *adv*: **to be ~** (*person: at home*) estar en casa; (*work*) estar; (*train, ship, plane*) haber llegado; (*in fashion*) estar de moda; **she'll be ~ later today** llegará más tarde hoy; **to ask sb ~** hacer pasar a uno; **to run/limp etc ~** entrar corriendo/cojeando *etc*

♦ *n*: **the ~s and outs** (*of proposal, situation etc*) los detalles

in. *abbr* = inch

inability [ɪnəˈbɪlɪtɪ] *n*: **~ (to do)** incapacidad *f* (de hacer)

inaccurate [ɪnˈækjʊrət] *adj* inexacto, incorrecto

inadequate [ɪnˈædɪkwət] *adj* (income, reply etc) insuficiente; (person) incapaz

inadvertently [ɪnədˈvɜːtntlɪ] *adv* por descuido

inadvisable [ɪnədˈvaɪzəbl] *adj* poco aconsejable

inane [ɪˈneɪn] *adj* necio, fatuo

inanimate [ɪnˈænɪmət] *adj* inanimado

inappropriate [ɪnəˈprəʊprɪət] *adj* inadecuado; (improper) poco oportuno

inarticulate [ɪnɑːˈtɪkjʊlət] *adj* (person) incapaz de expresarse; (speech) mal pronunciado

inasmuch as [ɪnəzˈmʌtʃ-] *conj* puesto que, ya que

inauguration [ɪnɔːgjʊˈreɪʃən] *n* ceremonia de apertura

inborn [ɪnˈbɔːn] *adj* (quality) innato

inbred [ɪnˈbred] *adj* innato; (family) engendrado por endogamia

Inc. *abbr* (US: = incorporated) S.A.

incapable [ɪnˈkeɪpəbl] *adj* incapaz

incapacitate [ɪnkəˈpæsɪteɪt] *vt*: **to ~ sb** incapacitar a uno

incense [*n* ˈɪnsens, *vb* ɪnˈsens] *n* incienso ♦ *vt* (anger) indignar, encolerizar

incentive [ɪnˈsentɪv] *n* incentivo, estímulo

incessant [ɪnˈsesnt] *adj* incesante, continuo; **~ly** *adv* constantemente

incest [ˈɪnsest] *n* incesto

inch [ɪntʃ] *n* pulgada; **to be within an ~ of** estar a dos dedos de; **he didn't give an ~** no dio concesión alguna

incident [ˈɪnsɪdnt] *n* incidente *m*

incidental [ɪnsɪˈdentl] *adj* accesorio; **~ to** relacionado con; **~ly** [-ˈdentlɪ] *adv* (by the way) a propósito

incite [ɪnˈsaɪt] *vt* provocar

inclination [ɪnklɪˈneɪʃən] *n* (tendency)

tendencia, inclinación *f*; (desire) deseo; (disposition) propensión *f*

incline [*n* ˈɪnklaɪn, *vb* ɪnˈklaɪn] *n* pendiente *m*, cuesta ♦ *vt* (head) poner de lado ♦ *vi* inclinarse; **to be ~d to** (tend) ser propenso a

include [ɪnˈkluːd] *vt* (incorporate) incluir; (in letter) adjuntar; **including** *prep* incluso, inclusive

inclusion [ɪnˈkluːʒən] *n* inclusión *f*

inclusive [ɪnˈkluːsɪv] *adj* inclusivo; **~ of tax** incluidos los impuestos

income [ˈɪnkʌm] *n* (earned) ingresos *mpl*; (from property etc) renta; (from investment etc) rédito; **~ tax** *n* impuesto sobre la renta

incoming [ˈɪnkʌmɪŋ] *adj* (flight, government etc) entrante

incomparable [ɪnˈkɒmpərəbl] *adj* incomparable, sin par

incompatible [ɪnkəmˈpætɪbl] *adj* incompatible

incompetent [ɪnˈkɒmpɪtənt] *adj* incompetente

incomplete [ɪnkəmˈpliːt] *adj* (partial) achievement etc) incompleto; (unfinished: painting etc) inacabado

incongruous [ɪnˈkɒŋgrʊəs] *adj* (strange) discordante; (inappropriate) incongruente

inconsiderate [ɪnkənˈsɪdərət] *adj* desconsiderado

inconsistent [ɪnkənˈsɪstənt] *adj* inconsecuente; (contradictory) incongruente; **~ with** (que) no concuerda con

inconspicuous [ɪnkənˈspɪkjʊəs] *adj* (colour, building etc) discreto; (person) que llama poco la atención

inconvenience [ɪnkənˈviːnjəns] *n* (no trouble) molestia, incomodidad *f* ♦ *vt* incomodar

inconvenient [ɪnkənˈviːnjənt] *adj* incómodo, poco práctico; (time, place, visitor) inoportuno

incorporate [ɪnˈkɔːpəreɪt] *vt* incorporar; (contain) comprender (*add*) agregar; **~d** *adj*: **~d company** (*US*) ≈ sociedad *f* anónima

incorrect [ɪnkəˈrɛkt] *adj* incorrecto

increase [*n* ˈɪnkriːs, *vb* ɪnˈkriːs] *n* aumento ♦ *vi* aumentar; (*grow*) crecer; (*price*) subir ♦ *vt* aumentar; (*price*) subir; **increasing** *adj* creciente; **increasingly** *adv* cada vez más, más y más

incredible [ɪnˈkrɛdɪbl] *adj* increíble

incubator [ˈɪnkjubeɪtə*] *n* incubadora

incumbent [ɪnˈkʌmbənt] *adj*: **it is ~ on him to ...** le incumbe ...

incur [ɪnˈkɜː*] *vt* (*expenditure*) incurrir; (*loss*) sufrir; (*anger, disapproval*) provocar

indebted [ɪnˈdɛtɪd] *adj*: **to be ~ to sb** estar agradecido a uno

indecent [ɪnˈdiːsnt] *adj* indecente; **~ assault** (*BRIT*) *n* atentado contra el pudor; **~ exposure** *n* exhibicionismo

indecisive [ɪndɪˈsaɪsɪv] *adj* indeciso

indeed [ɪnˈdiːd] *adv* efectivamente, en realidad; (*in fact*) en efecto; (*furthermore*) es más; **yes ~!** ¡claro que sí!

indefinitely [ɪnˈdɛfɪnɪtlɪ] *adv* (*wait*) indefinidamente

indemnity [ɪnˈdɛmnɪtɪ] *n* (*insurance*) indemnidad *f*; (*compensation*) indemnización *f*

independence [ɪndɪˈpɛndns] *n* independencia

Independence Day

El cuatro de julio es **Independence Day,** *la fiesta nacional de Estados Unidos, que se celebra en conmemoración de la Declaración de Independencia, escrita por Thomas Jefferson y aprobada en 1776. En ella se proclamaba la independencia total de Gran Bretaña de las trece colonias americanas que serían el origen de los Estados Unidos de América.*

---

independent [ɪndɪˈpɛndənt] *adj*

independiente

index [ˈɪndɛks] (*pl* **~es**) *n* (*in book*) índice *m*; (: *in library etc*) catálogo; (*pl* **indices**: *ratio, sign*) exponente *m*; **~ card** *n* ficha; **~ed** (*US*) *adj* = **~linked**; **~ finger** *n* índice *m*; **~linked** (*BRIT*) *adj* vinculado al índice del coste de la vida

India [ˈɪndɪə] *n* la India; **~n** *adj*, *n* indio/a *m/f*; **Red ~n** *n* piel roja *m/f*; **~Ocean** *n*: **the ~n Ocean** el Océano Índico

indicate [ˈɪndɪkeɪt] *vt* indicar; **indication** [-ˈkeɪʃən] *n* indicio, señal *f*; **indicative** [ɪnˈdɪkətɪv] *adj*: **to be indicative of** indicar; **indicator** *n* indicador *m*; (*AUT*) intermitente *m*

indices [ˈɪndɪsiːz] *npl of* **index**

indictment [ɪnˈdaɪtmənt] *n* acusación *f*

indifferent [ɪnˈdɪfrənt] *adj* indiferente; (*mediocre*) regular

indigenous [ɪnˈdɪdʒɪnəs] *adj* indígena

indigestion [ɪndɪˈdʒɛstʃən] *n* indigestión *f*

indignant [ɪnˈdɪɡnənt] *adj*: **to be ~ at sth/with sb** indignarse por algo/con uno

indigo [ˈɪndɪɡəu] *adj* de color añil ♦ *n* añil *m*

indirect [ɪndɪˈrɛkt] *adj* indirecto

indiscreet [ɪndɪsˈkriːt] *adj* indiscreto, imprudente

indiscriminate [ɪndɪsˈkrɪmɪnət] *adj* indiscriminado

indisputable [ɪndɪsˈpjuːtəbl] *adj* incontestable

indistinct [ɪndɪsˈtɪŋkt] *adj* (*noise, memory etc*) confuso

individual [ɪndɪˈvɪdjuəl] *n* individuo ♦ *adj* individual; (*personal*) personal; (*particular*) particular; **~ly** *adv* (*singly*) individualmente

indoctrinate [ɪnˈdɔktrɪneɪt] *vt* adoctrinar

indoor [ˈɪndɔː*] *adj* (*swimming pool*) cubierto; (*plant*) de interior; (*sport*) bajo cubierta; **~s** [ɪn'dɔːz] *adv* dentro

induce [ɪn'djuːs] *vt* inducir, persuadir; (*bring about*) producir; (*birth*) provocar; **~ment** *n* (*incentive*) incentivo; (*pej: bribe*) soborno

indulge [ɪn'dʌldʒ] *vt* (*whim*) satisfacer; (*person*) complacer; (*child*) mimar ♦ *vi*: **to ~ in** darse el gusto de; **~nce** *n* vicio; (*leniency*) indulgencia; **~nt** *adj* indulgente

industrial [ɪn'dʌstrɪəl] *adj* industrial; **~ action** *n* huelga; **~ estate** (*BRIT*) *n* polígono (*SP*) *o* zona (*AM*) industrial; **~ist** *n* industrial *m/f*; **~ize** *vt* industrializar; **~ park** (*US*) *n* = **~ estate**

industrious [ɪn'dʌstrɪəs] *adj* trabajador(a); (*student*) aplicado

industry ['ɪndəstrɪ] *n* industria; (*diligence*) aplicación *f*

inebriated [ɪ'niːbrɪeɪtɪd] *adj* borracho

inedible [ɪn'edɪbl] *adj* incomible; (*poisonous*) no comestible

ineffective [ɪnɪ'fektɪv] *adj* ineficaz, inútil

ineffectual [ɪnɪ'fektʃuəl] *adj* = **ineffective**

inefficient [ɪnɪ'fɪʃənt] *adj* ineficaz, ineficiente

inept [ɪ'nept] *adj* incompetente

inequality [ɪnɪ'kwɔlɪtɪ] *n* desigualdad *f*

inert [ɪ'nɜːt] *adj* inerte, inactivo; (*immobile*) inmóvil

inescapable [ɪnɪ'skeɪpəbl] *adj* ineludible

inevitable [ɪn'evɪtəbl] *adj* inevitable; **inevitably** *adv* inevitablemente

inexcusable [ɪnɪks'kjuːzəbl] *adj* imperdonable

inexpensive [ɪnɪk'spensɪv] *adj* económico

inexperienced [ɪnɪk'spɪərɪənst] *adj* inexperto

infallible [ɪn'fælɪbl] *adj* infalible

infamous ['ɪnfəməs] *adj* infame

infancy ['ɪnfənsɪ] *n* infancia

infant ['ɪnfənt] *n* niño/a; (*baby*) niño

pequeño, bebé *m*; (*pej*) aniñado

infantry ['ɪnfəntrɪ] *n* infantería

infant school (*BRIT*) *n* parvulario

infatuated [ɪn'fætjueɪtɪd] *adj*: **~ with** (*in love*) loco por

infatuation [ɪnfætju'eɪʃən] *n* enamoramiento, pasión *f*

infect [ɪn'fekt] *vt* (*wound*) infectar; (*food*) contaminar; (*person, animal*) contagiar; **~ion** [ɪn'fekʃən] *n* infección *f*; (*fig*) contagio; **~ious** [ɪn'fekʃəs] *adj* (*also fig*) contagioso

infer [ɪn'fɜː*] *vt* deducir, inferir

inferior [ɪn'fɪərɪə*] *adj*, *n* inferior *m/f*; **~ity** [-rɪ'ɔrɪtɪ] *n* inferioridad *f*

infertile [ɪn'fɜːtaɪl] *adj* estéril; (*person*) infecundo

infested [ɪn'festɪd] *adj*: **~ with** plagado de

in-fighting *n* (*fig*) lucha(s) *f(pl)* interna(s)

infinite ['ɪnfɪnɪt] *adj* infinito

infinitive [ɪn'fɪnɪtɪv] *n* infinitivo

infinity [ɪn'fɪnɪtɪ] *n* infinito; (*an ~*) infinidad *f*

infirmary [ɪn'fɜːmərɪ] *n* hospital *m*

inflamed [ɪn'fleɪmd] *adj*: **to become ~** inflamarse

inflammable [ɪn'flæməbl] *adj* inflamable

inflammation [ɪnflə'meɪʃən] *n* inflamación *f*

inflatable [ɪn'fleɪtəbl] *adj* (*ball, boat*) inflable

inflate [ɪn'fleɪt] *vt* (*tyre, price etc*) inflar; (*fig*) hinchar; **inflation** [ɪn'fleɪʃən] *n* (*ECON*) inflación *f*

inflexible [ɪn'fleksəbl] *adj* (*rule*) rígido; (*person*) inflexible

inflict [ɪn'flɪkt] *vt*: **to ~ sth on sb** infligir algo en uno

influence ['ɪnfluəns] *n* influencia ♦ *vt* influir en, influenciar; **under the ~ of alcohol** en estado de embriaguez; **~tial** [-'enʃl] *adj* influyente

influenza [ɪnflu'enzə] *n* gripe *f*

influx ['ɪnflʌks] *n* afluencia

inform [ɪnˈfɔːm] vt: **to ~ sb of sth**
informar a uno sobre de algo ♦ vi:
to ~ on sb delatar a uno

informal [ɪnˈfɔːməl] adj (manner, tone)
familiar; (dress, interview, occasion)
informal; (visit, meeting) extraoficial;
~ity [-ˈmælɪtɪ] n informalidad f;
sencillez f

informant [ɪnˈfɔːmənt] n informante
m/f

information [ɪnfəˈmeɪʃən] n
información f; (knowledge)
conocimientos mpl; **a piece of ~** un
dato; **~ desk** n (mostrador m de)
información f; **~ office** n información f

informative [ɪnˈfɔːmətɪv] adj
informativo

informer [ɪnˈfɔːmə*] n (also: police ~)
soplón/ona m/f

infra-red [ɪnfrəˈred] adj infrarrojo

infrastructure [ˈɪnfrəstrʌktʃə*] n (of
system etc) infraestructura f

infringe [ɪnˈfrɪndʒ] vt infringir, violar
♦ vi: **to ~ on** abusar de; **~ment** n
infracción f; (of rights) usurpación f

infuriating [ɪnˈfjuərɪeɪtɪŋ] adj (habit,
noise) enloquecedor(a)

ingenious [ɪnˈdʒiːnjəs] adj ingenioso;
ingenuity [-dʒɪˈnjuːɪtɪ] n ingeniosidad
f

ingenuous [ɪnˈdʒenjuəs] adj ingenuo

ingot [ˈɪŋɡət] n lingote m, barra

ingrained [ɪnˈɡreɪnd] adj arraigado

ingratiate [ɪnˈɡreɪʃɪeɪt] vt: **to ~ o.s.
with** congraciarse con

ingredient [ɪnˈɡriːdɪənt] n ingrediente
m

inhabit [ɪnˈhæbɪt] vt vivir en; **~ant** n
habitante m/f

inhale [ɪnˈheɪl] vt inhalar ♦ vi (breathe
in) aspirar; (in smoking) tragar

inherent [ɪnˈhɪərənt] adj: **~ in** or **to**
inherente a

inherit [ɪnˈherɪt] vt heredar; **~ance** n
herencia f; (fig) patrimonio

inhibit [ɪnˈhɪbɪt] vt inhibir, impedir;
~ed adj (PSYCH) cohibido; **~ion**

[-ˈbɪʃən] n cohibición f

inhospitable [ɪnhɔsˈpɪtəbl] adj
(person) inhospitalario; (place)
inhóspito

inhuman [ɪnˈhjuːmən] adj inhumano

initial [ɪˈnɪʃl] adj primero ♦ n inicial f
♦ vt firmar con las iniciales; **~s** npl (as
signature) iniciales fpl; (abbreviation)
siglas fpl; **~ly** adv al principio

initiate [ɪˈnɪʃɪeɪt] vt iniciar; **to
~ proceedings against sb** (LAW)
entablar proceso contra uno

initiative [ɪˈnɪʃətɪv] n iniciativa

inject [ɪnˈdʒekt] vt inyectar; **to ~ sb
with sth** inyectar algo a uno; **~ion**
[ɪnˈdʒekʃən] n inyección f

injunction [ɪnˈdʒʌŋkʃən] n interdicto

injure [ˈɪndʒə*] vt (hurt) herir, lastimar;
(fig: reputation etc) perjudicar; **~d** adj
(person, arm) herido, lastimado; **injury**
n herida, lesión f; (wrong) perjuicio,
daño; **injury time** n (SPORT) (tiempo
de) descuento

injustice [ɪnˈdʒʌstɪs] n injusticia

ink [ɪŋk] n tinta

inkling [ˈɪŋklɪŋ] n sospecha; (idea) idea

inlaid [ˈɪnleɪd] adj (with wood, gems
etc) incrustado

inland [adj ˈɪnlənd, adv ɪnˈlænd] adj
(waterway, port etc) interior ♦ adv tierra
adentro; **I~ Revenue** (BRIT) n
departamento de impuestos; ≈
Hacienda (SP)

in-laws npl suegros mpl

inlet [ˈɪnlɛt] n (GEO) ensenada, cala;
(TECH) admisión f, entrada

inmate [ˈɪnmeɪt] n (in prison) preso/a;
presidiario/a; (in asylum) internado/a

inn [ɪn] n posada, mesón m

innate [ɪˈneɪt] adj innato

inner [ˈɪnə*] adj (courtyard, calm)
interior; (feelings) íntimo; **~ city** n
barrios deprimidos del centro de una
ciudad; **~ tube** n (of tyre) cámara (SP),
llanta (AM)

innings [ˈɪnɪŋz] n (CRICKET) entrada,
turno

innocent [ˈɪnəsnt] *adj* inocente
innocuous [ɪˈnɒkjuəs] *adj* inocuo
innovation [ɪnəuˈveɪʃən] *n* novedad *f*
innuendo [ɪnjuˈɛndəu] (*pl* **-es**) *n* indirecta
inoculation [ɪnɒkjuˈleɪʃən] *n* inoculación *f*
in-patient *n* paciente *m/f* interno/a *f*
input [ˈɪnput] *n* entrada; (*of resources*) inversión *f*; (*COMPUT*) entrada de datos
inquest [ˈɪnkwɛst] *n* (*coroner's*) encuesta judicial
inquire [ɪnˈkwaɪə*] *vi* preguntar ♦ *vt*: **to ~ whether** preguntar si; **to ~ about** (*person*) preguntar por; (*fact*) informarse de; **~ into** *vt fus* investigar, indagar; **inquiry** *n* pregunta; (*investigation*) investigación *f*, pesquisa; "**Inquiries**" "Información"; **inquiry office** (*BRIT*) *n* oficina de información
inquisitive [ɪnˈkwɪzɪtɪv] *adj* (*curious*) curioso
ins. *abbr* = **inches**
insane [ɪnˈseɪn] *adj* loco; (*MED*) demente
insanity [ɪnˈsænɪtɪ] *n* demencia, locura
inscription [ɪnˈskrɪpʃən] *n* inscripción *f*; (*in book*) dedicatoria
inscrutable [ɪnˈskruːtəbl] *adj* inescrutable, insondable
insect [ˈɪnsɛkt] *n* insecto; **~icide** [ɪnˈsɛktɪsaɪd] *n* insecticida *m*; **~ repellent** *n* loción *f* contra insectos
insecure [ɪnsɪˈkjuə*] *adj* inseguro
insemination [ɪnsɛmɪˈneɪʃən] *n*: **artificial ~** inseminación *f* artificial
insensitive [ɪnˈsɛnsɪtɪv] *adj* insensible
insert [*vb* ɪnˈsɜːt, *n* ˈɪnsɜːt] *vt* (*into sth*) introducir ♦ *n* encarte *m*; **~ion** [ɪnˈsɜːʃən] *n* inserción *f*
in-service [ˈɪnsɜːvɪs] *adj* (*training, course*) a cargo de la empresa
inshore [ɪnˈʃɔː*] *adj* de bajura ♦ *adv* (*be*) cerca de la orilla; (*move*) hacia la orilla
inside [ɪnˈsaɪd] *n* interior *m* ♦ *adj* interior, interno ♦ *adv* (*be*) (por)

dentro; (*go*) hacia dentro ♦ *prep* dentro de; (*of time*): **~ 10 minutes** en menos de 10 minutos; **~s** *npl* (*inf: stomach*) tripas *fpl*; **~ information** *n* información *f* confidencial; **~ lane** *n* (*AUT: in Britain*) carril *m* izquierdo; (: *in US, Europe etc*) carril *m* derecho; **~ out** *adv* (*turn*) al revés; (*know*) a fondo
insider dealing, insider trading *n* (*STOCK EXCHANGE*) abuso de información privilegiada
insight [ˈɪnsaɪt] *n* perspicacia
insignificant [ɪnsɪgˈnɪfɪknt] *adj* insignificante
insincere [ɪnsɪnˈsɪə*] *adj* poco sincero
insinuate [ɪnˈsɪnjueɪt] *vt* insinuar
insipid [ɪnˈsɪpɪd] *adj* soso, insulso
insist [ɪnˈsɪst] *vi* insistir; **to ~ on** insistir en; **to ~ that** insistir en que; (*claim*) exigir que; **~ent** *adj* insistente; (*noise, action*) persistente
insole [ˈɪnsəul] *n* plantilla
insolent [ˈɪnsələnt] *adj* insolente, descarado
insomnia [ɪnˈsɒmnɪə] *n* insomnio
inspect [ɪnˈspɛkt] *vt* inspeccionar, examinar; (*troops*) pasar revista a; **~ion** [ɪnˈspɛkʃən] *n* inspección *f*, examen *m*; (*of troops*) revista; **~or** *n* inspector(a) *m/f*; (*BRIT: on buses, trains*) revisor(a) *m/f*
inspiration [ɪnspəˈreɪʃən] *n* inspiración *f*; **inspire** [ɪnˈspaɪə*] *vt* inspirar
instability [ɪnstəˈbɪlɪtɪ] *n* inestabilidad *f*
install [ɪnˈstɔːl] *vt* instalar; (*official*) nombrar; **~ation** [ɪnstəˈleɪʃən] *n* instalación *f*
instalment [ɪnˈstɔːlmənt] (*US* **installment**) *n* plazo; (*of story*) entrega; (*of TV serial etc*) capítulo; **in ~s** (*pay, receive*) a plazos
instance [ˈɪnstəns] *n* ejemplo, caso; **for ~** por ejemplo; **in the first ~** en primer lugar
instant [ˈɪnstənt] *n* instante *m*, momento ♦ *adj* inmediato; (*coffee etc*)

instantáneo; **~ly** adv en seguida

instead [ɪn'sted] adv en cambio; **~ of** en lugar de, en vez de

instep ['ɪnstep] n empeine m

instil [ɪn'stɪl] vt: **to ~ sth into** inculcar algo a

instinct ['ɪnstɪŋkt] n instinto

institute ['ɪnstɪtjuːt] n instituto; (professional body) colegio ♦ vt (begin) iniciar, empezar; (proceedings) entablar; (system, rule) establecer

institution [ɪnstɪ'tjuːʃən] n institución f; (MED: home) asilo; (: asylum) manicomio; (of system etc) establecimiento; (of custom) iniciación f

instruct [ɪn'strʌkt] vt: **to ~ sb in sth** instruir a uno en o sobre algo; **to ~ sb to do sth** dar instrucciones a uno de hacer algo; **~ion** [-ʃən] n (teaching) instrucción f; **~ions** npl (orders) órdenes fpl; **~ions (for use)** modo de empleo; **~or** n instructor(a) m/f

instrument ['ɪnstrəmənt] n instrumento; **~al** [-'mentl] adj (MUS) instrumental; **to be ~al in** ser (el) artífice de; **~ panel** n tablero (de instrumentos)

insufficient [ɪnsə'fɪʃənt] adj insuficiente

insular ['ɪnsjʊlə*] adj insular; (person) estrecho de miras

insulate ['ɪnsjuleɪt] vt aislar; **insulation** [-'leɪʃən] n aislamiento

insulin ['ɪnsjʊlɪn] n insulina

insult [n 'ɪnsʌlt, vb ɪn'sʌlt] n insulto ♦ vt insultar; **~ing** adj insultante

insurance [ɪn'ʃuərəns] n seguro; **fire/ life ~** seguro contra incendios/sobre la vida; **~ agent** n agente m/f de seguros; **~ policy** n póliza (de seguros)

insure [ɪn'ʃuə*] vt asegurar

intact [ɪn'tækt] adj íntegro, intacto; (unharmed) intacto

intake ['ɪnteɪk] n (of food) ingestión f; (of air) consumo; (BRIT: SCOL): **an ~ of 200 a year** 200 matriculados al año

integral ['ɪntɪɡrəl] adj (whole) íntegro; (part) integrante

integrate ['ɪntɪɡreɪt] vt integrar ♦ vi integrarse

integrity [ɪn'teɡrɪtɪ] n honradez f, rectitud f

intellect ['ɪntəlekt] n intelecto; **~ual** [-'lektjuəl] adj, n intelectual m/f

intelligence [ɪn'telɪdʒəns] n inteligencia

intelligent [ɪn'telɪdʒənt] adj inteligente

intelligible [ɪn'telɪdʒɪbl] adj inteligible, comprensible

intend [ɪn'tend] vt (gift etc): **to ~ sth for** destinar algo a; **to ~ to do sth** tener intención de o pensar hacer algo

intense [ɪn'tens] adj intenso; **~ly** adv (extremely) sumamente

intensify [ɪn'tensɪfaɪ] vt intensificar; (increase) aumentar

intensive [ɪn'tensɪv] adj intensivo; **~ care unit** n unidad f de vigilancia intensiva

intent [ɪn'tent] n propósito; (LAW) premeditación f ♦ adj (absorbed) absorto; (attentive) atento; **to all ~s and purposes** prácticamente; **to be ~ on doing sth** estar resuelto a hacer algo

intention [ɪn'tenʃən] n intención f, propósito; **~al** adj deliberado; **~ally** adv a propósito

intently [ɪn'tentlɪ] adv atentamente, fijamente

interact [ɪntər'ækt] vi influirse mutuamente; **~ive** adj (COMPUT) interactivo

interchange ['ɪntətʃeɪndʒ] n intercambio; (on motorway) intersección f; **~able** adj intercambiable

intercom ['ɪntəkɒm] n interfono

intercourse ['ɪntəkɔːs] n (sexual) relaciones fpl sexuales

interest ['ɪntrɪst] n (also COMM) interés m ♦ vt interesar; **to be ~ed in**

interesarse por; **~ing** adj interesante;
~ rate n tipo o tasa de interés

interface ['ɪntəfeɪs] n (COMPUT)
junción f

interfere [ɪntə'fɪə*] vi: **to ~ in**
entrometerse en; **to ~ with** (hinder)
estorbar; (damage) estropear

interference [ɪntə'fɪərəns] n
intromisión f; (RADIO, TV) interferencia

interim ['ɪntərɪm] n: **in the ~** en el
ínterin ♦ adj provisional

interior [ɪn'tɪərɪə*] n interior m ♦ adj
interior; **~ designer** n interiorista m/f

interjection [ɪntə'dʒekʃən] n
interposición f; (LING) interjección f

interlock [ɪntə'lɔk] vi entrelazarse

interlude ['ɪntəluːd] n intervalo;
(THEATRE) intermedio

intermediate [ɪntə'miːdɪət] adj
intermedio

intermission [ɪntə'mɪʃən] n
intermisión f; (THEATRE) descanso

intern [vb ɪn'təːn, n 'ɪntəːn] vt internar
♦ n (US) interno/a

internal [ɪn'təːnl] adj (layout, pipes,
security) interior; (injury, structure,
memo) internal; **~ly** adv: **"not to be
taken ~ly"** "uso externo";
I~ Revenue Service (US) n
departamento de impuestos; ≈
Hacienda (SP)

international [ɪntə'næʃənl] adj
internacional ♦ n (BRIT: match) partido
internacional

Internet ['ɪntənet] n: **the ~** Internet m
or f; **~ café** n cibercafé m; **~ Service
Provider** n proveedor m de (acceso a)
Internet

interplay ['ɪntəpleɪ] n interacción f

interpret [ɪn'təːprɪt] vt interpretar;
(translate) traducir; (understand)
entender ♦ vi hacer de intérprete; **~er** n
intérprete m/f

interrogate [ɪn'terəʊgeɪt] vt
interrogar; **interrogation** [-'geɪʃən] n
interrogatorio

interrupt [ɪntə'rʌpt] vt, vi interrumpir;

~ion [-'rʌpʃən] n interrupción f

intersect [ɪntə'sekt] vi (roads) cruzarse;
~ion [-'sekʃən] n (of roads) cruce m

intersperse [ɪntə'spəːs] vt: **to ~ with**
salpicar de

intertwine [ɪntə'twaɪn] vt entrelazarse

interval ['ɪntəvl] n intervalo; (BRIT:
THEATRE, SPORT) descanso; (: SCOL)
recreo; **at ~s** a ratos, de vez en
cuando

intervene [ɪntə'viːn] vi intervenir;
(event) interponerse; (time) transcurrir;
intervention n intervención f

interview [ɪn'təvjuː] n entrevista ♦ vt
entrevistarse con; **~er** n
entrevistador(a) m/f

intestine [ɪn'testɪn] n intestino

intimacy ['ɪntɪməsɪ] n intimidad f

intimate [adj 'ɪntɪmət, vb 'ɪntɪmeɪt]
adj íntimo; (friendship) estrecho;
(knowledge) profundo ♦ vt dar a
entender

into ['ɪntuː] prep en; (towards) a;
(inside) hacia el interior de; **~ 3
pieces/French** en 3 pedazos/al
francés

intolerable [ɪn'tɔlərəbl] adj
intolerable, insoportable

intolerant [ɪn'tɔlərənt] adj: **~ (of)**
intolerante (con o para)

intoxicated [ɪn'tɔksɪkeɪtɪd] adj
embriagado

intractable [ɪn'træktəbl] adj (person)
intratable; (problem) espinoso

intransitive [ɪn'trænsɪtɪv] adj
intransitivo

intravenous [ɪntrə'viːnəs] adj
intravenoso

in-tray n bandeja de entrada

intricate ['ɪntrɪkət] adj (design, pattern)
intrincado

intrigue [ɪn'triːg] n intriga ♦ vt
fascinar; **intriguing** adj fascinante

intrinsic [ɪn'trɪnsɪk] adj intrínseco

introduce [ɪntrə'djuːs] vt introducir,
meter; (speaker, TV show etc) presentar;

to ~ sb (to sb) presentar uno (a
otro); **to ~ sb to** (pastime, technique)
introducir a uno a; **introduction**
[-'dʌkʃən] n introducción f; (of person)
presentación f; **introductory**
[-'dʌktərɪ] adj introductorio; (lesson,
offer) de introducción

introvert ['ɪntrəvɜːt] n introvertido/a
♦ adj (also: ~ed) introvertido

intrude [ɪn'truːd] vi (person)
entrometerse; **to ~ on** estorbar; **~r** n
intruso/a; **intrusion** [-ʒən] n invasión f

intuition [ɪntjuː'ɪʃən] n intuición f

inundate ['ɪnʌndeɪt] vt: **to ~ with**
inundar de

invade [ɪn'veɪd] vt invadir

invalid [n 'ɪnvəlɪd, adj ɪn'vælɪd] n
(MED) minusválido/a ♦ adj (not valid)
inválido, nulo

invaluable [ɪn'væljuəbl] adj
inestimable

invariable [ɪn'vɛərɪəbl] adj invariable

invent [ɪn'vɛnt] vt inventar; **~ion**
[ɪn'vɛnʃən] n invento; (lie) ficción f,
mentira; **~ive** adj inventivo; **~or** n
inventor(a) m/f

inventory ['ɪnvəntrɪ] n inventario

invert [ɪn'vɜːt] vt invertir

inverted commas (BRIT) npl comillas
fpl

invest [ɪn'vɛst] vt invertir ♦ vi: **to ~ in**
(company etc) invertir dinero en; (fig:
sth useful) comprar

investigate [ɪn'vɛstɪgeɪt] vt investigar;
investigation [-'geɪʃən] n
investigación f, pesquisa

investment [ɪn'vɛstmənt] n inversión
f

investor [ɪn'vɛstə*] n inversionista m/f

invigilator [ɪn'vɪdʒɪleɪtə*] n persona
que vigila en un examen

invigorating [ɪn'vɪgəreɪtɪŋ] adj
vigorizante

invisible [ɪn'vɪzɪbl] adj invisible

invitation [ɪnvɪ'teɪʃən] n invitación f

invite [ɪn'vaɪt] vt invitar; (opinions etc)
solicitar, pedir; **inviting** adj atractivo

(food) apetitoso

invoice ['ɪnvɔɪs] n factura ♦ vt facturar

involuntary [ɪn'vɔləntrɪ] adj
involuntario

involve [ɪn'vɔlv] vt suponer, implicar;
tener que ver con; (concern, affect)
corresponder; **to ~ sb (in sth)**
comprometer a uno (con algo); **~d** adj
complicado; **to be ~d in** (take part)
tomar parte en; (be engrossed) estar
muy metido en; **~ment** n
participación f, dedicación f

inward ['ɪnwəd] adj (movement)
interior, interno; (thought, feeling)
íntimo; **~(s)** adv hacia dentro

I/O abbr (COMPUT = input/output)
entrada/salida

iodine ['aɪəudiːn] n yodo

ion ['aɪən] n ion m; **ioniser** ['aɪənaɪzə*]
n ionizador m

iota [aɪ'əutə] n jota, ápice m

IOU n abbr (= I owe you) pagaré m

IQ n abbr (= intelligence quotient)
cociente m intelectual

IRA n abbr (= Irish Republican Army) IRA
m

Iran [ɪ'rɑːn] n Irán m; **~ian** [ɪ'reɪnɪən]
adj, n iraní m/f

Iraq [ɪ'rɑːk] n Iraq; **~i** adj, n iraquí m/f

irate [aɪ'reɪt] adj enojado, airado

Ireland ['aɪələnd] n Irlanda

iris ['aɪrɪs] n (pl **~es**) (ANAT) iris m;
(BOT) lirio

Irish ['aɪrɪʃ] adj irlandés/esa ♦ npl: **the
~** los irlandeses; **~man/woman** (irreg)
n irlandés/esa m/f; **~ Sea** n: **the
~ Sea** el mar de Irlanda

iron ['aɪən] n hierro; (for clothes)
plancha ♦ cpd de hierro ♦ vt (clothes)
planchar; **~ out** vt (fig) allanar

ironic(al) [aɪ'rɔnɪk(l)] adj irónico

ironing ['aɪənɪŋ] n (activity) planchado;
(clothes: ironed) ropa planchada; (: to
be ironed) ropa por planchar; **~ board**
n tabla de planchar

ironmonger's (shop) ['aɪənmʌŋgəz]
(BRIT) n ferretería, quincallería

irony 444 **I.U.D.**

irony ['aɪrənɪ] n ironía

irrational [ɪ'ræʃənl] adj irracional

irreconcilable [ɪrekən'saɪləbl] adj (ideas) incompatible; (enemies) irreconciliable

irregular [ɪ'regjulə*] adj irregular; (surface) desigual; (action, event) anómalo; (behaviour) poco ortodoxo

irrelevant [ɪ'reləvənt] adj fuera de lugar, inoportuno

irresolute [ɪ'rezəluːt] adj indeciso

irrespective [ɪrɪ'spektɪv]: ~ of prep sin tener en cuenta, no importa

irresponsible [ɪrɪ'spɒnsɪbl] adj (act) irresponsable; (person) poco serio

irrigate ['ɪrɪgeɪt] vt regar; **irrigation** [-'geɪʃən] n riego

irritable ['ɪrɪtəbl] adj (person) de mal humor

irritate ['ɪrɪteɪt] vt fastidiar; (MED) picar; **irritating** adj fastidioso; **irritation** [-'teɪʃən] n fastidio; enfado; picazón f

IRS (US) n abbr = Internal Revenue Service

is [ɪz] vb see be

Islam ['ɪzlɑːm] n Islam m; ~ic [ɪz'læmɪk] adj islámico

island ['aɪlənd] n isla; ~er n isleño/a

isle [aɪl] n isla

isn't ['ɪznt] = is not

isolate ['aɪsəleɪt] vt aislar; ~d adj aislado; **isolation** [-'leɪʃən] n aislamiento

ISP n abbr = Internet Service Provider

Israel ['ɪzreɪl] n Israel m; ~i [ɪz'reɪlɪ] adj, n israelí m/f

issue ['ɪsjuː] n (problem, subject) cuestión f; (outcome) resultado; (of banknotes etc) emisión f; (of newspaper etc) edición f ♦ vt (rations, equipment) distribuir, repartir; (orders) dar; (certificate, passport) expedir; (decree) promulgar; (magazine) publicar; (cheques) extender; (banknotes, stamps) emitir; **at** ~ en cuestión; **to take** ~ **with sb (over)** estar en desacuerdo

con uno (sobre); **to make an** ~ **of sth** hacer una cuestión de algo

Istanbul [ɪstæn'buːl] n Estambul m

KEYWORD

it [ɪt] pron 1 (specific: subject: not generally translated) él/ella; (: direct object) lo, la; (: indirect object) le; (after prep) él/ella; (abstract concept) ello; ~'s **on the table** está en la mesa; **I can't find** ~ no lo (or la) encuentro; **give** ~ **to me** dámelo (or dámela); **I spoke to him about** ~ le hablé del asunto; **what did you learn from** ~? ¿qué aprendiste de él (or ella)?; **did you go to** ~? (party, concert etc) ¿fuiste?

2 (impersonal): **it's raining** llueve, está lloviendo; ~'s **6 o'clock/the 10th of August** son las 6/es el 10 de agosto; **how far is** ~? — ~'s **10 miles/2 hours on the train** ¿a qué distancia está? — a 10 millas/2 horas en tren; **who is** ~? — ~'s **me** ¿quién es? — soy yo

Italian [ɪ'tæljən] adj italiano ♦ n italiano/a; (LING) italiano

italics [ɪ'tælɪks] npl cursiva

Italy ['ɪtəlɪ] n Italia

itch [ɪtʃ] n picazón f ♦ vi (part of body) picar; **to** ~ **to do sth** rabiar por hacer algo; ~**y** adj: **my hand is** ~**y** me pica la mano

it'd ['ɪtd] = **it would; it had**

item ['aɪtəm] n artículo; (on agenda) asunto (a tratar); (also: **news** ~) noticia; ~**ize** vt detallar

itinerary [aɪ'tɪnərərɪ] n itinerario

it'll ['ɪtl] = **it will; it shall**

its [ɪts] adj su; sus pl

it's [ɪts] = **it is; it has**

itself [ɪt'self] pron (reflexive) sí mismo/a; (emphatic) él mismo/ella misma

ITV n abbr (BRIT: = Independent Television) cadena de televisión comercial independiente del Estado

I.U.D. n abbr (= intra-uterine device)

DIU m

I've [aɪv] = **I have**

ivory ['aɪvərɪ] n marfil m

ivy ['aɪvɪ] n (BOT) hiedra

J, j

jab [dʒæb] vt: **to ~ sth into sth** clavar algo en algo ♦ n (inf) pinchazo

jack [dʒæk] n (AUT) gato; (CARDS) sota; **~ up** vt (AUT) levantar con gato

jackal ['dʒækl] n (ZOOL) chacal m

jacket ['dʒækɪt] n chaqueta, americana, saco (AM); (of book) sobrecubierta

jack: ~-knife vi colear; **~ plug** n (ELEC) enchufe m de clavija; **~pot** n premio gordo

jaded ['dʒeɪdɪd] adj (tired) cansado; (fed-up) hastiado

jagged ['dʒægɪd] adj dentado

jail [dʒeɪl] n cárcel f ♦ vt encarcelar

jam [dʒæm] n mermelada; (also: traffic ~) embotellamiento; (inf: difficulty) apuro ♦ vt (passage etc) obstruir; (mechanism, drawer etc) atascar; (RADIO) interferir ♦ vi atascarse, trabarse; **to ~ sth into sth** meter algo a la fuerza en algo

Jamaica [dʒə'meɪkə] n Jamaica

jangle ['dʒæŋgl] vi entrechocar (ruidosamente)

janitor ['dʒænɪtə*] n (caretaker) portero, conserje m

January ['dʒænjuərɪ] n enero

Japan [dʒə'pæn] n (el) Japón; **~ese** [dʒæpə'niːz] adj japonés/esa ♦ n inv japonés/esa m/f; (LING) japonés m

jar [dʒɑ:*] n tarro, bote m ♦ vi (sound) chirriar; (colours) desentonar

jargon ['dʒɑːgən] n jerga

jasmine ['dʒæzmɪn] n jazmín m

jaundice ['dʒɔːndɪs] n ictericia

jaunt [dʒɔːnt] n excursión f

javelin ['dʒævlɪn] n jabalina

jaw [dʒɔː] n mandíbula

jay [dʒeɪ] n (ZOOL) arrendajo

jaywalker ['dʒeɪwɔːkə*] n peatón/ona m/f imprudente

jazz [dʒæz] n jazz m; **~ up** vt (liven up) animar, avivar

jealous ['dʒeləs] adj celoso; (envious) envidioso; **~y** n celos mpl; envidia

jeans [dʒiːnz] npl vaqueros mpl, tejanos mpl

Jeep ® [dʒiːp] n jeep m

jeer [dʒɪə*] vi: **to ~ (at)** (mock) mofarse (de)

jelly ['dʒelɪ] n (jam) jalea; (dessert etc) gelatina; **~fish** n inv medusa (SP), aguaviva (AM)

jeopardy ['dʒepədɪ] n: **to be in ~** estar en peligro

jerk [dʒɜːk] n (jolt) sacudida; (wrench) tirón m; (inf) imbécil m/f ♦ vt tirar bruscamente de ♦ vi (vehicle) traquetear

jersey ['dʒɜːzɪ] n jersey m; (fabric) (tejido de) punto

Jesus ['dʒiːzəs] n Jesús m

jet [dʒet] n (of gas, liquid) chorro; (AVIAT) avión m a reacción; **~-black** adj negro como el azabache; **~ engine** n motor m a reacción; **~ lag** n desorientación f después de un largo vuelo

jettison ['dʒetɪsn] vt desechar

jetty ['dʒetɪ] n muelle m, embarcadero

Jew [dʒuː] n judío

jewel ['dʒuːəl] n joya; (in watch) rubí m; **~ler** (US **~er**) n joyero/a; **~ler's (shop)** (US **~ry store**) n joyería; **~lery** (US **~ry**) n joyas fpl, alhajas fpl

Jewess ['dʒuːɪs] n judía

Jewish ['dʒuːɪʃ] adj judío

jibe [dʒaɪb] n mofa

jiffy ['dʒɪfɪ] (inf) n: **in a ~** en un santiamén

jigsaw ['dʒɪgsɔː] n (also: ~ puzzle) rompecabezas m inv, puzle m

jilt [dʒɪlt] vt dejar plantado a

jingle ['dʒɪŋgl] n musiquilla ♦ vi tintinear

jinx [dʒɪŋks] n: **there's a ~ on it** está

gafado

jitters ['dʒɪtəz] (inf) npl: **to get the ~** ponerse nervioso

job [dʒɔb] n (task) tarea; (post) empleo; **it's not my ~** no me incumbe a mí; **it's a good ~ that ...** menos mal que ...; **just the ~!** ¡estupendo!; **~ centre** (BRIT) n oficina estatal de colocaciones; **~less** adj sin trabajo

jockey ['dʒɔkɪ] n jockey m/f ♦ vi: **~ for position** maniobrar para conseguir una posición

jog [dʒɔg] vt empujar (ligeramente) ♦ vi (run) hacer footing; **to ~ sb's memory** refrescar la memoria a uno; **~ along** vi (fig) ir tirando; **~ging** n footing m

join [dʒɔɪn] vt (things) juntar, unir; (club) hacerse socio de; (POL: party) afiliarse a; (queue) ponerse en; (meet: people) reunirse con ♦ vi (roads) juntarse; (rivers) confluir ♦ n juntura; **~ in** vi tomar parte, participar ♦ vt fus tomar parte o participar en; **~ up** vi reunirse; (MIL) alistarse

joiner ['dʒɔɪnə*] (BRIT) n carpintero/a; **~y** n carpintería

joint [dʒɔɪnt] n (TECH) junta, unión f; (ANAT) articulación f; (BRIT: CULIN) pieza de carne (para asar); (inf: place) tugurio; (: of cannabis) porro ♦ adj (common) común; (combined) combinado; **~ account** (with bank etc) cuenta común

joke [dʒəuk] n chiste m; (also: practical ~) broma ♦ vi bromear; **to play a ~ on** gastar una broma a; **~r** n (CARDS) comodín m

jolly ['dʒɔlɪ] adj (merry) alegre; (enjoyable) divertido ♦ adv (BRIT: inf) muy, terriblemente

jolt [dʒəult] n (jerk) sacudida f; (shock) susto ♦ vt (physically) sacudir; (emotionally) asustar

jostle ['dʒɔsl] vt dar empellones a, codear

jot [dʒɔt] n: **not one ~** ni jota, ni

pizca; **~ down** vt apuntar; **~ter** (BRIT) n bloc m

journal ['dʒɜːnl] n (magazine) revista; (diary) periódico, diario; **~ism** n periodismo; **~ist** n periodista m/f, reportero/a

journey ['dʒɜːnɪ] n viaje m; (distance covered) trayecto

jovial ['dʒəuvɪəl] adj risueño, jovial

joy [dʒɔɪ] n alegría; **~ful** adj alegre; **~ous** adj alegre; **~ ride** n (illegal) paseo en coche robado; **~rider** n gamberro que roba un coche para dar una vuelta y luego abandonarlo; **~ stick** n (AVIAT) palanca de mando; (COMPUT) palanca de control

JP n abbr = **Justice of the Peace**

Jr abbr = **junior**

jubilant ['dʒuːbɪlnt] adj jubiloso

judge [dʒʌdʒ] n juez m/f; (fig: expert) perito ♦ vt juzgar; (consider) considerar; **judg(e)ment** n juicio

judiciary [dʒuː'dɪʃɪərɪ] n poder m judicial

judicious [dʒuː'dɪʃəs] adj juicioso

judo ['dʒuːdəu] n judo m

jug [dʒʌg] n jarra

juggernaut ['dʒʌgənɔːt] (BRIT) n (huge truck) trailer m

juggle ['dʒʌgl] vi hacer juegos malabares; **~r** n malabarista m/f

juice [dʒuːs] n zumo, jugo (esp AM); **juicy** adj jugoso

jukebox ['dʒuːkbɔks] n máquina de discos

July [dʒuː'laɪ] n julio

jumble ['dʒʌmbl] n revoltijo ♦ vt (also: ~ up) revolver; **~ sale** (BRIT) n venta de objetos usados con fines benéficos

---

jumble sale

Los **jumble sales** *son unos mercadillos que se organizan con fines benéficos en los locales de un colegio, iglesia u otro centro público. En ellos puede comprarse todo tipo de artículos baratos de segunda mano, sobre todo*

ropa, juguetes, libros, vajillas o
muebles.

jumbo (jet) ['dʒʌmbəʊ-] n jumbo
jump [dʒʌmp] vi saltar, dar saltos;
(with fear etc) pegar un bote; (increase)
aumentar ♦ vt saltar ♦ n salto; aumento;
to ~ the queue (BRIT) colarse
jumper ['dʒʌmpə*] n (BRIT: pullover)
suéter m, jersey m; (US: dress) mandil
m; **~ cables** (US) npl = **jump leads**
jump leads (BRIT) npl cables mpl
puente de batería
jumpy ['dʒʌmpɪ] (inf) adj nervioso
Jun. abbr = **junior**
junction ['dʒʌŋkʃən] n (BRIT: of roads)
cruce m; (RAIL) empalme m
juncture ['dʒʌŋktʃə*] n: **at this ~** en
este momento, en esta coyuntura
June [dʒu:n] n junio
jungle ['dʒʌŋgl] n selva, jungla
junior ['dʒu:nɪə*] adj (in age) menor,
más joven; (brother/sister etc): **7 years
her ~** siete años menor que ella;
(position) subalterno ♦ n menor m/f,
joven m/f; **~ school** (BRIT) n escuela
primaria
junk [dʒʌŋk] n (cheap goods) baratijas
fpl; (rubbish) basura; **~ food** n
alimentos preparados y envasados de
escaso valor nutritivo
junkie ['dʒʌŋkɪ] (inf) n drogadicto/a,
yonqui m/f
junk mail n propaganda de buzón
junk shop n tienda de objetos usados
Junr abbr = **junior**
juror ['dʒʊərə*] n jurado
jury ['dʒʊərɪ] n jurado
just [dʒʌst] adj justo ♦ adv (exactly)
exactamente; (only) sólo, solamente;
he's ~ done it/left acaba de
hacerlo/irse; **~ right** perfecto; **~ two
o'clock** las dos en punto; **she's ~ as
clever as you** (ella) es tan lista como
tú; **~ as well that ...** menos mal que
...; **~ as he was leaving** en el
momento en que se marchaba;

~ before/enough justo antes/lo
suficiente; **~ here** aquí mismo; **he
~ missed** por poco falló; **~ listen to
this** escucha esto un
momento
justice ['dʒʌstɪs] n justicia; (US: judge)
juez m; **to do ~ to** (fig) hacer justicia
a; **J~ of the Peace** n juez de paz
justify ['dʒʌstɪfaɪ] vt justificar; (text)
alinear
jut [dʒʌt] vi (also: **~ out**) sobresalir
juvenile ['dʒu:vənaɪl] adj (court) de
menores; (humour, mentality) infantil
♦ n menor m de edad

K, k

K abbr (= one thousand) mil; (=
kilobyte) kilobyte m, kiloocteto
kangaroo [kæŋgə'ru:] n canguro
karate [kə'rɑ:tɪ] n karate m
kebab [kə'bæb] n pincho moruno
keel [ki:l] n quilla; **on an even ~** (fig)
en equilibrio
keen [ki:n] adj (interest, desire) grande,
vivo; (eye, intelligence) agudo;
(competition) reñido; (edge) afilado;
(eager) entusiasta; **to be ~ to do** or
on doing sth tener muchas ganas de
hacer algo; **to be ~ on sth/sb**
interesarse por algo/uno
keep [ki:p] (pt, pp kept) vt (preserve,
store) guardar; (hold back) quedarse
con; (maintain) mantener; (detain)
detener; (shop) ser propietario de;
(feed: family etc) mantener; (promise)
cumplir; (chickens, bees etc) criar;
(accounts) llevar; (diary) escribir;
(prevent): **to ~ sb from doing sth**
impedir a uno hacer algo ♦ vi (food)
conservarse; (remain) seguir, continuar
♦ n (of castle) torreón m; (food etc)
comida, subsistencia; (inf): **for ~s** para
siempre; **to ~ doing sth** seguir
haciendo algo; **to ~ sb happy** tener a
uno contento; **to ~ a place tidy**

mantener un lugar limpio; **to ~ sth to o.s.** guardar algo para sí mismo; **to ~ sth (back) from sb** ocultar algo a uno; **to ~ time** (clock) mantener la hora exacta ♦ vi: **to ~ on doing** seguir o continuar haciendo; **to ~ on (about sth)** no parar de hablar (de algo); **~ out** vi (stay out) permanecer fuera; "**~ out**" "prohibida la entrada"; **~ up** vt mantener, conservar ♦ vi no retrasarse; **to ~ up with** (pace) ir al paso de; (level) mantenerse a la altura de; **~er** n guardián/ana m/f; **~fit** n gimnasia (para mantenerse en forma); **~ing** n (care) cuidado; **in ~ing with** de acuerdo con; **~sake** n recuerdo

kennel ['kɛnl] n perrera; **~s** npl residencia canina

Kenya ['kɛnjə] n Kenia

kept [kɛpt] pt, pp of **keep**

kerb [kɜːb] (BRIT) n bordillo

kernel ['kɜːnl] n (nut) almendra; (fig) meollo

ketchup ['kɛtʃəp] n salsa de tomate, catsup m

kettle ['kɛtl] n hervidor m de agua; **~ drum** n (MUS) timbal m

key [kiː] n llave f; (MUS) tono; (of piano, typewriter) tecla ♦ adj (issue etc) clave inv ♦ vt (also: **~ in**) teclear; **~board** n teclado; **~ed up** adj (person) nervioso; **~hole** n ojo (de la cerradura); **~hole surgery** n cirugía cerrada, cirugía no invasiva; **~note** n (MUS) tónica; (of speech) punto principal o clave; **~ring** n llavero

khaki ['kɑːkɪ] n caqui

kick [kɪk] vt dar una patada o un puntapié a; (inf: habit) quitarse de ♦ vi (horse) dar coces ♦ n patada; puntapié m; (of animal) coz f; (thrill): **he does it for ~s** lo hace por pura diversión; **~ off** vi (SPORT) hacer el saque inicial

kid [kɪd] n (inf: child) chiquillo m; (animal) cabrito; (leather) cabritilla ♦ vi (inf) bromear

kidnap ['kɪdnæp] vt secuestrar; **~per** n

secuestrador(a) m/f; **~ping** n secuestro

kidney ['kɪdnɪ] n riñón m

kill [kɪl] vt matar; (murder) asesinar ♦ n matanza; **to ~ time** matar el tiempo; **~er** n asesino/a; **~ing** n (one) asesinato; (several) matanza; **to make a ~ing** (fig) hacer su agosto; **~joy** (BRIT) n aguafiestas m/f inv

kiln [kɪln] n horno

kilo ['kiːləu] n kilo; **~byte** n (COMPUT) kilobyte m, kilococteto; **~gram(me)** ['kɪləgræm] n kilo, kilogramo; **~metre** ['kɪləmiːtə*] (US **~meter**) n kilómetro; **~watt** ['kɪləwɔt] n kilovatio

kilt [kɪlt] n falda escocesa

kin [kɪn] n see **next**

kind [kaɪnd] adj amable, atento ♦ n clase f, especie f; (species) género; **in ~** (COMM) en especie; **a ~ of** una especie de; **to be two of a ~** ser tal para cual

kindergarten ['kɪndəgɑːtn] n jardín m de la infancia

kind-hearted adj bondadoso, de buen corazón

kindle ['kɪndl] vt encender; (arouse) despertar

kindly ['kaɪndlɪ] adj bondadoso, cariñoso ♦ adv bondadosamente, amablemente; **will you ~ ...** sea usted tan amable de ...

kindness ['kaɪndnɪs] n (quality) bondad f, amabilidad f; (act) favor m

king [kɪŋ] n rey m; **~dom** n reino; **~fisher** n martín m pescador; **~size** adj de tamaño extra

kiosk ['kiːɔsk] n quiosco; (BRIT: TEL) cabina

kipper ['kɪpə*] n arenque m ahumado

kiss [kɪs] n beso ♦ vt besar; **to ~ (each other)** besarse; **~ of life** n respiración f boca a boca

kit [kɪt] n (equipment) equipo; (tools etc) (caja de) herramientas fpl; (assembly) juego de armar

kitchen ['kɪtʃɪn] n cocina; **~ sink** n fregadero

kite [kaɪt] n (toy) cometa

kitten ['kɪtn] n gatito/a

kitty ['kɪtɪ] n (funds) fondo común

km abbr (= kilometre) km

knack [næk] n: **to have the ~ of doing sth** tener el don de hacer algo

knapsack ['næpsæk] n mochila

knead [niːd] vt amasar

knee [niː] n rodilla; **~cap** n rótula

kneel [niːl] (pt, pp **knelt**) vi (also: **~ down**) arrodillarse

knew [njuː] pt of **know**

knickers ['nɪkəz] npl (BRIT) bragas fpl

knife [naɪf] (pl **knives**) n cuchillo ♦ vt acuchillar

knight [naɪt] n caballero m; (CHESS) caballo; **~hood** (BRIT) n (title): **to receive a ~hood** recibir el título de Sir

knit [nɪt] vt tejer, tricotar ♦ vi (wool) hacer punto, tricotar; (bones) soldarse; **to ~ one's brows** fruncir el ceño; **~ting** n labor f de punto; **~ting machine** n máquina de tricotar; **~ting needle** n aguja de hacer punto; **~wear** n prendas fpl de punto

knives [naɪvz] npl of **knife**

knob [nɔb] n (of door) tirador m; (of stick) puño; (on radio, TV) botón m

knock [nɔk] vt (strike) golpear; (bump into) chocar contra; (inf) criticar ♦ vi (at door etc): **to ~ at/on** llamar a ♦ n golpe m; (on door) llamada; **~ down** vt atropellar; **~ off** vi (inf) (finish) salir del trabajo ♦ vt (from price) descontar; (inf: steal) birlar; **~ out** vt dejar sin sentido; (BOXING) poner fuera de combate, dejar K.O.; (in competition) eliminar; **~ over** vt (object) tirar; (person) atropellar; **~er** n (on door) aldabón m; **~out** n (BOXING) K.O. m, knockout m ♦ cpd (competition etc) eliminatorio

knot [nɔt] n nudo m ♦ vt anudar

know [nəʊ] (pt **knew**, pp **known**) vt (facts) saber; (be acquainted with) conocer; (recognize) reconocer;

to ~ how to swim saber nadar; **to ~ about** or **of sb/sth** saber de uno/algo; **~-all** n sabelotodo m/f; **~-how** n conocimientos mpl; **~ing** adj (look) de complicidad; (purposely) adrede; (smile, look) con complicidad

knowledge ['nɔlɪdʒ] n conocimiento; (learning) saber m, conocimientos mpl; **~able** adj entendido

knuckle ['nʌkl] n nudillo

Koran [kɔ'rɑːn] n Corán m

Korea [kə'rɪə] n Corea

kosher ['kəʊʃə*] adj autorizado por la ley judía

Kosovo ['kɔsəvəʊ] n Kosovo m

L, l

L (BRIT) abbr = **learner driver**

l. abbr (= litre) l

lab [læb] n abbr = **laboratory**

label ['leɪbl] n etiqueta ♦ vt poner etiqueta a

labor etc ['leɪbə*] (US) = **labour**

laboratory [lə'bɔrətərɪ] n laboratorio

laborious [lə'bɔːrɪəs] adj penoso

labour ['leɪbə*] (US **labor**) n (hard work) trabajo; (~ force) mano f de obra; (MED): **to be in ~** estar de parto ♦ vi: **to ~ (at sth)** trabajar (en algo) ♦ vt: **to ~ a point** insistir en un punto; **L~, the L~ party** (BRIT) el partido laborista, los laboristas mpl; **~ed** adj (breathing) fatigoso; **~er** n peón m; **farm ~er** peón m; (day ~er) jornalero

lace [leɪs] n encaje m; (of shoe etc) cordón m ♦ vt (shoes: also: **~ up**) atarse (los zapatos)

lack [læk] n (absence) falta ♦ vt faltarle a uno, carecer de; **through** or **for ~ of** por falta de; **to be ~ing** faltar, no haber; **to be ~ing in sth** faltarle a uno algo

lacquer ['lækə*] n laca

lad [læd] n muchacho, chico

ladder ['lædə*] n escalera (de mano); (BRIT: in tights) carrera

laden ['leɪdn] adj: ~ (with) cargado (de)

ladle ['leɪdl] n cucharón m

lady ['leɪdɪ] n señora; (dignified, graceful) dama; "ladies and gentlemen ..." "señoras y caballeros ..."; **young ~** señorita; **the ladies' (room)** los servicios de señoras; **~bird** (US **~bug**) n mariquita; **~like** adj fino; **L~ship** n: **your L~ship** su Señoría

lag [læg] n retraso ♦ vi (also: ~ **behind**) retrasarse, quedarse atrás ♦ vt (pipes) revestir

lager ['lɑːgə*] n cerveza (rubia)

lagoon [lə'guːn] n laguna

laid [leɪd] pt, pp of **lay**; **~ back** (inf) adj relajado; **~ up** adj: **to be ~ up (with)** tener que guardar cama (a causa de)

lain [leɪn] pp of **lie**

lake [leɪk] n lago

lamb [læm] n cordero; (meat) (carne f de) cordero; **~ chop** n chuleta de cordero; **lambswool** n lana de cordero

lame [leɪm] adj cojo; (excuse) poco convincente

lament [lə'ment] n quejo ♦ vt lamentarse de

laminated ['læmɪneɪtɪd] adj (metal) laminado; (wood) contrachapado; (surface) plastificado

lamp [læmp] n lámpara; **~post** (BRIT) n (poste m de) farol m; **~shade** n pantalla

lance [lɑːns] vt (MED) abrir con lanceta

land [lænd] n tierra; (country) país m; (piece of ~) terreno; (estate) tierras fpl, finca ♦ vi (from ship) desembarcar; (AVIAT) aterrizar; (fig: fall) caer, terminar ♦ vt (passengers, goods) desembarcar; **to ~ sb with sth** (inf) hacer cargar a uno con algo; **~ up** vi: **to ~ up in/at** ir a parar a/en; **~fill site** ['lændfɪl-] n vertedero; **~ing** n aterrizaje m; (of staircase) rellano; **~ing**

gear n (AVIAT) tren m de aterrizaje; **~lady** n (of rented house, pub etc) dueña; **~lord** n propietario; (of pub etc) patrón m; **~mark** n lugar m conocido; **to be a ~mark** (fig) marcar un hito histórico; **~owner** n terrateniente m/f; **~scape** n paisaje m; **~scape gardener** n arquitecto de jardines; **~slide** n (GEO) corrimiento de tierras; (fig: POL) victoria arrolladora

lane [leɪn] n (in country) camino; (AUT) carril m; (in race) calle f

language ['læŋgwɪdʒ] n lenguaje m; (national tongue) idioma m, lengua; **bad ~** palabrotas fpl; **~ laboratory** n laboratorio de idiomas

lank [læŋk] adj (hair) lacio

lanky ['læŋkɪ] adj larguirucho

lantern ['læntn] n linterna, farol m

lap [læp] n (of track) vuelta; (of body) regazo; **to sit on sb's ~** sentarse en las rodillas de uno ♦ vt (also: ~ **up**) beber a lengüetadas ♦ vi (waves) chapotear; **~ up** vt (fig) tragarse

lapel [lə'pel] n solapa

Lapland ['læplænd] n Laponia

lapse [læps] n fallo; (moral) desliz m; (of time) intervalo ♦ vi (expire) caducar; (time) pasar, transcurrir; **to ~ into bad habits** caer en malos hábitos

laptop (computer) ['læptɔp-] n (ordenador m) portátil m

larch [lɑːtʃ] n alerce m

lard [lɑːd] n manteca (de cerdo)

larder ['lɑːdə*] n despensa

large [lɑːdʒ] adj grande; **at ~** (free) en libertad; (generally) en general; **~ly** adv (mostly) en su mayor parte; (introducing reason) en gran parte; **~-scale** adj (map) en gran escala; (fig) importante

lark [lɑːk] n (bird) alondra; (joke) broma

laryngitis [lærɪn'dʒaɪtɪs] n laringitis f

laser ['leɪzə*] n láser m; **~ printer** n impresora (por) láser

lash [læʃ] n latigazo; (also: **eye~**) pestaña; vt azotar; (tie): **to ~ to/ together** atar a/atar; **~ out** vi: **to ~**

~ out (at sb) (*hit*) arremeter (contra uno); **to ~ out against sb** lanzar invectivas contra uno

lass [læs] (*BRIT*) n chica

lasso [læ'suː] n lazo

last [lɑːst] adj último; (*end: of series etc*) final ♦ adv (*most recently*) la última vez; (*finally*) por último ♦ vi durar; (*continue*) continuar, seguir; **~ night** anoche; **~ week** la semana pasada; **at ~** por fin; **~ but one** penúltimo; **~-ditch** adj (*attempt*) último, desesperado; **~ing** adj duradero; **~ly** adv por último, finalmente; **~-minute** adj de última hora

latch [lætʃ] n pestillo

late [leɪt] adj (*far on: in time, process etc*) al final de; (*not on time*) tarde, atrasado; (*dead*) fallecido ♦ adv tarde; (*behind time, schedule*) con retraso; **of ~** últimamente; **~ at night** a última hora de la noche; **in ~ May** hacia fines de mayo; **the ~ Mr X** el difunto Sr X; **~comer** n recién llegado/a; **~ly** adv últimamente; **~r** adj (*date etc*) posterior; (*version etc*) más reciente ♦ adv más tarde, después; **~r** [ˈleɪtst] adj último; **at the ~st** a más tardar

lathe [leɪð] n torno

lather [ˈlɑːðə*] n espuma (de jabón) ♦ vt enjabonar

Latin [ˈlætɪn] n latín m ♦ adj latino; **~ America** n América Latina; **~ American** adj, n latinoamericano/a

latitude [ˈlætɪtjuːd] n latitud f; (*fig*) libertad f

latter [ˈlætə*] adj último; (*of two*) segundo ♦ n: **the ~** el último, éste; **~ly** adv últimamente

laudable [ˈlɔːdəbl] adj loable

laugh [lɑːf] n risa ♦ vi reír(se); (**to do sth for a ~** (*hacer algo*) en broma; **~ at** vt fus reírse de; **~ off** vt tomar algo a risa; **~able** adj ridículo; **~ing stock** n: **the ~ing stock of** el hazmerreír de el; **~ter** n risa

launch [lɔːntʃ] n lanzamiento m; (*boat*)

lancha ♦ vt (*ship*) botar; (*rocket etc*)

lanzar ♦ vt (*fig*) comenzar; **~ into** vt fus

lanzarse a; **~(ing) pad** n plataforma de lanzamiento

launder [ˈlɔːndə*] vt lavar

Launderette ® [lɔːnˈdrɛt] (*BRIT*) n lavandería (automática)

Laundromat ® [ˈlɔːndrəmæt] (*US*) n = **Launderette**

laundry [ˈlɔːndrɪ] n (*dirty*) ropa sucia; (*clean*) colada; (*room*) lavadero

lavatory [ˈlævətərɪ] n water m

lavender [ˈlævəndə*] n lavanda

lavish [ˈlævɪʃ] adj (*amount*) abundante; (*person*): **~ with** pródigo en ♦ vt: **to ~ sth on sb** colmar a uno de algo

law [lɔː] n ley f; (*SCOL*) derecho; (*a rule*) regla; (*professions connected with ~*) jurisprudencia; **~-abiding** adj respetuoso de la ley; **~ and order** n orden m público; **~ court** n tribunal m (de justicia); **~ful** adj legítimo, lícito; **~less** adj (*action*) criminal

lawn [lɔːn] n césped m; **~mower** n cortacésped m; **~ tennis** n tenis m sobre hierba

law school n (*US*) facultad f de derecho

lawsuit [ˈlɔːsuːt] n pleito

lawyer [ˈlɔːjə*] n abogado/a; (*for sales, wills etc*) notario/a

lax [læks] adj laxo

laxative [ˈlæksətɪv] n laxante m

lay [leɪ] (*pt, pp laid*) pt of **lie** ♦ adj laico; (*not expert*) lego ♦ vt (*place*) colocar; (*eggs, table*) poner; (*cable*) tender; (*carpet*) extender; **~ aside** or **by** vt dejar a un lado; **~ down** vt (*pen etc*) dejar; (*rules etc*) establecer; **to ~ down the law** imponer las normas; **~ off** vt (*workers*) despedir; **~ on** vt (*meal, facilities*) proveer; **~ out** vt (*spread out*) disponer, exponer; **~about** (*inf*) n vago; **~-by** n (*BRIT: AUT*) área de aparcamiento

layer [ˈleɪə*] n capa

layman [ˈleɪmən] (*irreg*) n lego

layout ['leɪaut] n (design) plan m, trazado; (PRESS) composición f

laze [leɪz] vi (also: ~ about) holgazanear

lazy ['leɪzɪ] adj perezoso, vago; (movement) lento

lb. abbr = **pound** (weight)

lead¹ [li:d] (pt, pp **led**) n (front position) delantera f; (clue) pista; (ELEC) cable m; (for dog) correa; (THEATRE) papel m principal ♦ vt (walk etc in front of) ir a la cabeza de; (guide): **to ~ sb somewhere** conducir a uno a algún sitio; (be leader of) dirigir; (start, guide: activity) protagonizar ♦ vi (road, pipe etc) conducir a; (SPORT) ir primero; **to be in the ~** (SPORT) llevar la delantera; (fig) ir a la cabeza; **to ~ the way** (also fig) llevar la delantera; **~ away** vt llevar; **~ back** vt (person, route) llevar de vuelta; **~ on** vt (tease) engañar; **~ to** vt fus producir, provocar; **~ up to** vt fus (events) conducir a; (in conversation) preparar el terreno para

lead² [led] n (metal) plomo; (in pencil) mina; **~ed petrol** n gasolina con plomo

leader ['li:də*] n jefe/a m/f, líder m; (SPORT) líder m; **~ship** n dirección f; (position) mando; (quality) iniciativa

leading ['li:dɪŋ] adj (main) principal; (first) primero; (front) delantero; **~ lady** n (THEATRE) primera actriz f; **~ light** n (person) figura principal; **~ man** (irreg) n (THEATRE) primer galán m

lead singer [li:d-] n cantante m/f

leaf [li:f] (pl **leaves**) n hoja ♦ vi: **to ~ through** hojear; **to turn over a new ~** reformarse

leaflet ['li:flɪt] n folleto

league [li:g] n sociedad f; (FOOTBALL) liga; **to be in ~ with** haberse confabulado con

leak [li:k] n (of liquid, gas) escape m, fuga; (in pipe) agujero; (in roof) gotera; (in security) filtración f ♦ vi (shoes, ship) hacer agua; (pipe) tener (un) escape;

(roof) gotear; (liquid, gas) escaparse, fugarse; (fig) divulgarse ♦ vt (fig) filtrar

lean [li:n] adj (thin) flaco; (meat) magro ♦ vt: **to ~ sth on sth** apoyar algo en algo ♦ vi (slope) inclinarse; **to ~ against** apoyarse contra; **to ~ on** apoyarse en; **~ back/forward** vi inclinarse hacia atrás/adelante; **~ out** vi asomarse; **~ over** vi inclinarse; **~ing** n: **~ing (towards)** inclinación f (hacia); **leant** [lent] pt, pp of **lean**

leap [li:p] (pt, pp **leaped** or **leapt**) n salto ♦ vi saltar; **~frog** n pídola; **~ year** n año bisiesto

learn [lə:n] (pt, pp **learned** or **learnt**) vt aprender ♦ vi aprender; **to ~ about sth** enterarse de algo; **to ~ to do sth** aprender a hacer algo; **~ed** ['lə:nɪd] adj erudito; **~er** n (BRIT: also: **~er driver**) principiante m/f; **~ing** n el saber m, conocimientos mpl

lease [li:s] n arriendo ♦ vt arrendar

leash [li:ʃ] n correa

least [li:st] adj: **the ~** (slightest) el menor o el más pequeño; (smallest amount of) mínimo ♦ adv (+ vb) menos; (+ adj): **the ~ expensive** el/la menos costoso/a; **the ~ possible effort** el menor esfuerzo posible; **at ~** por lo menos, al menos; **you could at ~ have written** por lo menos podías haber escrito; **not in the ~** en absoluto

leather ['leðə*] n cuero

leave [li:v] (pt, pp **left**) vt dejar; (go away from) abandonar; (place etc: permanently) salir de ♦ vi irse; (train etc) salir ♦ vt salir; **to ~ sth to sb** (money etc) legar algo a uno; (responsibility etc) encargar a uno de algo; **to be left** quedar, sobrar; **there's some milk left over** sobra o queda algo de leche; **on ~** de permiso; **~ behind** vt (on purpose) dejar; (accidentally) dejarse; **~ out** vt omitir; **~ of absence** n permiso de ausentarse

leaves [liːvz] npl of **leaf**

Lebanon ['lɛbənən] n: **the ~** el Líbano

lecherous ['lɛtʃərəs] (pej) adj lascivo

lecture ['lɛktʃə*] n conferencia f; (SCOL) clase f ♦ vi dar una clase ♦ vt (scold): **to ~ sb on** or **about sth** echar una reprimenda a uno por algo; **to give a ~ on** dar una conferencia sobre; **~r** n conferenciante m/f; (BRIT: at university) profesor(a) m/f

led [lɛd] pt, pp of **lead**

ledge [lɛdʒ] n repisa; (of window) alféizar m; (of mountain) saliente m

ledger ['lɛdʒə*] n libro mayor

leech [liːtʃ] n sanguijuela

leek [liːk] n puerro

leer [lɪə*] vi: **to ~ at sb** mirar de manera lasciva a uno

leeway ['liːweɪ] n (fig): **to have some ~** tener cierta libertad de acción

left [lɛft] pt, pp of **leave** ♦ adj izquierdo; (remaining): **there are 2 ~** quedan dos ♦ n izquierda ♦ adv a la izquierda; **on** or **to the ~** a la izquierda; **the L~** (POL) la izquierda; **~-handed** adj zurdo; **the ~-hand side** n la izquierda; **~-luggage (office)** (BRIT) n consigna; **~-overs** npl sobras fpl; **~-wing** adj (POL) de izquierdas, izquierdista

leg [lɛg] n pierna; (of animal, chair) pata; (trouser ~) pernera; (CULIN: of lamb) pierna; (of chicken) pata; (of journey) etapa

legacy ['lɛgəsɪ] n herencia

legal ['liːgl] adj (permitted by law) lícito; (of law) legal; **~ holiday** (US) n fiesta oficial; **~ize** vt legalizar; **~ly** adv legalmente; **~ tender** n moneda de curso legal

legend ['lɛdʒənd] n (also fig: person) leyenda

legislation [lɛdʒɪs'leɪʃən] n legislación f

legislature ['lɛdʒɪslətʃə*] n cuerpo legislativo

legitimate [lɪ'dʒɪtɪmət] adj legítimo

leg-room n espacio para las piernas

leisure ['lɛʒə*] n ocio, tiempo libre m; **at ~** con tranquilidad; **~ centre** n centro de recreo; **~ly** adj sin prisa; lento

lemon ['lɛmən] n limón m; **~ade** n (fizzy) gaseosa; **~ tea** n té m con limón

lend [lɛnd] (pt, pp **lent**) vt: **to ~ sth to sb** prestar algo a alguien; **~ing library** n biblioteca de préstamo

length [lɛŋθ] n (size) largo, longitud f; (distance): **the ~ of** todo lo largo de; (of swimming pool, cloth) largo; (of wood, string) trozo; (amount of time) duración f; **at ~** (at last) por fin, finalmente; (lengthily) largamente; **~en** vt alargar ♦ vi alargarse; **~ways** adv a lo largo; **~y** adj largo, extenso

lenient ['liːnɪənt] adj indulgente

lens [lɛnz] n (of spectacles) lente f; (of camera) objetivo

Lent [lɛnt] n Cuaresma

lent [lɛnt] pt, pp of **lend**

lentil ['lɛntl] n lenteja

Leo ['liːəu] n Leo

leotard ['liːətɑːd] n mallas fpl

leprosy ['lɛprəsɪ] n lepra

lesbian ['lɛzbɪən] n lesbiana

less [lɛs] adj (in size, degree etc) menor; (in quality) menos ♦ pron, adv menos ♦ prep: **~ tax/10% discount** menos impuestos/el 10 por ciento de descuento; **~ than half** menos de la mitad; **~ than ever** menos que nunca; **~ and ~** cada vez menos; **the ~ he works ...** cuanto menos trabaja ...; **~en** vi disminuir, reducirse ♦ vt disminuir, reducir; **~er** ['lɛsə*] adj menor; **to a ~er extent** en menor grado

lesson ['lɛsn] n clase f; (warning) lección f

let [lɛt] (pt, pp **let**) vt (allow) dejar, permitir; (BRIT: lease) alquilar; **to ~ sb do sth** dejar que uno haga algo; **to ~ sb know sth** comunicar algo a uno; **~'s go** ¡vamos!; **~ him come** que venga; **"to ~"** "se alquila"; **~ down** vt (tyre) desinflar; (disappoint) defraudar; **~ go** vi, vt soltar; **~ in** vt dejar entrar; (visitor etc) hacer pasar; **~ off** vt (culprit) dejar escapar; (gun) disparar; (bomb) accionar; (firework) hacer estallar; **~ on** (inf) vt divulgar; **~ out** vt dejar salir; (sound) soltar; **~ up** vi amainar, disminuir

lethal ['li:θl] adj (weapon) mortífero; (poison, wound) mortal

letter ['letə*] n (of alphabet) letra; (correspondence) carta; **~ bomb** n carta-bomba; **~box** (BRIT) n buzón m; **~ing** n letras fpl

lettuce ['letɪs] n lechuga

let-up n disminución f

leukaemia [lu:'ki:mɪə] (US **leukemia**) n leucemia

level ['levl] adj (flat) llano ♦ adv: **to draw ~ with** llegar a la altura de ♦ n nivel m; (height) altura ♦ vt nivelar; allanar; (destroy: building) derribar; (: forest) arrasar; **to be ~ with** estar a nivel de; **"A" ~s** (BRIT) npl ≈ exámenes mpl de bachillerato superior, B.U.P.; **"O" ~s** (BRIT) npl ≈ exámenes mpl de octavo de básica; **on the ~** (fig: honest) serio; **~ off** or **out** vi (prices etc) estabilizarse; **~ crossing** (BRIT) n paso a nivel; **~-headed** adj sensato

lever ['li:və*] n (also fig) palanca ♦ vt: **to ~ up** levantar con palanca; **~age** n (using bar etc) apalancamiento; (fig: influence) influencia

levy ['levɪ] n impuesto ♦ vt exigir, recaudar

lewd [lu:d] adj lascivo; (joke) obsceno, colorado (AM)

liability [laɪə'bɪlɪtɪ] n (pej: person, thing) estorbo, lastre m; (JUR: responsibility) responsabilidad f; **liabilities** npl (COMM) pasivo

liable ['laɪəbl] adj (subject): **~ to** sujeto a; (responsible): **~ for** responsable de; (likely): **~ to do** propenso a hacer

liaise [lɪ'eɪz] vi: **to ~ with** enlazar con;

liaison [lɪ'eɪzɔn] n (coordination)

enlace m; (affair) relaciones fpl amorosas

liar ['laɪə*] n mentiroso/a

libel ['laɪbl] n calumnia ♦ vt calumniar

liberal ['lɪbərl] adj liberal; (offer, amount etc) generoso

liberate ['lɪbəreɪt] vt (people: from poverty etc) librar; (prisoner) libertar; (country) liberar

liberty ['lɪbətɪ] n libertad f; (criminal): **to be at ~** estar en libertad; **to be at ~ to do** estar libre para hacer; **to take the ~ of doing sth** tomarse la libertad de hacer algo

Libra ['li:brə] n Libra

librarian [laɪ'brɛərɪən] n bibliotecario/a

library ['laɪbrərɪ] n biblioteca

libretto [lɪ'brɛtəu] n libreto

Libya ['lɪbɪə] n Libia; **~n** adj, n libio/a m/f

lice [laɪs] npl of **louse**

licence ['laɪsəns] (US **license**) n licencia; (permit) permiso; also: **driving ~**, (US) **driver's ~**) carnet m de conducir (SP), permiso (AM)

license ['laɪsəns] n (US) = **licence** ♦ vt autorizar, dar permiso a; **~d** adj (for alcohol) autorizado para vender bebidas alcohólicas; (car) matriculado; **~ plate** (US) n placa (de matrícula)

lick [lɪk] vt lamer; (inf: defeat) dar una paliza a; **to ~ one's lips** relamerse

licorice ['lɪkərɪs] (US) n = **liquorice**

lid [lɪd] n (of box, case) tapa; (of pan) tapadera

lido ['laɪdəu] n (BRIT) piscina

lie [laɪ] (pt **lay**, pp **lain**) vi (rest) estar echado, estar acostado; (of object: be situated) estar, encontrarse; (tell lies: pt, pp lied) mentir ♦ n mentira; **to ~ low** (fig) mantenerse a escondidas; **~ about** or **around** vi (things) estar tirado; (BRIT: people) estar tumbado; **~-down** (BRIT) n: **to have a ~-down** echarse (una siesta); **~-in** (BRIT) n: **to have a ~-in** quedarse en la cama

lieu [lu:] n: **in ~ of** prep en lugar de

lieutenant [lef'tenənt, (US) lu:'tenənt] n (MIL) teniente m

life [laif] (pl **lives**) n vida; **to come to** ~ animarse; ~ **assurance** (BRIT) n seguro de vida; ~ **belt** (BRIT) n salvavidas m inv; ~ **boat** n lancha de socorro; ~ **guard** n vigilante m/f, socorrista m/f; ~ **insurance** n = ~ **assurance**; ~ **jacket** n chaleco salvavidas; ~ **less** adj sin vida; (dull) soso; ~ **like** adj (model etc) que parece vivo; (realistic) realista; ~ **long** adj de toda la vida; ~ **preserver** (US) n cinturón m/chaleco salvavidas; ~ **sentence** n cadena perpetua; ~ **size** adj de tamaño natural; ~ **span** n vida; ~ **style** n estilo de vida; ~ **support system** n (MED) sistema m de respiración asistida; ~ **time** n (of person) vida; (of thing) período de vida

lift [lift] vt levantar; (end: ban, rule) levantar, suprimir ♦ vi (fog) disiparse ♦ n (BRIT: machine) ascensor m; **to give sb a** ~ (BRIT) llevar a uno en el coche; ~ **off** n despegue m

light [lait] (pt, pp **lighted** or **lit**) n luz f; (lamp) luz f, lámpara; (AUT) faro; (for cigarette etc) have you got a ~? ¿tienes fuego? ♦ vt (candle, cigarette, fire) encender (SP), prender (AM); (room) alumbrar ♦ adj (colour) claro; (not heavy, also fig) ligero; (room) con mucha luz; (gentle, graceful) ágil; ~ **s** npl (traffic ~s) semáforos mpl; **to come to** ~ salir a luz; **in the** ~ **of** (new evidence etc) a la luz de; ~ **up** vi (smoke) encender un cigarrillo; (face) iluminarse ♦ vt (illuminate) iluminar, alumbrar; (set fire to) encender; ~ **bulb** n bombilla (SP), foco (AM); ~ **en** vt (make less heavy) aligerar; ~ **er** n (also: cigarette ~ er) encendedor m, mechero; ~ **headed** adj (dizzy) mareado; (excited) exaltado; ~ **hearted** adj (person) alegre; (remark etc) divertido; ~ **house** n faro; ~ **ing** n (system) alumbrado; ~ **ly** adv ligeramente; (not

seriously) con poca seriedad; **to get off** ~ **ly** ser castigado con poca severidad; ~ **ness** n (in weight) ligereza

lightning ['laitniŋ] n relámpago; rayo; ~ **conductor** (US ~ **rod**) n pararrayos m inv

light: ~ **pen** n lápiz m óptico; ~ **weight** adj (suit) ligero ♦ n (BOXING) peso ligero; ~ **year** n año luz

like [laik] vt querer a uno ♦ prep como ♦ adj parecido, semejante ♦ n: **and the** ~ y otros por el estilo; **his** ~ **s and dislikes** sus gustos y aversiones; **I would** ~, **I'd** ~ me gustaría; (for purchase) quisiera; **would you** ~ **a coffee?** ¿te apetece un café?; **I** ~ **swimming** me gusta nadar; **she** ~ **s apples** le gustan las manzanas; **to look** ~ **sb/sth** parecerse a alguien/ algo; **what does it look/taste/ sound** ~? ¿cómo es/a qué sabe/cómo suena?; **that's just** ~ **him** es muy de él, es característico de él; **do it** ~ **this** hazlo así; **it is nothing** ~ ... no tiene parecido alguno con ...; ~ **able** adj simpático, agradable

likelihood ['laiklihud] n probabilidad f

likely ['laikli] adj probable; **he's** ~ **to leave** es probable que se vaya; **not** ~! ¡ni hablar!

likeness ['laiknis] n semejanza, parecido; **that's a good** ~ se parece mucho

likewise ['laikwaiz] adv igualmente; **to do** ~ hacer lo mismo

liking ['laikiŋ] n: ~ **(for)** (person) cariño (a); (thing) afición (a); **to be to sb's** ~ ser del gusto de uno

lilac ['lailək] n (tree) lilo; (flower) lila

lily ['lili] n lirio, azucena; ~ **of the valley** n lirio de los valles

limb [lim] n miembro

limber ['limbə*]: **to** ~ **up** vi (SPORT) hacer ejercicios de calentamiento

limbo ['limbəu] n: **to be in** ~ (fig) quedar a la expectativa

lime [laim] n (tree) limero; (fruit) lima;

(GEO) cal f

limelight ['laɪmlaɪt] n: to be in the ~ (fig) estar en el centro de atención

limerick ['lɪmərɪk] n especie de poema humorístico

limestone ['laɪmstəʊn] n piedra caliza

limit ['lɪmɪt] n límite m ♦ vt limitar; ~ed adj limitado; to be ~ed to limitarse a; ~ed (liability) company (BRIT) n sociedad f anónima

limousine ['lɪməziːn] n limusina

limp [lɪmp] n: to have a ~ tener cojera ♦ vi cojear ♦ adj flojo; (material) fláccido

limpet ['lɪmpɪt] n lapa

line [laɪn] n línea; (rope) cuerda; (for fishing) sedal m; (wire) hilo; (row, series) fila, hilera; (of writing) renglón m, línea; (of song) verso; (on face) arruga; (RAIL) vía ♦ vt (road etc) llenar; (SEWING) forrar; to ~ the streets llenar las aceras; in ~ with alineado con; (according to) de acuerdo con; ~ up vi hacer cola ♦ vt alinear; (prepare) preparar; organizar

lined [laɪnd] adj (face) arrugado; (paper) rayado

linen ['lɪnɪn] n ropa blanca; (cloth) lino

liner ['laɪnə*] n vapor m de línea, transatlántico m; (for bin) bolsa de basura)

linesman ['laɪnzmən] n (SPORT) juez m de línea

line-up n (US: queue) cola; (SPORT) alineación f

linger ['lɪŋgə*] vi retrasarse, tardar en marcharse; (smell, tradition) persistir

lingerie ['lænʒəri:] n lencería

linguist ['lɪŋgwɪst] n lingüista m/f; ~ics n lingüística

lining ['laɪnɪŋ] n forro; (ANAT) (membrana) mucosa

link [lɪŋk] n (of a chain) eslabón m; (relationship) relación f, vínculo ♦ vt vincular, unir; (associate): to ~ with or to relacionar con; ~s npl (GOLF) campo de golf; ~ up vt acoplar ♦ vi unirse

lino ['laɪnəʊ] n = linoleum

linoleum [lɪ'nəʊlɪəm] n linóleo

lion ['laɪən] n león m; ~ess n leona

lip [lɪp] n labio

liposuction ['lɪpəʊsʌkʃən] n liposucción f

lip: ~read vi leer los labios; ~ salve n crema protectora para labios; ~ service n: to pay ~ service to sth (pej) prometer algo de boquilla; ~stick n lápiz m de labios, carmín m

liqueur [lɪ'kjuə*] n licor m

liquid ['lɪkwɪd] adj, n líquido; ~ize [-aɪz] vt (CULIN) licuar; ~izer [-aɪzə*] n licuadora

liquor ['lɪkə*] n licor m, bebidas fpl alcohólicas

liquorice ['lɪkərɪs] (BRIT) n regaliz m

liquor store (US) n bodega, tienda de vinos y bebidas alcohólicas

Lisbon ['lɪzbən] n Lisboa

lisp [lɪsp] n ceceo ♦ vi cecear

list [lɪst] n lista ♦ vt (mention) enumerar; (put on a list) poner en una lista; ~ed building (BRIT) n monumento declarado de interés histórico-artístico

listen ['lɪsn] vi escuchar, oír; to ~ to sb/sth escuchar a uno/algo; ~er n oyente m/f; (RADIO) radioyente m/f

listless ['lɪstlɪs] adj apático, indiferente

lit [lɪt] pt, pp of **light**

liter ['li:tə*] (US) n = **litre**

literacy ['lɪtərəsɪ] n capacidad f de leer y escribir

literal ['lɪtərl] adj literal

literary ['lɪtərərɪ] adj literario

literate ['lɪtərət] adj que sabe leer y escribir; (educated) culto

literature ['lɪtərɪtʃə*] n literatura; (brochures etc) folletos mpl

lithe [laɪð] adj ágil

litigation [lɪtɪ'geɪʃən] n litigio

litre ['li:tə*] (US **liter**) n litro

litter ['lɪtə*] n (rubbish) basura; (young animals) camada, cría; ~ bin (BRIT) n papelera; ~ed adj: ~ed with (scattered) lleno de

little ['lɪtl] adj (small) pequeño; (not much) poco ♦ adv poco; a ~ un poco (de); ~ **house/bird** casita/pajarito; a ~ **bit** un poquito; ~ **by** ~ poco a poco; ~ **finger** n dedo meñique

live¹ [laɪv] adj (animal) vivo; (wire) conectado; (broadcast) en directo; (shell) cargado

live² [lɪv] vi vivir; ~ **down** vt hacer olvidar; ~ **on** vt fus (food, salary) vivir de; ~ **together** vi vivir juntos; ~ **up to** vt fus (fulfil) cumplir con

livelihood ['laɪvlɪhʊd] n sustento

lively ['laɪvlɪ] adj vivo; (interesting: place, book etc) animado

liven up ['laɪvn-] vt animar ♦ vi animarse

liver ['lɪvə*] n hígado

lives [laɪvz] npl of **life**

livestock ['laɪvstɔk] n ganado

livid ['lɪvɪd] adj lívido; (furious) furioso

living ['lɪvɪŋ] adj (alive) vivo ♦ n: to **earn** or **make a** ~ ganarse la vida; ~ **conditions** npl condiciones fpl de vida; ~ **room** n sala de (estar); ~ **standards** npl nivel m de vida; ~ **wage** n jornal m suficiente para vivir

lizard ['lɪzəd] n lagarto; (small) lagartija

load [ləʊd] n carga; (weight) peso ♦ vt (COMPUT) cargar; (also: ~ **up**): to ~ **(with)** cargar (con or de); a ~ **of rubbish** (inf) tonterías fpl; a ~ **of**, ~**s of** (fig) (gran) cantidad de, montones de; ~**ed** adj (vehicle): to be ~**ed** with estar cargado de; (question) intencionado; (inf: rich) forrado (de dinero)

loaf [ləʊf] (pl **loaves**) n (barra de) pan m

loan [ləʊn] n préstamo ♦ vt prestar; **on** ~ prestado

loath [ləʊθ] adj: to be ~ to do sth estar poco dispuesto a hacer algo

loathe [ləʊð] vt aborrecer; (person) odiar; **loathing** n aversión f; odio

loaves [ləʊvz] npl of **loaf**

lobby ['lɔbɪ] n vestíbulo, sala de

espera; (POL: pressure group) grupo de presión ♦ vt presionar

lobster ['lɔbstə*] n langosta

local ['ləʊkl] adj local ♦ n (pub) bar m; **the ~s** los vecinos, los del lugar; ~ **anaesthetic** n (MED) anestesia local; ~ **authority** n municipio, ayuntamiento (SP); ~ **call** n (TEL) llamada local; ~ **government** n gobierno municipal; **~ity** ['kælɪtɪ] n localidad f; **~ly** ['kəlɪ] adv en la vecindad; por aquí

locate [ləʊ'keɪt] vt (find) localizar; (situate) situar; to be ~**d in** estar situado en

location [ləʊ'keɪʃən] n situación f; **on** ~ (CINEMA) en exteriores

loch [lɔx] n lago

lock [lɔk] n (of door, box) cerradura; (of canal) esclusa; (of hair) mechón m ♦ vt (with key) cerrar (con llave) ♦ vi (door etc) cerrarse (con llave); (wheels) trabarse; ~ **in** vt encerrar; ~ **out** vt (person) cerrar la puerta a; ~ **up** vt (criminal) meter en la cárcel; (mental patient) encerrar; (house) cerrar (con llave) ♦ vi echar la llave

locker ['lɔkə*] n casillero

locket ['lɔkɪt] n medallón m

locksmith ['lɔksmɪθ] n cerrajero/a

lockup ['lɔkʌp] n (jail, cell) cárcel f

locum ['ləʊkəm] n (MED) interino/a

locust ['ləʊkəst] n langosta

lodge [lɔdʒ] n casita del (guarda) ♦ vi (person): to ~ **(with)** alojarse (en casa de); (bullet, bone) incrustarse ♦ vt presentar; **~r** n huésped(a) m/f

lodgings ['lɔdʒɪŋz] npl alojamiento

loft [lɔft] n desván m

lofty ['lɔftɪ] adj (noble) sublime; (haughty) altanero

log [lɔg] n (of wood) leño, tronco; (written account) diario ♦ vt anotar; ~ **in** or **on** vi (COMPUT) entrar en el sistema; ~ **off** or **out** vi (COMPUT) salir del sistema

logbook ['lɔgbʊk] n (NAUT) diario de a bordo; (AVIAT) libro de vuelo; (of car) documentación f (del coche (SP) or carro (AM))

loggerheads ['lɔɡǝhɛdz] npl: to be at ~ (with) estar en desacuerdo (con)

logic ['lɔdʒɪk] n lógica; **~al** adj lógico

logo ['lǝuɡǝu] n logotipo

loin [lɔɪn] n (CULIN) lomo, solomillo

loiter ['lɔɪtǝ*] vi (linger) entretenerse

loll [lɔl] vi (also: ~ about) repantigarse

lollipop ['lɔlɪpɔp] n chupa-chups ® m inv, pirulí m; ~ **man/lady** (BRIT irreg) n persona encargada de ayudar a los niños a cruzar la calle

---

lollipop man/lollipop lady

En el Reino Unido, se llama **lollipop man** o **lollipop lady** a la persona que se ocupa de parar el tráfico en los alrededores de los colegios para que los niños crucen sin peligro. Suelen ser personas ya jubiladas, vestidas con una gabardina de color llamativo y llevan una señal de stop portátil, la cual recuerda por su forma a una piruleta, y de ahí su nombre.

London ['lʌndǝn] n Londres; **~er** n londinense m/f

lone [lǝun] adj solitario

loneliness ['lǝunlɪnɪs] n soledad f; aislamiento

lonely ['lǝunlɪ] adj (situation) solitario; (person) solo; (place) aislado

long [lɔŋ] adj largo ♦ adv mucho tiempo, largamente ♦ vi: to ~ **for sth** anhelar algo; so or as ~ as mientras, con tal que; **don't be ~!** ¡no tardes!, ¡vuelve pronto!; **how ~ is the street?** ¿cuánto tiene la calle de largo?; **how ~ is the lesson?** ¿cuánto dura la clase?; **6 metres ~** que mide 6 metros, de 6 metros de largo; **6 months ~** que dura 6 meses, de 6 meses de duración; **all night ~** toda la noche; **he no ~er comes** ya no viene; **~ before** mucho antes; **before ~** (+ future) dentro de poco; (+ past)

poco tiempo después; **at ~ last** al fin, por fin; **~-distance** adj (race) de larga distancia; (call) interurbano; **~-haired** adj de pelo largo; **~-hand** n escritura sin abreviaturas; **~-ing** n anhelo, ansia; (nostalgia) nostalgia ♦ adj anhelante

longitude ['lɔŋɡɪtju:d] n longitud f

long: **~ jump** n salto de longitud; **~-life** adj (batteries) de larga duración; (milk) uperizado; **~-lost** adj desaparecido hace mucho tiempo; **~-range** adj (plan) de gran alcance; (missile) de largo alcance; **~-sighted** (BRIT) adj présbita; **~-standing** adj de mucho tiempo; **~-suffering** adj sufrido; **~-term** adj a largo plazo; **~ wave** n onda larga; **~-winded** adj prolijo

loo [lu:] (BRIT: inf) n wáter m

look [lʊk] vi mirar; (seem) parecer; (building etc): to ~ **south/on to the sea** dar al sur/al mar ♦ n (gen): to **have a ~** mirar; (glance) mirada; (appearance) aire m, aspecto; **~s** npl (good ~s) belleza; ~ (here)! (expressing annoyance etc) ¡oye!; ~! (expressing surprise) ¡mira!; **~ after** vt fus (care for) cuidar a; (deal with) encargarse de; **~ at** vt fus mirar; (read quickly) echar un vistazo a; **~ back** vi mirar hacia atrás; **~ down on** vt fus (fig) despreciar, mirar con desprecio; **~ for** vt fus buscar; **~ forward to** vt fus esperar con ilusión; (in letters): **we ~ forward to hearing from you** quedamos a la espera de sus gratas noticias; **~ into** vt investigar; **~ on** vi mirar (como espectador); **~ out** vi (beware): tener cuidado; **~ out for** vt fus (seek) buscar; (await) esperar; **~ round** vi volver la cabeza; **~ through** vt fus (examine) examinar; **~ to** vt fus (rely on) contar con; **~ up** vi mirar hacia arriba; (improve) mejorar ♦ vt (word) buscar; **~ up to** vt fus admirar; **~-out** n (tower etc) puesto de observación; (person)

vigía m/f; **to be on the ~-out for sth**
estar al acecho de algo

loom [luːm] *vi*: **~ (up)** *(threaten)* surgir,
amenazar; *(event: approach)*
aproximarse

loony ['luːnɪ] *(inf) n, adj* loco/a *m/f*

loop [luːp] *n* lazo ♦ *vt*: **to ~ sth round
sth** pasar algo alrededor de algo;
~hole *n* escapatoria

loose [luːs] *adj* suelto; *(clothes)* ancho;
(morals, discipline) relajado; **to be on
the ~** estar en libertad; **to be at a
~ end** *or* **at ~ ends** *(US)* no saber qué
hacer; **~ change** *n* cambio;
~ chippings *npl (on road)* gravilla
suelta; **~ly** *adv* libremente,
aproximadamente; **~n** *vt* aflojar

loot [luːt] *n* botín *m* ♦ *vt* saquear

lop off [lɒp-] *vt (branches)* podar

lop-sided *adj* torcido

lord [lɔːd] *n* señor *m*; **L~ Smith** Lord
Smith; **the L~** el Señor; **my ~** *(to
bishop)* Ilustrísima; *(to noble etc)* Señor;
good L~! ¡Dios mío!; **the (House of)
L~s** *(BRIT)* la Cámara de los Lores;
~ship *n*: **your L~ship** su Señoría

lore [lɔː*] *n* tradiciones *fpl*

lorry ['lɒrɪ] *(BRIT) n* camión *m*;
~ driver *n* camionero/a

lose [luːz] *(pt, pp lost) vt* perder ♦ *vi*
perder, ser vencido; *(clock)*
atrasarse; **~r** *n* perdedor(a) *m/f*

loss [lɒs] *n* pérdida; **heavy ~es** *(MIL)*
grandes pérdidas; **to be at a ~** no
saber qué hacer; **to make a ~** sufrir
pérdidas

lost [lɒst] *pt, pp of* **lose** ♦ *adj* perdido;
~ property *(US* **~ and found)** *n*
objetos *mpl* perdidos

lot [lɒt] *n (group: of things)* grupo; *(at
auctions)* lote *m*; **the ~** el todo, todos;
a ~ *(large number: of books etc)*
muchos; *(a great deal)* mucho,
bastante; **a ~ of, ~s of** mucho(s) *(pl)*; **I
read a ~** leo bastante; **to draw ~s
(for sth)** echar suertes (para decidir
algo)

lotion ['ləʊʃən] *n* loción *f*

lottery ['lɒtərɪ] *n* lotería *f*

loud [laʊd] *adj (voice, sound)* fuerte;
(laugh, shout) estrepitoso;
(condemnation etc) enérgico; *(gaudy)*
chillón/ona ♦ *adv (speak etc)* fuerte;
out ~ en voz alta; **~hailer** *(BRIT) n*
megáfono; **~ly** *adv* fuerte;
(aloud) en voz alta; **~speaker** *n*
altavoz *m*

lounge [laʊndʒ] *n* salón *m*, sala (de
estar); *(at airport etc)* sala; *(BRIT: also:
~-bar)* salón-bar *m* ♦ *vi (also: ~ about
or around)* reposar, holgazanear

louse [laʊs] *(pl* **lice)** *n* piojo

lousy ['laʊzɪ] *(inf) adj (bad quality)*
malísimo, asqueroso; *(ill)* fatal

lout [laʊt] *n* gamberro/a

lovable ['lʌvəbl] *adj* amable, simpático

love [lʌv] *n (romantic, sexual)* amor *m*;
(kind, caring) cariño ♦ *vt* amar, querer;
(thing, activity) encantarle a uno;
"~ from Anne" *(on letter)* "un abrazo
(de) Anne"; **to ~** *to* encantarle a
uno hacer; **to be/fall in ~ with** estar
enamorado/enamorarse de; **to make
~** hacer el amor; **"15 ~"** *(TENNIS)* "15 a cero";
I ~ paella me encanta la paella; **~
affair** *n* aventura sentimental; **~
letter** *n* carta de amor; **~ life** *n* vida
sentimental

lovely ['lʌvlɪ] *adj (delightful)*
encantador(a); *(beautiful)* precioso

lover ['lʌvə*] *n* amante *m/f*; *(person in
love)* enamorado/a; *(amateur)*: **a ~ of**
un(a) aficionado/a *or* un(a) amante de

loving ['lʌvɪŋ] *adj* amoroso, cariñoso;
(action) tierno

low [ləʊ] *adj, adv* bajo ♦ *n
(METEOROLOGY)* área de baja presión; **to
be ~ on** *(supplies etc)* andar mal de;
to feel ~ sentirse deprimido; **to turn
(down) ~** bajar; **~-alcohol** *adj* de
bajo contenido en alcohol; **~-calorie**
adj bajo en calorías; **~-cut** *adj (dress)*
escotado

lower ['ləuə*] *adj* más bajo; (*less important*) menos importante ♦ *vt* bajar; (*reduce*) reducir ♦ *vr*: **to ~ o.s. to** (*fig*) rebajarse a

low: **~-fat** *adj* (*milk, cheese*) desnatado; (*diet*) bajo en calorías; **~lands** *npl* (GEO) tierras *fpl* bajas; **~ly** *adj* humilde, inferior; **~ season** *n* la temporada baja

loyal ['lɔɪəl] *adj* leal; **~ty** *n* lealtad *f*; **~ty card** *n* tarjeta de cliente

lozenge ['lɒzɪndʒ] *n* (MED) pastilla

L.P. *n abbr* (= *long-playing record*) elepé *m*

L-plates ['el-] (BRIT) *npl* placas *fpl* de aprendiz de conductor

L-Plates

En el Reino Unido las personas que están aprendiendo a conducir deben llevar en la parte delantera y trasera de su vehículo unas placas blancas con una L en rojo conocidas como L-Plates (de learner). No es necesario que asistan a clases teóricas sino que, desde el principio, se les entrega un carnet de conducir provisional ("provisional driving licence") para que realicen sus prácticas, aunque no pueden circular por las autopistas y deben ir siempre acompañadas por un conductor con carnet definitivo ("full driving licence").

Ltd *abbr* (= *limited company*) S.A.

lubricate ['luːbrɪkeɪt] *vt* lubricar

luck [lʌk] *n* suerte *f*; **bad ~** mala suerte; **good ~!** ¡que tengas suerte!, ¡suerte!; **bad** *or* **hard** *or* **tough ~!** ¡qué pena!; **~ily** *adv* afortunadamente; **~y** *adj* afortunado; (*at cards etc*) con suerte; (*object*) que trae suerte

ludicrous ['luːdɪkrəs] *adj* absurdo

lug [lʌg] *vt* (*drag*) arrastrar

luggage ['lʌgɪdʒ] *n* equipaje *m*; **~ rack** *n* (*on car*) baca, portaequipajes *m inv*

lukewarm ['luːkwɔːm] *adj* tibio

lull [lʌl] *n* tregua ♦ *vt*: **to ~ sb to sleep** arrullar a uno; **to ~ sb into a false sense of security** dar a alguien una falsa sensación de seguridad

lullaby ['lʌləbaɪ] *n* nana

lumbago [lʌm'beɪgəu] *n* lumbago

lumber ['lʌmbə*] *n* (*junk*) trastos *mpl* viejos; (*wood*) maderos *mpl*; **~ with** *vt*: **to be ~ed with** tener que cargar con algo; **~jack** *n* maderero

luminous ['luːmɪnəs] *adj* luminoso

lump [lʌmp] *n* terrón *m*; (*fragment*) trozo; (*swelling*) bulto ♦ *vt* (*also*: **~ together**) juntar; **~ sum** *n* suma global; **~y** *adj* (*sauce*) lleno de grumos; (*mattress*) lleno de bultos

lunatic ['luːnətɪk] *adj* loco

lunch [lʌntʃ] *n* almuerzo, comida ♦ *vi* almorzar

luncheon ['lʌntʃən] *n* almuerzo; **~ voucher** (BRIT) *n* vale *m* de comida

lunch time *n* hora de comer

lung [lʌŋ] *n* pulmón *m*

lunge [lʌndʒ] *vi* (*also*: **~ forward**) abalanzarse; **to ~ at** arremeter contra

lurch [lɜːtʃ] *vi* dar sacudidas ♦ *n* sacudida; **to leave sb in the ~** dejar a uno plantado

lure [luə*] *n* (*attraction*) atracción *f* ♦ *vt* convencer con engaños

lurid ['luərɪd] *adj* (*colour*) chillón/ona; (*account*) espeluznante

lurk [lɜːk] *vi* (*person, animal*) estar al acecho; (*fig*) acechar

luscious ['lʌʃəs] *adj* (*attractive: person, thing*) precioso; (*food*) delicioso

lush [lʌʃ] *adj* exuberante

lust [lʌst] *n* lujuria; (*greed*) codicia

lustre ['lʌstə*] (US **luster**) *n* lustre *m*, brillo

lusty ['lʌstɪ] *adj* robusto, fuerte

Luxembourg ['lʌksəmbɜːg] *n* Luxemburgo

luxuriant [lʌg'zjuərɪənt] *adj* exuberante

luxurious [lʌg'zjuərɪəs] *adj* lujoso

luxury ['lʌkʃərɪ] n lujo ♦ cpd de lujo
lying ['laɪɪŋ] n mentiras fpl ♦ adj mentiroso
lyrical ['lɪrɪkl] adj lírico
lyrics ['lɪrɪks] npl (of song) letra

M, m

m. abbr = **metre; mile; million**
M.A. abbr = **Master of Arts**
mac [mæk] n (BRIT) impermeable m
macaroni [mækə'rəʊnɪ] n macarrones mpl
machine [mə'ʃiːn] n máquina ♦ vt (dress etc) coser a máquina, (TECH) hacer a máquina; **~ gun** n ametralladora; **~ language** n (COMPUT) lenguaje m máquina; **~ry** n maquinaria; (fig) mecanismo
macho ['mætʃəʊ] adj machista
mackerel ['mækrl] n inv caballa
mackintosh ['mækɪntɒʃ] (BRIT) n impermeable m
mad [mæd] adj loco; (idea) disparatado; (angry) furioso; (keen): **to be ~ about sth** volverse loco por algo
madam ['mædəm] n señora
madden ['mædn] vt volver loco
made [meɪd] pt, pp of **make**
Madeira [mə'dɪərə] n (GEO) Madera; (wine) vino de Madera
made-to-measure [BRIT] adj hecho a la medida
madly ['mædlɪ] adv locamente
madman ['mædmən] (irreg) n loco
madness ['mædnɪs] n locura
Madrid [mə'drɪd] n Madrid
magazine [mægə'ziːn] n revista; (RADIO, TV) programa m magazina
maggot ['mægət] n gusano
magic ['mædʒɪk] n magia ♦ adj mágico; **~al** adj mágico; (conjurer) prestidigitador(a) m/f
magistrate ['mædʒɪstreɪt] n juez m/f (municipal)

magnet ['mægnɪt] n imán m; **~ic** [-'netɪk] adj magnético; (personality) atrayente
magnificent [mæg'nɪfɪsənt] adj magnífico
magnify ['mægnɪfaɪ] vt (object) ampliar; (sound) aumentar; **~ing glass** n lupa
magpie ['mægpaɪ] n urraca
mahogany [mə'hɒgənɪ] n caoba
maid [meɪd] n criada; **old ~** (pej) solterona
maiden ['meɪdn] n doncella ♦ adj (aunt etc) solterona; (speech, voyage) inaugural; **~ name** n nombre m de soltera
mail [meɪl] n correo; (letters) cartas fpl ♦ vt echar al correo; **~box** (US) n buzón m; **~ing list** n lista de direcciones; **~-order** n pedido postal
maim [meɪm] vt mutilar, lisiar
main [meɪn] adj principal, mayor ♦ n (pipe) cañería maestra; (US) red f eléctrica; **the ~s** npl (BRIT: ELEC) la red eléctrica; **in the ~** = en general; **~frame** n (COMPUT) ordenador m central; **~land** n tierra firme; **~ly** adv principalmente; **~ road** n carretera; **~stay** n (fig) pilar m; **~stream** n corriente f principal
maintain [meɪn'teɪn] vt mantener; **maintenance** ['meɪntənəns] n mantenimiento; (LAW) manutención f
maize [meɪz] (BRIT) n maíz m (SP), choclo (AM)
majestic [mə'dʒestɪk] adj majestuoso
majesty ['mædʒɪstɪ] n majestad f; (title): **Your M~** Su Majestad
major ['meɪdʒər] n (MIL) comandante m ♦ adj principal; (MUS) mayor
Majorca [mə'jɔːkə] n Mallorca
majority [mə'dʒɒrɪtɪ] n mayoría
make [meɪk] (pt, pp **made**) vt hacer; (manufacture) fabricar; (mistake) cometer; (speech) pronunciar; (cause to be): **to ~ sb sad** poner triste a alguien; (force): **to ~ sb do sth**

obligar a alguien a hacer algo; (earn) ganar; (equal): **2 and 2 ~ 4** 2 y 2 son 4 ♦ n marca; **to ~ the bed** hacer la cama; **to ~ a fool of sb** poner a alguien en ridículo; **to ~ a profit/loss** obtener ganancias/sufrir pérdidas; **to ~ it** (arrive) llegar; (achieve sth) tener éxito; **what time do you ~ it?** ¿qué hora tienes?; **to ~ do with** contentarse con; **~ for** vt fus (place) dirigirse a; **~ out** vt (decipher) descifrar; (understand) entender; (see) distinguir; (cheque) extender; **~ up** vt (invent) inventar; (prepare) hacer; (constitute) constituir ♦ vi reconciliarse; (with cosmetics) maquillarse; **~ up for** vt fus compensar; **~-believe** n ficción f, invención f; **~r** n fabricante m/f; (of film, programme) autor(a) m/f; **~-shift** adj improvisado; **~-up** n maquillaje m; **~-up remover** n desmaquillador m

making ['meɪkɪŋ] n (fig): **in the ~** en vías de formación; **to have the ~s of** (person) tener madera de

Malaysia [mə'leɪʒə] n Malasia, Malaysia

male [meɪl] n (BIOL) macho ♦ adj (sex, attitude) masculino; (child etc) varón

malfunction [mæl'fʌŋkʃən] n mal funcionamiento

malice ['mælɪs] n malicia; **malicious** [mə'lɪʃəs] adj malicioso; rencoroso

malignant [mə'lɪgnənt] adj (MED) maligno

mall [mɔːl] n (also: shopping ~) centro comercial

mallet ['mælɪt] n mazo

malnutrition [mælnju:'trɪʃən] n desnutrición f

malpractice [mæl'præktɪs] n negligencia profesional

malt [mɔːlt] n malta; (whisky) whisky m de malta

Malta ['mɔːltə] n Malta; **Maltese** [-'tiːz] adj, n inv maltés/esa m/f

mammal ['mæml] n mamífero

mammoth ['mæməθ] n mamut m

♦ adj gigantesco

man [mæn] (pl **men**) n hombre m; (~kind) el hombre n (NAUT) tripular; (MIL) guarnecer; (operate: machine) manejar; **an old ~** un viejo; **~ and wife** marido y mujer

manage ['mænɪdʒ] vi arreglárselas, ir tirando ♦ vt (be in charge of) dirigir; (control: person) manejar; (: ship) gobernar; **~able** adj manejable; **~ment** n dirección f; **~r** n director(a) m/f; (of pop star) mánayer m/f; (SPORT) entrenador m/f; **~ress** n directora; entrenadora; **~rial** [-ə'dʒɪərɪəl] adj directivo; **managing director** n director(a) m/f general

mandarin ['mændərɪn] n (also: ~ orange) mandarina; (person) mandarín n

mandatory ['mændətərɪ] adj obligatorio

mane [meɪn] n (of horse) crin f; (of lion) melena

maneuver [mə'nu:və*] (US) = manoeuvre

manfully ['mænfəlɪ] adv valientemente

mangle ['mæŋgl] vt mutilar, destrozar

man: ~handle vt maltratar; **~hole** n agujero de acceso; **~hood** n edad f viril; (state) virilidad f; **~-hour** n hora-hombre f; **~hunt** n (POLICE) búsqueda y captura

mania ['meɪnɪə] n manía; **~c** ['meɪnɪæk] n maníaco/a; (fig) maniático

manic ['mænɪk] adj frenético; **~-depressive** n maníaco/a depresivo/a

manicure ['mænɪkjuə*] n manicura

manifest ['mænɪfest] vt manifestar, mostrar ♦ adj manifiesto

manifesto [mænɪ'festəu] n manifiesto

manipulate [mə'nɪpjuleɪt] vt manipular

man: ~kind [mæn'kaɪnd] n humanidad f, género humano; **~ly** adj varonil; **~-made** adj artificial

manner ['mænə*] n manera, modo;

(*behaviour*) conducta, manera de ser;
(*type*): **all ~ of things** toda clase de
cosas; **~s** npl (*behaviour*) modales mpl;
bad ~s mala educación; **~ism** n
peculiaridad f de lenguaje (*or de
comportamiento*)
manoeuvre [mə'nu:və*] (*US
maneuver) vt, vi maniobrar ♦ n
maniobra
manor ['mænə*] n (*also*: ~ **house**) casa
solariega
manpower ['mænpauə*] n mano f de
obra
mansion ['mænʃən] n palacio, casa
grande
manslaughter ['mænslɔ:tə*] n
homicidio no premeditado
mantelpiece ['mæntlpi:s] n repisa,
chimenea
manual ['mænjuəl] adj manual ♦ n
manual m
manufacture [mænju'fæktʃə*] vt
fabricar ♦ n fabricación f; **~r** n
fabricante m/f
manure [mə'njuə*] n estiércol m
manuscript ['mænjuskrɪpt] n
manuscrito
many ['mɛnɪ] adj, pron muchos/as; **a
great ~** muchísimos, un buen número
de; **~ a time** muchas veces
map [mæp] n mapa m; **to ~ out** vt
proyectar
maple ['meɪpl] n arce m (*SP*), maple m
(*AM*)
mar [mɑː*] vt estropear
marathon ['mærəθən] n maratón f
marble ['mɑːbl] n mármol m, (*toy*)
canica
March [mɑːtʃ] n marzo
march [mɑːtʃ] vi (*MIL*) marchar;
(*demonstrators*) manifestarse ♦ n
marcha; (*demonstration*) manifestación
f
mare [mɛə*] n yegua
margarine [mɑːdʒə'riːn] n margarina
margin ['mɑːdʒɪn] n margen m;
(*COMM: profit ~*) margen m de

beneficios; **~al** adj marginal; **~al seat**
n (*POL*) escaño electoral difícil de
asegurar
marigold ['mærɪgəuld] n caléndula
marijuana [mærɪ'wɑːnə] n marijuana
marina [mə'riːnə] n puerto deportivo
marinate ['mærɪneɪt] vt marinar
marine [mə'riːn] adj marino ♦ n
soldado de marina
marital ['mærɪtl] adj matrimonial;
~ status estado civil
marjoram ['mɑːdʒərəm] n mejorana
mark [mɑːk] n marca, señal f; (*in snow,
mud etc*) huella; (*stain*) mancha; (*BRIT:
SCOL*) nota; (*currency*) marco ♦ vt
marcar; manchar; (*damage: furniture*)
rayar; (*indicate: place etc*) señalar; (*BRIT:
SCOL*) calificar, corregir; **to ~ time**
marcar el paso; (*fig*) marcar(se) un
ritmo; **~ed** adj (*obvious*) marcado,
acusado; **~er** n (*sign*) marcador m;
(*bookmark*) señal f (de libro)
market ['mɑːkɪt] n mercado ♦ vt
(*COMM*) comercializar; **~ garden** (*BRIT*)
n huerto; **~ing** n márketing m; **~place**
n mercado; **~ research** n análisis m
inv de mercados
marksman ['mɑːksmən] n tirador m
marmalade ['mɑːməleɪd] n
mermelada de naranja
maroon [mə'ruːn] vt: **to be ~ed**
quedar aislado; (*fig*) quedar
abandonado
marquee [mɑː'kiː] n entoldado
marriage ['mærɪdʒ] n (*relationship,
institution*) matrimonio; (*wedding*)
boda; (*act*) casamiento; **~ certificate**
n partida de casamiento
married ['mærɪd] adj casado; (*life, love*)
conyugal
marrow ['mærəu] n médula;
(*vegetable*) calabacín m
marry ['mærɪ] vt casarse con; (*subj:
father, priest etc*) casar ♦ vi (*also: get
married*) casarse
Mars [mɑːz] n Marte m
marsh [mɑːʃ] n pantano; (*salt ~*)

marisma

marshal ['mɑːʃl] n (MIL) mariscal m; (at sports meeting etc) oficial m; (US: of police, fire department) jefe/a m/f ♦ vt (thoughts etc) ordenar; (soldiers) formar

marshy ['mɑːʃɪ] adj pantanoso

martial law ['mɑːʃl-] n ley f marcial

martyr ['mɑːtə*] n mártir m/f; **~dom** n martirio

marvel ['mɑːvl] n maravilla, prodigio ♦ vi: **to ~ (at)** maravillarse (de); **~lous** (US **~ous**) adj maravilloso

Marxist ['mɑːksɪst] adj, n marxista m/f

marzipan ['mɑːzɪpæn] n mazapán m

mascara [mæs'kɑːrə] n rímel m

masculine ['mæskjulɪn] adj masculino

mash [mæʃ] vt machacar; **~ed potatoes** npl puré m de patatas (SP) or papas (AM)

mask [mɑːsk] n máscara ♦ vt (cover): **to ~ one's face** ocultarse la cara; (hide: feelings) esconder

mason ['meɪsn] n (also: stone~) albañil m; (also: free~) masón m; **~ry** n (in building) mampostería

masquerade [mæskə'reɪd] vi: **to ~ as** disfrazarse de, hacerse pasar por

mass [mæs] n (people) muchedumbre f; (of air, liquid etc) masa; (of detail, figures etc) gran cantidad f; (REL) misa ♦ cpd masivo ♦ vi reunirse; concentrarse; **the ~es** npl las masas; **~es of** (inf) montones de

massacre ['mæsəkə*] n masacre f

massage ['mæsɑːʒ] n masaje m ♦ vt dar masaje en

masseur [mæ'sə:*] n masajista m

masseuse [mæ'sə:z] n masajista f

massive ['mæsɪv] adj enorme; (support, changes) masivo

mass media n medios mpl de comunicación

mass production n fabricación f en serie

mast [mɑːst] n (NAUT) mástil m; (RADIO etc) torre f

master ['mɑːstə*] n (of servant) amo;

(of situation) dueño, maestro; (in primary school) maestro; (in secondary school) profesor m; (title for boys): **M~ X** Señorito X ♦ vt dominar; **M~ of Arts/Science** n licenciatura superior en Letras/Ciencias; **~ly** adj magistral; **~mind** n inteligencia superior ♦ vt dirigir, planear; **~piece** n obra maestra; **~y** n maestría

mat [mæt] n estera; (also: door~) felpudo; (also: table ~) salvamanteles m inv, posavasos m inv ♦ adj = **matt**

match [mætʃ] n cerilla, fósforo; (game) partido; (equal) igual m/f ♦ vt (go well with) hacer juego con; (equal) igualar; (correspond to) corresponderse con; (pair: also: ~ up) casar con ♦ vi hacer juego; **to be a good ~** hacer juego; **~box** n caja de cerillas; **~ing** adj que hace juego

mate [meɪt] n (work~) colega m/f; (inf: friend) amigo/a; (animal) macho m/ hembra f; (in merchant navy) segundo de a bordo ♦ vi acoplarse, aparearse ♦ vt aparear

material [mə'tɪərɪəl] n (substance) materia; (information) material m; (cloth) tela, tejido ♦ adj material; (important) esencial; **~s** npl materiales mpl

maternal [mə'tə:nl] adj maternal

maternity [mə'tə:nɪtɪ] n maternidad f; **~ dress** n vestido premamá

math [mæθ] (US) n = **mathematics**

mathematical [mæθə'mætɪkl] adj matemático

mathematician [mæθəmə'tɪʃən] n matemático/a

mathematics [mæθə'mætɪks] n matemáticas fpl

maths [mæθs] (BRIT) n = **mathematics**

matinée ['mætɪneɪ] n sesión f de tarde

matrices ['meɪtrɪsiːz] npl of **matrix**

matriculation [mətrɪkju'leɪʃən] n (formalización f de) matrícula

matrimony ['mætrɪmənɪ] n

matrimonio

matrix ['meɪtrɪks] (*pl* **matrices**) *n* matriz *f*

matron ['meɪtrən] *n* enfermera *f* jefe; (*in school*) ama de llaves

mat(t) [mæt] *adj* mate

matted ['mætɪd] *adj* enmarañado

matter ['mætə*] *n* cuestión *f*, asunto; (*PHYSICS*) sustancia, materia; (*reading ~*) material *m*; (*MED: pus*) pus *m* ♦ *vi* importar; **~s** *npl* (*affairs*) asuntos *mpl*, temas *mpl*; **it doesn't ~** no importa; **what's the ~?** ¿qué pasa?; **no ~ what** pase lo que pase; **as a ~ of course** por rutina; **as a ~ of fact** de hecho; **~-of-fact** *adj* prosaico, práctico

mattress ['mætrɪs] *n* colchón *m*

mature [mə'tjuə*] *adj* maduro ♦ *vi* madurar; **maturity** *n* madurez *f*

maul [mɔːl] *vt* magullar

mauve [məuv] *adj* de color malva (*SP*) or guinda (*AM*)

maximum ['mæksɪməm] (*pl* **maxima**) *adj* máximo ♦ *n* máximo

May [meɪ] *n* mayo

may [meɪ] (*conditional*: **might**) *vi* (*indicating possibility*): **he ~ come** puede que venga; (*be allowed to*): **I smoke?** ¿puedo fumar?; (*wishes*): **~ God bless you!** ¡que Dios te bendiga!; **you ~ as well go** bien puedes irte

maybe ['meɪbiː] *adv* quizá(s)

May Day *n* el primero de Mayo

mayhem ['meɪhem] *n* caos *m* total

mayonnaise [meɪə'neɪz] *n* mayonesa

mayor [meə*] *n* alcalde *m*; **~ess** *n* alcaldesa

maze [meɪz] *n* laberinto

M.D. *abbr* = **Doctor of Medicine**

me [miː] *pron* (*direct*) me; (*stressed*, *after pron*) mí; (*after prep*) mí; **¿me oyes?; he heard ME!** me oyó a mí; **it's ~** soy yo; **give them to ~** dámelos; **las**; **with/without ~** conmigo/sin mí

meadow ['medəu] *n* prado, pradera

meagre ['miːgə*] (*US* **meager**) *adj*

escaso, pobre

meal [miːl] *n* comida; (*flour*) harina; **~time** *n* hora de comer

mean [miːn] (*pt, pp* **meant**) *adj* (*with money*) tacaño; (*unkind*) mezquino, malo; (*shabby*) humilde; (*average*) medio ♦ *vt* (*signify*) querer decir, significar; (*refer to*) referirse a; (*intend*): **to ~ to do sth** pensar o pretender hacer algo ♦ *n* medio, término medio; **~s** *npl* (*way*) medio, manera; (*money*) recursos *mpl*, medios *mpl*; **by ~s of** mediante, por medio de; **by all ~s!** ¡naturalmente!, ¡claro que sí!; **do you ~ it?** ¿lo dices en serio?; **what do you ~?** ¿qué quiere decir?; **to be meant for sb/sth** ser para uno/algo

meander [mi'ændə*] *vi* (*river*) serpentear

meaning ['miːnɪŋ] *n* significado, sentido; (*purpose*) sentido, propósito; **~ful** *adj* significativo; **~less** *adj* sin sentido

meanness ['miːnnɪs] *n* (*with money*) tacañería; (*unkindness*) maldad *f*, mezquindad *f*; (*shabbiness*) humildad *f*

meant [ment] *pt, pp of* **mean**

meantime ['miːntaɪm] *adv* (*also*: *in the ~*) mientras tanto

meanwhile ['miːnwaɪl] *adv* = **meantime**

measles ['miːzlz] *n* sarampión *m*

measure ['meʒə*] *vt, vi n* medida; (*ruler*) regla; **~ments** *npl* medidas *fpl*

meat [miːt] *n* carne *f*; **cold ~** fiambre *m*; **~ball** *n* albóndiga; **~ pie** *n* pastel *m* de carne

Mecca ['mekə] *n* La Meca

mechanic [mɪ'kænɪk] *n* mecánico/a; **~s** *n* mecánica ♦ *npl* mecanismo; **~al** *adj* mecánico

mechanism ['mekənɪzəm] *n* mecanismo

medal ['medl] *n* medalla; **~lion** [mɪ'dælɪən] *n* medallón *m*; **~list** (**~ist**) *n* (*SPORT*) medallista *m/f*

meddle ['mɛdl] vi: **to ~ in** entrometerse en; **to ~ with sth** manosear algo

media ['miːdɪə] npl medios mpl de comunicación ♦ npl of **medium**

mediaeval [mɛdɪ'iːvl] adj = **medieval**

mediate ['miːdɪeɪt] vi mediar; **mediator** n intermediario/a, mediador(a) m/f

Medicaid ® ['mɛdɪkeɪd] (US) n programa de ayuda médica para los pobres

medical ['mɛdɪkl] adj médico ♦ n reconocimiento médico

Medicare ® ['mɛdɪkɛə*] (US) n programa de ayuda médica para los ancianos

medication [mɛdɪ'keɪʃən] n medicación f

medicine ['mɛdsɪn] n medicina; (drug) medicamento

medieval [mɛdɪ'iːvl] adj medieval

mediocre [miːdɪ'əukə*] adj mediocre

meditate ['mɛdɪteɪt] vi meditar

Mediterranean [mɛdɪtə'reɪnɪən] adj mediterráneo; **the ~ (Sea)** el (Mar) Mediterráneo

medium ['miːdɪəm] adj mediano, regular ♦ n (means) medio; (pl mediums: person) médium m/f; **~ wave** n onda media

meek [miːk] adj manso, sumiso

meet [miːt] (pt, pp met) vt encontrar; (accidentally) encontrarse con, tropezar con; (by arrangement) reunirse con; (for the first time) conocer; (go and fetch) ir a buscar; (opponent) enfrentarse con; (obligations) cumplir; (encounter: problem) hacer frente a; (need) satisfacer ♦ vi encontrarse; (in session) reunirse; (join: objects) unirse; (for the first time) conocerse ♦ vt fus (difficulty) tropezar con; **to ~ with success** tener éxito; **~ing** n encuentro; (arranged) cita, compromiso; (business ~ing) reunión f; (POL) mitin m

megabyte ['mɛgəbaɪt] n (COMPUT) megabyte m, megaocteto

megaphone ['mɛgəfəun] n megáfono

melancholy ['mɛlənkəlɪ] n melancolía ♦ adj melancólico

mellow ['mɛləu] adj (wine) añejo; (sound, colour) suave ♦ vi (person) ablandar

melody ['mɛlədɪ] n melodía

melon ['mɛlən] n melón m

melt [mɛlt] vi (metal) fundirse; (snow) derretirse ♦ vt fundir; **~down** n (in nuclear reactor) fusión f de un reactor (nuclear); **~ing pot** n (fig) crisol m

member ['mɛmbə*] n (gen, ANAT) miembro; (of club) socio/a; **M~ of Parliament** (BRIT) diputado/a; **M~ of the European Parliament** (BRIT) eurodiputado/a; **M~ of the Scottish Parliament** (BRIT) diputado/a del Parlamento escocés; **~ship** n (members) número de miembros; (state) filiación f; **~ship card** n carnet m de socio

memento [mə'mɛntəu] n recuerdo

memo ['mɛməu] n apunte m, nota

memoirs ['mɛmwɑːz] npl memorias fpl

memorandum [mɛmə'rændəm] (pl **memoranda**) n apunte m, nota; (official note) acta

memorial [mɪ'mɔːrɪəl] n monumento conmemorativo ♦ adj conmemorativo

memorize ['mɛməraɪz] vt aprender de memoria

memory ['mɛmərɪ] n (also: COMPUT) memoria; (instance) recuerdo; (of dead person): **in ~ of** a la memoria de

men [mɛn] npl of **man**

menace ['mɛnəs] n amenaza ♦ vt amenazar; **menacing** adj amenazador(a)

mend [mɛnd] vt reparar, arreglar; (darn) zurcir ♦ vi reponerse ♦ n arreglo, reparación f; zurcido ♦ n: **to be on the ~** ir mejorando; **to ~ one's ways** enmendarse; **~ing** n reparación f; (clothes) ropa por remendar

meningitis [mɛnɪn'dʒaɪtɪs] n meningitis f

menopause ['menəupɔːz] n
menopausia

menstruation [menstru'eɪʃən] n
menstruación f

mental ['mentl] adj mental; **~ity**
[-'tælɪt] n mentalidad f

mention ['menʃən] n mención f ♦ vt
mencionar; (speak of) hablar de; **don't
~ it!** ¡de nada!

menu ['menjuː] n (set ~) menú m;
(printed) carta; (COMPUT) menú m

MEP n abbr = **Member of the
European Parliament**

merchandise ['mɜːtʃəndaɪz] n
mercancías fpl

merchant ['mɜːtʃənt] n comerciante
m/f; **~ bank** (BRIT) n banco comercial;
~ navy (US **~ marine**) n marina
mercante

merciful ['mɜːsɪful] adj compasivo;
(fortunate) afortunado

merciless ['mɜːsɪlɪs] adj despiadado

mercury ['mɜːkjurɪ] n mercurio

mercy ['mɜːsɪ] n compasión f; (REL)
misericordia; **at the ~ of** a la merced
de

merely ['mɪəlɪ] adv simplemente, sólo

merge [mɜːdʒ] vt (join) unir ♦ vi
unirse; (COMM) fusionarse; (colours etc)
fundirse; **~r** n (COMM) fusión f

meringue [mə'ræŋ] n merengue m

merit ['merɪt] n mérito ♦ vt merecer

mermaid ['mɜːmeɪd] n sirena

merry ['merɪ] adj alegre;
M~ Christmas! ¡Felices Pascuas!; **~-
go-round** n tiovivo

mesh [meʃ] n malla

mesmerize ['mezməraɪz] vt hipnotizar

mess [mes] n (muddle: of situation)
confusión f; (: of room) revoltijo m; (dirt)
porquería f; (MIL) comedor m; **~ about
or around** (inf) vi perder el tiempo;
(pass the time) entretenerse; **~ about
or around with** (inf) vt fus divertirse
con; **~ up** (spoil) estropear; (dirty)
ensuciar

message ['mesɪdʒ] n recado, mensaje

messenger ['mesɪndʒə*] n
mensajero/a

Messrs abbr (on letters: = Messieurs)
Sres

messy ['mesɪ] adj (dirty) sucio; (untidy)
desordenado

met [met] pt, pp of **meet**

metal ['metl] n metal m; **~lic** [-'tælɪk]
adj metálico

metaphor ['metəfə*] n metáfora

meteor ['miːtɪə*] n meteoro; **~ite**
[-aɪt] n meteorito

meteorology [miːtɪə'rɔlədʒɪ] n
meteorología

meter ['miːtə*] n (instrument) contador
m; (US: unit) = **metre** ♦ vt (US: POST)
franquear

method ['meθəd] n método

meths [meθs] (BRIT), **methylated
spirit** ['meθɪleɪtɪd-] (BRIT) n alcohol m
metilado or desnaturalizado

metre ['miːtə*] (US **meter**) n metro

metric ['metrɪk] adj métrico

metropolitan [metrə'pɔlɪtən] adj
metropolitano; **the M~ Police** (BRIT)
la policía londinense

mettle ['metl] n: **to be on one's ~**
estar dispuesto a mostrar todo lo que
uno vale

mew [mjuː] vi (cat) maullar

mews [mjuːz] n: **~ flat** (BRIT) piso
acondicionado en antiguos establos o
cocheras

Mexican ['meksɪkən] adj, n mejicano/a
m/f, mexicano/a m/f

Mexico ['meksɪkəu] n Méjico (SP),
México (AM); **~ City** n Ciudad f de
Méjico or México

miaow [miː'au] vi maullar

mice [maɪs] npl of **mouse**

micro... ['maɪkrəu] prefix micro...;
~chip n microplaqueta; **~(computer)**
n microordenador m; **~phone** n
micrófono; **~processor** n
microprocesador m; **~scope** n
microscopio; **~wave** n (also: **~wave**

oven) horno microondas

mid [mɪd] *adj*: **in ~ May** a mediados de mayo; **in ~ afternoon** a media tarde; **in ~ air** en el aire; **~day** *n* mediodía *m*

middle ['mɪdl] *n* centro; (*half-way point*) medio; (*waist*) cintura ♦ *adj* de en medio; (*course, way*) intermedio; **in the ~ of the night** en plena noche; **~-aged** *adj* de mediana edad; **the M~ Ages** *npl* la Edad Media; **~class** *adj* de clase media; **the ~ class(es)** *n(pl)* la clase media; **M~ East** *n* Oriente *m* Medio; **~man** *n* intermediario *m*; **~ name** *n* segundo nombre; **~-of-the-road** *adj* moderado; **~weight** *n* (BOXING) peso medio

middling ['mɪdlɪŋ] *adj* mediano

midge [mɪdʒ] *n* mosquito

midget ['mɪdʒɪt] *n* enano/a

Midlands ['mɪdləndz] *npl*: **the ~** la región central de Inglaterra

midnight ['mɪdnaɪt] *n* medianoche *f*

midst [mɪdst] *n*: **in the ~ of** (*crowd*) en medio de; (*situation, action*) en mitad de

midsummer [mɪd'sʌmə*] *n*: **in ~** en pleno verano

midway [mɪd'weɪ] *adj, adv*: **~ (between)** a medio camino (entre); **~ through** a la mitad de (de)

midweek [mɪd'wi:k] *adv* entre semana

midwife ['mɪdwaɪf] (*pl* **midwives**) *n* comadrona, partera

might [maɪt] *vb see* **may** ♦ *n* fuerza, poder *m*; **~y** *adj* fuerte, poderoso

migraine ['mi:greɪn] *n* jaqueca

migrant ['maɪgrənt] *n adj* (*bird*) migratorio; (*worker*) emigrante

migrate [maɪ'greɪt] *vi* emigrar

mike [maɪk] *n abbr* (= *microphone*) micro

mild [maɪld] *adj* (*person*) apacible; (*climate*) templado; (*slight*) ligero; (*taste*) suave; (*illness*) leve; **~ly** *adv* ligeramente; suavemente; **to put it**

~ly para no decir más

mile [maɪl] *n* milla; **~age** *n* número de millas, ≈ kilometraje *m*; **~ometer** [maɪ'lɔmɪtə*] *n* cuentakilómetros *m inv*; **~stone** *n* mojón *m*

militant ['mɪlɪtnt] *adj, n* militante *m/f*

military ['mɪlɪtərɪ] *adj* militar

militia [mɪ'lɪʃə] *n* milicia

milk [mɪlk] *n* leche *f* ♦ *vt* (*cow*) ordeñar; (*fig*) chupar; **~ chocolate** *n* chocolate *m* con leche; **~man** (*irreg*) *n* lechero; **~ shake** *n* batido, malteada (AM); **~y** *adj* lechoso; **M~y Way** *n* Vía Láctea

mill [mɪl] *n* (*windmill etc*) molino; (*coffee ~*) molinillo; (*factory*) fábrica ♦ *vt* moler ♦ *vi* (*also:* **~ about**) arremolinarse

millennium [mɪ'lenɪəm] (*pl* **~s** *or* **millennia**) *n* milenio, milenario

miller ['mɪlə*] *n* molinero

milli... ['mɪlɪ] *prefix*: **~gram(me)** *n* miligramo; **~metre** (US **~meter**) *n* milímetro

million ['mɪljən] *n* millón *m*; **a ~ times** un millón de veces; **~aire** [-jə'nɛə*] *n* millonario/a

milometer [maɪ'lɔmɪtə*] (BRIT) *n* = **mileometer**

mime [maɪm] *n* mímica; (*actor*) mimo/a ♦ *vt* remedar ♦ *vi* actuar de mimo

mimic ['mɪmɪk] *n* imitador(a) *m/f* ♦ *adj* mímico ♦ *vt* remedar, imitar

min. *abbr* = **minimum**; **minute(s)**

mince [mɪns] *vt* picar ♦ *n* (BRIT: CULIN) carne *f* picada; **~meat** *n* conserva de fruta picada; (US: *meat*) carne *f* picada; **~ pie** *n* empanadilla rellena de fruta picada; **~r** *n* picadora de carne

mind [maɪnd] *n* mente *f*; (*intellect*) intelecto; (*contrasted with matter*) espíritu *m* ♦ *vt* (*attend to, look after*) ocuparse de, cuidar; (*be careful of*) tener cuidado con; (*object to*): **I don't ~ the noise** no me molesta el ruido; **it is on my ~** me preocupa; **to bear**

sth in ~ tomar or tener algo en cuenta; **to make up one's ~** decidirse; **I don't ~** me es igual; **~ you, ...** te advierto que ...; **never ~!** ¡es igual!, ¡no importa!; (don't worry) ¡no te preocupes!; **"~ the step"** "cuidado con el escalón"; **~er** n guardaespaldas m inv; (child ~er) n niñera; **~ful** adj: **~ful of** consciente de; **~less** adj (crime) sin motivo; (work) de autómata

mine[1] [main] pron el mío/la mía etc; **a friend of ~** un(a) amigo/a mío/mía ♦ adj: **this book is ~** este libro es mío

mine[2] [main] n mina ♦ vt (coal) extraer; (bomb: beach etc) minar; **~field** n campo de minas; **miner** n minero/a

mineral ['mɪnərəl] adj mineral ♦ n mineral m; **~s** npl (BRIT: soft drinks) refrescos mpl; **~ water** n agua mineral

mingle ['mɪŋgl] vi: **to ~ with** mezclarse con

miniature ['mɪnətʃə*] adj (en) miniatura ♦ n miniatura

minibus ['mɪnɪbʌs] n microbús m

Minidisc ® ['mɪnɪdɪsk] n minidisco

minimal ['mɪnɪml] adj mínimo

minimize ['mɪnɪmaɪz] vt minimizar; (play down) empequeñecer

minimum ['mɪnɪməm] (pl **minima**) n, adj mínimo

mining ['maɪnɪŋ] n explotación f minera

miniskirt ['mɪnɪskə:t] n minifalda

minister ['mɪnɪstə*] n (BRIT: POL) ministro/a (SP), secretario/a (AM); (REL) pastor m ♦ vi: **to ~** to atender a

ministry ['mɪnɪstrɪ] n (BRIT: POL) ministerio (SP), secretaría (AM); (REL) sacerdocio

mink [mɪŋk] n visón m

minnow ['mɪnəu] n pececillo (de agua dulce)

minor ['maɪnə*] adj (repairs, injuries) leve; (poet, planet) menor; (MUS) menor ♦ n (LAW) menor m de edad

Minorca [mɪ'nɔ:kə] n Menorca

minority [maɪ'nɔrɪtɪ] n minoría

mint [mɪnt] n (plant) menta, hierbabuena; (sweet) caramelo de menta ♦ vt (coins) acuñar; **the (Royal) M~,** (US) **M~** la Casa de la Moneda; **in ~ condition** en perfecto estado

minus ['maɪnəs] n (also: **~ sign**) signo de menos ♦ prep menos; **12 ~ 6 equals 6** 12 menos 6 son 6; **~ 24°C** menos 24 grados

minute[1] ['mɪnɪt] n minuto; (fig) momento; **~s** npl (of meeting) actas fpl; **at the last ~** a última hora

minute[2] [maɪ'nju:t] adj diminuto; (search) minucioso

miracle ['mɪrəkl] n milagro

mirage ['mɪrɑ:ʒ] n espejismo

mirror ['mɪrə*] n espejo; (in car) retrovisor m

mirth [mə:θ] n alegría

misadventure [mɪsəd'ventʃə*] n desgracia

misapprehension [mɪsæprɪ'henʃən] n equivocación f

misappropriate [mɪsə'prəuprɪeɪt] vt malversar

misbehave [mɪsbɪ'heɪv] vi portarse mal

miscalculate [mɪs'kælkjuleɪt] vt calcular mal

miscarriage [mɪs'kærɪdʒ] n (MED) aborto; **~ of justice** error m judicial

miscellaneous [mɪsɪ'leɪnɪəs] adj varios/as, diversos/as

mischief ['mɪstʃɪf] n travesuras fpl, diabluras fpl; (maliciousness) malicia; **mischievous** [-tʃɪvəs] adj travieso

misconception [mɪskən'sepʃən] n idea equivocada; (wrong idea)

misconduct [mɪs'kɔndʌkt] n mala conducta; **professional ~** falta profesional

misdemeanour [mɪsdɪ'mi:nə*] (US **misdemeanor**) n delito, ofensa

miser ['maɪzə*] n avaro/a

miserable ['mɪzərəbl] adj (unhappy)

triste, desgraciado; (*unpleasant, contemptible*) miserable

miserly ['maɪzəlɪ] *adj* avariento, tacaño

misery ['mɪzərɪ] *n* tristeza; (*wretchedness*) miseria, desdicha

misfire [mɪs'faɪə*] *vi* fallar

misfit ['mɪsfɪt] *n* inadaptado/a

misfortune [mɪs'fɔːtʃən] *n* desgracia

misgiving [mɪs'gɪvɪŋ] *n* (*apprehension*) presentimiento; **to have ~s about sth** tener dudas acerca de algo

misguided [mɪs'gaɪdɪd] *adj* equivocado

mishandle [mɪs'hændl] *vt* (*mismanage*) manejar mal

mishap [mɪs'hæp] *n* desgracia, contratiempo

misinform [mɪsɪn'fɔːm] *vt* informar mal

misinterpret [mɪsɪn'təːprɪt] *vt* interpretar mal

misjudge [mɪs'dʒʌdʒ] *vt* juzgar mal

mislay [mɪs'leɪ] (*irreg*) *vt* extraviar, perder

mislead [mɪs'liːd] (*irreg*) *vt* llevar a conclusiones erróneas; **~ing** *adj* engañoso

mismanage [mɪs'mænɪdʒ] *vt* administrar mal

misplace [mɪs'pleɪs] *vt* extraviar

misprint ['mɪsprɪnt] *n* errata, error *m* de imprenta

Miss [mɪs] *n* Señorita

miss [mɪs] *vt* (*train etc*) perder; (*fail to hit: target*) errar; (*regret the absence of*): **I ~ him** (yo) le echo de menos or a faltar; (*fail to see*): **you can't ~ it** no tiene pérdida ♦ *vi* fallar ♦ *n* (*shot*) tiro fallido or perdido; **~ out** (*BRIT*) *vt* omitir

misshapen [mɪs'ʃeɪpən] *adj* deforme

missile ['mɪsaɪl] *n* (*AVIAT*) misil *m*; (*object thrown*) proyectil *m*

missing ['mɪsɪŋ] *adj* (*pupil*) ausente; (*thing*) perdido; (*MIL*): **~ in action** desaparecido en combate

mission ['mɪʃən] *n* misión *f*; (*official*

representation) delegación *f*; **~ary** *n* misionero/a

mist [mɪst] *n* (*light*) neblina; (*heavy*) niebla; (*at sea*) bruma ♦ *vi* (*eyes: also*: ~ **over**, ~ **up**) llenarse de lágrimas; (*BRIT: windows: also*: ~ **over**, ~ **up**) empañarse

mistake [mɪs'teɪk] (*vt: irreg*) *n* error *m* ♦ *vt* entender mal; **by ~** por equivocación; **to make a ~** equivocarse; **to ~ A for B** confundir A con B; **mistaken** *pp* of **mistake** ♦ *adj* equivocado; **to be mistaken** equivocarse, engañarse

mister ['mɪstə*] (*inf*) *n* señor *m*; *see* **Mr**

mistletoe ['mɪsltəu] *n* muérdago

mistook [mɪs'tuk] *pt* of **mistake**

mistress ['mɪstrɪs] *n* (*lover*) amante *f*; (*of house*) señora (de la casa); (*BRIT: in primary school*) maestra; (*in secondary school*) profesora; (*of situation*) dueña

mistrust [mɪs'trʌst] *vt* desconfiar de

misty ['mɪstɪ] *adj* (*day*) de niebla; (*glasses etc*) empañado

misunderstand [mɪsʌndə'stænd] (*irreg*) *vt, vi* entender mal; **~ing** *n* malentendido

misuse [*n* mɪs'juːs, *vb* mɪs'juːz] *n* mal uso; (*of power*) abuso; (*of funds*) malversación *f* ♦ *vt* abusar de; malversar

mitt(en) ['mɪt(n)] *n* manopla

mix [mɪks] *vt* mezclar; (*combine*) unir ♦ *vi* mezclarse; (*people*) llevarse bien ♦ *n* mezcla; **~ up** *vt* mezclar; (*confuse*) confundir; **~ed** *adj* mixto; (*feelings etc*) encontrado; **~ed-up** *adj* (*confused*) confuso, revuelto; **~er** *n* (*for food*) licuadora; (*for drinks*) coctelera; (*person*): **he's a good ~er** tiene don de gentes; **~ture** *n* mezcla; (*also*: **cough ~ture**) jarabe *m*; **~-up** *n* confusión *f*

mm *abbr* (= *millimetre*) mm

moan [məun] *n* gemido ♦ *vi* gemir; (*inf: complain*): **to ~ (about)** quejarse (de)

moat [məʊt] n foso
mob [mɒb] n multitud f ♦ vt acosar
mobile [ˈməʊbaɪl] adj móvil m; **~ home** n caravana; **~ phone** n teléfono portátil
mock [mɒk] vt (ridicule) ridiculizar; (laugh at) burlarse de ♦ adj fingido; **~ exam** examen preparatorio antes de los exámenes oficiales; **~ery** n burla; **~ up** n maqueta
mod [mɒd] adj see **convenience**
mode [məʊd] n modo
model [ˈmɒdl] n modelo; (fashion ~, artist's ~) modelo m/f ♦ adj modelo ♦ vt (with clay etc) modelar (copy): **to o.s. on** tomar como modelo a ♦ vi ser modelo; **to ~ clothes** pasar modelos, ser modelo; **~ railway** n ferrocarril m de juguete
modem [ˈməʊdəm] n módem m
moderate [adj ˈmɒdərət, vb ˈmɒdəreɪt] adj moderado/a ♦ vi moderarse, calmarse ♦ vt moderar
modern [ˈmɒdən] adj moderno; **~ize** vt modernizar
modest [ˈmɒdɪst] adj modesto; (small) módico; **~y** n modestia
modify [ˈmɒdɪfaɪ] vt modificar
mogul [ˈməʊgəl] n (fig) magnate m
mohair [ˈməʊhɛə*] n mohair m
moist [mɔɪst] adj húmedo; **~en** [ˈmɔɪsn] vt humedecer; **~ure** [ˈmɔɪstʃə*] n humedad f; **~urizer** [ˈmɔɪstʃəraɪzə*] n crema hidratante
molar [ˈməʊlə*] n muela
mold [məʊld] (US) n, vt = **mould**
mole [məʊl] n (animal, spy) topo; (spot) lunar m
molest [məʊˈlest] vt importunar; (assault sexually) abusar sexualmente de
mollycoddle [ˈmɒlɪkɒdl] vt mimar
molt [məʊlt] (US) vi = **moult**
molten [ˈməʊltən] adj fundido; (lava) líquido
mom [mɒm] (US) n = **mum**
moment [ˈməʊmənt] n momento; **at**

the ~ de momento, por ahora; **~ary** adj momentáneo; **~ous** [-ˈmentəs] adj trascendental, importante
momentum [məʊˈmentəm] n momento; (fig) ímpetu m; **to gather ~** cobrar velocidad; (fig) ganar fuerza
mommy [ˈmɒmɪ] (US) n = **mummy**
Monaco [ˈmɒnəkəʊ] n Mónaco
monarch [ˈmɒnək] n monarca m/f; **~y** n monarquía
monastery [ˈmɒnəstərɪ] n monasterio
Monday [ˈmʌndɪ] n lunes m inv
monetary [ˈmʌnɪtərɪ] adj monetario
money [ˈmʌnɪ] n dinero; (currency) moneda; **to make ~** ganar dinero; **~ order** n giro; **~-spinner** (inf) n: **to be a ~-spinner** dar mucho dinero
mongrel [ˈmʌŋgrəl] n (dog) perro mestizo
monitor [ˈmɒnɪtə*] n (SCOL) monitor m; (also: television ~) receptor m de control; (of computer) monitor m ♦ vt controlar
monk [mʌŋk] n monje m
monkey [ˈmʌŋkɪ] n mono; **~ nut** (BRIT) n cacahuete m (SP), maní m (AM); **~ wrench** n llave f inglesa
monopoly [məˈnɒpəlɪ] n monopolio
monotone [ˈmɒnətəʊn] n voz f (or tono) monocorde
monotonous [məˈnɒtənəs] adj monótono
monsoon [mɒnˈsuːn] n monzón m
monster [ˈmɒnstə*] n monstruo
monstrous [ˈmɒnstrəs] adj (huge) enorme; (atrocious, ugly) monstruoso
month [mʌnθ] n mes m; **~ly** adj mensual ♦ adv mensualmente
monument [ˈmɒnjʊmənt] n monumento
moo [muː] vi mugir
mood [muːd] n humor m; (of crowd, group) clima m; **to be in a good/bad ~** estar de buen/mal humor; **~y** adj (changeable) de humor variable; (sullen) malhumorado
moon [muːn] n luna; **~light** n luz f de

la luna; **~lighting** n pluriempleo; **~lit** adj: **a ~lit night** una noche de luna

Moor [muə*] n moro/a

moor [muə*] n páramo ♦ vt (ship) amarrar ♦ vi echar las amarras

Moorish ['muərɪʃ] adj moro; (architecture) árabe, morisco

moorland ['muələnd] n páramo, brezal m

moose [mu:s] n inv alce m

mop [mɔp] n fregona; (of hair) greña, melena ♦ vt fregar; **~ up** vt limpiar

mope [məup] vi estar o andar deprimido

moped ['məuped] n ciclomotor m

moral ['mɔrl] adj moral ♦ n moraleja; **~s** npl moralidad f, moral f

morale [mɔ'rɑ:l] n moral f

morality [mə'rælɪt] n moralidad f

morass [mə'ræs] n pantano

KEYWORD

---

most [məust] adj **1** (greater in number etc) más; **~ people/work than before** más gente/trabajo que antes **2** (additional) más; **do you want (some) ~ tea?** ¿quieres más té?; **is there any ~ wine?** ¿queda vino?; **it'll take a few ~ weeks** tardará unas semanas más; **it's 2 kms ~ to the house** faltan 2 kms para la casa; **~ time/letters than we expected** más tiempo del que/más cartas de las que esperábamos

♦ pron (greater amount, additional amount) más; **~ than 10** más de 10; **it cost ~ than the other one/than we expected** costó más o más de lo que esperábamos; **is there any ~?** ¿hay más?; **many/much ~** muchos(as)/mucho(a) más

♦ adv más; **~ dangerous/easily (than)** más peligroso/fácilmente (que); **~ and ~ expensive** cada vez más caro; **~ or less** más o menos; **~ than ever** más que nunca

---

moreover [mɔ:'rəuvə*] adv además, por otra parte

morning ['mɔ:nɪŋ] n mañana; (early ~) madrugada ♦ cpd matutino, de la mañana; **in the ~** por la mañana; **7 o'clock in the ~** las 7 de la mañana; **~ sickness** n náuseas fpl matutinas

Morocco [mə'rɔkəu] n Marruecos m

moron ['mɔ:rɔn] (inf) n imbécil m/f

morphine ['mɔ:fi:n] n morfina

Morse [mɔ:s] n (also: **~ code**) (código) Morse

morsel ['mɔ:sl] n (of food) bocado

mortar ['mɔ:tə*] n argamasa

mortgage ['mɔ:ɡɪdʒ] n hipoteca ♦ vt hipotecar; **~ company** (US) n ≈ banco hipotecario

mortuary ['mɔ:tjuəri] n depósito de cadáveres

Moscow ['mɔskəu] n Moscú

Moslem ['mɔzləm] adj, n = **Muslim**

mosque [mɔsk] n mezquita

mosquito [mɔs'ki:təu] (pl **~es**) n mosquito (SP), zancudo (AM)

moss [mɔs] n musgo

most [məust] adj la mayor parte de, la mayoría de ♦ pron la mayor parte, la mayoría ♦ adv el más; (very) muy; **the** (also: + adj) **el más; ~ of them** la mayor parte de ellos; **I saw the ~** yo vi el que más; **at the (very) ~** a lo sumo, todo lo más; **to make the ~ of** aprovechar (al máximo); **a ~ interesting book** un libro interesantísimo; **~ly** adv en su mayor parte, principalmente

MOT (BRIT) n abbr (= Ministry of Transport): **the ~ (test)** inspección (anual) obligatoria de coches y camiones

motel [məu'tel] n motel m

moth [mɔθ] n mariposa nocturna; (clothes ~) polilla

mother ['mʌðə*] n madre f ♦ adj materno ♦ vt (care for) cuidar (como una madre); **~hood** n maternidad f; **~-in-law** n suegra; **~ly** adj maternal;

~-of-pearl n nácar m; **~-to-be** n
futura madre f; **~ tongue** n lengua
materna

motion ['məʊʃən] n movimiento;
(gesture) además m, señal f; (at
meeting) moción f ♦ vt, vi: **to ~ (to) sb
to do sth** hacer señas a uno para que
haga algo; **~less** adj inmóvil;
~ picture n película

motivated ['məʊtɪveɪtɪd] adj
motivado

motive ['məʊtɪv] n motivo

motley ['mɒtlɪ] adj variado

motor ['məʊtə*] n motor m; (BRIT: inf:
vehicle) coche m (SP), carro (AM),
automóvil m ♦ adj motor (f: motora or
motriz); **~bike** n moto f; **~boat** n
lancha motora; **~car** (BRIT) n coche m,
carro, automóvil m; **~cycle** n
motocicleta; **~cycle racing** n
motociclismo; **~cyclist** n motociclista
m/f; **~ing** (BRIT) n automovilismo; **~ist**
n conductor(a) m/f, automovilista m/f;
~ racing (BRIT) n carreras fpl de
coches, automovilismo; **~ vehicle** n
automóvil m; **~way** (BRIT) n autopista

mottled ['mɒtld] adj abigarrado

motto ['mɒtəʊ] (pl **~es**) n lema m,
(watchword) consigna

mould [məʊld] (US **mold**) n molde m,
(mildew) moho ♦ vt moldear; (fig)
formar; **~y** adj enmohecido

moult [məʊlt] (US **molt**) vi mudar la
piel (or las plumas)

mound [maʊnd] n montón m,
montículo

mount [maʊnt] n monte m ♦ vt
montar, subir a; (jewel) engarzar;
(picture) enmarcar; (exhibition etc)
organizar ♦ vi (increase) aumentar;
~ up vi aumentar

mountain ['maʊntɪn] n montaña
♦ cpd de montaña; **~ bike** n bicicleta
de montaña; **~eer** [-'nɪə*] n
montañero/a (SP), andinista m/f (AM);
~eering [-'nɪərɪŋ] n montañismo,
andinismo; **~ous** adj montañoso

~ rescue team n equipo de rescate
de montaña; **~side** n ladera de la
montaña

mourn [mɔːn] vt llorar, lamentar ♦ vi:
to ~ for llorar la muerte de; **~er** n
doliente m/f; dolorido/a; **~ing** n luto;
in ~ing de luto

mouse [maʊs] (pl **mice**) n (ZOOL,
COMPUT) ratón m; **~ mat** n (COMPUT)
alfombrilla; **~trap** n ratonera

mousse [muːs] n (CULIN) crema
batida; (for hair) espuma (moldeadora)

moustache [məs'tɑːʃ] (US **mustache**)
n bigote m

mousy ['maʊsɪ] adj (hair) pardusco

mouth [maʊθ, pl maʊðz] n boca; (of
river) desembocadura; **~ful** n bocado;
~ organ n armónica; **~piece** n (of
musical instrument) boquilla;
(spokesman) portavoz m/f; **~wash** n
enjuague m; **~watering** adj apetitoso

movable ['muːvəbl] adj movible

move [muːv] n (movement)
movimiento; (in game) jugada; (: turn
to play) turno; (change: of house)
mudanza; (: of job) cambio de trabajo
♦ vt mover; (emotionally) conmover;
(POL: resolution etc) proponer ♦ vi
moverse; (traffic) circular; (also:
~ house) trasladarse, mudarse; **to ~ sb
to do sth** mover a uno a hacer algo;
to get a ~ on darse prisa; **~ about** or
around vi moverse; (travel) viajar;
~ along vi avanzar, adelantarse;
~ away vi alejarse; **~ back** vi
retroceder; **~ forward** vi avanzar; **~ in**
vi (to a house) instalarse; (police,
soldiers) intervenir; **~ on** vi ponerse en
camino; **~ out** vi (of house) mudarse;
~ over vi apartarse, hacer sitio; **~ up**
vi (employee) ser ascendido

moveable ['muːvəbl] adj = **movable**

movement ['muːvmənt] n
movimiento

movie ['muːvɪ] n película; **to go to
the ~s** ir al cine

moving ['muːvɪŋ] adj (emotional)

conmovedor(a); (that moves) móvil

mow [məu] (pt **mowed**
or **mown**) vt (grass, corn) cortar,
segar; ~ **down** vt (shoot) acribillar; ~**er**
n (also: lawn~er) cortacéspedes m inv

MP n abbr = **Member of Parliament**

m.p.h. abbr = **miles per hour** (60 m.p.h.
= 96 k.p.h.)

Mr ['mɪstə*] (US **Mr.**) n: ~ **Smith** (el)
Sr. Smith

Mrs ['mɪsɪz] (US **Mrs.**) n: ~ **Smith** (la)
Sra. Smith

Ms [mɪz] (US **Ms.**) n (= Miss or Mrs):
~ **Smith** (la) Sr(t)a. Smith

M.Sc. abbr = **Master of Science**

MSP n abbr = **Member of the
Scottish Parliament**

much [mʌtʃ] adj mucho ♦ adv mucho;
(before vb) muy ♦ n or pron mucho;
how ~ is it? ¿cuánto es?, ¿cuánto
cuesta?; **too ~** demasiado; **it's not ~**
no es mucho; **as ~ as** tanto como;
however ~ he tries por mucho que
se esfuerce

muck [mʌk] n suciedad f; ~ **about** or
around (inf) vi perder el tiempo;
(enjoy o.s.) entretenerse; ~ **up** (inf) vt
arruinar, estropear

mud [mʌd] n barro, lodo

muddle ['mʌdl] n desorden m,
confusión f; (mix-up) embrollo, lío ♦ vt
(also: ~ up) embrollar, confundir;
~ **through** vi salir del paso

muddy ['mʌdɪ] adj fangoso, cubierto
de lodo

mudguard ['mʌdgɑːd] n guardabarros
m inv

muffin ['mʌfɪn] n panecillo dulce

muffle ['mʌfl] vt (sound) amortiguar;
(against cold) embozar; ~**d** adj (noise
etc) amortiguado, apagado; ~**r** (US) n
(AUT) silenciador m

mug [mʌg] n taza grande (sin platillo);
(for beer) jarra; (inf: face) jeta f
(assault) asaltar; ~**ging** n asalto

muggy ['mʌgɪ] adj bochornoso

mule [mjuːl] n mula

multi... [mʌltɪ] prefix multi...

multi-level ['mʌltɪ'levl] (US) adj =
multistorey

multiple ['mʌltɪpl] adj múltiple ♦ n
múltiplo; ~ **sclerosis** n esclerosis f
múltiple

multiplex cinema ['mʌltɪpleks-] n
multicines mpl

multiplication [mʌltɪplɪ'keɪʃən] n
multiplicación f

multiply ['mʌltɪplaɪ] vt multiplicar ♦ vi
multiplicarse

multistorey [mʌltɪ'stɔːrɪ] (BRIT) adj de
muchos pisos

multitude ['mʌltɪtjuːd] n multitud f

mum [mʌm] (BRIT: inf) n mamá ♦ adj:
to keep ~ mantener la boca cerrada

mumble ['mʌmbl] vt, vi hablar entre
dientes, refunfuñar

mummy ['mʌmɪ] n (BRIT: mother)
mamá; (embalmed) momia

mumps [mʌmps] n paperas fpl

munch [mʌntʃ] vt, vi mascar

mundane [mʌn'deɪn] adj trivial

municipal [mjuː'nɪsɪpl] adj municipal

murder ['mɜːdə*] n asesinato; (in law)
homicidio ♦ vt asesinar, matar; ~**er/
ess** n asesino/a; ~**ous** adj homicida

murky ['mɜːkɪ] adj (water) turbio;
(street, night) lóbrego

murmur ['mɜːmə*] n murmullo ♦ vt, vi
murmurar

muscle ['mʌsl] n músculo; (fig:
strength) garra, fuerza; ~ **in** vi
entrometerse; **muscular**
['mʌskjulə*] adj muscular; (person) musculoso

muse [mjuːz] vi meditar ♦ n musa

museum [mjuː'zɪəm] n museo

mushroom ['mʌʃrum] n seta, hongo;
(CULIN) champiñón m ♦ vi crecer de la
noche a la mañana

music ['mjuːzɪk] n música; ~**al** adj
musical; (sound) melodioso; (person)
con talento musical ♦ n (show)
comedia musical; ~**al instrument** n
instrumento musical; ~ **hall** n teatro
de variedades; ~**ian** [-'zɪʃən] n

músico/a

Muslim ['mʌzlɪm] *adj, n* musulmán/
ana *m/f*

muslin ['mʌzlɪn] *n* muselina

mussel ['mʌsl] *n* mejillón *m*

must [mʌst] *aux vb (obligation)*: **I ~ do
it** debo hacerlo, tengo que hacerlo;
(probability): **he ~ be there by now**
ya debe (de) estar allí ♦ *n*: **it's a ~ es**
imprescindible

mustache ['mʌstæʃ] *(US) n =
moustache*

mustard ['mʌstəd] *n* mostaza

muster ['mʌstə*] *vt* juntar, reunir

mustn't ['mʌsnt] = **must not**

mute [mjuːt] *adj, n* mudo/a *m/f*

muted ['mjuːtɪd] *adj* callado/a; *(colour)*
apagado

mutiny ['mjuːtɪnɪ] *n* motín *m* ♦ *vi*
amotinarse

mutter ['mʌtə*] *vt, vi* murmurar

mutton ['mʌtn] *n* carne *f* de cordero

mutual ['mjuːtʃuəl] *adj* mutuo;
(interest) común; **~ly** *adv* mutuamente

muzzle ['mʌzl] *n* hocico; *(for dog)*
bozal *m*; *(of gun)* boca ♦ *vt (dog)* poner
un bozal a

my [maɪ] *adj* mis(s); **~ house/
brother/sisters** mi casa/mi
hermano/mis hermanas; **I've washed
~ hair/cut ~ finger** me he lavado el
pelo/cortado un dedo; **is this ~ pen
or yours?** ¿es este bolígrafo mío o
tuyo?

myself [maɪˈself] *pron (reflexive)* me;
(emphatic) yo mismo; *(after prep)* mí
(mismo); *see also* **oneself**

mysterious [mɪsˈtɪərɪəs] *adj* misterioso

mystery ['mɪstərɪ] *n* misterio

mystify ['mɪstɪfaɪ] *vt (perplex)* dejar
perplejo

myth [mɪθ] *n* mito

N, n

n/a *abbr* (= *not applicable*) no interesa

nag [næg] *vt (scold)* regañar; **~ging** *adj
(doubt)* persistente; *(pain)* continuo

nail [neɪl] *n (human)* uña; *(metal)* clavo
♦ *vt clavar*; **to ~ sth to sth** clavar algo
en algo; **to ~ sb down to doing sth**
comprometer a uno a que haga algo;
~brush *n* cepillo para las uñas; **~file** *n*
lima para las uñas; **~ polish** *n* esmalte
m or laca para las uñas; **~ polish
remover** *n* quitaesmalte *m*;
~ scissors *npl* tijeras *fpl* para las uñas;
~ varnish *(BRIT) n* = **~ polish**

naïve [naɪˈiːv] *adj* ingenuo

naked ['neɪkɪd] *adj (nude)* desnudo;
(flame) expuesto al aire

name [neɪm] *n* nombre *m*; *(surname)*
apellido; *(reputation)* fama, renombre
m ♦ *vt (child)* poner nombre a;
(criminal) identificar; *(price, date etc)*
fijar; **what's your ~?** ¿cómo se
llama?; **by ~** de nombre; **in the ~ of**
en nombre de; **to give one's ~ and
address** dar sus señas; **~ly** *adv* a
saber; **~sake** *n* tocayo/a

nanny ['nænɪ] *n* niñera

nap [næp] *n (sleep)* sueñecito, siesta

nape [neɪp] *n*: **~ of the neck** nuca,
cogote *m*

napkin ['næpkɪn] *n (also: table ~)*
servilleta

nappy ['næpɪ] *n (BRIT)* pañal *m*;
~ rash *n* prurito

narcotic [naːˈkɔtɪk] *adj, n* narcótico

narrow ['nærəu] *adj* estrecho, angosto;
(fig: majority etc) corto; *(: ideas etc)*
estrecho ♦ *vi (road)* estrecharse;
(diminish) reducirse; **to have a
~ escape** escaparse por los pelos; **to
~ sth down** reducir algo; **~ly** *adv
(miss)* por poco; **~-minded** *adj* de
miras estrechas

nasty ['nɑːstɪ] *adj (remark)* feo;

(person) antipático; (revolting: taste, smell) asqueroso; (wound, disease etc) peligroso, grave
nation ['neɪʃən] n nación f
national ['næʃənl] adj, n nacional m/f; ~ **dress** n vestido nacional; **N~ Health Service** (BRIT) n servicio nacional de salud pública; ≈ Insalud m (SP); **N~ Insurance** (BRIT) n seguro social nacional; ~**ism** n nacionalismo; ~**ist** adj, n nacionalista m/f; ~**ity** [-'nælɪtɪ] n nacionalidad f; ~**ize** vt nacionalizar; ~**ly** adv (nationwide) en escala nacional; (as a nation) nacionalmente, como nación; ~ **park** (BRIT) n parque m nacional
nationwide ['neɪʃənwaɪd] adj en escala o a nivel nacional
native ['neɪtɪv] n (local inhabitant) natural m/f, nativo/a ♦ adj (indigenous) indígena; (country) natal; (innate) natural, innato; **a ~ of Russia** un(a) natural m/f de Rusia; **a ~ speaker of French** un hablante nativo de francés; **N~ American** adj, n americano/a indígena, amerindio/a; ~ **language** n lengua materna
Nativity [nə'tɪvɪtɪ] n: **the ~** Navidad f
NATO ['neɪtəu] n abbr (= North Atlantic Treaty Organization) OTAN f
natural ['nætʃrəl] adj natural; ~**ly** adv (speak etc) naturalmente; (of course) desde luego, por supuesto
nature ['neɪtʃə*] n (also: N~) naturaleza; (group, sort) género, clase f; (character) carácter m, genio; **by ~** por o de naturaleza
naught [nɔːt] n = nought
naughty ['nɔːtɪ] adj (child) travieso
nausea ['nɔːsɪə] n náuseas fpl
nautical ['nɔːtɪkl] adj náutico, marítimo; (mile) marino
naval ['neɪvl] adj naval, de marina; ~ **officer** n oficial m/f de marina
nave [neɪv] n nave f
navel ['neɪvl] n ombligo
navigate ['nævɪgeɪt] vt gobernar ♦ vi

navegar; (AUT) ir de copiloto
navigation [-'geɪʃən] n (action) navegación f; (science) náutica
navigator n navegador m/f, navegante m/f; (AUT) copiloto m/f
navvy ['nævɪ] (BRIT) n peón m caminero
navy ['neɪvɪ] n marina de guerra; (ships) armada, flota; ~**(-blue)** adj azul marino
Nazi ['nɑːtsɪ] n nazi m/f
NB abbr (= nota bene) nótese
near [nɪə*] adj (place, relation) cercano; (time) próximo ♦ adv cerca ♦ prep (also: ~ to: space) cerca de, junto a; (: time) cerca de ♦ vt acercarse a, aproximarse a; ~**by** [nɪə'baɪ] adj cercano, próximo ♦ adv cerca; ~**ly** adv casi, por poco; **I ~ly fell** por poco me caigo; ~ **miss** n tiro cercano; ~**side** n (AUT: in Britain) lado izquierdo; (: in US, Europe etc) lado derecho; ~**sighted** adj miope, corto de vista
neat [niːt] adj (place) ordenado, bien cuidado; (person) pulcro; (plan) ingenioso; (spirits) solo; ~**ly** adv (tidily) con esmero; (skilfully) ingeniosamente
necessarily ['nesɪsrɪlɪ] adv necesariamente
necessary ['nesɪsrɪ] adj necesario, preciso
necessitate [nɪ'sesɪteɪt] vt hacer necesario
necessity [nɪ'sesɪtɪ] n necesidad f; **necessities** npl artículos mpl de primera necesidad
neck [nek] n (of person, garment, bottle) cuello; (of animal) pescuezo ♦ vi (inf) besuquearse; ~ **and ~** parejos; ~**lace** ['neklɪs] n collar m; ~**line** n escote m; ~**tie** ['nektaɪ] n corbata
née [neɪ] adj: ~ **Scott** de soltera Scott
need [niːd] n (lack) escasez f, falta; (necessity) necesidad f ♦ vt (require) necesitar; **I ~ to do it** tengo que o debo hacerlo; **you don't ~ to go** no hace falta que (te) vayas

needle ['niːdl] n aguja ♦ vt (fig: inf) picar, fastidiar
needless ['niːdlɪs] adj innecesario; **~ to say** huelga decir que
needlework ['niːdlwəːk] n (activity) costura, labor f de aguja
needn't ['niːdnt] = **need not**
needy ['niːdɪ] adj necesitado
negative ['nɛɡətɪv] n (PHOT) negativo; (LING) negación f ♦ adj negativo; **~ equity** n situación que se da cuando el valor de la vivienda es menor que el de la hipoteca que pesa sobre ella
neglect [nɪ'ɡlɛkt] vt (one's duty) faltar a, no cumplir con; (child) descuidar, desatender ♦ n (of house, garden etc) abandono; (of child) desatención f; (of duty) incumplimiento
negligee ['nɛɡlɪʒeɪ] n (nightgown) salto de cama
negotiate [nɪ'ɡəʊʃɪeɪt] vt (treaty, loan) negociar; (obstacle) franquear; (bend in road) tomar ♦ vi: **to ~ (with)** negociar (con); **negotiation** [-'eɪʃən] n negociación f, gestión f
neigh [neɪ] vi relinchar
neighbour ['neɪbə*] (US **neighbor**) n vecino/a; **~hood** n (place) vecindad f, barrio; (people) vecindario; **~ing** adj vecino; **~ly** adj (person) amable; (attitude) de buen vecino
neither ['naɪðə*] adj ni ♦ conj: **I didn't move and ~ did John** no me he movido, ni Juan tampoco ♦ pron ninguno, ni uno ni otro ♦ adv: **~ good nor bad** ni bueno ni malo; **~ is true** ninguno/a de los/las dos es cierto/a
neon ['niːɔn] n neón m; **~ light** n lámpara de neón
nephew ['nɛvjuː] n sobrino
nerve [nəːv] n (ANAT) nervio; (courage) valor m; (impudence) descaro, frescura; **a fit of ~s** un ataque de nervios; **~-racking** adj desquiciante
nervous ['nəːvəs] adj (anxious, ANAT) nervioso; (timid) tímido, miedoso; **~ breakdown** n crisis f nerviosa

nest [nɛst] n (of bird) nido; (wasp's) ~ avispero ♦ vi anidar; **~ egg** n (fig) ahorros mpl
nestle ['nɛsl] vi: **to ~ down** acurrucarse
net [nɛt] n (gen) red f; (fabric) tul m ♦ adj (COMM) neto, líquido ♦ vt coger (SP) o agarrar (AM) con red; (SPORT) marcar; **the N~** (Internet) la Red; **~ball** n básquet m
Netherlands ['nɛðələndz] npl: **the ~** los Países Bajos
nett [nɛt] adj = **net**
netting ['nɛtɪŋ] n red f, redes fpl
nettle ['nɛtl] n ortiga
network ['nɛtwəːk] n red f
neurotic [njuə'rɔtɪk] adj neurótico/a
neuter ['njuːtə*] adj (LING) neutro ♦ vt castrar, capar
neutral ['njuːtrəl] adj (person) neutral; (colour etc, ELEC) neutro ♦ n (AUT) punto muerto; **~ize** vt neutralizar
never ['nɛvə*] adv nunca, jamás; **I ~ went** no fui nunca; **~ in my life** jamás en la vida; see also **mind**; **~-ending** adj interminable, sin fin; **~theless** [nɛvəðə'lɛs] adv sin embargo, no obstante
new [njuː] adj nuevo; (brand new) a estrenar; (recent) reciente; **N~ Age** n Nueva Era; **~born** adj recién nacido; **~comer** ['njuːkʌmə*] n recién venido/a o llegado/a; **~fangled** (pej) adj modernísimo; **~found** adj (friend) nuevo; (enthusiasm) recién adquirido; **~ly** adv nuevamente, recién; **~ly-weds** npl recién casados mpl
news [njuːz] n noticias fpl; **a piece of ~** una noticia; **the ~** (RADIO, TV) las noticias fpl; **~ agency** n agencia de noticias; **~agent** (BRIT) n vendedor(a) m/f de periódicos; **~caster** n presentador(a) m/f, locutor(a) m/f; **~ flash** n noticia de última hora; **~letter** n hoja informativa, boletín m; **~paper** n periódico, diario; **~print** n papel m de periódico; **~reader** =

~caster n ~ **reel** n noticiario; ~ **stand** n quiosco or puesto de periódicos

newt [njuːt] n tritón m

New Year n Año Nuevo; **~'s Day** n Día m de Año Nuevo; **~'s Eve** n Nochevieja

New York [njuː'jɔːk] n Nueva York

New Zealand [njuː'ziːlənd] n Nueva Zelanda; **~er** n neozelandés/esa m/f

next [nekst] adj (house, room) vecino; (bus stop, meeting) próximo m; (following: page etc) siguiente ♦ adv después m; **the ~ day** el día siguiente; **~ time** la próxima vez; **~ year** el año próximo or que viene; **~ to** junto a, al lado de; **~ to nothing** casi nada; **~ please!** ¡el siguiente! **~ door** adv en la casa de al lado ♦ adj vecino, de al lado; **~-of-kin** n pariente m más cercano

NHS n abbr = **National Health Service**

nib [nɪb] n plumilla

nibble ['nɪbl] vt mordisquear, mordiscar

Nicaragua [nɪkə'ræɡjuə] n Nicaragua; **~n** adj, n nicaragüense m/f

nice [naɪs] adj (likeable) simpático; (kind) amable; (pleasant) agradable; (attractive) bonito, mono, lindo (AM); **~ly** adv amablemente, bien

nick [nɪk] n (wound) rasguño; (cut, indentation) mella, muesca ♦ vt (inf) birlar, robar; **in the ~ of time** justo a tiempo

nickel ['nɪkl] n níquel m; (US) moneda de 5 centavos

nickname ['nɪkneɪm] n apodo, mote m ♦ vt apodar

nicotine ['nɪkətiːn] n nicotina

niece [niːs] n sobrina

Nigeria [naɪ'dʒɪərɪə] n Nigeria; **~n** adj, n nigeriano/a m/f

niggling ['nɪɡlɪŋ] adj (trifling) nimio, insignificante; (annoying) molesto

night [naɪt] n noche f; (evening) tarde f; **the ~ before last** anteanoche; **at ~,** **by ~** de noche, por la noche; **~cap** n

(drink) bebida que se toma antes de acostarse; **~ club** n cabaret m; **~dress** (BRIT) n camisón m; **~fall** n anochecer m; **~gown** n = **~dress**; **~ie** [naɪti] n = **~dress**

nightingale ['naɪtɪŋɡeɪl] n ruiseñor m

night: ~life n vida nocturna; **~ly** adj de todas las noches ♦ adv todas las noches, cada noche; **~mare** n pesadilla; **~ porter** n portero de noche; **~ school** n clase(s f(pl) nocturna(s); **~shift** n turno nocturno or de noche; **~-time** n noche f; **~ watchman** n vigilante m nocturno

nil [nɪl] (BRIT) n (SPORT) cero, nada

Nile [naɪl] n: **the ~** el Nilo

nimble ['nɪmbl] adj (agile) ágil, ligero; (skilful) diestro

nine [naɪn] num nueve; **~teen** num diecinueve, diez y nueve; **~ty** num noventa

ninth [naɪnθ] adj noveno

nip [nɪp] vt (pinch) pellizcar; (bite) morder

nipple ['nɪpl] n pezón m

nitrogen ['naɪtrədʒən] n nitrógeno

KEYWORD

no [nəʊ] (pl **~es**) adv (opposite of "yes") no; **are you coming?** — (**I'm not**) ¿vienes? — no; **would you like some more?** — **~ thank you** ¿quieres más? — no gracias ♦ adj (not any): **I have ~ money/time/books** no tengo dinero/tiempo/libros; **~ other man would have done it** ningún otro lo hubiera hecho; **"~ entry"** "prohibido el paso"; **"~ smoking"** "prohibido fumar"

♦ n no m

---

nobility [nəʊ'bɪlɪtɪ] n nobleza

noble ['nəʊbl] adj noble

nobody ['nəʊbədɪ] pron nadie

nod [nɒd] vi saludar con la cabeza; (in agreement) decir que sí con la cabeza; (doze) dar cabezadas ♦ vt: **to ~ one's**

head inclinar la cabeza ♦ n inclinación f de cabeza; **~ off** vi dar cabezadas
noise [nɔɪz] n ruido; (din) escándalo, estrépito; **noisy** adj ruidoso; (child) escandaloso
nominate ['nɔmɪneɪt] vt (propose) proponer; (appoint) nombrar; **nominee** [-'niː] n candidato/a
non... [nɔn] prefix no, des..., in...; **~alcoholic** adj no alcohólico; **~chalant** adj indiferente; **~committal** adj evasivo; **~descript** adj soso
none [nʌn] pron ninguno/a ♦ adv de ninguna manera; **~ of you** ninguno de vosotros; **I've ~ left** no me queda ninguno/a; **he's ~ the worse for it** no le ha hecho ningún mal
nonentity [nɔ'nɛntɪtɪ] n cero a la izquierda, nulidad f
nonetheless [nʌnðə'lɛs] adv sin embargo, no obstante
non-existent adj inexistente
non-fiction n literatura no novelesca
nonplussed [nɔn'plʌst] adj perplejo
nonsense ['nɔnsəns] n tonterías fpl, disparates fpl; **~!** ¡qué tonterías!
non: ~-smoker n no fumador(a) m/f; **~-smoking** adj (de) no fumador; **~-stick** adj (pan, surface) antiadherente; **~-stop** adj continuo; (RAIL) directo ♦ adv sin parar
noodles ['nuːdlz] npl tallarines mpl
nook [nuk] n: **~s and crannies** escondrijos mpl
noon [nuːn] n mediodía m
no-one pron = **nobody**
noose [nuːs] n (hangman's) dogal m
nor [nɔː] conj = **neither** ♦ adv see **neither**
norm [nɔːm] n norma
normal ['nɔːml] adj normal; **~ly** adv normalmente
north [nɔːθ] n norte m ♦ adj del norte, norteño ♦ adv al o hacia el norte; **N~ Africa** n África del Norte; **N~ America** n América del Norte; **~east** n nor(d)este m; **~erly** ['nɔːðəlɪ]

adj (point, direction) norteño; **~ern** ['nɔːðən] adj norteño, del norte; **N~ern Ireland** n Irlanda del Norte; **N~ Pole** n Polo Norte; **N~ Sea** n Mar m del Norte; **~ward(s)** ['nɔːθwəd(z)] adv hacia el norte; **~-west** n nor(d)oeste m
Norway ['nɔːweɪ] n Noruega; **Norwegian** [-'wiːdʒən] adj noruego/a ♦ n noruego/a; (LING) noruego
nose [nəuz] n (ANAT) nariz f; (ZOOL) hocico; (sense of smell) olfato ♦ vi: **to ~ about** curiosear; **~bleed** n hemorragia nasal; **~-dive** n (of plane: deliberate) picado vertical; (: involuntary) caída en picado; **~y** (inf) adj curioso, fisgón/ona
nostalgia [nɔs'tældʒɪə] n nostalgia
nostril ['nɔstrɪl] n ventana de la nariz
nosy ['nəuzɪ] (inf) adj = **nosey**
not [nɔt] adv no; **~ that** ... no es que ...; **it's too late, isn't it?** es demasiado tarde, ¿verdad o no?; **~ yet/now** todavía/ahora no; **why ~?** ¿por qué no?; see also **all**; **only**
notably ['nəutəblɪ] adv especialmente
notary ['nəutərɪ] n notario/a
notch [nɔtʃ] n muesca, corte m
note [nəut] n (MUS, record, letter) nota; (banknote) billete m; (tone) tono ♦ vt (observe) notar, observar; (write down) apuntar, anotar; **~book** n libreta, cuaderno; **~d** ['nəutɪd] adj célebre, conocido; **~pad** n bloc de notas; **~paper** n papel m para cartas
nothing ['nʌθɪŋ] n nada; (zero) cero; **he does ~** no hace nada; **~ new** nada nuevo; **~ much** no mucho; **for ~** (free) gratis, sin pago; (in vain) en balde
notice ['nəutɪs] n (announcement) anuncio; (warning) aviso; (dismissal) despido; (resignation) dimisión f; (period of time) plazo ♦ vt (observe) notar, observar; **to bring sth to sb's ~** (attention) llamar la atención de uno sobre algo; **to take ~ of** tomar nota de, prestar atención a; **at short ~** con

poca anticipación; **until further ~**
hasta nuevo aviso; **to hand in one's
~** dimitir; **~able** adj evidente, obvio;
~ board (BRIT) n tablón m de anuncios

notify ['nəutɪfaɪ] vt: **to ~ sb (of sth)**
comunicar (algo) a uno

notion ['nəuʃən] n idea; (opinion)
opinión f

notorious [nəu'tɔːrɪəs] adj notorio

nougat ['nuːgɑː] n turrón m

nought [nɔːt] n cero

noun [naun] n nombre m, sustantivo

nourish ['nʌrɪʃ] vt nutrir; (fig)
alimentar; **~ing** adj nutritivo; **~ment**
n alimento, sustento

novel ['nɔvl] n novela ♦ adj (new)
nuevo, original; (unexpected) insólito;
~ist n novelista m/f; **~ty** n novedad f

November [nəu'vembə*] n noviembre
m

novice ['nɔvɪs] n (REL) novicio/a

now [nau] adv (at the present time)
ahora; (these days) actualmente, hoy
día ♦ conj: **~ (that)** ya que, ahora que;
right ~ ahora mismo; **by ~** ya; **just ~**
ahora mismo; **~ and then, ~ and
again** de vez en cuando; **from ~ on** de
ahora en adelante; **~adays**
['nauədeɪz] adv hoy (en) día,
actualmente

nowhere ['nəuwɛə*] adv (direction) a
ninguna parte; (location) en ninguna
parte

nozzle ['nɔzl] n boquilla

nuance ['njuːɑːns] n matiz m

nuclear ['njuːklɪə*] adj nuclear

nucleus ['njuːklɪəs] (pl **nuclei**) n
núcleo

nude [njuːd] adj, n desnudo/a m/f; **in
the ~** desnudo

nudge [nʌdʒ] vt dar un codazo a

nudist ['njuːdɪst] n nudista m/f

nuisance ['njuːsns] n molestia,
fastidio; (person) pesado, latoso; **what
a ~!** ¡qué lata!

null [nʌl] adj: **~ and void** nulo y sin
efecto

numb [nʌm] adj: **~ with cold/fear**
entumecido por el frío/paralizado por
miedo

number ['nʌmbə*] n número;
(quantity) cantidad f ♦ vt (pages etc)
numerar, poner número a; (amount to)
sumar, ascender a; **to be ~ed among**
figurar entre; **a ~ of** varios, algunos;
they were ten in ~ eran diez;
~ plate (BRIT) n matrícula, placa

numeral ['njuːmərəl] n número, cifra

numerate ['njuːmərɪt] adj competente
en la aritmética

numerous ['njuːmərəs] adj numeroso

nun [nʌn] n monja, religiosa

nurse [nəːs] n enfermero/a; (also:
~maid) niñera ♦ vt (patient) cuidar,
atender

nursery ['nəːsəri] n (institution)
guardería infantil; (room) cuarto de los
niños; (for plants) criadero, semillero;
~ rhyme n canción f infantil;
~ school n parvulario, escuela de
párvulos; **~ slope** (BRIT) n (SKI) cuesta
para principiantes

nursing ['nəːsɪŋ] n (profession)
profesión f de enfermera; (care)
asistencia, cuidado; **~ home** n clínica
de reposo

nut [nʌt] n (TECH) tuerca; (BOT) nuez f;
~crackers npl cascanueces m inv

nutmeg ['nʌtmeg] n nuez f moscada

nutritious [njuː'trɪʃəs] adj nutritivo,
alimenticio

nuts [nʌts] (inf) adj loco

nutshell ['nʌtʃel] n: **in a ~** en
resumidas cuentas

nylon ['naɪlɔn] n nilón m ♦ adj de
nilón

O, o

oak [əuk] n roble m ♦ adj de roble

O.A.P. (BRIT) n abbr = **old-age
pensioner**

oar [ɔː*] n remo

oasis [əu'eɪsɪs] (pl **oases**) n oasis m inv
oath [əuθ] n juramento; (swear word) palabrota; **on** (BRIT) or **under ~** bajo juramento
oatmeal ['əutmiːl] n harina de avena
oats [əuts] n avena
obedience [ə'biːdɪəns] n obediencia
obedient [ə'biːdɪənt] adj obediente
obey [ə'beɪ] vt obedecer; (instructions, regulations) cumplir
obituary [ə'bɪtjuərɪ] n necrología
object [n 'ɔbdʒɪkt, vb əb'dʒekt] n objeto; (purpose) objeto, propósito; (LING) objeto ♦ vi: **to ~** estar en contra de; (proposal) oponerse a; **to ~ that** objetar que; **expense is no ~** no importa cuánto cuesta; **I ~!** ¡yo protesto!; **to ~ion** [əb'dʒekʃən] n protesta; **I have no ~ion to ...** no tengo inconveniente en que ...; **~ionable** [əb'dʒekʃənəbl] adj desagradable; (conduct) censurable; **~ive** adj, n objetivo
obligation [ɔblɪ'geɪʃən] n obligación f; (debt) deber m; **without ~** sin compromiso
oblige [ə'blaɪdʒ] vt (do a favour for) complacer, hacer un favor a; **to ~ sb to do sth** forzar or obligar a uno a hacer algo; **to be ~d to sb for sth** estarle agradecido a uno por algo; **obliging** adj servicial, atento
oblique [ə'bliːk] adj oblicuo; (allusion) indirecto
obliterate [ə'blɪtəreɪt] vt borrar
oblivion [ə'blɪvɪən] n olvido; **oblivious** [-ɪəs] adj: **oblivious of** inconsciente de
oblong ['ɔblɔŋ] adj rectangular ♦ n rectángulo
obnoxious [əb'nɔkʃəs] adj odioso, detestable; (smell) nauseabundo
oboe ['əubəu] n oboe m
obscene [əb'siːn] adj obsceno
obscure [əb'skjuə*] adj oscuro ♦ vt oscurecer; (hide: sun) esconder
observant [əb'zəːvnt] adj

observador(a)
observation [ɔbzə'veɪʃən] n observación f; (MED) examen m
observe [əb'zəːv] vt observar; (rule) cumplir; **~r** n observador(a) m/f
obsess [əb'ses] vt obsesionar; **~ive** adj obsesivo; obsesionante
obsolete ['ɔbsəliːt] adj: **to be ~** estar en desuso
obstacle ['ɔbstəkl] n obstáculo; (nuisance) estorbo; **~ race** n carrera de obstáculos
obstinate ['ɔbstɪnɪt] adj terco, porfiado; (determined) obstinado
obstruct [əb'strʌkt] vt obstruir; (hinder) estorbar, obstaculizar; **~ion** [əb'strʌkʃən] n (action) obstrucción f; (object) estorbo, obstáculo
obtain [əb'teɪn] vt obtener; (achieve) conseguir
obvious ['ɔbvɪəs] adj obvio, evidente; **~ly** adv evidentemente, naturalmente; **~ly not** por supuesto que no
occasion [ə'keɪʒən] n oportunidad f, ocasión f; (event) acontecimiento; **~al** adj poco frecuente, ocasional; **~ally** adv de vez en cuando
occupant ['ɔkjupənt] n (of house) inquilino/a; (of car) ocupante m/f
occupation [ɔkju'peɪʃən] n ocupación f; (job) trabajo; (pastime) ocupaciones fpl; **~al hazard** n riesgo profesional
occupier ['ɔkjupaɪə*] n inquilino/a
occupy ['ɔkjupaɪ] vt (seat, post, time) ocupar; (house) habitar; **to ~ o.s. in doing** pasar el tiempo haciendo
occur [ə'kəː*] vi pasar, suceder; **to ~ to sb** ocurrírsele a uno; **~rence** [ə'kʌrəns] n acontecimiento; (existence) existencia
ocean ['əuʃən] n océano
o'clock [ə'klɔk] adv: **it is 5 ~** son las 5
OCR n abbr = **optical character recognition/reader**
October [ɔk'təubə*] n octubre m
octopus ['ɔktəpəs] n pulpo
odd [ɔd] adj extraño, raro; (number)

impar; (sock, shoe etc) suelto; **60-~** 60
y pico; **at ~ times** de vez en cuando;
to be the ~ one out estar de más;
~ity n rareza; (person) excentricidad;
~job man n chico para todo; **~ jobs**
npl bricolaje m; **~ly** adv curiosamente,
extrañamente; see also **enough**;
~ments npl (COMM) retales mpl; **~s** npl
(in betting) puntos mpl de ventaja; **it
makes no ~s** da lo mismo; **at ~s**
reñidos/as; **~s and ends** minucias fpl

odometer [ɔ'dɔmɪtə*] (US) n
cuentakilómetros m inv

odour ['əudə*] (US **odor**) n olor m;
(unpleasant) hedor m

of [ɔv, əv] prep **1** (gen) de; **a friend
~ ours** un amigo nuestro; **a boy ~ 10**
un chico de 10 años; **that was kind
~ you** eso fue muy amable por o de
tu parte
2 (expressing quantity, amount, dates
etc) de; **a kilo ~ flour** un kilo de
harina; **there were 3 ~ them** había
tres; **3 ~ us went** tres de nosotros
fuimos; **the 5th ~ July** el 5 de julio
3 (from, out of) de; **made ~ wood**
(hecho) de madera

off [ɔf] adj, adv (engine) desconectado;
(light) apagado; (tap) cerrado; (BRIT:
food: bad) pasado, malo; (: milk)
cortado; (cancelled) cancelado ♦ prep
de; **to be ~** (to leave) irse, marcharse;
to be ~ sick estar enfermo o de baja;
a day ~ un día libre o sin trabajar; **to
have an ~ day** tener un día malo; **he
had his coat ~** se había quitado el
abrigo; **10% ~** (COMM) (con el) 10%
de descuento; **5 km ~ (the road)** a 5
km (de la carretera); **~ the coast**
frente a la costa; **I'm ~ meat** (no
longer eat/like it) paso de la carne; **on
the ~ chance** por si acaso; **~ and on**
de vez en cuando

offal ['ɔfl] (BRIT) n (CULIN) menudencias

fpl

off-colour [ɔf'kʌlə*] (BRIT) adj (ill)
indispuesto

offence [ə'fɛns] (US **offense**) n (crime)
delito; **to take ~ at** ofenderse por

offend [ə'fɛnd] vt (person) ofender; **~er**
n delincuente m/f

offensive [ə'fɛnsɪv] adj ofensivo; (smell
etc) repugnante ♦ n (MIL) ofensiva

offer ['ɔfə*] n oferta, ofrecimiento;
(proposal) propuesta ♦ vt ofrecer;
(opportunity) facilitar; **"on ~"** (COMM)
"en oferta"; **~ing** n ofrenda

offhand [ɔf'hænd] adj informal ♦ adv
de improviso

office ['ɔfɪs] n (place) oficina; (room)
despacho; (position) carga, oficio;
doctor's ~ (US) consultorio; **to take ~**
entrar en funciones; **~ automation** n
ofimática, buromática; **~ block** (US
~ building) n bloque m de oficinas;
~ hours npl horas fpl de oficina; (US:
MED) horas fpl de consulta

officer ['ɔfɪsə*] n (MIL etc) oficial m/f;
(also: police **~**) agente m/f de policía;
(of organization) director(a) m/f

office worker n oficinista m/f

official [ə'fɪʃl] adj oficial, autorizado
♦ n funcionario, oficial m

offing ['ɔfɪŋ] n: **in the ~** (fig) en
perspectiva

off-licence (BRIT) n (shop) bodega,
tienda de vinos y bebidas alcohólicas;
~-line adj, adv (COMPUT) fuera de
línea; **~-peak** adj (electricity) de banda
económica; (ticket) billete de precio
reducido por viajar fuera de las horas
punta; **~-putting** (BRIT) adj (person)
asqueroso; (remark) desalentador(a);
~-season adj, adv fuera de temporada

En el Reino Unido la venta de bebidas
alcohólicas está estrictamente
regulada y se necesita una licencia
especial, con la que cuentan los bares,
restaurantes y los establecimientos de

off-licence, *los únicos lugares en donde se pueden adquirir bebidas alcohólicas para su consumo fuera del local, de donde viene su nombre. También venden bebidas no alcohólicas, tabaco, chocolatinas, patatas fritas, etc. y a menudo forman parte de una cadena nacional.*

offset ['ɔfset] (*irreg*) *vt* contrarrestar, compensar

offshoot ['ɔfʃuːt] *n* (*fig*) ramificación *f*

offshore [ɔf'ʃɔː*] *adj* (*breeze, island*) costera; (*fishing*) de bajura

offside ['ɔf'saɪd] *adj* (*SPORT*) fuera de juego; (*AUT*: *in UK*) del lado derecho; (: *in US, Europe etc*) del lado izquierdo

offspring ['ɔfsprɪŋ] *n inv* descendencia

off: ~**stage** *adv* entre bastidores; ~**the-peg** (*US* ~**the-rack**) *adv* confeccionado/a; ~**white** *adj* color crudo

often ['ɔfn] *adv* a menudo, con frecuencia; **how ~ do you go?** ¿cada cuánto vas?

oh [əu] *excl* ¡ah!

oil [ɔɪl] *n* aceite *m*; (*petroleum*) petróleo *m*; (*for heating*) aceite *m* combustible ♦ *vt* engrasar; ~**can** *n* lata de aceite; ~**field** *n* campo petrolífero; ~ **filter** *n* (*AUT*) filtro de aceite; ~ **painting** *n* pintura al óleo; ~ **rig** *n* torre *f* de perforación; ~ **tanker** *n* petrolero; (*truck*) camión *m* cisterna; ~ **well** *n* pozo de (petróleo); ~**y** *adj* aceitoso; (*food*) grasiento

ointment ['ɔɪntmənt] *n* ungüento

O.K., okay ['əu'keɪ] *excl* O.K., ¡está bien!, ¡vale! (*SP*) ♦ *adj* bien ♦ *vt* dar el visto bueno a

old [əuld] *adj* viejo; (*former*) antiguo; **how ~ are you?** ¿cuántos años tienes?, ¿qué edad tienes?; **he's 10 years ~** tiene 10 años; ~**er brother** hermano mayor; ~ **age** *n* vejez *f*; ~-**fashioned** *adj* anticuado, pasado de

moda

olive ['ɔlɪv] *n* (*fruit*) aceituna; (*tree*) olivo ♦ *adj* (*also*: ~-**green**) verde oliva; ~ **oil** *n* aceite *m* de oliva

Olympic [əu'lɪmpɪk] *adj* olímpico; **the ~ Games, the ~s** las Olimpíadas

omelet(te) ['ɔmlɪt] *n* tortilla (*SP*), tortilla de huevo (*AM*)

omen ['əumən] *n* presagio

ominous ['ɔmɪnəs] *adj* de mal agüero, amenazador/a

omit [əu'mɪt] *vt* omitir

on [ɔn] *prep* **1** (*indicating position*) en; sobre; ~ **the wall** en la pared; **it's ~ the table** está sobre *or* en la mesa; ~ **the left** a la izquierda

2 (*indicating means, method, condition etc*): ~ **foot** a pie; ~ **the train/plane** (*go*) en tren/avión; (*be*) en el tren/avión; ~ **the radio/television/telephone** por *or* en la radio/televisión/al teléfono; **to be ~ drugs** drogarse; (*MED*) estar a tratamiento; **to be ~ holiday/business** estar de vacaciones/en viaje de negocios

3 (*referring to time*): ~ **Friday** el viernes; ~ **Fridays** los viernes; ~ **June 20th** el 20 de junio; **a week ~ Friday** del viernes en una semana; ~ **arrival** al llegar; ~ **seeing this** al ver esto

4 (*about, concerning*) sobre, acerca de; **a book ~ physics** un libro de *or* sobre física

♦ *adv* **1** (*referring to dress*): **to have one's coat ~** tener *or* llevar el abrigo puesto; **she put her gloves ~** se puso los guantes

2 (*referring to covering*): "**screw the lid ~ tightly**" "cerrar bien la tapa"

3 (*further, continuously*): **to walk** *etc* ~ seguir caminando *etc*

♦ *adj* **1** (*functioning, in operation*): *machine, radio, TV, light*) encendido/a (*SP*), prendido/a (*AM*); (: *tap*) abierto/a; (: *brakes*) echado/a, puesto/a; **is the**

meeting still ~? (in progress) ¿todavía continúa la reunión?; (not cancelled) ¿va a haber reunión al fin?; **there's a good film ~ at the cinema** ponen una buena película en el cine

2: that's not ~! (inf: not possible) ¡eso ni hablar!; (: not acceptable) ¡eso no se hace!

once [wʌns] adv una vez; (formerly) antiguamente ♦ conj una vez que; **~ he had left/it was done** una vez que se había marchado se hizo; **at ~** en seguida, inmediatamente; (simultaneously) a la vez; **~ a week** una vez por semana; **~ more** otra vez; **~ and for all** de una vez por todas; **~ upon a time** érase una vez

oncoming ['ɔnkʌmɪŋ] adj (traffic) que viene de frente

KEYWORD

one [wʌn] num un(o)/una; **~ hundred and fifty** ciento cincuenta; **~ by ~** uno a uno
♦ adj **1** (sole) único; **the ~ book which** el único libro que; **the ~ man who** el único que
2 (same) mismo/a; **they came in the ~ car** vinieron en un solo coche
♦ pron **1**: **this ~** éste/ésta; **that ~** ése/ésa; (more remote) aquél/aquélla; **I've already got (a red) ~** ya tengo uno/a (rojo/a); **~ by ~** uno/a por uno/a
2: **~ another** (sp), se (+ el uno al otro, unos a otros etc); **do you two ever see ~ another?** ¿vosotros dos os veis alguna vez? (sp), ¿con vsn ustedes dos alguna vez?; **the boys didn't dare look at ~ another** los chicos no se atrevieron a mirarse (el uno al otro); **they all kissed ~ another** se besaron unos a otros
3 (impers): **never knows** nunca se sabe; **to cut ~'s finger** cortarse el dedo; **~ needs to eat** hay que comer

one: ~-day excursion (us) n billete m de ida y vuelta en un día; **~-man** adj (business) individual; **~-man band** n hombre-orquesta m; **~-off** (BRIT: inf) n (event) acontecimiento único

oneself [wʌn'sɛlf] pron (reflexive) se; (after prep) sí; (emphatic) uno/a mismo, a; **to hurt ~** hacerse daño; **to keep sth for ~** guardarse algo; **to talk to ~** hablar solo

one: ~-sided adj (argument) parcial; **~-to-~** adj (relationship) de dos; **~-way** adj (street) de sentido único

ongoing ['ɔngəʊɪŋ] adj continuo

onion ['ʌnjən] n cebolla

on-line adj (COMPUT) en línea

onlooker ['ɔnlʊkə*] n espectador(a) m/f

only ['əʊnlɪ] adv solamente, sólo ♦ adj único, solo ♦ conj solamente que, pero; **an ~ child** un hijo único; **not only ... but also ...** no sólo ... sino también ...

onset ['ɔnsɛt] n comienzo

onshore ['ɔnʃɔ:*] adj (wind) que sopla del mar hacia la tierra

onslaught ['ɔnslɔ:t] n ataque m, embestida

onto ['ɔntu] prep = **on to**

onward(s) ['ɔnwəd(z)] adv (move) (hacia) adelante; **from that time ~** desde entonces en adelante

onyx ['ɔnɪks] n ónice m

ooze [u:z] vi rezumar

opaque [əʊ'peɪk] adj opaco

OPEC ['əʊpɛk] n abbr (= Organization of Petroleum-Exporting Countries) OPEP f

open ['əʊpn] adj abierto; (car) descubierto; (road, view) despejado; (meeting) público; (admiration) manifiesto ♦ vt abrir ♦ vi abrirse; (book etc: commence) comenzar; **in the ~ (air)** al aire libre; **~ on to** vt fus (subj: room, door) dar a; **~ up** vt abrir ♦ vi abrirse, empezar; **~ing** n abertura ♦ adj (start) comienzo; (opportunity) oportunidad f

~ing hours npl horario de apertura; **~ learning** n enseñanza flexible a tiempo parcial; **~ly** adv abiertamente; **~-minded** adj imparcial; **~-necked** adj (shirt) desabrochado; sin corbata; **~-plan** adj: **~-plan office** gran oficina sin particiones

---

Open University

La **Open University**, fundada en 1969, está especializada en impartir cursos a distancia que no exigen una dedicación exclusiva. Cuenta con sus propios materiales de apoyo, entre ellos programas de radio y televisión emitidos por la BBC y para conseguir los créditos de la licenciatura, es necesaria la presentación de unos trabajos y la asistencia a los cursos de verano.

---

opera ['ɔpərə] n ópera; **~ house** n teatro de la ópera

operate ['ɔpəreɪt] vt (machine) hacer funcionar; (company) dirigir ♦ vi funcionar; **to ~ on sb** (MED) operar a uno

operatic [ɔpə'rætɪk] adj de ópera

operating table ['ɔpəreɪtɪŋ-] n mesa de operaciones

operating theatre n sala de operaciones

operation [ɔpə'reɪʃən] n operación f; (of machine) funcionamiento; **to be in ~** estar funcionando or en funcionamiento; **to have an ~** (MED) ser operado; **~al** adj operacional, en buen estado

operative ['ɔpərətɪv] adj en vigor

operator ['ɔpəreɪtə*] n (of machine) maquinista m/f, operario/a; (TEL) operador(a) m/f, telefonista m/f

opinion [ə'pɪnɪən] n opinión f; **in my ~** en mi opinión, a mi juicio; **~ated** adj testarudo; **~ poll** n encuesta, sondeo

opponent [ə'pəunənt] n adversario/a, contrincante m/f

opportunity [ɔpə'tjuːnɪtɪ] n oportunidad f; **to take the ~ of doing** aprovechar la ocasión para hacer

oppose [ə'pəuz] vt oponerse a; **to be ~d to sth** oponerse a algo; **as ~d to** a diferencia de; **opposing** adj opuesto, contrario

opposite ['ɔpəzɪt] adj opuesto, contrario a; (house etc) de enfrente ♦ adv en frente ♦ prep en frente de, frente a ♦ n lo contrario

opposition [ɔpə'zɪʃən] n oposición f

oppressive [ə'presɪv] adj opresivo; (weather) agobiante

opt [ɔpt] vi: **to ~ for** optar por; **to ~ to do** optar por hacer; **~ out** vi: **to ~ out of** optar por no hacer

optical ['ɔptɪkl] adj óptico

optician [ɔp'tɪʃən] n óptico m/f

optimist ['ɔptɪmɪst] n optimista m/f; **~ic** [-'mɪstɪk] adj optimista

option ['ɔpʃən] n opción f; **~al** adj facultativo, discrecional

or [ɔː*] conj o; (before o, ho) u; (with negative): **he hasn't seen ~ heard anything** no ha visto ni oído nada; **~ else** si no

oral ['ɔːrəl] adj oral ♦ n examen m oral

orange ['ɔrɪndʒ] n (fruit) naranja ♦ adj color naranja

orbit ['ɔːbɪt] n órbita ♦ vt, vi orbitar

orchard ['ɔːtʃəd] n huerto

orchestra ['ɔːkɪstrə] n orquesta; (US: seating) platea

orchid ['ɔːkɪd] n orquídea

ordain [ɔː'deɪn] vt (REL) ordenar, decretar

ordeal [ɔː'diːl] n experiencia horrorosa

order ['ɔːdə*] n orden m; (command) orden f; (good ~) buen estado; (COMM) pedido ♦ vt (also: put in ~) arreglar, poner en orden; (COMM) pedir; (command) mandar, ordenar; **in ~** en orden; (of document) en regla; (working) **~** en funcionamiento; **in ~ to do/that** para hacer/que; **on ~**

(COMM) pedido; **to be out of ~** estar desordenado; (*not working*) no funcionar; **to ~ sb to do sth** mandar a uno hacer algo; **~ form** n hoja de pedido; **~ly** n (MIL) ordenanza m; (MED) enfermero/a (auxiliar) m; **~** adj ordenado

ordinary ['ɔːdɪnrɪ] adj corriente, normal; (pej) común y corriente; **out of the ~** fuera de lo común

Ordnance Survey ['ɔːdnəns-] (BRIT) n servicio oficial de topografía

ore [ɔː*] n mineral m

organ ['ɔːgən] n órgano; **~ic** [ɔː'gænɪk] adj orgánico; **~ism** n organismo

organization [ɔːgənaɪ'zeɪʃən] n organización f

organize ['ɔːgənaɪz] vt organizar; **~r** n organizador(a) m/f

orgasm ['ɔːgæzəm] n orgasmo

orgy ['ɔːdʒɪ] n orgía

Orient ['ɔːrɪənt] n Oriente m; **oriental** [-'entl] adj oriental

orientate ['ɔːrɪənteɪt] vt: **to ~ o.s.** orientarse

origin ['ɒrɪdʒɪn] n origen m

original [ə'rɪdʒɪnl] adj original; (first) primero; (earlier) primitivo ♦ n original m; **~ly** adv al principio

originate [ə'rɪdʒɪneɪt] vi: **to ~ from, to ~ in** surgir de, tener su origen en

Orkneys ['ɔːknɪz] npl: **the ~** (also: the Orkney Islands) las Orcadas

ornament ['ɔːnəmənt] n adorno; (trinket) chuchería; **~al** [-'mentl] adj decorativo, de adorno

ornate [ɔː'neɪt] adj muy ornado, vistoso

orphan ['ɔːfən] n huérfano/a

orthopaedic [ɔːθə'piːdɪk] (US **orthopedic**) adj ortopédico

ostensibly [ɔs'tensɪblɪ] adv aparentemente

ostentatious [ɔsten'teɪʃəs] adj ostentoso

osteopath ['ɔstɪəpæθ] n osteópata m/f

ostracize ['ɔstrəsaɪz] vt hacer el vacío a

ostrich ['ɔstrɪtʃ] n avestruz m

other ['ʌðə*] adj otro ♦ pron: **the ~ (one)** el/la otro/a ♦ adv: **~ than** aparte de; **~s** (= people) otros; **the ~ day** el otro día; **~wise** adv de otra manera ♦ conj (if not) si no

otter ['ɔtə*] n nutria

ouch [autʃ] excl ¡ay!

ought [ɔːt] (pt ought) aux vb: **I ~ to do it** debería hacerlo; **this ~ to have been corrected** esto debiera haberse corregido; **he ~ to win** (probability) debe or debiera ganar

ounce [auns] n onza (28.35g)

our ['auə*] adj nuestro; see also **my**; **~s** pron (el) nuestro/(la) nuestra etc; see also **mine[1]**; **~selves** pron pl (reflexive, after prep) nosotros; (emphatic) nosotros mismos; see also **oneself**

oust [aust] vt desalojar

out [aut] adv fuera, afuera; (not at home) fuera (de casa); (light, fire) apagado; **~ there** allí fuera; **he's ~** (absent) no está, ha salido; **to be ~ in one's calculations** equivocarse (en sus cálculos); **to run ~** salir corriendo; **~ loud** en alta voz; **~ of** (outside) fuera de; (because of: anger etc) por; **~ of petrol** sin gasolina; **"~ of order"** "no funciona"; **~-and-~** adj (liar, thief etc) redomado, empedernido; **~back** n interior m; **~board** adj: **~board motor** (motor m) fuera borda m; **~break** n (of war) comienzo; (of disease) epidemia; (of violence etc) ola; **~burst** n explosión f, arranque m; **~cast** n paria m/f; **~come** n resultado; **~crop** n (of rock) afloramiento m; **~cry** n protestas fpl; **~dated** adj anticuado, fuera de moda; **~do** (irreg) vt superar; **~door** adj exterior, de aire libre; (clothes) de calle; **~doors** adv al aire libre

outer ['autə*] adj exterior, externo; **~ space** n espacio exterior

outfit ['aʊtfɪt] n (clothes) conjunto m; **~going** adj (character) extrovertido; (retiring: president etc) saliente; **~goings** (BRIT) npl gastos mpl; **~grow** (irreg) vt: **he has ~grown his clothes** su ropa le queda pequeña ya; **~house** n dependencia; **~ing** n excursión f, paseo

out: ~law n proscrito ♦ vt proscribir; **~lay** n inversión f; **~let** n salida; (of pipe) desagüe m; (US: ELEC) toma de corriente; (also: retail ~let) punto de venta; **~line** n (shape) contorno, perfil m; (sketch, plan) esbozo ♦ vt (plan etc) esbozar; **in ~line** (fig) a grandes rasgos; **~live** vt sobrevivir a, durar más que; **~look** n (fig: prospects) perspectivas fpl, (: for weather) pronóstico; **~lying** adj remoto, aislado; **~moded** adj anticuado, pasado de moda; **~number** vt superar en número; **~of-date** adj (passport) caducado; (clothes) pasado de moda; **~-of-the-way** adj apartado; **~patient** n paciente m/f externo/a; **~post** n puesto avanzado; **~put** n (volumen m de) producción f, rendimiento; (COMPUT) salida

outrage ['aʊtreɪdʒ] n escándalo; (atrocity) atrocidad f ♦ vt ultrajar; **~ous** [-'reɪdʒəs] adj monstruoso

outright [adv aʊt'raɪt, adj 'aʊtraɪt] adv (ask, deny) francamente; (refuse) rotundamente; (win) de manera absoluta; (be killed) en el acto ♦ adj franco; rotundo

outset ['aʊtset] n principio

outside [aʊt'saɪd] n exterior m ♦ adj exterior, externo ♦ adv fuera ♦ prep fuera de; (beyond) más allá de; **at the ~** (fig) a lo sumo; **~ lane** n (AUT: in Britain) carril m de la derecha; (: in US, Europe etc) carril m de la izquierda; **~ line** n (TEL) línea (exterior); **~r** n (stranger) extraño, forastero

out: ~size adj (clothes) de talla grande; **~skirts** npl alrededores mpl, afueras

fpl; **~spoken** adj muy franco; **~standing** adj excepcional, destacado; (remaining) pendiente; **~stay** vt: **to ~stay one's welcome** quedarse más de la cuenta; **~stretched** adj (hand) extendido; **~strip** vt (competitors, demand) dejar atrás, aventajar; **~tray** n bandeja de salida

outward ['aʊtwəd] adj (sign, appearances) externo; (journey) de ida; **~ly** adv por fuera

outweigh [aʊt'weɪ] vt pesar más que

outwit [aʊt'wɪt] vt ser más listo que

oval ['əʊvl] adj ovalado ♦ n óvalo

ovary ['əʊvərɪ] n ovario

oven ['ʌvn] n horno; **~proof** adj resistente al horno

over ['əʊvə*] adv encima, por encima ♦ adj (or adv) (finished) terminado; (surplus) de sobra ♦ prep (por) encima de; (above) sobre; (on the other side of) al otro lado de; (more than) más de; (during) durante; **~ here** (por) aquí; **~ there** (por) allí o allá; **all ~** (everywhere) por todas partes; **and ~ (again)** una y otra vez; **~ and above** además de; **to ask sb ~** invitar a uno a casa; **to bend ~** inclinarse

overall [adj, n 'əʊvərɔːl, adv əʊvər'ɔːl] adj (length etc) total; (study) de conjunto ♦ adv en conjunto ♦ n (BRIT) guardapolvo; **~s** npl mono (SP), overol m (AM)

over: ~awe vt: **to be ~awed (by)** quedar impresionado (con); **~balance** vi perder el equilibrio; **~board** adv (NAUT) por la borda; **~book** [əʊvə'bʊk] vt sobrereservar

overcast ['əʊvəkɑːst] adj encapotado

overcharge [əʊvə'tʃɑːdʒ] vt: **to ~ sb** cobrar un precio excesivo a uno

overcoat ['əʊvəkəʊt] n abrigo, sobretodo

overcome [əʊvə'kʌm] (irreg) vt vencer; (difficulty) superar

over: ~crowded adj atestado de gente; (city, country) superpoblado;

~do (irreg) vt exagerar; (overcook) cocer demasiado; **to ~do it** (work etc) pasarse; **~dose** n sobredosis f; **~draft** n saldo deudor; **~drawn** adj (account) en descubierto; **~due** adj retrasado; **~estimate** [əuvə'estimeit] vt sobreestimar

overflow [vb əuvə'fləu, n 'əuvəfləu] vi desbordarse ♦ n (also: ~ pipe) (cañería de) desagüe m

overgrown [əuvə'grəun] adj (garden) invadido por la vegetación

overhaul [vb əuvə'hɔːl, n 'əuvəhɔːl] vt revisar, repasar ♦ n revisión f

overhead [adv əuvə'hed, adj, n 'əuvəhed] adv por encima de la cabeza ♦ adj (cable) aéreo ♦ n (US) = **~s; ~s** npl (expenses) gastos mpl generales

over: ~hear (irreg) vt oír por casualidad; **~heat** vi (engine) recalentarse; **~joyed** adj encantado, lleno de alegría

overland ['əuvəlænd] adj, adv por tierra

overlap [əuvə'læp] vi traslaparse

over: ~leaf adv al dorso; **~load** vt sobrecargar; **~look** vt (have view of) dar a, tener vistas a; (miss: by mistake) pasar por alto; (excuse) perdonar

overnight [əuvə'nait] adv durante la noche; (fig) de la noche a la mañana ♦ adj de noche; **to stay ~** pasar la noche

overpass ['əuvəpɑːs] (US) n paso superior

overpower [əuvə'pauə*] vt dominar; (fig) embargar; **~ing** adj (heat) agobiante; (smell) penetrante

over: ~rate vt sobreestimar; **~ride** (irreg) vt no hacer caso de; **~riding** adj predominante; **~rule** vt (decision) anular; (claim) denegar; **~run** (irreg) vt (country) invadir; (time limit) rebasar, exceder

overseas [əuvə'siːz] adv (abroad: live) en el extranjero; (: travel) al extranjero ♦ adj (trade) exterior; (visitor)

extranjero

overshadow [əuvə'ʃædəu] vt: **to be ~ed by** estar a la sombra de

overshoot [əuvə'ʃuːt] (irreg) vt excederse

oversight ['əuvəsait] n descuido

oversleep [əuvə'sliːp] (irreg) vi quedarse dormido

overstep [əuvə'step] vt: **to ~ the mark** pasarse de la raya

overt [əu'vɜːt] adj abierto

overtake [əuvə'teik] (irreg) vt sobrepasar; (BRIT: AUT) adelantar

over: ~throw (irreg) vt (government) derrocar; **~time** n horas fpl extraordinarias; **~tone** n (fig) tono

overture ['əuvətʃuə*] n (MUS) obertura; (fig) preludio

over: ~turn vt volcar; (fig: plan) desbaratar; (: government) derrocar ♦ vi volcar; **~weight** adj demasiado gordo o pesado; **~whelm** vt aplastar; (subj: emotion) sobrecoger; **~whelming** adj (victory, defeat) arrollador(a); (feeling) irresistible; **~work** vi trabajar demasiado; **~wrought** [əuvə'rɔːt] adj sobreexcitado

owe [əu] vt: **to ~ sb sth, to ~ sth to sb** deber algo a uno; **owing to** prep debido a, por causa de

owl [aul] n búho, lechuza

own [əun] vt tener, poseer ♦ adj propio; **a room of my ~** una habitación propia; **to get one's ~ back** tomar revancha; **on one's ~** solo, a solas; **~ up** vi confesar; **~er** n dueño/a; **~ership** n posesión f

ox [ɔks] (pl **~en**) n buey m; **~tail** n: **~tail soup** sopa de rabo de buey

oxygen ['ɔksidʒən] n oxígeno

oyster ['ɔistə*] n ostra

oz. abbr = **ounce(s)**

ozone ['əuzəun]: **~ friendly** adj que no daña la capa de ozono; **~ hole** n agujero m de/en la capa de ozono; **~ layer** n capa f de ozono

P, p

p [pi:] abbr = **penny; pence**

P.A. n abbr = **personal assistant;
public address system**

p.a. abbr = **per annum**

pa [pɑː] (inf) n papá m

pace [peɪs] n paso ♦ vi: **to ~ up and
down** pasearse de un lado a otro; **to
keep ~ with** llevar el mismo paso
que; **~maker** n (MED) regulador m
cardíaco, marcapasos m inv; (SPORT:
also: **~setter**) liebre f

Pacific [pə'sɪfɪk] n: **the ~ (Ocean)** el
(Océano) Pacífico

pack [pæk] n (packet) paquete m; (of
hounds) jauría; (of people) manada,
bando; (of cards) baraja; (bundle) fardo;
(US: of cigarettes) paquete m; (back ~)
mochila ♦ vt (fill) llenar; (in suitcase etc)
meter, poner; (cram) llenar, atestar; **to
~ (one's bags)** hacer la maleta; **to
~ sb off** despachar a uno; **~ it in!** (inf)
¡déjalo!

package ['pækɪdʒ] n paquete m;
(bulky) bulto; (also: **~ deal**) acuerdo
global; **~ holiday** n vacaciones fpl
organizadas; **~ tour** n viaje m
organizado

packed lunch n almuerzo frío

packet ['pækɪt] n paquete m

packing ['pækɪŋ] n embalaje m;
~ case n cajón m de embalaje

pact [pækt] n pacto

pad [pæd] n (of paper) bloc m;
(cushion) cojinete m; (inf: home) casa
♦ vt rellenar; **~ding** n (material) relleno

paddle ['pædl] n (oar) canalete m; (US:
for table tennis) paleta ♦ vt impulsar
con canalete ♦ vi (with feet) chapotear;
paddling pool (BRIT) n estanque m
de juegos

paddock ['pædək] n corral m

padlock ['pædlɒk] n candado

paediatrics [piːdɪ'ætrɪks] (US

pediatrics) n pediatría

pagan ['peɪgən] adj, n pagano/a m/f

page [peɪdʒ] n (of book) página; (of
newspaper) plana; (also: **~ boy**) paje m
♦ vt (in hotel etc) llamar por altavoz a

pageant ['pædʒənt] n (procession)
desfile m; (show) espectáculo; **~ry** n
pompa

pager ['peɪdʒə*] n (TEL) busca m

paging device ['peɪdʒɪŋ-] n = **pager**

paid [peɪd] pt, pp of **pay** ♦ adj (work)
remunerado; (holiday) pagado; (official
etc) a sueldo; **to put ~ to** (BRIT)
acabar con

pail [peɪl] n cubo, balde m

pain [peɪn] n dolor m; **to be in ~**
sufrir; **to take ~s to do sth** tomarse
grandes molestias en hacer algo; **~ed**
adj (expression) afligido; **~ful** adj
doloroso; (difficult) penoso;
(disagreeable) desagradable; **~fully** adv
(fig: very) terriblemente; **~killer** n
analgésico; **~less** adj no causa
dolor; **~staking** ['peɪnzteɪkɪn] adj
(person) concienzudo, esmerado

paint [peɪnt] n pintura ♦ vt pintar; **to
~ the door blue** pintar la puerta de
azul; **~brush** n (artist's) pincel m;
(decorator's) brocha; **~er** n pintor(a);
~ing n pintura; **~work** n pintura

pair [peə*] n (of shoes, gloves etc) par
m; (of people) pareja; **a ~ of scissors**
unas tijeras; **a ~ of trousers** unos
pantalones, un pantalón

pajamas [pə'dʒɑːməz] (US) npl pijama
m

Pakistan [pɑːkɪ'stɑːn] n Paquistán m;
~i adj, n paquistaní m/f

pal [pæl] (inf) n compinche m/f,
compañero/a

palace ['pæləs] n palacio

palatable ['pælɪtəbl] adj sabroso

palate ['pælɪt] n paladar m

pale [peɪl] adj (gen) pálido; (colour)
claro ♦ n: **to be beyond the ~**
pasarse de la raya

Palestine ['pælɪstaɪn] n Palestina;

Palestinian [-'tɪnɪən] adj, n palestino/a m/f

palette ['pælɪt] n paleta f

pall [pɔːl] vi perder el sabor

pallet ['pælɪt] n (for goods) pallet m

pallid ['pælɪd] adj pálido

palm [pɑːm] n (ANAT) palma; (also: ~ tree) palmera, palma ♦ vt: **to ~ sth off on sb** (inf) encajar algo a uno; **P~ Sunday** n Domingo de Ramos

paltry ['pɔːltrɪ] adj irrisorio

pamper ['pæmpə*] vt mimar

pamphlet ['pæmflət] n folleto

pan [pæn] n (also: sauce~) cacerola, cazuela, olla; (also: frying ~) sartén f

Panama ['pænəmɑː] n Panamá m; **the ~ Canal** el Canal de Panamá

pancake ['pænkeɪk] n crepe f

panda ['pændə] n panda m; **~ car** (BRIT) n coche m Z (SP)

pandemonium [pændɪ'məʊnɪəm] n jaleo

pander ['pændə*] vi: **to ~ to** complacer a

pane [peɪn] n cristal m

panel ['pænl] n (of wood etc) panel m; (RADIO, TV) panel m de invitados; **~ling** (US **~ing**) n paneles mpl

pang [pæŋ] n: **a ~ of regret** (una punzada de) remordimiento; **hunger ~s** dolores mpl del hambre

panic ['pænɪk] n (terror m) pánico ♦ vi dejarse llevar por el pánico; **~ky** adj (person) asustadizo; **~-stricken** adj preso de pánico

pansy ['pænzɪ] n (BOT) pensamiento; (inf: pej) maricón m

pant [pænt] vi jadear

panther ['pænθə*] n pantera

panties ['pæntɪz] npl bragas fpl, pantis mpl

pantihose ['pæntɪhəʊz] (US) n pantimedias fpl

pantomime ['pæntəmaɪm] (BRIT) n revista musical representada en Navidad, basada en cuentos de hadas

---

Pantomime

En época navideña se ponen en escena en los teatros británicos las llamadas **pantomimes**, que son versiones libres de cuentos tradicionales como Aladino o El gato con botas. En ella nunca faltan personajes como la dama "dame", papel que siempre interpreta un actor, el protagonista joven "principal boy", normalmente interpretado por una actriz, y el malvado "villain". Es un espectáculo familiar en el que se anima al público a participar y aunque va dirigido principalmente a los niños, cuenta con grandes dosis de humor para adultos.

---

pantry ['pæntrɪ] n despensa

pants [pænts] n (BRIT: underwear: woman's) bragas fpl; (: man's) calzoncillos mpl; (US: trousers) pantalones mpl

paper ['peɪpə*] n papel m; (also: news~) periódico, diario; (academic essay) ensayo; (exam) examen m ♦ de papel ♦ vt empapelar (SP), tapizar (AM); **~s** npl (also: identity ~s) papeles mpl, documentos mpl; **~back** n libro en rústica; **~ bag** n bolsa de papel; **~ clip** n clip m; **~ hankie** n pañuelo de papel; **~weight** n pisapapeles m inv; **~work** n trabajo administrativo

paprika ['pæprɪkə] n pimentón m

par [pɑː*] n par f; (GOLF) par m; **to be on a ~ with** estar a la par con

parachute ['pærəʃuːt] n paracaídas m inv

parade [pə'reɪd] n desfile m ♦ vt (show off) hacer alarde de ♦ vi desfilar; (MIL) pasar revista

paradise ['pærədaɪs] n paraíso

paradox ['pærədɒks] n paradoja; **~ically** [-'dɒksɪklɪ] adv paradójicamente

paraffin ['pærəfɪn] (BRIT) n (also: ~ oil)

parafina

paragon ['pærəgən] n modelo

paragraph ['pærəgra:f] n párrafo

parallel ['pærəlel] adj en paralelo; (fig) semejante ♦ n (line) paralela; (fig, GEO) paralelo

paralyse ['pærəlaɪz] vt paralizar

paralysis [pə'rælɪsɪs] n parálisis f inv

paralyze ['pærəlaɪz] (US) vt = paralyse

paramount ['pærəmaunt] adj: of ~ importance de suma importancia

paranoid ['pærənɔɪd] adj (person, feeling) paranoico

paraphernalia [pærəfə'neɪlɪə] n (gear) avíos mpl

parasite ['pærəsaɪt] n parásito/a

parasol ['pærəsɔl] n sombrilla, quitasol m

paratrooper ['pærətru:pə*] n paracaidista m/f

parcel ['pɑ:sl] n paquete m ♦ vt (also: ~ up) empaquetar, embalar

parched ['pɑ:tʃt] adj (person) muerto de sed

parchment ['pɑ:tʃmənt] n pergamino

pardon ['pɑ:dn] n (LAW) indulto ♦ vt perdonar; ~ me!, I beg your ~! (I'm sorry!) ¡perdone usted!; **(I beg your) ~?, ~ me?** (US) (what did you say?) ¿cómo?

parent ['pɛərənt] n (mother) madre f; (father) padre m; **~s** npl padres mpl; **~al** [pə'rɛntl] adj paternal/maternal

parenthesis [pə'rɛnθɪsɪs] (pl **parentheses** [pə'rɛnθɪsi:z]) n paréntesis m inv

Paris ['pærɪs] n París

parish ['pærɪʃ] n parroquia

Parisian [pə'rɪzɪən] adj, n parisiense m/f

park [pɑ:k] n parque m ♦ vt aparcar, estacionar ♦ vi aparcar, estacionarse

parking ['pɑ:kɪŋ] n aparcamiento, estacionamiento; **"no ~"** "prohibido estacionarse"; **~ lot** (US) n parking m; **~ meter** n parquímetro; **~ ticket** n multa de aparcamiento

parliament ['pɑ:ləmənt] n parlamento; (Spanish) Cortes fpl; **~ary** [-'mɛntəri] adj parlamentario

Parliament

El Parlamento británico
(**Parliament**) tiene como sede el
palacio de Westminster, también
llamado "Houses of Parliament" y
consta de dos cámaras. La Cámara de
los Comunes ("House of Commons",
compuesta por 650 diputados
(**Members of Parliament**) elegidos
por sufragio universal en su respectiva
circunscripción electoral
(**constituency**), se reúne 175 días al
año y sus sesiones son moderadas por
el Presidente de la Cámara
(**Speaker**). La cámara alta es la
Cámara de los Lores ("House of
Lords") y está formada por miembros
que han sido nombrados por el
monarca o que han heredado su
escaño. Su poder es limitado, aunque
actúa como tribunal supremo de
apelación, excepto en Escocia.

parlour ['pɑ:lə*] (US **parlor**) n sala de recibo, salón m, living m (AM)

parochial [pə'rəukɪəl] (pej) adj de miras estrechas

parole [pə'rəul] n: **on ~** libre bajo palabra

parquet ['pɑ:keɪ] n: **~ floor(ing)** parquet m

parrot ['pærət] n loro, papagayo

parry ['pærɪ] vt parar

parsley ['pɑ:slɪ] n perejil m

parsnip ['pɑ:snɪp] n chirivía

parson ['pɑ:sn] n cura m

part [pɑ:t] n (gen, MUS) parte f; (bit) trozo; (of machine) pieza; (THEATRE etc) papel m; (of serial) entrega; (US: in hair) raya ♦ adv = **partly** ♦ vt separar ♦ vi (people) separarse; (crowd) apartarse; **to take ~ in** tomar parte or participar en; **to take sth in good ~** tomar algo

en buena parte; **to take sb's ~**
defender a uno; **for my ~** por mi
parte; **for the most ~** en su mayor
parte; **to ~ one's hair** hacerse la raya;
~ with vt fus ceder, entregar; (money)
pagar; **~ exchange** (BRIT) n: **in
~ exchange** como parte del pago
partial ['pɑːʃl] adj parcial; **to be ~ to**
ser aficionado a
participant [pɑːˈtɪsɪpənt] n (in
competition) concursante m/f; (in
campaign etc) participante m/f
participate [pɑːˈtɪsɪpeɪt] vi: **to ~ in**
participar en; **participation** [-ˈpeɪʃən]
n participación f
participle ['pɑːtɪsɪpl] n participio
particle ['pɑːtɪkl] n partícula; (of dust)
grano
particular [pəˈtɪkjulə*] adj (special)
particular; (concrete) concreto; (given)
determinado; (fussy) quisquilloso;
(demanding) exigente; **~s** npl
(information) datos mpl; (details)
pormenores mpl; **in ~** en particular;
~ly adv (in particular) sobre todo;
(difficult, good etc) especialmente
parting ['pɑːtɪŋ] n (act of separation)
f; (farewell) despedida; (BRIT: in hair)
raya ♦ adj (farewell) despedida
partisan [pɑːtɪˈzæn] adj partidista ♦ n
partidario/a
partition [pɑːˈtɪʃən] n (POL) división f;
(wall) tabique m
partly ['pɑːtlɪ] adv en parte
partner ['pɑːtnə*] n (COMM) socio/a;
(SPORT, at dance) pareja; (spouse)
cónyuge m/f; (lover) compañero/a;
~ship n asociación f; (COMM) sociedad
f
partridge ['pɑːtrɪdʒ] n perdiz f
part-time adj, adv a tiempo parcial
party ['pɑːtɪ] n (POL) partido; (team)
(celebration) fiesta; (group) grupo;
(LAW) parte f interesada ♦ cpd (POL) de
partido; **~ dress** n vestido de fiesta
pass [pɑːs] vt (time, object) pasar;
(place) pasar por; (overtake) rebasar;

(exam) aprobar; (approve) aprobar ♦ vi
pasar; (SCOL) aprobar, ser aprobado
♦ n (permit) permiso; (membership
card) carnet m; (in mountains) puerto,
desfiladero; (SPORT) pase m; (SCOL: also:
~ mark): **to get a ~ in** aprobar en; **to
~ sth through sth** pasar algo por
algo; **to make a ~ at sb** (inf) hacer
proposiciones a uno; **~ away** vi
fallecer; **~ by** vi pasar ♦ vt (ignore)
pasar por alto; **~ for** vt fus pasar por;
~ on vt transmitir; **~ out** vi
desmayarse; **~ up** vt (opportunity)
renunciar a; **~able** adj (road)
transitable; (tolerable) pasable
passage ['pæsɪdʒ] n (also: ~way)
pasillo; (act of passing) tránsito; (fare, in
book) pasaje m; (by boat) travesía;
(ANAT) tubo
passbook ['pɑːsbuk] n libreta de
banco
passenger ['pæsɪndʒə*] n pasajero/a,
viajero/a
passer-by [pɑːsəˈbaɪ] n transeúnte m/f
passing ['pɑːsɪŋ] adj pasajero; **in ~** de
paso; **~ place** n (AUT) apartadero
passion ['pæʃən] n pasión f; **~ate** adj
apasionado
passive ['pæsɪv] adj (gen, also LING)
pasivo; **~ smoking** n efectos del
tabaco en fumadores pasivos
Passover ['pɑːsəuvə*] n Pascua (de los
judíos)
passport ['pɑːspɔːt] n pasaporte m;
~ control n control m de pasaporte;
~ office n oficina de pasaportes
password ['pɑːswɜːd] n contraseña
past [pɑːst] prep (in front of) por
delante de; (further than) más allá de;
(later than) después de ♦ adj (gone by)
pasado; (president etc) antiguo ♦ n (time)
pasado; (of person) antecedentes mpl;
he's ~ forty tiene más de cuarenta
años; **ten/quarter ~ eight** las ocho y
diez/cuarto; **for the ~ few/3 days**
durante los últimos días/últimos 3 días;
to run ~ sb pasar a uno corriendo

pasta ['pæstə] n pasta
paste [peɪst] n pasta; (glue) engrudo
♦ vt pegar
pasteurized ['pæstəraɪzd] adj
pasteurizado
pastille ['pæstl] n pastilla
pastime ['pɑːstaɪm] n pasatiempo
pastry ['peɪstrɪ] n (dough) pasta; (cake)
pastel m
pasture ['pɑːstʃə*] n pasto
pasty¹ ['pæstɪ] n empanada
pasty² ['peɪstɪ] adj (complexion) pálido
pat [pæt] vt dar una palmadita a; (dog
etc) acariciar
patch [pætʃ] n (of material, eye ~)
parche m; (mended part) remiendo;
(of land) terreno ♦ vt remendar; (to go
through) a bad ~ (pasar por) una
mala racha; ~ up vt reparar; (quarrel)
hacer las paces en; ~work n labor m
de retazos; ~y adj desigual
pâté ['pæteɪ] n paté m
patent ['peɪtnt] n patente f ♦ vt
patentar ♦ adj patente, evidente;
~ leather n charol m
paternal [pə'tɜːnl] adj paternal;
(relation) paterno
path [pɑːθ] n camino, sendero; (trail,
track) pista; (of missile) trayectoria
pathetic [pə'θetɪk] adj patético,
lastimoso; (very bad) malísimo
pathological [pæθə'lɒdʒɪkəl] adj
patológico
pathway ['pɑːθweɪ] n sendero, vereda
patience ['peɪʃns] n paciencia; (BRIT:
CARDS) solitario
patient ['peɪʃnt] n paciente m/f ♦ adj
paciente, sufrido
patio ['pætɪəu] n patio
patriot ['peɪtrɪət] n patriota m/f; ~ic
[pætrɪ'ɒtɪk] adj patriótico
patrol [pə'trəul] n patrulla ♦ vt
patrullar por; ~ car n coche m patrulla;
~man (US irreg) n policía m
patron ['peɪtrən] n (in shop) cliente
m/f; (of charity) patrocinador(a) m/f;
~ of the arts mecenas m; ~ize

['pætrənaɪz] vt (shop) ser cliente de;
(artist etc) proteger; (look down on)
condescender con; ~ saint n santo/a
patrón/ona m/f
patter ['pætə*] n golpeteo; (sales talk)
labia ♦ vi (rain) tamborilear
pattern ['pætən] n (SEWING) patrón m;
(design) dibujo
pauper ['pɔːpə*] n pobre m/f
pause [pɔːz] n pausa ♦ vi hacer una
pausa
pave [peɪv] vt pavimentar; to ~ the
way for preparar el terreno para
pavement ['peɪvmənt] (BRIT) n acera
(SP), vereda (AM)
pavilion [pə'vɪlɪən] n caseta
paving ['peɪvɪŋ] n pavimento,
enlosado; ~ stone n losa
paw [pɔː] n pata
pawn [pɔːn] n (CHESS) peón m; (fig)
instrumento ♦ vt empeñar; ~ broker
n prestamista m/f; ~shop n monte de
piedad
pay [peɪ] (pt, pp paid) n (wage etc)
sueldo, salario ♦ vt pagar ♦ vi (be
profitable) rendir; to ~ attention (to)
prestar atención a; to ~ sb a visit
hacer una visita a uno; to ~ one's
respects to sb presentar sus respetos
a uno; ~ back vt (money) reembolsar;
(person) pagar; ~ for vt fus pagar; ~ in
vt ingresar; ~ off vt saldar ♦ vi (scheme,
decision) dar resultado; ~ up vt pagar
(de mala gana); ~able adj: ~able to
pagadero a; ~ day n día m de paga;
~ee n portador(a) m/f; ~ envelope
(US) n = ~ packet; ~ment n pago;
monthly ~ment mensualidad f;
~ packet (BRIT) n sobre m (de paga);
~ phone n teléfono público; ~roll n
nómina; ~ slip n recibo de sueldo;
~ television n televisión f de pago
PC n abbr = personal computer;
(BRIT) = police constable ♦ adv abbr
= politically correct
p.c. abbr = per cent
pea [piː] n guisante m (SP), chícharo

peace |piːs| n paz f; (calm) tranquilidad f; **~ful** adj (gentle) pacífico; (calm) tranquilo, sosegado

peach |piːtʃ| n melocotón m (SP), durazno (AM)

peacock |ˈpiːkɔk| n pavo real

peak |piːk| n (of mountain) cumbre f, cima; (of cap) visera; (fig) cumbre f; **~ hours** npl, **~ period** n horas fpl punta

peal |piːl| n (of bells) repique m; **~ of laughter** carcajada

peanut |ˈpiːnʌt| n cacahuete m (SP), maní m (AM); **~ butter** manteca de cacahuete or maní

pear |peə*| n pera

pearl |pəːl| n perla

peasant |ˈpeznt| n campesino/a

peat |piːt| n turba

pebble |ˈpebl| n guijarro

peck |pek| vt (also: **~ at**) picotear ♦ n picotazo; (kiss) besito; **~ing order** n orden m de jerarquía; **~ish** (BRIT: inf) adj: **I feel ~ish** tengo ganas de picar algo

peculiar |pɪˈkjuːlɪə*| adj (odd) extraño, raro; (typical) propio, característico; **~ to** propio de

pedal |ˈpedl| n pedal m ♦ vi pedalear

pedantic |pɪˈdæntɪk| adj pedante

peddler |ˈpedlə*| n: **drug ~** traficante m/f; camello

pedestrian |pɪˈdestrɪən| n peatón/ona m/f ♦ adj pedestre; **~ crossing** (BRIT) n paso de peatones; **~ precinct** (BRIT), **~ zone** (US) n zona peatonal

pediatrics |piːdɪˈætrɪks| (US) n = **paediatrics**

pedigree |ˈpedɪgriː| n genealogía; (of animal) raza, pedigrí ♦ cpd (animal) de raza, de casta

pee |piː| (inf) vi mear

peek |piːk| vi mirar a hurtadillas

peel |piːl| n piel f; (of orange, lemon) cáscara; (: removed) peladuras fpl ♦ vt pelar ♦ vi (paint etc) desconcharse; (wallpaper) despegarse, desprenderse; (skin) pelar

peep |piːp| n (BRIT: look) mirada furtiva; (sound) pío ♦ vi (BRIT: look) mirar furtivamente; **~ out** vi salir (un poco); **~hole** n mirilla

peer |pɪə*| vi: **to ~ at** escudriñar ♦ n (noble) par m; (equal) igual m; (contemporary) contemporáneo/a; **~age** n nobleza

peeved |piːvd| adj enojado

peg |peg| n (for coat etc) gancho, colgadero; (BRIT: also: **clothes ~**) pinza

Pekingese |piːkɪˈniːz| n (dog) pequinés/esa m/f

pelican |ˈpelɪkən| n pelícano; **~ crossing** (BRIT) n (AUT) paso de peatones señalizado

pellet |ˈpelɪt| n bolita; (bullet) perdigón m

pelt |pelt| vt: **to ~ sb with sth** arrojarle algo a uno ♦ vi (rain) llover a cántaros; (inf: run) correr ♦ n pellejo

pen |pen| n (fountain) pluma; (ballpoint) bolígrafo; (for sheep) redil m

penal |ˈpiːnl| adj penal; **~ize** vt castigar

penalty |ˈpenltɪ| n (gen) pena; (fine) multa; **~ (kick)** (FOOTBALL) penalty m; (RUGBY) golpe m de castigo

penance |ˈpenəns| n penitencia

pence |pens| npl of **penny**

pencil |ˈpensl| n lápiz m, lapicero (AM); **~ case** n estuche m; **~ sharpener** n sacapuntas m inv

pendant |ˈpendnt| n pendiente m

pending |ˈpendɪŋ| prep antes de ♦ adj pendiente

pendulum |ˈpendjuləm| n péndulo

penetrate |ˈpenɪtreɪt| vt penetrar

penfriend |ˈpenfrend| (BRIT) n amigo/a por carta

penguin |ˈpeŋgwɪn| n pingüino

penicillin |penɪˈsɪlɪn| n penicilina

peninsula |pəˈnɪnsjulə| n península

penis |ˈpiːnɪs| n pene m

penitentiary [penɪˈtenʃərɪ] (US) n cárcel f, presidio

penknife [ˈpennaɪf] n navaja

pen name n seudónimo

penniless [ˈpenɪlɪs] adj sin dinero

penny [ˈpenɪ] (pl **pennies** or (BRIT) **pence**) n penique m; (US) centavo

penpal [ˈpenpæl] n amigo/a por carta

pension [ˈpenʃən] n (state benefit) jubilación f; **~er** (BRIT) n jubilado/a; **~ fund** n caja o fondo de pensiones

pentagon [ˈpentəgən] n: **the P~** (US: POL) el Pentágono

Pentagon

Se conoce como **Pentagon** al edificio de planta pentagonal que acoge las dependencias del Ministerio de Defensa estadounidense ("Department of Defense") en Arlington, Virginia. En lenguaje periodístico se aplica también a la dirección militar del país.

Pentecost [ˈpentɪkɒst] n Pentecostés m

penthouse [ˈpenthaus] n ático de lujo

pent-up [ˈpentʌp] adj reprimido

people [ˈpiːpl] npl gente f; (citizens) pueblo, ciudadanos mpl; (POL): **the ~** el pueblo ♦ n (nation, race) pueblo, nación f; **several ~ came** vinieron varias personas; **~ say that ...** dice la gente que ...

pep [pep] (inf): **~ up** vt animar

pepper [ˈpepə*] n (spice) pimienta; (vegetable) pimiento ♦ vt: **to ~ with** (fig) salpicar de; **~mint** n (sweet) pastilla de menta

peptalk [ˈpeptɔːk] n: **to give sb a ~** darle a uno una inyección de ánimo

per [pɜː*] prep por; **~ day/person** por día/persona; **~ annum** al año; **~ capita** adj, adv per cápita

perceive [pəˈsiːv] vt percibir; (realize) darse cuenta de

per cent n por ciento

percentage [pəˈsentɪdʒ] n porcentaje m

perception [pəˈsepʃən] n percepción f; (insight) perspicacia; (opinion etc) opinión f; **perceptive** [-ˈseptɪv] adj perspicaz

perch [pɜːtʃ] n (fish) perca; (for bird) percha ♦ vi: **to ~ (on)** (bird) posarse (en); (person) encaramarse (en)

percolator [ˈpɜːkəleɪtə*] n (also: **coffee ~**) cafetera de filtro

perennial [pəˈrenɪəl] adj perenne

perfect [adj, n ˈpɜːfɪkt, vb pəˈfekt] adj perfecto ♦ n (also: **~ tense**) perfecto ♦ vt perfeccionar; **~ly** [ˈpɜːfɪktlɪ] adv perfectamente

perforate [ˈpɜːfəreɪt] vt perforar

perform [pəˈfɔːm] vt (carry out) realizar, llevar a cabo; (THEATRE) representar; (piece of music) interpretar ♦ vi (well, badly) funcionar; **~ance** n (of a play) representación f; (of actor, athlete etc) actuación f; (of car, engine, company) rendimiento; (of economy) resultado mpl; **~er** n (actor) actor m, actriz f

perfume [ˈpɜːfjuːm] n perfume m

perhaps [pəˈhæps] adv quizá(s), tal vez

peril [ˈperɪl] n peligro, riesgo

perimeter [pəˈrɪmɪtə*] n perímetro

period [ˈpɪərɪəd] n período; (SCOL) clase f; (full stop) punto; (MED) regla ♦ adj (costume, furniture) de época; **~ic(al)** [-ˈɔdɪk(l)] adj periódico; **~ical** [-ˈɔdɪkl] n periódico; **~ically** [-ˈɔdɪklɪ] adv de vez en cuando, cada cierto tiempo

peripheral [pəˈrɪfərəl] adj periférico ♦ n (COMPUT) periférico, unidad f periférica

perish [ˈperɪʃ] vi perecer; (decay) echarse a perder; **~able** adj perecedero

perjury [ˈpɜːdʒərɪ] n (LAW) perjurio

perk [pɜːk] n extra m; **~ up** vi (cheer up) animarse

perm [pɜːm] n permanente f

permanent ['pə:mənənt] adj permanente

permeate ['pə:mɪeɪt] vi penetrar, trascender ♦ vt penetrar, trascender a

permissible [pə'mɪsɪbl] adj permisible, lícito

permission [pə'mɪʃən] n permiso f

permissive [pə'mɪsɪv] adj permisivo

permit [n 'pə:mɪt, vt pə'mɪt] n permiso, licencia ♦ vt permitir

perplex [pə'pleks] vt dejar perplejo

persecute ['pə:sɪkju:t] vt perseguir

persevere [pə:sɪ'vɪə*] vi persistir

Persian ['pə:ʃən] adj, n persa m/f; the ~ **Gulf** el Golfo Pérsico

persist [pə'sɪst] vi: to ~ (in doing sth) persistir (en hacer algo); ~ence n empeño f; ~ent adj (determined) porfiado

person ['pə:sn] n persona; in ~ en persona; ~al adj personal; individual; (visit) en persona; ~al assistant n ayudante m/f personal; ~al column n anuncios mpl personales; ~al computer n ordenador m personal; ~ality [-'nælɪtɪ] n personalidad f; ~ally adv personalmente; (in person) en persona; to take sth ~ally tomarse algo a mal; ~al organizer n agenda; ~al stereo n Walkman ® m; ~ify [-'sɔnɪfaɪ] vt encarnar

personnel [pə:sə'nel] n personal m

perspective [pə'spektɪv] n perspectiva

Perspex ® ['pə:speks] n plexiglás ® m

perspiration [pə:spɪ'reɪʃən] n transpiración f

persuade [pə'sweɪd] vt: to ~ sb to do sth persuadir a uno para que haga algo

Peru [pə'ru:] n el Perú; **Peruvian** adj, n peruano/a m/f

perverse [pə'və:s] adj perverso; (wayward) travieso

pervert [n pə'və:t, vb pə'və:t] n pervertido/a m/f ♦ vt pervertir; (truth, sb's words) tergiversar

pessimist ['pesɪmɪst] n pesimista m/f;

~**ic** [-'mɪstɪk] adj pesimista

pest [pest] n (insect) insecto nocivo; (fig) lata, molestia

pester ['pestə*] vt molestar, acosar

pesticide ['pestɪsaɪd] n pesticida m

pet [pet] n animal m doméstico ♦ cpd favorito ♦ vt acariciar; **teacher's** ~ favorito/a (del profesor); ~ **hate** manía

petal ['petl] n pétalo

peter ['pi:tə*]: to ~ **out** vi agotarse, acabarse

petite [pə'ti:t] adj chiquita

petition [pə'tɪʃən] n petición f

petrified ['petrɪfaɪd] adj horrorizado

petrol ['petrəl] (BRIT) n gasolina; **two/ four-star** ~ gasolina normal/súper; ~ **can** n bidón m de gasolina

petroleum [pə'trəuliəm] n petróleo

petrol: ~ **pump** (BRIT) n (in garage) surtidor m de gasolina; ~ **station** (BRIT) n gasolinera; ~ **tank** (BRIT) n depósito (de gasolina)

petticoat ['petɪkəut] n enaguas fpl

petty ['petɪ] adj (mean) mezquino; (unimportant) insignificante; ~ **cash** n dinero para gastos menores; ~ **officer** n contramaestre m

petulant ['petjulənt] adj malhumorado

pew [pju:] n banco

pewter ['pju:tə*] n peltre m

phantom ['fæntəm] n fantasma m

pharmacist ['fɑ:məsɪst] n farmacéutico/a

pharmacy ['fɑ:məsɪ] n farmacia

phase [feɪz] n fase f ♦ vt: to ~ **sth in/ out** introducir/retirar algo por etapas

Ph.D. abbr = **Doctor of Philosophy**

pheasant ['feznt] n faisán m

phenomenon [fə'nɔmɪnən] (pl **phenomena**) n fenómeno

philanthropist [fɪ'lænθrəpɪst] n filántropo/a

Philippines ['fɪlɪpi:nz] npl: the ~ las Filipinas

philosopher [fɪ'lɔsəfə*] n filósofo/a

philosophy [fɪ'lɔsəfɪ] n filosofía

phobia ['fəubjə] n fobia

phone [fəun] n teléfono ♦ vt telefonear, llamar por teléfono; **to be on the ~** tener teléfono; (be calling) estar hablando por teléfono; **~ back** vt, vi volver a llamar; **~ up** vt, vi llamar por teléfono; **~ book** n guía telefónica; **~ booth** n cabina telefónica; **~ box** (BRIT) n = **~ booth**; **~ call** n llamada (telefónica); **~card** n teletarjeta; **~-in** (BRIT) n (RADIO, TV) programa m de participación (telefónica)

phonetics [fəˈnɛtɪks] n fonética

phoney [ˈfəunɪ] adj falso

photo [ˈfəutəu] n foto f; **~copier** n fotocopiadora; **~copy** n fotocopia ♦ vt fotocopiar

photograph [ˈfəutəgrɑːf] n fotografía ♦ vt fotografiar; **~er** [fəˈtɔgrəfə*] n fotógrafo; **~y** [fəˈtɔgrəfɪ] n fotografía

phrase [freɪz] n frase f ♦ vt expresar; **~ book** n libro de frases

physical [ˈfɪzɪkl] adj físico; **~ education** n educación f física; **~ly** adv físicamente

physician [fɪˈzɪʃən] n médico/a

physicist [ˈfɪzɪsɪst] n físico/a

physics [ˈfɪzɪks] n física

physiotherapy [fɪzɪəuˈθerəpɪ] n fisioterapia

physique [fɪˈziːk] n físico

pianist [ˈpiːənɪst] n pianista m/f

piano [pɪˈænəu] n piano

pick [pɪk] n (tool: also: ~-axe) pico, piqueta ♦ vt (select) elegir, escoger; (gather) coger (SP), recoger; (remove, take out) sacar, quitar; (lock) abrir con ganzúa; **take your ~** escoja lo que quiera; **the ~ of** lo mejor de; **to ~ one's nose/teeth** hurgarse las narices/limpiarse los dientes; **to ~ a quarrel with sb** meterse con alguien; **~ at** vt fus: **to ~ at one's food** comer con poco apetito; **~ on** vt fus (person) meterse con; **~ out** vt escoger; (distinguish) identificar; **~ up** vi (improve: sales) ir mejor; (: patient) reponerse; (: FINANCE) recobrarse ♦ vt

recoger; (learn) aprender; (POLICE: arrest) detener; (person: for sex) ligar; (RADIO) captar; **to ~ up speed** acelerarse; **to ~ o.s. up** levantarse

picket [ˈpɪkɪt] n piquete m ♦ vt piquetear

pickle [ˈpɪkl] n (also: ~s: as condiment) escabeche m; (fig: mess) apuro ♦ vt encurtir

pickpocket [ˈpɪkpɔkɪt] n carterista m/f

pickup [ˈpɪkʌp] n (small truck) furgoneta

picnic [ˈpɪknɪk] n merienda ♦ vi ir de merienda; **~ area** n zona de picnic; (AUT) área de descanso

picture [ˈpɪktʃə*] n (gen) cuadro; (painting) pintura; (photograph) fotografía; (TV) imagen f; (film) película; (fig: description) descripción f; (: situation) situación f ♦ vt (imagine) imaginar; **~s** npl: **the ~s** (BRIT) el cine; **~ book** n libro de dibujos

picturesque [pɪktʃəˈresk] adj pintoresco

pie [paɪ] n (of fruit) pastel m; (open) tarta; (small: of meat) empanada

piece [piːs] n pedazo, trozo; (of cake) trozo; (item): **a ~ of clothing/ furniture/advice** una prenda (de vestir)/un mueble/un consejo ♦ vt: **to ~ together** juntar; (TECH) armar; **to take to ~s** desmontar; **~meal** adv poco a poco; **~work** n trabajo a destajo

pie chart n gráfico de sectores or tarta

pier [pɪə*] n muelle m, embarcadero

pierce [pɪəs] vt perforar

piercing [ˈpɪəsɪŋ] adj penetrante

pig [pɪg] n cerdo (SP), puerco (SP), chancho (AM); (pej: unkind person) asqueroso; (: greedy person) glotón/ona m/f

pigeon [ˈpɪdʒən] n paloma; (as food) pichón m; **~hole** n casilla

piggy bank [ˈpɪgɪ-] n hucha (en forma de cerdito)

pig: ~headed [ˈpɪgˈhɛdɪd] adj terco,

testarudo; ~let ['pɪglɪt] *n* cochinillo;
~skin *n* piel *f* de cerdo; **~sty** ['pɪgstaɪ]
n pocilga; **~tail** (*girl's*) trenza *f*
(*Chinese, TAUR*) coleta

pike [paɪk] *n* (*fish*) lucio

pilchard ['pɪltʃəd] *n* sardina

pile [paɪl] *n* montón *m*; (*of carpet,
cloth*) pelo ♦ *vt* (*also: ~ up*) amontonar;
(*fig*) acumular ♦ *vi* (*also: ~ up*)
amontonarse; acumularse; **~ into** *vt
fus* (*car*) meterse en; **~s** [paɪlz] *npl*
(*MED*) almorranas *fpl*, hemorroides *mpl*;
~up *n* (*AUT*) accidente *m* múltiple

pilfering ['pɪlfərɪŋ] *n* ratería

pilgrim ['pɪlgrɪm] *n* peregrino/a; **~age**
n peregrinaje *f*, romería

pill [pɪl] *n* píldora; **the ~** la píldora

pillage ['pɪlɪdʒ] *vt* pillar, saquear

pillar ['pɪlə*] *n* pilar *m*; **~ box** (*BRIT*) *n*
buzón *m*

pillion ['pɪljən] *n* (*of motorcycle*)
asiento trasero

pillow ['pɪləʊ] *n* almohada; **~case** *n*
funda

pilot ['paɪlət] *n* piloto ♦ *cpd* (*scheme
etc*) piloto ♦ *vt* pilotar; **~ light** *n* piloto

pimp [pɪmp] *n* chulo (*SP*), cafiche *m*
(*AM*)

pimple ['pɪmpl] *n* grano

PIN *n abbr* (*= personal identification
number*) número personal

pin [pɪn] *n* alfiler *m* ♦ *vt* prender (con
alfiler); **~s and needles** hormigueo;
to ~ sb down (*fig*) hacer que uno
concrete; **to ~ sth on sb** (*fig*) colgarle
a uno el sambenito de algo

pinafore ['pɪnəfɔ:*] *n* delantal *m*;
~ dress (*BRIT*) *n* mandil *m*

pinball ['pɪnbɔ:l] *n* mesa americana

pincers ['pɪnsəz] *npl* pinzas *fpl*, tenazas
fpl

pinch [pɪntʃ] *n* (*of salt etc*) pizca ♦ *vt*
pellizcar; (*inf: steal*) birlar; **at a ~** en
caso de apuro

pincushion ['pɪnkʊʃən] *n* acerico

pine [paɪn] *n* (*also: ~ tree, wood*) pino
♦ *vi*: **to ~ for** suspirar por; **~ away** *vi*

morirse de pena

pineapple ['paɪnæpl] *n* piña, ananás *m*

ping [pɪŋ] *n* (*noise*) sonido agudo; **~-
pong** ® *n* pingpong ® *m*

pink [pɪŋk] *adj* rosado, (color de) rosa
♦ *n* (*colour*) rosa; (*BOT*) clavel *m*,
clavellina

pinpoint ['pɪnpɔɪnt] *vt* precisar

pint [paɪnt] *n* pinta (*BRIT* = 568cc; *US*
= 473cc); (*BRIT: inf: of beer*) pinta de
cerveza, ≈ jarra (*SP*)

pin-up *n* fotografía erótica

pioneer [paɪə'nɪə*] *n* pionero/a

pious ['paɪəs] *adj* piadoso, devoto

pip [pɪp] *n* (*seed*) pepita; **the ~s** (*BRIT*)
la señal

pipe [paɪp] *n* tubo, caño; (*for smoking*)
pipa ♦ *vt* conducir en cañerías; **~s** *npl*
(*gen*) cañería; (*also: bag~s*) gaita;
~ cleaner *n* limpiapipas *m inv*;
~ dream *n* sueño imposible; **~line** *n*
(*for oil*) oleoducto; (*for gas*) gasoducto;
~r *n* gaitero/a

piping ['paɪpɪŋ] *adv*: **to be ~ hot** estar
que quema

piquant ['pi:kənt] *adj* picante; (*fig*)
agudo

pique [pi:k] *n* pique *m*, resentimiento

pirate ['paɪərət] *n* pirata *m/f* ♦ *vt*
(*cassette, book*) piratear; **~ radio** (*BRIT*)
n emisora pirata

Pisces ['paɪsi:z] *n* Piscis *m*

piss [pɪs] (*inf!*) *vi* mear; **~ed** (*inf!*) *adj*
(*drunk*) borracho

pistol ['pɪstl] *n* pistola

piston ['pɪstən] *n* pistón *m*, émbolo

pit [pɪt] *n* hoyo; (*also: coal ~*) mina; (*in
garage*) foso de reparación; (*also:
orchestra ~*) platea ♦ *vt*: **to ~ one's
wits against sb** medir fuerzas con
uno; **~s** *npl* (*AUT*) box *m*

pitch [pɪtʃ] *n* (*MUS*) tono; (*BRIT: SPORT*)
campo, terreno; (*tar*) brea
♦ *vt* (*throw*) arrojar, lanzar ♦ *vi* (*fall*)
caer(se); **to ~ a tent** montar una
tienda (de campaña); **~-black** *adj*
negro como boca de lobo; **~ed battle**

n batalla campal

pitfall ['pɪtfɔːl] n riesgo

pith [pɪθ] n (of orange) médula

pithy ['pɪθɪ] adj (fig) jugoso

pitiful ['pɪtɪful] adj (touching)
lastimoso, conmovedor(a)

pitiless ['pɪtɪlɪs] adj despiadado

pittance ['pɪtns] n miseria

pity ['pɪtɪ] n compasión f, piedad f ♦ vt
compadecer(se de); **what a ~!** ¡qué
pena!

pizza ['piːtsə] n pizza

placard ['plækɑːd] n letrero; (in march
etc) pancarta

placate [plə'keɪt] vt apaciguar

place [pleɪs] n lugar m, sitio; (seat)
plaza, asiento; (post) puesto; (home):
at/to his ~ en/a su casa; (role: in
society etc) papel m ♦ vt (object) poner,
colocar; (identify) reconocer; **to take ~**
tener lugar; **to be ~d** (in race, exam)
colocarse; **out of ~** (not suitable) fuera
de lugar; **in the first ~** en primer
lugar; **to change ~s with sb**
cambiarse de sitio con uno; **~ of birth**
lugar m de nacimiento

placid ['plæsɪd] adj apacible

plague [pleɪg] n plaga; (MED) peste f
♦ vt (fig) acosar, atormentar

plaice [pleɪs] n inv platija

plaid [plæd] n (material) tartán m

plain [pleɪn] adj (unpatterned) liso;
(clear) claro, evidente; (simple) sencillo;
(not handsome) poco atractivo ♦ adv
claramente ♦ n llano, llanura;
~ chocolate n chocolate m amargo;
~clothes adj (police) vestido de
paisano; **~ly** adv claramente

plaintiff ['pleɪntɪf] n demandante m/f

plait [plæt] n trenza

plan [plæn] n (drawing) plano; (scheme)
plan m, proyecto ♦ vt proyectar,
planificar ♦ vi hacer proyectos; **to ~ to
do** pensar hacer

plane [pleɪn] n (AVIAT) avión m; (MATH,
fig) plano; (also: ~ tree) plátano; (tool)
cepillo

planet ['plænɪt] n planeta m

plank [plæŋk] n tabla

planner ['plænə*] n planificador(a) m/f

planning ['plænɪŋ] n planificación f;
family ~ planificación familiar;
~ permission n permiso para realizar
obras

plant [plɑːnt] n planta; (machinery)
maquinaria; (factory) fábrica ♦ vt
plantar; (field) sembrar; (cover) colocar

plaster ['plɑːstə*] n (for walls) yeso;
(also: ~ of Paris) yeso mate; (BRIT: also:
sticking ~) tirita (SP), esparadrapo,
curita (AM) ♦ vt enyesar; (cover): **to
~ with** llenar o cubrir de; **~ed** (inf)
adj borracho; **~er** n yesero

plastic ['plæstɪk] n plástico ♦ adj de
plástico; **~ bag** n bolsa de plástico

Plasticine ® ['plæstɪsiːn] (n) (BRIT)
plastilina ®

plastic surgery n cirujía plástica

plate [pleɪt] n (dish) plato; (metal, in
book) lámina; (dental ~) placa de
dentadura postiza

plateau ['plætəʊ] (pl ~s or ~x) n
meseta, altiplanicie f

plateaux ['plætəʊz] npl of **plateau**

plate glass n vidrio cilindrado

platform ['plætfɔːm] n (RAIL) andén m;
(stage, BRIT: on bus) plataforma; (at
meeting) tribuna; (POL) programa m
(electoral)

platinum ['plætɪnəm] adj, n platino

platoon [plə'tuːn] n pelotón m

platter ['plætə*] n fuente f

plausible ['plɔːzɪbl] adj verosímil;
(person) convincente

play [pleɪ] n (THEATRE) obra, comedia
♦ vt (game) jugar; (compete against)
jugar contra; (instrument) tocar; (part:
in play etc) hacer el papel de; (tape,
record) poner ♦ vi jugar; (band) tocar;
(tape, record) sonar; **to ~ safe** ir a lo
seguro; **~ down** vt quitar importancia
a; **~ up** vi (cause trouble) dar guerra;
~boy n playboy m; **~er** n jugador(a)
m/f; (THEATRE) actor/actriz m/f; (MUS)

músico/a; ~ful adj juguetón/ona;
~ground n (in school) patio de recreo;
(in park) parque m infantil; ~group n
jardín m de niños; ~ing card n naipe
m, carta; ~ing field n campo de
deportes; ~mate n compañero/a de
juego; ~-off n (SPORT) (partido de)
desempate m; ~pen n corral m;
~thing n juguete m; ~time n (SCOL)
recreo; ~wright n dramaturgo/a

plc abbr (= public limited company) ≈
S.A.

plea [pli:] n súplica, petición f; (LAW)
alegato, defensa; ~ bargaining n
(LAW) acuerdo entre fiscal y defensor
para agilizar los trámites judiciales

plead [pli:d] vt (LAW): to ~ sb's case
defender a uno; (give as excuse) poner
como pretexto ♦ vi (LAW) declararse;
(beg): to ~ with sb suplicar or rogar a
uno

pleasant ['pleznt] adj agradable; ~ries
npl cortesías fpl

please [pli:z] excl ¡por favor! ♦ vt (give
pleasure to) dar gusto a, agradar ♦ vi
(think fit): do as you ~ haz lo que
quieras; ~ yourself! (inf) ¡haz lo que
quieras!, ¡como quieras!; ~d adj
(happy) alegre, contento; ~d (with)
satisfecho (de); ~d to meet you
¡encantado!, ¡tanto gusto!; pleasing
adj agradable, grato

pleasure ['pleʒə*] n placer m, gusto;
"it's a ~" "el gusto es mío"

pleat [pli:t] n pliegue m

pledge [pledʒ] n (promise) promesa,
voto ♦ vt prometer

plentiful ['plentiful] adj copioso,
abundante

plenty ['plenti] n: ~ of mucho(s)/a(s)

pliable ['plaɪəbl] adj flexible

pliers ['plaɪəz] npl alicates mpl, tenazas
fpl

plight [plaɪt] n situación f difícil

plimsolls ['plɪmsəlz] (BRIT) npl zapatos
mpl de tenis

plinth [plɪnθ] n plinto

plod [plɒd] vi caminar con paso
pesado; (fig) trabajar laboriosamente

plonk [plɒŋk] (inf) n (BRIT: wine) vino
peleón ♦ vt: to ~ sth down dejar caer
algo

plot [plɒt] n (scheme) complot m,
conjura; (of story, play) argumento; (of
land) terreno, lote m (AM) ♦ vt (mark
out) trazar; (conspire) tramar, urdir ♦ vi
conspirar

plough [plau] (US plow) n arado ♦ vt
(earth) arar; to ~ money into invertir
dinero en; ~ through vt fus (crowd)
abrirse paso por la fuerza por;
~man's lunch (BRIT) n almuerzo de
pub a base de pan, queso y encurtidos

pluck [plʌk] vt (fruit) coger (SP),
recoger (AM); (musical instrument)
puntear; (bird) desplumar; (eyebrows)
depilar; to ~ up courage hacer de
tripas corazón

plug [plʌg] n tapón m; (ELEC) enchufe
m, clavija; (AUT: also: spark(ing) ~) bujía
♦ vt (hole) tapar; (inf: advertise) dar
publicidad a; ~ in vt (ELEC) enchufar

plum [plʌm] n (fruit) ciruela

plumb [plʌm] vt: to ~ the depths of
alcanzar los mayores extremos de

plumber ['plʌmə*] n fontanero/a (SP),
plomero/a (AM)

plumbing ['plʌmɪŋ] n (trade)
fontanería, plomería; (piping) cañería

plummet ['plʌmɪt] vi: to ~ (down)
caer a plomo

plump [plʌmp] adj rechoncho, rollizo
♦ vi: to ~ for (inf: choose) optar por;
~ up vt mullir

plunder ['plʌndə*] vt pillar, saquear

plunge [plʌndʒ] n zambullida ♦ vt
sumergir, hundir ♦ vi (fall) caer; (dive)
saltar; (person) arrojarse; to take the ~
lanzarse; plunging adj: plunging
neckline escote m pronunciado

pluperfect [plu:'pə:fɪkt] n
pluscuamperfecto

plural ['plʊərl] adj plural ♦ n plural m

plus [plʌs] n (also: ~ sign) signo más

♦ prep más, y, además de; **ten/ twenty ~** más de diez/veinte

plush [plʌʃ] adj lujoso

plutonium [pluː'təʊnɪəm] n plutonio

ply [plaɪ] vt (a trade) ejercer **♦** vi (ship) ir y venir **♦** n (of wool, rope) cabo; **to ~ sb with drink** insistir en ofrecer a uno muchas copas; **~wood** n madera contrachapada

P.M. n abbr = **Prime Minister**

p.m. adv abbr (= post meridiem) de la tarde o noche

pneumatic [njuː'mætɪk] adj neumático; **~ drill** n martillo neumático

pneumonia [njuː'məʊnɪə] n pulmonía

poach [pəʊtʃ] vt (cook) escalfar; (steal) cazar (or pescar) en vedado **♦** vi cazar (or pescar) en vedado; **~ed** adj escalfado; **~er** n cazador/a m/f furtivo/a

P.O. Box n abbr = **Post Office Box**

pocket ['pɒkɪt] n bolsillo; (fig: small area) bolsa **♦** vt meter en el bolsillo; (steal) embolsar; **to be out of ~** (BRIT) salir perdiendo; **~book** (US) n cartera; **~ calculator** n calculadora de bolsillo; **~ knife** n navaja; **~ money** n asignación f

pod [pɒd] n vaina

podgy ['pɒdʒɪ] adj gordinflón/ona

podiatrist [pɔ'diːatrɪst] (US) n pedicuro/a

poem ['pəʊɪm] n poema m

poet ['pəʊɪt] n poeta m/f; **~ic** [-'ɛtɪk] adj poético; **~ry** n poesía

poignant ['pɔɪnjənt] adj conmovedor(a)

point [pɔɪnt] n punto; (tip) punta; (purpose) fin m, propósito m; (use) utilidad f; (significant part) lo significativo; (moment) momento; (ELEC) toma de corriente; (also: decimal ~): **2 ~ 3 (2.3)** dos coma tres (2,3) **♦** vt señalar; (gun etc): **to ~ sth at sb** apuntar algo a uno **♦** vi: **to ~ at** señalar; **~s** npl (AUT) contactos mpl;

(RAIL) agujas fpl; **to be on the ~ of doing sth** estar a punto de hacer algo; **to make a ~ of** poner empeño en; **to get/miss the ~** comprender/ no comprender; **to come to the ~** ir al meollo; **there's no ~ (in doing)** no tiene sentido (hacer); **~ out** vt señalar; **to ~** vt fus (fig) indicar, señalar; **~-blank** adv (say, refuse) sin más hablar; (also: **at ~-blank range**) a quemarropa; **~ed** adj (shape) puntiagudo, afilado; (remark) intencionado; **~edly** adv intencionadamente; **~er** n (needle) aguja, indicador m; **~less** adj sin sentido; **~ of view** n punto de vista

poise [pɔɪz] n aplomo, elegancia

poison ['pɔɪzn] n veneno **♦** vt envenenar; **~ing** n envenenamiento; **~ous** adj venenoso; (fumes etc) tóxico

poke [pəʊk] vt (jab with finger, stick etc) empujar; (put): **to ~ sth in(to)** introducir algo en; **~ about** vi fisgonear

poker ['pəʊkə*] n atizador m; (CARDS) póker m

poky ['pəʊkɪ] adj estrecho

Poland ['pəʊlənd] n Polonia

polar ['pəʊlə*] adj polar; **~ bear** n oso polar

Pole [pəʊl] n polaco/a

pole [pəʊl] n palo; (fixed) poste m; (GEO) polo; **~ bean** (US) n ≈ judía verde; **~ vault** n salto con pértiga

police [pə'liːs] n policía **♦** vt vigilar; **~ car** n coche-patrulla m; **~man** (irreg) n policía m, guardia m; **~ state** n estado policial; **~ station** n comisaría; **~woman** (irreg) n mujer f policía

policy ['pɒlɪsɪ] n política; (also: insurance ~) póliza

polio ['pəʊlɪəʊ] n polio f

Polish ['pəʊlɪʃ] adj polaco **♦** n (LING) polaco

polish ['pɒlɪʃ] n (for shoes) betún m; (for floor) cera (de lustrar); (shine) brillo, lustre m; (fig: refinement) educación f **♦** vt (shoes) limpiar; (make

shiny) pulir, sacar brillo a; ~ off vt
(food) despachar; ~ed adj (fig: person)
elegante

polite [pə'laɪt] adj cortés, atento;
~ness n cortesía

political [pə'lɪtɪkl] adj político; ~ly adv
políticamente; ~ correct
políticamente correcto

politician [pɔlɪ'tɪʃən] n político/a

politics ['pɔlɪtɪks] n política

poll [pəul] n (election) votación f; (also:
opinion ~) sondeo, encuesta ♦ vt
encuestar; (votes) obtener

pollen ['pɔlən] n polen m

polling day ['pəulɪŋ-] n día m de
elecciones

polling station n centro electoral

pollute [pə'lu:t] vt contaminar

pollution [pə'lu:ʃən] n polución f,
contaminación f del medio ambiente

polo ['pəuləu] n (sport) polo; ~-
necked adj de cuello vuelto; ~ shirt n
polo, niqui m

polyester [pɔlɪ'estə*] n poliéster m

polystyrene [pɔlɪ'staɪri:n] n
poliestireno

polythene ['pɔlɪθi:n] (BRIT) n politeno

pomegranate ['pɔmɪgrænɪt] n
granada

pomp [pɔmp] n pompa

pompous ['pɔmpəs] adj pomposo

pond [pɔnd] n (natural) charca;
(artificial) estanque m

ponder ['pɔndə*] vt meditar

ponderous ['pɔndərəs] adj pesado

pong [pɔŋ] (BRIT: inf) n hedor m

pony ['pəunɪ] n poney m, jaca, potro
(AM); ~tail n cola de caballo;
~ trekking (BRIT) n excursión f a
caballo

poodle ['pu:dl] n caniche m

pool [pu:l] n (natural) charca; (also:
swimming ~) piscina (SP), alberca (AM);
(fig: of light etc) charco; (SPORT)
chapolín m ♦ vt juntar; ~s npl (football
~s) quinielas fpl; typing ~ servicio de
mecanografía

poor [puə*] adj pobre; (bad) de mala
calidad ♦ npl: the ~ los pobres; ~ly adj
mal, enfermo ♦ adv mal

pop [pɔp] n (sound) ruido seco; (MUS)
(música) pop m; (inf: father) papá m;
(drink) gaseosa ♦ vt (put quickly) meter
(de prisa) ♦ vi reventar; (cork) saltar;
~ in/out vi entrar/salir un momento;
~ up vi aparecer inesperadamente;
~corn n palomitas fpl

pope [pəup] n papa m

poplar ['pɔplə*] n álamo

popper ['pɔpə*] (BRIT) n automático

poppy ['pɔpɪ] n amapola

Popsicle ® ['pɔpsɪkl] (US) n polo

pop star n estrella del pop

populace ['pɔpjuləs] n pueblo, plebe f

popular ['pɔpjulə*] adj popular

population [pɔpju'leɪʃən] n población
f

porcelain ['pɔːslɪn] n porcelana

porch [pɔːtʃ] n pórtico, entrada; (US)
veranda

porcupine ['pɔːkjupaɪn] n puerco m
espín

pore [pɔː*] n poro ♦ vi: to ~ over
engolfarse en

pork [pɔːk] n carne f de cerdo (SP) or
chancho (AM)

pornography [pɔː'nɔgrəfɪ] n
pornografía

porpoise ['pɔːpəs] n marsopa

porridge ['pɔrɪdʒ] n gachas fpl de
avena

port [pɔːt] n puerto; (NAUT: left side)
babor m; (wine) vino de Oporto; ~ of
call puerto de escala

portable ['pɔːtəbl] adj portátil

porter ['pɔːtə*] n (for luggage)
maletero; (doorkeeper) portero/a,
conserje m/f

portfolio [pɔːt'fəuliəu] n cartera

porthole ['pɔːthəul] n portilla

portion ['pɔːʃən] n porción f; (of food)
ración f

portrait ['pɔːtreɪt] n retrato

portray [pɔː'treɪ] vt retratar; (subj:

actor) representar

Portugal [ˈpɔːtjugl] n Portugal m

Portuguese [pɔːtjuˈgiːz] adj
portugués/esa ♦ n inv portugués/esa
m/f; (LING) portugués m

pose [pəuz] n postura, actitud f ♦ vi
(pretend): **to ~** hacerse pasar por
♦ vt (question) plantear; **to ~ for** posar
para

posh [pɔʃ] (inf) adj elegante, de lujo

position [pəˈzɪʃən] n posición f; (job)
puesto; (situation) situación f ♦ vt
colocar

positive [ˈpɔzɪtɪv] adj positivo; (certain)
seguro; (definite) definitivo

possess [pəˈzɛs] vt poseer; **~ion**
[pəˈzɛʃən] n posesión f; **~ions** npl
(belongings) pertenencias fpl

possibility [pɔsɪˈbɪlɪtɪ] n posibilidad f

possible [ˈpɔsɪbl] adj posible; **as big
as ~** lo más grande posible; **possibly**
adv posiblemente; **I cannot possibly
come** me es imposible venir

post [pəust] n (BRIT: system) correos
mpl; (BRIT: letters, delivery) correo; (job,
situation) puesto; (pole) poste m ♦ vt
(BRIT: send by post) echar al correo;
(BRIT: appoint): **to ~** enviar a; **~age**
n porte m, franqueo; **~age stamp** n
sello de correos; **~al** adj postal, de
correos; **~al order** n giro postal; **~box**
(BRIT) n buzón m; **~card** n tarjeta
postal; **~code** (BRIT) n código postal

postdate [pəustˈdeɪt] vt (cheque)
poner fecha adelantada a

poster [ˈpəustə*] n cartel m

poste restante [pəustˈrɛstɑ̃nt] (BRIT)
n lista de correos

postgraduate [pəustˈgrædjuət] n
posgraduado/a

posthumous [ˈpɔstjuməs] adj
póstumo

postman [ˈpəustmən] (irreg) n cartero

postmark [ˈpəustmɑːk] n matasellos m

post-mortem [-ˈmɔːtəm] n autopsia f

post office n (building) oficina de

correos m; (organization): **the Post
Office** Administración f General de
Correos; **Post Office Box** n apartado
postal (SP), casilla de correos (AM)

postpone [pəsˈpəun] vt aplazar

postscript [ˈpəustskrɪpt] n posdata

posture [ˈpɔstʃə*] n postura, actitud f

postwar [pəustˈwɔː*] adj de la
posguerra

posy [ˈpəuzi] n ramillete m (de flores)

pot [pɔt] n (for cooking) olla; (tea~)
tetera; (coffee~) cafetera; (for flowers)
maceta; (for jam) tarro, pote m; (inf:
marijuana) chocolate m ♦ vt (plant)
poner en tiesto; **to go to ~** (inf) irse al
traste

potato [pəˈteɪtəu] (pl **~es**) n patata
(SP), papa (AM); **~ peeler** n pelapatatas
m inv

potent [ˈpəutnt] adj potente,
poderoso; (drink) fuerte

potential [pəˈtɛnʃl] adj potencial,
posible ♦ n potencial m; **~ly** adv en
potencia

pothole [ˈpɔthəul] n (in road) bache
m; (BRIT: underground) gruta; **~ling**
(BRIT) n: **to go potholing**
dedicarse a la espeleología

potluck [pɔtˈlʌk] n: **to take ~** tomar
lo que haya

potted [ˈpɔtɪd] adj (food) en conserva;
(plant) en tiesto o maceta; (shortened)
resumido

potter [ˈpɔtə*] n alfarero/a ♦ vi: **to
~ around, ~ about** (BRIT) hacer
trabajitos; **~y** n cerámica; (factory)
alfarería

potty [ˈpɔti] n orinal m de niño

pouch [pautʃ] n (ZOOL) bolsa; (for
tobacco) petaca

poultry [ˈpəultri] n aves fpl de corral;
(meat) pollo

pounce [pauns] vi: **to ~ on**
precipitarse sobre

pound [paund] n libra (weight = 453g
or 16oz; money = 100 pence) ♦ vt
(beat) golpear; (crush) machacar ♦

(*heart*) latir; **~ sterling** *n* libra esterlina

pour [pɔ:*] *vt* echar; (*tea etc*) servir ♦ *vi* correr, fluir; **to ~ sb a drink** servirle a uno una copa; **~ away or off** *vt* vaciar, verter; **~ in** *vi* (*people*) entrar en tropel; **~ out** *vi* salir en tropel ♦ *vt* (*drink*) echar, servir; (*fig*): **to ~ out one's feelings** desahogarse; **~ing** *adj*: **~ing rain** lluvia torrencial

pout [paut] *vi* hacer pucheros

poverty [ˈpɔvəti] *n* pobreza, miseria; **~-stricken** *adj* necesitado

powder [ˈpaudə*] *n* polvo; (*face ~*) polvos *mpl* ♦ *vt* polvorear; **to ~ one's face** empolvarse la cara; (*compact ~*) polvera; **~ed milk** *n* leche *f* en polvo; **~ room** *n* aseos *mpl*

power [ˈpauə*] *n* poder *m*; (*strength*) fuerza; (*nation, TECH*) potencia; (*drive*) empuje *m*; (*ELEC*) fuerza, energía ♦ *vt* impulsar; **to be in ~** (*POL*) estar en el poder; **~ cut** (*BRIT*) *n* apagón *m*; **~ed** *adj*: **~ed by** impulsado por; **~ failure** *n* = **~ cut; ~ful** *adj* poderoso; (*engine*) potente; (*speech etc*) convincente; **~less** *adj*: **~less (to do)** incapaz (de hacer); **~ point** (*BRIT*) *n* enchufe *m*; **~ station** *n* central *f* eléctrica

p.p. *abbr* (= *per procurationem*): **~ J. Smith** p.p. (por poder de) J. Smith; (= *pages*) págs

PR *n abbr* = **public relations**

practical [ˈpræktɪkl] *adj* práctico; **~ity** [-ˈkælɪtɪ] *n* factibilidad *f*; **~ joke** *n* broma pesada; **~ly** *adv* (*almost*) casi

practice [ˈpræktɪs] *n* (*habit*) costumbre *f*; (*exercise*) práctica, ejercicio; (*training*) adiestramiento; (*MED: of profession*) práctica, ejercicio; (*MED, LAW: business*) consulta ♦ *vt, vi* (*US*) = **practise**; **in ~** (*in reality*) en la práctica; **out of ~** desentrenado

practise [ˈpræktɪs] (*US* **practice**) *vt* (*carry out*) practicar; (*profession*) ejercer; (*train at*) practicar ♦ *vi* ejercer; (*train*) practicar; **practising** *adj* (*Christian etc*) practicante; (*lawyer*) en

ejercicio

practitioner [prækˈtɪʃənə*] *n* (*MED*) médico/a

prairie [ˈprɛərɪ] *n* pampa

praise [preɪz] *n* alabanza(s) *f(pl)*, elogio(s) *m(pl)* ♦ *vt* alabar, elogiar; **~worthy** *adj* loable

pram [præm] (*BRIT*) *n* cochecito de niño

prank [præŋk] *n* travesura

prawn [prɔ:n] *n* gamba; **~ cocktail** *n* cóctel *m* de gambas

pray [preɪ] *vi* rezar

prayer [prɛə*] *n* oración *f*, rezo; (*entreaty*) ruego, súplica

preach [pri:tʃ] *vi* (*also fig*) predicar; **~er** *n* predicador(a) *m/f*

precaution [prɪˈkɔ:ʃən] *n* precaución *f*, precaución

precede [prɪˈsi:d] *vt, vi* preceder

precedent [ˈprɛsɪdənt] *n* precedente *m*

preceding [prɪˈsi:dɪŋ] *adj* anterior

precinct [ˈpri:sɪŋkt] *n* recinto; **~s** *npl* contornos *mpl*; **pedestrian ~** (*BRIT*) zona peatonal; **shopping ~** (*BRIT*) centro comercial

precious [ˈprɛʃəs] *adj* precioso

precipitate [prɪˈsɪpɪteɪt] *vt* precipitar

precise [prɪˈsaɪs] *adj* preciso, exacto; **~ly** *adv* precisamente, exactamente

precocious [prɪˈkəuʃəs] *adj* precoz

precondition [prɪ:kənˈdɪʃən] *n* condición *f* previa

predecessor [ˈpri:dɪsɛsə*] *n* antecesor(a) *m/f*

predicament [prɪˈdɪkəmənt] *n* apuro

predict [prɪˈdɪkt] *vt* pronosticar; **~able** *adj* previsible; **~ion** [-ˈdɪkʃən] *n* predicción *f*

predominantly [prɪˈdɔmɪnəntlɪ] *adv* en su mayoría

pre-empt [prɪːˈɛmt] *vt* adelantarse a

preen [pri:n] *vt*: **to ~ itself** (*bird*) limpiarse (las plumas); **to ~ o.s.** pavonearse

preface [ˈprɛfəs] *n* prefacio

prefect [ˈpri:fɛkt] (*BRIT*) *n* (*in school*)

monitor(a) *m/f*

prefer [prɪ'fə:*] *vt* preferir; **to ~ doing** *or* **to do** preferir hacer; **~able** ['prefrəbl] *adj* preferible; **~ably** ['prefrəblɪ] *adv* de preferencia; **~ence** ['prefrəns] *n* preferencia; (*priority*) prioridad *f*; **~ential** [prefə'renʃəl] *adj* preferente

prefix ['pri:fɪks] *n* prefijo

pregnancy ['pregnənsɪ] *n* (*of woman*) embarazo; (*of animal*) preñez *f*

pregnant ['pregnənt] *adj* (*woman*) embarazada; (*animal*) preñada

prehistoric ['pri:hɪs'tɔrɪk] *adj* prehistórico

prejudice ['predʒudɪs] *n* prejuicio; **~d** *adj* (*person*) predispuesto

premarital ['pri:'mærɪtl] *adj* premarital

premature ['premətʃuə*] *adj* prematuro

premier ['premɪə*] *adj* primero, principal ♦ *n* (*POL*) primer(a) ministro/a

première ['premɪeə*] *n* estreno

premise ['premɪs] *n* premisa; **~s** *npl* (*of business etc*) local *m*; **on the ~s** en el lugar mismo

premium ['pri:mɪəm] *n* premio; (*insurance*) prima; **to be at a ~** ser muy solicitado; **~ bond** (*BRIT*) *n* bono del estado que participa en una lotería nacional

premonition [premə'nɪʃən] *n* presentimiento

preoccupied [pri:'ɔkjupaɪd] *adj* ensimismado

prep [prep] *n* (*SCOL*: *study*) deberes *mpl*

prepaid [pri:'peɪd] *adj* porte pagado

preparation [prepə'reɪʃən] *n* preparación *f*; **~s** *npl* preparativos *mpl*

preparatory [prɪ'pærətərɪ] *adj* preparatorio, preliminar; **~ school** *n* escuela preparatoria

prepare [prɪ'peə*] *vt* preparar, disponer; (*CULIN*) preparar ♦ *vi*: **to ~ for** (*action*) prepararse *o* disponerse para; (*event*) hacer preparativos para; **~d to** dispuesto a; **~d for** listo para

preposition [prepə'zɪʃən] *n* preposición *f*

preposterous [prɪ'pɔstərəs] *adj* absurdo, ridículo

prep school *n* = **preparatory school**

prerequisite [pri:'rekwɪzɪt] *n* requisito

Presbyterian [prezbɪ'tɪərɪən] *adj*, *n* presbiteriano/a *m/f*

preschool ['pri:'sku:l] *adj* preescolar

prescribe [prɪ'skraɪb] *vt* (*MED*) recetar

prescription [prɪ'skrɪpʃən] *n* (*MED*) receta

presence ['prezns] *n* presencia; **in sb's ~** en presencia de uno; **~ of mind** aplomo

present [*adj*, *n* 'preznt, *vb* prɪ'zent] *adj* (*in attendance*) presente; (*current*) actual ♦ *n* (*gift*) regalo; (*actuality*): **the ~** la actualidad, el presente ♦ *vt* (*introduce*, *describe*) presentar; (*expound*) exponer; (*give*) presentar, dar, ofrecer; (*THEATRE*) representar; **to give sb a ~** regalar algo a uno; **at ~** actualmente; **~able** [prɪ'zentəbl] *adj*: **to make o.s. ~able** arreglarse; **~ation** [-'teɪʃən] *n* presentación *f*; (*of report etc*) exposición *f*; (*formal ceremony*) entrega de un regalo; **~-day** *adj* actual; **~er** [prɪ'zentə*] *n* (*RADIO*, *TV*) locutor(a) *m/f*; **~ly** *adv* (*soon*) dentro de poco; (*now*) ahora

preservative [prɪ'zə:vətɪv] *n* conservante *m*

preserve [prɪ'zə:v] *vt* (*keep safe*) preservar, proteger; (*maintain*) mantener; (*food*) conservar ♦ *n* (*for game*) coto, vedado; (*often pl*: *jam*) conserva, confitura

president ['prezɪdənt] *n* presidente *m/f*; **~ial** [-'denʃl] *adj* presidencial

press [pres] *n* (*newspapers*): **the P~** la prensa; (*printer's*) imprenta; (*of button*) pulsación *f* ♦ *vt* empujar; (*button etc*) apretar; (*clothes*: *iron*) planchar; (*put pressure on*: *person*) presionar; (*insist*): **to ~ sth on sb** insistir en que uno acepte algo ♦ *vi* (*squeeze*) apretar;

(*pressurize*): **to ~ for** presionar por; **we are ~ed for time/money** estamos apurados de tiempo/dinero; **~ on** vi avanzar; (hurry) apretar el paso; **~ agency** n agencia de prensa; **~ conference** n rueda de prensa; **~ing** adj apremiante; **~ stud** (*BRIT*) n botón m de presión; **~-up** (*BRIT*) n plancha

pressure ['preʃə*] n presión f; **to put ~ on sb** presionar a uno; **~ cooker** n olla a presión; **~ gauge** n manómetro; **~ group** n grupo de presión; **pressurized** adj (*container*) a presión

prestige [pres'tiːʒ] n prestigio

presumably [prɪ'zjuːməblɪ] adv es de suponer que, cabe presumir que

presume [prɪ'zjuːm] vt: **to ~ (that)** presumir (que), suponer (que)

pretence [prɪ'tens] (*US* **pretense**) n fingimiento; **under false ~s** con engaños

pretend [prɪ'tend] vt, vi (*feign*) fingir

pretentious [prɪ'tenʃəs] adj presumido; (*ostentatious*) ostentoso, aparatoso

pretext ['priːtekst] n pretexto

pretty ['prɪtɪ] adj bonito (*SP*), lindo (*AM*) ♦ adv bastante

prevail [prɪ'veɪl] vi (*gain mastery*) prevalecer; (*be current*) predominar; **~ing** adj (*dominant*) predominante

prevalent ['prevələnt] adj (*widespread*) extendido

prevent [prɪ'vent] vt: **to ~ sb from doing sth** impedir a uno hacer algo; **to ~ sth from happening** evitar que ocurra algo; **~ative** adj = **preventive**; **~ive** adj preventivo

preview ['priːvjuː] n (*of film*) preestreno

previous ['priːvɪəs] adj previo, anterior; **~ly** adv antes

prewar [priː'wɔː*] adj de antes de la guerra

prey [preɪ] n presa ♦ vi: **to ~ on** (*feed on*) alimentarse de; **it was ~ing on**

his mind le preocupaba, le obsesionaba

price [praɪs] n precio ♦ vt (*goods*) fijar el precio de; **~less** adj que no tiene precio; **~ list** n tarifa

prick [prɪk] n (*sensation*) picadura ♦ vt pinchar; (*hurt*) picar; **to ~ up one's ears** aguzar el oído

prickle ['prɪkl] n (*sensation*) picor m; (*BOT*) espina; **prickly** adj espinoso; (*fig: person*) enojadizo; **prickly heat** n sarpullido causado por exceso de calor

pride [praɪd] n orgullo; (*pej*) soberbia ♦ vt: **to ~ o.s. on** enorgullecerse de

priest [priːst] n sacerdote m; **~hood** n sacerdocio

prim [prɪm] adj (*demure*) remilgado; (*prudish*) gazmoño

primarily ['praɪmərɪlɪ] adv ante todo

primary ['praɪmərɪ] adj (*first in importance*) principal ♦ n (*US: POL*) (elección f) primaria; **~ school** (*BRIT*) n escuela primaria

prime [praɪm] adj primero, principal; (*excellent*) selecto, de primera clase ♦ n: **in the ~ of life** en la flor de la vida ♦ vt (*wood, fig*) preparar; **~ example** ejemplo típico; **P~ Minister** n primer(a) ministro/a

primeval [praɪ'miːvəl] adj primitivo

primitive ['prɪmɪtɪv] adj primitivo; (*crude*) rudimentario

primrose ['prɪmrəʊz] n primavera, prímula

Primus (stove) ® ['praɪməs-] (*BRIT*) n hornillo de camping

prince [prɪns] n príncipe m

princess [prɪn'ses] n princesa

principal ['prɪnsɪpl] adj principal, mayor ♦ n director(a) m/f; **~ity** [-'pælɪtɪ] n principado

principle ['prɪnsɪpl] n principio; **in ~** en principio; **on ~** por principios

print [prɪnt] n (*foot~*) huella; (*finger~*) huella dactilar; (*letters*) letra de molde; (*fabric*) estampado, (*ART*) grabado; (*PHOT*) impresión f ♦ vt imprimir; (*cloth*) estampar; (*write in capitals*) escribir en letras de molde; **out of ~** agotado; **~ed matter** n impresos mpl; **~er** n (*person*) impresor(a) m/f; (*machine*) impresora; **~ing** n (*art*) imprenta; (*act*) impresión f; (*COMPUT*) impresión f

prior ['praɪə*] adj anterior, previo; (*more important*) más importante; **~ to** antes de

priority [praɪ'ɒrɪtɪ] n prioridad f; **to have ~ (over)** tener prioridad (sobre)

prison ['prɪzn] n cárcel f, prisión f ♦ cpd carcelario; **~er** n (*in prison*) preso/a; (*captured person*) prisionero/a; **~er-of-war** n prisionero de guerra

privacy ['prɪvəsɪ] n intimidad f

private ['praɪvɪt] adj (*personal*) particular; (*property, industry, discussion etc*) privado/a; (*person*) reservado/a; (*place*) tranquilo ♦ n soldado raso; (*on envelope*) "confidencial"; (*on door*) "prohibido el paso"; **in ~** en privado; **~ enterprise** n empresa privada; **~ eye** n detective m/f privado/a; **~ property** n propiedad f privada; **~ school** n colegio particular

privet ['prɪvɪt] n alheña

privilege ['prɪvɪlɪdʒ] n privilegio; (*prerogative*) prerrogativa

privy ['prɪvɪ] adj: **to be ~ to** estar enterado de

prize [praɪz] n premio ♦ adj de primera clase ♦ vt apreciar, estimar; **~-giving** n distribución f de premios; **~winner** n premiado/a

pro [prəu] n (*SPORT*) profesional m/f ♦ prep a favor de; **the ~s and cons** los pros y los contras

probability [prɒbə'bɪlɪtɪ] n probabilidad f; **in all ~** con toda probabilidad

probable ['prɒbəbl] adj probable

probably ['prɒbəblɪ] adv probablemente

probation [prə'beɪʃən] n: **on ~** (*employee*) a prueba; (*LAW*) en libertad

condicional

probe [prəub] n (*MED, SPACE*) sonda; (*enquiry*) encuesta, investigación f ♦ vt sondar; (*investigate*) investigar

problem ['prɒbləm] n problema m

procedure [prə'siːdʒə*] n procedimiento; (*bureaucratic*) trámites mpl

proceed [prə'siːd] vi (*do afterwards*): **to ~ to do sth** proceder a hacer algo; (*continue*): **to ~ (with)** continuar o seguir (con); (*LAW*) proceso; **~s** ['prəusiːdz] npl (*money*) ganancias fpl, ingresos mpl

process ['prəuses] n proceso ♦ vt tratar, elaborar; **~ing** n tratamiento, elaboración f; (*PHOT*) revelado

procession [prə'seʃən] n desfile m; (*funeral*) ~ cortejo fúnebre

pro-choice [prəu'tʃɔɪs] adj en favor del derecho a elegir de la madre

proclaim [prə'kleɪm] vt (*announce*) anunciar

procrastinate [prəu'kræstɪneɪt] vi demorarse

procure [prə'kjuə*] vt conseguir

prod [prɒd] vt empujar ♦ n empujón m

prodigy ['prɒdɪdʒɪ] n prodigio

produce [n 'prɒdjuːs, vt prə'djuːs] n (*AGR*) productos mpl agrícolas ♦ vt producir; (*play, film, programme*) presentar; **~r** n productor(a) m/f; (*of film, programme*) director(a) m/f; (*of record*) productor(a) m/f

product ['prɒdʌkt] n producto

production [prə'dʌkʃən] n producción f; (*THEATRE*) presentación f; **~ line** n línea de producción

productivity [prɒdʌk'tɪvɪtɪ] n productividad f

profession [prə'feʃən] n profesión f; **~al** adj profesional ♦ n profesional m/f; (*skilled person*) perito

professor [prə'fesə*] n (*BRIT*) catedrático/a; (*US, Canada*) profesor(a) m/f

proficient [prə'fɪʃənt] adj experto,

hábil
profile ['prəufaɪl] n perfil m
profit ['prɒfɪt] n (COMM) ganancia ♦ vi:
to ~ by or from aprovechar or sacar
provecho de; ~**ability** [-ə'bɪlɪtɪ] n
rentabilidad f; ~**able** adj (ECON)
rentable
profound [prə'faund] adj profundo
profusely [prə'fju:slɪ] adv
profusamente
programme ['prəugræm] (US
program) n programa m ♦ vt
programar; ~**r** (US **programer**) n
programador(a) m/f; **programming**
(US **programing**) n programación f
progress [n 'prəugres, vi prə'gres] n
progreso, vi prə'gres] n
progreso; (development) desarrollo ♦ vi
progresar, avanzar; in ~ en curso; ~**ive**
[-'gresɪv] adj progresivo; (person)
progresista
prohibit [prə'hɪbɪt] vt prohibir; to
~ **sb from doing sth** prohibir a uno
hacer algo; ~**ion** [-'bɪʃn] n prohibición
f; (US): **P~ion** Ley f Seca
project [n 'prɒdʒekt, vb prə'dʒekt] n
proyecto ♦ vt proyectar ♦ vi (stick out)
salir, sobresalir; ~**ion** [prə'dʒekʃn] n
proyección f; (overhang) saliente m;
~**or** [prə'dʒektə*] n proyector m
pro-life [prəu'laɪf] adj pro-vida
prolong [prə'lɒŋ] vt prolongar,
extender
prom [prɒm] n abbr = **promenade**;
(US: ball) baile m de gala

El ciclo de conciertos de música
clásica más conocido de Londres es el
llamado the **Proms** (promenade
concerts), que se celebra anualmente
en el Royal Albert Hall. Su nombre se
debe a que originalmente el público
paseaba durante las actuaciones,
costumbre que en la actualidad se
mantiene de forma simbólica,
permitiendo que parte de los
asistentes permanezcan de pie. En

Estados Unidos se llama **prom** a un
baile de gala en un centro de
educación secundaria o universitaria.

promenade [prɒmə'nɑːd] n (by sea)
paseo marítimo; ~ **concert** (BRIT)
concierto (en que parte del público
permanece de pie)
prominence ['prɒmɪnəns] n
importancia
prominent ['prɒmɪnənt] adj (standing
out) saliente; (important) eminente,
importante
promiscuous [prə'mɪskjuəs] adj
(sexually) promiscuo
promise ['prɒmɪs] n promesa ♦ vt, vi
prometer; **promising** adj
prometedor/a
promote [prə'məut] vt (employee)
ascender; (product, pop star) hacer
propaganda por; (ideas) fomentar; ~**r** n
(of event) promotor(a) m/f; (of cause
etc) impulsor(a) m/f; **promotion**
[-'məuʃən] n (advertising campaign)
campaña de promoción f; (in rank)
ascenso
prompt [prɒmpt] adj rápido ♦ adv: at
6 o'clock ~ a las seis en punto ♦ n
(COMPUT) aviso ♦ vt (urge) mover,
incitar; (when talking) instar; (THEATRE)
apuntar; to ~ **sb to do sth** instar a
uno a hacer algo; ~**ly** adv
rápidamente; (exactly) puntualmente
prone [prəun] adj (lying) postrado;
~ **to** propenso a
prong [prɒŋ] n diente m, punta
pronoun ['prəunaun] n pronombre m
pronounce [prə'nauns] vt pronunciar;
~**d** adj (marked) marcado
pronunciation [prənʌnsɪ'eɪʃən] n
pronunciación f
proof [pru:f] n prueba ♦ adj:
~ **against** a prueba de
prop [prɒp] n apoyo; (fig) sostén m ♦ vt
(also: ~ up) apoyar; (lean): to ~ **sth
against** apoyar algo contra
propaganda [prɒpə'gændə]

propaganda

propel [prə'pɛl] vt impulsar, propulsar; **~ler** n hélice f

propensity [prə'pɛnsɪtɪ] n propensión f

proper ['prɒpə*] adj (suited, right) propio; (exact) justo; (seemly) correcto, decente; (authentic) verdadero; (referring to place): **the village** = el pueblo mismo; **~ly** adv (adequately) correctamente; (decently) decentemente; **~ noun** n nombre m propio

property ['prɒpətɪ] n propiedad f; (personal) bienes mpl muebles; **~ owner** n dueño/a de propiedades

prophecy ['prɒfɪsɪ] n profecía

prophesy ['prɒfɪsaɪ] vt (fig) predecir

prophet ['prɒfɪt] n profeta m

proportion [prə'pɔːʃən] n proporción f; (share) parte f; **~al adj** (to) en proporción (con); **~al representation** n representación f proporcional; **~ate** adj: **~ate (to)** en proporción (con)

proposal [prə'pəuzl] n (offer of marriage) oferta f de matrimonio; (plan) proyecto

propose [prə'pəuz] vt proponer ♦ vi declararse; **to ~ to do** tener intención de hacer

proposition [prɒpə'zɪʃən] n propuesta f

proprietor [prə'praɪətə*] n propietario/a, dueño/a

propriety [prə'praɪətɪ] n decoro

pro rata [-'rɑːtə] adv a prorrateo

prose [prəuz] n prosa

prosecute ['prɒsɪkjuːt] vt (LAW) procesar; **prosecution** [-'kjuːʃən] n proceso, causa; (accusing side) acusación f; **prosecutor** n acusador(a) m/f; (also: **public prosecutor**) fiscal m

prospect [n 'prɒspɛkt, vb prə'spɛkt] n (possibility) posibilidad f; (outlook) perspectiva ♦ vi: **to ~ for** buscar; **~s** npl (for work etc) perspectivas fpl; **~ing** n prospección f; **~ive** [prə'spɛktɪv] adj futuro

prospectus [prə'spɛktəs] n prospecto

prosper ['prɒspə*] vi prosperar; **~ity** [-'spɛrɪtɪ] n prosperidad f; **~ous** adj próspero

prostitute ['prɒstɪtjuːt] n prostituta; (male) hombre que se dedica a la prostitución

protect [prə'tɛkt] vt proteger; **~ion** [-'tɛkʃən] n protección f; **~ive** adj protector(a)

protein ['prəutiːn] n proteína

protest [n 'prəutɛst, vb prə'tɛst] n protesta ♦ vi: **to ~ about** or **at/against** protestar de/contra ♦ vt (insist): **to ~ (that)** insistir en (que)

Protestant ['prɒtɪstənt] adj, n protestante m/f

protester [prə'tɛstə*] n manifestante m/f

protracted [prə'træktɪd] adj prolongado

protrude [prə'truːd] vi salir, sobresalir

proud [praud] adj orgulloso; (pej) soberbio, altanero

prove [pruːv] vt probar; (show) demostrar ♦ vi: **to ~ (to be) correct** resultar correcto; **to ~ o.s.** probar su valía

proverb ['prɒvɜːb] n refrán m

provide [prə'vaɪd] vt proporcionar, dar; **to ~ sb with sth** proveer a uno de algo; **~d (that)** conj con tal de que, a condición de que; **~ for** vt fus (person) mantener a; (problem etc) tener en cuenta; **providing** [prə'vaɪdɪŋ] conj: **providing (that)** a condición de que, con tal de que

province ['prɒvɪns] n provincia; (fig) esfera; **provincial** [prə'vɪnʃəl] adj provincial; (pej) provinciano

provision [prə'vɪʒən] n (supplying) suministro, abastecimiento; (of contract etc) disposición f; **~s** npl (food) comestibles mpl; **~al** adj provisional

proviso [prə'vaɪzəu] n condición f, estipulación f

provocative [prə'vɒkətɪv] adj

provocativo

provoke [prəˈvəuk] vt (cause) provocar, incitar; (anger) enojar

prowess [ˈprauis] n destreza

prowl [praul] vi (also: ~ about, ~ around) merodear ♦ n: **on the ~** de merodeo; **~er** n merodeador(a) m/f

proxy [ˈprɔksi] n: **by ~** por poderes

prudent [ˈpruːdənt] adj prudente

prune [pruːn] n ciruela pasa ♦ vt podar

pry [prai] vi: **to ~ (into)** entrometerse (en)

PS n abbr (= postscript) P.D.

psalm [sɑːm] n salmo

pseudonym [ˈsjuːdəunim] n seudónimo

psyche [ˈsaiki] n psique f

psychiatric [saikiˈætrik] adj psiquiátrico

psychiatrist [saiˈkaiətrist] n psiquiatra m/f

psychic [ˈsaikik] adj (also: ~al) psíquico

psychoanalyse [saikəuˈænəlaiz] vt psicoanalizar; **psychoanalysis** [-əˈnælisis] n psicoanálisis m inv

psychological [saikəˈlɔdʒikl] adj psicológico

psychologist [saiˈkɔlədʒist] n psicólogo/a

psychology [saiˈkɔlədʒi] n psicología

PTO abbr (= please turn over) sigue

pub [pʌb] n abbr (= public house) pub m, bar m

---

pub

Un pub es un local público donde se pueden consumir bebidas alcohólicas. La estricta regulación sobre la venta de alcohol prohíbe que se sirva a menores de 18 años y controla las horas de apertura, aunque éstas son más flexibles desde hace unos años. El pub es, además, un lugar de encuentro donde se sirven comidas ligeras o se juega a los dardos o al billar, entre otras actividades.

---

puberty [ˈpjuːbəti] n pubertad f

public [ˈpʌblik] adj público ♦ n: **the ~** el público; **in ~** en público; **to make ~** hacer público; **to ~ address system** n megafonía

publican [ˈpʌblikən] n tabernero/a

publication [pʌbliˈkeiʃən] n publicación f

public: **~ company** n sociedad f anónima; **~ convenience** (BRIT) n aseos mpl públicos (SP), sanitarios mpl (AM); **~ holiday** n día de fiesta (SP), (día) feriado (AM); **~ house** (BRIT) n bar m, pub m

publicity [pʌbˈlisiti] n publicidad f

publicize [ˈpʌblisaiz] vt publicitar

publicly [ˈpʌblikli] adv públicamente, en público

public: **~ opinion** n opinión f pública; **~ relations** n relaciones fpl públicas; **~ school** n (BRIT) escuela privada; (US) instituto; **~-spirited** adj que tiene sentido del deber ciudadano; **~ transport** n transporte m público

publish [ˈpʌbliʃ] vt publicar; **~er** n (person) editor(a) m/f; (firm) editorial f; **~ing** n (industry) industria del libro

pub lunch n almuerzo que se sirve en un pub; **to go for a ~** almorzar o comer en un pub

pucker [ˈpʌkə*] vt (pleat) arrugar; (brow etc) fruncir

pudding [ˈpudiŋ] n pudín m; (BRIT: dessert) postre m; **black ~** n morcilla

puddle [ˈpʌdl] n charco

puff [pʌf] n soplo; (of smoke, air) bocanada; (of breathing) resoplido ♦ vt: **to ~ one's pipe** chupar la pipa ♦ vi (pant) jadear; **~ out** vt hinchar; **~ pastry** n hojaldre m; **~y** adj hinchado

pull [pul] n (tug): **to give sth a ~** un tirón a algo ♦ vt tirar de; (press: trigger) apretar; (haul) tirar, arrastrar; (close: curtain) echar o vt tirar; **to ~ to pieces** hacer pedazos; **to not ~ one's**

punches no andarse con bromas; **to ~ one's weight** hacer su parte; **to ~ o.s. together** sobreponerse; **to ~ sb's leg** tomar el pelo a uno; **~ apart** vt (break) romper; **~ down** vt (building) derribar; **~ in** vi (car etc) parar (junto a la acera); (train) llegar a la estación; **~ off** vt (deal etc) cerrar; **~ out** vi (car, train etc) salir ♦ vt sacar, arrancar; **~ over** vi (car) hacerse a un lado; **~ through** vi (MED) reponerse; **~ up** vi (stop) parar ♦ vt (raise) levantar; (uproot) arrancar, desarraigar

pulley ['pulɪ] n polea

pullover ['puləuvə*] n jersey m, suéter m

pulp [pʌlp] n (of fruit) pulpa

pulpit ['pulpɪt] n púlpito

pulsate [pʌl'seɪt] vi pulsar, latir

pulse [pʌls] n (ANAT) pulso; (rhythm) pulsación f; (BOT) legumbre f

pump [pʌmp] n bomba; (shoe) zapatilla ♦ vt sacar con una bomba; **~ up** vt inflar

pumpkin ['pʌmpkɪn] n calabaza

pun [pʌn] n juego de palabras

punch [pʌntʃ] n (blow) golpe m, puñetazo; (tool) punzón m; (drink) ponche m ♦ vt (hit): **to ~ sb/sth** dar un puñetazo a uno/algo; golpear a uno/algo; **~line** n palabras que rematan un chiste; **~-up** (BRIT: inf) n riña

punctual ['pʌŋktjuəl] adj puntual

punctuation [pʌŋktju'eɪʃən] n puntuación f

puncture ['pʌŋktʃə*] (BRIT) n pinchazo ♦ vt pinchar

pungent ['pʌndʒənt] adj acre

punish ['pʌnɪʃ] vt castigar; **~ment** n castigo

punk [pʌŋk] n (also: ~ rocker) punki m/f; (also: ~ rock) música punk; (US: inf: hoodlum) rufián m

punt [pʌnt] n (boat) batea

punter ['pʌntə*] (BRIT) n (gambler) jugador(a) m/f; (inf) cliente m/f

puny ['pju:nɪ] adj débil

pup [pʌp] n cachorro

pupil ['pju:pl] n alumno/a; (of eye) pupila

puppet ['pʌpɪt] n títere m

puppy ['pʌpɪ] n cachorro, perrito

purchase ['pə:tʃɪs] n compra ♦ vt comprar; **~r** n comprador(a) m/f

pure [pjuə*] adj puro

purée ['pjuəreɪ] n puré m

purely ['pjuəlɪ] adv puramente

purge [pə:dʒ] n (MED, POL) purga ♦ vt purgar

purify ['pjuərɪfaɪ] vt purificar, depurar

purple ['pə:pl] adj purpúreo; morado

purpose ['pə:pəs] n propósito; **on ~** a propósito, adrede; **~ful** adj resuelto, determinado

purr [pə:*] vi ronronear

purse [pə:s] n monedero; (US) bolsa (SP), cartera (AM) ♦ vt fruncir

pursue [pə'sju:] vt seguir; **~r** n perseguidor(a) m/f

pursuit [pə'sju:t] n (chase) caza; (occupation) actividad f

push [puʃ] n empuje m, empujón m; (of button) presión f; (drive) empuje m ♦ vt empujar; (button) apretar; (promote) promover ♦ vi empujar; (demand): **to ~** for luchar por; **~ aside** vt apartar con la mano; **~ off** (inf) vi largarse; **~ on** vi seguir adelante; **~ through** vi (crowd) abrirse paso a empujones ♦ vt (measure) despachar; **~ up** vt (total, prices) hacer subir; **~chair** (BRIT) n sillita de ruedas; **~er** n (drug ~er) traficante m/f de drogas; **~over** (inf) n: **it's a ~over** está tirado; **~-up** (US) n plancha; **~y** (pej) adj agresivo

puss [pus] n minino

pussy(-cat) ['pusɪ-] n = **puss**

put [put] (pt, pp put) vt (place) poner, colocar; (~ into) meter; (say) expresar; (a question) hacer; (estimate) estimar; **~ about** or **around** vt (rumour) diseminar; **~ across** vt (ideas etc) comunicar; **~ away** vt (store) guardar;

~ back vt (replace) devolver a su lugar; (postpone) aplazar; **~ by** vt (money) guardar; **~ down** vt (on ground) poner en el suelo; (animal) sacrificar; (in writing) apuntar; (revolt etc) sofocar; (attribute) atribuir; **to ~ down to** atribuir algo a; **~ forward** vt (ideas) presentar, proponer; **~ in** vt (complaint) presentar; (time) dedicar; **~ off** vt (postpone) aplazar; (discourage) desanimar; **~ on** vt ponerse; (light etc) encender; (play etc) presentar; (gain): **to ~ on weight** engordar; (brake) echar; (record, kettle etc) poner; (assume) adoptar; **~ out** vt (fire, light) apagar; (rubbish etc) sacar; (cat etc) echar; (one's hand) alargar; (inf: person): **to be ~ out** alterarse; **~ through** vt (TEL) poner; (plan etc) hacer aprobar; **~ up** vt (raise) levantar, alzar; (hang) colgar; (build) construir; (increase) aumentar; (accommodate) alojar; **~ up with** vt fus aguantar

putt [pʌt] n putt m, golpe m corto; **~ing green** n terreno m; minigolf m

putty ['pʌtɪ] n masilla

put-up ['putʌp] adj: **~ job** (BRIT) amaño

puzzle ['pʌzl] n rompecabezas m inv; (also: crossword ~) crucigrama m; (mystery) misterio ♦ vt dejar perplejo, confundir ♦ vi: **to ~ over sth** devanarse los sesos con algo; **puzzling** adj misterioso, extraño

pyjamas [pɪ'dʒɑ:məz] (BRIT) npl pijama m

pylon ['paɪlən] n torre f de conducción eléctrica

pyramid ['pɪrəmɪd] n pirámide f

Pyrenees [pɪrə'ni:z] npl: **the ~** los Pirineos

python ['paɪθən] n pitón m

Q, q

quack [kwæk] n graznido; (pej: doctor) curandero/a

quad [kwɔd] n abbr = **quadrangle**; **quadruplet**

quadrangle ['kwɔdræŋgl] n patio

quadruple [kwɔ'drupl] vt, vi cuadruplicar

quadruplets [kwɔ:'dru:plɪts] npl cuatrillizos/as

quail [kweɪl] n codorniz f ♦ vi: **to ~ at** or **before** amedrentarse ante

quaint [kweɪnt] adj extraño; (picturesque) pintoresco

quake [kweɪk] vi temblar ♦ n abbr = **earthquake**

Quaker ['kweɪkə*] n cuáquero/a

qualification [kwɔlɪfɪ'keɪʃən] n (ability) capacidad f; (often pl: diploma etc) título; (reservation) salvedad f

qualified ['kwɔlɪfaɪd] adj capacitado; (professionally) titulado; (limited) limitado

qualify ['kwɔlɪfaɪ] vt (make competent) capacitar; (modify) modificar ♦ vi (in competition): **to ~ (for)** calificarse (para); (pass examination(s)): **to ~ (as)** calificarse (de), graduarse (en); (be eligible): **to ~ (for)** reunir los requisitos (para)

quality ['kwɔlɪtɪ] n calidad f; (of person) cualidad f; **~ time** n tiempo dedicado a la familia y a los amigos

---

quality press

La expresión **quality press** *se refiere a los periódicos que dan un tratamiento serio de las noticias, ofreciendo información detallada sobre un amplio espectro de temas y un análisis en profundidad de la actualidad. Por su tamaño, considerablemente mayor que el de los* *periódicos sensacionalistas, se les conoce también como "broadsheets".*

qualm [kwɑːm] n escrúpulo

quandary ['kwɒndərɪ] n: **to be in a ~** tener dudas

quantity ['kwɒntɪtɪ] n cantidad f; **in ~** en grandes cantidades; **~ surveyor** n aparejador(a) m/f

quarantine ['kwɒrntiːn] n cuarentena

quarrel ['kwɒrl] n riña, pelea ♦ vi reñir, pelearse

quarry ['kwɒrɪ] n cantera

quart [kwɔːt] n ≈ litro

quarter ['kwɔːtə*] n cuarto, cuarta parte f; (US: coin) moneda de 25 centavos; (of year) trimestre m; (district) barrio ♦ vt dividir en cuartos; (MIL: lodge) alojar; **~s** npl (barracks) cuartel m; (living ~s) alojamiento; **a ~ of an hour** un cuarto de hora; **~ final** n cuarto de final; **~ly** adj trimestral ♦ adv cada 3 meses, trimestralmente

quartet(te) [kwɔː'tet] n cuarteto

quartz [kwɔːts] n cuarzo

quash [kwɒʃ] vt (verdict) anular

quaver ['kweɪvə*] (BRIT) n (MUS) corchea ♦ vi temblar

quay [kiː] n (also: ~side) muelle m

queasy ['kwiːzɪ] adj: **to feel ~** tener náuseas

queen [kwiːn] n reina; (CARDS etc) dama; **~ mother** n reina madre

queer [kwɪə*] adj raro, extraño ♦ n (inf: highly offensive) maricón m

quell [kwel] vt (feeling) calmar; (rebellion etc) sofocar

quench [kwentʃ] vt: **to ~ one's thirst** apagar la sed

query ['kwɪərɪ] n (question) pregunta ♦ vt dudar de

quest [kwest] n busca, búsqueda

question ['kwestʃən] n pregunta; (doubt) duda; (matter) asunto, cuestión f ♦ vt (doubt) dudar de; (interrogate) interrogar, hacer preguntas a; **beyond ~** fuera de toda duda; **out of the ~**

imposible; ni hablar; **~able** adj dudoso; **~ mark** n punto de interrogación; **~naire** [-'nɛə*] n cuestionario

queue [kjuː] (BRIT) n cola ♦ vi (also: ~ up) hacer cola

quibble ['kwɪbl] vi sutilizar

quick [kwɪk] adj rápido; (agile) ágil; (mind) listo ♦ n: **cut to the ~** (fig) herido en lo vivo; **be ~!** ¡date prisa!; **~en** vt apresurar ♦ vi apresurarse, darse prisa; **~ly** adv rápidamente, de prisa; **~sand** n arenas fpl movedizas; **~witted** adj perspicaz

quid [kwɪd] (BRIT: inf) n inv libra

quiet ['kwaɪət] adj (voice, music etc) bajo; (person, place) tranquilo; (ceremony) íntimo ♦ n silencio; (calm) tranquilidad f ♦ vt, vi (US) = **~en**; **~en** (also: ~en down) vi calmarse; (grow silent) callarse ♦ vt calmar; hacer callar; **~ly** adv tranquilamente, (silently) silenciosamente; **~ness** n silencio; tranquilidad f

quilt [kwɪlt] n edredón m

quin [kwɪn] n abbr = **quintuplet**

quintet(te) [kwɪn'tet] n quinteto

quintuplets [kwɪn'tjuːplɪts] npl quintillizos/as

quip [kwɪp] n pulla

quirk [kwəːk] n peculiaridad f; (accident) casualidad f

quit [kwɪt] (pt, pp quit or quitted) vt dejar, abandonar; (premises) desocupar ♦ vi (give up) renunciar; (resign) dimitir

quite [kwaɪt] adv (rather) bastante; (entirely) completamente; **that's not ~ big enough** no acaba de ser lo bastante grande; **~ a few of them** un buen número de ellos; **~ (so)!** ¡así es!, ¡exactamente!

quits [kwɪts] adj: **~ (with)** en paz (con); **let's call it ~** dejémoslo en tablas

quiver ['kwɪvə*] vi estremecerse

quiz [kwɪz] n concurso ♦ vt interrogar; **~zical** adj burlón(ona)

quota [ˈkwəʊtə] n cuota
quotation [kwəʊˈteɪʃən] n cita; (estimate) presupuesto; **~ marks** npl comillas fpl
quote [kwəʊt] n cita; (estimate) presupuesto ♦ vt citar; (price) cotizar ♦ vi: **to ~ from** citar de; **~s** npl (inverted commas) comillas fpl

R, r

rabbi [ˈræbaɪ] n rabino
rabbit [ˈræbɪt] n conejo; **~ hutch** n conejera
rabble [ˈræbl] n (pej) chusma, populacho
rabies [ˈreɪbiːz] n rabia
RAC (BRIT) n abbr = **Royal Automobile Club**
rac(c)oon [rəˈkuːn] n mapache m
race [reɪs] n carrera; (species) raza ♦ vt (horse) hacer correr; (engine) acelerar ♦ vi (compete) competir; (run) correr; (pulse) latir a ritmo acelerado; **~ car** (US) n = **racing car**; **~ car driver** (US) n = **racing driver**; **~course** n hipódromo; **~horse** n caballo de carreras; **~track** n pista; (for cars) autódromo
racial [ˈreɪʃl] adj racial
racing [ˈreɪsɪŋ] n carreras fpl; **~ car** (BRIT) n coche m de carreras; **~ driver** (BRIT) n corredor/a m/f de coches
racism [ˈreɪsɪzəm] n racismo; **racist** [-sɪst] adj, n racista m/f
rack [ræk] n (also: luggage ~) rejilla; (shelf) estante m; (also: roof ~) baca, portaequipajes m inv; (dish ~) escurreplatos m inv; (clothes ~) percha ♦ vt atormentar; **to ~ one's brains** devanarse los sesos
racket [ˈrækɪt] n (for tennis) raqueta; (noise) ruido, estrépito; (swindle) estafa, timo
racquet [ˈrækɪt] n raqueta
racy [ˈreɪsɪ] adj picante, salado

radar [ˈreɪdɑː*] n radar m
radiant [ˈreɪdɪənt] adj radiante (de felicidad)
radiate [ˈreɪdɪeɪt] vt (heat) radiar; (emotion) irradiar ♦ vi (lines) extenderse
radiation [reɪdɪˈeɪʃən] n radiación f
radiator [ˈreɪdɪeɪtə*] n radiador m
radical [ˈrædɪkl] adj radical
radii [ˈreɪdɪaɪ] npl of **radius**
radio [ˈreɪdɪəʊ] n radio f; **on the ~** por radio
radio... [reɪdɪəʊ] prefix: **~active** adj radioactivo; **~graphy** [reɪdɪˈɔgrəfɪ] n radiografía; **~logy** [reɪdɪˈɔlədʒɪ] n radiología
radio station n emisora
radiotherapy [-ˈθerəpɪ] n radioterapia
radish [ˈrædɪʃ] n rábano
radius [ˈreɪdɪəs] (pl **radii**) n radio
RAF n abbr = **Royal Air Force**
raffle [ˈræfl] n rifa, sorteo
raft [rɑːft] n balsa; (also: life ~) balsa salvavidas
rafter [ˈrɑːftə*] n viga
rag [ræg] n (piece of cloth) trapo; (torn cloth) harapo; (pej: newspaper) periodicucho; (for charity) actividades estudiantiles benéficas; **~s** npl (torn clothes) harapos mpl; **~ doll** n muñeca de trapo
rage [reɪdʒ] n rabia, furor m ♦ vi (person) rabiar, estar furioso; (storm) bramar; **it's all the ~** (very fashionable) está muy de moda
ragged [ˈrægɪd] adj (edge) desigual, mellado; (appearance) andrajoso, harapiento
raid [reɪd] n (MIL) incursión f; (criminal) asalto; (by police) redada ♦ vt invadir, atacar; asaltar
rail [reɪl] n (on stair) barandilla, pasamanos m inv; (on bridge, balcony) pretil m; (of ship) barandilla; (also: towel ~) toallero; **~s** npl (RAIL) vía; **by ~** por ferrocarril; **~ing(s)** n(pl) vallado; **~road** (US) n = **~way**; **~way** (BRIT) n ferrocarril m, vía férrea; **~way line**

(BRIT) n línea (de ferrocarril);
~wayman (BRIT irreg) n ferroviario;
~way station (BRIT) n estación f de
ferrocarril

rain [reɪn] n lluvia ♦ vi llover; **in the ~**
bajo la lluvia; **it's ~ing** llueve, está
lloviendo; **~bow** n arco iris; **~coat** n
impermeable m; **~drop** n gota de
lluvia; **~fall** n lluvia; **~forest** n selvas
fpl tropicales; **~y** adj lluvioso

raise [reɪz] n aumento ♦ vt levantar;
(increase) aumentar; (improve: morale)
subir; (: standards) mejorar; (doubts)
suscitar; (a question) plantear; (cattle,
family) criar; (crop) cultivar; (army)
reclutar; (loan) obtener; **to ~ one's
voice** levantar la voz

raisin ['reɪzn] n pasa de Corinto

rake [reɪk] n (tool) rastrillo; (person)
libertino ♦ vt (garden) rastrillar

rally ['rælɪ] n (POL etc) reunión f, mitin
m; (AUT) rallye m; (TENNIS) peloteo ♦ vt
reunir ♦ vi recuperarse; **~ round** vt fus
reunir ♦ vt recuperarse; (fig) dar apoyo a

RAM [ræm] n abbr (= random access
memory) RAM f

ram [ræm] n carnero; (also: battering ~)
ariete m ♦ vt (crash land) dar contra,
chocar con; (push: fist etc) empujar con
fuerza

ramble ['ræmbl] n caminata, excursión
f en el campo ♦ vi (pej: also: ~ on)
divagar; **~r** n excursionista m/f; (BOT)
trepadera; **rambling** adj (speech)
inconexo; (house) laberíntico; (BOT)
trepador(a)

ramp [ræmp] n rampa; **on/off ~** (US:
AUT) vía de acceso/salida

rampage [ræm'peɪdʒ] n: **to be on
the ~** desmandarse ♦ vi: **they went
rampaging through the town**
recorrieron la ciudad armando alboroto

rampant ['ræmpənt] adj (disease etc):
to be ~ estar extendiéndose mucho

ram raid vt atracar (rompiendo el
escaparate con un coche)

ramshackle ['ræmʃækl] adj

destartalado

ran [ræn] pt of **run**

ranch [rɑ:ntʃ] n hacienda, estancia;
~er n ganadero

rancid ['rænsɪd] adj rancio

rancour ['ræŋkə*] (US **rancor**) n rencor
m

random ['rændəm] adj fortuito, sin
orden; (COMPUT, MATH) aleatorio ♦ n:
at ~ al azar

randy ['rændɪ] (BRIT: inf) adj cachondo

rang [ræŋ] pt of **ring**

range [reɪndʒ] n (of mountains) cadena
de montañas, cordillera; (of missile)
alcance m; (of voice) registro; (series)
serie f; (of products) surtido; (MIL: also:
shooting ~) campo de tiro; (also:
kitchen ~) fogón m ♦ vt (place) colocar;
(arrange) arreglar ♦ vi: **to ~ over**
(extend) extenderse por; **to ~ from ...
to ...** oscilar entre ... y ...

ranger [reɪndʒə*] n guardabosques m
inv

rank [ræŋk] n (row) fila; (MIL) rango;
(status) categoría; (BRIT: also: taxi ~)
parada de taxis ♦ vi: **to ~ among**
figurar entre ♦ adj fétido, rancio; **the
~ and file** (fig) la base

ransack ['rænsæk] vt (search) registrar;
(plunder) saquear

ransom ['rænsəm] n rescate m; **to
hold to ~** (fig) hacer chantaje a

rant [rænt] vi divagar, desvariar

rap [ræp] vt golpear, dar un golpecito
en ♦ n (music) rap m

rape [reɪp] n violación f; (BOT) colza
♦ vt violar; **~ (seed) oil** n aceite m de
colza

rapid ['ræpɪd] adj rápido; **~ity**
[rə'pɪdɪtɪ] n rapidez f; **~s** npl (GEO)
rápidos mpl

rapist ['reɪpɪst] n violador m

rapport [ræ'pɔ:*] n simpatía

rapturous ['ræptʃərəs] adj extático

rare [reə*] adj raro, poco común;
(CULIN: steak) poco hecho

rarely ['reəlɪ] adv pocas veces

raring ['rɛərɪŋ] adj: **to be ~ to go** (inf) tener muchas ganas de empezar

rascal ['rɑːskl] n pillo, pícaro

rash [ræʃ] adj imprudente, precipitado ♦ n (MED) sarpullido, erupción f (cutánea); (of events) serie f

rasher ['ræʃə*] n lonja

raspberry ['rɑːzbərɪ] n frambuesa

rasping ['rɑːspɪŋ] adj: **a ~ noise** un ruido áspero

rat [ræt] n rata

rate [reɪt] n (ratio) razón f; (price) precio; (: of hotel etc) tarifa; (of interest) tipo; (speed) velocidad f ♦ vt (value) tasar; (estimate) estimar; **~s** npl (BRIT: property tax) impuesto municipal; (fees) tarifa; **to ~ sth/sb as** considerar algo/a uno como; **~able value** (BRIT) n valor m impuesto; **~payer** (BRIT) n contribuyente m/f

rather ['rɑːðə*] adv: **it's ~ expensive** es algo caro; (too much) es demasiado caro; (to some extent) más bien; **there's ~ a lot** hay bastante; **I would** or **I'd ~ go** preferiría ir; **or ~ mejor** dicho

rating ['reɪtɪŋ] n tasación f; (score) índice m; (of ship) clase f; **~s** npl (RADIO, TV) niveles mpl de audiencia

ratio ['reɪʃɪəu] n razón f; **in the ~ of 100 to 1** a razón de 100 a 1

ration ['ræʃən] n ración f; **~s** npl víveres mpl ♦ vt racionar

rational ['ræʃənl] adj (solution, reasoning) lógico, razonable; (person) cuerdo, sensato; **~e** [-'nɑːl] n razón f fundamental; **~ize** vt justificar

rat race n lucha incesante por la supervivencia

rattle ['rætl] n golpeteo; (of train etc) traqueteo; (for baby) sonaja, sonajero ♦ vi castañetear; (car, bus): **to ~ along** traquetear ♦ vt hacer sonar agitando; **~snake** n serpiente f de cascabel

raucous ['rɔːkəs] adj estridente, ronco

ravage ['rævɪdʒ] vt hacer estragos en, destrozar; **~s** npl estragos mpl

rave [reɪv] vi (in anger) encolerizarse; (with enthusiasm) entusiasmarse; (MED) delirar, desvariar ♦ n (inf: party) rave m

raven ['reɪvn] n cuervo

ravenous ['rævənəs] adj hambriento

ravine [rə'viːn] n barranco

raving ['reɪvɪŋ] adj: **~ lunatic** loco/a de atar

ravishing ['rævɪʃɪŋ] adj encantador(a)

raw [rɔː] adj crudo; (not processed) bruto; (sore) vivo; (inexperienced) novato, inexperto; **~ deal** (inf) n injusticia; **~ material** n materia prima

ray [reɪ] n rayo; **~ of hope** (rayo de) esperanza

raze [reɪz] vt arrasar

razor ['reɪzə*] n (open) navaja; (safety ~) máquina de afeitar; (electric ~) máquina (eléctrica) de afeitar; **~ blade** n hoja de afeitar

Rd abbr = **road**

re [riː] prep con referencia a

reach [riːtʃ] n alcance m; (of river etc) extensión f entre dos recodos ♦ vt alcanzar, llegar a; (achieve) lograr ♦ vi extenderse; **within ~** al alcance (de la mano); **out of ~** fuera del alcance; **~ out** vt (hand) tender ♦ vi: **to ~ out for sth** alargar or tender la mano para tomar algo

react [riː'ækt] vi reaccionar; **~ion** [-'ækʃən] n reacción f

reactor [riː'æktə*] n (also: nuclear ~) reactor m (nuclear)

read [riːd, pt, pp red] (pt, pp **read**) vi leer ♦ vt leer; (understand) entender; (study) estudiar; **~ out** vt leer en alta voz; **~able** adj (writing) legible; (book) leíble; **~er** n lector(a) m/f; (BRIT: at university) profesor(a) m/f adjunto/a; **~ership** n (of paper etc) (número de) lectores mpl

readily ['rɛdɪlɪ] adv (willingly) de buena gana; (easily) fácilmente; (quickly) en seguida

readiness ['rɛdɪnɪs] n buena voluntad f; (preparedness) preparación f; **in ~**

reading ['ri:dɪŋ] n lectura; (on instrument) indicación f

ready ['rɛdɪ] adj listo, preparado; (willing) dispuesto; (available) disponible ♦ adv: **~-cooked** listo para comer ♦ n: **at the ~** (MIL) listo para tirar; **to get ~** vi prepararse ♦ vt preparar; **~-made** adj confeccionado; **~-to-wear** adj confeccionado

real [rɪəl] adj verdadero, auténtico; **in ~ terms** en términos reales; **~ estate** n bienes mpl raíces; **~istic** [-'lɪstɪk] adj realista

reality [ri:'ælɪtɪ] n realidad f

realization [rɪəlaɪ'zeɪʃən] n comprensión f; (fulfilment, COMM) realización f

realize ['rɪəlaɪz] vt (understand) darse cuenta de

really ['rɪəlɪ] adv realmente; (for emphasis) verdaderamente; (actually): **what ~ happened** lo que pasó en realidad; **~?** ¿de veras?; **~!** (annoyance) ¡vamos!, ¡por favor!

realm [rɛlm] n reino; (fig) esfera

realtor ® ['rɪəltɔ:*] (US) n corredor(a) m/f de bienes raíces

reap [ri:p] vt segar; (fig) cosechar, recoger

reappear [ri:ə'pɪə*] vi reaparecer

rear [rɪə*] adj trasero ♦ n parte f trasera ♦ vt (cattle, family) criar ♦ vi (also: **~ up**) (animal) encabritarse; **~guard** n retaguardia

rearmament [ri:'ɑ:məmənt] n rearme m

rearrange [ri:ə'reɪndʒ] vt ordenar o arreglar de nuevo

rear-view mirror n (AUT) (espejo) retrovisor m

reason ['ri:zn] n razón f ♦ vi: **to ~ with sb** tratar de que uno entre en razón; **it stands to ~ that** es lógico que; **~able** adj razonable; (sensible) sensato; **~ably** adv razonablemente; **~ing** n razonamiento, argumentos mpl

reassurance [ri:ə'ʃuərəns] n consuelo

reassure [ri:ə'ʃuə*] vt tranquilizar, alentar; **to ~ sb that** tranquilizar a uno asegurando que

rebate ['ri:beɪt] n (on tax etc) desgravación f

rebel [n 'rɛbl, vi rɪ'bɛl] n rebelde m/f ♦ vi rebelarse, sublevarse; **~lious** [rɪ'bɛljəs] adj rebelde; (child) revoltoso

rebirth [ri:'bə:θ] n renacimiento

rebound [vi rɪ'baund, n 'ri:baund] vi (ball) rebotar ♦ n rebote m; **on the ~** (also fig) de rebote

rebuff [rɪ'bʌf] n desaire m, rechazo

rebuild [ri:'bɪld] (irreg) vt reconstruir

rebuke [rɪ'bju:k] n reprimenda ♦ vt reprender

rebut [rɪ'bʌt] vt rebatir

recall [vb rɪ'kɔ:l, n 'ri:kɔ:l] vt (remember) recordar; (ambassador etc) retirar ♦ n recuerdo; retirada

recap ['ri:kæp], **recapitulate** [ri:kə'pɪtjuleɪt] vt, vi recapitular

rec'd abbr (= received) rbdo

recede [rɪ'si:d] vi (memory) irse o borrándose; (hair) retroceder;
receding adj (forehead, chin) huidizo; **to have a receding hairline** tener entradas

receipt [rɪ'si:t] n (document) recibo; (for parcel etc) acuse m de recibo; (act of receiving) recepción f; **~s** npl (COMM) ingresos mpl

receive [rɪ'si:v] vt recibir; (guest) acoger; (wound) sufrir; **~r** n (TEL) auricular m; (RADIO) receptor m; (of stolen goods) perista m/f; (COMM) administrador m jurídico

recent ['ri:snt] adj reciente; **~ly** adv recientemente; **~ly arrived** recién llegado

receptacle [rɪ'sɛptɪkl] n receptáculo

reception [rɪ'sɛpʃən] n recepción f; (welcome) acogida; **~ desk** n recepción f; **~ist** n recepcionista f

recess [rɪ'sɛs] n (in room) hueco; (for bed) nicho; (secret place) escondrijo;

(POL etc: holiday) clausura

recession [rɪˈsɛʃən] n recesión f

recipe [ˈrɛsɪpɪ] n receta; (for disaster, success) fórmula

recipient [rɪˈsɪpɪənt] n recibidor(a) m/f; (of letter) destinatario/a

recital [rɪˈsaɪtl] n recital m

recite [rɪˈsaɪt] vt (poem) recitar

reckless [ˈrɛkləs] adj temerario, imprudente; (driving, driver) peligroso; ~ly adv imprudentemente; de modo peligroso

reckon [ˈrɛkən] vt calcular; (consider) considerar; (think): I ~ that ... me parece que ...; ~ on vt fus contar con; ~ing n cálculo

reclaim [rɪˈkleɪm] vt (land, waste) recuperar; (land: from sea) rescatar; (demand back) reclamar

reclamation [rɛkləˈmeɪʃən] n (of land) acondicionamiento de tierras

recline [rɪˈklaɪn] vi reclinarse; **reclining** adj (seat) reclinable

recluse [rɪˈkluːs] n recluso/a

recognition [rɛkəgˈnɪʃən] n reconocimiento m; **transformed beyond** ~ irreconocible

recognizable [ˈrɛkəgnaɪzəbl] adj: ~ (by) reconocible (por)

recognize [ˈrɛkəgnaɪz] vt: to ~ (by/ as) reconocer (por/como)

recoil [vi rɪˈkɔɪl, n ˈriːkɔɪl] vi (person): to ~ from doing sth retraerse de hacer algo ♦ n (of gun) retroceso

recollect [rɛkəˈlɛkt] vt recordar, acordarse de; ~ion [-ˈlɛkʃən] n recuerdo

recommend [rɛkəˈmɛnd] vt recomendar

reconcile [ˈrɛkənsaɪl] vt (two people) reconciliar; (two facts) compaginar; to ~ o.s. to sth conformarse a algo

recondition [riːkənˈdɪʃən] vt (machine) reacondicionar

reconnoitre [rɛkəˈnɔɪtə*] (US **reconnoiter**) vt, vi (MIL) reconocer

reconsider [riːkənˈsɪdə*] vt repensar

reconstruct [riːkənˈstrʌkt] vt reconstruir

record [n ˈrɛkɔːd, vt rɪˈkɔːd] n (MUS) disco; (of meeting etc) acta; (register) registro, partida; (file) archivo; (also: criminal ~) antecedentes mpl; (written) expediente m; (SPORT, COMPUT) récord m ♦ vt (register); (MUS: song etc) grabar; **in ~ time** en un tiempo récord; **off the** ~ adj no oficial ♦ adv confidencialmente; ~ **card** n (in file) ficha; ~ed **delivery** (BRIT) n (POST) entrega con acuse de recibo; ~er n (MUS) flauta de pico; ~ **holder** n (SPORT) actual poseedor(a) m/f del récord; ~ing n (MUS) grabación f; ~ **player** n tocadiscos m inv

recount [rɪˈkaunt] vt contar

re-count [ˈriːkaunt] n (POL: of votes) segundo escrutinio

recoup [rɪˈkuːp] vt: to ~ **one's losses** recuperar las pérdidas

recourse [rɪˈkɔːs] n: to have ~ to recurrir a

recover [rɪˈkʌvə*] vt recuperar ♦ vi (from illness, shock) recuperarse; ~y n recuperación f

recreation [rɛkrɪˈeɪʃən] n recreo; ~al adj de recreo; ~al **drug** droga recreativa

recruit [rɪˈkruːt] n recluta m/f ♦ vt reclutar; (staff) contratar

rectangle [ˈrɛktæŋgl] n rectángulo; **rectangular** [-ˈtæŋgjulə*] adj rectangular

rectify [ˈrɛktɪfaɪ] vt rectificar

rector [ˈrɛktə*] n (REL) párroco; ~y n casa del párroco

recuperate [rɪˈkuːpəreɪt] vi reponerse, restablecerse

recur [rɪˈkəː*] vi repetirse; (pain, illness) producirse de nuevo; ~rence [rɪˈkarəns] n repetición f; ~rent [rɪˈkarənt] adj repetido

recycle [riːˈsaɪkl] vt reciclar

red [rɛd] n rojo ♦ adj rojo; (hair) pelirrojo; (wine) tinto; **to be in the** ~

(*account*) estar en números rojos; (*business*) tener un saldo negativo; **to give sb the ~ carpet treatment** recibir a uno con todos los honores; **R~ Cross** n Cruz f Roja; **~currant** n grosella roja; **~den** vt enrojecer ♦ vi enrojecerse

redeem [rɪ'diːm] vt redimir; (*promises*) cumplir; (*sth in pawn*) desempeñar; (*fig, also* REL) rescatar; **~ing ~ing feature** rasgo bueno o favorable

redeploy [riːdɪ'plɔɪ] vt (*resources*) reorganizar

red: **~-haired** adj pelirrojo; **~-handed** adj: **to be caught ~-handed** cogerse (SP) or pillarse (AM) con las manos en la masa; **~head** n pelirrojo/a; **~ herring** n (fig) pista falsa; **~-hot** adj candente

redirect [riːdaɪ'rekt] vt (*mail*) reexpedir

red light n: **to go through a ~** (AUT) pasar la luz roja; **red-light district** n barrio chino

redo [riː'duː] (*irreg*) vt rehacer

redress [rɪ'dres] vt reparar

Red Sea n: **the ~** el mar Rojo

redskin ['redskɪn] n piel roja m/f

red tape n (fig) trámites mpl

reduce [rɪ'djuːs] vt reducir; **to ~ sb to tears** hacer llorar a uno; **to ~d to begging** no quedarle a uno otro remedio que pedir limosna; **"~ speed now"** (AUT) "reduzca la velocidad"; **at a ~d price** (*of goods*) (a precio) rebajado; **reduction** [rɪ'dʌkʃən] n reducción f; (*of price*) rebaja; (*discount*) descuento; (*smaller-scale copy*) copia reducida

redundancy [rɪ'dʌndənsɪ] n (*dismissal*) despido; (*unemployment*) desempleo

redundant [rɪ'dʌndnt] adj (*worker*) parado, sin trabajo; (*detail, object*) superfluo; **to be made ~** quedar(se) sin trabajo

reed [riːd] n (BOT) junco, caña; (MUS) lengüeta

reef [riːf] n (*at sea*) arrecife m

reek [riːk] vi: **to ~ (of)** apestar (a)

reel [riːl] n carrete m, bobina; (*of film*) rollo; (*dance*) baile m escocés ♦ vt (*also: ~ up*) devanar; (*also: ~ in*) sacar ♦ vi (*sway*) tambalear(se)

ref [ref] (*inf*) n abbr = **referee**

refectory [rɪ'fektərɪ] n comedor m

refer [rɪ'fəː] vt (*send: patient*) referir; (: *matter*) remitir ♦ vi: **to ~ to** (*allude to*) referirse a, aludir a; (*apply to*) relacionarse con; (*consult*) consultar

referee [refə'riː] n árbitro; (BRIT: *for job application*): **to be a ~ for sb** proporcionar referencias a uno ♦ vt (*match*) arbitrar en

reference ['refrəns] n referencia; (*for job application: letter*) carta de recomendación; **with ~ to** (COMM: *in letter*) me remito a; **~ book** n libro de consulta; **~ number** n número de referencia

refill [vt rɪ'fɪl, n 'riːfɪl] vt rellenar ♦ n repuesto, recambio

refine [rɪ'faɪn] vt refinar; **~d** adj (*person*) fino; **~ment** n cultura, educación f; (*of system*) refinamiento

reflect [rɪ'flekt] vt reflejar ♦ vi (*think*) reflexionar, pensar; **it ~s badly/well on him** le perjudica/le hace honor; **~ion** ['flekʃən] n (*act*) reflexión f; (*image*) reflejo; (*criticism*) crítica; **on ~ion** pensándolo bien; **~or** n (AUT) captafaros m inv; (*of light, heat*) reflector m

reflex [rɪ'fleks] adj, n reflejo; **~ive** [rɪ'fleksɪv] adj (LING) reflexivo

reform [rɪ'fɔːm] n reforma ♦ vt reformar; **~atory** (US) n reformatorio

refrain [rɪ'freɪn] vi: **to ~ from doing** abstenerse de hacer ♦ n estribillo

refresh [rɪ'freʃ] vt refrescar; **~er course** (BRIT) n curso de repaso; **~ing** adj refrescante; **~ments** npl refrescos mpl

refrigerator [rɪ'frɪdʒəreɪtə*] n nevera (SP), refrigeradora (AM)

refuel [riː'fjuəl] vi repostar (combustible)

refuge [ˈrɛfjuːdʒ] n refugio, asilo; **to take ~ in** refugiarse en

refugee [rɛfjuˈdʒiː] n refugiado/a

refund [n ˈriːfʌnd, vb rɪˈfʌnd] n reembolso ♦ vt devolver, reembolsar

refurbish [riːˈfɜːbɪʃ] vt restaurar, renovar

refusal [rɪˈfjuːzəl] n negativa; **to have first ~ on** tener la primera opción a

refuse[1] [ˈrɛfjuːs] n basura; **~ collection** recolección f de basuras

refuse[2] [rɪˈfjuːz] vt rechazar; (invitation) declinar; (permission) denegar ♦ vi: **to ~ to do sth** negarse a hacer algo; (horse) rehusar

regain [rɪˈgeɪn] vt recobrar, recuperar

regal [ˈriːgl] adj regio, real

regard [rɪˈgɑːd] n mirada; (esteem) respeto; (attention) consideración f ♦ vt (consider) considerar; **to give one's ~s to** saludar de su parte a; **"with kindest ~s"** "con muchos recuerdos"; **~ing, as ~s, with ~ to** con respecto a, en cuanto a; **~less** adv a pesar de todo; **~less of** sin reparar en

régime [reɪˈʒiːm] n régimen m

regiment [ˈrɛdʒɪmənt] n regimiento; **~al** [-ˈmɛntl] adj militar

region [ˈriːdʒən] n región f; **in the ~ of** (fig) alrededor de; **~al** adj regional

register [ˈrɛdʒɪstə*] n registro ♦ vt registrar; (birth) declarar; (car) matricular; (letter) certificar; (subj: instrument) marcar, indicar ♦ vi (at hotel) registrarse; (as student) matricularse; (make impression) producir impresión; **~ed** adj (letter, parcel) certificado; **~ed trademark** n marca registrada

registrar [ˈrɛdʒɪstrɑː*] n secretario/a (del registro civil)

registration [rɛdʒɪsˈtreɪʃən] n (act) declaración f; (AUT: also: ~ number) matrícula

registry [ˈrɛdʒɪstrɪ] n registro; **~ office** (BRIT) n registro civil; **to get married**

in a ~ office casarse por lo civil

regret [rɪˈgrɛt] n sentimiento, pesar m ♦ vt sentir, lamentar; **~fully** adv con pesar; **~table** adj lamentable

regular [ˈrɛgjulə*] adj regular; (soldier) profesional; (usual) habitual; (: doctor) de cabecera ♦ n (in client etc) cliente/a m/f habitual; **~ly** adv con regularidad; (often) repetidas veces

regulate [ˈrɛgjuleɪt] vt controlar; **regulation** [-ˈleɪʃən] n (rule) regla, reglamento

rehearsal [rɪˈhɜːsəl] n ensayo

rehearse [rɪˈhɜːs] vt ensayar

reign [reɪn] n reinado; (fig) predominio ♦ vi reinar; (fig) imperar

reimburse [riːɪmˈbɜːs] vt reembolsar

rein [reɪn] n (for horse) rienda

reindeer [ˈreɪndɪə*] n inv reno

reinforce [riːɪnˈfɔːs] vt reforzar; **~d concrete** n hormigón m armado; **~ments** npl (MIL) refuerzos mpl

reinstate [riːɪnˈsteɪt] vt reintegrar; (tax, law) reinstaurar

reiterate [riːˈɪtəreɪt] vt reiterar, repetir

reject [n ˈriːdʒɛkt, vb rɪˈdʒɛkt] n (thing) desecho ♦ vt rechazar; (suggestion) descartar; (coin) expulsar; **~ion** [rɪˈdʒɛkʃən] n rechazo

rejoice [rɪˈdʒɔɪs] vi: **to ~ at** or **over** regocijarse or alegrarse de

rejuvenate [rɪˈdʒuːvəneɪt] vt rejuvenecer

relapse [rɪˈlæps] n recaída

relate [rɪˈleɪt] vt (tell) contar, relatar; (connect) relacionar ♦ vi relacionarse; **~d** adj afín; (person) emparentado; **~d to** (subject) relacionado con; **relating to** prep referente a

relation [rɪˈleɪʃən] n (person) familiar m/f, pariente/a m/f; (link) relación f; **~s** npl (relatives) familiares mpl; **~ship** n relación f; (personal) relaciones fpl; (also: family ~ship) parentesco

relative [ˈrɛlətɪv] n pariente/a m/f, familiar m/f ♦ adj relativo; **~ly** adv (comparatively) relativamente

relax [rɪ'læks] vi descansar; (unwind) relajarse ♦ vt (one's grip) soltar, aflojar; (control) relajar; (mind, person) descansar; **~ation** [riːlæk'seɪʃən] n descanso; (of rule, control) relajamiento; (entertainment) diversión f; **~ed** adj relajado; (tranquil) tranquilo; **~ing** adj relajante

relay ['riːleɪ] n (race) carrera de relevos ♦ vt (RADIO, TV) retransmitir

release [rɪ'liːs] n (liberation) liberación f; (from prison) puesta en libertad; (of gas etc) escape m; (of film etc) estreno; (of record) lanzamiento ♦ vt (prisoner) poner en libertad; (gas) despedir, arrojar; (from wreckage) soltar; (catch, spring etc) desenganchar; (film) estrenar; (book) publicar; (news) difundir

relegate ['relɪgeɪt] vt relegar; (BRIT: SPORT): **to be ~d to** bajar a

relent [rɪ'lent] vi ablandarse; **~less** adj implacable

relevant ['reləvənt] adj (fact) pertinente, al caso; **~ to** relacionado con

reliable [rɪ'laɪəbl] adj (person, firm) de confianza, de fiar; (method, machine) seguro; (source) fidedigno; **reliably** adv: **to be reliably informed that ...** saber de fuente fidedigna que ...

reliance [rɪ'laɪəns] n: **~ (on)** dependencia f

relic ['relɪk] n (REL) reliquia f; (of the past) vestigio

relief [rɪ'liːf] n (from pain, anxiety) alivio; (help, supplies) socorro, ayuda; (ART, GEO) relieve m

relieve [rɪ'liːv] vt (pain) aliviar; (bring help to) ayudar, socorrer; (take over from) sustituir; (: guard) relevar; **to ~ sb of sth** quitar algo a uno; **to ~ o.s.** hacer sus necesidades

religion [rɪ'lɪdʒən] n religión f; **religious** adj religioso

relinquish [rɪ'lɪŋkwɪʃ] vt abandonar; (plan, habit) renunciar a

relish ['relɪʃ] n (CULIN) salsa;

(enjoyment) entusiasmo f (food etc) saborear; (enjoy): **to ~ sth** hacerle mucha ilusión a uno algo

relocate [riːləʊ'keɪt] vt cambiar de lugar, mudar ♦ vi mudarse

reluctance [rɪ'lʌktəns] n renuencia

reluctant [rɪ'lʌktənt] adj renuente; **~ly** adv de mala gana

rely on [rɪ'laɪ-] vt fus depender de; (trust) contar con

remain [rɪ'meɪn] vi (survive) quedar; (be left) sobrar; (continue) quedar(se), permanecer; **~der** n resto; **~ing** adj que queda(n); (surviving) restante(s); **~s** npl restos mpl

remand [rɪ'mɑːnd] n: **on ~** detenido (bajo custodia) ♦ vt: **to be ~ed in custody** quedar detenido bajo custodia; **~ home** (BRIT) n reformatorio

remark [rɪ'mɑːk] n comentario ♦ vt comentar; **~able** adj (outstanding) extraordinario

remarry [riː'mærɪ] vi volver a casarse

remedial [rɪ'miːdɪəl] adj de recuperación

remedy ['remədɪ] n remedio ♦ vt remediar, curar

remember [rɪ'membə*] vt recordar, acordarse de; (bear in mind) tener presente; (send greetings to): **~ me to him** dale recuerdos de mi parte; **remembrance** n recuerdo; **R~ Day** n ≈ día en el que se recuerda a los caídos en las dos guerras mundiales

┌─────────────────────────┐
│ **Remembrance Day** │
└─────────────────────────┘

En el Reino Unido el domingo más próximo al 11 de noviembre se conoce como **Remembrance Sunday** o **Remembrance Day**, aniversario de la firma del armisticio de 1918 que puso fin a la Primera Guerra Mundial. Ese día, a las once de la mañana (hora en que se firmó el armisticio), se recuerda a los que murieron en las dos guerras mundiales con dos minutos de silencio ante los monumentos a los caídos. Allí se colocan coronas de amapolas, flor que también se suele llevar prendida en el pecho tras pagar un donativo destinado a los inválidos de guerra.

---

remind [rɪ'maɪnd] vt: to ~ sb to do sth recordar a uno que haga algo; to ~ sb of sth (of fact) recordar algo a uno; she ~s me of her mother me recuerda a su madre; ~er n notificación f; (memento) recuerdo

reminisce [rɛmɪ'nɪs] vi recordar (viejas historias); **reminiscent** adj: to be reminiscent of sth recordar algo

remiss [rɪ'mɪs] adj descuidado; it was ~ of him fue un descuido de su parte

remission [rɪ'mɪʃən] n remisión f; (of prison sentence) disminución f de pena; (REL) perdón m

remit [rɪ'mɪt] vt (send: money) remitir, enviar; ~tance n remesa, envío

remnant ['rɛmnənt] n resto; (of cloth) retal m; ~s npl (COMM) restos mpl de serie

remorse [rɪ'mɔːs] n remordimientos mpl; ~ful adj arrepentido; ~less adj (fig) implacable, inexorable

remote [rɪ'məut] adj (distant) lejano; (person) distante; ~ control n telecontrol m; ~ly adv remotamente; (slightly) levemente

remould [riː'məuld] (BRIT) n (tyre) neumático or llanta (AM) recauchutado f

removable [rɪ'muːvəbl] adj (detachable) separable

removal [rɪ'muːvəl] n (taking away) el quitar; (BRIT: from house) mudanza; (from office: dismissal) destitución f; (MED) extirpación f; ~ van (BRIT) n camión m de mudanzas

remove [rɪ'muːv] vt quitar; (employee) destituir; (name: from list) tachar, borrar; (doubt) disipar; (abuse)

suprimir, acabar con; (MED) extirpar

Renaissance [rɪ'neɪsɑːns] n: the ~ el Renacimiento

render ['rɛndə*] vt (thanks) dar; (aid) proporcionar, prestar; (make): to ~ sth useless hacer algo inútil; ~ing n (MUS etc) interpretación f

rendezvous ['rɒndɪvuː] n cita

renew [rɪ'njuː] vt renovar; (resume) reanudar; (loan etc) prorrogar; ~able adj renovable; ~al n reanudación f; prórroga

renounce [rɪ'nauns] vt renunciar a; (right, inheritance) renunciar

renovate ['rɛnəveɪt] vt renovar

renown [rɪ'naun] n renombre m; ~ed adj renombrado

rent [rɛnt] n (for house) arriendo, renta ♦ vt alquilar; ~al n (for television, car) alquiler m

rep [rɛp] n abbr = **representative**; **repertory**

repair [rɪ'pɛə*] n reparación f, compostura ♦ vt reparar, componer; (shoes) remendar; in good/bad ~ en buen/mal estado; ~ kit n caja de herramientas

repatriate [riː'pætrɪeɪt] vt repatriar

repay [riː'peɪ] (irreg) vt (money) devolver, reembolsar; (person) pagar; (debt) liquidar; (sb's efforts) devolver, corresponder a; ~ment n reembolso, devolución f; (sum of money) recompensa

repeal [rɪ'piːl] n revocación f ♦ vt revocar

repeat [rɪ'piːt] n (RADIO, TV) reposición f ♦ vt repetir ♦ vi repetirse; ~edly adv repetidas veces

repel [rɪ'pɛl] vt (drive away) rechazar; (disgust) repugnar; ~lent adj repugnante ♦ n: insect ~lent crema (or loción f) anti-insectos

repent [rɪ'pɛnt] vi: to ~ (of) arrepentirse (de); ~ance n arrepentimiento

repercussions [riːpə'kʌʃənz] npl

consecuencias fpl

repertory ['repətərɪ] n (also: ~ theatre) teatro de repertorio

repetition [repɪ'tɪʃən] n repetición f

repetitive [rɪ'petɪtɪv] adj repetitivo

replace [rɪ'pleɪs] vt (put back) devolver a su sitio; (take the place of) reemplazar, sustituir; **~ment** n (act) reposición f; (thing) recambio; (person) suplente m/f

replay ['riːpleɪ] n (SPORT) desempate m; (of tape, film) repetición f

replenish [rɪ'plenɪʃ] vt rellenar; (stock etc) reponer

replica ['replɪkə] n copia, reproducción f (exacta)

reply [rɪ'plaɪ] n respuesta, contestación f ♦ vi contestar, responder

report [rɪ'pɔːt] n informe m; (PRESS etc) reportaje m; (BRIT: also: school ~) boletín m escolar; (of gun) estallido ♦ vt informar de; (PRESS etc) hacer un reportaje sobre; (notify: accident, culprit) denunciar ♦ vi (make a report) presentar un informe; (present o.s.): to ~ (to sb) presentarse (ante uno); ~ card n (US, Scottish) cartilla f escolar; ~edly adv según se dice; ~er n periodista m/f

repose [rɪ'pəuz] n: **in ~** (face, mouth) en reposo

reprehensible [reprɪ'hensɪbl] adj reprensible, censurable

represent [reprɪ'zent] vt representar; (COMM) ser agente de; (describe): to ~ sth as describir algo como; ~ation [-'teɪʃən] n representación f; ~ations npl (protest) quejas fpl; ~ative n representante m/f; (US: POL) diputado/a m/f ♦ adj representativo

repress [rɪ'pres] vt reprimir; ~ion [-'preʃən] n represión f

reprieve [rɪ'priːv] n (LAW) indulto; (fig) alivio

reprisals [rɪ'praɪzlz] npl represalias fpl

reproach [rɪ'prəutʃ] n reproche m ♦ vt: to ~ sb for sth reprochar algo a uno;

~ful adj de reproche, de acusación

reproduce [riːprə'djuːs] vt reproducir ♦ vi reproducirse; **reproduction** [-'dʌkʃən] n reproducción f

reproof [rɪ'pruːf] n: to ~ sb for sth reprochar algo a uno

reptile ['reptaɪl] n reptil m

republic [rɪ'pʌblɪk] n república; ~an adj, n republicano/a m/f

repudiate [rɪ'pjuːdɪeɪt] vt rechazar; (violence etc) repudiar

repulsive [rɪ'pʌlsɪv] adj repulsivo

reputable ['repjutəbl] adj (make etc) de renombre

reputation [repju'teɪʃən] n reputación f

reputed [rɪ'pjuːtɪd] adj supuesto; ~ly adv según dicen or se dice

request [rɪ'kwest] n petición f; (formal) solicitud f ♦ vt: to ~ sth of or from sb solicitar algo a uno; ~ stop (BRIT) n parada discrecional

require [rɪ'kwaɪə*] vt (need: subj: person) necesitar, tener necesidad de; (: thing, situation) exigir; (want) pedir; to ~ sb to do sth pedir a uno que haga algo; ~ment n requisito; (need) necesidad f

requisition [rekwɪ'zɪʃən] n: ~ (for) solicitud f (de) ♦ vt (MIL) requisar

rescue ['reskjuː] n rescate m ♦ vt rescatar; ~ party n expedición f de salvamento; ~r n salvador m/f

research [rɪ'sɜːtʃ] n investigaciones fpl ♦ vt investigar; ~er n investigador(a) m/f

resemblance [rɪ'zembləns] n parecido

resemble [rɪ'zembl] vt parecerse a

resent [rɪ'zent] vt tomar a mal; ~ful adj resentido; ~ment n resentimiento

reservation [rezə'veɪʃən] n reserva

reserve [rɪ'zɜːv] n reserva; (SPORT) reserva; (SPORT) reservar; ~s npl (MIL) reserva; **in ~** de reserva; ~d adj reservado

reshuffle [riː'ʃʌfl] n: **Cabinet ~** (POL) remodelación f del gabinete

residence ['rezidəns] n (formal: home) domicilio; (length of stay) permanencia; ~ **permit** n (BRIT) n permiso de permanencia

resident ['rezidənt] n (of area) vecino/a; (in hotel) huésped/a m/f ♦ adj (population) permanente; (doctor) residente; **~ial** [-'denʃəl] adj residencial

residue ['rezidjuː] n resto

resign [rɪ'zaɪn] vt renunciar a ♦ vi dimitir; **to ~ o.s.** to (situation) resignarse a; **~ation** [rezɪg'neɪʃən] n dimisión f; (state of mind) resignación f; **~ed** adj resignado

resilient [rɪ'zɪlɪənt] adj (material) elástico; (person) resistente

resist [rɪ'zɪst] vt resistir, oponerse a; **~ance** n resistencia

resolute ['rezəluːt] adj resuelto; (refusal) tajante

resolution [rezə'luːʃən] n (gen) resolución f

resolve [rɪ'zɔlv] n resolución f ♦ vt resolver ♦ vi: **to ~ to do** resolver hacer; **~d** adj resuelto

resort [rɪ'zɔːt] n (town) centro turístico; (recourse) recurso ♦ vi: **to ~ to** recurrir a; **in the last ~** como último recurso

resounding [rɪ'zaundɪŋ] adj sonoro, (fig) clamoroso

resource [rɪ'sɔːs] n recurso; **~s** npl recursos mpl; **~ful** adj despabilado, ingenioso

respect [rɪs'pekt] n respeto ♦ vt respetar; **~s** npl recuerdos mpl, saludos mpl; **with ~ to** con respeto a; **in this ~** en cuanto a eso; **~able** adj respetable; (large: amount) apreciable; (passable) tolerable; **~ful** adj respetuoso

respective [rɪs'pektɪv] adj respectivo; **~ly** adv respectivamente

respite ['respaɪt] n respiro

respond [rɪs'pɔnd] vi responder; (react) reaccionar; **response** [-'pɔns] n respuesta; reacción f

responsibility [rɪspɔnsɪ'bɪlɪtɪ] n

responsabilidad f

responsible [rɪs'pɔnsɪbl] adj (character) serio, formal; (job) de confianza; (liable): **~ (for)** responsable (de)

responsive [rɪs'pɔnsɪv] adj sensible

rest [rest] n descanso, reposo; (MUS, pause) pausa, silencio; (support) apoyo; (remainder) resto ♦ vi descansar; (be supported): **to ~ on** descansar sobre ♦ vt (lean): **to ~ sth on/against** apoyar algo en o sobre/contra; **the ~ of them** (people, objects) los demás; **it ~s with him to ...** depende de él o que ...

restaurant ['restərɔn] n restaurante m; **~ car** (BRIT) n (RAIL) coche-comedor m

restful ['restful] adj descansado, tranquilo

rest home n residencia para jubilados

restive ['restɪv] adj inquieto; (horse) rebelón(ona)

restless ['restlɪs] adj inquieto

restoration [restə'reɪʃən] n restauración f; devolución f

restore [rɪ'stɔː*] vt (building) restaurar; (sth stolen) devolver; (health) restablecer; (to power) volver a poner a

restrain [rɪs'treɪn] vt (feeling) contener, refrenar; (person): **to ~ (from doing)** disuadir (de hacer); **~ed** adj reservado; **~t** n (restriction) restricción f; (moderation) moderación f; (of manner) reserva

restrict [rɪs'trɪkt] vt restringir, limitar; **~ion** [-kʃən] n restricción f, limitación f; **~ive** adj restrictivo

rest room n (US) n aseos mpl

result [rɪ'zʌlt] n resultado ♦ vi: **to ~ in** terminar en, tener por resultado; **as a ~ of** a consecuencia de

resume [rɪ'zjuːm] vt reanudar ♦ vi comenzar de nuevo

résumé ['reɪzjuːmeɪ] n resumen m; (US) currículum m

resumption [rɪ'zʌmpʃən] n reanudación f

resurgence [rɪ'səːdʒəns] *n* resurgimiento

resurrection [rezəˈrekʃən] *n* resurrección *f*

resuscitate [rɪ'sʌsɪteɪt] *vt (MED)* resucitar

retail ['riːteɪl] *adj, adv* al por menor; **~r** *n* detallista *m/f*; **~ price** *n* precio de venta al público

retain [rɪ'teɪn] *vt (keep)* retener, conservar; **~er** *n (fee)* anticipo

retaliate [rɪ'tælɪeɪt] *vi*: **to ~ (against)** tomar represalias (contra); **retaliation** [-'eɪʃən] *n* represalias *fpl*

retarded [rɪ'tɑːdɪd] *adj* retrasado

retch [retʃ] *vi* dársele a uno arcadas

retentive [rɪ'tentɪv] *adj (memory)* retentivo

retire [rɪ'taɪə*] *vi (give up work)* jubilarse; *(withdraw)* retirarse; *(go to bed)* acostarse; **~d** *adj (person)* jubilado; **~ment** *n (giving up work: state)* retiro; *(: act)* jubilación *f*

retiring *adj (leaving)* saliente; *(shy)* retraído

retort [rɪ'tɔːt] *vi* contestar

retrace [riː'treɪs] *vt*: **to ~ one's steps** volver sobre sus pasos, desandar lo andado

retract [rɪ'trækt] *vt (statement)* retirar; *(claws)* retraer; *(undercarriage, aerial)* replegar

retrain [riː'treɪn] *vt* reciclar; **~ing** *n* readaptación *f* profesional

retread ['riːtred] *n* neumático *(SP)* o llanta *(AM)* recauchutado/a

retreat [rɪ'triːt] *n (place)* retiro; *(MIL)* retirada *f* ♦ *vi* retirarse

retribution [retrɪ'bjuːʃən] *n* desquite *m*

retrieval [rɪ'triːvəl] *n* recuperación *f*

retrieve [rɪ'triːv] *vt* recobrar; *(situation, honour)* salvar; *(COMPUT)* recuperar; *(error)* reparar; **~r** *n* perro cobrador

retrospect ['retrəspekt] *n*: **in ~** retrospectivamente; **~ive** [-'spektɪv] *adj* retrospectivo; *(law)* retroactivo

return [rɪ'təːn] *n (going or coming back)* vuelta, regreso; *(of sth stolen etc)* devolución *f*; *(FINANCE: from land, shares)* ganancia, ingresos *mpl* ♦ *cpd (journey)* de regreso; *(BRIT: ticket)* de ida y vuelta; *(match)* de vuelta ♦ *vi (person etc: come or go back)* volver, regresar; *(symptoms etc)* reaparecer; *(regain)*: **to ~ to** recuperar ♦ *vt* devolver; *(favour, love etc)* corresponder a; *(verdict)* pronunciar; *(POL: candidate)* elegir; **~s** *npl (COMM)* ingresos *mpl*; **in ~ (for)** a cambio (de); **by ~ of post** a vuelta de correo; **many happy ~s (of the day)!** ¡feliz cumpleaños!

reunion [riː'juːnɪən] *n (of family)* reunión *f*; *(of two people, school)* reencuentro

reunite [riːjuː'naɪt] *vt* reunir; *(reconcile)* reconciliar

rev [rev] *(AUT) n abbr* (= *revolution*) revolución *f* ♦ *vt (also:* **~ up**) acelerar

reveal [rɪ'viːl] *vt* revelar; **~ing** *adj* revelador(a)

revel ['revl] *vi*: **to ~ in sth/in doing sth** gozar de algo/con hacer algo

revenge [rɪ'vendʒ] *n* venganza; **to take ~ on** vengarse de

revenue ['revənjuː] *n* ingresos *mpl*, rentas *fpl*

reverberate [rɪ'vəːbəreɪt] *vi (sound)* resonar, retumbar; *(fig: shock)* repercutir

reverence ['revərəns] *n* reverencia

Reverend ['revərənd] *adj (in titles)*: **the ~ John Smith** *(Anglican)* el Reverendo John Smith; *(Catholic)* el Padre John Smith; *(Protestant)* el Pastor John Smith

reversal [rɪ'vəːsl] *n (of order)* inversión *f*; *(of direction, policy)* cambio; *(of decision)* revocación *f*

reverse [rɪ'vəːs] *n (opposite)* contrario; *(back: of cloth)* revés *m*; *(: of coin)* reverso; *(: of paper)* dorso; *(AUT: also:* **~ gear**) marcha atrás; *(setback)* revés *m*

◆ adj (order) inverso; (direction) contrario; (process) opuesto ◆ vt (decision, AUT) dar marcha atrás a; (position, function) invertir ◆ vi (BRIT: AUT) dar marcha atrás; **~-charge call** (BRIT) n llamada a cobro revertido; **reversing lights** (BRIT) npl (AUT) luces fpl de retroceso

revert |rɪ'vɜːt| vi: **to ~** volver a

review |rɪ'vjuː| n (magazine, MIL) revista; (of book, film) reseña; (US: examination) repaso, examen m ◆ vt repasar, examinar; (MIL) pasar revista a; (book, film) reseñar; **~er** n crítico/a

revise |rɪ'vaɪz| vt (manuscript) corregir; (opinion) modificar; (price, procedure) revisar ◆ vi (study) repasar; **revision** |rɪ'vɪʒn| n corrección f; modificación f; (for exam) repaso

revival |rɪ'vaɪvl| n (recovery) reanimación f; (of interest) renacimiento m; (THEATRE) reestreno; (of faith) despertar m

revive |rɪ'vaɪv| vt resucitar; (custom) restablecer; (hope) despertar; (play) reestrenar ◆ vi (person) volver en sí; (business) reactivar

revolt |rɪ'vəʊlt| n rebelión f ◆ vi rebelarse, sublevarse ◆ vt dar asco a, repugnar; **~ing** adj asqueroso, repugnante

revolution |revə'luːʃən| n revolución f; **~ary** adj, n revolucionario/a m/f; **~ize** vt revolucionar

revolve |rɪ'vɒlv| vi dar vueltas, girar; (life, discussion): **to ~ (a)round** girar en torno a

revolver |rɪ'vɒlvə*| n revólver m

revolving |rɪ'vɒlvɪŋ| adj (chair, door etc) giratorio

revue |rɪ'vjuː| n (THEATRE) revista

revulsion |rɪ'vʌlʃən| n asco, repugnancia

reward |rɪ'wɔːd| n premio, recompensa f ◆ vt: **to ~ (for)** recompensar o premiar (por); **~ing** adj (fig) valioso

rewind |riː'waɪnd| (irreg) vt rebobinar

rewire |riː'waɪə*| vt (house) renovar la instalación eléctrica de

rheumatism |'ruːmətɪzəm| n reumatismo, reúma m

Rhine |raɪn| n: **the ~** el (río) Rin

rhinoceros |raɪ'nɒsərəs| n rinoceronte m

rhododendron |rəʊdə'dendrn| n rododendro

Rhone |rəʊn| n: **the ~** el (río) Ródano

rhubarb |'ruːbɑːb| n ruibarbo

rhyme |raɪm| n rima; (verse) poesía

rhythm |'rɪðm| n ritmo

rib |rɪb| n (ANAT) costilla ◆ vt (mock) tomar el pelo a

ribbon |'rɪbən| n cinta; **in ~s** (torn) hecho trizas

rice |raɪs| n arroz m; **~ pudding** n arroz m con leche

rich |rɪtʃ| adj rico; (soil) fértil; (food) pesado; (: sweet) empalagoso; (abundant): **~ in** (minerals etc) rico en; **the ~** npl los ricos; **~es** npl riqueza; **~ly** adv ricamente; (deserved, earned) bien

rickets |'rɪkɪts| n raquitismo

rid |rɪd| (pt, pp rid) vt: **to ~ sb of sth** librar a uno de algo; **to get ~ of** deshacerse o desembarazarse de

ridden |'rɪdn| pp of ride

riddle |'rɪdl| n (puzzle) acertijo; (mystery) enigma m, misterio ◆ vt: **to be ~d with** ser lleno o plagado de

ride |raɪd| (pt rode, pp ridden) n paseo; (distance covered) viaje m, recorrido ◆ vi (as sport) montar; (go somewhere: on horse, bicycle) dar un paseo, pasearse; (travel: on bicycle, motorcycle, bus) viajar ◆ vt (a horse) montar a; (a bicycle, motorcycle) andar en; (distance) recorrer; **to take sb for a ~** (fig) engañar a uno; **~r** n (on horse) jinete/a m/f; (on bicycle) ciclista m/f; (on motorcycle) motociclista m/f

ridge |rɪdʒ| n (of hill) cresta; (of roof) caballete m; (wrinkle) arruga

ridicule [ˈrɪdɪkjuːl] n irrisión f, burla
♦ vt poner en ridículo, burlarse de;
ridiculous [-ˈdɪkjuləs] adj ridículo

riding [ˈraɪdɪŋ] n equitación f; **I like ~**
me gusta montar a caballo; **~ school**
n escuela de equitación

rife [raɪf] adj: **to be ~** ser muy común;
to be ~ with abundar en

riffraff [ˈrɪfræf] n gentuza

rifle [ˈraɪfl] n rifle m, fusil m ♦ vt
saquear; **~ through** (papers)
registrar; **~ range** n campo de tiro; (at
fair) tiro al blanco

rift [rɪft] n rifle m, fusil m ♦ vt
(fig:
disagreement) desavenencia

rig [rɪg] n (also: oil ~: at sea) plataforma
petrolera ♦ vt (election etc) amañar;
~ out (BRIT) vt disfrazar; **~ up** vt
improvisar; **~ging** n (NAUT) aparejo

right [raɪt] adj (correct) correcto,
exacto; (suitable) indicado, debido;
(proper) apropiado; (just) justo; (morally
good) bueno; (not left) derecho ♦ n
bueno; (title, claim) derecho (not left)
derecha ♦ adv bien, correctamente;
(not left) a la derecha; (exactly): **~ now**
ahora mismo ♦ vt enderezar; (correct)
corregir ♦ excl ¡bueno!, ¡está bien!; **to
be ~** (person) tener razón; (answer) estar
correcto; **is that the ~ time?** (of
clock) ¿es esa la hora buena?; **by ~s** en
justicia; **on the ~** a la derecha; **to be
in the ~** tener razón; **~ away** en
seguida; **~ in the middle**
exactamente en el centro; **~ angle** n
ángulo recto; **~eous** [ˈraɪtʃəs] adj
justado, honrado; (anger) justificado;
~ful adj legítimo; **~-handed** adj
diestro; **~-hand man** n brazo
derecho; **~-hand side** n derecha; **~ly**
adv correctamente, debidamente; (with
reason) con razón; **~ of way** n (on
path etc) derecho de paso; (AUT)
prioridad f; **~-wing** adj (POL)
derechista

rigid [ˈrɪdʒɪd] adj rígido; (person, ideas)
inflexible

rigmarole [ˈrɪgmərəʊl] n galimatías m
inv

rigorous [ˈrɪgərəs] adj riguroso

rile [raɪl] vt irritar

rim [rɪm] n borde m; (of spectacles) aro;
(of wheel) llanta

rind [raɪnd] n (of bacon) corteza; (of
lemon etc) cáscara; (of cheese) costra

ring [rɪŋ] (pt rang, pp rung) n (of
metal) aro; (on finger) anillo; (of people)
corro; (of objects) círculo; (gang)
banda; (for boxing) cuadrilátero; (of
circus) pista; (bull ~) ruedo, plaza;
(sound of bell) toque m ♦ vi (on
telephone) llamar por teléfono; (bell)
repicar; (doorbell, phone) sonar; (also:
~ out) sonar; (ears) zumbar ♦ vt (BRIT:
TEL) llamar, telefonear, hacer
sonar; (doorbell) tocar; **to give sb a ~**
(BRIT: TEL) llamar o telefonear a
alguien; **~ back** (BRIT) vt, vi (TEL)
devolver la llamada; **~ off** (BRIT) vi
(TEL) colgar, cortar la comunicación;
~ up (BRIT) vt (TEL) llamar, telefonear;
~ing n (of bell) repique m; (of phone)
el sonar; (in ears) zumbido; **~ing tone**
n (TEL) tono de llamada; **~leader** n (of
gang) cabecilla m; **~lets** [ˈrɪŋlɪts] npl
rizos mpl, bucles mpl; **~ road** (BRIT) n
carretera periférica or de circunvalación

rink [rɪŋk] n (also: ice ~) pista de hielo

rinse [rɪns] n aclarado; (dye) tinte m
♦ vt aclarar; (mouth) enjuagar

riot [ˈraɪət] n motín m, disturbio ♦ vi
amotinarse; **to run ~** desmandarse;
~ous adj alborotado; (party) bullicioso

rip [rɪp] n rasgón m, rasgadura ♦ vt
rasgar, desgarrar ♦ vi rasgarse,
desgarrarse; **~cord** n cabo de desgarre

ripe [raɪp] adj maduro; **~n** vt madurar;
(cheese) curar ♦ vi madurar

ripple [ˈrɪpl] n onda, rizo; (sound)
murmullo ♦ vi rizarse

rise [raɪz] (pt rose, pp risen) n (slope)
cuesta, pendiente f; (hill) altura; (BRIT:
in wages) aumento; (in prices,
temperature) subida; (fig: to power etc)

ascenso ♦ vi subir; (waters) crecer; (sun, moon) salir; (person: from bed etc) levantarse; (also: ~ up: rebel) sublevarse; (in rank) ascender; **to give ~ to** dar lugar o origen a; **to ~ to the occasion** ponerse a la altura de las circunstancias; **risen** ['rɪzn] pp of **rise**; **rising** adj (increasing: number) creciente; (: prices) en aumento o alza; (tide) creciente; (sun, moon) naciente

risk [rɪsk] n riesgo, peligro ♦ vt arriesgar; (run the ~ of) exponerse a; **to take** or **run the ~ of doing** correr el riesgo de hacer; **at ~** en peligro; **at one's own ~** bajo su propia responsabilidad; **~y** adj arriesgado, peligroso

rissole ['rɪsəul] n croqueta

rite [raɪt] n rito; **last ~s** exequias fpl

ritual ['rɪtjuəl] adj ritual ♦ n ritual m, rito

rival ['raɪvl] n rival m/f; (in business) competidor(a) m/f ♦ adj rival, opuesto ♦ vt competir con; **~ry** n competencia

river ['rɪvə*] n río ♦ cpd (port) del río; (traffic) fluvial; **up/down~** río arriba/abajo; **~bank** n orilla (del río); **~bed** n lecho, cauce m

rivet ['rɪvɪt] n roblón m, remache m ♦ vt (fig) captar

Riviera [rɪvɪ'eərə] n: **the (French) ~** la Costa Azul (francesa)

road [rəud] n camino; (motorway etc) carretera; (in town) calle f ♦ cpd (accident) de tráfico; **major/minor ~** carretera principal/secundaria; **~ accident** n accidente m de tráfico; **~block** n barricada; **~hog** n loco/a del volante; **~ map** n mapa m de carreteras; **~ rage** n agresividad en la carretera; **~ safety** n seguridad f vial; **~side** n borde m (del camino); **~sign** n señal f de tráfico; **~ user** n usuario/a de la vía pública; **~way** n calzada; **~works** npl obras fpl; **~worthy** adj (car) en buen estado para circular

roam [rəum] vi vagar

roar [rɔ:*] n rugido, (of vehicle, storm) estruendo; (of laughter) carcajada ♦ vi rugir; hacer estruendo; **to ~ with laughter** reírse a carcajadas; **to do a ~ing trade** hacer buen negocio

roast [rəust] n carne f asada, asado ♦ vt asar; (coffee) tostar; **~ beef** n rosbif m

rob [rɔb] vt robar; **to ~ sb of sth** robar algo a uno; (fig: deprive) quitar algo a uno; **~ber** n ladrón/ona m/f; **~bery** n robo

robe [rəub] n (for ceremony etc) toga; (also: bath~, US) albornoz m

robin ['rɔbɪn] n petirrojo

robot ['rəubɔt] n robot m

robust [rəu'bʌst] adj robusto, fuerte

rock [rɔk] n roca; (boulder) peña, peñasco; (: small stone) piedrecita; (BRIT: sweet) ≈ pirulí ♦ vt (swing gently: cradle) balancear, mecer; (: child) arrullar; (shake) sacudir ♦ vi mecerse, balancearse; sacudirse; **on the ~s** (drink) con hielo; (marriage etc) en ruinas; **~ and roll** n rocanrol m; **~-bottom** n (fig) punto más bajo; **~ery** n cuadro alpino

rocket ['rɔkɪt] n cohete m

rocking ['rɔkɪŋ]: **~ chair** n mecedora; **~ horse** n caballo de balancín

rocky ['rɔkɪ] adj rocoso

rod [rɔd] n vara, varilla; (also: fishing ~) caña

rode [rəud] pt of **ride**

rodent ['rəudnt] n roedor m

roe [rəu] n (species: also: ~ deer) corzo; (of fish: hard/soft) hueva/lecha

rogue [rəug] n pícaro, pillo

role [rəul] n papel m

roll [rəul] n rollo; (of bank notes) fajo; (also: bread ~) panecillo; (register, list) lista, nómina; (sound: of drums etc) redoble m ♦ vt hacer rodar; (also: ~ up: string) enrollar; (: sleeves) arremangar; (cigarette) liar; (also: ~ out: pastry) aplanar; (flatten: road, lawn) apisonar ♦ vi rodar; (drum) redoblar; (ship) balancearse; **~ about** or **around** vi (*person*) revolcarse; (*object*) rodar (por); **~ by** vi (*time*) pasar; **~ over** vi dar una vuelta; **~ up** vi (*fig: arrive*) aparecer ♦ vt (*carpet*) arrollar; **~ call** n: **to take a ~ call** pasar lista; **~er** n rodillo; (*wheel*) rueda; (*for road*) apisonadora; (*for hair*) rulo; **~erblade** la patín m (en línea); **~er coaster** n montaña rusa; **~er skates** npl patines mpl de rueda

rolling ['rəulɪŋ] *adj* (*landscape*) ondulado; **~ pin** n rodillo (de cocina); **~ stock** n (*RAIL*) material m rodante

ROM [rɔm] n abbr (*COMPUT: = read only memory*) ROM f

Roman ['rəumən] *adj* romano/a; **~ Catholic** *adj, n* católico/a m/f (romano/a)

romance [rə'mæns] n (*love affair*) amor m; (*charm*) lo romántico; (*novel*) novela de amor

Romania [ru:'meɪnɪə] n = **Rumania**

Roman numeral n número romano

romantic [rə'mæntɪk] *adj* romántico

Rome [rəum] n Roma

romp [rɔmp] n retozo, juego ♦ vi (*also: ~ about*) jugar, brincar

rompers ['rɔmpəz] npl pelele m

roof [ru:f] (*pl* **~s**) n (*gen*) techo; (*of house*) techo, tejado ♦ vt techar, poner techo a; **the ~ of the mouth** el paladar; **~ing** n techumbre f; **~ rack** n (*AUT*) baca, portaequipajes m inv

rook [ruk] n (*bird*) graja; (*CHESS*) torre f

room [ru:m] n cuarto, habitación f, pieza (*esp AM*); (*also: bed~*) dormitorio; (*in school etc*) sala; (*space, scope*) sitio, cabida; **~s** npl (*lodging*) alojamiento; **"~s to let", "~s for rent"** (*US*) "se alquilan cuartos"; **single/double ~** habitación individual/doble o para dos personas; **~ing house** (*US*) n pensión f; **~mate** n compañero/a de cuarto; **~ service** n servicio de habitaciones; **~y** *adj* espacioso; (*garment*) amplio

roost [ru:st] vi pasar la noche

rooster ['ru:stə*] n gallo

root [ru:t] n raíz f ♦ vi arraigarse; **~ about** vi (*fig*) buscar y rebuscar; **~ for** vt fus (*support*) apoyar a; **~ out** vt desarraigar

rope [rəup] n cuerda; (*NAUT*) cable m ♦ vt (*tie*) atar or amarrar con cuerda; (*climbers: also: ~ together*) encordarse; (*an area: also: ~ off*) acordonar; **to know the ~s** (*fig*) conocer los trucos (del oficio); **~ in** vt (*fig*): **to ~ sb in** persuadir a uno a tomar parte

rosary ['rəuzərɪ] n rosario

rose [rəuz] pt of **rise** ♦ n rosa; (*shrub*) rosal m; (*on watering can*) roseta

rosé ['rəuzeɪ] n vino rosado

rosebud ['rəuzbʌd] n capullo de rosa

rosebush ['rəuzbʌʃ] n rosal m

rosemary ['rəuzmərɪ] n romero

roster ['rɔstə*] n: **duty ~** lista de deberes

rostrum ['rɔstrəm] n tribuna

rosy ['rəuzɪ] *adj* rosado, sonrosado; **a ~ future** un futuro prometedor

rot [rɔt] n podredumbre f; (*fig: pej*) tonterías fpl ♦ vt pudrir ♦ vi pudrirse

rota ['rəutə] n (*sistema m de*) turnos mpl

rotary ['rəutərɪ] *adj* rotativo

rotate [rəu'teɪt] vt (*revolve*) hacer girar, dar vueltas a; (*jobs*) alternar ♦ vi girar, dar vueltas; **rotating** *adj* rotativo

rotation [-'teɪʃən] n rotación f

rotten ['rɔtn] *adj* (*meat*) podrido; (*dishonest*) corrompido; (*inf: bad*) pocho; **to feel ~** (*ill*) sentirse fatal

rotund [rəu'tʌnd] *adj* regordete

rouble ['ru:bl] (*US* **ruble**) n rublo

rough [rʌf] *adj* (*skin, surface*) áspero; (*terrain*) quebrado; (*road*) desigual; (*voice*) bronco; (*person, manner*) tosco, grosero; (*weather*) borrascoso; (*treatment*) brutal; (*sea*) picado; (*town, area*) peligroso; (*cloth*) basto; (*plan*) preliminar; (*guess*) aproximado ♦ n (*GOLF*): **in the ~** en las hierbas altas; **to ~ it** vivir sin comodidades; **to sleep ~**

(BRIT) pasar la noche al raso; **~age** n fibra(s) f(pl); **~-and-ready** adj improvisado; **~ copy** n borrador m; **~ draft** n = copy; **~ly** adv (handle) torpemente; (make) toscamente; (speak) groseramente; (approximately) aproximadamente; **~ness** n (of surface) aspereza; (of person) rudeza

roulette [ruːˈlet] n ruleta

Rumania [ruːˈmeɪnɪə] n = Rumania

round [raund] adj redondo ♦ n círculo; (BRIT: of toast) rebanada; (of policeman) ronda; (of milkman) recorrido; (of doctor) visitas fpl; (game: of cards, in competition) partida; (of ammunition) cartucho; (BOXING) asalto; (of talks) ronda ♦ vt (corner) doblar ♦ prep alrededor de; (surrounding): **~ his neck/the table** en su cuello/alrededor de la mesa; (in a circular movement): **to move ~ the room/sail ~ the world** dar una vuelta a la habitación/ circunnavegar el mundo; (in various directions): **to move ~ a room/house** moverse por toda la habitación/casa; (approximately): **~ about** alrededor de; **the long way ~** por el camino menos directo; **all year ~** durante todo el año; **it's just ~ the corner** (fig) está a la vuelta de la esquina; **the clock** adv las 24 horas; **to go ~ to sb's (house)** ir a casa de uno; **to go ~ the back** pasar por atrás; **enough to go ~** bastante (para todos); **a ~ of applause** una salva de aplausos; **a ~ of drinks/ sandwiches** una ronda de bebidas/ bocadillos; **~ off** vt (speech etc) acabar, poner término a; **~ up** vt (cattle) acorralar; (people) reunir; (price) redondear; **~about** n (BRIT) n (AUT) isleta; (at fair) tiovivo ♦ adj (route, means) indirecto; **~ers** n (game) juego similar al béisbol; **~ly** adv (fig) rotundamente; **~ trip** n viaje m de ida y vuelta; **~up** n rodeo; (of criminals) redada; (of news) resumen m

rouse [rauz] vt (wake up) despertar; (stir up) suscitar; **rousing** adj (cheer, welcome) caluroso

route [ruːt] n ruta, camino; (of bus) recorrido; (of shipping) derrota

routine [ruːˈtiːn] adj rutinario ♦ n rutina; (THEATRE) número

rove [rəuv] vt vagar o errar por

row¹ [rəu] n (line) fila, hilera; (KNITTING) pasada ♦ vi (in boat) remar ♦ vt conducir remando; **4 days in a ~** 4 días seguidos

row² [rau] n (racket) escándalo; (dispute) bronca, pelea; (scolding) regaño ♦ vi pelear(se)

rowboat [ˈrəubəut] (US) n bote m de remos

rowdy [ˈraudɪ] adj (person: noisy) ruidoso; (occasion) alborotado

rowing [ˈrəuɪŋ] n remo; **~ boat** (BRIT) n bote m de remos

royal [ˈrɔɪəl] adj real; **R~ Air Force** n Fuerzas fpl Aéreas Británicas; **~ty** n (~ persons) familia real; (payment to author) derechos mpl de autor

rpm abbr (= revs per minute) r.p.m.

R.S.V.P. abbr (= répondez s'il vous plaît) SRC

Rt. Hon. abbr (BRIT: = Right Honourable) título honorífico de diputado

rub [rʌb] vt frotar; (scrub) restregar ♦ n: **to give sth a ~** frotar algo; **to ~ sb up** o (US) **sb the wrong way** entrarle uno por mal ojo; **~ off** vi borrarse; **~ off on** vt fus influir en; **~ out** vt borrar

rubber [ˈrʌbə*] n caucho, goma; (BRIT: eraser) goma de borrar; **~ band** n goma, gomita; **~ plant** n ficus m

rubbish [ˈrʌbɪʃ] n basura; (waste) desperdicios mpl; (fig: pej) tonterías fpl; (junk) pacotilla; **~ bin** (BRIT) n cubo (SP) o bote m (AM) de la basura; **~ dump** n vertedero, basurero

rubble [ˈrʌbl] n escombros mpl

ruble [ˈruːbl] (US) n = rouble

ruby [ˈruːbɪ] n rubí m

rucksack ['rʌksæk] n mochila

rudder ['rʌdə*] n timón m

ruddy ['rʌdɪ] adj (face) rubicundo; (inf: damned) condenado

rude [ru:d] adj (impolite: person) mal educado; (: word, manners) grosero; (crude) crudo; (indecent) indecente; **~ness** n descortesía

ruffle ['rʌfl] vt (hair) despeinar; (clothes) arrugar; **to get ~d** (fig: person) alterarse

rug [rʌg] n alfombra; (BRIT: blanket) manta

rugby ['rʌgbɪ] n (also: ~ football) rugby m

rugged ['rʌgɪd] adj (landscape) accidentado; (features) robusto

ruin ['ru:ɪn] n ruina ♦ vt arruinar; (spoil) estropear; **~s** npl ruinas fpl, restos mpl

rule [ru:l] n (norm) norma, costumbre f; (regulation, ruler) regla; (government) dominio ♦ vt (country, person) gobernar ♦ vi gobernar; (LAW) fallar; **as a ~** por regla general; **~ out** vt excluir; **~d** adj (paper) rayado; **~r** n (sovereign) soberano; (for measuring) regla; **ruling** adj (party) gobernante; (class) dirigente ♦ n (LAW) fallo, decisión f

rum [rʌm] n ron m

Rumania [ru:'meɪnɪə] n Rumanía; **~n** adj rumano/a ♦ n rumano/a m/f; (LING) rumano

rumble ['rʌmbl] n (noise) ruido sordo ♦ vi retumbar, hacer un ruido sordo; (stomach, pipe) sonar

rummage ['rʌmɪdʒ] vi (search) hurgar

rumour ['ru:mə*] (US rumor) n rumor m ♦ vt: **it is ~ed that** ... se rumorea que ...

rump [rʌmp] n (of animal) ancas fpl, grupa; **~ steak** n filete m de lomo

rumpus ['rʌmpəs] n lío, jaleo

run [rʌn] (pt ran, pp run) n (fast pace): **at a ~** corriendo; (SPORT, in tights) carrera; (outing) paseo, excursión f; (distance travelled) trayecto; (series)

serie f; (THEATRE) temporada; (SKI) pista ♦ vt correr; (operate: business) dirigir; (: competition, course) organizar; (: hotel, house) administrar, llevar; (COMPUT) ejecutar; (pass: hand) pasar; (PRESS: feature) publicar ♦ vi correr; (work: machine) funcionar, marchar; (bus, train: operate) circular; (: travel) ir; (continue: play) seguir; (: contract) ser válido; (flow: river) fluir; (colours, washing) desteñirse; (in election) ser candidato; (ticket) hubo mucha demanda de; **in the long ~** a la larga; **on the ~** en fuga; **I'll ~ you to the station** te llevaré a la estación (en coche); **to ~ a risk** correr un riesgo; **to ~ a bath** llenar la bañera; **~ about or around** vi (children) correr por todos lados; **~ across** vt fus (find) dar o topar con; **~ away** vi huir; **~ down** vt (production) ir reduciendo; (factory) ir restringiendo la producción en; (subj: car) atropellar; (criticize) criticar; **to be ~ down** (person: tired) estar debilitado; **~ in** (BRIT) vt (car) rodar; **~ into** vt fus (meet: person, trouble) tropezar con; (collide with) chocar con; **~ off** vt (water) dejar correr; (copies) sacar ♦ vi huir corriendo; **~ out** vi (person) salir corriendo; (liquid) irse; (lease) caducar, vencer; (money etc) acabarse; **~ out of** vt fus quedar sin; **~ over** vt (AUT) atropellar ♦ vt fus (revise) repasar; **~ through** vt fus (instructions) repasar; **~ up** vt (debt) contraer; **to ~ up against** (difficulties) tropezar con; **~away** adj (person) desbocado; (truck) sin frenos; (child) escapado de casa

rung [rʌŋ] pp of **ring** ♦ n (of ladder) escalón m, peldaño

runner ['rʌnə*] n (in race: person) corredor(a) m/f; (: horse) caballo; (on sledge) patín m; (on machine) carril m; **~ bean** (BRIT) n judía verde; **~-up** n subcampeón/ona m/f

running ['rʌnɪŋ] n (sport) atletismo;

(business) administración f ♦ adj (water, costs) corriente; (commentary) continuo; **to be in/out of the ~ for sth** tener/no tener posibilidades de ganar algo; **6 days** = 6 días seguidos; **~ commentary** n (TV, RADIO) comentario en directo; (on guided tour etc) comentario detallado; **~ costs** npl gastos mpl corrientes

runny ['rʌnɪ] adj fluido; (nose, eyes) gastante

run-of-the-mill adj común y corriente

runt [rʌnt] n (also pej) redrojo, enano

run-up n: **~ to** (election etc) período previo a

runway ['rʌnweɪ] n (AVIAT) pista de aterrizaje

rural ['rʊərl] adj rural

rush [rʌʃ] n ímpetu m; (hurry) prisa; (COMM) demanda repentina; (current) corriente f fuerte; (of feeling) torrente; (BOT) junco ♦ vt apresurar; (work) hacer de prisa ♦ vi correr, precipitarse; **~ hour** n horas fpl punta

rusk [rʌsk] n bizcocho tostado

Russia ['rʌʃə] n Rusia; **~n** adj ruso/a ♦ n ruso a m/f; (LING) ruso

rust [rʌst] n herrumbre f, moho ♦ vi oxidarse

rustic ['rʌstɪk] adj rústico

rustle ['rʌsl] vi susurrar ♦ vt (paper) hacer crujir

rustproof ['rʌstpruːf] adj inoxidable

rusty ['rʌstɪ] adj oxidado

rut [rʌt] n surco; (ZOOL) celo; **to be in a ~** ser esclavo de la rutina

ruthless ['ruːθlɪs] adj despiadado

rye [raɪ] n centeno

S, s

Sabbath ['sæbəθ] n domingo; (Jewish) sábado

sabotage ['sæbətɑːʒ] n sabotaje m ♦ vt sabotear

saccharin(e) ['sækərɪn] n sacarina

sachet ['sæʃeɪ] n sobrecito

sack [sæk] n (bag) saco, costal m ♦ vt (dismiss) despedir; (plunder) saquear; **to get the ~** ser despedido; **~ing** n despido; (material) arpillera

sacred ['seɪkrɪd] adj sagrado, santo

sacrifice ['sækrɪfaɪs] n sacrificio ♦ vt sacrificar

sad [sæd] adj (unhappy) triste; (deplorable) lamentable

saddle ['sædl] n silla (de montar); (of cycle) sillín m ♦ vt (horse) ensillar; **to be ~d with sth** (inf) quedar cargado con algo; **~bag** n alforja

sadistic [sə'dɪstɪk] adj sádico

sadly ['sædlɪ] adv lamentablemente; **to be ~ lacking in** estar por desgracia carente de

sadness ['sædnɪs] n tristeza

s.a.e. abbr (= stamped addressed envelope) sobre con las propias señas de uno y con sello

safari [sə'fɑːrɪ] n safari m

safe [seɪf] adj (out of danger) fuera de peligro; (not dangerous, sure) seguro; (unharmed) ileso ♦ n caja de caudales, caja fuerte; **~ and sound** sano y salvo; **(just) to be on the ~ side** para mayor seguridad; **~-conduct** n salvoconducto; **~-deposit** n (vault) cámara acorazada; (box) caja de seguridad; **~guard** n protección f, garantía ♦ vt proteger, defender; **~keeping** n custodia; **~ly** adv seguramente, con seguridad; **to arrive ~ly** llegar bien; **~ sex** n sexo seguro o sin riesgo

safety ['seɪftɪ] n seguridad f; **~ belt** n cinturón m (de seguridad); **~ pin** n imperdible m (SP), seguro (AM); **~ valve** n válvula de seguridad

saffron ['sæfrən] n azafrán m

sag [sæg] vi aflojarse

sage [seɪdʒ] n (herb) salvia; (man) sabio

Sagittarius [sædʒɪ'tɛərɪəs] n Sagitario

Sahara [sə'hɑːrə] n: **the ~** (Desert) el (desierto del) Sáhara

said [sed] *pt, pp of* **say**

sail [seɪl] *n* (on boat) vela; (trip): **to go for a ~** dar un paseo en barco ♦ *vt* (boat) gobernar ♦ *vi* (travel: ship) navegar; (SPORT) hacer vela; (begin voyage) salir; **they ~ed into Copenhagen** arribaron a Copenhague; **~ through** *vt fus* (exam) aprobar sin ningún problema; **~boat** (US) *n* velero, barco de vela; **~ing** *n* (SPORT) vela; **to go ~ing** hacer vela; **~ing boat** *n* barco de vela; **~ing ship** *n* velero; **~or** *n* marinero, marino

saint [seɪnt] *n* santo; **~ly** *adj* santo

sake [seɪk] *n*: **for the ~ of** por

salad ['sæləd] *n* ensalada; **~ bowl** *n* ensaladera; **~ cream** (BRIT) *n* (especie *f* de) mayonesa; **~ dressing** *n* aliño

salary ['sælərɪ] *n* sueldo

sale [seɪl] *n* venta; (at reduced prices) liquidación *f*, saldo; (auction) subasta; **~s** *npl* (total amount sold) ventas *fpl*, facturación *f*; **"for ~"** "se vende"; **on ~** en venta; **on ~ or return** (goods) venta por reposición; **~room** *n* sala de subastas; **~s assistant** (US **~s clerk**) *n* dependiente/a *m/f*; **salesman/woman** (irreg) *n* (in shop) dependiente/a *m/f*; (representative) viajante *m/f*

salmon ['sæmən] *n inv* salmón *m*

salon [sə'lu:n] *n* (hairdressing ~) peluquería; (beauty ~) salón *m* de belleza

saloon [sə'lu:n] *n* (US) bar *m*, taberna; (BRIT: AUT) (coche *m* de) turismo; (ship's lounge) cámara, salón *m*

salt [sɔlt] *n* sal *f* ♦ *vt* salar; (put ~ on) poner sal en; **~ cellar** *n* salero; **~water** *adj* de agua salada; **~y** *adj* salado

salute [sə'lu:t] *n* saludo; (of guns) salva ♦ *vt* saludar

salvage ['sælvɪdʒ] *n* (saving) salvamento, recuperación *f*; (things saved) objetos *mpl* salvados ♦ *vt* salvar

salvation [sæl'veɪʃən] *n* salvación *f*;

S~ Army *n* Ejército de Salvación

same [seɪm] *adj* mismo ♦ *pron*: **the ~** el/la mismo/a; (*likewise*) lo mismo; **the ~ book as** el mismo libro que; **at the ~ time** (at the ~ moment) al mismo tiempo; (*yet*) sin embargo; **all** *or* **just the ~** sin embargo, aun así; **to do the ~ (as sb)** hacer lo mismo (que uno); **the ~ to you!** ¡igualmente!

sample ['sɑ:mpl] *n* muestra ♦ *vt* (food) probar; (wine) catar

sanction ['sæŋkʃən] *n* aprobación *f* ♦ *vt* sancionar; aprobar; **~s** *npl* (POL) sanciones *fpl*

sanctity ['sæŋktɪtɪ] *n* santidad *f*; (inviolability) inviolabilidad *f*

sanctuary ['sæŋktjuərɪ] *n* santuario; (refuge) asilo, refugio; (for wildlife) reserva

sand [sænd] *n* arena; (beach) playa ♦ *vt* (also: ~ down) lijar

sandal ['sændl] *n* sandalia

sand: **~box** (US) *n* = **~pit**; **~castle** *n* castillo de arena; **~ dune** *n* duna; **~paper** *n* papel *m* de lija; **~pit** *n* (for children) cajón *m* de arena; **~stone** *n* piedra arenisca

sandwich ['sændwɪtʃ] *n* bocadillo (SP), sandwich *m*, emparedado (AM) ♦ *vt* intercalar; **~ed between** apretujado entre; **cheese/ham ~** sandwich de queso/jamón; **~ course** (BRIT) *n* curso de medio tiempo

sandy ['sændɪ] *adj* arenoso; (colour) rojizo

sane [seɪn] *adj* cuerdo; (sensible) sensato

sang [sæŋ] *pt of* **sing**

sanitary ['sænɪtərɪ] *adj* sanitario; (clean) higiénico; **~ towel** (US **~ napkin**) *n* paño higiénico, compresa

sanitation [sænɪ'teɪʃən] *n* (in house) servicios *mpl* higiénicos; (in town) servicio de desinfección; **~ department** (US) *n* departamento de limpieza y recogida de basuras

sanity ['sænɪtɪ] *n* cordura; (of

judgment) sensatez f

sank [sæŋk] *pt of* **sink**

Santa Claus [sæntə'klɔːz] *n* San Nicolás, Papá Noel

sap [sæp] *n* (*of plants*) savia ♦ *vt* (*strength*) minar, agotar

sapling ['sæplɪŋ] *n* árbol nuevo *or* joven

sapphire ['sæfaɪə*] *n* zafiro

sarcasm ['sɑːkæzm] *n* sarcasmo

sardine [sɑː'diːn] *n* sardina

Sardinia [sɑː'dɪnɪə] *n* Cerdeña

sash [sæʃ] *n* faja

sat [sæt] *pt, pp of* **sit**

Satan ['seɪtn] *n* Satanás *m*

satchel ['sætʃl] *n* (*child's*) cartera (SP), mochila (AM)

satellite ['sætəlaɪt] *n* satélite *m*; **~ dish** *n* antena de televisión por satélite; **~ television** *n* televisión f vía satélite

satin ['sætɪn] *n* raso ♦ *adj* de raso

satire ['sætaɪə*] *n* sátira

satisfaction [sætɪs'fækʃən] *n* satisfacción f

satisfactory [sætɪs'fæktərɪ] *adj* satisfactorio

satisfy ['sætɪsfaɪ] *vt* satisfacer; (*convince*) convencer; **~ing** *adj* satisfactorio

Saturday ['sætədɪ] *n* sábado

sauce [sɔːs] *n* salsa; (*sweet*) crema; jarabe *m*; **~pan** *n* cacerola, olla

saucer ['sɔːsə*] *n* platillo

Saudi ['saʊdɪ]: **~ Arabia** *n* Arabia Saudí *or* Saudita; **~ (Arabian)** *adj*, *n* saudí *m/f*, saudita *m/f*

sauna ['sɔːnə] *n* sauna

saunter ['sɔːntə*] *vi*: **to ~ in/out** entrar/salir sin prisa

sausage ['sɔsɪdʒ] *n* salchicha; **~ roll** *n* empanadita de salchicha

sauté ['səʊteɪ] *adj* salteado

savage ['sævɪdʒ] *adj* (*cruel, fierce*) feroz, furioso; (*primitive*) salvaje ♦ *n* salvaje *m/f* ♦ *vt* (*attack*) embestir

save [seɪv] *vt* (*rescue*) salvar, rescatar; (*money, time*) ahorrar; (*put by, keep*:

seat) guardar; (COMPUT) salvar (y guardar); (*avoid: trouble*) evitar; (SPORT) parar ♦ *vi* (*also: ~ up*) ahorrar ♦ *n* (SPORT) parada ♦ *prep* salvo, excepto

saving ['seɪvɪŋ] *n* (*on price etc*) economía ♦ *adj*: **the ~ grace of** el único mérito de; **~s** *npl* ahorros *mpl*; **~s account** *n* cuenta de ahorros; **~s bank** *n* caja de ahorros

saviour ['seɪvjə*] (US **savior**) *n* salvador/a *m/f*

savour ['seɪvə*] (US **savor**) *vt* saborear; **~y** *adj* sabroso; (*dish: not sweet*) salado

saw [sɔː] (*pt* **sawed**, *pp* **sawed** *or* **sawn**) *pt of* **see** ♦ *n* (*tool*) sierra ♦ *vt* serrar; **~dust** *n* (a)serrín *m*; **~mill** *n* aserradero; **~n-off shotgun** *n* escopeta de cañones recortados

saxophone ['sæksəfəʊn] *n* saxófono

say [seɪ] (*pt, pp* **said**) *n*: **to have one's ~** expresar su opinión ♦ *vt* decir; **to have a** *or* **some ~ in sth** tener voz *or* tener que ver en algo; **to ~ yes/no** decir que sí/no; **could you ~ that again?** ¿podría repetir eso?; **that is to ~** es decir; **that goes without ~ing** ni que decir tiene; **~ing** *n* dicho, refrán *m*

scab [skæb] *n* costra; (*pej*) esquirol *m*

scaffold ['skæfəʊld] *n* cadalso; **~ing** *n* andamio, andamiaje *m*

scald [skɔːld] *n* escaldadura ♦ *vt* escaldar

scale [skeɪl] *n* (*gen, MUS*) escala; (*of fish*) escama; (*of salaries, fees etc*) escalafón *m* ♦ *vt* (*mountain*) escalar; (*tree*) trepar; **~s** *npl* (*for weighing: small*) balanza; (*: large*) báscula; **on a large ~** en gran escala; **~ of charges** *n* tarifa, lista de precios; **~ down** *vt* reducir a escala

scallop ['skɒləp] *n* (ZOOL) venera; (SEWING) festón *m*

scalp [skælp] *n* cabellera ♦ *vt* escalpar

scampi ['skæmpɪ] *npl* gambas *fpl*

scan [skæn] *vt* (*examine*) escudriñar; (*glance at quickly*) dar un vistazo a; (TV,

RADAR) explorar, registrar ♦ *n* (MED): **to have a ~** pasar por el escáner

scandal ['skændl] *n* escándalo; (*gossip*) chismes *mpl*

Scandinavia [skændı'neıvıə] *n* Escandinavia *f*; **~n** *adj, n* escandinavo/a *m/f*

scant [skænt] *adj* escaso; **~y** *adj* (*meal*) insuficiente; (*clothes*) ligero

scapegoat ['skeıpgəut] *n* cabeza de turco, chivo expiatorio

scar [skɑː] *n* cicatriz *f*; (*fig*) señal *f* ♦ *vt* dejar señales en

scarce [skɛəs] *adj* escaso; **to make o.s. ~** (*inf*) esfumarse; **~ly** *adv* apenas; **scarcity** *n* escasez *f*

scare [skɛə*] *n* susto, sobresalto; (*panic*) pánico ♦ *vt* asustar, espantar; **to ~ sb stiff** dar a uno un susto de muerte; **bomb ~** amenaza de bomba; **~ off** *or* **away** *vt* ahuyentar; **~crow** *n* espantapájaros *m inv*; **~d** *adj*: **to be ~d** estar asustado

scarf [skɑːf] (*pl* **~s** *or* **scarves**) *n* (*long*) bufanda; (*square*) pañuelo

scarlet ['skɑːlıt] *adj* escarlata; **~ fever** *n* escarlatina

scarves [skɑːvz] *npl of* **scarf**

scary ['skɛərı] (*inf*) *adj* espeluznante

scathing ['skeıðıŋ] *adj* mordaz

scatter ['skætə*] *vt* (*spread*) esparcir, desparramar; (*put to flight*) dispersar ♦ *vi* desparramarse; dispersarse; **~brained** *adj* ligero de cascos

scavenger ['skævəndʒə*] *n* (*person*) basurero/a

scenario [sı'nɑːrıəu] *n* (*THEATRE*) argumento; (*CINEMA*) guión *m*; (*fig*) escenario

scene [siːn] *n* (*THEATRE, fig etc*) escena; (*of crime etc*) escenario; (*view*) panorama *m*; (*fuss*) escándalo; **~ry** *n* (*THEATRE*) decorado; (*landscape*) paisaje *m*; **scenic** *adj* pintoresco

scent [sent] *n* perfume *m*, olor *m*; (*fig: track*) rastro, pista

sceptic ['skɛptık] (*US* **skeptic**) *n*

escéptico/a; **~al** *adj* escéptico

sceptre ['sɛptə*] (*US* **scepter**) *n* cetro

schedule ['ʃɛdjuːl, (*US*) 'skɛdjuːl] *n* (*timetable*) horario; (*of events*) programa *m*; (*list*) lista ♦ *vt* (*visit*) fijar la hora de; **to arrive on ~** llegar a la hora debida; **to be ahead of/behind ~** estar adelantado/en retraso; **~d flight** *n* vuelo regular

scheme [skiːm] *n* (*plan*) plan *m*, proyecto; (*plot*) intriga; (*arrangement*) disposición *f*; (*pension ~ etc*) sistema *m* ♦ *vi* (*intrigue*) intrigar; **scheming** *adj* intrigante ♦ *n* intrigas *fpl*

schizophrenic [skıtsə'frɛnık] *adj* esquizofrénico

scholar ['skɒlə*] *n* (*pupil*) alumno/a; (*learned person*) sabio/a, erudito/a; **~ship** *n* erudición *f*; (*grant*) beca

school [skuːl] *n* escuela, colegio; (*in university*) facultad *f* ♦ *cpd* escolar; **~ age** *n* edad *f* escolar; **~book** *n* libro de texto; **~boy** *n* alumno; **~ children** *npl* alumnos *mpl*; **~girl** *n* alumna; **~ing** *n* enseñanza; **~master/mistress** *n* (*primary*) maestro/a; (*secondary*) profesor(a) *m/f*; **~teacher** *n* (*primary*) maestro/a; (*secondary*) profesor(a) *m/f*

schooner ['skuːnə*] *n* (*ship*) goleta

sciatica [saı'ætıkə] *n* ciática

science ['saıəns] *n* ciencia; **~ fiction** *n* ciencia-ficción *f*; **scientific** [-'tıfık] *adj* científico; **scientist** *n* científico/a

scissors ['sızəz] *npl* tijeras *fpl*; **a pair of ~** unas tijeras

scoff [skɒf] *vt* (*BRIT: inf: eat*) engullir ♦ *vi*: **to ~ (at)** (*mock*) mofarse (de)

scold [skəuld] *vt* regañar

scone [skɒn] *n* pastel de pan

scoop [skuːp] *n* (*for flour etc*) pala; (*PRESS*) exclusiva *f*; **~ out** *vt* excavar; **~ up** *vt* recoger

scooter ['skuːtə*] *n* moto *f*; (*toy*) patinete *m*

scope [skəup] *n* (*of plan*) ámbito; (*of person*) competencia; (*opportunity*) libertad *f* de acción

scorch [skɔːtʃ] vt (clothes) chamuscar; (earth, grass) quemar, secar

score [skɔː*] n (points etc) puntuación f; (MUS) partitura f; (twenty) veintena ♦ vt (goal, point) ganar; (mark) rayar; (achieve: success) conseguir ♦ vi marcar un tanto; (FOOTBALL) marcar (un) gol; (keep score) llevar el tanteo; ~**s of** (lots) decenas de; **on that** ~ en lo que se refiere a eso; **to** ~ **6 out of 10** obtener una puntuación de 6 sobre 10; ~ **out** vt tachar; ~ **over** vt fus obtener una victoria sobre; ~**board** n marcador m

scorn [skɔːn] n desprecio; ~**ful** adj desdeñoso, despreciativo

Scorpio [ˈskɔːpɪəʊ] n Escorpión m

scorpion [ˈskɔːpɪən] n alacrán m

Scot [skɒt] n escocés/esa m/f

Scotch [skɒtʃ] n whisky m escocés

Scotland [ˈskɒtlənd] n Escocia

Scots [skɒts] adj escocés/esa; ~**man/woman** (irreg) n escocés/esa m/f

Scottish [ˈskɒtɪʃ] adj escocés/esa; **Scottish Parliament** n Parlamento escocés

scoundrel [ˈskaʊndrl] n canalla m/f, sinvergüenza m/f

scout [skaʊt] n (MIL, also: boy ~) explorador m; **girl** ~ (US) niña exploradora; ~ **around** vi reconocer el terreno

scowl [skaʊl] vi fruncir el ceño; **to** ~ **at sb** mirar con ceño a uno

scrabble [ˈskræbl] vi (claw): **to** ~ **(at)** arañar; (also: ~ **around**: search) revolver todo buscando ♦ n: **S~** ® Scrabble ® m

scraggy [ˈskrægɪ] adj descarnado

scram [skræm] (inf) vi largarse

scramble [ˈskræmbl] n (climb) subida (difícil); (struggle) pelea ♦ vi: **to** ~ **through/out** abrirse paso/salir con dificultad; **to** ~ **for** pelear por; ~**d eggs** npl huevos mpl revueltos

scrap [skræp] n (bit) pedacito, pizca; (fight) riña, bronca; (also: ~ **iron**) chatarra, hierro viejo ♦ vt (discard) desechar, descartar ♦ vi reñir, armar

(una) bronca; ~**s** npl (waste) sobras fpl, desperdicios mpl; ~**book** n álbum m de recortes; ~ **dealer** n chatarrero/a

scrape [skreɪp] n: **to get into a** ~ meterse en un lío ♦ vt raspar; (skin etc) rasguñar; (~ against) rozar ♦ vi: **to** ~ **through** (exam) aprobar por los pelos; ~ **together** vt (money) juntar

scrap: ~ **heap** n (fig): **to be on the** ~ **heap** estar acabado; ~ **merchant** (BRIT) n chatarrero/a; ~ **paper** n pedazos mpl de papel

scratch [skrætʃ] n rasguño; (from claw) arañazo ♦ cpd: ~ **team** equipo improvisado ♦ vt (paint, car) rayar; (with claw, nail) rasguñar, arañar; (rub: nose etc) rascarse ♦ vi rascarse; **to start from** ~ partir de cero; **to be up to** ~ cumplir con los requisitos

scrawl [skrɔːl] n garabatos mpl ♦ vi hacer garabatos

scrawny [ˈskrɔːnɪ] adj flaco

scream [skriːm] n chillido ♦ vi chillar

screech [skriːtʃ] vi chirriar

screen [skriːn] n (CINEMA, TV) pantalla; (movable barrier) biombo ♦ vt (conceal) tapar; (from the wind etc) proteger; (film) proyectar; (candidates etc) investigar a; ~**ing** n (MED) investigación f médica; ~**play** n guión m; ~ **saver** n (COMPUT) protector m de pantalla

screw [skruː] n tornillo ♦ vt (also: ~ **in**) atornillar; ~ **up** vt (paper etc) arrugar; **to** ~ **up one's eyes** arrugar el entrecejo; ~**driver** n destornillador m

scribble [ˈskrɪbl] n garabatos mpl ♦ vt, vi garabatear

script [skrɪpt] n (CINEMA etc) guión m; (writing) escritura, letra

Scripture(s) [ˈskrɪptʃə*(z)] n(pl) Sagrada Escritura

scroll [skrəʊl] n rollo

scrounge [skraʊndʒ] (inf) vt: **to** ~ **sth off or from sb** obtener algo de uno de gorra; ~ **n on the** ~ de gorra; ~**r** n gorrón/ona m/f

scrub [skrʌb] n (land) maleza ♦ vt fregar, restregar; (inf: reject) cancelar, anular

scruff [skrʌf] n: **by the ~ of the neck** por el pescuezo

scruffy ['skrʌfɪ] adj desaliñado, piojoso

scrum(mage) ['skrʌm(mɪdʒ)] n (RUGBY) melée f

scruple ['skruːpl] n (gen pl) escrúpulo

scrutinize ['skruːtɪnaɪz] vt escudriñar; (votes) escrutar; **scrutiny** ['skruːtɪnɪ] n escrutinio, examen m

scuff [skʌf] vt (shoes, floor) rayar

scuffle ['skʌfl] n refriega

sculptor ['skʌlptə*] n escultor(a) m/f

sculpture ['skʌlptʃə*] n escultura

scum [skʌm] n (on liquid) espuma; (pej: people) escoria

scurry ['skʌrɪ] vi correr; **to ~ off** escabullirse

scuttle ['skʌtl] n (also: coal ~) cubo, carbonera ♦ vt (ship) barrenar ♦ vi to **~ away, ~ off** escabullirse

scythe [saɪð] n guadaña

SDP (BRIT) n abbr = **Social Democratic Party**

sea [siː] n mar m ♦ cpd de mar, marítimo; **by ~** (travel) en barco; **on the ~** (boat) en el mar; (town) junto al mar; **to be all at ~** (fig) estar despistado; **out to ~, at ~** en alta mar; **~board** n litoral m; **~food** n mariscos mpl; **~ front** n paseo marítimo; **~going** adj de altura; **~gull** n gaviota

seal [siːl] n (animal) foca; (stamp) sello ♦ vt (close) cerrar; **~ off** vt (area) acordonar

sea level n nivel m del mar

sea lion n león m marino

seam [siːm] n costura; (of metal) juntura; (of coal) veta, filón m

seaman ['siːmən] (irreg) n marinero

seance ['seɪɔns] n sesión f de espiritismo

seaplane ['siːpleɪn] n hidroavión m

seaport ['siːpɔːt] n puerto de mar

search [sɜːtʃ] n (for person, thing) busca, búsqueda; (COMPUT) búsqueda; (inspection: of sb's home) registro ♦ vt (look in) buscar en; (examine) examinar; (person, place) registrar ♦ vi: **to ~ for** buscar; **in ~ of** en busca de; **~ through** vt fus registrar; **~ engine** n (COMPUT) buscador m; **~ing** adj penetrante; **~light** n reflector m; **~ party** n pelotón m de salvamento; **~ warrant** n mandamiento (judicial)

sea: **~shore** n playa, orilla del mar; **~sick** adj mareado; **~side** n playa, orilla del mar; **~side resort** n centro turístico costero

season ['siːzn] n (of year) estación f, (sporting etc) temporada; (of films etc) ciclo ♦ vt (food) sazonar; **in/out of ~** en sazón/fuera de temporada; **~al** adj estacional; **~ed** adj (fig) experimentado; **~ing** n condimento, aderezo; **~ ticket** n abono

seat [siːt] n (in bus, train) asiento; (chair) silla; (PARLIAMENT) escaño; (buttocks) culo, trasero; (of trousers) culera ♦ vt sentar; (have room for) tener cabida para; **to be ~ed** sentarse; **~ belt** n cinturón m de seguridad

sea: **~ water** n agua del mar; **~weed** n alga marina; **~worthy** adj en condiciones de navegar

sec. abbr = **second(s)**

secluded [sɪ'kluːdɪd] adj retirado

seclusion [sɪ'kluːʒən] n reclusión f

second ['sekənd] adj segundo ♦ adv en segundo lugar ♦ n segundo; (AUT: also: ~ gear) segunda; (COMM) artículo con algún desperfecto; (BRIT: SCOL: degree) título de licenciado con calificación de notable ♦ vt (motion) apoyar; **~ary** adj secundario; **~ary school** n escuela secundaria; **~-class** adj de segunda clase ♦ adv (RAIL) en segunda; **~-hand** adj de segunda mano, usado; **~ hand** n (on clock) segundero; **~ly** adv en segundo lugar; **~ment** [sɪ'kɔndmənt] n (BRIT) traslado

temporal; **~-rate** adj de segunda
categoría; **~ thoughts** npl: **to have
~ thoughts** cambiar de opinión; **on
~ thoughts** or **thought** (US)
pensándolo bien

secrecy ['si:krəsɪ] n secreto

secret ['si:krɪt] adj, n secreto; **in ~** en
secreto

secretarial [sekrɪ'teərɪəl] adj de
secretario; (course, staff) de
secretariado

secretary ['sekrətərɪ] n secretario/a;
S~ of State (for) (BRIT: POL) Ministro
(de)

secretive ['si:krətɪv] adj reservado,
• sigiloso

secretly ['si:krɪtlɪ] adv en secreto

sect [sekt] n secta; **~arian** [-'teərɪən]
adj sectario

section ['sekʃən] n sección f; (part)
parte f; (of document) artículo; (of
opinion) sector m; (cross-~) corte m
transversal

sector ['sektə*] n sector m

secular ['sekjulə*] adj secular, seglar

secure [sɪ'kjuə*] adj seguro; (firmly
fixed) firme, fijo ♦ vt (fix) asegurar,
afianzar; (get) conseguir

security [sɪ'kjuərɪtɪ] n seguridad f; (for
loan) fianza; (: object) prenda

sedate [sɪ'deɪt] adj tranquilo ♦ vt tratar
con sedantes

sedation [sɪ'deɪʃən] n (MED) sedación f

sedative ['sedɪtɪv] n sedante m,
sedativo

seduce [sɪ'dju:s] vt seducir; **seduction**
[-'dʌkʃən] n seducción f; **seductive**
[-'dʌktɪv] adj seductor(a)

see [si:] (pt **saw**, pp **seen**) vt ver;
(accompany): **to ~ sb to the door**
acompañar a uno a la puerta;
(understand) ver, comprender ♦ vi ver
♦ n (arz)obispado; **to ~ that** (ensure)
asegurar que; **you soon!** ¡hasta
pronto!; **~ about** vt fus atender a,
encargarse de; **~ off** vt despedir;
~ through vt fus (fig) calar ♦ vt (plan)

llevar a cabo; **~ to** vt fus atender a,
encargarse de

seed [si:d] n semilla; (in fruit) pepita;
(fig: gen pl) germen m; (TENNIS etc)
preseleccionado/a; **to go to ~** (plant)
granar; (fig) descuidarse; **~ling** n
planta de semillero; **~y** adj (shabby)
desaseado, raído

seeing ['si:ɪŋ] conj: **~ (that)** visto que,
en vista de que

seek [si:k] (pt, pp **sought**) vt buscar;
(post) solicitar

seem [si:m] vi parecer; **there ~s to be
...** parece que hay ...; **~ingly** adv
aparentemente, según parece

seen [si:n] pp of **see**

seep [si:p] vi filtrarse

seesaw ['si:sɔ:] n subibaja

seethe [si:ð] vi hervir; **to ~ with
anger** estar furioso

see-through adj transparente

segment ['segmənt] n (part) sección f;
(of orange) gajo

segregate ['segrigeɪt] vt segregar

seize [si:z] vt (grasp) agarrar, asir; (take
possession of) secuestrar; (: territory)
apoderarse de; (opportunity)
aprovecharse de; **~ (up)on** vt fus
aprovechar; **~ up** vi (TECH) agarrotarse

seizure ['si:ʒə*] n (MED) ataque m,
(LAW, of power) incautación f

seldom ['seldəm] adv rara vez

select [sɪ'lekt] adj selecto, escogido
♦ vt escoger, elegir; (SPORT)
seleccionar; **~ion** [-'lekʃən] n selección
f, elección f; (COMM) surtido

self [self] (pl **selves**) n uno mismo; **the
~** el yo ♦ prefix auto...; **~-assured** adj
seguro de sí mismo; **~-catering** (BRIT)
adj (flat etc) con cocina; **~-centred** (US
~-centered) adj egocéntrico; **~-
confidence** n confianza en sí mismo;
~-conscious adj cohibido; **~-
contained** (BRIT) adj (flat) con entrada
particular; **~-control** n autodominio;
~-defence (US **~-defense**) n defensa
propia; **~-discipline** n autodisciplina;

~-employed adj que trabaja por cuenta propia; **~-evident** adj patente; **~-governing** adj autónomo; **~-indulgent** adj autocomplaciente; **~-interest** n egoísmo; **~ish** adj egoísta; **~ishness** n egoísmo; **~less** adj desinteresado; **~-made** adj: **~-made man** hombre m que se ha hecho a sí mismo; **~-pity** n lástima de sí mismo; **~-portrait** n autorretrato; **~-possessed** adj sereno, dueño de sí mismo; **~-preservation** n propia conservación f; **~-respect** n amor m propio; **~-righteous** adj santurrón/ona; **~-sacrifice** n abnegación f; **~-satisfied** adj satisfecho de sí mismo; **~-service** adj de autoservicio; **~-sufficient** adj autosuficiente; **~-taught** adj autodidacta

sell [sel] (pt, pp **sold**) vt vender ♦ vi venderse; **to ~ at** or **for £10** venderse a 10 libras; **~ off** vt liquidar; **~ out** vi: **to ~ out of tickets/milk** vender todas las entradas/toda la leche; **~-by date** n fecha de caducidad; **~er** n vendedor(a) m/f; **~ing price** n precio de venta

Sellotape ® ['seləʊteɪp] (BRIT) n cinta adhesiva, celo (SP), scotch (AM)

selves [selvz] npl of **self**

semblance ['sembləns] n apariencia f

semen ['siːmən] n semen m

semester [sɪ'mestə*] (US) n semestre m

semi... [semi] prefix semi..., medio...; **~circle** n semicírculo; **~colon** n punto y coma; **~conductor** n semiconductor m; **~detached (house)** n (casa) semiseparada; **~final** n semifinal m

seminar ['semɪnɑː*] n seminario

seminary ['semɪnərɪ] n (REL) seminario

semiskilled ['semɪskɪld] adj (work, worker) semi-cualificado

semi-skimmed (milk) n leche semidesnatada

senate ['senɪt] n senado; **senator** n senador(a) m/f

send [send] (pt, pp **sent**) vt mandar,

enviar; (signal) transmitir; **~ away** vt despachar; **~ away for** vt fus pedir; **~ back** vt devolver; **~ for** vt fus mandar traer; **~ off** vt (goods) despachar; (BRIT: SPORT: player) expulsar; **~ out** vt (invitation) mandar; (signal) emitir; **~ up** vt (person, price) hacer subir; (BRIT: parody) parodiar; **~er** n remitente m/f; **~off** n: **a good ~off** una buena despedida

senior ['siːnɪə*] adj (older) mayor, más viejo; (: on staff) de más antigüedad; (of higher rank) superior; **~ citizen** n persona de la tercera edad; **~ity** [-'ɒrɪtɪ] n antigüedad f

sensation [sen'seɪʃən] n sensación f; **~al** adj sensacional

sense [sens] n (faculty, meaning) sentido; (feeling) sensación f; (good ~) sentido común, juicio ♦ vt sentir, percibir; **it makes ~** tiene sentido; **~less** adj estúpido, insensato; (unconscious) sin conocimiento; **~ of humour** n sentido del humor

sensible ['sensɪbl] adj sensato; (reasonable) razonable, lógico

sensitive ['sensɪtɪv] adj sensible; (touchy) susceptible

sensual ['sensjuəl] adj sensual

sensuous ['sensjuəs] adj sensual

sent [sent] pt, pp of **send**

sentence ['sentns] n (LING) oración f; (LAW) sentencia, fallo ♦ vt: **to ~ sb to death/to 5 years (in prison)** condenar a uno a muerte/a 5 años de cárcel

sentiment ['sentɪmənt] n sentimiento; (opinion) opinión f; **~al** [-'mentl] adj sentimental

sentry ['sentrɪ] n centinela m

separate [adj 'seprɪt, vb 'sepəreɪt] adj separado; (distinct) distinto ♦ vt separar; (part) dividir ♦ vi separarse; **~s** npl (clothes) coordinados mpl; **~ly** adv por separado; **separation** [-'reɪʃən] n separación f

September [sep'tembə*] n

se(p)tiembre m

septic ['septik] adj séptico; ~ **tank** n fosa séptica

sequel ['si:kwl] n consecuencia, resultado; (of story) continuación f

sequence ['si:kwəns] n sucesión f, serie f; (CINEMA) secuencia

sequin ['si:kwin] n lentejuela

serene [sɪ'ri:n] adj sereno, tranquilo

sergeant ['sɑ:dʒənt] n sargento

serial ['sɪərɪəl] n (TV) telenovela, serie f televisiva; (BOOK) serie f; **~ize** vt emitir como serial; **~ killer** n asesino/a múltiple; **~ number** n número de serie

series ['sɪəriz] n inv serie f

serious ['sɪərɪəs] adj serio; (grave) grave; **~ly** adv en serio; (ill, wounded etc) gravemente

sermon ['sɜ:mən] n sermón m

serrated [sɪ'reɪtɪd] adj serrado, dentellado

serum ['sɪərəm] n suero

servant ['sɜ:vənt] n servidor/a m/f; (house ~) criado/a

serve [sɜ:v] vt servir; (customer) atender; (subj: train) pasar por; (apprenticeship) hacer; (prison term) cumplir ♦ vi (also: at table) servir; (TENNIS) sacar; **to ~ as/for/to do** servir de/para/para hacer ♦ n (TENNIS) saque m; **it ~s him right** se lo tiene merecido; **~ out** vt (food) servir; **~ up** vt = ~ out

service ['sɜ:vɪs] n servicio; (REL) misa; (AUT) mantenimiento; (dishes etc) juego ♦ vt (car etc) revisar; (: repair) reparar; **the S~s** npl las fuerzas armadas; **to be of ~ to sb** ser útil a uno; **~ included/not included** servicio incluido/no incluido; **~able** adj servible, utilizable; **~ area** n (on motorway) area de servicio; **~ charge** n (BRIT) n servicio; **~man** n militar m; **~ station** n estación f de servicio

serviette [sɜ:vɪ'et] (BRIT) n servilleta

session ['seʃən] n sesión f; **to be in ~** estar en sesión

set [set] n (pt, pp **set**) n juego; (RADIO)

aparato; (TV) televisor m; (of utensils) batería; (of cutlery) cubierto; (of books) colección f; (TENNIS) set m; (group of people) grupo; (CINEMA) plató m; (THEATRE) decorado; (HAIRDRESSING) marcado ♦ adj (fixed) fijo; (ready) listo ♦ vt (place) poner, colocar; (fix) fijar; (adjust) ajustar, arreglar; (decide: rules etc) establecer, decidir ♦ vi (sun) ponerse; (jam, jelly) cuajarse; (concrete) fraguar; (bone) componerse; **to be ~ on doing sth** estar empeñado en hacer algo; **to ~ to music** poner música a; **to ~ on fire** incendiar, poner fuego a; **to ~ free** poner en libertad; **to ~ sth going** poner algo en marcha; **to ~ sail** zarpar, hacerse a la vela; **~ about** vt fus ponerse a; **~ aside** vt poner aparte, dejar de lado; (money, time) reservar; **~ back** vt (cost): **to ~ sb back £5** costar a uno cinco libras; (: in time): **to ~ back (by)** retrasar (por); **~ off** vi partir ♦ vt (bomb) hacer estallar; (events) poner en marcha; (show up well) hacer resaltar; **~ out** vi partir ♦ vt (arrange) disponer; (state) exponer; **to ~ out to do sth** proponerse hacer algo; **~ up** vt establecer; **~back** n revés m, contratiempo; **~ menu** n menú m

settee [se'ti:] n sofá m

setting ['setɪŋ] n (scenery) marco; (position) disposición f; (of sun) puesta; (of jewel) engaste m, montadura

settle ['setl] vt (argument) resolver; (accounts) ajustar, liquidar; (MED: calm) calmar, sosegar ♦ vi (dust etc) depositarse; (weather) serenarse; (also: ~ down) instalarse; tranquilizarse; **to ~ for sth** convenir en aceptar algo; **to ~ on sth** decidirse por algo; **~ in** vi instalarse; **~ up** vi: **to ~ up with sb** ajustar cuentas con uno; **~ment** n (payment) liquidación f; (agreement) acuerdo, convenio; (village etc) pueblo; **~r** n colono/a, colonizador(a) m/f

setup ['setʌp] n sistema m; (situation)

situación f

seven ['sevn] num siete; **~teen**
num diez y siete, dieciséte; **~th** num
séptimo; **~ty** num setenta

sever ['sevə*] vt cortar; (relations)
romper

several ['sevrəl] adj, pron varios/as m/
fpl, algunos/as m/fpl; **~ of us** varios de
nosotros

severance ['sevərəns] n (of relations)
ruptura; **~ pay** n indemnización f por
despido

severe [sɪ'vɪə*] adj severo; (serious)
grave; (hard) duro; (pain) intenso;
severity [sɪ'verɪtɪ] n severidad f;
gravedad f; intensidad f

sew [səu] (pt sewed, pp sewn) vt, vi
coser; **~ up** vt coser, zurcir

sewage ['suːɪdʒ] n aguas fpl residuales

sewer ['suːə*] n alcantarilla, cloaca

sewing ['səuɪŋ] n costura; **~ machine**
n máquina de coser

sewn [səun] pp of sew

sex [seks] n sexo; (lovemaking): **to
have ~** hacer el amor; **~ist** adj, n
sexista m/f; **~ual** ['seksjuəl] adj sexual;
~y adj sexy

shabby ['ʃæbɪ] adj (person)
desharrapado; (clothes) raído, gastado;
(behaviour) ruin inv

shack [ʃæk] n choza, chabola

shackles ['ʃæklz] npl grillos mpl,
grilletes mpl

shade [ʃeɪd] n sombra; (for lamp)
pantalla; (for eyes) visera; (of colour)
matiz m, tonalidad f; (small quantity): **a
~ (too big/more)** un poquitín
(grande/más) ♦ vt (eyes)
proteger del sol; **in the ~** en la sombra

shadow ['ʃædəu] n sombra ♦ vt
(follow) seguir y vigilar; **~ cabinet**
(BRIT) n (POL) gabinete paralelo formado
por el partido de oposición; **~y** adj
oscuro; (dim) indistinto

shady ['ʃeɪdɪ] adj sombreado; (fig:
dishonest) sospechoso; (: deal) turbio

shaft [ʃɑːft] n (of arrow, spear) astil m;

(AUT, TECH) eje m, árbol m; (of mine)
pozo; (of lift) hueco, caja; (of light) rayo

shaggy ['ʃægɪ] adj peludo

shake [ʃeɪk] (pt shook, pp shaken) vt
sacudir; (building) hacer temblar;
(bottle, cocktail) agitar ♦ vi (tremble)
temblar; **to ~ one's head** (in refusal)
negar con la cabeza; (in dismay) mover
o menear la cabeza, incrédulo; **to
~ hands with sb** estrechar la mano o
uno; **~ off** vt sacudirse; (fig) deshacerse
de; **~ up** vt agitar; (fig) reorganizar;
shaky adj (hand, voice) trémulo;
(building) inestable

shall [ʃæl] aux vb: **~ I help you?**
¿quieres que te ayude?; **I'll buy three,
~ I?** compro tres, ¿no te parece?

shallow ['ʃæləu] adj poco profundo;
(fig) superficial

sham [ʃæm] n fraude m, engaño ♦ vt
fingir, simular

shambles ['ʃæmblz] n confusión f

shame [ʃeɪm] n vergüenza f ♦ vt
avergonzar; **it is a ~ that/to do** es
una lástima que/hacer; **what a ~!**
¡qué lástima!; **~ful** adj vergonzoso;
~less adj desvergonzado

shampoo [ʃæm'puː] n champú m ♦ vt
lavar con champú; **~ and set** n lavado
y marcado

shamrock ['ʃæmrɔk] n trébol m
(emblema nacional irlandés)

shandy ['ʃændɪ] n mezcla de cerveza
con gaseosa

shan't [ʃɑːnt] = shall not

shantytown ['ʃæntɪtaun] n barrio de
chabolas

shape [ʃeɪp] n forma ♦ vt formar, dar
forma a; (sb's ideas) formar; (sb's life)
determinar; **to take ~** tomar forma,
perfilarse; **~ up** vi (events) desarrollarse; (person)
formarse; **~-d** suffix: **heart~d** en
forma de corazón; **~less** adj informe,
sin forma definida; **~ly** adj (body etc)
esbelto

share [ʃeə*] n (part) parte f, porción f;
(contribution) cuota; (COMM) acción f

♦ vt dividir; (have in common)
compartir; **to ~ out (among or
between)** repartir (entre); **~holder**
(BRIT) n accionista m f

shark [ʃɑːk] n tiburón m

sharp [ʃɑːp] adj (blade, nose) afilado;
(point) puntiagudo; (outline) definido;
(pain) intenso; (MUS) desafinado;
(contrast) marcado; (voice) agudo;
(person: quick-witted) astuto;
(: dishonest) poco escrupuloso ♦ n
(MUS) sostenido ♦ adv: **at 2 o'clock**
a las 2 en punto; **~en** vt afilar; (pencil)
sacar punta a; (fig) agudizar; **~ener** n
(also: pencil ~ener) sacapuntas m inv;
~-eyed adj de vista aguda; **~ly** adv
(turn, stop) bruscamente; (stand out,
contrast) claramente; (criticize, retort)
severamente

shatter [ˈʃætə*] vt hacer añicos or
pedazos; (fig: ruin) destruir, acabar con
♦ vi hacerse añicos

shave [ʃeɪv] vt afeitar, rasurar ♦ vi
afeitarse, rasurarse ♦ n: **to have a ~**
afeitarse; **~r** n (also: electric ~r)
máquina de afeitar (eléctrica)

shaving [ˈʃeɪvɪŋ] n (action) el afeitarse,
rasurado; **~s** npl (of wood etc) virutas
fpl; **~ brush** n brocha (de afeitar);
~ cream n crema de afeitar; **~ foam**
n espuma de afeitar

shawl [ʃɔːl] n chal m

she [ʃiː] pron ella; **~-cat** n gata

sheaf [ʃiːf] (pl **sheaves**) n (of corn)
gavilla; (of papers) fajo

shear [ʃɪə*] (pt **sheared**, pp **sheared**
or **shorn**) vt esquilar, trasquilar; **~s** npl
(for hedge) tijeras fpl de jardín

sheath [ʃiːθ] n vaina; (contraceptive)
preservativo

sheaves [ʃiːvz] npl of **sheaf**

shed [ʃed] (pt, pp **shed**) n cobertizo
♦ vt (skin) mudar; (tears, blood)
derramar; (load) derramar; (workers)
despedir

she'd [ʃiːd] = **she had; she would**

sheen [ʃiːn] n brillo, lustre m

sheep [ʃiːp] n inv oveja; **~dog** n perro
pastor; **~skin** n piel f de carnero

sheer [ʃɪə*] adj (utter) puro, completo;
(steep) escarpado; (material) diáfano
♦ adv verticalmente

sheet [ʃiːt] n (on bed) sábana; (of
paper) hoja; (of glass, metal) lámina; (of
ice) capa

sheik(h) [ʃeɪk] n jeque m

shelf [ʃelf] (pl **shelves**) n estante m

shell [ʃel] n (on beach) concha; (of egg,
nut etc) cáscara; (explosive) proyectil m,
obús m; (of building) armazón f ♦ vt
(peas) desvainar; (MIL) bombardear

she'll [ʃiːl] = **she will; she shall**

shellfish [ˈʃelfɪʃ] n inv crustáceo; (as
food) mariscos mpl

shell suit n chándal m de calle

shelter [ˈʃeltə*] n abrigo, refugio ♦ vt
(aid) amparar, proteger; (give lodging
to) abrigar ♦ vi abrigarse, refugiarse;
~ed adj (life) protegido; (spot)
abrigado; **~ed housing** n viviendas
vigiladas para ancianos y minusválidos

shelve [ʃelv] vt (fig) aplazar; **~s** npl of
shelf

shepherd [ˈʃepəd] n pastor m ♦ vt
(guide) guiar, conducir; **~'s pie** (BRIT)
n pastel de carne y patatas

sherry [ˈʃerɪ] n jerez m

she's [ʃiːz] = **she is; she has**

Shetland [ˈʃetlənd] n (also: the ~s, the
~ **Isles**) las Islas de Zetlandia

shield [ʃiːld] n escudo; (protection)
blindaje m ♦ vt: **to ~ (from)** proteger
(de)

shift [ʃɪft] n (change) cambio; (at work)
turno ♦ vt trasladar; (remove) quitar
♦ vi moverse; **~ work** n trabajo a
turnos; **~y** adj tramposo; (eyes) furtivo

shimmer [ˈʃɪmə*] n reflejo trémulo

shin [ʃɪn] n espinilla

shine [ʃaɪn] (pt, pp **shone**) n brillo,
lustre m ♦ vi brillar, relucir ♦ vt (shoes)
lustrar, sacar brillo a; **to ~ a torch on
sth** dirigir una linterna hacia algo

shingle [ˈʃɪŋgl] n (on beach) guijarros

mpl, **~s** n (MED) herpes mpl o fpl

shiny [ˈʃaɪnɪ] adj brillante, lustroso

ship [ʃɪp] n buque m, barco m ♦ vt (goods) embarcar; (send) transportar o enviar por vía marítima; **~building** n construcción f de buques; **~ment** n (goods) envío; **~ping** n (act) embarque m; (traffic) buques mpl; **~wreck** n naufragio ♦ vt: **to be ~wrecked** naufragar; **~yard** n astillero

shire [ˈʃaɪə*] (BRIT) n condado

shirt [ʃəːt] n camisa; **in (one's) ~ sleeves** en mangas de camisa

shit [ʃɪt] (inf!) excl ¡mierda! (!)

shiver [ˈʃɪvə*] n escalofrío ♦ vi temblar, estremecerse; (with cold) tiritar

shoal [ʃəʊl] n (of fish) banco; (fig: also: **~s**) tropel m

shock [ʃɔk] n (impact) choque m; (ELEC) descarga (eléctrica); (emotional) conmoción f; (start) sobresalto, susto; (MED) postración f nerviosa ♦ vt dar un susto a; (offend) escandalizar; **~ absorber** n amortiguador m; **~ing** adj (awful) espantoso; (outrageous) escandaloso

shoddy [ˈʃɔdɪ] adj de pacotilla

shoe [ʃuː] (pt, pp shod) n zapato m; (for horse) herradura ♦ vt (horse) herrar; **~brush** n cepillo para zapatos; **~lace** n cordón m; **~ polish** n betún m; **~shop** n zapatería; **~string** n (fig): **on a ~string** con muy poco dinero

shone [ʃɔn] pt, pp of shine

shook [ʃʊk] pt of shake

shoot [ʃuːt] (pt, pp shot) n (on branch, seedling) retoño, vástago ♦ vt disparar; (kill) matar a tiros; (wound) pegar un tiro; (execute) fusilar; (film) rodar, filmar ♦ vi (FOOTBALL) chutar; **~ down** vt (plane) derribar; **~ in/out** vi entrar corriendo/salir disparado; **~ up** vi (prices) dispararse; **~ing** n (shots) tiros mpl; (HUNTING) caza con escopeta; **~ing star** n estrella fugaz

shop [ʃɔp] n tienda; (workshop) taller m ♦ vi (also: **go ~ping**) ir de compras;

~ assistant (BRIT) n dependiente/a m/f; **~ floor** (BRIT) n (fig) taller m, fábrica; **~keeper** n tendero/a; **~lifting** n mechería; **~per** n comprador(a) m/f; **~ping** n (goods) compras fpl; **~ping bag** n bolsa (de compras); **~ping centre** (US **~ping center**) n centro comercial; **~soiled** adj deteriorado; **~ steward** (BRIT) n (INDUSTRY) enlace m sindical; **~ window** n escaparate m (SP), vidriera (AM)

shore [ʃɔː*] n orilla ♦ vt: **to ~ (up)** reforzar; **on ~** en tierra

shorn [ʃɔːn] pp of shear

short [ʃɔːt] adj corto; (in time) breve, de corta duración; (person) bajo; (curt) brusco, seco; (insufficient) insuficiente; **(a pair of) ~s** (unos) pantalones mpl cortos; **to be ~ of sth** estar falto de algo; **in ~** en pocas palabras; **~ of doing** ... fuera de hacer ...; **it is ~ for** es la forma abreviada de; **to cut ~** (speech, visit) interrumpir, terminar inesperadamente; **everything ~ of** ... todo menos ...; **to fall ~ of** no alcanzar; **to run ~** de quedarse a uno poco; **to stop ~** pararen seco; **to stop ~ of** detenerse antes de; **~age** n: **a ~age** of una falta de; **~bread** n especie de mantecada; **~change** vt no dar el cambio completo a; **~circuit** n cortocircuito; **~coming** n defecto, deficiencia; **~(crust) pastry** (BRIT) n pasta quebradiza; **~cut** n atajo; **~en** vt acortar; (visit) interrumpir; **~fall** n déficit m; **~hand** (BRIT) n taquigrafía; **~hand typist** (BRIT) n taquimecanógrafo/a; **~ list** (BRIT) n (for job) lista de candidatos escogidos; **~lived** adj efímero; **~ly** adv en breve, dentro de poco; **~sighted** (BRIT) adj miope; (fig) imprudente; **~staffed** adj: **to be ~staffed** estar falto de personal; **~ story** n cuento; **~tempered** adj enojadizo; **~term** adj (effect) a corto plazo; **~wave** n (RADIO) onda corta

shot [ʃɔt] pt, pp of shoot ♦ n (sound)

tiro, disparo; (*try*) tentativa; (*injection*) inyección f; (*PHOT*) toma, fotografía; **to be a good/poor ~** (*person*) tener buena/mala puntería; **like a ~** (*without any delay*) como un rayo; **~gun** n escopeta

should [ʃud] *aux vb*: **I ~ go now** debo irme ahora; **he ~ be there now** debe de haber llegado (ya); **I ~ go if I were you** yo en tu lugar me iría; **I ~ like to** me gustaría

shoulder ['ʃəʊldə*] n hombro ♦ vt (*fig*) cargar con; **~ bag** n cartera de bandolera; **~ blade** n omóplato

shouldn't ['ʃudnt] = **should not**

shout [ʃaut] n grito ♦ vt gritar ♦ vi gritar, dar voces; **~ down** vt acallar a gritos; **~ing** n griterío

shove [ʃʌv] n empujón m ♦ vt empujar; (*inf*: *put*) **to ~ sth** in meter algo a empellones; **~ off** (*inf*) vi largarse

shovel ['ʃʌvl] n pala; (*mechanical*) excavadora ♦ vt mover con pala

show [ʃəʊ] (*pt* **showed**, *pp* **shown**) n (*of emotion*) demostración f; (*semblance*) apariencia; (*exhibition*) exposición f; (*THEATRE*) función f, espectáculo; (*TV*) show m ♦ vt mostrar, enseñar; (*courage etc*) manifestar; (*exhibit*) exponer; (*film*) proyectar ♦ vi mostrarse; (*appear*) aparecer; **for ~** para impresionar; **on ~** (*exhibits etc*) expuesto; **~ in** vt (*person*) hacer pasar; **~ off** (*pej*) vi presumir ♦ vt (*display*) lucir; (*pej*) hacer gala de; **~ out** vt **to ~ sb out** acompañar a uno a la puerta; **~ up** vi (*stand out*) destacar; (*inf*: *turn up*) aparecer ♦ vt (*unmask*) desenmascarar; **~ business** n mundo del espectáculo; **~down** n enfrentamiento (final)

shower ['ʃaʊə*] n (*rain*) chaparrón m, chubasco; (*of stones etc*) lluvia; (*for bathing*) ducha (*SP*), regadera (*AM*) ♦ vi llover ♦ vt (*fig*): **to ~ sb with sth** colmar a uno de algo; **to have a ~** ducharse; **~proof** *adj* impermeable

showing ['ʃəʊɪŋ] n (*of film*) proyección f

show jumping n hípica

shown [ʃəʊn] *pp* of **show**

show: ~-off (*inf*) n (*person*) presumido/a; **~piece** n (*of exhibition etc*) objeto cumbre; **~room** n sala de muestras

shrank [ʃræŋk] *pt* of **shrink**

shrapnel ['ʃræpnl] n metralla

shred [ʃred] n (*gen pl*) triza, jirón m ♦ vt (*also*: *CULIN*) desmenuzar; **~der** n (*vegetable ~der*) picadora; (*document ~der*) trituradora (de papel)

shrewd [ʃruːd] *adj* astuto

shriek [ʃriːk] n chillido ♦ vi chillar

shrill [ʃrɪl] *adj* agudo, estridente

shrimp [ʃrɪmp] n camarón m

shrine [ʃraɪn] n santuario, sepulcro

shrink [ʃrɪŋk] (*pt* **shrank**, *pp* **shrunk**) vi encogerse; (*be reduced*) reducirse; (*also*: *~ away*) retroceder ♦ vt encoger ♦ n (*inf*: *pej*) loquero/a; **to ~ from (doing) sth** no atreverse a hacer algo; **~wrap** vt embalar con película de plástico

shrivel ['ʃrɪvl] (*also*: *~ up*) vt (*dry*) secar ♦ vi secarse

shroud [ʃraud] n sudario ♦ vt: **~ed in mystery** envuelto en el misterio

Shrove Tuesday ['ʃrəʊv-] n martes m de carnaval

shrub [ʃrʌb] n arbusto; **~bery** n arbustos mpl

shrug [ʃrʌg] n encogimiento de hombros ♦ vt, vi: **to ~ (one's shoulders)** encogerse de hombros; **~ off** vt negar importancia a

shrunk [ʃrʌŋk] *pp* of **shrink**

shudder ['ʃʌdə*] n estremecimiento, escalofrío ♦ vi estremecerse

shuffle ['ʃʌfl] vt (*cards*) barajar ♦ vi: **to ~ (one's feet)** arrastrar los pies

shun [ʃʌn] vt rehuir, esquivar

shunt [ʃʌnt] vt (*train*) maniobrar; (*object*) empujar

shut [ʃʌt] (*pt, pp* **shut**) vt cerrar ♦ vi

cerrarse; **~ down** vt, vi cerrar; **~ off** vt
(supply etc) cortar; **~ up** n (inf: keep
quiet) callarse ♦ vt (close) cerrar;
(silence) hacer callar; **~ter** n
contraventana; (PHOT) obturador m

shuttle ['ʃʌtl] n lanzadera; (also:
~ service) servicio rápido y continuo
entre dos puntos: (: AVIAT) puente m
aéreo; **~cock** n volante m;
~ diplomacy n viajes mpl
diplomáticos

shy [ʃaɪ] adj tímido; **~ness** n timidez f

Sicily ['sɪsɪlɪ] n Sicilia

sick [sɪk] adj (ill) enfermo; (nauseated)
mareado; (humour) negro; (vomiting):
to be ~ (BRIT) vomitar; **to feel ~** tener
náuseas; **to be ~** of (fig) estar harto
de; **~ bay** n enfermería; **~en** vt dar
asco a; ♦ vi (fig) asquearse;
~ening adj (fig) asqueroso

sickle ['sɪkl] n hoz f

sick: **~ leave** n baja por enfermedad;
~ly adj enfermizo; (smell)
nauseabundo; **~ness** n enfermedad f,
mal m; (vomiting) náuseas fpl; **~ pay**
n subsidio de enfermedad

side [saɪd] n (gen) lado; (of body)
costado; (of lake) orilla; (of hill) ladera;
(team) equipo; ♦ adj (door, entrance)
lateral ♦ vi: **to ~ with sb** tomar el
partido de uno; **by the ~ of** al lado
de; **~ by ~** juntos/as; **from ~ to ~** de
un lado para otro; **from all ~s** de
todos lados; **to take ~s (with)** tomar
partido (con); **~board** n aparador m;
~boards (BRIT) npl = **~burns**;
~burns npl patillas fpl; **~ effect** n efecto
secundario; **~light** n (AUT) luz f lateral;
~line n (SPORT) línea de banda; (fig)
empleo suplementario; **~long** adj de
soslayo; **~ order** n plato de
acompañamiento; **~ show** n (stall)
caseta; **~step** vt (fig) esquivar;
~ street n calle f lateral; **~track** vt
(fig) desviar de su asunto; **~walk** n
(US) n acera; **~ways** adv de lado

siding ['saɪdɪŋ] n (RAIL) apartadero, vía

muerta

siege [siːdʒ] n cerco, sitio

sieve [sɪv] n colador n ♦ vt cribar

sift [sɪft] vt cribar; (fig: information)
escudriñar

sigh [saɪ] n suspiro ♦ vi suspirar

sight [saɪt] n (faculty) vista; (spectacle)
espectáculo; (on gun) mira, alza ♦ vt
divisar; **in ~** a la vista; **out of ~** fuera
de (la) vista; **on ~** (shoot) sin previo
aviso; **~seeing** n excursionismo,
turismo; **to go ~seeing** hacer turismo

sign [saɪn] n (with hand) señal f, seña;
(trace) huella, rastro; (notice) letrero;
(written) signo ♦ vt firmar; (SPORT)
fichar; **to ~ sth over to sb** hacer el
traspaso de algo a uno; **~ on** vi (BRIT:
as unemployed) registrarse como
desempleado; (for course) inscribirse
♦ vt (MIL) alistar; (employee) contratar;
~ up vi (MIL) alistarse; (for course)
inscribirse ♦ vt (player) fichar

signal ['sɪgnl] n señal f ♦ vi señalizar
♦ vt (person) hacer señas a; (message)
comunicar por señales; **~man** (irreg) n
(RAIL) guardavía m

signature ['sɪgnətʃə*] n firma; **~ tune**
n sintonía de apertura de un programa

signet ring ['sɪgnət-] n anillo de sello

significance [sɪg'nɪfɪkəns] n
(importance) trascendencia

significant [sɪg'nɪfɪkənt] adj
significativo; (important) trascendente

signify ['sɪgnɪfaɪ] vt significar

sign language n lenguaje m para
sordomudos

signpost ['saɪnpəust] n indicador m

silence ['saɪlns] n silencio ♦ vt acallar;
(guns) reducir al silencio; **~r** n (on gun,
BRIT: AUT) silenciador m

silent ['saɪlnt] adj silencioso; (not
speaking) callado; (film) mudo; **to
remain ~** guardar silencio; **~ partner**
n (COMM) socio a comanditario/a

silhouette [sɪluː'et] n silueta

silicon chip ['sɪlɪkən-] n plaqueta de
silicio

silk [sɪlk] n seda ♦ adj de seda; **~y** adj sedoso

silly ['sɪlɪ] adj (person) tonto; (idea) absurdo

silt [sɪlt] n sedimento

silver ['sɪlvə*] n plata; (money) moneda suelta ♦ adj de plata; (colour) plateado; **~ paper** (BRIT) n papel m de plata; **~-plated** adj plateado; **~smith** n platero/a; **~ware** n plata; **~y** adj argentino

similar ['sɪmɪlə*] adj: **~ (to)** parecido or semejante (a); **~ity** [-'lærɪtɪ] n semejanza; **~ly** adv del mismo modo

simmer ['sɪmə*] vi hervir a fuego lento

simple ['sɪmpl] adj (easy) sencillo; (foolish, COMM: interest) simple; **simplicity** [-'plɪsɪtɪ] n sencillez f; **simplify** ['sɪmplɪfaɪ] vt simplificar; **simply** ['sɪmplɪ] adv (live, talk) sencillamente; (just, merely) sólo

simulate ['sɪmjuleɪt] vt fingir, simular; **~d** adj simulado; (fur) de imitación

simultaneous [sɪməl'teɪnɪəs] adj simultáneo; **~ly** adv simultáneamente

sin [sɪn] n pecado ♦ vi pecar

since [sɪns] adv desde entonces, después ♦ prep desde ♦ conj (time) desde que; (because) ya que, puesto que; **~ then, ever ~** desde entonces

sincere [sɪn'sɪə*] adj sincero; **~ly** adv: **yours ~ly** (in letters) le saluda atentamente; **sincerity** [-'serɪtɪ] n sinceridad f

sinew ['sɪnju:] n tendón m

sing [sɪŋ] (pt **sang**, pp **sung**) vt, vi cantar

Singapore [sɪŋə'pɔː*] n Singapur m

singe [sɪndʒ] vt chamuscar

singer ['sɪŋə*] n cantante m/f

singing ['sɪŋɪŋ] n canto

single ['sɪŋgl] adj único, solo; (unmarried) soltero; (not double) simple, sencillo ♦ n (BRIT: also: **~ ticket**) billete m sencillo; (record) sencillo, single m; **~s** npl (TENNIS) individual m; **~ out** vt (choose) escoger; **~ bed** cama

individual; **~-breasted** adj recto; **~ file** n: **in ~ file** en fila de uno; **~-handed** adv sin ayuda; **~-minded** adj resuelto, firme; **~ parent** n padre m soltero, madre f soltera (o divorciado etc); **~ parent family** familia monoparental; **~ room** n cuarto individual

singly ['sɪŋglɪ] adv uno por uno

singular ['sɪŋgjulə*] adj (odd) raro, extraño; (outstanding) excepcional ♦ n (LING) singular m

sinister ['sɪnɪstə*] adj siniestro

sink [sɪŋk] (pt **sank**, pp **sunk**) n fregadero ♦ vt (ship) hundir, echar a pique; (foundations) excavar ♦ vi (gen) hundirse; **to ~ sth into** hundir algo en; **~ in** vi (fig) penetrar, calar

sinner ['sɪnə*] n pecador/a m/f

sinus ['saɪnəs] n (ANAT) seno

sip [sɪp] n sorbo ♦ vt sorber, beber a sorbitos

siphon ['saɪfən] n sifón m; **~ off** vt desviar

sir [sɜː*] n señor m; S~ **John Smith** Sir John Smith; **yes ~** sí, señor

siren ['saɪərn] n sirena

sirloin ['sɜːlɔɪn] n (also: **~ steak**) solomillo

sister ['sɪstə*] n hermana; (BRIT: nurse) enfermera jefe; **~-in-law** n cuñada

sit [sɪt] (pt, pp **sat**) vi sentarse; (be sitting) estar sentado; (assembly) reunirse; (for painter) posar ♦ vt (exam) presentarse a; **~ down** vi sentarse; **~ in on** vt fus asistir a; **~ up** vi incorporarse; (not go to bed) velar

sitcom ['sɪtkɒm] n abbr (= situation comedy) comedia de situación

site [saɪt] n sitio; (also: building **~**) solar m ♦ vt situar

sit-in n (demonstration) sentada

sitting ['sɪtɪŋ] n (of assembly etc) sesión f; (in canteen) turno; **~ room** n sala de estar

situated ['sɪtjueɪtɪd] adj situado

situation [sɪtju'eɪʃən] n situación f;

"~s vacant" (BRIT) "ofrecen trabajo"

six [sɪks] num seis; **~teen** num diez y seis, dieciséis; **~th** num sexto; **~ty** num sesenta

size [saɪz] n tamaño; (extent) extensión f; (of clothing) talla; (of shoes) número; **~ up** vt formarse una idea de; **~able** adj importante, considerable

sizzle ['sɪzl] vi crepitar

skate [skeɪt] n patín m e (fish: pl inv) raya ♦ vi patinar; **~board** n monopatín m; **~boarding** n monopatín m; **~r** n patinador(a) m/f; **skating** n patinaje m; **skating rink** n pista de patinaje

skeleton ['skɛlɪtn] n esqueleto; (TECH) armazón f; (outline) esquema m; **~ staff** n personal m reducido

skeptic etc ['skɛptɪk] (US) = **sceptic**

sketch [skɛtʃ] n (drawing) dibujo; (outline) esbozo, bosquejo; (THEATRE) sketch m ♦ vt dibujar; (plan etc also: ~ out) esbozar; **~ book** n libro de dibujos; **~y** adj incompleto

skewer ['skjuːə*] n broqueta

ski [skiː] n esquí m ♦ vi esquiar; **~ boot** n bota de esquí

skid [skɪd] n patinazo ♦ vi patinar

ski: ~er n esquiador(a) m/f; **~ing** n esquí m; **~ jump** n salto con esquís

skilful ['skɪlful] (BRIT) adj diestro, experto

ski lift n telesilla m, telesquí m

skill [skɪl] n destreza, pericia, técnica; **~ed** adj hábil, diestro; (worker) cualificado; **~full** (US) adj = **skilful**

skim [skɪm] vt (milk) desnatar; (glide over) rozar, rasar ♦ vi: to ~ through (book) hojear; **~med milk** n leche f desnatada

skimp [skɪmp] vt (also: ~ on: work) chapucear; (cloth etc) escatimar; **~y** adj escaso; (skirt) muy corto

skin [skɪn] n piel f; (complexion) cutis m ♦ vt (fruit etc) pelar; (animal) despellejar; **~ cancer** n cáncer m de piel; **~-deep** adj superficial; **~ diving** n buceo; **~ny** adj flaco; **~tight** adj (dress etc) muy ajustado

skip [skɪp] n brinco, salto; (BRIT: container) contenedor m ♦ vi brincar; (with rope) saltar a la comba ♦ vt saltarse

ski: ~ pass n forfait m (de esquí); **~ pole** n bastón m de esquiar

skipper ['skɪpə*] n (NAUT, SPORT) capitán m

skipping rope ['skɪpɪŋ-] (BRIT) n comba

skirmish ['skɜːmɪʃ] n escaramuza

skirt [skɜːt] n falda (SP), pollera (AM) ♦ vt (go round) ladear; **~ing board** (BRIT) n rodapié m

ski slope n pista de esquí

ski suit n traje m de esquiar

ski tow n remonte m

skittle ['skɪtl] n bolo; **~s** n (game) boliche m

skive [skaɪv] (BRIT: inf) vi gandulear

skull [skʌl] n calavera; (ANAT) cráneo

skunk [skʌŋk] n mofeta

sky [skaɪ] n cielo; **~light** n tragaluz m, claraboya; **~scraper** n rascacielos m inv

slab [slæb] n (stone) bloque m; (flat) losa; (of cake) trozo

slack [slæk] adj (loose) flojo; (slow) de poca actividad; (careless) descuidado; **~s** npl pantalones mpl; **~en** (also: ~en off) vi aflojarse ♦ vt aflojar; (speed) disminuir

slag heap [slæg-] n escorial m, escombrera

slag off (BRIT: inf) vt poner como un trapo

slam [slæm] vt (throw) arrojar (violentamente); (criticize) criticar duramente ♦ vi (door) cerrarse de golpe; **to ~ the door** dar un portazo

slander ['slɑːndə*] n calumnia, difamación f

slang [slæŋ] n argot m; (jargon) jerga

slant [slɑːnt] n sesgo, inclinación f; (fig) interpretación f; **~ed** adj (fig) parcial; **~ing** adj inclinado; (eyes) rasgado

slap |slæp| n palmada; (in face) bofetada ♦ vt dar una palmada or bofetada a; (paint etc): **to ~ sth on sth** embadurnar algo con algo ♦ adv (directly) exactamente, directamente; **~dash** adj descuidado; **~stick** n comedia de golpe y porrazo; **~-up** adj: **a ~-up meal** (BRIT) un banquetazo, una comilona

slash |slæʃ| vt acuchillar; (fig: prices) fulminar

slat |slæt| n tablilla, listón m

slate |sleɪt| n pizarra ♦ vt (fig: criticize) criticar duramente

slaughter |'slɔ:tə*| n (of animals) matanza; (of people) carnicería ♦ vt matar; **~house** n matadero

Slav |slɑ:v| adj eslavo

slave |sleɪv| n esclavo/a ♦ vi (also: ~ away) sudar tinta; **~ry** n esclavitud f

slay |sleɪ| (pt slew, pp slain) vt matar

sleazy |'sli:zɪ| adj de mala fama

sledge |sledʒ| n trineo; **~hammer** n mazo

sleek |sli:k| adj (shiny) lustroso; (car etc) elegante

sleep |sli:p| (pt, pp slept) n sueño ♦ vi dormir; **to go to ~** quedarse dormido; **~ around** vi acostarse con cualquiera; **~ in** vi (oversleep) quedarse dormido; **~er** n (person) durmiente m/f; (BRIT: RAIL: on track) traviesa; (: train) coche-cama m; **~ing bag** n saco de dormir; **~ing car** n coche-cama m; **~ing partner** (BRIT) n (COMM) socio comanditario; **~ing pill** n somnífero; **~less** adj: **a ~less night** una noche en blanco; **~walker** n sonámbulo/a; **~y** adj soñoliento; (place) soporífero

sleet |sli:t| n aguanieve f

sleeve |sli:v| n manga; (TECH) manguito; (of record) portada; **~less** adj sin mangas

sleigh |sleɪ| n trineo

sleight |slaɪt| n: **~ of hand** escamoteo

slender |'slendə*| adj delgado; (means)

escaso

slept |slept| pt, pp of **sleep**

slew |slu:| pt of **slay** ♦ vi (BRIT: veer) torcerse

slice |slaɪs| n (of meat) tajada; (of bread) rebanada; (of lemon) rodaja; (utensil) pala ♦ vt cortar (en tajos); rebanar

slick |slɪk| adj (skilful) hábil, diestro; (clever) astuto ♦ n (also: oil ~) marea negra

slide |slaɪd| (pt, pp slid) n (movement) descenso, desprendimiento; (in playground) tobogán m; (PHOT) diapositiva; (BRIT: also: hair ~) pasador m ♦ vt correr, deslizar ♦ vi (slip) resbalarse; (glide) deslizarse; **sliding** adj (door) corredizo; **sliding scale** n escala móvil

slight |slaɪt| adj (slim) delgado; (frail) delicado; (pain etc) leve; (trivial) insignificante; (small) pequeño ♦ n desaire m ♦ vt (insult) ofender, desairar; **not in the ~est** en absoluto; **~ly** adv ligeramente, un poco

slim |slɪm| adj delgado, esbelto; (fig: chance) remoto ♦ vi adelgazar

slime |slaɪm| n limo, cieno

slimming |'slɪmɪŋ| n adelgazamiento

slimy |'slaɪmɪ| adj cenagoso

sling |slɪŋ| (pt, pp slung) n (MED) cabestrillo; (weapon) honda ♦ vt tirar, arrojar

slip |slɪp| n (slide) resbalón m; (mistake) descuido; (underskirt) combinación f; (of paper) papelito ♦ vt (slide) deslizar ♦ vi deslizarse; (stumble) resbalar(se); (decline) decaer; (move smoothly): **to ~ into/out of** (room etc) introducirse en/salirse de; **to give sb the ~** eludir a uno; **a ~ of the tongue** un lapsus; **to ~ sth on/off** ponerse/quitarse algo; **~ away** vi escabullirse; **~ in** vt meter ♦ vi meterse; **~ out** vi (go out) salir (un momento); **~ up** vi (make mistake) equivocarse; meter la pata; **~ped disc** n vértebra dislocada

slipper ['slɪpə*] n zapatilla, pantufla
slippery ['slɪpərɪ] adj resbaladizo
slip: ~ **road** (BRIT) n carretera de acceso; ~**up** n (error) desliz m; ~**way** n grada, gradas fpl
slit [slɪt] (pt, pp **slit**) n raja; (cut) corte m ♦ vt rajar; cortar
slither ['slɪðə*] vi deslizarse
sliver ['slɪvə*] n (of glass, wood) astilla f; (of cheese etc) raja
slob [slɒb] (inf) n abandonado/a
slog [slɒg] (BRIT) vi sudar tinta; **it was a** ~ costó trabajo (hacerlo)
slogan ['sləʊgən] n eslogan m, lema m
slope [sləʊp] n (up) cuesta, pendiente f; (down) declive m; (side of mountain) falda, vertiente m ♦ vi: **to** ~ **down** estar en declive; **to** ~ **up** inclinarse
sloping adj en pendiente; en declive; (writing) inclinado
sloppy ['slɒpɪ] adj (work) descuidado; (appearance) desaliñado
slot [slɒt] n ranura ♦ vt: **to** ~ **into** encajar en
slot machine n (BRIT: vending machine) distribuidor m automático; (for gambling) tragaperras m inv
slouch [slaʊtʃ] vi andar etc con los hombros caídos
Slovenia [sləʊ'viːnɪə] n Eslovenia
slovenly ['slʌvənlɪ] adj desaliñado, desaseado; (careless) descuidado
slow [sləʊ] adj lento; (not clever) lerdo; (watch): **to be** ~ atrasar ♦ adv lentamente, despacio ♦ vt, vi (also: ~ **down**, ~ **up**) retardar; "~" (road sign) "disminuir velocidad"; ~**down** (US) n huelga de manos caídas; ~**ly** adv lentamente, despacio; **in** ~ **motion** a cámara lenta
sludge [slʌdʒ] n lodo, fango
slug [slʌg] n babosa; (bullet) posta; ~**gish** adj lento; (person) perezoso
sluice [sluːs] n (gate) esclusa; (channel) canal m
slum [slʌm] n casucha
slump [slʌmp] n (economic) depresión

slung [slʌŋ] pt, pp of **sling**
slur [slɜː*] n: **to cast a** ~ **on** insultar ♦ vt (speech) pronunciar mal
slush [slʌʃ] n nieve f a medio derretir
slut [slʌt] n putona
sly [slaɪ] adj astuto; (smile) taimado
smack [smæk] n bofetada ♦ vt dar con la mano a; (child, on face) abofetear ♦ vi: **to** ~ **of** saber a, oler a
small [smɔːl] adj pequeño; ~ **ads** (BRIT) npl anuncios mpl por palabras; ~ **change** n suelto, cambio; ~**holder** (BRIT) n granjero/a, parcelero/a; ~ **hours** npl: **in the** ~ **hours** a las altas horas (de la noche); ~**pox** n viruela; ~ **talk** n cháchara
smart [smɑːt] adj elegante; (clever) listo, inteligente; (quick) rápido, vivo ♦ vi escocer, picar; ~**en up** vi arreglarse ♦ vt arreglar
smash [smæʃ] n (also: ~**up**) choque m; (MUS) exitazo ♦ vt (break) hacer pedazos; (car etc) estrellar; (SPORT: record) batir ♦ vi hacerse pedazos; (against wall etc) estrellarse; ~**ing** (inf) adj estupendo
smattering ['smætərɪŋ] n: **a** ~ **of** algo de
smear [smɪə*] n mancha; (MED) frotis m inv ♦ vt untar; ~ **campaign** n campaña de desprestigio
smell [smel] (pt, pp **smelt** or **smelled**) n olor m; (sense) olfato ♦ vt, vi oler; ~**y** adj maloliente
smile [smaɪl] n sonrisa ♦ vi sonreír
smirk [smɜːk] n sonrisa falsa or afectada
smith [smɪθ] n herrero; ~**y** ['smɪðɪ] n herrería
smog [smɒg] n esmog m
smoke [sməʊk] n humo ♦ vi fumar; (chimney) echar humo ♦ vt (cigarettes) fumar; ~**d** adj (bacon, glass) ahumado; ~**r** n fumador/a m/f; (RAIL) coche m fumador; ~ **screen** n cortina de humo; ~ **shop** (US) n estanco (SP),

tabaquería (AM); **smoking** n: "**no smoking**" "prohibido fumar"; **smoky** adj (room) lleno de humo; (taste) ahumado

smolder ['sməuldə*] (US) vi = **smoulder**

smooth [smu:ð] adj liso; (sea) tranquilo; (flavour, movement) suave; (sauce) fino; (person: pej) meloso ♦ vt (also: ~ out) alisar; (creases, difficulties) allanar

smother ['smʌðə*] vt sofocar; (repress) contener

smoulder ['sməuldə*] (US smolder) vi arder sin llama

smudge [smʌdʒ] n mancha ♦ vt manchar

smug [smʌg] adj presumido; orondo

smuggle ['smʌgl] vt pasar de contrabando; ~r n contrabandista m/f; **smuggling** n contrabando

smutty ['smʌtɪ] adj (fig) verde, obsceno

snack [snæk] n bocado; ~ **bar** n cafetería

snag [snæg] n problema m

snail [sneɪl] n caracol m

snake [sneɪk] n serpiente f

snap [snæp] n (sound) chasquido; (photograph) foto f ♦ adj (decision) instantáneo ♦ vt (break) quebrar; (fingers) castañetear ♦ vi quebrarse; (fig: speak sharply) contestar bruscamente; **to ~ shut** cerrarse de golpe; ~ **at** vt fus (subj: dog) intentar morder; ~ **off** vi partirse; ~ **up** vt agarrar; ~ **fastener** (US) n botón m de presión; ~**py** (inf) adj (answer) instantáneo; (slogan) conciso; **make it ~py!** (hurry up) ¡date prisa!; ~**shot** n foto f (instantánea)

snare [snɛə*] n trampa

snarl [snɑ:l] vi gruñir

snatch [snætʃ] n (small piece) fragmento ♦ vt (~ away) arrebatar; (fig) agarrar; **to ~ some sleep** encontrar tiempo para dormir

sneak [sni:k] (pt (US) snuck) vi: **to ~ in/out** entrar/salir a hurtadillas ♦ (inf) soplón/ona m/f; **to ~ up on sb** aparecérsele de improviso a uno; ~**ers** npl zapatos mpl de lona; ~**y** adj furtivo

sneer [snɪə*] vi reír con sarcasmo; (mock): **to ~ at** burlarse de

sneeze [sni:z] vi estornudar

sniff [snɪf] vi sollozar ♦ vt husmear, oler; (drugs) esnifar

snigger ['snɪgə*] vi reírse con disimulo

snip [snɪp] n tijeretazo; (inf: bargain) ganga ♦ vt tijeretear

sniper ['snaɪpə*] n tirador(a) m/f

snippet ['snɪpɪt] n retazo

snob [snɔb] n (e)snob m/f; ~**bery** n (e)snobismo; ~**bish** adj (e)snob

snooker ['snu:kə*] n especie de billar

snoop [snu:p] vi: **to ~ about** fisgonear

snooze [snu:z] n siesta ♦ vi echar una siesta

snore [snɔ:*] n ronquido ♦ vi roncar

snorkel ['snɔ:kl] n (tubo) respirador m

snort [snɔ:t] n bufido ♦ vi bufar

snout [snaut] n hocico, morro

snow [snəu] n nieve f ♦ vi nevar; ~**ball** n bola de nieve ♦ vi (fig) agrandirse, ampliarse; ~**bound** adj bloqueado por la nieve; ~**drift** n ventisquero; ~**drop** n campanilla; ~**fall** n nevada; ~**flake** n copo de nieve; ~**man** (irreg) n figura de nieve; ~**plough** (US ~**plow**) n quitanieves m inv; ~**shoe** n raqueta (de nieve); ~**storm** n nevada, nevasca

snub [snʌb] vt (person) desairar ♦ n desaire m, repulsa; ~-**nosed** adj chato

snuff [snʌf] n rapé m

snug [snʌg] adj (cosy) cómodo; (fitted) ajustado

snuggle ['snʌgl] vi: **to ~ up to sb** arrimarse a uno

KEYWORD

so [səu] adv **1** (thus, likewise) así, de este modo; **if ~ de ser así; I like swimming — do I** a mí me gusta nadar — a mí también; **I've got work**

to do — has Paul tengo trabajo que hacer — Paul también; **it's 5 o'clock — ~ it is!** son las cinco ¡pues es verdad!; **I hope/think ~** espero/creo que sí; **~ far** hasta ahora; (*in past*) hasta este momento **2** (*in comparisons etc: to such a degree*) tan; **~ quickly (that)** tan rápido (que); **~ big (that)** tan grande (que); **she's not ~ clever as her brother** no es tan lista como su hermano; **we were ~ worried** estábamos preocupadísimos **3: ~ much** *adj, adv* tanto; **~ many** tantos/as **4** (*phrases*) **10 or ~** unos 10, 10 o así; **~ long!** (*inf: goodbye*) ¡hasta luego! ♦ *conj* **1** (*expressing purpose*): **~ as to do** para hacer; **~ (that)** para que + *sub* **2** (*expressing result*) así que; **~ you see, I could have gone** así que ya ves, (yo) podría haber ido

soak [sǝuk] *vt* (*drench*) empapar; (*steep in water*) remojar ♦ *vi* remojarse, estar a remojo; **~ in** *vi* penetrar; **~ up** *vt* absorber

soap [sǝup] *n* jabón *m*; **~flakes** *npl* escamas *fpl* de jabón; **~ opera** *n* telenovela; **~ powder** *n* jabón *m* en polvo; **~y** *adj* jabonoso

soar [sɔ:*] *vi* (*on wings*) remontarse; (*rocket, prices*) disparar se; (*building etc*) elevarse

sob [sɔb] *n* sollozo ♦ *vi* sollozar

sober ['sǝubǝ*] *adj* (*serious*) serio; (*not drunk*) sobrio; (*colour, style*) discreto; **~ up** *vt* quitar la borrachera

so-called *adj* así llamado

soccer ['sɔkǝ*] *n* fútbol *m*

social ['sǝuʃl] *adj* social ♦ *n* velada, fiesta; **~ club** *n* club *m*; **~ism** *n* socialismo; **~ist** *adj, n* socialista *m/f*; **~ize** *vi*: **to ~ize (with)** alternar (con); **~ly** *adv* socialmente; **~ security** *n* seguridad *f* social; **~ work** *n* asistencia social; **~ worker** *n* asistente/a *m/f*

social

society [sǝ'saɪǝtɪ] *n* sociedad *f*; (*club*) asociación *f*; (*also: high ~*) alta sociedad

sociology [sǝusɪ'ɔlǝdʒɪ] *n* sociología

sock [sɔk] *n* calcetín *m* (SP), media (AM)

socket ['sɔkɪt] *n* cavidad *f*; (BRIT: ELEC) enchufe *m*

sod [sɔd] *n* (*of earth*) césped *m*; (BRIT: *inf!*) cabrón/ona *m/f* (!)

soda ['sǝudǝ] *n* (CHEM) sosa; (*also: ~ water*) soda; (US: *also: ~ pop*) gaseosa

sofa ['sǝufǝ] *n* sofá *m*

soft [sɔft] *adj* (*lenient, not hard*) blando; (*gentle, not bright*) suave; **~ drink** *n* bebida no alcohólica; **~en** ['sɔfn] *vt* ablandar; suavizar; (*effect*) amortiguar ♦ *vi* ablandarse; suavizarse; **~ly** *adv* suavemente; (*gently*) delicadamente, con delicadeza; **~ness** *n* blandura; suavidad *f*; **~ware** *n* (COMPUT) software *m*

soggy ['sɔgɪ] *adj* empapado

soil [sɔɪl] *n* (*earth*) tierra, suelo ♦ *vt* ensuciar; **~ed** *adj* sucio

solar ['sǝulǝ*] *adj*: **~ energy** *n* energía solar; **~ panel** *n* panel *m* solar

sold [sǝuld] *pt, pp* of **sell**; **~ out** (COMM) agotado

solder ['sǝuldǝ*] *vt* soldar ♦ *n* soldadura

soldier ['sǝuldʒǝ*] *n* soldado; (*army man*) militar *m*

sole [sǝul] *n* (*of foot*) planta; (*of shoe*) suela; (*fish: pl inv*) lenguado ♦ *adj* único

solemn ['sɔlǝm] *adj* solemne

sole trader *n* (COMM) comerciante *m* exclusivo

solicit [sǝ'lɪsɪt] *vt* (*request*) solicitar ♦ *vi* (*prostitute*) importunar

solicitor [sǝ'lɪsɪtǝ*] *n* (BRIT) *n* (*for wills etc*) ≈ notario/a; (*in court*) ≈ abogado/a

solid ['sɔlɪd] *adj* sólido; (*gold etc*) macizo ♦ *n* sólido; **~s** *npl* (*food*) alimentos *mpl* sólidos

solidarity [sɔlɪ'dærɪtɪ] n solidaridad f
solitary ['sɔlɪtərɪ] adj solitario, solo;
~ **confinement** n incomunicación f
solo ['səʊləʊ] n solo ♦ adv (fly) en
solitario; **~ist** n solista m/f
soluble ['sɔljʊbl] adj soluble
solution [sə'luːʃən] n solución f
solve [sɔlv] vt resolver, solucionar
solvent ['sɔlvənt] adj (COMM) solvente
♦ n (CHEM) solvente m

KEYWORD

some [sʌm] adj 1 (a certain amount or
number of): ~ **tea/water/biscuits** té/
agua/(unas) galletas; **there's ~ milk
in the fridge** hay leche en el frigo;
there were ~ people outside había
algunas personas fuera; **I've got
~ money, but not much** tengo algo
de dinero, pero no mucho
2 (certain: in contrasts) algunos/as;
~ **people say that ...** hay quien dice
que ...; ~ **films were excellent, but
most were mediocre** hubo películas
excelentes, pero la mayoría fueron
mediocres
3 (unspecified): ~ **woman was
asking for you** una mujer estuvo
preguntando por ti; **he was asking
for ~ book (or other)** pedía un libro;
~ **day** algún día; ~ **day next week**
un día de la semana que viene
♦ pron 1 (a certain number): **I've got ~**
(books etc) tengo algunos/as
2 (a certain amount) algo; **I've got ~**
(money, milk) tengo algo; **could I
have ~ of that cheese?** ¿me puede
dar un poco de ese queso?; **I've read
~ of the book** he leído parte del libro
♦ adv: ~ **10 people** unas 10 personas,
una decena de personas

some: **~body** ['sʌmbədɪ] pron =
someone; **~how** adv de alguna
manera; (for some reason) por una u
otra razón; **~one** pron alguien; **~place**
(US) adv = **somewhere**

somersault ['sʌməsɔːlt] n (deliberate)
salto mortal; (accidental) vuelco ♦ vi
dar un salto mortal; dar vuelcos
some: **~thing** pron algo; **would you
like ~thing to eat/drink?** ¿te
gustaría cenar/tomar algo?; **~time** adv
(in future) algún día, en algún
momento; (in past): **~time last
month** durante el mes pasado;
~times adv a veces; **~what** adv algo;
~where adv (be) en alguna parte; (go)
a alguna parte; **~where else** (be) en
otra parte; (go) a otra parte
son [sʌn] n hijo
song [sɔŋ] n canción f
son-in-law n yerno
soon [suːn] adv pronto, dentro de
poco; **~ afterwards** poco después; see
also **as;** **~er** adv (time) antes, más
temprano; (preference): **I would ~er
do that** preferiría hacer eso; **~er or
later** tarde o temprano
soot [sut] n hollín m
soothe [suːð] vt tranquilizar; (pain)
aliviar
sophisticated [sə'fɪstɪkeɪtɪd] adj
sofisticado
sophomore ['sɔfəmɔː*] (US) n
estudiante m/f de segundo año
sopping ['sɔpɪŋ] adj: ~ (wet)
empapado
soppy ['sɔpɪ] (pej) adj tonto
soprano [sə'prɑːnəʊ] n soprano f
sorcerer ['sɔːsərə*] n hechicero
sore [sɔː*] adj (painful) doloroso, que
duele ♦ n llaga; **~ly** adv: **I am ~ly
tempted to** estoy muy tentado a
sorrow ['sɔrəʊ] n pena, dolor m; **~s**
npl pesares mpl; **~ful** adj triste
sorry ['sɔrɪ] adj (regretful) arrepentido;
(condition, excuse) lastimoso; ~!
¡perdón!, ¡perdone!; ~? ¿cómo?; **to
feel ~ for sb** tener lástima a uno; **I
feel ~ for him** me da lástima
sort [sɔːt] n clase f, género, tipo ♦ vt
(also: ~ out: papers) clasificar;
(: problems) arreglar, solucionar; **~ing**

office n sala de batalla
SOS n SOS m
so-so adv regular, así así
soufflé ['suːfleɪ] n suflé m
sought [sɔːt] pt, pp of **seek**
soul [səul] n alma; **~ful** adj lleno de sentimiento
sound [saund] adj (noise) sonido, ruido; (volume: on TV etc) volumen m; (GEO) estrecho ♦ adj (healthy) sano; (safe, not damaged) en buen estado; (reliable: person) digno de confianza; (sensible) sensato, razonable; (secure: investment) seguro ♦ adv: **~ asleep** profundamente dormido ♦ vt (alarm) sonar ♦ vi sonar, resonar; (fig: seem) parecer; **to ~ like** sonar a; **~ out** vt sondear; **~ barrier** n barrera del sonido; **~bite** n cita jugosa; **~ effects** npl efectos mpl sonoros; **~ly** adv (sleep) profundamente; (defeated) completamente; **~proof** adj insonorizado ♦ vt; **~track** n (of film) banda sonora
soup [suːp] n (thick) sopa; (thin) caldo; **~ plate** n plato sopero; **~spoon** n cuchara sopera
sour ['sauə*] adj agrio; (milk) cortado; **it's ~ grapes** (fig) están verdes
source [sɔːs] n fuente f
south [sauθ] n sur m ♦ adj del sur, sureño ♦ adv al sur, hacia el sur; **S~ Africa** n África del Sur; **S~ African** adj, n sudafricano/a m/f; **S~ America** n América del Sur, Sudamérica; **S~ American** adj, n sudamericano/a m/f; **~-east** n sudeste m; **~erly** ['sʌðəlɪ] adj sur; (from the ~) del sur; **~ern** ['sʌðən] adj del sur, meridional; **S~ Pole** n Polo Sur; **~ward(s)** adv hacia el sur; **~-west** n suroeste m
souvenir [suːvə'nɪə*] n recuerdo
sovereign ['sɔvrɪn] adj, n soberano/a m/f; **~ty** n soberanía
soviet ['səuvɪət] adj soviético; **the S~ Union** la Unión Soviética

sow[1] [səu] (pt **sowed**, pp **sown**) vt sembrar
sow[2] [sau] n cerda (SP), puerca (SP), chancha (AM)
soy [sɔɪ] (US) n = **soya**
soya ['sɔɪə] (BRIT) n soja; **~ bean** n haba de soja; **~ sauce** n salsa de soja
spa [spɑː] n balneario
space [speɪs] n espacio; (room) sitio ♦ cpd espacial ♦ vt (also: **~ out**) espaciar; **~craft** n nave f espacial; **~man/woman** (irreg) n astronauta m/f, cosmonauta m/f; **~ship** n = **~craft**; **spacing** n espaciado
spacious ['speɪʃəs] adj amplio
spade [speɪd] n (tool) pala, laya; **~s** npl (CARDS: British) picas fpl; (: Spanish) espadas fpl
spaghetti [spə'getɪ] n espaguetis mpl, fideos mpl
Spain [speɪn] n España
span [spæn] n (of bird, plane) envergadura; (of arch) luz f; (in time) lapso ♦ vt extenderse sobre, cruzar; (fig) abarcar
Spaniard ['spænjəd] n español(a) m/f
spaniel ['spænjəl] n perro de aguas
Spanish ['spænɪʃ] adj español(a) ♦ n (LING) español m, castellano; **the ~** npl los españoles
spank [spæŋk] vt zurrar
spanner ['spænə*] (BRIT) n llave f (inglesa)
spare [speə*] adj de reserva; (surplus) sobrante, de más ♦ n = **~ part** ♦ vt (do without) pasarse sin; (refrain from hurting) perdonar; **to ~** (surplus) sobrante, de sobra; **~ part** n pieza de repuesto; **~ time** n tiempo libre; **~ wheel** n (AUT) rueda de recambio
sparingly ['speərɪŋlɪ] adv con moderación
spark [spɑːk] n chispa; (fig) chispazo; **~(ing) plug** n bujía
sparkle ['spɑːkl] n centelleo, destello ♦ vi (shine) relucir, brillar; **sparkling** adj (eyes, conversation) brillante; (wine)

espumoso; (*mineral water*) con gas
sparrow ['spærəu] *n* gorrión *m*
sparse [spɑ:s] *adj* esparcido, escaso
spartan ['spɑ:tən] *adj* (*fig*) espartano
spasm ['spæzəm] *n* (*MED*) espasmo
spastic ['spæstɪk] *n* espástico/a
spat [spæt] *pt, pp of* **spit**
spate [speɪt] *n* (*fig*): **a ~ of** un torrente
de
spawn [spɔ:n] *vi* desovar, frezar ♦ *n*
huevas *fpl*
speak [spi:k] (*pt* **spoke**, *pp* **spoken**)
vt (*language*) hablar; (*truth*) decir ♦ *vi*
hablar; (*make a speech*) intervenir; **to
~ to sb/of** or **about sth** hablar con
uno/de o sobre algo; **~ up!** ¡habla
fuerte!; **~er** *n* (*in public*) orador(a) *m/f*;
(*also:* loud~er) altavoz *m*; (*for stereo etc*)
bafle *m*; (*POL*): **the S~er** (*BRIT*) el
Presidente de la Cámara de los
Comunes; (*US*) el Presidente del Congreso
spear [spɪə*] *n* lanza ♦ *vt* alancear;
~head *vt* (*attack etc*) encabezar
spec [spek] (*inf*) *n*: **on ~** como
especulación
special ['speʃl] *adj* especial; (*edition etc*)
extraordinario; (*delivery*) urgente; **~ist**
n especialista *m/f*; **~ity** [speʃɪ'ælɪtɪ]
(*BRIT*) *n* especialidad *f*; **~ize** *vi*: **to ~ize
(in)** especializarse (en); **~ly** *adv* sobre
todo, en particular; **~ty** (*US*) *n* = **~ity**
species ['spi:ʃi:z] *n inv* especie *f*
specific [spə'sɪfɪk] *adj* específico; **~ally**
adv específicamente
specify ['spesɪfaɪ] *vt, vi* especificar,
precisar
specimen ['spesɪmən] *n* ejemplar *m*;
(*MED: of urine*) espécimen *m* (*: of blood*)
muestra
speck [spek] *n* grano, mota
speckled ['spekld] *adj* moteado
specs [speks] (*inf*) *npl* gafas *fpl* (*SP*),
anteojos *mpl*
spectacle ['spektəkl] *n* espectáculo; **~s**
npl (*BRIT: glasses*) gafas *fpl* (*SP*),
anteojos *mpl*; **spectacular** [-'tækjulə*]
adj espectacular; (*success*)

impresionante
spectator [spek'teɪtə*] *n* espectador(a)
m/f
spectrum ['spektrəm] (*pl* **spectra**) *n*
espectro
speculate ['spekjuleɪt] *vi*: **to ~ (on)**
especular (en); **speculation**
[spekju'leɪʃən] *n* especulación *f*
speech [spi:tʃ] *n* (*faculty*) habla; (*formal
talk*) discurso; (*spoken language*)
lenguaje *m*; **~less** *adj* mudo,
estupefacto; **~ therapist** *n* especialista
m/f que corrige defectos de pronunciación en
los niños
speed [spi:d] *n* velocidad *f*; (*haste*)
prisa; (*promptness*) rapidez *f*; **at full** or
top ~ a máxima velocidad; **~ up** *vi*
acelerarse ♦ *vt* acelerar; **~boat** *n*
lancha motora; **~ily** *adv* rápido,
rápidamente; **~ing** (*AUT*) exceso de
velocidad; **~ limit** *n* límite *m* de
velocidad, velocidad *f* máxima;
~ometer [spɪ'dɒmɪtə*] *n* velocímetro;
~way *n* (*sport*) pista de carrera; **~y** *adj*
(*fast*) veloz, rápido; (*prompt*) pronto
spell [spel] (*pt, pp* **spelt** (*BRIT*) or
spelled) *n* (*also: magic ~*) encanto,
hechizo; (*period of time*) rato, período
♦ *vt* deletrear; (*fig*) anunciar, presagiar;
to cast a ~ on sb hechizar a uno; **he
can't ~** pone faltas de ortografía;
~bound *adj* embelesado, hechizado;
~ing *n* ortografía
spend [spend] (*pt, pp* **spent**) *vt*
(*money*) gastar; (*time*) pasar; (*life*)
dedicar; **~thrift** *n* derrochador(a) *m/f*,
pródigo/a
sperm [spɜ:m] *n* esperma
sphere [sfɪə*] *n* esfera
sphinx [sfɪŋks] *n* esfinge *f*
spice [spaɪs] *n* especia ♦ *vt*
condimentar
spicy ['spaɪsɪ] *adj* picante
spider ['spaɪdə*] *n* araña
spike [spaɪk] *n* (*point*) punta; (*BOT*)
espiga
spill [spɪl] (*pt, pp* **spilt** or **spilled**) *vt*

derramar, verter ♦ vi derramarse; **to ~ over** desbordarse

spin [spɪn] n (AVIAT) barrena; (trip in car) paseo (en coche); (on ball) efecto ♦ vt (wool etc) hilar; (ball etc) hacer girar ♦ vi girar, dar vueltas

spinach ['spɪnɪtʃ] n espinaca; (as food) espinacas fpl

spinal ['spaɪnl] adj espinal; **~ cord** n columna vertebral

spin doctor n informador(a) parcial al servicio de un partido político etc

spin-dryer (BRIT) n secador m centrífugo

spine [spaɪn] n espinazo, columna vertebral; (thorn) espina; **~less** adj (fig) débil, pusilánime

spinning ['spɪnɪŋ] n hilandería; **~ top** n peonza

spin-off n derivado, producto secundario

spinster ['spɪnstə*] n soltera

spiral ['spaɪərl] n espiral ♦ vi (fig: prices) subir desorbitadamente; **~ staircase** n escalera de caracol

spire ['spaɪə*] n aguja, chapitel m

spirit ['spɪrɪt] n (soul) alma f; (ghost) fantasma m; (attitude, sense) espíritu m; (courage) valor m, ánimo; **~s** npl (drink) licor(es) m(pl); **in good ~s** alegre, de buen ánimo; **~ed** adj enérgico, vigoroso

spiritual ['spɪrɪtjuəl] adj espiritual ♦ n espiritual m

spit [spɪt] (pt, pp spat) n (for roasting) asador m, espetón m; (saliva) saliva ♦ vi escupir; (sound) chisporrotear; (rain) lloviznar

spite [spaɪt] n rencor m, ojeriza ♦ vt causar pena a, mortificar; **in ~ of** a pesar de, pese a; **~ful** adj rencoroso, malévolo

spittle ['spɪtl] n saliva, baba

splash [splæʃ] n (sound) chapoteo; (of colour) mancha ♦ vt salpicar ♦ vi (also: ~ about) chapotear

spleen [spli:n] n (ANAT) bazo

splendid ['splendɪd] adj espléndido

splint [splɪnt] n tablilla

splinter ['splɪntə*] n (of wood etc) astilla; (in finger) espigón m ♦ vi astillarse, hacer astillas

split [splɪt] (pt, pp split) n hendedura, raja; (fig) división f; (POL) escisión f ♦ vt partir, rajar; (party) dividir; (share) repartir ♦ vi dividirse, escindirse; **~ up** vi (couple) separarse; (meeting) acabarse

spoil [spɔɪl] (pt, pp spoilt or spoiled) vt (damage) dañar; (mar) estropear; (child) mimar, consentir; **~s** npl despojo, botín m; **~sport** n aguafiestas m inv

spoke [spəuk] pt of **speak** ♦ n rayo, radio

spoken ['spəukn] pp of **speak**

spokesman ['spəuksmən] (irreg) n portavoz m; **spokeswoman** ['spəukswumən] (irreg) n portavoz f

sponge [spʌndʒ] n esponja; (also: ~ cake) bizcocho ♦ vt (wash) lavar con esponja ♦ vi: **to ~ off or on sb** vivir a costa de uno; **~ bag** (BRIT) n esponjera

sponsor ['spɒnsə*] n patrocinador(a) m/f ♦ vt (applicant, proposal etc) proponer; **~ship** n patrocinio

spontaneous [spɒn'teɪnɪəs] adj espontáneo

spooky ['spu:kɪ] (inf) adj espeluznante, horripilante

spool [spu:l] n carrete m

spoon [spu:n] n cuchara; **~-feed** vt dar de comer con cuchara a; (fig) tratar como un niño a; **~ful** n cucharada

sport [spɔ:t] n deporte m; (person): **to be a good ~** ser muy majo ♦ vt (wear) lucir, ostentar; **~ing** adj deportivo; (generous) caballeroso; **to give sb a ~ing chance** darle a uno una (buena) oportunidad; **~ jacket** (US) n = **~s jacket**; **~s car** n coche m deportivo; **~s jacket** (BRIT) n chaqueta deportiva; **~sman** (irreg) n deportista m;

~smanship n deportividad f; **~swear** n trajes mpl de deporte or sport; **~swoman** (irreg) n deportista; **~y** adj deportista

spot [spɔt] n sitio, lugar m; (dot: on pattern) punto, mancha; (pimple) grano; (RADIO) cuña publicitaria; (TV) espacio publicitario; (small amount): **a ~ of** un poquito de ♦ vt (notice) notar, observar; **on the ~** allí mismo; **~ check** n reconocimiento rápido; **~less** adj perfectamente limpio; **~light** n foco, reflector m; (AUT) faro auxiliar; **~ted** adj (pattern) de puntos; **~ty** adj (face) con granos

spouse [spauz] n cónyuge m/f

spout [spaut] n (of jug) pico; (of pipe) caño ♦ vi salir en chorro

sprain [spreɪn] n torcedura ♦ vt: **to ~ one's ankle/wrist** torcerse el tobillo/la muñeca

sprang [spræŋ] pt of **spring**

sprawl [sprɔ:l] vi tumbarse

spray [spreɪ] n rociada; (of sea) espuma; (container) atomizador m; (for paint etc) pistola rociadora; (of flowers) ramita ♦ vt rociar; (crops) regar

spread [spred] (pt, pp spread) n extensión f; (for bread etc) pasta para untar; (inf: food) comilona ♦ vt extender; (butter) untar; (wings, sails) desplegar; (work, wealth) repartir; (scatter) esparcir ♦ vi (also: ~ out: stain) extenderse; (news) diseminarse; **~ out** vi (move apart) separarse; **~-eagled** adj a pata tendida; **~sheet** n hoja electrónica or de cálculo

spree [spri:] n: **to go on a ~** ir de juerga

sprightly [ˈspraɪtlɪ] adj vivo, enérgico

spring [sprɪŋ] (pt sprang, pp sprung) n (season) primavera; (leap) salto, brinco; (coiled metal) resorte m; (of water) fuente f, manantial m ♦ vi saltar, brincar; **~ up** vi (problem: appear) aparecer; (problem) surgir; **~board** n trampolín m; **~-clean(ing)** n limpieza

general; **~time** n primavera

sprinkle [ˈsprɪŋkl] vt (pour: liquid) rociar; (: salt, sugar) espolvorear; **to ~ water etc on, ~ with water etc** rociar or salpicar de agua etc; **~r** n (for lawn) rociadera; (to put out fire) aparato de rociadura automática

sprint [sprɪnt] n esprint m ♦ vi esprintar

sprout [spraut] vi brotar, retoñar; **(Brussels) ~s** npl coles fpl de Bruselas

spruce [spru:s] n inv (BOT) pícea ♦ adj aseado, pulcro

sprung [sprʌŋ] pp of **spring**

spun [spʌn] pt, pp of **spin**

spur [spə:*] n espuela; (fig) estímulo, aguijón m ♦ vt (also: ~ on) estimular, incitar; **on the ~ of the moment** de improviso

spurious [ˈspjuərɪəs] adj falso

spurn [spə:n] vt desdeñar, rechazar

spurt [spə:t] n chorro; (of energy) arrebato ♦ vi chorrear

spy [spaɪ] n espía m/f ♦ vi: **to ~ on** espiar a ♦ vt (see) divisar, lograr ver; **~ing** n espionaje m

sq. abbr = **square**

squabble [ˈskwɔbl] vi reñir, pelear

squad [skwɔd] n (MIL) pelotón m; (POLICE) brigada; (SPORT) equipo

squadron [ˈskwɔdrən] n (MIL) escuadrón m; (AVIAT, NAUT) escuadra

squalid [ˈskwɔlɪd] adj vil; (fig: sordid) sórdido

squall [skwɔ:l] n (storm) chubasco; (wind) ráfaga

squalor [ˈskwɔlə*] n miseria

squander [ˈskwɔndə*] vt (money) derrochar, despilfarrar; (chances) desperdiciar

square [skwɛə*] n cuadro, (in town) plaza; (inf: person) carca m/f ♦ adj cuadrado; (inf: ideas, tastes) trasnochado ♦ vt (arrange) arreglar; (MATH) cuadrar; (reconcile) compaginar; **all ~** igual(es); **to have a ~ meal** comer caliente; **2 metres ~** 2 metros

en cuadro; **2 ~ metres** 2 metros
cuadrados; **~ly** adv de lleno
squash [skwɔʃ] n (BRIT: drink):
lemon/orange ~ zumo m o jugo
(AM) de limón/naranja; (US: BOT)
calabacín m, frontenis m ♦ vt aplastar
squat [skwɔt] adj achaparrado ♦ vi
(also: ~ **down**) agacharse, sentarse en
cuclillas; **~ter** n persona que ocupa
ilegalmente una casa
squeak [skwi:k] vi (hinge) chirriar,
rechinar; (mouse) chillar
squeal [skwi:l] vi chillar, dar gritos
agudos
squeamish ['skwi:mɪʃ] adj delicado,
remilgado
squeeze [skwi:z] n presión f; (of hand)
apretón m; (COMM) restricción f ♦ vt
(hand, arm) apretar; **~ out** vt exprimir
squelch [skweltʃ] vi chapotear
squid [skwɪd] n inv calamar m; (CULIN)
calamares mpl
squiggle ['skwɪɡl] n garabato
squint [skwɪnt] vi bizquear, ser bizco
♦ n (MED) estrabismo
squirm [skwə:m] vi retorcerse,
revolverse
squirrel ['skwɪrəl] n ardilla
squirt [skwə:t] vi salir a chorros ♦ vt
chiscar
Sr abbr = **senior**
St abbr = **saint**; **street**
stab [stæb] n (with knife) puñalada; (of
pain) pinchazo; (inf: try): **to have a
~ at (doing) sth** intentar (hacer) algo
♦ vt apuñalar
stable ['steɪbl] adj estable ♦ n cuadra,
caballeriza
stack [stæk] n montón m, pila ♦ vt
amontonar, apilar
stadium ['steɪdiəm] n estadio
staff [stɑ:f] n (work force) personal m,
plantilla; (BRIT: SCOL) cuerpo docente
♦ vt proveer de personal
stag [stæg] n ciervo, venado
stage [steɪdʒ] n escena; (point) etapa;

(platform) plataforma; (profession): **the
~** el teatro ♦ vt (play) poner en escena,
representar; (organize) montar,
organizar; **in ~s** por etapas; **~coach** n
diligencia; **~ manager** n director(a)
m/f de escena
stagger ['stægə*] vi tambalearse ♦ vt
(amaze) asombrar; (hours, holidays)
escalonar; **~ing** adj asombroso
stagnant ['stæɡnənt] adj estancado
stag party n despedida de soltero
staid [steɪd] adj serio, formal
stain [steɪn] n mancha; (colouring)
tintura ♦ vt manchar; (wood) teñir; **~ed
glass window** n vidriera de colores;
~less steel n acero inoxidable;
~ remover n quitamanchas m inv
stair [stɛə*] n (step) peldaño, escalón
m; **~s** npl escaleras fpl; **~case** n =
~way; **~way** n escalera
stake [steɪk] n estaca, poste m; (COMM)
interés m; (BETTING) apuesta ♦ vt
(money) apostar; (life) arriesgar;
(reputation) poner en juego; (claim)
presentar una reclamación; **to be at ~**
estar en juego
stale [steɪl] adj (bread) duro; (food)
pasado; (smell) rancio; (beer) agrio
stalemate ['steɪlmeɪt] n tablas fpl (en
ahogado); (fig) estancamiento
stalk [stɔ:k] n tallo, caña ♦ vt acechar,
cazar al acecho; **~ off** vi irse airado
stall [stɔ:l] n (in market) puesto; (in
stable) casilla (de establo) ♦ vt (AUT)
calar; (fig) dar largas a ♦ vi (AUT)
calarse; (fig) andarse con rodeos; **~s**
npl (BRIT: in cinema, theatre) butacas fpl
stallion ['stæliən] n semental m
stamina ['stæmɪnə] n resistencia
stammer ['stæmə*] n tartamudeo ♦ vi
tartamudear
stamp [stæmp] n sello (SP), estampilla
(AM); (mark, also fig) marca, huella; (on
document) timbre m ♦ vi (also: ~ one's
foot) patear ♦ vt (mark) marcar; (letter)
poner sellos o estampillas en; (with
rubber ~) sellar; **~ album** n álbum m

para sellos o estampillas; **~ collecting** n filatelia

stampede [stæm'pi:d] n estampida

stance [stæns] n postura

stand [stænd] (pt, pp **stood**) n (position) posición f, postura; (for taxis) parada; (hall ~) perchero; (music ~) atril m; (SPORT) tribuna; (at exhibition) stand m ♦ vi (be) estar, encontrarse; (be on foot) estar de pie; (rise) levantarse; (remain) quedar en pie; (in election) presentar candidatura ♦ vt (place) poner, colocar; (withstand) aguantar, soportar; (invite) to invitar; **to make a ~** (fig) mantener una postura firme; **to ~ for parliament** (BRIT) presentarse (como candidato) a las elecciones; **~ by** vi (be ready) estar listo ♦ vt fus (opinion) aferrarse a; (person) apoyar; **~ down** vi (withdraw) ceder el puesto; **~ for** vt fus (signify) significar; (tolerate) aguantar, permitir; **~ in for** vt fus suplir a; **~ out** vi (be prominent) destacarse; **~ up** vi levantarse, ponerse de pie; **~ up for** vt fus defender; **~ up to** vt fus hacer frente a

standard ['stændəd] n patrón m, norma; (level) nivel m; (flag) estandarte m ♦ adj (size etc) normal, corriente; (text) básico; **~s** npl (morals) valores mpl morales; **~ lamp** (BRIT) n lámpara de pie; **~ of living** n nivel m de vida

stand-by ['stændbaɪ] n (reserve) recurso seguro; **to be on ~** estar sobre aviso; **~ ticket** n (AVIAT) (billete m) standby m

stand-in ['stændɪn] n suplente m/f

standing ['stændɪŋ] adj (on foot) de pie, en pie; (permanent) permanente ♦ n reputación f; **of many years' ~** que lleva muchos años; **~ joke** n broma permanente; **~ order** n (BRIT) (at bank) orden f de pago permanente; **~ room** n sitio para estar de pie

stand: **~point** n punto de vista; **~still** n: **at a ~still** (industry, traffic) paralizado; (car) parado; **to come to**

a ~still quedar paralizado; pararse

stank [stæŋk] pt of **stink**

staple ['steɪpl] n (for papers) grapa ♦ adj (food etc) básico ♦ vt grapar; **~r** n grapadora

star [stɑ:*] n estrella; (celebrity) estrella, astro m (THEATRE, CINEMA) ser el/la protagonista de; **the ~s** npl (ASTROLOGY) el horóscopo

starboard ['stɑ:bəd] n estribor m

starch [stɑ:tʃ] n almidón m

stardom ['stɑ:dəm] n estrellato

stare [stɛə*] n mirada fija ♦ vi: **to ~ at** mirar fijo

starfish ['stɑ:fɪʃ] n estrella de mar

stark [stɑ:k] adj (bleak) severo, escueto ♦ adv: **~ naked** en cueros

starling ['stɑ:lɪŋ] n estornino

starry ['stɑ:rɪ] adj estrellado; **~-eyed** adj (innocent) inocentón/ona, ingenuo

start [stɑ:t] n principio, comienzo; (departure) salida; (sudden movement) salto, sobresalto; (advantage) ventaja ♦ vt empezar, comenzar; (cause) causar; (found) fundar; (engine) poner en marcha ♦ vi empezar, comenzar; (with fright) asustarse, sobresaltarse; (train etc) salir; **to ~ doing** or **to do sth** empezar a hacer algo; **~ off** vi empezar, comenzar; (leave) salir, ponerse en camino; **~ up** vi comenzar; (car) ponerse en marcha ♦ vt comenzar; poner en marcha; **~er** n (AUT) botón m de arranque; (SPORT: official) juez m/f de salida; (BRIT: CULIN) entrada; **~ing point** n punto de partida

startle ['stɑ:tl] vt asustar, sobrecoger; **startling** adj alarmante

starvation [stɑ:'veɪʃən] n hambre f

starve [stɑ:v] vi tener mucha hambre; (to death) morir de hambre ♦ vt hacer pasar hambre

state [steɪt] n estado ♦ vt (say, declare) afirmar; **the S~s** los Estados Unidos; **to be in a ~** estar agitado; **~ly** adj majestuoso, imponente; **~ly home** n casa señorial, casa solariega; **~ment** n afirmación f; **~sman** (irreg) n estadista m

static ['stætɪk] n (RADIO) parásitos mpl ♦ adj estático; **~ electricity** n estática f

station ['steɪʃən] n (gen) estación f; (RADIO) emisora; (rank) posición f social ♦ vt colocar, situar; (MIL) apostar

stationary ['steɪʃnərɪ] adj estacionario, fijo

stationer ['steɪʃənə*] n papelero/a; **~'s (shop)** (BRIT) n papelería; **~y** [-nərɪ] n papel m de escribir, artículos mpl de escritorio

station master n (RAIL) jefe m de estación

station wagon (US) n ranchera f

statistic [stə'tɪstɪk] n estadística; **~s** n (science) estadística

statue ['stætju:] n estatua

status ['steɪtəs] n estado; (reputation) estatus m; **~ symbol** n símbolo m de prestigio

statute ['stætju:t] n estatuto, ley f; **statutory** adj estatutario

staunch [stɔ:ntʃ] adj leal, incondicional

stay [steɪ] n estancia ♦ vi quedar(se); (as guest) hospedarse; **to ~ put** seguir en el mismo sitio; **to ~ the night/5 days** pasar la noche/estar 5 días; **~ behind** vi quedar atrás; **~ in** vi quedarse en casa; **~ on** vi quedarse; **~ out** vi (of house) no volver a casa; (on strike) permanecer en huelga; **~ up** vi (at night) velar, no acostarse; **~ing power** n aguante m

stead [sted] n: **in sb's ~** en lugar de uno; **to stand sb in good ~** ser muy útil a uno

steadfast ['stedfɑ:st] adj firme, resuelto

steadily ['stedɪlɪ] adv constantemente; (firmly) firmemente, fijamente; (work, walk) sin parar; (gaze) fijamente

steady ['stedɪ] adj (firm) firme; (regular) regular; (person, character) sensato, juicioso; (boyfriend) formal; (look, voice)

tranquilo ♦ vt (stabilize) estabilizar; (nerves) calmar

steak [steɪk] n (gen) filete m; (beef) bistec m

steal [sti:l] (pt **stole**, pp **stolen**) vt robar ♦ vi robar; (move secretly) andar a hurtadillas

stealth [stelθ] n: **by ~** a escondidas, sigilosamente; **~y** adj cauteloso, sigiloso

steam [sti:m] n vapor m; (mist) vaho, humo ♦ vt (CULIN) cocer al vapor ♦ vi echar vapor; **~ engine** n máquina de vapor; **~er** n (buque m de) vapor m; **~roller** n apisonadora; **~ship** n = **~er**; **~y** adj (room) lleno de vapor; (window) empañado; (heat, atmosphere) bochornoso

steel [sti:l] n acero ♦ adj de acero; **~works** n acería

steep [sti:p] adj escarpado, abrupto; (stair) empinado; (price) exorbitante, excesivo ♦ vt empapar, remojar

steeple ['sti:pl] n aguja; **~chase** n carrera de obstáculos

steer [stɪə*] vt (car) conducir (SP); manejar (AM); (person) dirigir ♦ vi conducir, manejar; **~ing** (AUT) dirección f; **~ing wheel** n volante m

stem [stem] n (of plant) tallo; (of glass) pie m ♦ vt detener; (blood) restañar; **~ from** vt fus ser consecuencia de

stench [stentʃ] n hedor m

stencil ['stensl] n (pattern) plantilla ♦ vt hacer un cliché de

stenographer [ste'nɔgrəfə*] (US) n taquígrafo/a

step [step] n paso; (on stair) peldaño, escalón m ♦ vi: **to ~ forward/back** dar un paso adelante/hacia atrás; **~s** npl (BRIT) = **~ladder; in/out of ~ (with)** acorde/en disonancia (con); **~ down** vi (fig) retirarse; **~ on** vt fus pisar; **~ up** vt (increase) aumentar; **~brother** n hermanastro; **~daughter** n hijastra; **~father** n padrastro; **~ladder** n escalera doble or de tijera;

~mother n madrastra; **~ping stone** n pasadera; **~sister** n hermanastra; **~son** n hijastro

stereo ['stɪərɪəʊ] n estéreo ♦ adj (also: **~phonic**) estéreo, estereofónico

sterile ['sterail] adj estéril; **sterilize** ['sterilaiz] vt esterilizar

sterling ['stɜ:lɪŋ] adj (silver) de ley ♦ n (ECON) (libras fpl) esterlinas fpl; **one pound ~** una libra esterlina

stern [stɜ:n] adj severo, austero ♦ n (NAUT) popa

stew [stju:] n cocido (SP), estofado (SP), guisado (AM) ♦ vt estofar, guisar; (fruit) cocer

steward ['stju:əd] n camarero; **~ess** n (esp on plane) azafata

stick [stɪk] (pt, pp **stuck**) n palo; (of dynamite) barreno; (as weapon) porra; (walking ~) bastón m ♦ vt (glue) pegar; (inf: put) meter; (: tolerate) aguantar, soportar; (thrust): **to ~ sth into** clavar or hincar algo en n ♦ vi pegarse; (be unmoveable) quedarse parado; (in mind) quedarse grabado; **~ out** vi sobresalir; **~ up** vi sobresalir; **~ up for** vt fus defender; **~er** n (label) etiqueta engomada; (with slogan) pegatina; **~ing plaster** n esparadrapo

stick-up ['stɪkʌp] (inf) n asalto, atraco

sticky ['stɪkɪ] adj pegajoso; (label) engomado; (fig) difícil

stiff [stɪf] adj rígido, tieso; (hard) duro; (manner) estirado; (difficult) difícil; (person) inflexible; (price) exorbitante ♦ adv: **scared/bored ~** muerto de miedo/aburrimiento; **~en** vi (muscles etc) agarrotarse; (~ neck) n tortícolis m inv; **~ness** n rigidez f, tiesura

stifle ['staɪfl] vt ahogar, sofocar; **stifling** adj (heat) sofocante, bochornoso

stigma ['stɪgmə] n (fig) estigma m

stile [stail] n portillo, portilla

stiletto [stɪ'letəʊ] (BRIT) n (also: ~ **heel**) tacón m de aguja

still [stɪl] adj inmóvil, quieto ♦ adv

todavía; (even) aún; (nonetheless) sin embargo, aun así; **~born** adj nacido muerto; **~ life** n naturaleza muerta

stilt [stɪlt] n zanco; (pile) pilar m, soporte m

stilted ['stɪltɪd] adj afectado

stimulate ['stɪmjʊleɪt] vt estimular

stimulus ['stɪmjʊləs] (pl **stimuli**) n estímulo, incentivo

sting [stɪŋ] (pt, pp **stung**) n picadura; (pain) escozor m, picazón f; (organ) aguijón m ♦ vt, vi picar

stingy ['stɪndʒɪ] adj tacaño

stink [stɪŋk] (pt **stank**, pp **stunk**) n hedor m, tufo ♦ vi heder, apestar; **~ing** adj hediondo, fétido; (fig: inf) horrible

stint [stɪnt] n tarea, trabajo ♦ vi: **to ~ on** escatimar

stir [stɜ:] n (fig: agitation) conmoción f ♦ vt (tea etc) remover; (fig: emotions) provocar ♦ vi moverse; **~ up** vt (trouble) fomentar

stirrup ['stɪrəp] n estribo

stitch [stɪtʃ] n (SEWING) puntada; (KNITTING) punto; (MED) punto (de sutura); (pain) punzada ♦ vt coser; (MED) suturar

stoat [stəʊt] n armiño

stock [stɒk] n (COMM: reserves) existencias fpl, stock m; (: selection) surtido; (AGR) ganado, ganadería; (CULIN) caldo; (descent) raza, estirpe f; (FINANCE) capital m ♦ adj (fig: reply etc) clásico ♦ vt (have in ~) tener existencias de; **~s and shares** acciones y valores; **in ~** en existencia or almacén; **out of ~** agotado; **to take ~ of** (fig) assessor, examinar; **~ up with** vt fus abastecerse de; **~broker** ['stɒkbrəʊkə*] n agente m/f or corredor(a) m/f de bolsa; **~ cube** (BRIT) n pastilla de caldo; **~ exchange** n bolsa

stocking ['stɒkɪŋ] n media

stock-: **~ market** n bolsa (de valores); **~pile** n reserva ♦ vt acumular, almacenar; **~taking** (BRIT) n (COMM) inventario

stocky ['stɔkɪ] adj (strong) robusto; (short) achaparrado

stodgy ['stɔdʒɪ] adj indigesto, pesado

stoke [stəuk] vt atizar

stole [stəul] pt of **steal ♦** n estola

stolen ['stəuln] pp of **steal**

stomach ['stʌmək] n (ANAT) estómago; (belly) vientre m ♦ vt tragar, aguantar; **~ache** n dolor m de estómago

stone [stəun] n piedra; (in fruit) hueso; = 6.348 kg; 14 libras ♦ adj de piedra ♦ vt apedrear; (fruit) deshuesar; **~-cold** adj helado; **~-deaf** adj sordo como una tapia; **~work** n (art) cantería; **stony** adj pedregoso; (fig) frío

stood [stud] pt, pp of **stand**

stool [stu:l] n taburete m

stoop [stu:p] vi (also: ~ down) doblarse, agacharse; (also: have a ~) ser cargado de espaldas

stop [stɔp] n parada; (in punctuation) punto ♦ vt parar, detener; (break off) suspender; (block: pay) suspender; (: cheque) invalidar; (also: put a ~ to) poner término a ♦ vi pararse, detenerse; (end) acabarse; **to ~ doing sth** dejar de hacer algo; **~ dead** vi pararse en seco; **~ off** vi interrumpir el viaje; **~ up** vt (hole) tapar; **~gap** n (person) interino/a; (thing) recurso provisional; **~over** n parada; (AVIAT) escala

stoppage ['stɔpɪdʒ] n (strike) paro; (blockage) obstrucción f

stopper ['stɔpə*] n tapón m

stop press n noticias fpl de última hora

stopwatch ['stɔpwɔtʃ] n cronómetro

storage ['stɔ:rɪdʒ] n almacenaje m; **~ heater** n acumulador m

store [stɔ:*] n (stock) provisión f; (depot: BRIT: large shop) almacén m; (US) tienda; (reserve) reserva, repuesto ♦ vt almacenar; **~s** npl víveres mpl; **in ~** (fig): **to be in ~ for sb** esperarle a

uno; **~ up** vt acumular; **~room** n despensa

storey ['stɔ:rɪ] (US **story**) n piso

stork [stɔ:k] n cigüeña

storm [stɔ:m] n tormenta; (fig: of applause) salva; (: of criticism) nube f ♦ vi (fig) rabiar ♦ vt tomar por asalto; **~y** adj tempestuoso

story ['stɔ:rɪ] n historia; (lie) mentira; (US) = **storey**; **~book** n libro de cuentos

stout [staut] adj (strong) sólido; (fat) gordo, corpulento; (resolute) resuelto ♦ n cerveza negra

stove [stəuv] n (for cooking) cocina; (for heating) estufa

stow [stəu] vt (also: ~ away) meter, poner; (NAUT) estibar; **~away** n polizón/ona m/f

straggle ['strægl] vi (houses etc) extenderse; (lag behind) rezagarse

straight [streɪt] adj recto, derecho; (frank) franco, directo; (simple) sencillo ♦ adv derecho, directamente; (drink) sin mezcla; **to put o get sth ~** dejar algo en claro; **~ away, ~ off** en seguida; **~en** vt (also: ~en out) enderezar, poner derecho; **~-faced** adj serio; **~forward** adj (simple) sencillo; (honest) honrado, franco

strain [streɪn] n tensión f; (TECH) presión f; (MED) torcedura; (breed) tipo, variedad f ♦ vt (back etc) torcerse; (resources) agotar; (stretch) estirar; (food, tea) colar; **~s** npl (MUS) son m; **~ed** adj (muscle) torcido; (laugh) forzado; (relations) tenso; **~er** n colador m

strait [streɪt] n (GEO) estrecho; **to be in dire ~s** pasar grandes apuros; **~jacket** n camisa de fuerza; **~-laced** adj mojigato, gazmoño

strand [strænd] n (of thread) hebra; (of hair) trenza; (of rope) ramal m

stranded ['strændɪd] adj (person: without money) desamparado; (: without transport) colgado

strange |streɪndʒ| adj (not known) desconocido; (odd) extraño, raro; **~ly** adv de un modo raro; see also **enough**; **~r** n correa/a; (from another area) forastero/a

strangle |ˈstræŋgl| vt estrangular; **~hold** n (fig) dominio completo

strap |stræp| n correa; (of slip, dress) tirante m

strategic |strəˈtiːdʒɪk| adj estratégico

strategy |ˈstrætɪdʒɪ| n estrategia

straw |strɔː| n paja; (drinking ~) caña, pajita; **that's the last ~!** ¡eso es el colmo!

strawberry |ˈstrɔːbərɪ| n fresa (SP), frutilla (AM)

stray |streɪ| adj (animal) extraviado; (bullet) perdido; (scattered) disperso ♦ vi extraviarse, perderse

streak |striːk| n raya; (in hair) raya ♦ vt rayar ♦ vi: **to ~ past** pasar como un rayo

stream |striːm| n riachuelo, arroyo; (of people, vehicles) riada, caravana; (of smoke, insults etc) chorro ♦ vt (scol) dividir en grupos por habilidad ♦ vi correr, fluir; **to ~ in/out** (people) entrar/salir en tropel

streamer |ˈstriːmə*| n serpentina

streamlined |ˈstriːmlaɪnd| adj aerodinámico

street |striːt| n calle f; **~car** (US) n tranvía m; **~ lamp** n farol m; **~ plan** n plano; **~wise** (inf) adj que tiene mucha calle

strength |streŋθ| n fuerza; (of girder, knot etc) resistencia; (fig: power) poder m; **~en** vt fortalecer, reforzar

strenuous |ˈstrenjuəs| adj (energetic, determined) enérgico

stress |stres| n presión f; (mental strain) estrés m; (accent) acento ♦ vt subrayar, recalcar; (syllable) acentuar

stretch |stretʃ| n (of sand etc) trecho ♦ vi estirarse; (extend): **to ~ to** or **as far as** extenderse hasta ♦ vt extender, estirar; (make demands on) exigir el

máximo esfuerzo a; **~ out** vi tenderse ♦ vt (arm etc) extender; (spread) estirar

stretcher |ˈstretʃə*| n camilla

strewn |struːn| adj: **~ with** cubierto or sembrado de

stricken |ˈstrɪkən| adj (person) herido; (city, industry etc) condenado; **~ with** (disease) afectado por

strict |strɪkt| adj severo; (exact) estricto; **~ly** adv severamente; estrictamente

stride |straɪd| (pt **strode**, pp **stridden**) n zancada, tranco ♦ vi dar zancadas, andar a trancos

strife |straɪf| n lucha

strike |straɪk| (pt, pp **struck**) n huelga; (of oil etc) descubrimiento; (attack) ataque m ♦ vt golpear, pegar; (oil etc) descubrir; (bargain, deal) cerrar ♦ vi declarar la huelga; (attack) atacar; (clock) dar la hora; on **~** (workers) en huelga; **to ~ a match** encender un fósforo; **~ down** vt derribar; **~ up** vt (MUS) empezar a tocar; (conversation) entablar; (friendship) trabar; **~r** n huelguista m/f; (SPORT) delantero; **striking** adj llamativo

string |strɪŋ| (pt, pp **strung**) n (gen) cuerda; (row) hilera ♦ vt: **to ~ together** ensartar; **to ~ out** extenderse; **the ~s** npl (MUS) los instrumentos de cuerda; **to pull ~s** (fig) mover palancas; **~ bean** n judía verde, habichuela; **~(ed) instrument** n (MUS) instrumento de cuerda

stringent |ˈstrɪndʒənt| adj riguroso, severo

strip |strɪp| n tira; (of land) franja; (of metal) cinta, lámina ♦ vt desnudar; (paint) quitar; (also: **~ down**: machine) desmontar ♦ vi desnudarse; **~ cartoon** n tira cómica (SP), historieta (AM)

stripe |straɪp| n raya; (MIL) galón m; **~d** adj a rayas, rayado

strip lighting n alumbrado fluorescente

stripper |ˈstrɪpə*| n artista m/f de

striptease

strive [straɪv] (pt **strove**, pp **striven**) vi: **to ~ for sth/to do sth** luchar por conseguir/hacer algo

strode [strəud] pt of **stride**

stroke [strəuk] n (blow) golpe m; (SWIMMING) brazada; (MED) apoplejía; (of paintbrush) toque m ♦ vt acariciar; **at a ~** de un solo golpe

stroll [strəul] n paseo, vuelta ♦ vi dar un paseo or una vuelta; **~er** (US) n (for child) sillita de ruedas

strong [strɔŋ] adj fuerte; **they are 50 ~** son 50; **~hold** n fortaleza; (fig) baluarte m; **~ly** adv fuertemente, con fuerza; (believe) firmemente; **~room** n cámara acorazada

strove [strəuv] pt of **strive**

struck [strʌk] pt, pp of **strike**

structure ['strʌktʃəʳ] n estructura; (building) construcción f

struggle ['strʌgl] n lucha ♦ vi luchar

strum [strʌm] vt (guitar) rasguear

strung [strʌŋ] pt, pp of **string**

strut [strʌt] n puntal m ♦ vi pavonearse

stub [stʌb] n (of ticket etc) talón m; (of cigarette) colilla; **to ~ one's toe on sth** dar con el dedo (del pie) contra algo; **~ out** vt apagar

stubble ['stʌbl] n rastrojo; (on chin) barba (incipiente)

stubborn ['stʌbən] adj terco, testarudo

stuck [stʌk] pt, pp of **stick** ♦ adj (jammed) atascado; **~-up** adj engreído, presumido

stud [stʌd] n (shirt ~) corchete m; (of boot) taco; (earring) pendiente m (de bolita); (also: ~ farm) caballeriza; (also: ~ horse) caballo semental ♦ vt (fig): **~ded with** salpicado de

student ['stju:dənt] n estudiante m/f ♦ adj estudiantil; **~ driver** (US) n aprendiz(a) m/f

studio ['stju:dɪəu] n estudio; (artist's) taller m; **~ flat** (US **~ apartment**) n estudio

studious ['stju:dɪəs] adj estudioso;

(studied) calculado; **~ly** adv (carefully) con esmero

study ['stʌdɪ] n estudio ♦ vt estudiar; (examine) examinar, investigar ♦ vi estudiar

stuff [stʌf] n materia; (substance) material m, sustancia; (things) cosas fpl ♦ vt llenar; (CULIN) rellenar; (animals) disecar; (inf: push) meter; **~ing** n relleno; **~y** adj (room) mal ventilado; (person) de miras estrechas

stumble ['stʌmbl] vi tropezar, dar un traspié; **to ~ across, ~ on** (fig) tropezar con; **stumbling block** n tropiezo, obstáculo

stump [stʌmp] n (of tree) tocón m; (of limb) muñón m ♦ vt: **to be ~ed for an answer** no saber qué contestar

stun [stʌn] vt dejar sin sentido

stung [stʌŋ] pt, pp of **sting**

stunk [stʌŋk] pp of **stink**

stunning ['stʌnɪŋ] adj (fig: news) pasmoso; (: outfit etc) sensacional

stunt [stʌnt] n (in film) escena peligrosa; (publicity ~) truco publicitario; **~man** (irreg) n doble m

stupid ['stju:pɪd] adj estúpido, tonto; **~ity** [-'pɪdɪti] n estupidez f

sturdy ['stɜ:dɪ] adj robusto, fuerte

stutter ['stʌtəʳ] n tartamudeo ♦ vi tartamudear

sty [staɪ] n (for pigs) pocilga

stye [staɪ] n (MED) orzuelo

style [staɪl] n estilo; **stylish** adj elegante, a la moda

stylus ['staɪləs] n aguja

suave [swɑ:v] adj cortés

sub... [sʌb] prefix sub...; **~conscious** adj subconsciente; **~contract** vt subcontratar; **~divide** vt subdividir

subdue [səb'dju:] vt sojuzgar; (passions) dominar; **~d** adj (light) tenue; (person) sumiso, manso

subject [n 'sʌbdʒɪkt, vb səb'dʒɛkt] n súbdito; (SCOL) asignatura ♦ (matter) tema m; (GRAMMAR) sujeto ♦ vt: **to ~ sb to sth** someter a uno a algo; **to**

be ~ to (law) estar sujeto a; (subj: person) ser propenso a; **~ive** [-'dʒɛktɪv] adj subjetivo; **~ matter** n (content) contenido

sublet [sʌb'lɛt] vt subarrendar

submarine [sʌbmə'ri:n] n submarino

submerge [səb'mɜ:dʒ] vt sumergir ♦ vi sumergirse

submissive [səb'mɪsɪv] adj sumiso

submit [səb'mɪt] vt someter ♦ vi: **to ~ to sth** someterse a algo

subnormal [sʌb'nɔ:məl] adj anormal

subordinate [sə'bɔ:dɪnət] adj, n subordinado/a f

subpoena [səb'pi:nə] n (LAW) citación f

subscribe [səb'skraɪb] vi suscribir; **to ~ to** (opinion, fund) suscribir, aprobar; (newspaper) suscribirse a; **~r** n (to periodical) suscriptor(a) m/f; (to telephone) abonado/a

subscription [səb'skrɪpʃən] n abono; (to magazine) suscripción

subsequent ['sʌbsɪkwənt] adj subsiguiente, posterior; **~ly** adv posteriormente, más tarde

subside [səb'saɪd] vi hundirse; (flood) bajar; (wind) amainar; **subsidence** [-'saɪdns] n hundimiento; (in road) socavón m

subsidiary [səb'sɪdɪərɪ] adj secundario ♦ n sucursal f, filial f

subsidize ['sʌbsɪdaɪz] vt subvencionar

subsidy ['sʌbsɪdɪ] n subvención f

subsistence [səb'sɪstəns] n subsistencia; **~ allowance** n salario mínimo

substance ['sʌbstəns] n sustancia

substantial [səb'stænʃl] adj sustancial, sustancioso; (fig) importante

substantiate [səb'stænʃɪeɪt] vt comprobar

substitute ['sʌbstɪtju:t] n (person) suplente m/f; (thing) sustituto ♦ vt: **to ~ A for B** sustituir A por B, reemplazar B por A

subtitle ['sʌbtaɪtl] n subtítulo

subtle ['sʌtl] adj sutil; **~ty** n sutileza

subtotal [sʌb'təʊtl] n total m parcial

subtract [səb'trækt] vt restar, sustraer; **~ion** [-'trækʃən] n resta, sustracción f

suburb ['sʌbɜ:b] n barrio residencial; **the ~s** las afueras de (la ciudad); **~an** [sə'bɜ:bən] adj suburbano; (train etc) de cercanías; **~ia** [sə'bɜ:bɪə] n barrios mpl residenciales

subway ['sʌbweɪ] n (BRIT) paso subterráneo o inferior; (US) metro

succeed [sək'si:d] vi (person) tener éxito; (plan) salir bien ♦ vt suceder a; **to ~ in doing** lograr hacer; **~ing** adj (following) sucesivo

success [sək'sɛs] n éxito; **~ful** adj exitoso; (business) próspero; **to be ~ful (in doing)** lograr (hacer); **~fully** adv con éxito

succession [sək'sɛʃən] n sucesión f, serie f

successive [sək'sɛsɪv] adj sucesivo, consecutivo

succinct [sək'sɪŋkt] adj sucinto

such [sʌtʃ] adj tal, semejante; (of that kind): **~ a book** tal libro; (so much): **~ courage** tanto valor ♦ adv tan; **a long trip** un viaje tan largo; **~ a lot of** tanto(s)/a(s); **~ as** (like) tal como; **as ~** como tal; **~-and-~** adj tal o cual

suck [sʌk] vt chupar; (bottle) sorber; (breast) mamar; **~er** n (ZOOL) ventosa; (inf) bobo, primo

suction ['sʌkʃən] n succión f

Sudan [su'dæn] n Sudán m

sudden ['sʌdn] adj (rapid) repentino, súbito; (unexpected) imprevisto; **all of a ~** de repente; **~ly** adv de repente

suds [sʌdz] npl espuma de jabón

sue [su:] vt demandar

suede [sweɪd] n ante m (SP), gamuza (AM)

suet ['su:ɪt] n sebo

Suez ['su:ɪz] n: **the ~ Canal** el Canal de Suez

suffer ['sʌfə*] vt sufrir, padecer; (tolerate) aguantar, soportar ♦ vi sufrir;

to ~ from (*illness etc*) padecer; **~er** *n* víctima; (MED) enfermo/a; **~ing** *n* sufrimiento

sufficient [sə'fɪʃənt] *adj* suficiente, bastante; **~ly** *ad* suficientemente, bastante

suffocate ['sʌfəkeɪt] *vi* ahogarse, asfixiarse; **suffocation** [-'keɪʃən] *n* asfixia

sugar ['ʃugə*] *n* azúcar *m* ♦ *vt* echar azúcar a, azucarar; **~ beet** *n* remolacha; **~ cane** *n* caña de azúcar

suggest [sə'dʒɛst] *vt* sugerir; **~ion** [-'dʒɛstʃən] *n* sugerencia; **~ive** (*pej*) *adj* indecente

suicide ['suɪsaɪd] *n* suicidio; (*person*) suicida *m/f*; *see also* **commit**

suit [suːt] *n* (*man's*) traje *m*; (*woman's*) conjunto; (LAW) pleito; (CARDS) palo ♦ *vt* convenir; (*clothes*) sentar a, ir bien a; (*adapt*): **to ~ sth to** adaptar o ajustar algo a; **well ~ed** (*well matched: couple*) hecho el uno para el otro; **~able** *adj* conveniente; (*apt*) indicado; **~ably** *adv* convenientemente, (*impressed*) apropiadamente

suitcase ['suːtkeɪs] *n* maleta (SP), valija (AM)

suite [swiːt] *n* (*of rooms, MUS*) suite *f*; (*furniture*): **bedroom/dining room ~** (*juego de*) dormitorio/comedor

suitor ['suːtə*] *n* pretendiente *m*

sulfur ['sʌlfə*] (US) *n* = **sulphur**

sulk [sʌlk] *vi* estar de mal humor; **~y** *adj* malhumorado

sullen ['sʌlən] *adj* hosco, malhumorado

sulphur ['sʌlfə*] (US **sulfur**) *n* azufre *m*

sultana [sʌl'tɑːnə] *n* (*fruit*) pasa de Esmirna

sultry ['sʌltrɪ] *adj* (*weather*) bochornoso

sum [sʌm] *n* suma; (*total*) total *m*; **~ up** *vt* resumir ♦ *vi* hacer un resumen

summarize ['sʌməraɪz] *vt* resumir

summary ['sʌmərɪ] *n* resumen *m* ♦ *adj* (*justice*) sumario

summer ['sʌmə*] *n* verano ♦ *cpd* de verano; **in ~** en verano; **~ holidays** *npl* vacaciones *fpl* de verano; **~house** *n* (*in garden*) cenador *m*, glorieta; **~time** *n* (*season*) verano; **~ time** *n* (*by clock*) hora de verano

summit ['sʌmɪt] *n* cima, cumbre *f*; (*also: ~ conference, ~ meeting*) (*conferencia*) cumbre *f*

summon ['sʌmən] *vt* (*person*) llamar; (*meeting*) convocar; (LAW) citar; **~ up** *vt* (*courage*) armarse de; **~s** *n* llamamiento, llamada ♦ *vt* (LAW) citar

sump [sʌmp] (BRIT) *n* (AUT) cárter *m*

sumptuous ['sʌmptjuəs] *adj* suntuoso

sun [sʌn] *n* sol *m*; **~bathe** *vi* tomar el sol; **~block** *n* filtro solar; **~burn** *n* (*painful*) quemadura; (*tan*) bronceado; **~burnt** *adj* quemado por el sol

Sunday ['sʌndɪ] *n* domingo; **~ school** *n* catequesis *f* dominical

sundial ['sʌndaɪəl] *n* reloj *m* de sol

sundown ['sʌndaun] *n* anochecer *m*

sundry ['sʌndrɪ] *adj* varios/as, diversos/as; **all and ~** todos sin excepción; **sundries** *npl* géneros *mpl* diversos

sunflower ['sʌnflauə*] *n* girasol *m*

sung [sʌŋ] *pp* of **sing**

sunglasses ['sʌnglɑːsɪz] *npl* gafas *fpl* (SP) *or* anteojos *mpl* de sol

sunk [sʌŋk] *pp* of **sink**

sun: ~light *n* luz *f* del sol; **~lit** *adj* iluminado por el sol; **~ny** *adj* soleado; (*day*) de sol; (*fig*) alegre; **~rise** *n* salida del sol; **~ roof** *n* (AUT) techo corredizo; **~screen** *n* protector *m* solar; **~set** *n* puesta del sol; **~shade** *n* (*over table*) sombrilla; **~shine** *n* sol *m*; **~stroke** *n* insolación *f*; **~tan** *n* bronceado; **~tan oil** *n* aceite *m* bronceador

super ['suːpə*] (*inf*) *adj* genial

superannuation [suːpərænjʊ'eɪʃən] *n* cuota de jubilación

superb [suː'pəːb] *adj* magnífico, espléndido

supercilious [suːpə'sɪlɪəs] *adj* altanero

superfluous [suˈpəːfluəs] adj superfluo, de sobra

superhuman [suːpəˈhjuːmən] adj sobrehumano

superimpose [ˈsuːpərɪmˈpəuz] vt sobreponer

superintendent [suːpərɪnˈtendənt] n director(a) m/f; (POLICE) comisario m/f

superior [suˈpɪərɪə*] adj superior; (smug) desdeñoso ♦ n superior m; **~ity** [-ˈɔrɪtɪ] n superioridad f

superlative [suˈpəːlətɪv] n superlativo m

superman [ˈsuːpəmæn] n (irreg) superhombre m

supermarket [ˈsuːpəmɑːkɪt] n supermercado

supernatural [suːpəˈnætʃərəl] adj sobrenatural ♦ n: **the ~** lo sobrenatural

superpower [ˈsuːpəpauə*] n (POL) superpotencia

supersede [suːpəˈsiːd] vt suplantar

superstar [ˈsuːpəstɑː*] n gran estrella

superstition [suːpəˈstɪʃən] n superstición f

superstitious [suːpəˈstɪʃəs] adj supersticioso

supertanker [ˈsuːpətæŋkə*] n superpetrolero

supervise [ˈsuːpəvaɪz] vt supervisar; **supervision** [-ˈvɪʒən] n supervisión f; **supervisor** n supervisor(a) m/f

supper [ˈsʌpə*] n cena

supple [ˈsʌpl] adj flexible

supplement [n ˈsʌplɪmənt, vb sʌplɪˈment] n suplemento ♦ vt suplir; **~ary** [-ˈmentərɪ] adj suplementario; **~ary benefit** (BRIT) n subsidio suplementario de la seguridad social

supplier [səˈplaɪə*] n (COMM) distribuidor(a) m/f

supply [səˈplaɪ] vt (provide) suministrar; (equip): **to ~ (with)** proveer de ♦ n provisión f; (gas, water etc) suministro; **supplies** npl (food) víveres mpl; (MIL) pertrechos mpl; **~ teacher** n profesor(a) m/f suplente

support [səˈpɔːt] n apoyo, (TECH) soporte m ♦ vt apoyar; (financially) mantener; (uphold, TECH) sostener; **~er**

n (POL etc) partidario/a; (SPORT) aficionado/a

suppose [səˈpəuz] vt suponer; (imagine) imaginarse; (duty): **to be ~d to do sth** deber hacer algo; **~dly** [səˈpəuzɪdlɪ] adv supongo que; **supposing** conj en caso de que

suppress [səˈpres] vt suprimir; (yawn) ahogar

supreme [suˈpriːm] adj supremo

surcharge [ˈsəːtʃɑːdʒ] n sobretasa, recargo

sure [ʃuə*] adj seguro; (definite, convinced) cierto; **to make ~ of sth/that** asegurarse de algo/asegurar que; **~!** (of course) ¡claro!, ¡por supuesto!; **~ enough** efectivamente; **~ly** adv (certainly) seguramente

surf [səːf] n olas fpl

surface [ˈsəːfɪs] n superficie f ♦ vt (road) revestir ♦ vi (also fig) salir a la superficie; **by ~ mail** por vía terrestre

surfboard [ˈsəːfbɔːd] n tabla (de surf)

surfeit [ˈsəːfɪt] n: **a ~ of** un exceso de

surfing [ˈsəːfɪŋ] n surf m

surge [səːdʒ] n oleada, oleaje m ♦ vi (wave) romper; (people) avanzar en tropel

surgeon [ˈsəːdʒən] n cirujano/a

surgery [ˈsəːdʒərɪ] n cirugía; (BRIT: room) consultorio; **~ hours** (BRIT) npl horas fpl de consulta

surgical [ˈsəːdʒɪkl] adj quirúrgico; **~ spirit** (BRIT) n alcohol m de 90°

surname [ˈsəːneɪm] n apellido

surpass [səːˈpɑːs] vt superar, exceder

surplus [ˈsəːpləs] n excedente m; (COMM) superávit m ♦ adj excedente, sobrante

surprise [səˈpraɪz] n sorpresa ♦ vt sorprender; **surprising** adj sorprendente; **surprisingly** adv: **it was surprisingly easy** me costó sorprendió lo fácil que fue

surrender [səˈrendə*] n rendición f, entrega ♦ vi rendirse, entregarse

surreptitious [sʌrəpˈtɪʃəs] adj

subrepticio

surrogate ['sʌrəgɪt] n sucedáneo; ~ **mother** n madre f portadora

surround [sə'raund] vt rodear, circundar; (MIL etc) cercar; **~ing** adj circundante; **~ings** npl alrededores mpl, cercanías fpl

surveillance [sə:'veɪləns] n vigilancia

survey [n 'sə:veɪ, vb sə:'veɪ] n inspección f, reconocimiento; (inquiry) encuesta ♦ vt examinar, inspeccionar; (look at) mirar, contemplar; **~or** n agrimensor(a) m/f

survival [sə'vaɪvl] n supervivencia

survive [sə'vaɪv] vi sobrevivir; (custom etc) perdurar ♦ vt sobrevivir a; **survivor** n superviviente m/f

susceptible [sə'sɛptəbl] adj: ~ (to) (disease) susceptible a; (flattery) sensible (a)

suspect [adj, n 'sʌspɛkt, vb sə'spɛkt] adj, n sospechoso/a m/f ♦ vt (person) sospechar de; (think) sospechar

suspend [səs'pɛnd] vt suspender; **~ed sentence** n (LAW) libertad f condicional; **~er belt** n portaligas m inv; **~ers** npl (BRIT) ligas fpl; (US) tirantes mpl

suspense [səs'pɛns] n incertidumbre f, duda; (in film etc) suspense m; **to keep sb in ~** mantener a uno en suspense

suspension [səs'pɛnʃən] n (gen, AUT) suspensión f; (of driving licence) privación f; **~ bridge** n puente m colgante

suspicion [səs'pɪʃən] n sospecha; (distrust) recelo; **suspicious** [-ʃəs] adj receloso; (causing suspicion) sospechoso

sustain [səs'teɪn] vt sostener, apoyar; (suffer) sufrir, padecer; **~able** adj sostenible; **~ed** adj (effort) sostenido

sustenance ['sʌstɪnəns] n sustento

swab [swɔb] n (MED) algodón m

swagger ['swægə*] vi pavonearse

swallow ['swɔləu] n (bird) golondrina ♦ vt tragar; (fig, pride) tragarse; **~ up** vt (savings etc) consumir

swam [swæm] pt of **swim**

swamp [swɔmp] n pantano, ciénaga ♦ vt (with water etc) inundar; (fig) abrumar, agobiar; **~y** adj pantanoso

swan [swɔn] n cisne m

swap [swɔp] n canje m, intercambio ♦ vt: **to ~ (for)** cambiar (por)

swarm [swɔ:m] n (of bees) enjambre m; (fig) multitud f ♦ vi (bees) formar un enjambre; (people) pulular; **to be ~ing with** ser un hervidero de

swastika ['swɔstɪkə] n esvástica

swat [swɔt] vt aplastar

sway [sweɪ] vi mecerse, balancearse ♦ vt (influence) mover, influir en

swear [swɛə*] (pt swore, pp sworn) vi (curse) maldecir; (promise) jurar ♦ vt jurar; **~word** n taco, palabrota

sweat [swɛt] n sudor m ♦ vi sudar

sweater ['swɛtə*] n suéter m

sweatshirt ['swɛtʃə:t] n suéter m

sweaty ['swɛtɪ] adj sudoroso

Swede [swi:d] n sueco/a

swede [swi:d] (BRIT) n nabo

Sweden ['swi:dn] n Suecia; **Swedish** ['swi:dɪʃ] adj sueco ♦ n (LING) sueco

sweep [swi:p] (pt, pp swept) n (act) barrido; (also: chimney ~) deshollinador/a m/f ♦ vt barrer; (with arm) empujar; (subj: current) arrastrar ♦ vi barrer; (arm etc) moverse rápidamente; (wind) soplar con violencia; **~ away** vt barrer; **~ past** vi pasar majestuosamente; **~ up** vi barrer; **~ing** adj (gesture) dramático; (generalized: statement) generalizado

sweet [swi:t] n (candy) dulce m, caramelo; (BRIT: pudding) postre m ♦ adj dulce; (fig: kind) dulce, amable; (: attractive) mono; **~corn** n maíz m; **~en** vt (add sugar to) poner azúcar a; (person) endulzar; **~heart** n novio/a; **~ness** n dulzura; **~ pea** n guisante m de olor

swell [swɛl] (pt swelled, pp swollen or swelled) n (of sea) marejada, oleaje m ♦ adj (US: inf: excellent) estupendo, fenomenal ♦ vt hinchar, inflar ♦ vi (also: ~ up) hincharse; (numbers) aumentar; (sound, feeling) ir aumentando; **~ing** n (MED) hinchazón f

sweltering ['sweltərɪŋ] adj sofocante, de mucho calor

swept [swept] pt, pp of **sweep**

swerve [swəːv] vi desviarse bruscamente

swift [swɪft] n (bird) vencejo ♦ adj rápido, veloz; **~ly** adv rápidamente

swig [swɪg] (inf) n (drink) trago

swill [swɪl] n (also: ~ out, ~ down) lavar, limpiar con agua

swim [swɪm] (pt **swam**, pp **swum**) n: **to go for a ~** ir a nadar o a bañarse ♦ vi nadar; (head, room) dar vueltas ♦ vt nadar; (the Channel etc) cruzar a nado; **~mer** n nadador(a) m/f; **~ming** n natación f; **~ming cap** n gorro de baño; **~ming costume** (BRIT) n bañador m, traje m de baño; **~ming pool** n piscina (SP), alberca (AM); **~ming trunks** npl bañador m (de hombre); **~suit** n = **~ming costume**

swindle ['swɪndl] n estafa ♦ vt estafar

swine [swaɪn] (inf!) canalla (!)

swing [swɪŋ] (pt, pp **swung**) n (in playground) columpio; (movement) balanceo, vaivén m; (change of direction) viraje m; (rhythm) ritmo ♦ vt balancear; (also: ~ round) voltear, girar ♦ vi balancearse, columpiarse; (also: ~ round) dar media vuelta; **to be in full ~** estar en plena marcha; **~ bridge** n puente m giratorio; **~ door** (US **~ing door**) n puerta giratoria

swingeing ['swɪndʒɪŋ] (BRIT) adj (cuts) atroz

swipe [swaɪp] vt (hit) golpear fuerte; (inf: steal) guindar

swirl [swəːl] vi arremolinarse

Swiss [swɪs] adj, n inv suizo/a m/f

switch [swɪtʃ] n (for light etc) interruptor m; (change) cambio ♦ vt (change) cambiar de; **~ off** vt apagar;

(engine) parar; **~ on** vt encender (SP), prender (AM); (engine, machine) arrancar; **~board** n (TEL) centralita (de teléfonos) (SP), conmutador m (AM)

Switzerland ['swɪtsələnd] n Suiza

swivel ['swɪvl] vi (also: ~ round) girar

swollen ['swəulən] pp of **swell**

swoon [swuːn] vi desmayarse

swoop [swuːp] n (by police etc) redada ♦ vi (also: ~ down) calarse

swop [swɔp] = **swap**

sword [sɔːd] n espada; **~fish** n pez m espada

swore [swɔː*] pt of **swear**

sworn [swɔːn] pp of **swear** ♦ adj (statement) bajo juramento; (enemy) implacable

swot [swɔt] (BRIT) vt, vi empollar

swum [swʌm] pp of **swim**

swung [swʌŋ] pt, pp of **swing**

sycamore ['sɪkəmɔː*] n sicomoro

syllable ['sɪləbl] n sílaba

syllabus ['sɪləbəs] n programa m de estudios

symbol ['sɪmbl] n símbolo

symmetry ['sɪmɪtrɪ] n simetría

sympathetic [sɪmpə'θetɪk] adj (understanding) comprensivo; (likeable) simpático; (showing support): **~ to(wards)** bien dispuesto hacia

sympathize ['sɪmpəθaɪz] vi: **to ~ with** (person) compadecerse de; (feelings) comprender; (cause) apoyar; **~r** n (POL) simpatizante m/f

sympathy ['sɪmpəθɪ] n (pity) compasión f; **sympathies** npl (tendencies) tendencias fpl; **with our deepest ~** nuestro más sentido pésame; **in ~** en solidaridad

symphony ['sɪmfənɪ] n sinfonía

symptom ['sɪmptəm] n síntoma m, indicio

synagogue ['sɪnəgɒg] n sinagoga

syndicate ['sɪndɪkɪt] n (gen) sindicato; (of newspapers) agencia (de noticias)

syndrome ['sɪndrəum] n síndrome m

synopsis [sɪ'nɒpsɪs] (pl **synopses**) n

sinopsis f inv

synthesis ['sɪnθəsɪs] n (pl **syntheses**) n síntesis f inv

synthetic [sɪn'θetɪk] adj sintético

syphilis ['sɪfɪlɪs] n sífilis f

syphon ['saɪfən] = **siphon**

Syria ['sɪrɪə] n Siria; **~n** adj, n sirio/a

syringe [sɪ'rɪndʒ] n jeringa

syrup ['sɪrəp] n jarabe m; (also: golden ~) almíbar m

system ['sɪstəm] n sistema m; (ANAT) organismo; **~atic** [-'mætɪk] adj sistemático, metódico; **~ disk** n (COMPUT) disco del sistema; **~s analyst** n analista m/f de sistemas

T, t

ta [tɑ:] (BRIT: inf) excl ¡gracias!

tab [tæb] n lengüeta; (label) etiqueta; **to keep ~s on** (fig) vigilar

tabby ['tæbɪ] n (also: ~ cat) gato atigrado

table ['teɪbl] n mesa; (of statistics etc) cuadro, tabla ♦ vt (BRIT: motion etc) presentar; **to lay** or **set the ~** poner la mesa; **~cloth** n mantel m; **~ of contents** n índice m de materias; **~ d'hôte** [tɑ:bl'dəut] adj del menú; **~ lamp** n lámpara de mesa; **~mat** n (for plate) posaplatos m inv; (for hot dish) salvamantel m; **~spoon** n cuchara de servir; (also: ~spoonful: as measurement) cucharada

tablet ['tæblɪt] n (MED) pastilla, comprimido; (of stone) lápida

table tennis n ping-pong m, tenis m de mesa

table wine n vino de mesa

tabloid ['tæblɔɪd] n periódico popular sensacionalista

tabloid press

El término **tabloid press** o **tabloids** se usa para referirse a la prensa popular británica, por el tamaño más pequeño de los periódicos. A diferencia de los de la llamada **quality press**, estas publicaciones se caracterizan por un lenguaje sencillo, una presentación llamativa y un contenido sensacionalista, centrado a veces en los escándalos financieros y sexuales de los famosos, por lo que también reciben el nombre peyorativo de "gutter press".

tack [tæk] n (nail) tachuela; (fig) rumbo ♦ vt (nail) clavar con tachuelas; (stitch) hilvanar ♦ vi virar

tackle ['tækl] n (fishing ~) aparejo (de pescar); (for lifting) aparejo ♦ vt (difficulty) enfrentarse con; (challenge: person) hacer frente a; (grapple with) agarrar; (FOOTBALL) cargar; (RUGBY) placar

tacky ['tækɪ] adj pegajoso; (pej) cutre

tact [tækt] n tacto, discreción f; **~ful** adj discreto, diplomático

tactics ['tæktɪks] n, pl táctica

tactless ['tæktlɪs] adj indiscreto

tadpole ['tædpəul] n renacuajo

tag [tæg] n (label) etiqueta; **~ along** vi ir (o venir) también

tail [teɪl] n cola; (of shirt, coat) faldón m ♦ vt (follow) vigilar a; **~s** npl (formal suit) levita; **~ away** vi (in size, quality etc) ir disminuyendo; **~ off** vi = **~ away**; **~back** (BRIT) n (AUT) cola; **~ end** n cola, parte f final; **~gate** n (AUT) puerta trasera

tailor ['teɪlə*] n sastre m; **~ing** n (cut) corte m; (craft) sastrería; **~-made** adj (also fig) hecho a la medida

tailwind ['teɪlwɪnd] n viento de cola

tainted ['teɪntɪd] adj (food) pasado; (water, air) contaminado; (fig) manchado

take [teɪk] (pt took, pp taken) vt tomar; (grab) coger (SP), agarrar (AM); (gain: prize) ganar; (require: effort, courage) exigir; (tolerate: pain etc) aguantar; (hold: passengers etc) tener cabida para; (accompany, bring, carry) llevar; (exam) presentarse a; **~ sth from** (drawer etc) sacar algo de; (person) quitar algo a; **I ~ it that ...** supongo que ...; **~ after** vt fus parecerse a; **~ apart** vt desmontar; **~ away** vt (remove) quitar; (carry off) llevar; (MATH) restar; **~ back** vt (return) devolver; (one's words) retractarse de; **~ down** vt (building) derribar; (letter etc) apuntar; **~ in** vt (deceive) engañar; (understand) entender; (include) abarcar; (lodger) acoger, recibir; **~ off** vi (AVIAT) despegar ♦ vt (remove) quitar; **~ on** vt (work) aceptar; (employee) contratar; (opponent) desafiar; **~ out** vt sacar; **~ over** vt (business) tomar posesión de; (country) tomar el poder ♦ vi: **to ~ over from sb** reemplazar a uno; **~ to** vt fus (person) coger cariño a, encariñarse con; (activity) aficionarse a; **~ up** vt (a dress) acortar; (occupy: time, space) ocupar; (engage in: hobby etc) dedicarse a; (accept): **to ~ sb up on** aceptar; **~away** (BRIT) adj (food) para llevar ♦ n tienda (or restaurante m) de comida para llevar; **~off** n (AVIAT) despegue m; **~out** (US) n = **~away**; **~over** n (COMM) absorción f

takings ['teɪkɪnz] npl (COMM) ingresos mpl

talc [tælk] n (also: **~um powder**) (polvos de) talco

tale [teɪl] n (story) cuento, (account) relación f; **to tell ~s** (fig) chivarse

talent ['tælnt] n talento; **~ed** adj de talento

talk [tɔːk] n charla, (conversation) conversación f; (gossip) habladurías fpl, chismes mpl ♦ vi hablar; **~s** npl (POL etc) conversaciones fpl; **to ~ about** hablar de; **to ~ sb into doing sth** convencer a uno para que haga algo; **to ~ sb out of doing sth** disuadir a uno de que haga algo; **~ shop** hablar del trabajo; **~ over** vt discutir;

~ative adj hablador(a); **~ show** n programa m de entrevistas

tall [tɔːl] adj alto; (object) grande; **to be 6 feet ~** (person) ≈ medir 1 metro 80

tally ['tælɪ] n cuenta ♦ vi: **to ~ (with)** corresponder (con)

talon ['tælən] n garra

tambourine [tæmbə'riːn] n pandereta

tame [teɪm] adj domesticado; (fig) mediocre

tamper ['tæmpə*] vi: **to ~ with** tocar, andar con

tampon ['tæmpən] n tampón m

tan [tæn] n (also: sun~) bronceado ♦ vi ponerse moreno ♦ adj (colour) marrón

tang [tæŋ] n sabor m fuerte

tangent ['tændʒənt] n (MATH) tangente f; **to go off at a ~** (fig) salirse por la tangente

tangerine [tændʒə'riːn] n mandarina

tangle ['tæŋɡl] n enredo; **to get in(to) a ~** enredarse

tank [tæŋk] n (water ~) depósito, tanque m; (for fish) acuario; (MIL) tanque m

tanker ['tæŋkə*] n (ship) buque m cisterna; (truck) camión m cisterna

tanned [tænd] adj (skin) moreno

tantalizing ['tæntəlaɪzɪŋ] adj tentador(a)

tantamount ['tæntəmaunt] adj: **~ to** equivalente a

tantrum ['tæntrəm] n rabieta

tap [tæp] n (BRIT: on sink etc) grifo (SP), canilla (AM); (gas ~) llave f; (gentle blow) golpecito ♦ vt (hit gently) dar golpecitos en; (resources) utilizar, explotar; (telephone) intervenir; **on ~** (fig: resources) a mano; **~ dancing** n claqué m

tape [teɪp] n (also: magnetic ~) cinta magnética; (cassette) cassette f, cinta; (sticky ~) cinta adhesiva; (for tying) cinta ♦ vt (record) grabar (en cinta); (stick with ~) pegar con cinta adhesiva; **~ deck** n grabadora; **~ measure** n cinta métrica, metro

taper ['teɪpə*] n cirio ♦ vi afilarse

tape recorder n grabadora

tapestry ['tæpɪstrɪ] n (object) tapiz m; (art) tapicería

tar [tɑː] n alquitrán m, brea

target ['tɑːgɪt] n (gen) blanco

tariff ['tærɪf] n (on goods) arancel m; (BRIT: in hotels etc) tarifa

tarmac ['tɑːmæk] n (BRIT: on road) asfaltado; (AVIAT) pista (de aterrizaje)

tarnish ['tɑːnɪʃ] vt deslustrar

tarpaulin [tɑː'pɔːlɪn] n lona impermeabilizada

tarragon ['tærəgən] n estragón m

tart [tɑːt] n (CULIN) tarta; (BRIT: inf: prostitute) puta ♦ adj agrio, ácido; ~ **up** (BRIT: inf) vt (building) remozar; **to ~ o.s. up** acicalarse

tartan ['tɑːtn] n tejido escocés m

tartar ['tɑːtə*] n (on teeth) sarro; **~(e) sauce** n salsa tártara

task [tɑːsk] n tarea; **to take to ~** reprender; **~ force** n (MIL, POLICE) grupo de operaciones

taste [teɪst] n (sense) gusto; (flavour) sabor m; (also: after~) sabor m, dejo; (sample): **have a ~!** ¡pruébalo! ♦ vt (also fig) probar ♦ vi: **to ~ of** or **like** (fish, garlic etc) saber a; **you can ~ the garlic (in it)** se nota el sabor a ajo; **in good/bad ~** de buen/mal gusto; **~ful** adj de buen gusto; **~less** adj (food) soso; (remark etc) de mal gusto; **tasty** adj sabroso, rico

tatters ['tætəz] npl: **in ~** hecho jirones

tattoo [tə'tuː] n tatuaje m; (spectacle) espectáculo militar ♦ vt tatuar

tatty ['tætɪ] (BRIT: inf) adj cochambroso

taught [tɔːt] pt, pp of teach

taunt [tɔːnt] n burla ♦ vt burlarse de

Taurus ['tɔːrəs] n Tauro

taut [tɔːt] adj tirante, tenso

tax [tæks] n impuesto ♦ vt gravar (con un impuesto); (fig: memory) poner a prueba (: patience) agotar; **~able** adj

(income) gravable; **~ation** [-'seɪʃən] n impuestos mpl; **~ avoidance** n evasión f de impuestos; **~ disc** (BRIT) (AUT) pegatina del impuesto de circulación; **~ evasion** n evasión f fiscal; **~-free** adj libre de impuestos

taxi ['tæksɪ] n taxi m ♦ vi (AVIAT) rodar por la pista; **~ driver** n taxista m/f; **~ rank** (BRIT) n = **~ stand**; **~ stand** n parada de taxis

tax: **~ payer** n contribuyente m/f; **~ relief** n desgravación f fiscal; **~ return** n declaración f de ingresos

TB n abbr = **tuberculosis**

tea [tiː] n té m; (BRIT: meal) ≈ merienda (SP); cena; **high ~** (BRIT) merienda-cena (SP); **~ bag** n bolsita de té; **~ break** (BRIT) n descanso para el té

teach [tiːtʃ] (pt, pp taught) vt: **to ~ sb sth, ~ sth to sb** enseñar algo a uno ♦ vi (be a teacher) ser profesor(a), enseñar; **~er** n (in secondary school) profesor/a m/f; (in primary school) maestro/a, profesor/a de EGB; **~ing** n enseñanza

tea cosy n cubretetera m

teacup ['tiːkʌp] n taza para el té

teak [tiːk] n (madera) de teca

team [tiːm] n equipo; (of horses) tiro; **~work** n trabajo en equipo

teapot ['tiːpɔt] n tetera

tear¹ [tɪə*] n lágrima; **in ~s** llorando

tear² [tɛə*] (pt tore, pp torn) n rasgón m, desgarrón m ♦ vt romper, rasgar ♦ vi rasgarse; **~ along** vi (rush) precipitarse; **~ up** vt (sheet of paper etc) romper

tearful ['tɪəful] adj lloroso

tear gas ['tɪə-] n gas m lacrimógeno

tearoom ['tiːruːm] n salón m de té

tease [tiːz] vt tomar el pelo a

tea set n servicio de té

teaspoon n cucharita; (also: ~ful: as measurement) cucharadita

teat [tiːt] n (of bottle) tetina

teatime ['tiːtaɪm] n hora del té

tea towel (BRIT) n paño de cocina
f(pl)

technical ['tɛknɪkl] adj técnico; ~ **college** (BRIT) n ~ escuela de artes y oficios (SP); ~**ity** [-'kælɪtɪ] n (point of law) formalismo m; (detail) detalle m técnico; ~**ly** adv en teoría; (regarding technique) técnicamente

technician [tɛk'nɪʃn] n técnico/a

technique [tɛk'niːk] n técnica

technological [tɛknə'lɔdʒɪkl] adj tecnológico

technology [tɛk'nɔlədʒɪ] n tecnología f

teddy (bear) ['tɛdɪ-] n osito de felpa

tedious ['tiːdɪəs] adj pesado, aburrido

teem [tiːm] vi: to ~ **with** rebosar de; **it is ~ing (with rain)** llueve a cántaros

teenage ['tiːneɪdʒ] adj (fashions etc) juvenil; (children) quinceañero; ~**r** n quinceañero/a

teens [tiːnz] npl: **to be in one's ~** ser adolescente

tee-shirt ['tiːʃəːt] n = **T-shirt**

teeter ['tiːtə'] vi balancearse; (fig): **to ~ on the edge of** estar al borde de

teeth [tiːθ] npl of **tooth**

teethe [tiːð] vi echar los dientes

teething ['tiːðɪŋ]: ~ **ring** n mordedor m; ~ **troubles** npl (fig) dificultades fpl iniciales

teetotal ['tiː'təutl] adj abstemio

telegram ['tɛlɪgræm] n telegrama m

telegraph ['tɛlɪgrɑːf] n telégrafo; ~ **pole** n poste m telegráfico

telepathy [tə'lɛpəθɪ] n telepatía

telephone ['tɛlɪfəun] n teléfono ♦ vt llamar por teléfono, telefonear; (message) dar por teléfono; **to be on the ~** (talking) hablar por teléfono; (possessing) ~ tener teléfono; ~ **booth** n cabina telefónica; ~ **box** (BRIT) n = ~ **booth**; ~ **call** n llamada (telefónica); ~ **directory** n guía (telefónica); ~ **number** n número de teléfono; **telephonist** [tə'lɛfənɪst] (BRIT) n telefonista m/f

telesales ['tɛlɪseɪlz] npl televenta(s)

telescope ['tɛlɪskəup] n telescopio

television ['tɛlɪvɪʒən] n televisión f; **on ~** en la televisión; ~ **set** n televisor m

teleworking ['tɛlɪwəːkɪŋ] n teletrabajo

tell [tɛl] (pt, pp **told**) vt decir; (relate: story) contar; (distinguish): **to ~ sth from** distinguir algo de ♦ vi (talk): **to ~ (of)** contar; (have effect) tener efecto; **to ~ sb to do sth** mandar a uno hacer algo; ~ **off** vt: **to ~ sb off** regañar a uno; ~**er** n (in bank) cajero/a; ~**ing** adj (remark, detail) revelador(a); ~**tale** adj (sign) indicador(a)

telly ['tɛlɪ] (BRIT: inf) n abbr (= television) tele f

temp [tɛmp] n abbr (BRIT: = temporary) temporero/a

temper ['tɛmpə'] n (nature) carácter m; (mood) humor m; (bad ~) (mal) genio; (fit of anger) acceso de ira ♦ vt (moderate) moderar; **to be in a ~** estar furioso; **to lose one's ~** enfadarse, enojarse

temperament ['tɛmprəmənt] n (nature) temperamento

temperate ['tɛmprət] adj (climate etc) templado

temperature ['tɛmprətʃə'] n temperatura; **to have** o **run a ~** tener fiebre

temple ['tɛmpl] n (building) templo; (ANAT) sien f

tempo ['tɛmpəu] (pl **tempos** or **tempi**) n (MUS) tempo, tiempo; (fig) ritmo

temporarily ['tɛmpərərɪlɪ] adv temporalmente

temporary ['tɛmpərərɪ] adj provisional; (passing) transitorio; (worker) temporero; (job) temporal

tempt [tɛmpt] vt tentar; **to ~ sb into doing sth** tentar o inducir a uno a hacer algo; ~**ation** [-'teɪʃən] n tentación f; ~**ing** adj tentador(a); (food) apetitoso/a

ten [tɛn] num diez

tenacity [tə'næsɪtɪ] n tenacidad f

tenancy ['tenənsɪ] n arrendamiento, alquiler m

tenant ['tenənt] n inquilino/a

tend [tend] vt cuidar ♦ vi: **to ~ to do sth** tener tendencia a hacer algo

tendency ['tendənsɪ] n tendencia

tender ['tendə*] adj (person, care) tierno, cariñoso; (meat) tierno; (sore) sensible ♦ n (COMM: offer) oferta; (money): **legal ~** moneda de curso legal ♦ vt ofrecer; **~ness** n ternura; (of meat) blandura

tenement ['tenəmənt] n casa de pisos (SP)

tennis ['tenɪs] n tenis m; **~ ball** n pelota de tenis; **~ court** n cancha de tenis; **~ player** n tenista m/f; **~ racket** n raqueta de tenis

tenor ['tenə*] n (MUS) tenor m

tenpin bowling ['tenpɪn-] n (juego de los) bolos

tense [tens] adj (person) nervioso; (moment, atmosphere) tenso; (muscle) tenso, en tensión ♦ n (LING) tiempo

tension ['tenʃən] n tensión f

tent [tent] n tienda (de campaña) (SP), carpa (AM)

tentative ['tentətɪv] adj (person, smile) indeciso; (conclusion, plans) provisional

tenterhooks ['tentəhuks] npl: **on ~** sobre ascuas

tenth [tenθ] num décimo

tent peg n clavija, estaca

tent pole n mástil m

tenuous ['tenjuəs] adj tenue

tenure ['tenjuə*] n (of land etc) tenencia; (of office) ejercicio

tepid ['tepɪd] adj tibio

term [tə:m] n (word) término; (period) período; (SCOL) trimestre m ♦ vt llamar; **~s** npl (conditions, COMM) condiciones fpl; **in the short/long ~** a corto/largo plazo; **to be on good ~s with sb** llevarse bien con uno; **to come to ~s with** (problem) aceptar

terminal ['tə:mɪnl] adj (disease) mortal; (patient) terminal ♦ n (ELEC)

borne m; (COMPUT) terminal m; (also: **air ~**) terminal f; (BRIT: also: **coach ~**) (estación f) terminal f

terminate ['tə:mɪneɪt] vt terminar

terminus ['tə:mɪnəs] (pl **termini**) n término, (estación f) terminal f

terrace ['terəs] n terraza; (BRIT: row of houses) hilera de casas adosadas; the **~s** (BRIT: SPORT) las gradas fpl; **~d** adj (garden) en terrazas; (house) adosado

terrain [te'reɪn] n terreno

terrible ['terɪbl] adj terrible, horrible; (inf) atroz; **terribly** adv terriblemente; (very badly) malísimamente

terrier ['terɪə*] n terrier m

terrific [tə'rɪfɪk] adj (very great) tremendo; (wonderful) fantástico, fenomenal

terrify ['terɪfaɪ] vt aterrorizar

territory ['terɪtərɪ] n (also fig) territorio

terror ['terə*] n terror m; **~ism** n terrorismo; **~ist** n terrorista m/f

test [test] n (gen, CHEM) prueba; (MED) examen m; (SCOL) examen m, test m; (also: driving ~) examen m de conducir ♦ vt probar, poner a prueba; (MED, SCOL) examinar

testament ['testəmənt] n testamento; the **Old/New T~** el Antiguo/Nuevo Testamento

testicle ['testɪkl] n testículo

testify ['testɪfaɪ] vi (LAW) prestar declaración; **to ~ to sth** atestiguar algo

testimony ['testɪmənɪ] n (LAW) testimonio

test: ~ match n (CRICKET, RUGBY) partido internacional; **~ tube** n probeta

tetanus ['tetənəs] n tétano

tether ['teðə*] vt atar (con una cuerda) ♦ n: **to be at the end of one's ~** no aguantar más

text [tekst] n texto; **~book** n libro de texto

textiles ['tekstaɪlz] npl textiles mpl; (textile industry) industria textil

texture ['tekstʃə*] n textura
Thailand ['taɪlænd] n Tailandia
Thames [temz] n: **the ~** el (río)
Támesis
than [ðæn] conj (in comparisons):
more ~ 10/once she ~ más de 10/una vez;
I have more/less ~ you/Paul tengo
más/menos que tú/Paul; **she is older
~ you think** es mayor de lo que
piensas
thank [θæŋk] vt dar las gracias a,
agradecer; **~ you (very much)**
muchas gracias; **~ God!** ¡gracias a
Dios!; **~s** npl gracias fpl ♦ excl (also:
many ~s, ~s a lot) ¡gracias!; **~s to** prep
gracias a; **~ful** adj: **~ful (for)**
agradecido (por); **~less** adj ingrato;
T~sgiving (Day) n día m de Acción
de Gracias

Thanksgiving (Day)

En Estados Unidos el cuarto jueves de
noviembre es **Thanksgiving Day**,
fiesta oficial en la que se recuerda la
celebración que hicieron los primeros
colonos norteamericanos ("Pilgrims" o
"Pilgrim Fathers") tras la estupenda
cosecha de 1621, por la que se dan
gracias a Dios. En Canadá se celebra
una fiesta semejante el segundo lunes
de octubre, aunque no está
relacionada con dicha fecha histórica.

KEYWORD

that [ðæt] (pl **those**) adj
(demonstrative) ese/a, pl esos/as; (more
remote) aquel/aquella, pl aquellos/as;
leave those books on the table
deja esos libros sobre la mesa; **~ one**
ése/ésa; (more remote) aquél/aquélla;
~ one over there ése/ésa de ahí;
aquél/aquélla de allí
♦ pron 1 (demonstrative) ése/a, pl
ésos/as; (neuter) eso; (more remote)
aquél/aquélla, pl aquéllos/as; (neuter)
aquello; **what's ~?** ¿qué es eso (or

aquello)?; **who's ~?** ¿quién es ése/a
(or aquél/aquélla)?; **is ~ you?** ¿eres
tú?; **will you eat all ~?** ¿vas a comer
todo eso?; **~'s my house** ésa es mi
casa; **~'s what he said** eso es lo que
dijo; **~ is** (to say) es decir
2 (relative: subject, object) que; (with
preposition) que etc, el/la cual etc, el/la cual
etc; **the book (~) I read** el libro que
leí; **the books ~ are in the library**
los libros que están en la biblioteca; **all
(~) I have** todo lo que tengo; **the
box (~) I put it in** la caja en la que or
donde lo puse; **the people (~) I
spoke to** la gente con la que hablé
3 (relative: of time) que; **the day (~)
he came** el día (en) que vino
♦ conj que; **he thought ~ I was ill**
creyó que yo estaba enfermo
♦ adv (demonstrative): **I can't work
~ much** no puedo trabajar tanto; **I
didn't realise it was ~ bad** no creí
que fuera tan malo; **~ high** así de alto

thatched [θætʃt] adj (roof) de paja;
(cottage) con tejado de paja
thaw [θɔ:] n deshielo ♦ vi (ice)
derretirse; (food) descongelarse ♦ vt
(food) descongelar

KEYWORD

the [ðiː, ðə] def art 1 (gen) el, f la, pl
los, fpl las (NB = el immediately before f
n beginning with stressed (h)a; a+ el =
al; de+ el = del); **boy/girl** el chico/
la chica; **~ books/flowers** los libros/
las flores; **to ~ postman/from
~ drawer** al cartero/del cajón; **I
haven't ~ time/money** no tengo
tiempo/dinero
2 (+ adj to form n) los; lo; **~ rich and
~ poor** los ricos y los pobres; **to
attempt ~ impossible** intentar lo
imposible
3 (in titles): **Elizabeth ~ First** Isabel
primera; **Peter ~ Great** Pedro el
Grande

4 (in comparisons): **~ more he works ~ more he earns** cuanto más trabaja más gana

theatre ['θɪətə*] (US **theater**) n teatro; (also: lecture ~) aula; (MED: also: **operating ~**) quirófano; **~goer** n aficionado/a al teatro

theatrical [θɪ'ætrɪkl] adj teatral

theft [θɛft] n robo

their [ðɛə*] adj su; **~s** pron (el) suyo/ (la) suya etc; see also **my; mine**[1]

them [ðɛm, ðəm] pron (direct) los/las; (indirect) les; (stressed, after prep) ellos/ ellas; see also **me**

theme [θi:m] n tema m; **~ park** n parque de atracciones (en torno a un tema central); **~ song** n tema m (musical)

themselves [ðəm'sɛlvz] pl pron (subject) ellos mismos/ellas mismas; (complement) se; (after prep) sí (mismos/as); see also **oneself**

then [ðɛn] adv (at that time) entonces; (next) después; (later) luego, después; (and also) además ♦ conj (therefore) en ese caso, entonces ♦ adj: **the ~ president** el entonces presidente; **by ~** para entonces; **from ~ on** desde entonces

theology [θɪ'ɔlədʒɪ] n teología

theory ['θɪərɪ] n teoría

therapist ['θɛrəpɪst] n terapeuta m/f

therapy ['θɛrəpɪ] n terapia

_____
KEYWORD
_____

there [ðɛə*] adv **1**: **~ is, ~ are** hay; **~ is no-one here/no bread left** no hay nadie aquí/no queda pan; **~ has been an accident** ha habido un accidente

2 (referring to place) ahí; (distant) allí; **it's ~** está ahí; **put it in/on/up/ down** ~ ponlo ahí dentro/encima/ arriba/abajo; **I want that book ~** quiero ese libro de ahí; **he is!** ¡ahí

está!

3: **~, ~** (esp to child) ea, ea

there: **~abouts** adv por ahí; **~after** adv después; **~by** adv así, de ese modo; **~fore** adv por lo tanto; **~'s = there is; there has**

thermal ['θə:ml] adj termal; (paper) térmico

thermometer [θə'mɔmɪtə*] n termómetro

Thermos ® ['θə:məs] n (also: **~ flask**) termo

thermostat ['θə:məustæt] n termostato

thesaurus [θɪ'sɔ:rəs] n tesoro

these [ði:z] pl adj estos/as ♦ pl pron éstos/as

thesis ['θi:sɪs] (pl **theses**) n tesis f inv

they [ðeɪ] pl pron ellos/ellas; (stressed) ellos (mismos)/ellas (mismas); **~ say that ...** (it is said that) se dice que ...; **~'d = they had; they would; ~'ll = they shall; they will; ~'re = they are; ~'ve = they have**

thick [θɪk] adj (in consistency) espeso; (in size) grueso; (stupid) torpe ♦ n: **in the ~ of the battle** en lo más reñido de la batalla; **it's 20 cm ~** tiene 20 cm de espesor; **~en** vi espesarse ♦ vt (sauce etc) espesar; **~ness** n espesor m; grueso; **~set** adj fornido

thief [θi:f] (pl **thieves**) n ladrón/ona m/f

thigh [θaɪ] n muslo

thimble ['θɪmbl] n dedal m

thin [θɪn] adj (person, animal) flaco; (in size) delgado; (in consistency) poco espeso; (hair, crowd) escaso ♦ vt: **to ~ (down)** diluir

thing [θɪŋ] n cosa; (object) objeto, artículo; (matter) asunto; (mania): **to have a ~ about sb/sth** estar obsesionado con uno/algo; **~s** npl (belongings) efectos mpl (personales); **the best ~ would be to ...** lo mejor sería ...; **how are ~s?** ¿qué tal?

think [θɪŋk] (*pt, pp* **thought**) *vi* pensar ♦ *vt* pensar, creer; **what did you ~ of them?** ¿qué te parecieron?; **to ~ about sth/sb** pensar en algo/uno; **I'll ~ about it** lo pensaré; **to ~ of doing sth** pensar en hacer algo; **I ~ so/not** creo que sí/no; **to ~ well of sb** tener buen concepto de uno; **~ over** *vt* reflexionar sobre, meditar; **~ up** *vt* (*plan etc*) idear; **~ tank** *n* gabinete *m* de estrategia

thinly ['θɪnlɪ] *adv* (*cut*) fino; (*spread*) ligeramente

third [θəːd] *adj* (*before n*) tercer(a); (*following n*) tercero/a ♦ *n* tercero/a; (*fraction*) tercio; (*BRIT: SCOL: degree*) título de licenciado con calificación de aprobado; **~ly** *adv* en tercer lugar; **~ party insurance** (*BRIT*) *n* seguro contra terceros; **~-rate** *adj* (de calidad) mediocre; **T~ World** *n* Tercer Mundo

thirst [θəːst] *n* sed *f*; **~y** *adj* (*person, animal*) sediento; (*work*) que da sed; **to be ~y** tener sed

thirteen ['θəː'tiːn] *num* trece

thirty ['θəːtɪ] *num* treinta

this [ðɪs] (*pl* **these**) *adj* (*demonstrative*) este/a; (*pl*) estos/as; (*neuter*) esto; **~ man/woman** este hombre/esta mujer; **these children/flowers** estos chicos/estas flores; **~ one (here)** éste/a, esto (de aquí) ♦ *pron* (*demonstrative*) éste/a; (*pl*) éstos/as; (*neuter*) esto; **who is ~?** ¿quién es éste/ésta?; **what is ~?** ¿qué es esto?; **~ is where I live** aquí vivo; **~ is what he said** esto es lo que dijo; **~ is Mr Brown** (*in introductions*) le presento al Sr. Brown; (*photo*) éste es el Sr. Brown; (*on telephone*) habla el Sr. Brown ♦ *adv* (*demonstrative*): **~ high/long** *etc* así de alto/largo *etc*; **~ far** hasta aquí

thistle ['θɪsl] *n* cardo

thorn [θɔːn] *n* espina

thorough ['θʌrə] *adj* (*search*) minucioso; (*wash*) a fondo; (*knowledge, research*) profundo; (*person*) meticuloso; **~-bred** *adj* (*horse*) de pura sangre; **~fare** *n* calle *f*; **"no ~fare"** "prohibido el paso"; **~ly** *adv* (*search*) minuciosamente; (*study*) profundamente; (*wash*) a fondo; (*utterly: bad, wet etc*) completamente, totalmente

those [ðəuz] *pl adj* esos/esas; (*more remote*) aquellos/as ♦ *pron* ésos/ésas; (*more remote*) aquéllos/as

though [ðəu] *conj* aunque ♦ *adv* sin embargo

thought [θɔːt] *pt, pp of* **think** ♦ *n* pensamiento; (*opinion*) opinión *f*; **~ful** *adj* pensativo; (*serious*) serio; (*considerate*) atento; **~less** *adj* desconsiderado

thousand ['θauzənd] *num* mil; **two ~** dos mil; **~s of** miles de; **~th** *num* milésimo

thrash [θræʃ] *vt* azotar; (*defeat*) derrotar; **~ about** *or* **around** *vi* debatirse; **~ out** *vt* discutir a fondo

thread [θred] *n* hilo; (*of screw*) rosca ♦ *vt* (*needle*) enhebrar; **~bare** *adj* raído

threat [θret] *n* amenaza; **~en** *vi* amenazar ♦ *vt*: **to ~en sb with/to do** amenazar a uno con/con hacer

three [θriː] *num* tres; **~-dimensional** *adj* tridimensional; **~-piece suit** *n* traje *m* de tres piezas; **~-piece suite** *n* tresillo; **~-ply** (*wool*) de tres cabos

threshold ['θreʃhəuld] *n* umbral *m*

threw [θruː] *pt of* **throw**

thrifty ['θrɪftɪ] *adj* económico

thrill [θrɪl] *n* (*excitement*) emoción *f*; (*shudder*) estremecimiento ♦ *vt* emocionar; **to be ~ed** (*with gift etc*) estar encantado; **~er** *n* novela (*or* obra *or* película) de suspense; **~ing** *adj* emocionante

thrive [θraɪv] (*pt, pp* **thrived**) *vi* (*grow*) crecer; (*do well*): **to ~ on sth** sentarse muy bien a uno algo; **thriving** *adj*

tormento ♦ vt atormentar; (fig: annoy)
fastidiar

torn [tɔːn] pp of **tear²**

torrent ['tɔrnt] n torrente m

tortoise ['tɔːtəs] n tortuga; **~shell**
['tɔːtəʃel] adj de carey

torture ['tɔːtʃə*] n tortura ♦ vt torturar;
(fig) atormentar

Tory ['tɔːrɪ] (BRIT) adj, n (POL)
conservador(a) m/f

toss [tɔs] vt tirar, echar; (one's head)
sacudir; **to ~ a coin** echar a cara o
cruz; **to ~ up for sth** jugar a cara o
cruz algo; **to ~ and turn** (in bed) dar
vueltas

tot [tɔt] n (BRIT: drink) copita; (child)
nene/a m/f

total ['təutl] adj total, entero;
(emphatic: failure etc) completo, total
♦ n total m, suma ♦ vt (add up) sumar;
(amount to) ascender a; **~ly** adv
totalmente

touch [tʌtʃ] n tacto; (contact) contacto
♦ vt tocar; (emotionally) conmover; **a
~ of** (fig) un poquito de; **to get in
~ with sb** ponerse en contacto con
uno; **to lose ~** (friends) perder
contacto; **~ on** vt fus (topic) aludir
(brevemente) a; **~ up** vt (paint)
retocar; **~-and-go** adj arriesgado;
~down n aterrizaje m; (on sea)
amerizaje m; (US: FOOTBALL) ensayo;
~ed adj (moved) conmovido; **~ing** adj
(moving) conmovedor(a); **~line** n
(SPORT) línea de banda; **~y** adj (person)
quisquilloso

tough [tʌf] adj (material) resistente;
(meat) duro; (problem etc) difícil;
(policy, stance) inflexible; (person)
fuerte; **~en** vt endurecer

toupée ['tuːpeɪ] n peluca

tour ['tuə*] n viaje m, vuelta; (also:
package ~) viaje m todo comprendido;
(of town, museum) visita; (by band etc)
gira ♦ vt recorrer, visitar; **~ guide** n
guía m turístico, guía f turística

tourism ['tuərɪzm] n turismo

tourist ['tuərɪst] n turista m/f ♦ cpd
turístico; **~ office** n oficina de turismo

tousled ['tauzld] adj (hair) despeinado

tout [taut] vi: **to ~ for business**
solicitar clientes ♦ n (also: ticket ~)
revendedor(a) m/f

tow [təu] vt remolcar; **"on or in** (US)
~" (AUT) "a remolque"

toward(s) [tə'wɔːd(z)] prep hacia;
(attitude) respecto a, con; (purpose)
para

towel ['tauəl] n toalla; **~ling** n (fabric)
felpa; **~ rail** (US **~ rack**) n toallero

tower ['tauə*] n torre f; **~ block** (BRIT)
n torre f (de pisos); **~ing** adj muy alto,
imponente

town [taun] n ciudad f; **to go to ~** ir a
la ciudad; (fig) echar la casa por la
ventana; **~ centre** n centro de la
ciudad; **~ council** n ayuntamiento,
consejo municipal; **~ hall** n
ayuntamiento; **~ plan** n plano de la
ciudad; **~ planning** n urbanismo

towrope ['təurəup] n cable m de
remolque

tow truck (US) n camión m grúa

toy [tɔɪ] n juguete m; **~ with** vt fus
jugar con; (idea) acariciar; **~shop** n
juguetería

trace [treɪs] n rastro ♦ vt (draw) trazar,
delinear; (locate) encontrar; (follow)
seguir la pista de; **tracing paper** n
papel m de calco

track [træk] n (mark) huella, pista;
(path: gen) camino, senda; (: of bullet
etc) trayectoria; (: of suspect, animal)
pista, rastro; (RAIL) vía; (SPORT) pista;
(on tape, record) canción f ♦ vt seguir la
pista de; **to keep ~ of** mantenerse al
tanto de seguir; **~ down** vt (prey)
seguir el rastro de; (sth lost) encontrar;
~suit n chándal M

tract [trækt] n (GEO) región f

traction ['trækʃən] n (power) tracción f;
in ~ (MED) en tracción

tractor ['træktə*] n tractor m

trade [treɪd] n comercio; (skill, job)

oficio ♦ vi negociar, comerciar ♦ vt
(exchange): **to ~ sth (for sth)** cambiar
algo (por algo); **~ in** vt (old car etc)
ofrecer como parte del pago; **~ fair** n
feria comercial; **~mark** n marca de
fábrica; **~ name** n marca registrada;
~r n comerciante m/f; **~sman** (irreg) n
(shopkeeper) tendero; **~ union** n
sindicato; **~ unionist** n sindicalista m/f

tradition [trə'dɪʃən] n tradición f; **~al**
adj tradicional

traffic ['træfɪk] n (gen, AUT) tráfico,
circulación f, circulación (AM) ♦ vi: **to ~ in**
(pej: liquor, drugs) traficar en; **~ circle**
(US) n isleta; **~ jam** n embotellamiento;
~ lights npl semáforo; **~ warden** n
guardia m/f de tráfico

tragedy ['trædʒədɪ] n tragedia

tragic ['trædʒɪk] adj trágico

trail [treɪl] n (tracks) rastro, pista; (path)
camino, sendero; (dust, smoke) estela
♦ vt (drag) arrastrar; (follow) seguir la
pista de ♦ vi arrastrar; (in contest etc) ir
perdiendo; **~ behind** vi quedar a la
zaga; **~er** n (AUT) remolque m;
(caravan) caravana; (CINEMA) trailer m,
avance m; **~er truck** (US) n trailer m

train [treɪn] n tren m; (of dress) cola;
(series) serie f ♦ vt (educate, teach skills
to) formar; (sportsman) entrenar; (dog)
adiestrar; (point: gun etc): **to ~ on**
apuntar a ♦ vi (SPORT) entrenarse;
(learn a skill): **to ~ as a teacher** etc
estudiar para profesor etc; **one's ~ of
thought** el razonamiento de uno; **~ed**
adj (worker) cualificado; (animal)
amaestrado; **~ee** [treɪ'niː] n
aprendiz(a) m/f; **~er** n (SPORT: coach)
entrenador(a) m/f; (: shoe): **~ers**
zapatillas fpl (de deporte); (of animals)
domador(a) m/f; **~ing** n (for a career)
entrenamiento; **to be in ~ing** (SPORT)
estar entrenando; **~ing college** n
(gen) colegio de formación profesional;
(for teachers) escuela de formación del
profesorado; **~ing shoes** npl zapatillas
fpl (de deporte)

trait [treɪt] n rasgo

traitor ['treɪtə*] n traidor(a) m/f

tram [træm] (BRIT) n (also: **~car**) tranvía
m

tramp [træmp] n (person) vagabundo/
a; (inf: pej: woman) puta

trample ['træmpl] vt: **to ~ (underfoot)** pisotear

trampoline ['træmpəliːn] n trampolín
m

tranquil ['træŋkwɪl] adj tranquilo;
~lizer n (MED) tranquilizante m

transact [træn'zækt] vt (business)
despachar; **~ion** [-'zækʃən] n
transacción f, operación f

transfer [n 'trænsfə*, vb træns'fə:*] n
(of employees) traslado; (of money,
power) transferencia; (SPORT) traspaso;
(picture, design) calcomanía ♦ vt
trasladar; transferir; **to ~ the charges**
(BRIT: TEL) llamar a cobro revertido

transform [træns'fɔːm] vt transformar

transfusion [træns'fjuːʒən] n
transfusión f

transient ['trænzɪənt] adj transitorio

transistor [træn'zɪstə*] n (ELEC)
transistor m; **~ radio** n transistor m

transit ['trænzɪt] n: **in ~** en tránsito

transitive ['trænzɪtɪv] adj (LING)
transitivo

transit lounge n sala de tránsito

translate [trænz'leɪt] vt traducir;
translation [-'leɪʃən] n traducción f;
translator n traductor(a) m/f

transmit [trænz'mɪt] vt transmitir;
~ter n transmisor m

transparency [træns'pɛərnsɪ] n
transparencia; (BRIT: PHOT) diapositiva

transparent [træns'pærnt] adj
transparente

transpire [træns'paɪə*] vi (turn out)
resultar; (happen) ocurrir, suceder; **it
~d that ...** se supo que ...

transplant [træns'plɑːnt] vt (MED)
transplante m

transport [n 'trænspɔːt, vt træns'pɔːt]
n transporte m; (car) coche m (SP),

carro (AM), automóvil m ♦ vt
transportar; **~ation** [-'teɪʃən] n
transporte m; **~ café** (BRIT) n bar-
restaurant m de carretera

transvestite [trænz'vestaɪt] n travestí
m/f

trap [træp] n (snare, trick) trampa;
(carriage) cabriolé m ♦ vt coger (SP) o
agarrar (AM) en una trampa; (trick)
engañar; (confine) atrapar; **~ door** n
escotilla

trapeze [trə'piːz] n trapecio

trappings ['træpɪnz] npl adornos mpl

trash [træʃ] n (rubbish) basura; (pej):
the book/film is ~ el libro/la película
no vale nada; (nonsense) tonterías fpl;
~ can (US) n cubo o balde m (AM)
de la basura

travel ['trævl] n el viajar ♦ vi viajar ♦ vt
(distance) recorrer; **~s** npl (journeys)
viajes mpl; **~ agent** n agente m/f de
viajes; **~ler** (US **~er**) n viajero/a; **~ler's
cheque** (US **~er's check**) n cheque m
de viajero; **~ling** (US **~ing**) n los viajes,
el viajar; **~ sickness** n mareo

trawler ['trɔːlə*] n pesquero de
arrastre

tray [treɪ] n bandeja; (on desk) cajón m

treacherous ['tretʃərəs] adj traidor,
traicionero; (dangerous) peligroso

treacle ['triːkl] n (BRIT) melaza

tread [tred] (pt trod, pp trodden) n
(step) paso, pisada; (sound) ruido de
pasos; (of stair) escalón m; (of tyre)
banda de rodadura ♦ vi pisar; **~ on** vt
fus pisar

treason ['triːzn] n traición f

treasure ['treʒə*] n (also fig) tesoro
♦ vt (value: object, friendship) apreciar;
(: memory) guardar

treasurer ['treʒərə*] n tesorero/a

treasury ['treʒərɪ] n: the **T~** el
Ministerio de Hacienda

treat [triːt] n (present) regalo ♦ vt
tratar; **to ~ sb to sth** invitar a uno a
algo

treatment ['triːtmənt] n tratamiento

treaty ['triːtɪ] n tratado

treble ['trebl] adj triple ♦ vt triplicar
♦ vi triplicarse; **~ clef** n (MUS) clave f
de sol

tree [triː] n árbol m; **~ trunk** tronco
(de árbol)

trek [trek] n (long journey) viaje m largo
y difícil; (tiring walk) caminata

trellis ['trelɪs] n enrejado

tremble ['trembl] vi temblar

tremendous [trɪ'mendəs] adj
tremendo, enorme; (excellent)
estupendo

tremor ['tremə*] n temblor m; (also:
earth ~) temblor m de tierra

trench [trentʃ] n zanja

trend [trend] n (tendency) tendencia;
(of events) curso; (fashion) moda; **~y**
adj de moda

trespass ['trespəs] vi: **to ~ on** entrar
sin permiso en; **"no ~ing"** "prohibido
el paso"

trestle ['tresl] n caballete m

trial ['traɪəl] n (LAW) juicio, proceso;
(test: of machine etc) prueba; **~s** npl
(hardships) dificultades fpl; **by ~ and
error** a fuerza de probar

triangle ['traɪæŋgl] n (MATH, MUS)
triángulo

tribe [traɪb] n tribu f

tribunal [traɪ'bjuːnl] n tribunal m

tributary ['trɪbjutərɪ] n (river) afluente
m

tribute ['trɪbjuːt] n homenaje m,
tributo; **to pay ~ to** rendir homenaje
a

trick [trɪk] n (skill, knack) tino, truco;
(conjuring ~) truco; (joke) broma;
(CARDS) baza ♦ vt engañar; **to play a
~ on sb** gastar una broma a uno; **that
should do the ~** a ver si funciona así;
~ery n engaño

trickle ['trɪkl] n (of water etc) goteo
♦ vi gotear

tricky ['trɪkɪ] adj difícil; delicado

tricycle ['traɪsɪkl] n triciclo

trifle ['traɪfl] n bagatela; (CULIN) dulce

de bizcocho borracho, gelatina, fruta y natillas ♦ adj: **a ~ long** un poquito largo; **trifling** adj insignificante

trigger ['trɪgə*] n (of gun) gatillo; **~ off** vt desencadenar

trim [trɪm] adj (house, garden) en buen estado; (person, figure) esbelto ♦ vt (haircut etc) recorte m; (cut) guarnición f ♦ (neaten) arreglar; (cut) recortar; (decorate) adornar; (NAUT: a sail) orientar; **~mings** npl (CULIN) guarnición f

trip [trɪp] n viaje m; (excursion) excursión f; (stumble) traspié m ♦ vi (stumble) tropezar; (go lightly) andar a paso ligero; **on a ~** de viaje; **~ up** vi tropezar, caerse ♦ vt hacer tropezar or caer

tripe [traɪp] n (CULIN) callos mpl

triple ['trɪpl] adj triple; **triplets** ['trɪplɪts] npl trillizos/as mpl/fpl;

triplicate ['trɪplɪkət] n: **in triplicate** por triplicado

trite [traɪt] adj trillado

triumph ['traɪʌmf] n triunfo ♦ vi: **to ~ (over)** vencer; **~ant** [traɪˈʌmfənt] adj (team etc) vencedor(a); (wave, return) triunfal

trivia ['trɪvɪə] npl trivialidades fpl

trivial ['trɪvɪəl] adj insignificante; (commonplace) banal

trod [trɒd] pt of **tread**

trodden ['trɒdn] pp of **tread**

trolley ['trɒlɪ] n carrito; (also: ~ bus) trolebús m

trombone [trɒmˈbəun] n trombón m

troop [truːp] n grupo, banda; **~s** npl (MIL) tropas fpl; **~ in/out** vi entrar/salir en tropel; **~ing the colour** n (ceremony) presentación f de la bandera

trophy ['trəufɪ] n trofeo

tropical ['trɒpɪkl] adj tropical

trot [trɒt] n trote m ♦ vi trotar; **on the ~** (BRIT: fig) seguidos/as

trouble ['trʌbl] n problema m, dificultad f; (worry) preocupación f;

(bother, effort) molestia, esfuerzo; (unrest) inquietud f; (MED) ~ problemas mpl gástricos etc ♦ vt (disturb) molestar; (worry) preocupar, inquietar ♦ vi: **to ~ to do sth** molestarse en hacer algo; **~s** npl (POL etc) conflictos mpl; (personal) problemas mpl; **to be in ~** estar en un apuro; **it's no ~!** ¡no es molestia (ninguna)!; **what's the ~?** (with broken TV etc) ¿cuál es el problema?; (doctor to patient) ¿qué pasa?; **~d** adj (person) preocupado; (country, epoch, life) agitado; **~maker** n agitador/a m/f; (child) alborotador m; **~shooter** n (in conflict) conciliador(a) m/f; **~some** adj molesto

trough [trɒf] n (also: drinking ~) abrevadero; (also: feeding ~) comedero; (depression) depresión f

troupe [truːp] n grupo

trousers ['trauzəz] npl pantalones mpl; **short ~** pantalones mpl cortos

trousseau ['truːsəu] (pl **~x** or **~s**) n ajuar m

trout [traut] n inv trucha

trowel ['trauəl] n (of gardener) palita; (of builder) paleta

truant ['truːənt] n: **to play ~** (BRIT) hacer novillos

truce [truːs] n tregua

truck [trʌk] n (lorry) camión m; (RAIL) vagón m; **~ driver** n camionero; **~ farm** (US) n huerto

true [truː] adj verdadero; (accurate) exacto; (genuine) auténtico; (faithful) fiel; **to come ~** realizarse

truffle ['trʌfl] n trufa

truly ['truːlɪ] adv (really) realmente; (truthfully) verdaderamente; (faithfully) **yours ~** (in letter) le saluda atentamente

trump [trʌmp] n triunfo

trumpet ['trʌmpɪt] n trompeta

truncheon ['trʌntʃən] n porra

trundle ['trʌndl] vi: **to ~ along** vi sin prisas

trunk [trʌŋk] n (of tree, person) tronco m; (of elephant) trompa f; (case) baúl m; (US: AUT) maletero; ~s npl (also: swimming ~s) bañador m (de hombre)

truss [trʌs] vt: ~ (up) atar

trust [trʌst] n confianza f; (responsibility) responsabilidad f; (LAW) fideicomiso ♦ vt (rely on) tener confianza en; (hope) esperar; (entrust): **to ~ sth to sb** confiar algo a uno; **to take sth on ~** aceptar algo a ojos cerrados; **~ed** adj de confianza; **~ee** [trʌs'tiː] n (LAW) fideicomisario; (of school) administrador m; **~ful** adj confiado; **~ing** adj confiado; **~worthy** adj digno de confianza

truth [truːθ, pl truːðz] n verdad f; **~ful** adj veraz

try [traɪ] n tentativa f, intento; (RUGBY) ensayo ♦ vt (attempt) intentar; (test: also: ~ out) probar, someter a prueba; (LAW) juzgar, procesar; (strain: patience) hacer perder ♦ vi probar; **to have a ~** probar suerte; **to do sth** intentar hacer algo; ~ **again!** ¡vuelve a probar!; ~ **harder!** ¡esfuérzate más!; **well, I tried** al menos lo intenté; ~ **on** vt (clothes) probarse; **~ing** adj (experience) cansado; (person) pesado

T-shirt ['tiːʃəːt] n camiseta

T-square n regla en T

tub [tʌb] n cubo (SP), balde m (AM); (bath) tina, bañera

tube [tjuːb] n tubo; (BRIT: underground) metro; (for tyre) cámara de aire

tuberculosis [tjubəːkjuˈləusɪs] n tuberculosis f inv

tube station (BRIT) n estación f de metro

tubular ['tjuːbjulə*] adj tubular

TUC (BRIT) n abbr (= Trades Union Congress) federación nacional de sindicatos

tuck [tʌk] vt (put) poner; ~ **away** vt (money) guardar; (building): **to be ~ed away** esconderse, ocultarse; ~ **in** vt

meter dentro; (child) arropar ♦ vi (eat) comer con apetito; ~ **up** vt (child) arropar; ~ **shop** n (SCOL) tienda; ≈ bar m (del colegio) (SP)

Tuesday ['tjuːzdɪ] n martes m inv

tuft [tʌft] n mechón m; (of grass etc) manojo

tug [tʌg] n (ship) remolcador m ♦ vt tirar de; **~-of-war** n lucha de tiro de cuerda; (fig) tira y afloja m

tuition [tjuːˈɪʃən] n (BRIT) enseñanza; (: private ~) clases fpl particulares; (US: school fees) matrícula

tulip ['tjuːlɪp] n tulipán m

tumble ['tʌmbl] n (fall) caída ♦ vi caer; **to ~ to sth** (inf) caer en la cuenta de algo; **~down** adj destartalado; ~ **dryer** (BRIT) n secadora

tumbler ['tʌmblə*] n (glass) vaso

tummy ['tʌmɪ] n (inf) barriga, tripa

tumour ['tjuːmə*] (US **tumor**) n tumor m

tuna ['tjuːnə] n inv (also: ~ fish) atún m

tune [tjuːn] n melodía ♦ vt (MUS) afinar; (RADIO, TV, AUT) sintonizar; **to be in/out of ~** (instrument) estar afinado/desafinado; (singer) cantar afinadamente/desafinar; **to be in/out of ~ with** (fig) estar de acuerdo/en desacuerdo con; ~ **in** vi: **to ~ in (to)** (RADIO, TV) sintonizar (con); ~ **up** vi (musician) afinar (su instrumento); **~ful** adj melodioso; **~r** n: **piano ~r** afinador/a m/f de pianos

tunic ['tjuːnɪk] n túnica

Tunisia [tjuːˈnɪzɪə] n Túnez m

tunnel ['tʌnl] n túnel m; (in mine) galería ♦ vi construir un túnel/una galería

turban ['təːbən] n turbante m

turbulent ['təːbjulənt] adj turbulento

tureen [təˈriːn] n sopera

turf [təːf] n césped m; (clod) tepe m ♦ vt cubrir con césped; ~ **out** (inf) vt echar a la calle

Turk [təːk] n turco/a

Turkey ['təːkɪ] n Turquía

turkey ['tɜːkɪ] n pavo
Turkish ['tɜːkɪʃ] adj, n turco
turmoil ['tɜːmɔɪl] n: **in ~** revuelto
turn [tɜːn] n turno; (in road) curva; (of mind, events) rumbo; (THEATRE) número; (MED) ataque m ♦ vt girar, volver; (collar, steak) dar la vuelta a; (page) pasar; (change): **to ~ sth into** convertir algo en ♦ vi volver; (person: look back) volverse; (reverse direction) dar la vuelta; (milk) cortarse; (become): **to ~ nasty/forty** ponerse feo/cumplir los cuarenta; **a good ~** un favor; **it gave me quite a ~** me dio un susto; **"no left ~"** (AUT) "prohibido girar a la izquierda"; **it's your ~** te toca a ti; **in ~** por turnos; **to take ~s (at)** turnarse (en); **~ away** vi apartar la vista ♦ vi rechazar; **~ back** vi volverse atrás ♦ vt hacer retroceder; (clock) retrasar; **~ down** vt (refuse) rechazar; (reduce) bajar; (fold) doblar; **~ in** vi (inf: go to bed) acostarse ♦ vt (fold) doblar hacia dentro; **~ off** vi (from road) desviarse ♦ vt (light, radio etc) apagar; (tap) cerrar; (engine) parar; **~ on** vt (light, radio etc) encender (SP), prender (AM); (tap) abrir; (engine) poner en marcha; **~ out** vt (light, gas) apagar; (produce) producir ♦ vi (appear) concurrir; **to ~ out to be ...** resultar ser ...; **~ over** vi (person) volverse ♦ vt (object) dar la vuelta a; (page) volver; **~ round** vi volverse; (rotate) girar; **~ up** vi (person) llegar, presentarse; (lost object) aparecer ♦ vt (gen) subir; **~ing** n (in road) vuelta; **~ing point** n (fig) momento decisivo
turnip ['tɜːnɪp] n nabo
turn: **~out** n concurrencia; **~over** n (COMM: amount of money) volumen m de ventas; (: of goods) movimiento; **~pike** (US) n autopista de peaje; **~stile** n torniquete m; **~table** n plato; **~up** (BRIT) n (on trousers) vuelta
turpentine ['tɜːpəntaɪn] n (also: turps) trementina

turquoise ['tɜːkwɔɪz] n (stone) turquesa ♦ adj color turquesa
turret ['tʌrɪt] n torreón m
turtle ['tɜːtl] n galápago; **~neck (sweater)** n jersey m de cuello vuelto
tusk [tʌsk] n colmillo
tutor ['tjuːtə*] n profesor(a) m/f; **~ial** [-'tɔːrɪəl] n (SCOL) seminario
tuxedo [tʌk'siːdəu] (US) n smóking m, esmoquin m
TV [tiː'viː] n abbr (= television) tele f
twang [twæŋ] n (of instrument) punteado; (of voice) timbre m nasal
tweezers ['twiːzəz] npl pinzas fpl (de depilar)
twelfth [twelfθ] num duodécimo
twelve [twelv] num doce; **at ~ o'clock** (midday) a mediodía; (midnight) a medianoche
twentieth ['twentɪɪθ] adj vigésimo
twenty ['twentɪ] num veinte
twice [twaɪs] adv dos veces; **~ as much** dos veces más
twiddle ['twɪdl] vi: **to ~ (with) sth** dar vueltas a algo; **to ~ one's thumbs** (fig) estar mano sobre mano
twig [twɪg] n ramita
twilight ['twaɪlaɪt] n crepúsculo
twin [twɪn] adj, n gemelo/a m/f ♦ vt hermanar; **~-bedded room** n habitación f doble
twine [twaɪn] n bramante m ♦ vi (plant) enroscarse
twinge [twɪndʒ] n (of pain) punzada; (of conscience) remordimiento
twinkle ['twɪŋkl] vi centellear; (eyes) brillar
twirl [twɜːl] vt dar vueltas a ♦ vi dar vueltas
twist [twɪst] n (action) torsión f; (in road, coil) vuelta; (in wire, flex) doblez f; (in story) giro ♦ vt torcer; (weave) trenzar; (roll around) enrollar; (fig) deformar ♦ vi serpentear
twit [twɪt] (inf) n tonto
twitch [twɪtʃ] n (pull) tirón m; (nervous) tic m ♦ vi crisparse

two [tu:] *num* dos; **to put ~ and ~ together** (*fig*) atar cabos; **~-door** *adj* (AUT) de dos puertas; **~-faced** *adj* (*pej: person*) falso; **~fold** *adv*: **to increase ~fold** doblarse; **~-piece (suit)** *n* traje m de dos piezas; **~-piece (swimsuit)** *n* dos piezas m *inv*, bikini m; **~some** *n* (*people*) pareja; **~-way** *adj*: **~-way traffic** circulación f de dos sentidos

tycoon [taɪˈkuːn] *n*: **(business) ~** magnate m

type [taɪp] *n* (*category*) tipo, género; (*model*) tipo; (TYP) tipo, letra ♦ *vt* (*letter etc*) escribir a máquina; **~cast** *adj* (*actor*) encasillado; **~face** *n* letra; **~script** *n* texto mecanografiado; **~writer** *n* máquina de escribir; **~written** *adj* mecanografiado

typhoid [ˈtaɪfɔɪd] *n* tifoidea

typical [ˈtɪpɪkl] *adj* típico

typing [ˈtaɪpɪŋ] *n* mecanografía

typist [ˈtaɪpɪst] *n* mecanógrafo/a

tyrant [ˈtaɪərnt] *n* tirano/a

tyre [ˈtaɪə*] (US **tire**) *n* neumático (SP), llanta (AM); **~ pressure** *n* presión f de los neumáticos

U, u

U-bend [ˈjuːbend] *n* (AUT, *in pipe*) recodo

udder [ˈʌdə*] *n* ubre f

UFO [ˈjuːfəu] *n abbr* = (*unidentified flying object*) OVNI m

ugh [ə:h] *excl* ¡uf!

ugly [ˈʌglɪ] *adj* feo; (*dangerous*) peligroso

UHT *abbr*: **~ milk** leche f UHT, leche f uperizada

UK *n abbr* = **United Kingdom**

ulcer [ˈʌlsə*] *n* úlcera; (*mouth ~*) llaga

Ulster [ˈʌlstə*] *n* Ulster m

ulterior [ʌlˈtɪərɪə*] *adj*: **~ motive** segundas intenciones *fpl*

ultimate [ˈʌltɪmət] *adj* último, final;

(*greatest*) máximo; **~ly** *adv* (*in the end*) por último, al final; (*fundamentally*) a o en fin de cuentas

umbilical cord [ʌmˈbɪlɪkl-] *n* cordón m umbilical

umbrella [ʌmˈbrelə] *n* paraguas m *inv*; (*for sun*) sombrilla

umpire [ˈʌmpaɪə*] *n* árbitro

umpteen [ʌmpˈtiːn] *adj* enésimos/as; **~th** *adj*: **for the ~th time** por enésima vez

UN *n abbr* (= United Nations) NN. UU.

unable [ʌnˈeɪbl] *adj*: **to be ~ to do sth** no poder hacer algo

unaccompanied [ʌnəˈkʌmpənɪd] *adj* no acompañado; (*song*) sin acompañamiento

unaccustomed [ʌnəˈkʌstəmd] *adj*: **to be ~ to** no estar acostumbrado a

unanimous [juːˈnænɪməs] *adj* unánime

unarmed [ʌnˈɑːmd] *adj* (*defenceless*) inerme; (*without weapon*) desarmado

unattached [ʌnəˈtætʃt] *adj* (*person*) soltero y sin compromiso; (*part etc*) suelto

unattended [ʌnəˈtendɪd] *adj* desatendido

unattractive [ʌnəˈtræktɪv] *adj* poco atractivo

unauthorized [ʌnˈɔːθəraɪzd] *adj* no autorizado

unavoidable [ʌnəˈvɔɪdəbl] *adj* inevitable

unaware [ʌnəˈwɛə*] *adj*: **to be ~ of** ignorar; **~s** *adv* de improviso

unbalanced [ʌnˈbælənst] *adj* (*report*) poco objetivo; (*mentally*) trastornado

unbearable [ʌnˈbɛərəbl] *adj* insoportable

unbeatable [ʌnˈbiːtəbl] *adj* (*team*) invencible; (*price*) inmejorable; (*quality*) insuperable

unbelievable [ʌnbɪˈliːvəbl] *adj* increíble

unbend [ʌnˈbend] (*irreg*) *vi* (*relax*) relajarse ♦ *vt* (*wire*) enderezar

unbiased [ʌn'baɪəst] *adj* imparcial

unborn [ʌn'bɔːn] *adj* que va a nacer

unbroken [ʌn'brəukən] *adj* (*seal*) intacto; (*series*) continuo; (*record*) no batido; (*spirit*) indómito

unbutton [ʌn'bʌtn] *vt* desabrochar

uncalled-for [ʌn'kɔːldfɔː*] *adj* gratuito, inmerecido

uncanny [ʌn'kænɪ] *adj* extraño

unceremonious ['ʌnserɪ'məunɪəs] *adj* (*abrupt, rude*) brusco, hosco

uncertain [ʌn'sɜːtn] *adj* incierto; (*indecisive*) indeciso

unchanged [ʌn'tʃeɪndʒd] *adj* igual, sin cambios

uncivilized [ʌn'sɪvɪlaɪzd] *adj* inculto; (*fig: behaviour etc*) bárbaro; (*hour*) inoportuno

uncle [ʌŋkl] *n* tío

uncomfortable [ʌn'kʌmfətəbl] *adj* incómodo; (*uneasy*) inquieto

uncommon [ʌn'kɔmən] *adj* poco común, raro

uncompromising [ʌn'kɔmprəmaɪzɪŋ] *adj* intransigente

unconcerned [ʌnkən'sɜːnd] *adj* indiferente, despreocupado

unconditional [ʌnkən'dɪʃənl] *adj* incondicional

unconscious [ʌn'kɔnʃəs] *adj* sin sentido; (*unaware*): **to be ~ of** no darse cuenta de ♦ *n*: **the ~** el inconsciente

uncontrollable [ʌnkən'trəuləbl] *adj* (*child etc*) incontrolable; (*temper*) indomable; (*laughter*) incontenible

unconventional [ʌnkən'venʃənl] *adj* poco convencional

uncouth [ʌn'kuːθ] *adj* grosero, inculto

uncover [ʌn'kʌvə*] *vt* descubrir; (*take lid off*) destapar

undecided [ʌndɪ'saɪdɪd] *adj* (*character*) indeciso; (*question*) no resuelto

under ['ʌndə*] *prep* debajo de; (*less than*) menos de; (*according to*) según, de acuerdo con; (*sb's leadership*) bajo

♦ *adv* debajo, abajo; **~ there** allí abajo; **~ repair** en reparación

under... ['ʌndə*] *prefix* sub; **~age** *adj* menor de edad; (*drinking etc*) de los menores de edad; **~carriage** (*BRIT*) *n* (*AVIAT*) tren *m* de aterrizaje; **~charge** *vt* cobrar menos de la cuenta; **~clothes** *npl* ropa interior (*SP*) or íntima (*AM*); **~coat** *n* (*paint*) primera mano; **~cover** *adj* clandestino; **~current** *n* (*fig*) corriente *f* oculta; **~cut** *vt irreg* vender más barato que; **~developed** *adj* subdesarrollado; **~dog** *n* desvalido/a; **~done** *adj* (*CULIN*) poco hecho; **~estimate** *vt* subestimar; **~exposed** *adj* (*PHOT*) subexpuesto; **~fed** *adj* subalimentado; **~foot** *adv* con los pies; **~go** *vt irreg* sufrir; (*treatment*) recibir; **~graduate** *n* estudiante *m/f*; **~ground** *n* (*BRIT: railway*) metro; (*POL*) movimiento clandestino ♦ *adj* (*car park*) subterráneo ♦ *adv* (*work*) en la clandestinidad; **~growth** *n* maleza; **~hand(ed)** *adj* (*fig*) socarrón; **~lie** *vt irreg* (*fig*) ser la razón fundamental de; **~line** *vt* subrayar; **~mine** *vt* socavar, minar; **~neath** [ʌndə'niːθ] *adv* debajo ♦ *prep* debajo de, bajo; **~paid** *adj* mal pagado; **~pants** *npl* calzoncillos *mpl*; **~pass** (*BRIT*) *n* paso subterráneo; **~privileged** *adj* desposeído; **~rate** *vt* menospreciar, subestimar; **~shirt** (*US*) *n* camiseta; **~shorts** (*US*) *npl* calzoncillos *mpl*; **~side** *n* parte *f* inferior; **~skirt** (*BRIT*) *n* enaguas *fpl*

understand [ʌndə'stænd] (*irreg*) *vt, vi* entender, comprender; (*assume*) tener entendido; **~able** *adj* comprensible; **~ing** *adj* comprensivo ♦ *n* comprensión *f*, entendimiento; (*agreement*) acuerdo

understatement ['ʌndəsteɪtmənt] *n* modestia (excesiva); **that's an ~!** ¡eso es decir poco!

understood [ʌndə'stud] *pt, pp of* **understand** ♦ *adj* (*agreed*) acordado, (implied): **it is ~ that** se sobreentiende que

understudy ['ʌndəstʌdɪ] n suplente m/f

undertake [ʌndə'teɪk] (irreg) vt emprender; **to ~ to do sth** comprometerse a hacer algo

undertaker ['ʌndəteɪkə*] n director(a) m/f de pompas fúnebres

undertaking ['ʌndəteɪkɪŋ] n empresa; (promise) promesa

under: **~tone** n: **in an ~tone** en voz baja; **~water** adv bajo el agua ♦ adj submarino; **~wear** n ropa interior (SP) or íntima (AM); **~world** n (of crime) hampa, inframundo; **~writer** n (INSURANCE) asegurador(a) m/f

undesirable [ʌndɪ'zaɪərəbl] adj (person) indeseable; (thing) poco aconsejable

undo [ʌn'duː] (irreg) vt (laces) desatar; (button etc) desabrochar; (spoil) deshacer; **~ing** n ruina, perdición f

undoubted [ʌn'dautɪd] adj indubable

undress [ʌn'drɛs] vi desnudarse

undulating ['ʌndjuleɪtɪŋ] adj ondulante

unduly [ʌn'djuːlɪ] adv excesivamente, demasiado

unearth [ʌn'ɜːθ] vt desenterrar

unearthly [ʌn'ɜːθlɪ] adj (hour) inverosímil

uneasy [ʌn'iːzɪ] adj intranquilo, preocupado; (feeling) desagradable; (peace) inseguro

uneducated [ʌn'ɛdjukeɪtɪd] adj ignorante, inculto

unemployed [ʌnɪm'plɔɪd] adj parado, sin trabajo ♦ npl: **the ~** los parados

unemployment [ʌnɪm'plɔɪmənt] n paro, desempleo

unending [ʌn'ɛndɪŋ] adj interminable

unerring [ʌn'ɜːrɪŋ] adj infalible

uneven [ʌn'iːvn] adj desigual; (road etc) lleno de baches

unexpected [ʌnɪk'spɛktɪd] adj inesperado; **~ly** adv inesperadamente

unfailing [ʌn'feɪlɪŋ] adj (support)

indefectible; (energy) inagotable

unfair [ʌn'fɛə*] adj: **~ (to sb)** injusto (con uno)

unfaithful [ʌn'feɪθful] adj infiel

unfamiliar [ʌnfə'mɪlɪə*] adj extraño, desconocido; **to be ~ with** desconocer

unfashionable [ʌn'fæʃnəbl] adj pasado or fuera de moda

unfasten [ʌn'fɑːsn] vt (knot) desatar; (dress) desabrochar; (open) abrir

unfavourable [ʌn'feɪvərəbl] (US **unfavorable**) adj desfavorable

unfeeling [ʌn'fiːlɪŋ] adj insensible

unfinished [ʌn'fɪnɪʃt] adj inacabado, sin terminar

unfit [ʌn'fɪt] adj bajo de forma; (incompetent): **~ (for)** incapaz de; **~ for work** no apto para trabajar

unfold [ʌn'fəuld] vt desdoblar ♦ vi abrirse

unforeseen ['ʌnfɔː'siːn] adj imprevisto

unforgettable [ʌnfə'gɛtəbl] adj inolvidable

unfortunate [ʌn'fɔːtʃnət] adj desgraciado; (event, remark) inoportuno; **~ly** adv desgraciadamente

unfounded [ʌn'faundɪd] adj infundado

unfriendly [ʌn'frɛndlɪ] adj antipático; (behaviour, remark) hostil, poco amigable

ungainly [ʌn'geɪnlɪ] adj desgarbado

ungodly [ʌn'gɔdlɪ] adj: **at an ~ hour** a una hora inverosímil

ungrateful [ʌn'greɪtful] adj ingrato

unhappiness [ʌn'hæpɪnɪs] n tristeza, desdicha

unhappy [ʌn'hæpɪ] adj (sad) triste, (unfortunate) desgraciado; (childhood) infeliz; **~ about/with** (arrangements etc) poco contento con, descontento de

unharmed [ʌn'hɑːmd] adj ileso

unhealthy [ʌn'hɛlθɪ] adj (place) malsano; (person) enfermizo; (fig: interest) morboso

unheard-of adj inaudito, sin precedente

unhurt [ʌnˈhɜːt] adj ileso

unidentified [ʌnaɪˈdentɪfaɪd] adj no identificado, sin identificar; see also UFO

uniform [ˈjuːnɪfɔːm] n uniforme m ♦ adj uniforme

unify [ˈjuːnɪfaɪ] vt unificar, unir

uninhabited [ʌnɪnˈhæbɪtɪd] adj desierto

unintentional [ʌnɪnˈtenʃənəl] adj involuntario

union [ˈjuːnjən] n unión f; (also: trade ~) sindicato ♦ cpd sindical; **U~ Jack** n bandera del Reino Unido

unique [juːˈniːk] adj único

unison [ˈjuːnɪsn] n: **in ~** (speak, reply, sing) al unísono

unit [ˈjuːnɪt] n unidad f; (section: of furniture etc) elemento; (team) grupo; **kitchen ~** módulo de cocina

unite [juːˈnaɪt] vt unir ♦ vi unirse; **~d** adj unido; (effort) conjunto; **U~d Kingdom** n Reino Unido; **U~d Nations (Organization)** n Naciones fpl Unidas; **U~d States (of America)** n Estados mpl Unidos

unit trust (BRIT) n bono fiduciario

unity [ˈjuːnɪtɪ] n unidad f

universe [ˈjuːnɪvɜːs] n universo

university [juːnɪˈvɜːsɪtɪ] n universidad f

unjust [ʌnˈdʒʌst] adj injusto

unkempt [ʌnˈkempt] adj (appearance) descuidado; (hair) despeinado

unkind [ʌnˈkaɪnd] adj poco amable; (behaviour, comment) cruel

unknown [ʌnˈnəun] adj desconocido

unlawful [ʌnˈlɔːful] adj ilegal, ilícito

unleaded [ʌnˈledɪd] adj (petrol, fuel) sin plombo

unless [ʌnˈles] conj a menos que; **~ he comes** a menos que venga; **~ otherwise stated** salvo indicación contraria

unlike [ʌnˈlaɪk] adj (not alike) distinto

de or a; (not like) poco propio de ♦ prep a diferencia de

unlikely [ʌnˈlaɪklɪ] adj improbable; (unexpected) inverosímil

unlimited [ʌnˈlɪmɪtɪd] adj ilimitado

unlisted [ʌnˈlɪstɪd] (US) adj (TEL) que no consta en la guía

unload [ʌnˈləud] vt descargar

unlock [ʌnˈlɔk] vt abrir (con llave)

unlucky [ʌnˈlʌkɪ] adj desgraciado; (object, number) que da mala suerte; **to be ~** tener mala suerte

unmarried [ʌnˈmærɪd] adj soltero

unmistak(e)able [ʌnmɪsˈteɪkəbl] adj inconfundible

unnatural [ʌnˈnætʃrəl] adj (gen) antinatural; (manner) afectado; (habit) perverso

unnecessary [ʌnˈnesəsrɪ] adj innecesario, inútil

unnoticed [ʌnˈnəutɪst] adj: **to go or pass ~** pasar desapercibido

UNO [ˈjuːnəu] n abbr (= United Nations Organization) ONU f

unobtainable [ʌnəbˈteɪnəbl] adj inconseguible; (TEL) inexistente

unobtrusive [ʌnəbˈtruːsɪv] adj discreto

unofficial [ʌnəˈfɪʃl] adj no oficial; (news) sin confirmar

unorthodox [ʌnˈɔːθədɔks] adj poco ortodoxo; (REL) heterodoxo

unpack [ʌnˈpæk] vi deshacer las maletas ♦ vt deshacer

unpalatable [ʌnˈpælətəbl] adj incomible; (truth) desagradable

unparalleled [ʌnˈpærəleld] adj (unequalled) incomparable

unpleasant [ʌnˈpleznt] adj (disagreeable) desagradable; (person, manner) antipático

unplug [ʌnˈplʌg] vt desenchufar, desconectar

unpopular [ʌnˈpɔpjulə*] adj impopular, poco popular

unprecedented [ʌnˈpresɪdəntɪd] adj sin precedentes

unpredictable [ʌnprɪ'dɪktəbl] adj imprevisible

unprofessional [ʌnprə'feʃənl] adj (attitude, conduct) poco ético

unqualified [ʌn'kwɔlɪfaɪd] adj sin título, no cualificado; (success) total

unquestionably [ʌn'kwestʃənəblɪ] adv indiscutiblemente

unreal [ʌn'rɪəl] adj irreal; (extraordinary) increíble

unrealistic [ʌnrɪə'lɪstɪk] adj poco realista

unreasonable [ʌn'riːznəbl] adj irrazonable; (demand) excesivo

unrelated [ʌnrɪ'leɪtɪd] adj sin relación; (family) no emparentado

unreliable [ʌnrɪ'laɪəbl] adj (person) informal; (machine) poco fiable

unremitting [ʌnrɪ'mɪtɪŋ] adj constante

unreservedly [ʌnrɪ'zɜːvɪdlɪ] adv sin reserva

unrest [ʌn'rest] n inquietud f, malestar m; (POL) disturbios mpl

unroll [ʌn'rəul] vt desenrollar

unruly [ʌn'ruːlɪ] adj indisciplinado

unsafe [ʌn'seɪf] adj peligroso

unsaid [ʌn'sed] adj: to leave sth ~ dejar algo sin decir

unsatisfactory ['ʌnsætɪs'fæktərɪ] adj poco satisfactorio

unsavoury [ʌn'seɪvərɪ] (US **unsavory**) adj (fig) repugnante

unscrew [ʌn'skruː] vt destornillar

unscrupulous [ʌn'skruːpjuləs] adj sin escrúpulos

unsettled [ʌn'setld] adj inquieto, intranquilo; (weather) variable

unshaven [ʌn'ʃeɪvn] adj sin afeitar

unsightly [ʌn'saɪtlɪ] adj feo

unskilled [ʌn'skɪld] adj (work) no especializado; (worker) no cualificado

unspeakable [ʌn'spiːkəbl] adj indecible; (awful) incalificable

unstable [ʌn'steɪbl] adj inestable

unsteady [ʌn'stedɪ] adj inestable

unstuck [ʌn'stʌk] adj: to come ~

despegarse; (fig) fracasar

unsuccessful [ʌnsək'sesful] adj (attempt) infructuoso; (writer, proposal) sin éxito; **to be ~** (in attempting sth) no tener éxito, fracasar; **~ly** adv en vano, sin éxito

unsuitable [ʌn'suːtəbl] adj inapropiado; (time) inoportuno

unsure [ʌn'ʃuə*] adj inseguro, poco seguro

unsuspecting ['ʌnsəs'pektɪŋ] adj desprevenido

unsympathetic [ʌnsɪmpə'θetɪk] adj poco comprensivo; (unlikeable) antipático

unthinkable [ʌn'θɪŋkəbl] adj inconcebible, impensable

untidy [ʌn'taɪdɪ] adj (room) desordenado; (appearance) desaliñado

untie [ʌn'taɪ] vt desatar

until [ʌn'tɪl] prep hasta ♦ conj hasta que; **~ he comes** hasta que venga; **~ now** hasta ahora; **~ then** hasta entonces

untimely [ʌn'taɪmlɪ] adj inoportuno; (death) prematuro

untold [ʌn'təuld] adj (story) nunca contado; (suffering) indecible; (wealth) incalculable

untoward [ʌntə'wɔːd] adj adverso

unused [ʌn'juːzd] adj sin usar

unusual [ʌn'juːʒuəl] adj insólito, poco común; (exceptional) inusitado

unveil [ʌn'veɪl] vt (statue) descubrir

unwanted [ʌn'wɒntɪd] adj (clothing) viejo; (pregnancy) no deseado

unwelcome [ʌn'welkəm] adj inoportuno; (news) desagradable

unwell [ʌn'wel] adj: to be/feel ~ estar indispuesto/sentirse mal

unwieldy [ʌn'wiːldɪ] adj difícil de manejar

unwilling [ʌn'wɪlɪŋ] adj: to be ~ to do sth estar poco dispuesto a hacer algo; **~ly** adv de mala gana

unwind [ʌn'waɪnd] (irreg: like **wind²**) vt desenvolver ♦ vi (relax) relajarse

unwise [ʌn'waɪz] *adj* imprudente
unwitting [ʌn'wɪtɪŋ] *adj* inconsciente
unworthy [ʌn'wɜ:ðɪ] *adj* indigno
unwrap [ʌn'ræp] *vt* desenvolver
unwritten [ʌn'rɪtn] *adj* (*agreement*) tácito; (*rules, law*) no escrito

---

KEYWORD

up [ʌp] *prep*: **to go/be ~** sth subir/ estar subido en algo; **he went ~ the stairs/the hill** subió las escaleras/la colina; **we walked/climbed ~ the hill** subimos la colina; **they live further ~ the street** viven más arriba en la calle; **go ~ that road and turn left** sigue por esa calle y gira a la izquierda
♦ *adv* **1** (*upwards, higher*) más arriba; **~ in the mountains** en lo alto (de la montaña); **put it a bit higher ~** ponlo un poco más arriba en algo; **~ there** ahí or allí arriba; **~ above** en lo alto, por encima, arriba
2: **to be ~** (*out of bed*) estar levantado; (*prices, level*) haber subido
3: **~ to** (*as far as*) hasta; **~ to now** hasta ahora or la fecha
4: **to be ~ to** (*depending on*): **it's ~ to you** depende de ti; **he's not ~ to it** (*job, task etc*) no es capaz de hacerlo; **his work is not ~ to the required standard** su trabajo no da la talla; (*inf: be doing*): **what is he ~ to?** ¿que estará tramando?
♦ *n*: **~s and downs** altibajos *mpl*

upbringing ['ʌpbrɪŋɪŋ] *n* educación *f*
update [ʌp'deɪt] *vt* poner al día
upgrade [ʌp'greɪd] *vt* (*house*) modernizar; (*employee*) ascender
upheaval [ʌp'hi:vl] *n* trastornos *mpl*; (*POL*) agitación *f*
uphill [ʌp'hɪl] *adj* cuesta arriba; (*fig: task*) penoso, difícil ♦ *adv*: **to go ~** ir cuesta arriba
uphold [ʌp'həʊld] (*irreg*) *vt* defender
upholstery [ʌp'həʊlstərɪ] *n* tapicería

upkeep ['ʌpki:p] *n* mantenimiento
upon [ə'pɒn] *prep* sobre
upper ['ʌpə*] *adj* superior, de arriba
♦ *n* (*of shoe: also*: **~s**) empeine *m*; **~ class** *n* de clase alta; **~ hand** *n*: **to have the ~ hand** tener la sartén por el mango; **~most** *adj* el más alto; **what was ~most in my mind** lo que me preocupaba más
upright ['ʌpraɪt] *adj* derecho; (*vertical*) vertical; (*fig*) honrado
uprising ['ʌpraɪzɪŋ] *n* sublevación *f*
uproar ['ʌprɔ:*] *n* escándalo
uproot [ʌp'ru:t] *vt* (*also fig*) desarraigar
upset [*n* 'ʌpset, *vb, adj* ʌp'set] *n* (*to plan etc*) revés *m*, contratiempo; (*MED*) trastorno ♦ (*irreg*) *vt* (*glass etc*) volcar; (*plan*) alterar; (*person*) molestar, disgustar ♦ *adj* molesto, disgustado; (*stomach*) revuelto
upshot ['ʌpʃɒt] *n* resultado
upside-down *adv* al revés; **to turn a place ~** (*fig*) revolverlo todo
upstairs [ʌp'steəz] *adv* arriba ♦ *adj* (*room*) de arriba ♦ *n* el piso superior
upstart ['ʌpsta:t] *n* advenedizo
upstream [ʌp'stri:m] *adv* río arriba
uptake [ʌp'teɪk] *n*: **to be quick/slow on the ~** ser muy listo/torpe
uptight [ʌp'taɪt] *adj* tenso, nervioso
up-to-date *adj* al día
upturn ['ʌptɜ:n] *n* (*in luck*) mejora; (*COMM: in market*) resurgimiento económico
upward ['ʌpwəd] *adj* ascendente; **~(s)** *adv* hacia arriba; (*more than*): **~(s) of** más de

urban ['ɜ:bən] *adj* urbano
urchin ['ɜ:tʃɪn] *n* pilluelo, golfillo
urge [ɜ:dʒ] *n* (*impulse*) deseo ♦ *vt*: **to ~ sb to do sth** animar a uno a hacer algo
urgent ['ɜ:dʒənt] *adj* urgente; (*voice*) perentorio
urinate ['jʊərɪneɪt] *vi* orinar
urine ['jʊərɪn] *n* orina, orines *mpl*
urn [ɜ:n] *n* urna; (*also*: **tea ~**) cacharro

metálico grande para hacer té

Uruguay [ˈjʊərəgwaɪ] *n* (el) Uruguay; **~an** [-ˈgwaɪən] *adj*, *n* uruguayo/a *m/f*

US *n abbr* (= *United States*) EE. UU.

us [ʌs] *pron* nos; (*after prep*) nosotros/ as; *see also* **me**

USA *n abbr* (= *United States of America*) EE. UU.

usage [ˈjuːzɪdʒ] *n* (LING) uso

use [*n* juːs, *vb* juːz] *n* uso, empleo; (*usefulness*) utilidad ♦ *vt* usar, emplear; **she ~d to do it** (ella) solía *or* acostumbraba hacerlo; **in ~** en uso; **out of ~** en desuso; **to be of ~** servir; **it's no ~** (*pointless*) es inútil; (*not useful*) no sirve; **to be ~d to** estar acostumbrado a, acostumbrar; **~ up** *vt* (*food*) consumir; (*money*) gastar; **~d** *adj* (*car*) usado; **~ful** *adj* útil; **~fulness** *n* utilidad *f*; **~less** *adj* (*unusable*) inservible; (*pointless*) inútil; (*person*) inepto; **~r** *n* usuario/a; **~r-friendly** *adj* (*computer*) amistoso

usher [ˈʌʃə*] *n* (*at wedding*) ujier *m*; **~ette** [-ˈret] *n* (*in cinema*) acomodadora

USSR *n* (HIST): **the ~** la URSS

usual [ˈjuːʒuəl] *adj* normal, corriente; **as ~** como de costumbre; **~ly** *adv* normalmente

utensil [juːˈtɛnsl] *n* utensilio; **kitchen ~s** batería de cocina

uterus [ˈjuːtərəs] *n* útero

utility [juːˈtɪlɪtɪ] *n* utilidad *f*; (*public ~*) (empresa *f* de) servicio público; **~ room** *n* ofis *m*

utilize [ˈjuːtɪlaɪz] *vt* utilizar

utmost [ˈʌtməʊst] *adj* mayor ♦ *n*: **to do one's ~** hacer todo lo posible

utter [ˈʌtə*] *adj* total, completo ♦ *vt* pronunciar, proferir; **~ly** *adv* completamente, totalmente

U-turn [ˈjuːˈtɜːn] *n* viraje *m* en redondo

V, v

v. *abbr* = **verse**; **versus**; (= *volt*) v; (= *vide*) véase

vacancy [ˈveɪkənsɪ] *n* (BRIT: *job*) vacante *f*; (*room*) habitación *f* libre; **"no vacancies"** "completo"

vacant [ˈveɪkənt] *adj* desocupado, libre; (*expression*) distraído

vacate [vəˈkeɪt] *vt* (*house, room*) desocupar; (*job*) dejar (vacante)

vacation [vəˈkeɪʃən] *n* vacaciones *fpl*

vaccinate [ˈvæksɪneɪt] *vt* vacunar

vaccine [ˈvæksiːn] *n* vacuna

vacuum [ˈvækjum] *n* vacío; **~ cleaner** *n* aspiradora; **~flask** (BRIT) *n* termo; **~-packed** *adj* empaquetado al vacío

vagina [vəˈdʒaɪnə] *n* vagina

vagrant [ˈveɪɡrnt] *n* vagabundo/a

vague [veɪɡ] *adj* vago; (*memory*) borroso; (*ambiguous*) impreciso; (*person: absent-minded*) distraído; (: *evasive*): **to be ~** no decir las cosas claramente; **~ly** *adv* vagamente, distraídamente; con evasivas

vain [veɪn] *adj* (*conceited*) presumido; (*useless*) vano, inútil; **in ~** en vano

valentine [ˈvæləntaɪn] *n* (*also*: **~ card**) tarjeta del Día de los Enamorados

valet [ˈvæleɪ] *n* ayuda *m* de cámara

valid [ˈvælɪd] *adj* válido; (*ticket*) valedero; (*law*) vigente

valley [ˈvælɪ] *n* valle *m*

valuable [ˈvæljuəbl] *adj* (*jewel*) de valor; (*time*) valioso; **~s** *npl* objetos *mpl* de valor

valuation [væljuˈeɪʃən] *n* tasación *f*, valuación *f*; (*judgement of quality*) valoración *f*

value [ˈvæljuː] *n* valor *m*; (*importance*) importancia ♦ *vt* (*fix price of*) tasar, valorar; (*esteem*) apreciar; **~s** *npl* (*principles*) principios *mpl*; **~ added tax** (BRIT) *n* impuesto sobre el valor añadido; **~d** adj (appreciated) apreciado

valve [vælv] n válvula

van [væn] n (AUT) furgoneta (SP), camioneta (AM)

vandal [vændl] n vándalo/a; **~ism** n vandalismo; **~ize** vt dañar, destruir

vanilla [və'nɪlə] n vainilla

vanish [vænɪʃ] vi desaparecer

vanity [vænɪtɪ] n vanidad

vantage point [vɑːntɪdʒ-] n (for views) punto panorámico

vapour ['veɪpə*] (US vapor) n vapor m; (on breath, window) vaho

variable [veərɪəbl] adj variable

variation [veərɪ'eɪʃən] n variación f

varicose [værɪkəus] adj: **~ veins** varices fpl

varied [veərɪd] adj variado

variety [və'raɪətɪ] n (diversity) diversidad f; (type) variedad f; **~ show** n espectáculo de variedades

various [veərɪəs] adj (several: people) varios/as; (reasons) diversos/as

varnish [vɑːnɪʃ] n (gen) barniz m; (nail ~) esmalte m ♦ vt barnizar; (nails) pintar (con esmalte)

vary [veərɪ] vt variar; (change) cambiar ♦ vi variar

vase [vɑːz] n florero

Vaseline ® [væsɪliːn] n vaselina ®

vast [vɑːst] adj enorme

VAT [væt] (BRIT) n abbr (= value added tax) IVA m

vat [væt] n tina, tinaja

Vatican [vætɪkən] n: **the ~** el Vaticano

vault [vɔːlt] n (of roof) bóveda; (tomb) panteón m; (in bank) cámara acorazada ♦ vt (also: **~ over**) saltar (por encima de)

vaunted [vɔːntɪd] adj: **much ~** cacareado, alardeado

VCR n abbr = **video cassette recorder**

VD n abbr = **venereal disease**

VDU n abbr (= visual display unit) UPV f

veal [viːl] n ternera

veer [vɪə*] vi (vehicle) virar; (wind) girar

vegan [viːgən] n vegetariano/a estricto/a, vegetaliano/a

vegeburger [vedʒɪbɜːgə*] n hamburguesa vegetal

vegetable [vedʒtəbl] n (BOT) vegetal m; (edible plant) legumbre f, hortaliza ♦ adj vegetal; **~s** npl (cooked) verduras fpl

vegetarian [vedʒɪ'teərɪən] adj, n vegetariano/a m/f

vehement [viːɪmənt] adj vehemente, apasionado

vehicle [viːɪkl] n vehículo; (fig) medio

veil [veɪl] n velo ♦ vt velar; **~ed** adj (fig) velado

vein [veɪn] n vena; (of ore etc) veta

velocity [vɪ'lɔsɪtɪ] n velocidad f

velvet [velvɪt] n terciopelo

vending machine [vendɪŋ-] n distribuidor m automático

veneer [və'nɪə*] n chapa, enchapado; (fig) barniz m

venereal disease [vɪ'nɪərɪəl-] n enfermedad f venérea

Venetian blind [vɪ'niːʃən-] n persiana

Venezuela [venɪ'zweɪlə] n Venezuela; **~n** adj, n venezolano/a m/f

vengeance [vendʒəns] n venganza; **with a ~** (fig) con creces

venison [venɪsn] n carne f de venado

venom [venəm] n veneno; (bitterness) odio; **~ous** adj venenoso; lleno de odio

vent [vent] n (in jacket) respiradero; (in wall) rejilla (de ventilación) ♦ vt (fig: feelings) desahogar

ventilator [ventɪleɪtə*] n ventilador m

venture [ventʃə*] n empresa ♦ vt (opinion) ofrecer ♦ vi arriesgarse, lanzarse; **business ~** empresa comercial

venue [venjuː] n lugar m

veranda(h) [və'rændə] n terraza

verb [vɜːb] n verbo; **~al** adj verbal

verbatim [vɜː'beɪtɪm] adj, adv palabra por palabra

verdict ['vɜːdɪkt] n veredicto, fallo; (fig) opinión f, juicio

verge [vɜːdʒ] (BRIT) n borde m; **"soft ~s"** (AUT) "arcén m no asfaltado"; **to be on the ~ of doing sth** estar a punto de hacer algo; **~ on** vt fus rayar en

verify ['verɪfaɪ] vt comprobar, verificar

vermin ['vɜːmɪn] npl (animals) alimañas fpl; (insects, fig) parásitos mpl

vermouth ['vɜːməθ] n vermut m

versatile ['vɜːsətaɪl] adj (person) polifacético; (machine, tool etc) versátil

verse [vɜːs] n poesía; (stanza) estrofa; (in bible) versículo

version ['vɜːʃən] n versión f

versus ['vɜːsəs] prep contra

vertebra ['vɜːtɪbrə] (pl **~e**) n vértebra

vertical ['vɜːtɪkl] adj vertical

verve [vɜːv] n brío

very ['verɪ] adv muy ♦ adj: **the ~ book which** el mismo libro que; **the ~ last** el último de todos; **at the ~ least** al menos; **~ much** muchísimo

vessel ['vesl] n (ship) barco; (container) vasija; see **blood**

vest [vest] n (BRIT) camiseta; (US: waistcoat) chaleco; **~ed interests** npl (COMM) intereses mpl creados

vet [vet] vt (candidate) investigar ♦ n abbr (BRIT) = **veterinary surgeon**

veteran ['vetərn] n veterano

veterinary surgeon ['vetrɪnərɪ] (us **veterinarian**) n veterinario/a m/f

veto ['viːtəu] (pl **~es**) n veto ♦ vt prohibir, vetar

vex [veks] vt fastidiar; **~ed** adj (question) controvertido

VHF abbr (= very high frequency) muy alta frecuencia

via ['vaɪə] prep por, por medio de

vibrant ['vaɪbrənt] adj (lively) animado; (bright) vivo; (voice) vibrante

vibrate [vaɪ'breɪt] vi vibrar

vicar ['vɪkə*] n párroco (de la Iglesia Anglicana); **~age** n parroquia

vice [vaɪs] n (evil) vicio; (TECH) torno de banco

vice- [vaɪs] prefix vice-; **~-chairman** n vicepresidente m

vice squad n brigada antivicio

vice versa ['vaɪsɪ'vɜːsə] adv viceversa

vicinity [vɪ'sɪnɪtɪ] n: **in the ~ (of)** cercano (a)

vicious ['vɪʃəs] adj (attack) violento; (words) cruel; (horse, dog) resabido; **~ circle** n círculo vicioso

victim ['vɪktɪm] n víctima

victor ['vɪktə*] n vencedor(a) m/f

victory ['vɪktərɪ] n victoria

video ['vɪdɪəu] cpd video ♦ n (~ film) videofilm m; (also: ~ cassette) videocassette f; (also: ~ cassette recorder) magnetoscopio; **~ game** n videojuego; **~ tape** n cinta de vídeo

vie [vaɪ] vi: **to ~ with sb for sth** competir (con uno por algo)

Vienna [vɪ'enə] n Viena

Vietnam [vjet'næm] n Vietnam m; **~ese** [-nə'miːz] n inv, adj vietnamita m/f

view [vjuː] n (outlook) perspectiva; (opinion) opinión f, criterio ♦ vt (look at) mirar; (fig) considerar; **on ~** (in museum etc) expuesto; **in full ~ (of)** en plena vista (de); **in ~ of the weather/the fact that** en vista del tiempo/del hecho de que; **in my ~** en mi opinión; **~er** n espectador(a) m/f; (TV) telespectador(a) m/f; **~finder** n visor m de imagen; **~point** n (attitude) punto de vista; (place) mirador m

vigour ['vɪgə*] (US **vigor**) n energía, vigor m

vile [vaɪl] adj vil, infame; (smell) asqueroso; (temper) endemoniado

villa ['vɪlə] n (country house) casa de campo; (suburban house) chalet m

village ['vɪlɪdʒ] n aldea; **~r** n aldeano/a

villain ['vɪlən] n (scoundrel) malvado/a; (in novel) malo; (BRIT: criminal) maleante m/f

vindicate ['vɪndɪkeɪt] vt vindicar, justificar

vindictive [vɪn'dɪktɪv] *adj* vengativo
vine [vaɪn] *n* vid *f*
vinegar ['vɪnɪɡə*] *n* vinagre *m*
vineyard ['vɪnjɑ:d] *n* viña, viñedo
vintage ['vɪntɪdʒ] *n* (*year*) vendimia, cosecha ♦ *cpd* de época; **~ wine** *n* vino añejo
vinyl ['vaɪnl] *n* vinilo
viola [vɪ'əulə] *n* (*MUS*) viola
violate ['vaɪəleɪt] *vt* violar
violence ['vaɪələns] *n* violencia
violent ['vaɪələnt] *adj* violento; (*intense*) intenso
violet ['vaɪələt] *adj* violado, violeta ♦ *n* (*plant*) violeta
violin [vaɪə'lɪn] *n* violín *m*; **~ist** *n* violinista *m/f*
VIP *n abbr* (= *very important person*) VIP *m*
virgin ['vɜ:dʒɪn] *n* virgen *f*
Virgo ['vɜ:ɡəu] *n* Virgo
virtually ['vɜ:tjuəlɪ] *adv* prácticamente
virtual reality ['vɜ:tjuəl-] *n* (*COMPUT*) mundo or realidad *f* virtual
virtue ['vɜ:tju:] *n* virtud *f*; (*advantage*) ventaja; **by ~ of** en virtud de
virtuous ['vɜ:tjuəs] *adj* virtuoso
virus ['vaɪərəs] *n* (*also: COMPUT*) virus *m*
visa ['vi:zə] *n* visado (*SP*), visa (*AM*)
visible ['vɪzəbl] *adj* visible
vision ['vɪʒən] *n* (*sight*) vista; (*foresight*, *in dream*) visión *f*
visit ['vɪzɪt] *n* visita ♦ *vt* (*person*: *us*: *also:* **~ with**) visitar, hacer una visita a; (*place*) ir a, (ir a) conocer; **~ing hours** *npl* (*in hospital etc*) horas *fpl* de visita; **~or** *n* (*in museum*) visitante *m/f*; (*invited to house*) visita; (*tourist*) turista *m/f*
visor ['vaɪzə*] *n* visera
visual ['vɪzjuəl] *adj* visual; **~ aid** *n* medio visual; **~ display unit** *n* unidad *f* de presentación visual; **~ize** *vt* imaginarse
vital ['vaɪtl] *adj* (*essential*) esencial, imprescindible; (*dynamic*) dinámico; (*organ*) vital; **~ly** *adv*: **~ly important**

de primera importancia; **~ statistics** *npl* (*fig*) medidas *fpl* vitales
vitamin ['vɪtəmɪn] *n* vitamina
vivacious [vɪ'veɪʃəs] *adj* vivaz, alegre
vivid ['vɪvɪd] *adj* (*account*) gráfico; (*light*) intenso; (*imagination*, *memory*) vivo; **~ly** *adv* gráficamente; (*remember*) como si fuera hoy
V-neck ['vi:nek] *n* cuello de pico
vocabulary [vəu'kæbjulərɪ] *n* vocabulario
vocal ['vəukl] *adj* vocal; (*articulate*) elocuente; **~ cords** *npl* cuerdas *fpl* vocales
vocation [vəu'keɪʃən] *n* vocación *f*; **~al** *adj* profesional
vodka ['vɔdkə] *n* vodka *m*
vogue [vəuɡ] *n*: **in ~** en boga
voice [vɔɪs] *n* voz *f* ♦ *vt* expresar; **~ mail** *n* fonobuzón *m*
void [vɔɪd] *n* vacío; (*hole*) hueco ♦ *adj* (*invalid*) nulo, inválido; (*empty*): **~ of** carente o desprovisto de
volatile ['vɔlətaɪl] *adj* (*situation*) inestable; (*person*) voluble; (*liquid*) volátil
volcano [vɔl'keɪnəu] (*pl* **~es**) *n* volcán *m*
volition [və'lɪʃən] *n*: **of one's own ~** de su propia voluntad
volley ['vɔlɪ] *n* (*of gunfire*) descarga; (*of stones etc*) lluvia; (*fig*) torrente *m*; (*TENNIS etc*) volea; **~ball** *n* vol(e)ibol *m*
volt [vəult] *n* voltio; **~age** *n* voltaje *m*
volume ['vɔlju:m] *n* (*gen*) volumen *m*; (*book*) tomo
voluntary ['vɔləntərɪ] *adj* voluntario
volunteer [vɔlən'tɪə*] *n* voluntario ♦ *vt* (*information*) ofrecer ♦ *vi* ofrecerse (de voluntario); **to ~ to do** ofrecerse a hacer
vomit ['vɔmɪt] *n* vómito ♦ *vt*, *vi* vomitar
vote [vəut] *n* voto; (*votes cast*) votación *f*; (*right to ~*) derecho de votar; (*franchise*) sufragio ♦ *vt* (*chairman*) elegir; (*propose*): **to ~ that** proponer

que ♦ vi votar, ir a votar; **~ of thanks** voto de gracias; **~r** n votante m/f; **voting** n votación f

vouch [vautʃ]: **to ~ for** vt fus garantizar, responder de

voucher ['vautʃə*] n (for meal, petrol) vale m

vow [vau] n voto ♦ vt: **to ~ to do/ that** jurar hacer/que

vowel ['vauəl] n vocal f

voyage ['vɔidʒ] n viaje m

vulgar ['vʌlgə*] adj (rude) ordinario, grosero; (in bad taste) de mal gusto; **~ity** [-'gæriti] n grosería; (in bad taste) de mal gusto

vulnerable ['vʌlnərəbl] adj vulnerable

vulture ['vʌltʃə*] n buitre m

W, w

wad [wɔd] n bolita; (of banknotes etc) fajo

waddle ['wɔdl] vi anadear

wade [weid] vi: **to ~ through** (water) vadear; (fig: book) leer con dificultad; **wading pool** (US) n piscina para niños

wafer ['weifə*] n galleta, barquillo

waffle ['wɔfl] n (CULIN) gofre m ♦ vi dar el rollo

waft [wɔft] vt llevar por el aire ♦ vi flotar

wag [wæg] vt menear, agitar ♦ vi moverse, menearse

wage [weidʒ] n (also: **~s**) sueldo, salario ♦ vt: **to ~ war** hacer la guerra; **~ earner** n asalariado/a; **~ packet** n sobre m de paga

wager ['weidʒə*] n apuesta

wag(g)on ['wægən] n (horse-drawn) carro; (BRIT: RAIL) vagón m

wail [weil] n gemido ♦ vi gemir

waist [weist] n cintura, talle m; **~coat** (BRIT) n chaleco; **~line** n talle m

wait [weit] n (interval) pausa ♦ vi esperar; **to lie in ~ for** acechar a; **I can't ~ to** (fig) estoy deseando; **to ~ for** esperar (a); **~ behind** vi

quedarse; **~ on** vt fus servir a; **~er** n camarero; **~ing** n: "**no ~ing**" (BRIT: AUT) "prohibido estacionarse"; **~ing list** n lista de espera; **~ing room** n sala de espera; **~ress** n camarera

waive [weiv] vt suspender

wake [weik] (pt **woke** or **waked**, pp **woken** or **waked**) vt (also: **~ up**) despertar ♦ vi (also: **~ up**) despertarse ♦ n (for dead person) vela, velatorio; (NAUT) estela; **waken** vt, vi = **wake**

Wales [weilz] n País m de Gales; **the Prince of ~** el príncipe de Gales

walk [wɔ:k] n (stroll) paseo; (hike) excursión f a pie, caminata; (gait) paso, andar m; (in park etc) paseo, alameda ♦ vi andar, caminar; (for pleasure, exercise) pasear ♦ vt (distance) recorrer a pie, andar; (dog) pasear; **10 minutes' ~ from here** a 10 minutos de aquí andando; **people from all ~s of life** gente de todas las esferas; **~ out** vi (audience) salir; (workers) declararse en huelga; **~ out on** (inf) vt fus abandonar; **~er** n (person) paseante m/f, caminante m/f; **~ie-talkie** ['wɔ:kɪ'tɔ:kɪ] n walkie-talkie m; **~ing** n el andar; **~ing shoes** npl zapatos mpl para andar; **~ing stick** n bastón m; **W~man** ® ['wɔ:kmən] n Walkman ® m; **~out** n huelga; **~over** (inf) n: **it was a ~over** fue pan comido; **~way** n paseo

wall [wɔ:l] n pared f; (exterior) muro; (city ~ etc) muralla; **~ed** adj amurallado; (garden) con tapia

wallet ['wɔlit] n cartera (SP), billetera (AM)

wallflower ['wɔ:lflauə*] n alhelí m; **to be a ~** (fig) comer pavo

wallow ['wɔləu] vi revolcarse

wallpaper ['wɔ:lpeipə*] n papel m pintado ♦ vt empapelar

walnut ['wɔ:lnʌt] n nuez f; (tree) nogal m

walrus ['wɔ:lrəs] (pl ~ or **~es**) n morsa

waltz [wɔ:lts] n vals m ♦ vi bailar el

vals

wand |wɒnd| n (also: magic ~) varita (mágica)

wander |'wɒndə*| vi (person) vagar; deambular; (thoughts) divagar ♦ vt recorrer, vagar por

wane |weɪn| vi menguar

wangle |'wæŋgl| (BRIT: inf) vt agenciarse

want |wɒnt| vt querer, desear; (need) necesitar ♦ n: for ~ of por falta de; ~s npl (needs) necesidades fpl; to ~ to do querer hacer; to ~ sb to do sth querer que uno haga algo; ~ed adj (criminal) buscado; "~ed" (in advertisements) "se busca"; ~ing adj: to be found ~ing no estar a la altura de las circunstancias

war |wɔ:*| n guerra; to make ~ (on) (also fig) declarar la guerra (a)

ward |wɔ:d| n (in hospital) sala; (POL) distrito electoral; (LAW: child: also: ~ of court) pupilo/a; ~ off vt (blow) desviar, parar; (attack) rechazar

warden |'wɔ:dn| n (BRIT: of institution) director(a) m/f; (of park, game reserve) guardián/ana m/f; (BRIT: also: traffic ~) guardia m/f

warder |'wɔ:də*| (BRIT) n guardián/ana m/f, carcelero/a

wardrobe |'wɔ:drəub| n armario, guardarropa, ropero (esp AM)

warehouse |'weəhaus| n almacén m, depósito

wares |weəz| npl mercancías fpl

warfare |'wɔ:feə*| n guerra

warhead |'wɔ:hed| n cabeza armada

warily |'weərɪlɪ| adv con cautela, cautelosamente

warm |wɔ:m| adj caliente; (thanks) efusivo; (clothes etc) abrigado; (welcome, day) caluroso; it's ~ hace calor; I'm ~ tengo calor; to ~ up vi (room) calentarse; (person) entrar en calor; (athlete) hacer ejercicios de calentamiento ♦ vt calentar; ~-hearted adj afectuoso; ~ly adv

afectuosamente; ~th n calor m

warn |wɔ:n| vt avisar, advertir; ~ing n aviso, advertencia; ~ing light n luz f de advertencia; ~ing triangle n (AUT) triángulo señalizador

warp |wɔ:p| vt (wood) combarse ♦ vi combar; (mind) pervertir

warrant |'wɒrnt| n autorización f; (LAW: to arrest) orden f de detención; (: to search) mandamiento de registro

warranty |'wɒrəntɪ| n garantía

warren |'wɒrən| n (of rabbits) madriguera; (fig) laberinto

warrior |'wɒrɪə*| n guerrero/a

Warsaw |'wɔ:sɔ:| n Varsovia

warship |'wɔ:ʃɪp| n buque m o barco m de guerra

wart |wɔ:t| n verruga

wartime |'wɔ:taɪm| n: in ~ en tiempos de guerra, en la guerra

wary |'weərɪ| adj cauteloso

was |wɒz| pt of be

wash |wɒʃ| vt lavar ♦ vi lavarse; (sea etc) to ~ against/over sth llegar hasta/cubrir algo ♦ n (clothes etc) lavado; (of ship) estela; to have a ~ lavarse; ~ away vt (stain) quitar lavando; (subj: river etc) llevarse; ~ off vi quitarse (al lavar); ~ up vi (BRIT) fregar los platos; (US) lavarse; ~able adj lavable; ~basin (US ~bowl) n lavabo; ~ cloth (US) n manopla; ~er n (TECH) arandela; ~ing n (dirty) ropa sucia; (clean) colada; ~ing machine n lavadora; ~ing powder (BRIT) n detergente m (en polvo)

Washington |'wɒʃɪŋtən| n Washington m

wash: ~ing-up (BRIT) n fregado, platos mpl (para fregar); ~ing-up liquid (BRIT) n líquido lavavajillas; ~-out (inf) n fracaso; ~room (US) n servicios mpl

wasn't |'wɒznt| = was not

wasp |wɒsp| n avispa

wastage |'weɪstɪdʒ| n desgaste m; (loss) pérdida

waste |weɪst| n derroche m,

despilfarro; (*of time*) pérdida; (*food*) sobras *fpl*; (*rubbish*) basura; desperdicios *mpl* ♦ *adj* (*material*) de desecho; (*left over*) sobrante; (*land*) baldío, descampado ♦ *vt* malgastar, derrochar; (*time*) perder; (*opportunity*) desperdiciar; ~ **s** *npl* (*area of land*) tierras *fpl* baldías; ~ **away** *vi* consumirse; ~ **disposal unit** (*BRIT*) *n* triturador *m* de basura; ~**ful** *adj* derrochador(a); (*process*) antieconómico; ~ **ground** (*BRIT*) *n* terreno baldío; ~ **paper basket** *n* papelera; ~ **pipe** *n* tubo de desagüe

watch [wɔtʃ] *n* (*also*: *wrist*~) reloj *m*; (*MIL*: *group of guards*) centinela *m*; (*act*) vigilancia; (*NAUT*: *spell of duty*) guardia ♦ *vt* (*look at*) mirar, observar; (: *match*, *programme*) ver; (*spy on*, *guard*) vigilar; (*be careful of*) cuidarse de, tener cuidado de ♦ *vi* ver, mirar; (*keep guard*) montar guardia; ~ **out** *vi* cuidarse, tener cuidado; ~**dog** *n* perro guardián; (*fig*) persona u organismo encargado de asegurarse de que las empresas actúan dentro de la legalidad; ~**ful** *adj* vigilante, sobre aviso; ~**maker** *n* relojero/a; ~**man** (*irreg*) *n see* **night-**; ~ **strap** *n* pulsera (de reloj)

water [ˈwɔːtə*] *n* agua ♦ *vt* (*plant*) regar ♦ *vi* (*eyes*) llorar; (*mouth*) hacerse la boca agua; ~ **down** *vt* (*milk etc*) aguar; (*fig*: *story*) dulcificar, diluir; ~ **closet** *n* wáter *m*; ~**colour** *n* acuarela; ~**cress** *n* berro; ~**fall** *n* cascada, salto de agua; ~ **heater** *n* calentador *m* de agua; ~**ing can** *n* regadera; ~ **lily** *n* nenúfar *m*; ~**line** *n* (*NAUT*) línea de flotación; ~**logged** *adj* (*ground*) inundado; ~ **main** *n* cañería del agua; ~**melon** *n* sandía; ~**proof** *adj* impermeable; ~**shed** *n* (*GEO*) cuenca; (*fig*) momento crítico; ~**skiing** *n* esquí *m* acuático; ~**tight** *adj* hermético; ~**way** *n* vía fluvial o navegable; ~**works** *n* central *f* depuradora; ~**y** (*coffee etc*) aguado;

(*eyes*) lloroso

watt [wɔt] *n* vatio

wave [weɪv] *n* (*of hand*) señal *f* con la mano; (*on water*) ola; (*RADIO*, *in hair*) onda; (*fig*) oleada ♦ *vi* agitar la mano; (*flag etc*) ondear ♦ *vt* (*handkerchief*, *gun*) agitar; ~**length** *n* longitud *f* de onda

waver [ˈweɪvə*] *vi* (*voice*, *love etc*) flaquear; (*person*) vacilar

wavy [ˈweɪvɪ] *adj* ondulado

wax [wæks] *n* cera ♦ *vt* (*moon*) crecer; ~ **paper** (*US*) *n* papel *m* apergaminado; ~**works** *n* museo de cera ♦ *npl* figuras *fpl* de cera

way [weɪ] *n* camino; (*distance*) trayecto, recorrido; (*direction*) dirección *f*, sentido; (*manner*) modo, manera; (*habit*) costumbre *f*; **which ~?** — **this ~** ¿por dónde?, ¿en qué dirección? — por aquí; **on the ~** (*en route*) en (el) camino; **to be on one's ~** estar en camino; **to be in the ~** bloquear el camino; (*fig*) estorbar; **to go out of one's ~ to do sth** desvivirse por hacer algo; **under ~** en marcha; **to lose one's ~** extraviarse; **in a ~** en cierto modo or sentido; **no ~!** (*inf*) ¡de eso nada!; **by the ~ ...** a propósito ...; **"~ in"** (*BRIT*) "entrada"; **"~ out"** (*BRIT*) "salida"; **the ~ back** el camino de vuelta; **"give ~"** (*BRIT*: *AUT*) "ceda el paso"

waylay [weɪˈleɪ] (*irreg*) *vt* salir al paso a

wayward [ˈweɪwəd] *adj* díscolo

W.C. *n* (*BRIT*) wáter *m*

we [wiː] *pl pron* nosotros/as

weak [wiːk] *adj* débil, flojo; (*tea etc*) claro; ~**en** *vi* debilitarse; (*give way*) ceder ♦ *vt* debilitar; ~**ling** *n* debilucho/a; (*morally*) persona de poco carácter; ~**ness** *n* debilidad *f*; (*fault*) punto débil; **to have a ~ness for** tener debilidad por

wealth [welθ] *n* riqueza; (*of details*) abundancia; ~**y** *adj* rico

wean [wiːn] *vt* destetar

weapon ['wɛpən] n arma

wear [wɛə*] (pt **wore**, pp **worn**) n (use) uso; (deterioration through use) desgaste m; (clothing): **sports/baby~** ropa de deportes/de niños ♦ vt (clothes) llevar; (damage: through use) gastar, usar ♦ vi (last) durar; (rub through etc) desgastarse; **evening ~** ropa de etiqueta; **~ away** vt gastar ♦ vi desgastarse; **~ down** vt gastar; (strength) agotar; **~ off** vi (pain etc) pasar, desaparecer; **~ out** vt desgastar; (person, strength) agotar; **~ and tear** n desgaste m

weary ['wɪərɪ] adj cansado; (dispirited) abatido ♦ vi: **to ~ of** cansarse de

weasel ['wi:zl] n (ZOOL) comadreja

weather ['wɛðə*] n tiempo ♦ vt (storm, crisis) hacer frente a; **under the ~** (fig: ill) indispuesto, pachucho; **~-beaten** adj (skin) curtido; (building) deteriorado por la intemperie; **~cock** n veleta; **~ forecast** n boletín m meteorológico; **~man** (irreg: inf) n hombre m del tiempo; **~ vane** n = **~cock**

weave [wi:v] (pt **wove**, pp **woven**) vt (cloth) tejer; (fig) entretejer; **~r** n tejedor(a) m/f; **weaving** n tejeduría

web [wɛb] n (of spider) telaraña; (on duck's foot) membrana; (network) red f; **the (World Wide) W~** el or la Web

website ['wɛbsaɪt] n espacio Web

wed [wɛd] (pt, pp **wedded**) vt casar ♦ vi casarse

we'd [wi:d] = **we had; we would**

wedding ['wɛdɪŋ] n boda, casamiento; **silver/golden ~ (anniversary)** bodas fpl de plata/de oro; **~ day** n día m de la boda; **~ dress** n traje m de novia; **~ present** n regalo de boda; **~ ring** n alianza

wedge [wɛdʒ] n (of wood etc) cuña; (of cake) trozo ♦ vt acuñar; (push) apretar

Wednesday ['wɛnzdɪ] n miércoles m inv

wee [wi:] (Scottish) adj pequeñito

weed [wi:d] n mala hierba, maleza ♦ vt escardar, desherbar; **~killer** n herbicida m; **~y** adj (person) mequetréfico

week [wi:k] n semana; **a ~ today/on Friday** de hoy/del viernes en ocho días; **~day** n día m laborable; **~end** n fin m de semana; **~ly** adv semanalmente, cada semana ♦ adj semanal ♦ n semanario

weep [wi:p] (pt, pp **wept**) vi, vt llorar; **~ing willow** n sauce m llorón

weigh [weɪ] vt, vi pesar; **~ anchor** levar anclas; **~ down** vt sobrecargar; (fig) agobiar; **~ up** vt sopesar

weight [weɪt] n peso; (metal ~) pesa; **to lose/put on ~** adelgazar/engordar; **~ing** n (allowance): **(London) ~ing** dietas (por residir en Londres); **~lifter** n levantador m de pesas; **~y** adj pesado; (matters) de relevancia or peso

weir [wɪə*] n presa

weird [wɪəd] adj raro, extraño

welcome ['wɛlkəm] adj bienvenido ♦ n bienvenida ♦ vt dar la bienvenida a; (be glad of) alegrarse de; **thank you — you're ~** gracias — de nada

weld [wɛld] n soldadura ♦ vt soldar

welfare ['wɛlfɛə*] n bienestar m; (social aid) asistencia social; **~ state** n estado del bienestar

well [wɛl] n fuente f, pozo ♦ adv bien ♦ adj: **to be ~** estar bien (de salud) ♦ excl ¡vaya!, ¡bueno!; **as ~** también; **as ~ as** además de; **~ done!** ¡bien hecho!; **get ~ soon!** ¡que te mejores pronto!; **to do ~** (business) ir bien; (person) tener éxito; **~ up** vi (tears) saltar

we'll [wi:l] = **we will; we shall**

well: ~-behaved adj bueno; **~-being** n bienestar m; **~-built** adj (person) fornido; **~-deserved** adj merecido; **~-dressed** adj bien vestido; **~-groomed** adj de buena presencia; **~-heeled** (inf) adj (wealthy) rico

wellingtons ['wɛlɪŋtənz] npl (also: **wellington boots**) botas fpl de goma

well: ~-known adj (person) conocido;

~-mannered adj educado; **~-meaning** adj bienintencionado; **~-off** adj acomodado; **~-read** adj leído; **~-to-do** adj acomodado; **~-wisher** n admirador(a) m/f

Welsh [welʃ] adj galés/esa ♦ n (LING) galés m; **the ~** npl los galeses; **the ~ Assembly** el Parlamento galés; **~man** (irreg) n galés m; **~ rarebit** n pan m con queso tostado; **~woman** (irreg) n galesa

went [went] pt of **go**

wept [wept] pt, pp of **weep**

were [wəː*] pt of **be**

we're [wɪə*] = **we are**

weren't [wəːnt] = **were not**

west [west] n oeste m ♦ adj occidental, del oeste ♦ adv al or hacia el oeste; **the W~** el Oeste, el Occidente; **W~ Country** (BRIT) n: **the W~ Country** el suroeste de Inglaterra; **~erly** adj occidental; (wind) del oeste; **~ern** adj occidental ♦ n (CINEMA) película del oeste; **W~ Germany** n Alemania Occidental; **W~ Indian** adj, n Antillano/a m/f; **W~ Indies** npl Antillas fpl; **~ward(s)** adv hacia el oeste

wet [wet] adj (damp) húmedo; (~ through) mojado; (rainy) lluvioso ♦ (BRIT) n (POL) conservador/a m/f moderado/a; **to get ~** mojarse; **"~ paint"** "recién pintado"; **~suit** n traje m térmico

we've [wiːv] = **we have**

whack [wæk] vt dar un buen golpe a

whale [weil] n (ZOOL) ballena

wharf [wɔːf](pl **wharves**) n muelle m

KEYWORD
---

what [wɔt] adj **1** (in direct/indirect questions) qué; **~ size is he?** ¿qué talla usa?; **~ colour/shape is it?** ¿de qué color/forma es?

2 (in exclamations): **~ a mess!** ¡qué desastre!; **~ a fool I am!** ¡qué tonto soy!

♦ pron **1** (interrogative) qué; **~ are you

doing?** ¿qué haces or estás haciendo?; **~ is happening?** ¿qué pasa or está pasando?; **~ is it called?** ¿cómo se llama?; **~ about me?** ¿y yo qué?; **~ about doing ...?** ¿qué tal si hacemos ...?

2 (relative) lo que; **I saw ~ you did/was on the table** lo vi lo que hiciste/había en la mesa

♦ excl (disbelieving) ¡cómo!; **~, no coffee!** ¡que no hay café!

whatever [wɔt'evə*] adj: **~ book you choose** cualquier libro que elijas ♦ pron: **do ~ is necessary** haga lo que sea necesario; **~ happens** pase lo que pase; **no reason ~** or **whatsoever** ninguna razón sea la que sea; **nothing ~** nada en absoluto

whatsoever [wɔtsəu'evə*] adj see **whatever**

wheat [wiːt] n trigo

wheedle ['wiːdl] vt: **to ~ sb into doing sth** engatusar a uno para que haga algo; **to ~ sth out of sb** sonsacar algo a uno

wheel [wiːl] n rueda; (AUT: also: steering ~) volante m; (NAUT) timón m ♦ vt (pram etc) empujar ♦ vi (also: ~ round) dar la vuelta, girar; **~barrow** n carretilla; **~chair** n silla de ruedas; **~ clamp** n (AUT) cepo

wheeze [wiːz] vi resollar

KEYWORD
---

when [wen] adv cuando; **~ did it happen?** ¿cuándo ocurrió?; **I know ~ it happened** sé cuándo ocurrió

♦ conj **1** (at, during, after the time that) cuando; **be careful ~ you cross the road** ten cuidado al cruzar la calle; **that was ~ I needed you** fue entonces que te necesité

2 (on, at which): **on the day ~ I met him** el día en que lo conocí

3 (whereas) cuando

whenever [wɛnˈɛvə*] conj cuando; (every time that) cada vez que ♦ adv cuando sea

where [wɛə*] adv dónde ♦ conj donde; **this is ~** aquí es donde; **~abouts** adv dónde ♦ n: **nobody knows his ~abouts** nadie conoce su paradero, **~as** conj visto que, mientras; **~by** pron por lo cual; **wherever** [-ˈɛvə*] conj dondequiera que; (interrogative) dónde; **~withal** n recursos mpl

whether [ˈwɛðə*] conj si; **I don't know ~ to accept or not** no sé si aceptar o no; **~ you go or not** vayas o no vayas

KEYWORD

which [wɪtʃ] adj 1 (interrogative: direct, indirect) qué; **~ picture(s) do you want?** ¿qué cuadro(s) quieres?; **~ one?** ¿cuál?

2 **in ~ case** en cuyo caso; **we got there at 8 pm, by ~ time the cinema was full** llegamos allí a las 8, cuando el cine estaba lleno
♦ pron 1 (interrogative) cuál; **I don't mind ~** el/la que sea

2 (relative: replacing noun) que; (: replacing clause) lo que; (: after preposition) (el/la) que etc, el/la cual etc; **the apple ~ you ate/~ is on the table** la manzana que comiste/que está en la mesa; **the chair on ~ you are sitting** la silla en la que estás sentado; **he said he knew, ~ is true/I feared** dijo que lo sabía, lo cual or lo que es cierto/me temía

whichever [wɪtʃˈɛvə*] adj: **take ~ book you prefer** coja (SP) el libro que prefiera; **~ book you take** cualquier libro que coja

while [waɪl] n rato, momento ♦ conj mientras; (although) aunque; **for a ~** durante algún tiempo; **~ away** vt pasar

whim [wɪm] n capricho

whimper [ˈwɪmpə*] n sollozo ♦ vi lloriquear

whimsical [ˈwɪmzɪkl] adj (person) caprichoso; (look) juguetón/ona

whine [waɪn] n (of pain) gemido; (of engine) zumbido; (of siren) aullido ♦ vi gemir; zumbar; (fig: complain) gimotear

whip [wɪp] n (POL: person) encargado de la disciplina partidaria en el parlamento ♦ vt azotar; (CULIN) batir; (move quickly): **to ~ sth out/off** sacar/quitar algo de un tirón; **~ped cream** n nata or crema montada; **~round** n (BRIT) n colecta

whirl [wə:l] vt hacer girar, dar vueltas a ♦ vi girar, dar vueltas; (leaves etc) arremolinarse; **~pool** n remolino; **~wind** n torbellino

whirr [wə:*] vi zumbar

whisk [wɪsk] n (CULIN) batidor m ♦ vt (CULIN) batir; **to ~ sb away or off** llevar volando a uno

whiskers [ˈwɪskəz] npl (of animal) bigotes mpl; (of man) patillas fpl

whiskey [ˈwɪskɪ] (US, Ireland) n = **whisky**

whisky [ˈwɪskɪ] n whisky m

whisper [ˈwɪspə*] n susurro ♦ vi, vt susurrar

whistle [ˈwɪsl] n (sound) silbido; (object) silbato ♦ vi silbar

white [waɪt] adj blanco; (pale) pálido ♦ n blanco; (of egg) clara; **~ coffee** (BRIT) n café m con leche; **~collar worker** n oficinista m/f; **~ elephant** n (fig) maula; **~ lie** n mentirilla; **~ness** n blancura; **~ noise** n sonido blanco; **~ paper** n (POL) libro rojo; **~wash** n (paint) jalbegue m, cal f ♦ vt (also fig) blanquear

whiting [ˈwaɪtɪŋ] n inv (fish) pescadilla

Whitsun [ˈwɪtsn] n pentecostés m

whizz [wɪz] vi: **to ~ past or by** pasar a toda velocidad; **~ kid** (inf) n prodigio

who [hu:] *pron* **1** (*interrogative*) quién; ~ **is it?, ~'s there?** ¿quién es?; **are you looking for?** ¿a quién buscas?; **I told her ~ I was** le dije quién era yo **2** (*relative*) que; **the man/woman ~ spoke to me** el hombre/la mujer que habló conmigo; **those ~ can swim** los que saben *or* sepan nadar

whodun(n)it [hu:'dʌnɪt] (*inf*) *n* novela policíaca

whoever [hu:'ɛvə*] *pron*: ~ **finds it** cualquiera *or* quienquiera que lo encuentre; **~ you like** pregunta a quien quieras; **~ he marries** no importa con quién se case

whole [həul] *adj* (*entire*) todo, entero; (*not broken*) intacto ♦ *n* todo; (*all*): **the ~ of the town** toda la ciudad, la ciudad entera ♦ *n* (*total*) total *m*; (*sum*) conjunto; **on the ~, as a ~** en general; **~food(s)** *n(pl)* alimento(s) *m(pl)* integral(es); **~hearted** *adj* sincero, cordial; **~meal** *adj* integral; **~sale** *n* venta al por mayor ♦ *adj* al por mayor; (*fig: destruction*) sistemático; **~saler** *n* mayorista *m/f*; **~some** *adj* sano; **~wheat** *adj* = **~meal; wholly** *adv* totalmente, enteramente

whom [hu:m] *pron* **1** (*interrogative*): ~ **did you see?** ¿a quién viste?; **to ~ did you give it?** ¿a quién se lo diste?; **tell me from ~ you received it** dígame de quién lo recibí **2** (*relative*) que; **to ~** a quien; **of ~** de quien(es), del/de la que *etc*; **the man ~ I saw/to ~ I wrote** el hombre que vi/a quien escribí; **the lady about/with ~ I was talking** la señora de (la) que/con quien *or* (la) que hablaba

whooping cough ['hu:pɪŋ-] *n* tos *f* ferina

whore [hɔ:*] (*inf: pej*) *n* puta

whose [hu:z] *adj* **1** (*possessive: interrogative*): ~ **book is this?, ~ is this book?** ¿de quién es este libro?; ~ **pencil have you taken?** ¿de quién es el lápiz que has cogido?; ~ **daughter are you?** ¿de quién eres hija? **2** (*possessive: relative*) cuyo/a, *pl* cuyos/as; **the man ~ son you rescued** el hombre cuyo hijo rescataste; **those ~ passports I have** aquellas personas cuyos pasaportes tengo; **the woman ~ car was stolen** la mujer a quien le robaron el coche ♦ *pron* de quién; ~ **is this?** ¿de quién es esto?; **I know ~ it is** sé de quién es

why [waɪ] *adv* por qué; ~ **not?** ¿por qué no?; ~ **not do it now?** ¿por qué no lo haces (*or* hacemos *etc*) ahora? ♦ *conj*: **I wonder ~ he said that** me pregunto por qué dijo eso; **that's not ~ I'm here** no es por eso (por lo) que estoy aquí; **the reason ~** la razón por la que ♦ *excl* (*expressing surprise, shock, annoyance*) ¡hombre!, ¡vaya! (*explaining*): ~, **it's you!** ¡hombre, eres tú!; ~, **that's impossible** ¡pero sí eso es imposible!

wicked ['wɪkɪd] *adj* malvado, cruel

wicket ['wɪkɪt] *n* (CRICKET: *stumps*) palos *mpl* mpl; (: *grass area*) terreno de juego

wide [waɪd] *adj* ancho; (*area, knowledge*) vasto, grande; (*choice*) amplio ♦ *adv*: **to open ~** abrir de par en par; **to shoot ~** errar el tiro; **~-**

angle lens n objetivo de gran angular; **~-awake** adj bien despierto; **~ly** adv (travelled) mucho; (spaced) muy; **it is ~ly believed/known that** ... mucha gente piensa/sabe que ...; **~n** vt ensanchar; (experience) ampliar ♦ vi ensancharse; **~ open** adj abierto de par en par; **~spread** adj extendido, general

widow ['wɪdəu] n viuda; **~ed** adj viudo; **~er** n viudo

width [wɪdθ] n anchura; (of cloth) ancho

wield [wiːld] vt (sword) blandir; (power) ejercer

wife [waɪf] (pl **wives**) n mujer f, esposa

wig [wɪg] n peluca

wiggle ['wɪgl] vt menear

wild [waɪld] adj (animal) salvaje; (plant) silvestre; (person) furioso, violento; (idea) descabellado; (rough: sea) bravo; (: land) agreste; (: weather) muy revuelto; **~s** npl regiones fpl salvajes, tierras fpl vírgenes; **~erness** ['wɪldənɪs] n desierto; **~life** n fauna; **~ly** adv (behave) locamente; (lash out) a diestro y siniestro; (guess) a lo loco; (happy) a más no poder

wilful ['wɪlful] (US **willful**) adj (action) deliberado; (obstinate) testarudo

---

KEYWORD

---

will [wɪl] aux vb **1** (forming future tense): **I ~ finish it tomorrow** lo terminaré or voy a terminar mañana; **I ~ have finished it by tomorrow** lo habré terminado para mañana; **you do it? — yes I ~/no I won't** ¿lo harás? — sí/no

2 (in conjectures, predictions): **he ~** or **he'll be there by now** ya habrá or debe (de) haber llegado; **that ~ be the postman** será or debe ser el cartero

3 (in commands, requests, offers): **~ you be quiet!** ¿quieres callarte?;

~ you help me? ¿quieres ayudarme?; **~ you have a cup of tea?** ¿te apetece un té?; **I won't put up with it!** ¡no lo soporto!
♦ vt (pt, pp **willed**): **to ~ sb to do sth** desear que alguien haga algo; **he ~ed himself to go on** con gran fuerza de voluntad, continuó
♦ n voluntad f; (testament) testamento

willing ['wɪlɪŋ] adj (with goodwill) de buena voluntad; (enthusiastic) entusiasta; **he's ~ to do it** está dispuesto a hacerlo; **~ly** adv con mucho gusto; **~ness** n buena voluntad

willow ['wɪləu] n sauce m

willpower ['wɪlpauə*] n fuerza de voluntad

willy-nilly [wɪlɪ'nɪlɪ] adv quiérase o no

wilt [wɪlt] vi marchitarse

win [wɪn] (pt, pp **won**) n victoria, triunfo ♦ vt ganar; (obtain) conseguir, lograr ♦ vi ganar; **~ over** vt convencer a; **~ round** (BRIT) vt = **~ over**

wince [wɪns] vi encogerse

winch [wɪntʃ] n torno

wind¹ [wɪnd] n, (MED) gases mpl ♦ vt (take breath away from) dejar sin aliento a

wind² [waɪnd] (pt, pp **wound**) vt enrollar; (wrap) envolver; (clock, toy) dar cuerda a ♦ vi (road, river) serpentear; **~ up** vt (clock) dar cuerda a; (debate, meeting) concluir, terminar

windfall ['wɪndfɔːl] n golpe m de suerte

winding ['waɪndɪŋ] adj (road) tortuoso; (staircase) de caracol

wind instrument [wɪnd-] n (MUS) instrumento de viento

windmill ['wɪndmɪl] n molino de viento

window ['wɪndəu] n ventana; (in car, train) ventanilla; (in shop etc) escaparate m (SP), vitrina (AM); **~ box** n jardinera de ventana; **~ cleaner** n

(person) limpiador m de cristales;
~ ledge n alféizar m, repisa; **~ pane** n
cristal m; **~ seat** n asiento junto a la
ventana; **~~shopping**: **to go ~~
shopping** ir de escaparates; **~sill** n
alféizar m, repisa

windpipe ['wɪndpaɪp] n tráquea f
wind power n energía eólica
windscreen ['wɪndskri:n] (US
windshield) n parabrisas m inv;
~ washer n lavaparabrisas m inv;
~ wiper n limpiaparabrisas m inv
windswept ['wɪndswept] adj azotado
por el viento
windy ['wɪndɪ] adj de mucho viento;
it's ~ hace viento
wine [waɪn] n vino; **~ bar** n enoteca;
~ cellar n bodega; **~ glass** n copa
(para vino); **~ list** n lista de vinos;
~ waiter n escanciador m
wing [wɪŋ] n ala; (AUT) aleta;
(THEATRE) bastidores mpl; **~er** n (SPORT)
extremo
wink [wɪŋk] n guiño, pestañeo ♦ vi
guiñar, pestañear
winner ['wɪnə*] n ganador(a) m/f
winning ['wɪnɪŋ] adj (team)
ganador(a); (goal) decisivo; (smile)
encantador(a); **~s** npl ganancias fpl
winter ['wɪntə*] n invierno ♦ vi
invernar; **wintry** ['wɪntrɪ] adj invernal
wipe [waɪp] n: **to give sth a ~** pasar
un trapo sobre algo ♦ vt limpiar; (tape)
borrar; **~ off** vt limpiar con un trapo;
(remove) quitar; **~ out** vt (debt)
liquidar; (memory) borrar; (destroy)
destruir; **~ up** vt limpiar
wire [waɪə*] n alambre m; (ELEC) cable
m (eléctrico); (TEL) telegrama m ♦ vt
(house) poner la instalación eléctrica
en; (also: **~ up**) conectar; (person:
telegram) telegrafiar
wiring ['waɪərɪŋ] n instalación f
eléctrica
wiry ['waɪərɪ] adj (person) enjuto y
fuerte; (hair) crespo
wisdom ['wɪzdəm] n sabiduría, saber

m; (good sense) cordura; **~ tooth** n
muela del juicio
wise [waɪz] adj sabio; (sensible) juicioso
...wise [waɪz] suffix: **time~** en cuanto a
or respecto al tiempo
wish [wɪʃ] n deseo ♦ vt querer; **best
~es** (on birthday etc) felicidades fpl;
with best ~es (in letter) saludos mpl,
recuerdos mpl; **to ~ sb goodbye**
despedirse de uno; **he ~ed me well**
me deseó mucha suerte; **to ~ to do/
sb to do sth** querer hacer/que
alguien haga algo; **to ~ for** desear;
~ful adj: **it's ~ful thinking** eso sería
soñar
wisp [wɪsp] n mechón m; (of smoke)
voluta
wistful ['wɪstful] adj pensativo
wit [wɪt] n ingenio, gracia; (person)
inteligencia; (person) chistoso/a
witch [wɪtʃ] n bruja; **~craft** n brujería;
~hunt n (fig) caza de brujas

KEYWORD

with [wɪð, wɪθ] prep **1** (accompanying,
in the company of) con (con+ mí, ti, sí
= conmigo, contigo, consigo); **I was
~ him** estaba con él; **we stayed
~ friends** nos quedamos en casa de
unos amigos; **I'm (not) ~ you**
(understand) (no) te entiendo; **to be
~ it** (inf: person: up-to-date) estar al
tanto; (: alert) ser despabilado
2 (descriptive, indicating manner etc)
con; de; **a room ~ a view** una
habitación con vistas; **the man ~ the
grey hat/blue eyes** el hombre del
sombrero gris/de los ojos azules; **red
~ anger** rojo de ira; **to shake ~ fear**
temblar de miedo; **to fill sth ~ water**
llenar algo de agua

withdraw [wɪθ'drɔ:] (irreg) vt retirar,
sacar ♦ vi retirarse; **to ~ money (from
the bank)** retirar fondos (del banco);
~al n retirada; (of money) reintegro;
~al symptoms npl (MED) síndrome m

de abstinencia; **~n** adj (person) reservado, introvertido

wither ['wɪðə*] vi marchitarse

withhold [wɪθ'həuld] (irreg) vt (money) retener; (decision) aplazar; (permission) negar; (information) ocultar

within [wɪð'ɪn] prep dentro de ♦ adv dentro; **~ reach (of)** al alcance (de); **~ sight (of)** a la vista (de); **the ~ week** antes de acabar la semana; **~ a mile (of)** a menos de una milla (de)

without [wɪð'aut] prep sin; **to go ~ sth** pasar sin algo

withstand [wɪθ'stænd] (irreg) vt resistir a

witness ['wɪtnɪs] n testigo m/f ♦ vt (event) presenciar; (document) atestiguar la veracidad de; **to bear ~ to** (fig) ser testimonio de; **~ box** n tribuna de los testigos; **~ stand** (US) n = **~ box**

witty ['wɪtɪ] adj ingenioso

wives [waɪvz] npl of **wife**

wk abbr = **week**

wobble ['wɒbl] vi temblar; (chair) cojear

woe [wəu] n desgracia

woke [wəuk] pt of **wake**

woken ['wəukən] pp of **wake**

wolf [wulf] n lobo; **wolves** [wulvz] npl of **wolf**

woman ['wumən] (pl **women**) n mujer f; **~ doctor** n médica; **women's lib** (inf: pej) n liberación f de la mujer; **~ly** adj femenino

womb [wu:m] n matriz f, útero

women ['wɪmɪn] npl of **woman**

won [wʌn] pt, pp of **win**

wonder ['wʌndə*] n maravilla, prodigio; (feeling) asombro ♦ vi: **to ~ whether/why** preguntarse si/por qué; **to ~ at** asombrarse de; **to ~ about** pensar sobre or en; **it's no ~ (that)** no es de extrañarse (que + subjun); **~ful** adj maravilloso

won't [wəunt] = **will not**

wood [wud] n (timber) madera; (forest)

bosque m; **~ carving** n (act) tallado en madera; (object) talla en madera; **~ed** adj arbolado; **~en** adj de madera; (fig) inexpresivo; **~pecker** n pájaro carpintero; **~wind** n (MUS) instrumentos mpl de viento de madera; **~work** n carpintería; **~worm** n carcoma

wool [wul] n lana; **to pull the ~ over sb's eyes** (fig) engatusar a uno; **~en** (US), **~len**; **~ien** adj de lana; **~lens** npl géneros mpl de lana; **~ly** adj lanudo, de lana; (fig: ideas) confuso; **~y** (US) adj = **~ly**

word [wə:d] n palabra; (news) noticia; (promise) palabra (de honor) ♦ vt redactar; **in other ~s** en otras palabras; **to break/keep one's ~** faltar a la palabra/cumplir la promesa; **to have ~s with sb** reñir con uno; **~ing** n redacción f; **~ processing** n proceso de textos; **~ processor** n procesador m de textos

wore [wɔ:*] pt of **wear**

work [wə:k] n (gen, job) empleo, trabajo; (ART, LITERATURE) obra ♦ vi trabajar; (mechanism) funcionar, marchar; (medicine) ser eficaz, surtir efecto ♦ vt (shape) trabajar; (stone etc) tallar; (mine etc) explotar; (machine) manejar, hacer funcionar; **~s** n (BRIT: factory) fábrica ♦ npl (of clock, machine) mecanismo; **to be out of ~** estar parado, no tener trabajo; **to ~ loose** (part) desprenderse; (knot) aflojarse; **~ on** vt fus trabajar en, dedicarse a; (principle) basarse en; **~ out** vi (plans etc) salir bien, funcionar ♦ vt (problem) resolver; (plan) elaborar; **it ~s out at £100** suma 100 libras; **~ up** vt: **to get ~ed up** excitarse; **~able** adj (solution) práctico, factible; **~aholic** [wə:kə'hɒlɪk] n trabajador(a) obsesivo/a m/f; **~er** n trabajador(a) m/f, obrero/a; **~force** n mano f de obra; **~ing class** n clase f obrera; **~ing-class** adj obrero; **~ing order** n: **in ~ing order**

en funcionamiento; **~man** n (irreg)
obrero; **~manship** n habilidad f,
trabajo; **~sheet** n hoja de trabajo;
~shop n taller m; **~ station** n puesto
or estación f de trabajo; **~to-rule** n
(BRIT) n huelga de celo

world [wɜːld] n mundo ♦ cpd
(champion) del mundo; (power, war)
mundial; **to think the ~ of sb** (fig)
tener un concepto muy alto de uno;
~ly adj mundano; **~-wide** adj
mundial, universal; **W~-Wide Web** n:
the **W~-Wide Web** el World Wide
Web

worm [wɜːm] n (also: earth~) lombriz f

worn [wɔːn] pp of wear ♦ adj usado;
~-out adj (object) gastado; (person)
rendido, agotado

worried ['wʌrɪd] adj preocupado

worry ['wʌrɪ] n preocupación f ♦ vt
preocupar, inquietar ♦ vi preocuparse;
~ing adj inquietante

worse [wɜːs] adj, adv peor ♦ n lo peor;
a change for the ~ un
empeoramiento; **~n** vt, vi empeorar;
~ off adj (financially): **to be ~ off**
tener menos dinero; (fig): **you'll be
~ off this way** de esta forma estarás
peor que nunca

worship ['wɜːʃɪp] n adoración f ♦ vt
adorar; **Your W~** (BRIT: to mayor)
señor alcalde; (: to judge) señor juez

worst [wɜːst] adj, adv peor ♦ n lo peor;
at ~ en lo peor de los casos

worth [wɜːθ] n valor m ♦ adj: **to be ~**
valer; **it's ~ it** vale or merece la pena;
to be ~ one's while (to do) merecer
la pena (hacer); **~less** adj sin valor;
(useless) inútil; **~while** adj (activity)
que merece la pena; (cause) loable

worthy ['wɜːðɪ] adj respetable;
(motive) honesto; **~ of** digno de

KEYWORD

would [wʊd] aux vb **1** (conditional
tense): **if you asked him he ~ do it**
si se lo pidieras, lo haría; **if you had**

asked him he **~ have done it** si se
lo hubieras pedido, lo habría or hubiera
hecho

2 (in offers, invitations, requests): **~ you
like a biscuit?** ¿quieres una galleta?;
(formal) ¿querría una galleta?; **~ you
ask him to come in?** ¿quiere hacerle
pasar?; **~ you open the window
please?** ¿quiere or podría abrir la
ventana, por favor?

3 (in indirect speech): **I said I ~ do it**
dije que lo haría

4 (emphatic): **it WOULD have to snow
today!** ¡tenía que nevar precisamente
hoy!

5 (insistence): **she ~n't behave** no
quiso comportarse bien

6 (conjecture): **it ~ have been
midnight** sería medianoche; **it
~ seem so** parece ser que sí

7 (indicating habit): **he ~ go there on
Mondays** iba allí los lunes

would-be (pej) adj presunto

wouldn't ['wʊdnt] = **would not**

wound¹ [wuːnd] n herida ♦ vt herir

wound² [waʊnd] pt, pp of **wind**

wove [wəʊv] pt of **weave**

woven ['wəʊvən] pp of **weave**

wrap [ræp] vt (also: ~ up) envolver;
~per n (on chocolate) envoltura;
(BRIT: of book) sobrecubierta; **~ping paper** n
papel m de envolver; (fancy) papel m
de regalo

wreak [riːk] vt: **to ~ havoc (on)** hacer
estragos (en); **to ~ vengeance
(on)** vengarse (de)

wreath [riːθ, pl riːðz] n (funeral ~)
corona

wreck [rek] n (ship: destruction)
naufragio; (: remains) restos mpl del
barco; (pej: person) ruina f (car etc)
destrozar; (chances) arruinar; **~age** n
restos mpl; (of building) escombros mpl

wren [ren] n (ZOOL) reyezuelo

wrench [rentʃ] n (TECH) llave f inglesa;
(tug) tirón m; (fig) dolor m ♦ vt

arrancar; **to ~ sth from sb** arrebatar algo violentamente a uno

wrestle ['resl] vi: **to ~ (with sb)** luchar (con or contra uno); **~r** n luchador(a) m/f (de lucha libre); **wrestling** n lucha libre

wretched ['retʃid] adj miserable

wriggle ['rɪɡl] vi (also: **~ about**) menearse, retorcerse

wring [rɪŋ] (pt, pp **wrung**) vt retorcer; (wet clothes) escurrir; (fig): **to ~ sth out of sb** sacar algo por la fuerza a uno

wrinkle ['rɪŋkl] n arruga ♦ vt arrugar ♦ vi arrugarse

wrist [rɪst] n muñeca; **~watch** n reloj m de pulsera

writ [rɪt] n mandato judicial

write [raɪt] (pt **wrote**, pp **written**) vt escribir; (cheque) extender ♦ vi escribir; **~ down** vt escribir; (note) apuntar; **~ off** vt (debt) borrar (como incobrable); (fig) desechar por inútil; **~ out** vt escribir; **~ up** vt redactar; **~off** n siniestro total; **~r** n escritor(a) m/f

writhe [raɪð] vi retorcerse

writing ['raɪtɪŋ] n escritura; (hand-~) letra; (of author) obras fpl; **in ~** por escrito; **~ paper** n papel m de escribir

written ['rɪtn] pp of **write**

wrong [rɔŋ] adj (wicked) malo; (unfair) injusto; (incorrect) equivocado, incorrecto; (not suitable) inoportuno, inconveniente; (reverse) del revés ♦ adv equivocadamente ♦ n injusticia ♦ vt ser injusto con; **you are ~ to do it** haces mal en hacerlo; **you are ~ about that, you've got it ~** en eso estás equivocado; **to be in the ~** no tener razón, tener la culpa; **what's ~?** ¿qué pasa?; **to go ~** (person) equivocarse; (plan) salir mal; (machine) estropearse; **~ful** adj injusto; **~ly** adv mal, incorrectamente; (by mistake) por error; **~ number** n (TEL): **you've got the ~ number** se ha equivocado de

número

wrote [rəʊt] pt of **write**

wrought iron [rɔːt-] n hierro forjado

wrung [rʌŋ] pt, pp of **wring**

wt. abbr = **weight**

WWW n abbr (= World Wide Web) WWW m

X, x

Xmas ['eksməs] n abbr = **Christmas**

X-ray ['eksreɪ] n radiografía ♦ vt radiografiar, sacar radiografías de

xylophone ['zaɪləfəʊn] n xilófono

Y, y

yacht [jɔt] n yate m; **~ing** n (sport) balandrismo; **~sman/woman** (irreg) n balandrista m/f

Yank [jæŋk] (pej) n yanqui m/f

Yankee ['jæŋkɪ] (pej) n = **Yank**

yap [jæp] vi (dog) aullar

yard [jɑːd] n patio; (measure) yarda; **~stick** n (fig) criterio, norma

yarn [jɑːn] n hilo; (tale) cuento, historia

yawn [jɔːn] n bostezo ♦ vi bostezar; **~ing** adj (gap) muy abierto

yd(s). abbr = **yard(s)**

yeah [jeə] (inf) adv sí

year [jɪə*] n año; **to be 8 ~s old** tener 8 años; **an eight-~-old child** un niño de ocho años (de edad); **~ly** adj anual ♦ adv anualmente, cada año

yearn [jɜːn] vi: **to ~ for sth** añorar algo, suspirar por algo

yeast [jiːst] n levadura

yell [jel] n grito, alarido ♦ vi gritar

yellow ['jeləʊ] adj amarillo

yelp [jelp] n aullido ♦ vi aullar

yes [jes] adv sí ♦ n sí; **to say/ answer ~** decir/contestar que sí

yesterday ['jestədɪ] adv ayer ♦ n ayer m; **~ morning/evening** ayer por la mañana/tarde; **all day ~** todo el día de ayer

yet [jɛt] *adv* ya; *(negative)* todavía
♦ *conj* sin embargo, a pesar de todo; **it
is not finished →** todavía no está
acabado; **the best →** el/la mejor hasta
ahora; **as →** hasta ahora, todavía

yew [ju:] *n* tejo

yield [ji:ld] *n (AGR)* cosecha; *(COMM)*
rendimiento ♦ *vt* ceder; *(results)*
producir, dar; *(profit)* rendir ♦ *vi*
rendirse, ceder; *(US: AUT)* ceder el paso

YMCA *n abbr (= Young Men's Christian
Association)* Asociación f de Jóvenes
Cristianos

yog(h)ourt ['jəʊgət] *n* yogur *m*

yog(h)urt ['jəʊgət] *n* = **yog(h)ourt**

yoke [jəʊk] *n* yugo

yolk [jəʊk] *n* yema (de huevo)

KEYWORD

---

you [ju:] *pron* **1** *(subject: familiar)* tú, *pl*
vosotros/as *(SP)*, ustedes *(AM)*; *(polite)*
usted, *pl* ustedes; **→ are very kind**
eres/es *etc* muy amable; **→ Spanish
enjoy your food** a vosotros *(or* ustedes*)*
los españoles os *(or* les*)* gusta la
comida; **→ and I will go** iremos tú y yo
2 *(object: direct: familiar)* te *pl* os *(SP)*,
les *(AM)*; *(polite)* le, *pl* les, f la, *pl* las; **I
know →** te/le *etc* conozco
3 *(object: indirect: familiar)* te, *pl* os *(SP)*,
les *(AM)*; *(polite)* le, *pl* les; **I gave the
letter to →** yesterday te/os *etc* di la
carta ayer
4 *(stressed)*: **I told you to do it** te dije
a ti que lo hicieras, es a ti a quien dije
que lo hicieras; *see also* **3, 5**
5 *(after prep: NB: con+ ti = contigo)*:
(familiar) ti, *pl* vosotros/as *(SP)*, ustedes
(AM); *(: polite)* usted, *pl* ustedes; **it's
for →** es para ti/vosotros *etc*
6 *(comparisons: familiar)* tú, *pl*
vosotros/as *(SP)*, ustedes *(AM)*; *(: polite)*
usted, *pl* ustedes; **she's younger
than →** es más joven que tú/vosotros
etc
7 *(impersonal: one)*: **fresh air does**

→ good el aire puro (te) hace bien; **→
never know** nunca se sabe; **→ can't
do that!** ¡eso no se hace!

---

you'd [ju:d] = **you had; you would**

you'll [ju:l] = **you will; you shall**

young [jʌŋ] *adj* joven ♦ *npl (of animal)*
cría; *(people)*: **the →** los jóvenes, la
juventud; **→er** *adj (brother etc)* menor;
→ster *n* joven *m/f*

your [jɔ:*] *adj* tu; *(pl)* vuestro; *(formal)*
su; *see also* **my**

you're [juə*] = **you are**

yours [jɔ:z] *pron* tuyo; *(pl)* vuestro;
(formal) suyo; *see also* **faithfully**;
mine¹; sincerely

yourself [jɔ:'sɛlf] *pron* tú mismo;
(complement) te; *(after prep)* tí
(mismo); *(formal)* usted mismo;
(: complement) se; *(: after prep)* sí
(mismo); **yourselves** *pl pron* vosotros
mismos; *(after prep)* vosotros (mismos);
(formal) ustedes (mismos);
(: complement) se; *(: after prep)* sí
mismos; *see also* **oneself**

youth [ju:θ, *pl* ju:ðz] *n* juventud f;
(young man) joven *m*; **→ club** club *m*
juvenil; **→ful** *adj* juvenil; **→ hostel** *n*
albergue *m* de juventud

you've [ju:v] = **you have**

Yugoslav ['ju:gəʊslɑ:v] *adj, n*
yugo(e)slavo/a *m/f*

Yugoslavia [ju:gəʊ'slɑ:vɪə] *n*
Yugoslavia

yuppie ['jʌpɪ] *(inf) adj, n* yupi *m/f*,
yupy *m/f*

YWCA *n abbr (= Young Women's
Christian Association)* Asociación f de
Jóvenes Cristianas

Z, z

zany ['zeɪnɪ] *adj* estrafalario

zap [zæp] *vt (COMPUT)* borrar

zeal [zi:l] *n* celo, entusiasmo; **~ous**
['zɛləs] *adj* celoso, entusiasta

zebra ['ziːbrə] n cebra; ~ **crossing** (BRIT) n paso de peatones

zero ['zɪərəu] n cero

zest [zɛst] n ánimo, vivacidad f; (of orange) piel f

zigzag ['zɪgzæg] n zigzag m ♦ vi zigzaguear, hacer eses

zinc [zɪŋk] n cinc m, zinc m

zip [zɪp] n (also: ~ fastener, (US) ~per) cremallera (SP), cierre m (AM) ♦ vt (also:

~ up) cerrar la cremallera de; ~ **code** (US) n código postal

zodiac ['zəudɪæk] n zodíaco

zone [zəun] n zona

zoo [zuː] n (jardín m) zoo m

zoology [zuːˈɔlədʒɪ] n zoología

zoom [zuːm] vi: to ~ **past** pasar zumbando; ~ **lens** n zoom m

zucchini [zuːˈkiːnɪ] (US) n(pl) calabacín(ines) m(pl)

SPANISH VERB TABLES

1 Gerund. **2** Imperative. **3** Present. **4** Preterite. **5** Future. **6** Present subjunctive. **7** Imperfect subjunctive. **8** Past participle. **9** Imperfect. *Etc* indicates that the irregular root is used for all persons of the tense, *e.g.* **oír: 6** oiga, oigas, oigamos, oigáis, oigan.

agradecer 3 agradezco **6** agradezca *etc*

aprobar 2 aprueba **3** apruebo, apruebas, aprueba, aprueban **6** apruebe, apruebes, apruebe, aprueben

atravesar 2 atraviesa **3** atravieso, atraviesas, atraviesan **6** atraviese, atravieses, atraviese, atraviesen

caber 3 quepo **4** cupe, cupiste, cupo, cupimos, cupisteis, cupieron **5** cabré *etc* **6** quepa *etc* **7** cupiera *etc*

caer 1 cayendo **3** caigo **4** cayó, cayeron **6** caiga *etc* **7** cayera *etc*

cerrar 2 cierra **3** cierro, cierras, cierra, cierran **6** cierre, cierres, cierre, cierren

COMER 1 comiendo **2** come, comed **3** como, comes, come comemos, coméis, comen **4** comí, comiste, comió, comimos, comisteis, comieron **5** comeré, comerás, comerá, comeremos, comeréis, comerán **6** coma, comas, coma, comamos, comáis, coman **7** comiera, comieras, comiera, comiéramos, comierais, comieran **8** comido **9** comía, comías, comía, comíamos, comíais, comían

conocer 3 conozco **6** conozca *etc*

contar 2 cuenta **3** cuento, cuentas, cuenta, cuentan **6** cuente, cuentes, cuente, cuenten

dar 3 doy **4** di, diste, dio, dimos, disteis, dieron **7** diera *etc*

decir 2 di **3** digo **4** dije, dijiste, dijo, diimos, dijisteis, dijeron **5** diré *etc* **6** diga *etc* **7** dijera *etc* **8** dicho

despertar 2 despierta **3** despierto, despiertas, despierta, despiertan **6** despierte, despiertes, despierte, despierten

divertir 1 divirtiendo **2** divierte **3** divierto, diviertes, divierte, divierten **4** divirtió, divirtieron **6** divierta, diviertas, divierta, divirtamos, divirtáis, diviertan **7** divirtiera *etc*

dormir 1 durmiendo **2** duerme **3** duermo, duermes, duerme, duermen **4** durmió, durmieron **6** duerma, duermas, duerma, durmamos, durmáis, duerman **7** durmiera *etc*

empezar 2 empieza **3** empiezo, empiezas, empieza, empiezan **4** empecé **6** empiece, empieces, empiece, empecemos, empecéis, empiecen

entender 2 entiende **3** entiendo, entiendes, entiende, entienden **6** entienda, entiendas, entienda, entiendan

ESTAR 2 está **3** estoy, estás, está, están **4** estuve, estuviste, estuvo, estuvimos, estuvisteis, estuvieron **6** esté, estés, esté, estén **7** estuviera *etc*

HABER 3 he, has, ha, hemos, han **4** hube, hubiste, hubo, hubimos, hubisteis, hubieron **5** habré *etc* **6** haya *etc* **7** hubiera *etc*

HABLAR 1 hablando **2** habla,

hablad 3 hablo, hablas, habla, hablamos, habláis, hablan 4 hablé, hablaste, habló, hablamos, hablasteis, hablaron 5 hablaré, hablarás, hablará, hablaremos, hablaréis, hablarán 6 hable, hables, hable, hablemos, habléis, hablen 7 hablara, hablaras, hablara, habláramos, hablarais, hablaran 8 hablado 9 hablaba, hablabas, hablaba, hablábamos, hablabais, hablaban

hacer 2 haz 3 hago 4 hice, hiciste, hizo, hicimos, hicisteis, hicieron 5 haré etc 6 haga 7 hiciera etc 8 hecho

instruir 1 instruyendo 2 instruye 3 instruyo, instruyes, instruye, instruimos, instruís, instruyen 4 instruyó, instruyeron 6 instruya etc 7 instruyera etc

ir 1 yendo 2 ve 3 voy, vas, va, vamos, vais, van 4 fui, fuiste, fue, fuimos, fuisteis, fueron 6 vaya, vayas, vaya, vayamos, vayáis, vayan 7 fuera etc 9 iba, ibas, iba, íbamos, ibais, iban

jugar 2 juega 3 juego, juegas, juega, juegan 4 jugué 6 juegue etc

leer 1 leyendo 4 leyó, leyeron 7 leyera etc

morir 1 muriendo 2 muere 3 muero, mueres, muere, mueren 4 murió, murieron 6 muera, mueras, muera, muramos, muráis, mueran 7 muriera etc 8 muerto

mover 2 mueve 3 muevo, mueves, mueve, mueven 6 mueva, muevas, mueva, muevan

negar 2 niega 3 niego, niegas, niega, niegan 4 negué 6 niegue, niegues, niegue, neguemos, neguéis, nieguen

ofrecer 3 ofrezco 6 ofrezca etc

oír 1 oyendo 2 oye 3 oigo, oyes, oye, oyen 4 oyó, oyeron 6 oiga etc

7 oyera etc

oler 2 huele 3 huelo, hueles, huele, huelen 6 huela, huelas, huela, huelan

parecer 3 parezco 6 parezca etc

pedir 1 pidiendo 2 pide 3 pido, pides, pide, piden 4 pidió, pidieron 6 pida etc 7 pidiera etc

pensar 2 piensa 3 pienso, piensas, piensa, piensan 6 piense, pienses, piense, piensen

perder 2 pierde 3 pierdo, pierdes, pierde, pierden 6 pierda, pierdas, pierda, pierdan

poder 1 pudiendo 2 puede 3 puedo, puedes, puede, pueden 4 pude, pudiste, pudo, pudimos, pudisteis, pudieron 5 podré etc 6 pueda, puedas, pueda, puedan 7 pudiera etc

poner 2 pon 3 pongo 4 puse, pusiste, puso, pusimos, pusisteis, pusieron 5 pondré etc 6 ponga etc 7 pusiera etc 8 puesto

preferir 1 prefiriendo 2 prefiere 3 prefiero, prefieres, prefiere, prefieren 4 prefirió, prefirieron 6 prefiera, prefieras, prefiera, prefiramos, prefiráis, prefieran 7 prefiriera etc

querer 2 quiere 3 quiero, quieres, quiere, quieren 4 quise, quisiste, quiso, quisimos, quisisteis, quisieron 5 querré etc 6 quiera, quieras, quiera, quieran 7 quisiera etc

reír 2 ríe 3 río, ríes, ríe, ríen 4 rio, rieron 6 ría, rías, ría, riamos, riáis, rían 7 riera etc

repetir 1 repitiendo 2 repite 3 repito, repites, repite, repiten 4 repitió, repitieron 6 repita etc 7 repitiera etc

rogar 2 ruega 3 ruego, ruegas, ruega, ruegan 4 rogué 6 ruegue, ruegues, ruegue, roguemos,

612

roguéis, rueguen

saber 3 sé 4 supe, supiste, supo, supimos, supisteis, supieron 5 sabré *etc* 6 sepa *etc* 7 supiera *etc*

salir 2 sal 3 salgo 5 saldré *etc* 6 salga *etc*

seguir 1 siguiendo 2 sigue 3 sigo, sigues, sigue, siguen 4 siguió, siguieron 6 siga *etc* 7 siguiera *etc*

sentar 2 sienta 3 siento, sientas, sienta, sientan 6 siente, sientes, siente, sienten

sentir 1 sintiendo 2 siente 3 siento, sientes, siente, sienten 4 sintió, sintieron 6 sienta, sientas, sienta, sintamos, sintáis, sientan 7 sintiera *etc*

SER 2 sé 3 soy, eres, es, somos, sois, son 4 fui, fuiste, fue, fuimos, fuisteis, fueron 6 sea *etc* 7 fuera *etc* 9 era, eras, era, éramos, erais, eran

servir 1 sirviendo 2 sirve 3 sirvo, sirves, sirve, sirven 4 sirvió, sirvieron 6 sirva *etc* 7 sirviera *etc*

soñar 2 sueña 3 sueño, sueñas, sueña, sueñan 6 sueñe, sueñes, sueñe, sueñen

tener 2 ten 3 tengo, tienes, tiene, tienen 4 tuve, tuviste, tuvo, tuvimos, tuvisteis, tuvieron 5 tendré *etc* 6 tenga *etc* 7 tuviera *etc*

traer 1 trayendo 3 traigo 4 traje, trajiste, trajo, trajimos, trajisteis, trajeron 6 traiga *etc* 7 trajera *etc*

valer 2 val 3 valgo 5 valdré *etc* 6 valga *etc*

venir 2 ven 3 vengo, vienes, viene, vienen 4 vine, viniste, vino, vinimos, vinisteis, vinieron 5 vendré *etc* 6 venga *etc* 7 viniera *etc*

ver 3 veo 6 vea *etc* 8 veía *etc*

vestir 1 vistiendo 2 viste 3 visto, vistes, viste, visten 4 vistió, vistieron 6 vista *etc* 7 vistiera *etc*

VIVIR 1 viviendo 2 vive, vivid 3 vivo, vives, vive, vivimos, vivís, viven 4 viví, viviste, vivió, vivimos, vivisteis, vivieron 5 viviré, vivirás, vivirá, viviremos, viviréis, vivirán 6 viva, vivas, viva, vivamos, viváis, vivan 7 viviera, vivieras, viviera, viviéramos, vivierais, vivieran 8 vivido 9 vivía, vivías, vivíamos, vivías, vivían

volver 2 vuelve 3 vuelvo, vuelves, vuelve, vuelven 6 vuelva, vuelvas, vuelva, vuelvan 8 vuelto

VERBOS IRREGULARES EN INGLÉS

present	pt	pp	present	pt	pp
arise	arose	arisen	dig	dug	dug
awake	awoke	awaked	do (3rd	did	done
be (am, is,	was,	been	person;		
are;	were		he/she/		
being)			it/does)		
bear	bore	born(e)	draw	drew	drawn
beat	beat	beaten	dream	dreamed,	dreamed,
become	became	become		dreamt	dreamt
begin	began	begun	drink	drank	drunk
behold	beheld	beheld	drive	drove	driven
bend	bent	bent	dwell	dwelt	dwelt
beset	beset	beset	eat	ate	eaten
bet	bet, betted	bet, betted	fall	fell	fallen
bid	bid,	bid,	feed	fed	fed
	bade	bidden	feel	felt	felt
bind	bound	bound	fight	fought	fought
bite	bit	bitten	find	found	found
bleed	bled	bled	flee	fled	fled
blow	blew	blown	fling	flung	flung
break	broke	broken	fly (flies)	flew	flown
breed	bred	bred	forbid	forbade	forbidden
bring	brought	brought	forecast	forecast	forecast
build	built	built	forget	forgot	forgotten
burn	burnt,	burnt,	forgive	forgave	forgiven
	burned	burned	forsake	forsook	forsaken
burst	burst	burst	freeze	froze	frozen
buy	bought	bought	get	got	got, (US)
can	could	(been			gotten
		able)	give	gave	given
cast	cast	cast	go (goes)	went	gone
catch	caught	caught	grind	ground	ground
choose	chose	chosen	grow	grew	grown
cling	clung	clung	hang	hung,	hung,
come	came	come		hanged	hanged
cost	cost	cost	have (has;	had	had
creep	crept	crept	having)		
cut	cut	cut	hear	heard	heard
deal	dealt	dealt	hide	hid	hidden

614

present	pt	pp	present	pt	pp
hit	hit	hit	**seek**	sought	sought
hold	held	held	**sell**	sold	sold
hurt	hurt	hurt	**send**	sent	sent
keep	kept	kept	**set**	set	set
kneel	knelt,	knelt,	**shake**	shook	shaken
	kneeled	kneeled	**shall**	should	—
know	knew	known	**shear**	sheared	shorn,
lay	laid	laid			sheared
lead	led	led	**shed**	shed	shed
lean	leant,	leant,	**shine**	shone	shone
	leaned	leaned	**shoot**	shot	shot
leap	leapt,	leapt,	**show**	showed	shown
	leaped	leaped	**shrink**	shrank	shrunk
learn	learnt,	learnt,	**shut**	shut	shut
	learned	learned	**sing**	sang	sung
leave	left	left	**sink**	sank	sunk
lend	lent	lent	**sit**	sat	sat
let	let	let	**slay**	slew	slain
lie (lying)	lay	lain	**sleep**	slept	slept
light	lit, lighted	lit, lighted	**slide**	slid	slid
lose	lost	lost	**sling**	slung	slung
make	made	made	**slit**	slit	slit
may	might	—	**smell**	smelt,	smelt,
mean	meant	meant		smelled	smelled
meet	met	met	**sow**	sowed	sown,
mistake	mistook	mistaken			sowed
mow	mowed	mown,	**speak**	spoke	spoken
		mowed	**speed**	sped,	sped,
must	(had to)	(had to)		speeded	speeded
pay	paid	paid	**spell**	spelt,	spelt,
put	put	put		spelled	spelled
quit	quit,	quit,	**spend**	spent	spent
	quitted	quitted	**spill**	spilt,	spilt,
read	read	read		spilled	spilled
rid	rid	rid	**spin**	spun	spun
ride	rode	ridden	**spit**	spat	spat
ring	rang	rung	**split**	split	split
rise	rose	risen	**spoil**	spoiled,	spoiled,
run	ran	run		spoilt	spoilt
saw	sawed	sawn	**spread**	spread	spread
say	said	said	**spring**	sprang	sprung
see	saw	seen	**stand**	stood	stood

present	pt	pp	present	pt	pp
steal	stole	stolen	**tell**	told	told
stick	stuck	stuck	**think**	thought	thought
sting	stung	stung	**throw**	threw	thrown
stink	stank	stunk	**thrust**	thrust	thrust
stride	strode	stridden	**tread**	trod	trodden
strike	struck	struck, stricken	**wake**	woke, waked	woken, waked
strive	strove	striven	**wear**	wore	worn
swear	swore	sworn	**weave**	wove, weaved	woven, weaved
sweep	swept	swept			
swell	swelled	swollen, swelled	**wed**	wedded, wed	wedded, wed
swim	swam	swum	**weep**	wept	wept
swing	swung	swung	**win**	won	won
take	took	taken	**wind**	wound	wound
teach	taught	taught	**wring**	wrung	wrung
tear	tore	torn	**write**	wrote	written

LOS NÚMEROS

NUMBERS

un, uno(a)	1	one
dos	2	two
tres	3	three
cuatro	4	four
cinco	5	five
seis	6	six
siete	7	seven
ocho	8	eight
nueve	9	nine
diez	10	ten
once	11	eleven
doce	12	twelve
trece	13	thirteen
catorce	14	fourteen
quince	15	fifteen
dieciséis	16	sixteen
diecisiete	17	seventeen
dieciocho	18	eighteen
diecinueve	19	nineteen
veinte	20	twenty
veintiuno	21	twenty-one
veintidós	22	twenty-two
treinta	30	thirty
treinta y uno(a)	31	thirty-one
treinta y dos	32	thirty-two
cuarenta	40	forty
cincuenta	50	fifty
sesenta	60	sixty
setenta	70	seventy
ochenta	80	eighty
noventa	90	ninety
cien, ciento	100	a hundred, one hundred
ciento uno(a)	101	a hundred and one
doscientos(as)	200	two hundred
doscientos(as) uno(a)	201	two hundred and one
trescientos(as)	300	three hundred
cuatrocientos(as)	400	four hundred
quinientos(as)	500	five hundred
seiscientos(as)	600	six hundred
setecientos(as)	700	seven hundred
ochocientos(as)	800	eight hundred
novecientos(as)	900	nine hundred
mil	1 000	a thousand
mil dos	1 002	a thousand and two
cinco mil	5 000	five thousand
un millón	1 000 000	a million

LOS NÚMEROS

NUMBERS

primer, primero(a), 1º, 1ᵉʳ (1ª, 1ᵉʳᵃ)	first, 1st
segundo(a) 2º (2ª)	second, 2nd
tercer, tercero(a), 3º (3ª)	third, 3rd
cuarto(a), 4º (4ª)	fourth, 4th
quinto(a), 5º (5ª)	fifth, 5th
sexto(a), 6º (6ª)	sixth, 6th
séptimo(a)	seventh
octavo(a)	eighth
noveno(a)	ninth
décimo(a)	tenth
undécimo(a)	eleventh
duodécimo(a)	twelfth
decimotercio(a)	thirteenth
decimocuarto(a)	fourteenth
decimoquinto(a)	fifteenth
decimosexto(a)	sixteenth
vigésimo(a)	twentieth
vigésimo(a) primero(a)	twenty-first
trigésimo(a)	thirtieth
centésimo(a)	hundredth
centésimo(a) primero(a)	hundred-and-first
milésimo(a)	thousandth

Números Quebrados etc

Fractions etc

un medio	a half
un tercio	a third
un cuarto	a quarter
un quinto	a fifth
cero coma cinco, 0,5	(nought) point five, 0.5
diez por cien(to)	ten per cent

N.B. In Spanish the ordinal numbers from 1 to 10 are commonly used; from 11 to 20 rather less; above 21 they are rarely written and almost never heard in speech. The custom is to replace the forms for 21 and above by the cardinal number.

LA HORA

THE TIME

¿qué hora es?

what time is it?

es/son

it's o *it is*

medianoche, las doce (de la noche)	midnight, twelve p.m.
la una (de la madrugada)	one o'clock (in the morning), one (a.m.)
la una y cinco	five past one
la una y diez	ten past one
la una y cuarto *or* quince	a quarter past one, one fifteen
la una y veinticinco	twenty-five past one, one twenty-five
la una y media *or* treinta	half-past one, one thirty
las dos menos veinticinco, la una treinta y cinco	twenty-five to two, one thirty-five
las dos menos veinte, la una cuarenta	twenty to two, one forty
las dos menos cuarto, la una cuarenta y cinco	a quarter to two, one forty-five
las dos menos diez, la una cincuenta	ten to two, one fifty
mediodía, las doce (de la tarde)	twelve o'clock, midday, noon
la una (de la tarde)	one o'clock (in the afternoon), one (p.m.)
las siete (de la tarde)	seven o'clock (in the evening), seven (p.m.)

¿a qué hora?

(at) what time?

a medianoche	at midnight
a las siete	at seven o'clock
en veinte minutos	in twenty minutes
hace quince minutos	fifteen minutes ago

LA FECHA

DATES

hoy	today
todos los días	every day
ayer	yesterday
esta mañana	this morning
mañana por la noche	tomorrow night
anteanoche; antes de ayer por la noche	the night before last
antes de ayer; anteayer	the day before yesterday
anoche	last night
hace dos días/seis años	2 days/six years ago
mañana por la tarde	tomorrow afternoon
pasado mañana	the day after tomorrow
todos los jueves, el jueves	every Thursday, on Thursday
va los viernes	he goes on Fridays
"miércoles cerrado"	"closed on Wednesdays"
de lunes a viernes	from Monday to Friday
para el jueves	by Thursday
un sábado de marzo	one Saturday in March
dentro de una semana	in a week's time
dentro de dos martes	a week next/on Tuesday/Tuesday week
el domingo que viene	next Sunday
esta semana/la semana que viene/la semana pasada	this/next/last week
dentro de dos semanas	in 2 weeks or a fortnight
dentro de tres lunes	two weeks on Monday
el primer/último viernes del mes	the first/last Friday of the month
el mes que viene	next month
el año pasado	last year
el uno de junio, el primero de junio (*LAM*)	the 1st of June, June first
el dos de octubre	the 2nd of October, October 2nd
nací en 1987	I was born in 1987
su cumpleaños es el 5 de junio	his birthday is on June 5th (*BRIT*) or 5th June (*US*)
el 18 de agosto	on 18th August (*BRIT*) or August 18th (*US*)
en el 96	in '96
en la primavera del 94	in the Spring of '94
del 19 al 3	from the 19th to the 3rd
¿qué fecha es hoy?, ¿a cuanto estamos?	what's the date?, what date is it today?

LA FECHA

hoy es 15, estamos a quince

mil novecientos ochenta y ocho

hoy hace 10 años
a final de mes
a final de mes
diariamente/semanalmente/
  mensualmente
anualmente
dos veces a la semana/dos veces al
  mes/dos veces al año
dos veces al mes
en el año 2006 (dos mil seis)
4 a. de C.
79 d. de C.
en el siglo XIII
en o durante los (años) 80
a mediados de la década de los 70
en mil novecientos noventa y
  tantos

DATES

today's date is the 15th, today is
  the 15th
1988 - nineteen (hundred and)
  eighty-eight
10 years to the day
at the end of the month
at the month end (*ACCOUNTS*)
daily/weekly/monthly

annually
twice a week/month/year

bi-monthly
in the year 2006
4 B.C., B.C. 4
79 A.D., A.D. 79
in the 13th century
in *or* during the 1980s
in the mid seventies
in 1990 something

HEADINGS OF LETTERS

9 de octubre de 1995

9th October 1995 *or* 9 October
  1995

PESOS Y MEDIDAS
CONVERSION CHARTS

In the weight and length charts the middle figure can be either metric or imperial. Thus 3.3 feet = 1 metre, 1 foot = 0.3 metres, and so on.

feet		metres	inches		cm	lbs		kg
3.3	1	0.3	0.39	1	2.54	2.2	1	0.45
6.6	2	0.61	0.79	2	5.08	4.4	2	0.91
9.9	3	0.91	1.18	3	7.62	6.6	3	1.4
13.1	4	1.22	1.57	4	10.6	8.8	4	1.8
16.4	5	1.52	1.97	5	12.7	11.0	5	2.2
19.7	6	1.83	2.36	6	15.2	13.2	6	2.7
23.0	7	2.13	2.76	7	17.8	15.4	7	3.2
26.2	8	2.44	3.15	8	20.3	17.6	8	3.6
29.5	9	2.74	3.54	9	22.9	19.8	9	4.1
32.9	10	3.05	3.9	10	25.4	22.0	10	4.5
			4.3	11	27.9			
			4.7	12	30.1			

°C	0	5	10	15	17	20	22	24	26	28	30	35	37	38	40	50	100
°F	32	41	50	59	63	68	72	75	79	82	86	95	98.4	100	104	122	212

Km	10	20	30	40	50	60	70	80	90	100	110	120
Miles	6.2	12.4	18.6	24.9	31.0	37.3	43.5	49.7	56.0	62.0	68.3	74.6

Liquids

gallons	1.1	2.2	3.3	4.4	5.5	pints	0.44	0.88	1.76
litres	5	10	15	20	25	litres	0.25	0.5	1

próspero

throat [θrəʊt] n garganta; **to have a sore ~** tener dolor de garganta

throb [θrɒb] vi latir; (pain) dar punzadas, vibrar

throes [θrəʊz] npl: **in the ~ of** en medio de

throne [θrəʊn] n trono

throng [θrɒŋ] n multitud f, muchedumbre f ♦ vt agolparse en

throttle ['θrɒtl] n (AUT) acelerador m ♦ vt estrangular

through [θruː] prep por, a través de; (time) durante; (by means of) por medio de, mediante; (owing to) gracias a ♦ adj (ticket, train) directo ♦ adv completamente, de parte a parte; de principio a fin; **to put sb ~ to sb** (TEL) poner o pasar a uno con uno; **to be ~** (TEL) tener comunicación f; (have finished) haber terminado; **"no ~ road"** (BRIT) "calle sin salida"; **~out** prep (place) por todas partes de, por todo; (time) durante todo ♦ adv por o en todas partes

throw [θrəʊ] (pt **threw**, pp **thrown**) n tiro; (SPORT) lanzamiento ♦ vt tirar, echar; (SPORT) lanzar; (rider) derribar; (fig) desconcertar; **to ~ a party** dar una fiesta; **~ away** vt tirar; (money) derrochar; **~ off** vt deshacerse de; **~ out** vt tirar; (person) echar; expulsar; **~ up** vi vomitar; **~away** adj para tirar, desechable; (remark) hecho de paso; **~-in** n (SPORT) saque m

thru [θruː] (US) = **through**

thrush [θrʌʃ] n zorzal m, tordo

thrust [θrʌst] (pt, pp **thrust**) vt empujar (con fuerza)

thud [θʌd] n golpe m sordo

thug [θʌg] n gamberro m

thumb [θʌm] n (ANAT) pulgar m; **to ~ a lift** hacer autostop; **~ through** vt fus hojear; **~tack** (US) n chincheta (SP)

thump [θʌmp] n golpe m; (sound) ruido seco o sordo ♦ vt golpear ♦ vi

(heart etc) palpitar

thunder ['θʌndə*] n trueno ♦ vi tronar; (train etc): **to ~ past** pasar como un trueno; **~bolt** n rayo; **~clap** n trueno; **~storm** n tormenta; **~y** adj tormentoso

Thursday ['θəːzdɪ] n jueves m inv

thus [ðʌs] adv así, de este modo

thyme [taɪm] n tomillo

thyroid ['θaɪrɔɪd] n (also: ~ gland) tiroides m inv

tic [tɪk] n tic m

tick [tɪk] n (sound: of clock) tictac m; (mark) palomita; (ZOOL) garrapata; (BRIT: inf): **in a ~** en un instante ♦ vi hacer tictac ♦ vt marcar; **~ off** vt marcar; (person) reñir; **~ over** vi (engine) girar en marcha lenta; (fig) tirando

ticket ['tɪkɪt] n billete m (SP), tíquet m, boleto (AM); (for cinema etc) entrada (SP), boleto (AM); (in shop: on goods) etiqueta; (for raffle) papeleta; (for library) tarjeta; (parking ~) multa por estacionamiento ilegal; **~ collector** n revisor(a) m/f; **~ office** n (THEATRE) taquilla (SP), boletería (AM); (RAIL) despacho de billetes (SP) o boletos (AM)

tickle ['tɪkl] vt hacer cosquillas a ♦ vi hacer cosquillas; **ticklish** adj (person) cosquilloso; (problem) delicado

tidal ['taɪdl] adj de marea; **~ wave** n maremoto

tidbit ['tɪdbɪt] (US) n = **titbit**

tiddlywinks ['tɪdlɪwɪŋks] n juego infantil con fichas de plástico

tide [taɪd] n marea; (fig: of events etc) curso, marcha; **~ over** vt (help out) ayudar a salir del apuro

tidy ['taɪdɪ] adj (room etc) ordenado; (dress, work) limpio; (person) (bien) arreglado ♦ vt (also: **~ up**) poner en orden

tie [taɪ] n (string etc) atadura; (BRIT: also: **neck~**) corbata; (fig: link) vínculo, lazo; (SPORT etc: draw) empate m ♦ vt atar ♦ vi (SPORT etc) empatar; **to ~ in a bow** atar con un lazo; **to ~ a knot in sth** hacer un nudo en algo; **~ down** vt (fig: person: restrict) sujetar; (: to price, date etc) obligar a; **~ up** vt (parcel) envolver; (dog, person) atar; (arrangements) concluir; **to be ~d up** (busy) estar ocupado

tier [tɪə*] n grada; (of cake) piso

tiger ['taɪgə*] n tigre m

tight [taɪt] adj (rope) tirante; (money) escaso; (clothes) ajustado; (shoes, schedule) apretado; (budget) ajustado; (security) estricto; (inf: drunk) borracho ♦ adv (squeeze) muy fuerte; (shut) bien; **~en** vt (rope) estirar; (screw, grip) apretar; (security) reforzar ♦ vi estirarse; apretarse; **~-fisted** adj tacaño; **~ly** adv (grasp) muy fuerte; **~rope** n cuerda floja; **~s** (BRIT) npl panti mpl

tile [taɪl] n (on roof) teja; (on floor) baldosa; (on wall) azulejo; **~d** adj de tejas; embaldosado; (wall) alicatado

till [tɪl] n caja (registradora) ♦ vt (land) cultivar ♦ prep, conj = **until**

tilt [tɪlt] vt inclinar ♦ vi inclinarse

timber ['tɪmbə*] n (material) madera

time [taɪm] n tiempo; (epoch: often pl) época; (by clock) hora; (moment) momento; (occasion) vez f; (MUS) compás m ♦ vt calcular o medir el tiempo de; (race) cronometrar; (remark, visit etc) elegir el momento para; **a long ~** mucho tiempo; **4 at a ~** de 4 en 4; **4 a la vez; for the ~ being** de momento, por ahora; **from ~ to ~** de vez en cuando; **at ~s** a veces; **in ~** (soon enough) a tiempo; (after some time) con el tiempo; (MUS) al compás; **in a week's ~** dentro de una semana; **in no ~** en un abrir y cerrar de ojos; **any ~** cuando sea; **on ~** a tiempo; **5 ~s 5** 5 por 5; **what ~ is it?** ¿qué hora es?; **to have a good ~** pasarlo bien, divertirse; **~ bomb** n bomba de efecto retardado; **~less** adj eterno; **~ limit** n

plazo; **~ly** adj oportuno; **~ off** n tiempo libre; **~r** n (in kitchen etc) programador m horario; **~ scale** (BRIT) n escala de tiempo; **~-share** n apartamento (or casa) a tiempo compartido; **~ switch** (BRIT) n interruptor m (horario); **~table** n horario; **~ zone** n huso horario

timid ['tɪmɪd] adj tímido

timing ['taɪmɪŋ] n (SPORT) cronometraje m; **the ~ of his resignation** el momento que eligió para dimitir

tin [tɪn] n estaño; (also: ~ **plate**) hojalata; (BRIT: can) lata; **~foil** n papel m de estaño

tinge [tɪndʒ] n matiz m ♦ vt: **~d with** teñido de

tingle ['tɪŋgl] vi (person): **to ~ (with)** estremecerse (de); (hands etc) hormiguear

tinker ['tɪŋkə*]: **~ with** vt fus jugar con, tocar

tinned [tɪnd] (BRIT) adj (food) en lata, en conserva

tin opener [-əupnə*] (BRIT) n abrelatas m inv

tinsel ['tɪnsl] n (guirnalda de) espumillón m

tint [tɪnt] n matiz m; (for hair) tinte m; **~ed** adj (hair) teñido; (glass, spectacles) ahumado

tiny ['taɪnɪ] adj minúsculo, pequeñito

tip [tɪp] n (end) punta; (gratuity) propina; (BRIT: for rubbish) vertedero; (advice) consejo ♦ vt (waiter) dar una propina a; (tilt) inclinar; (empty: also: ~ **out**) vaciar, echar; (overturn: also: ~ **over**) volcar; **~-off** n (hint) advertencia; **~ped** (BRIT) adj (cigarette) con filtro

Tipp-Ex ® [tɪpeks] n Tipp-Ex ® m

tipsy ['tɪpsɪ] (inf) adj alegre, mareado

tiptoe ['tɪptəu]: **on ~** de puntillas

tire ['taɪə*] n (US) = **tyre** ♦ vi (gen) cansarse; (become bored) aburrirse; **~d** adj cansado; **to be ~d of**

sth estar harto de algo; **~less** adj
incansable; **~some** adj aburrido;
tiring adj cansado

tissue ['tɪʃuː] n tejido; (paper
handkerchief) pañuelo de papel,
kleenex ® m; **~ paper** n papel m de
seda

tit [tɪt] n (bird) herrerillo común; **to
give ~ for tat** dar ojo por ojo

titbit ['tɪtbɪt] n (food)
golosina; (news) noticia sabrosa

title ['taɪtl] n título; **~ deed** n (LAW)
título de propiedad; **~ role** n papel m
principal

TM abbr = trademark

KEYWORD

to [tuː, tə] prep 1 (direction) a; **to go
~ France/London/school/the
station** ir a Francia/Londres/al
colegio/a la estación; **to go ~
Claude's/the doctor's** ir a casa de
Claude/al médico; **the road ~
Edinburgh** la carretera de
Edimburgo

2 (as far as) hasta, a; **from here ~
London** de aquí a ó hasta Londres;
to count ~ 10 contar hasta 10; **from
40 ~ 50 people** entre 40 y 50
personas

3 (with expressions of time): **a
quarter/twenty ~ 5** las 5 menos
cuarto/veinte

4 (for, of): **the key ~ the front door**
la llave de la puerta principal; **she is
secretary ~ the director** es la
secretaria del director; **a letter ~ his
wife** una carta a o para su mujer

5 (expressing indirect object): **to give
sth ~ sb** darle algo a alguien; **to talk
~ sb** hablar con alguien; **to be a
danger ~ sb** ser un peligro para
alguien; **to carry out repairs ~ sth**
hacer reparaciones en algo

6 (in relation to): **3 goals ~ 2** 3 goles a
2; **30 miles ~ the gallon** = 9,4 litros
a los cien (kms)

7 (purpose, result): **to come ~ sb's
aid** venir en auxilio o ayuda de
alguien; **to sentence sb ~ death**
condenar a uno a muerte; **my great
surprise** con gran sorpresa mía

♦ with vb 1 (simple infin): **to go/eat** ir/
comer

2 (following another vb): **to want/
try/start ~ do** querer/intentar/
empezar a hacer; see also relevant vb

3 (with vb omitted): **I don't want ~** no
quiero

4 (purpose, result) para; **I did it ~ help
you** lo hice para ayudarte; **he came
~ see you** vino a verte

5 (equivalent to relative clause): **I have
things ~ do** tengo cosas que hacer;
the main thing is ~ try lo principal
es intentarlo

6 (after adj etc): **ready ~ go** listo para
irse; **too old ~ ...** demasiado viejo
(como) para ...

♦ adv: **pull/push the door ~** tirar
de/empujar la puerta

---

toad [təud] n sapo; **~stool** n hongo
venenoso

toast [təust] n (CULIN) tostada; (drink,
speech) brindis m ♦ vt (CULIN) tostar;
(drink to) brindar por; **~er** n tostador
m

tobacco [tə'bækəu] n tabaco; **~nist** n
estanquero/a (SP), tabaquero/a (AM);
~nist's (shop) (BRIT) n estanco (SP),
tabaquería (AM)

toboggan [tə'bɔgən] n tobogán m

today [tə'deɪ] adv, n (also fig) hoy m

toddler ['tɔdlə*] n niño/a (que
empieza a andar)

toe [təu] n dedo (del pie); (of shoe)
punta; **to the line** (fig) conformarse;
~nail n uña del pie

toffee ['tɔfi] n toffee m; **~ apple** (BRIT)
n manzana acaramelada

together [tə'geðə*] adv juntos; (at
same time) al mismo tiempo, a la vez;
~ with junto con

toil ['tɔɪl] n trabajo duro, labor f ♦ vi trabajar duramente

toilet ['tɔɪlət] n retrete m; (BRIT: room) servicios mpl (SP), wáter m (SP), sanitario (AM) ♦ cpd (soap etc) de aseo; ~ **paper** n papel m higiénico; ~**ries** npl artículos mpl de tocador; ~ **roll** n rollo de papel higiénico

token ['təukən] n (sign) señal f, muestra; (souvenir) recuerdo; (disc) ficha ♦ adj (strike, payment etc) simbólico; **book/record** ~ (BRIT) vale m para comprar libros/discos; **gift** ~ (BRIT) vale-regalo

Tokyo ['təukjəu] n Tokio, Tokío

told [təuld] pt, pp of **tell**

tolerable ['tɔlərəbl] adj (bearable) soportable; (fairly good) pasable

tolerant ['tɔlərnt] adj: ~ **of** tolerante con

tolerate ['tɔlərest] vt tolerar

toll [təul] n (of casualties) número de víctimas; (tax, charge) peaje m ♦ vi (bell) doblar

tomato [tə'mɑ:təu] (pl ~es) n tomate m

tomb [tu:m] n tumba

tomboy ['tɔmbɔɪ] n marimacho

tombstone ['tu:mstəun] n lápida

tomcat ['tɔmkæt] n gato macho

tomorrow [tə'mɔrəu] adv, n (also: fig) mañana; **the day after** ~ pasado mañana; ~ **morning** mañana por la mañana

ton [tʌn] n tonelada (BRIT = 1016 kg; US = 907 kg); (metric ~) tonelada métrica; ~**s of** (inf) montones de

tone [təun] n tono ♦ vi armonizar; ~ **down** vt (criticism) suavizar; (colour) atenuar; ~ **up** vt (muscles) tonificar; ~-**deaf** adj con mal oído

tongs [tɔŋz] npl (for coal) tenazas fpl; (curling ~) tenacillas fpl

tongue [tʌŋ] n lengua; ~ **in cheek** irónicamente; ~-**tied** adj (fig) mudo; ~-**twister** n trabalenguas m inv

tonic ['tɔnɪk] n (MED, also fig) tónico; (also: ~ **water**) (agua) tónica

tonight [tə'naɪt] adv, n esta noche; esta tarde

tonsil ['tɔnsl] n amígdala; ~**litis** [-'laɪtɪs] n amigdalitis f

too [tu:] adv (excessively) demasiado; (also) también; ~ **much** demasiado; ~ **many** demasiados/as

took [tuk] pt of **take**

tool [tu:l] n herramienta; ~ **box** n caja de herramientas

toot [tu:t] n pitido ♦ vi tocar el pito

tooth [tu:θ] (pl **teeth**) n (ANAT, TECH) diente m; (molar) muela; ~**ache** n dolor m de muelas; ~**brush** n cepillo de dientes; ~**paste** n pasta de dientes; ~**pick** n palillo

top [tɔp] n (of mountain) cumbre f, cima; (of tree) copa; (of head) coronilla; (of ladder, page) lo alto; (of table) superficie f; (of cupboard) parte f de arriba; (lid: of box) tapa; (: of bottle, jar) tapón m; (of list etc) cabeza; (toy) peonza; (garment) blusa; camiseta ♦ adj de arriba; (in rank) principal, primero; (best) mejor ♦ vt (exceed) exceder; (be first in) encabezar; **on** ~ **of** (above) sobre, encima de; (in addition to) además de; **from** ~ **to bottom** de pies a cabeza; ~ **off** (US) = ~ **up**; ~ **up** vt llenar; ~ **floor** n último piso; ~ **hat** n sombrero de copa; ~-**heavy** adj (object) mal equilibrado

topic ['tɔpɪk] n tema m; ~**al** adj actual

top: ~-**less** adj (bather, bikini) topless inv; ~-**level** adj (talks) al más alto nivel; ~**most** adj más alto

topple ['tɔpl] vt derribar ♦ vi caerse

top-secret adj de alto secreto

topsy-turvy ['tɔpsɪ'tɜ:vɪ] adj al revés ♦ adv patas arriba

torch [tɔ:tʃ] n antorcha; (BRIT: electric) linterna

tore [tɔ:*] pt of **tear**²

torment [n 'tɔ:mɛnt, vt tɔ:'mɛnt]